THE ROUGH GUIDE TO
GREECE
WITHDRAWN

This fifteenth edition updated by

**Nick Edwards, John Fisher, Rebecca Hall,
John Malathronas and Martin Zatko**

Contents

Introduction to
Greece

Despite the media battering its economic reputation has endured, Greece remains a premier-league travel destination. Its incredible historic sites span four millennia, encompassing both the legendary and the obscure. Its convoluted coastline is punctuated by superb beaches, while its mountainous interior urges you to dust off your hiking boots and explore. Yet perhaps its greatest riches are the islands, ranging from backwaters where the boat calls twice a week to resorts as cosmopolitan as any in the Mediterranean.

For anyone with a cultural bone in their body, Greece cannot fail to inspire. Minoans, Romans, Arabs, Latin Crusaders, Venetians, Slavs, Albanians and Turks have all left their mark, and almost every town or village has a link to the **past**, whether it's a delicately crumbling temple to Aphrodite, a forbidding Venetian fort or a dusty Byzantine monastery decorated with exquisite frescoes. And you'll be spoilt for choice when it comes to museums stuffed to bursting with classical sculpture and archeological treasures.

But the call to cultural duty will never be too overwhelming on a Greek holiday. The **hedonistic pleasures** of languor and warmth – swimming in balmy seas at dusk, talking and drinking under the stars – are just as appealing. Greek **cuisine** and wine production are going through a renaissance, with many young chefs and wine growers returning from abroad laden with ideas, while the genuine **welcome** you'll receive at the simplest taverna is often enough to get you booking next year's break as soon as you return home.

Whatever you come here for, it's clear that Greece needs its tourists like never before: although the country's titanic **debt crisis** (see p.788) seems to have abated, at least in the short term, tourism has been the main engine of the Greek economy since 2013 during its struggle through a long, painful recession. Since the first edition of this guide was published in 1982, one thing has undoubtedly remained unchanged – Greece can offer surprises and a true sense of discovery to even the most demanding traveller.

ABOVE THE PARTHENON, ATHENS **OPPOSITE** BEACH, KÁRPATHOS

Where to go

Sprawling, globalized **Athens** is an obligatory, almost unavoidable introduction to Greece: home to over a third of the population, it is on first acquaintance a nightmare for many, but should not be dismissed so quickly. The city is currently enjoying a resurgence as a short-break destination, and, aside from the show-stopping Acropolis, it offers a truly metropolitan range of cultural diversions, from museums to concerts, well-stocked shops, gourmet restaurants and stimulating clubs, plus an excellent transport infrastructure – a visible legacy of the 2004 Olympics. **Thessaloníki**, the metropolis of the north, has emerged in its own right as a lively, sophisticated place, with restaurants and nightlife to match that of Athens, Byzantine monuments compensating for a lack of "ancient" ones, and a tremendous capacity among the city's inhabitants for enjoying life.

Apart from these cities, the **mainland** shows its best side in the well-preserved **classical ruins** of Mycenae, Olympia and Delphi, the frescoed Byzantine churches and monasteries at Mount Áthos, Metéora, Ósios Loukás, Kastoriá, Árta and Mystra, the massive **fortified towns** of Monemvasiá, Náfplio, Koróni and Methóni, the distinctive architecture of Zagóri and the Máni, and the long, **sandy beaches** of the **Peloponnese** and the Pelion peninsula. Perhaps more surprisingly, the mainland mountains offer some of the best and least-exploited **hiking**, rafting, canyoning and **skiing** in Europe.

Out in the Aegean or Ionian seas, you're more spoilt for choice. The best strategy for first-time visitors can be to sample assorted islands from nearby archipelagos – the Dodecanese, the Cyclades, the Sporades, and the Argo-Saronic are all reasonably well

FACT FILE

• Out of a total Greek **population** of 11.3 million, nearly one-tenth is immigrants, half of whom are from Albania. There are also large Greek communities in the US, Australia (Melbourne is the third-largest "Greek" city) and the UK.

• No point in Greece is more than 137km from water. Greece has about 14,400km of **coastline**, the tenth longest in the world.

• **Tourism** is the country's main foreign-currency earner, with twenty-nine million visitors from overseas in 2016; export of **agricultural products** – especially olive oil and olives, citrus, wine and raisins – is another key industry.

• With over 370 brands, anise-flavoured **ouzo** is Greece's most famous and popular beverage. Come the evening, the Greeks sip it with a little ice and water while tucking into mezédhes. *Stin uyeiá sou!* (Cheers!)

• **Easter** is the biggest date on the Greek calendar. Instead of chocolate eggs, locals exchange hard-boiled ones painted red.

connected with each other, while the northeast Aegean and Ionian groups are best visited in single trips. If time and money are short, the best place to head for is well-preserved **Ýdhra** in the **Argo-Saronic Gulf**, just a short ride from Pireás (the main port of Athens), but an utterly different place once the day-cruises have gone. Similarly, **Kéa**, one hour away from Lávrio, easily reached from the Athens International airport, has a Neoclassical charm, more akin to nineteenth-century Greece than the whitewashed tourist resorts of the Aegean. Among the rest, cataclysmically volcanic **Santoríni** (Thíra) and **Mýkonos**, with its perfectly preserved harbour town, rank as must-see spectacles, but fertile, mountainous **Náxos**, dramatic cliff-sided **Folégandhros** or gently rolling **Sífnos** have more life independent of cruise-ship tourism and seem more amenable to long stays. **Crete** could (and does) fill an entire Rough Guide to itself: the highlights here are Knossós and the nearby archeological museum in Iráklio, the other Minoan palaces at Phaestos and Ayía Triádha, and the west in general – the proud city of Haniá, with its hinterland extending to the relatively unspoilt southwest coast, reached via the fabled Samarian gorge. **Rhodes**, with its UNESCO World Heritage old town, is capital of the **Dodecanese**, but picturesque, Neoclassical Sými opposite, and austere, volcanic Pátmos, the island of Revelation, are far more manageable. Though somewhat marred by recent waves of migration, Híos with its striking medieval architecture, and balmy, traditional, olive-cloaked Lesvos are still worth visiting and offer great value. The **Ionian islands** are often dismissed as package-holiday territory, but their Venetian-style architecture, especially evident in Corfu and neighbouring Paxí, make them well worth seeking out.

When to go

If anything is god-given to the Greeks, it is their **climate** (see p.52). Most places are far more agreeable outside the mid-July to end of August peak season, when soaring temperatures, plus crowds of foreigners and locals alike, can be overpowering. You won't miss out on **warm weather** if you come in **June or September**, excellent times almost everywhere but particularly on the islands. An exception to this, however, is the north mainland coast – notably the Halkidhikí peninsula – and the islands of Samothráki and

DIVINE INSPIRATION

A high proportion of the ancient sites still seen in Greece today were built as shrines and temples to the **gods**, primarily the twelve who lived on Mount Olympus. **Zeus**, the lord of the heavens and supreme power; **Hera**, his wife and sister, goddess of fertility; **Athena**, the goddess of wisdom, patron of crafts and fearless warrior; **Apollo**, the god of music, of prophecy and the arts; his sister **Artemis**, the virgin huntress and goddess of childbirth; **Poseidon**, the god of the sea; beautiful **Aphrodite**, goddess of love and desire; **Hermes**, the messenger who leads the souls of the dead to the underworld; **Hephaestus**, the god of craftsmen; **Ares**, the god of war; **Demeter**, the goddess of crops and female fertility; and **Dionysus**, god of wine and intoxication. Worshipped, feared and admired, they formed the basis for the ancient Greek religion until paganism was banned by the Romans in AD 391.

Thássos, which only really bloom during **July and August**. In **October** you will almost certainly hit a stormy spell, especially in western Greece or in the mountains, but for most of that month the "little summer of Áyios Dhimítrios" (the Greek equivalent of **Indian summer**) prevails, and the southerly Dodecanese and Crete are extremely pleasant. Autumn in general is beautiful; the light is softer than in summer, the sea often balmier than the air and the colours subtler.

December to March are the coldest and least reliably sunny months, though even then there are many crystal-clear, fine days. The more northerly latitudes and high altitudes endure far colder and wetter conditions, with the mountains themselves under snow from November to May. The **mildest winter** climate is found on Rhodes, or in the southeastern parts of Crete. As spring slowly warms up, **April** is still uncertain, though superb for wild flowers, green landscapes and photography; by **May** the weather is more settled and predictable, and Crete, the Peloponnese, the Ionian islands and the Cyclades are perhaps at their best, even if the sea is still cold for swimming.

Other factors that affect timing for Greek travels have to do with the level of tourism and the amenities provided. Service standards occasionally slip under peak season pressure, and room prices on the islands can rocket. If you can only visit during midsummer, it is wise to reserve a package well in advance, buy any ferry tickets beforehand or plan your itinerary off the beaten track. You might choose, for instance, to explore the less obvious parts of Thessaly, Epirus and the northern mainland, or island-hop with an eye for the remoter places.

Out of season on the islands you will have to contend with much reduced ferry and plane services plus fairly skeletal facilities when you arrive. You will, however, find reasonable service on main routes and at least one hotel and taverna open in the port or main town of all but the tiniest isles. On the mainland, winter travel poses no special difficulties except, of course, in mountain villages either cut off by snow in mid-winter or (at weekends especially) monopolized by avid Greek skiers, especially in the central Peloponnese.

Author picks

Our authors travelled the length and breadth of Greece, teasing out the best beaches, sampling the tastiest meze and exploring countless ancient ruins. Here are their highlights:

Unique Ólymbos Traditions are fading fast in the mountain village of Ólymbos (p.544) on Kárpathos but you may still spot some women wearing distinctive, brightly coloured costumes.

Down the hatch Once confined to parts of northern Greece, the fiery spirit *tsípouro* (p.41) has become the tipple of choice for many all over the country.

Multicultural Greece Thrace is one of the most culturally diverse regions, with Xánthi (p.317), Komotiní (p.320) and surroundings full of Muslim, Pomak and Roma folk.

Ahead of its time The Antikythira Mechanism (p.85) in the Athens Archeological Museum is one of the world's most intriguing exhibits.

Best sunset Most tourists to Santorini make for Ía, but the sunset views from Akrotíri (p.443) at the croissant-shaped island's southwestern tip are better and far less crowded.

City break Haniá (p.494), Crete's second city, has daily flights from northern Europe, tremendous boutique hotels, and great food and atmosphere: what more could you ask for?

Byzantine wonders Set among almond trees and rolling hills, the Ósios Loukás monastery (p.213), close to Delphi, is home to some of the country's finest Byzantine mosaics.

Fabulous fast food A proper Greek *yíros pítta*, stuffed with lamb, tomatoes, onion, salad and a few fries, is the greatest fast food yet invented.

Most underrated resort With five excellent sandy beaches, a fishing village vibe and prices well below Greek-island averages, Finikoúnda in the southern Peloponnese is the ultimate family destination (p.181).

> Our author recommendations don't end here. We've flagged up our favourite places – a perfectly sited hotel, an atmospheric café, a special restaurant – throughout the guide, highlighted with the ★ symbol.

FROM TOP WOMEN IN TRADITIONAL DRESS, ÓLYMBOS, KÁRPATHOS; YÍROS; ÓSIOS LOUKÁS MONASTERY

25

things not to miss

It's not possible to see everything that Greece has to offer in one trip – and we don't suggest you try. What follows, in no particular order, is a selective taste of the region's highlights, including beautiful beaches, outstanding treks and fascinating ancient sites. All highlights have a page reference to take you straight into the Guide, where you can find out more. Coloured numbers refer to chapters in the Guide section.

1 ÍA, SANTORÍNI
Page 441

If there are 1000 things to do before you die, having a sundowner overlooking Santoríni's crater would near the top of the list.

2 SHIPWRECK BAY, ZÁKYNTHOS
Page 761

Lie back and enjoy the unforgettable scenery of one of Greece's poster beaches.

3 THE METÉORA MONASTERIES
Page 240

Rising like ecclesiastical eagles' nests, these monasteries are among the most awe-inspiring religious sites on earth.

4 ÝDHRA
Page 344

The bare granite cliffs of Ýdhra (aka Hydra) soon part to reveal the fabulous horseshoe of its harbour, perhaps the most scenic in Greece.

5 WINE TASTING
Pages 443 & 462

There's much more to Greek wine than dodgy retsina and you should visit at least one vineyard while you're here.

6 KNOSSÓS PALACE, CRETE
Page 459

Restored, vividly coloured and ultimately the most exciting of Crete's Minoan palaces – simply the best.

7 THE PELION PENINSULA
Page 225

Billed as the Greek Tuscany, this region has it all: lush countryside, excellent beaches, character-packed villages and superb treks.

8 NIKOS TAVERNA, MÝKONOS
Page 393

Experience the most frenetic nightlife east of Ibiza at the party capital of the Greek summer.

9 MYSTRA
Page 160

A ghost town that provides a time capsule for the modern tourist to step through to the Byzantine age.

10 SAMARIÁ GORGE, CRETE
Page 501

The 16km descent of this lush and leafy gorge enclosed by towering rock faces is an unforgettable hike.

11 MEZÉDHES
Page 41

For a true taste of Greece, tuck into a mezédhes (meze) platter of starters and dips accompanied by a glass of ouzo or *tsípouro*.

12 THE PRÉSPA LAKES
Page 292

Once a contentious border area, these lakes have been left alone for decades resulting in an almost pristine haven for birdlife.

13 LION GATE AT MYCENAE
Page 136

The imposing relief of lions guarding the main entrance to the Citadel of Mycenae is, incredibly, thirty-odd centuries old.

14 THE ACROPOLIS, ATHENS
Page 65

This small rock with its spectacular ruins is a cultural icon and a symbol of the birth of Western civilization.

15

15 DELPHI
Page 206

Located in an unbeatable natural setting, this ancient site has retained its inscrutable mystique through the centuries.

16 KEFALONIÁ
Page 740

Famous as the setting for *Captain Corelli's Mandolin*, Kefaloniá remains a firm favourite.

17 EASTER
Page 45

The biggest festival in Greece, Easter combines devout Orthodox belief with joyful spring celebrations.

18 WINDSURFING
Page 47

There are very few places on the islands where you can't turn a windy day to your advantage, especially off Lefkádha in the Ionians or Náxos, Páros and Ándhros in the Cyclades.

19 RHODES
Page 514

Once home to the ancient Colossus and the medieval Knights of St John, this is one of the most captivating islands in Greece.

16

17

18

19

Itineraries

Although there are as many itineraries as there are Greek islands, we've put together four inspiring routes. These include a shortlist of the Classical sites, island-hopping in the Cyclades (the ultimate summer experience), a Cretan odyssey and, for Greece aficionados, the road less travelled.

CLASSICAL GREECE

Take your own Grand Tour of Greece's Classical wonders and you'll be a budding archeologist in no time. Each stop tells you something new about one of the world's greatest and most influential civilizations. With your own vehicle, two weeks should be enough to see all these sites.

❶ Athens The birthplace of many of the most famous examples of Classical Greek architecture and home to incredible museums. **See p.56**

❷ Soúnion Watch the sunset from the Temple of Poseidon at the tip of the Attican peninsula and you'll see a view unchanged in centuries. **See p.119**

❸ Kórinthos Visit Ancient Corinth and the fortifications of Acrocorinth, a huge, barren rock crowned by a great fortress. **See p.132**

❹ Mycenae The city that gave its name to a civilization whose Homeric heroes have become household names. **See p.135**

❺ Olympia Sportsground of the ancients whose competitive motto "Faster, higher, longer" is as relevant today as it was then. **See p.187**

❻ Delphi The site of the famous oracle has lost none of its mystique, seamlessly blending into the landscape. **See p.206**

ISLAND-HOPPING

Thanks to quick and frequent ferry links, the Cyclades are the best island group to hop between. While you could do this trip in a couple of weeks, three would allow a more leisurely pace.

❶ Ándhros Green, fertile, culturally exciting and with a fantastic selection of beaches, this is a great introduction to the Cyclades. **See p.381**

❷ Mýkonos Party island for as many sensuous, fun-filled days as your body can take and your wallet can stand. **See p.390**

❸ Páros Choose between island experiences: peaceful hilltop retreats or nonstop happy hours and hangovers. **See p.403**

❹ Náxos The activity centre of the Cyclades, this is the place to go trekking, diving or kitesurfing. **See p.412**

❺ Santoríni It's camera-out time for the unforgettable spectacles around the crater, especially impressive at sunset. **See p.434**

❻ Mílos The place to join a boat ride around the island and swim in some of its inaccessible, kaleidoscopic beaches. **See p.373**

❼ Sérifos Quiet and good value with excellent beaches and a wonderful inland capital, this is a great place to chill out. **See p.364**

THE GREAT ISLAND

Ancient Minoan palaces, beautiful port towns, high mountains and plentiful beaches all make Crete more than just the biggest of the Greek islands. To explore properly, hire a car and give yourself a couple of weeks.

ABOVE ÍA, SANTORÍNI

❶ Haniá The island's sophisticated second city is the gateway to the mountains of the west, as well as a beautiful place to relax and people-watch. **See p.494**

❷ Loutró Accessible only on foot or by boat, Loutró is the perfect escape after you've hiked the Samariá Gorge. **See p.503**

❸ Réthymno A university city with an enchanting old town and a big, sandy beach right in the centre. **See p.483**

❹ Iráklio Crete's capital boasts a world-class archeological museum and is the easiest base from which to explore the ruins at Knossós. **See p.451**

❺ Áyios Nikólaos Home to the finest of Crete's luxury resort hotels, plus great food and nightlife. **See p.470**

❻ Káto Zákros A tiny, isolated seaside hamlet, with a lovely pebble beach and one of the four great Minoan palaces. **See p.480**

THE ROAD LESS TRAVELLED

Central and northern Greece barely feature on travel agent radars, but you'll find perhaps the most "Greek" places here. To really do these quirkier sights justice, you'll need at least two weeks with your own vehicle, longer if you're relying on public transport.

❶ The Pelion Wind your way down the hairpin roads of this spectacular peninsula, discovering lovely villages, quiet beaches and enjoying a beautifully cool climate. **See p.222**

❷ Píndhos Mountains The Píndhos mountain range offers rafting, skiing and one of the country's best treks along the 20km Víkos Gorge. **See p.243**

❸ Préspa Lakes One of Greece's prime locations for diverse birdlife, these peaceful lakes are bordered by several quaint villages where you can sample local lake fish. **See p.292**

❹ Xánthi This delightful town has one of Greece's most established Turkish minorities, as well as a colourful street market. **See p.317**

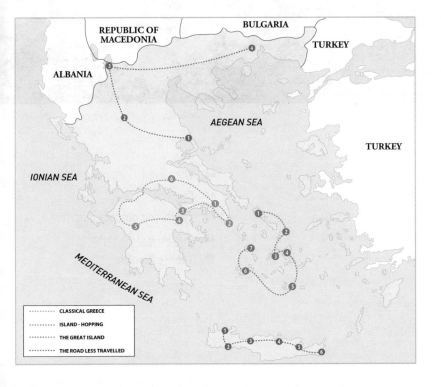

SPINÁLONGA, CRETE

Basics

Getting there

By far the easiest way to get to Greece is to fly, and there are direct flights to a variety of Greek destinations from all major UK airports. Even if your starting point is North America, Australia, New Zealand or South Africa, the most cost-effective route to Greece may well be to get to London, Amsterdam, Frankfurt or another Northern European hub, and pick up an onward flight from there.

Airfares are highest in July, August and during Easter week. But May, June and September are also popular, and since far fewer flights operate in winter, bargains are rare at any time.

Overland alternatives from the UK or Northern Europe involve at least three days of nonstop travel. If you want to take your time over the journey, **driving** or travelling **by train** can be enjoyable, although invariably more expensive than flying. We've included only brief details of these routes here.

When **buying flights** it always pays to shop around and bear in mind that many websites don't include charter or budget airlines in their results. Be aware too that a **package deal**, with accommodation included, can sometimes be as cheap as, or even cheaper than, a flight alone: there's no rule that says you have to use your accommodation every night, or even at all.

Flights from the UK and Ireland

Unless you book far in advance, there are few bargain **fares** to Greece. If you're heading **for Athens**, easyJet (W easyjet.com) can fly you direct **from Gatwick**, **Manchester** or **Edinburgh**, Ryanair (W ryanair.com) from **Stansted**, and Norwegian (W norwegian.com) from Gatwick for less than £50 each way, but you'll have to book early to find fares this cheap. Realistically their prices are little different from those of the traditional operators – British Airways (W britishairways.com) have frequent flights to Athens from **Heathrow**, Aegean (W aegeanair.com) from

Heathrow, Birmingham, Manchester and Edinburgh – and you can expect to pay £75–250 each way at most times of the year. From **Dublin**, Aer Lingus (W aerlingus.com) and Ryanair each have three direct flights a week in mid-summer, fewer in spring and autumn, with fares starting at around €70 each way, though you can easily pay three or four times that. Aer Lingus also flies direct to Corfu, and Ryanair to Haniá (Chania) in Crete.

Regional flights

If your destination is not Athens, or you are flying from a **regional airport**, there's a bewildering variety of options, though most of them operate only in the summer months (May–Sept). Many involve **charter flights**, most of which, in practice, work in much the same way as budget airlines. In addition to the airlines mentioned on p.33 (all of which also have regional flights), the main operators with whom you can book direct are Jet2 (W jet2.com), Thomas Cook (W thomascookairlines. com) and Thomson (W thomson.co.uk); others may be available indirectly, through travel agencies or third-party websites.

There are flights to many of the **Greek regional airports** (see map, pp.30–31) from Heathrow, Gatwick, Stansted, Luton and London City, as well as Birmingham, Bristol, East Midlands, Edinburgh, Glasgow, Leeds Bradford, Liverpool, Manchester and Newcastle. In addition to the obvious island airports, other handy destinations include mainland airports at Kalamáta (for the Peloponnese), Kavála (for Thássos), Vólos (for Mount Pílio and the Sporades) and Préveza (for Lefkádha). Thessaloníki (see p.268), Greece's second city, also has onward domestic connections throughout Greece.

Indirect flights and ferries

If you're heading for the islands, it may cost less to fly from London to Athens (or Thessaloníki) and get a **connecting domestic flight or ferry** (see Getting Around, p.25). Out of season, you may have no choice but to take an **indirect flight** in any case. From regional airports in the UK or from Ireland,

A BETTER KIND OF TRAVEL

At Rough Guides we are passionately committed to travel. We believe it helps us understand the world we live in and the people we share it with – and of course tourism is vital to many developing economies. But the scale of modern tourism has also damaged some places irreparably, and climate change is accelerated by most forms of transport, especially flying. All Rough Guides' flights are carbon-offset, and every year we donate money to a variety of environmental charities.

this usually means flying via London, while a multitude of Greek domestic destinations are accessible on connecting flights or ferries from Athens or Thessaloníki; Greek regional airports and major ferry routes are shown on our map (see p.30).

Flights from the US and Canada

Delta (W delta.com) operates **direct nonstop flights** from New York JFK to Athens, daily for most of the year, while American (W aa.com) flies five times a week from Philadelphia to Athens between May and October. Code-sharing airlines can quote through fares with one of the above, or a European partner, from **virtually every major US city**, connecting either in New York or a European hub such as London or Frankfurt.

Fares vary greatly, so it's worth doing some research on the internet, or using a good travel agent; book as far ahead as possible to get the best price. Round-trip prices range from US$700 out of season to $1400 in high summer; from the west coast, expect to pay ten to twenty percent more. Remember too that you may be better off getting a domestic flight to New York or Philadelphia and heading directly to Athens from there, or flying to London (beware of changing airports) or another European city and travelling on from there.

As with the US, airfares **from Canada** vary depending on where you start your journey and whether you take a direct service. Air Canada Rouge (W aircanada.com) flies daily to Athens out of Toronto and Montreal between May and October, while Air Transat (W airtransat.com) also has summer-only flights two or three times a week from Toronto and Montreal to Athens. Otherwise, you'll have to choose among one- or two-stop itineraries on a variety of European carriers, or perhaps Delta via New York; costs run from Can$800 round-trip in low season from Toronto to more than double that from Vancouver in high season.

Flights from Australia and New Zealand

There are **no direct flights** from Australia or New Zealand to Greece; you'll have to change in Southeast Asia, the Gulf or Europe. Tickets purchased direct from the airlines tend to be expensive; travel agents or Australia-based websites generally offer much better deals on fares and have the latest information on limited specials and stopovers.

Fares **from Australia** start from around Aus$1000, rising to around Aus$2600 depending on season, routing, validity, number of stopovers, etc. The shortest flights and best fares are generally with airlines like Emirates (W emirates.com), in partnership with Qantas (W qantas.com), and Etihad (W etihadairways.com) who fly you directly to Athens from their Gulf hubs, though you'll also find offers on Swiss (W swiss.com), KLM (W klm.com) and other European carriers. **From New Zealand**, prices are slightly higher: from around NZ$1200, rising to over NZ$3000 in high season.

Flights from South Africa

There are currently no direct flights from **South Africa** to Athens. Alternative routes include Emirates (W emirates.com) or Etihad (W etihadairways.com) via the Gulf, EgyptAir (W egyptair.com) via Cairo, or just about any of the major European airlines via their respective domestic hubs. Prices start at around R8000 return for a good low-season deal, to double that in high season or if the cheaper seats have gone.

FLIGHT AGENTS

Charter Flight Centre UK ☎ 020 8714 0010, W charterflights .co.uk. Booking for a huge range of charter flights from the UK and Ireland.
Flight Centre UK ☎ 0870 499 0040, Ireland ☎ 01 695 0365, US ☎ 1877 922 4732, Canada T1877 967 5302, Australia ☎ 133 133, New Zealand ☎ 0800 243 544, South Africa ☎ 0877 405 000; W flightcentre.com. Low-cost airfares worldwide from local agencies, plus rail passes and more.
North South Travel UK ☎ 01245 608 291, W northsouthtravel .co.uk. Friendly, competitive flight agency, offering discounted fares worldwide. Profits are used to support projects in the developing world, especially the promotion of sustainable tourism.
Skyscanner W skyscanner.net. Comprehensive flight search site that includes charter and budget airlines.
STA Travel UK ☎ 0333 321 0099, US ☎ 1800 781 4040, Australia ☎ 134 782, New Zealand ☎ 0800 474 400, South Africa ☎ 0861 781 781; W statravel.com. Worldwide specialists in independent travel; also student IDs, travel insurance, car rental, rail passes, and more. Good discounts for students and under-26s.
Trailfinders UK ☎ 020 7368 1200, Ireland ☎ 01 677 7888; W trailfinders.com. One of the best-informed and most efficient agents for independent travellers.
Travel CUTS Canada ☎ 1800 667 2887, W travelcuts.com. Popular, long-established student-travel organization, with good worldwide offers; not only for students.

Trains

As a result of the economic crisis, **Greek rail routes** have been greatly reduced, and for a while all international services were suspended. Travelling to Greece by train is possible, however, and the most practical route **from Britain** doesn't actually involve any Greek trains; you cross France and Italy by rail before embarking on the **ferry from Bari**, Brindisi, Ancona or Venice to the Ionian islands and Pátra (Patras), from where there are connecting buses to Athens (see box, below). If you're determined to go **all the way by train**, there are a number of routes across Europe to either Belgrade or Sofia, each of which has connections to Thessaloníki, from where you can get an onward train to Athens. The quickest route (though still slower and more expensive than using the ferry from Italy) is via Paris, Munich and Zagreb to Belgrade.

Either way, the journey to Athens from the UK takes **two days** at least and will almost always work out more expensive than flying. It also takes a fair bit of planning, since there's no through train and **tickets** have to be bought from several separate operators. However, you do have the chance to stop over on the way, while with an **InterRail** (for European residents only; W interrail.eu) or **Eurail** (for all others; W eurail.com) pass, you can take in Greece as part of a wider rail trip around Europe. Booking well in advance (essential in summer) and going for the cheapest seats on each leg, you can theoretically buy individual tickets for around £180 each way, to and from London, not including the incidental expenses along the way. Using rail passes will cost you more, but give far more flexibility. For full details, check out the Man in Seat 61 website (W seat61.com).

Car and ferry

Driving to Greece can be a pleasant proposition if you have plenty of time to dawdle along the way,

though fuel, toll and ferry costs ensure it's not a cheap option. It's only worth considering if you want to explore en route, or are going to stay for an extended period. The most popular **route** from the UK is down through France and Italy to catch one of the Adriatic ferries (see box, below); this is much the best way to get to western and southern Greece, the Ionian islands, and to Athens and most of the islands except those in the northeast Aegean. The far longer alternative through Germany, Austria, Slovenia, Croatia, Serbia and the FYROM only makes sense if you're heading to the north, or want to explore northern Greece on the way.

Tour operators

Every mainstream **tour operator** includes Greece in its portfolio. You'll find far more interesting alternatives, however, through the small **specialist agencies**. As well as traditional village-based accommodation and less-known islands, many also offer **walking** or **nature holidays** and other special interests such as **yoga**, **art** and above all **sailing**, with options ranging from shore-based clubs with dinghy tuition, through organized yacht flotillas to bareboat or skippered charters.

PACKAGE OPERATORS

Grecian Tours Australia ☎ 03 9663 3711, W greciantours.com.au. A variety of accommodation and sightseeing tours, plus flights.
Greek Sun Holidays UK ☎ 01732 740317, W greeksun.co.uk. Good-value package holidays mainly in smaller islands of the Dodecanese, northeast Aegean and Cyclades; also tailor-made island-hopping itineraries.
Hidden Greece UK ☎ 020 8758 4707, W hidden-greece.co.uk. Specialist agent putting together tailor-made packages to smaller destinations at reasonable prices.

ITALY–GREECE FERRIES

Sailing from **Italy to Greece**, you've a choice of four ports; ferries run year-round, but services are reduced December to April. The shortest routes and most frequent ferries link Bari and Brindisi with Corfu and other Ionian islands, Igoumenítsa (the port of the western Greek mainland) and Pátra (at the northwest tip of the Peloponnese). Ferries also sail from Venice and Ancona to Pátra via Igoumenítsa/Corfu. These longer routes are more expensive, but the extra cost closely matches what you'll pay in Italian motorway tolls and fuel to get further south. On most ferries, you can stop over in Corfu for no extra charge. For direct access to Athens and the Aegean islands head for Pátra, from where you can cut across country to Pireás.

The following companies operate ferries: schedule and booking details for all of them are also available at W openseas.gr.

ANEK/Superfast W www.anek.gr, W superfast.com. Ancona, Bari and Venice to Corfu, Igoumenítsa and Pátra.
Grimaldi Lines W www.grimaldi-lines.com. Ancona, Brindisi and Venice to Igoumenítsa and Pátra.
Minoan Lines W minoan.gr. Ancona and Venice to Igoumenítsa

and Pátra.
Red Star W albaniaferries.it. Brindisi to Corfu, Paxí, Kefaloniá and Zákynthos, some via Albania.
Ventouris Ferries W ventourisferries.it. Bari to Corfu, Igoumenítsa, Kefaloniá and Zákynthos.

Homeric Tours US ☎ 800 223 5570, ⓦ homerictours.com. Hotel packages, individual tours, escorted group tours and fly-drive deals. Good source of inexpensive flights.

Olympic Holidays UK ☎ 020 8492 6868, ⓦ olympicholidays.com. Huge package-holiday company specializing in Greece; all standards from cheap and cheerful to five-star, and often a good source of last-minute bargains and cheap flights.

Sun Island Tours Australia ☎ 1300 665 673, ⓦ sunislandtours .com.au. Greece specialist offering an assortment of island-hopping, fly-drives, cruises and guided land-tour options, as well as tailor-made.

Sunvil Holidays UK ☎ 020 8758 4758, ⓦ sunvil.co.uk. High-quality outfit with a wide range of holidays to all parts of the mainland and islands.

True Greece US ☎ 1 800 817 7098, ⓦ truegreece.com. Luxury hotels and villas, plus cruises, customized trips, weddings and more.

VILLA AND APARTMENT AGENTS

Cachet Travel UK ☎ 020 8847 8700, ⓦ cachet-travel.co.uk. Attractive range of villas and apartments in the more unspoilt parts of Crete, plus Híos, Sámos, Ikaría and Foúrni.

CV Villas UK ☎ 020 7563 7999, ⓦ cvvillas.com. High-quality villas across Greece, though principally in the Ionian islands and Crete.

Greek Islands Club UK ☎ 020 8232 9780, ⓦ www .gicthevillacollection.com. Specialist in upmarket villas with private pools, especially in the Ionian islands and Sporades.

Ionian Island Holidays UK ☎ 020 8459 0777, ⓦ ionianislandholidays.com. Villas and small hotels, not just in the Ionians but also in the Sporades and mainland.

Oliver's Travels UK ☎ 0800 133 7999, ⓦ oliverstravels.com. Stunning upmarket villas on Mýkonos and Santoríni as well as Crete, the Ionians and mainland.

Pure Crete UK ☎ 01444 880 404, ⓦ purecrete.com. Lovely, converted cottages and farmhouses in western Crete, plus walking, wildlife and other special-interest trips.

Simpson Travel UK ☎ 020 8392 5742, ⓦ simpsontravel.com. Classy villas, upmarket hotels and village hideaways in selected areas of the mainland and on Crete, the Ionians and Skópelos.

SMALL GROUP TOURS, YOGA AND ART HOLIDAYS

Hellenic Adventures US ☎ 1 800 851 6349 ⓦ hellenicadventures.com. Small-group escorted tours led by enthusiastic expert guides, as well as itineraries for independent travellers, cruises and other travel services.

Painting Alonissos UK ☎ 07766 906 483, ⓦ paintingalonissos .com. Painting holidays and art courses on the island of Alónissos.

Skyros Holidays UK ☎ 01983 865566, ⓦ skyros.com. Holistic yoga, dance, art, music, "personal growth" and more on the island of Skýros, as well as well-regarded writers' workshops.

Yoga Escapes UK ☎ 0207 584 9432, ⓦ yoga-escapes.com. Yoga retreats with 5-star accommodation in Mýkonos and Crete.

Yoga Rocks UK ☎ 020 3286 2586, ⓦ yogaholidaysgreece.com. Yoga courses in a beautifully isolated spot in southern Crete.

WALKING AND CYCLING

Classic Adventures US ☎ 800 777 8090, ⓦ classicadventures .com. Spring or autumn rural cycling tours crossing the north Peloponnese to Zákynthos and on Crete.

Cycle Greece US ☎ 800 867 1753, ⓦ cyclegreece.gr. Wide variety of bike tours on the mainland and islands, including cycle cruises, hopping between islands on a traditional sailing boat.

Explore Worldwide US ☎ 1 800 715 1746, Can ☎ 1 888 216 3401, UK ☎ 01252 883 760, Aus ☎ 1300 439 756, NZ ☎ 0800 269 263; ⓦ exploreworldwide.com. A wide variety of tours, many combining hiking with sailing between the islands.

Freewheeling Adventures Canada & US ☎ 800 672 0775, ⓦ freewheeling.ca. Eight-day cycling tours of Crete.

Hooked on Cycling UK ☎ 01506 635 399, ⓦ hookedoncycling .co.uk. Guided and self-guided cycle tours, including island-hopping on a private boat.

Inntravel UK ☎ 01653 617001, ⓦ inntravel.co.uk. Walking holidays to the mainland, Crete, Ionians and Cyclades.

Jonathan's Tours ⓦ guidedwalks.net. Family-run walking holidays on Crete, Corfu, Cyclades and Dodecanese.

Macs Adventure UK ☎ 0141530 5837, US ☎ 1 844 829 3969, ⓦ macsadventure.com. Self-guided walking tours in the Cyclades, Crete and mainland, plus cycling on Rhodes.

No Footprint Greece ☎ 0030 6976 761 492, ⓦ nofootprint.gr. Guided and self-guided walks in the Cyclades, Ionians and on Crete, with a focus on low impact tourism and the environment.

Ramblers Holidays UK ☎ 01707 331133, ⓦ ramblersholidays. co.uk. A huge variety of walking trips including spring hiking in Crete, Dodecanese island-hopping and combined island and mainland treks.

Walking Plus Greece ☎ 0030 22840 92117, US ☎ 347 815 5621, ⓦ walkingplus.co.uk. Guided and self-guided walks in the smaller Cyclades, which can be tailor-made, plus Greek language and culture classes.

WILDLIFE HOLIDAYS

Natural Greece Greece ☎ 0030 2130 46261, ⓦ natural-greece.gr. Birdwatching, bear-spotting, botanical and marine-eco (some including scuba) trips across the country.

Naturetrek UK ☎ 01962 733051, ⓦ naturetrek.co.uk. Fairly pricey but expertly led one- or two-week birdwatching and botanical tours in Crete, the Peloponnese. Lesvós and more.

The Travelling Naturalist UK ☎ 01305 267994, ⓦ naturalist. co.uk. Wildlife holiday company that runs excellent birding and wild-flower-spotting trips to Crete.

SAILING AND WATERSPORTS

Big Blue Swim UK ☎ 0113 216 9434, ⓦ thebigblueswim.com. Open-water swimming around Crete, Lefkádha and Santoríni.

Northwest Passage US ☎ 1 800 732 7328, ⓦ nwpassage.com. Excellent sea-kayaking tours in Crete and the islands; also yoga, climbing and hiking.

Nautilus Yachting UK ☎ 01732 867445, ⓦ nautilusyachting. com. Bareboat yacht charter, flotillas and sailing courses from a wide variety of marinas.

Neilson UK ☎ 0333 014 3351, ⓦ neilson.co.uk. Half a dozen excellent beach activity clubs, plus flotillas and bareboat charter.

Planet Windsurf UK ☎ 01273 921 001, ⓦ planetwindsurfholidays.com. Wind- and kitesurfing trips and instruction on Crete, Kárpathos, Kos, Rhodes, Sámos and Zákynthos, plus mountain-biking.

Seafarer UK ☎ 020 8324 3117, ⓦ seafarercruises.com. Small-boat island cruises, including tall-ship and mega-yacht vessels.

Sportif UK ☎ 01273 844919, ⓦ sportif.travel. Wind- and kitesurfing packages and instruction on Crete, Kos, Mýkonos, Rhodes, Sámos, Lésvos, Límnos and Kárpathos.

Swim Trek UK ☎ 01273 739 713, ⓦ swimtrek.com. Week-long open-water swimming tours in the Cyclades, Crete and Sporades, including the original island-hopping Cyclades trip.

Valef Yachts US ☎ 1 267 404 2415, ⓦ valefyachts.com. Small-boat cruises around the islands and luxury crewed yacht or motorboat charter.

Getting around

The standard overland public transport in Greece is the bus. Train networks are limited, even more so with recent cutbacks. Buses cover most primary routes on the mainland and provide basic connections on the islands. The best way to supplement buses is to rent a scooter, motorbike or car, especially on the islands where – in any substantial town or resort – you will find at least one rental outlet. Inter-island travel involves taking ferries, catamarans or the few remaining hydrofoils, which will eventually get you to any of the sixty-plus inhabited isles. Internal flights are mostly relatively expensive, but can save literally days of travel: Athens–Rhodes is just 2 hours return, versus 28 hours by boat.

By bus

Bus services on **major routes** are efficient and frequent, departing promptly at scheduled departure times. On **secondary roads** they're less regular, with long gaps, but even the remotest villages will be connected once or twice weekly to the provincial capital. On islands there are usually buses to connect the port and main town (if different) for ferry arrivals or departures. The national network is run by a syndicate of private operators based in each county, known as the **KTEL** (*Kratikó Tamío Ellinikón Leoforíon*; ☎ 14505 premium call charge and no national online timetable). In medium-sized or large towns there may be several scattered terminals for services in different directions, so make sure you have the right station for your departure.

From major departure points, **ticketing** is computerized, with assigned seating, and on inter-city lines such as Athens–Pátra buses often get fully booked at the *ekdhotíria* (ticket-issuing office); some regional KTEL companies have online booking, though it's no cheaper than buying from the ticket office on the day. On secondary rural/island routes, it's first-come, first-served, with some standing allowed, and tickets dispensed on the spot by a conductor (*ispráktoras*). Prices are fixed according to distance: Athens–Pátra costs €20.70 one-way, €30 return, though note that return tickets are not always cheaper than two one-way fares.

By train

The Greek mainland's railway network is run by **OSE** (*Organismós Sidherodhrómon Elládhos*; ☎ 14511, ⓦ trainose.gr); with a few exceptions, trains are slower than equivalent buses. However, they can be much cheaper – fifty percent less on non-express services (but much the same on express), even more if you buy a return ticket – and some lines are intrinsically enjoyable, such as the rack-and-pinion service between Dhiakoftó and Kalávryta in the Peloponnese (see p.197).

Timetables are available online or at station schedule boards or information counters. If you're starting a journey at a station with computerized facilities you can (at no extra cost) **reserve a seat**; a carriage and seat number will be printed on your ticket.

There are two basic **classes**: first and second, the latter about 25 percent cheaper, while first class includes a meal on certain routes. Express trains, called **Intercity** (IC on timetables), run between Alexandhroúpoli, Thessaloníki, Vólos, Kalambáka and Athens, though part of the line between Alexandhroúpoli and Thessaloníki is currently closed and served by replacement buses; also, if the line upgrade is ever completed, Pátra and Kalamáta, although currently all trains on this route terminate at Kiáto, with bus transfers completing the journey.

A second-class ticket on the IC service between Athens and Thessaloníki costs €45.40 in person, €34.70 online, with occasional much cheaper deals. The slower overnight train costs €25.10 (€19.20 online) for a seat, €47 (€41 online) for a sleeper.

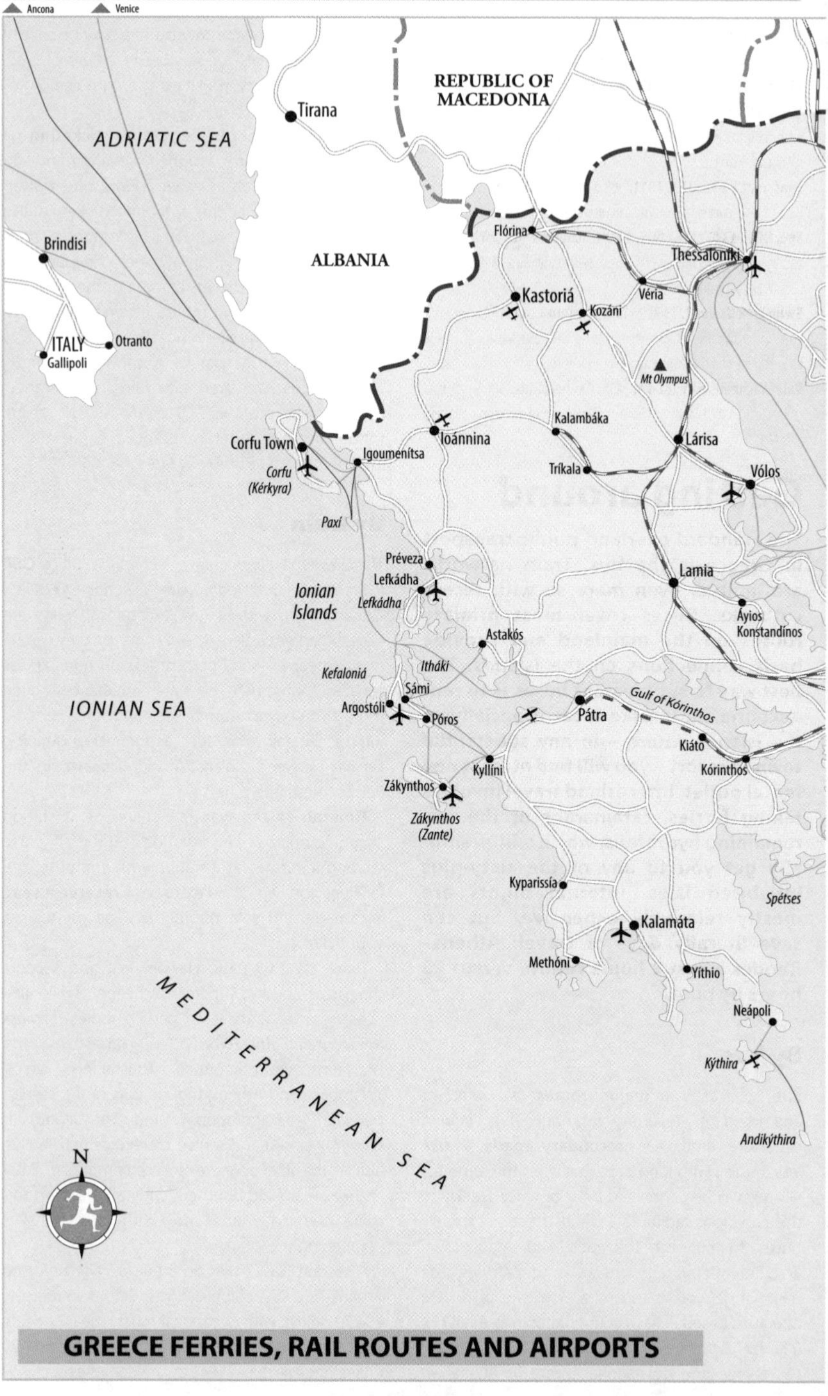

Ancona   Venice

Bari

ADRIATIC SEA

Tirana

REPUBLIC OF
MACEDONIA

ALBANIA

Brindisi

Flórina

Thessaloníki

Kastoriá

Kozáni

Véria

ITALY
Gallipoli

Otranto

Mt Olympus

Corfu Town

Igoumenítsa

Ioánnina

Kalambáka

Lárisa

Corfu
(Kérkyra)

Tríkala

Vólos

Paxí

Préveza

Lamía

Lefkádha

Ionian
Islands

Lefkádha

Áyios
Konstandínos

Astakós

Itháki

Kefaloniá

Sámi

Gulf of Kórinthos

IONIAN SEA

Argostóli

Pátra

Póros

Kiáto

Kyllíni

Kórinthos

Zákynthos

Zákynthos
(Zante)

Kyparissía

Spétses

Kalamáta

Methóni

Yíthio

Neápoli

Kýthira

N

Andikýthira

MEDITERRANEAN SEA

GREECE FERRIES, RAIL ROUTES AND AIRPORTS

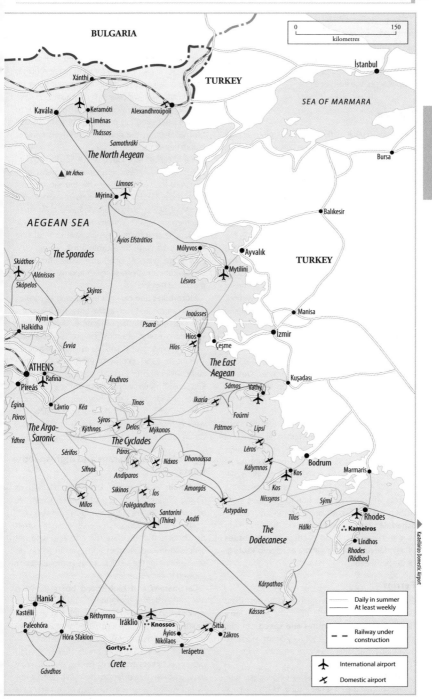

Tickets issued on board carry a fifty-percent penalty charge; by contrast, under-26s and over-60s get 25 percent **discounts** at off-peak seasons for non-express trains. **InterRail** and **Eurail pass holders** must secure reservations, and pay express supplements, like everyone else.

By sea

There are several varieties of sea-going vessels: **ordinary ferries**, which never exceed 17 knots; "**high-speed**" boats (*tahyplóö*) and catamarans, which usually carry cars, and are capable of reaching 27 knots; **hydrofoils**, similarly quick but which carry only passengers; **roll-on-roll-off** short-haul barges, nicknamed *pandófles* ("slippers"); and local **kaïkia**, small boats which do short hops and excursions in season.

Ferry connections are indicated both on the route **map** (see pp.30–31) and in the "Arrival and Departure" sections throughout this book, though the ongoing economic crisis means some minor routes are sometimes discontinued without warning. Schedules are also notoriously erratic and must be verified seasonally; details given are for departures between late June and early September. When sailing in season from **Pireás** to the Cyclades or Dodecanese, you should have a choice of at least two, sometimes three, daily departures. **Out-of-season** departure frequencies drop sharply, with less populated islands connected only two or three times weekly.

Reliable departure information is available from the local **port police** (*limenarhío*) at all island and mainland harbours of any size; around Athens there are offices at Pireás (☎210 455 0000), Rafína (☎22940 28888) and Lávrio (☎22920 25249). Busier port police have automated phone-answering services with an English option for schedule information. Many companies produce annual **schedule** booklets, which may not be adhered to as the season wears on – check their **websites** (if any) for current information, or refer to ⓦgtp.gr or ⓦopenseas.gr.

Ferries

Except for some subsidized peripheral routes where older rust-buckets are still used, the Greek **ferry fleet** is fairly modern. **Routes and speed** can vary enormously, however; a journey from Pireás to Santoríni, for instance, can take anything from five to ten hours.

Tickets are best bought a day before departure, unless you need to reserve a cabin berth or space for a car. During holiday periods – Christmas/New Year, the week before and after Easter, late July to early September – and around the dates of elections, ferries need to be booked at least ten days in advance. Ticketing for most major routes is computerized and you cannot **buy** your ticket on board, although booths on the quay sell last-minute tickets. Many companies allow you to reserve places and pay online, but tickets must still be picked up at the port at least fifteen minutes before departure.

The cheapest **fare class**, which you'll automatically be sold unless you specify otherwise, is *ikonomikí thési*, which gives you the run of most boats except for the upper-class restaurant and bar. Most newer boats seem designed to frustrate summertime travellers attempting to sleep on deck. For long overnight journeys, it's worth considering the few extra euros for a **cabin bunk**; second-class cabins are typically quadruple, while **first-class** double cabins with en-suite bathrooms can cost as much as a flight.

Motorbikes and cars get issued separate tickets, which can cost as much as five times the passenger fare, depending on size and journey duration – the shortest crossings are most expensive in comparison to a passenger ticket. For example, Keramotí–Thássos is €3.50 per person/€18 per car, while Sámos–Ikaría costs €10/€35 and Sámos–Pireás is €38.50/€80. It's really only worth taking a car to the larger islands like Crete, Rhodes, Híos, Lésvos, Sámos, Corfu or Kefaloniá, and only if staying a week or more. Otherwise, it is cheaper to leave your car on the mainland and rent another on arrival.

Hydrofoils, catamarans and high-speed boats

Hydrofoils – commonly known as *dhelfínia* or "Flying Dolphins" – are at least twice as expensive as ordinary ferries, although their network has been drastically reduced in recent years. The other drawback is that they are the first vessels to get cancelled in bad weather and even in moderate seas are not for the seasick-prone. Hydrofoils aren't allowed to carry scooters or bicycles.

Catamarans and high-speed boats (*tahýplia*) are ruthlessly air-conditioned, usually without deck seating and with Greek TV blaring at you from multiple screens – paying extra for *dhiakrikriméni thési* (upper class) merely gets you a better view. Car fares are the same as on the ferries, though passenger **tickets** are at least double a comparable ferry journey, ie similar to hydrofoil rates. Most hydrofoils and catamarans don't run October–April.

Small boats

In season, small boats known as **kaïkia** and **small ferries** sail between adjacent islands and to a few of the more obscure satellite islets. These are extremely useful and often very pleasant, but seldom cheaper than mainline services. The more consistent *kaïki* links are noted in the text, though the only firm information is to be had on the quayside. Swarms of **taxi boats** are a feature of many islands; these shuttle clients on set routes to remote beaches or ports which can only be reached arduously, if at all, overland. Costs on these can be pretty stiff, usually per person but occasionally per boat.

By plane

Scheduled Greek **domestic flights** are run by the merged partnership of Olympic Air (☎ 801 801 0101, ⓦ olympicair.com) and Aegean Airlines (☎ 801 112 0000, ⓦ aegeanair.com), as well as minor operators Sky Express (☎ 2810 223 800, ⓦ skyexpress.gr), Ellinair (☎ 2311 224 700; ⓦ ellinair.com), Astra Airlines (☎ 2310 489 390, ⓦ astra-airlines.gr) and Ryanair (ⓦ ryanair.com). Together they cover a broad network of island and mainland destinations, though most routes, especially on Aegean/Olympic, are to and from Athens or Thessaloníki. All four airlines are geared to web and call-centre **e-ticket sales**, as there are few walk-in town offices. Tickets bought through travel agencies attract a minimum €10 commission charge.

Fares to/between the islands usually cost at least double the price of a deck-class ferry journey, but on inter-island routes poorly served by boat (Rhodes–Sámos, for example), consider this time well bought, and indeed some subsidized peripheral routes cost less than a hydrofoil/catamaran journey.

Island flights are often full in peak season, so make **reservations** at least a month in advance. Waiting lists exist and are worth signing on to, as there are almost always cancellations. Small prop planes, which won't fly in strong winds or (in some cases) after dark, are used on many routes to less popular destinations. A 15kg baggage **weight limit** can be strictly enforced; if, however, you are connecting with an international flight or purchased your ticket outside Greece, you're allowed the standard 20–23kg limit.

By car, motorcycle and taxi

Greece is blessed with dramatic mountain and coastal scenery, which is undoubtedly a joy to drive through. You should, however, bear in mind that it has one of the highest fatal **accident rates** in Europe. Local driving habits can be atrocious; overtaking on bends, barging out from side roads and failing to signal manoeuvres are common practices. **Drunk driving** is also a major issue, especially on Sunday afternoons, public holidays or late at night.

Road conditions can be very poor, from bad surfaces and inadequate signposting to unmarked railway crossings. There is a limited but growing number of **motorways** on which tolls (€2–3) are levied, adding over €30, for example, on the drive from Athens to Thessaloníki. **Fuel**, whether regular unleaded (*amólyvdhi*), super or diesel, is currently over €1.50 per litre across the country, often €1.70-plus in remoter areas. Be aware that many petrol stations close after 8pm and on Sundays.

Parking in almost every mainland town, plus the biggest island centres, is uniformly a nightmare. **Pay-and-display** systems, plus residents-only schemes, are common, and it's often unclear where to obtain tickets.

Rules of the road

You **drive on the right** in Greece. Uphill drivers demand their **right of way**, as do the first to approach a one-lane bridge; **flashed headlights** usually mean the opposite of what they do in the UK or North America, here signifying that the other driver insists on coming through or overtaking. However, this gesture rapidly repeated from someone approaching means they're warning you

---

FIVE SCENIC DRIVES

Kefaloniá's west coast The route north from Argostóli allows vistas of the Lixoúri Peninsula, Mýrtos beach and picturesque Ássos; see p.747.

Sithonía circuit Making the clockwise circuit of Sithonía keeps imposing Mount Áthos in view for half the way; see p.301.

Arcadian mountains The Peloponnese is at its most bucolic on the drive through the Arcadian mountains west of Trípoli; see p.174.

Píndhos mountains The mountains and villages north of Ioánnina offer scenic splendour; see p.243.

Mount Psilorítis, Crete Drive via Anóyia and Margarítes for sweeping views of the fertile valleys around Mount Psilorítis; see p.469.

of a police control-point ahead. Bizarrely, there is no national law about who has the right of way at **roundabouts** – more often than not it is the vehicle entering the round-about, but proceed with care.

Seat-belt use (and wearing a helmet on scooters and motorcycles) is compulsory, and children under the age of 10 are not allowed to sit in the front seats of cars; infractions of these rules are punishable by fines. It's illegal to drive away from any kind of **accident** – or to move the vehicles before the police appear – and where serious injury has resulted to the other party you can be held at a police station for up to 24 hours.

Car rental

Car rental in Greece starts at around €250 a week in peak season for the smallest vehicle from a one-off outlet or local chain, including unlimited mileage, tax and insurance. At other times, at smaller local outfits, you can pay €25–30 a day, all inclusive, with even better **rates** for three days or more – or prebooked on the internet. Rates for open **jeeps** vary from €60 to €90 per day.

Rental prices in Greece almost never include **collision damage waiver** (CDW) and personal insurance. The CDW typically has a deductible charge of €400–700, which may be levied for even the tiniest scratch or missing mudguard. To avoid this, it is strongly recommended that you pay the €6–9 extra per day for full coverage. Frequent EU-based travellers should consider **annual excess insurance** through Insurance 4 Car Hire (Ⓦ insurance4carhire.com).

Most major agencies require a **credit card** to swipe as a deposit, though smaller companies on the islands may ask for cash payment upfront; minimum **age requirements** vary from 21 to 23. **Driving licences** issued by any European Economic Area state are honoured, but an **International Driving Permit** is required by all other drivers (despite claims by unscrupulous agencies). You can be arrested and charged if caught by the traffic police without an IDP, if required.

Avance, Antena, Auto Union, Payless, Kosmos, National/Alamo, Reliable, Tomaso and Eurodollar are dependable Greek, or smaller international, chains with branches in many towns; all are cheaper than Hertz, Sixt or Avis. Specific local recommendations are given in the Guide.

Bringing your own car

If you intend to **drive your own car to and within Greece**, remember that insurance contracted in any EU state is valid in any other, but in many cases this is only third-party cover. Competition in the industry is intense, however, so many UK insurers will throw in full, pan-European cover for free or for a nominal sum, for up to sixty days. Those with proof of AA/RAC/AAA membership are given free road assistance from ELPA, the Greek equivalent, which runs **breakdown services** on several of the larger islands; in an emergency ring ☎ 10400.

EU citizens bringing their own cars are free to drive in Greece for six months, or until their home-based road tax or insurance expires, whichever is first; keeping a car in Greece for longer entails more paperwork. **Non-EU nationals** will get a car entered in their passport; the carnet normally allows you to keep a vehicle in Greece for up to six months, exempt from road tax.

Scooter and motorcycle rental

Small **motor scooters** with automatic transmission, known in Greek as *mihanákia* or *papákia* (little ducks), are good transport for all but the steepest terrain. They're available for rent on many islands and in a few of the popular mainland resorts for €12–18 per day. Prices can be bargained down out of peak season, or for a longer rental period. Only models of 80cc and above are powerful enough for two riders in mountainous areas, which includes most islands.

True **motorbikes** (*mihanés*) with manual transmissions and safer tyres are less common. With the proper licence, bikes of 125cc and up are available in many resorts for around €20 per day. **Quads** are also increasingly offered – without doubt the most stupid-looking and impractical transport yet devised, and very unstable on turns – make sure helmets are supplied.

Reputable establishments demand a full **motorcycle driving licence** (Class B) for any engine over 80cc and sometimes even for 50cc models, which is the official legal requirement. You will sometimes have to leave your passport as a deposit. Failure to carry the correct licence on your person also attracts a stiff fine, though some agencies still demand this rather than a passport as security.

Many rental outfits will offer you (an often ill-fitting) **crash helmet** (*krános*), and some will make you sign a waiver of liability if you refuse it. Helmet-wearing is required by law, with a €185 fine for failure to do so; on some smaller islands the rule is laxly enforced, on others random police roadblocks do a brisk business in citations, to foreigners and locals alike.

Before riding off, always check the **brakes** and **electrics**; dealers often keep the front brakes far too loose, with the commendable intention of preventing you going over the handlebars. Make sure also that there's a kick-start as backup to the battery, since ignition switches commonly fail.

Taxis

Greek **taxis** are among the cheapest in the Mediterranean – so long as you get an honest driver who switches the meter on and doesn't use high-tech devices to doctor the reading. Use of the meter is mandatory within city or town limits, where Tariff 1 applies, while in rural areas or between midnight and 5am Tariff 2 is levied. On certain islands, set rates apply on specific fixed routes – these might only depart when full. Otherwise, throughout Greece the meter starts at €1.20, though the minimum **fare** is €3.40 (€3.16 in Athens and Thessaloníki). Baggage in the boot is charged at €0.40 per piece. Additionally, there are surcharges of €2.60–3.84 for leaving or entering an airport, and €1.07 for leaving a harbour area. If you summon a taxi by phone on spec, there's a €1.92 charge; the meter starts running from the moment the driver begins heading towards you. All categories of supplemental charges must be set out on a card affixed to the dashboard. For a week or so before and after Orthodox Easter, and Christmas, a *filodhórima* (gratuity) of about ten percent is levied.

By bike

Cycling in Greece is not such hard going as you might imagine (except in summer), especially on one of the mountain bikes that are now the rule at rental outfits; they rarely cost more than €8 a day. You do, however, need steady nerves, as roads are generally narrow with no verges or bike lanes, and Greek drivers are notoriously inconsiderate to cyclists.

If you have your own bike, consider taking it along by **train** or **plane** (it's free if within your 20–23kg international air allowance, but arrange it in writing with the airline beforehand to avoid huge charges at check-in). Once in Greece, you can take a bike for free on most ferries, in the guard's van on most trains (for a small fee), and in the luggage bays of buses. Bring any small spare parts, since specialist shops are rare.

Accommodation

There are vast numbers of beds available for tourists in Greece, and most of the year you can rely on simply turning up pretty much anywhere and finding something. At Easter and in July and August, however, you can run into problems unless you've booked in advance. The economic crisis and subsequent loss of domestic tourism has tended to depress prices, and what you pay may depend on how far you are willing to bargain.

In cities and mainland towns you'll probably stay in **hotels**, but in the resorts and islands the big hotels and self-catering complexes are mostly pre-booked by package-holiday companies for the whole season. Non-package visitors are more likely to find themselves staying in smaller, simpler places which usually describe themselves simply as "**rooms**", or as apartments or studios. Standards here can vary from spartan (though invariably clean) to luxurious, but the vast majority are purpose-built blocks where every room is air-conditioned, and where the minimal furnishings are well adapted to the local climate – at least in summer.

Seasons

There are typically three **seasons** which affect prices: October to April (low), May, June and September (mid) and July and August (high), while **Easter** and the first two weeks of August may be in a higher category still. Urban hotels with a predominantly business clientele tend to charge the same rates all year. Elsewhere, places that have significant domestic tourism, such as Náfplio, the Pelion or the Argo-Saronic islands, frequently charge significantly more at weekends.

Many of the smaller places offering rooms **close from October to April**, so in winter you may have to stay in hotels in the main towns or ports. On smaller islands, there may be just one hotel and a single taverna open year-round.

Hotels

The tourist police set official **star categories** for hotels, from five-star down; all except the top category have to keep within set price limits. You may still see the old letter system (L, luxury, is five-star, then A to E). Ratings correspond to the facilities available (lifts, dining room, pool etc), a box-ticking exercise which doesn't always reflect the actual quality of the hotel; there are plenty of 2-star hotels which are in practice smarter and more comfortable than 3-star outfits. A "boutique" category allows some hotels to escape the straitjacket on the grounds of location or historical significance.

ACCOMMODATION PRICES AND BOOKING

The price we quote is for the establishment's **cheapest double room in mid-season** – there may well be other rooms that cost more. Depending on where you are, the price may rocket in the first two weeks of August, sometimes by as much as double: for much of the year, however, you can expect to pay a bit less. In rooms establishments and the cheaper hotels, the price of a basic double room starts at around €20–25 a night out of season, though the same room may be €50 or more in August. For a bit more luxury and in more touristy areas, you'll probably be paying €40–50 in mid-season, €70–90 if you add a pool and other facilities; 5-star hotels charge €200 and above. In practice, the price is highly flexible, especially if you call direct or just turn up: if there's a spare room, they'll try to fill it.

By law, **prices must be displayed** on the back of the door of your room, or over the reception desk. You should never pay more than this, and in practice it is rare to pay as much as the sign says. If you feel you're being overcharged, threaten to make a report to the tourist office or police, who will generally take your side in such cases. The price is for the room only, except where otherwise indicated; fancier places often include breakfast in the price – we indicate this in the listing, but check when booking.

All the usual **online booking** engines operate in Greece, including Airbnb, and the majority of places have their own online booking. Even on Airbnb, most of the properties in tourist areas are regular commercial rooms or apartments: in theory, all accommodation has to be registered and pay tax. The vast majority of hoteliers prefer you to book direct, however, rather than pay commission to a third party, and will often offer a better deal for direct bookings.

Hotels with 2-star and below have only to provide the most rudimentary of continental **breakfasts** – sometimes optional for an extra charge – while 3-star and above will usually offer buffets with cheese, cold meats, eggs and cereals.

Single rooms are rare, and generally poor value – you'll often have to pay the full double-room price or haggle for a small discount; on the other hand, larger groups and families can almost always find triple and quadruple rooms, and more upmarket hotels may have **family suites** (two rooms sharing one bathroom), all of which can be very good value.

Private rooms and apartments

Many places categorized as apartments or rooms are every bit as comfortable as hotels, and in the lower price ranges are usually more congenial and better value. Traditionally, **rooms** (*dhomátia* – but usually marked by a "Rooms for Rent" or "Zimmer Frei" sign) were literally a room in someone's house, a bare space with a bed and a hook on the back of the door, where the sparse facilities were offset by the disarming hospitality you'd be offered as part of the family. Such places are now rare, however, and these days almost all are purpose-built (though many still family-run), with comfortable en-suites, air-conditioning and balconies – at the fancier end of the scale you'll find studio and apartment complexes with marble floors, pools, bars and children's playgrounds. Many have a variety of rooms at different prices, so ask to see the room first. Places described as **studios** usually have a small kitchenette, while **apartments** generally have at least one bedroom and separate kitchen/living room.

If you haven't already booked a room, you may find owners descending on ferry or bus arrivals to fill any space they have, sometimes with photos of their premises. This can be great, though you may find the rooms are much further than you had been led to believe, or bear no relation to the pictures. In some places, the practice has been outlawed. In the more developed island resorts, room owners may insist on a **minimum stay** of a few days, or even a week, especially in high season.

Rooms proprietors sometimes ask to keep your **passport**: ostensibly "for the tourist police", but in reality to prevent you leaving with an unpaid bill. They'll almost always return the documents should you ask for them.

Villas and longer-term rentals

Although one of the great dreams of Greek travel is finding an idyllic coastal villa and renting it for virtually nothing for a whole month, there's no chance at all of your dream coming true in modern Greece. All the best **villas** are contracted out to **agents** and let through **foreign operators**. Even if you do find one empty for a week or two, renting it locally usually costs far more than it would have done to arrange from home. There, specialist

---

AIR CONDITIONING, WI-FI AND HOT WATER

When checking out a room, always ask about the status of **air conditioning** and **hot water**. Almost all modern rooms and apartments have air conditioning (indicated by a/c in our listings), but it's sometimes an optional extra, in which case you'll be charged an additional €5 or so a night to use it. Hot water is always theoretically available, though there may not always be enough: rooftop solar heaters are popular and effective, but shared solar-powered tanks tend to run out in the post-beach shower crunch around 6–7pm, with no more available until the next day. A water heater, either as a backup or primary source, is more reliable. **Wi-fi** is ubiquitous, and almost always free – even the most basic places tend to have it, though the signal may not extend to every room, and it's often pretty slow.

---

operators (see p.27) represent some superb places, from simple to luxurious, and costs can be very reasonable, especially if shared between a few people.

However, if you do arrive and decide you want to drop roots for a while, you can still strike lucky if you don't mind avoiding the obvious coastal tourist spots, and are happy with relatively modest accommodation. Choose an untouristed village, get yourself known and ask about; you might still pick up a wonderful deal. **Out of season**, your chances are much better – even in touristy areas, between October and March (sometimes as late as April and May) you can bargain a very good rate, especially for stays of a month or more. **Travel agents** are a good source of information on what's available locally, and many rooms places have an apartment on the side or know someone with one to rent.

Hostels and backpackers

Over the years, most traditional youth **hostels** in Greece have closed down; competition from inexpensive rooms meant that they were simply not as cost-effective as elsewhere in Europe. However, those that survive are generally very good, and there's a new generation of youth-oriented **backpackers**, in the cities and more popular islands, big on social life and a party atmosphere. Few of them are members of any official organization – though an IYHF card or student ID may save you a few euros – and virtually none will have a curfew or any restrictive regulations. Prices for a dorm bed vary from €12 in a simple, traditional hostel to as much as €30 in high season in the fancier Athenian or island backpackers.

If you're planning to spend a few nights in hostels, **IYHF membership** is probably worthwhile. By no means all Greek hostels offer discounts, but there are other membership benefits – the card may be accepted as student ID, for example. You may be able to buy membership at official hostels;

otherwise, you can join at ⓦhihostels.com (and book official hostels) or apply via your local youth hostel association. To book hostels online try ⓦhostelworld.com, though note that many of the places on there are simply rooms, and not formal hostels.

Monasteries

Greek **monasteries** and **convents** have a tradition of putting up travellers (of the appropriate sex). On the mainland, this – steadily decreasing – practice is used mostly by villagers on pilgrimage; on the islands, monastic hospitality is less common, so check locally before heading out to a monastery for the night. Also, **dress modestly** – no shorts or short skirts – and try to **arrive early** in the evening, not later than 8pm or sunset (whichever is earlier). For men, the most exciting monastic experience is a visit to the "Monks' Republic" of Mount Áthos (see p.306), on the Halkidhikí peninsula, near Thessaloníki. This is, however, a far from casual travel option, involving a significant amount of advance planning and the securing of a permit.

Camping

Partly thanks to the economic crisis, Greek **camping** has undergone something of a revival in recent years. **Officially recognized campsites** range from ramshackle compounds on the islands to highly organized and rather soulless complexes, often dominated by camper vans. Most places cost in the region of €5–7 a night per person, plus €4–6 per tent and the same again for a car, or €7–10 per camper van; at the fanciest sites, rates for two people plus a tent can almost equal the price of a basic room. You will need at least a light sleeping bag, since even summer nights can get cool and damp. The website of the official Greek camping organization (ⓦwww.greececamping.gr) lists all authorized campsites, with booking for many of them.

SIX SPECIAL PLACES TO STAY

Kinsterna, Áyios Stéfanos, Monemvasiá An Ottoman judge's farmhouse around an old cistern, converted into a spa eco-retreat. See p.151

Kyrimai, Yeroliménas, Peloponnese An 1860s trading post and manor house turned into a unique luxury hotel. See p.170

Papaevangelou Hotel, Megálo Pápingo, Zagóri Traditional comfort brought up to date in a beautiful high mountain village. See p.254

Mount Áthos monasteries Though just for male visitors, staying with the monks here is an unforgettable experience. See p.309

Imaret, Kavála Beautifully converted medrese with pool, massage spa and original Ottoman features. See p.316

Kokkini Porta Rossa, Rhodes Six exquisite luxury suites in a tastefully renovated Turkish mansion; wonderful breakfast using local produce too. See p.522

Camping **outside an official campsite** (with or without a tent) is against the law – enforced in most tourist areas and on beaches. If you do camp rough, exercise sensitivity and discretion. Police will crack down on people camping (and especially littering) if a large community of campers develops. Off the beaten track nobody is very bothered, though it is always best to ask permission in the local taverna or café, and to be aware of rising crime, even in rural areas. If you want to camp near a beach, the best strategy is to find a sympathetic taverna, which in exchange for regular patronage will probably be willing to guard small valuables and let you use their facilities.

Food and drink

Although many visitors get by on moussaka or kalamári almost every night, there is a huge range to Greek cuisine, not least its wonderful mezédhes, seafood and juicy, fat olives. Despite depressed wages, most Greeks still eat out with friends or family at least once a week. The atmosphere is always relaxed and informal, with pretensions rare. Drinking is traditionally meant to accompany food, though a range of bars and clubs exists.

Breakfast

Greeks don't generally eat **breakfast**, more often opting for a mid-morning snack (see below). This is reflected in the abysmal quality of most hotel "continental" offerings, where waxy orange squash, stewed coffee, processed cheese and meats, plus pre-packaged butter, honey and jam (confusingly

called *marmeládha*), are the rule at all but the top establishments. There might be some fresh fruit, decent yoghurt and pure honey, if you are lucky. The only egg-and-bacon kinds of places are in resorts where foreigners congregate, or where there are returned North American- or Australian-Greeks. Such outlets can often be good value (€4–7 for the works, including coffee), especially if there's competition.

Picnics and snacks

Picnic ingredients are easily available at supermarkets, bakeries and greengrocers; sampling produce like cheese or olives is acceptable. Standard white **bread** is often of minimal nutritional value and inedible within a day of purchase, although rarer brown varieties such as *olikís* (wholemeal), *sikalísio* (rye bread) or *oktásporo* (multi-grain) fare better. Olives are ubiquitous; the Kalamáta and Ámfissa varieties usually surpass most local picks in quality.

Honey is the ideal topping for the famous local **yoghurt**, which is widely available in bulk. Sheep-milk yoghurt (*próvio*) is richer and sweeter than the more common cow's-milk. **Feta cheese** is found everywhere, often with a dozen varieties to choose from, made from goat's, sheep's or cow's milk in varying proportions. Harder *graviéra* is the second most popular cheese.

Greece imports very little produce from abroad, aside from bananas, the odd pineapple and a few mangoes. **Fruit** is relatively expensive and mainly available seasonally. Reliable picnic fruits include cherries (June–July); *krystália*, small, heavenly green pears (Sept–Nov); *vaniliés*, orange- or red-fleshed plums (July–Oct); and kiwi (Oct–May). Less portable, but succulent, are figs (mainly Aug–Sept). Salad **vegetables** are more reasonably priced; besides the famous, enormous tomatoes (June–Sept), there's a bewildering variety of cool-season greens, including rocket, dill, enormous spring onions and lettuces.

Restaurants

Greek cuisine and **restaurants** are usually straightforward and still largely affordable – typically €12–20 per person for a substantial meal with plenty of house wine. Even when preparation is basic, raw materials are usually wholesome and fresh. The best strategy is to **go where Greeks go**, often less obvious backstreet places that might not look much from outside but deliver the real deal. The two most common types of restaurant are the **estiatório** and the **taverna**. The main distinction is that the former is more commonly found in large towns and emphasizes the more complicated, oven-baked casserole dishes termed **mayireftá** (literally, "cooked").

As one might expect, the identikit tavernas at resorts dominated by foreigners tend to make less effort, bashing out speedily grilled meat with pre-cut chips and rice containing the odd pea. You should beware of **overcharging** and bill-padding at such establishments too. In towns, growing numbers of pretentious restaurants boast fancy decor and Greek nouvelle (or fusion) cuisine with speciality wine lists, while producing little of substance.

Greeks generally eat very late in the evening, rarely venturing out until after 9pm and often arriving at midnight or later. Consequently, most restaurants operate flexible hours, varying according to the level of custom, and thus the

FAST FOOD GREEK STYLE

Traditional hot **snacks** are still easy to come by, although they are being elbowed aside by Western fast food at both international and nationwide Greek chains such as *Goody's* (burgers, pasta and salad bar), *Everest*, *Grigoris* and *Theios Vanias* (baked pastries and baguette sandwiches), and various pizzerias. Still, thousands of kebab shops (*souvladzídhika*) churn out *souvlákia*, either as small shish on wooden sticks or as *yíros* – doner kebab with garnish in *pítta* bread. Other snacks include cheese pies (*tyrópites*), spinach pies (*spanokópites*) and, less commonly, minced-meat pies (*kreatópites*); these are found either at the baker's or some of the aforementioned chains.

opening times given throughout the listings should be viewed as approximate at best.

Estiatória

With their long hours and tiny profit margins, **estiatória** (sometimes known as *inomayiría*, "wine-and-cook-houses") are, alas, a vanishing breed. An *estiatório* will generally feature a variety of *mayireftá* such as moussaka, *pastítsio* (macaroni pie), meat or game stews, stuffed tomatoes or peppers, the oily vegetable casseroles called *ladherá*, plus oven-baked meat and fish. Usually you point at the steam trays to choose these dishes. Batches are cooked in the morning and then left to stand, which is why the food is often **lukewarm**; most such dishes are in fact enhanced by being allowed to steep in their own juice.

Tavernas and psistariés

Tavernas range from the glitzy and fashionable to rough-and-ready beachside ones with seating under a reed canopy. Really primitive ones have a very limited (often unwritten) menu, but the more elaborate ones will offer some of the main *mayireftá* dishes mentioned above, as well as standard taverna fare: **mezédhes** (hors d'oeuvres) or **orektiká** (appetizers) and **tis óras** (meat and fish, fried or grilled to order). **Psistariés** (grill-houses) serve spit-roasted lamb, pork, goat, chicken or *kokorétsi* (grilled offal roulade), and often *yíros* by the portion. They will usually have a limited selection of mezédhes and salads (*salátes*), but no *mayireftá*. In rural areas, roadside *psistariés* are often called *exohiká kéndra*.

The most common **mezédhes** are tzatzíki (yoghurt, garlic and cucumber dip), melitzanosa-láta (aubergine/eggplant dip), tyrokafterí/khtypití/kopanistí (spicy cheese dips), fried courgette/zucchini or aubergine/eggplant slices, yígandes (white haricot beans in hot tomato sauce), tyropi-tákia or spanakopitákia (small cheese or spinach pies), revythokeftédhes (chickpea patties similar to falafel), octopus salad and mavromátika (black-eyed peas).

Among **meats**, souvláki and chops are reliable choices; pork is usually better and cheaper than veal, especially as *pantséta* (pork belly). The best souvláki, not always available, is lamb; more commonly encountered are rib chops (*païdhákia*); lamb roasted in tin foil (*exohikó*) is another favourite. Keftédhes (breadcrumbed meatballs), biftékia (pure-meat patties) and the spicy, coarse-grain sausages called loukánika are cheap and good. Chicken is widely available but typically battery-farmed. Other

TAVERNA TIPS

Since the idea of **courses** is foreign to Greek cuisine, starters, main dishes and salads often arrive together unless you request otherwise. The best strategy is to order a selection of mezédhes and salads to share, in local fashion. Waiters encourage you to take *horiátiki saláta* – the so-called Greek **salad**, including feta cheese – because it is the most expensive. If you only want tomato and cucumber, ask for *angourodomáta*. Cabbage-carrot (*láhano-karóto*) and lettuce (*maroúli*) are the typical cool-season salads.

Bread is generally counted as part of the "cover" charge (€0.50–1 per person), so you have to pay for it even if you don't eat any. Though menu prices are supposedly inclusive of all taxes and service, an extra **tip** of around five percent or simple rounding up of the bill is a decent gesture if you've had good service.

dishes worth trying are stewed goat (*yídha vrastí*) or baked goat (*katsíki stó foúrno*) – goat in general is typically free-range and organic.

Fish and seafood

Seafood can be one of the highlights of a trip to Greece, though there are some tips to bear in mind. When ordering, the standard procedure is to go to the glass cooler and pick your specimen, then have it weighed (uncleaned) in your presence. Overcharging, especially where a printed menu is absent, is not uncommon; have weight and price confirmed clearly. Taverna owners often comply only minimally with the requirement to indicate when seafood is **frozen** – look for the abbreviation "kat", "k" or just an asterisk on the Greek-language side of the menu. If the price, almost invariably quoted by the kilo, seems too good to be true, it's almost certainly farmed. The choicest varieties, such as red mullet, *tsipoúra* (gilt-head bream), sea bass or *fangrí* (common bream), will be expensive if wild – €45–70 per kilo. Less esteemed species tend to cost €20–35 per kilo but are usually quoted at €6–9 per portion.

Fish caught in the summer months tend to be smaller and drier, and so are served with *ladholémono* (oil and lemon) sauce. An inexpensive May–

June treat is fresh, grilled or fried *bakaliáros* (hake). *Gávros* (anchovy), *atherína* (sand smelts) and *sardhélles* (sardines) are late-summer fixtures, at their best in the northeast Aegean. *Koliós* (mackerel) is excellent either grilled or baked in sauce. Especially in autumn you may find *psarósoupa* (fish soup) or *kakaviá* (bouillabaisse).

Cheaper **seafood** (*thalassiná*) such as fried baby squid (usually frozen); *thrápsalo* (large, grillable deep-water squid) and octopus are summer staples; often mussels, cockles and small prawns will also be offered at reasonable sums (€20–30 per kilo).

Wine

All tavernas will offer you a choice of bottled **wines**, and most have their own house variety: kept in barrels, sold in bulk (*varelísio* or *hýma*) by the quarter-, half- or full litre, and served in glass flagons or brightly coloured tin "monkey-cups". Per-litre prices depend on locale and quality, ranging from €4–5 (Thessaly, Skýros) to €10–12 (Santoríni, Rhodes). Non-resinated wine is almost always more than decent; some people add a dash of soda water or lemonade. Barrelled **retsina** – pine-resinated wine, often an acquired taste – is far less common than it used to be, though you will find bottled brands everywhere: Yeoryiadhi from Thessaloníki, Liokri from Aharía, and Malamatina from central Greece are all quaffable.

Among **bottled wines** available nationwide, Cambas Attikos, Zítsa and Rhodian CAIR products are good, inexpensive whites, while Boutari Naoussa and Kourtakis Apelia are decent, mid-range reds. For a better but still moderately priced red, choose either Boutari or Tsantali Merlot, or Averof Katoï from Epirus.

An increasing number of Greek **wineries** open their doors to visitors for **tastings and tours**, which are usually free or make a nominal charge. There are a number of **wine routes** on the mainland and

VEGETARIANS

Vegetarians will find scarcely any dedicated **meat-free restaurants** in Greece. That is not to say that they cannot enjoy excellent food, however. The best solution in tavernas or ouzerís is to assemble a meal from vegetarian mezédhes and salads and, in *estiatória* especially, keep an eye open for the delicious *ladherá*, vegetables baked in various sauces.

individual wineries dotted around the wine-producing islands such as Límnos, Lésvos, Santoríni, Kefaloniá, Náxos, Ikaría, Rhodes and Crete (see ⓦnewwinesofgreece.com). Curiously, island **red wines** are almost uniformly mediocre, so you are better off ordering mainland varieties from Carras on Halkidhikí, and various spots in the Peloponnese and Thessaly. Particularly notable vintages are mentioned throughout this Guide.

Other **premium microwineries** on the mainland whose products have long been fashionable, in both red and white, include the overrated Hatzimihali (central Greece), the outstanding Dhiamandakou (near Náoussa, red and white), Athanasiadhi (central Greece), Skouras (Argolid) and the two rival Lazaridhi vintners (Dhráma, east Macedonia), especially their superb Merlots. For any of these you can expect to pay €10–18 per bottle in a shop, double that at a taverna. The best available current **guide** to the emerging Greek domaines and vintners is Konstantinos Lazarakis' *The Wines of Greece*.

Finally, CAIR on Rhodes makes "**champagne**" ("naturally sparkling wine fermented en bouteille", says the label), in both brut and demi-sec versions. It's not Moët & Chandon by any means, but at about €7 per bottle, the quality is not bad.

Cafés and bars

A venerable institution, under attack from the onslaught of mass global culture, is the **kafenío**, still found in every Greek town but dying out or extinct in most resorts. In greater abundance, you'll encounter **patisseries** (*zaharoplastía*), swish modern **cafeterias** and **trendy bars**.

Kafenía, cafeterias and coffee

The **kafenío** (plural *kafenía*) is the traditional Greek coffee house. Although its main business is "Greek" (Middle Eastern) **coffee** – prepared unsweetened (*skétos* or *pikrós*), medium (*métrios*) or sweet (*glykós*) – it also serves instant coffee, ouzo, brandy, beer, sage-based tea known as *tsáï vounoú*, soft drinks and juices. Some *kafenía* close at siesta time, but many remain open from early in the morning until late at night. The chief summer socializing time for a pre-prandial ouzo is 6–8pm, immediately after the afternoon nap.

Cafeterias are the province of fancier varieties of coffee and **kafés frappé**, iced instant coffee with sugar and (optionally) condensed milk – uniquely Greek despite its French name. Like Greek coffee, it is always accompanied by a glass of water. *Freddoccino* is a cappuccino-based alternative to the traditional cold frappé. "Nes"(café) is the generic term for all instant **coffee**, regardless of brand. Thankfully, almost all cafeterias now offer a range of foreign-style coffees – filter, dubbed *fíltros* or *gallikós* (French); cappuccino; and espresso – at overseas prices. Alcohol is also served and many establishments morph into lively bars late at night.

Sweets and desserts

The **zaharoplastío**, a cross between café and patisserie, serves coffee, a limited range of alcohol, yoghurt with honey and sticky cakes. The better establishments offer an amazing variety of pastries, cream-and-chocolate confections, honey-soaked Greco–Turkish sweets like *baklavás*, *kataïfi* (honey-drenched "shredded wheat"), *loukoumádhes* (deep-fried batter puffs dusted with cinnamon and dipped in syrup), *galaktoboúreko* (custard pie) and so on. For more dairy-based products, seek out a **galaktopolío**, where you'll often find *rizógalo* (rice pudding), *kréma* (custard) and locally made *yiaoúrti* (yoghurt). Both *zaharoplastía* and *galaktopolía* are more family-oriented places than a *kafenío*. **Traditional specialities** include "spoon sweets" or *glyká koutalioú* (syrupy preserves of quince, grape, fig, citrus fruit or cherry).

Ice cream, sold principally at the parlours which have swept across Greece (Dhodhoni is the posh home-grown competition to Haägen-Dazs), can be very good and almost indistinguishable from Italian prototypes. A scoop (*baláki*) costs €1.50–2.

Ouzerís, mezedhopolía and spirits

Ouzerís (often called **tsipourádhika** in Vólos, Thessaloníki and increasingly elsewhere), found mainly in select neighbourhoods of larger islands and towns, specialize in ouzo or *tsípouro* and *mezédhes*. In some places you also find **mezedhopolía**, a bigger, more elaborate kind of ouzerí. These places are well worth trying for the marvellous variety of *mezédhes* they serve. In effect, several plates of *mezédhes* plus drinks will substitute for a more conventional meal at a taverna, though it works out more expensive if you have a healthy appetite. Faced with an often bewilderingly varied menu, you might opt for a **pikilía** (assortment) available in several sizes, the most expensive one usually featuring seafood.

Ouzo is served by the glass, to which you can add water from the accompanying glass or ice to taste. The next measure up is a *karafáki* – a 200ml vial, the favourite means of delivery for *tsípouro*. Once, every ouzo was automatically accompanied by a small plate of **mezédhes** on the house: cheese, cucumber, tomato, a few olives, sometimes octopus

---

THE STRONG STUFF

Ouzo, *tsípouro* (north mainland and increasingly nationwide) and **rakí** or *tsikoudhiá* (Crete) are simple spirits of up to 48 percent alcohol, distilled from the grape-mash residue of winemaking. The former is always flavoured with anise, the latter two are mostly unadulterated but may have a touch of anise, cinnamon, pear essence or fennel. There are nearly thirty brands of ouzo or *tsípouro*; the best are reckoned to be from Lésvos and Sámos islands, or Zítsa and Týrnavos on the mainland. Note that ouzo has the peculiar ability to bring back its effect when you drink water the morning after, so make sure you don't plan to do anything important (like driving) the next day.

---

or a couple of small fish. Nowadays, "**ouzomezés**" is a separate, pricier option. Often, however, this is "off-menu", but if you order a *karafáki* you will automatically be served a selection of basic snacks.

Bars, beer and mineral water

Bars (*barákia*) are ubiquitous across Greece, ranging from clones of Spanish bodegas and British pubs to musical beachside bars more active by day than at night. At their most sophisticated, however, they are well-executed theme venues in ex-industrial premises or Neoclassical houses, with both Greek and inter-national soundtracks. Many Greek bars have a half-life of about a year; the best way to find current hot spots, especially if they're more club than bar, is to look out for posters advertising bar-hosted events in the neighbourhood.

Shots and **cocktails** are invariably expensive at €5–8, except during well-advertised happy hours: beer in a bar will cost €4–6, up to €12 for imports in trendier parts of Athens. **Beers** are mostly foreign lagers made locally under licence at a handful of breweries on the mainland. **Local brands** include the palatable Fix from Athens, milder Mythos and Veryina from Komotiní. There is, however, a growing number of quality **microbreweries**: the original is Craft in Athens, who produce lager in three grades (blonde, "smoked" and black), as well as a red ale, and now distribute quite widely. Other highly rated but strictly local microbreweries have sprung up on Crete (Réthymno), Corfu, Híos and Santoríni. Genuinely **imported** German beers, such as Bitburger, Fisher and Warsteiner (plus a few British and Irish ones), are found in Athens, Thessaloníki and at busier resorts.

The ubiquitous Loutraki **mineral water** is not esteemed by the Greeks themselves, who prefer various brands from Crete and Epirus. In many tavernas there's been a backlash against plastic bottles, and you can now get mineral water in glass bottles. Souroti, Epsa and Sariza are the principal labels of naturally **sparkling** (*aerioúho*) water, in small bottles. Note that despite variable quality in taste **tap water** is essentially safe all over Greece, though persuading a restaurant to provide it can be difficult in some places, especially islands.

Health

There are no required inoculations for Greece, though it's wise to ensure you are up to date on tetanus and polio. The main health risks faced by visitors involve overexposure to the sun, overindulgence in food and drink, or bites and stings from insects and sea creatures.

EU nationals (including British citizens at the time of writing) are entitled to free medical care in Greece upon presentation of a European Health Insurance Card (see box opposite). The US, Canada, Australia and New Zealand have no formal healthcare agreements with Greece (other than allowing for free emergency trauma treatment), so insurance is highly recommended.

Doctors and hospitals

For serious medical attention, you'll find English-speaking **doctors** (mainly private) in all the bigger towns and resorts: if your hotel can't help, the tourist police or your consulate should be able to come up with some names. There are also **hospitals** in all the big cities; medical standards are high but, in state hospitals at least, you'll only get the most basic level of nursing care – locals depend on family for support. For an ambulance, phone ☎166.

Pharmacies, drugs and contraception

For minor complaints it's enough to go to the local **pharmacy** (*farmakío*). Greek pharmacists are highly trained and dispense a number of medicines which elsewhere could only be prescribed by a doctor. In the larger towns and resorts there'll usually be one who speaks good English. Pharmacies are usually closed evenings and Saturday mornings, but all should have a schedule on their door showing the night and weekend duty pharmacists in town.

If you regularly use any form of **prescription drug**, you should bring along a copy of the prescription, together with the generic name of the drug; this will help you replace it, and avoids problems with customs officials. Also, be aware that **codeine** is banned in Greece – if you import any you might find yourself in serious trouble, so check labels carefully; it's a major ingredient of Panadeine, Veganin, Solpadeine, Codis and Nurofen Plus, to name just a few.

Contraceptive pills are sold over the counter at larger pharmacies, though not necessarily the brands you may be used to; a good pharmacist should come up with a close match. **Condoms** are inexpensive and ubiquitous – just ask for *profylaktiká* (less formally, *plastiká* or *kapótes*) at any pharmacy, sundries store or corner *períptero* (kiosk). Sanitary towels and **tampons** are widely sold in supermarkets.

Common health problems

The main health problems experienced by visitors – including many blamed on the food – have to do with **overexposure to the sun**. To avoid these, cover up, wear a hat, and drink plenty of fluids to avoid any danger of **sunstroke**; remember that even hazy sun can burn. **Tap water** meets strict EU standards for safety, but high mineral content and less than perfect desalination on many islands can leave a brackish taste not suited to everyone. For that reason many people prefer to stick to bottled water (see opposite). **Hayfever** sufferers should be prepared for a pollen season earlier than in northern Europe, peaking in April and May.

Hazards of the sea

To avoid hazards in or by the sea, goggles or a dive mask for swimming and footwear for walking over wet or rough rocks are useful. You may have the bad luck to meet an armada of **jellyfish** (*tsoúkhtres*), especially in late summer; they come in various colours and sizes ranging from purple "pizzas" to invisible, minute creatures. Various over-the-counter remedies are sold in resort pharmacies to combat the sting, and baking soda or diluted ammonia also help to lessen the effects. Less vicious but far more common are spiny **sea urchins**, which infest rocky shorelines year-round. If you step on or graze against one, an effective way to remove the spines is with a needle (you can crudely sterilize it with heat from a cigarette lighter) and olive oil. If you don't remove the spines, they'll fester.

Bites and stings

Most of Greece's insects and reptiles are pretty benign, but there are a few that can give a painful bite. Much the most common are **mosquitoes**: you can buy repellent devices and sprays at any minimarket. On beaches, **sandflies** can also give a nasty (and potentially infection-carrying) sting. **Adders** (*ohiés*) and **scorpions** (*scorpii*) are found throughout Greece. Both are shy, but take care when climbing over drystone walls where snakes like to sun themselves, and – particularly when camping – don't put hands or feet in places, like shoes, where you haven't looked first.

Finally, in addition to munching its way through a fair amount of Greece's surviving pine forests, the pine processionary **caterpillar** – which takes its name from the long, nose-to-tail convoys – sports highly irritating hairs, with venom worse than a scorpion's. If you touch one, or even a tree trunk they've been on recently, you'll know all about it for a week, and the welts may require antihistamine to heal.

If you snap a **wild-fig shoot** while walking, avoid contact with the highly irritant **sap**. The immediate antidote to the active alkaloid is a mild acid – lemon juice or vinegar; left unneutralized, fig "milk" raises welts which take a month to heal.

The media

Greeks are great devourers of newsprint – although few would propose the Greek mass media as a paradigm of objective journalism. Papers are almost uniformly sensational, while state-run TV and radio are often biased in favour of whichever party happens to be in government. Foreign news is widely available, though, in the form of locally printed newspaper editions and TV news channels.

Newspapers and magazines

British newspapers are widely available in resorts and the larger towns at a cost of €2–4 for dailies, or €4–6 for Sunday editions. Many, including the *Times*, *Mail* and *Mirror*, have slimmed-down editions printed in Greece which are available the same day; others are likely to be a day old. In bigger newsagents you'll also be able to find *USA Today* and *Time* as well as the *International New York Times*, which has the bonus of including an abridged English edition of the same day's *Kathimerini*, a respected Greek daily, thus allowing you to keep up with Greek news too. From time to time you'll also find various English-language magazines aimed at visitors to Greece, though none seems to survive for long.

Radio

Greece's airwaves are cluttered with **local and regional stations**, many of which have plenty of music, often traditional. In popular areas, many of them have regular news bulletins and tourist information in English. The mountainous nature of much of the country, though, means that any sort of **radio reception** is tricky: if you're driving around, you'll find that you constantly have to retune. The two state-run networks are ER1 (a mix of news, talk and pop music) and ER2 (pop music).

The BBC World Service no longer broadcasts to Europe on short wave, though Voice of America can be picked up in places. Both of these and dozens of others are of course available as internet broadcasts, however, or via satellite TV channels.

Television

Greece's state-funded **TV stations**, ET1, NET and ET3, lag behind the private channels – notably Mega, Star, Alpha, Alter and Skai – in the ratings, though not necessarily in the quality of offerings. Most foreign films and serials are broadcast in their original language with Greek subtitles; there's almost always a choice of English-language movies and series from about 9pm onwards, although the closer you get to the end of the movie, the more adverts you'll encounter. Hotels and rooms places usually have TVs in the room, but reception can be poor: even where they advertise satellite, the only English-language channels this usually includes are CNN and BBC World.

Films

Greek **cinemas** show all the regular major release movies, which in the case of English-language titles will almost always be in English with Greek subtitles. In summer, wonderful **open-air screens** operate in all the big towns and many resorts. You may not hear much, thanks to crackly speakers and locals chatting throughout, but watching a movie under the stars on a warm night is simply a great experience.

Festivals

Most of the big Greek popular festivals have a religious basis, so they're observed in accordance with the Orthodox calendar: this means that Easter, for example, can fall as much as three weeks to either side of the Western festival.

On top of the main religious festivals, there are scores of local festivities, or **paniyíria**, celebrating the patron saint of the village church. Some of the more important are listed below; the *paramoní*, or **eve of the festival**, is often as significant as the day itself, and many of the events are actually celebrated on the night before. If you show up on the morning of the date given, you may find that you have missed most of the music, dancing and drinking. With some 330-odd possible saints' days, though, you're unlikely to travel round for long without stumbling on something. Local tourist offices should be able to fill you in on events in their area.

Easter

Easter is by far the most important festival of the Greek year. It is an excellent time to be in Greece, both for the beautiful and moving religious ceremonies and for the days of feasting and celebration which follow. If you make for a smallish village, you may well find yourself an honorary member for the period of the festival. This is a busy time for Greek tourists as well as international ones, however, so book ahead: for Easter dates, see below.

The first great ceremony takes place on **Good Friday** evening, as the Descent from the Cross is lamented in church. At dusk, the *Epitáfios*, Christ's funeral bier, lavishly decorated by the women of the parish, leaves the sanctuary and is paraded solemnly through the streets. Late **Saturday** evening sees the climax in a majestic Mass to celebrate Christ's triumphant return. At the stroke of midnight, all the lights in each crowded church are extinguished and the congregation plunged into the darkness until the priest lights the candles of the worshippers, intoning "*Dévte, lévete Fós*" ("Come, take the Light"). The burning candles are carried home through the streets; they are said to bring good fortune to the house if they arrive still burning.

The lighting of the flames is the signal for celebrations to start and the Lent fast to be broken. The traditional greeting, as fireworks and dynamite explode all around you in the street, is "*Khristós Anésti*" ("Christ is risen"), to which the response is "*Alithós Anésti*" ("Truly He is risen"). On **Easter Sunday** there's feasting on roast lamb.

The Greek equivalent of **Easter eggs** is hard-boiled eggs (painted red on Holy Thursday), which are baked into twisted, sweet, bread loaves (*tsourékia*) or distributed on Easter Sunday. People rap their eggs against their friends' eggs, and the owner of the last uncracked egg is considered lucky.

Name days

In Greece, everyone gets to celebrate their birthday twice. More important, in fact, than your actual birthday, is the "**Name Day**" of the saint who bears the same name. If your name isn't covered, no problem – your party is on All Saints' Day, eight weeks after Easter. If you learn that it's an acquaintance's name day, you wish them *Khrónia Pollá* (literally, "many years").

The big name day **celebrations** (Iannis/Ianna on Jan 7 or Yioryios on April 23, for example) can

involve thousands of people. Any church or chapel bearing the saint's name will mark the event – some smaller chapels will open just for this one day of the year – while if an entire village is named after the saint, you can almost guarantee a festival. To check out when your name day falls, see ⓦ namedays.gr.

Festival calendar

JANUARY

January 1: New Year's Day (Protokhroniá) In Greece this is the feast day of Áyios Vassílios (St Basil). The traditional New Year greeting is "Kalí Khroniá".

January 6: Epiphany (Theofánia/Tón Fóton) Marks the baptism of Jesus as well as the end of the twelve days of Christmas. Baptismal fonts, lakes, rivers and seas are blessed, especially harbours (such as Pireás), where the priest traditionally casts a crucifix into the water and local youths compete for the privilege of recovering it.

FEBRUARY/MARCH

Carnival (Apokriátika) Festivities span three weeks, climaxing during the seventh weekend before Easter. Pátra Carnival, with a chariot parade and costume parties, is one of the largest and most outrageous in the Mediterranean. Interesting, too, are the *boúles* (masked revels) which take place around Macedonia (particularly at Náoussa), Thrace (Xánthi), and the outrageous Goat Dance on Skýros in the Sporades. The Ionian islands, especially Kefaloniá, are also good for Carnival, as is Ayiássos on Lésvos, while Athenians celebrate by hitting each other on the head with plastic hammers.

Clean Monday (Katharí Dheftéra) The day after Carnival ends and the first day of Lent, 48 days before Easter, marks the start of fasting and is traditionally spent picnicking and flying kites.

March 25: Independence Day and the feast of the Annunciation (Evangelismós) Both a religious and a national holiday, with military parades and dancing to celebrate the beginning of the revolt against Ottoman rule in 1821, plus church services to honour the news given to Mary that she was to become the Mother of Christ. There are major festivities on Tínos, Ýdhra and any locality with a monastery or church named Evangelístria or Evangelismós.

APRIL/MAY

Easter (Páskha: April 28 2019; April 19 2020; May 2 2021) The most important festival of the Greek year (see above). The island of Ýdhra, with its alleged 360 churches and monasteries, is the prime Easter resort; other famous Easter celebrations are held at Corfu, Pyrgí on Híos, Ólympos on Kárpathos and St John's monastery on Pátmos, where on Holy Thursday the abbot washes the feet of twelve monks in the village square, in imitation of Christ doing the same for his disciples. Good Friday and Easter Monday are also public holidays.

April 23: The feast of St George (Áyios Yeóryios) St George, the patron of shepherds, is honoured with a big rural celebration, with much feasting and dancing at associated shrines and towns. If it falls during Lent, festivities are postponed until the Monday after Easter.

MAY/JUNE

May 1: May Day (Protomayiá) The great urban holiday when townspeople traditionally make for the countryside to picnic and fly kites, returning with bunches of wild flowers. Wreaths are hung on their doorways or balconies until they are burnt in bonfires on St John's Eve (June 23). There are also large demonstrations by the Left for Labour Day.

May 21: Feast of St Constantine and St Helen (Áyios Konstandínos & Ayía Eléni) Constantine, as emperor, championed Christianity in the Byzantine Empire; St Helen was his mother. There are firewalking ceremonies in certain Macedonian villages; elsewhere celebrated rather more conventionally as the name day for two of the more popular Christian names in Greece.

Whit Monday (Áyio Pnévma) Fifty days after Easter, sees services to commemorate the descent of the Holy Spirit to the assembled disciples. Many young Greeks take advantage of the long weekend, marking the start of summer, to head for the islands.

June 29 & 30: SS Peter and Paul (Áyios Pétros & Áyios Pávlos) The joint feast of two of the more widely celebrated name days is on June 29. Celebrations often run together with those for the Holy Apostles (Áyii Apóstoli), the following day.

JULY

July 17: Feast of St Margaret (Ayía Marína) A big event in rural areas, as she's an important protector of crops.

July 20: Feast of the Prophet Elijah (Profítis Ilías) Widely celebrated at the countless hilltop shrines of Profítis Ilías. The most famous is on Mount Taïyetos, near Spárti, with an overnight vigil.

July 26: St Paraskevi (Ayía Paraskeví) Celebrated in parishes or villages bearing that name, especially in Epirus.

AUGUST

August 6: Transfiguration of the Saviour (Metamórfosis toú Sotíros) Another excuse for celebrations, particularly at Khristós Ráhon

village on Ikaría, and at Plátanos on Léros. On Hálki the date is marked by messy food fights with flour, eggs and squid ink.

August 15: Assumption of the Blessed Virgin Mary (Apokímisis tís Panayías) This is the day when people traditionally return to their home village, and the heart of the holiday season, so in many places there will be no accommodation available. Even some Greeks resort to sleeping in the streets at the great pilgrimage to Tínos; also major festivities at Páros, at Ayiássos on Lésvos, and at Ólymbos on Kárpathos.

August 29: Beheading of John the Baptist (Apokefálisis toú Prodhrómou) Popular pilgrimages and celebrations at Vrykoúnda on Kárpathos.

SEPTEMBER

September 8: Birth of the Virgin Mary (Yénnisis tís Panayías) Special services in churches are dedicated to the event, and a double cause for rejoicing on Spétses where they also celebrate the anniversary of the battle of the straits of Spétses. Elsewhere, there's a pilgrimage of childless women to the monastery at Tsambíka, Rhodes.

September 14: Exaltation of the Cross (Ípsosis toú Stavroú) A last major summer festival, keenly observed on Hálki.

September 24: Feast of St John the Divine (Áyios Ioánnis Theológos) Observed on Níssyros and Pátmos, where at the saint's monastery there are solemn, beautiful liturgies the night before and early in the morning.

OCTOBER

October 26: Feast of St Demetrios (Áyios Dhimítrios) Another popular name day, particularly celebrated in Thessaloníki, of which he is the patron saint. In rural areas the new wine is traditionally broached on this day, a good excuse for general inebriation.

October 28: Óhi Day A national holiday with parades, folk dancing and speeches to commemorate prime minister Metaxas' one-word reply to Mussolini's 1940 ultimatum: "Ohi!" ("No!").

CULTURAL FESTIVALS

Throughout the summer you'll find **festivals** of music, dance and theatre at venues across Greece, with many of the events taking place at atmospheric outdoor venues. Some, in the resorts and islands, are unashamedly aimed at tourists, others more seriously artistic. The granddaddy of them all is the **Athens and Epidaurus Festival** (ⓦgreekfestival.gr; see p.112), which has been running every summer for over sixty years, incorporating everything from open-air performances of Classical drama in ancient theatres to jazz and contemporary art. Others include:

Dhimitría Cultural Festival, Thessaloníki Oct ⓦ dimitria .thessaloniki.gr

Domus Festival, Náxos July–early Sept ⓦ naxosfestival.com

Festival of the Aegean, Sýros July ⓦ festivaloftheaegean.com

Ioánnina Folk Festival July

Ippokrateia Festival, Kos July

Iráklio Festival, Crete July–Aug

Kalamáta Dance Festival July ⓦ kalamatadancefestival.gr

Kassándhra Festival, Halkidhikí (held jointly in Síviri and Áfytos) July–Aug ⓦ kassandrafestival.gr

Lefkádha Arts and Folklore festivals last week of Aug ⓦ liff.gr

Olympus Festival, Dhíon, Mt Olympus July–Aug ⓦ festivalolympou.gr

Pátra International Festival May–July ⓦ festivalpatras.gr

Pátra Film Festival Oct

Philippi Festival, Thássos July–Aug ⓦ philippifestival.gr

Réthymno Cretan Diet Festival July ⓦ www .cretandietfestival.gr

Sáni Jazz Festival, Halkidhikí July–Aug ⓦ sanifestival.gr

Santoríni Music Festival Sept

Thessaloníki International Film Festival Oct–Nov ⓦ www .filmfestival.gr

NOVEMBER

November 8: Feast of the Archangels Michael and Gabriel (Mihaíl & Gavríïl, or tón Taxiárhon) Marked by rites at the numerous churches named after them, particularly at the rural monastery of Taxiárhis on Sými, and the big monastery of Mandamádhos, Lésvos.

DECEMBER

December 6: Feast of St Nicholas (Áyios Nikólaos) The patron saint of seafarers, who has many chapels dedicated to him.

December 25 & 26: Christmas (Khristoúyenna) If less all-encompassing than Greek Easter, Christmas is still an important religious feast, one that increasingly comes with the usual commercial trappings: decorations, gifts and alarming outbreaks of plastic Santas on rooftops.

December 31: New Year's Eve (Paramoní Protohroniá) As on the other twelve days of Christmas, a few children still go door-to-door singing traditional carols for money. Adults tend to sit around playing cards, often for money. A special baked loaf, the *vassilópitta*, in which a coin is concealed to bring its finder good luck throughout the year, is cut at midnight.

Sports and outdoor pursuits

The Greek seashore offers endless scope for watersports, from waterskiing and parasailing to yachting and windsurfing. On land, the greatest attraction lies in hiking, through what is one of Europe's more impressive mountain terrains. Winter also sees possibilities for skiing at a number of underrated centres. As for spectator sports, the twin Greek obsessions are football (soccer) and basketball, with volleyball a close third.

Watersports

Windsurfing and **kitesurfing** are very popular around Greece: the country's bays and coves are ideal for beginners, with a few spectacularly windy spots for experts (see box below). Board rental rates are reasonable and instruction is generally also available. **Waterski** boats spend most of their time towing people around on bananas or other inflatables, though usually you can waterski or wakeboard as well, while **parasailing** (*parapént*) is also on offer at all the big resorts. **Jet skis** can be rented in many resorts, too, for a fifteen-minute burst of fuel-guzzling thrills.

A combination of steady winds, appealing seascapes and numerous natural harbours has long

---

SIX OF THE BEST WINDSURFING SPOTS

Kórthi, Ándros. See p.385
Kalafáti, Mýkonos. See p.395
Kouremónos, eastern Crete. See p.479
Prassoníssi, Rhodes. See p.529
Kokkári, Sámos. See p.612
Vassilikí, Lefkádha. See p.736

---

made Greece a tremendous place for **sailing**. All sorts of bareboat and flotilla yacht trips are on offer (see p.28), while dinghies, small cats and motorboats can be rented at many resorts. For yachting, spring and autumn are the most pleasant seasons; *meltémi* winds can make for nauseous sailing in July and August, when you'll also find far higher prices and crowded moorings. The Cyclades suffer particularly badly from the *meltémi*, and are also relatively short on facilities: better choices are to explore the Sporades from Skiáthos; to set out from Athens for the Argo-Saronic islands and north Peloponnese coast; or to sail around Corfu and the Ionians, though here winds can be very light.

Because of the potential for pilfering submerged antiquities, **scuba diving** is still restricted, though relaxation of the controls has led to a proliferation of dive centres across the mainland, Dodecanese, Ionians, Cyclades and Crete. There's not a huge amount of aquatic life surviving around Greece's over-fished shores, but you do get wonderfully clear water, while the rocky coast offers plenty of caves and hidden nooks to explore.

In the Peloponnese, central mainland and Epirus, there's much potential for **rafting** and **kayaking**, while **sea kayaks** can be rented on many islands. Specialist companies offer both sea kayaking and **wild swimming** holidays (see p.28)

Skiing

Skiing, which began on Mount Parnassós in the 1950s, is a comparative newcomer to Greece. With global warming, snow conditions are unpredictable at the southernmost resorts, and runs remain generally short. However, there are over **twenty ski centres** scattered about the mountains, and what they may lack in professionalism is often made up for by an easy-going, unpretentious après-ski scene. The season generally lasts from the beginning of January to the beginning of April, with a few extra weeks possible at either end, depending on snow conditions. No foreign package operators currently feature Greece among their offerings – it's very much a local, weekender scene.

The most developed of the resorts is Kelária-Fterólakkas on **Parnassós**, the legendary mountain near Delphi, though high winds often close the lifts. Other major ski centres include **Vórras** (Mount Kaïmaktsalán), near Édhessa; **Veloúhi** (Mount Tymfristós), near Karpeníssi in central Greece; **Helmós**, near Kalávryta on the Peloponnese; and **Vérmion**, near Náoussa in Macedonia.

Walking and cycling

If you have the time and stamina, **walking** is probably the single best way to see the remote back-country, with plenty of options from gentle strolls to long-distance mountain paths. This Guide includes some of the more accessible mountain hikes, as well as suggestions for more casual walks; there are also plenty of companies offering walking holidays (see p.28). Local **hiking guidebooks** are available in the more popular spots, though detailed **maps** (see p.53) may be better bought in advance.

Cycling is less popular with Greeks, but in an increasing number of resorts you can hire **bikes**. Many rental places also lead organized rides, varying from easy explorations of the countryside to serious rides up mountains, while specialist companies offer Greek cycling breaks (see p.28). Summer heat can be fierce, but there are great riding and walking conditions in spring and autumn.

Football and basketball

Football (soccer) is far and away the most popular sport in Greece – both in terms of participating and watching, its status strengthened still further by Greece's unexpected (and still unforgotten) emergence as Euro 2004 champions. The big teams are Panathanaïkós (W pao.gr); AEK of Athens (W aekfc .gr), now challenging at the top again after bankruptcy-enforced relegation to the third, amateur tier; Athens' Atrómitos (W atromitosfc.gr), now regular European qualifiers; Olympiakós of Pireás (W olympiacos.org); and PAOK of Thessaloníki (W paokfc.gr). Matches – usually Wednesday nights and Sunday afternoons – take place between September and May, and tickets are generally not too hard to come by at prices far lower than in the UK.

The national **basketball** team is one of Europe's strongest, while at club level, many of the football teams maintain basketball squads – Panathanaïkós are the most consistently successful.

Culture and etiquette

In many ways, Greece is a thoroughly integrated European country, and behaviour and social mores differ little from what you may be used to at home. Dig a little deeper, however, or travel to more remote, less touristed areas, and you'll find that traditional Greek ways survive to a gratifying degree. It's easy to accidentally give offence – but equally easy to avoid doing so by following a few simple tips, and to upgrade your status from that of tourist to xénos, a word that means both stranger and guest.

In general, Greeks are exceptionally friendly and curious, to an extent that can seem intrusive, certainly to a reserved Brit. Don't be surprised at being asked personal questions, even on short acquaintance, or having your personal space invaded. On the other hand, you're also likely to be **invited** to people's houses, often to meet a large extended family. Should you get such an invitation, you are not expected to be punctual – thirty minutes late is normal – and you should bring a small **gift**, usually flowers, or cakes from the local cake shop. If you're invited out to dinner, you can offer to **pay**, but it's very unlikely you'll be allowed to do so, and too much insistence could be construed as rude.

Dress codes and cultural hints

Though **dress codes** on the beach are entirely informal, they're much less so away from the sea; most Greeks will dress up to go out, and not doing so is considered slovenly at the least. There are quite a number of **nudist** beaches in remote spots, with plenty of locals enjoying them, but on family beaches, or those close to town or near a church (of which there are many along the Greek coast), even toplessness is often frowned on. Most monasteries and to a lesser extent churches impose a fairly strict **dress code** for visitors: no shorts, with women expected to cover their arms and wear skirts (though most Greek women visitors will be in trousers); the necessary wraps are often provided on the spot.

Two pieces of **body language** that can cause **unintentional offence** are hand gestures; don't hold your hand up, palm out, to anybody, and don't make an OK sign by forming a circle with your thumb and forefinger – both are extremely rude. Nodding and shaking your head for yes and no are also unlikely to be understood; Greeks use a slight forward inclination of the head for yes, a more vigorous backward nod for no.

Although **no-smoking zones** in restaurants, bars or public offices are beginning to be respected, Greeks are still among the heaviest smokers in Europe, and in outdoor spaces at least you're likely to be surrounded by people puffing away.

Bargaining and tipping

Most shops have fixed prices, so **bargaining** isn't a regular feature of tourist life. It is worth negotiating over rooms off-season, or for vehicle rental, especially for longer periods, but don't be aggressive about it; ask if they have a cheaper room, for example, rather than demanding a lower price. **Tipping** is not essential anywhere, though taxi drivers generally expect it from tourists and most service staff are very poorly paid. Restaurant bills incorporate a service charge; if you want to tip, rounding up the bill is usually sufficient.

Women and lone travellers

Thousands of **women** travel independently in Greece without harassment or intimidation. With the westernization of relationships between unmarried Greek men and women, almost all the traditional Mediterranean macho impetus for trying one's luck with foreign girls has faded. Foreign women are more at risk of **sexual assault** in certain notorious resorts (including Kávos in Corfu, Laganás in Zákynthos and Faliráki in Rhodes) by northern European men than by ill-intentioned locals. It is sensible not to bar-crawl alone or to accept late-night rides from strangers (**hitching** at any time is not advisable for lone female travellers). In more remote areas, intensely traditional villagers may wonder why women travelling alone are unaccom-

panied, and may not welcome their presence in exclusively male *kafenía*. Travelling with a man, you're more likely to be treated as a *xéni*.

Lone men need to be wary of being invited into bars in the largest mainland towns and island ports, in particular near Sýndagma in Athens; these bars are invariably staffed with hostesses (who may also be prostitutes) persuading you to treat them to drinks. At the end of the night you'll be landed with an outrageous bill, some of which goes towards the hostess's commission; physical threats are brought to bear on reluctant payers.

Travel essentials

Costs

The **cost of living** in Greece has increased astronomically since it joined the EU, particularly after the adoption of the euro and further increases in the VAT rate in 2011. Prices in shops and cafés now match or exceed those of many other EU member countries (including the UK). However, outside the chintzier resorts, travel remains affordable, with the aggregate cost of restaurant meals, short-term accommodation and public transport falling somewhere in between that of cheaper Spain or France and pricier Italy.

Prices depend on where and when you go. Pockets of the larger cities, the trendier tourist resorts and small islands (such as Sými, Ýdhra, Mýkonos, Paxí and Santoríni) are more expensive and costs everywhere increase sharply during July and August, Christmas, New Year and Easter.

On most islands a daily per-person **budget** of €50/£40/$64 will get you basic accommodation and meals, plus a short ferry or bus ride, as one of a couple. Camping would cut costs marginally. On €100/£80/$128 a day you could be living quite well, plus sharing the cost of renting a large motor-bike or small car. Note that **accommodation** costs (see box, p.36) vary greatly over the seasons.

A basic taverna **meal** with bulk wine or a beer costs around €12–20 per person. Add a better bottle of wine, pricier fish or fancier decor and it could be up to €20–30 a head; you'll rarely pay more than that, unless you are tricked into buying overpriced fish (see p.40). Even in the most developed resorts, with inflated "international" menus, there is often a basic but decent taverna where the locals eat.

Crime and personal safety

Greece is one of Europe's safest countries, with a **low crime rate** and a deserved reputation for honesty. Most of the time if you leave a bag or wallet at a café, you'll probably find it scrupulously looked after, pending your return. Nonetheless, theft and muggings are becoming increasingly common, especially in Athens, a trend only likely to be increased by the economic crisis. With this in mind, it's best to lock rooms and cars securely, and to keep your valuables hidden. Civil unrest, in the form of strikes and demonstrations, is also on the increase, but while this might inconvenience you, you'd be very unlucky to get caught up in any trouble as a visitor.

Though the chances are you'll never meet a member of the national **police force**, the Elliniki Astynomia, Greek cops expect respect, and many have little regard for foreigners. If you do need to go to the police, always try to do so through the **Tourist Police** (☏171), who should speak English and are used to dealing with visitors. You are required to carry suitable ID on you at all times – either a passport or a driving licence – though it's understood you probably won't have it at the beach, for example.

The most common causes of a brush with the law are beach nudity, camping outside authorized sites, **public inebriation** or lewd behaviour. In 2009, a large British stag group dressed as nuns was arrested in Mália and held for several days; they managed to combine extreme drunkenness with a lack of respect for the church. Also avoid taking **photos in forbidden areas** such as airports (see p.55).

Drug offences are treated as major crimes, particularly since there's a mushrooming local addiction problem. The maximum penalty for "causing the use of drugs by someone under 18", for example, is life imprisonment and an astronomical fine. Foreigners caught in possession of even small amounts of marijuana get long jail sentences if there's evidence that they've been supplying others.

Electricity

Voltage is 220 volts AC. Standard European two-pin plugs are used; **adaptors** should be bought before-hand in the UK, as they can be difficult to find locally; standard 5-, 6- or 7.5-amp models permit operation of a hairdryer or travel iron. Unless they're dual voltage, North American appliances will require both a step-down transformer and a plug adaptor (the latter easy to find in Greece).

Entrance fees

All the major **ancient sites**, like most **museums**, charge **entrance fees** ranging from €2–20, with an average fee of around €4. From November to March, entrance to all state-run sites and museums is half price (we have quoted the full summer price thoughout the Guide) and **free** on Sundays and public holidays.

Entry requirements

EU citizens (and most of those from European countries not in the EU) need only a valid **passport** or identity card to enter Greece and can stay indefi-nitely (see p.52), though the rules post-Brexit may change for UK nationals from 2019. US, Australian, New Zealand, Canadian and most non-EU Europeans can stay, as tourists, for ninety days (cumulative) in any six-month period. Such nationals arriving by flight or boat from another EU state party to the Schengen Agreement may not be stamped in routinely at minor Greek ports, so make sure this is done in order to avoid unpleasantness on exit. Your passport must be valid for three months after your arrival date.

Visitors from **non-EU** countries are currently not, in practice, being given extensions to tourist visas. You must leave not just Greece but the entire Schengen Group and stay out until the maximum 90-days-in-180 rule, as set forth above, is satisfied. If you **overstay** your time and then leave under your own power – i.e. are not deported – you'll be hit with a huge fine upon departure, and possibly be banned from re-entering for a lengthy period of time; no excuses will be entertained except (just maybe) a doctor's certificate stating you were immobilized in hospital. It cannot be overemphasized just how exigent Greek immigration officials have become on this issue.

Greek embassies abroad

Australia & New Zealand 9 Turrana St, Yarralumla, Canberra, ACT 2600 ☎ 02 6271 0100, ⓦ mfa.gr/canberra.

Canada 80 Maclaren St, Ottawa, ON K2P 0K6 ☎ 613 238 6271, ⓦ mfa.gr/canada/en/the-embassy.

Ireland 1 Upper Pembroke St, Dublin 2 ☎ 01 676 7254, ⓦ mfa.gr/dublin.

South Africa 323 North Village Lane, Hilside Lynwood 0081 ☎ 012 348 2352, ⓦ mfa.gr/pretoria.

UK 1A Holland Park, London W11 3TP ☎ 020 7229 3850, ⓦ mfa.gr/london.

USA 2217 Massachusetts Ave NW, Washington, DC 20008 ☎ 202 939 1300, ⓦ mfa.gr/washington.

Gay and lesbian travellers

Greece is deeply ambivalent about **homosexuality**: ghettoized as "to be expected" in the arts, theatre and music scenes but apt to be closeted elsewhere. "Out" gay Greeks are rare, and "out" local lesbians rarer still; foreign same-sex couples will be regarded in the provinces with some bemusement but accorded the same standard courtesy as straight foreigners – as long as they refrain from public displays of affection, taboo in rural areas. There is a sizeable **gay community** in Athens, Thessaloníki and Pátra, plus a fairly obvious scene at resorts like Ýdhra, Rhodes and Mýkonos. Skála Eressoú on Lésvos, the birthplace of Sappho, is unsurprisingly an international mecca for lesbians. Even in Athens, however, most gay nightlife is underground (often literally so in the siting of clubs), with no visible signage for nondescript premises.

Insurance

Despite the EU healthcare privileges that currently apply in Greece (see box, p.43), you should consider taking out an **insurance policy** before travelling, to cover against theft, loss, illness or injury. Before paying for a whole new policy, however, it's worth checking whether you are already covered: some home insurance policies may cover your possessions when overseas, and many private medical schemes (such as BUPA or WPA in the UK) offer coverage extensions for abroad. **Students** will often find that their student health coverage extends during the vacations.

Make any claim as soon as possible. If you have medical treatment, keep all receipts for medicines and treatment. If you have anything stolen or lost, you must obtain an **official statement** from the police or the airline which lost your bags – with numerous claims being fraudulent, most insurers won't even consider one unless you have a police report.

Internet

Other than in major cities and some towns, **internet cafés** have all but disappeared, due to the proliferation of **wi-fi**. Nearly all accommodation, most cafés (but not old-style *kafenía*) and an increasing number of tavernas offer free wi-fi to patrons, and an increasing number of municipalities are introducing free wi-fi hotspots.

Laundry

Laundries, or *plindíria*, in Greek, are available in the main resort towns; sometimes an attended service wash is available for little or no extra charge over the basic cost of €8–10 per wash and dry. Self-catering villas will usually be furnished with a drying line and a selection of plastic wash-tubs or a bucket. Most larger hotels have laundry services, but charges are steep.

ROUGH GUIDES TRAVEL INSURANCE

Rough Guides has teamed up with WorldNomads.com to offer great **travel insurance** deals. Policies are available to residents of over 150 countries, with cover for a wide range of adventure sports, 24hr emergency assistance, high levels of medical and evacuation cover and a stream of travel safety information. Roughguides.com users can take advantage of their policies online 24/7, from anywhere in the world – even if you're already travelling. And since plans often change when you're on the road, you can extend your policy and even claim online. Roughguides.com users who buy travel insurance with WorldNomads.com can also leave a positive footprint and donate to a community development project. For more information go to ⓦ roughguides.com/travel-insurance.

AVERAGE MONTHLY TEMPERATURES AND RAINFALL

	Jan	Feb	Mar	April	May	June	July	Aug	Sept	Oct	Nov	Dec
ATHENS												
Maximum (°C/°F)	13/55	14/57	16/61	20/68	25/77	30/86	33/91	33/91	29/84	24/75	19/66	15/59
Minimum (°C/°F)	6/43	7/45	8/46	11/52	16/61	20/68	23/73	23/73	19/66	15/59	12/54	8/46
Rainfall (mm)	62	37	37	23	23	14	6	7	7	51	56	71
THESSALONÍKI												
Maximum (°C/°F)	9/48	12/54	14/57	20/68	25/77	29/84	32/90	32/90	28/82	22/72	16/61	11/52
Minimum (°C/°F)	2/36	3/37	5/41	10/50	14/57	18/64	21/70	21/70	17/63	13/55	9/48	4/39
Rainfall (mm)	44	34	38	41	40	40	22	14	29	57	55	56
CRETE (IRÁKLIO)												
Maximum (°C/°F)	16/62	16/62	17/63	20/68	23/73	27/81	29/84	29/84	27/81	24/75	21/70	18/64
Minimum (°C/°F)	9/48	9/48	10/50	12/54	15/59	19/66	22/72	22/72	19/66	17/63	14/57	11/52
Rainfall (mm)	95	46	43	26	13	3	1	1	11	64	71	79
DODECANESE (RHODES)												
Maximum (°C/°F)	15/59	16/62	17/63	21/70	25/77	30/86	32/90	33/91	29/84	25/77	21/70	17/63
Minimum (°C/°F)	7/45	8/46	9/48	12/54	15/59	19/66	21/70	22/72	19/66	15/59	12/54	9/48
Rainfall (mm)	201	101	92	23	21	1	1	0	15	75	114	205
IONIANS (CORFU)												
Maximum (°C/°F)	14/57	15/59	16/62	19/66	23/73	28/82	31/88	32/91	28/82	23/73	19/66	16/61
Minimum (°C/°F)	6/43	6/43	8/46	10/50	13/55	17/63	19/66	19/66	17/63	14/57	11/52	8/46
Rainfall (mm)	196	132	100	70	41	14	4	20	95	184	237	259

Living in Greece

EU (and EEA) nationals are allowed to stay indefinitely in any EU state, but to avoid any problems – eg, in setting up a bank account – you should, after the third month of stay, get a **certificate of registration** (vevéosi engrafís). In 2019, UK nationals should check the official situation, which may change post-Brexit. Residence/work permits for **non-EU/non-EEA nationals** can only be obtained on application to a Greek embassy or consulate outside Greece; you have a much better chance of securing one if you are married to a Greek, are of Greek background by birth or have permanent-resident status in another EU state.

As for **work**, non-EU nationals of Greek descent and EU/EEA native speakers of English have a much better chance than anyone else. **Teaching English** at a private language school (frontistírio) is not as well paid as it used to be and is almost impossible to get into these days without a bona fide TEFL certificate.

Many people find **tourism-related work**, especially on the islands most dominated by foreign visitors; April and May are the best time to look around. Opportunities include being a rep for a package company, although they recruit the majority of staff from the home country; all you need is EU nationality and the appropriate language, though knowledge of Greek is a big plus. Jobs in bars or restaurants are a lot easier for women to come by than men. Another option if you have the requisite skills is to work for a **windsurfing** school or **scuba diving** operation.

Mail

Post offices are open Monday to Friday from 7.30am to 2pm, though certain main branches also open evenings and Saturday mornings. **Airmail letters** take 3–7 days to reach the rest of Europe, 5–12 days to North America, a little longer for Australia and New Zealand. Postal rates for all postcards are 80c; letters up to 20g cost 85c within the EU and 90c to all other overseas destinations. For a modest fee (about €3) you can shave a day or two off delivery time to any destination by using the **express service** (katepígonda). **Registered delivery** (systiméno) is also available for a similar amount but is slow unless coupled with express service. Stamps (grammatósima) are widely available at newsagents and other tourist shops, often for a small surcharge.

Parcels should (and often can) only be handled in the main provincial or county capitals. For non-EU/EEA destinations, always present your box open for inspection, and come prepared with tape and scissors.

Ordinary **post boxes** are bright yellow, express boxes dark red, but it's best to use those adjacent to an actual post office, since days may pass between collections at boxes elsewhere.

Maps

The most reliable **general touring maps** of Greece are those published by Athens-based Anavasi (**W**anavasi.gr), Road Editions (**W**travelbookstore.gr) and Orama (**W**oramaeditions.gr). Anavasi and Road Editions products are widely available in Greece at selected bookshops, as well as at petrol stations and general tourist shops countrywide. In Britain they are found at Stanfords (**T**020 7836 1321, **W**stanfords.co.uk) and the Hellenic Book Service (**T**020 7267 9499, **W**hellenicbookservice.com); in the US, they're sold through Omni Resources (**T**910 227 8300, **W**omnimap.com).

Hiking/topographical maps are gradually improving in quality and availability. Road Editions, in addition to their touring maps, produce 1:50,000 topographical maps for mainland mountain ranges, including Áthos, Pílio, Parnassós, Ólymbos, Taïyetos, Ágrafa and Íti, usually with rudimentary route directions in English. Anavasi publishes a series covering the mountains of central Greece (including Ólymbos) and Epirus, some on the Peloponnese, the White Mountains and Psilorítis on Crete and Mt Dhýrfis on Évvia.

Money

Greece's currency is the **euro** (€). Up-to-date **exchange rates** can be found on **W**xe.com. Euro notes come in denominations of 5, 10, 20, 50, 100, 200 and 500 euros, and coins in denominations of 1, 2, 5, 10, 20 and 50 cents and 1 and 2 euros. Avoid getting stuck with **counterfeit euro notes** (€100 and €200 ones abound). The best tests are done by the naked eye: genuine notes all have a hologram strip or (if over €50) patch at one end, there's a watermark at the other, plus a security thread embedded in the middle. Note that shopkeepers do not bother much with shortfalls of 10 cents or less, whether in their favour (especially) or yours.

Banks and exchange

Greek **banks** normally open Monday to Thursday 8.30am–2.30pm and Friday 8.30am–2pm. Always take your passport with you as proof of identity and expect long queues. Large hotels and some travel

agencies also provide a **foreign cash exchange service**, though with hefty commissions, as do a number of authorized brokers in Athens and other major tourist centres. When changing small amounts, choose bureaux that charge a flat percentage commission (usually 1 percent) rather than a high minimum. There are a small number of 24-hour automatic **foreign-note-changing machines**, but a high minimum commission tends to be deducted. There is no need to **purchase euros** beforehand unless you're arriving at some ungodly hour to one of the remoter frontier posts.

ATMs and debit/credit cards

Debit cards are the most common means of accessing funds while travelling, by withdrawing money from the vast network of Greek **ATMs**. Larger airports have at least one ATM in the arrivals hall and any town or island with a population larger than a few thousand (or substantial tourist traffic) also has them. Most accept Visa, MasterCard, Visa Electron, Plus and Cirrus cards; American Express holders are restricted to the ATMs of Alpha and National Bank. There is usually a charge of 2.25 percent on the sterling/dollar transaction value, plus a commission fee of a similar amount. Using **credit cards** at an ATM costs roughly the same; however, inflated interest accrues from the moment of use. When using a card, if you are given the option for the transaction to be calculated in euros or your home currency, always choose euros to avoid disadvantageous rates.

Major credit cards are not usually accepted by cheaper tavernas or hotels but they can be essential for renting cars. Major travel agents may also accept them, though a **three-percent surcharge** is often levied on the purchase of ferry tickets.

Opening hours and public holidays

It's difficult to generalize about Greek **opening hours**, which are notoriously erratic. Most shops open 8.30/9am and close for a long break at 2/2.30pm. Most places, except banks, reopen around 5.30/6pm for three hours or so, at least on Tuesday, Thursday and Friday. Tourist areas tend to adopt a more northern European timetable, with supermarkets and travel agencies, as well as the most important archeological sites and museums, more likely to stay open through-out the day. If you need to tackle **Greek bureaucracy**, don't count on getting anything essential done except from Monday to Friday, between 9.30am and 1pm.

PUBLIC HOLIDAYS

January 1 New Year's Day.
January 6 Epiphany.
February/March Clean Monday (*katharí dheftéra*), 7 weeks before Easter.
March 25 Independence Day.
April/May Good Friday and Easter Monday (see p.45 for dates).
May 1 May Day.
May/June Whit Monday, 7 weeks after Easter.
August 15 Assumption of the Virgin Mary.
October 28 Ohi Day (see p.46).
December 25/26 Christmas Day/Boxing Day.

As far as possible, times are quoted in the text for **tourist sites** but these change with exasperating frequency, especially since the economic crisis. Both winter and summer hours are quoted throughout the Guide, but to avoid disappointment, either phone ahead, check on the Greek Ministry of Culture website (Ⓦ odysseus.culture.gr), or time your visit during the core hours of 9am–2pm. **Monasteries** are generally open from approximately 9am to 1pm and 5 to 8pm (3.30–6.30pm in winter) for limited visits. Again, the opening times given for **restaurants**, **cafés** and **bars** can also be very flexible.

Phones

Three **mobile phone networks** operate in Greece: Vodafone, Cosmote and Q-Telecom/WIND. **Coverage** countrywide is good, though there are a few "dead" zones in the mountains, or on really remote islets. There are no roaming charges within the EU, so EU nationals pay the same price for calls, texts and data to numbers in their home country as they would at home; UK nationals should check the situation post-Brexit in 2019. For calling Greek numbers, however, you can save money by buying a **pay-as-you-go** SIM card (€15–20) from any of the mobile phone outlets. Top-up cards – starting from €8–10 – are available at all *períptera* (kiosks). North American users can only use tri-band phones in Greece.

Land lines and public phones are run by OTE who provide phonecards (*tilekártes*), available in denominations starting at €4, from kiosks and newsagents. If you plan on making lots of international calls, use a **calling card**, which involves calling a free access number from certain phone boxes or a fixed line (not a mobile) and then entering a twelve-digit code. OTE has its own scheme, but competitors generally prove cheaper. Avoid making calls direct **from hotel rooms**, as a large surcharge will be applied, though you will not be charged to access a free calling card number.

PHONE CODES AND NUMBERS

All Greek phone numbers require you to dial all ten digits, including the area code. Land lines begin with 2; mobiles begin with 6. All land-line exchanges are digital, and you should have few problems reaching any number from either overseas or within Greece. Mobile phone users are well looked after – there's even signal in the Athens metro.

PHONING GREECE FROM ABROAD
Dial ☎ 0030 + the full number

PHONING ABROAD FROM GREECE
Dial the country code (below) + area code (minus any initial 0) + number

Australia ☎ 0061	**Canada** ☎ 001	**Ireland** ☎ 00353
New Zealand ☎ 0064	**UK** ☎ 0044	**USA** ☎ 001
South Africa ☎ 0027		

GREEK PHONE PREFIXES
Local call rate ☎ 0801   **Toll-free/Freefone** ☎ 0800

USEFUL GREEK TELEPHONE NUMBERS

Ambulance ☎ 166	**Police/Emergency** ☎ 100
Fire brigade, urban ☎ 199	**Speaking clock** ☎ 141
Forest fire reporting ☎ 191	**Tourist police** ☎ 171 (Athens);
Operator ☎ 132 (Domestic);	☎ 210 171 (elsewhere)
☎ 139 (International)	

Photography

You can feel free to snap away at most places in Greece, although some **churches** display "No photography" signs, and museums and archeological sites may require **permits** at least for professional photographers. The main exception is around **airports** or **military installations** (usually clearly indicated with a "No pictures" sign). The ordeal of twelve British plane-spotters who processed slowly through Greek jails and courts in 2001–2 on espionage charges should be ample deterrent.

Time

Standard Greek time is two hours ahead of GMT. Along with the rest of Europe, the clocks move forward one hour onto **summer time** between the last Sunday in March and the last Sunday in October. For North America, the difference is usually seven hours for Eastern Standard Time, ten hours for Pacific Standard Time.

Toilets

Public toilets are usually in parks or squares, often subterranean; otherwise try a bus station. Except in tourist areas, public toilets tend to be filthy – it's best to use those in restaurants and bars. Remember that throughout Greece, you drop paper in the adjacent **wastebins**, not the toilet bowl.

Tourist information

The **National Tourist Organization of Greece** (Ellinikós Organismós Tourismoú, or EOT; Visit Greece, ⓦ visitgreece.gr) maintains offices in several European capitals and major cities around the world. It publishes an array of free, glossy pamphlets, invariably several years out of date, fine for getting a picture of where you want to go, though low on useful facts.

Within Greece, a lack of funding has led to the closure of all public EOT offices outside Athens and Rhodes, although administrative branches still exist. You can, however, often get information from **municipal tourist offices**, including advice on local attractions and public transport, as well as informal advice. In the absence of any of these, you can visit the **Tourist Police**, essentially a division (often just a single room) of the local police. They can sometimes provide you with lists of rooms to let, which they regulate, but they're really the place

to go if you have a **serious complaint** about a taxi, accommodation or eating establishment.

Greek national tourist offices abroad

UK & Ireland 4 Great Portland St, London W1W 8QJ ☏ 020 7495 9300, ⓔ info@gnto.co.uk.
USA 800 3rd Ave, New York, NY 10022 ☏ 212 421 5777, ⓔ info@ greektourism.com.

Travellers with disabilities

In general, **disabled** people are not especially well catered for in Greece, though, as EU-wide legislation is implemented, things are gradually improving. Wheelchair ramps and beeps for the sight-impaired are rare at pedestrian crossings, and outside Athens few buses are have disabled access. Only Athens airport, its metro and airline staff in general are wheelchair-friendly. Ancient monuments, one of the country's main attractions, are usually inaccessible or hazardous for anyone with impaired mobility.

The National Tourist Organization of Greece (see above) can help; they also publish a useful questionnaire that you can send to hotels or self-catering accommodation. Before purchasing **travel insurance**, ensure that pre-existing medical conditions are not excluded. A **medical certificate** of your fitness to travel is also useful; some airlines or insurance companies may insist on it.

Travelling with children

Children are worshipped and indulged in Greece, and present few problems when travelling. They are not segregated from adults at meal times, and early on in life are inducted into the typical late-night routine – kids at tavernas are expected to eat (and talk) like adults. Other than certain all-inclusive resorts with children's programmes, however, there are very few amusements specifically for them – certainly nothing like Disney World Paris. Water parks, tourist sites and other places of interest that are particularly child-friendly are noted throughout the guide.

Luxury hotels are more likely to offer some kind of **babysitting** or **crèche service**. All the same basic baby products that you can find at home are available in Greece, though some may be more expensive, so it can pay to load up on nappies, powders and creams before leaving home.

Most domestic ferry-boat companies and airlines offer child **discounts**, ranging from fifty percent to completely free depending on their age; hotels and rooms won't charge extra for infants, and levy a modest supplement for an extra bed.

Athens and around

THE PARTHENON

1

Athens and around

In Athens the past looms large – literally, in the shape of the mighty Acropolis that dominates almost every view, as well as on every visitor's itinerary. For all too many visitors, this is a city that happened two-and-a-half thousand years ago. Yet modern Athens has been transformed in the twenty-first century; home to over four million people, it's the vibrant capital of the nation and a place full of interest.

It's true that on first acquaintance, Athens is not a beautiful place – the scramble for growth in the decades after World War II, when the population grew from around 700,000 to close to its present level, was an architectural disaster. But, helped by huge **investment** of European funds and for the 2004 Olympics, the city has started to make the most of what it has, with new roads, rail and Metro, along with extensive **pedestrianization** in the centre. The views for which Athens was once famous have reappeared and, despite inevitable globalization and the appearance of all the usual high-street and fast-food chains, the city retains its character to a remarkable degree. Hectic modernity is always tempered with an air of intimacy and homeliness; as any Greek will tell you, Athens is merely the largest village in the country.

However often you've visited, the vestiges of the ancient Classical Greek city, most famously represented by the **Parthenon** and other remains that top the **Acropolis**, are an inevitable focus; along with the refurbished **National Archeological Museum**, the finest collection of Greek antiquities anywhere in the world, they should certainly be a priority. The majority of the several million visitors who pass through each year do little more; they never manage to escape the crowds and so see little of the Athens Athenians know. Take the time to explore some of the city's **neighbourhoods**, and you'll get far more out of it.

Above all, there's the sheer effervescence of the city. **Cafés** are packed day and night and the streets stay lively until 3 or 4am, with some of the best **bars and clubs** in the country. **Eating out** is great, and establishments range from traditional tavernas to gourmet restaurants. In summer, much of the action takes place outdoors, from dining on the street or clubbing on the beach to **open-air cinema**, **concerts** and **classical drama**. There's a diverse **shopping** scene, too, ranging from colourful bazaars and lively street markets to chic suburban malls crammed with the latest designer goods. And with good-value, extensive public transportation allied to inexpensive taxis, you'll have no difficulty getting around.

Outside Athens are more Classical sites – the **Temple of Poseidon at Soúnio**, sanctuaries at **Ramnous** and **Eleusis** (Elefsína), the burial mound from the great victory at **Marathon** – and there are also easily accessible **beaches** all around the coast.

TOWER OF THE WINDS

Highlights

❶ The Acropolis Rising above the city, the great rock of the Acropolis symbolizes not just Athens, but the birth of European civilization. **See p.65**

❷ Pláka Wander the narrow alleys and steep steps of this architecturally fascinating and vibrant quarter. **See p.74**

❸ Tower of the Winds Intriguing and elegant, this ancient clocktower is well worth seeking out. **See p.76**

❹ The bazaar Athens' raucous and colourful market area spills out into the streets all around the nineteenth-century covered food hall. **See p.83**

❺ National Archeological Museum The world's finest collection of ancient Greek art and sculpture. **See p.85**

❻ Café life Much of Athens' life is lived outdoors; check out the buzzing cafés of Thissío as the setting sun illuminates the Parthenon. **See p.106**

❼ Gázi The heart of Athens' nightlife, packed with bars, cafés and restaurants that are buzzing till late at night. **See p.109**

❽ Temple of Poseidon, Cape Soúnio Dramatic and evocative, this sanctuary to the sea god has been a shipping landmark for centuries. **See p.119**

HIGHLIGHTS ARE MARKED ON THE MAP ON P.60 & P.117

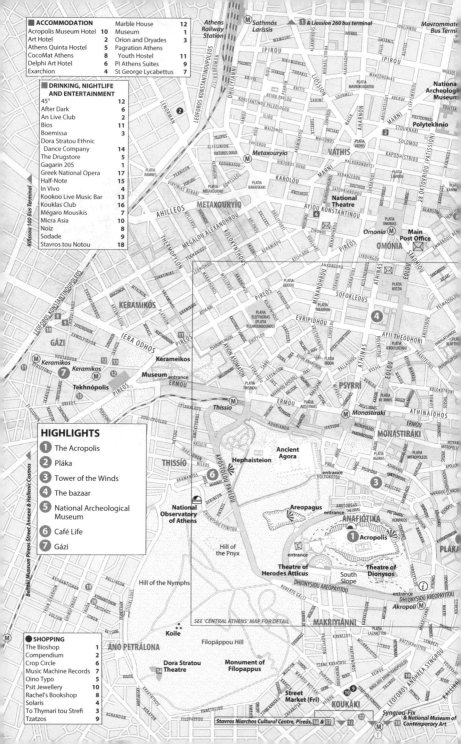

ATHENS

0   200

metres

Pedhío tou Áreos
(Pedhío Áreos Park)

ÁREOS

LEOFOROS ALEXANDRAS

Lófos tou Stréfi
(Stréfis Hill)

Panathinaikos
Stadium

EXÁRHIA

HARÍLAOU TRIKOÚPI

NEÁPOLI

Lykavitós
Theatre

HARÍLAOU TRIKOÚPI

IPPOKRÁTOUS

Áyios
Nikólaos

Christ
Church

Áyios
Yeóryios

Lykavitós
Hill

Funicular
Railway

US Embassy
Mégaro
Mousikís

Naval
Hospital

Alexándras
Hospital

Panepistímio

Friday
Market

Yennádhion
Library

Megaro Moussikis

British
Archeological
Society

Hospital

Aretaíaion
Hospital

Evangelismos
Hospital

KOLONÁKI

ILÍSIA

Hilton
Hotel

Ilissia
Park

SÝNTAGMA

Benáki
Museum

British
Council

Museum of
Cycladic Art

War
Museum

Syndagma

Evzones
Barracks

Evangelismos

Roman
Mosaic

Byzantine
Museum

Syndagma

Botanical
Museum

Aristotle's
Lyceum

National
Gardens

Mégaro
Maximou

Athens
Conservatory

LEOFOROS VASSILEOS YEORYIOU B

Presidential
Palace

Záppio

LEOFOROS VASSILEOS KONSTANTÍNOU

Zappeion
Gardens

Temple of
Olympian Zeus

Pangráti
Park

PANGRÁTI

Ardhittós
Hill

METS

Panathenaic
Stadium

Próto Nekrotafío
(First Cemetery)

Street
Market (Fri)

EATING	
Ambrosia	22
Andreas	8
Balsamakis (To Kotopoulo)	16
Butcher Shop	15
Chez Lucien	19
Da Capo	14
Dinner In The Sky	12
Filippou	10
Floral Books and Café	3
Gazohori	11
Ikio	13
Karavitis	18
Katsourbos	17
Lefka	2
Mama Tierra	7
Mystic Pizza	5
Oikonomou	20
Pinaleon	1
Rozalia	4
Spondi	21
Yiandes	6
Zahari ke Alati	9

1

Further afield, **Delphi** (see p.206) and the **islands** of the Saronic gulf (Chapter 5) are also within easy day-trip distance. Moving on is quick and easy, as scores of **ferries** and hydrofoils leave daily from the port at **Pireás** (Piraeus) and, somewhat less frequently, from the two other Attic ferry terminals at **Rafína** and **Lávrio**.

Brief history

Athens has been continuously inhabited for over seven thousand years. Its acropolis, commanding views of all seaward approaches and encircled by protective mountains, was a natural choice for prehistoric settlement and for the **Mycenaeans**, who established a palace-fortress on the rock. Gradually, Athens emerged as a city-state that dominated the region, ruled by kings who stood at the head of a land-owning aristocracy known as the *Eupatridae* (the "well-born"), who governed through a Council which met on the Areopagus – the Hill of Ares (see p.72).

The birth of democracy

As Athens grew wealthier, dissatisfaction with the rule of the *Eupatridae* grew, above all among a new middle class excluded from political life but forced to pay rent or taxes to the nobility. Among the reforms aimed at addressing this were new, fairer laws drawn up by **Draco** (whose "draconian" lawcode was published in 621 BC), and the appointment of **Solon** as ruler (594 BC), with a mandate to introduce sweeping economic and political reform. Although Solon's reforms laid the foundations of what eventually became Athenian democracy, they failed to stop internal unrest, and eventually **Peisistratos**, his cousin, seized power in the middle of the sixth century BC. Peisistratos is usually called a tyrant, but this simply means he seized power by force: thanks to his populist policies, he was in fact a well-liked and successful ruler who greatly expanded Athens' power, wealth and influence.

His sons **Hippias and Hipparchus** were less successful: Hipparchus was assassinated in 514 BC and Hippias overthrown in 510 BC. A new leader, **Kleisthenes**, took the opportunity for more radical change: he introduced ten classes or tribes based on place of residence, each of which elected fifty members to the *Boule* or Council of State, who decided on issues to be discussed by the full Assembly. The Assembly was open to all citizens and was both a legislature and a supreme court. This system was the basis of **Athenian democracy** and remained in place, little changed, right through to Roman times.

In around 500 BC, Athens sent troops to aid the Ionian Greeks of Asia Minor, who were rebelling against the Persian Empire; this in turn provoked a Persian invasion of Greece. In 490 BC, the Athenians and their allies defeated a far larger Persian force at the **Battle of Marathon** (see p.770). The Persians returned ten years later, when they captured and sacked Athens; much of the city was burned to the ground. That same year, however, a naval triumph at **Salamis** (see p.770) sealed victory over the Persians, and also secured Athens' position as Greece's leading city-state.

The rise and fall of Classical Athens

Perhaps the most startling aspect of Classical Athens is how suddenly it emerged to the glory for which we remember it – and how short its heyday proved to be. In the middle of the **fifth century BC**, Athens was little more than a country town in its street layout and buildings – a scattered jumble of single-storey houses or wattle huts, intersected by narrow lanes. On the Acropolis, a site reserved for the city's most sacred monuments, stood only the blackened ruins of temples and sanctuaries.

There was little to suggest that the city was entering a unique phase of its history in terms of power, prestige and creativity. But following the victory over the Persians at Salamis, Athens stood unchallenged for a generation. It grew rich on the export of olive oil and of silver from the mines of Attica, but above all it benefited from its control of the **Delian League**, an alliance of Greek city-states formed as insurance against Persian

THE ATHENIAN GOLDEN AGE

Under the democratic reforms of Pericles, a new and exalted notion of the **Athenian citizen** emerged. This was a man who could shoulder political responsibility while also playing a part in the **cultural and religious events** of the time. The latter assumed ever-increasing importance. The city's Panathenaic festival, which honoured the goddess Athena, was upgraded along the lines of the Olympic Games to include drama, music and athletic contests. The next five decades became the **Golden Age** of cultural development, during which the great dramatic works of Aeschylus, Sophocles and Euripides and the comedies of Aristophanes were written. Foreigners such as Herodotus, considered the inventor of history, and Anaxagoras, the philosopher, were drawn to live in the city. Thucydides wrote *The Peloponnesian War*, a pioneering work of documentation and analysis, while Socrates posed the problems of philosophy that were to exercise his follower Plato and to shape the discipline to the present day.

But it was the great civic **building programme** that became the most visible and powerful symbol of the age. Under the patronage of Pericles, the architects Iktinos, Mnesikles and Kallikrates, along with the sculptor Fidias, transformed the city. Their buildings included the Parthenon and Erechtheion on the Acropolis; the Hephaisteion and several *stoas* (arcades) around the Agora; a new *odeíon* (theatre) on the South Slope of the Acropolis hill; and, outside the city, the temples at Soúnio and Ramnous.

resurgence. The Athenians relocated the League's treasury from the island of Delos to their own acropolis, ostensibly on the grounds of safety, and with its revenues their leader **Pericles** (see p.772) was able to create the so-called **Golden Age** of the city. Great endowments were made for monumental construction, arts in all spheres were promoted, and – most significantly – it was all achieved under stable, **democratic rule**. The Delian League's wealth enabled office-holders to be properly paid, thereby making it possible for the poor to play a part in government.

The fatal mistake of the Athenian democracy, however, was allowing itself to be drawn into the **Peloponnesian War** (see p.772). Defeated, a demoralized Athens succumbed to a brief period of oligarchy, though it later recovered sufficiently to enter a new phase of democracy: the **age of Plato**. However, in 338 BC, Athens was again called to defend the Greek city-states, this time against the incursions of **Philip of Macedon**. Demosthenes, said to be as powerful an orator as Pericles, spurred the Athenians to fight, in alliance with the Thebans, at Chaeronea. There they were routed, in large part by the cavalry commanded by Philip's son, Alexander (later to become known as Alexander the Great), and Athens fell under the control of the **Macedonian Empire**.

The city continued to be favoured, particularly by **Alexander the Great**, a former pupil of Aristotle, who respected both Athenian culture and its democratic institutions. Following his death, however, came a more uncertain era, which saw both periods of independence and Macedonian rule, until 146 BC when the **Romans** (see box, p.76) swept through southern Greece and it was incorporated into the Roman province of Macedonia.

Christians and Turks

The emergence of **Christianity** was perhaps the most significant step in Athens' long decline from the glories of its Classical heyday. Having survived with little change through years of Roman rule, the city lost its pivotal role in the Roman–Greek world after the division of the Roman Empire into Eastern and Western halves, and the establishment of Byzantium (Constantinople, now Istanbul) as capital of the Eastern – **Byzantine** – empire. In 529 AD the city's temples, including the Parthenon, were reconsecrated as churches.

Athens rarely featured in the chronicles of the Middle Ages, as it passed through the hands of various foreign powers before the arrival in 1456 of **Sultan Mehmet II**, the Turkish conqueror of Constantinople. **Turkish Athens** was never much more than a

1

garrison town, occasionally (and much to the detriment of its Classical buildings) on the front line of battles with the Venetians and other Western powers. Although the Acropolis became the home of the Turkish governor and the Parthenon was used as a mosque, life in the village-like quarters around the Acropolis drifted back to a semi-rural existence.

Four centuries of Ottoman occupation followed until, in 1821, the Greeks of Athens rose and joined the **rebellion sweeping the country**. They occupied the Turkish quarters of the lower town – the current Pláka – and laid siege to the Acropolis. The Turks withdrew, but five years later were back to reoccupy the Acropolis fortifications, while the Greeks evacuated to the countryside. When the Ottoman garrison finally left in 1834, and the **Bavarian** architects of the new German-born monarch moved in, Athens, with a population of only five thousand, was at its nadir.

Modern Athens

Athens was not the first-choice **capital** of modern Greece: that honour went instead to Náfplio in the Peloponnese. In 1834, however, the new king Otto transferred the capital and court to Athens. The reasoning was almost purely symbolic: Athens was not only insignificant in terms of population and physical extent but was then at the edge of the territories of the new Greek state. Soon, while the archeologists stripped away all the Turkish and Frankish embellishments from the Acropolis, a city began to take shape: the grand Neoclassical plan was for processional avenues radiating out from great squares, a plan that can still be made out on maps but has long ago been subverted by the realities of daily life. **Pireás**, meanwhile, grew into a significant port again.

The first mass expansion of both municipalities came suddenly, in 1923, as the result of the tragic Greek–Turkish war in **Asia Minor** (see p.781). A million and a half "Greek" Christians arrived in Greece as refugees, and over half of them settled in Athens and Pireás; with a single stroke, this changed the whole make-up of the capital. The integration and survival of these new inhabitants is one of the great events of the city's history.

Athens was hit hard by German occupation in **World War II**: during the winter of 1941–42, there were an estimated two thousand deaths from starvation each day. In late 1944, when the Germans finally left, the capital saw the first skirmishes of **civil war**, and from 1946 to 1949 Athens was a virtual island, with road approaches to the Peloponnese and the north only tenuously kept open.

During the 1950s, the city again started to expand rapidly thanks to the growth of industry and massive **immigration** from the war-torn, impoverished countryside. By the late 1960s, Greater Athens covered a continuous area from the slopes of mounts Pendéli and Párnitha down to Pireás. Much of this development is unremittingly ugly, since old buildings were demolished wholesale in the name of a quick buck, particularly during the colonels' junta of 1967–74 (see p.784). Financial incentives encouraged homeowners to demolish their houses and replace them with **apartment blocks** up to six storeys high; almost everyone took advantage, and as a result most central streets seem like narrow canyons between these ugly, concrete blocks.

THE OLYMPIC LEGACY

The **2004 Olympics** can take much of the credit for getting Athens back on the map and regenerating the city's infrastructure. Successful as they were in many ways, however, the legacy of the Games is a bitter one. In the rush to be ready on time, many of the works went disastrously **over budget**, while inadequate planning means that few of the costly stadia have found any purpose in life since the Games finished. These decaying white elephants are a potent symbol of Greece's economic crisis and of the crazed rush to spend money that, ultimately, Greece never had.

Unrestrained **industrial development** on the outskirts was equally rampant.

Growth in recent decades has been much slower, but it's only in the last twenty years that much effort has gone in to improving the city's **environment**. Although Athens still lags far behind Paris or London in terms of open space, the evidence of recent efforts is apparent. What's left of the city's architectural heritage has been extensively restored; there's clean public transportation; new building is controlled and there's some interesting, radical modern architecture. Meanwhile, the economic crisis has a legacy of its own, in an extra-ordinary blossoming of graffiti art, especially on abandoned and boarded-up buildings.

Acropolis

The rock of the **Acropolis**, crowned by the dramatic ruins of the **Parthenon**, is one of the archetypal images of Western culture. The first time you see it, rising above the traffic or from a distant hill, is extraordinary: foreign, and yet utterly familiar. As in other Greek cities, the Acropolis itself is simply the highest point of the city, and this steep-sided, flat-topped crag of limestone, rising abruptly 100m from its surroundings, has made it the focus of Athens during every phase of its development. Easily defensible and with plentiful water, its initial attractions are obvious. Even now, with no function apart from tourism, it is the undeniable heart of the city, around which everything else clusters, glimpsed at almost every turn.

You can walk an entire circuit of the Acropolis and ancient Agora on **pedestrianized streets** which allow the monuments to be appreciated from almost every angle: in particular, the pedestrianization has provided spectacular terraces for

---

A BRIEF HISTORY OF THE ACROPOLIS

The Acropolis was home to one of the earliest known settlements in Greece, as early as 5000 BC. In **Mycenaean** times – around 1500 BC – it was fortified with Cyclopean walls (parts of which can still be seen), which enclosed a royal palace, and temples to the cult of Athena. By the ninth century BC, the Acropolis had become the heart of Athens, sheltering its principal public buildings which remained there until 510 BC, when the Oracle at Delphi ordered that the Acropolis should remain the **province of the gods**, unoccupied by humans.

Following the Persian sacking of Athens in 480 BC, a grand rebuilding project under the direction of the architect and sculptor **Fidias** created almost everything you see today in an incredibly short time: the Parthenon itself took only ten years to finish. The monuments survived unaltered for close to a thousand years, until in the reign of Emperor Justinian the temples were converted to **Christian** worship. Over the following centuries the uses became secular as well as religious, and embellishments increased, gradually obscuring the Classical designs. Fifteenth-century Italian princes held court in the Propylaia, and the same quarters were later used by the **Turks** as their commander's headquarters and as a gunpowder magazine.

The **Parthenon** underwent similar changes: from Greek to Roman temple and Byzantine church to Frankish cathedral before several centuries of use as a Turkish mosque. The **Erechtheion**, with its graceful female figures, saw service as a harem. A Venetian diplomat described the Acropolis in 1563 as "looming beneath a swarm of glittering golden crescents", with a minaret rising from the Parthenon. For all their changes in use, however, the buildings would still have resembled – very much more than today's bare ruins – the bustling and ornate ancient Acropolis, covered in sculpture and painted in bright colours.

Sadly, such images remain only in the prints and sketches of that period: the Acropolis buildings finally fell victim to the ravages of war, blown up during successive attempts by the Venetians to oust the Turks. In 1687, laying siege to the garrison, the Venetians ignited a Turkish gunpowder magazine in the Parthenon, and in the process blasted off its roof and set a **fire** that raged for two days and nights. The process of stripping down to the bare ruins seen today was completed by souvenir hunters and the efforts of the first archeologists (see box, p.70).

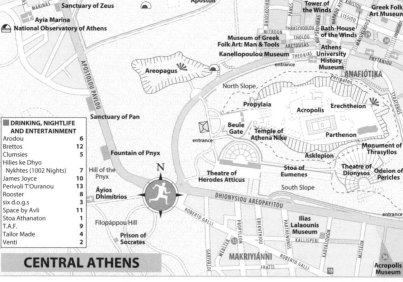

CENTRAL ATHENS

■ ACCOMMODATION					
Acropolis House	13	Fresh Hotel	1	Phardra	16
Alice Inn	14	Herodion	18	Phidias	10
Athens Backpackers	17	Hotel Grande		Student &	
Athens Center Square	2	Bretagne	7	Traveller's Inn	15
Attalos	4	InnAthens	11	Sweet Home	
City Circus	3	Metropolis	8	Athens	9
Electra Palace	12	O & B	5	Tempi	6

■ DRINKING, NIGHTLIFE AND ENTERTAINMENT	
Arodou	6
Brettos	12
Clumsies	5
Hilies ke Dhyo Nykhtes (1002 Nights)	7
James Joyce	10
Perivoli T'Ouranou	13
Rooster	8
six d.o.g.s	3
Space by Avli	11
Stoa Athanaton	1
T.A.F.	9
Tailor Made	4
Venti	2

Municipal Art Gallery
PLATIA THEATROU
Town Hall
PLATIA KOTZIA
PLATIA ELEFTHERIAS (PLATIA KOUMOUNDOUROU)
Fruit & Vegetable Bazaar
Meat & Seafood Market
PLATIA IEROU LOCHOU
AYII THEODHORI
Benáki Museum of Islamic Art
Museum of Traditional Pottery
Turkish Bath
Kerameikos
First Synagogue
PLATIA THISSIOU
Áyii Asómati
PLATIA IROON
PSYRRÍ
Thissio
AYIAS IRINIS
Áyia Irini
Kapnikaréa
Athens Flea Market
Monastiraki
MONASTIRÁKI
Herakleidon
Stoa of Zeus
Hephaisteion
Monument of Eponymous Heroes
Tholos
Ancient Agora
Odeion of Agrippa
Palace & Stoas
Áyii Apóstoli
Stoa of Attalos (Agora Museum)
Ceramics Collection
Hadrian's Library
Forum Ticket Office
Fethiye Mosque
Roman Forum
Tower of the Winds
Medresse
Popular Musical Instruments
Museum of Greek Folk Art Museum
Greek Folk Art Museum
Sanctuary of Zeus
Ayía Marína
National Observatory of Athens
Museum of Greek Folk Art: Man & Tools
Kanellopoulou Museum
Bath-House of the Winds
Athens University History Museum
Areopagus
ANAFIÓTIKA
Sanctuary of Pan
North Slope
Propylaia
Acropolis
Erechtheion
Beule Gate
Temple of Athena Nike
Parthenon
Monument of Thrasyllos
Asklepion
Theatre of Dionysos
Odeion of Pericles
Fountain of Pnyx
Hill of the Pnyx
Theatre of Herodes Atticus
Stoa of Eumenes
South Slope
Áyios Dhimítrios
DHIONYSIOU AREOPAYITOU
Filopáppou Hill
Prison of Socrates
MAKRIYÁNNI
Ilias Lalaounis Museum
Acropolis Museum

N

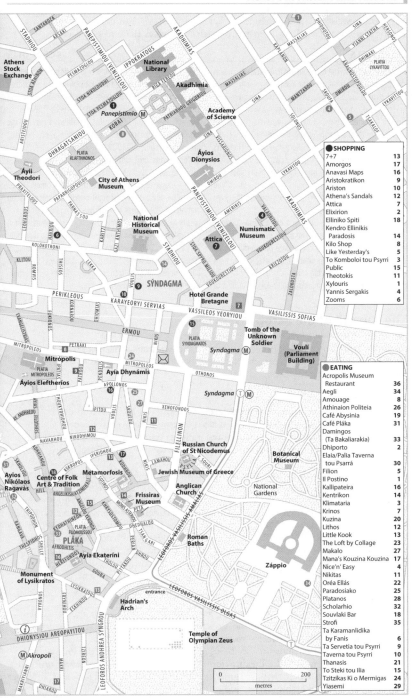

1

cafés to the west, in Thissío. On the other side, in Pláka, you may get a little lost among the jumble of alleys, but the rock itself is always there to guide you.

Tickets Entrance to the Acropolis archeological site, which includes the Parthenon, plus the South and North Slopes, costs €20 for a single visit. Alternatively, you can buy a joint ticket for €30, which is valid for up to seven visits over five days: it includes entrance to the Acropolis archeological site, the South and North Slopes, the Ancient Agora, the Ancient Agora Museum, the Roman Forum, Hadrian's Library, the Temple of Olympian Zeus, the Kerameikos archeological site and Aristotles Lyceum. Many sites also sell individual tickets (see accounts for prices), but if you want to visit several of the main sites, buying the joint ticket will work out cheaper.

Getting there To avoid the worst of the crowds, come very early in the day or late. The peak rush comes in late morning, when coach tours congregate before moving on to lunch elsewhere. The summit can be entered only from the west, where there's a big coach park at the bottom of the hill: bus #230 from Sýndagma will take you almost to

the entrance. On foot, the obvious approach is from Akrópoli Metro station to the south, along pedestrianized Dhionysíou Areopayítou past the Acropolis Museum, Theatre of Dionysos and Herodes Atticus Theatre (or through the South Slope site). Disabled access to the Acropolis is available via a lift on the north side (by arrangement only ☎ 210 321 4172).

Cafés, shops and cloakrooms You can buy water and sandwiches, as well as guidebooks, postcards and so on, from a couple of stands near the main ticket office. There's a handy branch of *Everest* right opposite Akrópoli Metro station (at the corner of Makriyiánni and Dhiakoú) and plenty of similar places around Monastiráki Metro station, plus cafés and tavernas nearby in almost every direction: Pláka (see p.103), Monastiráki (see p.104), Makriyiánni (see p.106) and Thissío (see p.106). Backpacks and large bags are not allowed in to the site – there's a cloakroom near the main ticket office.

The summit of the Acropolis

Daily 8am–8pm • €20, including entry to South and North slopes, or included in €30 joint ticket (see p.68)

As well as the iconic Parthenon, the **summit of the Acropolis** is home to the Erechtheion, the Temple of Athena Nike and the Propylaia, as well as lesser remains of many other ancient structures.

Propylaia

Today, as throughout history, the **Propylaia** are the gateway to the Acropolis. In Classical times, the Sacred Way extended along a steep ramp to this massive monumental double gatehouse; the modern path makes a more gradual, zigzagging ascent, passing first through an arched Roman entrance, the **Beule Gate**, added in the third century AD.

The Propylaia were constructed by Mnesikles from 437–432 BC, their axis and proportions aligned to balance the recently completed Parthenon. They – the name is the plural of *propylon*, or gateway, referring to the fact that there are two wings – were built from the same Pentelic marble (from Mount Pendéli, northeast of the city) as the temple, and in grandeur and architectural achievement are almost as impressive. In order to offset the difficulties of a sloping site, Mnesikles combined, for the first time, standard Doric columns with the taller and more delicate Ionic order. The ancient Athenians, awed by the fact that such wealth and craftsmanship should be used for a purely secular building, ranked this as their most prestigious monument.

The Panathenaic Way

The **Panathenaic Way** was the route of the great annual procession for ancient Athens' Panathenaic Festival, in honour of the city's patron goddess Athena. The procession – depicted on the Parthenon frieze – wound right through the Classical city from the gates now in the Kerameikos site (see p.89) via the North Slope and the Propylaia to the Parthenon and, finally, the Erechtheion. You can see traces of the ancient route just inside the Propylaia, where there are grooves cut for footholds in the rock and, to either side, niches for innumerable statues and offerings. In Classical times, it ran past a

10m-high bronze statue of Athena Promachos (Athena the Champion), whose base can just about be made out. Athena's spear and helmet were said to be visible to sailors approaching from as far away as Soúnio.

Close to the Propylaia too are the scant remains of a **Sanctuary of Artemis**. Although its function remains obscure, it is known that the precinct once housed a colossal bronze representation of the Wooden Horse of Troy. More noticeable is a nearby stretch of **Mycenaean wall** (running parallel to the Propylaia) that was incorporated into the Classical design.

Temple of Athena Nike

Simple and elegant, the **Temple of Athena Nike** stands on a precipitous platform overlooking Pireás and the Saronic Gulf. It has only recently reappeared, having been dismantled, cleaned and reconstructed. Not for the first time either: demolished by the Turks in the seventeenth century, the temple was reconstructed from its original blocks two hundred years later.

In myth, it was from the platform beside the temple that King Aegeus maintained a vigil for the safe return of his son Theseus from his mission to slay the Minotaur on Crete. Theseus, flushed with success, forgot his promise to swap the boat's black sails for white on his return. Seeing the black sails, Aegeus assumed his son had perished and, racked with grief, threw himself to his death.

Parthenon

The **Parthenon** temple was always intended to be a spectacular landmark and a symbol of the city's imperial confidence, and it was famous throughout the ancient world. Yet even in their wildest dreams, its creators could hardly have imagined that the ruins would come to symbolize the emergence of Western civilization – nor that, two-and-a-half millennia on, it would attract some two million tourists a year.

The first great building in Pericles' scheme, it was intended as a sanctuary for Athena and a home for her cult image – a colossal wooden statue by Fidias overlaid with ivory and gold plating, with precious gems as eyes and sporting an ivory gorgon's head on her breast. Originally the columns were brightly painted and surrounded by the finest sculpture of the Classical age, foremost among them the beautiful **Parthenon frieze** and pediments. Also brightly coloured, these are generally held to have depicted the Panathenaic procession, the birth of Athena and the struggles of Greeks to overcome giants, Amazons and centaurs. The greater part of the frieze, along with the central columns, were destroyed by the Venetian bombardment in 1687. The best surviving examples are in the British Museum in London (see box, p.70); the Acropolis Museum also has a few original pieces, as well as reconstructions of the whole thing.

To achieve the Parthenon's extraordinary and unequalled harmony of design, its architect, **Iktinos**, used every trick known to the Doric order of architecture. The building's proportions maintain a universal 9:4 ratio while all seemingly straight lines are in fact slightly **curved**, an optical illusion known as *entasis* (intensification). The columns (their profile bowed slightly to avoid seeming concave) are slanted inwards by 6cm, while each of the steps along the sides of the temple was made to incline just 12cm over a length of 70m.

FORTY YEARS OF SCAFFOLDING

If you see a photo of a pristine **Parthenon** standing against a clear sky, it is almost certainly an old one. For most of the twenty-first century the Acropolis buildings have been swathed in **scaffolding** and surrounded by **cranes** – at times some structures have even been removed altogether, to be cleaned and later replaced. Though originally intended to be complete in time for the 2004 Olympics, the work is now set to continue for the foreseeable future – some claim that it will be forty years before the job is complete.

1

THE ELGIN MARBLES

The controversy over the so-called Elgin Marbles has its origin in the activities of Western looters at the start of the nineteenth century: above all, the French ambassador **Fauvel**, who gathered antiquities for the Louvre, and **Lord Elgin**, who levered away sculptures from the Parthenon. As British Ambassador, Elgin obtained permission from the Turks to erect scaffolding, excavate and remove stones with inscriptions. He interpreted this concession as a licence to make off with almost all of the bas-reliefs from the Parthenon's frieze, most of its pedimental structures and a caryatid from the Erechtheion – all of which he later sold to the **British Museum**. While there were perhaps justifications for Elgin's action at the time – not least the Turks' tendency to use Parthenon stones in their lime kilns – his pilfering was controversial even then. Byron, for one, roundly disparaged his actions.

The Greeks hoped that the long-awaited completion of the new Acropolis Museum would create the perfect opportunity for the British Museum to bow to pressure and return the **Parthenon Marbles** (as they are always known here). But despite a campaign begun by the late Greek actress and culture minister Melina Mercouri in the 1980s, there is so far little sign of that happening; central to the British Museum's argument is that to return them would be to set a precedent that would empty virtually every museum in the world.

Erechtheion

To the north of the Parthenon stands the **Erechtheion**, the last of the great works of Pericles to be completed. Both Athena and the city's old patron of Poseidon-Erechtheus were worshipped here, in the most revered of the ancient temples. The site, according to myth, was that on which Athena and Poseidon held a contest, judged by their fellow Olympian gods; at the touch of Athena's spear, the first ever olive tree sprang from the ground, while Poseidon summoned forth a fountain of sea water. Athena won, and became patron of the city.

Today, the sacred objects within are long gone, but the elegant Ionic porticoes survive. By far the most striking feature, however, is the **Porch of the Caryatids**, whose columns form the tunics of six tall maidens. The ones *in situ* are replacements: five of the originals are in the Acropolis Museum, while a sixth was looted by Elgin – they are substituted here by casts in a different colour.

The South and North slopes

Daily 8am–8pm • Included in €20 Acropolis ticket, or €30 joint ticket (see p.68) • Ⓜ Akrópoli

Entrance to the **South Slope** site is either by a path leading around the side of the Acropolis near the main ticket office, or from below, off pedestrianized Leofóros Dhionysíou Areopayítou close to Ⓜ Akrópoli. A great deal of restoration and excavation work is ongoing here, including the opening up of a new area, the **North Slope**, on the eastern and northern edges of the rock, above Pláka.

Theatre of Dionysos

The **Theatre of Dionysos** is one of the most evocative locations in the city. Here the masterpieces of Aeschylus, Sophocles, Euripides and Aristophanes were first performed; it was also the venue in Classical times for the annual festival of tragic drama, where each Greek citizen would take his turn as member of the chorus. Founded in the sixth century BC and rebuilt in the fourth, the theatre could hold some 17,000 spectators – considerably more than Herodes Atticus' 5000–6000 seats. Twenty of the original 64 tiers survive. Most notable are the great marble thrones in the front row, each inscribed with the name of an official of the festival or of an important priest; in the middle sat the priest of Dionysos and on his right the representative of the Delphic Oracle. At the centre of the roped-off stage is a diamond **mosaic** of multicoloured marble, best seen from above, while to the rear are reliefs of episodes in the life of Dionysos flanked by two squatting Sileni, devotees of the satyrs.

1

Herodes Atticus Theatre

The dominant structure on the south side of the Acropolis – much more immediately obvious even than the Theatre of Dionysos – is the second-century Roman **Herodes Atticus Theatre** (Odeion of Herodes Atticus). This has been extensively restored for performances of music and Classical drama during the summer festival (see p.112) but is open only for shows; at other times, you'll have to be content with spying over the wall.

Stoa of Eumenes

Between the two theatres lie the foundations of the **Stoa of Eumenes**, originally a massive colonnade of stalls erected in the second century BC. Above the *stoa*, high up under the walls of the Acropolis, extend the ruins of the **Asklepion**, a sanctuary devoted to the healing god Asklepios and built around a sacred spring; restoration is ongoing.

Monument of Thrasyllos

Above the Theatre of Dionysos, you can see the entry to a huge cave, originally sacred to Artemis. It later housed choregic awards (to celebrate victory in drama contests; see p.75) won by the family of **Thrasyllos**, hence the name. The entrance was closed off around 320 BC with a marble facade, which is currently being restored. The cave was later converted to Christian use and became the chapel of Virgin Mary of the Rocks, but an ancient statue of Dionysos remained inside until it was removed by Lord Elgin (and is now in the British Museum), while the Classical structure survived almost unchanged until 1827, when it was blown up in a Turkish siege.

Peripatos

The **Peripatos** was the ancient street that ran around the north side of the Acropolis. Access to this side has only recently been opened up so that you can now walk right around the rock within the fenced site, starting above the Theatre of Dionysos and emerging by the entry to the main Acropolis site; there's also a new entrance from Pláka, by the Kannellopoulou museum.

There are no major monuments en route, but the numerous caves and springs help explain the strategic importance of the Acropolis. In one impressive cleft in the rock was a secret stairway leading up to the temples: this provided access to spring water in times of war, and was also used in rituals, when blindfolded initiates would be led this way. Nearby are numerous other caves and rock arches that had cult status in ancient times.

Acropolis Museum

Dhionysíou Areopayítou 15 • April–Oct Mon 8am–4pm, Tues–Thurs, Sat & Sun 8am–8pm, Fri 8am–10pm; Nov–March Mon–Thurs 9am–5pm, Fri 9am–10pm, Sat & Sun 9am–8pm; last admission 30min before closing • €5 • ⓦ theacropolismuseum.gr • ⓜ Akrópoli

The **Acropolis Museum**, opened in 2009, is a magnificent building, filled with beautiful objects, with a wonderful sense of space and light and a glass top storey with a direct view up to the Parthenon itself.

The remains of ancient Athens, uncovered during the building work, can be seen even before you enter, protected under glass flooring that continues through the ground floor. The displays proper start with a ramp described as the **Slopes of the Acropolis**, as that is where most of the pottery and other objects displayed here were found. At the top of the ramp are sculptures from the pediment of an early temple that stood on the site of the Parthenon, the Hekatompedon. Their surviving paintwork gives a good indication of the vivid colours originally used in temple decoration.

Statues dominate the **first floor**: the *Moschophoros*, a painted marble statue of a young man carrying a sacrificial calf, dated 570 BC, is one of the earliest examples of Greek art in marble. There's also an extensive collection of *Korai*, or statues of maidens. The

1

progression in style, from the simply contoured Doric clothing to the more elegant and voluminous Ionic designs, is fascinating; the figures' smiles also change subtly, becoming increasingly loose and natural.

On the **top floor**, a fifteen-minute video (alternately in English and Greek) offers a superb introduction to the Parthenon sculptures. The metopes and the frieze are set out around the outside of the hall, arranged as they would have been on the Parthenon itself; the pediments are displayed separately at each end of the gallery. Only a relatively small number are original (see box, p.70); the rest are represented by plaster copies which seem deliberately crude, to make a point (there are better copies in Akropoli Metro station, for example).

On the way back down through the museum are **statues** from the Temple of Athena Nike and the Erechtheion, including the original Caryatids. The sculptures from the parapet of the former, all depicting Athena Nike in various guises, include a particularly graceful and fluid sculpture known as *Iy Sandalizoméni*, which depicts her adjusting her sandal. Don't forget to check out the restaurant, too (see p.108).

Areopagus

Immediately below the entrance to the Acropolis • Free access

Metal steps as well as ancient, slippery, rock-hewn stairs ascend the low hill of the **Areopagus**, or "Hill of Ares". This was the site of the Council of Nobles and the Judicial Court under the aristocratic rule of ancient Athens; during the Classical period, the court lost its powers of government to the Assembly (held on the Pnyx) but it remained the court of criminal justice, dealing primarily with cases of homicide. In **myth**, it was also the site where Ares, God of War, was tried for the murder of one of Poseidon's sons; Aeschylus used the setting in *The Eumenides* for the trial of Orestes, who stood accused of murdering his mother, Clytemnestra. The Persians camped here during their siege of the Acropolis in 480 BC, and in the Roman era Saint Paul preached the "Sermon on an Unknown God" on the hill and won, among his converts, Dionysios "the Areopagite", who became the city's patron saint.

Today, there's little evidence of ancient grandeur beyond various steps and niches cut into the perilously slippery rock, and the hill is littered with cigarette butts and empty beer cans left by the crowds who come to rest after their exertions on the Acropolis and to enjoy the **views**. These, at least, are good – down over the Agora and towards the ancient cemetery of Kerameikos.

Ancient Agora

Daily 8am–3pm; last admission 15min before closing • €8, or included in €30 joint ticket (see p.68) • Ⓜ Monastiráki

The **ancient Agora**, or market, was the heart of Athenian city life from as early as 3000 BC. Approached either from the Acropolis, down the path skirting the Areopagus, or through the northern entrance on Adhrianoú, it is an extensive and confusing jumble of ruins, dating from various stages of building between the sixth century BC and the fifth century AD. As well as the **marketplace**, this was the chief **meeting place** of the city, where orators held forth, business was discussed and gossip exchanged – St Paul, for example, took the opportunity to meet and talk to Athenians here. It was also the first home of the democratic assembly before that moved to the Pnyx, and continued to be its meeting place when cases of ostracism (see p.74) were discussed for most of the Classical period.

Hephaisteion

The best overview of the Agora is from the exceptionally well-preserved **Hephaisteion**, or Temple of Hephaistos, where there's a terrace overlooking the rest of the site from

CLOCKWISE FROM TOP LEFT SNFCC (P.93); TOMB OF THE UNKNOWN SOLDIER (P.80); ACROPOLIS MUSEUM (P.71) >

1

the west. Here a plan shows the buildings as they were in 150 AD, and the various remains laid out in front of you make a great deal more sense with this to help (there are similar plans at the entrances). The temple itself was originally thought to be dedicated to Theseus, because his exploits are depicted on the frieze (hence Thissíon, which has given its name to the area); more recently it has been accepted that it actually honoured Hephaistos, patron of blacksmiths and metalworkers. It was one of the earliest buildings of Pericles' programme, but is now one of the least known – perhaps because it lacks the curvature and "lightness" of the Parthenon's design; the barrel-vaulted roof dates from a Byzantine conversion into the **church** of Saint George.

Áyii Apóstoli

The church of **Áyii Apóstoli** (the Holy Apostles), by the south entrance, is worth a look as you wander among the extensive foundations of the other Agora buildings. Inside are fragments of fresco, exposed during restoration of the eleventh-century shrine.

Stoa of Attalos

Same hours as Agora but opens at 11am Mon • €4 extra, or included in €30 joint ticket (see p.68)

For some background to the Agora, head for the **Stoa of Attalos**. Originally constructed around 158 BC, the Stoa was completely rebuilt between 1953 and 1956 and is, in every respect except colour, an entirely faithful reconstruction; with or without its original bright red and blue paint, it is undeniably spectacular.

A small **museum** occupies 10 of the 21 shops that formed the lower level of the building. It displays items found at the Agora site from the earliest Neolithic occupation to Roman and Byzantine times. Many of the early items come from burials, but as ever the highlights are from the Classical era, including some good red-figure pottery and a bronze Spartan shield. Look out for the *ostraka*, or pottery shards, with names written on them. At annual assemblies of the citizens, these would be handed in, and the individual with most votes banished, or **"ostracized"**, from the city for ten years.

Pláka

The largely pedestrianized area of **Pláka**, with its narrow lanes and stepped alleys climbing towards the Acropolis, is arguably the most attractive part of Athens and certainly the most popular with visitors; it's a welcome escape from the concrete blocks that dominate the rest of the metropolis. With scores of **cafés, restaurants and shops** to fill the time between museums and important sites such as the **Roman Forum**, it's an enjoyable place to wander.

An appealing approach to Pláka is to follow **Odhós Kydhathinéon**, a pedestrian walkway that starts near the **Anglican and Russian churches** on Odhós Filellínon. It leads gently downhill, past the Museum of Greek Folk Art, through café-crowded Platía Filomoússou Eterías, to Hadrian's street, **Odhós Adhrianoú**, which runs nearly the whole length of Pláka and on into Monastiráki and Thissío. These two are the main commercial and tourist streets of the district, with Adhrianoú increasingly tacky and downmarket as it approaches Platía Monastirakíou and the Flea Market.

Jewish Museum of Greece

Nikis 39 • Mon–Fri 9am–2.30pm, Sun 10am–2pm • €6 • ⓦ jewishmuseum.gr • Ⓜ Sýndagma

The **Jewish Museum of Greece** tells the story of Jews in Greece, elegantly presented in a series of dimly lit rooms, with plenty of explanation in English. Downstairs are art and religious paraphernalia, many of which are centuries old. The centrepiece is the reconstructed **synagogue of Pátra**, which dates from the 1920s, whose furnishings have been moved here en masse and remounted. Upstairs, more recent history includes

A SLICE OF OLD ATHENS: ANAFIÓTIKA

The main arteries of Pláka, above all Adhrianoú, home of the Manchester United beach towel and "Sex in Ancient Greece" playing cards, can become depressingly **touristy**. For a break, climb up into the jumble of streets and alleys that cling to the lower slopes of the northeast side of the Acropolis. Here, the whitewashed houses and ancient churches of the **Anafiótika** quarter proclaim a cheerfully architect-free zone. There's still the odd shop, and taverna tables are set out wherever a bit of flat ground can be found, but there are also plenty of hidden corners redolent of a quieter era. A particularly good view of this area can be had by following the paths that track around the base of the Acropolis, above the buildings.

World War II and the German occupation, when Greece's Jewish population was reduced from almost eighty thousand to less than ten thousand. There are features, too, on the part played by Jews in the Greek resistance and many stories of survival.

Frissiras Museum

Monís Asteríou 3 and 7 • Wed–Fri 10am–5pm, Sat & Sun 11am–5pm • €6 • ⓦ frissirasmuseum.com • Ⓜ Sýndagma or Akrópoli

The **Frissiras Museum**, housed in two beautifully renovated, Neoclassical buildings, is home to a significant **permanent modern art collection**. The museum has over three thousand works – mostly figurative painting plus a few sculptures, as well as a regular programme of exhibitions. The space at no. 7 houses the permanent exhibition, which includes plenty of names familiar to English-speakers – David Hockney, Peter Blake and Paula Rego among them – as well as many Greek and European artists. Temporary exhibitions, along with a fine shop and an elegant café, are a block away at no. 3.

Monument of Lysikratos

In the southeastern corner of Pláka, the **Monument of Lysikratos**, a stone-and-marble structure dating from 335 BC, rises from a small, triangular open area overlooked by a quiet café/taverna. It's near the end of Odhós Tripódhon, a relic of the ancient **Street of the Tripods**, where winners of drama competitions erected monuments to dedicate their trophies (in the form of tripod cauldrons) to Dionysos. The last survivor of these monuments, this example sports six Corinthian columns rising up to a marble dome on which, in a flourish of acanthus-leaf carvings, the winning tripod was placed.

In the seventeenth century, the monument became part of a Capuchin convent, which provided regular lodgings for European travellers – **Byron** is said to have written part of *Childe Harold* here, and the street beyond, Výronos, is named after him.

Ayía Ekateríni

Platía Ayía Ekateríni • Mon–Fri 7.30am–12.30pm & 5–6.30pm, Sat & Sun 5–10pm • Free • ☎ 210 322 8974 • Ⓜ Akrópoli

The church of **Ayía Ekateríni** – St Catherine's – is one of the few in Pláka that's routinely open. At its heart is an eleventh-century Byzantine original, although this has been pretty well hidden by later additions. You can see it most clearly from the back of the church, while in the courtyard in front are foundations of a Roman building. Inside, the over-restored frescoes look brand new, and there are plenty of glittering icons.

Athens University History Museum

Thólou 5 • Mon–Fri 9.30am–2.30pm; June–Sept also Mon & Wed 6–9pm • Free • ☎ 210 368 9500 • Ⓜ Monastiráki

High up under the Acropolis, the **Athens University History Museum**, site of Athens' first university, occupies a grand old mansion, one of the oldest in the city. The building itself is a large part of the attraction – in particular the scintillating views from

1

the top-floor terrace – but there's also a great collection of old scientific and medical instruments, sadly, labelled unfortunately in Greek only.

Kanellopoulou Museum

Theorías 12 • Tues–Sun 8am–3pm • Free • Ⓜ Monastiráki • ☎ 210 321 2313

Head for the highest street beneath the looming Acropolis walls, and you'll eventually emerge by the eclectic **Kanellopoulou Museum**, directly opposite the North Slope Acropolis entrance. This private collection includes a bit of everything – gilded icons, ancient jewellery, Classical-era pottery – and almost every object is a superb example of its kind.

Roman Forum

Entrance on Dhioskoúron • Daily: April–Oct 8am–8pm; Nov–March 8am–5pm • €2, or included in €30 joint ticket (see p.68) • Ⓜ Monastiráki

The **Roman Forum** was built during the reign of Julius Caesar and his successor Augustus as an extension of the older Agora. As today, its main entrance was on the west side, through the **Gate of Athena Archegetis**. This gate marked the end of a street leading up from the Greek Agora, and its four surviving columns give a vivid impression of the grandeur of the original portal. On the side facing the Acropolis, you can still make out an engraved edict announcing the rules and taxes on the sale of oil. At the opposite end of the Roman Forum, a second gateway is also easily made out, and between the two was the marketplace itself, surrounded by colonnades and shops, some of which have been excavated. Inside the fenced site, but just outside the market area to the east, are the foundations of public latrines dating from the first century AD.

Tower of the Winds

The best preserved and easily the most intriguing of the ruins inside the Forum site is the graceful octagonal structure known as the **Tower of the Winds**. This predates the Forum and stands just outside the main market area. Designed in the first century BC by Andronikos of Kyrrhos, a Syrian astronomer, it served as a compass, sundial, weather vane and water clock – the last of these powered by a stream from one of the Acropolis springs. Each face of the tower is adorned with a relief of a figure floating through the air, personifying the eight winds. Beneath each of these, it is still possible to make out the markings of eight sundials. On top of the building was a bronze weather vane in the form of the sea god Triton. In Ottoman times, dervishes used the tower as a *tekke* or ceremonial hall, terrifying their superstitious Orthodox neighbours with their chanting, music and whirling meditation.

ROMAN ATHENS

In 146 BC, the **Romans** ousted Athens' Macedonian rulers and incorporated the city into their vast new province of Achaia, whose capital was at Corinth. The city's status as a renowned seat of learning (Cicero and Horace were educated here) and great artistic centre ensured that it was treated with respect, and Athenian artists and architects were much in demand in Rome. Athens, though, was a backwater – there were few major construction projects, and what building there was tended to follow Classical Greek patterns.

The one Roman emperor who did spend a significant amount of time in Athens, and left his mark here, was **Hadrian** (reigned 117–138 AD). Among his grandiose monuments are Hadrian's Arch (see p.82), a magnificent and immense library (see p.79), and (though it had been begun centuries before) the Temple of Olympian Zeus (see p.82). A generation later, **Herodes Atticus**, a Roman senator who owned extensive lands in Marathon, became the city's last major benefactor of ancient times.

THE OTTOMAN LEGACY

Although they occupied the city for more than four hundred years, there are remarkably few **Ottoman relics in Athens**. Near the Roman Forum is a small cluster including the Fethiye Tzami (see p.77) and Medresse (see p.77), both of which can be viewed only from the outside, and the Bath-House of the Winds (see p.77); also worth checking out are the nearby ceramic collection of the Museum of Greek Folk Art (see p.79) and the Benáki Museum of Islamic Art (see p.89).

Fethiye Tzami (Mosque)

The oldest **mosque** in Athens, the **Fethiye Tzami**, built in 1458, occupies a corner of the Forum site. It was dedicated by Sultan Mehmet II, who conquered Constantinople in 1453 (*fethiye* means "conquest" in Turkish). There's a fine, porticoed entrance but, unfortunately, you can't see inside the restored building, as it's used as an archeological warehouse.

Medresse

Eólou, at Pelopídha

Outside the Forum site, more or less opposite the Tower of the Winds, the gateway and single dome of a **medresse**, an Islamic school, survive. During the last years of Ottoman rule and the early years of Greek independence, this building was used as a prison and was notorious for its harsh conditions; a plane tree in the courtyard was used for hangings. The prison was closed in the 1900s and the bulk of it torn down.

Museum of Greek Popular Musical Instruments

Dhioyénous 1–3 • Tues–Sun 8am–3pm • Free • ☎ 210 325 0198 • Ⓜ Monastiráki

The **Museum of Greek Popular Musical Instruments** traces the history of virtually every type of musical instrument that has ever been played in Greece. It's all attractively displayed in a fine mansion, with drums and wind instruments of all sorts (from crude bagpipes to clarinets) on the ground floor, lyras, fiddles, lutes and a profusion of stringed instruments upstairs. In the basement, there are more percussion and toy instruments. Reproductions of frescoes show the Byzantine antecedents of many instruments, and headphones are provided for sampling the music made by the various exhibits.

Bath-House of the Winds

Kirístou 8 • Wed–Mon 8am–3pm • €2; audio tour €1, plus deposit • Ⓦ melt.gr • Ⓜ Monastiráki

Close to the Fethiye Mosque is another Ottoman survival, the site of the **Bath-House of the Winds**. Constructed in the 1450s, the baths were in use, with many later additions, right up to 1965. The restored bath-house offers an insight into a part of Athens' past that is rarely glimpsed and well worth a look. Traditionally, the baths would have been used in shifts by men and women, although expansion in the nineteenth century provided the separate facilities you see today. The *tepidarium* and *caldarium*, fitted out in marble with domed roofs and skylights, are particularly beautiful. The underfloor and wall heating systems have been exposed in places, while upstairs there are photos and pictures of old Athens. Labelling throughout is in Greek only, but an **audio tour** is available. You can visit a working hammam in Thissío (see p.87).

The Museum of Greek Folk Art

Kiristou 8 • 8am–3pm; closed Tues • €2 • Ⓦ melt.gr • Ⓜ Sýndagma or Akrópoli

The **Folk Art Museum** is one of the most enjoyable in the city, even though it's let down somewhat by poor lighting and labelling. Its five floors are devoted to displays of

1

weaving, pottery, regional costumes, jewellery and embroidery along with other traditional Greek arts and crafts. The highlight, though, is on the first floor: a reconstructed room from a house on the island of Lesvós with a series of murals by the primitive artist **Theofilos** (1868–1934). These naive scenes from Greek folklore and history, especially the independence struggle, are wonderful, and typical of the artist, who was barely recognized in his lifetime and spent most of his career painting tavernas and cafés in exchange for food and board.

There are three other branches of the museum across the city: a tiny but fascinating section devoted to the world of work, entitled "**Man and Tools**" at Panós 22 (Tues–Sat 8am–3pm; €2), the **Bath-House of the Winds** (see p.77) and a **ceramics collection** housed inside a mosque (see opposite).

Monastiráki and Psyrrí

Monastiráki, to the north of Pláka, is substantially less touristy than its neighbour, though there are still plenty of sights and extensive opportunities for eating, drinking and shopping. The area gets its name from the little monastery church (*monastiráki*) on central **Platía Monastirakíou**. The square, with its handy Metro station, marks a return to the traffic and bustle of commercial Athens – it's full of fruit stalls, street performers, lottery vendors and kiosks. This neighbourhood has been a **marketplace** since Ottoman times, and it still preserves, in places, a bazaar atmosphere. The main market (see p.84) lies straight up Athinás from here, towards Omónia, but nearer at hand you'll see signs in either direction that proclaim you're entering the famous **Athens Flea Market**.

Psyrrí, northwest of Platía Monastirakíou, is a former working-class district that is now home to some of Athens' busiest nightlife as well as quirky shops and galleries. Around Odhós Sarrí, especially, **graffitti art** has been positively encouraged and there are some magical works on the crumbling buildings and metal-shuttered shop fronts around here. This is also a great place to **eat and drink**: between them, Monastiráki and Psyrrí probably have more places to eat per square metre than anywhere else in Athens.

Athens Flea Market

Most shops open daily all day, till late, though more traditional ones close for a siesta; genuine flea market on Sun mornings

These days the description of the streets around Platía Monastirakíou as **Athens Flea Market** is a bit of a misnomer – there's plenty of shopping, but mostly of a very conventional nature. **Odhós Pandhróssou**, to the east, is almost entirely geared to tourists, an extension (though not quite literally) of Adhrianoú. West of the square the flea market has more of its old character, and among the tourist tat you'll find shops full of handmade musical instruments, or stalls selling nothing but chess and *tavlí* (Greek backgammon) boards. Around Normánou and **Platía Avyssinías** shops specialize in furniture and junky antiques, while from here to Adhrianoú, the relics of a real flea market survive in hopeless jumble-sale rejects, touted by a cast of eccentrics (especially on Sun). **Odhós Adhrianoú** is at its most appealing at this end, with a couple of interesting antique shops and some shady cafés overlooking the Metro Lines, the Agora and the Acropolis.

The stretch of **Odhós Ermoú** on the edge of the flea market as it heads west from Platía Monastirakíou is the southern fringe of fashionable Psyrrí, and among the workaday old-fashioned furniture stores here are some interesting new designer and retro shops. In the other direction, as it heads up towards Sýndagma, the street is much more staid; in the pedestrianized upper section are familiar high-street chains and department stores.

Iridhanós River

Platía Monastirakíou • Ⓜ Monastiráki

The **Iridhanós River** (or Eridanos) runs across Athens from its source on Lykavitós hill, via Sýndagma and Monastiráki to Keramikós. Celebrated in Classical times, it had effectively been lost until the work on the Metro expansion uncovered its underground course early this century. Part of the ancient Greek and Roman system that turned it into an **underground drain** can be seen at Monastiráki Metro station, and through railings and glass paving from the platía above. The brick vaulting of these **ancient waterworks** constitutes some impressive engineering work and, in winter and spring, substantial amounts of water still course through.

Hadrian's Library

Entry on Áreos • Daily 8am–3pm • €2, or included in €30 joint ticket (see p.68) • ☎ 210 324 9350 • Ⓜ Monastiráki

Bordering the north end of the Forum site and stretching right through from Eólou to Áreos, **Hadrian's Library** was an enormous building that once enclosed a cloistered courtyard of a hundred columns. Despite the name, this was much more than just a library – it was a **cultural centre** that included art galleries, lecture halls and a great public space at its centre. The site is still being **excavated**; much of it has been built over many times, and a lot of what you can see today consists of the foundations and mosaic floors of later Byzantine churches. However, the entrance has been partly reconstructed, some of the original columns survive, and above all you get an excellent sense of the sheer scale of the original building, once enclosed by walls and covering an area even larger than the current site. The **Tetraconch Church**, for example, whose remains lie at the centre of the site, was built entirely within the library's internal courtyard.

Museum of Greek Folk Art: Ceramics Collection

Áreos 1 • 8am–3pm; closed Tues • €2 • Ⓦ melt.gr • Ⓜ Monastiráki

Squeezed between the walls of Hadrian's library and the shacks of Pandhróssou, the **Ceramics Collection** is housed in the former Mosque of Tzisdarákis. Built in 1759, the building has had a chequered life; it was converted to a barracks and then a jail after Greek independence, before it became the original home of the **Museum of Greek Folk Art** in 1918. Today, as a branch of that museum, it houses the **Kyriazópoulos collection** of ceramics – the legacy of a Thessaloníki professor. Good as it is, the collection is likely to excite you only if you have a particular interest in pottery; most will probably find the **mosque** itself, the only one in Athens open to the public, at least as big an attraction.

Though missing its minaret, and with a balcony added inside for the museum, plenty of **original features** remain. In the airy, domed space, look out for the striped *mihrab* (the niche indicating the direction of Mecca), a calligraphic inscription above the entrance that records the mosque's founder and date, and a series of niches used as extra *mihrabs* for occasions when worshippers could not fit into the main hall.

Kapnikaréa

Ermoú, at Kapnikaréas • Free access • ☎ 210 322 4462 • Ⓜ Monastiráki

The pretty Byzantine church of **Kapnikaréa** marks more or less the beginning of the upmarket shopping on Ermoú; it looks tiny, almost shrunken, in these high-rise, urban surroundings. Originally eleventh century, but with later additions, it has a lovely little dome and a gloomy interior in which you can just about make out the modern frescoes. The church is allegedly named after its founder, a tax collector: *kapnós* means smoke, and in the Byzantine era there was a tax on houses, known as the smoke tax.

1

Platía Mitropóleos and around

A welcome spot of calm among the busy shopping streets that surround it, **Platía Mitropóleos** – Cathedral Square – is home to not just one, but two cathedrals. The modern **Mitrópolis** is a large, clumsy nineteenth-century edifice; **Áyios Eleftheríos** alongside it is dwarfed by comparison but infinitely more attractive. There are also several other small churches nearby: look out especially for the dusty, tiny chapel of **Ayía Dhynámis** (though you're best off admiring it from the outside, as the building above looks like its about to collapse), crouching surreally beneath the concrete piers of the now abandoned Ministry of Education and Religion building on Odhós Mitropóleos, a short way up towards Sýndagma.

Áyios Eleftheríos

Platía Mitropóleos

There is said to have been a church where **Áyios Eleftheríos** now stands since the very earliest days of Christianity in Athens; what you see today dates from the twelfth century. Also known as Mikrí Mitropolí ("little cathedral"), it's a beautiful little structure, cobbled together with plain and carved blocks from earlier incarnations, some of which are almost certainly from that original church.

Sýndagma

All roads lead to **Sýndagma** – **Platía Syndágmatos**, or Constitution Square, to give it its full name: you'll almost inevitably find yourself here sooner or later for the Metro and bus connections. Roughly midway between the Acropolis and Lykavitós hill, with the Greek Parliament building (the Voulí) on its uphill side, and banks, offices and embassies clustered around, it's the **political and geographic heart** of Athens and still the principal venue for mass demonstrations and political rallies. The square's name derives from the fact that King Otto was forced by popular pressure to declare a formal constitution for the new Greek state from a palace balcony here in 1844.

Greek Parliament and the Tomb of the Unknown Soldier

Platía Syndágmatos • Not open to the public • Ⓜ Sýndagma

The **Voulí**, the **Greek Parliament**, presides over Platía Syndágmatos from its uphill (east) side. A vast, ochre-and-white Neoclassical structure, it was built as the royal palace for Greece's first monarch, the Bavarian King Otto, who moved in in 1842. In front of it, goose-stepping **evzónes** in tasselled caps, kilt and woolly leggings – a prettified version of traditional mountain costume – change their guard at regular intervals before the **Tomb of the Unknown Soldier**. On Sundays, just before 11am, a full band and the entire corps parade from the tomb to their barracks at the back of the National Gardens to the rhythm of innumerable camera shutters.

Hotel Grande Bretagne

Vasiléos Yeoryíou 1 • Ⓦ grandebretagne.gr • Ⓜ Sýndagma

Along with the Voulí, the vast **Hotel Grande Bretagne** – Athens' grandest – is just about the only building on Platía Syndágmatos to have survived postwar development. Past the impressive facade and uniformed doormen, the interior is magnificently opulent, as befits a grand hotel established in the late nineteenth century. It's worth taking a look inside or having a drink at one of the **bars**; recent renovations include a new rooftop pool, bar and restaurant with great views across the city.

The hotel has long been at the centre of Greek **political intrigue**. In one notorious episode, Winston Churchill narrowly avoided being blown up here on Christmas Day, 1944, when saboteurs from the Communist-led ELAS movement placed an enormous explosive charge in the drains. According to whom you believe, the bomb was either discovered in time by a kitchen employee, or removed by ELAS themselves when they realized that Churchill was one of their potential targets.

National Gardens

Entrances on Amalías, Vasilíssis Sofías and Iródhou Attikoú • Sunrise–sunset • Free • Ⓜ Sýndagma

The **National Gardens**, which spread out to the south and east of the Voulí, are the most refreshing acres in the city – not so much a flower garden as a luxuriant tangle of trees, whose shade and duck ponds provide palpable relief from the heat of summer. They were originally the private palace gardens, a pet project of Queen Amalia in the 1840s; supposedly the main duty of the minuscule Greek navy in its early days was the fetching of rare plants, often the gifts of other royal houses, from remote corners of the globe. Despite a major pre-Olympic clear-out, there's still something of an air of benign neglect here, with rampant undergrowth and signs that seem to take you round in circles. It's a great place for a picnic, though, or just a shady respite from the city streets. There's a children's **playground** (on the Záppio side) and a tiny **zoo** (signed *Irattikou*) with ostriches and some exotic fowl, though most of the cages these days are occupied by chickens, rabbits and domestic cats. The pretty building of the **Botanical Museum** occupies an elegant little pavilion nearby, though it was closed for refurbishment at the time of writing.

Presidential Palace

Iródhou Attikoú, at Vasiléos Yeoryíou B • Not open to the public • Ⓜ Sýndagma

Across the road from the east side of the National Gardens is the **Presidential Palace**, the royal residence until King Constantine's exile in 1967, where *evzónes* stand on sentry duty. Next door, the slightly more modest **Mégaro Maxímou** is the official residence of the prime minister.

Záppio

Grounds 24hr • Free • **Building** Only open to the public during exhibitions • Ⓦ zappeion.gr • Ⓜ Sýndagma

On the southern side of the National Gardens are the graceful crescent-shaped grounds of the **Záppio**. More formally laid out than the Gardens, the grounds are popular with evening and weekend strollers. The imposing Neoclassical building, originally built as an exhibition hall, has taken on prestigious roles such as headquarters of the Greek presidency of the European Union and of the 2004 Olympic: today, it hosts occasional exhibitions (see website for details).

Roman baths

Leóforos Amalías • Ⓜ Akrópoli or Sýndagma

Roman Athens expanded beyond the Classical Greek city to cover much of the area around the National Gardens. The most tangible evidence of this lies in a large **Roman baths** complex that was discovered during excavations for the Metro. It originally dates from the late third century AD, though it was substantially expanded over succeeding centuries. The baths, in which complete rooms have been well preserved, are now visible under a metal-and-perspex cover alongside the busy avenue of Leóforos Amalías, 100m or so north of Hadrian's Arch.

1

Hadrian's Arch

Leóforos Amalías • Free, unfenced • Ⓜ Akrópoli

Hadrian's Arch stands in splendid isolation across from one of the busiest road junctions in Athens, the meeting of Amalías and Syngroú. With the traffic roaring by, this is not somewhere you'll be tempted to linger, but it's definitely worth a look on your way to the Temple of Olympian Zeus. The arch, 18m high, was erected by the emperor to mark the edge of the Classical city and the beginning of his own. On the west side, its frieze – damaged and hard to make out – is inscribed, "This is Athens, the ancient city of Theseus", and on the other, "This is the City of Hadrian and not of Theseus". With so little that's ancient remaining around it, this doesn't make immediate sense, but you can look up, westwards, to the Acropolis and in the other direction see the columns of the great temple completed by Hadrian.

Temple of Olympian Zeus

Entrance on Vasilíssis Ólgas • Daily 8am–7pm • €2, or included in €30 joint ticket (see p.68) • Ⓜ Akrópoli

Directly behind Hadrian's Arch, the colossal pillars of the **Temple of Olympian Zeus** – also known as the **Olympieion** – stand in the middle of a huge, dusty clearing with excellent views of the Acropolis and constant traffic noise. One of the largest temples in the ancient world, and according to Livy, "the only temple on earth to do justice to the god", it was dedicated by Hadrian in 131 AD, almost seven hundred years after Peisistratos had begun work on it. Hadrian marked the occasion by contributing a statue of Zeus and a suitably monumental one of himself, although both have since been lost.

Today, just fifteen of the temple's original 104 **marble pillars** remain erect. To the north of the temple enclosure, by the site entrance, are various excavated remains including another impressive **Roman bath complex**. The south side of the enclosure overlooks a further area of excavation (not open to the public) where both Roman and much earlier buildings have been revealed.

The Grand Avenues

Northwest from Sýndagma, the broad and busy **grand avenues** of **Stadhíou**, **Panepistimíou** (officially called Venizélou) and **Akadhimías** head towards Platía Omonías. Initially lined with grandiose mansions, some converted to museums, squares with open vistas and opulent arcades with chichi shopping, they move steadily downmarket as you approach Omónia.

Museums

There are three museums around the grand avenues of rather specialist interest: the **National Historical Museum** (Stadhíou 13, Platía Kolokotróni; Tues–Sun 9am–2pm; €3, free on Sun; ⓦnhmuseum.gr), which focuses on Greek history from the fall of Constantinople to the reign of King Otto; the **City of Athens Museum** (Paparigopoúlou 7, on Platía Klafthmónos; Mon & Wed–Fri 9am–4pm, Sat & Sun 10am–3pm; €5; ⓦathenscitymuseum.gr), set in King Otto's 1830s residence; and the **Numismatic Museum** (Panepistimíou 12; Tues–Sun 8.30am–4pm; €3; ⓦenma.gr), which houses a collection of over 600,000 coins and related artefacts.

Platía Klafthmónos

Platía Klafthmónos offers a wonderful view towards three grand Neoclassical buildings on Panepistimíou. Here the planners' conceptualization of the capital of newly independent Greece can for once be seen more or less as they envisaged it – the nation's Classical heritage blends with modern, Western values. As you look up you'll see, from the left, the sober grey marble of the **National Library**, the rather racier

Akadhimía (University), enlivened by frescoes depicting King Otto surrounded by ancient Greek gods and heroes, and the over-the-top **Academy of Science** with its pediment friezes and giant statues of Athena and Apollo. The garish decoration gives an alarming impression of what the Classical monuments might have looked like when their paintwork was intact. Behind these buildings, on Akadhimías, is a major terminus for **city buses**, from where you can get a connection to almost anywhere in the city or its suburbs.

Platía Omónias and the bazaar

While Pláka and Sýndagma are resolutely geared to tourists and the Athenian well-heeled, **Platía Omonías** (Omónia Square) and its surroundings represent a much more gritty city. Here the grand avenues imagined by the nineteenth-century planners have been subverted by time and the realities of Athens' status as a commercial capital. If you head up from Monastiráki, you'll come to the **bazaar** area around Odhós Athinás, home to a bustling series of markets and small shops spilling out onto the street. Platía Omonías itself – brutal and shadeless – has little to offer in terms of aesthetics but it is the heart of Athens for a good portion of the population: a continuous turmoil of people and cars. Avoid walking around this area alone at night, and be sure to hide your valuables.

Bazaar

The city's **bazaar** area, concentrated on **Athinás** and **Eólou streets**, has a cosmopolitan ethnic mix as well as some of urban Athens' most compelling sights. It's also a neighbourhood that's been increasingly recolonized by the drug addicts and prostitutes who were cleared out for the 2004 Olympics – a process accelerated by the economic crisis.

Here the unsophisticated stores still reflect their origins in the Oriental **souk system** with each street selling certain goods. Hence the Monastiráki end of Athinás is dedicated to tools; food stores are gathered around the central market in the middle, especially along Evripídhou; there's glass to the west; paint and brasswork to the east; and clothes in Eólou and Ayíou Márkou. Always raucous and teeming with shoppers, *kouloúri* (bread-ring) sellers, gypsies and other vendors, the whole area is great free entertainment.

Meat and seafood market

Athinás • Mon–Sat 8am–3pm (liveliest in the morning)

The lively heart of the neighbourhood is the central **meat and seafood market**, which occupies almost an entire block bordered by Athinás, Evripídhou, Eólou and Sofokléous. The building itself is a grand nineteenth-century relic. Its fretted iron awnings shelter forests of carcasses and mounds of hearts, livers and ears – no place for the squeamish. In the middle section of the hall is the fish market, with all manner of bounty from the sea, squirming and glistening on the marble slabs.

Fruit and vegetable bazaar

Athinás • Mon–Sat 8am–3pm (liveliest in the morning)

Across Athinás is the colourful **fruit and vegetable** bazaar, surrounded by streets where grocers pile their stalls high with sacks of pulses, salt cod, barrels of olives and wheels of cheese. A clear sign of Athens' increasingly **multi-ethnic** character can be seen in the streets around Evripídhou just west of here, where a growing community from South Asia, predominantly Bengalis, gather around spice-rich minimarkets.

1

Odhós Eólou

Pedestrianized **Odhós Eólou** is far less frantic than parallel Athinás and benefits from café tables in the street and benches to rest on. Its gentler nature is also reflected by the goods sold here: where Athinás has power tools and raw meat, Eólou offers clothes and flowers.

Eólou itself follows the line of an ancient road, and the sight of the Acropolis as you approached Athens in ancient times must have been awe-inspiring. The views remain impressive today, with the Erechtheion's slender columns and pediment peeking over the edge of the crag at the bottom of the street.

Platía Ayías Irínis

The little square around the church of Ayía Iríni, at the southern end of Eólou, was traditionally home to Athens' **flower market**. There's still the odd stall selling flowers here, especially on Sunday morning, but **Platía Ayías Irínis** and the streets surrounding it have suddenly become uber-fashionable, and the majority of the flower sellers have been squeezed out by jewellery stalls, bars, clubs and restaurants, all of them packed day and night.

Platía Kotziá

At the northern end of Odhós Eólou, **Platía Kotziá** is a far more formal enclave, and one of the city's more impressive examples of Olympic refurbishment. Surrounded by the town hall and the weighty Neoclassical buildings of the National Bank, it's a rare glimpse of elegant old Athens, spoilt only by the crumbling modern blocks above the post office. In the middle of the square, a large section of **ancient road** has been uncovered and can be seen in a fenced-off site – numerous tombs and small buildings lie alongside it. Also on display, by the new Stock Exchange, is an ancient **city gate** discovered during building work; nearby, more sections of the ancient road and a drainage system are visible under glass pyramids in the middle of Eólou.

North of the centre

North of the centre, there's just one sight of any note, the fabulous **National Archeological Museum**, the finest collection of ancient Greek artefacts anywhere, and one of the world's greatest museums. That aside, it's a rewarding part of the city for a wander – restaurants, bars, cafés and bookshops abound, while **Exárhia** and adjacent **Neápoli** are among the city's liveliest neighbourhoods. Traditionally the home of anarchists, revolutionaries, artists and students, Exárhia is pretty tame

---

NOVEMBER 17: THE STUDENT UPRISING

In November 1973, students at **Athens Polytekhnío** launched a **protest** against the repressive regime of the **colonels**. The campaigners occupied the building and broadcasted calls for mass resistance from a pirate radio transmitter. Large numbers came to demonstrate support. The colonels' regime was determined to smash the protest and, on the night of November 17, **snipers** were positioned in neighbouring houses and ordered to fire into the courtyards while a tank broke down the entrance gate and the buildings were **stormed**. Even today nobody knows how many of the unarmed students were killed – estimates range from twenty to three hundred. The protest arguably marked the beginning of the end for the colonels; its anniversary is still commemorated by marches and sombre remembrance ceremonies, and the date is an iconic one; it's used, for example, by the November 17 terrorist group, which was active in Greece from 1975 to 2002. The Neoclassical Polytekhnío itself, alongside the National Archeological Museum, is not open for visits.

these days, but it's still the closest thing in central Athens to an "alternative" quarter. On Saturdays, locals flock to the colourful **street market** (around 7am–2pm) on Kallidhromíou. Just above, the little-visited **Stréfis Hill** provides some great views and a welcome break from the densely packed streets and dull apartment blocks surrounding it.

National Archeological Museum

Patission 44 • Mon 1–8pm, Tues–Sun 8am–8pm • €10 • Ⓦ namuseum.gr • Ⓜ Viktorías or Omónia; also dozens of buses, including trolleys #2 and #5 – look for those labelled *Mousseio*

The **National Archeological Museum** is an essential stop on any visit to Athens. However high your expectations, this unrivalled treasure-trove of ancient Greek art and sculpture seems to surpass them. The interior is surprisingly plain; there's nothing flashy at all about the displays, but they are clearly exhibited and well labelled. You could easily spend an entire morning or afternoon here, but it's equally possible to scoot round the highlights in an hour or two; arriving early in the morning or late in the afternoon should mean you won't be competing with the tour groups for space.

Mycenaean and Cycladic art

Directly ahead of you as you enter are the **Mycenaean halls**, which have always been the biggest crowd pullers. The gold **Mask of Agamemnon**, arguably the museum's most famous piece, is almost the first thing you see. Modern dating techniques offer convincing proof that the funerary mask actually belonged to some more ancient king, but crowds are still drawn by its correspondence with the Homeric myth and compelling expression.

Among the other highlights are a golden-horned **Bull's Head** displayed alongside a gold **Lion's Head**; gold jewellery, including a diadem and a gold-foil cover for the body of an infant from Grave III (the "Grave of the Women"); the **Acropolis Treasure** of gold goblets, signet rings and jewellery; the gold **Vafio** cups, with their scenes of wild bulls and long-tressed, narrow-waisted men; and dozens of examples of the Mycenaeans' consummate art – intricate, small-scale decoration of rings, cups, seals and inlaid daggers. There's work in silver, ivory, bronze and boars' tusks as well; there are baked tablets of Linear B, the earliest Greek writing (mainly accounting records) and Cretan-style frescoes depicting bull-vaulting and chariot-borne women watching spotted hounds in pursuit of boar. It's a truly exceptional display, and the gold shines as if it were in the window of a jeweller's shop.

Still earlier Greece is represented in the adjoining rooms. Room 5 covers **Neolithic pottery** and stone tools from Attica and elsewhere, and runs through to the early Bronze Age. The pottery shows sophisticated decoration from as early as 5000 BC, and there are many figurines, probably fertility symbols (judging by their phallic or pregnant nature), as well as simple gold ornaments. Room 6 is home to a large collection of **Cycladic art** from the Aegean islands. Many of these idols suggest the abstract forms of modern Cubist art – most strikingly in the much-reproduced **Man Playing a Lyre**.

Early sculpture

Sculpture makes up a large part of the museum's most important exhibits, and the pieces follow a broadly chronological arrangement around the main halls of the museum. Early highlights include a statue of a **kore** (maiden) from Merenda (Myrrhinous) in Attica, in room 11. Her elegantly pleated, belted *chiton* (dress) bears traces of the original paint and decoration of swastikas, flowers and geometric patterns. Nearby is a wonderful grave stele of a young *doryphoros* (spear-bearer) standing against a red background. Room 13 has the **Stele of a Young Warrior**, with delicately carved

1

beard, hair and tunic folds, and the **Kroisus kouros** (statue of an idealized youth), who looks as if he's been working out; both are from the late sixth century BC.

Classical art

Just a few highlights of the massive **Classical art** collection can be mentioned. Room 15 boasts a mid-fifth-century BC bronze **Statue of Poseidon**, dredged from the sea off Évvia in the 1920s. The god stands poised to throw his trident – weight on the front foot, athlete's body perfectly balanced, the model of idealized male beauty. A less dramatic, though no less important, piece in the same room is the **Eleusinian Relief**, showing the goddess of fertility, accompanied by her daughter Persephone, giving to mankind an ear of corn – symbol of the knowledge of agriculture and associated with the Mysteries of Eleusis (see box, p.123). In Room 20 is a small marble statue of **Athena**, a copy of the great cult statue that once stood in the Parthenon. It's a scary figure; the vast original, covered in gold and ivory, must have been extraordinary. The **Little Jockey of Artemission**, a delicate bronze figure that seems too small for his galloping horse, was found in the same shipwreck as the *Poseidon*. Room 28 has some fine fourth-century BC bronzes including the **Antikythira Youth**, thought to depict either Perseus or Paris, from yet another shipwreck, off Andikýthira, and the bronze head of a **Boxer**, burly and battered. Still more naturalistic, in room 29, is the third-century BC bronze head of a **Philosopher**, with furrowed brow and unkempt hair.

Later sculpture

The most reproduced of the **later sculptures** is a first-century AD statue of a naked and indulgent **Aphrodite** (room 30) about to rap Pan's knuckles for getting too fresh – a far cry (a long fall, some would say) from the reverent, idealizing portrayals of the gods in Classical times. There is also an extraordinary bronze equestrian portrait statue (without the horse) of the **Emperor Augustus**.

Minor collections

Less visited, but still extremely worthwhile, are the collections hidden away at the rear of the museum and upstairs. These include, downstairs, the **Stathatos collection**, with some truly exquisite jewellery; a wonderful **Egyptian** room; and the **bronze collection**. The last named is an exceptional display of thousands of items: weapons, figurines, axes, cauldrons, jewellery, mirrors, kitchen implements; even bronze sandals. Perhaps the highlight is the **Antikythira Mechanism**, at the far end. Dating from around 150–100 BC, it was discovered in a shipwreck off the island of Andikýthira in 1900, but modern scanning techniques have only recently revealed its full complexity. It is believed to be an astronomical computer capable of predicting the movements of stars and planets, and its sophisticated use of differential gears is unique – technologically, it was at least 1500 years ahead of its time.

Upstairs is a collection of hundreds of **vases**, if anything still more spectacular, with a full explanation of manufacturing techniques, changing styles of decoration and the uses of the different types of vessel. As ever, the highlights are from the Classical era. Up here, too, is a display on the excavations of Akrotíri on Santoríni (see p.443), including some of the famous **Minoan frescoes** discovered there.

Stréfis Hill

Just above **Exárhia**, a labyrinth of paths leads to the summit of **Stréfis Hill** (Lófos toú Stréfi), from where there are wonderful views – above all of the Acropolis with the Saronic Gulf and islands behind, but also across to nearby Lykavitós. Watch out for unguarded drops near the top, and stick to the main paths as you walk up, in order to avoid one of the more obvious signs of the area's alternative lifestyle – discarded hypodermics.

Western Athens

Some of the most interesting up-and-coming areas of Athens – **Thissío**, **Gázi**, **Keramikós** and **Roúf** – lie to the west of the centre, where the extension of Metro Line 3 has acted as a further spur to the pace of change. Nightlife and restaurants are the chief attractions here, but there's also a cluster of new museums and galleries. Here too is **Kerameikos**, site of a substantial section of the walls of ancient Athens and an important burial ground. South of Thissío, things are rather more traditional. The **hills of the Pnyx and Filopáppou** offer a pleasant, green escape from the city as well as fine views down over the Acropolis and Agora. On the west side of the hills, the residential zone of **Áno Petrálona** is a real delight, entirely untouristy, with some excellent tavernas and a great open-air cinema, though absolutely nothing in the way of sights.

Thissío

The cafés of **Thissío**, with tables set out on huge terraces above the Agora site, offer some of the finest views of the Acropolis, especially at night. Head south from Thissío Metro station and you can follow pedestrianized Apóstolou Pávlou past these terraces and right around the edge of the Ancient Agora and Acropolis sites. It's an especially rewarding walk in the early evening, when the setting sun illuminates this side of the rock, and the cafés start to fill with an anticipatory buzz. As you follow the street round, you'll notice a number of small excavations at the base of the hills on your right. First, immediately below the church of Ayía Marína, is a rocky area identified as the earliest known **Sanctuary of Zeus** in Attica; there's not a great deal to see through the fence, but it's clear that the rocks have been cut into terraces.

Sanctuary of Pan

Off Apóstolou Pávlou, on the lower slopes of the Pnyx just beyond the Thission open-air cinema • View through the fence

The cult of Pan was associated with caves, and at the **Sanctuary of Pan** you can see the opening to an underground chamber cut into the rock. Inside were found reliefs of Pan, a naked nymph and a dog. There's also a mosaic floor and, nearby, remains of an ancient road and two rock-cut, Classical-era houses.

Fountain of Pnyx

Off Apóstolou Pávlou, on the lower slopes of the Pnyx just beyond the Sanctuary of Pan • View through the fence

Under Peisistratos (see p.767), a water system was engineered, with subterranean pipes bringing water from springs to rock-cut cisterns that supplied the city. The so-called **Fountain of Pnyx** is believed to be one of those; behind a locked entrance is a chamber with a Roman mosaic floor where the water was collected. You can also see traces of the concrete used to seal the chamber during World War II, when valuable antiquities were stored inside.

A CITY WITH A VIEW

Athens is a city built on hills. Most famous is the **Acropolis** itself, which forms the backdrop to all the finest **views** of the city and whose summit also offers wonderful vistas across the metropolis and out to Pireás and the sea. But there are dozens of other viewpoints throughout Athens. Some of the finest views are from the café terraces of **Thissío**, packed in the early evening as the setting sun picks out the ancient monuments – try Athinaion Politeia (see p.106). There are other great views from Lykavitós Hill (see p.90), Odhós Eólou (see p.84), Filopáppou Hill (see p.88) and the roof-top bars at the Hotel Grande Bretagne (see p.101) and 45° (see p.109).

1

Filopáppou Hill

From around the junction of Apóstolou Pávlou and Dhionysíou Areopayítou, a network of paths leads up **Filopáppou Hill**, known in antiquity as the "Hill of the Muses". Its pine- and cypress-clad slopes provide fabulous views of the Acropolis and the city beyond, especially at sunset (although night- and even day-time muggings have occurred here, so take care). This strategic height has played an important, if generally sorry, role in the city's history: in 1687 it was from here that the shell which destroyed the roof of the Parthenon was lobbed; more recently, the colonels placed tanks on the slopes during their coup of 1967. The hill's summit is capped by a grandiose monument to a Roman senator and consul, Filopappus. To the west, paths lead across to Áno Petrálona and the Dora Stratou Theatre (see p.112) through the ancient district of **Koíle**. You can clearly see remnants of rock-cut houses here, as well as the ancient Koíle road, which led from the city to the port at Pireás, protected by the Long Walls; a vital strategic thoroughfare in antiquity.

Prison of Socrates

24hr (open access to the site, though you can't go inside)

On the way up Filopáppou Hill, signed off to the left, is the so-called **Prison of Socrates**, in actual fact the rear part of a house – age unknown but probably very ancient – with rooms cut into the rock. The main structure would have been in front, and you can still see holes for joists and beams, and part of a rock-cut stairway.

Áyios Dhimítrios

The main path up Filopáppou Hill follows a line of truncated ancient walls past the attractive Byzantine church of **Áyios Dhimítrios**. The church is much venerated because, the story goes, its patron saint (Dhimítrios "The Bomber") protected worshippers celebrating his saint's day here in 1656. The Turks planned to bombard the church, but instead "God sent a thunderbolt, exploding the powder and destroying their cannon, killing Yusuf Aga and his men". Inside, original Byzantine frescoes have been uncovered under later ones, the eyes of the saints gouged out.

Hill of the Pnyx

North of Filopáppou, with access on paths from Áyios Dhimítrios or up behind Thissío, rises the **Hill of the Pnyx**, an area used in Classical Athens as the meeting place for the **democratic assembly**, which gathered more than forty times a year. All male citizens could vote and, at least in theory, voice their opinions, though the assembly was harsh on inarticulate or foolish speakers. At the site, poorly signed but unmistakeable when you find it, a convenient semicircular terrace makes a natural spot from which to address the crowd. There are remains of the original walls, which formed the theatre-like court, and of *stoas* where the assembly would have taken refreshment, all with commanding Acropolis views.

Hill of the Nymphs

The **Hill of the Nymphs** (Lófos Nymfón) lies to the west of the Pnyx and Filopáppou, overlooking Áno Petrálona. Nymphs were associated with the dusty whirlwinds to which this hill is particularly prone and it is said to be the location of the fairy sequences in Shakespeare's *A Midsummer Night's Dream*. Slightly lower and quieter than its better-known neighbours, this is a peaceful, shaded place to wander, with vistas of the western suburbs, across Pireás and out to sea.

Benáki Museum of Islamic Art

Áyion Asomáton 22, at Dhípylou • Thurs–Sun 10am–6pm • €9, free Thurs • ⓦ www.benaki.gr • Ⓜ Thissío

Antónis Benákis, founder of the Benáki Museum (see p.91), spent much of his life in Egypt, and this museum, in a converted Neoclassical mansion, was created to house the collection he amassed there. Exhibits in the **Benáki Museum of Islamic Art** follow a chronological course up through the building, from the seventh century on the first floor to the nineteenth on the fourth. Throughout, there are beautiful, intricately decorated objects in almost every type of art: **ceramics** (especially tiles), **metalwork** and **wood** above all, but also textiles, jewellery, glass, scientific instruments, armour and more.

The highlights are on the **third floor**, from the sixteenth- and seventeenth-century Golden Age of the Ottoman Empire under Süleyman the Magnificent. Here is a reconstructed room from a Cairo mansion, complete with inlaid marble floor, sunken fountains and elaborate wooden window screens, as well as silk wall hangings (not from the mansion), shot with silver and gold thread.

There's a top-floor **café** overlooking the Kerameikos site and industrial Gázi beyond, as well as offering views of the Acropolis and Filopáppou. In the **basement**, you can examine a substantial chunk of the ancient city wall, almost 6m high, preserved during the building's restoration.

Kerameikos

Entrance on Ermoú • Daily 8am–8pm • €2, or included in €30 joint ticket (see p.68) • Ⓜ Thissío

The **Kerameikos** (or Keramikós) site, which encompasses one of the principal burial grounds of ancient Athens and a hefty section of the ancient wall, provides a fascinating and quiet retreat. Little visited, it has something of an oasis feel, with the lush Iridhanós channel, speckled with water lilies, flowing across the site from east to west.

To the right of the entrance is the stream and the double line of the **city wall**. Two roads pierced the wall here, and the gates that marked their entrance to the city have been excavated: the great **Dipylon Gate** was the busiest in the ancient city, where the road from Pireás, Eleusis and the north arrived; and the **Sacred Gate** was a ceremonial entrance where the Ierá Odhós, or Sacred Way, entered the city – it was used for the Eleusinian and Panathenaic processions.

Street of the Tombs

Branching off to the left from the Sacred Way is the **Street of the Tombs**, the old road to Pireás. In ancient Greece people were frequently buried alongside roads, and especially near gates, a practice at least partly related to the idea of death as a journey. This site, by the principal routes into the Classical city, was clearly a prestigious one, and numerous commemorative monuments to wealthy or distinguished Athenians have been excavated, their original stones reinstated or replaced by replicas. The flat, vertical **stelae** were the main funerary monuments of the Classical world; the **sarcophagi** that you see are later, from Hellenistic or Roman times. The large **tomb** with the massive semicircular base to the left of the path is the *Memorial of Dexileos*, the 20-year-old son of Lysanias of Thorikos, who was killed in action at Corinth in 394 BC. The adjacent plot contains the *Monument of Dionysios of Kollytos*, in the shape of a pillar stele supporting a bull carved from Pentelic marble.

Museum

The site **museum** is a lovely, cool, marble-floored space displaying finds from the site and related material, above all stelae and grave markers. There are also many poignant **funerary offerings** – toys from child burials, gold jewellery and beautiful small objects of all sorts. The ceramics are particularly fine and include lovely dishes with horses on their lids (*pyxides*) from the early eighth century BC and some stunning fifth-century BC black-and-red figure pottery.

1

Gázi

Gázi, to the west of Kerameikos, is a former industrial area where the reinvention of the old gasworks as the **Tekhnópolis** cultural centre (Pireós 100; Mon–Fri 8am–9pm, Sat & Sun 9am–10pm, later for special events; ⓦtechnopolis-athens .com; ⓜ Keramikós) has helped spark a rush of hip bars and restaurants. Inside the cultural centre is the **Industrial Gas Museum** (Tues–Sun: Mid-Oct to mid-April 10am–8pm; mid-April to mid-Oct 10am–6pm; free), while the area has also seen the emergence of other exhibition sites such as the **Benáki Museum Pireos Street Annexe** (Pireós 138; Tues, Wed & Fri–Sun 11am–9pm, Thurs 11am–11pm; €6–8, free Thurs; ⓦbenaki.gr; ⓜ Petrálona, or many buses along Pireós including #049, #B18 and trolley #21). By day the streets tend to be deserted, though after dark the surrounding area comes alive: it's safe enough, but late at night you may want to take a taxi here.

Hellenic Cosmos

Pireós 254 • mid-June to end-Sept Tues–Fri & Sun 10am–3pm; end-Sept to mid-June Tues–Thurs 9am–1.30pm, Fri 9am–8pm, Sat 11am–4pm, Sun 10am–6pm • €4–9 • ⓦhellenic-cosmos.gr • ⓜ Kallithea, bus #049 or #914

A cultural centre, exhibition space and above all interactive multimedia theatre, the **Helenic Cosmos** has at its heart a futuristic domed **planetarium** in which video-game-like interactive movies are shown. The best of them are a tour of the ancient Agora and of Classical Olympia, complete with the Olympic games; live English commentary can be provided. It's ideal, above all, for kids and is often busy with Greek school parties. There are also temporary exhibitions, often with a scientific theme.

Kolonáki and the museum quarter

Kolonáki is the city's most chic central address and shopping area. Walk up from Sýndagma, past the jewellery stores on Voukourestíou, and you can almost smell the money. It's also from Kolonáki that a funicular hauls you up **Lykavitós Hill**, where some of the best views of the city can be enjoyed. The neighbourhood's lower limits are defined by the streets of Akadhimías and Vassilísis Sofías, where grand Neoclassical palaces house embassies and **museums**.

Lykavitós Hill

Funicular daily 9am–2.30am; every 30min, more frequent at busy times • €5 one way, €7 return • The funicular base is at Odhós Aristípou, near the top of Ploutárhou; though it doesn't look far from Kolonáki Square, it's a steep ascent to walk here through the stepped residential streets – or you can take bus #060 which starts at the terminus beside the National Archeological Museum and has stops on Akadhimías

Lykavitós Hill offers tremendous views, particularly from late afternoon onwards – on a clear day, you can see the mountains of the Peloponnese. After dark, the shimmering lights of Athens spread right across the Attica basin. To get to the summit, you can take the **funicular** or you can walk. The principal **path** up the hill begins from the western end of Aristípou above Platía Dhexamenís, and it rambles up through woods to the top. It's not as long or as hard a walk as it looks – easily done in twenty minutes – though the top half offers little shade.

On the summit, the brilliantly white chapel of **Áyios Yióryios** dominates – a spectacular place to celebrate the saint's name-day if you're in Athens at the time. Just below it, *Orizontes* (ⓦorizonteslycabettus.gr) is a very expensive restaurant with an equally expensive café, both of which enjoy spectacular views. Over to the east a second, slightly lower peak is dominated by the open-air **Lykavitós Theatre**, which is used mainly for concerts from May to October.

Platía Kolonakíou

1

The heart of Kolonáki is a square officially called Platía Filikís Eterías, but known to all as **Platía Kolonakíou**, after the ancient "little column" that hides in the trees on the southwest side. Dotted around the square are kiosks which stock foreign papers and magazines, or in the library of the **British Council** on the south side of the square you can check out the British press for free. The surrounding cafés are almost invariably packed with Gucci-clad shoppers – you'll find better value if you move away from the square a little. In the dozens of small, upmarket **shops** the accent is firmly on fashion and designer gear.

Benáki Museum

Koumbári 1, at Vassilísis Sofías • Wed & Fri 9am–5pm, Thurs & Sat 9am–midnight, Sun 9am–3pm; shop also open Mon • €9, free Thurs • Ⓦ benaki.gr • Ⓜ Evangelismós or Sýndagma, plus many buses including trolleys #3, #7 & #8

The often overlooked but fascinating **Benáki Museum** houses a private collection donated to the state in the 1950s by **Antónis Benákis**, a wealthy cotton merchant. Its exhibits range from Mycenaean jewellery and Classical ceramics through to costumes and folk artefacts, as well as memorabilia of the Greek War of Independence. It's a microcosm of almost every other Athens Museum, gathered into one building.

Highlights include the Euboea Treasure and other early gold jewellery; some very early Greek Gospels, rescued by Greek refugees from Asia Minor in 1922; two magnificent reception rooms, wood-carved and gilded, from eighteenth-century Macedonia; and unique historical material on the Cretan statesman Eleftherios Venizelos and the Cretan Revolution. An additional attraction, especially if you've been dodging traffic all day, is the **second-floor café**, whose terrace has views over the nearby National Gardens. The museum **shop** is also excellent, with some of the best posters and postcards in the city.

Museum of Cycladic Art

Neofýtou Dhouká 4 • Mon, Wed, Fri & Sat 10am–5pm, Thurs 10am–8pm, Sun 11am–5pm • €7, half-price Mon • Ⓦ cycladic.gr • Ⓜ Evangelismós, plus many buses including trolleys #3, #7 & #8

The small, private **Museum of Cycladic Art** is a beautifully presented collection that includes objects from the Cycladic civilization (third millennium BC, from the islands of the Cyclades group), pre-Minoan Bronze Age (second millennium BC) and the period from the fall of Mycenae to around 700 BC, plus a selection of Archaic, Classical and Hellenistic pottery.

The **Cycladic** objects are on the first floor – above all, distinctive marble bowls and folded-arm figurines (mostly female) with sloping wedge heads whose style influenced twentieth-century artists like Moore, Picasso and Brancusi. The exact purpose of the effigies is unknown but, given their frequent discovery in grave-barrows, it's possible that they were spirit-world guides for the deceased, or representations of the Earth Goddess. Their clean, white simplicity is in fact misleading, for they would originally have been painted. Look closely, and you can see that many still bear traces of colour.

Of the ancient Greek art on the upper floors, the highlight is the superb black-figure pottery, especially a collection of painted **Classical-era** bowls, many of which show two unrelated scenes on opposite sides – for example, one of the star exhibits depicts revellers on one face and three men in cloaks conversing on the other.

On the ground floor and basement there's a tiny children's area and a good **shop**, as well as a pleasant **café** (with vegetarian choices) in an internal courtyard. A covered walkway connects to the nineteenth-century **Stathatos House**, magnificently restored as an extension for temporary exhibitions.

1

Byzantine Museum

Vassilísis Sofías 22 • Daily 8am–8pm • €8 • ⓦ byzantinemuseum.gr • Ⓜ Evangelismós, plus many buses including trolleys #3, #7 & #8

Excellently displayed in a beautiful building, the **Byzantine Museum** is mainly concerned with Christian art, but the collection is far more wide-ranging than that might lead you to expect. Exhibits start with art from the very earliest days of Christianity – the fish and dove motifs can't disguise the extremely close parallels with Classical Greek objects. There are displays on everyday Byzantine life; reconstructions of parts of early churches (mosaic floors and chunks of masonry, some even from the Christian Parthenon); a Coptic section with antique clothing, such as leather shoes decorated with gold leaf; and tombs, in some of which offerings were left, again a reminder of a pagan heritage.

But the highlights are the **icons**, the earliest of which are from the thirteenth and fourteenth centuries. There are dozens of lovely examples, many of them double-sided, some mounted to be carried in procession, and you can follow the development of their style from the simplicity of the earliest to the Renaissance-influenced art of the sixteenth century. Alongside the icons are some fine **frescoes** including an entire dome reconstructed inside the museum. The *Ilissia Café* in the museum grounds is a good place for a coffee break.

Aristotle's Lyceum

Vassilísis Sofías • Daily 8am–8pm • €4, or included in €30 joint ticket (see p.68) • Ⓜ Evangelismós, plus many buses including trolleys #3, #7 & #8

Located in a pleasant park, around which you can wander freely, the remains of **Aristotle's Lyceum** have been excavated alongside the Byzantine Museum. Dating from the fourth-century BC, it's one of Ancient Athens oldest schools, where Aristotle taught for thirteen years and to which Socrates was a frequent visitor – though, today, it's little more than a ruin.

War Museum

Rizári 2, at Vassilísis Sofías • Nov–March 9am–5pm; April–Oct 9am–7pm • €4 • ⓦ warmuseum.gr • Ⓜ Evangelismós, plus many buses including trolleys #3, #7 & #8

The only "cultural" endowment of the 1967–74 junta, the **War Museum** becomes predictably militaristic and right-wing as it approaches modern events: the Asia Minor campaign, Greek forces in Korea, Cyprus and so on. However, the bulk of the collection consists of **weaponry and uniforms**, with a large collection of eighteenth- and nineteenth-century swords and handguns, and a particular concentration on the World War II era. Earlier times are also covered with displays on changing warfare from Mycenae through to the Byzantines and Turks, and an array of models of the acropolises and castles of Greece, both Classical and medieval. Outside are artillery pieces and planes, including a full-scale model of the *Daedalus*, one of the first-ever military aircraft, which dropped bombs on Turkish positions in December 1912 during the Balkan Wars.

Southern Athens

There are very few sights south of the centre, but the easily accessible quiet residential districts here are full of character and home to excellent restaurants and cafés that see few tourists. Immediately south of the Acropolis lies upmarket **Makriyiánni**, revitalized by the presence of the Acropolis Museum; adjacent **Koukáki** is a plainer neighbourhood with numerous hotels and good local places to eat. **Mets**, a steep hillside area on the other side of busy Syngroú avenue, and neighbouring **Pangráti** have a wealth of small, homely tavernas and *mezedhopolía*. The latter also boasts buzzing local nightlife and good shops along Imittoú avenue, as well as an impressive street market every Friday (around 7am–2pm) on Odhós Arhimídhous, off Platía Plastíra. Southern Athens is also home to two new additions to Athens' cultural life, the **National Museum of Contemporary Art** and the **Stavros Niarchos Cultural Centre.**

National Museum of Contemporary Art

Kallirrois & Amvrosiou Frantzi • Tues, Wed & Fri–Sun 11am–9pm, Thurs 11am–11pm • €8 • Ⓦ www.emst.gr • Ⓜ Syngroú-Fix

Opened in 2016 in the vast, sleek former Fix brewery, the **National Museum of Contemporary Art** is home to some 1100 artworks by Greek and international artists, such as Jan Fabre and the Albanian artist Edi Hila. Two floors of the museum are devoted to this permanent collection, while the remaining space features visiting exhibitions by international artists, working in a wide range of media on themes as diverse as gender discrimination, the occupation of Palastine and issues of border crossings, diaspora and cultural exchange. The museum's top-floor café has great views out to the Acropolis and Parthanon.

The Panathenaic Stadium

Vassiléos Konstantínou • Daily: March–Oct 8am–7pm; Nov–Feb 8am–5pm • €5 • Ⓦ panathenaicstadium.gr • Tram Záppio, plus buses including trolley #2, or walk via the Záppio gardens]

The old Olympic Stadium or **Panathenaic Stadium** (also dubbed Kalimármaro, "White Marble") is a nineteenth-century reconstruction on Roman foundations, slotted tightly between the pine-covered spurs of Ardhittós hill. Originally marked out in the fourth century BC for the Panathenaic **athletic contests**, it became an arena for **gladiatorial blood sports** under the reign of Emperor Hadrian. The Roman senator Herodes Atticus later refurbished the entire stadium; the white marble from the sixty thousand seats was to provide the city with a convenient quarry through the ensuing seventeen centuries.

The stadium's reconstruction dates from the modern revival of the **Olympic Games** in 1896, paid for by another wealthy benefactor, the Alexandrian Greek Yiorgos Averoff. Its appearance and pristine whiteness must be very much as it was when first reopened under the Roman senator. Though the bends are too tight for major modern events, it's still used by local athletes (there are early-morning jogging sessions), and marks the finishing point of the annual Athens Marathon.

The Stavros Niarchos Cultural Centre

Leoforos Andhrea Syngrou 364, Kallithea • Daily: April–Oct 9am–midnight; Nov–March 6am–8pm • Free • Ⓦ snfcc.org • Tram Tzitzifies, and buses #B2 or #550 from Central Athens. Shuttle buses run from Ⓜ Syntagma during special events

Some 4.5km from Athens centre, near Faliro Bay, the **Stavros Niarchos Cultural Centre** is a new arts and cultural complex that sits within 42 acres of parkland. Designed by award-winning architect Renzo Piano at a cost of more than €500 millon, it is home to the Greek National Opera and the Greek National Library, both cleverly housed underground beneath a sloping, green, living roof with panaramic views over to the sea and the Acropolis from the top. The beautifully landscaped grounds are home to herb and vegetable gardens plus a seawater canal, where visitors can learn to sail or kayak, and regular activities are held including tango lessons at night and outdoor cinema screenings in the summer.

Pireás

PIREÁS (Piraeus) has been Athens' port since Classical times, when the so-called Long Walls, scattered remnants of which can still be seen, were built to connect it to the city. Today it's a substantial metropolis in its own right. The port and its **island ferries** are the reason most people come here; if you're spending any time, though, the real attractions of the place are around the small-boat harbours of **Zéa Marina** and

1

Mikrolímano, on the opposite side of the small peninsula. Here, the upscale residential areas are alive with attractive waterfront cafés, bars and restaurants, which offer some of the best seafood in town, and there's an excellent archeological museum.

ARRIVAL AND DEPARTURE | PIREÁS

By Metro The best way to travel between the port and central Athens is on Metro Line 1; it takes about 30min from Omónia.

By bus Bus #40 (roughly every 10min daily 5am–midnight, hourly 1–5am) runs to and from Sýndagma, while #49 from Omónia (roughly every 15min daily 5am–midnight, hourly 1–5am) will drop you slightly closer to the ferries. Allow at

least an hour though. From the airport, you can take express bus #X96 (around 1hr 20min).

By taxi Taxis from the centre of Athens cost about €15 at day tariff, though it can be hard to hail one going the other way amid the throng disgorging from a ferry.

By ferry Hundreds of ferries leave Pireás daily (see p.97).

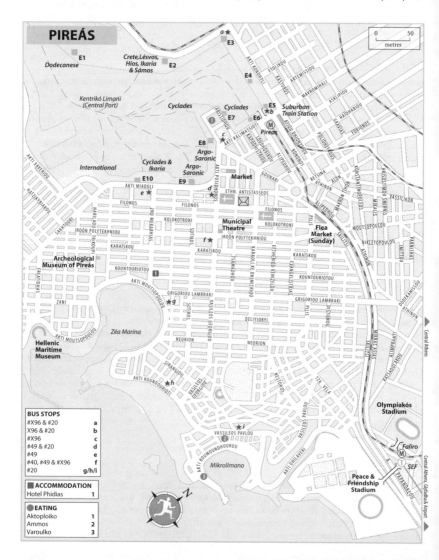

PIREÁS

0   50
metres

Dodecanese — E1
Crete, Lésvos, Híos, Ikaría & Sámos — E2
a ★ E3
E4
Kentrikó Limáni (Central Port)
Cyclades
Cyclades — E5
★ b
E7
E6
Suburban Train Station
M Pireás
International
Cyclades & Ikaría
Argo-Saronic
E8
E10
E9
Argo-Saronic
e ★
d ★
Market
ETHN. ANTISTASSEOS
Municipal Theatre
Flea Market (Sunday)
f ★
Archeological Museum of Pireás
1
★ g
Zéa Marina
Hellenic Maritime Museum
★ h
Olympiakós Stadium
Faliro
SEF
★ i
VASSILEOS PAVLOU
Mikrolímano
Peace & Friendship Stadium
Central Athens
Central Athens, Glyfádha & Airport

BUS STOPS
#X96 & #20	a
X96 & #20	b
#X96	c
#49 & #20	d
#49	e
#40, #49 & #X96	f
#20	g/h/i

■ ACCOMMODATION
Hotel Phidias	1

● EATING
Aktoploiko	1
Ammos	2
Varoulko	3

CITY BEACHES

People swim from the rocks or sea wall almost anywhere on the coast southeast of Pireás – especially the older generation (the youth tend to head down towards the fleshpots and pay beaches of Glyfádha) – but the closest pleasant beach to the centre is **Edem**, reached by tram to the Edem or Báthis stops. A small patch of sand with cafés and tavernas, it's busy and urban but fine for a quick swim and sunbathe and, remarkably, has Blue Flag status. There are other free beaches near the Flisvós, Kalamáki and Zéfyros tram stops.

Brief history

The port at Pireás was founded at the beginning of the fifth century BC by **Themistocles**, who realized the potential of its three natural harbours. His work was consolidated by Pericles with the building of the **Long Walls** to protect the corridor to Athens, and the port remained active under Roman and Macedonian rulers. Subsequently, under Turkish control, the place declined to the extent that there was just one building here, a monastery, by the end of the War of Independence. From the 1830s on, though, Pireás grew by leaps and bounds. By World War I, it had become the nation's **predominant port**, its strategic position enhanced by the opening of the Suez and Corinth canals in 1862 and 1893 respectively. Like Athens itself, the port's great period of expansion began in 1923, with the exchange of populations with Turkey. Over a hundred thousand Asia Minor Greeks decided to settle in Pireás, which doubled the population almost overnight – and gave a boost to a pre-existing semi-underworld culture, whose enduring legacy was rembétika (see p.800), outcasts' music played in hashish dens along the waterside.

Archeological Museum of Pireás

Hariláou Trikoúpi 31 • Tues–Sun 8.30am–3pm • €3 • ☎ 210 452 1598 • Bus #1 from Sýndagma passes close by, or take local buses #300 or #904

The **Archeological Museum of Pireás** boasts an excellent collection, and merits a special trip for Classical enthusiasts. The displays begin upstairs, where one of the star exhibits is a bronze **kouros** (idealized male statue) of Apollo. Dating from 530–520 BC, this is the earliest known life-size bronze, here displayed with two similar but slightly later figures of Artemis and Athena. They were all found in 1959, in a storeroom, where they had supposedly been hidden in 86 BC, when the Roman general Sulla besieged Pireás.

Many other items in the museum were dragged from shipwrecks at the bottom of the harbour, including, in the last room on the ground floor, second-century AD **stone reliefs** of battles between Greeks and Amazons, apparently mass-produced for export to Rome (note the identical pieces). Other highlights include some very ancient musical instruments, and many funeral stelae and statues.

Small boat harbours

Local trolley #20, or walk from Ⓜ Fáliro/Tram SEF

On the opposite side of the Pireás peninsula from the mania of the port, separated by busy shopping streets, the residential districts around the **small boat harbours** have a calm and elegant atmosphere. At **Zéa Marina** (aka Pasalimáni), the principal port of ancient Athens, you can admire monstrous gin palaces moored beneath swish apartments. The boats at **Mikrolímano** (known to many locals as Turkolímano) are more modest, and the harbour itself is prettier, with dozens of cafés and restaurants at which to sit and enjoy it. Between the two harbours there's a small **beach** (bus #20) – it's not Athens' finest, but pleasant enough if you have a few hours to kill between ferries.

1

ARRIVAL AND DEPARTURE

ATHENS

BY PLANE

Eleftheríos Venizélos (Athens International) Airport Located at Spáta, 33km southeast of the city, Athens' modern and efficient airport (☎ 210 353 0000, ⓦ aia.gr) has facilities including free wi-fi (max 1hr), ATMs and banks with money-changing facilities on all levels, the usual array of travel agencies and car rental places, plus a municipal tourist office (daily 8am–8pm) and pricey luggage storage with Pacific (☎ 210 353 0160, ⓦ pacifictravel.gr). Aegean (ⓦ www.aegeanair .com), Astra (ⓦ astra-airlines.gr), Olympic (ⓦ olympicair.com), Ryanair (ⓦ ryanair.com) and Sky Express (ⓦ skyexpress.gr) operate daily domestic flights in summer. Refer to individual destinations for flight frequencies and journey times.

Domestic destinations Alexandhroúpoli; Astypálea; Haniá (Chania, Crete); Híos; Ikaría; Ioánnina; Iráklio (Heraklion, Crete); Kálimnos; Kárpathos; Kastoriá; Kavála; Kefaloniá; Kérkyra (Corfu); Kos; Kozáni; Kýthira; Léros; Límnos; Mílos; Mýkonos; Mytilíni (Lésvos); Náxos; Páros; Rhodes; Sámos; Santoríni; Sitía (Crete); Skiáthos; Skýros; Sýros; Thessaloníki and Zákynthos.

FROM THE AIRPORT INTO TOWN

By Metro and rail The Metro and suburban trains share a station at the airport, and departures for both are displayed in the terminals. Metro Line 3 takes you straight into the heart of the city in 45min (every 30min, 6.30am–11.30pm; single €10, 48hr return €18, discounts for multiple tickets) where you can change to the other lines at either Monastiráki or Sýndagma. The suburban train (same fares) offers direct trains to the northern suburbs and Corinth, but for Laríssis station in the centre and Pireás you have to change at SKA, or to Metro Line 1 at Neratzíotissa.

By bus Buses can be slower than the Metro (1hr–1hr 30min), especially at rush hour, but they're also cheaper, more frequent (3–4 per hr during the day, every 30min through the night), run all night and offer direct links to other parts of the city: the #X95 runs to Sýndagma square; #X96 to the port at Pireás via Glyfádha and the beach suburbs; #X93 to the bus stations. Tickets cost €6 from a booth beside the stops or on board – be sure to validate your ticket once on the bus. There are also regional bus services to the port of Rafína (19 daily, 4.50am–10.20pm; €5, buy ticket on the bus). Electronic boards in the airport show all bus departures.

By taxi Taxis can take anything from 35min to 1hr 35min (at rush hour) to reach the centre; there's a fixed fare to the centre of €35, or €50 at night, and no extras should be added. The fare to Ráfina should be similar, Pireás or Lávrio €10–15 more.

BY TRAIN

Laríssis station Athens' main terminus, northwest of Platía Omonías, is on Metro Line 2 (Stathmós Laríssis, also known as Lárissa); this is the most convenient way to get into central Athens, or to anywhere else on the Metro system including the port of Pireás (though many trains continue direct to Pireás). Alternatively, the #1 trolley bus heads from Laríssis for Omónia, Sýndagma and on past Akrópoli Metro station (close to the Acropolis) into Koukáki. And of course there are also taxis; no journey within the centre should cost more than €7. There are often huge queues for train tickets, so book in advance at the office at Sína 6 (off Panepistimíou), online (ⓦ trainose.gr) or call central reservations on ☎ 1110.

Suburban destinations Kórinthos (change at SKA; hourly 6am–10pm; 1hr 30min).

Main line destinations Halkídha (21 daily; 1hr 30min); Thessaloníki (7 daily; 5hr 25min) via Thíva (Thebes; 1hr) and Lárissa (4hr).

BY BUS

Athens has two principal bus terminals, at Kifissoú 100 and Liossíon 260, and a smaller terminus at Mavrommatéon. International buses use a variety of stops, though most commonly Kifissoú 100 or the train station.

Kifissoú 100 Northwest of the centre, this station serves routes to northern Greece and the Peloponnese. Bus #051 (usually every 10min 5am–11.30pm) runs between here and the corner of Zínonos and Menándhrou, just off Omónia square.

Destinations Árgos (12 daily; 1hr 45min); Árta (8 daily; 5hr 30min); Corfu (3 daily; 9hr); Igoumenítsa (4 daily; 7hr); Ioánnina (9 daily; 6hr 45min); Kalamáta (13 daily; 4hr); Kefaloniá (3–4 daily; 7hr); Kórinthos (hourly; 1hr 10min); Lefkádha (5 daily; 5hr 10min); Mycenae/Náfplio (hourly; 2hr 30min); Olympia (2 daily; 5hr 30min); Pátra (every 30min; 3hr); Pýlos (2 daily; 5hr 30min); Pýrgos (9 daily; 5hr 30min); Spárti (11 daily; 3hr 30min); Thessaloníki (13 daily; 6hr 15min); Trípoli (15 daily; 2hr 15min); Zákynthos (4 daily; 5hr).

Liossíon 260 Slightly further out to the north of Kifissoú 100, this station generally serves routes to central Greece. Buses #A11 and #B11 (usually every 10min 5.30am–11.30pm) run to Faviérou at the corner of Máyer, not far from Omónia; or walk (about 6min) to Ag. Nikolaos on Metro Line 1.

Destinations Áyios Konstandínos (hourly; 2hr 30min); Delphi (6–8 daily; 3hr); Halkídha (every 30min; 1hr 10min); Kalampaka from Meteora (6 daily; 5hr 30min); Karpeníssi (3 daily; 4hr 30min); Kými, for Skýros ferries (1 daily, connecting with ferry; 5hr); Lamía (hourly; 2hr 15min); Lárissa (7 daily; 4hr 30min); Thiva/Thebes (hourly; 1hr 35min); Tríkala (6 daily; 4hr 30min); Vólos (10–12 daily; 4hr 50min).

1

Mavrommatéon If you're travelling within the state of Attica – for example from the ports at Lávrio or Rafína – you'll use this terminus at the southwest corner of the Pedhíon Áreos Park. This is very close to Ⓜ Viktorías, and there are dozens of buses heading down Patissíon (aka 28 Oktovríou) past the National Archeological Museum towards the centre.

Destinations Lávrio (every 30min 5.45am–6.45pm, less frequent till 10.30pm; 1hr 30min); Marathon (every 30min; 1hr 20min); Pórto Ráfti (hourly; 1hr 30min); Rafína (every 30min; 1hr); Soúnio via the coast (hourly on the half-hour, 6.30am–7.30pm; 2hr) or inland route (via Lávrio; hourly 5.45am–6.45pm; 1hr 45min).

BY FERRY

The vast majority of ferries, hydrofoils and catamarans leave from the port of Pireás, but there are also smaller ferry terminals at Rafína and Lávrio.

PIREÁS

A comprehensive list of ferries from Pireás is hard to find: even the tourist office simply look up individual queries online (at ⓦ openseas.gr).

Tickets There's no need to buy tickets for conventional ferries before you get here, unless you want a berth in a cabin or are taking a car on board; during Greek holidays (Aug and Easter especially) these can be hard to get and it's worth booking in advance – the big companies have online booking. Hydrofoil and fast catamaran reservations are also a good idea at busy times, especially Fri night/Sat morning out of Athens, and Sun evening coming back. In general, though, the best plan is simply to get to Pireás early and check with some of the dozens of shipping agents around the Metro station and along the quayside Platía Karaïskáki (there are plenty of agents in central Athens, too). Most of these act only for particular lines, so for a full picture you will need to ask at three or four outlets.

Departure points Boats for different destinations leave from a variety of points around the main harbour: it can be helpful to know the gate number, though these are primarily for drivers. Free, airport-style buses run from gate E5, near the Metro, as far as E1, for the big ferries to Crete, the Dodecanese and the northwest. The main gates and departure points are marked on our map, but always check with the ticket agent, as on any given day a ferry may dock in an unexpected spot. They all display signs showing their destination and departure time; you can't buy tickets on the boat, but there's usually a ticket hut on the quayside nearby.

RAFÍNA

The port of Rafína (see p.120), about 30km from central Athens, has fast ferries and catamarans to the Cyclades as well as to Marmári on nearby Évvia. It is connected by KTEL bus with the Mavrommatéon terminal in Athens (every 30min; 1hr) and also has direct buses to the airport (12 daily; 40min). There are ticket agents all round the port, and the bus terminal is right on the seafront, facing the open sea; get your ticket on the bus. The vast majority of ferries leave either early morning or late afternoon. The following departure details are for peak season only. Ferry timetables are highly seasonal and very complicated, so do check details before you leave.

Destinations Peak season departures include: Ándhros (at least 6–7 daily; 1hr 55min); Íos (Sat–Thurs 1 daily; 5hr 45min); Mýkonos (at least 8 daily; 2hr 30min–4hr 40min); Náxos (1–2 daily; 4hr 25min–6hr 15min); Páros (1–2 daily; 2hr 35min–3hr 30min); Santoríni (1 daily; 6hr 45min); Tínos (7–8 daily; 2hr–3hr 45min).

LÁVRIO

Lávrio lies close to the southern tip of Attica, some 60km from the centre of Athens. Its ferries mainly serve Kéa and Kýthnos, but there are also services twice or more a week to the northeast Aegean and to many of the Cycladic islands via Sýros. KTEL buses run between Lávrio and the airport (20 daily; 30min), as well as the Mavrommatéon terminal in Athens (hourly; 1hr 40min). As for Rafína, times below are for peak season and can vary wildly at different times of the year.

Destinations Peak season departures include: Áyios Efstrátios (4 weekly; 7hr 30min–11hr 20min); Folégandhros (1 weekly; 15hr); Íos (1 weekly; 11hr 35min); Kavála (3 weekly; 14hr–14hr 30min); Kéa (3–5 daily; 1hr); Kímolos (2 weekly; 11hr); Kýthnos (2–3 daily; 1hr 40min–2hr 45min); Límnos (4 weekly; 10hr–12hr 50min); Mílos (2 weekly; 12hr 20min–15hr 45min); Náxos (1 weekly; 9hr 40min); Páros (2 weekly; 8hr 20min); Síkinos (1 weekly; 12hr 15min); Sýros (2 weekly; 5hr).

INFORMATION AND TOURS

Greek National Tourist Office Dhionysíou Areopayítou 18–20, just by the entrance to the South Slope of the Acropolis (Mon–Fri 9am–8pm, Sat & Sun 10am–4pm; Ⓜ Akrópoli). This is a useful first stop and they have a good free map as well as information sheets on current museum and site opening hours, bus schedules and so on.

Athens City Tourism Provides a manned infopoint at the airport and an excellent website, ⓦ thisisathens.org – check out the interactive maps.

Open-top bus tours City Sightseeing (☎ 210 922 0604, ⓦ citysightseeing.gr) and Athens City Tour (☎ 210 881 5207, ⓦ athensopentour.com) offer very similar open-top bus tours of Athens, for similar prices (€18–20 adults, €8

1

children; discounts online). The tours start from Sýndagma square at least every 30min, last about 90min (an extended version for €22 also takes in Pireás) and you can hop off and on at numerous stops along the way. Kids may prefer the Happy Train (☏ 213 039 0888, ⓦ athenshappytrain.com), which leaves from Ermoú at the corner of Sýndagma square on an hour-long trip around the centre (€6 adults, €4 children).

Walking tours There are walking tours aplenty, specializing in themes such as food, architecture, history and street-art: Alternative Tours of Athens (☏ 210 322 6713, ⓦ atathens.org) is strong on street art around the city; Greeking.Me (☏ 694 207 0899, ⓦ greeking.me) offers Greek dance classes, culinary experiences and tours for kids; while family-run Livin' Lovin' (☏ 210 807 7073, ⓦ livinlovin.gr) runs archeological tours around the centre and walks around authentic Athenian neighbourhoods to see daily life in action, such as the local street market.

Bike and Segway tours Athens by Bike (Tziréon 16 at Dhionysíou Areopayítou; from €30; ☏ 213 042 0724, ⓦ athensbybike.gr; ⓜ Akrópoli) offers 3hr bike tours of the city. Alternatively, you can cruise the pedestrian streets around the Acropolis or National Gardens with Athens Segway Tours (Eskhínou 9; ☏ 210 322 2500, ⓦ athenssegwaytours.com; €59/2hr; ⓜ Akrópoli), or take a three-wheeled trike trip with Scooterise (Chatzichristou 18; ☏ 216 700 3277, ⓦ scooterise.com; ⓜ Akrópoli) who offer a variety of tours from Athens Highlights (€32/1hr), Food Safari (€42/2hr 30min) or along the Athens Riviera Coast (€58/3hr 30min).

GETTING AROUND

Athens is served by slow but ubiquitous **buses**, a fast, mostly modern **Metro** system, and a **tram** service that runs from the centre to the beach suburbs. Combined public transport passes for these are a good idea (see below). **Taxis** are also plentiful and, for short journeys in town, exceptionally cheap. **Driving** is a traffic-crazed nightmare, and parking far worse: you're strongly advised not to try and drive around the city centre.

BY PUBLIC TRANSPORT

Tickets Athens has recently introduced an electronic ticketing system using a paper smartcard called the Ath.ena ticket (ⓦ athenstransport.com/tickets), which is valid on the city's buses, trolleybuses, trams, Metro and the suburban railway in central Athens (everything except the airport route beyond Doukissis Plakentias and some long-distance bus lines). The ticket can be bought at any Metro or suburban train station and loaded with five journeys (€7), eleven journeys (€14), a one-day unlimited pass (€4.50), a three-day pass (€9) or a five-day pass (€22): it can be recharged as often as you like. Tickets are valid from the first day they are used and must be scanned at the start of your journey – in the machines by the gates at Metro stations, or on board buses and trams. Those staying in Athens long-term may find it cheaper to get the plastic Ath.ena card, which can be loaded with all the above tickets or a thirty-day pass (€30) or a ninety-day pass (€85), though you'll need to show a passport and provide a photo to get it.

BY METRO

The expanded Metro system is much the easiest way to get around central Athens; it's fast, quiet and user-friendly. Trains run from roughly 5.30am till midnight (later on Line 1). When travelling on the Metro, you need to know the final stop in the direction you're heading, as that is how the platforms are identified; there are plenty of maps in the stations. For further information try ⓦ stasy.gr.

Lines There are three lines: Line 1 (green; Pireás to Kifissiá) is the original section, with useful stops in the centre at Thissío, Monastiráki, Omónia and Viktorías; Line 2 (red; Anthoúpoli to Ellinikó) has central stops at Omónia, Sýndagma and Akrópoli at the foot of the Acropolis; and Line 3 (blue; Ag Marína to the airport) passes through Monastiráki and Sýndagma.

Stations Some of the new stations are attractions in their own right, as they display artefacts discovered during excavation (numerous important discoveries were made) and other items of local interest. Sýndagma and Akrópoli are particularly interesting central ones.

BY BUS

The bus network in Athens is extensive, but it's also crowded and confusing. Most buses run from around 5am till midnight, and just a few – including those to the airport and to Pireás – continue all night.

Routes Routes, where relevant, are detailed in the individual accounts in this chapter, and there are helpful information

---

MIND YOUR STEP!

Athens' traffic is chaotic, but generally observant of traffic signals, so stick to official crossings when you cross the road. If anything, **pedestrian streets** are more hazardous since, while generally free of cars, they are by no means traffic-free – mopeds and motorbikes see them as their property too. Potholed **pavements** are an additional danger – though much of the time parked cars force you to walk in the road anyway.

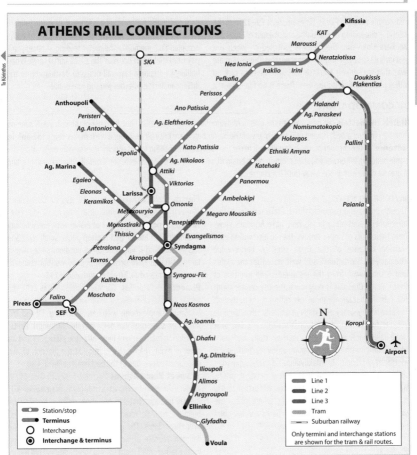

ATHENS RAIL CONNECTIONS

Legend:

- Station/stop
- **Terminus**
- Interchange
- **Interchange & terminus**

- Line 1
- Line 2
- Line 3
- Tram
- Suburban railway

Only termini and interchange stations are shown for the tram & rail routes.

N

---

boots at most of the major stops. Easiest to use are the trolleybuses: #1 connects Laríssis train station with Omónia, Sýndagma and Koukáki; #2, #4, #5, #9, #11 and #15 all link Sýndagma with Omónia and the National Archeological Museum. There's excellent city bus information at ⓦ oasa.gr.

BY TRAM

Athens' tram network is a great way to get to the coastal suburbs and the beach. Trams run from around 5.30am to 1am, or 2.30am on Fri and Sat. Numbers are displayed on the front of the tram and are worth checking, as the electronic boards at the stations are erratic. Trams don't automatically stop at every station, so push the bell if you're on board, or wave it down if you're on the platform. Check ⓦ stasy.gr for details.

Lines The tram runs from Leofóros Amalías just off Sýndagma to the coast, where it branches. To the right it heads northwest towards Pireás, terminating at SEF (the Stádhio Eirínis ké Filías or Peace and Friendship Stadium), an interchange with Metro Line 1 at Fáliro and within walking distance of Pireás's leisure harbours. Left, the tram lines run southwest along the coast to Glyfádha and Voúla. There are effectively three lines – #1, from Sýndagma to SEF; #2, from Sýndagma to Voúla; and #3, from SEF to Voúla.

TAXIS

All officially licensed cars are yellow and have a red-on-white number plate. You can wave them down on the street, pick them up at ranks in most of the major travel termini and central squares, phone for one, or use Taxibeat, an Athens-specific app similar to Uber.

Costs Athenian taxis are cheap – trips around the city centre rarely cost above €5, so for a group of three or four they are little more than the Metro. Longer trips are also

1

reasonable value: to Pireás, for example, is €9–12 from the centre – depending on the traffic and amount of luggage. **Meters** Make sure the meter is switched on when you get in. If it's "not working", find another taxi. One legitimate way that taxi-drivers increase their income is to pick up other passengers along the way. There is no fare-sharing:

each passenger (or group of passengers) pays the full fare for their journey. So if you're picked up by an already-occupied taxi, memorize the meter reading at once; you'll pay from that point on, plus the €1.20 initial tariff. When hailing an occupied taxi, call out your destination, so the driver can decide whether you suit him or not.

ACCOMMODATION

Hotels and **hostels** can be packed to the gills in midsummer – Aug especially – but for most of the year you'll have no problem finding a bed. Having said that, many of the better hotels are busy all year round, so it makes sense to **book in advance**. In the cheaper places especially, ask to see the room before booking in – standards vary greatly even within the same building. Wherever you stay, rooms tend to be small, and noise can be a problem; you'll get slightly better value, and a greater chance of peace, away from the centre.

WHERE TO STAY

Though pricey and commercialized, Pláka remains highly atmospheric, and many hotels here have Acropolis views from their roofs or upper storeys; they're also within easy walking distance of the main sites. A better-value alternative is Monastiráki, still well placed for the sights and a short walk from the restaurants and nightlife of Psyrrí. Platía Omonías is very much the city centre; south towards the bazaar are some interesting options, though the area is very sleazy, especially at night. North of Omónia you are further out of the tourist mainstream, but near good-value local restaurants, cinemas, clubs and bars. Immediately south of the Acropolis, easily reached via the Metro at Akrópoli, is Makriyiánni, a very upmarket residential neighbourhood with a few good, if pricey, hotels and arguably the city's best hostel. Further south, it merges into more earthy Koukáki, where prices are significantly lower. Over in Pangráti, there's another good hostel with a much quieter atmosphere.

PLÁKA
HOTELS
Acropolis House Kódhrou 6 ☎210 322 2344, ⓦ acropolishouse.gr; ⓜ Sýndagma; map pp.66–67. A rambling, slightly dilapidated, family-run 150-year-old mansion, much loved by its regulars, most of whom are academics who often leave behind books for guests to read. The furnishings are individual, and some of its 20 rooms have (sole use) bathrooms across the hall; there's a/c throughout. Discounts available for longer stays. Breakfast included. **€80**

★**Alice Inn** Tsatsou Konstadinou 9 ☎210 323 7139, ⓦ aliceinnathens.com; ⓜ Akrópoli; map pp.66–67. A hip and funky B&B with four suites in a Neoclassical house, in the centre of Pláka. It's bright and spacious with quirky furnishings throughout, and a kitchen on the lower floor to prepare snacks. There's a roof terrace with Acropolis views and one of the suites has its own patio garden. If you're a large party, it's also possible to rent the whole house out. Breakfast included. **€95**

Electra Palace Nikodhímou 18 ☎210 337 0000, ⓦ electrahotels.gr; ⓜ Sýndagma; map pp.66–67. Five-star luxury right in the heart of Pláka, with every facility including both indoor and rooftop pools, small gym and sauna. Stunning if you have an upper-floor suite, whose large balconies have great Acropolis views, but standard rooms are rather dull. Breakfast included. **€215**

Phaedra Herefóndos 16, at Adhrianoú ☎210 323 8461, ⓦ hotelphaedra.com; ⓜ Akrópoli; map pp.66–67. Small, simple rooms with bare tiled floors, TV and a/c, not all en suite (but you get a private bathroom). Polite, welcoming management looks after the place well and it's quiet at night, thanks to a location at the junction of two pedestrian alleys. One of the best deals in Pláka. **€80**

★**Sweet Home Athens** Patroou 5 ☎210 322 9029, ⓦ sweethomehotel.gr; ⓜ Sýndagma; map pp.66–67. A small boutique hotel in a lovingly restored Neoclassical building, with six rooms (including doubles and triples) over three floors. The geranium-clad balconies, plus the wooden staircase, artwork and various antiquities make up for the rather small room sizes in this traditional old home. Breakfast included. **€135**

HOSTEL
Student & Traveller's Inn Kydhathinéon 16 ☎210 324 4808, ⓦ studenttravellersinn.com; ⓜ Akrópolí/Sýndagma; map pp.66–67. Very friendly, perennially popular travellers' meeting place, clean and well run though a bit dated and not always the quietest spot. Small courtyard breakfast area/bar, luggage storage, laundry and travel agency. Rooms range from eight-bed dorms to private doubles, some en suite, some shared bath; triples, four-bed and female-only dorms also available. Dorm **€18**, double **€54**

MONISTIRÁKI AND PSYRRÍ
HOTELS
Attalos Athinás 29 ☎210 321 2801, ⓦ attaloshotel .com; ⓜ Monastiráki; map pp.66–67. Modern from the outside but traditional within, the *Attalos* has bright,

comfortable rooms (some triples available), well insulated from the noisy street, all with a/c and TV. Some balcony rooms on the upper floors have great views, but rooms facing the internal courtyard at the back are generally larger and quieter. There's also a roof-terrace bar in the evenings. Breakfast included. **€100**

Metropolis Mitropóleos 46 ☎210 321 7469, ⓦhotelmetropolis.gr; ⓂSýndagma/Monastiráki; map pp.66–67. Right by the cathedral, the friendly *Metropolis* has simple, plainly furnished rooms with vinyl floors, each with a good-size balcony, a/c and TV: some have shared bathrooms. The upper floors offer Acropolis views. **€121**

★O&B Leokoríou 7 ☎210 331 2950, ⓦoandbhotel .com; ⓂThissío; map pp.66–67. Understated designer hotel with exceptional service and just 22 rooms including a couple of large suites with private terrace and Acropolis views. All rooms have satellite TV, classy bathrooms and toiletries, plus DVD and CD players with a library of titles to borrow. Friendly, comfortable and elegant, plus a great location on the fringes of Psyrrí. Breakfast included. **€140**

★Tempi Eólou 29 ☎210 321 3175, ⓦtempihotel.gr; Ⓜ Monastiráki; map pp.66–67. A long-time favourite with budget travellers, this family-run place has 24 simple a/c rooms, some tiny and half with shared facilities. Service is exceptionally friendly and there's a book exchange, free luggage store, 24-hour reception, a shared kitchen, plus a handy affiliated travel agency. **€57**

HOSTEL

City Circus Sarrí 16 ☎213 023 7244, ⓦcitycircus.gr; Ⓜ Thissío; map pp.66–67. Super-cool hostel with en-suite dorms (mixed or female-only), classy communal areas and excellent facilities including a bar and bike hire. There's custom-made wooden furniture alongside retro pieces in the dorms and rooms, and plenty of social life, though the relative luxury comes at a price. Breakfast included. Dorm **€29**, double **€90**

APARTMENTS

★Boutique Athens ☎6985 083 556, ⓦboutiqueathens.com. One-to four-bedroom apartments across Athens, with the highest concentration in Monistiráki and Psyrrí. They're all extremely comfortable and generously equipped, with interesting art on the walls; highly recommended as an alternative to cramped hotel rooms. Minimum stay usually two nights; breakfast included. **€80**

SÝNDAGMA

Hotel Grande Bretagne Vassíléos Yioryíou 1, Platía Sýndagma ☎210 333 0000, ⓦgrandebretagne.gr; Ⓜ Sýndagma; map pp.66–67. If someone else is paying, try to get them to put you up at the *Grande Bretagne*, the

grandest of all Athens' hotels with the finest location in town. Refurbished for the Olympics, it really is magnificent, with every conceivable facility. The crisis has seen prices drop dramatically, with many special offers; even so, treatments in the spa cost more than a night at many hotels. Breakfast included. **€330**

★innAthens G Souri, 3 ☎210 325 8555, ⓦinnathens .com; Ⓜ Sýndagma; map pp.66–67. Shaped like a triangle around a gorgeous courtyard with a lemon tree at its centre, this boutique hotel has 22 suites with quirky furnishings such as off-cuts of marble for tables and sink backsplashes. Although in a relatively busy neighbourhood, it's a quiet oasis after a day's sightseeing. Breakfast included. **€150**

OMÓNIA AND THE BAZAAR

HOTELS

Athens Center Square Arostogítonos 15 ☎210 321 1770, ⓦathenscentresquarehotel.gr; Ⓜ Omónia/ Monastiráki; map pp.66–67. A budget boutique hotel directly above the fruit and vegetable market, handy for Psyrrí too. Smallish but very well-appointed rooms with a/c and flat-screen TV, some with balconies; very good online deals often available. Breakfast included. **€110**

Delphi Art Hotel Ayíou Konstandínou 27 ☎210 524 4004, ⓦdelphiarthotel.com; Ⓜ Omónia; map pp.60–61. Right by the National Theatre and Áyios Konstantínos church, this rather dated 1930s mansion has Art Nouveau touches and eclectic, individual furnishings, plus jacuzzi baths in some rooms. Wi-fi costs extra. **€75**

Fresh Hotel Sofokléous 26 ☎210 524 8511, ⓦfreshhotel.gr; Ⓜ Omónia; map pp.66–67. Gay-friendly, glossy, designer hotel in the heart of the market area, with lavish use of colour, elegant furnishings and great lighting and bathrooms – though the cutting-edge design is perhaps starting to lose its edge, and some rooms are tiny. Facilities include bike hire and an elegant rooftop pool, bar and restaurant (open to non-residents). Breakfast included. **€145**

HOSTEL

Athens Quinta Hostel Methonis 13 ☎693 651 3026, ⓦathens-quinta.hotelsathens.org; Ⓜ Panepistimiou; map pp.60–61. In a beautifully restored Neoclassical manor house near the university district, this hostel has 3- and 6-bed dorms, some with en-suite bathrooms and balconies, plus double rooms. The vintage furniture is somewhat dated, but there's a lovely courtyard to relax in and laundry facilities. Dorm **€22**, double **€45**

NORTH OF THE CENTRE

HOTELS

Art Hotel Márni 27 ☎210 524 0501, ⓦarthotelathens .gr; Ⓜ Omónia; map pp.60–61. Not the greatest location

1

– on a rather noisy, scruffy street – but a very pleasant boutique hotel in a refurbished 1920s building with individually designed rooms. Thoughtful touches include Korres toiletries in the marble bathrooms, and there's a substantial buffet breakfast included. **€80**

Exarchion Themistokléous 55, Platía Exarhíon ☎ 210 380 0731, ⓦ exarchion.com; Ⓜ Omónia; map pp.60–61. This big, 1960s high-rise is a great deal less fancy inside than you might imagine. Still, it's good value if you want to be at the heart of Exárhia's nightlife. The simple rooms have TV, a/c and fridge, and the upper floors are quieter, with better views. **€60**

Museum Bouboulínas 16 ☎ 210 380 5611, ⓦ museumhotel.gr; Ⓜ Viktorías/Omónia; map pp.60–61. Very pleasant, international-style hotel (part of the Best Western chain), right behind the National Archeological Museum and the Polytekhnío. Rooms in the new wing, which has triples, quads and small suites, are more luxurious but slightly more expensive. **€70**

Orion and Dryades Emmanouíl Benáki 105, at Anexartisías ☎ 210 382 7362, ⓦ orion-dryades.com; Ⓜ Viktorías/Omónia; map pp.60–61. Quiet, well-run twin hotels across from the Stréfis Hill – a steep uphill walk from almost anywhere. Reception is in the cheaper *Orion*, which has shared bathrooms, a kitchen, and a communal area on the roof with an amazing view of central Athens. All rooms in the *Dryades* are en suite with a/c and TV; wi-fi costs extra. *Orion* **€60** *Dryades* **€80**

WEST OF THE CENTRE

Phidias Apostólou Pávlou 39 ☎ 210 345 9511, ⓦ phidias.gr; Ⓜ Thissío; map pp.66–67. In an enviable location in Thissío overlooking the Acropolis, at the heart of a fashionable area crammed with designer cafés, the *Phidias* has cosy if rather dated rooms, almost all of which have balconies and fabulous views. The hotel also boasts a great café. Breakfast included. **€160**

KOLONÁKI

★**Coco-Mat** Patriarchou Ioakim 36 ☎ 210 723 0000, ⓦ cocomatathens.gr; map pp.60–61. Run by a Greek designer bedding company, this luxury hotel has 42 rooms and some suites in a renovated 1935 building above the company's flagship store. The hotel focuses its efforts on an excellent night's sleep, with super-comfy mattresses, bathrooms containing natural products, plus a lavender-filled pillow at turndown time. The roof terrace offers sweeping views across the city and a cleverly designed wall mural. Breakfast using locally sourced products is included. **€160**

St George Lycabettus Kleoménous 2 ☎ 210 729 0711, ⓦ sglycabettus.gr; map pp.60–61. A luxury hotel and an Athenian classic, positioned high on Lykavitós Hill overlooking the city. There's abundant marble and leather in the public areas, a welcome rooftop pool and fashionable bars

and restaurant, popular with wealthy young Athenians. Some of the rooms are rather small, however, and there's no point staying here if you don't pay extra for the view. Breakfast included. **€245**

SOUTHERN ATHENS
HOTELS

★**Acropolis Museum Boutique Hotel** Syngrou Ave 48 ☎ 210 924 9050, ⓦ acropolismuseumhotel.com; Ⓜ Syngroú-Fix; map pp.60–61. Walking distance from the Acropolis, this boutique hotel has 22 rooms over three floors with high ceilings, ornate furnishings, wooden floors and comfortable mattress toppers. Ask for a room not facing the street if you're a light sleeper. Breakfast included. **€148**

Herodion Robérto Gálli 4 ☎ 210 923 6832, ⓦ herodion.gr; Ⓜ Akrópoli; map pp.66–67. Though it's not quite as luxurious as the exterior and lobby suggest, this lovely four-star hotel enjoys an enviable position right behind the Acropolis. The roof terrace looks almost straight down to the south slope of the Acropolis. Breakfast included. **€220**

Marble House Cul-de-sac off A. Zínni 35A ☎ 210 923 4058, ⓦ marblehouse.gr; Ⓜ Syngroú-Fix; map pp.60–61. The best value in Koukáki, this family-run, friendly *pension* offers simple rooms, some without private bathroom with fans or a/c (for extra charge); there are also two self-catering studios for longer stays. It's often full, so call ahead. **€49**

HOSTELS

★**Athens Backpackers** Mákri 12 ☎ 210 922 4044, ⓦ backpackers.gr; Ⓜ Akrópoli; map pp.66–67. Very central Athenian–Australian-run hostel with few frills, but clean mixed or female-only dorms (3-, 4- and 6-bed) with shared or en-suite bathrooms, plus a 2-person self-contained apartment. There's also a communal kitchen, laundrette, bar, fabulous rooftop view and great atmosphere. Breakfast included. April–Oct. Dorm **€28**, apartment **€110**

Pagration Athens Youth Hostel Dhamáreos 75, Pangráti ☎ 210 751 9530; trolleys #2 and #11 from Omónia via Sýndagma, bus #203 or #204 or (15–20min walk) Ⓜ Evangelismós; map pp.60–61. A bit out of the way in a decent, quiet neighbourhood with plenty of local restaurants and nightlife, this friendly, good value hostel has 5-, 6-, 8- and 9-bed mixed dorms. There's free use of the kitchen and communal area with TV, but they charge for using the washing machine and hot water. There's no sign on the door, so look for the green gate. Dorm **€12**

APARTMENTS

Pi Athens Suites Fokianou 4 ☎ 210 751 2345, ⓦ piathens.com; Ⓜ Syntagma; map pp.60–61. Four rooms, one apartment and one suite (with Acropolis view) sleeping 2–5 people in a central location, right by the Panathenaic Stadium and National Gardens. It has a great rooftop terrace with views to the Acropolis and a small courtyard by the reception. There's also free parking next door. Breakfast included. Double €122, suite €156

PIREÁS

Phidias Pireas Kountouriotou 189, Pireás ☎ 210 429 6480, ⍟ hotelphidias.gr; Ⓜ Pireás; map p.94. It's easy to get from the centre to Pireás, but if you have a early departure or late ferry arrival, this hotel is a solid option. On a quiet street, 300 metres from the port and the trendy Pasalimani Marina, it has a range of clean and functional

rooms with large beds, though somewhat lacking in personality. €80

AIRPORT

St. Thomas B&B St. Thomas 21, Peania ☎ 210 602 9367, ⍟ stay-in-athens.com. It's only about 40min by train or metro to the centre of Athens, but if you need to stay near the airport, this family run B&B is a great choice. About 10 min from the airport, it has four rooms (one family sized), an outdoor swimming pool and airport pick-up and drop-off. It gets a lot of repeats clientele, so book ahead. Breakfast included. €85

EATING AND DRINKING

Athens has the best and the most varied **restaurants** and **tavernas** in Greece. Fast-food and takeaway places are also plentiful – the usual international chains keep a relatively low profile, and there are plenty of more authentic alternatives. **Reservations** are rarely necessary (the simpler places can usually squeeze in an extra table if necessary) – though it's worth calling ahead at the fancier restaurants, or if you're planning a special trip across town.

WHERE TO EAT

While Pláka's hills and narrow lanes can provide a pleasant, romantic evening setting, they also tend to be marred by high prices, aggressive touts and general tourist hype. Still in the centre, lively and fashionable areas like Psyrrí, Monastiráki and Thissío (or Gázi a little further afield) are where the locals go for a meal out. Omónia is business territory and a great place to grab a quick (or long) lunch. For better value and traditional food, it's worth striking out into the ring of neighbourhoods around, all of which have plenty of local tavernas: Exárhia, Neápoli, Áno Petrálona, Pangráti, Koukáki or the more upmarket Kolonáki are all good bets. On the coast, the big attraction, not surprisingly, is fish. The pleasure harbours of Pireás, especially, are a favourite Sunday lunchtime destination.

PLÁKA

CAFÉS

Café Pláka Tripódhon 1, ☎ 210 322 0388; map pp.66–67. This convenient, not too touristy, comfortable café serves crêpes (€6.50–8), sandwiches and ice cream, plus free wi-fi and a roof terrace on which to enjoy them. Daily till late.

★ **Kallipateira** Astiggos 8, ☎ 210 321 4152; map pp.66–67. In a Neoclassical building on a pedestrianized street in the heart of Pláka, this is where young Athenians hang out. It serves traditional, simple light lunches and dinners at decent prices (oven baked chicken and salad €6; lentils and salad €5.50), and at weekends you can hear rembetika (Greek blues music). Daily noon–2am.

Yiasemi Mnisikléous ☎ 2130 417 937, ⍟ yiasemi.gr; map pp.66–67. A café-bistro on a steep, stepped street, *Yiasemi* is almost always packed with locals. If there are no tables on the street, check inside, where stairs lead up to a

lesser-known outdoor terrace. There are hot drinks and fresh juices, big breakfast for €8 and inexpensive lunchtime specials (many vegetarian, such as cheese pie with black-eye pea salad) for €5. Daily 10am–2am.

RESTAURANTS

Damingos (Ta Bakaliarakia) Kydhathinéon 41 ☎ 210 323 5084; map pp.66–67. Open since 1865 and tucked away in a basement, this place has dour service, but the old-fashioned style (hefty barrels in the back room filled with the family's home vintages, including a memorable retsina), and the excellent *bakaliáro skordhaliá* (deep-fried cod with garlic sauce) for which it is famed make up for it. It's cheap, too, with starters, such as fried haloumi €3–5, and mains €7–10. Best in winter. Mon–Fri 5pm–midnight, Sat & Sun from noon; closed Aug.

Elaia/Palia Taverna tou Psarrá Erekhthéos 16, at Erotókritou ☎ 210 324 9512/321 8733; map pp.66–67. Though they appear to be separate restaurants, these two share a menu and kitchen; given that, the best place to sit is on the roof terrace at *Elaia* for wonderful views; there are also plenty of tables below, both inside and on a tree-shaded and bougainvillea-draped pedestrian cross-roads. You're best making a meal of the mezédhes (€6–9), which include the usual tzatziki, fried cheese and dolmades as well as seafood and fish concoctions. There's live music Thurs–Sat evenings and Sun lunchtime. Mon–Sat 1pm–1am, Sun from noon.

Paradosiako Apollonos 4 ☎ 210 321 4121; map pp.66–67. On a busy street, this small place serves excellent, unpretentious, fresh Greek food, including good vegetarian options like fava and chickpea casserole and fish such as sea bream; it's reasonably priced at around €25 per person including drinks. There's just three or four tables on the pavement, and a similar number inside. Mon–Sat 11.30am–midnight.

1

Platanos Dhioyénous 4 ☎ 210 322 0666; map pp.66–67. Established in 1932, and it feels like there's been little change to the staff or menu at this taverna since. There's outdoor summer seating in a quiet square under the plane tree from which it takes its name, and reasonably priced traditional dishes such as roast lamb with artichokes or with spinach and potatoes (all €9.50), washed down with cloudy wine from vast barrels. Cash only. Daily noon–4.30pm, Mon–Sat also 7.30pm–midnight.

★**Scholarhio** Tripódhon 14 ☎ 210 324 7605, ⓦ scholarhio.gr; map pp.66–67. Attractive, split-level ouzerí with a popular summer terrace, sheltered from the street. It has a great selection of mezédhes (all €3–7) brought out on trays so that you can point to the ones that you fancy. Especially good are the flaming sausages, bouréki (thin pastry filled with ham and cheese) and grilled aubergine. The house red wine is also palatable and cheap. All-inclusive deals at €15 a head. Daily 11am–2am.

MONASTIRÁKI AND PSYRRÍ

CAFÉS

★**Little Kook** Karaiskaki 17 ☎ 210 321 4144; map pp.66–67. This fairy-tale themed coffee shop is great for kids and adults alike: the staff wear costumes – Alice in Wonderland is a favourite – and the desserts are to-die-for. It's not cheap, at €8 for a slice of cake, but you're paying for the ambiance. Daily 11am–12am.

Oréa Ellás Mitrópoleos 59 or Pandhróssou ☎ 210 321 3023; map pp.66–67. Tucked away on the upper floor of the Kendro Ellinikis Paradosis store, this old-fashioned café serving coffee and desserts such as baklava (€7) offers a welcome escape from the crowded flea market. There's also a great view of the rooftops of Pláka on the slope towards the Acropolis. Daily 8am–1am.

★**Ta Servetia tou Psyrri** Eskhýlou 3 ☎ 210 324 5862; map pp.66–67. All the rage with locals for its traditional desserts and sticky cakes such as Kiunefe – a filo pastry dish with cream cheese and buffalo cream (€8), washed down with tea, coffee or ouzo. It's the place to head for Greek desserts. Mon–Thurs & Sun 10am–2am, Fri & Sat till 4am.

RESTAURANTS

★**Café Abysinia** Kynétou 7, Platía Avysinnías ☎ 210 321 7047; map pp.66–67. With two floors and a delicious, modern take on traditional Greek cooking (wild boar meatballs, €15, for example, or mussel pilaf for €10.50), Café Abysinia is always busy, with a local alternative crowd. Though more expensive than many, it's still decent value, and there's live music most weekday evenings and weekend lunchtimes. Tues–Sat 11am–1am, Sun till 7pm.

Kuzina Adhrianoú 9 ☎ 210 324 0133, ⓦ www.kuzina.gr; map pp.66–67. Far more adventurous than the average Greek taverna, Kuzina's fusion cooking offers starters varying from Greek staples like octopus to lamb spring rolls and crab cakes; mains tend to the exotic – mussels with saffron, ouzo, fennel and feta (€12) or twelve-hour roasted pork with lime and basil cream (€15). The simpler lunch menu has main dishes from €7.50–10. Daily lunch and dinner.

Lithos Aisópou 17 ☎ 210 324 7797, ⓦ lithospsiri.gr; map pp.66–67. Lively restaurant where locals enjoy a modern take on Greek classics and live music every night (and weekend lunchtimes). Excellent cheese or fennel pies to start (around €5), followed perhaps by lamb with honey and thyme (€15), octopus, or seafood risotto (around €10). Daily lunch and dinner.

★**Manas Kouzina-Kouzina** Aiolou 27 ☎ 210 325 2335; map pp.66–67. This excellent value family restaurant, "Mother's Kitchen", serves slow-cooked, traditional Greek dishes made from locally sourced ingredients: expect dishes such as Mana's famous vegetarian moussaka (€7), or bifteki thalasinon (seafood patties from Patmos; €9) and rosto Naxos (pork with orange sauce; €9). Tables outside on the bustling pedestrianized square have Acropolis views, but for a cosier atmosphere eat inside with the Greek regulars. Often there's live traditional music at the weekends, too. Daily 8am–12am.

Nikitas Ayíon Anaryíron 19 ☎ 210 325 2591; map pp.66–67. A survivor from the days before Psyrrí was fashionable, and by far the least expensive option here, with no-nonsense simple fare such as grilled meats and daily specials like chickpeas with orange, plus great chips. Expect to pay €9–10 per person. Mon–Thurs & Sun 10am–7pm, Fri & Sat 11am–midnight.

Souvlaki Bar Thissíou 15 ☎ 210 515 0550; map pp.66–67. Modern take on a classic souvladzídhika (kebab shop), close to Thissío Metro. Great yíros (€2.50) and souvláki (including veggie versions; portion €6.50–8.50) in designer surroundings, plus excellent burgers (€6.50–9) and more. Daily lunch and dinner till late.

Taverna tou Psyrri Eskhýlou 12 ☎ 210 321 4923; map pp.66–67. Crowded out by its flashier neighbours, this is one of the oldest restaurants in Psyrrí: it still serves good food, though, with starters like stuffed aubergine for €4 and simple dishes including moussaka and meatballs for €5.50. Check out the daily specials, too, with traditional country dishes like rabbit stifádho (stew) or an earthy goat soup (€7). Daily lunch and dinner.

Thanasis Mitrópoleos 69 ☎ 210 324 4705; map pp.66–67. Reckoned to serve the best souvláki and yíros in this part of Athens. Inexpensive at around €5–9, it's always packed with locals at lunchtime: there's no booking, so you'll have to fight for a table. Daily 9.30am–1am.

SÝNDAGMA

CAFÉS

Aegli Café In the National Gardens, by the Záppio; map pp.66–67. One of Athens' most historic cafés, where

Athenians from all walks of life mix: politicians, actors, fashion designers, you name it. It serves delicious desserts (€12) and fresh juices (€6) plus a range of cocktails (from €10) – they are pricey due to its location and the Acropolis views, but it's worth visiting once. Daily 9am–midnight.

★ **The Loft by Collage** Kapnikareas 3 ☎ 697 330 0290; map pp.66–67. With an events space on the top floor, the huge open-plan café and bar at street level attracts young Athenian entrepreneurs and students using the wi-fi to study. It serves a range of dishes with mains such as chicken and cheddar burrito (€8) and desserts including orange pie with cream (€5.50) and salted caramel cheesecake (€5.50). Vegan dishes also available. Mon–Thurs & Sun 9:30am–2am, Fri–Sat till 4am.

RESTAURANTS

Kentrikon Kolokotróni 3 ☎ 210 323 2482, ⓦ estiatorio -kentrikon.gr; map pp.66–67. Elegant, old-fashioned restaurant with attentive staff, on a shady, quiet corner close to Sýntagma. Classy and classic, it attracts an elderly, well-dressed clientele, so you might not fit in in T-shirt and shorts, but the traditional lunchtime food is delicious and far from expensive: veal with green beans for €11, or roast chicken €9.50. Mon–Sat noon–6pm.

★ **Makalo** Níkis 23 ☎ 211 406 7032; map pp.66–67. Excellent café and restaurant, with waiters in traditional costume, serving light dishes such as couscous with goats cheese (€7.50), mains such as salmon fillet with courgette (€13) and huge dishes of pasta with courgette cream sauce (€8.50), plus healthy salads, meat dishes from €9.50, and a good range of wines. Mon–Sat noon–11pm, Sun 1pm–5pm.

Tzitzikas Ki O Mermigas Mitrópoleos 12–14 ☎ 210 324 7607; map pp.66–67. One of a small chain of very popular Athenian restaurants, the *"Ant and the Grasshopper"* is designed to look like a village store. They serve traditional Greek dishes with a modern twist, plus excellent salads and dishes like kid with rosemary and raki (€11), and their signature dish-chicken *mastihato (€15)*. Great ambience, and always busy with locals and tourists. Definitely reserve. Daily noon–midnight.

OMÓNIA AND THE BAZAAR

CAFÉS

Amouage Galeria Koraï, off Platía Koraï; map pp.66–67. The Galeria Koraï is full of cafés and fast-food places – including the likes of *Starbucks* and *McDonald's* – as well as more local places like this, where they serve crêpes (€3–6), sandwiches, hot dogs and juices. Mon–Sat all day till early evening.

Krinos Eólou 87, behind the central market; map pp.66–67. *Krinos* has been operating since 1922, and is still the place for old-fashioned treats like *loukoumádhes* (doughnut-like puffs soaked in syrup; €3 with coffee) and *bougátsa* as well as flaky, sesame-topped *tirópittes*,

sandwiches and ice creams. Mon, Wed & Sat 7.30am–3.30pm, Tues, Thurs & Fri till 8.30pm.

RESTAURANTS

Andreas Themistokléous 18 ☎ 210 382 1522; map pp.60–61. A popular venue for long weekday lunches, this traditional ouzerí specializes in fish dishes, such as mussels and octopus fritters; mezes are typically around €5 – check the daily specials, too. Live music Thurs–Sat. Mon–Sat lunch and dinner, Sun lunch only.

Dhiporto Theátrou, at Sokrátous ☎ 210 321 1463; map pp.66–67. *Dhiporto* has a rather unusual entrance: two brown-painted metal trapdoors in the pavement open to a steep stairway down into a basement that feels like it belongs in an Athens of fifty years ago. Simple, inexpensive Greek food – chickpea soup, Greek salad, fried fish – washed down with retsina is enjoyed by market workers as well as tourists and office suits. As the afternoon wears on, impromptu music often breaks out. Mon–Sat 6am–6pm.

Klimataria Platía Theátrou 2 ☎ 210 321 6629, ⓦ klimataria.gr; map pp.66–67. Friendly, old-fashioned taverna serving ample portions of traditional fare at reasonable prices (mains around €8). The daily specials usually feature excellent vegetable dishes plus daily roast meats. Barrels of wine are the only decoration, but there's open courtyard seating in summer and live music at the end of the week. Daily lunch, Fri & Sat also dinner.

Mama Tierra Akadamias 84 ☎ 211 411 4420, ⓦ mamatierra.gr; map pp.60–61. Its name means "mother earth" in Spanish, and this restaurant specializes in vegetarian and vegan dishes that combine Mediterranean, Asian and Middle Eastern flavours and spices. Expect such as hummus with sweet potato (€4.20) and falafel platter (€6.50). Mon–Thurs noon–9pm, Fri noon–10pm, Sat 1pm–10pm.

★ **Ta Karamanlidika by Fanis** Sokrátous & Evripídou 1 ☎ 210 325 4184; map pp.66–67. In the heart of the Bazaar area, *Ta Karamanlidika* is an excellent deli and mezédhes restaurant that makes your mouth water from the minute you set foot inside. On display are meats sourced from regions around Greece plus aged cheeses, while the mezédhes include spicy sausage (€3) and Pastirma pie with filo pastry served with eggs (€6). Mon–Sat noon–11pm.

NORTHERN ATHENS

CAFÉS

Floral Books and Cafe Themistokléous 80, Platía Exarhíon ☎ 210 380 0070, ⓦ floralcafe.gr; map pp.60–61. Very popular with students and academics, this spacious and comfortable bookstore/café has free wi-fi and regular live music. Coffee, juices and snacks such as toasted sandwiches (€4) are served during the day, and there's more of a cocktail bar atmosphere at night. Daily 9am–3am.

1

RESTAURANTS

Lefka Mavromiháli 121 ☎ 210 361 4038; map pp.60–61. Beloved old taverna with great *fáva* (hummus-like bean purée), black-eyed beans, baked and grilled meat like lamb with oregano, plus barrelled retsina: expect to pay around €10 per person. There's lovely summer seating in a huge garden enclosed by barrels. Mon–Sat lunch and dinner, Sun lunch only.

Mystic Pizza Emmanouíl Benáki 76 ☎ 210 383 9500, ⓦ mystic.com.gr; map pp.60–61. Tiny, unpretentious place serving pasta and salads as well as excellent pizzas (mostly €8–9). The flour they use is made from hemp (cannabis) seeds, which they claim has both health and environmental benefits. Takeaway and delivery service, too. Mon–Fri 1pm–1am, Sat & Sun from 7pm.

Pinaleon Mavromiháli 152 ☎ 210 644 0945; map pp.60–61. A classic old-style taverna serving rich *mezédhes* and meaty main courses (€7–10), washed down with excellent organic wine. Daily dinner only 8pm–midnight; closed June–Sept.

Rozalia Valtetsíou 54 ☎ 210 330 2133, ⓦ rozalia.gr; map pp.60–61. Ever-popular mid-range taverna, serving excellent chicken and highly palatable barrelled wine. Order *mezédhes* (mostly €3.50–7) from the tray, while the waiters thread their way through the throng; there's also a regular menu of grilled fish and meat (€10.50–13). Garden seating in summer. Daily noon–midnight.

★ Yiandes Valtetsíou 44 ☎ 210 330 1369; map pp.60–61. Excellent modern Greek cuisine, with influences from around the world and organic ingredients, served in a pleasant courtyard next to the Riviera open-air cinema. Greek-style quesadillas (€6) are particularly good, or try the knuckle of pork with beer sauce (€12). Daily 1pm–1am.

WESTERN ATHENS

CAFÉ

Athinaion Politeia Akamántos 1, at Apóstolou Pávlou, Thissío ☎ 210 341 3795, ⓦ athinaionpoliteia.gr; map pp.66–67. Housed in an old mansion, in an enviable position with great views from the terrace towards the Acropolis, this is a popular meeting place and a decent spot to relax over a frappé. Light meals such as chicken meatballs with ginger (€7), and mains such as ravioli stuffed with pumpkin (€11.50) are also served. Daily 9am–3am.

RESTAURANTS

Butcher Shop Persefónis 19, Gázi ☎ 210 341 3440; map pp.60–61. As the name and the decor suggest, this is not one for vegetarians (though the next door fish restaurant, *Sardelles*, is under the same management and can serve to the same tables). There are all sorts of high-quality meat, from lamb chops (€15.40) to game (€12),

plus a huge variety of burgers (€10–12.50), exotic sausages (€7.50–9) and fancy *yíros* (with shank and pancetta of free-range pork, €11.50). Great chips, too. Daily noon–2am.

Chez Lucien Tróon 32, Áno Petrálona ☎ 210 346 4236; map pp.60–61. Excellent French bistro with a short menu of authentic, well-prepared dishes, such as potatoes au gratin or duck (mains €15–25) plus a set menu for €23. You may have to wait – there are no reservations – and/or share a table. Tues–Sat 8.30pm–2am; closed Aug.

Dinner in the Sky Iakchou & Voutadon, Gázi/Technopolis ☎ 694 539 6509, ⓦ dinnerinthesky.gr; map pp.60–61. A table of 22 people, plus the chef, is lifted into the air by crane for an amazing view across the city as you eat. The set menu features dishes such as cucumber and mango soup, shrimp saganaki and chocolate mousse: it's not cheap at €120 per person, but you're paying for the experience. Avoid, if you're scared of heights. Daily 8pm–11pm.

Gazohori Dhekeléon 2–6 ☎ 210 342 4044, ⓦ gazohori.gr; map pp.60–61. A big, busy place whose tables spread halfway down the street, *Gazohori* attracts a typically young crowd. Traditional meze such as stuffed vine leaves, taramasalata and moussaka are served on marble-topped tables, and wine comes in tin jugs. Prices are reasonable: a large *pikilía* (meze selection) costs €16. Daily lunch and dinner.

★ Oikonomou Tróon 41, at Kydhantidhón, Áno Petrálona ☎ 210 346 7555; map pp.60–61. Wonderful, traditional taverna where home-cooked food is served to packed pavement tables in summer. There's no menu, just a dozen or so inexpensive daily specials such as *pastitsio* (like lasagne, but with tubed pasta) for €6: check out what others are eating as the waiters may not know the names of some of the dishes in English. Mon–Sat dinner only.

★ To Steki tou Ilia Eptahálkou 5, Thissío ☎ 210 345 8052; map pp.66–67. Simple, inexpensive place on a pedestrianized street above the Metro tracks. It's renowned for some of the finest lamb chops in the city (€12) and gets so busy that the owners have opened a second branch 200m further down (at Thessaloníkis 7). Tables on the street in summer. Mon–Sat noon–midnight, Sun noon–7pm.

KOLONÁKI

CAFÉS

Da Capo Tsákalof 1 ☎ 210 360 2497; map pp.60–61. One of the most popular of the many establishments on this pedestrianized street, just north of Kolonáki square, the chic, self-service *Da Capo* serves the best cappuccino in Athens (€4), plus snacks such as brioche sandwiches (€5). Daily 6.30am–10pm.

1

Filion Skoufá 34 ☎ 210 361 2850; map pp.66–67. A local institution for coffee, cakes, omelettes, salads and breakfasts (€5–10): it's busy at all times of day, with a more sober crowd than the average Kolonáki café. Daily 8am–midnight.

RESTAURANTS

Balsamakis (To Kotopoulo) Platía Kolonakíou, north side ☎ 210 360 6725; map pp.60–61. As the name indicates (*kotópoulo* means chicken), this tiny hole-in-the-wall, with just a few tables on the pavement, is *the* place for juicy, crispy, rotisserie-style poultry (chicken and chips €6.50); they also do kebabs and *yíros*. It's strictly no-frills, lit by fluorescent lights and packed with people at all hours. Mon–Sat 11am–11pm.

Filippou Xenokrátous 19 ☎ 210 721 6390; map pp.60–61. This old-time taverna has been refurbished, with an elegant interior, though the menu hasn't changed much; you can still check out the simmering pots and casseroles in the kitchen, or find favourites like pork in lemon sauce or rabbit with wine sauce for around €8, as well as some more ambitious, modern Greek dishes. Relatively formal; liveliest at lunchtime. Mon–Sat 1–5pm, Mon–Fri also 8.30pm–midnight.

★**Ikio** Ploútarhou 15 ☎ 210 725 9216; map pp.60–61. The name means "homely", and this busy, reasonably priced neighbourhood restaurant serves a modern take on Greek classics and a short menu of daily specials, such as chicken meatballs with "arab pie" and yoghurt sauce (€10), plus pasta and salads. Mon–Sat 1pm–12.30am.

★**Il Postino** Grivéon 3, in alleyway off Skoufá ☎ 210 364 1414; map pp.66–67. Good-value modern Italian osteria serving freshly made pasta (from €9; spaghetti *vongole* €14) and simple Italian dishes (homemade gnocchi with gorgonzola and prosciutto €12) in a friendly, bustling room. Mon–Thurs 6.30pm–1am, Sat from 1am, Sun from 6pm.

Nice 'n' Easy Skoufá 60 ☎ 210 361 7201, ⓦ niceneasy .gr; map pp.66–67. Very popular with locals and tourists alike, this organic restaurant has a film-star-themed contemporary Mediterranean cuisine menu. It breeds its own water buffalo on an organic farm in Northern Greece for dishes such as the gluten-free 'Marvin Gay' burger (€8.50) or 'Bruce Lee' spring rolls (€7.50). Daily 9am–1am.

Zahari ke Alati Anapiron Polemou 22 ☎ 210 380 1253, ⓦ zaxarialati.gr; map pp.60–61. "Sugar and Salt" bistro-bar, near Lykavitós Hill, serves upmarket Mediterranean-influenced dinners such as grilled salmon with walnut and orange sauce (€18) and aubergine ravioli with ratatouille (€10.50). Upstairs is a superb cocktail bar. Tues–Sat 7pm–2am, Sun 1pm–2am.

SOUTHERN ATHENS

CAFÉ

★**Acropolis Museum Restaurant** Acropolis Museum, Dhionysíou Areopayítou ☎ 210 900 0915, ⓦ theacropolismuseum.gr; map pp.66–67. Café serving light meals such as octopus with pasta (€12.50) and baked red beans with sausage & fennel (€8), as well as salads, cakes and drinks – the quality is superb and prices reasonable. There's a large, cool, internal area and a shaded terrace looking towards the Parthenon. Don't go to the ground-floor café; instead, grab a free pass to the second floor where the menu is the same but with views of the Acropolis. Mon 8am–4pm, Tues–Thurs 8am–8pm, Fri 8am–midnight, Sat & Sun 8am–8pm.

RESTAURANTS

Ambrosia Dhrákou 3–5, Koukáki ☎ 210 922 0281; map pp.60–61. A friendly *psistaría* packed with locals, especially on summer nights when the tables spill out into the pedestrian walkway. Food is inexpensive, simple and delicious – succulent grilled chicken, pork chops, kebabs and Greek salads (€6–10) – and the service friendly and attentive. Daily lunch and dinner.

Karavitis Arktínou 33, at Pafsaníou, Pangráti ☎ 210 751 5155; map pp.60–61. This crumbling single-storey building, surrounded by high-rises, looks like a dump from the outside, but inside it's a cheery old-style taverna, dating back to 1926. It serves barrel wine, *mezédhes* such as fried courgettes, and simple clay-cooked main courses including lamb chops (€8–12.50). In summer, there's outdoor seating in an enclosed garden. Mon–Thurs 8pm–midnight, Fri & Sat 8pm–12.30am, Sun 1.30pm–12.30am.

★**Katsourbos** Amínta 2, Pangráti ☎ 210 722 2167, ⓦ katsourbos.gr; map pp.60–61. Cretan food is fashionable in Athens, and this modern-looking place serves tasty food created from ingredients sourced from the island – try the baked Cretan Cheese with honey or lamb in lemon sauce. Relatively expensive (around €25–30 a head), but worth it. Daily lunch and dinner.

Spondi Pýrronos 5, just off Platía Varnáva, Pangráti ☎ 210 756 4021, ⓦ spondi.gr; map pp.60–61. Long-time contender for the title of Athens' best restaurant, *Spondi* has two Michelin stars to show for the efforts of French chef Arnaud Bignon, and serves superb French-influenced cuisine in a lovingly restored bourgeois mansion. With starters such as frogs legs in tandoori powder (€37) and mains such as pigeon with celery and hazelnut purée plus polenta flavoured with hay (€48), it's not cheap, but it's worth it for a special occasion. Tasting menus including wine are €73 and €156; booking essential. Daily 8pm–11.45pm.

Strofi Robérto Gálli 25, Makriyiánni ☎ 210 921 4130, ⓦ strofi.gr; map pp.66–67. A refurbished, upmarket taverna, whose chief attraction is a roof terrace with great, close-up Acropolis views. Dishes like pork in lemon sauce with rice (€13.50) or kid with tomato and thyme on noodles (€16.50) seem especially delicious from a rooftop table. Daily noon–1am.

PIREÁS

If you're looking for food to take on board a ferry, or breakfast, you'll find numerous places around the market area and near the Metro station, as well as all along the waterfront. There are plenty of bakeries and *souvláki* joints here, including a handy branch of *Everest* on the corner of Aktí Kalimassióti by the Metro. Otherwise, there's little good food in the port area, but some superb fish tavernas over at Mikrolímano.

CAFÉ

Aktoploiko Aktí Tsélegi 4; map p.94. Less manic than most places around the port, with tables outside on a pedestrianized part of the waterfront just off Platía Karaïskáki, this café serves breakfast and light meals – *souvláki*, salads, pasta – throughout the day (€10–15). Daily morning till late.

RESTAURANTS

Ammos Aktí Koumoundoúrou 44, Mikrolímano ☎ 210 422 1868 ⓦ ammosmikrolimano.gr; map p.94. In contrast to the high-luxe places around it, *Ammos* has more of an islandy feel, with hand-painted tables and beach scenes, plus lower prices and a younger crowd than its neighbours. It serves mainly fish (breaded haddock bites €7.60; stuffed squid €13.40; grilled octopus €11), and a wide variety of meze such as feta with honey (€6.50) and fried peppers (€4.80). Reservations recommended at weekends. Daily lunch and dinner.

★**Varoulko** Akti Koumoundourou 52, Pireas ☎ 210 522 8400, ⓦ varoulko.gr; map p.94. Run by Chef Lefteris Lazarou, who has earned a Michelin star every year since 2002, this seafood restaurant in Piraeus' Mikrolimano Marina isn't over-elaborate or pretentious. However, you can expect to pay about €70 per head for a meal, with starters like squid with basil pesto on a potato nest and mains such as sea bream with cauliflower mousse. Daily 1pm–1am.

NIGHTLIFE

In the city centre, the most vibrant nightlife is in **Psyrrí** and adjoining **Platía Ayías Irínis**, **Gázi** and **Thissío** but there are **bars** and **clubs** almost everywhere, mostly kicking off around 10pm or later. Bars listed here mostly focus on music or morph into clubs after midnight, and there are also plenty of cafés that function as bars at night. Some central Athens air-conditioned clubs remain open year-round, but in **summer** the scene really moves out to the long stretch of coast from Fáliro to Várkiza, where huge temporary clubs operate on and around the beaches. If you head out, bear in mind you'll have to pay the taxi fare plus admission fee, which usually includes a free drink.

BARS

Arodou Miaoúli 22, at Protoyénous ☎ 210 321 6774; map pp.66–67. Miaoúli, leading up from the Metro into Psyrrí, is packed with bars and crowded with people every evening. *Arodou* is right at the heart – a hugely popular place with plenty of space both outside and in. Drink prices are very reasonable, and excellent, well-priced meze (€2.50–6; shared plates from €9) are also available. Daily till late.

★**45°** Iákhou 18, Gázi ☎ 210 347 7729; map pp.60–61. A big, lively, rock-music-based bar/club that's loud and fun, and one of the longest-established places in Gázi. Opens relatively early, and there's a rooftop terrace with Acropolis views. Tues–Sun 9pm till late.

Bios Pireós 84, Gázi ☎ 210 342 5335, ⓦ bios.gr; map pp.60–61. Boho art space/café/bar/club with frequent performance art, live music and experimental theatre. There's something going on here most evenings, and a basement dance space with late-night avant-garde sounds. Daily morning till late.

Brettos Kydhathinéon 41 ⓦ brettosplaka.com; map pp.66–67. *Brettos* was originally a store selling the products of their own family distillery, a simple, unpretentious place with barrels along one wall and a huge range of bottles, backlit at night, along another.

They still sell bottles (from €3.50), but now the main business is as a bar, open all day for ouzo and meze and with a great selection of Greek wines by the glass. Daily 10am–2am.

James Joyce Ástigos 12 ☎ 210 323 5055, ⓦ jjoyceirishpubathens.com; map pp.66–67. Every city has its Irish pub – and this central Athens version is a friendly place with great atmosphere, well-kept Guinness (as well as any other drink you might care to name), Sky Sports and regular live acoustic music. There's also good pub-style food including steaks (€18), burgers (€9.50), and chicken wings (€8). Mon–Thurs & Sun 10am–1am, Fri & Sat till 3am.

Clumsies Praxitelous 30, Psyrri ☎ 210 323 2682, ⓦ theclumsies.gr; map pp.66–67. All-day cocktail bar in an old Venetian-style house, which serves breakfast (French toast for €6.50), and mains such as steak sandwich (€9). The cocktails are pricey (€10–44), but the atmosphere is worth it – you can even hire the private Room with your own barman. Themed nights often held. Daily 10am–2am; event hours vary.

Micra Asia Konstantinoupóleos 70, Gázi ☎ 210 346 9139; map pp.60–61. Old house converted to a bar with several floors, including roof space. There's an Ottoman

1

theme, with a downstairs meze bar (€10–15) and chilled music to match. Occasional exhibitions, and DJs at weekends playing electro, hip-hop, R&B and house. Daily 10pm till late.

six d.o.g.s Avramiótou 6, Monastiráki ☎ 210 321 0150, Ⓦ sixdogs.gr; map pp.66–67. This place is almost impossible to define, with performance and art spaces plus a garden and bar serving great cocktails (€5–12). It aims to host at least one event a day, which might be anything from a DJ set or live band to performance art. Always worth a look. Daily 10am–late.

★T.A.F. Normanou 5, Monastiráki ☎ 210 323 8757, Ⓦ theartfoundation.metamatic.gr; map pp.66–67. Blink and you'll miss this hidden bar in a former prison in the heart of the Flea Market. Just look for the wooden door and don't be afraid to go in – you'll come across a courtyard with various art exhibitions housed in the buildings surrounding it. It's an oasis from the bustling centre, and serves great cocktails too (€7–15). Daily 10am–3am.

Tailor Made Platía Ayías Irínis 2, Monastiráki ☎ 213 004 9645; map pp.66–67. Great coffee, but it's really about the nightlife here, with inventive cocktails and resident DJs Thurs–Mon nights. Mon–Thurs 8am–2am, Fri & Sat 8am–4am, Sun 9am–2am.

CLUBS
DOWNTOWN
Space by Avli Iraklidhón 14, Thissío ☎ 210 347 0900; map pp.66–67. In the heart of the Thissío bar area, this daytime café/bar on three floors evolves at night into a funky club with jazz and soul music. Daily lunchtime till late.

Venti Lepeniótou 20, Psyrrí ☎ 210 325 4504; map pp.66–67. Elegant, upmarket bar/club/restaurant around a courtyard with opening glass roof. Dance music gets going after midnight. Daily 9pm–3am.

SUMMER BEACH CLUBS
The House Project Balux Café Possidhónos 58 ☎ 210 898 3577, Ⓦ baluxcafe.com; tram Kolymvitirio. *Balux* is a large beach house with various spaces to eat, relax in the quiet library or outside on the sun loungers (€7) by the sea. Check the website for its summer club events. No entrance fee. Summer daily 9am–3am.

Bolivar Aktí tou Ilíou, off Possidhónos ☎ 6980 392 325, Ⓦ bolivar.gr; tram Kalamáki. All-day beach bar, on an organized beach with good facilities; club nights starting from around 10pm on Fri and Sat, sometimes during the week too; entry varies from free to around €15. Summer daily morning till late.

GAY AND LESBIAN VENUES

Athens' **gay scene** is mostly very discreet, but the city has its share of bars and clubs; most, these days, are in Gázi. Athens Pride takes place in the first week of June (Ⓦ athenspride.eu).

Koukles Club Zan Moreas 32, Siggrou ☎ 210 694 755 7443; map pp.60–61. Drag and cabaret club with nightly shows of vibrant performances and comedy. Mon–Fri midnight–4am Sat & Sun midnight–5am.

Noiz Konstantinoupóleos 78, Gázi ☎ 210 346 7850; map pp.60–61. Lesbian bar/club with good international sounds and a welcoming atmosphere. Daily 10pm–4am.

Rooster Platía Ayías Irínis 4, Monastiráki ☎ 210 346 0677, Ⓦ roostercafe.gr; map pp.66–67. All-day gay café/bar serving breakfasts (€5.50–7.50), coffee (€3.50),

a huge variety of teas (€3.50), smoothies (€4.50–5.50) and light meals, including pizza (€8), at the heart of Athens' buzziest square. Daily 9am–3am.

Sodade 2 Triptolémou 10, Gázi ☎ 210 346 8657, Ⓦ facebook.com/Sodade2; map pp.60–61. Both lesbian- and gay-friendly, *Sodade* attracts a stylish crowd and plays great music – one room for Greek and mainstream, the other progressive, house and R&B. There are many more gay bars and clubs in the immediate surrounds. Mon–Fri & Sun 11pm–4am, Fri & Sat till 6am.

WHAT'S ON WHEN
Sources of information on **what's on** in English are limited. There are some listings in a number of free monthly or weekly publications distributed to hotels, but these are partial and not always accurate; slightly better are the weekly *Athens Views* (published Fri), with movie listings and coverage of major events, or the daily local edition of the *International New York Times*. Listings including music, clubs, restaurants and bars can be found in local weekly *Athinorama*, but in Greek only. Look out, too, for **free weeklies** like *Lifo* and *Athens Voice* (again, Greek only), which can be picked up in galleries, record shops and the like. **Specialist record shops** (see p.115) are also good sources of information in themselves – they frequently display posters and sell tickets for rock, jazz or festival concerts.

ENTERTAINMENT

Live traditional **Greek music** is one of the capital's big attractions, but you have to visit during winter to see the best acts; in summer many musicians head off to tour the islands. From October to May is also when the major **classical music**, **ballet** and **drama** performances are staged, and the **sporting** calendar is at its busiest. On the other hand, summer is the **festival** season. Most significant is the **Athens & Epidaurus Festival** (June–Sept) of dance, music and ancient drama, but there are also annual rock, jazz and blues events.

LIVE GREEK MUSIC

Boemissa Solomoú 13–15, Exárhia ☎210 383 8803, ⓦboemissa.gr; map pp.60–61. Rembétika and laïká (see p.800) place popular with university students, who jam the dancefloor and aisles, and inevitably end up writhing on the tabletops as well. A good company of musicians play music from all regions of Greece. Entry, unlimited wine and some meaty mezédhes all for €16. Reservations recommended. Tues–Sun 11pm–4am.

Hilies Ke Dhyo Nykhtes (1002 Nights) Karaïskáki 10, Psyrrí ☎210 331 7293, ⓦ1002nyxtes.gr; map pp.66–67. Live music venue that's also a bar and restaurant with a Middle Eastern theme. Expect Arabic-inspired dishes such as Iskender kebab (€9) or kebab with aubergine (€10), plus traditional Greek music which explores its eastern roots – legendary Irish lyra player Ross Daly is a regular. Entry free, up to €10 for events. Most nights 10.30pm till late.

Perivoli T'Ouranou Lysikrátous 19, Pláka ☎210 323 5517, ⓦperivoli-touranou.gr; map pp.66–67. Traditional rembétika club on the edge of Pláka (so they are used to tourists) with regular appearances by classy performer Babis Tsertsos. Entry varies, but even when free they make up for it on the food and drink – €10 a beer, €25–30 for main courses. Oct–June Fri & Sat 9.30pm till late.

Stoa Athanaton Sofokléous 19, in the meat market ☎210 321 4362; map pp.66–67. Music here is fronted by *bouzoúki* (see p.800) veterans Hondronakos and company. There's good taverna food at reasonable prices, but expensive drinks; the taverna is open year-round, and for lunch, but music is only in the winter plus some summer weekends, starting close to midnight and continuing into the early hours. Mon–Sat 3–7.30pm & 9pm–4am.

LIVE ROCK

The indigenous Greek rock scene is small but still manages to support a number of local bands, while Athenian rock enthusiasts tend to be knowledgeable to the point of obsession. For rock bars, clubs and record shops, Exárhia is the place to be. Major inter-national bands generally appear in the summer to play open-air venues.

After Dark Dhidhótou 31 & Ippokrátous, Exárhia ☎210 360 6460; map pp.60–61. Rock, blues and soul, plus the occasional live performance by Greek indie bands to a young crowd. Entry typically €5. Tues–Thurs doors 10.30pm, Fri & Sat midnight.

The Drugstore Arachovis 10 & Ippokratous 69, Exárhia ☎210 6979 709 743, ⓦdrugstoreathens. com; ⓜ Panepistimio; map pp.60–61. Not strickly speaking a rock club, but it does host live rock bands (see website for upcoming events) and guests can bring their own music to play. The walls are adorned with vintage "drugstore" finds (hence the name). There's no entry fee –expect to pay €16 for a 1 litre jug of cocktail, or "package drinks" ie: 8 drinks (spirits, wines and beers) for €19.50, which is cheaper than buying lots of individual drinks. Hours vary.

An Live Club Solomoú 13–15, Exárhia ☎210 330 5056, ⓦanclub.gr; map pp.60–61. Basement club featuring live performances by local and lesser-known foreign rock bands. Entry typically €6–12. Doors 9pm.

Gagarin 205 Liossíon 205, Attikís ☎210 854 7601, ⓦgagarin205.gr; ⓜ Attikís; map pp.60–61. Some way north, but probably the finest venue for live rock in Athens, where around two thousand fans can crowd in to see the best touring indie bands as well as local talent and club nights. Entry around €20. Hours vary.

Kookoo Live Music Bar Iákhou 17, Gázi ☎210 345 0930, ⓦkookoo.gr; map pp.60–61. Fun live music venue featuring young Greek alternative and rock musicians in an enjoyably sweaty space. Entry typically €12 including a drink. Hours vary.

Stavros tou Notou Tharípou 37, Néos Kósmos ☎210 922 6975, ⓦstn.gr; ⓜ Syngroú-Fix; map pp.60–61. One of the liveliest rock clubs in town, this place mostly features Greek artists, but also plenty of touring foreigners. Entry typically €15, including first drink. Hours vary.

LIVE JAZZ AND LATIN

Jazz has only a small following in Greece, but there are still some good clubs that can attract touring bands of inter-national repute. The major events take place as part of the Jazz and Blues Festival at the end of June; information and tickets are available from the Athens Festival box office (see p.112) and some record stores.

Half-Note Trivonianoú 17, Mets ☎210 921 3310, ⓦhalfnote.gr; map pp.60–61. Athens' premier jazz club, with live jazz most nights and frequent big-name touring performers. Entry €25–30 (Mon €20), drinks €10. Oct–June doors most weeknights 9.30pm, Fri & Sat 10.30pm.

In Vivo Hariláou Trikoúpi 79, Neápoli ☎210 382 2103,

1

THE ATHENS AND EPIDAURUS FESTIVAL

The annual **Athens and Epidaurus Festival** encompasses a broad spectrum of cultural events: most famously, ancient Greek theatre (performed in modern Greek at the Herodes Atticus Theatre on the South Slope of the Acropolis), but also modern theatre, traditional and contemporary dance, classical music, jazz, traditional Greek music and even a smattering of rock.

The **Herodes Atticus Theatre** (see p.71) is a memorable place to watch a performance on a warm summer's evening – avoid the cheapest seats, though, unless you bring a pair of binoculars and a cushion. Other festival venues include the open-air **Lykavitós Theatre** on Lykavitós Hill, and the two ancient theatres at **Epidaurus** (see p.144). For the latter, you can buy inclusive trips from Athens from the festival box office, either by coach or boat – the two-hour boat trip includes dinner on board on the way home.

Performances run from late May right to early October, although the exact dates vary each year. If you can, book in advance (on ☎ 210 327 2000 or ⊛ greekfestival.gr); **tickets** go on sale online and at the box office three weeks before the event. Programmes are available online and from tourist offices or from the **festival box office** in the arcade at Panepistimíou 39 (Mon–Fri 8.30am–4pm, Sat 9am–2.30pm). There are also box offices at the Herodes Atticus Theatre (daily 9am–2pm & 6–9pm) and Epidaurus (Mon–Thurs 9am–7pm, Fri & Sat 9am–9pm) for events at those venues only.

⊛ invivoclub.gr; map pp.60–61. Classy blues, jazz and rock acts at an intimate, friendly venue. Entry €6–15. Oct–June Fri & Sat doors 8pm, acts 11pm.

DANCE AND CLASSICAL MUSIC

Classical music and opera are primarily winter pursuits, though you will find a pared-down schedule at the main venues in summer and at the Athens & Epidaurus Festival (see below).

Dora Stratou Ethnic Dance Company Filopáppou Hill ☎ 210 324 4395, ⊛ grdance.org; ⊕ Petrálona or Akrópoli; map pp.60–61. The Dora Stratou company's show in their own open-air theatre combines traditional music, authentic Greek dancing and original handmade costumes for an experience you'd be hard put to encounter in many years' travelling around Greece. Tickets (€15) can almost always be picked up at the door: dance classes are also available from €40. Performances late May to late Sept Wed–Fri 9.30pm, Sat & Sun 8.15pm.

Greek National Opera, Stavros Niarchos Foundation Cultural Centre, Leoforos Andhrea Syngrou 364 ☎ 213 088 5700, ⊛ nationalopera.gr; map pp.60–61. Opera features here primarily, but there are also ballet and classical concerts. Oct–July.

Mégaro Mousikís Leofóros Vassilísis Sofías, at Kókkali ☎ 210 728 2333, ⊛ www.megaron.gr; ⊕ Mégaro Mousikís; map pp.60–61. Athens' premier concert hall hosts a variety of events year-round, though the most prestigious classical performances are during the winter. Performance times vary.

FILM

Athens is a great place to catch a movie. In summer, dozens of outdoor screens spring up in every neighbourhood; they make for a quintessentially Greek film-going experience. Outdoor screens tend to concentrate on art-house and alternative offerings, classics and themed festival seasons. There are also plenty of regular indoor cinemas including a number in the centre, though many of these, with no air conditioning, close from mid-May to October. Films are almost always shown in the original language, with Greek subtitles, though you may never hear the soundtrack above the din of locals cracking *passatémpo* (pumpkin seeds), drinking and chatting (sit near a speaker if you want to hear). Snack-bars serve sandwiches, popcorn, pizza, beer and wine.

Cine Paris Kydhathinéon 22, Pláka ☎ 210 322 2071, ⊛ cineparis.gr. Outdoor screen in a rooftop setting with side view of the Acropolis, right in the heart of town, with first-run mainstream movies and the odd classic.

Thission Apostólou Pávlou 7, Thissío ☎ 210 342 0864 ⊛ cine-thisio.gr. Old-fashioned outdoor summer theatre, with an Acropolis view; shows mainly arty new releases.

Village Entertainment Park Thívon 228, halfway between the centre and Pireás ☎ 210 427 8600, ⊛ www.villagecinemas.gr; bus #B18 from Omónia. This twenty-screen multiplex in a huge shopping centre is Athens' largest; the same group has smaller multiscreens in Pángrati, Fáliro and Maroúsi.

Zefyros Tróön 36, Áno Petrálona ☎ 210 346 2677. Smarter than most, trendy Zefyros shows art-house and foreign-language movies as well as mainstream classics. A particular favourite of Athenian thirtysomethings.

SHOPPING

Shopping in Athens is decidedly schizophrenic. On the one hand, the **bazaar area** is an extraordinary jumble of little specialist shops and stalls, and almost every neighbourhood still hosts a weekly **street market**. On the other hand, the

1

upmarket shopping areas of the city centre, and the **malls** and fashion emporia of the ritzier suburbs, are as glossy and expensive as any in Europe. Somewhere between the extremes, in the city centre you'll find endless *stoas*, covered arcades off the main streets full of little shops. Some have been expensively refurbished and house cafés and designer-label stores; most, though, are a little dilapidated, and many still specialize in a single product – books here, computer equipment there, spectacles in another.

HANDICRAFTS, ANTIQUES AND GIFTS

Greek handicrafts are not particularly cheap, but the standard of workmanship is usually very high. In addition to the stores listed below, several museums have excellent shops, including the National Archeological Museum (see p.85), Benáki Museum (see p.91) and Cycladic Art Museum (see p.91).

Amorgos Kódhrou 3, Pláka ☎210 324 3836, Ⓦamorgosart.gr; map pp.66–67. A small, old-fashioned shop filled with an eclectic collection of tasteful wood-carvings, needlework, lamps, lace, shadow puppets and other handicrafts. Mon–Fri 11am–8.30pm, Sat till 3.30pm.

Elliniko Spiti Kekropós 14, just off Adhrianoú, Pláka ☎210 323 5924; map pp.66–67. Amazing artworks and pieces of furniture created from found materials, especially driftwood but also metal and marble. Probably too big to take home (for your wallet as well as your suitcase), but well worth a look. Mon–Fri 10am–2pm & 4–8pm.

Kendro Ellinikis Paradosis entrances at Mitropóleos 59 and Pandhróssou 36, Monastiráki. As the name, "Centre of Hellenic Tradition", suggests, this upstairs emporium has a wide selection of traditional arts and crafts, especially ceramics and woodcarving, all at reasonable prices and with little hard sell from the assistants. Even better is a selection of old Greek film posters, postcards and the like. Daily 10am–5pm.

Theotokis Normánou 7, Monastiráki ☎210 331 1638; map pp.66–67. One of a number of quirky antique/junk shops in this narrow street in the flea market. Prints, posters, postcards, old radios, typewriters, military uniforms: if you're looking for something specific, you might be in luck – it's amazing what they can find among their stock. Mon–Sat 10am–6pm.

To Komboloi tou Psyrri Ayíon Anaryíron 13, Psyrrí ☎210 324 3012; map pp.66–67. A lovely little shop selling worry beads (*komboloi*) in every conceivable shape and size, plus hand-made jewellery and crafts. Daily 10am–10pm.

FASHION AND JEWELLERY

You'll find familiar international clothes brands in the main shopping area of Ermoú below Sýndagma, and in the many malls in the suburbs. For high fashion, head to Kolonáki, where there are dozens of small boutiques in the narrow streets around the Platía. For something more alternative, wander over into adjoining Exárhia.

Athena's Sandals Normánou 7, Monastiráki ☎210 331 1925, Ⓦmelissinos-sandals.gr; map pp.66–67.

Stavros Melissinos, the "poet sandal-maker", was an Athens institution – The Beatles, Anthony Quinn and Sophia Loren were among his celebrity clients. Now retired, his daughter carries on his tradition, with interesting leather-work of all kinds (belts, bags, slippers) alongside the sandals, while his son has a rival store nearby, at Aghías Théklas 2. Mon, Wed, Sat & Sun 10am–6pm, Tues, Thurs & Fri till 8pm.

Attica Panepistimíou 9, Sýndagma ☎211 180 2600, Ⓦatticadps.gr; map pp.66–67. Athens' prime fashion department store, with the finest window displays in the city and a huge branch of upmarket café *Zonar's* on the ground floor. Convenient if you want to do everything under one roof, especially in the summer when it's hot, though the designer labels include little you wouldn't find at home. Mon–Fri 10am–9pm, Sat 10am–7pm.

Crop Circle Themistokléous 52 & 66, Exárhia ☎210 381 4509, Ⓦcropcircle.gr; map pp.60–61. Reasonably priced boutique selling both men's and women's clothing, along with jewellery and accessories. It's at the heart of "alternative" Exárhia and very much in that style – unconventional T-shirts and ethnic-print skirts and dresses. Mon–Fri 10am–6pm.

Kilo Shop Ermoú 120, Psyrrí ☎210 323 7203, Ⓦkilo-shop.gr; map pp.66–67. Standing out among the fashionable postmodern stores at the Psyrrí end of Ermoú, Kilo Shop sells clothing, vintage and new, for men and women, by weight. Simply choose what you want from the huge stock, and weigh it to determine the price. Mon–Sat 10am–8.30pm, Sun till 8pm.

Like Yesterday's Protoyénous 16, Psyrrí ☎216 70 04 810, Ⓦfacebook.com/likeyesterdays2ndhand; map pp.66–67. Classy little vintage clothing store in an up-and-coming Psyrrí alley. Mon, Wed & Sun 11am–4pm, Tues, Thurs & Fri till 8pm, Sat till 6pm.

Psit Veïkóu 9, Makriyiánni ☎210 923 5093, Ⓦpsitjewellery.com; map pp.60–61. Quirky and inexpensive jewellery is on sale here, as well as cards and ceramics, hand-made by designer Katerina Stamati; several other small, creative shops are nearby. Tues, Thurs & Fri 11am–2pm & 5–8pm, Wed & Sat 11am–3pm.

Yannis Sergakis Valaoritou 5, Kolonáki ☎210 363 0041, Ⓦyannissergakis.com; map pp.66–67. Set in the heart of well-heeled Kolonáki, this shop is the place to treat

1

BAZAARS AND MARKETS

Even on a purely visual level, the **central bazaar** and nearby flower market are well worth a visit, while the surrounding streets, especially Evripídhou, are full of wonderfully aromatic little shops selling herbs and nuts, and others concentrating on supplies for a peasant way of life that seems entirely at odds with modern Athens – rope, corks, bottles and preserving jars. On Sunday mornings from around 6am until 2pm, between Monastiráki and Thissío Metro stations, you will find a **flea market** of authentic Greek junk (used phone cards and the like) spread out on the pavements, especially along the Metro Lines towards the Thissío end of Adhrianoú.

Usually running from 7am to 2pm, **street markets** are inexpensive and enjoyable; they sell household items and dry goods, as well as fresh fruit and vegetables, dried herbs and nuts. Some of the best and most central ones are listed below:

Mondays Hánsen in Patissíon (Ⓜ Áyios Eleftheríos).
Tuesdays Lésvou in Kypséli (Ⓜ Viktorías); Láskou in Pangráti (trolley #2 or #11).
Fridays Xenokrátous in Kolonáki; Dhragoúmi in Ilísia (Ⓜ Evangelismós/Mégaro Mousikís); Tsámi Karatássou in Koukáki (Ⓜ Akrópoli); and Arhimídhous in Mets, behind the Panathenaic Stadium.
Saturdays Plakendías in Ambelókipi (Ⓜ Ambelókipi); Kallidhromíou in Exárhia.

yourself to jewellery made by award-winning designer Yannis Sergaki. Tues, Thurs & Fri 9.30am–8.30pm, Mon & Wed 9.30am–4pm & Sat 10.30am–5pm.

Zooms Praxítelous 7, Sýndagma; map pp.66–67. Fashionable women's and children's clothing in the midst of a traditional area of haberdashery and electrical stores. Mon–Fri 9am–5pm, Sat 10am–4pm.

FOOD AND DRINK

Aristokratikon Voúlis 7, Sýndagma ☎ 210 322 0546, ⓦ aristokratikon.com; map pp.66–67. An old Athenian favourite selling upmarket traditional Greek chocolates (try the chocolate-covered prunes) as well as much-coveted pistachios, sugared almonds and sour cherry jam. A token from here is always welcome when visiting someone's home. Mon–Fri 8am–-9pm, Sat till 4pm.

Ariston Voúlis 10, Sýndagma ☎ 210 322 7626; map pp.66–67. An old-fashioned bakery famous above all for its savoury pies, though they also serve excellent-value sweet ones too, as well as biscuits, cakes and fruit jelly sweets. Mon, Wed & Sat 7am–6pm, Tues, Thurs & Fri 7.30am–9pm.

The Bioshop Veuku Ave 30, Galatsi ☎ 210 222 0519, ⓦ bioshop.gr; map pp.60–61. Opened in 1993, this is one of Greece's first natural stores selling organic food, women's cosmetics, household cleaning products and aromatherapy oils. Mon–Fri 9am–2.30pm and 5pm–9pm, Sat 9am–3pm.

Elixirion Evripídhou 41, central bazaar ☎ 210 321 5141, ⓦ elixir.com.gr; map pp.66–67. Old-fashioned store with magnificent original fittings. Herbs, dried fruit and garlic hang from the ceiling, and you can buy teas, spices, grinders, dried fruits and honey. Mon–Wed & Sat 7.30am–5pm, Thurs & Fri till 3.30pm.

Oino Typo Hariláou Trikoúpi 98, Neápoli ☎ 210 361 6274; map pp.60–61. Excellent wine merchant with over fifty varieties of Greece's famous barrelled wines (you can fill your own container), as well as 1200 international bottled types. Mon–Sat 10am–10pm.

To Thymari tou Strefi Kallidhromíou 51A, Neápoli ☎ 210 330 0384; map pp.60–61. A lovely retro *pantopolío* (corner store, literally a store that sells everything) selling traditional Greek preserves, honey, nuts, dried fruit, cheese, olives and olive oil among much else. Great for edible souvenirs and gifts. Mon & Wed 9am–4pm, Tues, Thurs & Fri 9am–2pm & 5–8pm, Sat 10am–6pm.

Tzatzos Veïkou 45, Koukáki ☎ 210 923 1456; map pp.60–61. Koukáki boasts some of the finest *zaharoplastía* (cake shops) in Athens, and Tzatsos is one of the best of them: try the traditional *kadaifi* and *baklava*. Mon–Sat 7am–2pm & 5–10pm.

BOOKS AND MAPS

Anavasi Maps Voúlis 32, Sýndagma ☎ 210 321 8104, ⓦ anavasi.gr; map pp.66–67. Here, at the store of the Greek map publisher, they sell mainly their own excellent regional maps of Greece, but also a few others to fill the gaps. Mon & Wed 9.30am–5.30pm, Tues, Thurs & Fri 9.30am–8.30pm, Sat 10am–4.30pm.

Compendium Alikarnassoú 8, Metaxouryío ☎ 210 383 2139, ⓦ compendium.gr; map pp.60–61. Long-established English-language bookshop, where there's a small secondhand section and noticeboards for travellers and residents, as well as regular poetry readings and other events. Mon–Sat 9am–3pm.

Public Karagiorgi Servias 1, Syntagma ☎ 210 818 1333, ⓦ public.gr; map pp.66–67. Spread over five or six levels, this bookshop is one of a popular chain of selling international books of all varieties (fiction, non-fiction), as well as electronics such as laptops and stationary. The rooftop café on the top floor offers phenomenal views of the Constitution Square and the countryside beyond. Mon–Fri 9am–9pm, Sat 9am–8pm.

Rachel's Bookshop Ploutarchou 22, Kolonaki ☎ 210 721 1442; map pp.60–61. This cute bookshop near the British Embassy is a great choice for lovers of Greek history, archeology and mythology: it also sells a wide selection of Greek recipe books. Books in Greek and English, plus other languages if you're lucky. Mon–Fri 9am–9pm.

Solaris Botási 6, Exárhia ☎ 210 384 1065, ⊛ solaris.gr; map pp.60–61. The place to come for comics old and new, as well as graphic novels, models of characters and other paraphernalia. Mon, Wed & Sat 9am–3.30pm, Tues, Thurs & Fri 9am–2.30pm & 5–8.30pm.

MUSIC

You'll find mainstream music stores in any of the main shopping areas; below are listings for places to explore

Greek sounds, as well as classic vinyl. There are dozens of specialist music stores, especially in Exárhia.

7+7 Iféstou 22, Monastiráki ☎ 210 321 4032, ⊛ 7plus7. gr; map pp.66–67. A choice selection of old and new rock, heavy metal, punk, Greek music and more on vinyl and CD. Nearby, in the flea market, are several other record and secondhand bookshops. Mon–Sat 10am–6pm.

Music Machine Records Dhidhótou 16, Exárhia ☎ 210 361 2376; map pp.60–61. This shop hosts a fine collection of classic vinyl and posters, along with high-end hi-fis, new and secondhand. A cool place with good music. Mon & Wed 10am–4pm, Tues, Thurs & Fri 10am–2pm & 5–8pm, Sat 10am–6pm.

Xylouris Panepistimíou 39 in Stoa Pesmazoglóu, Omónia ☎ 210 322 2711, ⊛ xilouris.gr; map pp.66–67. Run by the widow of the late, great Cretan singer Nikos Xylouris, this old-fashioned store is one of the best places for finding Greek pop, folk and Cretan music. There are several other excellent music stores in the same arcade. Mon & Wed 9am–3pm, Tues, Thurs & Fri 9am–2pm & 5–8pm, Sat 10am–4pm.

DIRECTORY

Banks and currency exchange Normal banking hours are Mon–Thurs 8am–2.30pm and Fri till 2pm, and just about all banks can exchange money during those hours; several banks with longer hours can be found around Sýndagma, plus there are numerous currency exchange places (generally with worse rates) in Pláka and around Sýndagma, and hotels will change money at a worse rate still. Almost every bank in the centre has an ATM.

Bike, scooter and motorbike rental For mountain bikes, try Athens by Bike (Tziréon 16, at Dhionysíou Areopayítou; ☎ 2130 423 922, ⊛ athensbybike.gr). For motorized wheels, Motorent (Kavalóti 4, at Robérto Gálli; ☎ 210 923 4939, ⊛ motorent.blogspot.co.uk). Both are in Makriyiánni, near Metro Akrópoli.

Car rental The vast majority of downtown car rental offices are on Leofóros Syngroú, mostly in the first section close to the Temple of Olympian Zeus. They include Avance at no. 40–42 (☎ 210 920 0100, ⊛ avance.gr); Europcar, no. 25 (☎ 210 921 1444, ⊛ europcar.com); Hertz, no. 12 (☎ 210 922 0102, ⊛ hertz.gr/en/athens) and Kosmos, no. 9 (☎ 210 923 4695, ⊛ kosmos-carrental.com). The local companies are generally cheaper; if you turn up in person and compare prices, you can often haggle a better rate.

Doctors and hospitals The largest central hospital is Evangelismós at Ipsilándhou 45, Kolonáki (☎ 210 720 1000; ⓜ Evangelismós). Check ⊛ www.athensinfoguide. com/genhospitals.htm for a list of hospital addresses and practitioners. Most doctors speak at least some English, and medical care is generally very good, though nursing and aftercare tend to rely on the help of family. SOS doctors (☎ 1016) offer an emergency call-out service from €75.

Embassies and consulates Most major embassies are in Kolonáki or Ambelókipi, on or not far from Leofóros Vassilísis Sofías. They include: Australia (Level 6, Thon Building, cnr Kifissiás & Alexandhrás, Ambelókipi; ☎ 210 870 4000, ⊛ greece.embassy.gov.au; ⓜ Ambelókipi); Canada (Ioánnou Yennadhíou 4; ☎ 210 727 3400, ⊛ athens.gc.ca; ⓜ Evangelismós); Ireland (Vassiléos Konstantínou 7, in Pangráti near the Panathenaic Stadium; ☎ 210 723 2771, ⊛ embassyofireland.gr); New Zealand honorary consulate (Kifissiás 76, Maroúsi; ☎ 210 692 4136; ⓜ Panormóu); South Africa (Kifissiás 60, Maroúsi; ☎ 210 617 8020; ⓜ Panormóu); UK (Ploutárhou 1, Kolonáki; ☎ 210 727 2600, ⊛ ukingreece.fco.gov.uk; ⓜ Evangelismós); USA (Vassilísis Sofías 91; ☎ 210 720 2414, ⊛ athens.usembassy.gov; ⓜ Mégaro Mousikís).

Emergencies European emergency number ☎ 112; Ambulance ☎ 166; Fire ☎ 199; Police ☎ 100; Tourist police ☎ 171; SOS doctors ☎ 1016. For details of emergency hospitals and duty doctors and pharmacies call ☎ 1434.

Internet cafés There's free municipal wi-fi in many parts of Athens, including Sýndagma square and the port at Pireás, as well as in many hotels and cafés. Among the more central and reliable internet cafés are: Bits & Bytes (Kapnikaréas 19, off Adhrianoú, Pláka; 24hr; ☎ 210 381 3234, ⊛ bnb.gr); Athens Internet (Veíkou 3a, Koukáki; 24hr; ☎ 210 923 5811, ⊛ athensinternet.gr); and Ivis Travel (Mitropóleos 5, Sýndagma; daily 8am–10pm; ☎ 210 324 3365, ⊛ ivis.gr).

Laundry Most hotels will do laundry, but charge a fortune for it. Laundromats that do service washes include National (Apóllonos 17, Pláka; Mon & Wed 8am–5pm, Tues, Thurs & Fri till 8pm; €4 per kilo, min. €8; also offers dry cleaning);

1

Athens Launderette (Veïkou 3a, Koukáki; 24hr; €7 per load); Y&Y (Víktoros Ougó 18, next to the International Youth Hostel; daily 8am–8pm; €6 load); and a nameless place at Makriyiánni 33, near the Acropolis Museum (Mon–Fri 8am–8pm, Sat till 5pm; €9 load).

Luggage storage Best arranged with your hotel; many places will keep the bulk of your luggage for free or for a nominal amount while you head off to the islands. Otherwise Athens Internet Café (Veïkou 3a, Koukáki; ☎210 923 5811; 24hr) charges €3 per day; Pacific Travel at the airport is handy short-term, but charges upwards of €9 per day.

Pharmacies There are a number of large general pharmacies (*farmakía*) around Omónia, especially on 28 Oktovríou (Patissíon) and Panepistimíou; many also sell homeopathic remedies. Standard hours are Mon & Wed 8am–2.30pm, Tues, Thurs & Fri 8am–2pm & 5.30–8.30pm. A list of places open out of hours is on display at many pharmacies, or call ☎1434.

Police Dial ☎100 for emergencies (☎112 from a mobile), or ☎171 for the Tourist Police; for thefts,

problems with hotel overcharging, etc, it's the latter you should contact.

Post offices (*Tahydhromía*) For ordinary letters and parcels up to 2kg, the branch on Sýndagma (cnr Mitropóleos) is open Mon–Fri 7.30am–8.30pm, Sat 7.30am–2.30pm, Sun 9am–1.30pm. There are machines selling stamps and phonecards. To send heavier parcels, use the post office at Mitropóleos 60, near the cathedral (Mon–Fri 7.30am–8pm), or at Koumoundhoúrou 29 by the National Theatre, Omónia. There are also major branches near Omónia at Eólou 100 (the central office for poste restante) and on Platía Kótzia. Queues can be enormous, so be sure you're at the right counter – there are often separate ones (with shorter queues) for stamps and parcels.

Turkish bath At the corner of Melidhóni and Áyion Asomáton in Thissío, Hammam (Mon–Fri 12.30–10pm, Sat & Sun 10am–10pm; ⓦhammam.gr) is a modern interpretation of the traditional Turkish hammam, combined with modern spa treatments.

Around Athens: Attica

Attica (Attikí), the region encompassing the capital, is not much explored by tourists – only the great romantic ruin of the **Temple of Poseidon** at **Cape Soúnio** and the beaches immediately outside Athens are at all well known. The rest, if seen at all, tends to be en route to somewhere else – the airport or the Peloponnese or to the ports of **Rafína** or **Lávrio**.

At first sight, the neglect is not surprising; the mountains of **Imittós**, **Pendéli** and **Párnitha**, which surround Athens on three sides, are progressively less successful in confining the urban sprawl, while the routes out of the city are unenticing to say the least. Yet a day-trip or two, or a brief circuit by car, can make a pleasant and rewarding break, with much of Greece to be seen in microcosm within an hour or two of the capital. There are rewarding archeological sites at **Eleusis** and **Ramnous** as well as Soúnio, and **beaches** almost everywhere you turn, though none remote enough to avoid the Athenian hordes. Combine a couple of these with a meal at one of the scores of seaside *psarotavérnas* (fish restaurants), always packed out on summer weekends, and you've got a more than worthwhile day out.

The Apollo Coast

Athens' coastline is often overlooked by visitors, who are here for their Classical fix and off to the islands for beaches. For Athenians, though, it's an essential summertime safety valve, and they head down here in droves: not just for beaches, but for cafés, restaurants, nightlife and shopping. In an area dubbed the "**Apollo Coast**", the southern suburbs form an almost unbroken line along the coast all the way from Pireás to Vouliagméni and Várkiza, some 20km away. Buses and the tram make it easy to head down to the beach for a quick swim and be back in the centre just a couple of hours later; astonishingly, the water almost everywhere is clean and crystal clear.

Beyond Várkiza, the coast road rapidly becomes much emptier and the countryside more barren. At **Saronídha**, the furthest outpost for city buses (#E22), roughly halfway from Várkiza to Soúnio, there's a large sandy beach with a gently shelving bottom, very

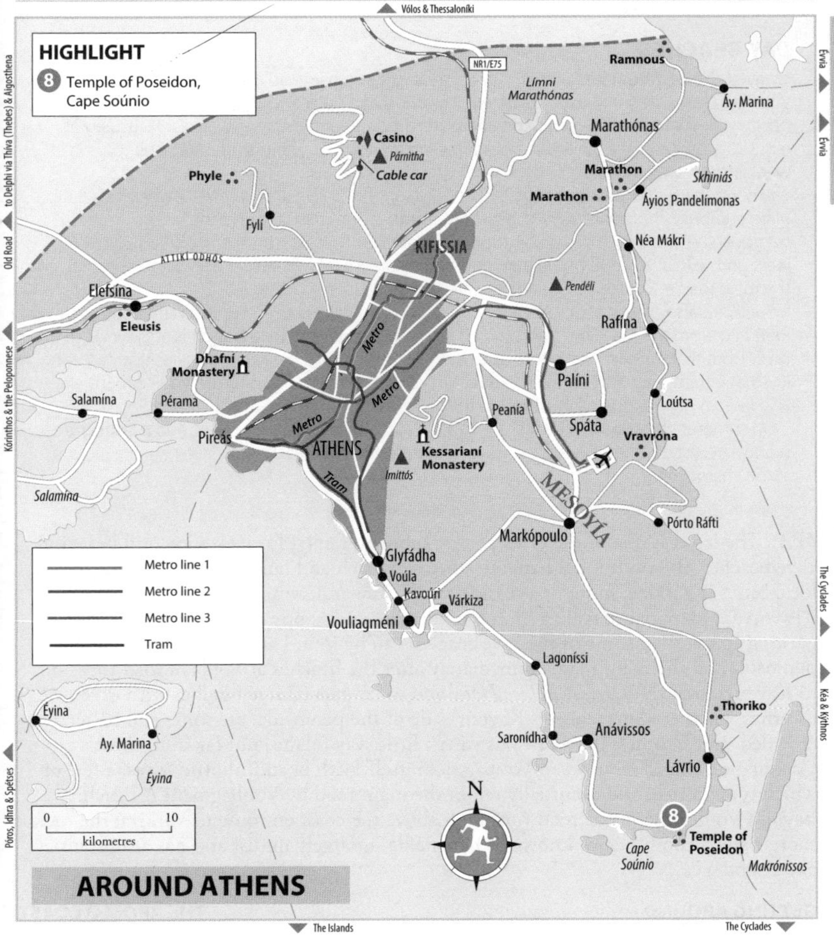

HIGHLIGHT

8 Temple of Poseidon, Cape Soúnio

Metro line 1
Metro line 2
Metro line 3
Tram

0 ___ 10
kilometres

AROUND ATHENS

N

popular with windsurfers. Neighbouring **Anávissos** has a row of *psarotavérnas* along its more sheltered southern beach. Further still, the coast starts to get rockier and the road more winding, as it looks out on small islands offshore, until finally you begin to catch glimpses of the Temple of Poseidon ahead.

Glyfádha

City buses #A2, #B2, #A3, #B3 and #E22 from the centre of Athens, and #A1, #G1 or #X96 from Pireás; the tram also heads here from Athens' centre or Pireás

The heart of the city's summer suburban playground – for shopping, clubbing, dining or posing on the beach – is **Glyfádha**, a bizarre mix of glitz and suburbia. At weekends, half of Athens seems to decamp down here. The epicentre is around the crescent of **Leofóros Angélou Metáxa**, lined with shops and malls, with the tram running down the centre and streets of cafés and restaurants heading off on either side.

Vouliagméni peninsula

Glyfádha merges almost indistinguishably into its neighbour **Voúla** (accessible by tram), and then into quieter, more upmarket **Kavoúri** and **Vouliagméni** (buses #A3 and

1

PAY BEACHES

Many of the best **beaches** within easy reach of Athens charge an **admission fee**, which gets you clean sand, lifeguards, somewhere to buy food and drink and other facilities including beach volleyball, massage, fun parks and watersports. Loungers are also available, usually at extra cost. Some of the fanciest, in Glyfádha and Vouliagméni, charge up to €12 per person at weekends; more basic places cost €4–7.

Among the better **pay beaches** are: Asteria (summer daily 8am–8pm; €10, weekends €30), a glam and busy choice right in the heart of Glyfádha, with many facilities including trampolining and beach volleyball; more basic are South Coast (summer daily 8am–7pm; €4, weekends €7), at the end of the tram line, and Vouliagméni A (summer daily 8am–8pm; €4), on the main road in Vouliagméni, with few facilities but a lovely setting.

There are also plenty of places to swim for free, though this may mean from the rocks, or a long hike from the road. The best sandy beach with sections of **free beach** is at Skhiniás (see p.121), but that's a long way out on the northeast Attic coast. The sands at Áyios Kósmas, at Ag. Kosmas 2 tram stop, and the twin beaches in Voúla, between Glyfádha and Vouliagméni, are also free; they have good sand, though the facilities are a little run-down.

On summer weekends, all beaches – and the roads to them – are packed, and **parking** is a nightmare, especially in Glyfádha and Vouliagméni; the pay beaches all have parking, though some charge extra.

#B3). The latter is one of the city's posher suburbs, famed for its lagoon and beautiful cove beaches, the traditional hangout of Athens' rich and famous. Last stop for the local buses is **Várkiza**, more of a seaside resort pure and simple.

If you are prepared to walk a bit, or are driving and happy to battle the locals for parking space, then some of the best beaches can be found around the **Vouliagméni peninsula**, off the main road. Immediately after the beaches at Voúla, a road turns off to Kavoúri, past the *Divani Palace Hotel* and some packed free beaches with excellent tavernas. Further along, on this Kavoúri side of the peninsula, are some still better, less crowded, free beaches: the #114 bus runs a little way inland, not far from these. Carrying on round, you get to Vouliagméni itself, with beautiful little coves, a few of which remain free, and eventually rejoin the main road by Vouliagméni A Beach. Beyond Vouliagméni, the road runs high above the coast en route to Várkiza; the rocky shore a steep climb below, known as **Limanákia**, is largely nudist and has a substantial gay attendance.

GETTING AROUND   THE APOLLO COAST

By bus Local bus services #114 (route Glyfádha–Kavoúri–Vouliagméni) and #115/6 (route Glyfádha–Vouliagméni–Várkiza) are useful.

EATING AND DRINKING

GLYFÁDHA

George's Steak House Konstantinoupoléos 4 ☎ 210 894 6020, ⓦ georgessteakhouse.gr. Despite the name, this is a fairly traditional Greek grill-house. It's large, reasonably priced and very popular; try the excellent lamb chops (€12) and meatballs (€7.20). You'll find it on a side street crowded with restaurants, close to the main Platía Katráki tram stop. Daily noon–midnight.

Molly Malone's Yiannitsopoúlou 8 ☎ 210 894 4247, ⓦ mollymalones.gr. Irish-run pub offering a warm welcome, cold Guinness and distinctively Irish–Greek craic. Good food too, ranging from tortilla nachos (€8) and chicken wings (€7.50) to steak and Guiness pie (€10.50). Daily noon–late.

Vincenzo Yiannitsopoúlou 1, Platía Espéridhon ☎ 210 894 1310, ⓦ vincenzoglyfada.gr. Good, reasonably priced Italian fare including excellent pizzas (€5–12) from a wood oven; live jazz Thurs evenings. Daily noon–1.30am.

VOULIAGMÉNI

Akti Possidhónos 6 ☎ 210 896 0448. On the main road just beyond the Vouliagméni peninsula, with waterfront tables and great views, this is a top-class fish taverna. Fish is expensive and so is Vouliagméni; by those standards, €50–60 a head is reasonable value. Waterfront tables are very heavily in demand; booking essential. Daily lunch and dinner.

★**Island** Limanakia Vouliagménis; km27 on Athens–Soúnio road between Vouliagméni and

Várkiza ☎210 965 3563, ⓦislandclubrestaurant.gr. Beautiful bar-restaurant/club with a breathtaking clifftop setting; very chic and not as expensive as you might expect, at €15–25 for a main course. They serve modern Mediterranean food and have a sushi lounge. Booking essential, especially at weekends. May–Oct Mon–Thurs & Sun 9pm–3am, Fri & Sat till 6am (club from 11pm).

Cape Soúnio

Aktí Souníou – **Cape Soúnio** – the southern tip of Attica, some 70km from the city centre, is one of the most imposing spots in Greece. For centuries it was a landmark for boats sailing between Pireás and the islands, and an equally dramatic vantage point from which to look out over the Aegean. On its tip stands the fifth-century BC **Temple of Poseidon**, built in the time of Pericles as part of a major sanctuary to the sea god.

Below the promontory are several **coves** – the most sheltered is a five-minute walk east from the car park and site entrance. The main Soúnio beach, a short distance to the north, is more crowded, but has a couple of tavernas at the far end.

ARRIVAL AND DEPARTURE CAPE SOÚNIO

By bus Orange KTEL Attikis buses leave Athens from the Mavrommatéon terminal (see p.97). For Soúnio via the coast, there are 8–9 departures daily (7.05am–7pm; roughly 2hr; €6.90); there's also a more central (but in summer, very busy) stop 10min later on Filellínon, south of Sýndagma (cnr of Xenofóndos). On the less attractive but marginally cheaper (€5.70) inland route via Lávrio, there are departures every two hours from 5.45am to 3.45pm. Returns are every two hours (7.10am–6.30pm), alternately via the coast or inland. There are also direct buses between Lávrio and the airport.

By car Drivers can take either route described above or complete a circuit, but there's little to see in the interior, where the road takes you via the airport and the toll motorway.

Temple of Poseidon
Daily 9am–sunset • €8

The **Temple of Poseidon** owes much of its fame to Lord Byron, who visited in 1810, carved his name on the nearest pillar (an unfortunate and much-copied precedent, which means the temple is now roped off) and immortalized the place in verse:

Place me on Sunium's marbled steep,
Where nothing, save the waves and I,
May hear our mutual murmurs sweep;
There, swan-like, let me sing and die:
A land of slaves shall ne'er be mine –
Dash down yon cup of Samian wine!

from Don Juan

In summer, at least, there is little hope of silent solitude, unless you visit first thing, before the tour groups arrive. But the setting is still wonderful – on a clear day, the **view** takes in the islands of Kéa, Kýthnos and Sérifos to the southeast, Égina and the Peloponnese to the west – and the temple is as evocative a ruin as any in Greece. Doric in style, it was probably built by the architect of the Hephaisteion in the Athens Agora. That it is so admired and visited is in part due to its position, but also perhaps to its picturesque state of ruin.

The rest of the site is subject to new **excavation**, which aims to highlight the fact that this was not just a temple, but also a powerful **fortress** protecting Athens from the sea; boats were kept in readiness here at all times to repel invaders. There are remains of a fortification wall around the sanctuary, as well as a propylaion (entrance hall), *stoa* and cuttings for two shipsheds. To the north are the foundations of a small **Temple of Athena**.

1

EATING AND DRINKING

Akroyiali Soúnio beach ☎ 22920 39107. Right down by the water, this beachside taverna has both character and history – a number of illustrious Greek guests have dined here. The food, mainly fish, is simple but cooked to perfection (as ever, the fish is priced by weight; around €45 per kilo for lobster, for example), but there are cheaper options such as delicious stuffed kalamári (€12). Daily 11am–11pm.

The east coast

Central Attica is by the airport and its associated motorways, and though there are still villages with Byzantine churches and countryside where wine is made, there's little incentive, when heading **east**, to stop before the **coast**. The shoreline is popular with weekending Athenians and the site of many second homes. Almost due east of Athens lies the port of **Rafína**, and to the north of here are **Marathon** and the isolated site of ancient **Ramnous**, as well as some relatively uncrowded beaches. South of Rafína, the coast is less attractive, with continuous development all the way down through **Loútsa** (aka Artemis) towards **Pórto Ráfti** (hourly buses from Athens 5.45am–7.45pm); it is also directly beneath the airport flight path.

ARRIVAL AND DEPARTURE

THE EAST COAST

By bus KTEL buses to the east coast leave from the Mavrommatéon terminal (see p.97). Main services include those to Rafína, Marathon, Ayía Marína (at least 5 daily; connects with ferries to Évvia), and Pórto Ráfti and Avláki (hourly, 5.45am–7.45pm).

By car The main route for drivers is straight out on Messoyíon (following airport signs) onto the eastbound Leofóros Marathónos, which heads straight for Rafína and Marathon.

Rafína

Buses from Athens daily every 30min (5.40am–10.30pm; 1hr 10 min; €2.60)

The port of **RAFÍNA** has fast **ferries** and **catamarans** to the Cyclades, as well as to nearby Évvia. Many Athenians have summer homes overlooking the attractive, rocky coast, but the beaches are tricky to reach even with a car. Ferries aside, the port's chief attraction is is a line of excellent harbourfront **seafood restaurants**, cafés and fishmongers, with a ringside view of the marine comings and goings. The pedestrianized square above the harbour is also a lively place, ringed with cafés and cheaper eating options.

Marathon

Sites and museum Tues–Sun 8am–3pm • Joint ticket €6 • Buses run daily from Athens to Marathónas (6am–10.30pm approx every 30min; €4.10), passing close by the major battle sites; the Tÿmfos Marathóna is about 1km east of the main road, 4km before Marathónas, and the Tomb of the Plateians is 1km west of the road, a little further on

The site of the **battle of Marathon**, the most famous and arguably most important military victory in Athenian history, lies not far from the unenticing village of **MARATHÓNAS**, 42km from Athens. In 490 BC, a force of 9000 Athenians and 1000 of their Plataian allies defeated a 25,000-strong Persian army at Marathon. After the victory, a runner was sent to Athens to declare the news: having run the first marathon, he delivered his message and dropped dead. Just 192 Athenians died in the battle (compared to some 6000 Persians), and the burial mound where they were laid, the **Tÿmfos Marathóna** can still be seen. It is a quietly impressive monument, though surrounded now by one-way roads installed for the Olympic marathon race.

The **Mound of the Plataians**, where the eleven Plataians (including a 10-year-old boy) who died in the battle of Marathon were laid to rest, is on the road to the village of Vranás; there's a small, modern **archeological museum** in the village, near the feet of the mountains.

THE BATTLE OF MARATHON

For the Athenians, victory in the **Battle of Marathon** set the seal on their democracy and marked the start of a new self-confident era. And indeed, it was the most remarkable of victories.

The Athenian army, with their allies the Plataeans, fearful of the Persians' superior numbers and of their cavalry and archers, held a defensive position astride the mountain pass leading into the plain of Marathon for five days, waiting for Spartan reinforcements. On the fifth day, the Persians gave up hope of joining battle at Marathon and embarked their cavalry to advance on Athens by sea, sending their infantry forwards to cover the operation. With the Persian forces divided, Athenian general **Miltiades** saw his opportunity, Spartan help or no, and sent his hoplites racing downhill to get quickly under the hail of Persian arrows and engage their infantry in close combat. The Athenian centre was kept weak while the wings were reinforced, so that when the Persians broke through the centre of the charging line, the momentum of the Greek wings soon engulfed them on either side and to the rear. The Persians fell into disorder and were beaten into the marshes and the sea, with seven ships lost.

The remainder of the Persian force sailed round **Cape Sounio** to land within sight of the Acropolis, but Miltiades had brought the army back to Athens by forced march and stood ready to meet the enemy again. That astonishing burst of energy – 10,000 men marching 26 miles in full armour after fighting one battle, ready to fight another – overwhelmed the Persians' morale, and their expedition returned to Asia.

Áyios Pandelímonas

Four buses a day (three on Sun) run from the Mavrommatéon terminal

ÁYIOS PANDELÍMONAS, also known as Paralía Marathónas, lies straight on past the Týmfos Marathóna. The beach isn't that great – though there's plenty of room to spread out – but a string of waterfront fish tavernas ensure plenty of local visitors in summer.

Skhiniás

Four buses a day run along the road behind the beach, where there are a number of stops

The best **beach** in the region – some would say the best in the Athens area – lies north of Marathon at **SKHINIÁS**, a long, pine-backed strand with shallow water, big enough to allow some chance of escaping the crowds. At the southern end there's a certain amount of development with sections of free beach, plus several cordoned-off sections of pay-beach offering cafés, showers, loungers and watersports. The central section of Skhiniás beach, beyond the Olympic rowing and kayaking centre, is the least developed, with numerous tracks leading through the pines from the road to the sand. At the northern end there's more low-key development, mainly in the form of cafés and scattered **tavernas** on the sand.

Ramnous

Around 20km northeast of Marathónas • 6am–4pm 5 daily • €4.70 • Not realistically accessible by public transport, unless you're prepared to take a bus from Athens' Mavrommatéon terminal to Ayía Marína and hitch from the junction, some 5km from the site

The little-visited ruins of **Ramnous** occupy an isolated, atmospheric site above the sea, with magnificent views across the strait to Évvia. The site was an Athenian lookout point from the earliest times, and remains can be clearly seen continuing way below the fenced site, all the way down to the rocky shore. Within the site, the principal ruin is a Doric **Temple of Nemesis**, goddess of divine retribution. Pausanias records that the invading Persians incurred her wrath by their presumption in bringing with them a giant marble block upon which they intended to commemorate their victory. They met their nemesis, however, at the battle of Marathon, and the Athenians used the marble to create a statue instead. There are also the remains of a smaller temple dedicated to Themis, goddess of justice, and a section of ancient road.

1

ACTIVITIES

THE EAST COAST

Karavi Southern end of Skhiniás beach ☎22940 55950, ⓦkaravi.gr. The best of Skhiniás's organized beaches, with free entry, lifeguard, loungers, volleyball courts and windsurf hire and lessons, as well as a decent bar and restaurant. Summer daily 9am–9pm.

ACCOMMODATION AND EATING

RAFÍNA

Hotel Avra Arafinidhón Alón 3 ☎22940 22780, ⓦhotelavra.gr. Occupying a prime position high above the harbour, this business-style designer hotel has luxury rooms and suites, many with sea views. Include buffet breakfast. **€90**

Ouzerí Limeni Platía Plastíra 17 ☎22940 24750. The best choice on the lively pedestrianized square above the harbour, with excellent meze, such as stuffed vine leaves (€5.50) and grilled meat or chicken standards (€7), for less than you'll pay down at the harbour. Tues–Sun lunch and dinner.

Ta Kavoúria tou Asimáki Rafína harbour ☎22940 24551. The pick of Rafína's seafood restaurants is the first you'll come to as you descend towards the harbour from the square; though it looks fancier than its neighbours, it's no more expensive – kalamári, for example, costs €12. Head for the roof terrace, with a great view of the harbour activity. Daily noon–midnight.

ÁYIOS PANDELÍMONAS

Tria Adhelfia Beach road 1km north of the centre ☎22940 56461. Simple seafood taverna in a stunning waterfront position, with white tables on a whitewashed terrace which gets packed on a sunny weekend. Try the shrimp *saganáki* (€10) or lobster spaghetti (€20). May, June, Sept & Oct Sat & Sun lunch only; July & Aug daily lunch and dinner.

SKHINIÁS

Delphini Northern end of Skhiniás beach ☎22940 63253. Simple, busy taverna at the heart of life at this end of Skhiniás beach, which serves local catch of the day, and mezes dishes for about €10 per person. Daily roughly 11am–late.

West to the Peloponnese

The route from the centre of Athens towards **Kórinthos** (Corinth) follows the ancient Ierá Odhós – the Sacred Way – as far as Elefsína, ancient Eleusis. There's nothing sacred about it these days, though: this is as ugly a road as any in Greece, traversing an industrial wasteland. For the first 30km or so you have little sense of leaving Athens, whose western suburbs merge into Elefsína and then Mégara. Offshore lies **Salamína** (ancient Salamis; see box, p.331), these days just another suburb. The Attikí Odhós motorway from the airport meets the road from Athens just outside Elefsína.

Beyond Elefsína, the **old road to Thebes and Delphi** heads northwest into the hills. This route is described in Chapter 3 (see p.206), and is highly worthwhile, with its detours to **ancient Aegosthena** and the tiny resort of **Pórto Yermenó**. Directly west, towards the **Corinth Canal** (see p.132) and the Peloponnese, there are shingle beaches along the old coastal road at Kinéta and Áyii Theódhori. This highway, with the Yeránia mountains to the north and those of the Peloponnese across the water, follows the route where Theseus slew the bandit Skiron and threw him off the cliffs to be eaten by a giant sea turtle.

ARRIVAL AND DEPARTURE

WEST TO THE PELOPONNESE

By bus Bus #A16 or #B16 from Platía Eleftherías (aka Platía Koumoundhoúrou) runs along the Sacred Way several times an hour and stops at Dhafní en route to Elefsína (the #G16 goes to Dhafní but not Elefsína).

By car The main road out of Athens towards Eleusis and Dhafní is the busy Leofóros Athinón, though it's also possible to follow the Ierá Odhós (Sacred Way) from the centre of town, which may have less traffic and certainly seems more appropriate.

Dhafní Monastery

Leofóros Athinón, 11km northwest of Athens • Tues & Fri 8am–3pm • Free; you may have to buzz for entry • Bus #A16, #B16 or #G16

The **Dhafní Monastery**, a beautiful example of Byzantine architecture, was badly damaged by an earthquake in 1999, and only reopened in 2011. Its **dome** showcases

THE MYSTERIES OF ELEUSIS

The ancient **Mysteries** had an effect on their initiates that was easily the equal of any modern cult. Established in Mycenaean times, perhaps as early as 1500 BC, the cult centred on **Demeter**, the goddess of corn, and her daughter Persephone, whose annual descent into and resurrection from the underworld came to symbolize the rebirth of the crops and the miracle of fertility. By the fifth century BC, the cult had developed into a sophisticated annual festival which attracted up to thirty thousand people every autumn from all over the Greek world. The ceremonies lasted nine days: the **Sacred Objects** (identity unknown) were taken to Athens, where they were stored in the Ancient Agora for four days. Various rituals took place in the city, many on the Acropolis but also mass bathing and purification in the sea at Fáliro. Finally, a vast procession brought the objects back, following the Sacred Way to the sanctuary at Eleusis. Here initiates took part in the final rituals of *legomena* (things said), *dhromena* (things done) and *dheiknumena* (things shown). One theory suggests that these rituals involved drinking a fungus-infused potion which produced similar effects to those of modern **psychedelic drugs**. The Mysteries survived well into the Christian era, but eventually fell victim to the new orthodoxy.

Demeter is said to have threatened to render the land permanently barren if her worship at Eleusis ceased. Looking at the ecological havoc wreaked by the area's industry, it would seem that the curse has been fulfilled.

some stunning eleventh-century **mosaics**, considered among the artistic masterpieces of the Middle Ages; the monastery's mosaics include depictions of the Life of Christ, the Prophets, and the *Pandokrátor* (Christ in Majesty) in the dome itself. The restored mosaics, glistening with gold, are magnificent, and the stern Christ depicted here is a classic Orthodox image. A chamber next to the church has an excellent display on the monastery's history and restoration, along with close-up detail of the mosaics and identification of the saints and events depicted.

Eleusis

Elefsína, 18km northwest of Athens • Daily 8am–3pm • €6 • Bus #A16 or #B16 to Elefsína; ask the driver to set you down at the closest stop to the ruins – the terminal is a 10min walk back along the waterfront

The **Sanctuary of Demeter** at **Eleusis** was one of the most important in the ancient Greek world. For two millennia, the ritual ceremonies known as the Mysteries (see box above) were performed here. Today, the extensive **ruins** of the sanctuary occupy a low hill on the coast right in the heart of modern Elefsína.

On arrival, head straight for the **museum**, which features models of the sanctuary at various stages in its history: Eleusis is impressively large, with huge walls and gates, some of which date back to Mycenaean times, but the numerous eras of building can also be confusing, especially as signage is poor and mainly in Greek. Outside, the most important structure of ancient Eleusis was the **Telesterion**. This windowless Hall of Initiation lay at the heart of the cult, and it was here that the priests of Demeter would exhibit the **Sacred Objects** and speak "the Unutterable Words".

EATING AND DRINKING | ELEUSIS

Cyceon S Gióka 2, Elefsína ☎ 210 554 5401, ⓦ cyceon .gr. Directly opposite the entrance to the Eleusis archeological site, *Cyceon* café-bar is a cool spot (in every sense) to take a break. It serves dishes such as Cretan *dakos* (similar to Italian bruschetta) with feta (€6.50) and tortilla wrap with salmon and lettuce (€4). Daily 8.15am–2am.

The Peloponnese

ANCIENT THEATRE, EPIDAURUS

The Peloponnese

The cultural riches and natural beauty of the Peloponnese can hardly be overstated. This southern peninsula – technically an island since the cutting of the Corinth Canal – seems to have the best of almost everything Greek. Ancient sites include the Homeric palaces of Agamemnon at Mycenae and of Nestor at Pýlos, the best preserved of all Greek theatres at Epidaurus, and the lush sanctuary of Olympia, host to the Olympic Games for a millennium. The medieval remains are scarcely less rich, with the fabulous Venetian, Frankish and Turkish castles of Náfplio, Methóni and ancient Corinth; the strange battle towers and frescoed churches of the Máni; and the extraordinarily well-preserved Byzantine enclaves of Mystra and Monemvasiá.

Beyond this incredible profusion and density of cultural monuments, the Peloponnese is also a superb place to relax and wander. Its **beaches**, especially along the west and southwest coast, are among the finest in the country, and the **landscape** inland is superb – dominated by forested mountains cut by some of the most captivating valleys and **gorges** imaginable. Not for nothing did its heartland province of **Arcadia** become synonymous with the very concept of a Classical rural idyll.

The Peloponnese reveals its true character most clearly when you venture off the beaten track: to the likes of old Arcadian **hill towns** Karítena, Stemnítsa and Dhimitsána; to the **Máni tower villages** such as Váthia; at Voïdhokiliá and Elafónissos **beaches** in the south; or through the Vouraïkós Gorge on the old **rack-and-pinion railway**.

The region will amply repay any amount of time you spend here. The **Argolid**, the area richest in ancient history, is just a couple of hours from Athens, and if pushed you could complete a circuit of the main sights here – **Corinth**, **Mycenae** and **Epidaurus** – in a couple of days, making your base by the sea in **Náfplio**. Given an extra week, you could add in the two large sites of **Mystra** and **Olympia** at a more leisurely pace. To get to grips with all this, however, plus the southern peninsulas of the Máni and Messinía, and the hill towns of Arcadia, you'll need at least three weeks; the province is the size of Belgium.

If you were planning a combination of Peloponnese-plus-islands, then the **Argo-Saronic** or **Ionian islands** are most convenient (chapters 5 and 11 respectively). Of the Ionian islands, isolated **Kýthira** is covered in this chapter, since closest access is from the southern Peloponnese ports, but **Zákynthos** (see p.752) or **Kefaloniá** (see p.740) can be reached from the western port of Kyllíni, and Greece's second port city of **Pátra** is a gateway to eastern Italy.

Corinthian saints and sinners p.133	Blood feuds in the Máni p.166
Mycenaean murders p.136	Hiking the Výros Gorge p.173
Palamedes – cleverest of the Greeks p.140	Hiking near ancient Gortys p.176
Snakes alive: healing in ancient Greece p.145	Bassae's missing metopes p.178
	The battle of Navarino p.184
A Spartan upbringing p.158	Telemachus takes a bath p.185
Across the Langádha pass p.159	The Olympic Games p.189
The Mystra renaissance p.160	The Kalávryta Express (Odontotós) p.197

MANI COASTLINE - LIMENI VILLAGE

Highlights

❶ Mycenae The imposing palace of legend, site of priceless treasure and the alleged tomb of Agamemnon, who was murdered upon his return from the Trojan War. **See p.135**

❷ Náfplio With its gently fading nineteenth-century elegance, this port makes a picturesque base for exploring the Argolid. **See p.140**

❸ Epidaurus One of the most beautifully preserved of all ancient theatres, epitomizing the inspiring views and perfect acoustics for which the Greeks were renowned. **See p.144**

❹ Monemvasiá The Byzantines' impregnable stronghold – the "Gibraltar of the East" – is now a unique time bubble; stylish, low-key and traffic-free. **See p.149**

❺ Mystra A visually stunning medieval city, which once boasted a population of 20,000, preserves a superb assemblage of Byzantine frescoed churches. **See p.160**

❻ The Máni This rugged southern peninsula has inspired many visitors with its quirky tower houses and isolated churches. **See p.164**

❼ The Messenian Coast Mainland Greece's answer to the island beach holiday. **See p.181**

❽ Olympia Some 1400 years of the Olympic Games are laid bare along the verdant valley of the Alfiós, and the site's museum houses some of Greece's greatest sculptures. **See p.187**

HIGHLIGHTS ARE MARKED ON THE MAP ON PP.128–129

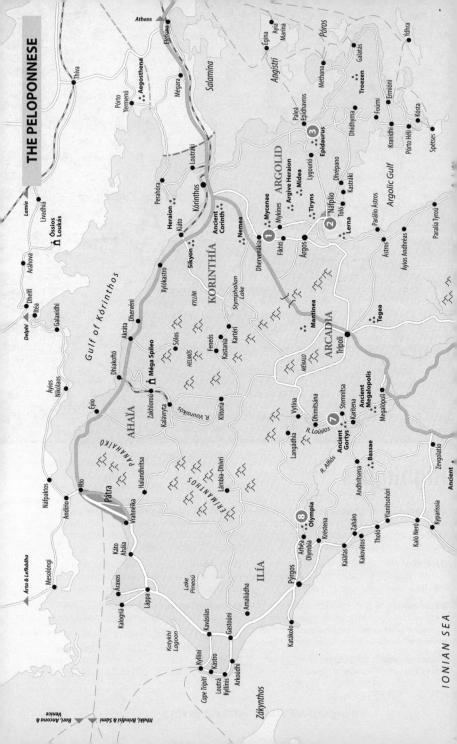

ARNONAS

LANGÁDHA PASS
Mystra
Ayios Ioánnis
Anavrytí

Kalamáta

TAÏYETOS

Kýparissi

Yérakas

Monemvasiá ④

Neápoli

Cape Maléas

Andikýthira

Marí

Yeráki

LAKONÍA

Skála

Krokeés

R. Evrótas

Molái

Pýrta

Arhángelos

Dounda

Elafónisos

Kýthira

Ayía Pelayía

Potamós

Dhiakófti

Avlémonas

Mylopótamos

Kapsáli

Hóra

Yíthio

Skoutári

Kótronas

Gulf of
Lakonía

Cape Ténaro

Ítylo
Langádha

MÁNI ⑥

Areópoli
Pýrgos Dhiroú

Kókkala

Yerolimnénas

Váthia

Vátika

Gulf of
Messíni

Kámbos

Kardhamýli

Stoúpa

Aviá

Messíni

Vélika
Análipsi

Petalídhi

Khráni

Finikoúnda

Koróni

Maráthi

Hóra

Korifássi

Yiálova

Pylos

Methóni

Nestor's
Palace

Sapiénza

Skhíza

M E D I T E R R A N E A N   S E A

N

0   25
kilometres

Brief history

The Peloponnese was home to some of the most powerful rulers in ancient Greece. During the **Mycenaean period** (around 2000–1100 BC), the peninsula hosted the legendary kingdoms of Agamemnon at Mycenae, Nestor at Pýlos and Menelaus at Sparta. In the **Dorian** and **Classical** eras, the region's principal city-state was Sparta, which, with its allies, brought down Athens in the ruinous Peloponnesian War. Under **Roman** rule, Corinth was the capital of the southern Greek province.

From the decline of the Roman Empire to the Ottoman conquest, the Peloponnese pursued a more complex, individual course from the rest of Greece. A succession of **occupations and conquests**, with attendant outposts and **castles**, left an extraordinary legacy of medieval remains. It retained a nominally Roman civilization well after colonial rule had dissipated, with Corinth at the fore until it was destroyed by two major **earthquakes** in the fourth and sixth centuries.

In the Middle Ages, the region was known as the **Moreas**, due to the resemblance of its outline to the leaf of a mulberry tree (*mouriá*). The **Byzantines** established their courts, castles and towns from the ninth century onward; their control, however, was only partial. The **Venetians** dominated the coast, and founded trading ports at Monemvasiá, Pýlos and Koróni which endured, for the most part, into the fifteenth century. The **Franks**, fresh from the sacking of Constantinople in the Fourth Crusade, arrived in 1204 and swiftly conquered large tracts of the peninsula, dividing it into feudal baronies under a prince of the Moreas.

Towards the mid-thirteenth century, there was a remarkable **Byzantine renaissance**, which spread from the court at Mystra to reassert control over the peninsula. A last flicker of "Greek" rule was eventually extinguished by the **Turkish conquest** between 1458 and 1460, and was to lie dormant, save for sporadic rebellions in the perennially intransigent Máni, until the nineteenth-century **Greek War of Independence**.

The nineteenth and twentieth centuries

The Peloponnese played a major part in the revolt against the Turks, with local heroes **Theodhoros Kolokotrónis** and **Petros Mavromihális** becoming important military leaders. At Pýlos, the international, but accidental, naval battle at **Navarino Bay** in 1827 decided the war, and the **first Greek parliament** was convened at Náfplio. After independence, however, power swiftly drained away from the Peloponnese to Athens, where it was to stay. The peninsula became disaffected, highlighted by the **assassination of Kapodhístrias**, the first Greek president, by Maniots in Náfplio.

Throughout the **nineteenth** and **early twentieth centuries**, the region developed important ports at Pátra, Kórinthos and Kalamáta, but its interior reverted to backwater status, which started a population decline that has continued up to the present. It was little disturbed until **World War II**, during which the area saw some of the worst German atrocities; there was much brave resistance in the mountains, but also some of the most shameful collaboration. The subsequent **civil war** left many of the towns polarized and physically in ruins; in its wake there was substantial **emigration** from both towns and countryside, to North America and Australia in particular. **Earthquakes** still cause considerable disruption, as at Kórinthos in 1981, Kalamáta in 1986, and Éyio in 1995.

ARRIVAL AND GETTING AROUND   THE PELOPONNESE

By bus Buses from Athens (daily, hourly; 1hr) to the Peloponnese run along the highway past Elefsína and over the Corinth Canal to the Isthmós KTEL station, 6km east of the modern town of Kórinthos. Most stop there (except for services to Kórinthos town) and then go on to Náfplio, Trípoli, Spárti, Kalamáta, Pýrgos and Pátra. If you don't have a direct service to the Peloponnesian towns, you'll have to change here.

By train Athens' commuter train network, the Proestiakós, runs hourly to Kiáto via Kórinthos (daily 6am–11pm; 1hr 30min), and makes a worthwhile alternative to the bus. There are works underway to extend the line to Patra, but currently you have to change at Kiáto onto an OSE shuttle bus for Patra. No other trains operate except the rack-and-pinion railway train to Kalávryta.

By car Drivers heading from Athens to the Peloponnese should take the express tollway to Elefsína/Kórinthos. Once on the peninsula, there are three highways: the Kórinthos–Kalamáta highway, which allows you to cross the Peloponnese diagonally in less than 2hr, albeit with several road tolls; the Kórinthos–Pátra highway; and the Olympic Highway from Pátra to Pýrgos. A branch off the Kórinthos–Kalamáta highway to Spárti was completed in 2017.

By boat Arrival for many on the Peloponnese is by hydrofoil from the Argo-Saronic islands (see p.326), linked with the ports of Ermióni and Pórto Héli (see p.146). For details and frequencies of services, which are drastically seasonal, check the Greek Travel Pages website, ⓦ gtp.gr. Pátra (see p.193) is the Peloponnese port of call for arrivals by ferry from Italy, as well as from Igoumenítsa on the mainland (see p.256) and from the Ionian islands (see p.706). There are also ferries from the island of Kýthira (see p.152) to and from Neápoli.

Corinth and around

Throughout Greek history, the Isthmus of Corinth, the mainland gateway to the Peloponnese, was strategically important, accounting for the great significance of the city of Corinth in the classical world. In modern times, this small strip of land was further enhanced, at least economically, by the cutting, at long last, of the **Corinth Canal**. The modern city of **Kórinthos**, the capital of its eponymous province, fails to live up to the historic hype – it's now little more than a minor transport hub. By contrast, the archeological site of **Ancient Corinth** is one of the high points of a visit to the Peloponnese, while the sanctuary of **ancient Nemea** is also an evocative spot.

Kórinthos

Like its ancient predecessor, **KÓRINTHOS** (modern Corinth) has been levelled on several occasions by **earthquakes** – most recently in 1981. Repaired and reconstructed, with buildings of characterless concrete, it is largely an industrial and agricultural centre, its economy bolstered by the drying and shipping of **currants**, for centuries one of Greece's most successful exports (the word "currant" itself derives from "Corinth"). The modern city has little to offer the outsider, so plan on moving on quickly if you land up here. That said, the pedestrianized centre has made what used to be a rather colourless Greek city much more lively and pleasant.

ARRIVAL AND INFORMATION   KÓRINTHOS

By bus The Kórinthos town KTEL bus station is a few blocks east of the centre, at Dimocratías 4 (☎ 27410 75410; ⓦ ktelkorinthias.gr).

Destinations Ancient Corinth (hourly; 20min); Athens (1–2hourly; 1hr 15min); Kiáto (Mon–Fri 2 hourly; 20min); Nemea (3–6 daily; 45min).

By train The Proastiakós train station is located about 3km southwest of town (☎ 21052 72000) alongside the Néa Ethnikí Odhós expressway; taxis to town are €4.

Destinations Athens (hourly; 1hr 15min); Kiáto (hourly; 15min).

Services You'll find various banks along northern Ethnikís Andístasis, and the main post office on Adhimándou, on the south side of the park. For car rental try Vasilopoulos at Adhimándou 39 (☎ 27410 25573; ⓦ cars-hire.gr), near the post office.

GETTING AROUND

By taxi Cabs wait along the Ethnikís Andístasis side of the park (☎ 27410 24844 or ☎ 27410 26900).

On foot The pedestrianized centre revolves around two parallel streets: Kolokotróni and Períandhrou.

ACCOMMODATION AND EATING

Blue Dolphin Camping Léheo, 6km west of Kórinthos ☎ 27410 25766, ⓦ camping-blue-dolphin. gr. Shady but basic beachside campsite: services include a mini-market, taverna and wi-fi. Take the bus to Vóha from Korinthos and ask the driver to drop you by the campsite. April–Oct. **€14**

★**Korinthos** Damaskinou 26 ☎ 27410 26701, ⓦ korinthoshotel.gr. Just a few metres from the marina, this medium-sized family hotel is plain, clean and very central. Rooms are en suite and have a/c and balconies, some with good views. Parking is available at the public car park behind the hotel. The buffet breakfast costs €5 extra. **€50**

Efeteio Kolokotróni 24 ☎ 27410 21777. Opposite the city courts, this is a 1950s-style ouzerí with a regular clientele of lawyers popping in for lunch. Try its famed kondosoúvli (pieces of chicken on a spit) for €8.50. Mon–Fri 11am–6pm, Sat 11am–7pm; closed August.

Corinth Canal

Cutting through the narrow isthmus that joins the Peloponnese to the mainland, the 6km **Corinth Canal** seems a very narrow strip of water when viewed from the bridge above, until a huge freighter from Pireás or cruise ship to the Ionian islands suddenly assumes toy-like dimensions as it passes nearly 80m below. Today, supertankers have tended to make it something of an anachronism, but it is still used by large vessels and remains a memorable sight. At the western end of the canal, by the old Kórinthos–Loutráki floating bridge, there are remains of the **diolkós**, a paved way along which a wheeled platform used to carry boats across the isthmus. In use from Roman times until the twelfth century, the boats were strapped onto the platform after being temporarily relieved of their cargo.

Brief history

The idea for a canal providing a short cut and safe passage between the Aegean and Ionian seas harks back at least to Roman times, when **Emperor Nero** himself performed the initial excavations with his little silver shovel, later heavily supplemented by Jewish slave labour. It was only in the 1890s, however, that the technology finally became available for cutting right across the 6km isthmus. Opened in July 1893, the canal, along with its near-contemporary Suez, helped establish Pireás as a **major Mediterranean port** and shipping centre.

ARRIVAL AND DEPARTURE	CORINTH CANAL
By car The national road passes directly over the canal, and the free car park is easy to spot. Look out for the cluster of tourist shops and restaurants, and you'll know you're there. **By bus** Almost all buses between the Peloponnese and elsewhere stop here.	Destinations Árgos (10–14 daily; 45min); Fichti for Mycenae (10–14 daily; 35min); Kalamáta (8 daily; 3hr 30min); Náflpio (10–14 daily; 1hr 10min); Pátra (every 30-45min; 2hr 30min); Spárti (9 daily; 2hr 30min); Trípoli (10–12 daily; 1hr).

Ancient Corinth

The ruins of **Ancient Corinth (Arhéa Kórinthos)**, which occupy an extensive site next to the village of the same name and 7km southwest of the modern city, are an essential stop. The site is split into a vast, impressively excavated city with the **Temple of Apollo** at its core, and even more compelling is the stunning acropolis site of **Acrocorinth**, towering 565m above the ancient city. To explore both you need a full day or an overnight stay – a much more agreeable option than staying in Kórinthos itself.

Brief history

Ancient Corinth was a key centre of the Greek and Roman worlds, whose possession meant the control of trade between northern Greece and the Peloponnese. Not surprisingly, therefore, the area's ancient and medieval history was one of invasions and power struggles that, in Classical times, was dominated by Corinth's **rivalry with Athens**, against whom it sided with Sparta in the Peloponnesian War.

After defeating the Greek city-states of the Achaean League, the Romans **razed** the city in 146 BC, before rebuilding it on a majestic scale in 44 BC under the command of Julius Caesar. Initially it was intended as a colony for veterans, but later became the **provincial capital**. Once again, Corinth grew rich on trade – with Rome to the west, and Syria and Egypt to the east. The city endured until rocked by two major **earthquakes**, in 375 and 521, which brought down the Roman buildings and again depopulated the site until a brief Byzantine revival in the eleventh century.

> **CORINTHIAN SAINTS AND SINNERS**
>
> Roman Corinth's reputation for wealth, fuelled by its trading access to luxury goods, was soon equalled by its appetite for **earthly pleasures** – including sex. Corinthian women were renowned for their beauty and much sought after as *hetairai* (courtesans); over a thousand sacred prostitutes served a temple to Aphrodite/Venus, on the acropolis of Acrocorinth. **St Paul** stayed in Corinth for eighteen months in 51–52 AD, though his attempts to reform the citizens' ways were met with rioting – tribulations recorded in his two **letters to the Corinthians**.

The site

Daily: summer 8am–8pm; winter 8am–3pm • €8

Entering from the north, you are in the **Roman agora**, an enormous marketplace flanked by the substantial foundations of a huge *stoa*, once a structure of several storeys, with 33 shops on the ground floor. Opposite the *stoa* is a *bema*, a marble platform used by **St Paul** in his defence against the charges brought against him by the Corinthians. At the far end are remains of a **basilica**, while the area behind the *bema* is strewn with the remnants of numerous Roman administrative buildings. Back across the agora, hidden in a swirl of broken marble and shattered architecture, there's a fascinating trace of the Greek city – a grille-covered **sacred spring**, at the base of a narrow flight of steps.

Fountain of Peirene

More substantial than the spring is the elaborate Roman **Fountain of Peirene**, which stands below the level of the agora, to the side of a wide, excavated stretch of the marble-paved **Lechaion Way** – the main approach to the city. The fountain house was, like many of Athens' Roman public buildings, the gift of the wealthy Athenian and friend of Emperor Hadrian, Herodes Atticus. Water still flows through the underground cisterns and supplies the modern village.

Temple of Apollo

Museum same hours as site • Entrance included in site admission

The real focus of the ancient site, though, is a rare survival from the Classical Greek era, the fifth-century BC **Temple of Apollo**, whose seven austere Doric columns stand slightly above the level of the forum, flanked by foundations of another marketplace and baths. Over to the west is the site **museum**, housing a large collection of domestic pieces, some good Greek and Roman mosaics from nearby, a frieze depicting some of the labours of Hercules, and a good number of Roman statues.

Other excavations

A number of miscellaneous smaller excavations surround the main site. To the west, just across the road from the enclosing wire, there are outlines of two **theatres**: a Roman **Odeon** (endowed by Herodes Atticus) and a larger Greek theatre, used by the Romans for gladiatorial battles. To the north are the inaccessible but visible remains of an **Asclepeion** (dedicated to the god of healing).

Acrocorinth

Daily Tues–Sun 8am–3pm • €2 • A hot 4km climb (nearly 1hr) or a 10min drive up from Ancient Corinth

Rising almost sheer above the lower town and the fertile plains, the medieval fortress of **Acrocorinth** is sited on an imposing mass of rock, still largely encircled by 2km of wall. Despite the long approach, a visit is unreservedly recommended. Looking down over the Saronic Gulf and the Gulf of Kórinthos, you get a real sense of its strategic importance. Amid the extensive remains is a jumble of chapels, mosques, houses and battlements, erected in turn by Greeks, Romans, Byzantines, Frankish crusaders, Venetians and Turks.

2

The Turkish remains are unusually substantial. Elsewhere in Greece, evidence of the Ottoman occupation has been removed or defaced, but here, at the start of the climb to the entrance, you can see the still-used **fountain of Hatzi Mustafa**, Christianized by the addition of great carved crosses. The outer of the citadel's **triple gates** is also largely Turkish; the middle is a combination of Venetian and Frankish; the inner, Byzantine, incorporating fourth-century BC towers. Within the citadel, the first summit (to the right) is enclosed by a **Frankish keep** – as striking as they come – which last saw action in 1828 during the War of Independence. Keeping along the track to the left, you pass some interesting (if perilous) cisterns, the remains of a Turkish bathhouse, and crumbling Byzantine chapels.

In the southeast corner of the citadel, hidden away in the lower ground, is the **upper Peirene spring**. This is not easy to find: look out for a narrow, overgrown entrance, from which a flight of iron stairs leads down some 5m to a metal screen. Here, broad stone steps descend into the dark depths, where a fourth-century BC arch stands guard over a **pool** of (non-potable) water that has never been known to dry up. To the north of the fountain, on the second and higher summit, is the site of the **Temple of Aphrodite**; after its days as a brothel, it saw use as a church, mosque and belvedere.

ARRIVAL AND DEPARTURE — ANCIENT CORINTH

By bus Buses to Arhéa Kórinthos village leave from Kórinthos every hour from 7am to 9pm (20min; €1.40) and return on the half hour.

ACCOMMODATION AND EATING

There is a scattering of rooms to rent in Arhéa Kórinthos village and plenty of tavernas along the fence that encloses the site.

★**Marinos Rooms** ☎&☏ 27410 31004, ⊛marinos-rooms.gr. A perennial Rough Guides favourite, this is a long-standing family-run hotel with huge rooms and a view of Acrocorinth. Breakfast included. There's great food in the taverna below too –try their 3-course €15 menu. Daily noon–11pm. **€55**

★**Yemelos** ☎ 27410 31361. Large taverna with quirky, kitsch Greek decor and a panoramic roof terrace overlooking the Temple of Apollo. Excellent meals feature the likes of grilled chicken, home-made pitta bread and fat juicy olives (mains €7). Daily 8am–late.

Nemea

Daily: winter 8am–3pm; summer 8am–8pm• €6, including museum • ☎ 27460 22739 • Bus runs from Kórinthos to Nemea (3–6 daily; 45min); ask to be dropped at Arhéa Neméa, a small village 300m west of the ruins

Nemea – home to the Lion of Hercules' (Herakles) first labour – is just 31km southwest of Kórinthos, off the road to Mycenae and Árgos. Like Olympia, Nemea held athletic games for the Greek world from the sixth century BC, until these were transferred to Árgos in 270 BC.

A sanctuary rather than a town, the principal remains at the **site** are of the **Temple of Nemean Zeus**, currently three slender Doric columns surrounded by other fallen and broken drums, but slowly being reassembled. Nearby are a **palaestra** with **baths** and a Christian **basilica**, built with blocks from the temple. There is also an excellent **museum**, with contextual models, displays relating to the biennial games and items from the area.

Outside the site, 500m east, is the **stadium**, which once seated forty thousand spectators. The vaulted entrance tunnel, now reconstructed, and complete with the graffiti of ancient athletes, is the oldest known. There is a guide available, written by archeologist Stephen Miller, who organized the (now quadrennial) **New Nemean Games** in 1996 as a non-commercial alternative to the Olympics; anyone can enter if they run barefoot and wear traditional tunics (⊛nemeangames.org).

Argolid

The region that you enter to the south and southeast of Corinth was once known as the **Argolid** (Argolídha in modern Greek), after the city of Árgos, which held sway here in the Pre-Classical era. This compact peninsula, its western boundary delineated by the main road south from Kórinthos, contains the greatest concentration of ancient sites in Greece. Within less than an hour's drive of each other are Agamemnon's fortress at **Mycenae**, the great theatre of **Epidaurus**, plus the magnificent hill fort at **Tiryns** and ancient **Árgos**.

In peak season, you may want to see the sites early or late in the day to realize their magic. When ruin-hopping palls, you can enjoy the urban pleasures of elegant **Náfplio**, and a handful of **beach resorts**.

Mycenae

Tucked into a fold of the hills just east of the road from Kórinthos to Árgos, Agamemnon's citadel at **MYCENAE** (Mykínes) fits the legend better than any other place in Greece. It was uncovered in 1874 by the German archeologist **Heinrich Schliemann** (who also excavated the site of Troy), impelled by his single-minded belief that there was a factual basis to Homer's epics. Schliemann's finds of brilliantly crafted gold and sophisticated tomb architecture bore out the accuracy of Homer's epithets of "well-built Mycenae, rich in gold". And with the accompaniment of the sound of bells drifting down from goats grazing on the hillsides, a stroll around the ramparts is still evocative of earlier times.

Brief history

The Mycenae-Árgos region is one of the longest occupied in Greece, with evidence of Neolithic settlements from around 3000 BC. But it is to the period from around 1550 to 1200 BC that the citadel of Mycenae and its associated drama belong. This period is known as **Mycenaean**, a term that covers not just the Mycenae region but a whole

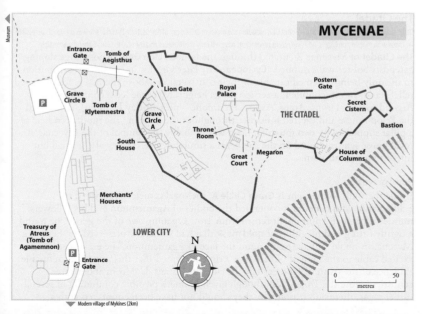

2

MYCENAEAN MURDERS

According to legend, the city of Mycenae was founded by Perseus, the slayer of Medusa the Gorgon, before it fell into the bloodied hands of the House of Atreus. **Atreus**, in an act of vengeance for his wife's seduction by his brother Thyestes, murdered Thyestes' sons, and fed them to their father. Not surprisingly, this incurred the wrath of the gods: Thyestes' daughter, Pelopia, subsequently bore her father a son, Aegisthus, who later murdered Atreus and restored Thyestes to the throne.

The next generation saw the gods' curse fall upon Atreus' son **Agamemnon**. On his return to Mycenae after commanding the Greek forces in the Trojan War – a role in which he had earlier consented to the sacrifice of his own daughter, Iphigeneia – he was killed in his bath by his wife Klytemnestra and her lover, Aegisthus, who had also killed his father. The tragic cycle was completed by Agamemnon's son, Orestes, who, egged on by his sister Elektra, took revenge by murdering his mother, Klytemnestra, and was pursued by the Furies until Athena finally lifted the curse on the dynasty.

Bronze Age civilization that flourished in southern Greece at the time, referred to in Homer's epics.

The **archeological remains** of Mycenae fit remarkably easily with the tales (see box above), at least if it is taken as a poetic rendering of dynastic struggles, or, as most scholars now believe it to be, a merging of stories from various periods. The buildings unearthed by Schliemann show signs of occupation from around 1950 BC, as well as two periods of intense disruption, around 1200 BC and again in 1100 BC – at which stage the town, though still prosperous, was **abandoned**.

No coherent explanation has been put forward for these events, but it seems that **war** among the rival kingdoms was a major factor in the Mycenaean decline. These struggles appear to have escalated as the civilization developed in the thirteenth century BC: excavations at Troy revealed the sacking of that city, quite possibly by forces led by a king from Mycenae, in 1240 BC. The Mycenae citadel seems to have been replanned, and heavily **fortified**, during this period.

The Citadel

Daily: summer 8am–8pm; winter 8am–3pm • €12, including the museum & Treasury of Atreus. Note that this site was previously accessible for those with mobility problems, however recent renovations have left only the museum and the way to Lion's Gate fully accessible.

The Citadel of Mycenae is entered through the famous **Lion Gate**, whose huge sloping gateposts bolster walls dubbed "**Cyclopean**" by later Greeks, in bewildered attribution to the only beings deemed capable of their construction. Above them, a graceful carved relief stands out in confident assertion: at its height, Mycenae led a confederation of Argolid towns (Tíryns, Árgos, Assine, Hermione – present-day Ermióni), dominated the Peloponnese and exerted influence throughout the Aegean. The motif seen here of a pillar supported by two muscular lions was probably the symbol of the Mycenaean royal house – a seal found on the site bears a similar device. There's also a small but interesting site **museum**.

Royal graves

Inside the walls to the right is **Grave Circle A**, the royal cemetery excavated by Schliemann, who believed it contained the bodies of Agamemnon and his followers, murdered on their triumphant return from Troy. Opening one of the graves, he found a tightly fitting and magnificent **gold mask** that had somehow preserved the flesh of a Mycenaean noble; "I have gazed upon the face of Agamemnon," he exclaimed in an excited cable to the king of Greece. For a time it seemed that this provided irrefutable evidence of the truth of Homer's tale. In fact, the burials date from about three centuries before the Trojan War, though given Homer's possible combining of several earlier sagas, there's no reason why they should not have been connected with a

Mycenaean king Agamemnon. They were certainly royal graves, for the finds, which are now displayed in the National Archeological Museum in Athens (see p.85), are among the richest that archeology has yet unearthed.

Royal Palace

Schliemann took the extensive **South House**, beyond the grave circle, to be the Palace of Agamemnon. However, a building much grander and more likely to be the **Royal Palace** was later discovered near the summit of the acropolis. Rebuilt in the thirteenth century BC, this is an impressively elaborate and evocative building complex; although the ruins are only at ground level, the different rooms are easily discernible. Like all Mycenaean palaces, it is centred around a **great court**: on the south side, a staircase would have led via an anteroom to the big rectangular **throne room**; on the east, a double porch gave access to the **megaron**, the grand reception hall with its traditional circular hearth. The small rooms to the north are believed to have been **royal apartments**, and in one of them the remains of a **red stuccoed bath** have led to its fanciful identification as the scene of Agamemnon's murder.

The secret cistern and merchants' houses

A salutary reminder of the nature of life in Mycenaean times is the **secret cistern** at the eastern end of the ramparts, created around 1225 BC. Whether it was designed to enable the citadel's occupants to withstand siege from outsiders, rival Mycenaeans or even an increasingly alienated peasantry is not known. Steps lead down to a deep underground spring; it's still possible to descend the whole way, though you'll need to have a torch and be sure-footed, since there's a drop to the water at the final turn of the twisting passageways. Nearby is the **House of Columns**, a large and stately building with the base of a stairway that once led to an upper storey.

Only the ruling Mycenaean elite could live within the citadel itself. Hence the main part of town lay outside the walls and, in fact, extensive remains of **merchants' houses** have been uncovered near to the road. Their contents included **inscribed tablets** (in Linear B, an early form of Greek) which detailed the spices used to scent oils, suggesting that the early Mycenaeans may have dabbled in the **perfume trade**. The discovery of the tablets has also shown that, here at least, writing was not limited to government scribes working in the royal palaces, as had previously been thought, and that around the citadel there may have been a commercial city of some size and wealth.

Tholos tombs

Alongside the merchants' houses are the remains of **Grave Circle B**, from around 1650 BC and possibly of an earlier, rival dynasty to those kings buried in Grave Circle A, and two **tholos** (circular chamber-type) **tombs**, identified by Schliemann as the **tombs of "Aegisthus" and "Klytemnestra"**. The former, closer to the Lion Gate, dates from around 1500 BC and has now collapsed, so is roped off; the latter dates from some two centuries later – thus corresponding with the Trojan timescale – and can still be entered.

Treasury of Atreus

Included in the Citadel ticket

Four hundred metres down the road from the Citadel site is another, far more startling, **tholos**, known as the **Treasury of Atreus** or – the currently preferred official name – **"Tomb of Agamemnon"**. This was certainly a royal burial vault at a late stage in Mycenae's history, contemporary with the "Tomb of Klytemnestra", so the attribution to Agamemnon is as good as any – if the king were indeed the historic leader of the Trojan expedition. Whoever it belonged to, this beehive-like structure, built without the use of mortar, is an impressive monument to Mycenaean building skills. Entering the tomb along a majestic 15m corridor, you arrive at the chamber doorway, above which is a great lintel formed by two immense slabs of stone – one of which, a staggering 9m long, is estimated to weigh 118 tonnes.

Mykínes

Unless you have your own transport, you might want to stay at the modern village of
MYKÍNES, 2km from the main Kórinthos–Árgos road and the small train station at
Fíkhti. It can be busy by day, but quietens down once the site has closed and the tour
buses depart. The archeological site is a 2km walk uphill from Mykínes centre.

ARRIVAL AND DEPARTURE   MYKÍNES

By bus Buses from Athens drop passengers at Fíkhti rather than at Mykínes village (taxi €5); local, unreliable buses from Árgos or Náfplio serve the village and the site.

Destinations Athens (10–13 daily; 2hr); Árgos (10–13 daily; 30min); Náfplio (10–13 daily; 1hr).

ACCOMMODATION

All the places listed below are along Mykínes village's single street, where you'll find an array of hotels and rooms for rent.

Atreus Camping ☎ 27510 76221, **@** atreus@otenet .gr. Friendly family-run site on the left as you enter the town from Fíkhti. Good facilities including washing machines and a nice pool. Great home cooking is on offer, too, at the restaurant (mains €6). Tents to rent if needed. March–Oct. **€15.80**
Le Petite Planète ☎ 27510 76240, **ⓦ** petite-planet .gr. At the top end of the village, this recently refurbished hotel is the nearest to the site, with a/c rooms, great views and a swimming pool. Dinner, which features organic produce, is available at the on-site restaurant. Breakfast

included. April–Oct. **€55**
La Belle Helène ☎ 27510 76225, **@** bellhel@otenet .gr. The second-oldest (1885) hotel in Greece, converted from the house used by Schliemann during his excavations. Rooms with the original layout (so none en suite) are named after famous guests who have slept in them like Karl Jung or Agatha Christie, although Schliemann's room is now a museum piece (daily 10am–6pm; €3, free to guests). Signatures in the visitors' books include Virginia Woolf, Sartre, Himmler and Goebbels. There's a good restaurant attached. Breakfast included. March–Nov. **€40**

EATING

Electra ☎ 27510 76447. Very welcoming, despite its bland decor and overweening size. The food (typical Greek fare) is all home-made and there's a very good three-course set menu for €10. Daily 9am–9pm.

Mykinaïko ☎ 27510 76245. Basic yet picturesque, this postcard-Greek taverna serves up reliable home-made dishes at very affordable prices (fresh Greek salads €4, set menus from €8). Daily noon–10pm.

Árgos

ÁRGOS, 12km south of the Mykínes junction, is said to be the oldest continuously
inhabited town in Greece (c.5000 years), although you wouldn't guess it from first
impressions. However, this busy trading centre has some pleasant squares and
Neoclassical buildings, and a brief stop is worthwhile for the excellent **museum** and
mainly **Roman ruins**.

Archeological Museum of Argos

Platía Ayíou Pétrou • Currently closed for renovations: call ☎ 27510 68819 to check re-opening times

The modern **Archeological Museum of Argos** makes an interesting detour after
Mycenae, with a good collection of Mycenaean tomb objects and armour as well as
extensive pottery finds. The region's Roman occupation is well represented here, in
sculpture and mosaics.

Agora

Tues–Sun 8am–3pm • Free • 10min walk down the Trípoli road from Árgos

Before leaving Árgos, visit the town's ancient **Agora**; from the market square take
Fidhónos, then Theátrou. The **site** is surprisingly extensive and excavations are
ongoing. The Classical Greek **theatre**, adapted by the Romans, looks oddly narrow
from the road, but climb up to the top and it feels immense. Estimated to have held
twenty thousand spectators – six thousand more than Epidaurus – it is matched on the

Greek mainland only by the theatres at Megalopolis and Dodóna. Alongside are the remains of an **Odeon** and **Roman baths**.

Castle of Lárissa

Free access • A steep walk up indistinct trails from the Agora, or via a winding uphill road from the village

Above the Agora looms the ancient **acropolis**, on a conical hill capped by the largely Frankish medieval **castle of Lárissa**, built on sixth-century BC foundations and later augmented by the Venetians and Turks. Massively walled, cisterned and guttered, the sprawling ruins offer wonderful views – a reward for the tough walk to get here.

2

By bus The station is at the eastern end of the city at the beginning of the Náfplio highway, about 1.5km from the centre.

Destinations Athens via Fíkhti for Mykínes (10–13 daily; 2hr); Náfplio (10–13 daily; 30min).

Tiryns

8km southeast of Argos • Daily 8am–3pm • €4 • ☎ 27520 22657

In Mycenaean times, the impressive fortress of **Tiryns** (**Tíryntha**) stood by the sea, commanding the coastal approaches to Árgos and Mycenae. The Aegean shore gradually receded, leaving it stranded on a low hillock, surrounded by citrus groves. History buffs considerate it a better Mycenaean site than Mycenae, though the setting is not as enchanting – which in part explains why this highly accessible, substantial site is undeservedly neglected and relatively empty of visitors. After the crowds at Mycenae, however, the opportunity to wander about Homer's "wall-girt Tiryns" in near-solitude is worth taking.

The site

The entrance to **the site** is on the far side of the fortress from the road, from where you can explore a restricted number of passages, staircases and the parts of the palace. The walls, 750m long and up to 7m thick, formed of huge Cyclopean stones, dominate the site; the Roman guidebook writer Pausanias found them "more amazing than the Pyramids" – a claim that seems a little exaggerated today. Despite this, the sophistication and defensive function of the citadel are evident as soon as you climb the **entrance ramp**. Wide enough to allow access to chariots, the ramp is angled to leave the right-hand, unshielded side of any invading force exposed for the entire ascent. The **gateways**, too, constitute a formidable barrier; the outer one would have been similar in design to Mycenae's Lion Gate.

Of the **palace** itself, only the limestone foundations survive, but the fact that they occupy a level site gives you a clearer idea of its structure than at hilly, boulder-strewn Mycenae. The walls would have been of sun-dried brick, stucco-covered and decorated with frescoes, fragments of which are now in the Náfplio museum. From the forecourt one enters a spacious **colonnaded court** with a round sacrificial altar in the middle. A typically Mycenaean double porch leads directly ahead to the **megaron** (great hall), where the base of a throne was found – it's now in the National Archeological Museum in Athens (see p.85). Sometime in the sixth century BC, part of the palace became the site of a **temple to Hera**, a structure whose column bases now pepper the ground. **Royal apartments** lead off on either side; the women's quarters are thought to have been to the right, while to the left is the bathroom, its floor – a huge, single flat stone – still intact.

A tower further off to the left of the megaron gives access to a **secret staircase**, as at Mycenae, which winds down to an inconspicuous **postern gate**. The walled-in **lower acropolis**, north of the megaron, is the site of two underground vaulted cisterns outside its far end, on the western side. The most stunning part of the site, however, is the stone-vaulted **galleria**, a covered walkway dating from c.1580BC on the eastern side.

Náfplio and around

NÁFPLIO (also sometimes known as Nafplia or Náfplion) is a rarity among Greek towns. A lively, beautifully sited place, it exudes a grand, occasionally slightly faded elegance, inherited from the days when it was the fledgling capital of modern Greece. The town is a popular year-round weekend retreat and remains by far the most attractive base for exploring the Argolid.

There's ample pleasure to be had in just wandering around: looking around the harbourfront, walking the coastal circuit, and, when you're feeling energetic, exploring the great twin fortresses of **Palamídhi** and **Akronafplía**. Náfplio also offers some of the peninsula's best **restaurants** and shops, plus facilities, including car rental. In the town itself there are a few minor sights, mainly part of its Turkish heritage, and some good **museums**. **Platía Syndágmatos**, the main square of the old town, is the focus of most interest. The nearest good **beach** is at **Karathónas**, and closer to the town is the one at **Arvanitiá**.

Brief history

The town's past certainly stretches back to prehistory, and parts of the **Akronafplía wall** bear witness to that fact, though little else remains dating to earlier than the Byzantine era. From the thirteenth century down to the early nineteenth, Náfplio, along with the rest of the region, became an object of contention among **invading forces**. Finally came the **Greek War of Independence**, and the city was named the **first capital**, from 1829 to 1834. It was also in Náfplio that the first president, Kapodhístrias, was assassinated by vengeful Maniot clansmen, and here, too, that the young Bavarian Prince Otto (Óthon), put forward by the European powers to be crowned as the first king of Greece, had his initial **royal residence** from 1833 to 1834. He is now commemorated by a locally unpopular statue.

Palamídhi

Daily: summer 8am–8pm; winter 8am–4.30pm • €8 • ☎ 27520 28036 • The most direct approach is from the end of Polyzoïdhou street, beside a Venetian bastion from where it's a very steep climb up 890-plus stone-hewn steps (in shade early morning); there is also a circuitous approach by car directly to the gate – follow the signs from the southeast end of town

The **Palamídhi**, Náfplio's principal **fort**, was a key military flashpoint of the War of Independence. The Greek commander Kolokotronis – of whom there's a majestically bewhiskered statue at Platía Kapodhístria – laid siege for over a year before finally gaining control. After independence, he was imprisoned in the same fortress by the new Greek government; wary of their attempts to curtail his powers, he had kidnapped four members of the parliament.

If coming via the somewhat challenging steep steps approach, as you reach the 216m summit you're confronted with a bewilderingly vast **complex**. Within the outer walls there are three self-contained castles, all of them built by the Venetians between 1711 and 1714, which accounts for the appearance of that city's symbol – the Lion of St Mark – above the various gateways. The middle fort, San Niccolo (Miltiádhes), was the one where Kolokotronis was incarcerated; it became a notorious **prison** during the 1947–51 civil war.

Akronafplía

24hr • Free

The **Akronafplía**, to the west of the Palamídhi, is a **fort** occupying the ancient acropolis, whose walls were adapted by three successive medieval restorers – hence the name. The

---

PALAMEDES – CLEVEREST OF THE GREEKS

Palamídhi fortress takes its name from Náfplio's most famous and most brilliant legendary son, **Palamedes**. According to mythology, he was responsible for a range of inventions including dice, lighthouses, measuring scales, an early form of chess and military formations for soldiers. He was killed by the Greeks at Troy, on charges of treachery trumped up by Odysseus, who regarded himself as the cleverest of the Greeks.

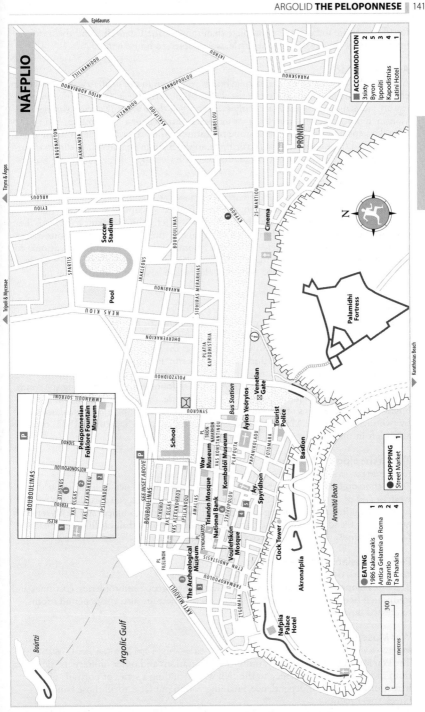

NÁFPLIO

Epidaurus

Tirins & Argos

Tripoli & Mycenae

Argolic Gulf

Bóurtzi

2

Karathónas Beach

Palamidhi Fortress

Pólnia

Cinema

Soccer Stadium

Pool

Peloponnesian Folklore Museum

Fountain

School

Bus Station

Venetian Gate

Tourist Police

Bastión

Ayios Yeóryios

War Museum

Komboloï Museum

Trianón Mosque

National Bank

Vouleftikón Mosque

Ay. Spyridhon

Clock Tower

Akronafplía

The Archeological Museum

Nafplia Palace Hotel

Aranitidha Beach

Arvanitiá Beach

N

ACCOMMODATION
3sixty	2
Byron	5
Ippoliti	3
Kapodístrias	4
Latíni Hotel	1

EATING
1986 Kakanarakis	1
Antica Gelateria di Roma	3
Byzantio	2
Ta Phanária	4

SHOPPING
Street Market	1

0   300
metres

fortifications are today far less complete than those of the Palamídhi, and the most intact section, the lower Torrione castle, was adapted to house hotels.

Arvanitiá beach

A fork in the access road to Akronafplía brings you down to the small **Arvanitiá beach**, an enjoyable enough spot to cool off in the shelter of the forts. It gets very crowded in peak season and is more pleasant in the early evening when there are only a few swimmers. Continue along the path from just past the beach entrance for a few minutes, and you can take steps down to some small stone platforms by the sea, or take the attractive paved route around the western end of Akronafplía, to the main town harbour. A dirt road to the southeast of Arvanitiá leads to Karathónas beach (see opposite), a 45-minute walk.

Boúrtzi

Daily every 30 min 8am–sunset • Return boat trip €4, from the northeastern end of Aktí Miaoúli.

The town's third **fort**, the much-photographed **Boúrtzi**, occupies the islet of Áyios Theódhoros, offshore from the harbour. Built in 1473 by the Venetians to control the shipping lane to the town and to much of Árgos bay, the castle has seen various uses in modern times – from the nineteenth-century home of the town's public executioner to a luxury hotel in the early twentieth century. In her autobiography *I Was Born Greek*, the actress and politician Melina Mercouri claimed to have consummated her first marriage there.

Ottoman sights

Near Platía Syndágmatos, three converted **Ottoman mosques** survive: one, the **Trianón**, in the southeast corner of the square, is an occasional theatre and cinema; another, the **Vouleftikón**, just off the southwest corner, was the modern Greek state's original Voulí (parliament building). A third, fronting nearby Plapoúta, was reconsecrated as the cathedral of **Áyios Yeóryios**, having started life as a Venetian Catholic church. Worth a quick look are a pair of handsome **Turkish fountains** – one abutting the south wall of the theatre-mosque, the other on Kapodhístria, opposite the church of Áyios Spyrídhon. On the steps of the latter, president **Ioannis Kapodhístrias** was assassinated by two members of the Mavromihális clan from the Máni in September 1831; there is a scar left in the stone by one of the bullets.

The Archeological Museum

Platia Syndágmatos • Tues–Sun 8am–3pm • €6 • ☎ 27520 27502

The **Archeological Museum** in Náfplio occupies a dignified Venetian mansion at the western end of Syndágmatos. It has some good collections, as you'd expect in a town near the Argolid sites, including a unique and more or less complete suit of **Mycenaean armour**, the Dendra panoply from around 1400 BC, wonderful, birdlike Mycenaean **female figurines**, and reconstructed **frescoes** from Tiryns.

Peloponnesian Folklore Museum

Vassiléos Alexándhrou 1 • Mon–Sat 9am–2.30pm, Sun 9.30am–3pm• €2 • ⓦ pli.gr

The fine **Peloponnesian Folklore Museum** features gorgeous embroideries, costumes and traditional household items from all over Greece. There are also entire period rooms, re-created down to the last detail.

War Museum

Amalías 22 • Nov–March Tues–Sat 9am–5pm, Sun 9.30am–5pm; April–Oct Tues–Sat 9am–7pm, Sun 9.30am–7pm • €3 • ☎ 27520 25591

The **War Museum** has weaponry, uniforms, illustrations and other military memorabilia from the War of Independence to the civil war, including a series of portraits of the heroes of the War of Independence, enabling you to put faces to all those familiar Greek street names.

Komboлóï Museum

Staïkopoúlou 25 • Oct–April Wed–Mon 9.30am–8pm; May–Sept daily 9.30am–8pm;• €2 • ⓦ komboloi.gr

The private labour of love that is the quirky **Komboлóï Museum** is unmissable. Its large collection of worry beads and rosaries from Greece, the Middle and Far East as well as Western Europe is comprehensive, entertaining and well researched.

Karathónas beach

4 morning bus services from Náfplio run daily in season

The closest proper beach to Náfplio is at **Karathónas**, a fishing hamlet just over the headland beyond the Palamídhi fortress, which can be reached by a short spur off the drive going up to the ramparts. A more direct dirt road, theoretically closed to traffic, around the base of the intervening cliffs, can make a pleasant 45-minute walk; however, women alone are occasionally pestered by local scooter drivers. The narrow **sandy beach** stretches for a couple of kilometres, and has a summer taverna at its far end.

2

ARRIVAL AND DEPARTURE   NÁFPLIO

By bus The KTEL bus station (☎ 27520 27323, ⓦ ktelargolida .gr) is at Syngroú 8, just south of the inter-locking squares, Platía Trión Navárhon and Platía Kapodhistría.

Destinations Árgos (every 30min; 20min); Athens (10–13 daily; 1hr 45min); Epidaurus (3–6 daily; 30min); Fichti for Mycenae (hourly; 45min); Kalamáta (2 weekly; 2 hrs); Pátra

(1 weekly; 2hr 30 min); Tiryns (every 30min; 10 min); Trípoli (1 daily; 1hr).

By car Finding a parking space near the old town is very difficult in summer – your best chance may be on the harbourfront, or if you're staying up near the Akronafplía, there are good options on top.

INFORMATION AND ACTIVITIES

Tourist office The tourist office is inside the City Hall, at Vasiléos Konstandínou 34 (Mon–Fri 9am–8pm, Sat, Sun 9am–1pm & 4–8pm; ☎ 27520 24444), and there's a useful website ⓦ all-about-nafplio.com.

Tourist police The helpful tourist police is on Koundourióti (daily 7.30am–9pm; ☎ 27520 98727).

Watersports Náfplio Diving Center ☎ 27520 27201, ⓦ nafpliodivingcenter.gr).

GETTING AROUND

By bike Nafplio Bikes, at Kyprou 2, rents and maintains bicycles (☎ 27520 97836, ⓦ nafplio-bike.gr).

By car and scooter Europcar, on Neas Kiou, rent cars and

mopeds (☎ 27520 59289).

By taxi There's a 24hr taxi rank opposite the bus station (☎ 27520 24120).

ACCOMMODATION

Accommodation in Náfplio is generally expensive, particularly in the old town, though out of season during the week most hotels drop their prices significantly.

3sixty Kolétti & Papanikoláou 26 ☎ 27525 00501 ⓦ 3sixtyhotel.gr. The original 1880s spiral staircase and contemporary silver sculptures at reception cry out "boutique", and the overall design – Versace sheets, mirrors turning into giant TV screens and real fireplaces – is exceptional. Its fine dining restaurant, open to all, is surprisingly affordable (burgers €12). Breakfast included. **€200**

Byron Plátonos 2 ☎ 27520 22351, ⓦ byronhotel.gr. A beautifully restored old mansion up steep steps above Áyios Spyrídhon church, which has expanded into a second neoclassical building. The cheaper rooms don't have views, but up your budget a little and you'll get either a balcony or a decent view. Breakfast included. **€60**

★ **Ippolíti** Ilía Miniáti & Aristídou 9 ☎ 27520 96088, ⓦ ippoliti.gr. The only hotel in the old town with a pool

and gym, this is a comfortable place that that succeeds in being luxurious without sacrificing the sought-after Náfplio atmosphere. Choose between a jacuzzi or a personal hammam cabin in your room. Breakfast included. **€120**

Kapodistrias Kokkínou 20 ☎ 27520 29366, ⓦ hotelkapodistrias.gr. Boutique hotel with individually decorated rooms, in a 200-year-old house just 50m from where Kapodhístrias met his end. Breakfast included. **€70**

Latini Hotel Óthonos 47 ☎ 27520 96470, ⓦ latinihotel .gr. A friendly, recently refurbished family-run hotel, with a nautical theme and spacious rooms right in the centre of the old town. Ask for a top-floor room for great views of Bourtzi. Breakfast included. **€55**

2

Marianna Potamiánou 9 ☎ 27520 24256, ⊛ hotelmarianna.gr. Restored house up by the Akronafplía fortress walls, with some of the best views in town from the terrace, where an organic breakfast is served – for €5 extra, it's very good value. There are new maisonettes and apartments on a courtyard below. Parking nearby. **€85**

EATING

Waterside Bouboulínas is lined with cafés, popular with Athens weekenders. A cosier place to start menu-gazing is Staïkopoúlou, where there are many enjoyable, if touristy, tavernas.

1986 Kakanarakis Vassilísis Ólgas 18 ☎ 27520 25371, ⊛ kakanarakis.gr. A lively, stylishly refurbished local favourite, serving a variety of appetisers (€5) plus dishes such as *kokkinistó* (meat simmered in tomato sauce) for €10. Daily noon–1am.

Antica Gelateria di Roma Farmakopoúlon 3 & Komninoú ☎ 27520 23520, ⊛ anticagelateria.com. Real home-made Italian ice cream pulls the crowds here and has done so since 1870. They offer a full range of other Italian sweets, as well, including soft *torrone* and almond *cantucci*, and some tempting coffee concoctions. Daily: Nov–March 9am–1am; April–Oct 8am–2am.

★ **Byzantio** Vassiléos Alexándhrou 15 ☎ 27520 21631, ⊛ taverna-byzantio.gr. This excellent taverna is on a quiet corner of a beautiful street, under a cloud of pink and purple bougainvillea. Specialities include home-made sausages, its own organic wine and an unfinishable meat meze platter. About €10 per person. Daily noon–11pm.

Ta Phanaria Staïkopoúlou 13 ☎ 27520 27141, ⊛ fanaria.gr. The place to try good seasonal cooking featuring local veg like aubergine baked with cheese filling (€5.50) and lots of grilled meat options, too (€11). Choose cosy seating indoors, or eat in the bougainvillea-covered courtyard. Daily noon–11pm.

SHOPPING

Street Market Along Kyprou, on the park side, up to 25 Martiou. Mostly food produce, but also clothes, housewares, ceramics and jewellery. Wed & Sat morning.

DIRECTORY

Banks These are concentrated around Platía Syndágmatos and along Amalías; most have ATMs.
Post office The main branch (Mon–Fri 7.30am–8.30pm) is on the northwest corner of Platía Kapodhistría.
Travel agent Staïkos Travel, at Bouboulínas 50 (☎ 27520 27950, ✉ staikostravel@naf.forthnet.gr.)

Epidaurus (Epídhavros)

Site Daily: summer 8am–8pm, winter 8am–5pm • €12, including theatre, museum and Asclepian Sanctuary • **Athens Festival performances** Fri & Sat evenings from June till the last weekend in Aug • €15–50; available in advance online (⊛ greekfestival.gr), in Athens (at the festival box offices ☎ 210 327 2000), or sometimes at the site (☎ 27530 22026) during the festival

EPIDAURUS is a major Greek site visited for its stunning **ancient theatre**, built around 330–320 BC. With its extraordinary acoustics, this has become a very popular venue for the annual **Athens Festival** productions on summer evenings. The works range from the ancient tragedies of Sophocles, Euripides and Aeschylus to operas and guest appearances by foreign theatre groups. Note that subsidies have been drastically cut with the crisis, meaning that fewer and fewer performances are taking place.

The theatre is just one component of what was one of the most important sanctuaries in the ancient world, dedicated to **Asclepios** (god of healing) and a site of pilgrimage for half a millennium, from the sixth century BC into Roman times. In addition to its medical activities, the sanctuary hosted a quadrennial festival, which followed the Isthmian Games.

The ancient theatre

Epidaurus's **ancient theatre** is the primary sight. With its backdrop of rolling hills, this 14,000-seat semicircle merges perfectly into the landscape, so well, in fact, that it was rediscovered and unearthed only in the nineteenth century. Constructed with mathematical precision, it has an extraordinary equilibrium and, as guides on the stage are forever demonstrating, near-perfect natural **acoustics** – such that you can hear coins, or even matches, dropped in the circular orchestra from the highest of the 54

SNAKES ALIVE: HEALING IN ANCIENT GREECE

Temples to **Asclepios**, god of medicine, were once found across ancient Greece, and his symbol, the **staff and serpent**, is still seen today on everything from ambulances to the logo of the World Health Organization. Although quite advanced surgical instruments have been found at Epidaurus, healing methods were far from conventional. Harmless **snakes** are believed to have been kept in the building and released at night to bestow a divinely curative forked-tongue lick. In other cases, snakes might have been used as a primitive kind of shock therapy for the mentally ill. The afflicted would have crawled in darkness through the maze-like Tholos (see below) guided by a crack of light towards the middle, where they would find themselves surrounded by writhing reptiles.

tiers of seats. Constructed of white limestone (red for the dignitaries in the front rows), the tiered seats have been repaired, though the beaten-earth stage has been retained, as in ancient times.

The museum

Most of the ruins visible today are just foundations – the sanctuary was looted by the Romans in 86 BC – but a visit to the **museum** helps identify some of the former buildings. The finds displayed show the progression of medical skills and cures used at the Asclepeion.

Asclepian Sanctuary

The **Asclepian sanctuary**, as large a site as Olympia or Delphi, holds considerable fascination, for the ruins are all of buildings with identifiable functions: hospitals for the sick, dwellings for the priest-physicians, and hotels and amusements for the fashionable visitors to the spa. The setting, a wooded valley thick with the scent of thyme and pine, is clearly that of a health farm.

The reasonably well-labelled **site** begins just past the museum, where there are remains of **Greek baths** and a huge **gymnasium** with scores of rooms leading off a great colonnaded court; in its centre the Romans built an **odeon**. To the southwest is the **stadium** used for the ancient games, while to the northeast, a small **sanctuary of Egyptian gods** suggests a strong influence on the medicine used at the site.

North of the stadium are the foundations of the **Temple of Asclepios**, and beside it a rectangular building known as the **Ávaton** or **Kimitírion**. Patients would sleep here to await a visitation from the healing god, commonly believed to assume the form of a serpent. The deep significance of the **serpent** at Epidaurus is elaborated in the circular **Tholos**, one of the best-preserved buildings on the site. Its inner foundation walls form a labyrinth, thought to have been used as a snakepit (see box, above). Another theory is that the labyrinth was used as an initiation chamber for the priests of Asclepios, who underwent a symbolic death and rebirth, a common theme in ancient religion.

ARRIVAL AND INFORMATION   EPIDAURUS

By bus Most people take in Epidaurus as a day-trip from Athens or Náfplio: there are also special buses to the site from Náfplio and Athens on show days (Athens ☎ 21051 34588; Náfplio ☎ 27520 27323). Buses only go up to the site June–Sept; the rest of the year they stop at *Café Tzaní*, 1.5km from the site.
Destinations Athens (2 daily; 2hr); Náfplio (2–4 daily; 45min).

ACCOMMODATION AND EATING

★**Leonidas** Paleá Epídhavros ☎ 27520 22115. Great traditional taverna serving the standard Greek dishes, with a garden out the back; you'd be wise to book ahead if your visit coincides with a performance at the ancient theatre. Actors eat here after shows, and photos on the wall feature the likes of François Mitterrand and Sir Peter Hall. Mains around €15. June–Sept daily 9am–3pm & 6pm–midnight.

Southwest Argolid

The roads across and around the southern tip of the Argolid are sensational scenic rides, though the handful of resorts here, such as **Toló** and **Pórto Héli**, lack character and are generally overdeveloped. They are, however, good bases for those who want to combine a beach holiday with ancient sightseeing.

Toló

Some 9km southeast of Náfplio, **TOLÓ** is a functioning fishing village with a long stretch of sandy beach that has made it very popular with package tour groups. Nevertheless, the old marina facing a bay punctuated by three small, pine-clad islands has considerable charm.

ARRIVAL AND INFORMATION   TOLÓ

By bus The bus station is by the harbour, with regular services from Náfplio (9–12 daily; 20min).

ACCOMMODATION

★Minoa Hotel Aktís 56 ☎27520 59207, ⓦminoanhotels.com/en. At the edge of the long beach close to the marina and right by the bus stop and public parking area, this three-star hotel is the best budget option in town. The buffet breakfast (included) and dinner are surprisingly good. Half board €15 extra. **€65**

Pórto Héli

Extensive, developed **PÓRTO HÉLI** has pretty waterfront views around a roughly circular bay, numerous accommodation options and is popular with yachters exploring the Argo-Saronic islands. It is much easier to come here by ferry from Pireás than by bus from Athens or even Náfplio.

ARRIVAL AND INFORMATION   PÓRTO HÉLI

By bus There are no direct buses from Náfplio to Pórto Héli. You must change buses at Kranídhi (3–4 daily Mon–Sat; 1hr) and then take the local bus to Porto Héli (3–4 daily; 30 min).
By ferry and hydrofoil The ferry and hydrofoil departure port is at the centre of the seafront.
Destinations Pireás (3–5 daily; 2hr 30min); Póros (1–3 daily; 2hr); Spétses (3–5 daily; 15min); Ýdhra (3–4 daily; 1hr).
By water-taxi Water-taxis run every 10–15min to Spétses, from Costa, 3km south of the port.
Tourist information Travel agent Hellenic Vision (☎27540 51544, ✉portoheli@hellenicvision.gr) on the war memorial square, books hydrofoils, rents cars and can find accommodation.

ACCOMMODATION

★Nautica Bay ☎27540 51415, ⓦwww .nauticabayhotel.gr. This is a well-equipped resort with a bar, a sizeable pool and a variety of activities, including tennis and volleyball courts, table tennis and miniature golf. There are nine buildings in total and most rooms have balconies with sea or pool views. Breakfast included. March–Sept. **€65**
Rozos ☎27540 51416, ⓦhotelrozos.com. Large, beige-coloured hotel with airy, comfortable rooms, all with sea-view balconies (although they also look down on the busy road in front). Breakfast included. April–Oct. **€65**

The east coast: south to Leonídhio

The **road south** closely follows the coastline, winding through empty, mountainous terrain. Considering its proximity to Náfplio – and Athens – the whole stretch is enjoyably low-key and comparatively unexploited. More popular with Greek holiday-makers than with foreign tourists, the few resorts along here may be fully booked well in advance for the mid-June to mid-August Greek school holidays.

Leonídhio and around

The first town of note that you come to, if you're heading south from Náfplion or Árgos, is **LEONÍDHIO** (Leonídhion in formal Greek). Gigantic ochre cliffs that wouldn't

FROM TOP MANI TOWERHOUSES (P.166); PHILIPPEION RUINS (P.188) >

look out of place in the deserts of the American Southwest or the Canary Islands provide a dramatic backdrop to this red-roofed market town, as it slopes down almost to the sea. This prosperous and traditional place sees little need to pander to tourists, most of whom head for the coast, either Leonídhio's diminutive port, **Pláka**, or the tiny neighbouring resort of **Poúlithra**.

Pláka

4km east of Leonídhio

2

PLÁKA, Leonídhio's port and beach, is a delightful place consisting of a harbour and some charming **sleeping** and **eating** options. It has a fine pebble beach, which in recent years has become popular with Greek and foreign tourists, plus a sporadic influx of yachters.

Poúlithra

3km south of Pláka

The small, attractive resort of **POÚLITHRA**, with little development, makes a relaxing staging post. Accommodation is generally easy to find and there are tavernas near the narrow strip of beach. From here, the road heads inland to small, isolated mountain villages, which lead down eventually to Monemvasiá.

Inland from Leonídhio

The route inland from **Leonídhio** climbing through the huge **Dhafnón gorge**, is worth taking for its own sake, although the views are even better if this route is covered in the reverse direction, descending through the gorge to Leonídhio.

ARRIVAL AND DEPARTURE — LEONÍDHIO AND AROUND

By bus Buses stop in Leonídhio to the right of the bridge over the river (T 27570 22255; W ktelarkadias.gr).
Destinations Athens (2–3 daily; 3hr); Pláka (July–Aug hourly; 10min) and Poúlithra (July–Aug Mon, Wed & Fri 2 daily; 15min); Tripoli (1–2 daily; 2hr 30min).

ACCOMMODATION AND EATING

PLÁKA

Dionysos T 27570 23455 E hoteldionysosplaka@gmail.com. Appealing small hotel with quirky decoration and friendly management, just steps away from the beach (opposite *Michel-Margaret*). All rooms have three beds and come with a/c, TV, plus balconies with sea views. Easter–Oct. €45

★**Michel-Margaret** T 27570 22379. Despite the foreign name, this taverna has been run by the Bekerou family = since 1830, with great attention to quality and service. Enjoy the views from the spacious terrace while savouring the cuisine: massive salads made with ingredients from their own farm (€6), Greek standards (moussaka €8) and fresh seafood (kalamári €9). Daily 9am–1am.

POÚLITHRA

Kyma T 27570 51250 or T 69327 89570, W kyma-poulithra.gr. Rooms and self-catering apartments are available here, in a garden setting, which is relatively lush for this arid region, 10m from the sea. Facilities include en-suite bathrooms, balconies and parking. June–Sept. €35

Mirtoön T 27570 51339. This simple, traditional taverna serves good Greek food from a standard menu, with dishes ranging from €5 to €8. Wash it down with the local rosé, served chilled in a terracotta jug, for about €3/half-litre. Dine inside or out on the sea-view terrace. Daily 10am–midnight.

The southeast

The isolated southeasternmost "finger" of the Peloponnese comprises a dramatic and underpopulated landscape of harsh mountains and poor, dry, rocky soil. The highlight here is the extraordinarily preserved Byzantine enclave of **Monemvasiá** – an essential visit for any tour of the southern Peloponnese. The rest of this slim peninsula is little visited by tourists, except for the area around **Neápoli**, the most southerly town in mainland Greece, which offers access to the islet of **Elafónissos**, just offshore, and to the larger island of **Kýthira**. This may begin to change now that the new highway is completed, joining the main Kalamata-Kórinthos motorway to Monemvasia and a new fast road from Monemvasiá to Neápoli.

Monemvasiá

MONEMVASIÁ, standing impregnable on a great island-like irruption of rock, was the medieval seaport and commercial centre of the Byzantine Peloponnese. Its modern mainland service town is called **Yéfira**, from which a 1km **causeway** takes visitors out to the medieval site. Divided into the inhabited lower town and the ruined upper town, it's a fascinating mix of atmospheric heritage, careful restoration and sympathetic redevelopment.

Fortified on all approaches, it was invariably the last outpost of the Peloponnese to fall to invaders, and was only ever taken through siege. Even today, it differs deeply in character from the nearby mainland.

Brief history

Founded by the **Byzantines** in the sixth century, Monemvasiá soon became an important port. It later served as the chief commercial port of the Despotate of Mystra and was for all practical purposes the Greek Byzantine capital, with a population of almost sixty thousand. Like Mystra, Monemvasiá had something of a golden age in the thirteenth century, when it was populated by a number of noble Byzantine families and reaped considerable wealth from estates inland, wine production (Malvasia, from which Malmsey wine comes) and from their own roving corsairs who preyed on shipping heading for the East.

When the rest of the Moreas fell to the Turks in 1460, Monemvasiá was able to seal itself off, placing itself first under the control of the papacy, later under the **Venetians**. Only in 1540 did the **Turks** gain control, after the Venetians had abandoned their garrison following the defeat of their navy at Préveza.

Monemvasiá was again thrust to the fore during the **War of Independence**, when, in July 1821, after a terrible siege and wholesale massacre of the Turkish inhabitants, it became the first of the major Turkish fortresses to fall. After the war, there was no longer any need for such strongholds and, with shipping moving to the Corinth Canal, the town drifted into a village existence, its buildings allowed to fall into ruin. By **World War II**, only eighty families remained. Today it enjoys a renaissance with a permanent population of a thousand, while much restoration work has been done to the houses, walls and many of the churches.

The rock: medieval Monemvasiá

From mainland Yéfira nothing can be seen of **medieval Monemvasiá** itself, which is built purely on the seaward face of **the rock**. Nor is anything revealed as you cross the causeway to the **kástro** (castle); but the 1km-long entrance road, used for parking, finally comes to a dead end at castellated walls. Once through the fortified entrance gate, narrow and tactically z-shaped, everything looms into view: in the **lower town**, clustered houses with tiled roofs and walled gardens, narrow stone streets, and distinctively Byzantine churches. High above, the extensive castle walls protect the **upper town** on the summit.

Lower town

The **lower town** once numbered forty churches and over eight hundred homes, an incredible mass of building, which explains the confusing labyrinth of alleys. A single main street – up and slightly to the left from the gateway – is lined with cafés, tavernas and souvenir shops.

At the end of this street is the lower town's main square, a beautiful public space, with a cannon and a well in its centre, and the setting for the great, vaulted **cathedral** (opening

2

hours erratic: free), built by the Byzantine emperor Andronikos II Komnenos when he made Monemvasiá a see in 1293. The largest medieval church in southern Greece, it is dedicated to Christ in Chains, Khristós Elkómenos. Inside, you can see one of the most important religious paintings in the Peloponnese, a large fourteenth-century icon of the Crucifixion to the right of the iconostasis: it was stolen in 1979, then recovered, damaged, a year later, but only returned to the church in 2011. Across the square is a domed eighteenth-century mosque, which according to local tradition was originally the church of Áyios Pétros. It now houses a small **museum** of local finds (summer Tues–Sun 8.30am–3pm; €2). Unusually for Ottoman Greece, the Christian cathedral was allowed to function during the occupation and did so beside this mosque.

Access by water is as limited as by land. In peaceful times, the town was supplied from the tiny external harbour, **Kourkoúla**, below the road as you approach the entrance gateway. The **Portello**, in town, down towards the sea, is a small gate in the sea wall; you can **swim** off the rocks here.

Upper town

The climb to the **upper town** is highly worthwhile – not least for the solitude, since most day-trippers stay down below – and it is less strenuous than it initially looks (20–30min depending on fitness). There are sheer drops from the rock face, and unfenced cisterns, so descend before dusk.

The fortifications, like those of the lower town, are substantially intact – even the **entrance gate** retains its iron slats. Within, the site is a ruin, unrestored and deserted though many structures are still recognizable, and there are information boards. The only building that is relatively complete, even though its outbuildings have long since crumbled to foundations, is the beautiful thirteenth-century **Ayía Sofía** (usually locked), a short distance up from the gateway. It was founded on the northern rim of the rock as a monastery by Andronikos II.

Beyond the church extend acres of ruins; in medieval times the population here was much greater than that of the lower town. Among the remains are the stumpy bases of Byzantine houses and public buildings, and, perhaps most striking, vast **cisterns** to ensure a water supply in time of siege. Its weak point was its food supply, which had to be entirely imported from the mainland. In the last siege, by Mavromihalis's Maniot army in the War of Independence, the Turks were reduced to eating rats and, so the propagandists claimed, Greek children.

Yéfira

YÉFIRA (now also labelled "Monemvasia" on road signs, to the consternation of the inhabitants of the rock itself) is little more than a straggle of hotels, rooms and restaurants serving the rock's tourist trade. It has a pebble beach, called Oúga, though for a proper swim, it's best to head 3–4km north along the coast to Porí. Alternatively, take a separate road to the very clean, northern, Kastráki beach, by the Cyclopean walls of ancient **Epidavros Limira**, where snorkellers can see further marble remains from the site, underwater, as well as the wreckage of a sunken German warship.

ARRIVAL AND INFORMATION

MONEMVASIÁ

By bus Buses arrive in the modern mainland village of Yéfira, from where a minibus shuttles across to the rock every 30min (Nov–April Mon–Thurs 8am–2pm, Fri–Sun 8am–10pm; May to mid-June & mid-Sept–Oct Mon–Fri 8am–10pm, Sat–Sun 8am–midnight; mid-June to mid-Sept daily 8am–midnight; €2.20). All buses connect with Spárti, although they are not timed to allow a day-visit from there.
Destinations Athens (3–4 daily 4hr); Spárti (3–4 daily; 1hr 30min).

Tourist information Travel agent Malvasia Travel (☎27320 61752) in Yéfira can help with rooms, bus tickets and car or scooter rental (Nov–March Mon–Fri 7am–3pm; May & Oct Mon–Fri 7am–3pm & 5–7pm; June–Aug 7am–3pm & 5–8.30pm).
Services Yéfira has a bank, three ATMs and a post office. There are no ATMs in the kastro.

ACCOMMODATION

Accommodation in the kástro itself is expensive and from June to Sept you should book months ahead. For cheaper hotel options, check out Yéfira.

MONEMVASIÁ

Byzantino ☎ 27320 61351, ⓦ hotelbyzantino.com. This elegant, historic property features a range of rooms with period details, some with balconies and sea views. All rooms come with a/c and vary widely in price depending on the view. Breakfast included. **€65**

Lazareto ☎ 27320 61992, ⓦ lazareto.gr. On the rock itself – 800m from the KTEL bus stop and about 1km from the Kastro gate – but in the formidable shadow of the kastro, this is a luxury resort complex with access to the sea, a pool, a spa and parking facilities. It's a collection of traditional stone buildings with comfortable, sleekly modern rooms shaded by mulberry trees. Try to book the suite in the restored Venetian tower. Breakfast included. **€135**

★ **Malvasia Traditional Hotels** ☎ 27320 61323, ⓦ malvasiahotel-traditional.gr. This well-appointed complex occupies three separate buildings between the main street and the sea as well as the more modern hotel *Malvasia* at the end of the main commercial road. Call first at the common reception, just after the main gateway and they will direct you to your building. Breakfast included. April–Oct. **€65**

YÉFIRA

Filoxenía ☎ 27320 61716, ⓦ filoxenia-monemvasia .gr. Located just north of the causeway, this modern hotel has comfortable rooms with a/c and large balconies with views of the sea and the rock. Prices almost double in high season. Breakfast included. **€40**

Flower of Monemvasia ☎ 27320 61395, ⓦ flower-hotel.gr. Just inland of the road, this pleasant, red-tile-roofed property has self-catering rooms with kitchenette, a/c and balconies with panoramic views. Great shoulder-season offers are available through the hotel website. Breakfast included. **€50**

★ **Kinsterna** Áyios Stéfanos ☎ 27320 66300, ⓦ kinsternahotel.gr. One of the finest hotels in Greece, this seventeenth-century manor has been converted to a luxury hotel and spa, overlooking the rock, some 8km south of Yéfira. With its period olive press, open cistern and grape-stomping vat, it's like staying in an open-air museum and well worth the price. Check the many special offers on its website. Breakfast included. **€210**

EATING

Chrisóvoulo Kástro ☎ 27320 62022, ⓦ chrisovoulo.gr. A snazzy, successful fine-dining place in the Kastro, 10m up some steep steps off the main commercial street (signposted). There's creative Greek cooking on the à la carte menu, as well as several four-course menus from €28. April–Oct daily 8.30am–midnight,

Matoúla Kástro ☎ 27320 61660, ⓦ matoula.gr. This family taverna, established in 1950, offers both excellent food and a leafy garden overlooking the sea. Main courses here hover around €8. Everything, including the plump *dolmádhes (€9)*, is home-made. Daily noon–11pm;

closed two weeks in winter.

To Kanoni Kástro ☎ 27320 61387. A friendly place in the main square that serves traditional Greek food but is better known for its Italian pizza and pasta dishes (€10–13). Try to book a table on the balcony overlooking the sea. March–Oct daily 8am–midnight.

Trata Yéfira ☎ 27320 62084. Just at the beginning of the causeway, this seafood ouzerí occupies an inviting converted fisherman's hut. The delicious fish soup starter is a meal in itself and the mussel pilau at €8 a veritable feast. Daily: May–Oct 8am–1am; Nov–April 10am–10pm.

Neápoli

NEÁPOLI (full name Neápoli Voïón), 42km south of Monemvasiá, is a mix of old buildings and modern Greek concrete behind a grey-sand beach with views of **Kýthira** and **Elafónissos** islands. The new road from the northeast has cut the journey time from Monemvasiá to Neápoli down to twenty minutes opening up this rarely visited part of Greece.

Neápoli **beach** extends northwest to Vigláfia village and the little harbour of **Poúnda**, some 12km west of Neápoli, with frequent vehicle ferry crossings over the short strait to Elafónissos island. To the left of Pounda ferry docks, and beyond the sand spit, lie the submerged ruins of **Pavlopétri**, an ancient city beneath the waves, that featured in a recent BBC documentary and has become a popular snorkelling destination.

ARRIVAL AND DEPARTURE

NEÁPOLI

By bus The KTEL bus station is on Leofóros Dhimokratías 7 (☎ 27340 23222).

Destinations Athens (3 daily; 6hr); Spárti (3 daily; 2hr 30min).

By ferry Ferries leave from the jetty at the junction of Voïon and Ayias Triadhas streets (☎ 276340 22228).

Ferry tickets are available from the office of the Vatika Bay Shipping Agency (☎ 27340 24004/29004, ⓦ vatikabay.gr) about 200m after entering the town from the north.

Destinations Andikýthira (June–Sept 1 weekly; 2hr 30min); Kýthira (June–Sept 1–2 daily; 1hr 15min).

GETTING AROUND

By taxi Taxis can be ordered on ☎ 27340 22590.

ACCOMMODATION

Aïvalí Akti Voïon 164 ☎ 27340 22287, ⓦ aivalihotel.gr. This clean, unpretentious hotel is right on the seafront, near the ferry for Kýthira. Rooms (completely refurbished in 2014) have a/c and balconies, all facing the water, though family suites look towards the back. Breakfast included. **€45**

Limina Mare Voïion 230 ☎ 27340 22236, ⓦ limiramare.gr. Elegant and comfortable hotel northwest of the waterfront, most of whose beautifully furnished rooms – some with four poster beds – come with views of Elafonissos opposite. Good garden restaurant, free parking and a large buffet breakfast included. **€70**

Elafónissos

Part of the mainland until 375 AD, when an earthquake separated it, **ELAFÓNISSOS** is just 19 square kilometres and gets very busy in the short summer season, when its 700-odd resident population is vastly outnumbered by visitors. The island's eponymous town is largely modern, but has plenty of hotels, plus some good fish tavernas.

One of the island's two surfaced roads leads 5km southeast to **Símos**, one of the best **beaches** in this part of Greece, a large double bay with fine pale sand heaped into dunes and views to Kýthira; a *kaïki* (boat) leaves from the town to Símos every morning in summer. To the southwest of town is the small, scattered settlement of Káto Nisí, and **Panayítsa** beach, quieter than Símos but almost as beautiful, with views to the Máni peninsula. There is a petrol station on the Panayítsa road.

ARRIVAL AND DEPARTURE

ELAFÓNISSOS

By ferry Ferries to the island leave from Poúnda docks, which are located 12km west of Neápoli (June–Sept 2 hourly; Oct–May every 1–2 hours; 10min; ☎ 27340 61117, ⓦ elafonissos.gr).

ACCOMMODATION AND EATING

ELAFÓNISSOS TOWN

Voúla ☎ 27340 61320 ⓦ voularesort.gr. A romantic resort with a large landscaped garden and rooms with designer furniture that feels secluded enough to appeal to couples, although it's located just 500m south of the ferry dock. Buffet breakfast included. Two nights minimum. May–Sept. **€70**

★**Menti Brothers** ☎ 27340 61263. This taverna, towards the end of the harbour, serves the freshest fish on the island – the catch of the day is chosen each

morning – at affordable prices. Their speciality is shrimp (€15). June–Sept daily noon–midnight.

SÍMOS

Simos Camping and Bungalows ☎ 27340 22672, ⓦ simoscamping.gr. Well-equipped campsite, 4km from the harbour, at the western end of the beach. There are bungalows (with a/c and fridges) as well as campsites, plus a minimarket and restaurant. May–Oct. Camping **€22**, bungalow **€60**

Kýthira

Isolated at the foot of the Peloponnese, the island of **KÝTHIRA** traditionally belongs to the Ionian islands, and shares their history of **Venetian** and, later, **British** rule; under the former it was known as Cerigo. For the most part, similarities end there. The island architecture of whitewashed houses and flat roofs looks more like that of the Cyclades. The landscape is different, too: wild scrub- and gorse-covered hills, or moorland sliced by deep valleys and ravines. Though badly affected by **emigration** tourism has brought some prosperity but most summer visitors are Greeks. For the few foreigners who reach Kýthira, it remains something of a refuge, with its undeveloped **beaches** a principal attraction.

2

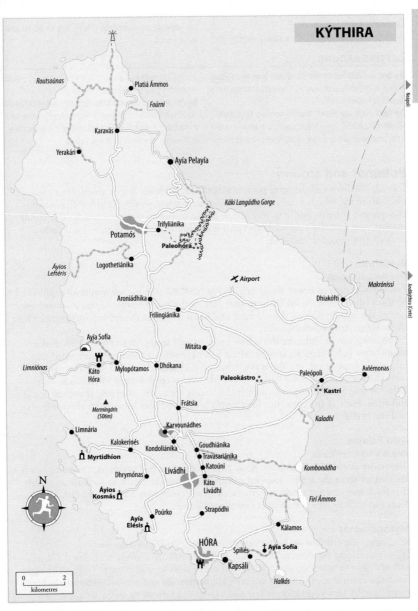

KÝTHIRA

Routsoúnas

Platiá Ámmos

Foúrni

Karavás

Yerakári

Ayía Pelayía

Náfpli

Káki Langádha Gorge

Trifyliánika

Potamós

Paleohóra

Áyios Leftéris

Logothetiánika

Airport

Makrónissi

Aroniádhika

Dhiakófti

Andíkythira (Crete)

Frilingiánika

Ayía Sofía

Mitáta

Limniónas

Káto Hóra

Mylopótamos

Dhókana

Avlémonas

Paleópoli

Paleokástro

Kastrí

Mermingáris
(506m)

Frátsia

Kaladhí

Limnária

Karvounádhes

Kalokerinés

Kondoliánika

Goudhiánika

Kombonádha

Myrtidhíon

Travasariánika

Katoúni

Dhrymónas

Livádhi

Firí Ámmos

Áyios Kosmás

Káto Livádhi

Poúrko

Strapódhi

Ayía Elésis

Kálamos

HÓRA

Spiliés

Ayía Sofía

Kapsáli

Halkós

N

0   2
kilometres

ARRIVAL AND INFORMATION

By air Kýthira's Alexander Onassis airport is deep in the interior, 8km southeast of Potamós (☎ 27360 33297): taxis to Livadhi cost €14 (☎ 27360 31160, ⓦ drakakistours.com).

Destinations Athens (1–2 daily; 45min).

By ferry The huge all-weather harbour at Dhiakófti is the arrival point for Neápoli and Andikýthira ferries (ⓦ kythera .gr). Dhiakófti has a sandy beach and a few places to stay, but most people move on quickly.

Destinations Andikýthira (high season 1 weekly; 2hr);

Neápoli (June–Sept 1–2 daily; 1hr 15min).

Information and services ⓦ kythera.gr is a useful website. Potamós town has tavernas, a bank ATM, a post office and petrol stations. Hóra has a couple of banks with ATMs and a post office on the main square. Drakakis Tours in Livadhi (☎ 27360 31160, ⓦ drakakistours.com) and El Greco at Ayía Pelayía (☎ 27360 33903, ⓦ elgrecotours.gr) can organize accommodation, ferry and air tickets plus excursions. A.

GETTING AROUND

By bus The only bus on the island runs from Ayía Pelayía (July & Aug 1 daily each way) to Hóra (40min) then on to Kapsáli (a further 10min).

By taxi There are fewer than 20 licensed taxis on the whole of the island, so make sure you have transport to and from your hotel pre-arranged. Taxis from the port charge

around €25 to Kapsáli and €18 to Potamós, but you should establish a price beforehand.

By car, motorbike and bike Panayotis, based in Kapsáli (☎ 27360 31004, ⓦ panayotis-rent-a-car.gr), rents cars, motorbikes, mountain bikes and scooters: it also has offices at Dhiakófti, the airport and Ayía Pelayía.

Potamós and around

Inland, northwest of the ferry port, is **POTAMÓS**, Kýthira's largest town. It's a pleasant, unspoilt place, which makes a perfect lunch stop when you're exploring the island, though you should choose to stay at one of the towns on or near a beach. The **Sunday market** here (usually around 8am–4pm) is the island's biggest event – local cafés provide live music to coincide.

Paleohóra

About 3km east of Potamós

Few people seem to know about or visit **PALEOHÓRA**, the ruined **medieval capital** of Kýthira (then called Áyios Dhimítrios), despite the fact that these remains constitute one of the best Byzantine sites around and boast a spectacular setting, surrounded by a sheer 100m drop on three sides.

The town was built in the thirteenth century, and when Mystra fell to the Turks, many of its noble families sought refuge here. Despite its seemingly concealed and impregnable position, the site was discovered and **sacked** in 1537 by Barbarossa, commander of the Turkish fleet, and the island's seven thousand inhabitants were killed or sold into slavery. The principal remains are of the surviving **churches**, some still with traces of **frescoes** (but kept firmly locked, so peer in through the windows), and the **castle**.

Ayía Pelayía

About 4km northeast of Potamós

The resort of **AYÍA PELAYÍA** has a good choice of **rooms** and **tavernas**; the main beaches are cleaner since the ferries stopped coming here, but the beach at Kalamítsa, a 2km dirt track away to the south, is better – the track continues on to the mouth of the Kakí Langádha gorge which offers excellent hiking.

Mylopótamos

Head south from Potamós for about 4km, then take the westbound turning for another couple of kilometres

It's worth taking the time to stop off at **MYLOPÓTAMOS**, a lovely traditional village and a shady oasis in summer, set in a wooded valley with a small stream. Follow the signs from the main square to find a series of old **watermills** and a small **waterfall**, hidden from view by lush vegetation where you can have a refreshing swim.

Ayía Sofía cave

June–Aug daily10am–5pm, though times are irregular; call first ☎ 27360 31213 /31731• €5 (includes guided tour) • A 30min signposted walk from Mylopótamos, or a short drive along a paved road off the Limniónas road

Most visitors come to Mylopótamos to see the **Ayía Sofía cave**, the largest and most impressive of a number of caverns on the island. The cave's entrance has been used as a **church** and has an iconostasis carved from the rock, with important Byzantine **frescoes** on it. Beyond, the cave system comprises a series of **chambers**, which reach 250m into the mountain, although the guided tour (in Greek and English) only takes in the more interesting outer chambers.

2

ACCOMMODATION AND EATING   POTAMÓS AND AROUND

POTAMÓS

★**Panaretos** ☎ 27360 34290. Traditional, lively taverna that dominates the central square, with indoor seating in the main restaurant below. Farm-to-table produce all year; try the tenderloin in thyme sauce or aubergines baked with local cheese. Mains (€13–15). Daily noon–midnight; Nov–March closed Sun.

AYÍA PELAYÍA

Kaleris ☎ 27360 33461. The chef here specializes in inventive, original versions of a whole range of Greek and Mediterranean dishes, such as chicken risotto with parmesan cheese. Expect to pay about €15/person. April–Oct daily noon–midnight.

★**Venardos** ☎ 27360 34100, ⓦ venardos-hotels.gr. Extensive hotel complex with hilltop views and just a short walk from the beach. Rooms range from standard doubles to suites and studios, and facilities include parking, a pool and spa, as well as hikes and excursions. Breakfast included. €60

MYLOPÓTAMOS

Plátanos ☎ 27360 33397. This shady café-taverna above the village spring with a beautifully painted ceiling makes a pleasant stop for a meal. It serves standard Greek main courses from €10, but it's the home-made local sweets such as avgokalamara (fried dough wraps in honey) that are the highlight. Easter–Oct daily 9am–1am.

Kapsáli and the south

KAPSÁLI, on the **south coast**, is largely devoted to summer tourism – in fact, much of it closes down from September to June. Most savvy foreign visitors to Kýthira in summer stay here, and it's a popular port of call for yachts, particularly since it is sheltered from the strong north winds of summer. Set behind double-coved beaches and looked over by a **castle**, as well as the tiny white **monastery** of Áyios Ioánnis Éngremmos perched high on grey cliffs, it is certainly memorable.

Hóra

HÓRA (or Kýthira Town), the island's picturesque capital, is a steep 2km haul above Kapsáli, and is quite somnolent in comparison. It enjoys an equally dramatic position, however, with its Cycladic-style houses tiered on the ridge leading to its very own Venetian **castle**. Below the castle are both the remains of older Byzantine walls and, in Mésa Voúrgo, numerous well-signed but securely locked Byzantine churches.

Archeological Museum

Tues–Sun: summer 8am–8pm; winter 8am–3pm • €4

Reopened in 2016 with a new permanent exhibition, the modern **Archeological Musuem** has walk-through multimedia displays covering the eras from 9000BC to Hellenistic times. The most interesting finds include the emblematic Lion of Kýthira, an Archaic-era marble lion statue (525–500BC), and those from the Minoan temple at Áyios Yeóryios, whose wealth of bronze statuettes constitutes the biggest such treasure haul outside Crete.

Hóra's castle

Daily 8am–7pm • Free

Hóra's castle is a must mostly for the breathtaking 360-degree **panorama** it affords over the entire area. Within the castle walls, most of the buildings are in ruins, except for the

2

paired churches of Panayía Myrtidhiótissa and the smaller Panayía Orfaní (Catholic and Orthodox respectively, under the Venetian occupation). There are spectacular **views** down to Kapsáli and out to sea to the chunk of inaccessible islet known as **Avgó** (Egg), legendary **birthplace of Aphrodite**. On its cliffs grow the endemic yellow-flowered everlasting *sempreviva*, used locally for making small dried flower arrangements (which you see for sale in every shop), symbol of the goddess's eternal beauty.

ACCOMMODATION AND EATING   KAPSÁLI AND THE SOUTH

In high season, you must book ahead in Kapsáli. Finding a hotel up in Hóra, away from the beach, is easier.

KAPSÁLI

Hýtra ☎ 27360 37200. This appealing harbourside taverna offers all the best of Greek traditional cookery with beachfront seating – expect dishes such as extraordinary stewed broad green beans in season, or satisfying eats such as burgers (€9). April–Oct daily 11am–11pm.

Porto Delfino ☎ 27360 31940, ⓦ portodelfino.gr. Individual bungalows, recently renovated in a great location overlooking Kapsáli with both sea and kástro views, an infinity pool, bar, garden and restaurant. Breakfast included. May–Oct. **€120**

HÓRA

Castello Apartments ☎ 27360 31069, ⓦ castelloapts-kythera.gr. This cheerful structure, on the Kapsáli side

of town, is in a garden setting with great views all around. The nine self-catering studios and one apartment are the epitome of tranquillity – some have balconies and views. **€40**

Margarita ☎ 27360 31711, ⓦ hotel-margarita.com. This beautiful, immaculately maintained 1840s mansion just below the main street offers wonderful views of the coast and the castle, and has very friendly and helpful staff. The buffet breakfast costs €10/person. Prices double in Aug. April–Oct. **€50**

Zorba's ☎ 27360 31655. By far the best value grill taverna in town – only €15 for a full meal, with specialities such as *kondosoúvli* (a kind of chicken kebab), served on a roof terrace. May–Sept daily 7pm–midnight.

Avlémonas

The prettiest destination on the east coast is **Avlémonas**, on a rocky bay at the top of this coast. It's a small **fishing port** with an end-of-the-world feel as you approach from a distance. It becomes much more attractive once reached, and has a remarkable coordination of colour schemes throughout the village. There is a small **Venetian fortress** and little coves with some of the clearest water around, fine for **swimming**.

ACCOMMODATION AND EATING   AVLÉMONAS

Maryianni ☎ 27360 33316, ⓦ maryianni.gr. This bright, pleasantly landscaped complex is the closest to the sea. Rooms are fully self-catering (including a washing machine) and offer great views from private terraces to the kastro, the sea or the garden. Book well in advance. **€80**

Sotiris ☎ 27360 33722. This taverna, with seating overlooking the sparkling little cove, offers a wide selection of fresh, well-prepared and decently priced fish dishes (around €65/kg). If you feel in a lavish mood, order the *astakomakaronádha* (lobster spaghetti). Daily noon–midnight.

Andikýthira

Thirteen kilometres to the south of Kýthira, the tiny, wind-blown 22-square-kilometre island of **ANDIKÝTHIRA** is linked to its bigger sister by a sporadic ferry service. Rocky and poor, and a site of political exile until 1964, the island only received electricity in 1984, but it has one remarkable claim to fame: the **Andikythera Mechanism** (see p.86). Local attractions include good birdlife (a bird observatory has been built in the old school at Lazianá) and flora, but it's not the place if you want company, with only 45 permanent residents (500 in the summer) divided among a scattering of settlements – mainly in **Potamós**, the harbour, and **Sohória**, the village. Ferries permitting, the **festival of Áyios Mýron** is held here on August 17 – an annual reunion jamboree for the Andikytheran diaspora.

Excavation work above Xeropótamos has revealed the site of ancient **Aigila**, a 75-acre fortress city of the Hellenistic period. At the harbour below are the remains of one of ancient Greece's best-preserved warship slipways, a *neosoikos*, carved out of the rock. The organization Dig Kythera (⊕krg.org.au) can arrange volunteer excavation work either at Andikýthira or Kýthira.

ARRIVAL AND INFORMATION

By ferry Andikýthira has, theoretically, a weekly summer connection with Kýthira (2hr), but landings are often impossible due to adverse weather.

ACCOMMODATION AND EATING

You can camp in the open anywhere on the island - hardcore campers only. There are a couple of tavernas and a village shop at Sohória, but you should bring plenty of supplies with you.

Antikythera Rooms Potamós ☎27360 33004. The only official accommodation on the island, this hostel-like set of rooms with shared bathroom is run by the local community. Call, and they may find you rooms rented by villagers, as well. June–Sept. €20

Spárti (Sparta) and around

The central core of the Peloponnese is the luxuriantly spreading Mount Ménalo; but due south, in the Lakonian Evrótas valley, are **Spárti** and its Byzantine companion, **Mystra**, both overlooked and sheltered from the west by the massive and astonishing wall of the **Taïyetos** mountain ridge. Spárti had a big role in the development of ancient Greece, while Mystra, arrayed in splendour on its own hillside, is one of the country's most compelling historical sites.

Spárti

Despite lying on the site of the ancient city-state of Sparta, modern **SPÁRTI**, capital of **Lakonía**, has few ancient ruins, and is today merely the administrative centre of a huge agricultural plain. Spárti's appeal lies in its very ordinariness – the pedestrianized side streets, café-lined squares and evening *vólta*. The reason for coming here is basically to see the Byzantine town of **Mystra**, 5km to the west, which once controlled great swaths of the medieval world.

Brief history

Commanding the Lakonian plain and fertile Evrótas valley from a series of low hills just west of the river, **ancient Sparta** was at the height of its power from the eighth to the fourth century BC, a period when its society was structured according to extremely harsh laws (see box, p.158). The ancient "capital" occupied more or less the site of today's town, though it was in fact less a city than a grouping of villages. **Lykurgos**, architect of the warlike Spartan constitution and society, declared that "it is men not walls that make a city".

The Spartans famously defeated Athens in the **Peloponnesian War** between 431 and 421 BC and later established colonies around the Greek world. They eventually lost hegemony through defeat to Thebes. A second period of prosperity came under the Romans – for whom this was an outpost in the south of Greece, with the Máni never properly subdued. However, from the third century AD Sparta declined, as nearby Mystra became the focus of Byzantine interest.

The annual September **Spartathlon**, a 246km run from Athens to Spárti, commemorates the messenger Pheidippides who ran the same route in 490 BC: the current course record is 20 hours and 25 minutes.

A SPARTAN UPBRINGING

As the blood-spattered 2006 film *300* confirms, the famously tough Spartans can still stir the imagination. In part, this stems from their legendary upbringing. Under a system known as the **agoge**, Spartan boys were rigorously trained by the state to develop physical toughness, loyalty and cunning. Babies judged unlikely to make the grade were left exposed on the slopes of Mount Taïyetos. Other boys were taken from their families at the age of seven to live in barracks. They were habitually underfed, so that they would learn to live off the land. At the age of twelve, they were required to form a sexual bond with a young Spartan soldier, who would act as their mentor. At eighteen, they would become provisional members of the army until the age of thirty, when it would finally be decided if they were worthy of **Spartan citizenship**. At this point they were expected to marry and produce offspring. The system was much admired in the ancient world, and boys from other city-states were sometimes sent here for their education.

Acropolis

Daily: April–Oct 8am–8pm; Nov–March 8am–3pm • Free

There are a few ruins to be seen to the north of the city. From the bold **Statue of Leonidas**, hero of Thermopylae, at the top of Paleológou, follow the track around and behind the modern stadium towards the old **acropolis**, tallest of the Spartan hills. An immense **theatre** here, built into the side of the hill, can be quite clearly traced, even though today most of its masonry has gone – hurriedly adapted for fortification when the Spartans' power declined and, later still, recycled for the building of Byzantine Mystra. Above the theatre, a sign marks a fragment of the **Temple of Athina Halkiakou**, while at the top of the acropolis sit the knee-high ruins of the tenth-century Byzantine church and monastery of **Ósios Níkon**.

Sanctuary of Artemis Orthia

24hr, though you can't walk inside the actual site • Free • ☎ 27310 23315

Out on the Trípoli road (Ton 118, just past the junction with Orthias Artémidhos), a track leads to the remains of the **Sanctuary of Artemis Orthia**. This was where Spartan boys underwent gruelling tests by flogging. The Roman geographer and travel writer **Pausanias** records that young men often perished under the lash, and the altar had to be splashed with blood before the goddess was satisfied. The Romans, addicts of morbid blood sports, revived the custom here – the main ruins are of the spectators' grandstand they built.

Archeological Museum

Cnr Lykoúrgou & Ayíoy Níkonos • Daily 8am–3pm • €2 • ☎ 27310 28575

All Spárti's moveable artefacts and mosaics have been transferred to the town's small **Archeological Museum**. Among its more interesting exhibits are a number of votive offerings found on the sanctuary site – sickles set in stone that were presented as prizes to the Spartan youths and solemnly rededicated to the goddess – and a fifth-century BC marble bust of a running Spartan hoplite, found on the acropolis and said to be Leonidas. There is a dramatic late sixth-century BC stele, with relief carvings on both sides, possibly of Menelaus with Helen and Agamemnon with Klytemnestra; the ends have carved snakes. Look out, too, for fragments of Hellenistic and Roman mosaics, and numerous small lead figurines, clay masks and bronze idols from the Artemis Orthia site.

Museum of the Olive and Greek Olive Oil

Óthonos–Amalías 129 • Wed–Mon: summer 10am–6pm; winter 10am–5pm • €3 • ☎ 27310 89315, ⓦ piop.gr

In the southwest corner of town, the informative **Museum of the Olive and Greek Olive Oil** is worth a visit for its insight into the love affair of the Greeks with the olive tree that has provided them with food, heat, soap and medicines for thousands of years. Of most interest are the olive tree fossils from fifty thousand years ago, as well as a fully functioning olive press from the nearby village of Xerokambi.

ARRIVAL AND INFORMATION

SPÁRTI AND AROUND

By bus The main bus terminal is on the eastern edge of town, at the far end of Lykoúrgou, though to reach the centre, alight earlier on Lykoúrgou, near the Archeological Museum. For bus info call ☎ 27310 26441.
Destinations Areópoli (3 daily; 2hr); Athens via Kórinthos (6–7 daily; 4hr); Kalamáta (1–2 daily; 2hr); Monemvasiá (3

daily; 1hr 30min); Mystra (6 daily; 30min); Neápoli (3 daily; 3hr); Trípoli (6–7 daily; 1hr); Pátra (1–2 daily; 6hr); Yeroliménas (2–3 daily; 3hr); Yíthio (5 daily; 1hr).
Services Most of the banks are on Paleológou. There is a good bookshop and map stockist near the corner of Paleológou and Lykoúrgou.

ACCOMMODATION

There are usually enough hotels to go around, many of them on the main avenue, Paleológou, though noise can be a problem here.

★**Dioscouri** Lycourgou 182 & Atreidon ☎ 27310 28484, ⓦ www.dioscouri.gr. The best budget option in town, in a good location with no lack of comfort. There's lots of space, art on the walls, large comfortable beds and parking possibilities – on top of that, the home-made buffet breakfast (included) is fantastic. €55
Maniatis Paleológou 72–76 ☎ 27310 22665, ⓦ www. maniatishotel.gr. Across the street from the Archeological Museum, this modern hotel – all glass and metal with blond wood trim – has good facilities: four lounge areas, a

bar and two restaurants. Rooms have spotless decor, a/c and some have views of the countryside. Buffet breakfast included. €70
Menelaïon Paleológou 91 ☎ 27310 26332, ⓦ menelaion.gr. Housed in a restored Neoclassical property this is a sleek, modern eco-friendly hotel with a bar, restaurant and swimming pool. All rooms come with high ceilings, double-glazing to prevent street noise and solar-powered hot water. Buffet breakfast included. €90

EATING AND DRINKING

★**Diethnes** Paleológou 105 ☎ 27310 28636. Long-established and reliably good, with an extensive menu of traditional Greek dishes; mains €8. There's plenty of atmosphere inside, with photographs of old Sparta on the walls, but you're best to head straight for the delightful garden filled with orange and lemon trees, and home to ten or so uninhibited terrapins. Daily 8am–late.
En Hatipi Hrysikou 27 ☎ 27310 26677. A local taverna where quality meat is grilled on hot coals,

service is friendly and relaxed, and the food tastes fantastic. Try as many dishes as you can (€6–7 for a burger). Daily noon–midnight.
Ministry Palaiologou 84 ☎ 2731 081288, ⓦ ministrymusichall.gr. Set in a former supermarket, this is a café, restaurant and cocktail bar all in one, depending on the time of day. It has convincing Moulin Rouge decor inside, while music in the evenings attract the Spartan youth. Cocktails €8. Daily 7am–late.

ACROSS THE LANGÁDHA PASS

The remote and wild **Langádha pass**, the 60km road over the **Taïyetos** mountain range from Spárti to Kalamáta, is a worthwhile scenic drive. With long uninhabited sections, it unveils a constant drama of peaks and precipitous drops, magnificent at all times but startling at sunrise; the pine forests suffered extensive damage in recent fires, but are showing signs of a comeback. This was the route Telemachus took in the *Odyssey* on his way from Nestor's palace near Pýlos (see p.183) to that of Menelaus at Sparta; his journey, by chariot, lasted a day. The road climbs steeply into the mountains and enters the **Gorge of Langádha**, a wild sequence of hairpins. The rock of Keádhas, high above the southern side of the road a short distance from the village, is where the Spartans used to leave their sick or puny babies to die. Above Keádhas is a **climbing park** with marked routes for rock climbers. At the **pass**, tracks and paths head north and south along the mountain ridge – peaks up to 1900m are accessible in a day's outing. On the Kalamáta side you enter the **Nédhondas Gorge** for the final zigzagging descent.

Mystra

Daily: summer 8am–8pm; winter 8am–3pm, though a lack of staff may mean earlier closing times, so it's best to call first and check • €12 • ☎ 27310 23315

MYSTRA is one of the most exciting and dramatic sites in the Peloponnese – a glorious, airy place, hugging a very steep, 280m foothill of Taïyetos. Winding up the lushly vegetated hillside is a remarkably intact Byzantine town that once sheltered a population of some twenty thousand, and through which you can now wander. Snaking alleys lead through monumental gates, past medieval houses and palaces, and above all into the **churches**, several of which yield superb if faded frescoes. The overall effect is of straying into a massive unearthing of architecture, painting and sculpture – and into a different age with a dramatically different mentality.

ARRIVAL AND ORIENTATION

By bus Buses run from Spárti to the *Xenia* café near the lower Mystra site entrance (6 daily; 30min; €2); they stop en route at the modern village of Néos Mystrás, 500m from the lower entrance.

Orientation The site of the Byzantine city comprises three main parts: the Káto Hóra (lower town), with the city's most important churches; the Áno Hóra (upper town), grouped around the vast shell of a royal palace; and the kástro (castle). There are two entrances to the site: one is at the base of the lower town: the other is 2km away, up near the kástro. A road loops up from the modern village of Néos Mystrás passing near both upper and lower entrances. Once inside, the site is well signposted.

ACCOMMODATION AND EATING

There are no accommodation or catering facilities at the site itself, so it's best to base yourself at nearby Néos Mystrás (see p.164) – a better, though more expensive option than Spárti, just for the relative quiet setting and easy access to the site. The nearest eating option is the *Xenia* café/restaurant, 250 metres or so outside the lower site entrance towards the town.

Brief history

In 1249, Guillaume II de Villehardouin, fourth **Frankish** prince of the Moreas, built a castle here – one of a trio of fortresses (the others at Monemvasiá and the Máni) designed to garrison his domain. The Franks, however, were driven out of Mystra by the **Byzantines** in 1262, and by the mid-fourteenth century this isolated triangle of land in the southeastern Peloponnese, which encompassed the old Spartan territories, became the **Despotate of Mystra**. This was the last province of the Greek Byzantine empire and, with Constantinople in terminal decay, its virtual capital.

During the next two centuries, Mystra was the focus of a defiant rebirth of Byzantine power before eventual subjugation by the Turks in 1460, seven years after the fall of Constantinople. Mystra remained in Turkish hands until 1687 when it was captured, briefly, by the **Venetians**. Decline set in with a second stage of Turkish control,

---

THE MYSTRA RENAISSANCE

Throughout the fourteenth century and the first decades of the fifteenth, Mystra was the principal **cultural and intellectual centre** of the Byzantine world. It attracted the finest Byzantine scholars and theologians and sponsored a **renaissance** in the arts. Most notable of the court scholars was the humanist philosopher **Gemisthus Plethon**, who revived and reinterpreted Plato's ideas, using them to support his own brand of revolutionary teachings, which included the assertions that land should be redistributed among labourers and that reason should be placed on a par with religion. Although his beliefs had limited impact in Mystra itself – whose monks excommunicated him – his followers, who taught in Italy after the fall of Mystra, exercised wide influence in Renaissance Florence and Rome.

More tangibly, Mystra also was home to the final flourish of **Byzantine architecture**, with the building of a magnificent palace for the despots and a perfect sequence of multi-domed and brilliantly frescoed churches.

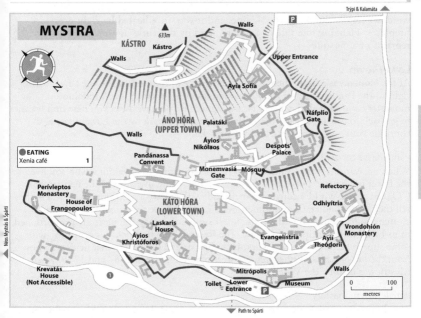

from 1715 onwards, culminating in the destruction that accompanied the **War of Independence**; the site was evacuated after fires in 1770 and 1825. **Restoration**, begun in the first decades of the twentieth century, was interrupted by the civil war – during which it was, for a while, a battle site – and renewed in earnest in the 1950s when the last inhabitants were relocated.

The kástro and Upper Town

The **kástro**, in the **Upper Town**, reached by a path direct from the upper gate, maintains the Frankish design of its original thirteenth-century construction. There is a walkway around most of the keep, with views of an intricate panorama of the town below. The castle itself was the court of Guillaume II de Villehardouin but in later years was used primarily as a citadel.

Ayía Sofía

Following a course downhill from the kástro, the first identifiable building you come to is the church of **Ayía Sofía** (1350). The chapel's finest feature is its floor, made from polychrome marble. Its frescoes, notably a *Pandokrátor* (Christ in Majesty) and *Nativity of the Virgin*, have survived reasonably well, protected until recent years by coatings of whitewash applied by the Turks, who adapted the building as a mosque.

Palatáki and the Despot's Palace

Heading down from Ayía Sofía, you have a choice of routes. The right fork winds past ruins of a Byzantine mansion, one of the oldest houses on the site, the **Palatáki** ("Small Palace"; 1250–1300), and **Áyios Nikólaos**, a large seventeenth-century building decorated with unsophisticated paintings. The left fork is more interesting, passing the fortified **Náfplio Gate**, which was the principal entrance to the upper town, and the vast, multistorey, Gothic-looking complex of the **Despots' Palace** (1249–1400). Most prominent among its numerous rooms is a great vaulted audience hall, built at right angles to the line of the building; its ostentatious windows regally dominate the skyline, and it was once heated by eight great fireplaces. Flanking one side of a square, used by the Turks as a marketplace, are the remains of a **mosque**.

Lower Town

At the **Monemvasiá Gate**, there is a further choice of routes down to the **Lower Town**: right to the Pandánassa and Perivléptos monasteries or left to the **Vrondohíou** monastery and cathedral, all very clearly signed. If you have a car, you may find it easier to go back to the upper gate, then drive down to and park by the Lower Gate and continue your visit from there (keep your ticket).

Pandánassa convent

When excavations were resumed in 1952, the last thirty or so families who still lived in the lower town were moved out to Néos Mystrás. Only five nuns of the **Pandánassa** ("Queen of the World") **convent** remain today; they have a reception room where they sell their own handicrafts and sometimes offer fresh juice to visitors. The convent's church, built in 1428, is perhaps the finest surviving in Mystra, perfectly proportioned in its blend of Byzantine and Gothic. The **frescoes** date from various centuries, with some superb fifteenth-century work, including one in the gallery that depicts scenes from the life of Christ. Other frescoes were painted between 1687 and 1715, when Mystra was held by the Venetians.

Perívleptos monastery

The diminutive **Perívleptos monastery** (1310), a single-domed church, partially carved out of the rock, contains Mystra's most complete cycle of frescoes, almost all of which date from the fourteenth century. They are in some ways finer than those of the Pandánassa; they blend an easy humanism with the spirituality of the Byzantine icon traditions. The position of each figure depended upon its sanctity, and so upon the dome the image of heaven is the *Pandokrátor* (the all-powerful Christ in glory after the Ascension); on the apse is the Virgin; and the higher expanses of wall portray scenes from the life of Christ. Prophets and saints could only appear on the lower walls, decreasing in importance according to their distance from the sanctuary.

Laskaris House

Along the path leading from Perívleptos to the lower gate are a couple of minor, much-restored churches, and, just above them, the **Laskaris House**, a mansion thought to have belonged to relatives of the emperors. Like the House of Frangopoulos, it is balconied; its ground floor probably served as stables. Close by, beside the path, is the old Marmara Turkish Fountain.

Mitrópolis

The **Mitrópolis** or cathedral, immediately beyond the gateway, is the oldest of Mystra's churches, built between 1270 and 1292. A marble slab set in its floor is carved with the double-headed eagle of Byzantium, commemorating the 1448 coronation of Constantine XI Paleologos, the last Eastern emperor; he was soon to perish, with his empire, in the Turkish sacking of Constantinople in 1453. A stone with red stains is said to mark where Bishop Ananias Lambadheris was murdered in 1760. Of the church's frescoes, the earliest, in the northeast aisle, depict the torture and burial of Áyios Dhimítrios, the saint to whom the church is dedicated. Opposite are frescoes illustrating the miracles of Christ and the life of the Virgin; more intimate and lighter of touch, they date from the last great years before Mystra's fall. Adjacent to the cathedral, a small **museum** contains various fragments of sculpture and pottery.

RUINS OF MYSTRA (P.161) >

2

Vrondohíou monastery

The **Vrondohíou monastery**, a short way uphill, was the centre of cultural and intellectual life in the fifteenth-century town – the cells of the monastery can still be discerned – and was also the burial place of the despots. Of its two attached churches, the furthest one, **Odhiyítria** (Afendikó; 1310), has been beautifully restored, revealing startlingly bold, fourteenth-century frescoes similar to those of Perívleptos.

Néos Mystrás

The pleasant roadside community of Néos Mystrás has a small square with several tavernas. It's crowded with tour buses by day but low-key at night, except at the end of August when the place buzzes with live music during the week-long annual *paniyíri* (fête).

ACCOMMODATION AND EATING   NÉOS MYSTRÁS

You will need to book ahead, or arrive early in the day, to find somewhere to stay.

Byzantion ☎ 27310 83309, ⓦ byzantionhotel.gr. This modern, congenial but basic, no-frills hotel on the main square has fairly large rooms with balconies, some with wonderful views of Mystra. Breakfast buffet included. April–Oct. €60

Castle View Camping ☎ 27310 83303, ⓦ castleview.gr. Laid-back campsite 300m from the main square on the Sparta road, shaded by olive and mulberry trees. Facilities include a pool, restaurant (main courses €7) and stone bungalows for 2 or 4 people with ensuite facilities. Cooked breakfast €6. April–Oct. Camping €15, bungalow €40

O Ellinas ☎ 27310 82666. A good quality but pricey taverna just off the main square with a leafy terrace on the side. The food is reliably good; for something a bit different, try the veal spaghetti (€8.50) or fried cod fillet with garlic aioli (€15), both house specialities. Daily 7am–midnight.

Máni

The southernmost peninsula of Greece, the **MÁNI** stretches from Yíthio in the east to Kardhamýli in the west and terminates at Cape Ténaro. It is a wild landscape, an arid Mediterranean counterpart to Cornwall or the Scottish Highlands, with a wildly idiosyncratic culture and history to match. Perhaps because of this independent spirit, the sense of hospitality is, like nearby Crete, as strong as anywhere in Greece.

The peninsula's spine, negotiated by road at just a few points, is the vast grey mass of **Mount Taïyetos** and its southern extension, **Sangiás**. The **Mésa Máni** – the part of the peninsula south of a line drawn between Ítylo and Vathý bay – is classic Máni territory, its jagged coast relieved only by the occasional cove, and its land a mass of rocks. Attractions include the coastal villages, like **Yeroliménas** on the west coast, or **Kótronas** on the east, as well as the remarkable caves at **Pýrgos Dhiroú**, but the pleasure is mainly in exploring the region's distinctive **tower-houses** and **churches**, and the solitude. The **Éxo Máni** – the somewhat more verdant coast up from Areópoli to Kalamáta, mostly in Messinía province – sees the emphasis shift to walking and beaches. **Stoúpa** and **Kardhamýli** are both attractive resorts, developed but far from spoilt. The road itself is an experience, threading up into the foothills of Taïyetos before looping back down to the sea. Patrick Leigh Fermor's classic *Mani: Travels in the Southern Peloponnese* (see p.806) is the definitive travelogue of the area.

You need at least three days to do the Máni justice, preferably with your own vehicle. Possible bases include Areópoli, or Yíthio, though the latter isn't typical of the region. Otherwise, pick a beach resort, such as Kardhamýli or, better yet, remote Yeroliménas.

GETTING AROUND   MÁNI

By bus There are several routes in season: Areópoli–Yeroliménas (2–4 daily; 30min), a service that sometimes continues to Álika–Váthia (a further 15min); Areópoli–Kótronas–Láyia (1–2 daily; 50min/1hr) and Areópoli–Ítylo (3 daily; 15min). In the Éxo Máni, the Kalamáta–Ítylo bus serves the coastal towns (2–4 daily; 1hr 30min). For detailed information call ☎ 27310 26441 (Spárti) or ☎ 27210 27172 (Kalamáta).

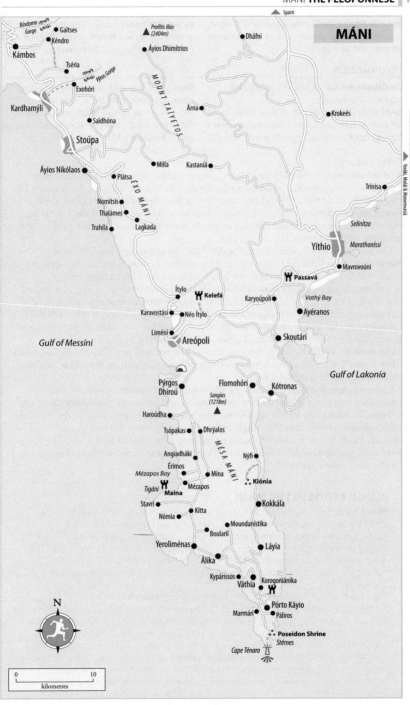

By car and motorbike Given the sporadic public transport, you really should consider renting a car or motorbike at Kalamáta, Yíthio or Stoúpa.

By taxi There are only a handful of taxis serving the region, generally negotiable, at Areópoli, Yeroliménas, Kótronas and Yíthio; a taxi from Areópoli to Váthia should cost €40.

INFORMATION

Tourist information The best website for planning your trip is ⓦ exploremani.gr.

Services There are banks with ATMs and well-stocked supermarkets in Areópoli, Kalamáta, Kardhamýli, Stoúpa and Yíthio, plus smaller markets in Pýrgos Dhiroú and Yeroliménas.

Maps A good, large-scale map is invaluable for navigating among the innumerable tiny settlements of the Mésa Máni. You can buy detailed walking maps in Kalamáta or Yíthio. A number of walking routes are signposted around Máni with useful map boards at the starting points.

Brief history

The **mountains** offer the key to Maniot history. Formidable natural barriers, they provided a refuge from, and bastion of resistance to, every occupying force of the last two millennia. **Christianity** did not take root in the interior until the ninth century (some five hundred years after the establishment of Byzantium) and the region was ruled by intense and violent internal tribalism, seen at its most extreme in the elaborate tradition of **blood feuds** (see box below).

The Turks, wisely, opted to control the Máni by granting a level of local **autonomy**, thus investing power in one or other clan whose leader they designated "bey" of the region. This system worked well until the nineteenth-century appointment of **Petrobey Mavromihalis**. With a power base at Liméni, he united the clans in revolution in March 1821, and his **Maniot army** was to prove vital to the success of the **War of Independence**. Mavromihalis swiftly fell out with the first president of the nation, Kapodhístrias, and, with other members of the clan, was imprisoned by the president at Náfplio – an act leading to the Kapodhístrias' **assassination** at the hands of Mavromihalis' brother and son. The monarchy fared little better until one of the king's German officers was sent to the Máni to enlist soldiers in a special Maniot militia.

In the twentieth century, ignored by the central government in Athens, this backwater area slipped into decline, with drastic and persistent **depopulation** of the villages. In places like Váthia and Kítta, which once held populations in the hundreds, the numbers are now down to single figures. Recently, there has been an influx of money, partly due to increased tourism, partly to membership in the EU. The result has been considerable refurbishment, with many postwar concrete houses acquiring "traditional" stone facings.

BLOOD FEUDS IN THE MÁNI

Blood feuds were the result of an intricate feudal society that seems to have developed across the Máni in the fourteenth century. After the arrival of refugee Byzantine families, the various clans developed **strongholds** in the tightly clustered villages. From these local forts, often marble-roofed towers, the clans conducted **vendettas** according to strict rules. The object was to destroy the tower and kill the male members of the opposing clan. The favoured method of attack was to smash the prestigious tower roofs; the forts consequently rose to four and five storeys.

Feuds would customarily be signalled by the ringing of **church bells**, and from this moment the adversaries would confine themselves to their towers, firing at each other with all available weaponry. The battles could last for years, even decades, with women (who were safe from attack) shuttling in food, ammunition and supplies. Truces were declared at harvest times; then, with business completed, the battle would recommence. The feuds lasted until either one side was annihilated or through **ritual surrender**, whereby a whole clan would file out to kiss the hands of enemy parents who had lost children in the feud; the victors would then dictate strict terms by which the vanquished could remain in the village.

Yíthio

YÍTHIO (Gythion), Sparta's ancient port, is the eastern gateway to the Máni peninsula, and one of the south's most attractive seaside towns in its own right. Its somewhat low-key harbour, with occasional ferries to Pireás and Kýthira, gives onto a graceful nineteenth-century waterside of tiled-roof houses – some of them now showing their age. In the bay, tethered by a long, narrow jetty, is the picturesque islet of **Marathoníssi**, with the long, sandy Mavrovoúni beach, some 4km south.

Marathoníssi

Marathoníssi islet is Yíthio's main attraction, with swimming possible off the rocks towards the lighthouse. Called **Kranae** in antiquity, it is here that Paris of Troy, having abducted Helen from Menelaus's palace at Sparta, dropped anchor, and the lovers spent their first night. Paris left his helmet there, from which the name Kranae derives. Amid the island's trees and scrub stands the restored **Tzanetákis** tower-fortress, built in around 1810 by the Turkish-appointed Bey of the Máni, to guard the harbour against his lawless countrymen.

Roman theatre

Open access • Free • Follow the road past the post office for about 300m until you reach the army barracks – the site stands just to the left, inside the outer gate

There are some impressive remains of a **Roman theatre** at the northeast end of the town. With most of its stone seats intact, and 50m in diameter, the theatre illustrates perfectly how buildings in Greece take on different guises through the ages: to one side is a Byzantine **church** (now ruined) which, in turn, functions as an outer wall of the **barracks**.

ARRIVAL AND DEPARTURE   YÍTHIO

By bus The bus station (☎ 27310 26441) is close to the centre of town; with your back to it, the main waterfront street, Vassiléos Pávlou, lies ahead of you.

Destinations Athens (6 daily; 4–5hr); Areópoli (3 daily; 30min); Ítylo (Mon–Sat 1 daily; 1hr); Spárti (6 daily; 50min); Yeroliménas (3 daily; 1hr).

INFORMATION

Services There are several banks and ATMs on Vassiléos Pávlou. Rozakis Travel Agency on the waterfront (☎ 27330 22207) rents out cars and can help with accommodation.
Bookshop The extensive Hasanakos bookshop at Larissiou

2 (☎ 27330 29128) is worth scouring for books on the area and has an exhibition of Greek shadow puppets on the first floor (free).
Taxi 24-hr service 27330 23400.

ACCOMMODATION

Finding accommodation shouldn't be hard, with a fair range in town – most hotels are along the waterfront, though some suffer from late-night noise from the many bars.

Aktaion Resort Selinitsa beach, 3.5km north of the centre ☎ 27330 29114, ⓦ aktaion-resort.com. Rooms and stone-built bungalows in a spacious luxury resort in the middle of a large fruit grove. There are two pools, a pool bar and great beach, plus sea views from balconies throughout. Breakfast included. June–Sept. Double **€100**, bungalow **€120**
Gythion Vassiléos Pávlou 33 ☎ 27330 23452, ⓦ gythionhotel.gr. A fine old (1864) hotel with period decorated rooms, all with 5m-high ceilings and views of the waterfront. Guests can use the Gythion Bay campsite's beach and private beach facilities. The excellent breakfast costs €6 and includes *tiganides* (fried doughsticks). **€40**

Leonidas Vassiléos Pávlou 17 ☎ 27330 22389, ⓔ hotelleonidasgytheio@gmail.com. Friendly Petros runs this very basic, unassuming hotel, with its Art-Deco-style entrance and spartan rooms, which nevertheless have a/c: most also have balconies with port views. **€40**
Meltemi Mavrovoúni beach, 3km from Yíthio ☎ 27330 23260, ⓦ campingmeltemi.gr. Nestled in a 25-acre olive grove, this large campsite faces a broad swathe of beach and clean sea. Facilities include a pool, minimarket, restaurant, washing machines and dryers, plus free wi-fi. April–Oct. **€17.50**

EATING

Saga Tzanetáki ☎ 27330 21358. Above-average (and pricy) fish taverna overlooking the Marathoníssi islet, and run by a friendly, knowledgeable French–Greek family. Choose your fish from the ice bucket knowing it arrived the same day, and be sure to try the fish soup as a starter (€9). Daily noon–midnight.

Yíthio to Areópoli

The **road from Yíthio** into the Máni runs slightly inland of the coast and the sandy, Blue-Flag **Mavrovoúni beach**, one of Greece's undiscovered delights. The route begins amid a fertile and gentle wooded landscape, running through tracts of citrus and olive groves and between hilltop towers, until, about 12km beyond Yíthio, the Máni suddenly asserts itself as the road enters a valley below the **Castle of Passavás**. Shortly after, a turning to the left leads down to an attractive long sandy beach at **Vathý Bay** (Vathý Ayéranou), which is popular with German tourists.

As you continue **towards Areópoli** from Passavás castle, the landscape remains fertile until the wild, scrubby mass of Mount Kouskoúni signals the final approach to the Mésa Máni. You enter another pass, with the **Castle of Kelefá** (see p.172) above to the north, and beyond it several southerly peaks of the Taïyetos ridge. Areópoli, as you wind down from the hills, inspires a real sense of arrival.

Areópoli and the west coast

An initially austere-looking town, **AREÓPOLI** (Aerópoli) sets an immediate mood for the region. Until the nineteenth century, it was secondary to Ítylo, 11km north and the western gateway to the Mésa Máni, but the modern road has made Areópoli, to all intents, the region's centre, and many of the stone buildings have now undergone renovation. Formerly Tsímova, its present name, meaning "town of Ares" (the god of war), was bestowed for its efforts during the War of Independence. It was here that Mavromihalis (commemorated by a statue in the main platía) declared the uprising.

The town's sights are archetypically Maniot in their anachronisms. The **Áyii Taxiárhes** cathedral, for example, has primitive reliefs above its doors that look twelfth century until you notice their date: 1798. Similarly, the tower-houses could readily be described as medieval, though most of them were built in the early 1800s. On its own, in a little platía, is the church of **Áyios Ioánnis**, the Mavromihalis' family church; the interior is lined with frescoes. Facing, there's a tiny but fascinating **Byzantine museum** (Tues–Sun 8am–3pm; €2; ☎ 27330 29531) in the Pikoulakis tower.

Dhiroú caves

5km beyond the village of Pýrgos Dhiroú, set beside the sea and a separate beach • Daily: summer 10am–6pm; winter 8.30am–3.30pm • €13; buy a ticket as soon as possible on arrival at the caves to give you a priority number for the tours – on mid-season weekends, you can wait 1hr or more for tickets, so arrive as early as possible in the day • ☎ 27330 52222 • Taxis from Areópoli will take you to the caves, then wait and take you back

Some 8km south of Areópoli, the road forks off to the **Dhiroú caves** – the Máni's major tourist attraction. Often referred to simply as "Spílea", they are very much a packaged attraction but worth a visit, especially on weekday afternoons when the wait is shorter. A visit consists of a thirty-minute punt around the underground waterways of the **Glyfádha (Vlyhádha) caves**, well lit and crammed with stalactites, whose reflections are a remarkable sight in the up to 20m deep water. You are then permitted a brief tour, on foot, of the **Alepótrypa caves** – huge chambers (one of them 100m by 60m) in which excavation has unearthed evidence of prehistoric occupation. Bring swimming gear to make the most of the adjacent beach.

The nearby **museum** (Tues–Sun 8.30am–3pm; €2), on a bend of the road, contains interesting Neolithic finds from the caves.

ARRIVAL AND INFORMATION

By bus Buses arrive and depart from the main square, Platía Athánatos; if you are heading north into Messinía, towards Kalamáta, you will need to change in Ítylo. Destinations Athens (3 daily; 6–7hr); Ítylo (Mon–Sat 3 daily; 20min); Kalamáta (2–4 daily changing at Ítylo; 1hr 30min–2hr 30min); Spárti (3 daily; 2hr); Yeroliménas (3 daily; 45min); Yíthio (3 daily; 45min).

Services On the main platía is a bank with an ATM and the post office. On the main road behind the square is a large supermarket for supplies (especially useful if heading on south).

ACCOMMODATION

Trapela ☏ 27330 52690, ⌨ trapela.gr. By the entrance to the city, this new small boutique hotel is furnished in the traditional Maniot style – a typical Areópoli mix of austere and cosy. It also has a garden and its own bar. Breakfast included. **€70**

EATING

Barba Petros ☏ 27330 51205. Unassuming spot off the cobbled street towards Áyii Taxiárhes, with lots of perfectly simmered vegetable dishes and stews to choose from; mains about €10. Daily: May–Oct noon–late; Nov–April noon–4pm.

To Katóï ☏ 27330 51201. An excellent taverna with rustic barrel-vaulted stone dining rooms, as well as atmospheric seating outside. The menu is deceptively standard, and inexpensive – the priciest item is only €9 – but the quality is extraordinary. Oven-roasted kid is a speciality. May–Oct Mon–Thurs 4pm–late, Fri–Sun noon–late.

Yeroliménas and the south

After the journey from Areópoli, **YEROLIMÉNAS** feels like a village in limbo, but it does make a good base for exploring the southern extremities of the Máni. There are a few **shops**, a **post office**, a couple of **cafés** and several **hotels**. It all feels very remote: the petrol station just by town is the southernmost of the peninsula.

South from Yeroliménas, the scenery becomes browner, treeless and more arid; a good road (and the bus) continues to **Álika**, where it divides. One fork leads east through the mountains to Láyia (see p.171), and the other continues southwards to **Váthia** and across the **Marmári isthmus** towards **Cape Ténaro**. Between Álika and Váthia there are good coves for swimming. One of the best is **Kypárissos**, reached by following a dry riverbed about midway to Váthia. On the headland above are scattered Roman remains of ancient Kaenipolis including (amid the walled fields) the excavated ruins of a sixth-century basilica.

Váthia

VÁTHIA, a photogenic group of tower-houses set uncompromisingly on a high hillside outcrop, is one of the most dramatic villages in the Mésa Máni. It features in Colonel Leake's account of his travels, one of the best sources on Greece in the early nineteenth century. He was warned to avoid going through the village in 1805, as a feud had been running between two families for the previous forty years. Today, it is the closest thing to a ghost town you are likely to find in Greece, mainly because the restored inn, which occupies a dozen tower-houses, has been bankrupt and inactive for several years.

Pórto Káyio

From Váthia, the road south to the cape edges around the mountain, before slowly descending to a couple of junctions. Left at the second one brings you steeply down to the beach and laidback hamlet of **PÓRTO KÁYIO** ("Bay of Quails"), 6km from Váthia. A pleasant short walk goes out to the **Áyios Nikólaos** chapel (usually closed) on the southeastern headland of the bay, while across the bay on the north side are the spectacular ruins of a **Turkish fortress** (open access; free) contemporary with Kelefá and the monastery of Korogoniánika.

Marmári

Above Pórto Káyio, the right branch of the road goes south along the headland, which is capped by the Grigorákis tower, to the pleasant, sandy **beaches** at the double bay of **MARMÁRI**. The picturesque hamlet itself straddles a promontory between the two bays and amounts to little more than a collection of accommodation options, some of them quite luxurious for such a desolate and stony spot.

On to Cape Ténaro

2

Starting from the left fork before Marmári, follow the surfaced road and signs for the fish taverna; pass a turning for Páliros and make your way along the final barren peninsula to Stérnes (Kokkinóyia). The road ends at a knoll crowned with the squat **Chapel of Asómati** (usually closed), constructed largely of materials from an ancient **temple of Poseidon**.

To the left (east) as you face the chapel is the little pebbly **Asómati Bay**; on the shore is a small **cave**, another addition to the list of mythical entrances to the underworld. To the right (west) of Asómati, the marked main path continues along the edge of another cove and through the metre-high foundations of a **Roman town** that grew up around the Poseidon shrine; there is even a mosaic in one structure. From here the old trail, which existed before the road was bulldozed, reappears as a walled path, allowing 180-degree views of the sea on its 25-minute course to the lighthouse on **Cape Ténaro**, the southernmost point of continental Europe.

ACCOMMODATION AND EATING   YEROLIMÉNAS AND THE SOUTH

The tip of the peninsula is so rocky and extreme that coming across any sign of civilization is almost a shock. Yet, somewhat surprisingly, there are enchanting places to stay and to eat – usually one and the same.

YEROLIMÉNAS

Akroyiali ☎ 27330 54204, ⓦ gerolimenas-hotels. com. An accommodation complex with rooms on the beach plus self-catering apartments (200m from the village) in traditional stone-built edifices. It also has its own excellent restaurant where the baked fish in lemon juice and olive oil takes some beating. Breakfast included. **€70**

★ Kyrimai ☎ 27330 54288, ⓦ kyrimai.gr. Ensconced at the southeastern end of the bay is this castle-like "country chic elegant" property in a restored 1870 trade centre, with a Maniot memorabilia library, a pool and very stylish rooms. Breakfast included. **€100**

PÓRTO KÁYIO

Akrotiri ☎ 27330 52013, ⓦ porto-kagio.gr. An attractive hotel with adjoining taverna that has an end-of-the-world feel about it, but is very welcoming. The food is simple and good, while each room is different and warmly inviting; all have a/c and some sea views. Breakfast included. Daily 9am–1am. **€55**

MARMÁRI

Marmari Paradise ☎ 27330 52101, ⓦ marmari paradise.com. A wonderful, traditional stone property with garden terraces, featuring stone rooms with sea views and a panoramic restaurant that serves Máni recipes (mains around €8). Breakfast and beach sunbeds included. Easter–Oct daily 7am–late. **€70**

East coast

The landscape of the **east coast**, the "sunward coast", is different from the western "shadow coast", and it's far less developed, though it offers some of the region's most spectacular views. It works best as a **scenic drive**, rather than a place to stay. There are few **beaches** and less coastal plain, but larger, more scattered and picturesque **villages** hanging on the hillsides. Road signs are fewer than in the west.

GETTING AROUND

By bus The east coast of the Mésa Máni is most easily approached from Areópoli, where there's a daily bus through Kótronas to Láyia.

By car or motorbike If you have your own transport,

or you're prepared to walk and hitch, there's satisfaction in doing a full loop of the peninsula, crossing over to Láyia from Yeroliménas (Álika) or Pórto Káyio.

Láyia

From the fork at Álika (see p.169), it's 10km by road to **LÁYIA**, one of the highest villages (400m) in the Mésa Máni. A turning off the road, not far above Álika, takes you to **Moundanístika**, the Máni's highest village – recommended for spectacular views. Láyia itself is a multi-towered village that perfectly exemplifies the feudal setup of the old Máni. Four families lived here, and their four independently sited settlements, each with its own church, survive. One of the taller towers, so the locals claim, was built overnight by four hundred men who hoped to gain an advantage at sunrise. Today, a council-owned café faces the main church, and the village shows healthy signs of revival, with the ongoing refurbishment of a number of houses.

Flomohóri and around

Some 30km northwards, passing views, towered hamlets and modest beaches, you reach **FLOMOHÓRI**. The land below is relatively fertile, and the village has maintained a reasonable population as well as an imposing group of tower-houses, one reckoned by some to be the Máni's highest. The way of life here survives as a bit of a time warp: the deeply traditional black dress of perpetual mourning is usual, and the locals are liable to regard you with an odd mix of amusement and bravado – as if you just stepped off a spaceship. You might feel the same.

Kótronas, a few kilometres downhill, feels less harsh than the rest of the Máni. It is still a working fishing village, and there's a sandy beach if you feel like a dip in the sea.

The Éxo (Outer) Máni: Areópoli to Kalamáta

The 40km of road into Messinía, between Areópoli (see p.168) and Kalamáta (see p.179), are as dramatic and beautiful as any in Greece, almost a corniche route between the **Taïyetos** ridge and the **Gulf of Messinía**. The first few settlements en route are classic Máni villages, their towers packed against the hillside. As you move north, with the road dropping to near sea level, there are several small appealing and popular resorts. For walkers, there is a reasonably well-preserved *kalderími* (cobbled footpath) running parallel to much of the paved route, with superb **gorge hikes** just east of Kardhamýli, a good base for local exploration and touring.

Liméni

The less austere Éxo Máni begins at **LIMÉNI**, Areópoli's tiny traditional port, which lies 3km to the north, in a dramatic location on the coast. Liméni consists of a handful of houses on a curve of sparkling sea, dominated by the restored **tower-house** of Petrobey Mavromihalis, now a luxury **hotel** (see below), though it resembles nothing so much as an English country parish church.

ACCOMMODATION AND EATING LIMÉNI

★**Pirgos Mavromichali** 📞 27330 51042, ⓦ pirgosmavromichali.gr. A luxury hotel in the refurbished historic tower-house of the legendary clan. It's a magical setting: white stone archways, secret stairways, glistening turquoise waters below, all enhanced at night by imaginative lighting. Bedrooms and suites are coolly sophisticated and perfectly appointed, and breakfast on the terrace is included. **€140**

Takis 📞 27330 51327. A well-regarded fish taverna next to *Pirgos Mavromichali*. It's perfect for a blowout meal (fresh fish costs around €65/kg), but you can also opt for more affordable taverna dishes – Greek salads go for €5. Mid-March to Oct daily 11pm–midnight; Nov to mid-March Fri–Sun only.

Ítylo and around

The village of **ÍTYLO** (Oítylo), 8km farther along the main road after the Liméni turn-off, has been experiencing a resurgence in fortunes, with many crumbling old houses now restored. In earlier times, Ítylo was the **capital** of the Máni, and from the sixteenth to the eighteenth centuries it was the region's most notorious base for **piracy** and **slave trading**. The Maniots traded efficiently in slaves; they sold Turks to Venetians, Venetians to Turks, and, at times of feud, the women of each other's clans to both. Irritated by the piracy and hoping to control the important pass to the north, the Turks built the sprawling **Castle of Kelefá** in 1670 (open access; free). It is just a kilometre's walk from Ítylo across a gorge, and its walls and bastions, built for a garrison of five hundred, are substantially intact. Also worth exploring is the **monastery of Dhekoúlou** (ⓦ monidekoulou.gr), down towards the coast; its setting is beautiful and there are some fine eighteenth-century frescoes in the chapel.

ACCOMMODATION AND EATING   ÍTYLO

There is not much choice of accommodation in Ítylo, so it's best to head down to the tiny hamlet of Néo Ítylo, where you'll find rooms to rent and a hotel on the beach: it's just round the bay from Ítylo's port, Karavostási.

Ítylo Néo Ítylo ☎ 27330 59222, ⓦ hotelitilo.gr. This comfortable stone-and-iron hotel is right on the beach and comes complete with a restaurant and a playground for kids. Breakfast included; special offers for longer stays. March–Oct. €120

Stoúpa

Some 20km north of Ítylo, **STOÚPA** is a first-rate resort and very popular with British holiday-makers and holiday-home owners. It has possibly the best sands along this coast, with two glorious **beaches** (Stoúpa and the smaller, deeper Kalogriá) separated by a headland, each sloping into the sea and superb for children. Submarine freshwater springs gush into the bay, keeping it unusually clean. A ten-minute walk to the north of Kalogriá beach is the delightful and often deserted cove of Dhelfíni. A further 600m brings you to the pebble beach of Fonéa, wrapped around a rock outcrop and tucked into a corner of the hillside. Stoúpa was home in 1917–18 to the wandering Cretan writer, Nikos Kazantzakis, who is said to have based the title character in *Zorba the Greek* on a worker at the lignite mine in nearby Pástrova.

Out of peak season, Stoúpa is certainly recommended, though in July and August, and any summer weekend, you may find the crowds a bit overwhelming and space at a premium.

ARRIVAL AND INFORMATION   STOÚPA

By bus The Kalamáta–Ítylo bus stops at the junctions at each end of town, but does not go in.
Destinations Ítylo (3–4 daily; 30min); Kalamáta (3 daily; 1hr).
By car If driving up from the south, you'll find that the main access road to town is well signed; it forks off about 1km away from the centre.
Tourist information The town's official website, ⓦ stoupa-greece.com, has plenty of useful information. There are five ATMs on the waterfront.

GETTING AROUND

By car Doufexis Travel (☎ 27210 77677, ⓦ doufexis.com) can organize car rental and find accommodation.
By taxi Stoúpa Taxi is on ☎ 27210 77477.

ACCOMMODATION AND EATING

Akroyiali Southern end of main beach ☎ 27210 77335. This taverna at the end of the beach not only serves well-prepared food, including seafood, but also has magical views after dark of the lights of the mountain villages above Stoúpa. Mains around €10, and EZA brewery beer €2.50 for 500ml. April–Oct daily 9am–midnight.
Kastro Middle of main beach ☎ 27210 64080 ⓦ hotel-kastro.gr. The best located hotel in Stoúpa, right on the beach with twelve tastefully decorated rooms around an internal patio complete with a fountain. It's worth paying extra for the sea-facing balconies. Beach umbrellas for guests €5. Continental breakfast is included; cooked English an extra €3pp. May–Oct. €70.
★ **Lefktron** In the middle of town, 50m from the beach ☎ 27210 77322, ⓦ lefktron-hotel.gr. Friendly and comfortable, this family-run hotel has rooms with a/c, fridges and balconies facing the pool. There's a well-stocked bar, three patios on different levels, parking spaces and foreign exchange facilities. Breakfast included. April–Oct. €80

Kardhamýli

KARDHAMÝLI, 8km north of Stoúpa, is a major resort by Peloponnese standards and suffers from the busy main road that splits it. The **beach** is good, though not sandy – a long pebble strip north of the village, backed by olive trees. This is where the author Patrick Leigh Fermor (see p.806) chose to make his home, and it's certainly one of the greenest and loveliest of places around – an excellent base for walkers (see box, below).

Inland from the platía, there's a nice walk up to "**Old Kardhamýli**", a partly restored citadel of nineteenth-century houses, gathered about the church of **Áyios Spyrídhon** with its unusual multistorey bell tower. Here in the church courtyard, Maniot chieftains Kolokotronis and Mourtzinos played human chess with their troops during the War of Independence. Further back, on the path up to Ayía Sofía, is a pair of ancient tombs, said to be of the **Dioskoúri** (the Gemini twins).

ARRIVAL AND INFORMATION   KARDHAMÝLI

By bus The bus station is by the central square at the northern end of town.
Destinations Kalamáta (3–4 daily; 1hr); Ítylo (4 daily; 1hr).
By car Driving up from the south, the main road passes

through town, just 2 blocks inland.
Services On the main road south of the platía, you'll find a bookshop and a post office (Mon–Fri 7.30am–2pm). There is an ATM at the bank, next to the bridge.

GETTING AROUND

By car To rent a car, try MyCarRentals at Kardhamýli (☎27210 64150, ⚙mycarrentals.gr).

By taxi Taxis are on ☎27210 74497/73433/74323.

ACCOMMODATION

Anniska On the seafront ☎27210 73601, ⚙anniska-liakoto.com. With easy sea access to a secluded rocky promontory, this property, belonging to an Australian-Greek, offers self-catering studios and apartments. Amenities include concierge service, wi-fi as well as free use of PCs, a panoramic terrace coffee bar and a garden patio. April–Oct. **€95**
★**Kalamitsi** 1km south of town ☎27210 73131-4, ⚙www.kalamitsi-hotel.gr. Apart from its great location, set among the orange groves just outside

Kardhamýli, this hotel is famous for its connection with British writers Patrick Leigh Fermor, whose house was in the adjoining property, and Bruce Chatwin, who wrote *Songlines* in what is now Room 1 in the annexe. Breakfast included. **€90**
Liakoto On the seafront ☎27210 73600, ⚙anniska-liakoto.com. Belonging to the same owner as *Anniska* (see above), this hotel is easily accessible from the main road with parking spaces and a pebble beach in front. The self-catering apartments, in dark wood and white marble, are

---

HIKING THE VÝROS GORGE

The giant **Výros Gorge** plunges down from the summit ridge of Taïyetos to meet the sea just north of Kardhamýli. Tracks penetrate the gorge from various directions and are well worth a day or two's exploration. From Kardhamýli, the *kalderími* from the citadel continues to the church and village of Ayía Sofía, and then proceeds on a mixture of tracks and lanes either across the plateau up to the hamlet of **Exohóri**, or down into the gorge, where **monasteries** nestle deep at the base of dramatic cliffs. An hour or so inland along the canyon, more cobbled ways lead up to either Tséria on the north bank (there's a taverna, but no accommodation) or back towards Exohóri on the south flank, about 10km from Kardhamýli. If you reach Exohóri, pay a visit to the church of **Áyios Nikólaos** (always closed), where the urn containing the ashes of writer Bruce Chatwin is buried outside, to the right of the sanctuary (unmarked). When he lived in Kardhamýli (see above), he used to walk 5km up to Exohóri and back down almost every day.

ACCOMMODATION AND EATING

Faraggi Exohóri ☎27210 73001, ✉hotel-faraggi@ hotmail.com. A large stone house with breath-taking views of the gorge and six simple, very tasteful rooms

with kitchenette. Well placed for walks, or just for enjoying the delicious food, drinks and the mountain heights from the roof terrace bar. Breakfast included. **€60**

arranged around the pool and all have at least partial sea views. April–Oct. **€110**

Elies Ritsá beach, 2km north of town ☎ 27210 73140, ⓦ elieshotel.gr. A complex of spacious self-catering stone studios, apartments and maisonettes in the middle of a 20-acre olive grove facing a gravel beach. It also has a fabulous restaurant where all the vegetables served are grown in its own garden: dishes averaging around €10.

Daily: March, April, Sept & Oct 8am–6pm; June–Aug 8am–10pm. **€110**

Notos ☎ 27210 73730, ⓦ notoshotel.gr. Tranquil and tastefully decorated, the two-person self-catering studios here come with all amenities you'd expect. The stone buildings are clustered in a hilly garden enclave, with wonderful views over the whole area. Three-night minimum for best rate. No breakfast. **€90**

EATING

Kiki Beach ☎ 27210 73148. This is one of the finest of the traditional tavernas here, and serves genuine Maniot dishes created from the freshest local produce. Stick to the dish of the day (around €8) and you won't be disappointed. March–Nov daily 8am–late.

★**Lela's** Near the harbour ☎ 27210 73730

ⓦ lelastaverna.com. This legendary, relaxing taverna has a flowery setting and serves wonderful food at moderate prices with traditional Maniot dishes from €8–10. The eponymous Lela, now deceased, was British travel writer Patrick Leigh Fermor's cook, and the taverna is run by one of her sons, following her recipes. April–Oct daily noon–11pm.

Arcadia

ARCADIA (Arkadhía), the heartland province of the Peloponnese, contains some of the most beautiful alpine landscapes in Greece. Dramatic hills are crowned by a string of medieval towns, and the occasional Classical antiquity. Beautiful **Karítena** is a picture-postcard hill town, but the best area of all is around **Stemnítsa** and **Dhimitsána**, where walkers are rewarded with the luxuriant **Loúsios Gorge**. Another hill town, **Andhrítsena**, attracts archeology buffs with the nearby **Temple of Bassae**, which is still spectacular though tented for restoration. The main transport hub of the region is **Trípoli**, a lively, if rather nondescript, town. **Wild fires** in 2000 and 2007 severely damaged the area's oak and fir woodland, though recovery is evident and the legendary beauty still holds, especially in spring, when the slopes are bright yellow with masses of broom plants.

Drivers should be aware that Arcadia's highways, some of the broadest and emptiest in the Peloponnese, are shared with sheep- and goat-herds moving their flocks.

Trípoli

TRÍPOLI is a major crossroads of the Peloponnese. Set in a huge upland plain and surrounded by spectacular mountains, the Arcadian capital is a large, modern town, and home to one of the country's biggest army barracks. Its altitude of 665m means an often markedly cooler summer climate and harsh winters. Medieval Tripolitsá was destroyed during the War of Independence, when the Greek forces, led by Kolokotronis, massacred the town's Turkish population in one of their worst atrocities.

The city doesn't pander to tourism and has few obvious attractions, but its youthful Greek exuberance is hard to match anywhere else in the Peloponnese, and there are far worse places to get stranded by bus schedules for the night. The traffic here can be chaotic, so you may wish to escape to the quiet greenery of **Platía Áreos** or **Kendrikí Platía**, whose shops and cafés seem frozen in the 1960s.

Panarcadic Archeological Museum

Evangelistrías 8 • Tues–Sun 8am–3pm • €2

Housed in a Neoclassical building designed by Ernst Ziller with a beautiful rose garden, the **Panarcadic Archeological Museum** is Trípoli's most interesting attraction. Its collection includes finds from all over Arcadia, from the Neolithic era to Roman times.

ARRIVAL AND DEPARTURE

TRÍPOLI

By bus The main bus terminal is at the top of Nafplíou St (☎2710 222 560, ⓦktelarkadias.gr). Destinations: Andhrítsena (1–2 daily; 1hr 30min); Athens (10–12 daily; 2hr 30min); Dhimitsána (1–2 daily; 1hr 30min); Kalamata (6 daily; 1hr 30min); Karítena (1–2 daily; 1hr); Monemvasia (2–3 daily; 2hr 30min); Náfplio, via Árgos (2 daily; 2hr); Pátra (1–2 daily; 3hr); Spárti (7–9 daily; 1hr); Stemnítsa (3 weekly; 1hr); Yíthio (5 daily; 1h 30min).

ACCOMMODATION AND EATING

Anaktorikon Ethnikís Andístasis 48 ☎2710 226 545, ⓦanaktorikon.gr. Tripoli's only four-star hotel, revamped in 2017, and incorporating a spa. Each room has individual furnishings and decor, although room 32 with its black marble bathroom is hard to beat. Breakfast included. **€80**

Mainalon Resort Platía Areos ☎2710 230 300, ⓦmainalonhotel.gr. Unashamedly decorated in carmine red, this 1936 hotel boasts sumptuous fin-de-siècle French cornices. It's worth paying the €10 extra for a room looking over Platia Areos. Breakfast and parking included. **€70**

EATING AND DRINKING

Tripoli's nightlife is at its buzziest in the pedestrianized streets around the small church of St Paul.

Villa Incognito Delligianni & Tassou Sehioti 43 ☎2710 222 111. The current "in" place in Trípoli – the massive lighting rigs, large mirrors and wooden tables and chairs almost distract from the very good international cuisine, with mains for €10–12. Booking recommended. Tues–Thurs 8pm–12.30am, Fri & Sat 1–5pm & 8pm–12.30am.

X2 Dariotou 18 ☎2710 226 010. This mezedhopolío attracts a thirty-something clientele, and serves the usual Greek staples, plus massive salads (€6), mezédhes featuring six kinds of local cheese (€3 each) and selected local wines at €2 a glass. Tues–Sat 1–5pm & 8.30pm–midnight.

Arcadian hill towns

West of Trípoli lies the best of Arcadia lies, with minor roads curling through a series of lush valleys and below the area's most exquisite **medieval hill towns**. The obvious first stop is lofty **Karítena**. Then the route to the northwest winds farther up around the edge of the Ménalo mountains to the delightful towns of **Stemnítsa** and **Dhimitsána**, from either of which you can explore the **Loúsios Gorge**, the remote site of **ancient Gortys** and the stunning eleventh-century **Monastery Ayíou Ioánnou Prodhrómou**, as well as additional ancient monasteries on up the gorge. Further west is the hill town of **Andhrítsena** and the nearby ancient **Temple of Bassae**. The hill towns offer plenty of great places to stay and, unlike other Greek resorts, are cheaper in the summer, as they cater mostly for the domestic ski tourism.

GETTING AROUND

ARCADIAN HILL TOWNS

By car and bus Having your own transport is pretty essential here, though there are limited buses from Trípoli (see opposite).
By taxi Taxis are not that expensive for travelling between towns, if you use a local one for the outward journey: try Dhimitsána ☎6977 575 955, ☎6955 050 212; Stemnítsa ☎6932 270 026; Karítena ☎6942 486 835; Andhrítsena ☎26260 22380.

ACTIVITIES

Whitewater rafting The *Alpin Club* (ⓦalpinclub.gr) organizes rafting trips down the River Alfiós.

Karítena

In a picturesque setting watching over the strategic Megalópoli–Andhrítsena, **KARÍTENA** provides one of the signature Arcadian images. Like many of the hill towns hereabouts, its history has Frankish, Byzantine and Turkish contributions. It was founded by the Byzantines in the seventh century and had attained a population of some twenty thousand when the Franks took it in 1209. Under their century-long rule, Karítena was the capital of a large barony under Geoffroy de Bruyères, the paragon of chivalry in the medieval ballad *The Chronicle of the Morea*, and probably the only well-liked Frankish overlord.

These days the village has a population of just a couple of hundred, but as recently as the beginning of the nineteenth century, there were at least ten times that figure.

Froúrio

Open access • Free

Up steps off the platía is the **Froúrio**, the castle built in 1245 by the Franks, with added Turkish towers. It was repaired by Theodhoros Kolokotronis and it was here that he held out against Ibrahim Pasha in 1826 and turned the tide of the War of Independence.

Medieval bridge and the River Alfiós

Don't miss Karítena's **medieval bridge** over the River Alfiós (Alpheus). To find it, stop on the south side of the modern bridge and follow a short track down, almost underneath the new span. The old structure is missing the central section, but is an intriguing sight nonetheless, with a small Byzantine chapel built into one of the central pillars. **Whitewater rafting** is organized near the bridge (see p.178).

Stemnítsa and around

Some 16km north of Karítena, the winter resort of **STEMNÍTSA** (Ypsoús on many maps) lies at an altitude of 1050m. It's divided by ravines into three distinct quarters: the **kástro** (the ancient acropolis hill, worth the walk up for the views), **Ayía Paraskeví** (east of the stream) and **Áyios Ioánnis** (west of the stream). For centuries, it was one of the premier **goldworking centres** of the Balkans and is still the location of Greece's premier gold- and silversmith school. Today, the winding main street is home to three different workshops that will handcraft jewellery to your own design – try Varveropoulos, in Ayía Paraskeví (📞6943 886 767, ✉g.varveropoulos@gmail.com).

Although much depopulated, Stemnítsa remains a fascinating town, with a small **folklore museum** and several quietly magnificent medieval churches: the seventeenth-century **basilica of Trión Ierarhón**, across the way from the museum, is the most accessible of them.

Folklore Museum

Just off the main road in Ayía Paraskeví • Wed–Fri 10am–1pm, Sat & Sun 10am–2pm • €1 • 📞 27950 81252, 🌐 stemnitsamuseum.gr

The ground floor of the **Folklore Museum** is devoted to mock-ups of the workshops of indigenous crafts such as candle-making, bell-casting, shoe-making and jewellery. The next floor up features re-creations of the salon of a well-to-do family and a humbler cottage. The top storey is taken up by the rather random collections of the Savopoulos

---

HIKING NEAR ANCIENT GORTYS

The farmland surrounding ancient Gortys belongs to the monks of the nearby **Prodhrómou Monastery**, who have carved a path along the **Loúsios Gorge** between Áyios Andhréas and the monastery. It's about a forty-minute walk up a well-graded trail following the stream. The monastery, stuck on to the cliff like a swallow's nest, is plainly visible a couple of hundred metres above the path. There are no more than five monks here, and one of them may show visitors the tiny, frescoed *katholikón*. Strict dress rules apply, with blanket-like clothing provided if necessary. The monastery is also accessible by an asphalt road that makes a circuitous 7km descent from the Stemnítsa–Dhimitsána road to a parking lot and newish chapel, and then it's a further 1km descent on foot along a steep path.

Beyond Prodhrómou, the path continues clearly to the outlying, well-signed monasteries of **Paleá** and then **Néa Filosófou** on the opposite side of the valley. The older (Paleá), dating from the tenth century, is merely a ruin and blends into the cliff against which it is flattened. The newer monastery (Néa, seventeenth-century) has been restored and recently expanded considerably, but retains frescoes from 1663 inside; there is a permanent caretaker monk. From here, paths follow the west then east banks of the river, to reach Dhimitsána via Paleohóri in under two hours.

family: plates by Avramides (a refugee from Asia Minor and ceramics master), textiles and costumes from all over Greece, weapons, copperware and eighteenth- and nineteenth-century icons.

Ancient Gortys
8km southeast of Stemnítsa • Open access • Free

Ancient Gortys is a charming site, set beside the rushing river known in ancient times as the Gortynios. The remains are widely strewn over the hillside on the west bank of the stream, but the main attraction, below contemporary ground level and not at all obvious until well to the west of the little Byzantine chapel of Áyios Andhréas (by the old bridge), is the huge excavation containing the remains of a **temple to Asclepios** and an adjoining **bath**, both dating from the fourth century BC. The most curious feature of the site is a circular **portico** enclosing round-backed seats, which most certainly would have been part of the therapeutic centre.

Dhimitsána

Some 11km north of Stemnítsa, **DHIMITSÁNA** has an immediately seductive appearance, its cobbled streets and tottering houses straddling a twin hillside overlooking the Loúsios River. Views from the village are stunning, and though quite a small resort, it has an excellent accommodation selection, as well as the best choice of tavernas in the area, making Dhimitsána a prime base for exploring the centre of the Peloponnese.

In the town, a half-dozen churches with tall, squarish belfries recall the extended Frankish, and especially Norman, tenure in this part of the Moreas during the thirteenth century. Yet no one should dispute the deep-dyed Greekness of Dhimitsána. It was the birthplace of **Archbishop Yermanos**, who first raised the flag of rebellion at Kalávryta in 1821, and of the hapless patriarch, **Grigoris V**, hanged in Constantinople upon the sultan's receiving news of the insurrection.

Open-Air Water-Power Museum
2km east of Dhimitsána • Wed–Mon: March to mid-Oct 10am–6pm; mid-Oct to Feb 9am–5pm • €3 • ☎ 27950 31630

The award-winning **Open-Air Water-Power Museum** has a reconstructed watermill, tannery and gunpowder mill, with exhibitions on the pre-industrial processes involved.

Andhrítsena and around

ANDHRÍTSENA, 28km west of Karítena along a beautiful route, is a traditional hill town and the base from which to visit the **Temple of Apollo Epikourios** at **Bassae** up in the mountains to the south. Though very much a roadside settlement today, Andhrítsena was a major urban centre during the years of Turkish occupation and the first century of independent Greece.

Temple of Apollo Epikourios
Summer daily 8am–8pm • €6 • Winter daily 8am–3pm • €3

Some 14km into the mountains south of Andhrítsena and well signposted stands a **World Heritage Site**, the fifth-century BC **Temple of Apollo Epikourios** at **BASSAE** (Vásses), which occupies one of the remotest, highest (1131m) and arguably most spectacular **sites** in Greece. One of the best-preserved Classical monuments in the country, it is thought to have been designed by Iktinos, architect of the Parthenon and the Hephaisteion (Thisseion) in Athens.

Unfortunately, to protect it from the elements during its complicated **restoration**, the magnificent temple is currently swathed in a gigantic marquee suspended from metal girders. The work, recounted in a video on site, is badly needed to keep the whole thing from tumbling, stone by stone, into the valley below and the marquee is quite a sight in itself. However, you may feel a bit disappointed at first sight, until you enter the tent and

2

BASSAE'S MISSING METOPES

Many of the Temple of Apollo Epikourios's stunning **metopes**, the marble frieze sculptures, as well as other fine pieces, were removed and installed in London's **British Museum** in 1814–15. Reportedly, an English archeologist bribed the local Ottoman pasha, who evidently did not consider preservation of the works of any importance. The metopes powerfully depict the battles of the Amazons, Lapiths and Centaurs, and they are on display in a special room with the controversial **Elgin Marbles** (see p.70), which, under similar circumstances, were boxed up and shipped to Britain in 1812.

---

are awestruck by the sheer scale and majesty of the structure. Even with its scaffolding, the temple is worth all the narrow, precipitous mountain roads it takes to get here.

ACCOMMODATION

KARÍTENA

Vrenthi ☎ 27910 31650, ⓦ vrenthi.gr. Located on the right just before the main square, this good-value café has rooms to rent at their nearby homely stone-built guesthouse that can sleep up to seven people. **€40**

STEMNÍTSA

★ **Mpelleiko** ☎ & ⓕ 27950 81286, ⓦ mpelleiko.gr. High above the town, overlooking the whole mountainous area, stands a marvellous stone mansion, beautifully converted into this unique guesthouse. The rooms are all different and cosy and come with a fireplace. Hearty buffet breakfast included. **€65**

Trikolonion ☎ 27950 29500, ⓦ trikoloniontcountry.gr. Just to the east of town is this very comfortable luxury resort in a converted nineteenth-century boarding school. The rooms have every amenity, and there's a gym/spa and free parking. Horse-riding and rafting trips arranged. Buffet breakfast included. **€75**

ARCADIAN HILL TOWNS

DHIMITSÁNA

Amanites ☎ 27950 31090, ⓦ amanites.gr. This beautiful stone building stands prominently just above the main road and has very comfortable rooms with spectacular views over the town and valley. The lovely owners are always ready to help, and the breakfast (included) features home-made treats. **€60**

★ **En Dimitsani** ☎ 27950 31748, ⓦ en-dimitsani.gr. Traditionally built in stone and wood, yet modern and luxurious, this Arcadian hotel manages to combine cosy rooms with functioning fireplaces (free wood) and great views over the Lusios gorge. There's parking – a rarity in Dhimitsána – and a great home-made breakfast included. **€70**

Xenonas Kazakou ☎ 27950 31660, ⓦ xenonaskazakou.gr. It's a steep schlep up from the main road, winding around past the old church, to this magnificent property, which is unbeatable for spacious comfort, friendliness and especially the breakfast cooked to order (included). **€60**

EATING

STEMNÍTSA

I Stemnitsa ☎ 27950 81371. The town's eponymous taverna turns out dishes in keeping with its wild mountain setting, with plenty of fresh produce, as well as game – try the country sausage (€7), or chopped grilled chicken (€6.50). Daily noon–10pm.

DHIMITSÁNA

Sto Kioupi ☎ 27950 31232, ⓦ stokioupi.gr. This very central and amiable restaurant has some tables with views down the valley, and an extensive menu featuring both meat and game dishes such as rabbit in garlic sauce (€11): there are also vegetarian specialities, including its

signature vegetable pie (€4.50). Daily 11am–11pm.

★ **Teuthis** ☎ 27950 31514. Near the main square, this elegant, rustic spot, with a functioning fireplace and friendly service, specializes in pork dishes – try the salt pork omelette, a local staple, or pork in a pot with mustard sauce, both €8. Daily noon–midnight.

To Steki tis Gefsis ☎ 27950 31424, ⓦ tostekitisgefsis.gr. With rifle displays on the walls, this "corner of taste", as it dubs itself, has gone for the full Greek Independence revolutionary chic. It fits well with the menu of coal-grilled meats (€12) and pork stews (€10) that the old warriors would have loved. Wed–Mon noon–midnight.

Messinía

The province of **Messinía** stretches from the western flank of the Taïyetos ridge across the plain of **Kalamáta** to include the hilly southwesternmost "finger" of the Peloponnese.

Green, fertile and luxuriant for the most part, it is ringed with a series of well-preserved castles overlooking some of the area's most expansive beaches. The towns of **Koróni**, **Methóni** and **Finikoúnda** and their beaches draw the crowds, while the pale curve of fine sand at the bay of **Voïdhokiliá**, near Pýlos, sandwiched between sea, rock and lagoon, is one of the most beautiful beaches in Greece. Messinía's notable archeological sites, such as **ancient Messene** west of Kalamáta and **Nestor's Palace** north of Pýlos, rarely see as many visitors as the Argolid sites.

Kalamáta and around

KALAMÁTA is by far the largest city in the southern Peloponnese, spreading for some 4km back from the sea and into the hills, and it provides quite a metropolitan shock after the small-town life of the rest of the region. As well as the best urban beach this side of Athens, it also boasts plenty of big-town facilities, decent tavernas and a pleasant historic centre. Synonymous for centuries with **olives** (and to a lesser extent figs), Kalamáta today has been boosted by a new international airport and is a resort in itself, as well as being the gateway to the Mani and the southwestern Peloponnese.

Brief history
The town flourished as a commercial centre during the Turkish period and became one of the first independent Greek towns in 1821; the first newspaper to be printed on Greek soil was produced here the same year. In 1986, Kalamáta was near the epicentre of a severe **earthquake** that killed twenty people and left twelve thousand families homeless. But for the fact that the quake struck in the early evening, when many people were outside, the death toll would have been much higher. As it was, large numbers of buildings were levelled throughout the town.

Old town
Kalamata's **old town** is small and attractive especially along its pedestrianized promenades flanked by fin-de-siècle houses. The typical **kástro** (Tues–Sun: winter 8am–3pm; summer 8am–8pm; €2) makes for a green stroll amid evocative ruins to a small, photogenic chapel. Below the castle, one of the region's most colourful produce **markets** (8am–3pm) takes place on Wednesdays and Saturdays, across the bridge from the bus station. The **Archeological Museum**, on Platía Agíon Apostólon (Mon 1.30–8pm, Tues–Sun 8am–8pm; €4), has a modest collection, with everything informatively labelled and panelled. Just in front, is the diminutive and delightful **Byzantine church** (daily 7.30am–2pm, 5–8pm; free), the oldest part of which dates from at least the twelfth century. Heading straight down towards the port, you'll walk through a pleasant city park, where an **open-air railway museum** (24hr; free) has retired locomotives and train cars lined up to admire.

Ancient Messene (Ithómi)
Daily: winter 9am–4pm; summer 8am–8pm • €12, including museum • ☎ 27240 51201, ⓦ ancientmessene.gr • Local bus to Mavromáti from Kalamáta twice daily

Located just 22km northwest of Kalamáta, the substantial remains of **ancient Messene** are spread out just below the village of Mavromáti. This former Messinian capital was founded in 371 BC, following the liberation of the area from Spartan hegemony. The space was originally girded by 9km of Cyclopean **ramparts**, and there are remnants of massive gates. Count on three hours for a complete walkabout. Besides the walls, sights include the agora, a restored theatre, a stadium with its columned entrance, a partial colonnade of the gymnasium, various temple bases and a large Asklepion. There's also a small **museum**, which houses a few very good pieces of statuary found here, including one of **Artemis Orthia**. Apart from some olive groves, most of the area is shadeless, and there are no services, so fill up water bottles at the lovely old **fountain** in the village before setting off.

2

ARRIVAL AND DEPARTURE KALAMÁTA

By air The airport (☏ 27210 69442), 8km west of Kalamáta on the highway to Messíni and Pýlos, is served by BA and seasonal charter and budget airlines from London and other UK regional airports. It featured in the 2013 film *Before Midnight*, and has an ATM and a helpful tourist office, open when flights are due. Buses to the centre leave every thirty minutes (€5.50); a taxi to the city is €42.

By bus The bus station (☏ 27210 28581; ⊛ ktelmessinias.gr) is at the top of Artemisías, about 1km north of the centre.

Destinations Ancient Messini (Mon–Fri 2 daily; 1hr); Athens (4 direct daily; 2hr 45min); Costa Navarino (7 daily;

1hr 15min); Finikoúnda (3 daily; 2hr); Ioánnina (3–4 weekly; 7hr); Kardhamýli (2–3 daily; 1hr); Kórinthos via Isthmós (6 daily; 3hr 15min–4hr); Koróni (4–6 daily; 1hr 30min); Messíni (1–2 hourly; 30min); Methóni (3–5 daily; 1hr 30min); Pátra (2 daily; 3hr–3hr 30min); Pýlos (5–7 daily; 1hr 20min); Pýrgos (2 daily; 2hr 30min); Spárti (1–2 daily, changing at Artemisia; 2hr–2hr 30min); Stoúpa (2–3 daily; 1hr 30min); Thessaloniki (3 weekly; 10–11hr); Trípoli (4 daily; 1hr 30min).

By car Driving through Kalamáta is easy, with good sign-posting.

INFORMATION

Tourist office The new municipal tourist office, at Aristomenous 28 (daily 9am–9pm; ☏ 27210 60754), is helpful and brimming with maps, brochures and books on the area. Birgit Ferger Travel at Ayiou Ioannou 3 (April–Nov 10am–2pm & 6.30pm–8pm; ☏ 27210 63395, ⊛ birgitfergertravel.com) is a useful travel agency run by an

enthusiastic German who lives in Kalamata and knows the area very well.

Services There are banks and ATMs all over the city. The post office is near the customs house beyond the park at the seaward end of Aristoménous (Mon–Fri 7.30am–2pm).

GETTING AROUND

By bus The local #1 bus (€1.30) starts from Platía 23-Martiou, about a 600m walk from the bus station, and heads south through the centre then runs the length of the seafront to *Hotel Filoxenia*.

By car There are many car rental places in town, including the reliable Verga Rent A Car, Farón 202 (☏ 27210 95190, ⊛ car-rental-kalamata.gr) and Avance

Rent A Car, Lycourgou 6-8 (☏ 27210 27211, ⊛ avance .gr). You can rent motorbikes from Bastakos, at Farón 139 (☏ 27210 26638).

By taxi Radio Taxis on ☏ 27210 21112 (24hr).

Activities Explore Messinia, Bouloukou 26 (☏ 69718 97640, ⊛ exploremessinia.com) organizes intrepid hikes, kayaking trips and river rafting.

ACCOMMODATION

★ **Elektra Hotel & Spa** Psaron 152, at Bouboulinas ☏ 27210 99100, ⊛ elektrahotelspa.gr. Convenient for the marina and the ferries, this swish hotel has the largest and most comfortable beds you are likely to sink into in Greece. There's a gym, rooftop pool, sauna and Turkish bath plus a dozen different spa treatments on offer, all adding up to a great stay. Breakfast included. **€100**

★ **Filoxenia Terma** Navarínou ☏ 27210 23343, ⊛ filoxeniakalamata.com. The best beach resort in Kalamata, and the only one where you don't have to cross the busy seafront road to get to the beach. It has large rooms with balconies, two pools, tennis courts, a sauna,

spa and gym, plus free parking. Buffet breakfast included; half board €25 extra. **€110**

Haïkos Navarínou 115 ☏ 27210 88902, ⊛ haikos.gr. A trim, modern hotel with plush rooms by the town beach. All rooms have balconies, a/c and wi-fi, but it's worth paying a little extra to get sea views. Free parking; breakfast included. **€90**

Rex Aristomenous 26 ☏ 27210 22334, ⊛ rexhotel.gr. Historic old-town hotel built in 1899. Rooms are on the small side, but fresh and well appointed, some with balconies, in a fine Neoclassical building facing the palm-lined promenade. There's also a restaurant and a café. Breakfast included. **€100**

EATING AND DRINKING

The west marina is where you'll find the top restaurants, while the Navarínou waterfront is a good place for popular cafés, bars and ice-cream parlours: the pedestrianized old town is the nightlife hub.

★ **Kannas** Poseidonos 12, Marina ☏ 27210 91596, ⊛ kannas.gr. Facing the water, with seating on a pretty terrace, this restaurant has good fish and pasta dishes. Try the shrimp risotto for €12. Daily noon–midnight.

Vino Banco Tapas Diós Ithómata 6 ☏ 27210 25160.

This tapas wine bar in the old town has taken Kalamáta by storm. They also serve larger dishes such as paella, and pride themselves on being "always open" – we can't guarantee such a claim, but have yet to see it closed. There's a lot going on, such as wine tastings and stand-up comedy to while away your time. Daily 8am–late.

Yachting Café Terma Marina ☎ 27210 87432. Lording it over the end of the marina, this two-storey restaurant with a sweeping terrace has some excellent dishes at low prices: large crepes (€4), pasta (€5) or a meat platter for two (€12). There are often live bands at weekends (free for diners). Daily 8am–late.

Koróni

KORÓNI, 40km southwest of Kalamáta, occupies one of the more picturesque locations in Greece, stacked against a fortified bluff and commanding grand views across the Messenian gulf. It's a place to relax on the beach, drink wine and amble about a countryside lush with vineyards and olive groves. The town is rustically beautiful with tiled and pastel-washed houses arrayed in a maze of stair-and-ramp streets that have changed little since the medieval **Venetian occupation** (1206–1500). Koróni, along with its sister fortress of **Methóni**, were the Venetians' oldest and longest-held possessions in the Peloponnese.

2

The citadel and beaches

Open access • Free

Koróni's **citadel** is one of the least martial-looking in Greece, crowning the town more like a large, pleasantly dilapidated garden. Part of the interior is given over to private houses and garden plots, but the greater part is occupied by the nunnery of **Timíou Prodhrómou**, whose chapels, outbuildings and flower-strewn gardens occupy nearly every bastion. Downhill from the citadel, you reach the rarely-crowded **Zánga beach**, which runs into **Mémi beach**, making a 2km stretch of sand with preternaturally clear water.

ARRIVAL AND INFORMATION

KORÓNI

By bus Buses terminate in the main square, one block back from the waterfront where the taxi rank is also located.

Destinations Athens (1 daily; 5hr); Kalamáta (4–6 daily; 1hr)

Services Koróni has two banks and ATMs, as well as a post office (Mon–Fri 7.30am–2pm).

ACCOMMODATION

★ Camvillia Vounaria ☎ 27250 42131, ⓦ camvillia .com. The new kid on the block aims high, with an infinity pool, gourmet restaurant, secluded beach access and designer rooms with stunning views over Messinia bay. Breakfast (cooked to order by the chef) included. Mid-May to Sept. **€130**

Diana Port ☎ 27250 22312, ⓦ dianahotel-koroni.gr. Located on a side street as you arrive at the port, this boutique property, totally renovated in 2017, has modern designer rooms any Koroni hotel would envy. May–Sept. **€50**

Koroni Camping 200m north of town ☎ 27250 22884, ⓦ koronicamping.com. Just 60m up from a sandy beach, this eucalyptus-shaded campsite sports a pool, a bar, an excellent restaurant (mains €5), a minimarket, washing machines and wi-fi. Skygazers can enjoy free use of a telescope. **€21**

EATING AND DRINKING

Bogris #2 Left of the port ☎ 27250 22947. This port-side taverna boasts a romantic garden courtyard. Check the day's offerings on the menu: there are always dozens of grills (€5–6) and a good meze selection. Daily noon–midnight.

Parthenon Port ☎ 27250 22146. This restaurant has the best location by the harbour and serves up a classic mix of Greek dishes, notably seafood. Good-value 3-course day menus for €10–12. Also serves breakfast. Feb–Nov daily 8am–midnight.

Finikoúnda

FINIKOÚNDA, 18km west of Koróni, is a small fishing village with seven superb beaches, some of which are in front of the various campsites. It is arguably the best-looking resort between Kalamáta and Yalova, and is popular with British package-holiday companies.

2

ARRIVAL AND ACTIVITIES

FINIKOÚNDA

By bus The bus station is by the village church but in high season buses don't enter the village and stop on the main highway by the entrance roundabout. Finikoúnda is served by the Kalamáta–Pýlos bus (3 daily; 2hr).

Boat trips Bebis cruises (☎ 6944 5654210) at the end of the harbour runs five-hour boat trips from Finikoúnda taking in the three surrounding islands Sapiénza, Schíza and Ayía Marína including a swim (€45pp; drinks on sale; no food provided).

ACCOMMODATION

★**Estía** 70m from the beach ☎ 27230 71116, ⓦ hotelestia.com. Run by a Canadian/Greek couple, this hotel has a roof terrace bar and large self-catering apartments with excellent cooking facilities and USB chargers. There's also a gym, plus aromatherapy treatments (€50/hr) and yoga classes on offer. May–Oct. **€70**

★**Finikes Camping** 2km west of the village ☎ 27230 28524, ⓦ finikescamping.gr. Set in the middle of nature, this shady campsite is situated along a beautiful beach and has rooms as well. Facilities include a minimarket, bar, restaurant info-kiosk, kitchen and good sanitation services. Greek PM Alexis Tsipras caused a stir when he stayed here for May Day in 2017. Camping **€14**, double **€40**

Fotis Apartments 150m from the beach ☎ 27230 28588, ⓦ www.finikoundaapartments.gr. This self-catering apartment complex around a central pool is quiet, friendly and owned by a chatty couple who may well share their home-made cakes with you. Every studio has a kitchenette and free wi-fi. May–Sept. **€50**

Korakakis Beach Beachfront ☎ 27230 71221, ⓔ korakaki@otenet.gr. Medium-sized, quirkily decorated hotel with a bar-restaurant: it also has self-catering bungalows at similar prices, 50m from the beach. Choose top-floor front rooms for maximum views. **€50**

Loutsa Camping 1km east of town ☎ 27230 71169, ⓦ loutsacamping.gr. This campsite offers ample shade and a garden setting, just steps from a breathtaking, wide sandy beach. There's a minimarket, taverna and free wi-fi, plus washing machines available on-site. Mid-May to mid-Oct. **€17**

EATING

Dionysos Harbourfront ☎ 27230 71229. The best taverna in town after *Elena*, its seafront location is both idyllic and relaxing. Best known for its grills, it also offers excellent lamb dishes such as *kléftiko*. Mains €7–9. Daily: March to mid-May & Oct to mid-Nov 6.30pm–midnight; mid-May to Sept noon–midnight.

★**Elena** End of the harbour ☎ 27230 71235, ⓔ elenfini@gmail.com. This taverna is one of the best in Messinia and counts several VIPs as regulars, including Lord Owen whose holiday home is nearby. They serve vegetables from their own garden and meat from their farm (mains €6–8). They also feature live rembétika music three times a week in season. Noon–midnight: May–Sept daily; Oct–April Fri & Sat only.

Methóni

METHÓNI is geared more conspicuously to tourism than Koróni and gets very crowded in season, but is still the best value resort along this coastline. The huge Venetian fortress here is as imposing and romantic as they come – massively bastioned, washed on three sides by the sea, and cut off from the land by a great moat. The modern town, which stretches inland for 1km northward, is full of charming back alleys and it meets the sea at a small, pleasant **beach** just on the east side of the citadel.

Methóni Fortress

Daily: winter 8am–3pm; summer 8am–8pm • €2

Once used to garrison knights on their way to the Crusades, **Methóni Fortress** is entered across the moat along a stone bridge. Inside are very extensive remains: a Venetian cathedral (the Venetians' Lion of St Mark emblem is ubiquitous), a Turkish bath, the foundations of dozens of houses, a strange pyramid-roofed stone structure, and some awesome, but mostly cordoned-off, underground passages. Walk around the walls, and you'll see a sea gate at the southern end, which leads out across a causeway to the **Boúrtzi**, a small fortified island that served as a prison and place of execution. The octagonal tower was built by the Turks in the sixteenth century to replace an earlier Venetian fortification.

ARRIVAL AND INFORMATION

By bus KTEL buses stop at the first forked junction in town. **Destinations** Athens (2 daily; 5hr); Finikoúnda (3 daily; 20min); Kalamáta (6–8 daily; 1hr 30min); Pýlos (3–5 daily; 20min).

Services There are two banks and two ATMs (one on Mézonos and one on Episkópou Grigoríou S). The post office is on Mezonos 40 (Mon–Fri 7.30am–2pm).

ACCOMMODATION

★**Niriides Luxury Villas** ☎27230 28787, ⓦniriidesmessiniahotel.gr. A no-expense-spared housing development 200m up from the end of the beach. It has two pools, landscaped gardens, parking, solar panels, parquet floors, and apartments (sleeping four) with fitted kitchens, American fridges, luxury beds and lots of space. Former guests include the US Ambassador and his entourage, who stayed here in 2016. Apartment €180, double €105

★**Ulysses Kyprou & Bouboulinas** ☎27230 31600, ⓦwww.ulysseshotel.com. Lovely family hotel with simple, clean rooms, galloping wi-fi, TV and fridge with free bottled water: the windows/balconies have mosquito netting. Decoration is by photographer-owner Nikos Markopoulos and the home-made breakfast is served in a large wine-shaded garden, where there are also yoga classes in the summer. March–Oct. €80

EATING

The best places to eat are around the castle gate, rather than on the beach square.

Klimataria ☎27230 31544. In a courtyard garden just down from the fortress, this taverna serves fresh, well-prepared dishes (including good, classically Greek veggie options), which you can pick out from the day's offerings. Mains €6–13. May–Oct daily noon–midnight.

Nikos ☎27230 31282. Just up from the beach square, this is a high-aspiring taverna with an Athenian chef who will fillet the fish in front of you. Vegetables are grown in the orchard opposite and olive oil comes from their own grove. Mains €10–12. Daily noon–midnight.

Pýlos and around

PÝLOS is a compact but surprisingly stylish town for rural Messinía; guarded by a pair of medieval castles, it occupies a superb position on one of the finest natural harbours in Greece, the almost landlocked **Navarino Bay**. The main pleasures of Pýlos are exploring the hillside alleys, waterside streets and fortress. Given the town's associations with the **Battle of Navarino**, and, more anciently, with Homer's "sandy Pýlos", the domain of wise **King Nestor** whose alleged palace (see opposite) has been excavated 16km to the north, it makes a good base for exploring this part of the Peloponnese, particularly if you have a car. If you're relying on public transport, you'll find that gaps in services make complex day-trips impractical.

Town centre

Shaded by a large plane tree and several of its offspring, **Platía Trión Navárhon** in Pýlos **town centre** is a beautiful public space, encircled by cafés and colonnaded shops. At its head is a **war memorial** commemorating the admirals Codrington, de Rigny and von Heyden, who commanded the British, French and Russian forces in the Battle of Navarino (see box opposite).

Niókastro (Néo Kástro)

Off Methoni Rd • Tues–Sun winter 8.30am–3pm; summer 8am–8pm • €6, includes museum.

The principal sight in town is the **Niókastro**. The huge "new castle" was built by the Turks in 1572, and you can walk around much of the 1.5km of arcaded battlements. For most of the eighteenth and nineteenth centuries, it served as a prison, and its inner courtyard was divided into a warren of narrow yards separated by high walls. The design was intended to keep **Máni** clansmen, the bulk of the prison population, from continuing their murderous vendettas inside. Pylos' small but interesting **Archeological museum** is in the Maison building inside the castle and showcases local finds from Neolithic to Roman times. They include the notable

2

THE BATTLE OF NAVARINO

In 1827, during the Greek War of Independence (see p.779), the Great Powers of Britain, France and Russia were attempting to force an armistice on the Turks, having established diplomatic relations with the Greek insurgents. To this end they sent a fleet of 27 warships to **Navarino Bay** below the town of Pýlos, where Ottoman leader Ibrahim Pasha had gathered his forces – 16,000 men in 89 ships. The declared intention was to coerce Ibrahim into leaving Messinía, which he had been raiding ruthlessly.

On the night of October 20, an Egyptian frigate, part of the Turks' supporting force, fired its cannons, and full-scale battle broke out. Without intending to take up arms for the Greeks, the "allies" responded to the attack and, extraordinarily, sank and destroyed 53 of the Turkish fleet without a single loss. There was considerable international embarrassment when news filtered through to the "victors", but the action had nevertheless effectively ended Turkish control of Greek waters and within a year **Greek independence** was secured and recognized.

Dioscouri twin bronzes plus some exquisitely crafted gold ornaments, precious stone necklaces and delicate glassware.

René Puaux Museum

Pylos Port • Tues–Sun winter 8.30am–3pm; summer 8am–8pm • €2

The appealing **René Puaux Museum**, in the former house of a Greek 1912 long jump Olympic champion, houses a surprisingly extensive collection of early nineteenth-century lithographs and cartoons on the Greek War of Independence. They belonged to the French journalist, philhellene and collector René Puaux (1878–1936), who donated them to the Greek state after his death.

Island of Sfaktiría

For tours of the bay (2hr; €15), contact Pylos Cruises at the port (☎ 27230 23155; 🌐 pyloscruises.gr) • Boat rental from Pylos Marine by the *Karalis Hotel* (☎ 69764 37515).

Memories of the Battle of Navarino can be evoked by a visit to the **island of Sfaktiría**. **Tours of the bay** land on Sfaktiria to visit various tombs of philhellenes, a chapel and memorials to Russian, British and French sailors. You can also hire a **boat** from the port and snorkel to see the remains of the Turkish fleet lying on the seabed of the island. Sfaktiría was also the site of a battle between a small group of Spartans under siege by the Athenians during the Peloponnesian War – one of the few times that Spartans have surrendered.

Yiálova

6km north of Pýlos

YIÁLOVA has tamarisk trees shading its sandy beach, and makes a delightful base for walkers, beach lovers or bird-watchers drawn by Voïdhokiliá beach and the adjoining nature reserve.

Paleókastro

At the end of the bay, 5km west of Yiálova

Pýlos's northern castle and ancient acropolis, **Paleókastro** (old castle), stands on a hill ridge almost touching the island of Sfaktiría. It has substantial walls and identifiable courtyards, a mix of Frankish and Venetian designs, set upon ancient foundations. It is currently out of bounds because of subsidence, but you can go up and take in the **view** over Voïdhokiliá, one of the finest beaches in the Peloponnese.

Voïdhokiliá beach

Voïdhokiliá beach is a spectacular crescent of white sand and turquoise waters 12km north of Pýlos. The **lagoon** behind the beach is an important bird conservation area, and vehicles are not allowed on the earth road around its eastern rim. Turtles still breed at Voïdhokiliá (and at the beaches of Romanoú and Máti, further north), and there's a tiny population – the only one in mainland Europe – of **chameleons** among the dune shrubs.

Spílaio toú Néstoros

A path from the southern Voïdhokiliá dunes ascends to the **Spílaio toú Néstoros** (Nestor's Cave), and then to Paleókastro. This impressive bat cave with a hole in the roof is fancifully identified as the grotto in which, according to the *Odyssey*, Nestor and Neleus kept their cows, and in which Hermes hid Apollo's cattle.

2

Nestor's Palace

17km from Pýlos • Winter daily 8am–3pm; summer Tues–Sun 8am–8pm • €6 • ☎ 27630 31437 • Buses from Pylos to Hóra stop at the site (4 daily; 20min).

Nestor's Palace is the best preserved of all the Mycenaean royal palaces. Flanked by deep, fertile valleys, the palace site looks out towards Navarino Bay – a location which perfectly suits the wise and peaceful king described in Homer's *Odyssey*. The site, which re-opened in 2016 after a three-year restoration, was discovered in 1939 but left virtually undisturbed until after World War II. The site's most important find was a group of 1200 **tablets** inscribed in **Linear B**, which, given their similarity to tablets discovered in Knossós (see p.459), proved conclusively that there was a link between the Mycenaean and Minoan civilizations. The tablets were baked hard in the fire that destroyed the palace at the time of the Dorian invasion, around 1200 BC, perhaps as little as one generation after the fall of Troy.

The site

The new 2300-square-metre steel structure that covers the main site and the elevated metal walkway above it were unveiled in late 2016 and work wonders for fully absorbing the scale and structure of Nestor's massive complex. Unlike most Greek sites, it's wheelchair accessible.

The buildings are in three principal groups: the **main palace** in the middle, an earlier and **smaller palace** on the left, and on the right **guardhouses** and an **arsenal**. The basic design will be familiar if you've been to Mycenae or Tiryns: an internal court, guarded by a sentry box, gives access to the main sections of the principal palace that contained some 45 rooms and halls.

On first entering the site, you climb on the walkway in front of the **propylon** in the shape of a letter H. The propylon leads through a double porch to the **megaron** (throne room), with its characteristic open hearth, directly ahead of the entrance. The finest of the frescoes was discovered here, depicting a griffin (perhaps the royal emblem) standing guard over the throne; that work is now in the museum at Hóra (see 186).

TELEMACHUS TAKES A BATH

King Nestor rates several mentions in Homer's epic, but the scene from *Odyssey* that is set here is the visit of **Telemachus**, son of Odysseus, who had journeyed from Ithaca to seek news of his father from the king. As Telemachus arrives at the beach, accompanied by the disguised goddess Athena, he comes upon **Nestor** with his sons and court sacrificing to Poseidon. The visitors are welcomed and feasted, "sitting on downy fleeces on the sand", and although the king has no news of Odysseus, he promises Telemachus a chariot so he can enquire from Menelaus at Sparta. First, however, the guests are taken back to the palace, where Telemachus is given a bath by Nestor's "youngest grown daughter, beautiful Polycaste", and emerges, anointed with oil, "with the body of an immortal". By some harmonious twist of fate, an actual **bathtub** was unearthed here, rendering the palace ruins as a whole potent ground for Homeric imaginings.

2

To the right of the megaron lies the famous **bathroom**, with its painted terracotta tub *in situ*, adjoining a smaller complex of rooms, centred on another, smaller, structure, identified as the **queen's megaron**. To the left of the here lie **pantries**, one of which yielded no fewer than 2853 kylikes (drinking vessels), a **canteen** and a **waiting room** for dignitaries with a stone bench still visible. Finally, as you go out behind the car park you can visit a **tholos tomb**, a smaller – but no less impressive – version of the famous ones at Mycenae.

The Archeological Museum

Signposted above the main square in Hóra (Hóra Trifylías), 4km northeast of Nestor's Palace • Tues–Sun 8.30am–3pm • €2 • ☎ 27630 31358 • If coming from Pylos by bus (see below), stop here first before visiting the site, and then walk the 45min downhill to Nestor's Palace.

A browse round the **Archeological Museum** adds significantly to a visit to Nestor's Palace. Pride of place in the display goes to the **palace fresco fragments**, one of which, bearing out Homer's descriptions, shows a warrior in a boar-tusk helmet. You can also see, in a small reproduction, the Nestor Palace's **mosaics** which are not displayed at the site. Lesser finds include much pottery – there are even a few 3300-year-old ceramic baby feeders – some beautiful **gold cups** and other everyday objects, such as loom weights, scales and combs, gathered both from the site and from other Mycenaean tombs in the region.

ARRIVAL, INFORMATION AND TOURS

By bus The bus station is on the main square (☎ 27230 22230). The ticket office keeps odd hours, though 8–11am every day is a good bet. Getting your bearings is easy, as the town is not large, and the main square facing the port is very much at its heart.

Destinations Athens (1 daily; 5hr); Finikoúnda (Mon–Sat 2–3 daily; 45min); Hóra (4 daily; 35min); Kalamáta (5–6 daily; 1hr); Methóni (3–5 daily; 20min); Yiálova (1–4 daily; 15min).

PÝLOS AND AROUND

By car Car rental is available through AutoUnion (☎ 27230 22393, ✉ info@kasimiotis.gr) on the Kalamáta road.

Services There are three banks with ATMs on the central square. The post office is just up from the bus station on Nileos St (Mon–Fri 7.30am–2.30pm).

Tours Nikos Lymberópoulos (☎ 6974 747 454, ✉ nikoslym@otenet.gr) is an English-speaking tour leader for wildlife expeditions and various hikes including Nestor's cave and Paleókastro (€20/person).

ACCOMMODATION

PÝLOS

Karalís Kalamátas 26 ☎ 27230 22960, ⊕ hotelkaralis. gr. Located up from the town centre, on the main road to the north, this is an attractive port-view hotel with comfortable modern rooms with balconies, some with jacuzzis. Breakfast included. **€70**

Karalís Beach Seafront below the castle ☎ 27230 23021, ⊕ karalisbeach.gr. This is the Karalís family's luxury property below the castle, right on the sea, with a comfortable mix of minimalist design and traditional decor. There's no beach though. Buffet breakfast included. April– Oct. **€90**

Miramare Tsamadou 3 Paralia ☎ 27230 22751, ⊕ miramarepylos.gr. Under new, enthusiastic management, this well-located hotel has basic rooms, but all have balconies with views, and the bathrooms were renovated in 2017. Models of ancient ships decorate the lobby, there's a well-stocked late bar and a few private parking spaces opposite. Breakfast, a buffet tour-de-force is included. April–Oct. **€70**

YIÁLOVA

Camping Erodios 500m west of town ☎ 27230 23269, ⊕ erodioss.gr. A modern campsite, with its own sandy beach and a restaurant, bar, minimarket, playground and washing machines. Of particular interest are the self-catering bungalows, as good as any hotel. Mid-April to mid-Oct. Camping **€16**, bungalow **€50**

Camping Navarino ☎ 27230 22973, ⊕ navarino-beach.gr. Large, walled campsite that looks and feels more like a resort. Superb sandy beach, shady palm trees, top-notch facilities, watersports and wi-fi; a good restaurant and supermarket complete the picture. Ten percent discount for stays over six days. April–Oct. **€16**

★ **Zoe Resort** Beach ☎ 27230 22025, ⊕ zoeresort.gr. An ever-improving eco-resort with spacious, self-catering apartments surrounded by an orchard full of orange, lemon and banana trees, right on the beach. There is also a large pool, a good restaurant (have a dessert, even if it means skipping a starter), a herb and veg garden and several ponds populated with frogs and goldfish. Best buffet breakfast in the area included. **€90**

EATING

PÝLOS

Grigoris ☎ 27230 22621. This warm welcoming, bustling place, at the edge of the port, is renowned for its grilled meats (€11–13) but also offers home-made cooked dishes (€6). Daily 10am–midnight.

Poseidonia ☎ 27230 23133. Many locals eat here for its inspired Greek cuisine – start with the soup or pie of the day (€3–4) and continue with variations on well-known Greek dishes. To top it all, there's a knockout wine list. Noon–midnight: April–Sept daily, Oct–March Fri & Sat.

YIÁLOVA

To Spitiko ☎ 27230 22138. This pleasant and friendly taverna is arguably the best on the Yalova promenade. It serves up a wide range of dishes, some of them Cypriot like their owner. For a memorable experience, try the *afélia*, pork in red wine (€7.50). Daily noon–midnight.

Olympia and Ilía

Dominated by the monumental archeological site of **Olympia**, gracing the fertile Alfiós valley, the sizeable province of **Ilía** comprises for the most part flat coastal plains with a series of undistinguished market towns, bordered on the west by long, fine, often underused **beaches**; the resort to head for here is **Arkoúdhi**.

Olympia

The historic associations and resonance of **OLYMPIA**, which for over a millennium hosted the most important **Panhellenic Games**, are rivalled only by Delphi or Mycenae. It is one of the largest ancient sites in Greece, spread beside the twin rivers of Alfiós (Alpheus) – the largest in the Peloponnese – and Kládhios, and overlooked by the Hill

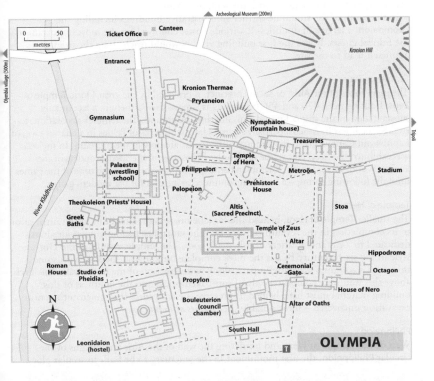

of Krónos. The site itself is picturesque, but the sheer quantity of ruined structures can give a confusing impression of their ancient grandeur and function. Despite the crowds, tour buses, souvenir shops and other trappings of mass tourism, it deserves a visit with at least an overnight stay at the modern village Arhéa (Ancient) Olymbía.

The site

Daily: summer 8am–8pm; winter 8.30am–3pm · €12, including the Archeological Museum, the Museum of the History of the Olympic Games in Antiquity and the Museum of the History of Excavations in Olympia · ☎ 26240 22517

From its beginnings, the **site** was a sanctuary, with a permanent population limited to the temple priests. At first the games took place within the sacred precinct, the walled, rectangular **Altis**, but as events became more sophisticated a new **stadium** was built adjoining it.

Gymnasium and official buildings

The **entrance** to the site, located just 200m from the village, leads along the west side of the Altis wall, past a group of public and official buildings. On the left, beyond some Roman baths, is the **Prytaneion**, the administrators' residence, where athletes stayed and feasted at official expense. On the right are the ruins of a **gymnasium** and a **palaestra** (wrestling school), used by the competitors during their obligatory month of pre-games training.

Beyond these stood the Priests' House, the **Theokoleion**, a substantial colonnaded building in whose southeast corner is a structure adapted as a Byzantine church. This was originally the **studio of Fidias**, the fifth-century BC sculptor responsible for the great gold and ivory cult statue in Olympia's Temple of Zeus. It was identified by following a description by Pausanias, and through the discovery of tools, moulds for the statue and a cup engraved with the sculptor's name.

To the south of the studio lie further administrative buildings including the **Leonidaion**, a large and doubtless luxurious hostel endowed for the most important of the festival guests. It was the first building visitors would reach along the original approach road to the site.

Temple of Zeus

The main focus of the **Altis**, or **sacred precinct**, is provided by the great Doric **Temple of Zeus**. Built between 470 and 456 BC, it was as large as the Parthenon, a fact quietly substantiated by the vast column drums littering the ground. The temple's decoration, too, rivalled the finest in Athens; partially recovered, its sculptures of Pelops in a chariot race, of Lapiths and Centaurs, and the Labours of Hercules, are now in the museum. In the *cella* was exhibited the (lost) cult statue of Zeus by Fidias, one of the seven wonders of the ancient world. Here, too, the **Olympian flame** was kept alight, from the time of the games until the following spring – a tradition continued at an altar for the modern games.

Temple of Hera

The smaller **Temple of Hera**, behind the Prytaneion, was the first built in the Altis; prior to its completion in the seventh century BC, the sanctuary had only open-air altars, dedicated to Zeus and a variety of other cult gods. The temple, rebuilt in the Doric style in the sixth century BC, is the most complete building on the site, with some thirty of its columns surviving in part, along with a section of the inner wall. The levels above this wall were composed only of sun-baked brick, and the lightness of this building material must have helped to preserve the sculptures that nineteenth-century excavation uncovered – most notably the *Hermes of Praxiteles*.

Philippeion

West of the Temple of Hera and bordering the wall of the Altis are remains of the circular **Philippeion**, the first monument in the sanctuary to be built to secular glory.

2

THE OLYMPIC GAMES

The origins of the games at Olympia are rooted in **legends** – often relating to the mythical hero Pelops, Zeus, or to Hercules. Historically, the contests probably began around the eleventh century BC, growing over the next two centuries from a local festival to the **quadrennial** celebration attended by states from throughout the Greek world. These great gatherings extended the games' importance and purpose well beyond the winning of olive wreaths; assembled under a strict **truce**, nobles and ambassadors negotiated treaties, while merchants did business and sculptors and poets sought commissions.

EVENTS

From the beginning, the main Olympic **events** were athletic. The earliest was a race over the course of the stadium – roughly 200m. Later came the introduction of two-lap (400m) and 24-lap (5000m) races, along with the most revered of the Olympiad events, the **pentathlon**. This encompassed running, jumping, discus and javelin events, and the competitors were gradually reduced to a final pair for a wrestling-and-boxing combat. It was, like much of these early Olympiads, a fairly brutal contest. One of the most prestigious events was the **pancratium**, where contestants fought each other, naked and unarmed, using any means except biting or gouging. Similarly, the **chariot races** were extreme tests of strength and control; only one team in twenty completed the 7km course.

RULES AND AWARDS

In the early Olympiads, the **rules** of competition were strict. Only free-born Greek males could take part, and the **rewards** of victory were entirely honorary: a palm, given to the victor immediately after the contest, and an olive branch, presented in a ceremony closing the games. As the games developed, however, the rules were loosened to allow participation by athletes from all parts of the Greek and Roman world. By the fourth century BC, when the games were at their peak, the athletes were virtually all **professionals**, heavily sponsored by their home states and, if they won at Olympia, commanding huge appearance money at games elsewhere. Under the Romans, commercialization accelerated and new events were introduced. Emperor Nero postponed the games by two years to 67 AD just so that he could compete in (and win) special singing and lyre-playing events.

DECLINE AND FALL

Notwithstanding Roman abuses, the Olympian tradition was popular enough to be maintained for another three centuries, and the games' eventual **closure** happened as a result of religious dogma rather than lack of support. In 393 AD **Emperor Theodosius**, recently converted to **Christianity**, suspended the games as part of a general crackdown on public pagan festivities. This suspension proved final, for Theodosius's successor ordered the destruction of the temples, a process completed by barbarian invasion, earthquakes and, lastly, by the Alfiós River changing its course to cover the sanctuary site. There it remained, covered by 7m of silt and sand, until the first excavation by German archeologists in the 1870s.

It was begun by Philip II to commemorate his victory at the Battle of Chaeronea (see p.207), which gave him control over the Greek mainland; the building may have been completed by his son, Alexander the Great.

Nymphaion (fountain house), treasuries and Metroön

To the east of the Hera temple is a small, second-century AD **Nymphaion**, or **fountain house**, the gift of the ubiquitous Herodes Atticus. Beyond, lining a terrace at the base of the Hill of Krónos, are the state **treasuries**, storage chambers for sacrificial items and sporting equipment used in the games. They are built in the form of temples, as at Delphi; the oldest and grandest, at the east end, belonged to Gela in Sicily. In front of the treasuries are the foundations of the **Metroön**, a fourth-century BC Doric temple dedicated to the mother of the gods.

Pelopeion

Between the temples of Hera and Zeus is a grove described by Pausanias, and identified as the **Pelopeion**. In addition to a cult altar to the Olympian hero, this enclosed a small mound formed by sacrificial ashes, among which excavations unearthed many of the terracotta finds in the museum. The sanctuary's principal altar, dedicated to Zeus, probably stood just to the east.

Bouleuterion (council chamber)

The ancient ceremonial entrance to the Altis was on the south side, below a long **stoa** taking up almost the entire east side of the precinct. At the corner was a house built by the Roman emperor Nero for his stay during the games. He also had the entrance remodelled as a triumphal arch, fit for his anticipated victories. Through the arch, just outside the precinct, stood the **Bouleuterion**, or **council chamber**, where before a great statue of Zeus the competitors took their oaths to observe the Olympian rules. These were not to be taken lightly: lining the way were bronze statues paid for with the fines exacted for foul play, bearing the name of the disgraced athlete, his father and city.

Stadium

The natural focus of the Olympic site is the 200m track of the **stadium** itself, entered by way of a long arched tunnel. The starting and finishing lines are still there, with the judges' thrones in the middle and seating ridges banked to either side. Originally unstructured, the stadium developed with the games' popularity, forming a model for others throughout the Greek and Roman world. The tiers here eventually accommodated up to twenty thousand spectators, with a smaller number on the southern slope overlooking the **hippodrome** where the chariot races were held. Even so, the seats were reserved for the wealthier strata of society. The ordinary populace – along with slaves and all women spectators – watched the events from the Hill of Krónos to the north, then a natural, treeless grandstand. The stadium was unearthed only in World War II, during a second phase of German excavations between 1941 and 1944, allegedly on the direct orders of Hitler.

Archeological Museum

200m north of the sanctuary • Daily: summer 8am–8pm; winter 8.30am–3pm • €12, including the site, the Museum of the History of the Olympic Games in Antiquity and the Museum of the History of Excavations in Olympia • ☎ 26240 22742

Olympia's site **Archeological Museum** contains some of the finest Classical and Roman sculptures in the country, all superbly displayed. The most famous of the individual sculptures are the **head of Hera** and the **Hermes of Praxiteles**, both dating from the fourth century BC and discovered in the Temple of Hera. The Hermes is one of the best preserved of all Classical sculptures, and remarkable in the easy informality of its pose; it retains traces of its original paint. On a grander scale is the **Nike of Paionios**, which was originally 10m high. Though no longer complete, it hints at how the sanctuary must once have appeared, crowded with statuary.

In the main hall of the museum is the centrepiece of the Olympia finds: statuary and sculpture reassembled from the **Temple of Zeus**. These include a delicately moulded frieze of the **Twelve Labours of Hercules**. Another from the east pediment depicts Zeus presiding over a famous **chariot race** between Pelops and King Oinamaos – the prize the hand of the king's daughter. The king (on the left of the frieze) was eventually defeated by Pelops (on the right), after – depending on the version – assistance from Zeus (depicted at the centre), magic steeds from Poseidon or, most un-Olympian, bribing Oinamaos's charioteer to tamper with the wheels.

The west pediment illustrates the **Battle of the Lapiths and Centaurs** at the wedding of King Peirithous of the Lapiths. This time, Apollo presides over the scene while Theseus helps the Lapiths defeat the drunken centaurs, depicted attacking the women and boy guests. Many of the metope fragments are today in the Louvre in Paris, and some of what you see here are plaster-cast copies.

The last rooms of the museum contain a collection of objects relating to the games – including *halteres* (jumping weights), discuses, weightlifters' stones and other sporting bits and pieces. Also displayed are a number of **funerary inscriptions**, including that of a boxer, Camelos of Alexandria, who died in the stadium after praying to Zeus for victory or death.

Arhéa Olymbía

ARHÉA OLYMBÍA is a village that has grown up simply to serve the excavations and tourist trade. It's almost literally a one-horse town – its main street, **Praxitéles Kondhýli**, is lined with shops, and there are just a few short side streets. Nevertheless, it is quite a pleasant place to stay and is preferable by far to Pýrgos, offering the prospect of good countryside walks along the Alfiós River and around the Hill of Krónos.

There are a few somewhat dutiful minor museums, worth a visit if you have time on your hands. The **Museum of the History of the Olympic Games in Antiquity** and the **Museum of the History of Excavations in Olympia** (both Mon 10am–5pm, Tues–Fri 8am–3pm; €12, including the site and the Archeological Museum) lie above the coach park at the eastern end of the village, en route to the main site.

ARRIVAL AND INFORMATION	**ARHÉA OLYMBÍA**

By bus The bus stop is behind the now unused train station within a block of Arhéa Olymbía village centre. Destinations from Arhéa Olymbía Athens (only through connections via Pýrgos, 7 daily; 5hr 30min); Pýrgos (7–12 daily; 30min).

Services Arhéa Olymbía has three banks on the main avenue and a post office at De Coubertin 2 (Mon–Fri 7.30am–2.30pm).

ACCOMMODATION

Europa Dhroúva 1 ☎ 26240 22650, ⓦ www .hoteleuropa.gr. A well-run and comfortable resort hotel situated near the top of the hill to the southwest. There's a large pool, ample parking and a very good restaurant. Excellent choice if you have a car, but if not it's a steep 10min walk from the main street. Breakfast included. **€90**

Kronio Tsoúreka 1 ☎ 26240 22188, ⓦ hotelkronio.gr. A comfortable, welcoming hotel with large, basic, airy rooms. As befits the town, the owner was a city marathon runner (and winner). Pick ups from Pyrgos can be arranged. Breakfast included. **€45**

Neda Karamanlí 1 ☎ 26240 22563, ⓦ www.hotelneda .gr. Well furnished and managed, this central hotel offers many extras for its price range such as rooms with bathtubs, a decent pool and large private parking area. Breakfast and wi-fi are included. **€70**

★**Pelops** Varelás 2 ☎ 26240 22543, ⓦ hotelpelops.gr. Run by a Greek–Australian couple, this pleasant hotel is situated on a square by the church. They offer a popular cooking course (€50 for half a day including the resulting meal), as well as courses in painting and creative writing in English. Sumptuous breakfast is available for €6. March–Oct. **€55**

EATING

The village is loaded with tavernas and kebab grills, but the best places are off the main drag.

★**Aegeon** Georgiou Douma ☎26240 22540. This unassuming place serves everything from baked lamb and roast chicken to pizza, but even dedicated carnivores should try the vegetarian stews made with fresh local produce. Mains €8–10. April–Nov daily 8am–midnight.

To Steki tou Vangeli Stefanopoúlou 13 ☎26240 22530. Excellent grill house highly recommended by locals and operated by a charming couple. They also supply takeaway dinners to the regional fire service based at Olympia. Try the grilled chicken with lemon & mustard sauce for €6 – and a litre of house wine costs just €4. Feb–Nov daily 6pm–1am.

Pýrgos

PÝRGOS is a large, modern business town and the capital of Ilía province. A public transport hub, it's pleasant enough in parts, though with little appeal for tourists. The town has a grim history. When the Germans withdrew at the end of World War II, it remained under the control of Greek Nazi collaborators. They negotiated a surrender with the Greek Resistance, who were met by gunfire as they entered the town. Full-scale battle erupted and for five days the town burned.

ARRIVAL AND DEPARTURE PÝRGOS

By bus The bus station is to the west of town (☎ 26210 20600, ⓦ ktelileias.gr).
Destinations Athens (9–11 daily; 5–7hr); Dhimitsana (1 daily; 1hr 30min); Kalamáta (5 weekly; 2hr 30min); Kyllíni (2–3 daily; 1hr); Olympia (7–12 daily; 30min); Pátra (7 daily; 2hr); Trípoli (5 daily; 2hr 30min).

ACCOMMODATION

Olympos Karkavitsa 2, at Patron ☎26210 33650, ⓦ hotelolympos.gr. This modern high-rise hotel has handsome rooms and is located right in the city centre, not far from parks and shopping. Facilities include satellite TV, car rental and private parking. Bathrooms are small, but some have hot tubs. Breakfast included. **€60**

Cape Tripití and around

About 25km to the north of Pýrgos, near the point where this most westerly coast of the Peloponnese forms **Cape Tripití**, is **ARKOÚDHI**, a compact village resort that has something of an island feel to it, and a fine sandy bay enclosed by a rocky promontory. Using Arkoúdhi as a base, it's worth taking time to drive or climb to the village of **Kástro**, at the centre of the cape.

Khlemoútsi Castle

Kástro • Tues–Sun: summer 8.30am–4pm; winter 8am–3pm • €4

Looming above Kástro village and visible from many kilometres around is the Frankish **Khlemoútsi Castle**, one of the best-preserved Venetian castles in Greece, with a vast hexagonal structure built (1220–23) by Geoffrey de Villehardouin. Its function was principally to control the province of Ahaïa, though it also served as a strategic fortress on the Adriatic. Haze permitting, there are sweeping views across the straits to Zákynthos, and even to Kefaloniá and Itháki, from the well-preserved and restored ramparts.

Kyllíni

Heading north from Kástro, you'll pass a rather clinical spa resort, **Loutra Kyllínis**, on the way to the northern tip of the cape. Here, the cheerless little port of **KYLLÍNI** has little more to offer than its **ferry connections** to Zákynthos and Kefaloniá.

ARRIVAL AND DEPARTURE CAPE TRIPITÍ AND AROUND

By bus KTEL buses from Athens and Pátra to Kyllíni continue on the ferry to Zákynthos (ⓦ ktel-zakynthos.gr).
Destinations from Kyllíni Athens (5 daily; 4hr); Pátra (5 daily; 1hr 30min).

By ferry Ferries from Kyllíni are run by the Ionian Group (Ⓦ ioniangroup.com) and Kefalonian Lines (Ⓦ kefalonianlines.com).
Destinations Póros, Kefaloniá (10 daily; 1hr 30min);

Zákynthos (10–12 daily; 1hr). These are summer frequencies; a heavily reduced service operates year-round.

ACCOMMODATION AND EATING

Almira Arkoúdhi ☎ 26230 96800, Ⓦ almira-hotel.gr. Luxury hotel and spa right on the sandy beach, this is a three-star with higher aspirations: there's a sauna, gym, pool and a lively beach bar-restaurant. Rooms with sea views are only slightly more expensive. Parking and breakfast included. **€80**

R.Q.D. Arkoúdhi ☎ 26230 96167, Ⓦ rqd.gr. Located right down on the beach, this is more of a bar than restaurant, though the food is gourmet and sometimes a bit pricey (pasta dishes go for as much as €18), and the atmosphere crackles with summer energy. June–Sept daily noon–midnight.

Pátra and Ahaïa

Capital of the large northern province of **Ahaïa**, **Pátra** is the largest city in the Peloponnese and third most populous in Greece. At first glance, it offers little to visitors. However, there are a few decent beaches including a sensational one at **Kalogriá**, and from the small town of **Dhiakoftó** you can opt for a trip on a picturesque rack-and-pinion railway which follows the dramatic **Vouraikós Gorge** up to **Kalávryta**, a ski centre.

Pátra

PÁTRA (Patras) is a major Greek port, from where you can catch ferries to Italy and Corfu. The pedestrianization of its centre has added much character to the town, and there are several new chic restaurants and cafés to while away your time until late in the evening. The relative lack of tourists and the presence of a large **university** makes Pátra a good place to meet Greeks outside a touristy environment. It's also home to Greece's largest and best known **carnival** (Ⓦ carnivalpatras.gr), which starts on St Anthony's Day (Jan 18) and ends on the Sun before Clean Monday (Katharí Dheftéra) with a 30,000-strong grand parade through the city centre attended by half a million people. The city is also the gateway to Kalogriá (see p.196), with its dunes and stunning beach.

Kástro

May–Sept Tues–Fri 8.30am–7pm, Sat & Sun 8.30am–3pm; Oct–April Tues–Fri 8am–5pm, Sat & Sun 8.30am–3pm • Free

The **Kástro**, a mainly Frankish–Byzantine and partly restored citadel fifteen minutes' walk up from the water, is not particularly exciting, but it is up and away from the city bustle, surrounded by a small park and with woodland beyond.

Turkish hammam

Boukaoúri 29 • Sept–May: women Mon, Wed &Fri 9am–2.30pm & 5–9pm, Tues, Thurs & Sat 2.30pm–5pm; Men Tues, Thurs & Sat 9am–2.30pm & 5–9pm, Mon & Wed 2.30pm–5pm • €6.30 • ☎ 2610 274 267

Just beneath the Kástro is Europe's oldest still-functioning **Turkish hammam**, built in 1400. After six hundred years it's still good for a steam, though the 1987 restoration left few original features.

Archeological Museum

Patras–Athens National Rd 38–40 • Summer daily 8am–8pm; winter Tues–Sun 8am–3pm • €4 • ☎ 2610 623 820

Located about 3km from the centre, at the north end of the city, the crisply contemporary **Archeological Museum** is second only in size to Athens' Acropolis Museum (see p.71). Themed exhibits include a vast quantity of everyday objects from Ahaïa dating from the Mycenaean to the Roman eras, most of which have been in

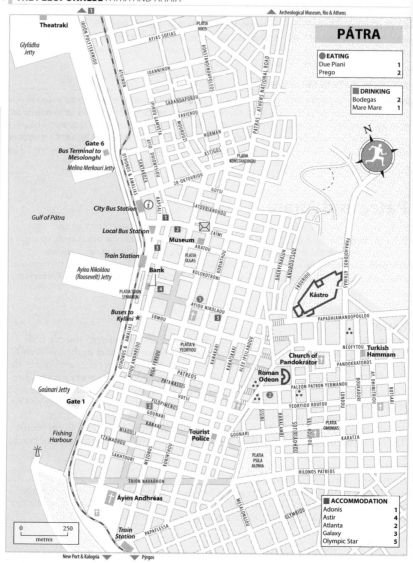

storage for the past thirty years. Though it houses one of Greece's biggest Roman mosaic collections, there's no single item of great import, and the whole approach can be a little too didactic for most.

New and old churches of Áyios Andhréas

Daily: new 7am–8pm, old 8am–1am; other times by appointment on ☎ 6947 154 907 • Free

The **new and old churches of Áyios Andhréas** (St Andrew) stand next to each other at the southwest end of the waterfront. The old basilica, restored in 1835, lies on the spot where St Andrew is said to have been martyred in 69 AD, and where an ancient temple to Demeter once stood. The saint's tomb is housed within, but the relics (returned by the Vatican in 1964, after the crusaders plundered it in 1204) are housed in the grand eclectic-style church built in 1903 with elements of Art Nouveau.

Roman Odeon

Platiá Áyios Yeóryios • Tues–Sun 8am–2.30pm • Free

The impressive **Roman Odeon**, dating from the first century AD and restored in 1956, lies in the north end of the square of Áyios Yeóryios (25 March). It was once the centre of ancient Pátra; ruins of the Roman stadium can also be seen on the south side of the square. The Odeon is still used occasionally for music performances during the summer.

Church of Pandokrátor

Pandokrátoros • Sun Mass only • Free

Further up from the Odeon, the **Church of Pandokrátor** is one of the most striking monuments in the city. Dating from 900 AD, its current multi-dome shape belies the fact that it was converted into the city mosque during the Ottoman era.

ARRIVAL AND DEPARTURE

PÁTRA

By bus The main bus station (☎ 2610 623 888, ⓦ ktelachaias .gr) is next to the InfoCenter Patras at Agora Argýri. Buses for Mesolóngi and Náfpaktos leave from the old Deck 5 at Iróon Polytechníou 42 (☎ 2610 421 205), about 15min walk north.
Destinations Athens (2 hourly, 3hr); Náfplio via Árgos (1 every Fri; 4hr); Éyio for Kalávryta (1 hourly; 1hr); Itéa, for Delphi (1–2 daily; 3–4hr); Ioánnina (1 daily; 4hr 30min); Kalamáta (2 daily; 4hr); Kalogriá (3–5 daily in season; 1hr 15min); Kyllíni (5 daily; 1hr 30min); Mesolóngi (6–9 daily; 1hr); Náfpaktos (Mon–Fri 7 daily; Sat 1 daily; 1hr); Pýrgos (8–10 daily; 2hr); Thessaloníki (2–3 daily; 7hr); Vólos (4 weekly; 6hr).

By train The train station, on Óthonos & Amalías, serves only the commuter line Pátra–Rio. The Proestiakós rail line to Athens is currently under construction: in the meantime, there are replacement buses to Kiáto, where you can pick up the Athens suburban train.

By ferry All ferries leave from Néo Limáni (New Port) at the south of the city. A taxi to the centre costs €5, and bus #18 will also take you through the centre to the KTEL station (hourly 10.30am–5.30pm; €1.30). Italy-bound ferries (see box, p.27) leave from early afternoon to midnight. You must check in at the agent's embarkation booth at least 2hr before departure (ⓦ patrasport.gr).
Destinations Ancona (2–3 daily; 22hr); Bari (1–2 daily; 15hr 30min); Brindisi (1–2 daily; 14hr 30min); Corfu (4–5 weekly; 7hr 30min); Igoumenítsa (3–5 daily; 6hr); Venice (1–2 weekly; 31hr).

By car Pátra is linked to the mainland by the suspension bridge across the gulf from Río to Andírio (5min; €13.30 car toll). If you're going beyond Pátra, you can take a fast bypass to the east. From Pátra you can reach Kórinthos in 1hr 30min along the national highway; the onward journey to Athens takes another 45min.

INFORMATION

Tourist office InfoCenter Patras at Agora Argýri Ayíou Andreou 12–14 (daily 7.30am–9pm; ☎ 2610 461 740, ⓦ patrasinfo.com) offers maps, info and free bike rental (3hr; passport/ID necessary). They also have a kiosk on Platía Trión Symmáhon (daily 8am–2pm).

GETTING AROUND

By bus Local buses go from Óthonos & Amalías north of the main bus station; tickets are also available from kiosks.
By car The traffic and one-way system in Pátra is no less frustrating for drivers than in Athens. Car rental is available from: Lalas (Ayíou Andhréou 1; ☎ 2610 273 667); Dirent A

Car (28 October 5; ☎ 2610 995 950); Avis (Óthonos Amalías 33; ☎ 2610 275 547); Avance (Ayíou Andhréou 6; ☎ 2610 621 360); Tsoulos (Kanári 55; ☎ 2610 992 803); Hertz (Aktí Dhymaíon 40; ☎ 2610 220 990); Lion Rental (Norman 18–20; ☎ 2610 275 677).

ACCOMMODATION

Adonis Kapsáli 9, at Zaïmi ☎ 2610 224 213, ⓦ adoniscityhotel.gr. This large high-rise hotel is well maintained, though showing its age, and rooms and bathrooms are small. It feels like a cheap overall option, but is conveniently located by the bus station. Breakfast included. **€40**
★**Astir** Ayíou Andhréou 16 ☎ 2610 277 502, ⓦ hotelastirpatras.gr. Pleasantly modernist styling in the

2

public spaces, handsome large rooms, great harbour views plus a rooftop terrace restaurant with a pool (summer only) and sauna make this the best choice in the centre of town. Breakfast and secure parking included. **€75**

Atlanta Zaïmi 10 ☎ 2610 278 627, ⓦ hotelatlanta.gr. Plain but central hotel, just across from the bus station, with small rooms, but decorwise a better choice than the similar *Adonis* (see p.195), which is further out. Smoking rooms available. Breakfast included. **€40**

★**Galaxy City Center** Ayíou Nikoláou 9 ☎ 2610 275

981, ⓦ galaxyhotel.com.gr. Well-placed for the nightlife, this hotel is clean and old-fashioned, with a sleek modern lobby and more than decent rooms with balconies, flat-screen TVs and galloping wi-fi. The rooms not facing the street are quieter. Breakfast €6. **€65**

Olympic Star Ayíou Nikoláou 46 ☎ 2610 622 939, ⓦ olympicstar.gr. Stylish hotel with large rooms, each with its own balcony, LCD TV, and bathroom with a classy jet shower. If you can afford it, ask for the suite – it's almost an apartment, and a bargain at €80. Breakfast included. **€45**

EATING

Stroll and choose among shoulder-to-shoulder bars and restaurants in the pedestrianized section along Ríga Feréou, Ayíou Nikoláou and Pandanássis streets.

Due Piani Ayíou Nikolaou 47 ☎ 2610 279 222. You can come here three times in the same day and find a very different crowd and atmosphere – it's a café in the mornings, swish restaurant during the day and a live and DJ venue in the evenings. Try the medium *poikilía* (a meze platter) for €12 if you dare. Daily 8am–2am.

Prego Ayíou Germanou 18 ☎ 2610 333 876. If you're feeling peckish late at night, this is the place to come. It has a stunning location opposite the Roman Odeon, plays reassuring lounge music and the mains only cost around €7. In the summer, the whole shebang moves to *Mare Mare* (see below). Oct–May daily 10am–4am; kitchen 1pm–1am.

DRINKING

Bodegas Riga Feraiou 147 ☎ 2610 221 113. Pricey-but-worth-it wine bar with food, situated on the main nightlife drag and serving a wide selection from local vineyards (glass €3–5). The food is good too: the veal burger with three-pepper sauce (€8) is delicious. Daily noon–1am.

Mare Mare Platia Terpsithéas ☎ 2610 428 851. The

team from *Prego* (see above) set up on the seafront in the summer offering the best sunset views in the city from their bar-restaurant (indifferent mains for around €13): book in advance if you're coming for the sunset and note that the service gets easily overwhelmed. Mid-May to Sept daily 11am–3am.

DIRECTORY

Banks and exchange There are plenty of banks and ATMs in Pátra.

Consulate Britain, Vótsi 2 ☎ 2610 277 329, ☎ 2610 225 334, ✉ patras@british-consulate.gr.

Post office Mézonos & Záïmi 23 ☎ 2610 620 644 (Mon–Fri 7.30am–8.30pm; Sat 7.30am–2.30pm).

Tourist police Goúnari 52 ☎ 2610 695 073 (daily 7am–11pm).

The north coast

The resorts and villages lining the **north coast** are modest, but at least not overdeveloped. Generally you'll find little more than a narrow strip of beach, a campsite, a few rooms for rent and a couple of seasonal tavernas. About 35km west of Pátra is **Kalogriá**, the best beach in the area. To the east is **Dhiakoftó**, from where you can stop for the old **Kalávryta railway** ride up into the picturesque **Vouraikós gorge** via quaint **Zakhloroú**. After Dhiakoftó, if you're unhurried, it's worth taking the old **coast road** along the Gulf of Kórinthos; this runs below the national highway, often right by the sea.

Kalogriá

KALOGRIÁ (locally Kalógria) is the best **beach** near Pátra: a 7km strand, partly naturist, bordered by a swathe of umbrella pine forests. A fair proportion of Pátra, including the gay community, descends here at the weekend. The whole area is protected as part of the 22-square-kilometre **Strofyliá Forest-Kotýkhi Wetland National Park**, which covers beach dunes, a pine, cedar and myrtle forest, as well as lagoons with their rare birdlife, and permanent development remains low-key.

Kalogriá is not actually a village – the nearest bona fide town is Metóhi – but rather a small cluster of tavernas and stores. Behind the hotels, the 200m outcrop Mávra Vouná has a number of hiking routes.

ARRIVAL AND INFORMATION   KALOGRIÁ

By bus Regular buses run from Pátra (3–5 daily in season; 1hr 15min) in the summer.
Tourist office There is an enthusiastic and helpful

information centre (Mon–Fri 8am–4pm; ☎ 26930 31651) for the park at nearby Láppa. They can also book guides for groups.

ACCOMMODATION

Kalogria Beach ☎ 26930 31380, ⓦ kalogriahotel.gr. Extensive but dated, this family resort on a stunning stretch of the beach has every sort of facility: a restaurant, beach sunbeds with umbrellas and three large pools. Wi-fi not available everywhere. Rate includes three meals a day. June–Sept. **€90**

★**Verde Al Mare** 350m from the beach ☎ 26930 31111, ⓦ verdealmare.gr. This is a great-looking boutique hotel-cum-resort with two good pools and an even better upmarket restaurant. They rent mountain bikes and offer bird-watching activities and guided tours of the national park. Breakfast included. **€88**

Río
Local bus #6 from Pátra (every 30min; 30min)

RÍO signals the beginning of swimmable water east of Pátra, though most travellers pass through for the **suspension bridge** across the gulf to Andírio (5min; €12.90 car toll).

Dhiakoftó
From **DHIAKOFTÓ** (officially Dhiakoptó) an old **rack-and-pinion railway**, the Kalávryta express (see box, below) heads south up into the **Vouraïkós gorge** and terminates at **Kalávryta**. Dhiakoftó itself is typically drab, but there's a narrow pebble beach along the eastern side.

ARRIVAL AND INFORMATION   DHIAKOFTÓ

By bus Athens–Pátra buses stop at Éyio about 10km west, from where local buses connect to Dhiakoftó (4–5 daily; 30min). A taxi costs about €18. In July and August there is

one direct bus a day (Mon–Fri) from Athens to Dhiakoftó (2hr) and Zakhloroú (2hr 30min).

ACCOMMODATION AND EATING

Chris Paul ☎ 26910 41715, ⓦ chrispaul-hotel.gr. Friendly and well-located hotel by the entrance of the rack-and-pinion railway, with a pool among a lemon and

orange grove. There's private parking, a café, and a/c, though it may be for heating rather than cooling. Breakfast included. **€50**

THE KALÁVRYTA EXPRESS (ODONTOTÓS)

The 22km **rack-and-pinion railway** from **Dhiakoftó** to **Kalávryta** (☎ 26910 43206, ⓦ odontotos.com) is a crazy feat of Italian engineering, rising at gradients of up to one in seven as it cuts inland through the Vouraïkós gorge. The journey can be hot, crowded and uncomfortable, but the route is a toy-train fantasy of tunnels, bridges and precipitous overhangs, and well worth experiencing.

The railway was built between 1889 and 1896 to bring minerals from the mountains to the sea. Its 1896 steam locomotives were replaced some years ago – one (O Moutzouris) remains by the line at Dhiakoftó station with other relics, and another at Kalávryta – but the track itself retains all the charm of its period. The tunnels, for example, have delicately carved window openings, and the narrow bridges zigzagging across the Vouraïkós seem engineered for sheer virtuosity.

It takes around 45 minutes to get from Dhiakoftó to **Zakhloroú** (listed on timetables as **Méga Spíleo**), and about another 20 minutes from there to Kalávryta. In peak season the ride is very popular, so plan to buy tickets in advance of your preferred departure (Mon–Fri 3 daily, Sat & Sun 5 daily; one way €9.50, return €19).

Zakhloroú

ZAKHLOROÚ is as perfect a train stop as could be imagined: a tiny hamlet echoing with the sound of the **Vouraïkós River**, which splits it into two neighbourhoods. It's a lovely, peaceful place with an old hotel (see below).

Méga Spiléou Monastery

Daily 8am–sunset • Museum €1 • ☎ 26920 23130 • 45min walk from Zakhloroú village, up a rough donkey track along the hillside • Usual monastery dress code applies

The eight-storey **Méga Spiléou Monastery** ("Great Cave") near Zakhloroú is the oldest monastery in Greece and spectacularly sited under a 120m cliff. The view of the gorge valley from the monastery is for many the principal attraction – sadly the monastery itself has been burned and rebuilt so many times that it now resembles nothing so much as a 1970s hotel – however, its treasury, arranged as a small **museum**, is outstanding. In the main **church**, among its icons is a charred black wax and mastic image of the Virgin, one of three in Greece said to be by the hand of St Luke (but probably from the tenth century); a smaller chapel houses a remarkable collection of body parts from various saints, all encased in precious materials. The monastery was founded by Saints Theodhoros and Simeon, after a vision by the shepherdess Euphrosyne in 362 AD led to the discovery of the icon in the cave (Ayíazma) behind the site of the later church.

ACCOMMODATION AND EATING   **ZAKHLOROÚ**

Olympios Zeus ☎ 26920 22595, ⊚ olympioszeus.gr. Built with traditional stone and wood, this luxury hotel caters for winter clients at the Helmós ski resort, so winter prices are higher. Worth staying overnight if you are going to Kalávryta for the grand views of Mt Helmós. Breakfast included. **€60**

Kalávryta

Despite its beautiful position amid gorgeous greenery at the end of the little train line, with Mount Helmós as a backdrop, **KALÁVRYTA** retains an air of both melancholy and poignancy due to its tragic history during **World War II**. On December 13, 1943, the town's German occupiers shot the entire male population over the age of twelve and set fire to the town, killing around seven hundred in reprisal for partisan activity. By the end of the war, the local death toll had risen to around twelve hundred.

Greeks come here out of a sense of **patriotic pilgrimage** – it's crowded with school parties during the week and with families at weekends – and the attitude to foreigners is business-like rather than overtly friendly. Still, the town tries hard to generate a resort feel; everything's well turned out, with lots of souvenir shops and cafés and restaurants, and from here there's a winding scenic road of 10km north to Méga Spiléou and on to the coast, as well as a road deep into Arcadia in the other direction.

Remembrance sights and shrines

The first and last sight you're likely to encounter is a mural, opposite the train station, that reads: "Kalávryta, founding member of the Union of Martyred Towns, appeals to all to fight for world peace." The left clocktower on the central church stands fixed at 2.34pm – the hour of the massacre. In the old primary school is the **Museum of the Sacrifice of the People of Kalávryta** (daily 9am–4pm; free), while outside of town is a shrine to those massacred, with the single word "Peace" (*Iríni*), as well as the historically significant **Ayías Lávras Monastery**.

Ayías Lávras Monastery

6km southwest of Kalávryta • Daily: summer 10am–1pm & 4–5pm; winter 10am–1pm & 3–4pm • Free

The tenth-century **monastery of Ayías Lávras** was the site where Yermanos, Archbishop of Pátra, raised the flag to signal the **War of Independence**. Destroyed in World War II, it has since been rebuilt and features a small historical **museum**.

ARRIVAL AND DEPARTURE

KALÁVRYTA

By bus The new bus station is 1km outside of town, on the road to Pounda; it's more convenient to get on and off the bus at the stop by the train station. For information & timetables call ☎ 26920 22224.

Destinations Athens (July–August 1 daily; 2hr 45min);

Éyio Éyio (1–2 daily; 2hr).

By train The train station is at Andréa Lóndou street, by Platía Fotéla in the centre of town.

Destinations Dhiakoftó (3–5 daily; 1hr).

ACCOMMODATION AND EATING

If you miss the last train out, you can stay at several hotels here, open all year since the town is a ski resort in winter. There are several adequate restaurants around the square as well as on the main pedestrian drag.

Filoxenia Ethnikís Andístasis 10 ☎ 26920 22422, ⓦ hotelfiloxenia.gr. This is a chalet-like hotel which verges on being luxurious, with good amenities, including wi-fi, and winter pluses such as a hammam, sauna and jacuzzi. Add forty percent to prices in winter. Breakfast included. **€50**

Stani 25th March 3 ☎ 26920 23000. Located off the main square, this taverna attracts more tourists than most, for good reason. Its menu consists of grilled and baked farm-to-table pork, lamb and goat dishes (€10). Daily noon–11pm.

The central mainland

THE METÉORA

The central mainland

The central mainland of Greece has long been thought of as the Greek heartland, the zone first liberated from the Turks. In fact, its most central province, Stereá Elládha, means literally "Solid Greece". For the visitor its most stellar attractions are the site of the ancient oracle at Delphi and, further north, the otherworldly rock-pinnacle monasteries of Metéora. Close to Delphi is Ósios Loukás monastery – containing the finest Byzantine mosaics in the country – and, to the south, the pleasant port resorts of Galaxídhi and Náfpaktos along the north shore of the Gulf of Kórinthos.

North of Delphi lies the vast agricultural plain of **Thessaly**, dotted with mostly drab market and industrial towns, but also boasting the mountainous **Pelion peninsula**, with its enticing villages, beaches and hiking options. On the east side of Thessaly lie the remote monasteries of the **Metéora** and the imposing **Píndhos Mountains**, which once formed the barrier with the eastern province of **Epirus**, the last region to shake off Turkish rule. The Píndhos range makes for scenic hiking opportunities and features the dramatic **Víkos Gorge**, reputedly Europe's deepest. The Epirot capital, lakeside **Ioánnina**, still evokes an exotic past. Nearby lies ancient **Dodóna**, the majestic site of Greece's first oracle, presided over by Zeus. Finally, the **west coast** is sprinkled with some good beaches and resorts along the Ionian Sea, as well as with more historic sites from every epoch. With your own transport (highly recommended) and careful planning, you can take in the central mainland's main sights and pleasures in a couple of weeks.

Delphi and Stereá Elládha

The inevitable magnet of the central province of **Stereá Elládha** is **Delphi**, 175km northwest of Athens. If you have your own transport, there are ample rewards in approaching it along the old road to **Thebes**, and you could also easily include the Byzantine monastery of **Ósios Loukás**. Legendary **Mount Parnassós** above Delphi offers skiing and walking opportunities depending on the season, while to the south, on the **Gulf of Kórinthos**, the port towns of **Galaxídhi** and **Náfpaktos** are good for a seaside sojourn. Further east, **Áyios Konstandínos** provides access to the island of Évvia, while heading inland brings you to Lamía and the mountainous **Karpeníssi Valley**.

TEMPLE OF APOLLO, DELPHI

Highlights

❶ Delphi Once home to the famous oracle, these spectacularly set ruins were believed in ancient times to be the centre of the earth. **See p.206**

❷ Ósios Loukás A splendidly positioned Byzantine monastery with vivid eleventh-century mosaics. **See p.213**

❸ The Pelion The mythical home of the centaurs offers hikes between mansion-filled villages clinging to wooded hillsides, plus fine beaches. **See p.222**

❹ The Metéora Expect mind-boggling scenery and exquisite Byzantine monasteries. **See p.236**

❺ Ioánnina The Ottoman citadel, lakefront and island associated with locally infamous hero/villain Ali Pasha. **See p.245**

❻ Zagóri A beguiling, thinly populated region that's home to brown bears and dazzling blue rivers. **See p.250**

❼ Víkos Gorge One of the longest and deepest in Europe and a worthy rival to its Cretan counterpart. **See p.252**

HIGHLIGHTS ARE MARKED ON THE MAP ON PP.204–205

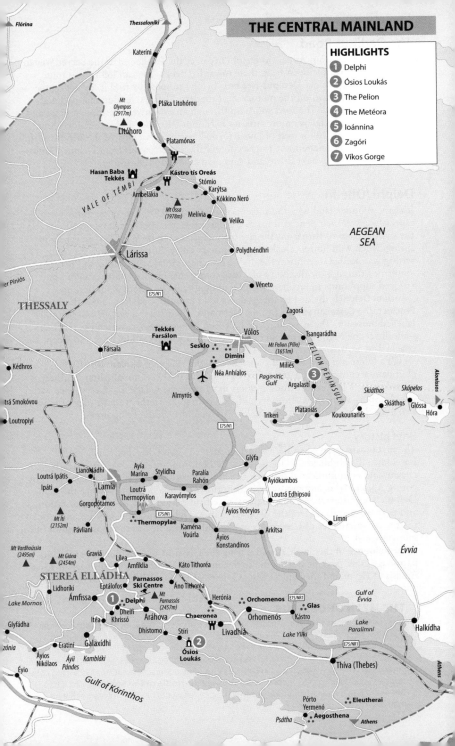

The Oedipus Road

The ancient road from Athens to Delphi began at the Parthenon as the **Sacred Way to Eleusis**, climbing northwest from there towards Thebes. You can follow this route, almost unchanged since **Oedipus** (see box, below) supposedly trod it, by taking the road signposted north off the motorway at modern Elefsína, leaving that polluted, chaotic port behind. The road winds up through an evocative landscape of pines and stony hills, becoming ever more striking as Mount Parnassós and its outriders loom overhead. Around 20km west of Livadia, you'll reach the vicinity of the **Triodos** (Triple Way) or **Oedipus junction**, the intersection of the ancient roads from Delphi, Daulis (today Dhávlia), Thebes (Thíva) and Ambrossos (modern Dhístomo).

Delphi (Dhelfí)

It's easy to understand why the ancients considered **DELPHI** the centre of the earth, especially given their penchant for awe-inspiring sacred spots. Framed on all sides by the soaring crags of Parnassós, the site truly captures the imagination, especially in spring, when wild flowers cloak the precipitous valley. But more than a stunning setting was needed to confirm the divine presence: sanctity, according to Plutarch, was confirmed through the discovery of a **rock chasm** that exuded strange vapours and reduced supplicants to incoherent – and undoubtedly prophetic – mutterings.

Ancient Delphi is divided by the Aráhova road into three adjacent **sites**: the **Sacred Precinct**, the **Castalian spring** and the **Marmaria**. There's also a well-lit and helpfully labelled **museum**. The attractions are best seen in two stages, covering the sanctuary – ideally at the beginning or end of the day, or (in winter) at lunchtime, to escape the coached-in crowds.

Half a kilometre away from the ancient site, the village of **Modern Dhelfí** offers abundant accommodation and eating options (see p.211). Though almost entirely geared to mass tourism (including skiers in winter), the village is a cheery place with jaw-dropping valley views from its cliff-side setting. From the western edge of town you'll see the blinking lights of Itéa, Galaxídhi, and even the Peloponnese.

Brief history

The **first oracle** established here was dedicated to Gaia ("Mother Earth") and Poseidon ("Earth Shaker"). The serpent Python, son of Gaia, dwelt in a nearby chasm, and communicated through the Pythian priestess. Python was later slain by young Apollo, who supposedly arrived in the form of a dolphin – hence the name Delphi. Thereafter, the **Pythian Games** were held periodically in commemoration, and perhaps also to placate the deposed deities. Delphi subsequently became one of the major sanctuaries of Greece, its oracle widely regarded as the most truthful in the known world.

The **influence** of the oracle spread during the Classical age of colonization and its patronage grew, peaking during the sixth century BC, with benefactors such as King Amasis of Egypt and the hapless King Croesus of Lydia. Delphi's wealth, however,

---

THE MYTH OF OEDIPUS

Pausanias identified this fateful Triodos junction (see above) as the site of **Oedipus**'s murder of his father, King Laius of Thebes. As the tale recounts, Oedipus was returning on foot from Delphi while Laius and his entourage were speeding towards him from the opposite direction on a chariot. Neither would give way, and in the ensuing altercation Oedipus killed them, ignorant of who they were. It was, in Pausanias' supreme understatement, "the beginning of his troubles". Continuing on to Thebes, Oedipus solved the **riddle of the Sphinx** – which had been ravaging the area – and took widowed Queen Jocasta as his wife – unaware that he was marrying his own mother.

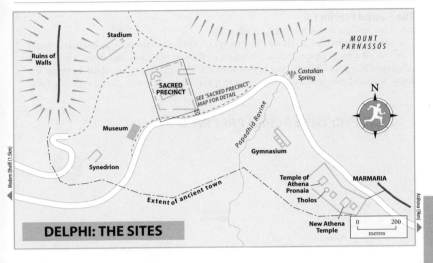

DELPHI: THE SITES

made it vulnerable to Greek rivalries; by the mid-fifth century BC, the oracle had become the object of a struggle between Athens, Phokia and Sparta, prompting a series of **Sacred Wars**. These culminated in Philip of Macedon invading southern Greece, crushing the city-states in 338 BC at the **Battle of Chaeronea**. Delphi's political intriguing was effectively over.

Under **Macedonian** and later **Roman** rule, the oracle's role became increasingly domestic, dispensing advice on marriages, loans, voyages and the like. The Romans thought little of its utterances, rather more of its treasure: Sulla plundered the sanctuary in 86 BC, and Nero, outraged when the oracle denounced him for murdering his mother, carted away five hundred bronze statues. Upon the proscription of paganism by Theodosius in 391 AD, the oracle ceased.

The sanctuary site was rediscovered towards the end of the seventeenth century and explored haphazardly from 1838 onwards; systematic **excavation** began only in 1892 when the French School of Archeology leased the land. There was initially little to be seen other than the outline of a stadium and theatre, but the inhabitants of Kastrí village, set amid the ruins, were evicted to a new town 1km west (now Modern Dhelfí), and digging commenced. By 1903, most of the excavations and reconstruction visible today had been completed.

THE WORLD'S SOOTHSAYER

For over a millennium, a steady stream of pilgrims converged on Delphi to seek divine direction in matters of war, worship, love or business. On arrival they would pay a set fee (the *pelanos*), sacrifice a goat, boar or even a bull, and – depending on the omens – wait to submit questions inscribed on lead tablets. The Pythian priestess, a village woman over fifty years of age, would chant her **prophecies** from a tripod positioned over the oracular chasm. An attendant priest would then "interpret" her utterings in hexameter verse.

Many **oracular answers** were pointedly ambiguous: Croesus, for example, was told that if he commenced war against Persia he would destroy a mighty empire; he did – his own. But the oracle would hardly have retained its popularity for so long without offering predominantly sound advice, largely because the Delphic priests were better informed than any others of the time. They were able to amass a wealth of political, economic and social information and, from the seventh century BC onwards, had their own network of agents throughout the Greek world.

The Sacred Precinct

Daily: summer 8am–8pm; winter 8am–6pm • €12, including museum

The **Sacred Precinct**, or Temenos (Sanctuary) of Apollo, is entered – as in ancient times – by way of a small **agora** enclosed by ruins of Roman porticoes and shops selling votive offerings. The paved **Sacred Way** begins after a few stairs, zigzagging uphill between the foundations of memorials and treasuries to the Temple of Apollo. Along each edge is a

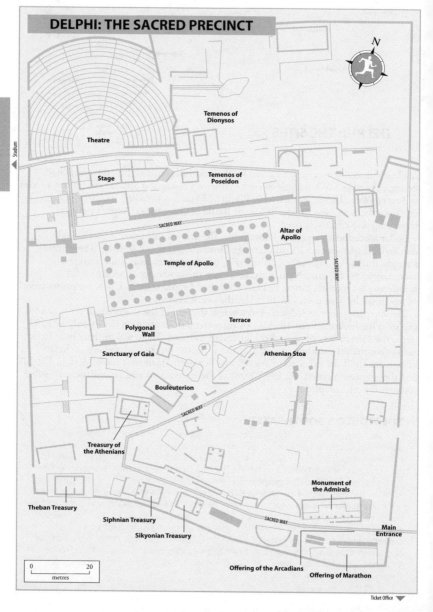

DELPHI: THE SACRED PRECINCT

N

Temenos of Dionysos

Theatre

Stage

Temenos of Poseidon

SACRED WAY

Altar of Apollo

Temple of Apollo

SACRED WAY

Terrace

Polygonal Wall

Sanctuary of Gaia

Athenian Stoa

Bouleuterion

SACRED WAY

Treasury of the Athenians

Monument of the Admirals

Theban Treasury

Siphnian Treasury

Sikyonian Treasury

SACRED WAY

Main Entrance

Offering of the Arcadians

Offering of Marathon

0   20
metres

Stadium

3

Ticket Office ▼

jumble of statue bases where gold, bronze and painted-marble figures once stood; Pliny counted more than three thousand on his visit, and that was after Nero's infamous raid.

The style and positioning of these **memorials** were dictated by more than religious zeal; many were used as a deliberate show of strength or as a direct insult against a rival Greek state. For instance, the Spartans celebrated their victory over Athens by erecting their **Monument of the Admirals** – a large recessed structure, which once held 37 bronze statues of gods and generals – directly opposite the Athenians' **Offering of Marathon**.

The Treasuries

Further up the path, past the Doric remains of the **Sikyonian Treasury** on the left, lie the foundations of the **Siphnian Treasury**, a grandiose Ionic temple erected in 525 BC. Ancient Siphnos (Sífnos) had rich gold mines and intended the building to be an unrivalled show of opulence. Above this is the **Treasury of the Athenians**, built, like the city's "offering", after Marathon (490 BC). It was reconstructed in 1904–06 by matching the inscriptions – including a hymn to Apollo with musical notation – that completely cover its blocks.

The Polygonal Wall and around

Next to the Treasury are the foundations of the **Bouleuterion**, or council house, a reminder that Delphi needed administrators, and above stretches the remarkable **Polygonal Wall** whose irregular interlocking blocks have withstood, intact, all earthquakes. It, too, is covered with inscriptions, mostly referring to the emancipation of slaves; Delphi was one of the few places where such freedom could be made official by an inscribed register. An incongruous outcrop of rock between the wall and the treasuries marks the original **Sanctuary of Gaia**.

The Temple of Apollo

Finally, the Sacred Way leads past the **Athenian Stoa** (which housed trophies from an Athenian naval victory of 506 BC) to the temple terrace where you're confronted with a large altar, erected by the island of Chios (Híos). The **Temple of Apollo** now visible dates from the mid-fourth century BC, two previous versions having succumbed to fire and earthquake. The French excavators found only foundations, but re-erected six of the Doric columns to illustrate the temple's dominance over the sanctuary. In the innermost part of the temple was the *adyton*, a subterranean cell at the mouth of the oracular chasm where the Pythian priestess officiated. No trace of cave or chasm has been found, nor any trance-inducing vapours, but it's conceivable that such a chasm did exist and was closed by later earthquakes. On the architrave of the temple were inscribed the maxims "Know Thyself" and "Moderation in All Things".

The theatre and stadium

The theatre and stadium used for the main events of the Pythian Festival occupy terraces above the temple. The **theatre**, built during the fourth century BC with a capacity of five thousand (the seats, sadly, are roped off), was associated with Dionysos, the god of ecstasy, the arts and wine, who ruled Delphi during the winter when the oracle was silent. A path leads up through cool pine groves to the **stadium** (its seats also off limits), artificially levelled in the fifth century BC to a length of 178m, though it was banked with stone seats (giving a capacity of seven thousand) only in Roman times – the gift, like so many other public buildings in Greece, of Herodes Atticus.

The museum

Mon 10am–5pm, Tues–Sun 8am–8pm • €12, including Sacred Precinct

Delphi's **museum** contains a rare and exquisite collection of sculpture spanning the Archaic to the Roman eras, matched only by finds on Athens' Acropolis. It also features pottery, bronze articles and friezes from the various treasuries and temple pediments, which give a good picture of the sanctuary's riches.

The most famous exhibit, with a room to itself at the south end of the galleries, is the **Charioteer**, one of the few surviving bronzes of the fifth century BC. It was unearthed in 1896 as part of the "Offering of Polyzalos", which toppled during the earthquake of 373 BC. The charioteer's eyes, made of onyx and set slightly askew, lend it a startling realism. Other major pieces include two huge **kouroi** from the sixth century BC, which betray clear Asiatic/Egyptian stylistic traits; a life-size, sixth-century BC votive **bull** fashioned from hammered silver and copper sheeting; and the elegant Ionic winged **Sphinx of the Naxians**, dating from 565 BC. In the same gallery, the **Siphnian frieze** depicts Zeus and other gods looking on as the Homeric heroes fight over the body of Patroclus. Another portion of this frieze shows a battle between gods and giants, including a lion graphically mauling a warrior.

The **Athenian Treasury** is represented by fragments of the **metopes** (friezes) depicting the labours of Hercules, the adventures of Theseus and a battle with Amazons. A group of three colossal if badly damaged **dancing women**, carved from Pentelic marble around an acanthus-topped column – probably a tripod stand – dates from the fourth century BC and is thought to represent the daughters of Kekrops. Among later works is an exquisite second-century AD figure of **Antinoös**, favourite of Roman emperor Hadrian.

The Castalian spring

Following the road east of the sanctuary, towards Aráhova, you reach a sharp bend. Just to the left, marked by niches for votive offerings and by the remains of an Archaic fountain-house, the celebrated **Castalian spring** still flows from a cleft – the legendary lair of Python.

Visitors to Delphi were obliged to **purify** themselves in its waters, usually by washing their hair, though murderers had to take the full plunge. **Lord Byron**, impressed by the legend that the waters nurtured poetic inspiration, also jumped in. This is no longer possible, since the spring is fenced off owing to sporadic rock falls from the cliffs.

The Marmaria

Daily: summer 7.30am–sunset; winter 8.30am–sunset • Free

Across and below the road from the spring is the **Marmaria** (*marmariá* means "marble quarry", after the medieval practice of filching the ancient blocks for private use).

The most conspicuous building in the precinct, easily visible from the road, is the **Tholos**, a fourth-century BC rotunda. Three of its dome-columns and their entablature have been rebuilt, but while these amply demonstrate the original beauty of the building (which is *the* postcard image of Delphi), its purpose remains a mystery.

At the entrance to the precinct stood the original **Temple of Athena Pronaia** ("Fore-Temple", in relation to the Apollo shrine), destroyed by the Persians and reconstructed during the fourth century BC beyond the Tholos; foundations of both structures can be traced. Outside the precinct on the northwest side (above the Marmaria) is a **gymnasium**, again built in the fourth century BC, but later enlarged by the Romans; prominent among the ruins is a circular plunge bath for athletes' refreshment after their exertions.

ARRIVAL AND DEPARTURE   **DELPHI**

By bus There are several daily buses from Athens to Delphi, so it is possible to visit Delphi as a day-trip, although it makes for a very long day of at least 5–6hr on the road (3hr each way). The KTEL bus stops at the eastern end of town, where the upper and lower streets link up. Westbound buses go to Ámfissa (for onward connections north), Itéa and (with a change) on to Náfpaktos, while eastbound services go to Aráhova and on to Athens. Since all coaches originate elsewhere, tickets (sold inside the *In Delphi* café, by the stop) are limited and can sell out quickly.

Destinations Athens (5–6 daily; 3hr); Ámfissa (7–8 daily; 45min); Aráhova (5–6 daily; 20min); Galaxídhi (3–4 daily; 45min); Itéa (7 daily; 30min); Lamía (1 daily; 2hr 30min); Pátra (1 daily; 4hr; also connections via Itéa); Thessaloniki (1 daily; 5hr).

By car As with buses, doing Delphi as a day-trip by car from Athens means spending hours on the road – on the whole it's best to spend a night in the vicinity. From Delphi, the E75/N1 motorway barrels north towards the Pelion,

HIKING TO THE CORYCIAN CAVE

The **Corycian Cave** (Korýkio Ándro) plays a significant part in Delphi mythology, since it was sacred to Pan and the nymphs, and they were the presiding deities of the oracle during winter, when Apollo abandoned the spot.

Allow a full day for this outing (4hr for ascent to cave, 3hr 30min back to Dhelfí) and take ample food and water. To reach the **trailhead** follow signposting up through Dhelfí village to the Museum of Delphic Festivals. Continue climbing from here to the highest point of the fence enclosing the sanctuary ruins. Where the track ends at a gate, take a trail on your left, initially marked by a black-and-yellow rectangle on a white background; these markers, repeated regularly, indicate the trail is part of the **E4 European long-distance route**.

Initially steep, the way soon flattens out on a grassy knoll overlooking the stadium, and continues along a ridge. Soon after, you join an ancient cobbled trail coming from inside the fenced precinct – the **Kakí Skála**, which zigzags up the slope above you in broad arcs. The path ends an hour-plus above the village, at the top of the **Phaedriades** cliffs. From one of several nearby rock pinnacles those guilty of sacrilege in ancient times were thrown to their deaths – a custom perhaps giving rise to the name Kakí Skála or "Evil Stairway".

E4 markers remain visible in the valley ahead of you as the principal route becomes a gravel track bearing northeast; ignore this and follow instead a metal sign pointing towards the cave, taking the right fork near the **Krokí spring** and watering troughs, with a complex of summer cottages on your right. This track, now intermittently paved, passes a picnic ground and a chapel (of Ayía Paraskeví) within fifteen minutes. Continue for some forty minutes beyond the chapel, heading gently downhill and passing another sign for the cave, until you emerge from the fir woods (2hr 40min from Dhelfí) with a view east and ahead to the rounded mass of the Yerondóvrahos peak (2367m) of the Parnassós massif.

Another fifteen minutes' walk brings you to a second chapel (of Ayía Triádha) on the left, with a spring and picnic ground. To the left rises a steep ridge, site of the ancient **Corycian cave**. Persevere along the road for five more minutes to where a white bilingual sign indicates a newer path, marked by orange paint splodges and red-triangle signs. After forty minutes' climb on this, you meet another dirt road; turn left and follow it five minutes more to the end, just below the conspicuous cave mouth at an altitude of 1370m.

In ancient times, the cave was the site of orgiastic rites in November, when women, acting as nymphs, made the long hike up from Delphi on the Kakí Skála by torchlight. If you look carefully with a torch you can find **ancient inscriptions** near the entrance; without artificial light you can't see more than 100m into the chilly, forbidding cavern. By the entrance you'll also notice a rock with a man-made circular indentation – possibly an ancient altar for libations.

skirting the coast part of the way, with Évvia visible just across the gulf. Another road leads southwest along the scenic Gulf of Kórinthos through Galaxídhi and Náfpaktos, with an optional link to the Peloponnese over the Andírio– Río bridge. A third, more remote, route leads west to mountainous Karpeníssi and then across the southernmost extensions of the Píndhos Mountains.

On a tour Organized day-trips to Delphi can be taken from Athens; prices vary wildly, but expect to pay in the region of €80, compared to around €33 return on the public bus.

INFORMATION

Tourist office There's a tourist office in Modern Dhelfí's town hall, on the lower main thoroughfare Vassiléos Pavloú kéh Fridheríkis (Mon–Fri 7.30am–2.30pm, Sat 8am–2pm; ☏ 22650 82900).

Services Modern Dhelfí has several ATMs, and a post office.

ACCOMMODATION

Given the quick visitor turnover and number of **hotels** and **pensions**, finding a vacancy is usually pretty easy. Try to get a room with a view – it's worth the slight extra fee. As an alternative to Dhelfí, consider staying just to the east in Aráhova (p.212), or down by the coast in Galaxídhi (p.214), especially if you have your own transport.

★**Acropole** Filellínon 13 ☏ 22650 82675, ⊚delphi. com.gr. On the quietest, lowest street of the village, this hotel's rooms feature wooden furniture and marble dresser tops, and there are three attic rooms with fireplaces: some rooms have unbeatable views over the Plistós Gorge (around €10 extra). Decent breakfasts (included) are served in the large-yet-cosy dining hall. **€60**

Fedriades Pávlou ké Fridheríkis 46 ☎ 22650 82370, ⓦ fedriades.com. Reasonable mid-range option in the busiest part of town. Some of the suites have spa baths, there's a simple buffet breakfast included, and you can borrow bikes for a quick tour around town. Guests get ten percent off food at *Epikouros* (see below), just across the road. **€55**

Orfeas Ifiyenías Syngroú 35 ☎ 22650 82077, ⓦ hotelorfeas.com. Very cheap, clean rooms on a quiet street just uphill from the busiest part of town. If you can, try to get one of the rooms on the top floor, which have sloping wooden ceilings and balconies overlooking the sea and mountains. **€32**

Pan Pávlou ké Fridheríkis 53 ☎ 22650 82294, ⓦ panartemis.gr. All rooms, including attic quads, are reasonably well appointed, with a/c and bathrooms with tubs; balconies have fine views to the gulf. Immediately opposite is the annexe, the *Artemis*, with rooms of equal standard, but no views. **€40**

Sibylla Pávlou ké Fridheríkis 9 ☎ 22650 82335, ⓦ sibylla-hotel.gr. Come here for clean, bright, small-to-medium-sized rooms; there are fans rather than a/c, but some balconies overlook the gorge, all the way down to the gulf. Breakfast included. **€26**

Varonos Vassiléos Pavlou 25 ☎ 22650 82345, ⓦ hotel-delphi.gr. Family-run and very friendly, with rooms decorated in honey tones. Comfort and cosiness are the key here, and some rooms have balconies with spectacular views down to the sea. **€45**

CAMPING

Apollon Camping 1.5km west along the road to Itéa ☎ 22650 82762, ⓦ apolloncamping.gr. This beautifully positioned site, with breathtaking views, has self-catering bungalows sleeping two, plus a pool, restaurant, minimarket, free transfers to Delphi and a playground: open all year. Camping **€15**, bungalow **€45**

EATING AND DRINKING

Restaurants in Dhelfí are generally overpriced, but are packed at mealtimes nonetheless. Most visitors are likely to have at least one meal here, so you may as well opt for a place with a view.

★**Epikouros** Pávlou ké Fridheríkis 33 ☎ 22650 83250, ⓦ epikouros.net. The best of the restaurants along the "killer view" strip, with a panorama gazing straight down to the gulf; in addition, prices are surprisingly reasonable considering the swanky air and good service. Try the grilled local formella cheese (€2.40), *dolmádhes* in lemon sauce (€4.60), or a hearty kléftiko (€11.50); try to come outside the obvious mealtimes in order to avoid the coach groups. Daily 11am–11pm.

Melopolio Pávlou ké Fridheríkis 14 ☎ 22650 83247. This café is one of those rare places where you'll usually see more locals than tourists. The ice creams are great, especially the pistachio (€1.50 per scoop), while good coffee and tasty baklava are also on offer, as well as some bottled Greek craft beer. Daily 7am–10pm.

Skalakia Isaia 11 ☎ 69442 07532. On the steps between the two main streets, this restaurant has a pleasing atmosphere at or after sundown, though service can be so-so. The rabbit, lamb and pork dishes (all around €9–12) are the best optiosn on the menu. Daily noon–11pm.

To Patriko Mas Apollonos Pávlou ké Fridheríkis 69 ☎ 22650 82150. Prime valley vistas make the outdoor tables here the place for sundown – but you may need to reserve in advance. As well as the regular meats and salads, they serve more left-field dishes, such as truffle risotto (€10.50), couscous (€6.50), salmon fillet (€18), or veggie moussaka (€7). There's also a good range of wine, plus some pricey house cocktails. Daily noon–midnight, usually only Fri–Sun in winter.

Aráhova

Just 11km east of Delphi, **ARÁHOVA** sits in the foothills of Mount Parnassós. The peaks rise from the town in tiers, sullied somewhat by the wide asphalt road built to reach the **ski resort** – a winter-weekend haunt of well-heeled Athenians. The town centre tends to be trendy, chic and pricey, rather like a Greek Aspen, with its comprehensive après-ski boutique commercialization. A small number of houses in Aráhova retain their vernacular architecture or have been restored in varying taste, flanking narrow, often stepped, lanes twisting north up the slope or poised to the south on the edge of the olive-tree-choked Plistós Gorge. The area is renowned for its strong purplish wines, *tsípouro*, honey, candied fruits and nuts, cheese (especially cylindrical *formélla*), the egg-rich noodles called *hilopíttes*, and woollen weavings, now mostly imported from elsewhere and/or machine-loomed. You'll find some handwoven exhibits – and basic tourist information – at the town's **Ethnographic Museum**, just off the main through-road at the western end of town.

SKIING ON PARNASSÓS

The two main **skiing** areas on the northwest flank of Mount Parnassós, **Keláría** and **Fterólakka** (23km and 29km from Aráhova respectively), are run jointly by the Parnassos Ski Centre (⦿parnassos-ski.gr). The top point for each is about 2200m, descending to 1600–1700m when conditions permit; the twenty or so runs are predominantly red-rated, and served by fourteen lifts, of which about half are bubble-chair type. Most **facilities** (and the biggest car park) are at Keláría, but Fterólakka has longer, more challenging runs.

Equipment is rented on a daily basis at the resort, or for longer term in Aráhova (which teems with seasonal sports equipment shops). Most visitors drive, but in season **shuttle buses** run here from Aráhova.The main problem is high **winds**, which often close the lifts, so check the forecast before setting off. The skiing season is generally from mid-December to April, rarely into May.

ARRIVAL AND INFORMATION

ARÁHOVA

By bus Buses stop at two locations along the main road as they pass through town: outside the Ethnographic Museum and just across from the car park near *Parnassos* restaurant, just off the main road.

Destinations Athens (5–6 daily; 2hr 40min); Dhelfí (5–6 daily; 20min).

Services The post office is a few paces from *Parnassos*, and there are several ATMs in the village.

ACCOMMODATION

In winter, particularly at weekends, **rooms** are at a premium in all senses, with prices more or less doubling.

Ariadne Komna Traka, a 5min walk uphill from the main road ⦿ 22670 31247, ⦿ariad.gr. Simple, stone-built guesthouse with reasonably fresh rooms equipped with a/c, a fridge, desk, coffee machine, TV, DVD player and fireplace. Balconied rooms have good views over the town's terracotta rooftops. The small bathrooms are a bit of a drawback. **€30**

★**Celena Maisonettes** Platía Lakka, midway along main road through town ⦿ 22670 31990, ⦿celena.gr. Smart duplex rooms (the beds are up a flight of wooden stairs) tucked behind a popular, cinema-themed café on the main street. Each one has its own colour scheme, plus a little

shaded seating area out the back. The corridors can get stuffy in summer, but rooms have a/c. Breakfast included. **€55**

Lykoria Filellinon, just west of the centre ⦿ 22670 31180, ⦿likoria.gr. Huge standard balconied doubles, plus a few suites with designer baths. Other amenities include a terrace garden and buffet breakfast (included) served in the cosy salon. Easy parking, too. **€50**

Maria Paradhosiakos Xenonas ⦿ 22670 31803. One of Aráhova's better restored inns, occupying a pair of lovely old buildings in the village centre with an array of doubles, triples and quads, replete with rustic mountain decor. **€45**

EATING AND DRINKING

★**Panayiota** Uphill from the main road, behind Áyios Yeóryios church ⦿ 22670 32735. Comfy chairs and tables are set out under poplar and plane trees to take advantage of this restaurant's unbeatable setting. The traditional cuisine is decent and well priced (€5–12 for main dishes). Service is good and there's usually a sweet offered on the house, in the Greek tradition. Daily noon–10pm; weekends only in summer.

To Kalderimi About 20 steps down from the main road (it's signposted in Greek) ⦿ 22670 31418. This atmospheric stone taverna is known for its traditional

meaty stews, pies and assortment of local starters. Main dishes €6–10. Daily lunch and dinner; closed mid-July to mid-Aug.

To Poloï Down from the crescent on the main road (signposted) ⦿ 22670 31151. Tourists rarely venture this far down (it's a steep path, especially getting back up), and simple staples here don't cost much (you can eat for under €5, if necessary) – the home-made *melizanosalata* (€2.75) and formella cheese (€2.20) are particularly tasty. Daily 11am–8pm.

Ósios Loukás monastery

6km east of Dhístomo • Daily: May 3–Sept 15 9am–6pm; rest of year 9am–5pm • €4 • There are buses from Dhelfí to the turn-off for Dhístomo, on the Livadhiá–Athens line (hourly; 35min), but nothing on to Stíri, the village 3.5km west of the monastery (the last 2.5km on a spur road), so you might have to walk, take a taxi or hitch

The **monastery of Ósios Loukás** was a precursor of the final flourish of **Byzantine art** found in the great churches at Mystra in the Peloponnese (see p.160). From an architectural or decorative standpoint it ranks as one of the great buildings of medieval Greece; the remote setting is exquisite as well, especially in February when the many local almond trees bloom. As you approach along the last stretch of road, Ósios Loukás suddenly appears on its shady terrace, overlooking the highest summits of the Elikónas range and a beautiful broad valley. The complex comprises two domed churches: the larger **katholikón** of Ósios Loukás (a local beatified hermit, Luke of Stiri, not the Evangelist) and the adjacent chapel of **Theotókos**.

A few monks still live in the cells around the courtyard, but the monastery is essentially a museum, with a shop on the grounds selling souvenirs and refreshments, including dozens of varieties of typically Greek sesame-based snacks. There are tables and chairs on the beautiful terrace, so you can take in the sweeping view while you enjoy them.

The katholikón

The design of the **katholikón**, built around 1040 to a cross-in-square plan, strongly influenced later churches at Dhafní and at Mystra. Externally it is unassuming, with rough brick-and-stone walls topped by a well-proportioned octagonal dome. The **interior**, however, is rich, with multicoloured-marble walls contrasting with gold-background mosaics on the high ceiling. Light filtering through alabaster windows reflects from the curved mosaic surfaces onto the marble walls and back, bringing out subtle shading.

The **mosaics** were damaged by an earthquake in 1659 and replaced at many points by unremarkable frescoes, but surviving examples testify to their glory. On the right as you enter the narthex are a majestic *Resurrection* and *Thomas Probing Christ's Wound*. The mosaic of the *Niptir* (*Washing of the Apostles' Feet*) on the far left (north side) of the narthex is one of the finest here, the expressions of the Apostles ranging between diffidence and surprise. This humanized approach is again illustrated by the *Baptism*, up in the northwest squinch (curved surface supporting the dome). Here Jesus reaches for the cross amid a swirling mass of water, an illusion of depth created by the curvature of the wall. On other squinches, the Christ Child reaches out to the High Priest Simeon in *The Presentation*, while in *The Nativity*, angels predominate rather than the usual shepherds. The church's original **frescoes** are confined to vaulted chambers at the corners of the cross plan and, though less imposing than the mosaics, employ subtle colours, notably in *Christ Walking towards the Baptism*.

The Theotókos chapel

The chapel of **Theotókos** ("God-Bearing", ie the Virgin Mary), built shortly after Luke's death, is nearly a century older than the *katholikón*. From outside it overshadows the main church with **elaborate brick decoration** culminating in a marble-panelled drum, but the interior seems mean by comparison, enlivened only by a couple of fine Corinthian capitals and the original floor mosaic, its colours now faint.

The crypt

Finally, do not miss the vivid **frescoes** in the **crypt** of the *katholikón*, entered on the lower south side of the building. It's not essential but you may wish to bring a torch, since illumination is limited to three small lights to preserve the colours of the post-Byzantine frescoes.

Galaxídhi

GALAXÍDHI is a charming port town appearing mirage-like out of an otherwise lifeless shore along the Gulf of Kórinthos, just 35km from Delphi. It makes a decent base for visiting **Delphi** (and, with your own transport, **Ósios Loukás**), and it's also worth at least

a day or two in its own right. Amazingly, given its size, Galaxídhi was once one of Greece's major harbours, with a fleet of over four hundred two- and three-masted *kaïkia* and schooners, trading as far afield as the UK. But shipowners failed to convert to steam power after 1890, and the town's prosperity vanished. Clusters of nineteenth-century shipowners' **mansions**, reminders of those heady days, reflect borrowings from Venice, testament to the sea captains' far-flung travels, and to their wealth. Despite some starts at gentrification, the town retains its authenticity, with an animated commercial high street (Nikólaou Máma) and a good range of places to eat and drink.

The old town

The **old town** stands on a raised headland, crowned by the eighteenth-century church of Ayía Paraskeví (the old basilica, not the more obvious belfried Áyios Nikólaos, patron saint of sailors). With its protected double harbour, the location proved irresistible to early settlers, which explains stretches of walls – all that's left of **ancient Chaleion** and its successor **Oianthe** – between the two churches and the water on the headland dividing the two anchorages. What you see dates from 1830 to 1870, as the town was largely destroyed during the War of Independence.

Nautical and Historical Museum

Just uphill from the main harbour • Tues–Sun 8.30am–3.30pm • €5 • ☎ 22650 41795

Galleries at the **Nautical and Historical Museum** provide a well-labelled gallop round this citadel-settlement in all eras, arranged clockwise. Ancient Chaleion is represented by painted pottery and a bronze folding mirror, then it's on to the chronicles of Galaxídhi – the place's name from Byzantine times onwards – and its half-dozen shipyards, mostly alongside the northwesterly Hirólakkas anchorage. The local two- and three-masters are followed from their birth – primitive, fascinating tools for shipbuilding and sail-making – to their all-too-frequent sudden violent death. Along the way are propeller-operated logs, wooden rattles to signal the change of watches, a *bouroú* or large shell used as a foghorn and – best of all – superb polychrome figureheads.

Beaches

Strolling or driving around the pine-covered headland flanking the southeastern harbour leads to tiny pebbly **coves** where most people swim. The closest "real" beaches are at the end of this road, or at **Kalafátis** just north of town, though neither is brilliant – harsh shingle underfoot and occasionally turbid water. With your own transport, head for better beaches at Ágios Vassílis (4km west) or Áyii Pándes (11km west).

ARRIVAL AND INFORMATION   GALAXÍDHI

By bus Buses stop on the southern edge of the landscaped, central Platía Iróon, in the middle of town. You can buy tickets from the café/bar by the stop – look for the one with green doors and window frames.
Destinations Athens (2–3 daily; 4hr, with connection likely in Ámfissa or Itéa); Delphi (2–3 daily; 1hr); Itéa (3–4 daily; 30min); Náfpaktos (3–4 daily; 1hr 45min); Pátra (2 daily; 2hr 15min); Thessaloniki (1 daily; 5hr).
Services Galaxídhi is large enough to support a post office, bank and a couple of ATMs; the nearest petrol station is about 2km away, on the main road heading east. There's also a weekly farmers' market (Thurs 7.30–10am).

ACCOMMODATION

Art Hotel Arhontiko Uphill from the jetty ☎ 22650 42292 or ☎ 6972 555 488, ⌨ archontikoarthotel.gr. This family-run eight-room hotel occupies a secluded spot in the northern part of town, beyond Hirólakkas. Features include easy parking, sea views, themed rooms (including one with a mirror on the ceiling) and self-catering facilities; breakfast (included) is served in the ground-floor salon or out in the rock-garden courtyard. **€70**

Café Liberty Harbourfront, eastern part of town ☎ 22650 41209. Cramped but surprisingly bright rooms above a harbourfront café, with TVs and clean en-suite bathrooms. Rooms at the front are the same price as those at the back, but have much better views. **€35**

Galaxa Mansion Above the northwest shore of Hirólakkas ☎ 22650 41620. Pretty hillside hotel with private parking; most of the rooms have some sort of water view (the best in town), and all have blue-and-white decor, fridges, phones and small bathrooms. There's also a popular garden terrace bar where breakfast (included) is served. €55

★**Ganimede** Nikólaou Gourgoúri 20 (southwest market street) ☎ 22650 41328, ⓦ ganimede.gr. Pleasant hotel under the energetic management of the Papalexis family since 2004. There are four doubles in the finely restored old house (best is #1), with fridges and satellite TV, and a family suite with loft and fireplace across the courtyard-garden. The breakfast (included) is

extremely good, with loads of local fruit, homemade preserves and scones. They also run cooking classes by appointment (€55 for one or two people). Double €60, family suite €150

Miramare Signposted off the main harbour road, eastern side of town ☎ 22650 41466, ⓦ ganimede. gr. Ganimede's sister hotel is modern and fresh, and right near the waterfront. There are five identical rooms, each with kitchenette, and an on-site dive school runs courses for accredited divers in July & Aug (from €35/person). €60

EATING AND DRINKING

The **tavernas** on the quay tend to be aimed at tourists, with correspondingly high prices – but it's a good spot for **drinks** after dark. For those with a sweet tooth, several shops sell local **pastries** on Nikoláou Máma, between Platía Iróön and lánthi.

Albatross Satha, up from the harbour on the street between the two churches ☎ 22650 42233. This authentic choice offers well-executed *mayireftá* from a short daily menu, which might stretch to octopus, spinach/cheese pie, rabbit stew, and pale *taramosaláta*. Most mains €7. Daily 10am–2pm & 7–11pm.

Kaffeneio On the harbour ☎ 22650 41315. The most appealing of the bars on the harbour, with outdoor seats facing the bobbing yachts – they also serve very generous measures of ouzo. Daily noon–1am.

★**O Bebelis** Mama Nikolou, two streets east of the *Ganimede* hotel ☎ 22650 41677. Vaguely

maritime-themed, this family-friendly taverna is decked out with model boats and does a good range of fresh local seafood – from sardines (€9 per plate) to grilled octopus (€10) and boiled mussels (€10), and the house speciality *samári* (pancetta in savoury sauce). A little pricier than the norm, but you usually get a free sweet for dessert. Daily 3.30pm–10.30pm.

Tasos On the harbour ☎ 22650 41291. A nice little seafood restaurant on the harbour that is less pushy that some of its neighbours. Ask what's fresh, or go for something simple like the vinagered octopus (€8). Daily noon–11pm.

Náfpaktos and around

The lively port town of **NÁFPAKTOS** (medieval Lepanto) is the largest settlement on the north shore of the Gulf of Korínthos, and the jumping-off point for the bridge to the Peloponnese. Some 2.9km in length, the bridge is easy to spot from the town's plane-tree-shaded seafront, which runs below a sprawling Venetian castle. The planes are nurtured by numerous running springs, which attest to water-rich **mountains** just inland. The town itself is centred on a delightful, crab-claw-shaped **harbour** – incredibly photogenic even by Greek standards, it sports a statue of Spanish author Cervantes (see box, p.218) on its western arm, and an old mosque on its eastern one. Náfpaktos also makes a good base for visiting the ancient sacred site of **Thermon**, dedicated to the twin gods Apollo and his sister Artemis.

The kástro

A 25min walk up from the centre • Tues–Sun 8am–3pm • €2

The rambling, pine-tufted **kástro** provides an impressive backdrop; most of it dates from the Venetians' fifteenth-century tenure. A complete tour is only possible by walking or driving 2.5km to the car park at the highest citadel, passing en route a couple of nice cafés with great views. At the summit are the remains of Byzantine baths and an Ottoman mosque, both converted into chapels. From here, the curtain walls plunge down to the sea at the harbour.

Beaches

Most of the town centre faces long, developed beaches. The more popular and less shaded west beach is **Psáni**, with its frontage road, Navmahías, lined with tavernas and

---

THE BATTLE OF LEPANTO

The **Battle of Lepanto** was fought just off Náfpaktos on October 7, 1571. An allied Christian armada commanded by John of Austria devastated an Ottoman fleet – the first European naval victory over the Turks since the death of the dreaded pirate-admiral Barbarossa. **Cervantes**, author of *Don Quixote*, lost his left arm to a cannonball during the conflict; a Spanish-erected statue honours him at the old harbour. But Western naval supremacy proved fleeting, since the Ottomans quickly replaced their ships and had already wrested Cyprus from the Venetians that same year.

---

hotels. To the east is **Grímbovo**, more tranquil and lined with trees (and with easier parking), where aqueducts bring mountain streams into gurgling fountains.

ARRIVAL AND INFORMATION

NÁFPAKTOS AND AROUND

By bus Náfpaktos has two bus stations: the KTEL Fokídhas on Asklipíou handles local services (as far as Antirrio to the west, and Itéa to the east), while long-distance services stop at the main terminal, 2km northeast of town.
Destinations Amfissa (3–4 daily; 2hr); Athens (2–3 daily; 3hr 30min); Dhelfí (3–4 daily; 3hr including a change in Itéa); Galaxídhi (3–4 daily; 1hr 30min); Lamía (2 daily; 3hr 30min); Kastraki (2–7 daily; 15min); Mesolóngi (1 daily Mon–Fri; 1hr 15min); Pátra (Mon–Fri 8 daily, Sat & Sun

1–2 daily; 1hr).
Activities Rafting House Outdoor Activities on Háni Baniás (☎26340 26436, ⓦraftinghouse.gr) offers 2hr-long rafting trips on the Évinos River, northwest of town (Oct–May; from €35/person) plus climbing, horseriding and hiking trips year-round. There's also excellent kitesurfing on offer just to the east of town; Junkpark (ⓦnafpaktoskitepark.blogspot.gr) can organize equipment hire.

ACCOMMODATION

Akti Karidaleos ☎26340 28464, ⓦakti.gr. East of the centre, with gulf views from about half the rooms, this pleasant place has a lobby cluttered with designer furniture and an airy, cheerful salon where breakfast (included) is served. Standard doubles have butler sinks and marble dresser tables, while the three palatial rooftop suites are worth the splurge. €̲5̲0̲

★**Apollon Library Suites** Athanassiadi Nova 18 ☎26340 38615, ⓦapollonlibrarysuites.com. This literature-themed hotel has twelve immaculate suites each with its own theme, and a mini-library stocked with books

pertaining to it. The breakfasts (included) are gigantic, and service top-notch; unusually for a Greek hotel, it's female-owned. €̲1̲0̲5̲
Ilion Daliáni 7 ☎26340 38088, ⓦnafpaktoshotel.gr. This hotel has the best views in town from its rooms – refurbished with mock-antique furniture and wood floors – and from the terrace bar, where hearty breakfasts (included) are served. It lies about 250m inland, in Botsaréïka at the base of the kástro, though it's a fair climb up with no easy parking nearby. €̲8̲0̲

EATING AND DRINKING

Most of Náfpaktos' **tavernas** line the beaches and are all fairly comparable in quality. Otherwise, the medieval harbour and the Stenopázaro lane just inland are full of *frappádhika* and **bars**, which constitute the town's nightlife.

Grillicious On the harbour ☎26340 28800. With seats facing the harbour walls, this serves regular grilled meat dishes, as well as a range of "dirty" burgers (€5.50) plus the usual wraps and skewers. Daily 1pm–1am.
Kastro On road to castle ☎26340 25121. Of the two cafés on the road heading up to the castle, this has the better vistas – enjoy a coffee and toast on its grassy terraces, with whopping views down to the centre and over

the sea, or swing by for an ouzo nightcap. Daily 10am–midnight.
Papoulis Pedestrian zone, near Fetiye mosque ☎26340 21578. This atmospheric place serves large portions of well-cooked food (try the mussels in a cheesy tomato sauce; €7); there's outside seating near the square, but try to nab one of the two indoor tables overlooking the gulf. Daily 10am–11pm.

Ancient Thermon

Around 46km northwest of Náfpaktos, and signed 1.5km southeast of Thérmo • Tues–Sun 8.30am–3pm • Free • Photography forbidden

Inland from Náfpaktos and close to the small town of Thérmo, **ancient Thermon** was the walled political capital and main religious sanctuary of the Aetolians. This modest site is still under excavation: the **main temple** (c.1000 BC), orientated north-to-south rather than the usual west-to-east, was dedicated to Apollo Thermios; just east lies an even older, smaller shrine to Apollo Lyseios, while to the northwest are foundations of an Artemis temple. South of the main temple the **sacred spring** still flows, still potable and, in season, full of frogs. The keeper will unlock the small, one-room **museum**, which is crammed with unlabelled objects.

Áyios Konstandínos

ÁYIOS KONSTANDÍNOS is the closest port to Athens for the Sporades islands, with daily catamaran or car-ferry departures to Skiáthos, Skópelos and Alónissos. It lies on the coastal **Athens–Lamía motorway** which offers spectacular views of the surrounding mountains. En route there are various links with the island of **Évvia** (see p.696): first at Halkídha (where there's a causeway), then by ferry at **Arkítsa**.

ARRIVAL AND DEPARTURE   ÁYIOS KONSTANDÍNOS

By bus The bus station is about 200m south of the ferry landing. As well as the regular buses to and from Athens' Liossíon terminal, there are also dedicated buses from central Athens in high season, timed to coincide with ferries, run by Alkyon Travel (☎210 383 2545, ⓦalkyontravel.gr) for Hellenic Seaways, and Jeta Tours (☎210 323 0582, ⓦjeta-tours.gr) for Anes Ferries.
Destinations Athens (hourly; 2hr 30min); Pátra (1 daily; 4hr).
By ferry In summer, Hellenic Seaways fast catamarans and ferries (☎21041 99000, ⓦhsw.gr) and Anes ferries (ⓦanes.gr) run to Alónissos, Skópelos and Skiáthos; prebooking is recommended. Edipsos Ferries (☎22260 23330, ⓦferriesedipsos.gr) also runs a frequent service from Arkítsa (16km east of Áyios Konstandínos) to Edhipsós on Évvia.
Destinations Alónissos (summer 1–2 daily; 3hr 25min–5hr); Skiáthos (summer 1–2 daily; 1hr 50min–3hr); Skópelos (summer 1–2 daily; 3hr–4hr 25min).

Lamía and around

LAMÍA, with a population of around fifty thousand, is a busy transport hub that inspires few overnight visitors. From here, most travellers head north toward Metéora, west to the mountainous Karpeníssi Valley, or east and then north to Vólos and the Pelion. To the southwest stands **Mount Íti** (2150m), one of the country's most beautiful mountains, and its national park, offering spectacular views of surrounding peaks, including Parnassós, while to the southeast lies the famous battle site of **Thermopylae** and its hot springs.

If you choose to stay in this city – or have to – you'll find Lamía's sprawling foothills setting attractive enough, and its main squares full of life and local colour, not to mention tavernas offering local cuisine.

ARRIVAL AND DEPARTURE   LAMÍA

By train The mainline train station is at Lianokládhi, 6km west of Lamía. Up to six buses per day make the journey from here into town, or it's around €6 by taxi.
Destinations Athens (8 daily; 2hr 30min); Lárissa (6 daily; 1hr 40min); Thessaloníki (6 daily; 3hr); Vólos (via Lárissa; 6 daily; 2hr 40min).
By bus The huge main bus station is on Taigetou, around 2km southeast of the centre.
Destinations Athens (around 14 daily; 2hr 30min); Delphi (1 daily; 2hr); Ioánnina (1 daily; 4hr 30min); Karpeníssi (at least 2 daily; 1hr); Larissa (at least 1 daily; 2hr); Tríkala (6 daily; 2hr 30min); Thessaloníki (at least 4 daily; 4hr); Vólos (1–2 daily; 2hr).

ACCOMMODATION AND EATING

Lamia is an almost inevitable connection if using public transport to see the region; if you have to spend the night, there are some acceptable options.

Athina Rozakis Angelis 41 ☎22310 20700. About 2km from the main bus station and 3km from the motorway, this large, modern hotel is handy for the centre and has helpful staff. Public rooms are rather bland, but guestrooms are large, clean and well appointed. Private parking extra. **€50**

Fitilis Platía Laou 6 ☎ 22310 26761. One of many on the main square, this restaurant specializes in the region's grilled meats, including goat and lamb, but also offers the usual non-meat plates and *mayireftá*. Expect to pay about €15–20/person. Daily lunch and dinner.

Thermopylae

Some 17km southeast of Lamía, just off the main motorway to Áyios Konstandínos, is the **Pass of Thermopylae** (Thermopýles), where a majestic **monument** commemorates Spartan King **Leonidas** and his entourage, who made their stand against Xerxes' thirty-thousand-strong Persian army in August 480 BC. The Spartans' bravery is described by Herodotus (and more recently, comic-book style, by Zack Snyder's film *300*): Leonidas held the pass, the only approach an army could take to enter Attica from Thessaly, for two days with a mixed force of seven thousand Spartans, Phokians, Thebans and helots. By night, however, Xerxes – tipped off by the traitor Ephialtes – sent an advance party along a little-used mountain trail and skirted the pass to attack the Greeks from behind. Leonidas ordered a retreat of the main army, but remained in place with a rearguard of about 2300, including three hundred Spartans (thus the film's title), to delay the Persians' progress. All but two of them fought to their deaths on the third day.

Loutrá Thermopylíon

Loutrá Thermopylíon, across the road from the gloriously heroic statue of Leonidas and midway through the pass, are thermal springs exploited since antiquity. Here you can bathe undisturbed in open-air hot cascades, while off to the side 500m away lies the grave mound of the fallen rearguard.

Mount Íti

To the southwest of Lamía, **Mount Íti** boasts one of the most beautiful of Greek national parks – along its green northeast slopes – which is also unusually accessible by Greek standards. The classic **full traverse** of the range from Ypáti to Pávliani, taking in the summit, takes about eleven hours, best spread over two days. The flat-topped peak of Pyrá ("the pyre") is where in legend Hercules immolated himself to escape the agony of the poisoned tunic which his wife Deinaneira had given him.

A rewarding **one-day outing** through Íti's sheer rock ramparts and lush meadows involves two overnights in Ypáti. The way uphill, starting from the square, is patchily marked with red paint splodges or square placards; the actual path from the top of the village leads in around four hours to an EOS refuge at **Trápeza** (usually locked, but with a spring nearby). From there you could return on a different path via Zapandólakka to Ypáti for a circular hike.

ARRIVAL AND INFORMATION   MOUNT ÍTI

By bus and train Frequent buses cover the 22km from Lamía to Ypáti, the usual trailhead (45min); be sure not to get off the bus at Loutrá Ypátis spa, 5km before Ypáti proper. These buses pass Lianokládhi station en route, so if you're travelling by train, you can bypass Lamía completely.

Maps Two topographic maps of Mount Íti are available, published by Road Editions (no. 43, 1:50,000, with route summaries in English) and Anavasi (Editions no. 10, 1:50,000), also with a useful booklet in bilingual text.

Karpeníssi Valley

West of Mount Íti, the **KARPENÍSSI VALLEY** is surrounded by dark fir forest and snow-fringed (Dec–May) mountains, a region promoted (with some justice) as "the Greek Switzerland". Skiing on **Mount Tymfristós** (**Veloúhi**) and springtime rafting or summer canyoning along local rivers are the main outdoor activities. Seasonal tourism, mostly domestic, is well established, such that accommodation prices in the area are also authentically Swiss, boosted by a clientele of wealthy Athenians and Thessalonians.

Karpeníssi

The main road in from Lamía, after scaling a spur of Mount Tymfristós, drops down to **KARPENÍSSI**; a 1400m tunnel below the snow line guarantees year-round access and spares drivers at least twice that distance of curvy road over the pass. Karpeníssi's site is spectacular – huddled at the base of the peak and head of the valley, which extends south all the way to wall-like Mount Panetolikó – but the town itself is entirely nondescript, having been destroyed in World War II by the Germans and again in the civil war. Snow conditions at the downhill **ski centre**, 11km above town, are variable as the twelve runs and four chair lifts have a top point of only 2048m. Gear is available to rent at the resort.

ARRIVAL AND DEPARTURE
KARPENÍSSI

By bus Arriving by public bus is inconvenient, since the KTEL bus station is 1.5km out on the bypass road, though shuttles occasionally do a run into town, along the main drag Zinopoúlou, to the central platía. In season, a daily "ski bus" connects the resort with Athens and Lamia; see ⓦ velouxi.gr for times.

Destinations Agrínio (1 daily; 3hr 30min); Athens (2–3 daily; 4hr 30min); Lamía (at least 2 daily; 1hr); Megálo/Mikró Horió (2 daily; 15min).
By car Parking in the centre is difficult and heavily controlled: all our accommodation listings have free parking.

ACCOMMODATION AND EATING

Anesis Zinopoúlou 50 ⓞ 22370 80700, ⓦ anesis.gr. A chalet-style spot, mainly worth it if you get one of the rooms with stunning valley views. Located on the edge of town, a 10min walk from the centre, with easy parking. Very substantial breakfast included. **€80**
Elvetia Zinopoúlou 17 ⓞ 22370 22465, ⓦ elvetiahotel. gr. Not much to look at from the outside, but attractive communal areas (including an arcaded stone-and-wood

bar and a sky-lit dining area), attention to detail and helpful management make up for somewhat small rooms. Breakfast included. **€42**
Panorama Ríga Feréou 18 ⓞ 22370 25976. This taverna has terrace-garden seating with views, and offers well-executed *mayireftá* and mountain grills among a wide range of menu choices (about €10–15/person). Daily lunch and dinner.

CLIMBING MOUNT KALIAKOÚDHA

The eight-hour **hike** up and down **Mount Kaliakoúdha** (2098m) is one of the most popular outings in the Karpeníssi Valley. There's a good, waymarked path much of the way to the top, but the final ascent conquers a pretty sharp grade and requires scrambling skills. The route and its features are shown reasonably accurately on Anavasi Editions 1:50,000 **map** no. 13, *Karpenisi Prousos*. With an early start, you'll polish off most of the 1250m altitude difference before the sun catches you.

From Megálo's square with its bars and cafés, head southeast, following painted red or yellow waymarks on walls until a proper path leaves the village. This passes one water source and climbs steadily through fir forest where many trees are dead or dying due to climate change, but the survivors provide welcome shade. About two hours above the village, and frequent crossing of the dirt track, the path ends temporarily just below the tree line at **Malakássa**, near the only other reliable **spring** this side of the mountain. You're forced onto the track for about another hour (unless you use some trail short cuts) to a saddle at the northeast flank of the peak. The track continues down and south towards Stournára and Pandavréhi (see p.221); for Kaliakoúdha, head west and relentlessly up, following red-paint waymarks. The trail is poor to nonexistent, often strewn with scree, but there's little danger of getting lost and on a fine day you'll have company. Just under an hour (roughly 4hr from the village) should see you on the **summit** with its trig point; staggering **views** over central Greece are your reward. Vardhoússia and Íti loom to the east; the Ágrafa region unfolds beyond Mount Tymfristós to the north-northeast; while Mount Panetolikó approximates the provincial border south-southwest.

Due south lies Stournára village in the Krikellopótamos Valley, poised just above **Pandavréhi**, the other big local attraction, where waterfalls pour year-round from the walls of a narrow gorge of the Krikellopótamos. As there are no reliable facilities in Stournára, most people visit Pandavréhi by car; from the signposted junction just below Megálo Horió, it's 23km there along the track system.

The Pelion peninsula

The hilly **PELION PENINSULA** confounds every stereotypical image of Greece, with its abundant fruit trees and dense forests and water gurgling up from fountains or aqueducts. Summer temperatures here can be a good 5°C cooler than on the baking plains nearby, and this finger of land is very popular with Greek tourists and more discerning foreign visitors drawn to its pretty **villages**, excellent **beaches** and **hiking routes** (see box, p.226).

The peninsula is dominated by **Mount Pelion** (Mount Pílio; 1651m), below which villages are spread out widely, linked by cobbled paths. The best concentration of traditional communities lies just north and east of **Vólos**, the main gateway to the region. The **west coast** down from Vólos to Áfyssos is less memorable, with

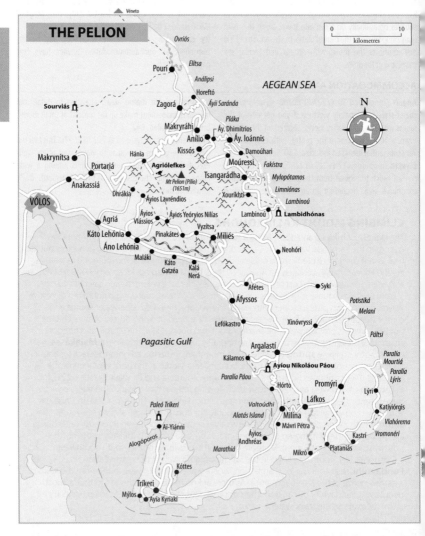

THE PELION

0 — 10 kilometres

Véneto

Ovriós

Elítsa

Pourí

Análipsi

Horeftó

AEGEAN SEA

Sourviás

Zagorá

Áyii Saránda

Pláka

Makryráhi

Áy. Dhimítrios

Anílio

Áy. Ioánnis

Makrynítsa

Hánia

Kissós

Damoúhari

Moúressi

Fakístra

Portariá

Agriólefkes

Tsangarádha

Mylopótamos

Anakassiá

Mt Pelion (Pílio) (1651m)

Limniónas

Dhrákia

Áyios Lavréndios

Xouríkhti

Lambinoú

VÓLOS

Agriá

Áyios Vlássios

Áyios Yeóryios Nilías

Lambinoú

Lambidhónas

Káto Lehónia

Pinakátes

Vyzítsa

Miliés

Áno Lehónia

Maláki

Káto Gatzéa

Kalá Nerá

Neohóri

Afétes

Sykí

Áfyssos

Potistiká

Melaní

Lefókastro

Xinóvryssi

Páltsi

Pagasitic Gulf

Argalastí

Paralía Mourtiá

Kálamos

Ayíou Nikoláou Páou

Paralía Lýris

Paralía Páou

Hórto

Promýri

Lýri

Láfkos

Katiyiórgis

Paleó Trikeri

Valtoúdhi

Milína

Vlahórema

Alatás Island

Áï-Yiánni

Mávri Pétra

Vromonéri

Alogóporos

Áyios Andhréas

Kastrí

Marathiá

Mikró

Plataniás

Kóttes

Trikeri

Mýlos

Áyia Kyriakí

concentrated development along the Pagasitic Gulf despite no decent beaches. The **far south**, relatively low-lying and sparsely populated, has just two major resorts – Plataniás and Milína – plus a few inland villages and the picturesque fishing port of Ayía Kyriakí at the extreme southwestern tip.

One of the great pleasures of the Pelion is staying in one of its many beautifully restored **traditional mansions**. The northwestern part of the peninsula is especially rich in these, and there are some good ones between Vyzítsa and Pinakátes: if you plan on visiting out of high season, make sure you book well in advance.

ARRIVAL AND GETTING AROUND   THE PELION PENINSULA

The natural gateway to the Pelion is Vólos (see p.below), and there are buses from there to most towns, albeit slow and infrequent. However, to take full advantage of the place in all its variety, it's essential to have your **own transport**.

By air Arriving fairly directly in the Pelion from overseas is possible, thanks to May–Oct charter flights to either Skiáthos (see p.672), or Néa Anhíalos airport near Vólos (see p.224).

By bus Buses to the east cover two main routes from Vólos (see p.224 for full details): to Zagorá, via Portariá, and Áyios Ioánnis, via Tsangarádha, with scarce services linking Zagorá and Tsangarádha to complete a loop. The far south is equally infrequently served, though

Makrynítsa and Vyzítsa in the west both have more frequent connections, as does Áfyssos. Sunday services are always more sparse.

By car Given the patchy bus services, a rental car is your best option. Note that driving is slow progress, since perilously narrow (and often rock-strewn) roads snake around ravine contours, seemingly never getting closer to villages just across the way. Car rental is available in Vólos (see p.224).

INFORMATION

Services Banks and petrol stations are found along the commercialized coastal road just out from Vólos. Otherwise, there are ATMs in Zagorá, Tsangarádha, Ayía Kyriakí and

Argalastí, and petrol stations in Zagorá, Argalastí, Ayía Kyriakí and elsewhere.

Vólos

Sitting at the northwest corner of the Pagasitic Gulf, the city of **VÓLOS** is a major port and looks promising enough based on the glittering view from the hillside as you approach. Close-up, however, the resolutely industrial outskirts and the mostly lacklustre centre evoke nothing of its mythological past as the spot from which Jason and the Argonauts embarked on their quest for the Golden Fleece.

With a population approaching 150,000, Vólos ranks as the fifth-largest Greek city, rebuilt in utilitarian style after a series of devastating earthquakes between 1947 and 1957, and now edging to its natural limits against the Pelion foothills. University of Thessaly students make it a lively place, and you could do worse than spend a few hours or even a night here while waiting for a bus into the Pelion or a boat to the Sporades islands, for which Vólos is the **main port**. The most attractive place to linger is along the eastern **waterfront esplanade**, between landscaped Platía Yeoryíou and the archeological museum.

Archeological Museum
Athanasaki 1 • Summer 8am–5pm; winter 8am–3pm • €3 • ☎ 24210 25285

At the far eastern end of the city's seafront, the **Archeological Museum** boasts exemplary labelling and well-lit galleries, one of which is reserved for changing exhibits. Highlights of the permanent collection include one of the best European assemblages of Neolithic (6500–3500 BC) figurines from various surrounding sites; faint but expressive painted grave stelae from Hellenistic Dimitrias depicting everyday scenarios of fifth-century BC life, with some inscriptions helpfully translated; and a massive quantity of items, including superb stone and gold jewellery, from tombs of all eras across Thessaly.

3

ARRIVAL AND INFORMATION

By air The nearest airport receiving overseas flights (but no domestic ones), is 26km southwest of the city, beyond Néa Anhíalos (Almyrós). Buses generally meet the charter flights, and transfer passengers to Vólos.

By train The train station is just off Platía Ríga Feréou, to the west of the city centre.

Destinations Athens (10 daily via Lárissa; 5–8hr); Lárissa (12 daily; 50min).

By bus The KTEL city bus terminal is on Sekéri, just off Grigoríou Lampráki, a 10min walk southwest of the main square, Platía Ríga Feréou; there's a taxi rank right outside. As well as the following destinations, there are also some services heading into the Pelion (see p.222).

Destinations Áfyssos (10 daily; 1hr); Athens (11 daily; 3hr 30min); Áyios Ioánnis (2–3 daily; 2hr 15min); Ioánnina (2–3 daily; 4hr); Katiyiórgis (Mon–Sat 1 daily; 2hr); Lárissa (10–12 daily; 1hr); Makrynítsa (6–7 daily; 50min); Miliés (4–5 daily; 1hr); Milína (3–5 daily; 1hr 30min); Plataniás (2–3 daily; 2hr); Thessaloníki (8 daily; 3hr); Tríkala (4 daily; 2hr 30min); Tríkeri (1–2 daily; 2hr 30min); Tsangarádha (2–3 daily; 1hr 45min); Vyzítsa (4–5 daily; 1hr 10min); Zagorá (2–3 daily; 2hr–2hr 30min).

VÓLOS

By car The city centre has pay-and-display parking – or try the large car park on Kontaratou. Car rental is widely available; agents include Avis, Argonaftón 41 (☎24210 28880); Budget, Grigoriou Lampraki 48 (☎24210 20473); and Hertz, at the airport (☎26950 24287).

By ferry In summer, Vólos has frequent car ferries to the Sporades, plus faster, passenger-only hydrofoils and catamarans. Hellenic Seaways (☎21041 99000, ⓦhellenicseaways.gr), Anes Ferries (☎22460 71444; ⓦanes.gr) and Aegean Flying Dolphins (☎21042 21766) run most of the routes, and the first two publish up-to-date timetables online.

Destinations Alónissos (1–2 daily car ferries in summer, 5hr; plus 1–3 daily passenger catamarans/hydrofoils, 2hr 25min–3hr 20min); Mantoudi, Évvia (1 daily; 5hr 30min–7hr 30min); Skiáthos (2–3 daily car ferries in summer; 2hr 15min–3hr; 2–3 daily passenger catamarans/hydrofoils, 1hr 15min–1hr 40min); Skópelos (1–2 daily car ferries in summer; 2hr 5min–3hr 35min; 1–2 daily passenger catamarans/hydrofoils in summer, 2hr–2hr 30min).

Tourist office Opposite the KTEL (Mon–Fri 8am–4pm; ☎24210 30930, ⓦvolosinfo.gr), this is one of the best tourist offices in mainland Greece.

ACCOMMODATION

Aegli Argonafton 24 ☎24210 24471, ⓦaegli.gr. Right by the port and close to the best restaurants and nightlife, this hotel has clean, simple rooms with high ceilings (though some lack daylight), plus a modern breakfast room (including) with stone-clad walls. **€75**

Anastasia On the edge of the square at Makedonias 38 ☎24210 85089, ⓦanastasiahotel.net. It's a long walk from the centre but this budget place has very clean and tidy rooms, some with balconies overlooking the pretty churchyard. **€38**

Jason Pávlou Melá 1 ☎24210 26075, ⓦjason-hotel.gr. Facing the waterfront, this basic, bright, plain hotel has double-glazed windows, a/c, a small elevator, free wi-fi and balconies. Rooms and bathrooms are generally on the small side but clean; ask to see a few before choosing. **€50**

Xenia Domotel Plastíra 1 ☎24210 92700, ⓦdomotel.gr. This crisply modern seafront luxury resort has a pool, spa, fitness centre, plush rooms in blue-green and white, plus free use of a laptop, and a copious buffet breakfast (included). **€95**

EATING AND DRINKING

Vólos specializes in the authentic **ouzerí** or *tsipourádhiko*, serving mezédhes washed down with ouzo or *tsípouro*, the all-but-identical spirit of the northern mainland. For something more contemporary, Kontarátou is lined with funky **wine bars** and **restaurants**, while there are stacks of bars and seafood restaurants along the waterfront, and a collection of international fast-food restaurants a block inland.

Grooove Kontarátou 40 ☎24210 33032. Very well stocked cocktail bar with drinks at €7–8 a glass, plus mountainous sandwiches and cheap tapas (from €3). Expect flickering candles, Rococo furniture and chilled dance music. Daily 9am–1am.

★**Mezen** Alonissou 8 ☎24210 20844. This small, back-alley *tsipourádhiko* has exploded in popularity of late, thanks to its successful – and award-winning – modern take on the humble bar. There's only one choice to make

here: do you want your *tsípouro* anise-flavoured, or not? For every one you order (around €4), you'll get a couple of meze plates included, often involving seafood, and all of sky-high quality. Almost perfect. Daily noon–midnight.

Papadis Argonafton 6 ☎24210 29360. The best of the waterfront seafood restaurants, its tables are often crammed with locals who come for the affordable shellfish, octopus and the like (€8–15 per dish). Daily 11am–1am.

The northwestern Pelion

Near Vólos, the villages of the **northwestern Pelion** provide a pleasant sampler of the peninsula – and are easy to get to if you're relying on public transport (or simply not a fan of long car journeys on winding roads). Closest to the city is **Anakassiá**, with its unique art museum, followed by **Portariá**, a buzzing little place that's lofty enough to boast wonderful vistas; from here, a half-hour walk will bring you to **Makrynítsa**, a marginally more refined village, where stone houses straggle picturesquely 200m down the mountainside.

Anakassiá

The village of (Iolkós), 4km out of Vólos, is still essentially a suburb, but it does offer a museum dedicated to the "naive" painter **Theophilos** (1873–1934). A prize eccentric, originally from Lésvos, Theophilos lived for long periods in Vólos, where he wandered around, often dressed as a historical hero, painting frescoes in exchange for a meal or pocket money. On the Pelion you find his murals in unlikely places, such as village tavernas, bakeries and *kafenía*.

Theophilos Museum

A 5min walk from the square (signposted) • Tues–Sun 8am–3pm, but may close unexpectedly • Free

The **Theophilos Museum** occupies the **Arhondikó Kondoú**, an eighteenth-century mansion whose first floor preserves much of Theophilos' earliest (1912–27) work, with unusually vivid colours thanks to restoration in recent decades. The Greek War of Independence – one of his favourite themes – features often, including such scenes as Patriarch Gregory's body being dumped into the Bosphorus, Admiral Tombazis setting the Ottoman flagship alight, and the taking of Tripoli, with the attendant massacre of Turkish civilians graphically shown. Nearer floor level, a bestiary features a bear-headed hippo (the painter never saw most of his animal subjects in the flesh).

Portariá

Just 12km from central Vólos, **PORTARIÁ** stares down over the city from an elevation of over 600m. Despite the profusion of guesthouses, and the fact that it's the portal to the Pelion, the village rarely feels over-busy, and there are some charming stone houses hereabouts. As ever, the village is centred around a central square presided over by a large plane tree – this one dates back to 1220.

Makrynítsa

Some 10km from Vólos, **MAKRYNÍTSA** was founded in 1204 by refugees from the Fourth Crusade's sacking of Constantinople, and comprises six churches plus a monastery, and various **traditional mansions** – many restored as accommodation. Most impressive of the churches are **Áyios Ioánnis**, next to the fountain on the shady main platía, and the beautiful eighteenth-century **monastery of Panayía Makrynítissa**, beneath the clocktower. The marble relief work on Áyios Ioánnis' apse, plus that on the fountain opposite, is among the best of its type in Greece.

The views are splendid from most points around the village, which is also the starting point for the trek to the **monastery of Sourviás** (see box, p.226).

ACCOMMODATION AND EATING   **THE NORTHWESTERN PELION**

MAKRYNÍTSA

Apolafsi ☎24280 90085. Most visitors stay on and around the main square to eat, but head just a short way down the hill to this family-run operation for a romantic atmosphere, super views and dishes made that morning by the grandmother – the menu changes daily, but usually features delicious baked aubergine with cheese (€7.50). Thurs–Mon 1pm–midnight.

Arhondiko Repana ☎24280 99067, ⓦarchontiko repana.gr. One of the finest of the Pelion's restored traditional mansions along the pedestrianized main street, this has rooms edging towards the twee but is the best value in the village. Great views, and breakfast included. **€72**

3

Karamarlis ☎24280 99570, ⓦarchontikakaramarlis
.gr. Hugging the hillside below the pedestrianized main
street, this warren-like restored mansion has good-quality
rooms, the best of which have high beds and sofas
overlooking the mountains. There's a quirky café-cum-
restaurant too. **€65**

PORTARIÁ

★**Kritsa** ☎24280 99121, ⓦhotel-kritsa.gr. This
restored mansion is one of the best places to stay on the
whole peninsula. Its stylish rooms, professional service
and central-square location make it a great deal even
without the award-winning breakfasts (included) –
prepare for a feast. This is also the best place to eat in the
village, with a menu full of affordable dishes, including
local specialities such as spetzofai (sausage and peppers
in tomato sauce; €8). There's also a decent wine menu,
and the water jugs are filled from a natural spring
spouting from beneath a 900-year-old tree. Daily mid-
morning until late. **€55**

Triantafillies ☎24280 99641, ⓦtriantafillies.gr. A
quiet, semi-rural restored mansion at the far edge of
town, with a handful of cosy rooms, a delightful pool
surrounded by flowers, and local dogs and cats popping
by to say hello. Breakfast (included) is superb, and a
small "happy hour" buffet of snacks, sweets and coffee is
offered as evening approaches. **€50**

The northeastern Pelion

The **northeastern Pelion** features the region's best – and most popular – beaches, and its
lushest scenery, particularly along the Aegean-facing **coast**. A relatively humid climate
and shady dells nurture exotic flowers such as hydrangeas, gardenias and camellias,
locally bred and sold at the roadside. The "county town" of the region is **Zagorá**,
self-proclaimed apple capital of Greece, though for most travellers it's best used as a
transport hub.

HIKING IN THE NORTHERN PELION

Until the 1950s, Pelion villages were linked exclusively by a dense network of **kalderímia** (old
cobbled paths). Subsequent road building bulldozed many or consigned them to disuse, and
neglected trails quickly became blocked by vegetation. Since the 1990s, however, committed
residents and village councils have mounted campaigns to clean, restore, mark and document
these superb **walking routes**, so that now the number of Pílio hiking opportunities is at least
stable rather than dwindling. The best **walking seasons** are late April to early June, and early
September to October; summer is hot and humid, and the winter mist and snow line in the
north can dip well below the villages.

MAKRYNÍTSA TO THE MONASTERY OF SOURVIÁS

Makrynítsa is the starting point for the three-and-a-half-hour trek (one way) to the deserted,
frescoed **monastery of Sourviás**, mostly on *kalderími* and path surface. The route starts from
a steep cement track west of the monastery of Ayíou Yerasímou, though trail resumes for most
of the way once Makrynítsa is out of sight.

THE TSANGARÁDHA LOOP

From Damoúhari on the east coast, you can follow the popular and rewarding walk to
Tsangarádha in 75 minutes (an increase in elevation of 500m), though most folk do it
downhill in under an hour. At the mouth of the ravine descending to the larger bay, a
spectacular *kalderími* begins its steep ascent, allowing glimpses of up to six villages
simultaneously, plus the Sporades on a clear day, from points en route. Then there is deep
shade, and a potable spring approaching Ayía Kyriakí; the path eventually emerges in the
Ayía Paraskeví quarter of Tsangarádha. You can make a loop of this route by continuing from
Tsangarádha for a further thirty minutes to Moúressi, and from there either taking the
45-minute descent to Damoúhari (look for the signposted start of the trail, on the bend in the
road just past the minimarket), or head down the twisty road (with several *kalderími*
short-cuts) to Áyios Ioánnis, from where it's a thirty-minute coastal walk back to Damoúhari.
You can start or finish this loop-route at any point, though the Damoúhari-to-Tsangarádha
stretch is best tackled uphill, since the gradient and surface make it tricky (not to mention
tough on the knees) going down.

Zagorá

The largest Pelion village, **ZAGORÁ** has a life more independent of tourism than others. Visitors often jump to unfavourable conclusions from the workaday main street where the bus calls; in fact, there are four well-preserved and architecturally varied parishes with handsome Neoclassical mansions, arrayed around a number of squares, strung out over 5km. Best are **Ayía Paraskeví** (Perahóra), with its pleasant, unvisited platía, and **Áyios Yeóryios**, whose platía boasts a large plane tree and beautiful eighteenth-century church.

Horeftó

Eight twisting kilometres down the mountain from Zagorá, **HOREFTÓ** makes an excellent coastal base. There is ample choice of **beaches**: a long, decent one in front of this former fishing village; secluded Áyii Saránda 2km south and two coves at Análipsi, just north – a brief hike brings you to the first cove, a little paradise popular with nudists and rough campers taking advantage of a spring behind the sand. Determined explorers can follow the coastal path for twenty minutes more to the northerly cove, road-accessible and rockier. There are also two hour-long *kalderímia* up to Zagorá, which can be combined to make an enjoyable loop.

Áyios Ioánnis

ÁYIOS IOÁNNIS is the main resort town on the Pelion's east coast. Numerous hotels and *dhomátia* were erected during the 1980s to a density no longer allowed, but despite this, finding a bed here in peak season can be as problematic as anywhere on the peninsula. The **beach** at Áyios Ioánnis is decent enough: there are windsurf boards to rent, while more ambitious watersports and activites can be booked through local travel agencies (see p.228).

Many visitors prefer to hike a few minutes north from Áyios Ioánnis to the next cove, where pebbly **Pláka beach** boasts crystal clear waters. Heading south for a few minutes –via a pedestrian bridge over a small stream – brings you to **Papá Neró beach**, essentially a continuation of Áyios Ioánnis, but quieter and popular with the camping and caravanning set; its dead-end shore road makes for a delightful post-sunset prom.

Damoúhari

South of Áyios Ioánnis, a narrow paved road leads up over a low ridge and down through olive groves to **DAMOÚHARI** hamlet, bordering a stage-set-perfect port which has, in fact, been used for several film shoots. The construction of a broader road down from Moúressi ended its seclusion, and villas have sprung up mushroom-like among the olive trees. However, cars are excluded from the shoreline, where there's a large pebble beach, the overgrown ruins of a Venetian castle, and several **tavernas**. It's also possible to hike from here to Tsangarádha (see box, opposite).

Tsangarádha

Generally unappealing on account of its size and distance from the sea, **TSANGARÁDHA** is the largest northeastern village after Zagorá, though it may not seem so at first, since it's also divided into four distinct quarters, strung along several kilometres of road. Each of these focuses on a namesake church and platía; the finest is **Ayía Paraskeví**, shaded by what is reputedly the heftiest plane tree in Greece – more than one thousand years old, and requiring eighteen men to encircle it.

Mylopótamos

From Taxiárhes Tsangarádha, you can follow a ninety-minute path, or a 7km hairpin road, down to **MYLOPÓTAMOS** and its two attractive (if hugely popular) pebble coves, where there is afternoon shade from caves and overhangs. The pair are separated by a naturally tunnelled rock, with a music bar just above. The craggy rocks and deep pools here make it a favourite spot with coasteering groups (see below).

Limniónas Beach

Southeast of Mylopótamos lies the attractive **Limniónas beach**. You can arrive on foot from Mylopótamos, but most people get there via Lambinoú village (no reliable facilities), from where a paved road leads 3km down past the restored eighteenth-century **Lambidhónas monastery**, which sports fine frescoes over the doors. Scenic Limniónas has a freshwater shower but no other reliable amenities. There's a romantic, out-of-the-way hotel option here (see below).

ACTIVITIES

Coasteering Pelion Active (☎ 69488 16202; ⓦ pelionactive.weebly.com) offers coasteering, rock-climbing and sea kayaking in Mylopótamos; most activities cost around €25 for a 2hr excursion.

THE NORTHEASTERN PELION

Sea kayaking and mountain biking Les Hirondelles at Áyios Ioánnis (☎ 24210 32171, ⓦ les-hirondelles.gr) can arrange a number of outdoor activities, including sea kayaking and mountain biking.

ACCOMMODATION

HOREFTÓ

Limanaki Rooms ☎ 24260 23421, ⓦ limanakirooms .gr. Right above the harbour at the southern end of the beach, on the road up to Agii Saranta, this good-value guesthouse has great views and decent rooms, despite the institutional feel in the corridors. Some rooms have kitchens, there's a BBQ area and a free-to-borrow boat for fishing trips. A fair hike up from beach but there's parking outside on the road. **€40**

ÁYIOS IOÁNNIS

Anesis ☎ 24260 31123, ⓦ hotelanesis.gr. Slightly set back from the street, so quieter than its neighbours, this simple hotel has a laid-back, slightly alternative atmosphere. The rooms are large and decorated in pastel tones, while breakfast (extra) is served on a terrace with sea views. **€40**

Kentrikon Boutique ☎ 24260 32200, ⓦ kentrikon -pelion.gr. One street back from the middle of the beach, this quiet, airy hotel has flowers and ornaments decorating the hallways plus a nice shady breakfast area out back. Standard doubles aren't anything special but the bigger executive rooms are surprisingly luxurious, with wooden floors, couches and cosy fireplace. Double **€85**, executive room **€150**

Sofokles ☎ 24260 31230, ⓦ sofokleshotel.com. Excellent value, this hotel is handily located towards the northern end of the beachfront. Plus points include sea views from most of the bright, airy rooms, and an attractive terrace-pool. **€65**

DAMOÚHARI

Kastro Studios ☎ 24260 49475. A good pick in this quiet enclave, with a clutch of self-catering units, most with balconies overlooking the harbour (go for those on the higher level, if possible), and a handy mini-market downstairs. **€50**

TSANGARÁDHA

Konaki ☎ 24260 49481. Located just south of the Ayía Paraskeví square but set back from the road. All rooms have fridges and views, some have balconies, and there's a pleasant basement breakfast area; rates also include use of the on-site sauna. **€70**

The Lost Unicorn ☎ 24260 49930, ⓦ lostunicornhotel .gr. Located in a 1890s building, this place scores as highly for its communal areas – kitted out like a British gentlemen's club – as for its eight antique-furnished, terrazzo-floored rooms. The pricey on-site restaurant (for guests only) transforms local products into French-and Italian-inspired dishes. April–Oct. **€85**

MOÚRESSI

The Old Silk Store ☎ 24260 49086 or ☎ 6937 156 780. With an English owner, this is not the most modern place but one of the most atmospheric by far, set in a beautiful restored nineteenth-century mansion with a lush garden, barbecue area, and high-ceilinged, wood-floored rooms. **€50**

MYLOPÓTAMOS

Diakoumis ☎ 24260 49203, ⓦ diakoumis.gr. Approaching Mylopótamos, these are the first rooms you come to and are among the best, just 1km from the beach. Accommodation is spread over two rambling buildings; each studio (2–3 people) or apartment (up to 5 people) is brightly decorated and comes with its own kitchen and spectacular views of the sea. **€45**

LIMNIÓNAS

★ **Faros** ☎ 24260 49994. North of Limniónas, at the very end of a rough, precipitous road, stands this very welcoming operation, in a secluded, leafy spot popular with hikers, beach-goers and horseriders. **€50**

EATING AND DRINKING

ÁYIOS IOÁNNIS

★ **Akti** ☎ 24260 31236. There are plenty of restaurants to choose from on the seafront strip, but this is the one that's most likely to be packed: with excellent dishes (like the delectable pastitsio; €8.50), gregarious service and fair prices, it has quickly become a favourite with locals and visitors alike. May–Sept 9am–midnight.

Paralos ☎ 24260 32052. Brightly coloured chairs mark out this chilled "all-day music bar", just off the main waterfront road near the *Sofokles* hotel (see opposite). Although it attracts a few coffee drinkers during the daytime, it only really gets going at night when DJs spin house tunes to a mostly youthful crowd. May–Sept daily 24hr, in theory.

DAMOÚHARI

★ **Karagatsi** ☎ 24260 49841. One of the best tavernas in the area, with bay views, especially romantic at sunset. The personable chef/owner here puts together big Greek salads and fresh fish dishes, including his own *taramosaláta*. You may wind up getting a guided tour of the kitchen, and the various dishes on offer (most €7–9). May–Sept daily 10am–11pm.

MYLOPÓTAMOS

Aggelika ☎ 24260 49588. Welcoming, efficient tavern (actually pronounced "Angelika") where the fresh fish is expensive, but other seafood, mezédhes and *mayireftá* are tasty and reasonably priced. €10–15/person. May–Sept daily 10.30am–8.30pm.

TSANGARÁDHA

0 Geyoeis On the approach road to *The Lost Unicorn* ☎ 6946 589 121. Traditional taverna serving good home-made salads and reasonable souvláki at affordable prices – around €7–8 for a main course, or €15 per person for a full meal with wine. Daily 10am–9pm.

ZAGORÁ

Thraka Ayía Kyriakí ☎ 24260 22322. Attractive taverna in the grounds of an even prettier eighteenth-century church, serving salads made with local apples (in season) and, the house speciality – local sausages cooked with peppers (€7). Daily 7.30am–midnight; closed Mon in winter.

The western Pelion

Lying in the rain shadow of the mountain, the **western Pelion** has a drier, more Mediterranean climate, with olives and arbutus predominating except in shady, damp ravines. The beaches, at least until Kalá Nerá, are far more developed than their natural endowments merit and lack the character of those on the east shore. Inland it is a different story, with pleasant foothill villages and decent bus services. **Vyzítsa** and **Pinakátes** in particular both make good bases for car tours or hiking.

Miliés

The sizeable village of **MILIÉS** (sometimes Miléës or Mileai) is the de facto hub of the area, its centre located just uphill from the main road linking the peninsula's east and west

---

THE PELION TRENÁKI

A prime west Pelion attraction is the *trenáki*, or **narrow-gauge railway**, which originally ran between Vólos and Miliés. The 60km line, in normal service until 1971, was laid out between 1894 and 1903 under the supervision of engineer Evaristo de Chirico, father of famous artist Giorgio de Chirico (which accounts for the little trains which chug across several of his paintings). To conquer the 2.8 percent gradient and numerous ravines between Áno Lehónia and Miliés, the elder de Chirico designed six multiple-span stone viaducts, tunnels and a riveted **iron trestle bridge**, all justly considered masterpieces of form and function. The bridge, some 700m west of the terminus below Miliés, spans a particularly deep gorge and can be crossed on a **pedestrian catwalk**; indeed, following the entire route down to Áno Lehónia is a popular 5hr 30min walk, with occasional springs en route.

You can ride on one of the original Belgian steam locomotives (since converted to diesel), during weekends and holidays between Easter and October (daily July & Aug), and several of the *belle epoque* stations have been restored. The **train** leaves Áno Lehónia (city bus #5 from Vólos) on the coast at 10am, taking ninety minutes to reach Miliés, from where it returns at 3pm. **Tickets** are currently €18 adults, €10 kids (round trip), and go on sale at 9.30am (start queuing at 9am), at either Vólos or Áno Lehónia. However, groups often book out the three carriages, so it's best to make enquiries at Vólos station a few days in advance.

coasts: it's also close to the eastern terminus of the peninsular railway (see box, p.229). An important cultural refuge during the eighteenth century, it retains some imposing mansions, and the Pelion's most interesting church, **Taxiárhis** (usually open around 6pm; free). Its eighteenth century narthex frescoes are some of the oldest and most unusual in the area: they include scenes from Noah's Flood (with two elephants boarding the Ark) and, in one corner, a three-ringed mandala showing the seasons, the zodiac and the cycle of human existence. With five wells under the floor and 48 clay urns secreted in the walls, the church's acoustics are superb, so it's occasionally used for concerts of sacred music.

Vyzítsa

VYZÍTSA, 3km west of Miliés and alive with water in streams and aqueducts, has a more open and less lived-in feel than either Makrynítsa or Miliés, though it, too, draws crowds of day-trippers in summer. It's also the nexus of pleasant trails, some of which can be combined into half-day **loop-hikes**. One that leads down to the sea in about two hours starts from the chapel of Zoödhóhou Piyís, just below Vyzítsa's platía, and follows a sporadically marked route that takes you around a vast landslip zone, and then across two ravines (bridges provided) followed by a brief stretch of farm track until dropping down to Kalá Nerá. Whatever your 3penchant for exploring the area, the famously picturesque hamlet makes an excellent base, with several accommodation options in converted mansions.

Pinakátes

PINAKÁTES, at the top of a densely forested ravine, was once among the least visited and most desolate of the west Pelion villages, following a 1955 phylloxera outbreak that ended its status as vineyard capital of the Pelion. No longer: the surfacing of roads that come in from three directions and trendy Greeks buying up crumbling mansions for restoration have seen to that. For now it remains a superbly atmospheric spot, with just enough food and accommodation to make it practicable for a sojourn.

ACCOMMODATION AND EATING   **THE WESTERN PELION**

There are more beautiful antique **mansions** to be found in this part of the Pelion, but also quite a few modern copycats, no less comfortable or charming for that. Booking ahead is often essential.

MILIÉS

Anna Na Ena Milo ☎ 24230 86889. The best coffee on the peninsula is available at this café just downhill from the clock tower. It's charmingly decorated with old movie posters and vintage advertising, and there's usually some wartime crooner or other on the sound system – sadly, the service often leaves something to be desired. Daily 9am–midnight.

O Palios Stathmos ☎ 24230 86425, ⓦ paliosstathmos.com. "The Old Station" is located, as the name implies, out by the old train station. The colourful, simple rooms here are worth it if you get a balconied front one with a nostalgic view of the quaint tracks. Breakfast is included in its traditional restaurant, which is also open for lunch and dinner (€10–15/ person). **€40**

Panorama ☎ 24230 86128. This simple grill occupies a vine-covered wedge-shaped building just above the platía, and is consistently good. Fresh vegetable pies and meats, average price/dish €7.50. Daily 10am–10pm.

VYZÍTSA

★Arhondiko Katerina ☎ 24230 86346, ⓦ archontikokaterina.gr. A handsome restored mansion, with homely touches all over – hand-made lace curtains, carved-wood furnishings and ceilings, a garden bursting with flowers, and (in some rooms) four-poster beds. Not to mention the gigantic breakfasts (included). **€55**

Balkonaki ☎ 24230 86321. Follow the steps up from the parking area to the lantern-lit square with three enormous trees, and on its uppermost tier you'll find this very simple, traditional taverna dishing up good salads as well as delicious lemon goat (€10). Daily 10am–midnight.

Stoïkos ☎ 24230 86406, ⓦ hotelstoikos.gr. The approach road from Miliés to the village is lined with inns, including this modern one constructed in the traditional way, where most of the well-executed rooms have wood-beam ceilings and views. Breakfast included. **€50**

RIGHT TAXIÁRHIS CHURCH, MILIÉS (P.229) >

PINAKÁTES

Dhrosia At the far western edge of Pinakátes ☎ 24230 86772. This taverna serves up good food, with free-range meat and poultry used where possible. Try the *dolmádhes* and *gídha lemonáti* (goat stew with lemon sauce), then wash it down with a jug of the deceptively potent red wine from some of the few surviving local vineyards. Expect to pay about €15/person. Daily 5pm–midnight.

★**Mansion Sakali** Towards the western end of the village ☎ 24230 86560, ✆ sakalihotel.gr. Thick stone walls keep the luxurious guest rooms at this 150-year-old mansion nice and cool, even in the hottest weather. Crisp cotton sheets and carved wooden fittings ramp up the comfort levels and there are great mountain views from the pool and terrace, where breakfast is served. **€135**

The southern Pelion

The **southern Pelion** is drier, lower and more stereotypically Mediterranean; the terrain overall is less dramatic, the villages more scattered. The region has been hit hard by forest fires – in particular a June 2007 blaze that burnt the entire coast from Argalastí to Áfyssos, and across the peninsula to Potistiká – such that the only undamaged pines grow around Neohóri, southeast of Miliés, and above Katiyiórgis. There are, however, interesting corners, and considerably less tourism inland, while a number of busy coastal resorts attract a mixed clientele of foreigners and Greeks. The area can be reached a little tortuously by bus or car from Vólos, or more directly by sea, via speedboats from Vólos.

Áfyssos

The first village you come to in the deep south, **ÁFYSSOS**, is by far the prettiest Pagasitic resort, laid out like a theatre, on hillside slopes with a shady waterfront square and a fairly broad, long crescent beach, lined with consistently vernacular structures: tavernas, private bungalows, small hotels and rooms. It's packed out in summer – with Greeks, especially – and you can forget about the teeming weekends. Its main claim to fame is that this was the very spot from which Jason and the Argonauts embarked in pursuit of the Golden Fleece.

Argalastí

ARGALASTÍ, an inland junction point, is the biggest place in the south, and close to the Pagasitic Gulf, with two **beaches** just a brief drive (or short walk) west. **Kálamos** is about the longest and sandiest on the Pagasitic side, but the road runs just behind it; there are dozens of apartments and two tavernas. Secluded **Paralía Páou**, reached by a different, dead-end road, is by contrast fine gravel, one of the best on the Pagasitic, but without amenities. En route there, stop at **Ayíou Nikoláou Páou monastery**, usually open to visitors who want to view its **frescoes**, which are dated to 1794; particularly fine are an Ancient of Days in the narthex dome, townscapes with ships, and a *Pandokrátor* in the sanctuary dome.

Hórto and Milína

Continuing south from Argalastí, you reach the sea again after 7km at **HÓRTO**, a quiet little resort largely insured against exploitation by its mediocre beaches. Just 3km further, **MILÍNA** seems far more commercialized; the beach is scanty, the norm for Pagasitic beaches, making it mostly a place to watch magnificent sunsets over the offshore islets and distant mainland ridges from one of the waterside **bar-cafés**.

Plataniás

Heading south eventually brings you to **PLATANIÁS** (or "Plataniá"), on the Pelion's south coast. One of the earliest Pelion beach resorts, Plataniás is essentially a collection of low-rises interspersed with restored vernacular houses. Named for the robust plane trees in the stream valley meeting the sea here, this is the biggest southern resort after Milína, with bus service from Vólos, and excursion *kaïkia* – on which you can arrange passage – calling most days from Skiáthos. The small beach is fine, but always busy; from the olive grove just inland, an obvious path, threading spectacularly above the coast, leads twelve minutes west to the much bigger and better strand of **Mikró**, with naturist covelets in between.

Tríkeri and Ayía Kyriakí

Until 1974 no road linked southwesterly **TRÍKERI** with the rest of the Pelion; though a broad highway now connects it with Milína in less than 45 minutes, this crab-claw-shaped peninsula still feels remote and insular. The hilltop village of **Tríkeri** ("Horió" in local parlance) has few amenities for outsiders so best carry on down the hill to its port town, **AYÍA KYRIAKÍ**. Transport by donkeys and mules is on the wane, but the 1500m *kalderími* that connects the two is still well used (drivers tackle a winding, 6km road). Ayía Kyriakí is still very much a working port with multicoloured fishing smacks at anchor, and is much the most attractive spot on this coast. It's also a very active shipbuilding centre; in the boatyard, a variety of craft are still built as they always have been, continuing the local seafaring tradition. Tourist facilities are few, perhaps because there's no really good beach nearby.

ACCOMMODATION AND EATING   THE SOUTHERN PELION

There are a few more restored eighteenth-century mansions here, but mostly the south features modern **self-catering resorts** and **modest rooms** for rent, more in keeping with the arid, more typically "Greek" landscape.

3

HÓRTO

Diplomats' Holidays ☏ 24230 65497, ⊚ diplomatsholidays.com. A mock-traditional complex of white, red-tile-roofed houses set amid garden greenery. Excellent facilities include a pool, tennis court and private beach, pebbly and small, but all yours. All accommodation is self-catering and comes with a/c and private verandas. April–Oct. **€42**

MILÍNA

★ **O Ikosimo** ☏ 24230 65217. Large stone house one street back from the sea, near the southern end of the beach, where the excellent rooms have small kitchenettes, balconies (some with great views) and fluffy white towels. The whole place has a fresh and welcoming feel, with art on the walls and light fittings made of old driftwood. Great value. **€50**

O Sakis ☏ 24230 66078. This seafront taverna at the southern end of the beach is one of the best in the area, and has the most genuinely Greek feel. You can assemble a tasty meal of seafood, two mezédhes and local wine for €14 – or fish for a bit more. Lots of meat dishes, too. Daily lunch and dinner.

PLATANIÁS

Camping Louisa ☏ 24230 71260, ⊚ camplouisa.gr/en. Located on the access road 600m inland, set amid forest and flowers and a certified organic farm, you'll find this rustic campsite. They offer full kitchen use as well as their own taverna plus 24hr hot showers and laundry facilities. Full range of information on activities that include kayaking, area hikes, spelunking, rock climbing, horseriding, mountain biking and fishing. Some sites have sea views. May–Sept. **€14**

Platanias ☏ 24230 71266, ⊚ hotelplatanias.com. Located east of the river mouth, right on the waterfront, this is the best and quietest option in Plataniás. Set in a rambling complex, all rooms have a kitchenette and balcony, and mostly mountain rather than sea views; they also have family rooms sleeping four and their own sea-front taverna (*To Steki*) on the ground floor. **€35**

AYÍA KYRIAKÍ

Agia Kyriaki ☏ 24230 91112, ⊚ agiakyriaki.gr. Follow the signposts a couple of streets up from the waterfront and you'll reach this attractive, five-bedroomed B&B set in its own quiet gardens. Breakfast (included) features home-made bread and marmalades. **€50**

Argo-Mythos Mylos ☏ 24230 91032, ⊚ argomythos.gr. This beautiful, well-managed hilltop resort, just 4km over the hill from Ayía Kyriakí, has it all: rooms and self-catering apartments with a/c and balconies, a swimming pool, a restaurant, and proximity to a cove with beach – plus fine views. **€75**

Mouragio ☏ 24210 45791. One of three traditional tavernas in a row, this is the most likely to be open all year. It serves all the usual Greek dishes, plus fresh catch-of-the-day, temptingly prepared and at excellent prices (€10–15/person). Daily 11am–11pm.

Lárissa and around

The third-largest city on the Greek mainland, and surrounded by a prosperous but dull landscape of wheat and corn fields, **LÁRISSA** is a major transport hub, as well as both marketplace and major garrison: army camps ring it, the airport remains monopolized by the Greek Air Force, and the southwestern part of the city is dominated by ranks of military housing. There's no real reason to stay here, unless your transport schedule requires it; if so, you'll find a city centre with an ancient theatre and the remains of an acropolis with archeological layers dating eight thousand years back to Neolithic times. In the modern centre, life focuses around three main squares and a park, all connected with part-pedestrianized roads, and usually teeming with students.

Travelling **north** from Lárissa, the motorway heads towards Thessaloníki via the renowned **Vale of Témbi**, between mounts Olympus and Óssa, before emerging on the coast. **West from Lárissa**, the road follows the River Piniós to **Tríkala**, a provincial capital with a fairly attractive centre and important Byzantine monuments nearby.

ARRIVAL AND DEPARTURE

LÁRISSA

By train The train station (☎ 24105 90143) lies south of the city centre, at Platia OSE. Long one of the ugliest stations in Greece, it's currently undergoing renovations.
Destinations Athens (6 daily; 4hr); Kalambáka (1 daily direct, 5 daily via Palaeofarsalos; 1hr 25min); Lianokládhi, for Lamía (6 daily; 1hr 40min); Thessaloníki (16 daily; 1hr 20min–2hr 40min); Tríkala (1 daily direct, 5 daily via Palaeofarsalos; 1hr 10min); Vólos (12 daily; 50min).

By bus The main KTEL station (☎ 24105 67600) is on Olýmbou, 100m north of Georgiadou, but all buses towards Tríkala leave from a station on Iróon Polytekhníou, south-west of the centre (☎ 24106 10124).
Destinations Athens (8 daily; 3hr 35min–4hr 15min); Kalambáka (3 daily; 1hr 20min); Thessaloníki (9 daily; 2hr); Tríkala (every 1–2hr; 1hr); Vólos (10–12 daily; 1hr).

ACTIVITIES

Rafting Olympos Trek (☎ 24109 21244, ⓦ olympostrek .gr) is a Lárissa-based operator offering rafting trips along the Vale of Témbi gorge with Grade IV rapids at Vernézi (€50 for 2hr 30min, or €35 for part of the route).

ACCOMMODATION AND EATING

The city's student population is well catered for with a string of lively, semi-swanky restaurants, bars and cafés, some of which have rather curious names – there's even a Café Bollocks.
Diethnes Platia OSE ☎ 24102 34210. Filled with businessfolk, Larissa's hotels can be expensive. This is one of the rare cheapies, conveniently located just north of the train station; rooms are plain and the beds a little hard, but it's not a bad place to stay. **€35**
Divani Palace Papanastassiou 19 ☎ 24102 52791, ⓦ divanilarissahotel.com. The smartest place in town, and just steps from the ancient theatre. It's not really

five-star, as claimed, but the service is good and there's an indoor pool and gym. Good walk-up rates are often available. **€100**
★**Klimax** Corner of Ifaistou and Venizelou ☎ 241052 51108, ⓦ klimax4.gr. Opposite the theatre, this beautiful, modern venue serves up some interesting options – try the Hiot specialities such as mastic spring water or grilled mastello cheese (€5.80), Italian with bruschetta or pasta (around €8 for the latter), or a chocolate soufflé for dessert. They also have a good range of bottled Greek beers (including Septem, Donkey and Chios), and Japanese whisky. Mon–Sat 8am–1am, Sun 9am–midnight.

The Vale of Témbi

The **Vale of Témbi**, for millennia inspiration to poets, is a gorge-like valley cut over the eons by the Piniós River, which runs for nearly 10km between steep cliffs of the Olympus (Ólymbos) and Óssa ranges. In antiquity it was sacred to Apollo and constituted one of the few practicable approaches into central Greece – being the route taken by both Xerxes and Alexander the Great.

At the beginning of the vale, on the northern side, a notable landmark is the **Hasa Baba Tekkés**, the domed remnant of a Turkish Dervish monastery (not open to visitors). Halfway through the vale (on the southeast flank) is another ruin, the **Kástro tís Oréas** ("of the Beautiful Maiden"), one of four local Frankish guardposts, while marking the northern end – and the border with Macedonia – is the Platamónas Crusader-built **fortress** (summer daily 8am–7pm; winter Tues–Fri 8.30am–5pm, Sat & Sun 8.30am–3pm; €2, buy tickets at top of hill).

Tríkala

TRÍKALA, home to a population of around fifty thousand, has a fairly charming centre and is reasonably easy to manoeuvre; like so many Greek municipalities, however, it's generally shabby and seems to be dusty even when it's raining. The town is evenly divided by the Lethéos River, a tributary of the Piniós – clean enough to harbour trout – and backed by the Kóziakas mountain range rising abruptly to the west. For most travellers, it's merely a staging post en route to the Metéora, with the rail line connecting Lárissa and Tríkala continuing to Kalambáka. Frequent buses also call from Lárissa, with additional services heading west over the mountains.

Tríkala was the capital of a nineteenth-century Ottoman province, and in the **Varoúsi** district – below the fortress clocktower at the north end of town – there are lanes with restored houses of variable quality from that era. The town's inner **fortress**, a Turkish and Byzantine adaptation of a fourth-century BC citadel, hosts attractive gardens and a terrace café. The liveliest part of town, encompassing what remains of the **old bazaar**, centres on the streets around the central, riverside **Platía Iróön Polytekhníou** with its statue of local hero Stefanos Sarafis, commander of ELAS from 1943 to 1945. Rembétika great Vassilis Tsitsanis (see p.800) also hailed from here, and he, too, is honoured by the street bearing his name, which heads east from the platía.

ARRIVAL AND DEPARTURE

TRÍKALA

By train The picturesque nineteenth-century station (☏ 24310 27214) is on Asklipiou, at the southern edge of town.
Destinations Athens (3 daily; 4hr 30min–7hr); Kalambáka (6 daily; 15min); Lárissa (1 daily direct, 5 daily via Palaeofarsalos; 1hr 5min); Thessaloníki (1 daily; 2hr 50min).
By bus Long-distance buses stop near the ring road, around 3.5km southeast of town and just off route 30. Destinations Athens (7 daily; 4hr 30min); Eláti (Mon–Fri

2 daily, Sat & Sun 1 daily; 1hr); Ioánnina (2 daily; 2hr 30min); Kalambáka (hourly 5am–10pm; 30min); Lárissa (roughly hourly; 1hr); Métsovo (2 daily; 2hr); Pýli (hourly; 20min); Thessaloníki (5 daily; 3hr); Vólos (2 daily; 2hr 30min).
By car Drivers should be mindful of the prevailing pay-and-display parking scheme, easily avoided by parking slightly out of the centre – or following signs to attended fee car parks.

ACCOMMODATION AND EATING

Ananti City Resort Loggaki, around 3km north of town ☏ 24310 63950, ⓦ anantiresort.gr. Sleek, minimal and with commanding hilltop views, this is by far the most luxurious place to stay around here. Rooms are all exposed concrete and comfy furnishings, with beds made from natural coconut fibres. There are two pools, a small gym and an excellent restaurant (mains around €16), where you can sip cocktails on the panoramic terrace. **€130**

Palia Istoria Ypsilanti 3 ☏ 24310 77627. A popular taverna (the name means the "Old Story") a couple of blocks north of the main square, with good prices (€10–12) for dishes such as sardines, grilled mushrooms, ostrich

steak, *imám baildí* and hot peppers. Wed–Mon noon–midnight.

Panellinion Platía Ríga Feréou ☏ 24310 73545, ⓦ hotelpanellinion.com. This Neoclassical beauty is Tríkala's most distinctive and historic mid-range hotel, away from traffic noise and gracing a mostly pedestrian area. It dates from 1914; during World War II it served as the Italian and German HQ. En-suite rooms are parquet-floored and a/c, some with balconies and small tubs; there's a mezzanine bar and a decent ground-floor restaurant, where breakfast (included) is served. **€55**

Pýli

Those interested in Byzantine architecture should visit **PÝLI**, 19km southwest of Tríkala, for the **thirteenth-century church** of Pórta Panayía, one of the unsung beauties of the region, in a superb setting at the mouth of a narrow gorge. A kilometre upstream from Pórta Panayía, easiest reached along the Pýli bank of the river, a graceful **medieval bridge**, built in 1514 by St Vissarionos, spans the Portaïkós at the point where it exits the gorge.

Pórta Panayía

Daily: summer 8am–noon & 4–8pm; winter 8am–noon & 3–5pm • Free • A 10min walk from Pýli village: bear left after crossing the river footbridge

Much of the current church of **Pórta Panayía** was completed in 1283 by Prince Ioannis Doukas of the Despotate of Epirus, atop an ancient Athena temple (its masonry liberally recycled into the walls); the domed narthex, Serbian-built, was added a century later. In the three-aisled Doukas section, perpendicular barrel vaults over a narrow transept and more generous nave lend antiseismic properties, with further support from six columns.

The highlights of the interior are two **mosaic icons** depicting the adult Christ plus the Virgin holding the Child right-handedly, contrary to the usual iconography. Slightly later **frescoes** have fared less well, either blackened by fires or long covered by plaster. The most interesting is the *Metastási* (Assumption) of the Virgin on the west wall, reflecting the church's August 23 festival and a late medieval Holy Trinity over the apse, showing Renaissance influence.

ARRIVAL AND ACCOMMODATION   PÝLI

By bus Pýli is served by hourly buses from Tríkala (20min).

Pyli ☎ 24340 23191. Very close to the church and surrounded by greenery, this is a cosy little guesthouse, especially in winter, when the fireplace crackles away in the lounge; in warmer months, they spread chairs around the terrace and surrounding lawns. The rooms are pretty, if a little overpriced. **€55**

The Metéora

The **monasteries of the METÉORA** are indisputably one of the great sights of Greece. These extraordinary buildings, perched on seemingly inaccessible rock pinnacles, occupy a valley just north of **Kalambáka**; *metéora* means "suspended in mid-air", while *kalabak* is an Ottoman Turkish word meaning cliff or pinnacle. Arriving at the town, you glimpse the closest of the monasteries, Ayíou Stefánou, firmly ensconced on a massive pedestal; beyond stretches a forest of greyish pinnacles and stubbier, rounded cliffs. These are remnants of river sediment which flowed into a prehistoric sea that covered the plain of Thessaly around 25 million years ago, subsequently moulded into bizarre shapes by the combined action of fissuring from tectonic-plate pressures, and erosion by the infant River Piniós.

Seeing the six inhabited monasteries of the Metéora requires at least a full day, which means staying at least one night, in either Kalambáka or **Kastráki**. Perhaps the ideal time to visit is out of season, when the leaves turn or snow blankets the pinnacles. During midsummer, the commercialization, traffic and crowds detract from the wild, spiritual aspect of the valley. In this period you're better off heading for less-visited monasteries such as Ayíou Nikoláou or Ayías Triádhos.

Brief history

Legend credits **St Athanasios**, founder of the earliest hermitage here (late 900s), with flying up the rocks on the back of an eagle. More prosaically, local villagers may have helped the original hermits up – with ropes and pulleys. Centuries later, in 1336 they were joined by two Athonite monks: **Gregorios** and his disciple **Athanasios**. Gregorios soon returned to Áthos, having ordered Athanasios to found a monastery. This Athanasios did around 1344, establishing Megálou Meteórou. Despite imposing a particularly austere rule he was quickly joined by other brothers, including (in 1381) **John Urod**, who renounced the throne of Serbia to become the monk Ioasaph.

Royal patronage was instrumental in endowing monasteries and hermitages, which multiplied on all the (relatively) accessible rocks to 24 institutions during the reign of Ottoman sultan Süleyman the Magnificent (1520–66). Money was provided

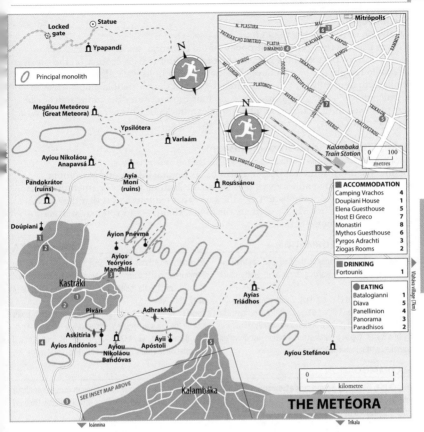

THE METÉORA

ACCOMMODATION

Camping Vrachos	4
Doupiani House	1
Elena Guesthouse	5
Host El Greco	7
Monastiri	8
Mythos Guesthouse	6
Pyrgos Adrachti	3
Ziogas Rooms	2

DRINKING

Fortounis	1

EATING

Batalogianni	1
Diava	5
Panellinion	4
Panorama	3
Paradhisos	2

by estates in distant Wallachia and Moldavia, as well as in Thessaly itself. It was largely the loss of land and revenues (particularly after the Greco-Turkish war) that brought about the **ruin of the monasteries** – although some were simply not built to withstand the centuries and gradually disintegrated in the harsh climatic conditions here.

By the late 1950s, there were just four active monasteries, struggling along with barely a dozen monks between them – an era chronicled in Patrick Leigh Fermor's *Roumeli*. Ironically, before being overtaken by **tourism** in the 1970s, the monasteries had begun to revive, attracting younger and more educated brothers; today about sixty monks and fifteen nuns dwell in the six extant foundations.

Kalambáka

KALAMBÁKA has pleasantly functional appeal, and its position right below the **Metéora** rocks guarantees regular awe-inspiring views – perhaps even from your hotel room. Though largely destroyed during World War II, a few prewar buildings remain in the upper reaches, closer to the rocks, from which point there are obvious footpaths heading up to the Metéora. Down on the main road, **Trikalon**, the majority of the town's places to eat and drink are centred on and between three main squares.

The Mitrópolis

Just off Lefkosias, at the northern edge of town, • Daily 8am–1pm & 4–6pm • €2

Kalambáka's eleventh-century **Mitrópolis**, or old cathedral, stands at the end of a bucolic road to the top of town. It was first erected in the sixth century on the site of an Apollo temple and incorporates Classical masonry in its walls. The interior is dominated, unusually for a Greek church, by a great double marble pulpit – like an Islamic *mimber* or oratory. Thirteenth- and fourteenth-century Byzantine frescoes are best preserved in the narthex, emphasizing the miracles of Christ (*Healing the Paralytic*, *The Storm on Galilee*, *Raising Lazarus*, *The Wedding at Cana*).

Natural History and Mushroom Museum

Pindou 20, just east of train station • Daily 10am–7pm • €5 • ☎ 24320 24959, ⓦ meteoramuseum.gr

Despite the unusual subject matter, Kalambáka's **Natural History and Mushroom Museum** is great fun and very well presented. The "natural history" element includes some three hundred stuffed animals – the somewhat tenuous link is that they all share habitats with mushrooms. Upstairs are the fungi exhibits – and you may well get to taste a few mushrooms at the end.

ARRIVAL AND INFORMATION

KALAMBÁKA

By train The train station is on the ring road, south of the centre and within easy walking distance of pretty much anywhere in town.

Destinations Athens (1 direct daily, 2 with connections; 4hr 40min–7hr); Laríssa (1 direct daily, 2 with connections; 1hr 20min); Thessaloníki (1 daily; 3hr); Tríkala (5 daily; 15min).

By bus Buses stop at a nondescript junction just downhill from the central Platía Dhimarhíou, on Ródhon.

Destinations Athens (7 daily; 5hr): Ioánnina (2 daily; 2hr 30min); Kastráki (hourly, 6am–10pm; 10min); Thessaloníki (5 daily; 4hr); Tríkala (hourly, 6am–10pm; 30min); Vólos (4 daily; 2hr 30min).

Tourist information A community information point just off the main square on Vlachava (Mon–Fri 8am–8pm, Sat 8am–2pm; ☎ 24323 50270) hands out limited information in English, including bus times and maps.

ACCOMMODATION

Arrivals may be met by **accommodation touts**; you are advised to ignore them, following numerous complaints about substandard rooms and price-fiddling. It's also best to avoid **hotels** on the main street, which are usually filled with coach tours and plagued by traffic noise despite double glazing.

Elena Guesthouse Kanari 3 ☎ 24320 77789. In a quiet part of town, very close to the start of the main hiking route up to the monasteries, this is a peaceful choice. The rooms are traditional in style yet rather plush, and all come with balconies. €55

Host El Greco Sidirodromo 5 ☎ 69738 17188, ⓦ hostelgreco.gr. The pick of the town's smattering of hostels – and not just for the clever name. The rooms here are all en suite (even the dorms), and if you're travelling as a pair, you'll barely pay any more for a twin; in addition, staff are adept at organizing things like vehicle rental, and they occasionally throw fun barbecues. Breakfast, towels and linen included. Dorm €14, twin €30

★**Monastiri** Nea Dimotiki Odos ☎ 24320 23952, ⓦ monastiri-guesthouse.gr. Located on the lower side of the train station, with views of the pinnacles, everything in this handsome stone mansion is done with perfect taste and sumptuous style. The hosts are welcoming, and extremely knowledgeable about hiking trails throughout the Metéora. Wonderful homemade breakfast (included) in the sunny parlour, with views. €62

Mythos Guesthouse Vlachava 20 (Platanos Square) ☎ 24320 23952, ⓦ mythos-guesthouse.com. Situated near the upper, old part of the town, the very cosy rooms in this fresh property have balconies with Metéora views. Facilities include en-suite bathrooms, free wi-fi, flat-screen TV, a/c and free parking, and there's an atmospheric taverna on the ground floor serving fresh traditional dishes using only local produce. Breakfast included. €50

EATING AND DRINKING

Diava Trikalon 98 ☎ 24320 24686. You most likely won't see the name of this grilled meat stop – look for a sign saying "Souvlaki Gyros" opposite the petrol station. Pleasingly simple, it's the best of the several fast-food spots on the main drag; you'll pay just €2 for a souvlaki wrap. Daily 5pm–midnight.

★**Fortounis** Vlachava 21 ☎24320 22555. Locals tend to eschew the touristy drinking holes on the strip, but this little spot near Mythos Guesthouse (see opposite) is packed with them every night. Prices are great – a half-litre of wine will set you back €3, and a glass of ouzo (including a tasty side-dish) just €2. Daily 9am–midnight.

Panellinion Platia Dimarhio ☎24320 24735. The pick of the "tourist restaurants" on the main drag, standing out for its cheery rustic-kitsch decor and average prices (mains €8–15). High-quality ingredients, home cooking and good brown bread, plus superb fresh-cut chips. Be sure to ask about the dishes of the day, which may include lamb with

oregano, lemon chicken, vegetable stews or casseroles, or another of the chef's family recipes – always based on whatever's in season. Seating inside and out. Daily noon–midnight.

Panorama Patriarcho Dimitrio 54 ☎24320 78128. Yes, this restaurant is a popular tour-bus stop, but so what – up on the rise west of town, the views are up there with the best in Greece. Given its clientele, the place remains friendly and good value, and if you play your cards right and avoid the mealtime rushes, you can enjoy your food in relative peace – try veal in a jug, with aubergine, potato and four kinds of cheese (€10). Daily 11.30am–midnight.

Kastráki

KASTRÁKI is a smaller, sloping village located on the way up to the pinnacles, twenty minutes' walk out of Kalambáka, along a busy and narrow road; in season there's a regular bus throughout the day. Almost rural in feel, it's far more low-key than Kalambáka, and arguably a better springboard for hiking among (or even climbing) the fifty-odd pinnacles which encircle the traditional houses here.

3

ACCOMMODATION   KASTRÁKI

As at Kalambáka it's worth avoiding the main road, where coaches rumble through much of the day (and scooters buzz along by night).

Camping Vrachos ☎24320 22293. Entering the downhill end of the village, you pass this well-equipped facility, with a pool, minimarket, restaurant and fairly reliable facilities (hot water for showers can run out). €17

Doupiani House ☎24320 77555, ⓦdoupianihouse .com. Well signposted left of the road, with superb views from the front-facing rooms; proprietors Thanassis and Toula serve breakfast (included) in Kastráki's finest hotel garden, and can point walkers to the start of various hikes. €73

Pyrgos Adrachti ☎24320 22275, ⓦhotel-adrachti.gr.

Built in 2007, this cosy, family-run property sits at the top of the old quarter – a steep drive up but there's ample parking on arrival. Their comfortable wood and stone rooms with a/c have some of the best views in the area. Free wi-fi and parking. Breakfast included. €60

Ziogas Rooms ☎24320 24037, ⓦziogasrooms.com. Located downhill and well back from the road, this place offers very simple balconied, marble-floored rooms with a/c and wi-fi, most with superb views, above a huge restaurant where guests have breakfast (extra). A little dated but okay for the money. Free parking. €40

EATING

Batalogianni ☎24320 23253. Largely ignored by the tourists, this little taverna, tucked into an alley near the main square, is worth tracking down for the mammoth

views from the tables in its back yard – try the *dolmádhes*, served in an odd lemon foam (€5). Daily noon–midnight.

HEALING HEADSCARVES

Visitors to Kastráki are often puzzled by the sight of brightly coloured **rags** hanging in a cave high above the village. This is the shrine of **Áyios Yeóryios Mandhilás** (Saint George of the Kerchiefs), and the "rags" are votive cloths, offerings to the saint. Legend has it that in the seventeenth century, during the Turkish occupation of Greece, a local Muslim landowner cut down some trees in the saint's sacred grove. As punishment, Saint George paralysed the man's hand; and he was only cured after he offered the saint his wife's veil or *yashmak*, the most precious gift a Muslim can give. In memory of that donation, once a year on April 23, a couple of hundred daredevil youths from neighbouring villages clamber up to hang new pieces of cloth and retrieve the old ones, a guarantee of good luck and good health in the coming year.

★**Paradhisos** ☎ 24320 22723. On the through road, with nice views and an award-winning owner-chef. As well as excellent *kokorétsi* and *biftéki*, it serves moussaka, *ravaní* and a good choice of veggie options; everything is fresh and local, with prices around €10–15/person. Daily 11am–midnight.

The monasteries

The four most visited monasteries and convents – **Megálou Meteórou, Ayíou Nikoláou, Varlaám** and **Roussánou** – are essentially museum-monuments. Only **Ayías Triádhos** and **Ayíou Stefánou** still function with a primarily religious purpose, though there has been a notable increase in devout Romanian and Russian Orthodox pilgrims. Service elevators have been installed for deliveries and visiting dignitaries, though access for most visitors is by extensive **stairways** carved into the rock in the early twentieth century.

Each monastery consists essentially of monks' cells focused round a central space, with chapels and refectories added on as possible – up, down and sideways – given the physical limitations of constructing on a rock pinnacle. The central church of each monastery, the *katholikón*, is usually elaborately decorated with beautiful and often quirky sixteenth- and seventeenth-century frescoes.

3

GETTING AROUND · THE MONASTERIES

By car There are paved roads right up to the entrances of all the monasteries, up from Kalambáka and through Kastráki. Each has a parking area, sometimes complete with souvenir stands and *kantínas* selling drinks and packaged snacks.

By bus In season there are up to four buses daily (at 9am, 11am, 1pm and 5pm) from Kalambáka up the road as far as Megálou Meteórou/Varlaám; even being taken just part-way will provide the necessary head start to make a hiking day manageable, and to fit in perhaps half the monasteries. The last bus back is at 6pm.

On a tour Plenty of agencies in Kalambáka sell bus tours – itineraries vary, but the regular ones visit the major monasteries and cost around €25. There are also sunset and hiking tours available.

On foot The main road is often narrow and busy with speeding cars, so follow the hiking directions – by using trails and dirt tracks you avoid most of the asphalt. If you're hiking between the monasteries, be sure to get a map; you'll most likely receive one from your accommodation, though offline apps such as Maps.me also feature most trails.

INFORMATION

Opening times Out of 24 original monasteries, only six can still be visited, and all keep different visiting hours/days. It's currently only possible to see them all in one day at weekends, because on any given weekday at least one monastery is closed. We have provided a schedule for each site, but it is always subject to change, so confirm opening days and times with your hotel or the community information point in Kalambáka (see p.238).

Entry charge Each monastery levies an admission charge of €3; student discounts are generally not given.

Dress code and photography All monasteries enforce dress codes: in theory, both sexes must cover their shoulders; women must wear a long skirt, not trousers' and men long trousers, not shorts. In practice, however, women should be fine with trousers, and men with shorts which at least cover the knee; skirts or wraps are often lent to female visitors, but don't rely on this. Photography and filming are strictly forbidden inside all monasteries, though taking shots of the surrounding terrain is fine.

METÉORA ACTIVITIES

Beyond visits to the monasteries themselves, the dramatic setting makes for exciting outdoor **activities**, especially **hiking**. In all, there are nearly seven hundred different trails among and around the monoliths, though many of them are far from an easy stroll and some are crumbling outright. In any case, if you go off-road, a good **map** is essential (see above), and don't hesitate to ask the locals about current conditions.

No Limits Konitsa ☎ 26550 23777, ⊕ nolimits .com.gr. Long-established Greek operator focusing on mountain and river adventures in Metéora and areas of the Píndhos range, especially the Zagóri. Activities include trekking, rappelling, rafting and mountain biking.

Ayíou Nikoláou Anapafsá

Daily except Fri: April–Oct 9am–3.30pm; Nov–March 9am–2pm • ☎ 24320 22375 • 20min on foot or 5min by car from Kastráki

The diminutive **Ayíou Nikoláou Anapafsá** is the closest monastery to Kastráki. The road leads to the base of the stairway-path (150 steps). This tiny, multilevelled structure has superb frescoes from 1527 by the Cretan painter Theophanes in its *katholikón* (main chapel). On the east wall of the naos over the window, a shocked disciple somersaults backwards at the *Transfiguration*, an ingenious use of the cramped space; in the *Denial of Peter* on the left door-arch as you enter the naos, the protagonists warm their hands over a fire in the pre-dawn, while above the *ierón* window is the *Sacrifice of Abraham*. On the west wall of the narthex, a stylite (column-dwelling hermit) perches in a wilderness populated by wild beasts, while an acolyte prepares to hoist up a supply basket – as would have been done just outside when the fresco was new. Other Desert Fathers rush to attend the funeral of St Ephraim the Syrian: some riding beasts, others – crippled or infirm – on litters or riding piggyback on the strong.

Megálou Meteórou

Daily except Tues: April–Oct 9am–5pm; Nov–March 9am–4pm • ☎ 24320 22278

The **Megálou Meteórou** (aka Great Meteoron and Metamorphosis) is the highest monastery – requiring a climb of nearly three hundred steps from its entrance – built on the Platýs Líthos ("Broad Rock") 615m above sea level. It enjoyed extensive privileges and dominated the area for centuries: in an eighteenth-century engraving (sold as a reproduction) it dwarfs its neighbours.

The katholikón

The monastery's cross-in-square **katholikón**, dedicated to the Transfiguration, is Metéora's most imposing; columns and beams support a lofty dome with a *Pandokrátor*. It was enlarged in the 1500s and 1600s and the original chapel, constructed by the Serbian Ioasaph in 1383, is now the *ierón* behind the intricately carved *témblon*. Frescoes, however, are much later (mid-sixteenth century) than at most other monasteries and artistically undistinguished; those in the narthex concentrate almost exclusively on grisly martyrdoms.

The cellar, refectory and kitchen

Elsewhere in this vast, arcaded cluster of buildings, the *kellári* (cellar) hosts an exhibit of rural impedimenta; and in the domed, vaulted refectory, still set with the traditional silver/pewter table service for monastic meals, a **museum** features exquisite carved-wood crosses and rare icons. The ancient smoke-blackened kitchen adjacent preserves its bread oven and soup-hearth.

Varlaám (Barlaam)

April–Oct daily except Fri 9am–4pm; Nov–March daily except Thurs & Fri 9am–4pm • ☎ 24320 22277

Varlaám is among the oldest monasteries, replacing a hermitage established by St Varlaam shortly after Athanasios' arrival. The present building, now home to a handful of monks and one of the most beautiful in the valley, was constructed by the Apsaras brothers from Ioánnina in 1540–44. To get up to it from the entrance point means climbing about 150 steps.

The katholikón and around

The monastery's **katholikón**, dedicated to Ayíon Pándon (All Saints), is small but glorious; it's supported by painted beams, its walls and pillars totally covered by frescoes (painted 1544–66) that are dominated by the great *Pandokrátor* of the inner dome. Among the more unusual are a beardless Christ Emmanuel in the right transept conch, and the Parliament of Angels on the left; on one pier, the Souls of the Righteous nestle in the Bosom of Abraham, while the Good Thief is admitted to Paradise. On the inner sanctuary wall, there's a vivid Crucifixion and a Dormition of the Virgin with, lower down, an angel severing the hands of the Impious Jew attempting to overturn her funeral bier. The treasury-museum features crucifixes and silver items; elsewhere the monks' original water barrel is on show.

The ascent tower

Varlaám prominently displays its old **ascent tower**, comprising a reception platform, well-worn windlass and original rope-basket. Until the 1930s the only way of reaching most Metéoran monasteries was by being hauled up in said rope-basket, or by equally perilous retractable ladders. A nineteenth-century abbot, asked how often the rope was changed, replied, "Only when it breaks." Steel cables eventually replaced ropes, and then steps were cut to all monasteries by order of the Bishop of Tríkala, unnerved by the vulnerability of his authority on visits. Today rope-baskets figure only as museum exhibits, having been supplanted by metal cage-buckets, as well as a hidden elevator or two.

Roussánou

Daily except Wed: April–Oct 9am–6pm; Nov–March 9am–2pm • ☎ 24320 22649

The convent of **Roussánou**, founded in 1545, has an extraordinary, much-photographed situation, its walls edging to sheer drops all around. After some 150 steps up, the final approach to the convent (today housing about a dozen nuns) is across a vertiginous bridge from an adjacent rock.

Inside, the narthex of its main chapel has particularly gruesome frescoes (1560) of martyrdom and judgement, the only respite from sundry beheadings, spearings, crushings, roastings and mutilations being the lions licking Daniel's feet in his imprisonment (left of the window); diagonally across the room, two not-so-friendly lions proceed to devour Saint Ignatios Theoforos. On the right of the transept there's a vivid *Transfiguration* and *Entry to Jerusalem*, while to the left are events after Christ's Resurrection. On the east of the wall dividing naos from narthex is an exceptionally vivid Apocalypse.

Ayías Triádhos

April–Oct daily except Thurs 9am–5pm; Nov–March daily except Wed & Thurs 9am–4pm • ☎ 24320 22220

Few tour buses stop at **Ayías Triádhos** (Holy Trinity) – despite it famously featuring in the 1981 James Bond film, *For Your Eyes Only* – and life remains essentially monastic, even if there are only three brothers to maintain it. The **approach** from the parking area consists of some 150 steps down and then another roughly 150 back up the other side of the sheer ravine that separates its pinnacle from the road. You finally emerge into a cheerful compound with small displays of kitchen/farm implements, plus an old ascent windlass.

The monastery

The seventeenth-century frescoes in the **katholikón** have been completely cleaned and restored, fully justifying a visit. On the west wall, the *Dormition* is flanked by the *Judgement of Pilate* and the *Transaction of Judas*, complete with the thirty pieces of silver and subsequent self-hanging. Like others at the Metéora, this church was built in two phases, as evidenced by two domes, each with a *Pandokrátor* (the one above the *témblon* is very fine), and two complete sets of Evangelists on the squinches. In the arch right of the *témblon* is a rare portrait of a beardless Christ Emmanuel, borne aloft by four seraphs; on the arch supports to the left appear the *Hospitality of Abraham* and *Christ the Righteous Judge*.

The trail to Kalambáka

Although Ayías Triádhos teeters above its deep ravine and the little garden ends in a precipitous drop, an obvious, well-signposted **path** leads from the bottom of the monastery's access steps back to the upper quarter of **Kalambáka**. This 1km descent, a partly cobbled, all-weather surface, is in good shape, and it ends adjacent to Kalambáka's fine, very early cathedral (see p.238).

Ayíou Stefánou

Daily except Mon: April–Oct 9am–1.30pm & 3.30–5.30pm; Nov–March 9.30am–1pm & 3–5pm • ☎ 24320 22279

Ayíou Stefánou, the last, easternmost monastery, is 1.5km along the road beyond Ayías Triádhos (no path short cuts), and it's the only one that requires no staircase climb to get to. Note that it's also the only one that closes at lunchtime. It's occupied by nuns keen to sell trinkets and memorabilia, but the buildings – bombed during World War II and then raided during the civil war – are disappointing: it's the obvious one to miss if you're short of time. That said, the fifteenth-century **refectory** contains an apsidal fresco of the Virgin, beyond the **museum** which is graced by a fine *Epitáfios* (Good Friday bier) covering embroidered in gold thread. The trail towards Kalambáka from Ayíou Stefánou is disused and dangerous – return to Ayías Triádhos to use the descending path described above.

The Píndhos Mountains

Continuing west from Metéora, you soon encounter the rugged peaks, forested ravines and turbulent rivers of the **Píndhos Mountains**. Over the centuries, this range has insulated the communities and culture here from outside interference, securing a large measure of autonomy even under Ottoman rule. Yet today it's the mountains themselves that provide the strongest attraction. Their physical beauty is stunning, with limestone peaks, dramatic **gorges** and dense forest contrasting with stone-built **villages** and arched packhorse **bridges**.

Roughly halfway over the mountains stands **Métsovo**, the most convenient venue for alpine life Greek-style, plus a taste of the local **Vlach** culture. Down on the plain below is the fascinating lakeside city of **Ioánnina**, capital of **Epirus**, the last region of Greece to be liberated from the Turks. Farther to the north, back up in the Píndhos mountains, authentic stone hamlets and the stunning **Víkos Gorge** provide unforgettable scenery and hiking opportunities.

Métsovo

MÉTSOVO lies just west of the Katára pass, 1km off the Vía Egnatía. It's a small, touristy alpine town occupying two sides of a plunging ravine and guarded by the forbidding peaks of the Píndhos range to the south and east. It's pretty enough, with tiers of eighteenth- and nineteenth-century stone houses spilling downhill to and past the main platía, where a few old men still loiter after Sunday Mass in traditional dress (black caps and pompom-topped shoes).

TAKE THE HIGH ROAD: THE KATÁRA PASS

West of Kalambáka, the 1694m **Katára Pass** carries the only high-altitude paved road across the central Píndhos Mountains, linking the regions of Thessaly and Epirus, which lie on either side. One of the most spectacular drives in the country, this centuries-old route switchbacks through folds in the enormous peaks rising more than 2300m around **Métsovo**. From November to April the pass is snowploughed – although these days the old, twisty road is entirely optional. Sixty enormous tunnels linked by long viaducts have been bored through the ridges here as part of the **Vía Egnatía** expressway, which now smoothly flows all the way to the west coast; you can't yet get on the expressway in Kalambáka, but a link road is being built.

If you avoid the high seasons (midsummer and Christmas/Easter weeks), stay overnight and take in the surroundings, the place can seem magical. In season, Métsovo makes a favourite target for tour buses full of Greeks, who are catered for by shops selling kitsch wooden souvenirs and "traditional" weavings (mostly mass-produced these days). Even the roof tiles of many traditional houses have been replaced with garish modern versions.

Nonetheless, it would be a shame to omit Métsovo altogether, for its history and status as the **Vlach "capital"** (see box, below) make it unique. Positioned astride the most viable route over the Píndhos, it secured a measure of independence, both political and economic, in the earliest days of Ottoman rule. Métsovo's continued prosperity and preservation of some traditions is largely due to **Baron Mihaïl Tositsas** (1888–1950), a Swiss banker and offspring of a local family, who left his colossal fortune to an endowment that supports industries, crafts and restoration work in and around the town.

Áyios Nikólaos

A 15–30min walk south of town • Daily 8.30am–1.30pm & 4–7.30pm • Donation and/or purchase expected

The main attraction in Métsovo's surroundings is the stone monastery of **Áyios Nikólaos**, signposted from the main platía but in fact thirty minutes' walk down just south of town; it is reached just off the path toward Anílio, in a dramatic position on a steep ravine. The monastery's *katholikón*, topped by a simple barrel vault, was built in the fourteenth century to an unconventional plan; what might once have been the narthex eventually became a *yinaikonítis* or women's gallery. Inside are some brilliantly coloured **frescoes** dating from 1702, cleaned and illuminated courtesy of the Tosítsa Foundation. A guardian family lives on the premises and receives visitors. You'll also be shown the monks' former cells, with insulating walls of mud and straw, and the abbot's less austere quarters.

ARRIVAL AND DEPARTURE   MÉTSOVO

By bus Métsovo is best reached from Ioánnina (2 daily; 1hr), with buses stopping on the main platía. Ioánnina–Trikala services (which also stop at Kalambaka) pass by Metsovo, but drop off at a lonely, taxi-less spot, a tricky 40min walk from town.

By car The old Kalambáka–Ioánnina highway is now superseded by the Vía Egnatía, which runs to the coast, linking Métsovo with Ioánnina and Igoumenítsa.

ACTIVITIES

Hiking There's great hiking in the spectacular countryside around Métsovo on the new, well-marked Ursa Trails, starting in town: one trail runs to the Anilo Ski Centre (11km one way; 8–10hr return), and another to Politsiora near the Metsovo Ski Centre (7.7km loop, 2–3hr return); if the latter isn't long enough, you can add on a loop to the Vale di Liosani (an extra 10km; 3hr). The handy Metsovo Ursa Trail app is available with all routes, and there are full and half marathons along the trails each year, at the end of May.

THE VLACHS

Europe's last semi-nomadic people, the **Vlachs**, have lived in the Píndhos Mountains for centuries. Each summer, the melting of the winter snows finds the vast slopes here coming alive with the sound of bells, as the Vlachs bring their flocks up from the plains to graze in the mountains. Though the ethnicity of the Vlachs (from the ancient Germanic word for "foreigner" *Walh*) is a subject of much scholarly debate, most claim to be descendants of Roman soldiers stationed here in classical times, and they speak a Latin-derived, unwritten **language** similar to modern Romanian – or, at least, those born before the mid-1970s do, with the language largely alien to younger generations. Today, although the Greek government keeps no records of ethnicity, it is estimated that perhaps forty thousand Vlachs live in small communities scattered throughout the Píndhos range, where you can still see **shepherds** wearing the distinctive goat-skin cape and wielding their fanciful crook. In the remotest areas, traditional Vlach **pagan beliefs** are only thinly overlaid with the Orthodox faith; many elderly women still have a black cross tattooed on their foreheads, to ward off the evil eye, and their gossip is rife with folktales of sorcery and curses.

ACCOMMODATION

Métsovo has a wide range of **accommodation**, with some twenty hotels plus quite a few *dhomátia*, nearly all en suite. Outside Christmas/Easter weeks, the local festival (July 26) or Aug, you should have little trouble in getting a bed or even bargaining indicated prices down.

Aroma Dryos Towards the eastern end of town ☎ 26560 29008, ⓦ aromadryos.gr. From the main square, signposts point the way to this design-focused hotel, built out of stone and oak. Although each of the sixteen rooms is different, they're all named after trees and most are similarly luxurious, with a balcony, fireplace and hydro-massage shower. The glitzy interiors might be a bit much for some, however. **€90**

Bitouni At the top of the main street ☎ 26560 41217, ⓦ hotelbitouni.com. Most rooms at this atmospherically gloomy hotel are wood-panelled, and some have balconies with valley views; there are attic suites, too, that sleep four. Simple breakfast included. **€35**

Galaxia Just above the main square ☎ 26560 41202, ⓦ hotel-galaxias-metsovo.gr. This very traditional, slate-roofed hotel has lots of natural wood in its eight large, comfortable rooms, three of which have fireplaces. Rooms with a balcony overlooking the square cost €10 extra. **€45**

EATING

Most **restaurants** here are generally part of hotels and *dhomátia*, and menus often feature traditional mountain dishes. **Wine** buffs may want to try the fabled Katóyi, available at restaurants, local shops and indeed across Greece. It's a moderately expensive limited bottling from vineyards along the Árakhthos River, though quality of the main Averoff label varies (the Ktima line is best).

Arhontiko ☎ 26560 42511. There's a real mountain feel to this cosy taverna, with its pine ceilings and walls, and woven-fabric cushions. The food is suitably hearty, with plenty of beans, leeks and the like on the menu, as well as various tasty pies (€4). Daily 10am–10pm.

Metsovorama ☎ 26560 42500. Coffee is a little expensive at this café (even a Greek coffee is €2.50), but it's worth it for the superlative views out across the mountains. Simple snacks and alcohol also available. Daily 9am–1am.

To Katoï ☎ 26560 42040. Named after the noted Métsovo red wine, this popular taverna occupies several wood-panelled rooms on the main square and is good for grills (€8–9) and all the Greek standards. Daily 11am–11pm.

Ioánnina and around

The provincial capital of Epirus, **IOÁNNINA** (vaguely pronounced "Yann-inna") boasts an idyllic setting, its old town jutting out into the great **Lake Pamvótis** along a rocky promontory, its fortifications punctuated by spindly minarets. From this base, **Ali Pasha** "the Lion of Ioánnina" (see box, p.247) carved from the Turkish domains a personal fiefdom that encompassed much of western Greece and present-day Albania: an act of rebellion that prefigured wider defiance in the Greeks' own **War of Independence**.

Although much of the city is modern and undistinguished (albeit home to a thriving university), the **old town** remains one of the most interesting in Greece. Stone-built **mosques** and a **synagogue** evoke the Ottoman era, and Ali Pasha's citadel, the **kástro**, survives more or less intact, its **inner citadel** now a museum park. In the lake, **Nissí island** has a car-free village and frescoed **monasteries**. Ioánnina is also a springboard for visits to the **caves of Pérama**, among the country's largest, off the northern shore of the lake, and a slightly longer excursion to the very ancient Oracle of Zeus at **Dodona**. Finally, the city is also the gateway to what is possibly the area's most rewarding corner, **Zagóri** (see p.250).

The kástro

In its heyday the **kástro's** walls dropped abruptly to the lake, and were moated on their landward (southwest) side. The moat has been filled in, and a quay-esplanade now extends below the lakeside ramparts, but there is still the sense of a citadel, with narrow alleys and bazaar-like shops.

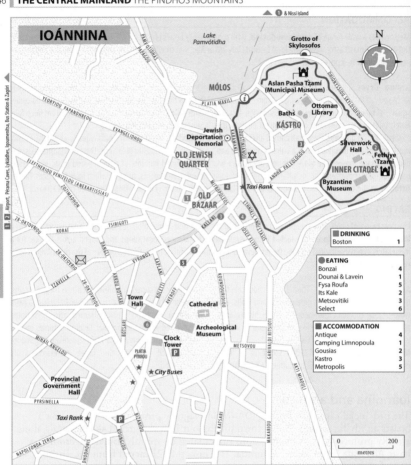

Municipal Museum

Daily 8.30am–4.30pm • €2 • ☎ 26510 26356

Signs inside point to the **Municipal Museum**, an elegantly arranged collection of Epirot costumes, guns, silverwork and Islamic art, housed in the well-preserved, floodlit **Aslan Pasha Tzamí**, thereby allowing a rare glimpse inside an intact Greek mosque. It dates from 1618 and was built on the site of an Orthodox cathedral that was pulled down in reprisal for a failed local revolt of 1611. The interior retains painted decoration in its dome and *mihrab* (niche indicating direction of Mecca), as well as a vividly coloured *mimber* or pulpit, nicely complementing a walnut and mother-of-pearl suite on display in the "Muslim section".

More poignant is a section devoted to synagogue rugs and tapestries donated by the dwindling Jewish community of about fifty.

The inner citadel (the Its Kale)

Its Kale Daily 7am–10pm • **Fethiye Tzamí** Tues–Sat 10.30am–3pm, Sun 10.30am–5pm • **Byzantine Museum** Mon noon–8pm, Tues–Sun 8am–8pm • **Silverwork Hall** Wed–Mon 10am–6pm • €3 ticket includes entrance to all the inner citadel sights; grounds free

Southeast of the Aslan Pasha Tzamí lies the **inner citadel**, signposted as **Its Kale**, a transliteration of its Turkish name – a kind of fortress within the fortress. The park-like grounds, with wonderful mountain views from this elevated spot, are occasionally used for concerts after-hours, and there's a large and pleasant terrace café-restaurant near the entrance, occupying the garrison's former mess.

Next to the old **Fethiye Tzamí** ("Victory Mosque") and its slim, rocket-like minaret – which occupy an upper corner – are two Ottoman graves, one of which, surmounted by an elegant wrought-iron cage, is probably that of Ali Pasha, while the other contains his first wife Emine and one son. The mosque itself, remodelled by Ali, was built atop the remains of a thirteenth-century cathedral.

Next to the mosque, on the site of Ali's vanished palace, where Byron was entertained, stands the arcaded so-called **Byzantine Museum**, a thin, largely post-Byzantine collection. The displays comprise masonry, coins, pottery, icons and colour prints of frescoes from various ages; the only actually Byzantine painting is a fresco fragment of *The Betrayal*.

A few paces down the hill, in the presumed treasury of Ali Pasha's seraglio, is the **Silverwork Hall**, containing important masterpieces of Ioánnina's centuries-old silver-working tradition.

The old bazaar and Jewish quarter

Apart from the kástro, the town's most enjoyable district is the **old bazaar and Jewish quarter**, a warren of narrow lanes and alleys between the citadel's main gate and Anexartissías avenue bounding it on the south. It retains a cluster of Ottoman-era buildings (including imposing mansions with ornate window grilles and founding inscriptions), as well as a scattering of copper- and tinsmiths, plus the silversmiths who were long a mainstay of the town's economy. Look out, too, for the gentrified *stoas*, off Anexartisías, which used to serve the old warehouses.

Nissí island

Waterbuses every 30min in summer, otherwise hourly (10min); last one back 10pm • €2 each way

The island of **Nissí** in **Lake Pamvótis** is connected by waterbuses from the Mólos quay on Platía Mavíli. Only islanders' cars are allowed, hauled across on a chain-barge to the

---

ALI PASHA – THE LION OF IOÁNNINA

As an "heroic rebel", the Muslim Albanian **Ali Pasha** assumes an ambivalent role – for his only consistent policy was that of ambition and self-interest. As frequent as his attacks on the Ottoman authorities were, he also engaged in acts of appalling savagery against his Greek subjects. Despite this, he is still held in some regard by locals for his perceived role as a **defier of Istanbul**, the common enemy – folk postcards of the man abound, and a platía in the citadel is named after him.

Ali was born in 1741 in Tepelene, now in modern Albania, and by 1787 had been made pasha of Tríkala as a reward for his efforts in the war against Austria. His ambitions, however, were larger, and the following year he **seized Ioánnina**, an important town since the thirteenth century, with a population of thirty thousand – probably the largest in Greece at the time. Paying perfunctory and sporadic tribute to the sultan, he operated from here for the next 33 years, allying himself in turn, as strategy required, with the Ottomans, the French or the British.

In 1809, when his dependence upon the sultan was nominal, Ali was visited by the young **Lord Byron**, whom he overwhelmed with hospitality and attention. Byron, impressed for his part with the rebel's daring and stature, and the lively revival of Greek culture in Ioánnina, commemorated the meeting in *Childe Harold*. This portrait that he draws, however, is ambiguous, since Byron well knew that behind Ali's splendid court and deceptively mild countenance were "deeds that lurk" and "stain him with disgrace".

Ali met a suitably grisly end. In 1821, the Ottoman sultan resolved to eliminate Ali's threat to his authority before tackling the Greek insurgency, and he sent an army of fifty thousand to capture him. Lured from the security of Ioánnina citadel with false promises of lenient surrender terms, he was ambushed, shot and decapitated, his head sent to Istanbul. The rest of Ali supposedly lies in the northeast corner of the inner citadel, in an artful tomb topped with a filigree-like frame.

mainland opposite. The pretty island village, founded during the sixteenth century by refugees from the Máni, is flanked by several **monasteries**, worthy targets for an afternoon's visit. By day the main lane leading up from the boat dock is crammed with stalls selling jewellery and kitsch souvenirs. Away from the busy restaurants, quiet descends with the sun setting vividly over the reed beds that fringe the island – though there is no accommodation on the island.

Lake Pamvótis itself is certainly idyllic-looking enough, and it's the region's largest lake, but run-off **pollution** is a serious, ongoing problem and most locals do not advise either swimming in its waters or eating its fish.

ARRIVAL AND DEPARTURE
IOÁNNINA

By air Ioánnina airport is on the road to Pérama, 5km northwest of the centre (frequent city buses link it with Platía Pýrrou in the city centre).

Destinations Athens (2 daily; 1hr).

By bus KTEL buses arrive and depart from the station on Yeoryiou Papandhreou (☎ 26510 26286), around 1km northwest of the centre.

Destinations Athens (5–6 daily; 7hr 30min); Igoumenítsa (5–6 daily; 2hr 30min); Kalambáka (2 daily; 2hr 30min); Lamía (1 daily; 4hr 30min); Métsovo (1–2 daily; 1hr); Monodhéndhri (Mon & Fri early

morning & early afternoon; 1hr); Pápingo (Tues early morning & early afternoon; 2hr); Párga (1 daily in summer; 3hr); Pátra (1 daily in summer; 3hr 30min); Préveza (6–8 daily; 2hr); Tríkala (2 daily; 2hr 30min); Thessaloníki (5–6 daily; 3hr); Vólos (3 daily; 4hr).

By car Most drivers arrive from the south via the Vía Egnatía expressway. The city's pay-and-display parking scheme only allows 2hr at a time – it's easiest to use the car parks shown on the map (p.246), or try for unregulated spaces in the kástro. Better still, choose a hotel with private parking.

GETTING AROUND AND ACTIVITIES

By bus Blue-and-white city buses leave from a cluster of stops below the central Platía Pýrrou, mostly on Bizaniou; buy tickets (€1.20) from adjacent booths beforehand, and validate them when boarding.

By car There are several car rental outlets on Dhodhónis: Avis (also at the airport) is at no. 71 (☎ 26510 46333), Budget at no. 109 (☎ 26510 43901) and Tomaso at no. 42

(☎ 26510 20000). Hertz is at the airport ☎ 26510 27400.

By taxi Local taxis are dark green; central ranks are marked on the map (p.246).

Activities Alpine Zone, based at Smyrnis 1 (☎ 26510 23222, ⊕ alpinezone.gr), offers rafting, canyoning, trekking and a full range of other activities in the Píndhos. A 4hr rafting trip along grade 2 rapids costs €25/person.

ACCOMMODATION

Ioánnina has some appealing restored mansions to stay in, though accommodation can be pricey here. There are cheaper options in the **Pérama** area, 5km away on the north shore of the lake, near some great caves (see opposite), and accessible by city bus (€1.20) or taxi (€5).

Antique Neoptolemou 8 ☎ 26510 39999, ⊕ hotelantique.gr. Set in a charming building, this is a real treat, with elaborately-designed rooms, including some duplexes. Management are friendly and knowledgeable, and a whopping buffet breakfast (included) is served in the stylish dining area – the enclosed courtyard is also a great place for coffee or wine. **€60**

Gousias Parados Katsimitrou, Pérama ☎ 26510 81943, ⊕ hotelgousias.gr. Surprisingly swanky rooms in Pérama, located (this could be a good or bad thing) out by the fields, a 10min walk north of the urban area. **€45**

★**Kastro** Andhroníkou Paleológou 57 ☎ 26510 22866, ⊕ hotelkastro.gr. Located at the base of the ramp up to the Its Kale, this classy, restored inn has seven rooms decorated in plush fabrics and soft tones. Two sleep three;

the rest sleep two, and all have a/c. Adequate street parking. **€65**

★**Metropolis** Avéroff 33 ☎ 26510 30004, ⊕ metropolishotel.gr. A grand 1930s building transformed into a state-of-the-art, design-oriented hotel, with young, English-speaking managers. Each of the rooms is unique, but all have gorgeously plump beds and cool, clutter-free interiors. Breakfast (included) is served in the ground-floor bistro. **€120**

CAMPING

Camping Limnopoula Kanari 10 ☎ 26510 25265. Unusual in being in town, this attractive lakeside option is well equipped and mosquito-free, though a bit cramped and more geared towards campervans than tents. To get here, walk 1500m west of Platía Mavíli. **€23**

SWEET TREATS IN IOÁNNINA

Ioánnina is the home of **bougátsa** (custard tart, served with a salty *kouloúra* or round biscuit), traditionally served fresh at breakfast time with sweet or savoury fillings. While you can find it all over Greece (especially the mainland), it's still best eaten in its home town – many local hotels serve *bougátsa* at breakfast, or try it at tiny *Select* (see below).

EATING

Ioánnina has numerous **restaurants**, including some non-Greek options – maybe welcome if you've been in the sticks for a while. Even locals admit that few of the town's restaurants are truly special, though the café selection is very decent.

CAFÉS

Dounai & Lavein Nissí island, a block inland from boat launch ☎ 69366 22948. If you're over on Nissí island, head for this super-chilled spot, good for coffee or a suck on a shisha (€5) as swallows play overhead. Daily 9.30am–midnight.

Its Kale Its Kale, on the approach to the Byzantine Museum ☎ 26510 64206. Nothing to do with the superfood, this castle café is a bustling, atmospheric spot with fine views, and ideal for a drink or light meal. Daily 9.30am–midnight.

Select Platía Dhimokratías 2. The best place in town for bougátsa (see box, above) is a comically retro affair – the unstylish decor of terrazzo floor and marble tables has remained essentially unchanged since the 1970s. A slab of the town's speciality will set you back €2.60. Daily 8am–10pm.

RESTAURANTS

Bonzai Giosef Eligia 11 ☎ 26510 48140. Asian restaurants aren't that common in the Greek hinterlands, especially ones as good as this. The food is reasonably authentic, including sushi rolls (from €5.20), Szechuan chicken (€7.80) and Peking duck (€11.80); consider dining up on the roof, under the stars. Open 1.30pm–12.30am.

Fysa Roufa Avéroff 55 ☎ 26510 70705. Head here for traditional *mayireftá* such as *patsás*, *mayirítsa*, baked fish, suckling pig and *spetzofáï* (€4–7 each). It's fresher-looking than most such venues, its decor including photos of Párga (the proprietor's birthplace), and Greek theatre actors. Open 24hr.

★**Metsovitiki Folia** Corner of Avéroff and Kallari ☎ 26510 22033. There are only a few items on the menu at this grill restaurant, but they're all cooked superbly – try some of the juiciest souvláki you'll ever eat (€6.50), and wash it down with some cheap local retsina (€3.50). Daily 1–11.30pm.

DRINKING AND ENTERTAINMENT

You'll find the busiest **nightlife** around Kallari, which is lined with boisterous bars with little to distinguish them in terms of drinks or music. However, the real late-night drinking happens in various alleys in the old metalworking district just to the west. There are **cinemas** around Platía Pýrrou, which usually host first-run films (nearly all in English, with subtitles), as does the Odeon five-screen at the Paralimnio Centre, out in Votanikós district. Various formal **music/theatre events** occur in midsummer; look out for posters around town or ask at your hotel.

Boston In an alley off Zappa ☎ 26513 07980. One of the funkiest places to drink in the centre, with a good line in designer cocktails (from €8.50). The music is usually chilled, with seats sprawling across the alley. Daily 8pm–4am.

The Pérama caves

5km north of Ioánnina • Daily 9am–5pm • €7 • ☎ 26510 81521 • City bus #16 to Pérama village; the caves are a 400m walk from here

The village of **Pérama** claims to have Greece's largest system of **caves**, extending for kilometres beneath a low hill. They were discovered during late 1940 by locals attempting to find shelter from Italian bombing raids. The one-hour mandatory **tours** of the complex are primarily in Greek (commentary repeated in passable English) and make some effort to educate, though there are the inevitable bawdy nicknames for various suggestively shaped formations.

Dodona: the Oracle of Zeus

22km southwest of Ioánnina • Daily 8am–3pm, may close at 6pm in midsummer • €2 • Take the Vía Egnatía west and follow the exit for "Dodhóni"; a round-trip by taxi from Ioánnina should cost about €55, including waiting time

Set in a broad, mountain-ringed valley, **Dodona** comprises the ruins and large **theatre** of the ancient **Oracle of Zeus**, Greece's first oracle – some of the site dates back as far as four millennia.

THE OAK TREE ORACLE

"Wintry Dodona" was mentioned by Homer, and religious activities here appear to have begun with the first Hellenic tribes who arrived in Epirus around 1900 BC. Herodotus records that the oracle was founded after the mythic arrival of a *peleiae* (either "dove" or "old woman" in ancient Greek) from Egypt, said to have alighted on an oak tree. In any case, the **oak tree** was certainly central to the cult with the oracle speaking through the rustling of its leaves, amplified by copper vessels suspended from its branches. These sounds would then be interpreted by frenzied priestesses and/or priests, who allegedly slept on the ground and never washed their feet.

Many **oracular inscriptions** were found when the site was first systematically dug in 1952, demonstrating not only the oracle's lingering influence even after its eclipse by Delphi, but also the fears and inadequacies motivating pilgrims of the era in such questions as: "Am I her children's father?" and "Has Peistos stolen the wool from the mattress?"

The impressive theatre was built during the reign of King Pyrrhus (297–272 BC), and was one of the largest in Greece, rivalled only by those at Argos and Megalopolis. The Romans added a protective wall and a drainage channel around the orchestra as adaptations for their blood sports. What's now visible is a meticulous late nineteenth-century **reconstruction**. Almost all except the stage area is off limits, though it's worth following a path around to the top of the *cavea* (seating curve) to fully savour the glorious setting, looking across a green, silent valley to Mount Tómaros. A grand entrance gate leads into the overgrown **acropolis**, with Hellenistic foundations up to 5m wide.

Beside the theatre, tiered against the same slope, are the foundations of a *bouleuterion*, beyond which lie the complex ruins of the **Sanctuary of Zeus**, site of the oracle itself. There was no temple per se until late in the fifth century BC; until then, worship had centred upon the **sacred oak**, inside a circle of votive tripods and cauldrons. The remains you can see today are adorned with a modern oak tree planted by a helpfully reverent archeologist. Nearby is a useful placard detailing the entire site.

Dodona occasionally hosts **musical and ancient drama performances** on summer weekends, though since 2000 these are staged on modern wooden bleachers rather than in the ancient theatre.

Zagóri and the Víkos Gorge

Few parts of Greece are more surprising or more beguiling than the part of the Píndhos Mountains known as **ZAGÓRI**. A wild, thinly populated region, it lies just to the north of Ioánnina. The beauty of its landscape is unquestionable: dense forest and rugged mountains are furrowed by foaming rivers and dotted with **traditional villages** (the Zagorohória), many sporting grand stone houses or *arhondiká*, dating from the late eighteenth century. Here, also, you can seek out evocative ancient **monasteries** set in improbably remote spots. **Wildlife** is impressive too: there's good bird-watching, increasing numbers of wolves, plus legally protected brown bears.

The best way to enjoy the countryside is by **hiking** the numerous paths connecting the villages. The most accessible and rewarding target is the magnificent UNESCO-protected **Víkos Gorge** (see box, p.252), while **mounts Gamíla** and **Smólikas** provide several days of serious trekking. Even if you don't plan on hiking, the area deserves some time. Its remoteness, traditional architecture and scenery all constitute a very different Greece to the popular tourist stereotype and, despite growing popularity, the area remains relatively unspoilt.

Monodhéndhri

Near the south end of the gorge, at 1150m elevation, stands handsome **MONODHÉNDHRI**, the main accommodation base in the area. The village survived

World War II more or less intact – though it's now slightly spoilt by tourist shops and parked coaches. Just off the flagstoned platía, with its giant tree, is the seventeenth-century church of **Áyios Minás**, which is usually kept locked.

Ayía Paraskeví

A wide, artlessly modern *kalderími* heads from the far end of the platía for 900m to the eagle's-nest monastery of **Ayía Paraskeví** (built 1412), teetering on the brink of the gorge (there's a small viewing platform just behind) and home to a small gift shop selling religious icons and bracelets to devotees. Those with a head for heights can continue around the adjacent cliff face along an exceedingly narrow and dangerous path to a stair-trail climbing to **Megáli Spiliá**, a secluded cave where villagers once barricaded themselves in times of danger. Although the views over the gorge from a natural balcony en route are spectacular, with all of Víkos spread vertiginously at your feet, be warned: at least one person has fallen to their death from this path.

The Pápingo villages

MEGÁLO PÁPINGO is the larger of the two paired **Pápingo villages**, comprising two distinct quarters of 25 or so houses each along a tributary of the Voïdhomátis. It has served as the location for Jonathan Nossiter's 2000 film *Signs and Wonders*, starring Charlotte Rampling, plus countless Greek advertising shoots. Even before this, Megálo was a haunt of wealthy, trendy Greeks, making it unrecommended in peak season,

3

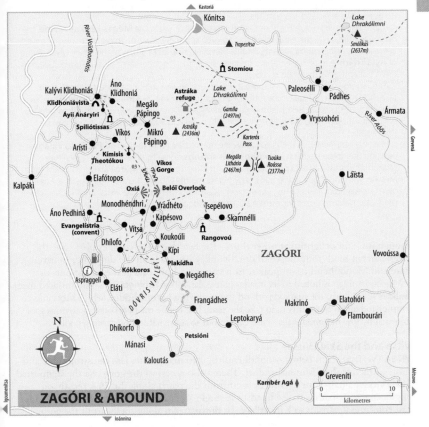

ZAGÓRI & AROUND

HIKING THE VÍKOS GORGE

The **Víkos Gorge** cuts right through the limestone uplands of Mount Gamíla for 20km, separating the villages of western and central Zagóri. With walls almost 1000m high in places, it's quite equal to the famous Samarian Gorge in Crete, and a **hike** through or around it is probably the highlight of a visit to the Zagóri.

Despite the gorge's popularity with hikers, and periodic bouts of trail maintenance, it's worth emphasizing that it is not a Sunday stroll. Bring proper, over-the-ankle **boots** and a leak-proof water container and walking poles or a stick (also useful for warding off guard dogs and belligerent cows). The best **maps** for the region are produced by Anavasi Editions (see p.53). Check **conditions** in advance of setting out. During April or early May, snowmelt often makes the Monodhéndhri end impassable, and following rainstorms the sides of the gorge are prone to landslides.

THE ROUTE

The most used **path down to the gorge** begins beside the Áyios Athanásios church in Monodhéndhri; a sign shows fairly accurate walking times of four and a half hours to Víkos village, six hours to either of the Pápingo villages. Once past Monodhéndhri's municipal amphitheatre, the path is cobbled for most of the forty minutes down to the riverbed, whose stony course you follow for another few minutes before shifting up the west bank, reaching the best viewpoint at a saddle ninety minutes from the village.

The entire route is waymarked, sometimes faintly, by red-paint dots and white-on-red stencilled metal diamonds. However, the surface underfoot is arduous, with some boulder-hopping in the gorge bed, metal or felled-branch ladders getting you over tricky bits on the bank, plus slippery, land-slid patches.

About two hours out of Monodhéndhri you draw even with the **Mégas Lákkos ravine**, the only major breach in the east wall of the gorge; a spring here has been piped to make it more useable in summer. Another thirty minutes' level walking takes you past the small, white shrine of **Ayía Triádha**; a further half-hour (around 3hr from Monodhéndhri) sees the gorge begin to open out and the sheer walls recede.

As the gorge widens you must make a choice. Continuing straight, the best-defined path takes you past the side trail to beautifully set eighteenth-century **Kímisis Theotókou** chapel. Beyond here, the route becomes a well-paved *kalderími*, climbing up and left to **Víkos** (Vitsikó; 870m elevation), four-plus hours from Monodhéndhri and also accessible by a 5km paved road from Arísti.

Most walkers, however, prefer to follow the marked O3 route to the two **Pápingo villages**, crossing the gorge bed at the **Voïdhomátis springs**, some three-and-a-half hours from Monodhéndhri. It's about two hours' walk from the springs up to Mikró Pápingo, slightly less to Megálo, with the divide in the trail nearly ninety minutes above the riverbed crossing. After an initial steep climb, there's a fine view down into the gorge near some weathered, tooth-like pinnacles, before the trail traverses a stable rockslide to the fork.

though it is still delightful at other times. The fact that large coaches can't scale the steep hairpin road from the Voïdhomátis valley has made all the difference between here and Monodhéndhri; in peak season you must leave cars at the village outskirts.

Megálo Pápingo is linked to its smaller namesake, **Mikró Pápingo**, by a 3km surfaced road; walkers should take the marked path off the road, via a historic bridge, which short cuts the journey to half an hour. If you do take the road, just before the bend – at an obvious spot adorned by low masoned walls – you can detour to some natural swimming pools.

Vítsa and the Skála Vítsas

VÍTSA (Vezítsa), 2km below Monodhéndhri, is to many tastes less claustrophobic and more attractive than Monodhéndhri. There's also access to the gorge via the signposted **Skála Vítsas**, a half-hour's gentle descent from the platía along the **Z9** – mostly on engineered stair-path – to the handsome single-arched **Mísiou bridge**; from there one can continue upstream to Kípi village, or downstream along the heart of the gorge.

Dhílofo

From either Vítsa or the Misíou bridge, the **Z15** leads south to **DHÍLOFO**, one of the most handsome Zagorian villages. The village has road access (though cars must be left at the outskirts). Alternatively, it makes for a rewarding hike. The path-start in Vítsa is trickier to find than the branch leading from the bridge, but once done it's a twenty-minute descent to a stream bed, where the Misíou branch links up, then a climb along a crumbled *kalderími* which peters out in flysch badlands. After another stream crossing, the path resumes before becoming a track to the outskirts of Dhílofo, just over an hour along.

Eláti

The village of **ELÁTI** (Boúltzi) is rather distant from the gorge, but there are fine views north to the peaks of Gamíla. From Dhílofo, walkers can continue down to Áyios Minás chapel on the main road and thence to Eláti on the **Z24**, but nearly half the way (1hr 30min) is along asphalt or bulldozer track, so you may as well come by car.

Dhíkorfo and the Kaloutás bridge

DHÍKORFO (Tzódhila) proves a beauty with its grand houses and unusual, minaret-like belfry of Áyios Minás church. Beyond the village the chief attraction is the enormous **triple-arched bridge** below **Kaloutás**, about 250m off the paved road by dirt track. All villages past Kaloutás were destroyed during World War II, but the road continues paved to Miliotádhes and thence the old Ioánnina–Métsovo highway – a useful short cut.

Áno Pedhiná

ÁNO PEDHINÁ (Soudhená), 3km west of Vítsa and Monodhéndhri, offers a few places with rooms and some superior hotels. At the base of the village stands the restored **convent of Evangelístria**, currently untenanted. Should you gain admission, you'll see the *katholikón*'s magnificent carved *témblon* and vivid, cleaned frescoes from 1793, though the structure is much older. Nearby Káto Pedhiná is home to **activity organizer** Compass Adventures (see below).

ARRIVAL AND INFORMATION
ZAGÓRI AND THE VÍKOS GORGE

By bus The bus from Ioánnina to Vítsa and Monodhéndhri leaves on Mon & Fri at 6.15am and 2pm. Buses leave Ioánnina for Dhílofo on Mon & Fri at 6am & 1.45pm, though they won't run if there are no passengers. On Tues there are two services from Ioánnina to the Pápingo villages (at 5.30am and 2.30pm) – the trip takes about an hour, and the buses then make immediate return trips.

By car Take care when driving: the steep, skinny roads are full of switchbacks, making distances deceptive, and potholes appear out of nowhere. Fill up before embarking on a long journey through the mountains as petrol stations are few and far between.

By taxi A taxi from Ioánnina to Monodhéndhri costs about €50.

Information If you're planning to spend a few days in the area, call first at the Northern Pindos National Park information centre, near the Eko petrol station on the park's western edge, around 2km northwest of Asprangeli (📞 26530 22245, 🌐 pindosnationalpark.gr). English-speaking staff, using a giant map of the area, can point out short cuts, give advice on spotting wildlife and provide you with information on walking in the hills.

ACTIVITIES

As well as the operators listed, Ioánnina-based Alpine Zone (see p.248) offers a range of activities in the area.

Hiking Compass Adventures, Káto (📞 6978 845 232, 🌐 compassadventures.gr) runs 6–7hr hikes of Víkos Gorge for €35/person (more if you're in a group of less than four) including an English-speaking guide and equipment. Also offers mountain biking and skiing.

Rafting Papigo Rafting (📞 6972 858 713, 🌐 papigorafting.gr) are a friendly local team running trips on grade 2 rapids that are well suited to families and beginners (€35/person including lunch and transfers from your hotel); trekking and ski tours also available.

ACCOMMODATION AND EATING

Monodhéndhri is the most popular **accommodation** base, but far from the only one. Every hamlet within spitting distance of the gorge has some form of rooms, and at least one taverna or snack-bar. You'll be lucky to get a room anywhere without prior booking from mid-July through to late Aug, and at weekends and official holidays the rest of the year.

MONODHÉNDHRI

Kikitsas ☎ 26530 71320. Located just up from the platía, one of three tavernas with seating all around the big tree, this friendly, family-run place serves up standard Greek fare as well as local specialities such as *alevrópitta* (a heavy dish made from dough, egg and cheese; €7.50), or simple cooked dishes like beans with spinach. Daily 10am–10pm.

Monodendri ☎ 26530 71300, ⓦ monodendrihotel. com. Sumptuously-decorated hotel near the northern end of the village; rooms have wooden floors and good-quality furnishings, and there's also a traditional-style restaurant with terrace-view seating. Breakfast included. **€60**

VÍTSA

Gia Gia Evgenia ☎ 26530 71971, ⓦ giagiaevgania.gr. On the southern approach to the village, this place has ten fresh, modern rooms with fireplace and TV; the one upstairs at the back is the best, with a small balcony affording tremendous views. Breakfast (included) is served in a nice bright room on the ground floor. **€65**

DHÍLOFO

★**Arhondiko Dhilofo** ☎ 26530 22455, ⓦ dilofo.eu. Quintessential Zagóri, this centuries-old mansion house has nine comfy, spick-and-span rooms, and the whole place is filled with treasures, about which the gregarious owner will happily hold forth. Breakfast (included) consists of home-made and locally-sourced products, and is something to look forward to on waking. **€50**

Lithos ☎ 26530 22600. A pleasant surprise in this homely village, this swanky little place has an odd sort of Greek gastropub feel. The house salad, made with beetroot and grilled cheese (€7), gives an idea of what the menu is about – well-presented, healthy food, often served with the best bread you'll find in the whole Zagóri. A good place for a nightcap, too. Daily noon–midnight.

ELÁTI

Driofillo ☎ 26530 71077, ⓦ driofillo.gr. Okay, it caters to the package-tourist crowd (and is a little bit soulless as a result), but this huge stone-built place offers excellent walk-up rates for its ten spacious and smart rooms, which have wooden floors, balconies and gleaming bathrooms. **€55**

★**Sta Riza** ☎ 26530 71550. A traditional taverna serving local *píttes*, vegetarian choices, such as the cheese ramekin with aubergine, and grills and casseroles, with good house wines and local *tsípouro*, all backed up by overly dramatic muzak. Local specialities include various game dishes, stewed with nuts and fruit. Great views over the gorge from the balconies. About €12/person. Daily 10.30–midnight.

ÁNO PEDHINÁ

Monopatia ☎ 26530 71116, ⓦ monopatiaresort.gr. Fifteen rooms and suites spread across some of the village's oldest buildings, elegantly restored with contemporary interiors and sandblasted until pearly white. The cheapest doubles are in a newer block and, although comfy, don't really compare with the luxurious studios higher up the hill. The on-site restaurant (Thurs–Sun dinner only), occupying a former stable decorated with the owner's art, serves good local trout and meats (mains around €15). Double **€95**, studio **€135**

Porfyron ☎ 26530 71579, ⓦ porfyron.com. Located beside Áyios Dhimítrios church, this lovingly restored mansion has very large rooms with painted or carved ceilings, antique furnishings and fireplaces; there's also a large garden and a taverna (mains about €15/person). Breakfast included. **€65**

MEGÁLO PÁPINGO

★**Astra** ☎ 26530 42108, ⓦ papigo.com. Close to the centre, on the road leading east out of the village, sits this lovely, ivy-clad house with views over the mountains; if it's not too busy, you'll have the chance to pick veggies for your own salad from the rambling garden. Order trout (€9) and it'll be fished out of the pond, cooked and served at your table. Even the local cheese is freshly sourced from mountain sheep. The leafy terrace here is the perfect place to sip wine and watch the sunset. They also have some perfectly comfortable rooms, spread across six properties. Daily 9am–11pm. **€65**

★**Papaevangelou** ☎ 26530 41135, ⓦ papaevangelou.gr. At the far north end of the village, this gorgeous guesthouse has homely, non-institutional rooms – many with fireplace – plus four self-catering studios amid well-tended gardens. The communal areas are family-friendly and the genial proprietor is multilingual. Superb breakfast included. **€75**

FROM TOP TRADITIONAL BRIDGE, ZAGÓRI (P.250); MÉTSOVO (P.243) >

The west coast

Starting just south of where the Vía Egnatía expressway ends, the **west coast** has some attractive **beaches** between Igoumenítsa and Préveza, among the best on the mainland outside of the Pelion. **Igoumenítsa** itself, the capital of Thesprotía province, is a purely functional ferry port. Attractive **Párga**, the most established beach resort on the stretch south, gets super packed-out in summer and at Easter, so is best in June or September. Just inland, there are worthwhile detours from the main route south: the intriguing **Nekromanteion of Acheron** evokes the legendary entrance to Hades; and the vast ruins of **Nikopolis** break the journey to **Préveza**, a low-key provincial capital at the mouth of the marshy Amvrakikós gulf. Down along the south coast, **Mesolónghi** is considered by Greeks to be a sacred spot, as the place where Lord Byron died while doing his part to liberate Greece from the Ottomans.

3

Igoumenítsa

IGOUMENÍTSA is Greece's third passenger port after Pireás and Pátra, with frequent ferries to **Corfu** and **Italy**. With the completion of the Vía Egnatía from Grevená to here, this unloved provincial capital has become the country's leading cargo port; a mega-terminal – part of the **New Port Egnatía** – for lorries dominates the harbour, and all shipping agencies have branches nearby, plus embarkation booths inside.

These seagoing functions and waterfront apart, Igoumenítsa is decidedly unappealing; it was levelled during World War II and rebuilt in bland utilitarian style. You should, hopefully, be able to get a ferry out immediately; every day in season there are sailings to Italy in the morning, and throughout the evening. If you end up stuck for the day, you're better off taking an excursion out of Igoumenítsa than hanging around this rather dodgy port town.

ARRIVAL AND INFORMATION   IGOUMENÍTSA

By bus The KTEL terminal is on Leoforos 49 Martiron, between the two ferry terminals.

Destinations Athens (3 daily, 8hr); Ioánnina (5–6 daily; 2hr 30min); Párga (Mon–Fri 2 daily; 1hr); Préveza (3 weekly in summer; 2hr 30min).

By ferry Almost all international ferries (see p.27) depart from the Egnatía port at the far south end of town, which is the western terminus of the Vía Egnatía – so drivers bound for Italy can skip the town altogether. Check in with the appropriate official agent's embarkation booth at least 2hr before departure, and book ahead in summer for cabins or vehicles. Domestic services to Corfu (with connections to Paxí) operate from

a quay 2km north; tickets for these services are purchased at waterside booths, which open an hour before departure.

International destinations Ancona (2–3 daily; 15hr); Bari (1–2 daily; 9–12hr); Brindisi (1–4 daily; 7–9hr); Venice (2 weekly; 24hr).

Domestic destinations Corfu Town (every 10–45min; 1hr 15min–2hr); Lefkími, Corfu (4–6 daily; 40min).

By car Accessing the town and the port areas via the new expressway couldn't be easier, with all the routes and ramps well signed in English. Drivers can use the free car park at the waterfront's north end.

ACCOMMODATION

Seleykos Palace On Mikras Asias, 3km north of town in Nea Selefkia ☎ 26650 23763. The nicest digs hereabouts, with a lovely outdoor pool, free parking and good-sized doubles with bright red bedspreads. Ask for a room at the front as these have sea views for the same price. You'll need a car to get there; call ahead as it often gets booked out by wedding parties. **€65**

Stavrodhromi Soulíou 16 ☎ 26650 22343, ⓦ stavrodromihotel.gr. The best budget choice – it's on the street leading diagonally uphill and northeast from Dimarhio square. Simple a/c rooms with small kitchenettes, plus a ground-floor bar-restaurant that sometimes hosts live music. **€40**

Párga and around

PÁRGA, 53km south of Igoumenítsa, has prospered thanks to its alluring setting on a lush coastline with a string of rocky islets offshore. Though concrete development has spread to the outskirts, the old centre, an arc of tiered houses set below a Norman-Venetian **kástro**, retains plenty of charm. Greeks love Párga for their holidays, and the little alleyways of the centre can become impossibly crowded with cars and people in midsummer and at Easter. That said, normal life just about continues, exemplified by older ladies in the traditional garb of black veil, braids and dark-blue kerchiefs. Visit in spring or autumn and you'll truly appreciate the atmosphere.

Brief history

Párga has an idiosyncratic history, being linked with the Ionian islands as much as with the mainland. From the 1300s to the 1700s, the port was a lone **Venetian** toehold in Epirus – the Venetian Lion of St Mark still adorns the kástro keep – and during this time a small Jewish community flourished here producing citrons (a lemon-like fruit used in Jewish ceremonies).

Later, the Napoleonic **French** briefly took Párga, leaving additional fortifications on the largest islet guarding the harbour. At the start of the nineteenth century, the town enjoyed autonomy under **Russian** protection, and lived from olive export, before being acquired by the **British**, who sold it on to **Ali Pasha**. Ali Pasha rebuilt all the local castles, while the townspeople, knowing his reputation, decamped to the Ionian islands on Good Friday 1819. The area was subsequently resettled by **Muslim Turks** who remained until the exchange of populations in 1923, when they were replaced in part by **Orthodox Greek** refugees.

The kástro

8am–12.30am • Free

The bluff-top Venetian **kástro** provides a haven from Párga's bustle; a long stair-street leads up to the crumbled, cypress-tufted ramparts, which offer excellent views. Restored barracks inside the castle boundary house a recommended café (see p.258); you can continue up a cobbled way to one of Ali Pasha's summer **palaces**, a warren of vaulted rooms and cisterns, with ruined, domed baths at the very summit.

The beaches

Párga's **beaches** line several consecutive bays, split by various headlands. The small, spring-chilled bay of **Kryonéri** lies opposite the islet studded with a monastery and Napoleonic fortifications, a 200m swim or pedalo from the town quay – you can usually even wade most of the way. Tiny but scenic **Gólfo beach**, the next (less clean) cove southeast, is reached by a narrow lane signposted for its eponymous taverna. Immediately northwest beyond the kástro lies **Váltos beach**, more than 1km in length as it arcs around to the eponymous hamlet; it can be reached on foot by the long ramp from the kástro gate, or by frequent water-taxis from the town dock (see p.258). **Lýkhnos beach**, 3km in the opposite (southeast) direction, is similarly huge; a shaded path through the olive groves from the far end of Kyronéri short-cuts the winding road in, or take a taxi-boat to spare yourself the walk.

ARRIVAL AND GETTING AROUND   PÁRGA

By bus The KTEL station – just a small booth – is up on the bypass road, near the start of Spýrou Livadhá (the way to Váltos).

Destinations Athens (3 daily; 7hr); Igoumenítsa (2 daily in summer; 1hr); Lárissa (1 daily except Sat; 4hr); Préveza (3–4 daily; 2hr); Thessaloníki (1 daily; 5hr).

By car or scooter Established car rental outlets include Avis, by the bus stop (☎26840 32732, ⓦavis.com); waterfront travel agencies rent scooters. Free parking is available at Kryonéri.

By taxi The main taxi rank is at the corner of Spýrou Livadhá and Alexándhrou Bánga. Fees are fixed and displayed on a board by the cars (you'll pay €7 to get from here to Lýkhnos, one way).

By water-taxi Water-taxis are available from the town dock; it's €4 return to Váltos (regular), and €9 to Lýkhnos (most going out in the morning and returning in the afternoon and evening).

On a tour A glut of agencies around town offer day-trips by boat to Paxos (€25), or inland to destinations including the Metéora (€40), the Vikos Gorge (€45) and even southern Albania (from €40).

ACCOMMODATION

Tour operators and regular visitors monopolize most of Párga's accommodation between mid-June and early September. Outside these seasons, however, you'll have ample choice on spec. **Rooms/studios** cluster in the lanes inland from Kryonéri, and the ridge of Tourkopázaro (officially Odhós Patatoúka), where premises have unbeatable views over Váltos beach. **Camping** is also available near several of the beach areas.

CENTRAL PÁRGA

Sol Kryonéri beach ☎ 26840 32332, ⓦ hotel-sol.eu. The most popular mid-range hotel in the area, with a prime beachfront location and a small outdoor pool. Ten of the twelve rooms here have a sea view and, during high season at least, all of them are booked up months (or even years) in advance; three-day minimum stay in high season. **€90**

Magda's Apartments On the road to Váltos ☎ 26840 31728, ⓦ magdas-hotel.com. A few minutes' walk uphill from town brings you to this mix of studios and superior apartments (usually let by the week), in a hillside garden with partial sea views, plus a terrace pool and two spas. Good breakfasts (extra), easy parking, and acoustic music sessions. English-speaking hosts Kostas and Spyros are ever helpful; unsurprisingly, three-month advance booking is usually necessary in high season. May to late Oct. **€65**

★Pension Nikos Vergos Agiou Athanasiou 8, Kryonéri ☎ 26840 31621, ⓦ parga-vergos.gr. Very clean, great-value rooms with black-and-white wall and floor patterns occasionally interrupted with flashes of marine blue. The smallest doubles are a little poky, but a few extra euros will buy you a little more space. One notch up gets you a studio with kitchenette and sea view. Double **€40**, studio **€70**

Villa Coralli Kryonéri ☎ 26840 31069, ⓦ villacoralli .com. This large and spacious hotel is right on the beach and has clean, well-appointed rooms and self-catering studios and apartments, all with balconies and either sea or hillside views. There's a large sea-view terrace for dining, and parking options not far away. Buffet breakfast included. Easter–Nov. **€55**

LÝKHNOS BEACH

★Lichnos Beach Lýkhnos ☎ 26840 31257, ⓦ lichnosbeach.gr. Set in large, grassy grounds that rarely feel over-busy, this is a slice of affordable luxury, and makes a good-value choice for families. There's a mix of standard rooms, studios and bungalows, plus a tennis court, pool and "private" beach with watersports facilities; half-board plans are available. There's free private parking and breakfast is included. **€120**

Lichnos Camping Lýkhnos, at the western end of the beach ☎ 26840 31171, ⓦ www.enjoy-lichnos.net. Centred on less congested Lýkhnos beach, this site offers both camping and self-catering apartments with sea-view balconies. They have their own taverna, as well, and the beach and watersports are handy. Campsites are in shady groves and some have views, too. Camping **€15**, apartment **€35**

EATING AND DRINKING

There are some thirty full-service **tavernas** around town, and though cooking is usually aimed squarely at the package trade, most offer **local wine** from the barrel. There's plenty of café society, too, nearly all places vying to offer all things to all people: restaurant, taverna, café, bar, breakfast spot. **Nightlife** centres around annually changing, semi-open-air **bars** on the east quay, with more bars along the steps to the kástro.

CENTRAL PÁRGA

★Café Citadel Kástro ☎ 26840 31267. High up above the quay within the kástro grounds and with views down over the water, this is a great, unpretentious spot for a nightcap while you listen to the cicadas and view the distant lapping of waves. Expect to pay a few euros for a small beer or glass of red, and about the same for a coffee. Daily 9am–12.30am.

Five Senses Beside Alfa Hotel, around 1km east of the harbour on Agiou Athanasiou. Make the long walk to this smart, open-sided restaurant for modern interpretations of classic Greek dishes, served with a touch of style. The seafood spaghetti (full of prawns, clams, scallops and kalamári; €12.50) is especially good. May–Oct daily 6.30–11.30pm.

Shanghai At western edge of waterfront ☎ 26840 32501. At the end of the strip, this has perhaps the best views in town; the name is a little misleading, since they have Indian curries (and an Indian chef), plus sushi, as well as Chinese dishes. Prices are fair, and on Tues and Thurs they offer gut-busting Chinese buffets (€13). May–Oct daily 6pm–midnight.

The Green Bakery Spýrou Livadhá 40 ☎26840 31400. Predating World War II, this café has a shady terrace which makes a pleasant spot for breakfast or brunch. Go for a mini *bougátsa* (€0.50) and espresso, a full breakfast (from €6.60), or home-made ice cream. Daily 7.30am–1am.

To Souli Anexartisias 45, on the waterfront ☎26840 31658. The oldest taverna in town, serving *mayireftá* standards and seafood (including fresh lobster every

day) – ask to see what's cooking (the fish moussaka is interesting; €14), or plump for something simple like fried kalamári (€9). May–Oct daily 10am–midnight.

LÝKHNOS BEACH

★**Porto Lichnos** At the top of the road to Lichnos Beach ☎26840 32684. Large, friendly restaurant offering an extensive menu of simple fare, plus panoramic views all the way down to the beach. Mains (around €10) include grilled chicken fillet with a side of chips and salad, or English-style fried breakfasts. A good place for an evening beer, too. May–Oct daily 6.30am–11.30pm.

Castle of Ayiá

Around 5km northwest of Parga • 8am–midnight • Free • Served by tourist trains from Kyronéri quay (4 daily; 2hr return; €8)

A short excursion leads to the diminutive **castle of Ayiá** (actually between Anthoússa and Ayiá), which is illuminated at night. The castle is more elaborate and intact than apparent from a distance, having been rebuilt in 1814 by Ali Pasha's Italian engineers. There's unrestricted access to the dungeons, the upper gallery and the roof, with its rusty cannons and superb views encompassing Paxí, Váltos beach, Ammoudhiá and Lefkádha.

Nekromanteion of Acheron

22km southeast of Párga • Daily 8.30am–3pm, may close later in summer • €2 • Best visited with your own transport; Mesopótamos is well signed, just 1km off the main coast highway

The **Nekromanteion of Acheron** stands on a rocky hill just above the village of **Mesopótamos**. According to mythology, the Underworld rivers Styx, Acheron and Cocytus flowed into a marshy lake here across which Charon rowed the dead to the gates of Hades. From Mycenaean to Roman times an elaborate **oracle** for consulting the departed existed somewhere nearby. The Acheron sanctuary never achieved the stature of Delphi or Dodona, but its fame was sufficient to warrant a mention in Homer where it becomes the site of Odysseus's visit to Hades.

A stand of trees marks the ostensible netherworld gateway. Homer spoke of poplars and willows, but today's cypresses are appropriate enough, being emblems of the dead across the Mediterranean. The ancient lake, which once made this spot an island, has now receded, though the mythological rivers still flow in the area, under different names.

The **ruins** in some ways correspond with descriptions of the oracle by ancient chroniclers, but based on archeological finds here, including such things as domestic pottery and catapult parts, the site is actually consistent with a fairly large agricultural enterprise that had occasion to defend itself against invaders – and, in fact, it has been dated to only Hellenistic times, the third or fourth century BC at the earliest, nearly a thousand years after Homer's account.

Préveza and around

At the mouth of the Amvrakikós Gulf, **PRÉVEZA** has undergone a transformation in recent years, and its **old bazaar quarter** and **waterfront**, now pedestrianized and full of appealing tavernas, are worth a look. Since international flights began serving Áktio airport, the town has had a partial facelift, and more character remains in the old quarter than at Párga. Préveza merits a stopover also for the nearby ruined Roman city of **Nikopolis**.

3

ARRIVAL AND DEPARTURE PRÉVEZA

By air Charters from destinations in northern Europe (including London and Manchester) arrive at nearby Áktio airport and generally have transport laid on to the various resorts; otherwise there are taxis for the 7km trip to town (set fee of €20). The airport itself is a cheerless, overcrowded shed with few facilities.

By bus The bus station is at the north edge of town, 1.5km out along route 21: there are sporadic shuttle buses into the centre, or it's an easy (if ugly) walk.

Destinations Athens (5 daily; 6hr); Ioánnina (6–8 daily; 2hr); Lefkádha (Mon–Sat 6 daily, 2 on Sun; 25min); Párga (3 daily; 2hr); Igoumenítsa (3 weekly; 2hr 30min).

By car A high-tech tunnel under the straits links Préveza and Áktio (3min; €3 cars, €5 campervans; no cyclists). Drivers from Párga or Préveza should follow signs for "Áktio" to find the entrance.

By taxi There's a taxi rank on the waterfront.

ACCOMMODATION AND EATING

It's worth staying in town overnight, as there is fairly lively nightlife on offer. A dozen **tavernas** (many dinner only) are scattered around the inland lanes and alleyways of old Préveza, with **cafés and bars** mostly lined up along the pedestrianized waterfront esplanade Venizélou. At night, bars and tavernas in the pedestrianized alleys of the old bazaar district, particularly around the fish-market building and the clocktower, come alive with locals, guests from surrounding resorts and denizens of yachts moored at the esplanade.

Amvrosios Grigoriou ☎ 26820 27192. Popular psarotaverna with plenty of Greek clientele, on the pedestrian alley between the Venetian clocktower and the shorefront drag. Fresh fish from just €5 per portion, and hearty salads too. Daily 10am–1am.

★**The Captain's House** Kariotraki 4–6 ☎ 26820 23915, ⓦ captainshousepreveza.gr. As the name suggests, this nineteenth-century mansion once belonged to a Greek captain, and has now been tastefully converted

into a top-end hotel with nine rooms, three of which are suites. There's a drawing room with books and maps on the local area, plus free parking and bikes available for guests to borrow. €95

Pension Alexandros Agiou Georgiou 27 ☎ 26820 23481. A twenty-minute walk from the centre, but nearer the beach, this is a very good value option, with large rooms in spacious grounds. €35

Nikopolis

NIKOPOLIS ("Victory City") was founded by Octavian on the site where his army had camped prior to the Battle of Actium: an ill-considered gesture that made little geographical sense. The settlement was on unstable ground, water had to be transported by aqueduct from the distant Loúros springs, and a population had to be forcibly imported from various towns. However, such a *folie de grandeur* was understandable. At **Actium** (modern Áktio), Octavian had first blockaded and then annihilated the combined fleets of Antony and Cleopatra, gathered there for the invasion of Italy. These events culminated in Octavian the general becoming Roman Emperor Augustus.

The subsequent history of Nikopolis is undistinguished, with much of its population drifting back to their homes, and the town suffering barbarian sackings as Rome declined. During the sixth century AD, it flourished briefly as a Byzantine city, but within four centuries it had vanished from the combined effect of earthquakes and Bulgar raids. Today the site, which is still being excavated, looks rather neglected – with tufts of long grass sprouting up between the ruins.

Archeological Museum

Around 5km north of Préveza on the road to the site • Daily: summer 8am–3pm; winter 8.30am–3pm • €3 • Buses from Préveza pass by the museum, but there is no regular stop

Architecturally minimalist, the small but well-presented museum offers good lighting and informative labelling for its finds, which include impressive marble carvings, stelae and inscriptions, as well as mosaics and a variety of pottery. Highlights include a marble relief depicting an erotic banquet scene and a fourth-century BC seated lion, life-size.

The site

Around 8km north of Préveza • Unrestricted access

The far-flung monuments begin 8km north of Préveza, on either side of the main road. The 2220-acre site is too scattered to tour on foot or by bus; hire a taxi in Préveza, or come by car – if you're going to or from Párga, you can stop by on the way.

Nikopolis is bounded on the south by a formidable stretch of sixth-century Byzantine **walls**, beyond which lie the **Dhométios basilica** (with covered-over mosaics) and the Roman **odeion** dating from the original construction of the city, well restored for use in the local summer festival. From the foundations of the sixth-century **basilica of Alkýsonos** just north of the main **baths**, it's 2km to the main **theatre**, west of which you can discern the sunken outline of the **stadium**, below Smyrtoúna village.

Astakós

ASTAKÓS ("Lobster") is a small port on the western mainland with frequent ferries to Kefaloniá and Itháki. Despite the name, there's no lobster served at any of the mediocre tavernas lining the quay; around the marketplace many Neoclassical buildings from the 1870s hint at a more prosperous past.

ARRIVAL AND DEPARTURE ASTAKÓS

By bus The KTEL bus station is at the end of the quay; buses from Athens (5hr) should coincide with ferry departures.

By ferry The ferry timetables to and from Kefaloniá and Itháki change from month to month throughout summer, but there are at least five weekly departures to each destination May–Oct; contact Ionion Pelagos (w ionionpelagos.com; ☎ 26460 38020) for the latest schedules.

ACCOMMODATION

Giannis Village Above town ☎ 69748 10800. Far better than the measly options in town, this place has large, modern-looking apartments (sleeping up to four) and a pool, with good vistas down to town and across the sea beyond. **€60**

Mesolóngi and around

Mesolóngi (also written as Missolongi or Messolongi), for most visitors, is irrevocably associated with **Lord Byron**, who died here to dramatic effect during the War of Independence (see box p.262). Otherwise it's a fairly shabby and unromantic place: rainy from autumn to spring, and comprised largely of drab, modern buildings between which locals enthusiastically cycle along a flat grid plan. To be fair, the town has been spruced up a bit, especially in the centre, but if you come here on pilgrimage, it's still best to move on the same day, most likely to Lefkádha island or the Peloponnese. More interesting than any town sight is a walk across the **Klísova lagoon**, past two **forts** that were vital defences against the Ottoman navy. The lagoon, with its salt-evaporation ponds and fish farms, attracts a variety of wading birds, especially in spring.

Gate of the Sortie

You enter the town from the northeast through the **Gate of the Sortie**, named after the April 12, 1826 break-out by nine thousand Greeks, ending the Ottomans' year-long siege. In one desperate dash they quit Mesolóngi, leaving a group of defenders to destroy it – and some three thousand civilians not capable of leaving – by firing the powder magazines. But those fleeing were betrayed, ambushed on nearby Mount Zygós; fewer than two thousand evaded massacre or capture and enslavement by an Albanian mercenary force.

3

BYRON IN MESOLÓNGI

Byron has been a Greek national **hero** ever since he became involved in the country's struggle for independence. Almost every town in the country has a street – Výronos – named after him; not a few men still answer to "Vyron" as a first name. He first passed through in 1809 when tyrannical local ruler Ali Pasha was at the height of his power, and the poet's tales of intrigue sent a shiver down romantic Western spines.

Later, in January 1824, Byron made his way to **Mesolóngi**, a squalid, inhospitable southwestern port amid lagoons – but also the western centre of **resistance** against the Ottomans. The poet, who had by then contributed his personal fame and fortune to the war effort, was enthusiastically greeted with a 21-gun salute, and made **commander** of the five-thousand-strong garrison, a role as much political as military. The Greek forces were divided into factions whose brigand-chieftains separately and persistently petitioned him for money. Occasionally Byron despaired: "Here we sit in this realm of mud and discord", read one of his journal entries. But while other Philhellenes returned home, disillusioned by the fractious, larcenous Greeks, or worn out by quasi-tropical Mesolóngi, he stayed.

On February 15 Byron caught a **fever**, possibly malaria, and two months later **died**; ironically, he became more valuable to the Greek cause dead than alive. News of the poet's demise, embellished to heroic proportions, reverberated across northern Europe; arguably it changed the course of the war in Greece. When Mesolóngi fell again to the Ottomans in spring 1826, there was outcry in the European press, and French and English forces were finally galvanized into sending a naval force that unintentionally engaged an Egyptian fleet at Navarino, striking a fatal blow against the Ottoman navy.

Garden of Heroes

Daily: summer 8am–9pm; winter 8am–6pm, but sometimes unaccountably closed • Free

Just inside the Gate of the Sortie, on the right, partly bounded by the remaining fortifications, is the **Kípos Iróön**, or "Garden of Heroes" – signposted in English as "Heroes' Tombs" – where a tumulus covers the bodies of the town's anonymous defenders. Beside the tomb of Souliot commander Markos Botsaris is a **statue of Byron**, erected in 1881, under which – despite apocryphal traditions – is buried neither the poet's heart nor lungs. Byron might conceivably have been offered the throne of an independent Greece: thus the relief of his coat of arms with a royal crown above. Among the palm trees and rusty cannon loom busts, obelisks and cenotaphs to an astonishing range of American, German and French Philhellenes, those Romantics who strove to free the Classical Greece of their ideals from the barbaric thrall of the Ottomans.

Museum of History and Art

Platía Bótsari • Mon–Fri 9am–1.30pm & 4–7pm, Sat & Sun 9am–1pm & 4–7pm, closes 6pm winter • Free • ☎ 26310 22134

Back on the central square, the Neoclassical town hall houses the small **Museum of History and Art** devoted to the revolution. There are some emotive paintings on the upper floor (including a copy of Delacroix's *Gate of the Sortie*), reproductions of period lithographs and a rather disparate (and desperate) collection of Byronia on the ground floor. Pride of place, by the entrance, goes to an original edition of Solomos's poem *Hymn to Liberty*, now the words of the national anthem.

ARRIVAL AND INFORMATION   MESOLÓNGI

By bus KTEL buses arrive where Chondrodimou meets Naupactus, close to the northern edge of the Garden of Heroes (see above). Local blue-and-white ones call at a little booth on Evgenidou.

Destinations Athens (9 daily; 3hr 30min); Ioánnina, via Agrínio (2–4 daily; 3hr); Náfpaktos (Mon–Fri 2 daily;

50min); Pátra (5–9 daily; 1hr).

By car Mesolóngi is linked to Ioánnina by the modern

Ionian Highway.

ACCOMMODATION AND EATING

The main concentration of **tavernas**, interspersed with a few bars, is along and around Athanasíou Razikótsika, a pedestrianized street one block south of car-free Hariláou Trikoúpi. In the narrow alleys linking these two broader streets are countless **bars** and **kafenía** – you'll find something to suit. Mesolóngi is especially noted for its eels, smoked or grilled; also famous is the local *avgotáraho* or *haviára*, caviar made from grey mullet roe.

Dimotroukas Chrosoupedou ☎ 26310 23237. Reliable taverna, operating here since the 1970s. Good for local fish specialities, including eel, as well as meats, salads and cooked dishes; you can eat well here for under €15. Tues–Sun noon–1am.

Mama's Bakery On the corner of Stavropoulou and Trikoúpi Spyrou ☎ 26310 24044. This bakery has a huge selection of baked goods (from €1), plus good coffee and excellent *gelato*. There's a seating area out the back with plenty of shade. Daily 6am–11pm.

Socrates Organic Village 5km north of the centre ☎ 26310 41141, ⓦ organic-village.gr. Options in town are pretty dire, so these apartments, a little way to the north, make a useful alternative. The friendly owners often bring along veggies from their organic gardens, and there's a pleasant pool and green grounds to relax in. €50

Theoxenia On the lagoon shore, just south of town ☎ 26310 22493, ⓦ theoxenia-hotel.gr. This small, landscaped complex by the lagoon is an upmarket, if impersonal, choice – convenient if you're driving, though the 1970s-vintage rooms are ripe for an overhaul. Breakfast included. €35

Tourlídha

A causeway extends 4km from Mesolóngi to the open sea at **TOURLÍDHA**, a hamlet of wood-plank and prefab summer cottages on stilts, plus a few **tavernas**. If you can stomach the intermittent stench from the nearby salt-ponds, you could swim from the packed-sand **beach**, which has showers and a few café-bars. It makes a picturesque, fun outing if you're visiting Mesolóngi.

EATING   TOURLÍDHA

Tourlidha ☎ 26310 24360. With tables on stilted walkways that extend out over the shimmering water, this café/bar/restaurant is a surprisingly cool place for a drink. It does a few good fish dishes too; a huge plate of spaghetti and prawns big enough for two people costs €15. Daily 11am–11pm.

The northern mainland

WHITE TOWER, THESSALONÍKI

The northern mainland

Greece's northern mainland is dominated by the provinces of Macedonia and Thrace. Each has been part of the modern Greek state for only around a century – Macedonia (Makedhonía) was surrendered by the Turks in 1913, while Greek sovereignty over western Thrace (Thráki) was not confirmed until 1923, and there is still a sizeable ethnic minority population (see box, p.317). Consequently, these two regions stand slightly apart from the rest of the country, an impression reinforced for visitors by architecture, scenery, customs and climate that seem more Balkan than typically Mediterranean. In fact, the region is relatively little known to outsiders, perhaps thanks to its capricious climate, lack of beach resorts and few charter flights. Yet northern Greece is one of the country's most rewarding areas to visit.

Mount Olympus, mythical abode of the gods, is a tempting target for hikers, while **Mount Áthos**, a Byzantine ecclesiastical idyll, is an unmissable attraction (at least for men, who are the only ones allowed here). The sybaritic capital of Macedonia, **Thessaloníki**, and the region's other main city, **Kavála**, are intriguing places; the former provides access to the beach-fringed peninsula of **Halkidhikí**. The north also has more outstandingly beautiful spots, especially the **Préspa National Park** in rugged western Macedonia and the bird-watchers' heaven of the **Kerkíni wetlands** to the east. The lakeside city of **Kastoriá** and the clifftop town of **Édhessa** are among Greece's most beguiling urban centres, thanks to a belated but determined attempt to restore some fine old buildings. Admittedly, the region's ancient sites are relatively modest, though there is one notable exception: the awe-inspiring Macedonian tombs discovered at **Vergina** in the 1970s, near the pleasant city of Véria. Not so well known are the Macedonian and Roman sites at **Pella**, with its fabulous mosaics, and at **Philippi**, St Paul's first stop in Greece. Few travellers on their way to Bulgaria or Turkey stray from the dull trunk road through **Thrace**, but there are places here that deserve more than just a meal stop, including the well-preserved town of **Xánthi**; a trio of minor archeological sites; the waterfowl reserves of the **Évros Delta**; and the **Dhadhiá Forest**, with its black vultures. **Alexandhroúpoli** is dull, but it rewards the curious with one of the best ethnological museums in the whole of Greece.

GETTING AROUND
NORTHERN MAINLAND

By train and bus Public transport in the north is somewhat limited. A few trains link some of the urban centres, but the railway line east from Thessaloníki curls unhelpfully inland, bypassing Kavála altogether and leaving buses or your own transport as the only alternatives for travelling along the coast. The KTEL bus network is pretty comprehensive, at least as far as getting to and from Thessaloníki, though not always between major towns.

By car The road system has improved beyond recognition in recent years, with the completion of the "Via Egnatia" highway, which now provides an uninterrupted link between the west coast and the Bulgarian and Turkish borders, as well as connecting to the upgraded Athens–Thessaloníki motorway.

PRESPA LAKE

Highlights

① Thessaloníki Balkan in atmosphere, Greece's second city offers historic monuments, great eating and a vibrant nightlife. **See p.268**

② Mount Olympus The mythical home of the gods; a three-day hike to the summit and back offers pristine scenery and riots of wild flowers. **See p.282**

③ Vergina Beguiling treasures unearthed in the poignant, beautifully displayed burial chambers of Macedonia's royal dynasty. **See p.288**

④ Édhessa Clifftop wooden houses and impeccably restored water mills make this one of Greece's most inviting towns. **See p.290**

⑤ Préspa lakes The reed-fringed shores of these lakes, which form the leading ornithological reserve in the region, are a haven for nature lovers. **See p.292**

⑥ Kastoriá Situated on a wooded headland jutting into the pewter-coloured Lake Orestiádha, this atmospheric town is the country's fur capital. **See p.294**

⑦ Mount Athos Timeless Orthodox monasteries set among unspoilt landscapes in a semi-independent republic run by monks. **See p.306**

⑧ Dhadhiá Oak and pine forests draped over volcanic ridges, home to black vultures and other rare raptors. **See p.324**

HIGHLIGHTS ARE MARKED ON THE MAP ON PP.268–269

Thessaloníki

Home to over a million people, Greece's second city, **THESSALONÍKI** – or **Salonica**, as it is was once known – stands apart from the rest of the country. Situated at the head of the Gulf of Thessaloníki, it seems open to the rest of the world, with a wide ethnic mix and an air of general prosperity, stimulated by a major university and a famously avant-garde live music and entertainment scene. The food is among the most highly rated in Greece and there are some very sophisticated restaurants, as well as wholesome traditional food on offer in a great number of old-fashioned Turkish-influenced ouzerís and tavernas.

The city has plenty to offer the visitor for two or three days, at least. There are substantial **Roman remains** and the many **churches** (see box, p.275) constitute a showcase of Orthodox architecture through the ages. You can catch glimpses of the Turkish city both in the walled Upper City and in the modern grid of streets below: isolated pockets of **Ottoman buildings**, many of them Islamic monuments, which miraculously survived the 1917 fire (see p.272). Modern Greek architecture is exemplified by Art Deco piles dating from the city's twentieth-century heyday, around the time of the first **International Trade Fair** in 1926, an event that continues to this

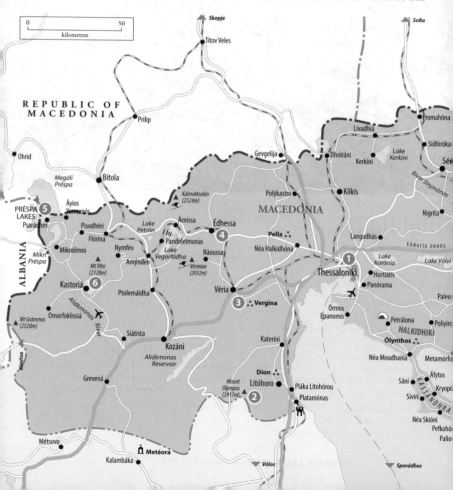

day. Thessaloníki's many and often excellent **museums** cover subjects as varied as Byzantine culture, the city's Jewish heritage, folklife, musical instruments, Atatürk (who was born here) and, more recently, modern art and photography.

Brief history

When King Cassander of Macedonia founded the city in 315 BC, he named it after his wife, Thessalonike, **Alexander the Great**'s half-sister, whose name in turn derived from the Macedons' decisive victory (*nike*) over the Thessalians. It soon became the region's cultural and trading centre, issuing its own coins, and when Rome conquered Macedonia in 146 BC, the city (under the name **Salonica**) became the natural and immediate choice of capital. Its fortunes and significance were boosted by the building of the Via Egnatia, the great road linking Rome (via Brindisi) with Byzantium and the East.

  Christianity had slow beginnings in the city. St Paul visited twice, and on the second occasion, in 56 AD, he stayed long enough to found a church, and later wrote the two Epistles to the Thessalonians, his congregation there. It was another three centuries, however, before the new religion took full root. **Galerius**, who acceded as eastern emperor upon Byzantium's break with Rome, provided the city with virtually all its

HIGHLIGHTS

1. Thessaloníki
2. Mount Olympus
3. Vergina
4. Édhessa
5. Préspa lakes
6. Kastoriá
7. Mount Athos
8. Dhadhiá

NORTHERN MAINLAND

surviving late Roman monuments. The first resident Christian emperor was **Theodosius** (reigned 379–95), who after his conversion issued the Edict of Salonica, which officially ended paganism.

Under Justinian's rule (527–65) Salonica became the second city of **Byzantium** after Constantinople, which it remained – under constant pressure from Goths and Slavs – until its sacking by Saracens in 904. The storming and sacking continued under

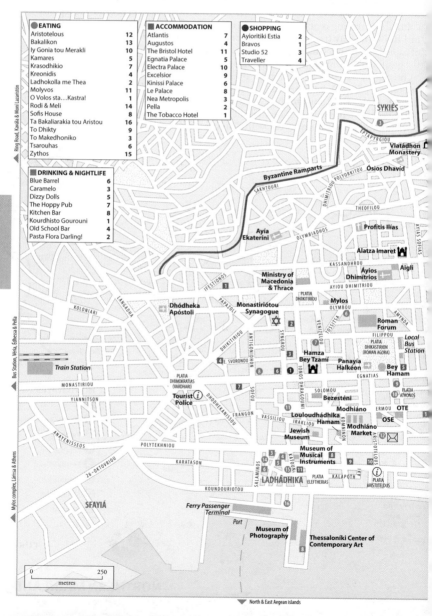

● EATING	
Aristotelous	12
Bakalikon	13
Iy Gonia tou Merakli	10
Kamares	5
Krasodhikio	7
Kreonidis	4
Ladhokolla me Thea	2
Molyvos	11
O Volos sta…Kastra!	1
Rodi & Meli	14
Sofis House	8
Ta Bakaliarakia tou Aristou	16
To Dhikty	9
To Makedhoniko	3
Tsarouhas	6
Zythos	15

■ ACCOMMODATION	
Atlantis	7
Augustos	4
The Bristol Hotel	11
Egnatia Palace	5
Electra Palace	10
Excelsior	9
Kinissi Palace	6
Le Palace	8
Nea Metropolis	3
Pella	2
The Tobacco Hotel	1

● SHOPPING	
Ayioritiki Estia	2
Bravos	1
Studio 52	3
Traveller	4

■ DRINKING & NIGHTLIFE	
Blue Barrel	6
Caramelo	3
Dizzy Dolls	5
The Hoppy Pub	7
Kitchen Bar	8
Kourdhisto Gourouni	1
Old School Bar	4
Pasta Flora Darling!	2

Map labels: Ring Road, Kavála & Moni Lazaristón; Bus Station, Véria, Édhessa & Pella; Mylos complex, Lárisa & Athens

SYKIÉS

Vlatádhon Monastery

Byzantine Ramparts

Ósios Dhavid

Ayía Ekateríni

Profítis Ilías

Alatza Imaret

Ministry of Macedonia & Thrace

Áyios Dhimítrios

Aigli

Dhódheka Apóstoli

Monastiriótou Synagogue

Mylos

Roman Forum

Local Bus Station

Train Station

Hamza Bey Tzamí

Panayía Halkéon

Bey Hamam

Tourist Police

Bezesténi

Modhiáno

OTE

Louloudhádhika Hamam

Modhiáno Market

OSE

Jewish Museum

Museum of Musical Instruments

LADHÁDHIKA

SFAYIÁ

Ferry Passenger Terminal

Port

Museum of Photography

Thessaloníki Center of Contemporary Art

Street labels: KOLONIARI, LANGADHA, DHIKITIRIOU, ANTIGONIDHON, E. SVORONOU, SYNGROU, IONOS DRAGOUMI, SOLOMOU, ERMOU, ARISTOTELOUS, KOLOKOTRONI, VENIZELOU, IOUSTITSA, OLYMBOU, AMYNDA, FILIPPOU, EGNATIAS, SOFOU, VASSILIOU, IRAKLIOU, MITROPOLEOS, KATOUNI, SALAMINOS, KALAPOTH, KOUNDOURIOTOU, KARATASON, POLYTEKHNIOU, 26-OKTOVRIOU, ANAYENISSEOS, YIANNITSON, MONASTIRIOU, DHODHEKANISSOU, FRANGON, KASSANDHROU, THEOFILOU, DHIMITRIOU POLYORKITOU, SAKHTOURI, EPTAPYRGIOU, IFESTIONOS, PAPAZOLI, AYIAS SOFIAS

PLATIA DHIMOKRATIAS (VARDHARI), PLATIA DHIKITIRIOU, PLATIA DHIKASTIRION (ROMAN AGORA), PLATIA ATHONOS, PLATIA ELEFTHERIAS, PLATIA ARISTOTELOUS

0 — 250 metres

▼ North & East Aegean islands

the Normans of Sicily (1185) and with the Fourth Crusade (1204), when the city became capital of the Latin Kingdom of Salonica. It was, however, restored to the Byzantine Empire of Nicea in 1246, and it reached a cultural "**golden age**" until Turkish conquest and occupation in 1430.

Thessaloníki was the premier **Ottoman Balkan city** when Athens was still a backwater. Its population was as varied as any in the region, with Greek Orthodox

THESSALONÍKI

Walls
PAPARESKA
Yedi Küle
EPTAPYRGIO
ÁNO PÓLI
POLYDHOROU
EPTAPYRGIOU
Chain Tower
N
Théatro Dhássous
TIMOTHEOU IGOUMENOU
IFIKRATOUS
PODHROMOU
AKROPOLEOS
MOREAS
AMFITRIONOS
KÁSTRA
Áyios Nikólaos Orfanós
PALEAS ATHINAS
AP. PAVLOU
KASTRON
TZOGAEOU
SARÁNDA EKKLISSIES
PL. PAVLOU MELA
ATHINAS
IOULIANOU
Atatürk's House
Central Hospital
AYIOU DHIMITRIOU
Kaftantzoglio Stadium
LEONIDHA IASSONIDHOU
ARMENOPOULOU
ARRIANOU
PLATIA AY. YEORYIOU
Rotónda
University
Panayía Ahirópiitos
Athos Pilgrims' Bureau
Arch of Galerius
ETHNIKIS
PLATIA SINDRIVANIOU
KONSTANDINOU KARAMANLI
Helexpo Exhibition Ground
Ayía Sofía
I. MIHAIL
DHIMITRIOU GOUNARI
DHELLIOU
MYSIS
ANGELAKI
MACK. KING
P. P. YERMANOU
IKTINOU
SVOLOU
IPODHROMIOU
FILIKIS ETERIAS
PAVLOU MELA
PLATIA NAVARINOU
TSIMISKI
Cathedral
MIT. IOSIF
MITROPOLEOS
Folk & Ethnological Museum of Macedonia
Archeological Museum of Thessaloniki
KAFTANZOGLOU
PROXENOU KOROMILA
LORI MARGARITI
E
Etería Makedhonikón Spoudhón
PLATIA H.A.N.TH.
Museum of Byzantine Culture
STRATOU
NIKIS
YERMANOU
Théatro Kípou
White Tower
PLATIA LEFKOU PYRGOU
Vassilikó Théatro
VELISSARIOU
VASSILEOS YEORYIOU
Thessaloníki Bay
MEGALOU ALEXANDHROU

4

Panorama & Theatro Damári

Ippokration Hospital

Christians in a distinct minority. Besides Ottoman Muslims, who called the city "Selanik", there were Slavs (who still know it as "Solun"), Albanians, Armenians and, following the Iberian expulsions after 1492, the largest European **Jewish community** of the age (see box, p.276).

The modern quality of Thessaloníki is due largely to a disastrous **fire** in 1917 which levelled most of the old plaster houses along a labyrinth of Ottoman lanes, including the entire Jewish quarter. The city was rebuilt, often in a special form of Art Deco style, over the following eight years, on a grid plan prepared under the supervision of French architect Ernest Hébrard, with long central avenues running parallel to the seafront and cross streets densely planted with trees. During **World War II** the city was occupied by the Nazis, who decimated the Jewish community. After the war, more reconstruction was necessary to repair bomb damage, though this was interrupted in 1978 by a severe **earthquake** that damaged many older buildings.

Thessaloníki's opulence has traditionally been epitomized by the locals' sartorial elegance, but the boom of the 1990s is long gone and an increasing number of boarded-up shops indicate Greece's continuing economic malaise. A permanent underclass lives in shantytowns near the port, and consists of Pontic or Black Sea Greeks, Albanians and eastern European refugees, as well as a growing community of Afghans, Kurds, Syrians and Africans.

Archeological Museum of Thessaloniki

M Andhrónikou 6 · Daily: mid-April to Oct 8am–8pm; Nov to mid-April 9am–4pm · €8 · ☎ 2310 830 538, ⓦ amth.gr

The refurbished **Archeological Museum of Thessaloniki** is undoubtedly the city's leading museum. Star billing goes to the marvellous **Gold of Macedon exhibition** in the south hall, which displays – and clearly labels in both English and Greek – many of the finds from the royal tombs of Philip II of Macedon (father of Alexander the Great) and others at the ancient Macedonian capital of Aegae, in Vergina (see p.288). They include startling amounts of gold and silver, such as masks, crowns, necklaces, earrings and bracelets, as well as pieces in ivory and bronze. The treasures here are beautiful, practical and of extraordinarily imaginative craftsmanship. Other highlights include the central gallery (opposite as you enter), which is devoted to rich grave **finds from ancient Sindos**, a few kilometres north of the modern city, while the left-hand wing is taken up by **Hellenistic and Roman art**, in particular some exquisite blown-glass birds, found in the tumuli, or *toúmbes*, which stud the plain around Thessaloníki.

Museum of Byzantine Culture

Leofóros Stratoú 2 · Daily: April–Oct 8am–8pm; Nov–March 9am–4pm · €8 · ☎ 2313 306 400, ⓦ mbp.gr

The prize-winning **Museum of Byzantine Culture**, in a handsome brick structure just east of the Archeological Museum, does a fine job of displaying the early Christian tombs and graves excavated in the city. The museum features rescued wall paintings that depict, among others, *Susannah and the Elders*, and a naked rower surrounded by sea creatures. Despite this and the faultless lighting and display techniques, most of the exhibits will appeal more to specialists than to lay visitors.

White Tower

East end of Leofóros Níkis · Tues–Sun 8.30am–3pm · €3 · ☎ 2310 267 832, ⓦ lpth.gr

Dominating the seafront promenade, the **White Tower** (Lefkós Pýrgos) is the city's graceful symbol. Originally known as the Lions' Tower and then the Fortress of Kalamariá, it formed a corner of the city's Byzantine and Ottoman defences before most of the walls were demolished, late in the nineteenth century. In 1890, a Jewish prisoner was given the task of whitewashing the tower, in exchange for his freedom, hence the new name, which stuck, even though it is now more of a buff colour. It was restored in 1985 for the city's 2300th birthday celebrations and has since been converted into a historical museum (Greek displays only).

Arch of Galerius

The **Arch of Galerius** dominates a pedestrianized square just off the eastern end of Egnatía. Along with the nearby Rotónda (see below), it originally formed part of a larger Roman complex which included palaces and a hippodrome. The mighty arch is the surviving span of a dome-surmounted arcade that once led towards the palaces. Built to commemorate the emperor's victories over the Persians in 297 AD, its piers contain weathered reliefs of the battle scenes interspersed with glorified poses of Galerius himself. The well-displayed remains of **Galerius's palace** can be viewed, below the modern street level, along pedestrianized Dhimitríou Goúnari, towards its southern extension, Platía Navarínou.

Rotónda (Áyios Yeóryios)

Platía Ayíou Yeoryíou • Tues–Sun 8.30am–3pm • Free • ☎ 2310 968 860

North of the great Arch of Galerius, the **Rotónda**, later converted into the church of **Áyios Yeóryios**, is the most striking single Roman monument in the city. It was designed, but never used, as an imperial mausoleum, possibly for Galerius himself. Consecrated for Christian use in the late fourth century, by the addition of a sanctuary, an apse, a narthex and rich mosaics, it later became one of the city's major **mosques**, from which period the minaret remains. The cavernous interior is stark, but some of the stunning mosaics remain in place.

Roman Forum

Platía Aristotélous • Daily: summer 8am–8pm; winter 8am–3pm • Free

Just north of leafy Platía Dhikastiríon, the **Roman Forum** has been undergoing gradual excavation for over a decade, so access is limited. In many ways, its layout is best observed from Olýmbou, the road behind, from where the shape of the *stoa*

OTTOMAN THESSALONÍKI

Despite years of neglect, the 1917 fire and the 1978 quake, Thessaloníki has quite a number of vestiges of **Ottoman architecture** to show, which are mostly within walking distance of Platía Dhikastiríon. At the eastern corner of the square itself stands the disused but well-preserved **Bey Hammam** or Parádhisos Baths (Mon–Fri 9am–9pm, Sat & Sun 8.30am–3pm; free; ☎ 2310 226 931), the oldest Turkish bathhouse in the city (1444) and in use until 1968. The doorway is surmounted by elaborate ornamentation, while inside, art exhibitions – often, paradoxically, with Byzantine themes – are held from time to time.

To the south of Platía Dhikastiríon lies the main **Turkish bazaar area**, bounded roughly by Egnatía, Dhragoúmi, Ayías Sofías and Tsimiskí. The most interesting bit, and a quiet midtown oasis, is a grid of lanes between Ayías Sofías and Aristotélous, devoted to selling crafts and cane furniture. Nearby, Ottoman monuments include the six-domed **Bezesténi**, the old covered valuables market, at the corner of Venizélou and Egnatía, which now houses jewellery and other shops. Directly opposite, on the north side of Egnatía, rather more modest stores occupy a prominent mosque, the fifteenth-century purpose-built – which is unusual, as most mosques in Ottoman Thessaloníki were converted churches – **Hamza Bey Tzamí**, now looking decidedly ramshackle.

Well to the north of Platía Dhikastiríon, beyond Áyios Dhimítrios basilica, is the seventeenth-century **Yeni Hammam**, now a summer cinema and music venue serving basic food, and better known as the Aigli (see p.280); and the fifteenth-century **Altaza Imaret**, which is tucked away in a quiet square diagonally opposite, sports a handsome portico and multiple domes.

(colonnaded walkway), with several remaining columns, is clear. The restored amphitheatre is used for occasional summer performances.

Atatürk's house

Apostólou Pávlou 17 • Daily 10am–5pm • Free • For admission contact the Turkish Consulate, next door (Ayíou Dhimitríou 151; Mon–Fri 9.30am–12.30pm; ☎ 2310 248 452)

In **Kástra**, as the lower fringes of the Upper Town are known, stands a pink nineteenth-century building in which **Kemal Atatürk**, creator and first president of the modern secular state of Turkey, was born in 1881. The consulate maintains **Atatürk's house** as a small **museum**, with its original fixtures and an interesting selection of Atatürk memorabilia. Due to tight security, you must apply for admission with your passport to the Turkish Consulate, next door.

Ayía Sofía

Between Egnatía and Platía Navarínou • Daily 7am–1pm & 5–6.30pm • Free • ☎ 2310 270 253

The heavily restored eighth-century church of **Ayía Sofía** is the finest of its kind in the city. Modelled on its more illustrious namesake in Constantinople, it replaced an older basilica, the only trace of which remains a few paces south: the below-street-level holy well of John the Baptist, originally a Roman *nymphaeum* (sacred fountain). Ayía Sofía's dome, 10m in diameter, bears a splendid **mosaic** of the *Ascension*, for which you'll need binoculars to see properly. Christ, borne up to the heavens by two angels, sits resplendent on a rainbow throne, his right hand extended in blessing; below, a wry inscription quotes Acts 1:11: "Ye men of Galilee, why stand ye gazing up into heaven?" The mosaic is ringed by fifteen figures: the Virgin attended by two angels, and the twelve Apostles reacting to the miracle. The dome was restored late in the 1980s; the rest of the interior decoration was plastered over after the 1917 fire.

Áyios Dhimítrios

Ayíou Dhimitríou • Church and crypt Mon 12.30–7pm, Tues–Sat 8am–8pm, Sun 10.30am–8pm • Free • ☎ 2310 968 843

The massive yet simple church of **Áyios Dhimítrios** was conceived in the fifth century but subsequently heavily restored. Far more impressive than the official cathedral down at Mitropóleos, this is the de facto cathedral of the city, with pride of place in Thessalonian hearts, and was almost entirely rebuilt after the 1917 fire. The church is dedicated to the city's patron saint and stands on the site of his martyrdom.

As the largest basilica in Greece, its immense interior cannot fail to inspire awe. Amid the multicoloured marble columns and vast extents of off-white plaster, six small surviving **mosaics**, mostly on the columns flanking the altar, make an easy focal point. Of these, four date back to the church's second reconstruction after the fire of 620. The astonishing seventh-century mosaic of *Áyios Dhimítrios Flanked by the Church's Two Founders*, on the inside of the south (right-hand) pier beside the steps to the crypt, and the adjacent mosaics of *Áyios Sérgios* and *Áyios Dhimítrios with a Deacon*, contrast well with their contemporary on the north column, a warm and humane mosaic of the saint with two young children.

The **crypt** contains the *martyrion* of the saint – probably an adaptation of the Roman baths in which he was imprisoned – and a whole exhibit of beautifully carved column capitals, labelled in Greek only and arrayed around a seven-columned fountain and collecting basin.

Áno Póli (Upper Town)

Above Odhós Kassándhrou, the street parallel to Ayíou Dhimitríou, rises the **Upper Town** or **Áno Póli**, the main surviving quarter of Ottoman Thessaloníki. Although

BYZANTINE CHURCHES

Almost all Thessaloníki's Byzantine churches are in the central districts or on the slopes heading up towards the Upper Town. Under the Turks, most of the buildings were converted for use as mosques, a process that obscured many of their original features and destroyed the majority of their frescoes and mosaics. Further damage came with the 1917 fire and, more recently, with the 1978 earthquake. Restoration seems a glacially slow process, meaning that many sanctuaries remain locked. Nevertheless, those below are all worth a visit and free to enter.

One of the most central is the eleventh-century **Panayía Halkéon** church (daily 7.30am–noon), a classic though rather unimaginative example of the "cross-in-square" form, nestling at the lush southwestern corner of Platía Dhikastiríon. Its interior contains fragmentary frescoes in the cupola and some fine icons.

Several blocks east, and tucked away just out of sight, north of Egnatía, is the restored, fifth-century, three-aisled basilica of **Panayía Ahiropíitos** (daily 7am–noon & 4.30–6.30pm), the oldest church in the city. It features arcades, monolithic columns and highly elaborate capitals – a popular development begun under Theodosius. Only the mosaics inside the arches survive; they depict birds, fruits and vegetation, in a rich Alexandrian style.

Around Áyios Dhimítrios (see p.280) are several more churches, which are utterly different in feel. To the west along Ayíou Dhimitríou is the church of **Dhódheka Apóstoli** (daily 8.30am–noon & 4–6pm), built in the twelfth century under the bold Renaissance influence of Mystra. Its five domes rise in perfect symmetry above walls of fine brickwork, while inside are glorious fourteenth-century mosaics, among the last executed in the Byzantine Empire. High up in the arches to the south, west and north of the dome respectively are a *Nativity*, an *Entry into Jerusalem*, a *Resurrection* and a *Transfiguration*.

A short climb up Ayías Sofías is **Ósios Dhavíd** (Mon–Sat 9am–noon & 4–6pm), a tiny fifth-century church on Odhós Timothéou. It doesn't really fit into any architectural progression, since the Ottomans demolished much of the building when converting it to a mosque. However, it has arguably the finest mosaic in the city, depicting a clean-shaven Christ Emmanuel appearing in a vision, with the four Rivers of Paradise, replete with fish, flowing beneath and lapping the feet of the prophets Ezekiel and Habakkuk.

Further east in Kástra, on Irodhótou, is fourteenth-century **Áyios Nikólaos Orfanós** (Tues–Sun 8.30am–2.45pm), a diminutive, much-altered basilica; the imaginative and well-preserved frescoes inside are the most accessible and expressive in the city. It also houses the unusual *Áyion Mandílion*, an image of Christ's head superimposed on a legendary Turin-style veil sent to an ancient king of Anatolian Edessa.

4

the streets here have long been swamped by new apartment buildings, they remain ramshackle and atmospheric, a labyrinth of timber-framed houses and winding steps.

Byzantine ramparts

Many of the older houses here have been bought up and restored, and it is justifiably one of the city's favourite after-dark destinations. Sections of the fourteenth-century **Byzantine ramparts**, constructed with brick and rubble on top of old Roman foundations, crop up all around the northern part of town. The best-preserved portion begins at a large circular keep, the Trigónion or **Chain Tower** (so called for its encircling ornamental moulding), in the northeast angle where the easterly city walls veer west. A much smaller circuit of walls rambles around the district of **Eptapýrgio** (Seven Towers), enclosing the old eponymous acropolis at the top end. For centuries, it served as the city's **prison** until abandoned as too inhumane in 1989; it is described as a sort of Greek Devil's Island in a number of plaintive old songs entitled *Yedi Küle*, the Turkish name for Eptapýrgio.

Jewish Museum

Ayíou Miná 11 • Mon–Fri 10am–3pm, Wed also 5–8pm, Sun 10am–2pm • €3 • ☎ 2310 250 406, ⊕ jmth.gr

Way down in the Bazaar quarter, an early twentieth-century house, which once belonged to a Jewish family, has been beautifully renovated to accommodate

THE JEWS OF THESSALONÍKI

In the early sixteenth century, after virtually all the Jews were **expelled** from Spain and Portugal, nearly half of the inhabitants of Thessaloníki, over eighty thousand people, were Jewish. For them "Salonik" or "Salonicco" ranked as a "Mother of Israel" and the community dominated the city's commercial, social and cultural life for some four hundred years, mostly tolerated by the Ottoman authorities, but often resented by the Greeks. The first waves of Jewish **emigration** to Palestine, western Europe and the United States began after World War I. Numbers had dropped to fewer than sixty thousand at the onset of World War II, during which all but a tiny fraction were **deported** from Platía Eleftherías to the concentration camps and immediate gassing. The vast Jewish **cemeteries** east of the city centre, among the world's largest, were desecrated in 1944; to add insult to injury, the area was later covered over by the new university and expanded trade-fair grounds in 1948. Thessaloníki's only surviving pre-Holocaust **synagogue** is the Monastiriótou at Syngroú 35, which has an imposing, if austere, facade; it's usually open for Friday-evening and Saturday-morning worship. At the very heart of the former Jewish district sprawls the Modhiáno, the still-functioning central meat, fish and produce **market**, named after the wealthy Jewish Modiano family which long owned it.

the impressive **Jewish Museum**. On the ground floor are a few precious remains and some moving photographic documentation of the city's Jewish **cemetery**, which contained half a million graves until it was vandalized by the Nazis. One outstanding item is a marble Roman **stele** from the third century, recycled as a Jewish tombstone for a member of the post-1492 Sephardic community from Iberia. In the middle of the courtyard is a finely sculpted fountain that once stood in a city synagogue. Upstairs, a well-presented **exhibition**, clearly labelled in Greek and English, traces the history of the Jewish presence from around 140 BC to the present day, and displays some of the few religious and secular items that miraculously survived the 1917 fire and the Holocaust.

The port-side museums

If you cross busy Koundouriótou, the harbour-end extension of Níkis, to the city's **port**, through Gate A, you'll find a set of dockside warehouses that have been converted into the city's latest arts complex, complete with bars and, bizarrely, a kindergarten. Sharing the same warehouse as the hermetic Cinema Museum, only of interest to Greek film buffs, is the outstanding **Museum of Photography** (Tues–Thurs, Sat & Sun 11am–7pm, Fri 11am–10pm; €2; ☎2310 566 716, ⓦwww.thmphoto.gr), which stages exhibitions by Greek and international photographers. Across the road in an unprepossessing breeze-block bunker, the **Thessaloniki Center of Contemporary Art** (Tues–Fri 10am–6pm, Sat & Sun 11am–7pm; €3; ☎2310 546 683, ⓦcact.gr) hosts exhibitions of paintings, often related to the city and its history.

Folk & Ethnological Museum of Macedonia

Vasilíssis Ólgas 68 • Mon, Tues, Fri–Sun 9am–3.30pm, Wed 9am–9pm • €2 • ☎2310 830 591, ⓦlemmth.gr • Buses #5, #6, #8 & #78

In the southeast of the city, the **Folk & Ethnological museum** is housed in the elegant early twentieth-century mansion of the **Modiano** family, one of several Jewish-built residences in the district. It is one of the best of its kind in Greece, with well-written commentaries (English and Greek) accompanying temporary exhibitions on housing, costumes, day-to-day work and crafts.

ARRIVAL AND DEPARTURE

THESSALONÍKI

By plane Thessaloníki "Makedonia" airport (☎ 2310 985 000, ⓦ thessalonikiairport.com) is 15km south of the city centre. City bus #78 (€2) shuttles from the airport to the KTEL bus terminal via the town centre all day (1–2 hourly), and #78N goes once an hour through the night. A taxi ride into town costs nearly €20, including extras (see p.35). There are numerous flight connections with major European cities and destinations all over Greece.

Domestic destinations Athens (13–15 daily; 50min); Haniá (Chania), Crete (1–2 daily; 1hr 30min); Híos (10 weekly; 1hr 10min); Iráklio (Heraklion), Crete (2–3 daily; 1hr 15min); Kalamáta (4 weekly; 1hr 10min); Kos (3 weekly; 1hr 30min); Lésvos (1–2 daily; 1hr 5min); Límnos (4 weekly; 45min); Rhodes (1–2 daily; 1hr 5min–1hr 20min); Sámos (1–2 daily; 1hr 20min); Santorini (3 weekly; 1hr 5min); Skýros (2 weekly; 45min); Sýros (2 weekly; 1hr 10min).

By train The train station is on the west side of town and has convenient bus links and a taxi rank. To buy tickets or make reservations in advance, the OSE office at Aristotélous 18 (Mon–Wed 9am–6pm, Thurs & Fri 9am–9pm; Sat 9am–3.30pm) is far more central and helpful than the station ticket-windows. At the time of writing the section of line east of Thessaloníki between Dhráma and Alexandhroúpoli is closed and a bus replacement service is in operation.

Destinations Alexandhroúpoli (2 daily; 6hr 5min–6hr 35min); Athens (6 daily; 5hr 10min–6hr); Édhessa (5 daily; 1hr 20min–1hr 30min); Flórina (3 daily; 2hr 30min); Komotiní (2 daily; 5hr 20min–6hr); Lárissa (16

daily; 1hr 20min–1hr 35min); Litóhoro (10 daily; 1hr); Véria (5 daily; 45min–1hr); Xánthi (2 daily; 4hr 50min–5hr 30min).

By bus Most KTEL buses arrive at the main terminal ("Makedonia"), 3km west of the city centre at Yiannitsón 194 (☎ 2310 500 111, ⓦ ktelmacedonia.gr); local buses #1, #31 & #78 go to the train station and Egnatía. All Halkidhikí buses leave from the dedicated KTEL Halkidhikís (☎ 2310 316 555, ⓦ ktel-chalkidikis.gr), 8km east of the city; bus #45 links the two terminals via the city centre, running the length of Egnatía.

Destinations from Makedonia Alexandhroúpoli (7–10 daily; 4hr); Athens (9 daily; 7hr); Édhessa (hourly; 1hr 45min); Flórina (6 daily; 2hr 30min); Igoumenítsa (2 daily; 5hr); Ioánnina (5–6 daily; 4hr); Kalambáka (5 daily; 4hr 30min); Kastoriá (6–7 daily; 2hr 30min); Kavála (hourly; 2hr–2hr 30min); Komotiní (7 daily; 3hr 15min); Litóhoro (11–12 daily; 1hr 15min); Pélla (hourly; 1hr); Véria (every 15–30min; 1hr); Vólos (8 daily; 3hr); Xanthi (9–10 daily; 2hr 30min).

Destinations from KTEL Halkidhikí Ierissós (4–6 daily; 2hr 30min); Kassándra (various resorts; 5–9 daily; 2–3hr); Ouranoúpoli (4–6 daily; 2hr 45min); Sithonía (various resorts; 3 daily; 2hr 30min–3hr 30min).

By ferry All ferries leave from the port located at the western end of the seafront. The most convenient agent is Ferry Traveller, inside the domestic passenger terminal (Mon–Fri 9am–6pm, Sat 10am–3pm; ☎ 2310 500 800, ⓦ ferrytraveller.gr). Destinations Daily June to mid-Sept: Skiáthos (2hr 30min), Skópelos (3hr) and Alónissos (3hr 30min).

INFORMATION

Information The helpful city tourist kiosk is on Platía Aristotélous (Mon–Fri: summer 9am–9pm; winter

9am–4.30pm; ☎ 2310 229 070), or try the useful website ⓦ saloniki.org.

GETTING AROUND

By bus The local bus system (ⓦ oasth.gr) is very comprehensive and user-friendly; many kiosks (*períptera*) sell single-ride tickets for €1, while a €1.20 ticket allows multiple transfers for up to 90min; each ticket type costs €0.10 extra from machines on board; a 24hr pass costs €3. Useful lines include #10 and #11, both of which ply the length of Egnatía/Karamanlí. From Platía Eleftherías, just behind the seafront, buses initially run east along Mitropóleos; line #5 takes you to the archeological and folklore museums, and #23 heads north through Kástra to the highest quarter, known as Eptapýrgio.

By taxi Taxis are plentiful and reliable; an average trip across the town centre will cost around €5.

By car It's best to use the attended fee-parking area that occupies all of Platía Eleftherías, where you pay on

exit. Otherwise, finding a kerbside space is tough, even in the suburbs; most city-centre street parking costs €1.50/hr, Mon–Fri 8am–8pm and Sat 8am–3pm – buy stripcards from a *períptero*. Nearly all streets are one way. Most car rental agencies are clustered near the fairgrounds and archeological museum on Angeláki, which is a good place to compare prices. The leading multinationals here have kiosks at the airport too, but unless you have booked a cheap online deal, prices are better from local firms, such as Macedonia at no. 9 (☎ 2310 241 119, ⓦ automotorental.gr) or Avance at no. 7 (☎ 2310 279 888, ⓦ avance.gr).

By metro A metro system has been under construction for years but the first section seems unlikely to be in operation before 2020, due to the economic climate and numerous archeological finds.

ACCOMMODATION

During the **International Trade Fair** (Sept) hotels add a twenty percent surcharge to the standard rate. This being a business-oriented city low season is June–Aug.

HOTELS
WESTERN EGNATÍA AREA

Atlantis Egnatía 14 ☎ 2310 540 131, ⓦ atlantishotel .com.gr. Old-style joint with high ceilings and period decor. Some of the newly furnished rooms still have shared bathrooms, and the ones at the back are the best deals. **€35**

★**Augustos** Ptoleméon 1 ☎ 2310 522 550, ⓦ augustos.gr. Charmingly renovated, welcoming 1920s hotel with arty decor, on a quiet corner near Egnatía; all the rooms have high ceilings and there is a spacious breakfast-lounge-cum-bar. **€40**

Kinissi Palace Egnatía 41 ☎ 2310 508 081, ⓦ kinissipalace.gr. The smartest hotel in the area, *Kinissi Palace* offers comfortable rooms with all mod cons but cramped bathrooms and noisy a/c. There's a sauna, hammam and massage service, plus a bar and a decent restaurant, the *Averof*. Breakfast included. **€60**

Nea Metropolis Syngroú 22 ☎ 2310 546 097, ⓦ www .neametropolis.gr. Relatively quiet for its location, this hotel is clean, reasonable value and well maintained; the smallish rooms are brightly furnished with fridges and quality TVs. Good online deals. **€45**

Pella Íonos Dhragoúmi 63 ☎ 2310 524 222, ⓦ pella-hotel.gr. A tall, narrow, modern hotel on a moderately quiet street, with pleasant, impeccably clean minimalist rooms and modern if smallish bathrooms. **€36**

The Tobacco Hotel (Davitel) Ayíou Dhimitríou 25 ☎ 2310 515 002, ⓦ davitel.gr. This former tobacco warehouse has sleek double-glazed rooms with contemporary decor and efficient a/c; complimentary breakfasts are served in a designer-rustic mezzanine salon. **€75**

REST OF THE CITY

The Bristol Hotel Oplopíou 2 ☎ 2310 506 500, ⓦ bristol.gr. Thessaloníki's original boutique hotel, with twenty period-furnished rooms and suites, in an impeccably restored 1870 building. There's a good Argentinian restaurant, and a lavish buffet breakfast is included. Best deals are online. **€120**

Egnatia Palace Egnatía 61 ☎ 2310 222 900, ⓦ egnatiapalace.gr. A smart hotel in a modern building with some Art Deco flourishes, *Egnatia Palace* has spacious rooms where the modish decor ranges from kitsch to stylish. There's a spa, and breakfast is included. Good summer deals. **€70**

Electra Palace Platía Aristotélous 9 ☎ 2310 294 000, ⓦ electrahotels.gr. In one of the town's most prestigious locations, and as palatial inside as out, this five-star hotel has large, lavishly furnished rooms and a good restaurant, albeit with a slightly dated air. **€140**

★**Excelsior** Mitropóleos 23 ☎ 2310 021 020, ⓦ excelsiorhotel.gr. Smart yet friendly boutique hotel in a lovely building with Neoclassical features, and lavishly furnished rooms. An outstanding buffet breakfast on the top floor is included, while a ground floor restaurant is also excellent. Good online deals. **€112**

Le Palace Tsimiskí 12 ☎ 2310 257 400, ⓦ lepalace .gr. Art Deco hotel whose stylish rooms are spacious and very comfortable. The lovely common areas include a mezzanine lounge and ground floor café and restaurant: a lavish buffet breakfast is included. Big online discounts. **€55**

EATING

There is a wealth of interesting places to eat in Thessaloníki, from authentic tavernas and eclectic ouzerís or *tsipourádhika* to quite sophisticated international restaurants. Areas particularly worth investigating are trendy **Ladhádhika**, near the port, and the web of streets between **Syngroú** and **Platía Athónos**. All the places listed are within walking distance, though to reach **Áno Póli** you can take the handy #23 bus. Check out ⓦ foodfestival.thessaloniki.gr for a list of restaurants that offer a €10 fixed menu on Tuesday evenings.

CITY CENTRE

Aristotelous Aristotélous 8 ☎ 2310 230 762. Tucked off the road behind wrought-iron gates, this stylish ouzerí with its fine, arcaded interior and courtyard specializes in excellent mezédhes for €4–10. Great *tsípouro*, too. Daily noon–1am; closed Sun pm and 1 week mid-Aug.

★**Bakalikon** Platía Navarínou 7 ☎ 2310 227 676, ⓦ mpakalikon.gr. With indoor and outdoor seating in a quiet corner of the square, this place does a good range of mezédes like cheese croquettes and main courses, both grilled and oven cooked. Fixed price €10 menu on Tues. Daily 11am–1am.

★**Iy Gonia tou Merakli** Avyerinoú 8 ☎ 2310 287 726. Inexpensive seafood, larger than average portions, a quality free dessert and highly palatable barrelled wine make this the best of several ouzerís in the atmospheric alleys around Platía Áthonos. Mezé plus drink deals for €4. Mon–Sat noon–2am.

Kamares Platía Ayíou Yeoryíou 11, by the Rotónda ☎ 2310 219 686. Excellent seafood, salads and grilled meat for €6–8, washed down by bulk wine from Límnos. In summer, you can sit outdoors beside the park. Daily 10am–1am, Sun till 6pm.

Krasodhikio Filíppou 18 ☎ 2310 239 031, ⓦ krasodikio .gr. A fine ouzerí serving a range of ample meat and seafood meals, as well as mezédhes, on the pavement in summer or in the cosy interior when it's cold. Usually has a great unlimited-food-and-drink menu for only €13. Daily noon–1.15am.

Molyvos Kapodhistríou 1 ☎ 2310 555 952, ⓦ molyvos .gr. Specialities from Crete, Lesvos, Cyclades and Istanbul mostly cost under €10 at this first-floor taverna-ouzerí, with an attached shop selling ouzo and olive oils. Daily noon–1am.

Rodi & Meli Eyíptou 5 ☎ 2310 521 952, ⓦ rodimeli.gr. Apart from the juicy lamb chops, steaks and some of the seafood, most items are under €10 at this sleek new Ladádika restaurant, which looks more expensive than it is. Extensive winelist available. Daily 11am–1am.

Sofis House Andigonídhon 4 ☎ 2310 525 501, ⓦ sofishouse.gr. Brightly lit and cavernous *estiatório* with two levels indoors and limited pavement seating. Oven dishes, such as beef in a rich tomato sauce, (around €5–7) feature strongly on the menu, plus there are grills and *souvláki*. Daily 10am–midnight.

Ta Bakaliarakia tou Aristou Katoúni 3, Ladhádhika ☎ 2310 542 906. Heaps of cod and chips, served on grease-proof paper for around €6–7, make this joint, in a pedestrianized port-side alley, quite memorable. There's a second branch one block away at Fasianoú 2. Daily 9am–7.30pm.

To Dhikty Dhímitsa 18, Platía Áthonos ☎ 2310 267 063, ⓦ todixti.gr. This popular spot, which bills itself as a traditional Voliot *tsipourádhiko*, specializes in seafood recipes such as *soupiés* (made with cuttlefish) for around €8.50, plus a wide range of other mezédhes. Fixed price €10 menu on Tues. Daily 11am–2am.

★**Tsarouhas** Olýmbou 78 ☎ 2310 271 621. Reputedly the best and certainly the most famous of the city's *patsatzídhika* (tripe restaurants), these guys churn out rich tripe-and-trotter soup for €8, as well as lots of other tasty *mayireftá* (casserole-type dishes) and Anatolian puddings. Fixed price €10 menu on Tues. 24hr; closed mid-July to mid-Aug.

Zythos Platía Katoúni 5, Ladhádhika ☎ 2310 540 284, ⓦ zithos.gr. Imaginative Greek cuisine is on offer here, mostly around €9, though the delicious *hungar begendi* (beef ragout with aubergine purée) goes for €13. Also has an excellent selection of wines and beers. Reservations recommended at weekends. Daily: food noon–9.30pm, drinks 10am–2am.

ÁNO PÓLI

Kreonidis Leofóros Óhi 4 ☎ 2310 206 006, ⓦ kreonidis .gr. This *psistariá* and ouzerí has tables overlooking the city and sea, where you can eat grills or mezédhes for under €10 while enjoying the splendid view from the balcony. Daily noon–1am.

Ladhokolla me Thea Kýprou 2 ☎ 2310 210 805. The popular practice of eating chunks of pork or lamb on greaseproof paper for €7–8, or much cheaper *souvláki*, is the way to go in this otherwise smart Áno Póli taverna. Tues–Sun noon–midnight.

★**O Volos sta…Kastra!** Gravías 1 ☎ 2310 210 819. A range of dips, salads, meats and fish, as well as seafood risotto and shrimp spaghetti (€12), can be enjoyed here, along with organic Cretan wine, ouzo or *tsípouro*. Mon–Thurs 2pm–midnight, Fri–Sun noon–midnight.

To Makedhoniko Y Papadhopoúlou 32, Sykiés ☎ 6940 993 850. Tucked inside the western city gate, this old-fashioned taverna with a triangular courtyard serves an excellent but limited range of grills, dips, salads and barrelled retsina. Stuff yourself and drink merrily for little over €10 per head. Live music on Fri & Sat evenings. Tues–Sun noon–midnight.

NIGHTLIFE

Apart from the almost unbroken line of expensive café-bars on the seafront road, **Leofóros Níkis**, and around **Platía Aristotélous**, the most fashionable nightlife is to be found in **Ladhádhika**, near the port. Bustling **Platía Navarínou** and the nearby pedestrianized streets, **Iktínou** and **Zefxídhou**, also contain some of the trendiest establishments in the city. During the warmer months, action mostly shifts to various glitzy, barn-like establishments lining the coast road out to **Kalamariá**, for which you'll need to take taxis.

★**Blue Barrel** Dhóxis 5, Ladhádhika ☎ 2314 009 130, ⓦ bluebarrel.gr. This joint is now one of the most popular places in town for live jazz, rock and blues, with a cool and fairly spacious interior and excellent sound system. Daily 9pm–late.

Caramelo Polytekhníou 14, Ladhádhika ☎ 6980 112 600. For an unabashed old-style rose-throwing live Greek experience, this *skyládhiko* is worth a try, though a bottle of whiskey costs €70 and wine €30. Daily 10pm–late.

Dizzy Dolls Eyíptou 5, Ladhádhika ☎ 2310 544 874. Full-on rock and goth sounds abound in this lively bar where instruments hang from sturdy wooden beams and Guinness and other beers are on tap. Daily 9pm–late.

★**The Hoppy Pub** Nikifórou Foká 6 ☎ 2310 269 203. Cosy and wonderful pub with a gentle rock vibe: it's run by a real ale expert, who ensures there is always a fantastic range of Greek and imported microbrews on tap, plus a huge stock of bottles. Daily 8.30am–2.30am.

Kitchen Bar Warehouse B, 2nd Port ☎ 2310 502 241. This cavernous warehouse conversion is now a top hangout, with a hi-tech indoor space and breezy seafront terrace that has sweeping city views as you sip a cocktail, eat a full-blown meal or just relax with a coffee. Daily 10am–2am.

Kourdhisto Gourouni Ayías Sofías 31 ☎ 2310 274 672. Several foreign brews are on tap and a bewildering range of bottled beers is available at this stylish bar, whose name means "Clockwork Pig"; there's indoor and outdoor seating

and a rather expensive food menu. Daily 11am–2am.

Old School Bar Orvílou 4, Ladhádhika ☎ 6982 749 597. Cracking place for proper "old school" hard rock in a friendly atmosphere created by people hell bent on having fun. Daily 9pm–3am.

★ **Pasta Flora Darling!** Zefxídhou 6 ☎ 2310 261 518. This small, crowded student favourite retains touches of eccentricity in its decor, with the odd gnome and abstract painting; good cocktails and vegetarian snacks too. Daily 10am–2am.

ENTERTAINMENT

THEATRE

Moní Lazaristón Kolokotróni 25, Stavroúpoli ☎ 2310 652 020, ⓦ monilazariston.gr. This arts complex and theatre was converted from a deconsecrated Catholic monastery. It's 2km north of the centre along Langadhá; buses #34 and #38 go there from Platía Dhikastiríon.

Mylos Andhréou Yeoryíou 56 ☎ 2310 551 836, ⓦ mylos. gr. A multifunctional cultural complex housed in an old flour mill some way west of the centre. Here you'll find a couple of bars, a live jazz café, a popular *tsipourádhiko*, a summer cinema, a theatre, concert halls and exhibition galleries.

State Theatre of Northern Greece Multiple venues ☎ 2315 200 000, ⓦ ntng.gr. Hosts winter events at Etería Makedhonikón Spoudhón or the ultramodern Vassilikó Théatro, both near the White Tower. In summer, things move to a number of outdoor venues: the Théatro Kípou, near the Archeological Museum; well up the hill at the

Théatro Dhássous, in the pines east of the upper town, with events from late June to mid-Sept; or the Théatro Damári in Triandhría district.

CINEMA

Thessaloníki is a cinephile city, never more so than during its annual film festival (ⓦ www.filmfestival.gr) in early Nov, and while open-air cinemas are now thin on the ground, they are worth seeking out in summer. Listings are given in the local papers, if your Greek can manage it.

Indoor cinemas Central ones include: Aristotelion, Ethnikís Ámynas 2 (☎ 2310 262 051); Kolosseon, V Olgas 150 (☎ 2310 834 996); Makedhonikon, cnr Ethnikís Ámynas and A Svólou (☎ 2310 261 727); and Olympion 1, Platía Aristotélous 10 (☎ 2310 378 404).

Summer open-air cinemas Aigli, outside the Yeni Hammam at Ayíou Nikoláou 3 (☎ 2310 270 016); and Natali, Megálou Alexándhrou 3 (☎ 2310 829 457).

SHOPPING

Ayioritiki Estia Egnatía 109 ☎ 2310 263 308, ⓦ agioritikiestia.gr. There are some books in English and lots of great Orthodox paraphenalia at this shop in front of the Mount Athos Pilgrims' Bureau (see p.309). Mon & Wed 9am–4pm, Tues, Thurs & Fri 9am–8pm, Sat 9am–2pm.

Bravos Egnatía 43 ☎ 2310 525 223, ⓦ bravossound.gr. This is the place to buy your *bouzoúki* or choose from a range of other quality traditional instruments. Mon–Fri 10am–7.30pm, Sat 10am–2pm.

Studio 52 D Goúnari 46 ☎ 2310 279 688, ⓦ www .studio52.gr. Basement shop packed to the gills with CDs and some vinyl, including a comprehensive range of all Greek genres and a fair bit of international stuff too. Mon, Wed & Sat 9.30am–4pm, Tues, Thurs & Fri 9.30am–9pm.

Traveller Proxénou Koromilá 48 ☎ 2310 275 215, ⓦ traveler.gr. Plenty of travel books in English, as well as maps and gifts. Mon–Fri 10am–3pm, Tues, Thurs & Fri also 5.30–9pm, Sat 10am–4pm.

DIRECTORY

Consulates Australia (Fragón 13; ☎ 2310 553 355); Canada (N Koundouriótou 19; ☎ 2310 256 350); Ireland (Platía Aristotélous 5; ☎ 2310 465 177); South Africa (Tsimiskí 51; ☎ 2310 489 386); UK (Tsimiskí 43; ☎ 2310 278 006); US (Tsimiskí 43, 7th floor; ☎ 2310 242 905).

Exchange For changing notes, use the 24hr automatic exchange machine at the National Bank on Platía Aristotélous 6.

Football Thessaloníki's biggest team is PAOK, whose stadium is in the east of the city at Toúmba, but the fans have a bad

reputation for violence. Its two big rivals are Aris, who play in Hariláou, also east of the centre, and Iraklis, whose Kaftantzoglou stadium is both the largest and most central.

Hospitals For minor trauma, use the Yeniko at Ethnikís Amynis 41 (☎ 2313 308 100); otherwise, head for the Ippokratio at Konstandinopóleos 49 (☎ 2313 312 000), in the eastern part of town.

Police The tourist police (daily 8am–2pm plus Tues, Thurs & Fri 5–9pm; ☎ 2310 554 871) are at Dhodhekaníssou 4, off Platía Dhimokratías.

THE FIRE-WALKERS OF LANGADHÁS

On May 21, the feast day of SS Constantine and Helen, villagers at **Langadhás**, 20km north of Thessaloníki, perform a ritual barefoot dance across a bed of burning coals known as the **anastenária**. While it has been suggested that they are remnants of a Dionysiac cult, devotees fiercely assert a purely **Christian tradition**. This seems to relate to a **fire**, around 1250, in the Thracian village of Kostí (now in Bulgaria), from where many of the inhabitants of Langadhás originate. Holy icons were heard groaning from the flames and were rescued by villagers, who emerged miraculously unburnt from the blazing church. The icons, passed down by their families, are believed to ensure protection during the fire walking. Equally important is piety and purity of heart: it is said that no one with any harboured grudges or unconfessed sins can pass through the coals unscathed.

Whatever the origin, the **rite** is still performed most years – lately as something of a tourist attraction, with an admission charge and repeat performances over the next two days. It is nevertheless eerie and impressive, beginning around 7pm with the lighting of a cone of hardwood logs. A couple of hours later, their embers are raked into a circle and, just before complete darkness, a traditional Macedonian *daoúli* drummer and two lyra players precede a group of about sixteen women and men into the arena. These *anastenáridhes* (literally "groaners"), in partial trance, then shuffle across the coals for about a quarter of an hour, somehow without requiring a trip to hospital at the end.

Post office The main branch is at V. Iraklíou 38 (Mon–Fri 7.30am–8pm, Sat 7.30am–2pm, Sun 9am–1.30pm). There are other post offices around the city: the most useful ones are at Ethnikís Amynis 9A and Ayíou Dhimitríou 98.
Travel agents Most general sales agents and consolidators cluster in the streets around Platía Eleftherías towards the port, such as Polizas Travel Services at Koundouriótou 21 (☎ 2310 521 221, ⊛ polizas.gr) or Caravel Travel Services at Leofóros Níkis 1 (☎ 2310 256 580, ⊛ caravel-travel.gr).

Pella

PELLA, 40km west of Thessaloníki, was the capital of Macedonia throughout its greatest period and the first capital of Greece after Philip II forcibly unified the country around 338 BC. It was founded some sixty years earlier by King Archelaos, who transferred the royal Macedonian court here from Aegae (see p.288). At that time it lay at the head of a broad lake, connected to the Thermaïkós gulf by a navigable river. The royal palace was decorated by the painter **Zeuxis** and was said to be the greatest artistic showplace since the time of Classical Athens. **Euripides** wrote and produced his last plays at the court, and here, too, **Aristotle** was to tutor the young Alexander the Great – born, like his father Philip II, in the city.

The site today is a worthwhile stopover en route to Édhessa and western Macedonia or as a day-trip from Thessaloníki. Its main treasures are a series of pebble **mosaics**, some in the museum, others *in situ*.

The site

Junction of the main road and the road into the village • Summer Mon noon–8pm, Tues–Sun 8am–8pm; winter Mon 11am–3pm, Tues–Sun 8am–3pm • €8 (includes museum) • ☎ 23820 32963 • Buses run here every 30min along the main Thessaloníki–Édhessa road

Today, Pella's ruins stand in the middle of a broad expanse of plain. The **site** was located by chance finds in 1957 and as yet has only been partially excavated. The **acropolis** at Pella is a low hill to the west of the modern village of Pélla. To the north of the road, at the main site, stand the low remains of a grand official building, probably a government office; it is divided into three large open courts, each enclosed by a *peristyle*, or portico (the columns of the central one have been re-erected), and bordered by wide streets with a sophisticated drainage system.

In the third court, three late fourth-century BC **mosaics** have been left in their original positions under sheltering canopies; one, a stag hunt, is complete, and is astounding in its dynamism and use of perspective. The others represent, respectively, the rape of Helen by Paris and his friends Phorbas and Theseus, and a fight between a Greek and an Amazon.

The museum

Hours same as site • €4, or €8 including site • ☎ 23820 32963

The excellent new **museum**, designed on the rectangular model of the ancient dwellings, stands up at the back of the modern village of Pélla. It showcases more spectacular **pebble mosaics** taken from the site, as well as rich grave finds from the two local necropolises, delicately worked terracotta figurines from a sanctuary of Aphrodite and Cybele, a large hoard of late Classical/early Hellenistic coins, and – on the rarely seen domestic level – metal door fittings: pivots, knocker plates and crude keys. The finds are all set within the context of life in the ancient capital, with detailed contextual displays, all of which are well translated.

Mount Olympus and around

The highest, most magical and most dramatic of all Greek mountains, **MOUNT OLYMPUS** – Ólymbos in Greek – rears straight up to 2917m from the coast and, when pollution allows, is visible from Thessaloníki, some 100km away to the northeast. Its summit was believed by the ancient Greeks to be the home of the gods, and it seems that quite a few locals still follow the old religion. Dense forests cover its lower slopes, and its **wild flowers** are unparalleled, even by Greek standards.

Climbing the mountain requires an early start (certainly pre-8am) for the three-hour ascent to Mýtikas, the highest peak, so it's best to stay overnight at one of the **refuges**. The peaks frequently cloud up by midday and you lose the view, to say nothing of the danger of catching one of Zeus's thunderbolts. Besides, nights at the refuge are fantastic: a log fire blazes, you watch the sun set on the peaks and dawn break over the Aegean, and you can usually see a multitude of stars.

ESSENTIALS   MOUNT OLYMPUS

Arrival To reach alpine Olympus, you've a choice of road or foot routes via Litóhoro (see p.282), the main village nearby. With your own vehicle, you can drive deep into the mountain along a fairly decent road, the first 11km of which is paved.

The climb To make the most of the mountain, you need to allow 2–3 days' hiking (see box, p.284), and be equipped with decent boots and warm clothing. No special expertise is necessary to get to the top in summer (mid-June to Oct), but it's a long hard pull and requires a good deal of stamina; winter climbs, of course, are another matter, with heavy snowfall adding to the challenge. At any time of year,

Olympus should be treated with respect: its weather is notoriously fickle, with sudden fogs or storms, and it regularly claims lives.

Maps and guides The best and most easily available commercial trekking map is Road Editions' *Olymbos* at 1:50,000, available from specialist map shops abroad, or in Athens and Thessaloníki; a good alternative is the same scale one that is co-produced by *Korfes* magazine. One of the other is usually available at local shops in Litóhoro. Two organizations, EOS and SEO (see p.284), can provide limited advice, as can 2917 in Thessaloníki (☎ 2310 914 654, ⓦ 2917.gr).

ACCOMMODATION AND EATING

Accommodation There are two staffed refuges on Mount Olympus (see p.284). **Meals** at both shelters are expensive, and mandatory since no cooking is allowed inside; bring more money than you think you'll need, as bad weather can ground you a day or two longer than planned. For sustenance while walking, buy food in Litóhoro, though water can wait until you're in the vicinity of the main trailhead at Priónia (see box, p.284).

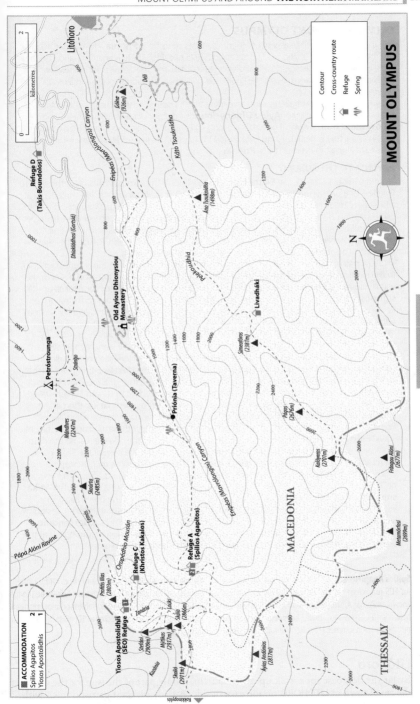

MOUNT OLYMPUS

ACCOMMODATION
Spílios Agápitos — 2
Yíosos Apostolídhis — 1

Litóhoro

Refuge D (Takís Boundólos)

Gólna (926m)
Déli

Enipéas (Mavrólongos) Canyon

Dhiakládhosi (Gortsiá)

Káto Tsoukníadha

Áno Tsoukníadha (1498m)

Petróstrounga

Old Ayíou Dhionysíou Monastery

Stavrós

Papadhiá

Mandhres (2247m)

Skoúrta (2485m)

Lemós

Priónia (Taverna)

Livadháki

Orooedhio Mousón

Skála

Zonária

Loúki

Skála (2866m)

Enipéas (Mavrólongos) Canyon

Skolió (2911m)

Mýtikas (2917m)

Stefáni (2909m)

Kazánia

Skála

Áyios Andónios (2817m)

Profítis Ilías (2803m)

Refuge C (Khrístos Kákalos)

Refuge A (Spílios Agápitos)

Yíosos Apostolídhis (SEO) Refuge

Símenfóros (2381m)

Págos (2676m)

Kalóyeros (2701m)

Frángou Alóni (2677m)

Metamórfosi (2691m)

MACEDONIA

THESSALY

Kokkinopilós

0 — kilometres — 2

Contour
Cross-country route
Refuge
Spring

N

4

CLIMBING MOUNT OLYMPUS

The main trailhead for the ascent of Mount Olympus starts from **Prió004nia** – just under 18km up the mountain on the sealed road from Litóhoro (€25 taxi ride). There is an information booth at km3, where (in high season) your nationality is recorded and you're given some literature advising you of the park rules. At the Prió004nia car park, there's a spring, toilets and a basic taverna (May–Oct).

If you're up for a real challenge and an early start, it's possible to **walk** from Litóhoro to Prió004nia via the monastery of **Ayíou Dhionysíou**. It's a delightful route (allow 4hrs) along the **E4 overland trail**, but you'll need basic hiking skills, as there are some scrambles over steep terrain and a few water crossings. From Ayíou Dhionysíou, it's just under an hour more upstream along the riverside E4 to **Prió004nia**.

PRIÓNIA TO THE SUMMIT

From the Prió004nia car park, the **E4 trail** carries on just uphill by a signpost that gives the time to *Refuge A* (see below) as two-and-a-half hours, though it actually takes more like three, even at a brisk pace. You cross a stream (last water before *Refuge A*; purification advisable) and start to climb steeply up through woods of beech and black pine. The continuation of the E4, this path is well trodden and marked: as you gain height, there are majestic views across the Enipéas (Mavrólongos) canyon to your left and to the peaks towering above you. *Refuge A* perches on the edge of an abrupt spur, surrounded by huge storm-beaten trees.

The E4 path continues behind the refuge (your final **water source** on the ascent), climbing to the left up a steep spur among the last of the trees. Ignore the initial right fork towards the usually unstaffed *Khristos Kakalos* hut (*Refuge C*), and within about an hour you'll reach a **signposted fork** above the tree line. Continuing straight on takes you across the range to Kokkinopylós village with the E4 waymarks, or with a slight deviation right to Mýtikas, via the ridge known as Kakí Skála (1hr 30min–2hr). An immediate right turn leads to the *Yiosos Apostolidhis* hut in one hour along the so-called Zonária trail, with the option after 45min of taking the very steep Loúki couloir left up to Mýtikas; if you do this, be wary of rock falls.

For the safer **Kakí Skála route**, continue up the right flank of the stony, featureless valley in front of you, with the Áyios Andónios peak up to your left. An hour's dull climb brings you to the summit ridge between the peaks of Skolió on the left and Skála on the right. You know you're there when one more step would tip you over a 500m sheer drop into the Kazánia chasm; take great care. The Kakí Skála ("Evil Stairway") begins in a narrow cleft on the right just short of the ridge; paint splashes mark the way. The route keeps just below the ridge, so you are protected from the drop into Kazánia. Even so, it's a tough scramble and not for those who don't like heights.

Kakí Skála begins with a rightward traverse to a narrow nick in the ridge revealing the drop to Kazánia – easily negotiated. Continue traversing right, skirting the base of the Skála peak, then climb leftwards up a steepish gully, made a little awkward by loose rock on sloping footholds. Bear right at the top over steep but reassuringly solid rock, and across a narrow neck. Step left around an awkward corner, and in front of you, scarcely 100m away, is **Mýtikas summit**, an airy, boulder-strewn platform with a trigonometric point, tin Greek flag and visitors' book. In reasonable conditions it's about forty minutes to the summit from the start of Kakí Skála, three hours from the refuge, or five-and-a-half hours from Prió004nia. **Descending** from Mýtikas, most climbers go back the way they came, with the option of turning left at the signpost for the *Yiosos Apostolidhis* hut (2hr 30min from Mýtikas by this route).

Spilios Agapitos ☎ 23520 81800, ⓦ mountolympus.gr. An EOS-run refuge, at an altitude of 2100m, commonly known as *Refuge A*, sleeping over 100. You can also camp here, with access to their bathroom. Reservations recommended in summer. May–Oct. Bunk **€10**, camping **€5**

Yiosos Apostolidhis ☎ 2310 224 710, ⓦ bit.ly/1IUAeJi. The SEO-managed hut at 2700m is open July–Sept, though its glassed-in porch is always available for climbers in need. Lights-out and outer door locked at 10pm, so bring a torch. Bunk **€10**

Litóhoro

By far the best base for a walk up the mountain, if only part of the way for the views, is the small town of **LITÓHORO** on the eastern side. A fairly pleasant garrison town with two huge army camps on the approach road, its setting, in good weather, affords intoxicating vistas into the heart of the range. Facilities have also improved greatly in recent years, as it has become a popular weekend getaway for Thessalonians.

ARRIVAL AND DEPARTURE

LITÓHORO

By train The train station is 5km away, down by the motorway, where you'll find taxis sometimes waiting, or you can walk 500m and pick up a bus just west of the motorway. There are regular trains to and from Thessaloníki (10 daily; 1hr).

By bus The KTEL bus station is at the central platía. Destinations Kateríni (hourly; 30min); Thessaloníki (11–12 daily; 1hr 15min).

By car Litóhoro has its own turn-off from the main Athens–Thessaloníki motorway, and ample street parking.

ACCOMMODATION

Enipeas Enipeos 2, behind the Xenios Dias ☎ 6932 952 511, ⊛ hotel-enipeas.gr. This beautifully situated hotel is welcoming and spotlessly clean. The upper rear rooms have fine views, while attic rooms (with skylight only) are cheaper. **€40**

Nireas Varikó Beach ☎ 23520 61290. One of two campsites on Varikó beach, *Nireas* offers shady pitches and decent shared facilities, including a restaurant and bar. June–Sept. **€12**

Olympus Mediterranean Dhionýsou 5 ☎ 23520 81831, ⊛ mediterraneanhotels.gr. Boasting a smart lobby in modernist style, a posh restaurant and twenty beautifully refurbished rooms, this is the town's most upmarket option. Breakfast included. **€99**

Summit Zero Gríitsa ☎ 23520 61406, ⊛ summitzero .gr. Set right on the beach, 5km from Litóhoro, this friendly family-run hostel has bunk beds for twenty people (split over four rooms) and spotless shared facilities. Dorm **€15**

Xenios Dias On the main square ☎ 23520 81234, ⊛ hotel-xeniosdias.gr. With views to equal those of the *Enipeas*, this place has smarter rooms, and a full bar in the fancy lobby. Breakfast included. **€65**

★**Xenonas Papanikolaou** N E Kítrous 1, signposted 100m from the square ☎ 23520 81236, ⊛ xenonas-papanikolaou.gr. Very central, but tucked in a quiet side street, this friendly and excellently appointed hostel has modernized, yet traditionally decorated rooms with a/c, central heating and cable TV. Superb value. **€45**

EATING AND DRINKING

★**Gastrodromio "En Olymbo"** Ayíou Nikoláou 36 ☎ 23520 21300, ⊛ gastrodromio.gr. Main courses such as rabbit or wild boar with plums cost €8–30 at this smart restaurant, while starters (€5–6) include dishes like chickpeas with mushrooms. Fine wine list, too. Daily 12.30–11.30pm.

Meze Meze Ayíou Nikoláou 40 ☎ 23520 82721. Bright and colourfully decorated restaurant serving a range of tasty mezédhes and some baked items, such as lamb with potatoes and cuttlefish in wine sauce (€8.50). Daily noon–11.30pm.

Neromylos Start of Enipéas canyon ☎ 23520 84141. The food at this lovely riverside spot is solid taverna

fare, with salads, dips and grills, all under €10, but the spectacular setting is unsurpassed. May–Sept daily 11am–11pm; Oct–April Fri–Sun only.

Papa Steve Pub Start of Enipéas canyon ☎ 23520 82118, ⊛ papasteve.gr. Since opening in 2015, this cosy bar in a lovely stone building has become the locals' favourite hangout for the inexpensive drinks and decent rock music. Daily noon–2am; Sat & Sun only in winter.

★**Pazari** Platía 3-Martíou ☎ 23520 82540. Extremely friendly ouzerí serving locally caught octopus and squid, as well as other fish and various mezédhes for around €5–7. Shows footie on TV too. Daily noon–midnight.

Dion

Ancient **DION**, in the foothills of Mount Olympus, outside the modern village of **Dhíon**, was the Macedonians' sacred city. At this site – a harbour before the river mouth silted up – the kingdom maintained its principal sanctuaries: to Zeus (from which the name Dion, or Dios, is derived) above all, but also to Demeter, Artemis, Asklepios and, later on, to foreign gods such as the Egyptian Isis and Serapis. Philip II and Alexander both came to sacrifice to Zeus here before their expeditions and battles. **Inscriptions** found at the sanctuaries referring to boundary disputes, treaties and other affairs of state suggest that the political and social importance of the city's festivals exceeded a purely Macedonian domain.

Most exciting for visitors, however, are the finds of **mosaics, temples and baths** that have been excavated since 1990 – work that remains in progress whenever funds allow.

These are not quite on a par with the Vergina tombs (see p.289), but still rank among the major discoveries of ancient Macedonian culture.

The site

Daily: April–Oct 8am–7pm; Nov–March 8am–3pm • €8, including the museum • ☎ 23510 53484, ⓦ ancientdion.org

The integrity of the **site** and its finds is due to the nature of the city's demise. At some point in the fifth century AD, a series of earthquakes prompted an evacuation of Dion, which was then swallowed up by a mudslide from the mountain. The place is still quite waterlogged, and constant pumping against the local aquifer is necessary; indeed the surrounding frog ponds and grazing geese lend it a delightfully bucolic air. The main visible excavations are of the vast **public baths** complex and, outside the city walls, the **sanctuaries** of Demeter and Aphrodite-Isis. In the latter, a small temple has been unearthed, along with its cult statue – a copy of which remains *in situ*. Two Christian **basilicas** attest to the town's later years as a Byzantine bishopric in the fourth and fifth centuries AD. An observation platform allows you to view the layout of the site more clearly.

The museum

Tues–Sun: April–Oct 8am–7pm; Nov–March 8.30am–3pm • €4, €8 including the site • ☎ 23510 53206, ⓦ ancientdion.org

In Dhíon village, the well-laid-out and refurbished **museum** houses most of the finds. In the basement, there are fascinating displays on **daily life**, including many tools and household goods such as pottery. The ground floor features **sculptures**, perfectly preserved by the mud, accompanied by various tombstones and altars. Finds from the villa of Dionysos are highlighted upstairs, along with the finest **mosaics** yet discovered at the site, including one of Medusa.

ARRIVAL AND DEPARTURE

DION

By bus Dhíon is 7km inland from Litóhoro beach and can be reached by #14 bus from Kateríni.

By car A direct, signposted, paved road links Dion to Litóhoro (see p.284), around 10km away.

ACCOMMODATION

Safetis Apartments 100m from the museum ☎ 23510 46272, ⓦ safetis.gr. Smart, comfortable studios of different sizes are available in this modern place with a leafy courtyard. Breakfast included. **€60**

Véria and Vergina

West of Thessaloníki, **VÉRIA** (ancient Berrhoea or Berea) is one of the more interesting northern Greek communities, thanks to its mixed Jewish, Muslim and Christian heritage. In the nineteenth century, the town became an important industrial centre, growing prosperous from flour and sesame milling as well as hide tanning. The pleasant modern town boasts an excellent new Byzantine Museum and a smattering of appealing religious edifices. There are also enough facilities to make it a reasonable base for visits to the excavations of ancient Aegae at **Vergina**.

The Archeological Museum

Leofóros Aníxeos 47 • Tues–Sun 8.30am–3pm • €2 • ☎ 23310 24972

Véria's modest **Archeological Museum** has three rooms on a single floor. Two of these display finds from the **Hellenistic** period: funerary relics in the shape of vases, weapons and jewellery are in the first, and sculptures, inscriptions and figurines in the second. The third room is devoted to sculptures and other remains from the **Roman** period, while the garden at the back has an impressive array of columns.

Byzantine Museum

Thomaïdhos 26 • Tues–Sun: April–Oct 8am–5pm; Nov–March 9am–5pm • €2 • ☎ 23310 25847

Véria's outstanding **Byzantine Museum** is housed in a beautifully restored nineteenth-century flour mill. It mostly comprises an exquisite display of icons – Véria was renowned for its painting workshops in the late Middle Ages – along with other treasures mainly from the Byzantine era, including coins. On the ground floor, a highly moving video, with English subtitles, records the history of the mill, its demise and its exemplary refurbishment.

Barboúta

What remains of the old **bazaar** straddles central Kendrikís, while downhill and to the west tumbles the riverside Ottoman quarter of **Barboúta** (aka Barboúti). Largely **Jewish** before the 1944 deportations annihilated the thousand-strong community, it is today being gentrified. The disused **synagogue** can be reached via Odhós Dhekátis Merarhías, past the conspicuous officers' club near Platía Oroloyíou. Situated on a plaza with a small amphitheatre, it is a long stone building with an awning over the door, which is sometimes left ajar, allowing you to look at the rambling, arcaded interior. One of the many handsome nineteenth-century mansions hereabouts, the impeccably restored **Arhondikó Béka**, currently houses the International Institute of Traditional Architecture.

Muslim Véria

Survivals of the **Muslim** presence in Véria are more numerous and conspicuous, but in a poor state of preservation, and you can't go inside them. Nevertheless, it is worth hunting down the twin hammam complex, **Dhídhymi Loutrónes**, at the end of Loutroú, the small **Ortá Tzamí** mosque just off Kendrikís, and the splendid **Medresé Tzamí** mosque on Márkou Bótsari.

Vergina

Daily: April–Oct 8am–8pm; Nov–March 9am–5pm • €12 • No photography • ☎ 23310 92347 • Bus from Véria (4–8 daily; 20min); parking around the site costs €1.50

One of Greece's most memorable attractions, **VERGINA**, 16km southeast of Véria, was the site of **Aegae**, the original **Macedonian royal capital** before its shift to Pella, and later the sanctuary and royal burial place of the Macedonian kings. It was here that **Philip II**, father of Alexander the Great, was assassinated, cremated and buried; tradition maintained that the dynasty would be destroyed if any king were buried elsewhere, as indeed happened after the death of Alexander in Asia. Until the site was unearthed in 1977, after decades of work by **Professor Manolis Andronikos**, Aegae had long been

---

LITTLE JERUSALEM

Christianity has a long and venerable history in Véria: St Paul preached here (Acts 17:10–14) on two occasions, between 50 and 60 AD, and a gaudy alcove shrine or "altar" of modern mosaics at the base of Mavromiháli marks the supposed spot of his sermons. Four dozen or so small **churches**, some medieval but mostly dating from the sixteenth to eighteenth centuries, are scattered around the town, earning it the moniker of **Little Jerusalem**. Under Ottoman rule, many were disguised as barns or warehouses, with small dormer windows rather than domes to admit light; but today, often surrounded by cleared spaces and well labelled, they're not hard to find. The only church regularly open, however, is the well-signposted **Resurrection of Christ**, or **Anastásseos Christoú** (Tues–Sun 8.30am–3pm; free), near the fork end of Mitropóleos, with fourteenth-century frescoes. The most striking images here are a *Dormition/Assumption* over the west door and on the north wall, a rare image of Christ mounting the Cross on a ladder.

assumed to be lost beneath modern Édhessa. The ruins of the **Palace of Palatítsia** are currently closed for renovations until at least 2020, while the **Macedonian Tomb** 500m uphill is closed indefinitely.

Royal Tombs

Under a tumulus, then just outside modern Veryína, Andronikos discovered several large Macedonian chamber tombs, known simply as the **Royal Tombs**. From outside, all that's visible is a low hillock with skylights and long ramps leading inside, but once underground in the climate-controlled bunker, you can admire the facades and doorways of the tombs, well illuminated behind glass. Finds from the site and tombs, the richest Greek trove since the discovery of Mycenae, are exhibited in the complex along with erudite texts in Greek and English. It's best to try to get here very early or visit at siesta time in order to avoid the crowds.

A clockwise tour takes you round the tombs in the order IV-I-II-III. **Tomb IV**, the so-called Doric, was looted in antiquity; so too was **Tomb I**, or the **Persephone tomb**, but it retained a delicate and exquisitely crafted **mural** of the rape of Persephone by Hades, the only complete example of an ancient Greek painting that has yet been found. **Tomb II**, that of **Philip II**, is a much grander vaulted affair, with a Doric facade adorned by a sumptuous painted **frieze** of Philip, Alexander and their retinue on a lion hunt. Incredibly, the tomb was discovered intact. Among its treasures on display are a marble sarcophagus containing a **gold ossuary** (*larnax*), its cover embossed with the sixteen-pointed star symbol of the royal line, and, more significantly, there are five small **ivory heads**, among them representations of both Philip II and Alexander. It was this clue, as well as the fact that the skull bore marks of a facial wound Philip was known to have sustained, that led to the identification of the tomb as his. Also on view are a fabulous **gold oak-leaf wreath** – so delicate it quivers – and a modest *larnax* (small coffin) found in the antechamber, presumed to contain the carefully wrapped bones and ashes of a Thracian queen or concubine.

Tomb III is thought to be that of Alexander IV, "the Great's" son, murdered in adolescence – thus the moniker **Prince's Tomb**. His bones were discovered in a silver vase. From the tomb frieze, a superb **miniature of Dionysos and his consort** is highlighted, while an excellent **video**, subtitled in English, brings the archeological finds to life.

ARRIVAL AND DEPARTURE

VÉRIA AND VERGINA

By bus The KTEL station is just off Venizélou, at the northern end of central Véria.

Destinations from Véria Athens (2 daily; 6hr 30min);

Édhessa (Mon–Fri 2 daily; 1hr); Thessaloníki (every 15min–1hr; 1hr); Vergina (4–8 daily; 20min).

ACCOMMODATION

VÉRIA

Makedonia Kondoyeorgáki 50 ☎ 23310 66902, ⓦ makedoniahotel.gr. Modern four-storey hotel with smart, functional rooms and an attractive roof garden with admirable views. Substantial breakfast included. **€60**

Villa Elia Eliás 10 ☎ 23310 26800, ⓦ hotel-villaelia.gr. Near the central Belvedere Park, this modern hotel, has compact, comfortable rooms, and there is a smart lounge. Breakfast included. **€58**

VERGINA

Hotel Aigon 250m from the Royal Tombs ☎ 23310 92524, ⓦ hotel-aigon.gr. Well designed hotel with plain but comfortable rooms and a quiet courtyard. Breakfast included. **€50**

Evridiki Guest House Just below the Macedonian Tomb ☎ 23310 92502, ⓦ evridiki.com.gr. The splendid location of this guesthouse and its welcoming owner add immeasurably to the attraction of the place. The simple first floor rooms have lovely rural views. March–Oct. **€45**

EATING AND DRINKING

Véria has a respectable smattering of decent **tavernas**. There is a cluster of trendy **bars** along Eliás and around Belvedere Park, while the pedestrianized area around Patriárhou Ioakeím is crammed full of noisy bars which come to life after dark. Vergina's restaurants are, unsurprisingly, mostly touristic.

VÉRIA

Elia Belvedere Park ☎ 23310 24676, ⓦ elia-veria.gr. A stylish restaurant with huge windows overlooking the plain: main dishes such as gnocchi, pasta and grilled meat go for €8–14. Daily 11am–midnight.

Marmita Edhéssis 2 ☎ 23310 26400. Keenly-priced central *mezedhopolío*, where dishes such as *keftedhákia* and grilled octopus cost around €5.50. Plenty of quality *tsípouro*, ouzo and bulk wine to sample. Daily 11am–1am.

Veryiotiko Thomaídhos 2 ☎ 23310 74139. The menu here is mostly predictable taverna fare, though in winter it occasionally serves the likes of wild boar with quinces for around €8–10. The summer terrace suffers from road noise. Daily noon–late.

VERGINA

Gonia Elia 100m up from the Royal Tombs ☎ 23310 92045. By far the most authentic of modern Veryína's restaurants, favoured by locals for its ample portions and simple but tasty grills such as *pantséta* (€6) or souvláki. Tues–Sun 11am–11pm.

Northwest Macedonia

The intriguing corner of **northwest Macedonia** includes the handsome towns of **Édhessa** and **Kozáni**. West of Édhessa is the attractive mountain village of **Nymféo**, where some of the pretty stone houses have been converted into classy accommodation, and the bird-rich **Préspa lakes**, both of which nestle in a strategic spot where Greece, Albania and the Republic of Macedonia meet. **Flórina**, the area's main urban centre, is of limited appeal but does have two notable museums. Seeing the area properly is really only viable if you have your own transport.

Édhessa

The main gateway to northwest Macedonia, **ÉDHESSA** is a delightful place atop an escarpment. Its modest fame is attributed to the waters that flow through the town. Descending from the mountains to the north these waters eventually cascade down a dramatic ravine, luxuriant with vegetation, to the plain below. Two noteworthy facts are that the area produces one percent of the world's **cherries** and that **Ho Chi Minh** served in the French colonial army here. Most of the town's architecture is humdrum, but the various stream-side parks and wide pedestrian pavements are a rare pleasure in Greece (Édhessa was a pioneer in pedestrianization), and it's an increasingly important centre for regional tourism.

Reptile House

Just south of the waterfalls • Daily: April–Oct 10am–5pm; Nov–March 11am–4pm • €2 • ☎ 23310 28626

The surprisingly fascinating, non-profit **Reptile House**, built from converted watermills, is one of the town's main attractions. The enthusiastic curator will explain all about the fifty-plus species housed here: most are snakes from different parts of the world – they have managed to breed boas here – but there are also tortoises, turtles and a collection of stuffed birds.

Mill of Flavours

Just south of the waterfalls • Daily 10am–4pm • €3 • ☎ 23310 20300

Beautifully converted from a stone sesame mill, the **Mill of Flavours** explains the stages of production of various local produce via displays and videos, then allows you to have a taste. You can also purchase some of the goodies.

Folklore Museum

Megálou Alexándhrou, Varósi district • Tues–Sun 10am–4pm • €2 • ☎ 23310 28787

Housed in an imposing mid-twentieth-century building, the delightful little **Folklore Museum** sits between the Áyii Pétros & Pávlos and Mitrópolis churches. Inside are displays of various household objects and traditional items of the kind that would once have graced every home in the district.

ARRIVAL AND INFORMATION
ÉDHESSA

By train The train station in the north of town serves Thessaloníki (5 daily; 1hr 20min–1hr 30min) and Flórina (3 daily; 1hr 10min).

By bus The main KTEL station is on the corner of Filíppou and Pávlou Melá and serves Thessaloníki (hourly; 1hr 30min), Véria (Mon–Fri 2 daily; 1hr), and other local destinations.

Tourist office The excellent visitor centre in the park at Garéfi and Pérdhika (Mon–Fri 10am–4pm, Sat & Sun 10am–6pm; ☎ 23810 20300, ⓦ edessacity.gr) is the best in the region. English-speaking staff provide useful bilingual leaflets and information about activities, such as trekking, rafting, kayaking and skiing in the surrounding region.

ACCOMMODATION

Alfa Egnatía 28 ☎ 23810 22221, ⓔ hotel-a@otenet. gr. Largely business-oriented hotel, where rooms in the more modern wing are smarter but a little more expensive. €40

Olympia 18-Oktovríou 51 ☎ 23810 23544. This typical 1960s-era hotel, with simply furnished and quiet rooms, is very convenient for the train station. As it's a one-man

show, you may have to wait a while. €30

★**Varosi** Arhieréos Meletíou 45–47, Varósi ☎ 23810 21865, ⓦ varosi.gr. This beautifully converted stone mansion boasts open fires and cosy rooms decorated in a vernacular style; delicious breakfasts are included, which are taken at the plusher *Varosi Four Seasons*, just up the road. €55

EATING AND DRINKING

★**Irtha & Edhessa** Cnr of Karaóli & Tsimiskí ☎ 23813 00660. Revamped taverna with a bright interior, serving high quality food. Try the Edessa salad with local *batsí* cheese, crispy fried parmesan and cherries (€5.50) or the beef *kefetdhákia* with *kása* topping, like bechamel but thicker. Daily 10am–2am.

Katarraktes Next to the waterfalls ☎ 23810 27810. A huge restaurant with ample indoor and patio seating, where you can get some tasty dishes, such as the superb *tsoblék kebab*, with beef, cheese, aubergine and potato in a

rich tomato sauce (€9). Daily 8am–10pm.

Psilos Vrahos Megálou Aléxandhrou 2 ☎ 23810 26118. Perched atop its namesake vantage point, this municipal café is worth a visit for a beer, coffee or fruit juice and the superb view. Daily 8am–midnight.

★**Stathmos** At the train station ☎ 23810 21110. The name means "Station", but this is no railway canteen; it's a fine taverna that serves meaty delights like liver with caramelised onions (most around €5), plus the full gamut of tasty mezédhes. Daily noon–2am.

Nymféo

Perched at 1300m, on the eastern flank of Mount Vítsi, some 85km southwest of Édhessa and 60km northeast of Kastoriá, lies the well-groomed mountain village of **NYMFÉO**, popular with prosperous young Greek professionals looking for alternative recreational activities far from the city. A kilometre northeast of the village lie the large forested compounds of the **Arcturos Bear Sanctuary**, which offers hourly twenty-minute guided tours (daily except Wed 10am–4.30pm; €6; ☎ 23860 41500, ⓦ arcturos.gr).

ACCOMMODATION AND EATING
NYMFÉO

As a trendy getaway, Nymféo has accommodation options that tends to be on the pricey side, especially during winter weekends, so try to visit during the week. The best and cheapest tavernas are in the village centre.

Ederne Centre of village ☎ 23860 31230, ⓦ enterne.gr. This professionally run inn offers simple, traditionally decorated rustic rooms, a welcoming lounge and self-catering facilities. Breakfast included. €60

★**La Moara** Uphill towards back of the village ☎ 23860 31377, ⓦ lamoara.gr. A luxurious mansion with tastefully appointed, modern rooms and state-of-the-art

bathrooms. Run by nationally renowned winemakers, the Boutari family, *La Moara*'s refined cuisine matches the cellar. Breakfast included. €75

Platia Centre of village ☎ 6947 153604. Appealing and reasonably priced restaurant, with cosy indoor seating, ideal for chilly winter evenings, and an outdoor terrace for the summer. Delights such as lamb *gástra* go for €8. Daily 10am–late.

Flórina

Surrounded by steep hills carpeted with beech woods, **FLÓRINA** lies only 13km from the border with the Macedonian Republic and is the nearest town with any albeit infrequent transport connections to the Préspa lakes (see below). Although the only attractive part of town is the immediate environs of the Sakouléva River, two **museums** warrant a visit.

Museum of Modern Art

Tagmatárkhou Fouledháki 8 • April–Oct Mon–Sat 6–9pm, Sun 10am–1pm; Nov–March Mon–Sat 5–8pm, Sun 10am–1pm • Free • ☎ 23850 29444

Flórina's impressive **Museum of Modern Art** is housed in a refurbished Neoclassical building half a block north of the river. With nearly five hundred works by over two hundred and fifty Greek painters, sculptors and engravers of the twentieth century, it boasts the best collection of contemporary art outside Athens.

Archeological Museum

Sidirodromikou Stathmou 3 • Tues–Sun 8am–3pm • €2 • ☎ 23850 28206

Just opposite the sleepy railway station, the **Archeological Museum** displays a modest collection of sculpture, votive reliefs and some artefacts from the Préspa lakeshores. These and other items found in the county of Florina date from Neotlithic to Byzantine times, and are spread across four rooms.

ARRIVAL AND DEPARTURE

FLÓRINA

By train The train station is on the east side of town. Destinations Édhessa (3 daily; 1hr 15min); Thessaloníki (3 daily; 2hr 45min).

By bus The KTEL bus station is at Makedhonomákou 10 (☎ 23850 22430), just north of the centre.

Destinations Áyios Yermanós, Préspes (2 on Wed only; 1hr); Athens (1 daily; 8hr); Édhessa (2–3 daily; 1hr); Kozáni (for Kastoriá; 5–6 daily; 1hr 45min); Thessaloníki (5 daily; 2hr 30min).

ACCOMMODATION AND EATING

Hotel Hellinis Pávlou Melá 31 ☎ 23850 22671, ⓦ www.hotel-hellinis.gr. This classic 1960s-style town hotel has been upgraded to make the rooms slightly more comfortable and contemporary. Very central and good value. €30

River Side Leofóros Eleftherías 68 ☎ 23850 25580. By the river, with views of the mountains, this place is split into two halves: the ground floor is a laidback café, while the upstairs restaurant serves interesting dishes like *thrápsalo* or prawns with *tsípouro* and red pepper for around €9. Daily 10am–midnight.

To Petrino Pávlou Melá 2 ☎ 23850 22560. Very popular *estiatório*, where they serve healthy portions of oven-baked goodies such as cumin-tinged *keftédhes* or beef *stifádho* at lunchtime and grills in the evening. Daily 10am–2am.

The Préspa lakes

A shimmering expanse of water riven by islets and ridges, the **PRÉSPA LAKES** are one of the Balkans' most important wildlife sanctuaries. Though not postcard-pretty, the basin, in the far northwest of Macedonia, has an eerie beauty that grows on you with further acquaintance. It also has a surprisingly turbulent history as a place of **exile** for troublesome noblemen during the Byzantine era and the scene of vicious local **battles** during the 1947–49 Greek Civil War.

Mikrí Préspa, the southerly lake, is mostly shallow (9m maximum depth) and reedy, with a narrow fjord curling west and just penetrating Albanian territory. The borders of Greece, Albania and the Republic of Macedonia meet in the middle of deeper **Megáli Préspa** and, especially during the early 1990s, it became a major exit corridor into Greece for Albanian refugees, who found work as illegal agricultural workers in the local bean and hay industry.

THE BIRDS OF PRÉSPA

The lakes are home to relatively few birds of prey, but you should see a fair number of **egrets**, **cormorants**, **crested grebes** and **pelicans**. This is one of the few breeding sites of both the white and Dalmatian pelican, which nest in the spring, and the chicks are out and about by summer. They feed partly on the large numbers of **snakes**, which include vipers, whip snakes and harmless water snakes (that you may encounter while swimming). Observation towers are available at Vromolímni and near Áyios Ahíllios, but dawn spent anywhere at the edge of the reed beds with a pair of binoculars will be immensely rewarding. Bear in mind, however, that you are not allowed to boat or wade into the reeds.

The core of the **national park**, established in 1971, barely encompasses Mikrí Préspa and its shores, but the peripheral zone extends well into the surrounding mountains and affords protection of sorts to foxes, wolves and even bears, which inhabit the area. The lakes have a dozen resident fish species, including *tsiróni*, a sort of freshwater sardine, and *grivádhi*, a kind of carp, but it's **birdlife** for which the Préspa basin is most famous.

Mikrolímni

MIKROLÍMNI, 5km up a side road off the main route into the valley, is a sleepy hamlet that might be your first conceivable stop. In the evening, you can look towards **sunsets** over reed beds and the snake-infested Vidhronísi (or Vitrinítsi) islet, though swimming isn't good here, or anywhere else on Mikrí Préspa for that matter.

Áyios Yermanós

ÁYIOS YERMANÓS, 4km to the right at the T-junction when the main Flórina–Kastoriá highway reaches Megáli Préspa, is a large village of tile-roofed houses, overlooking a patch of the lake in the distance and adjoining the hamlet of **Lemós**. It's worth making the trip up just to see two tiny late Byzantine churches, whose frescoes, dating from the time when the place belonged to the bishopric of Ohrid, display a marked Macedonian influence. Inside the lower church, **Áyios Athanásios** (seldom open), you can glimpse a dog-faced *St Christopher* among a line of saints opposite the door. Far more impressive, however, is the tiny, eleventh-century parish church of **Áyios Yermanós** up on the square, hidden behind a new monster awkwardly tacked onto it in 1882. The frescoes, skilfully retouched in 1743, can be lit; the switch is hidden in the narthex.

Koúla beach

At the far end of the wide causeway dividing the two lakes, 4km to the left from the T-junction, is **Koúla beach**, a motley cluster of what passes for tourist development hereabouts: a patch of reed-free sand from where you can swim in Megáli Préspa; a free but basic camping area, now bereft of its water tap; plus an army post.

Psarádhes

Reached by 6km of panoramic corniche road from a signposted turning near Koúla beach, the rickety village of **PSARÁDHES** makes for a pleasant stroll. Unfortunately, the wonderful old houses lining the lanes are increasingly derelict. It is sometimes possible to take a short **boat excursion** out onto the lake to see some of the lakeside monuments and churches, though this is not the best way to spot birdlife; there is no fixed schedule, so ask around.

Áyios Ahíllios

Two kilometres directly south of Koúla beach, the road soon brings you to a pontoon footbridge, 1500m in length, which leads across to the islet of **Áyios**

Ahíllios and its impoverished, almost deserted hamlet. A five-minute walk from the footbridge is the ruined Byzantine **basilica** of Áyios Ahíllios, while another ruin, a sixteenth-century **monastery**, Panayía Porfaras, lies at the southern end of the islet. For unrivalled views of Mikrí Préspa, climb up to the summit of the islet's hill.

ARRIVAL AND INFORMATION

PRÉSPA LAKES

By bus There are just two market buses on Wednesdays from Flórina (1hr), and nothing for the rest of the week, so in order to explore the region, you really need a vehicle.
Tourist office Áyios Yermanós has the informative Prespa National Forest Management Body (Mon–Sat 9am–2pm;

☎ 23870 51870), while in Lemós is the helpful Préspa information centre (daily 9.30am–7.30pm, staff permitting; ☎ 23850 51211, ⓦ www.spp.gr). Both focus on the wildlife of the national park.

ACCOMMODATION AND EATING

Préspa is becoming increasingly popular, so you'd be wise to reserve a room in advance during midsummer, especially at weekends. You can camp for free on Koúla beach. Look out for lake fish at the restaurants.

MIKROLÍMNI

★**ly Syndrofia** Psarádhes ☎ 23850 46107, ⓦ syntrofia-prespes.gr. A good spot to sample *fasoládha* (bean soup) or *saganáki* coated in sesame seeds and honey, as well as lake fish like *grivádhi*, unavailable elsewhere in Greece, for under €10, plus the proprietor's fine wine. There are also a few rooms (€40). Daily 11am–1am.
To Arhontiko Psarádhes ☎ 23850 46260. An effectively converted old stone house, this place offers decent en-suite rooms, the upper ones with lake views, and a warm welcome. Ask at *ly Akrolimnia* taverna in front. €35
Ta Psaradhika Tou Hassou Mikrolímni ☎ 23850 46803. Authentic local taverna which can rustle up simple grilled meat or fish for around €7, plus a limited but tasty range of starters and salads. Daily 11am–11pm.

ÁYIOS YERMANÓS

★**Agios Germanos** Áyios Yermanós ☎ 23850 51397, ⓦ prespa.com.gr. Centrally located near the small village square, this extremely welcoming guesthouse has traditional stone rooms and a convivial lounge, where the complimentary breakfast is served; evening meals on request. €55

To Tzaki Near the church, Áyios Yermanós ☎ 23850 51303. The best taverna in the village offers a good range of tasty *mayireftá* such as pork in wine sauce and baked aubergines, as well as succulent meat cooked in the *gástra* (clay oven) for €9. Daily noon–11pm.
Xenonas Prespes Just below the school, Áyios Yermanós ☎ 23850 51266. Plain yet cosy guesthouse with a friendly owner and simple but spotlessly clean rooms. Breakfast included. €50

LEMÓS

Mimallones Lemós ☎ 23850 51422, ⓦ mimallones.gr. Undoubtedly Préspa's smartest accommodation, this spacious modern hotel has large comfortably furnished rooms, a massive bar-cum-lounge and friendly management. Breakfast included. €50

ÁYIOS AHÍLLIOS

Ayios Ahillios Áyios Ahíllios hamlet ☎ 23850 46601, ⓦ agiosahilios.gr. Cosy rooms with some larger apartments available above the hotel's café and basic restaurant. It's well situated on a quiet islet, and can arrange activities such as hikes and canoeing. €45

Kastoriá

Set on a hilly, wooded peninsula extending deep into slate-coloured Lake Orestiádha, **KASTORIÁ** is one of the most interesting and attractive towns of mainland Greece. For centuries, it grew rich on the **fur trade**, using the pelts of local wild beavers (*kastóri* in Greek). Though these animals were trapped to extinction by the nineteenth century, Kastoriá still supports a considerable industry of furriers using a mixture of imported pelts and locally farmed beavers. You'll see pelts drying on racks, and fur megastores with a profusion of Russian signposting – a hint at the target market. The town also has a strong tradition of **rowing**, and rowers can be seen out on the lake most days. Even the Oxford and Cambridge Blues have been known to practise their strokes here.

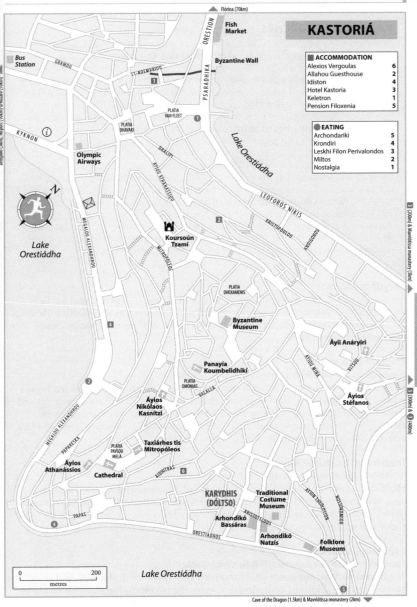

Flórina (70km)

Fish Market

Bus Station

Byzantine Wall

GRAMOU

ORESTION

PSARADHIKA

KASTORIÁ

ΠΤ-NOEMVRIOU

PLATIA VAN FLEET

PLATIA DHAVAKI

KYKNON

Olympic Airways

DRALIPI

AGIOU ATHANASSIOU

MITROPOLEOS

Koursoún Tzamí

Lake Orestiádha

LEOFOROS NIKIS

KRISTOPOULOU

ANDIGONIS

MEGALOU ALEXANDROU

PLATIA DHEXAMENIS

Byzantine Museum

Ayii Anáryiri

AGIOU MINA

Panayía Koumbelidhíki

PLATIA OMONIAS

VALALLA

Áyios Nikólaos Kasnítzi

Áyios Stéfanos

MEGALOU ALEXANDROU

PAPARESKA

PLATIA PAVLOU MELA

Taxiárhes tis Mitropóleos

Áyios Athanássios

Cathedral

ALDHITRAS

AGIOU THEOLOGOU

PAPAS

KARYDHIS (DÓLTSO)

ARISTOTELOUS

Traditional Costume Museum

Arhondikó Bassáras

ORESTIADHOS

Arhondikó Natzís

KOSMOMIOU

Folklore Museum

0   200
metres

Lake Orestiádha

Cave of the Dragon (1.5km) & Mavriótissa monastery (2km)

ACCOMMODATION	
Alexios Vergoulas	6
Allahou Guesthouse	2
Idiston	4
Hotel Kastoria	3
Keletron	1
Pension Filoxenia	5

EATING	
Archondariki	5
Krondiri	4
Leskhi Filon Perivalondos	3
Miltos	2
Nostalgia	1

(200m) & Mavriótissa monastery (3km)

(300m) & (400m)

4

For most visitors, however, Kastoriá's main appeal lies in traces of its former prosperity: dozens of splendid *arhondiká* – **mansions** of the old fur families – dating from the seventeenth to nineteenth centuries, plus some fifty Byzantine and medieval **churches**. About the only reminder of Muslim settlement is the minaret-less Koursoún Tzamí, marooned in a ridgetop car park; there's also a patch of an originally Byzantine fortification wall down on the neck of the peninsula.

KASTORIÁ'S CHURCHES

Of the town's many Byzantine churches, a handful are well worth seeking out. The excellent frescoes of the twelfth-century church of **Áyios Nikólaos Kasnítzi** were returned to their former glory during the late 1980s. The unusual epithet stems from the donor, who is shown with his wife on the narthex wall presenting a model of the church to Christ. Lower down are ranks of exclusively female saints, to console the women congregated in the narthex which long served as a women's gallery. High up on the west wall of the nave, the *Dormition* and the *Transfiguration* are in good condition, the former inexplicably backwards (the Virgin's head is usually to the left). **Taxiárhes tís Mitropóleos**, the oldest (ninth-century) church, was built on the foundations of an earlier pagan temple, of which recycled columns and capitals are visible. Its more prominent frescoes, such as that of the *Virgin Platytera and Adoring Archangels* in the conch of the apse, and a conventional *Dormition* on the west wall, are fourteenth century. In the north aisle is the tomb of Greek nationalist Pavlos Melas, assassinated by Bulgarians at a nearby village in 1906, and commemorated by street names across northern Greece. Lastly, there's the **Panayía Koumbelidhikí**, named because of its unusual dome (*kübe* in Turkish), which retains one startling and well-lit fresco: a portrayal – almost unique in Greece – of God the Father in a ceiling mural of the *Holy Trinity*. The building was constructed in stages, with the apse completed in the tenth century and the narthex in the fifteenth. The cylindrical dome was meticulously restored after being destroyed by Italian bombing in 1940.

Karýdhis (Dóltso)

For a sense of what Kastoriá must once have been during its heyday, head for the former lakeside quarter officially called **Karýdhis**, but better known as **Dóltso**. Among the notable mansions in the area are **Bassáras** and the well-restored **Natzís**, close together on Vyzandíon.

Folklore Museum

Kapetán Lázou 10 • Tues–Sat 10am–5pm, Sun from 11am • €2 • ☎ 24670 28603

The splendidly opulent seventeenth-century Aïvazís family mansion has been turned into a **Folklore Museum**. The house was inhabited until 1972, and its furnishings and most of its ceilings are in excellent repair, having miraculously survived German shelling; the Ottoman-style kiosk sports a set of stained-glass windows, three of them original, the others replaced by a local craftsman.

Traditional Costume Museum

Platia Dóltso • Daily 10am–noon & 4–6pm • Free

Housed in another notable villa, the Emmanouíl mansion, and run by the same organization as the Folklore museum, the **Traditional Costume Museum** has a magical display of traditional clothing from western Macedonia – and offers the chance to see another magnificent interior.

Byzantine Museum

Platía Dhexamenís • Tues–Sun 8.30am–3pm • €4 • ☎ 24670 26781, ⓦ bmk.gr

The **Byzantine Museum** wisely goes for quality over quantity in this well-lit if unimaginatively displayed collection that spans the twelfth to the sixteenth centuries. Highlights include an unusually expressive thirteenth-century icon of Áyios Nikólaos and a fourteenth-century Ayii Anaryiri, plus a later one depicting the life of St George. There are also a few double-sided icons, including a rare *Deposition*, intended for use in religious processions. Note that captions are in Greek only.

Lake Orestiádha

One of the most pleasant things to do in Kastoriá is to follow the narrow road along **Lake Orestiádha** to the **peninsula** to the east of town; at the tip, vehicles must circulate anticlockwise, but the route is mainly used by joggers and the odd walker. Although the lake itself is visibly polluted, **wildlife** still abounds – pelicans, swans, cormorants, frogs, tortoises and water snakes especially, and on a spring day numerous fish break water.

Mavriótissa monastery

Near the southeastern tip of the peninsula, some 3km from the *Hotel Kastoria* (see p.298).

Two churches are all that remain of the **Mavriótissa monastery**: a smaller fourteenth-century chapel, with fine frescoes of scenes from Christ's life, abuts the larger, wood-roofed eleventh-century *katholikón* on whose outer wall looms a well-preserved *Tree of Jesse*, which shows the genealogy of the Saviour.

Cave of the Dragon (Spiliá tou Dhrákou)

1.5km along the anticlockwise lakeshore route • Tues–Sun: summer 10am–6pm; winter 9am–5pm • €6; boat trips €4• ☎ 6957 591 303, ⓦ spilaiodrakoukast.gr

The **Dragon's Cave**, discovered in 1940 but only opened to the public in 2010, was given its name because the entrance resembles the mouth of a dragon, and an old legend claimed there was a resident one that spouted fire if anyone approached. The interior is festooned with an impressive array of stalagmites and stalactites, and there are some patches of lake within, around which walkways have been carefully constructed. Daily **boat trips** around the part of the lake run from the nearby jetty.

Dhispílio prehistoric lake settlement

5km from Kastoriá, in Dhispílio • Museum daily 9am–2pm & 5–8pm • €4 • ☎ 24670 21910

On the southern shore of the lake, in the village of Dhispílio, lie the remains of a fascinating **prehistoric lake settlement**, which is thought to date from around 5500–5000 BC, during the Neolithic period. First excavated in 1992, finds include a range of household goods and a wooden tablet, inscribed with an early linear script. A modern re-creation of the original **huts** and an **eco-museum** help bring to life what the area must have looked like in these distant times.

ARRIVAL AND INFORMATION   KASTORIÁ

By plane The airport (☎ 24670 21700) is 10km south of town, and the only destination served is Athens by Sky Express (2 weekly; 1hr 5min).

By bus The KTEL bus station is at A. Dhiákou 14 (☎ 24670 83633, ⓦ ktel-kastorias.gr), near the western edge of the peninsula.

Destinations Athens (3 daily; 7hr 30min); Ioánnina (4 weekly; 2hr 30min); Kozáni (for Flórina; 5 daily; 1hr);

Thessaloníki (6–7 daily; 2hr 30min).

By car A fee-parking scheme, operated by ticket machines, applies across much of the city centre; only a couple of the more expensive hotels have free or off-street parking.

Tourist office There is a municipal tourist kiosk (May–Sept 9am–9pm; ☎ 24670 26777) in the lakeside park, 150m from KTEL, but staffing problems mean it is often shut.

ACCOMMODATION

Many of Kastoriá's best hotels fill up at weekends, although a string of noisy, modern business hotels along the airport road takes care of the overspill and keeps prices reasonable. It's worth paying extra for the experience of staying in a converted mansion.

★**Alexios Vergoulas** Aïdhítras 14, Dóltso ☎ 24670 23415, ⓦ vergoulasmansion.gr. Delightful boutique hotel, housed in a handsome mid-nineteenth-century mansion. Rooms with a view are pricier but all are faultlessly decorated in traditional yet comfortable style, albeit with midget bathrooms. Breakfast included. **€70**

★**Allahou Guesthouse** Panayiás Faneroménis 18 ☎ 24670 27058, ⓦ allahou.gr. Beautifully converted

mansion with five brightly decorated and comfortably furnished rooms, plus an airy breakfast conservatory. Discount for *Rough Guide* readers. **€50**

Idiston Megálou Alexándhrou 91 ☎ 24670 22250, ⓦ idiston.gr. Self-catering apartments in a prime location above a cafeteria; the front rooms have lake views but those at the rear are quieter. Run by a returnee from Canada whose passion for his native town is contagious. Book well ahead. **€50**

4

Hotel Kastoria Leofóros Níkis 122 ☎ 24670 29453, ⓦ hotel-kastoria.gr. At the far end of the northern waterfront, one of the town's smartest hotels offers lake views from its pricier balconied, air-conditioned front rooms, plus free parking. **€40**

Keletron 11-Noemvríou 52 ☎ 24670 22525, ⓦ www.anastassiou-hotels.gr. Simple but perfectly adequate hotel with its entrance on a side street and some rooms overlooking leafy Platía Van Fleet. **€40**

Pension Filoxenia Y Paleológou 23 ☎ 24670 22162, ⓦ filoxeniakastoria.gr. Well located and thoughtfully decorated, this welcoming place has rooms of varying sizes; the pricier ones have lake views. Breakfast included. **€55**

EATING AND DRINKING

Archondariki Orestiádhos 87 ☎ 24670 26361. Delightfully located taverna with tables right next to the lake. Grilled meat and fish such as sardines or *gávros* cost in the region of €8–10. Daily 11.30am–midnight.

★ **Krondiri** Orestiádhos 13 ☎ 24670 28258. This stylish taverna dishes up some of the town's best food, especially fancy *mezédhes* like steamed veg with a mustard and orange sauce, plus succulent meat dishes for €6–8. There are some tables on the lakeshore in fine weather. Daily 11am–1am.

Leskhi Filon Perivalondos Tsardháki ☎ 24670 26300. The café of the Friends of the Environment is a great spot for a drink, with fine views of the northeastern lakeshore from its vantage point up near Profítis Ilías. Daily noon–midnight.

Miltos Megálou Aléxandhrou 125 ☎ 24670 29659. Best and oldest of the southern lakefront establishments, *Miltos* offers a great selection of soups, salads, dips, oven dishes and roasts, mostly well under €10. Daily 11am–1am.

Nostalgia Níkis 2 ☎ 24670 22630. All-round taverna with *mayireftá* (casserole-type dishes) such as coq au vin with mushrooms, as well as lots of grilled meat and a fine pork *tiganiá* (skillet), mostly under €10. Lake views from the patio seating. Daily noon–2am.

4

Halkidhikí

HALKIDHIKÍ begins at a perforated edge of shallow lakes east of Thessaloníki, then extends into three prongs of land – Kassándhra, Sithonía and Athos – trailing like tentacles into the northern Aegean Sea. **Kassándhra** and **Sithonía** host some of the busiest holiday resorts in Greece, drawing hordes from Thessaloníki and other parts of the north, as well as increasing numbers from eastern Europe. The beaches themselves consist of white sand, ranging in consistency from powder to coarse-grained.

Mount Athos, the easternmost peninsula, is in all ways separate, a "Holy Mountain" whose monastic population, semi-autonomous within the Greek state, **excludes all females** – even as visitors. The most that women can do is to glimpse the buildings from offshore cruise *kaïkia* sailing from the two small resorts on the periphery of the peninsula – Ierissós and Ouranoúpoli – on the "secular" part of the Athos peninsula.

ARRIVAL AND INFORMATION   HALKIDHIKÍ

By bus Buses run frequently to all the larger resorts. In spite of this, neither peninsula is that easy to travel around if you are dependent on public transport. You really have to pick a place and stay there, then perhaps rent a motorbike or car for excursions.

By car Both Kassándhra and Sithonía are connected to Thessaloníki by a four-lane expressway which ends at Néa Moudhaniá, a dull town and minor passenger port, from where a network of fast two-lane roads extends around their coastlines.

Information ⓦ halkidiki.com is moderately useful.

Kassándhra and around

Vaguely boot-shaped **KASSÁNDHRA**, the nearest of Halkidhikí's three peninsulas to Thessaloníki, is also by far the most developed. In 2006, extensive fires decimated almost the entire forest that once covered the central section of its spine, and this is only just beginning to recover. Most of the attractive **inland villages** date from the mid-nineteenth century, as the earlier ones were left deserted after their inhabitants were massacred during the 1821 War of Independence. On the coast, there were only a few small **fishing hamlets** here until after 1923, when the peninsula was resettled by

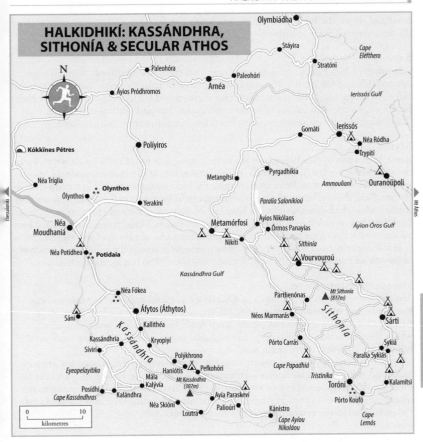

HALKIDHIKÍ: KASSÁNDHRA, SITHONÍA & SECULAR ATHOS

refugees from around the Sea of Marmara – these have since burgeoned into **holiday venues**. Many travellers choose to bypass Kassándhra and keep going to Sithonía or the top end of Athos.

Kókkines Pétres

Centre of modern village • Daily 9am–5pm • €7, guided tours only • ☎ 23730 71671, ⓦ petralona-cave.gr

Fifty kilometres southeast of Thessaloníki, en route to the Kassándhra peninsula and set among handsome mountain scenery, is **Kókkines Pétres** (Petralona Cave). The cave, whose name means "Red Stones", was discovered in 1959 by villagers from nearby Petrálona looking for water. Besides an impressive display of stalagmites and stalactites, the villagers – and, later, academics – found the fossilized remains of prehistoric animals and, most dramatic of all, a **Neanderthal skull**, all of which are displayed in a decent **museum** near the cave entrance. Note that no photography is allowed.

Néa Fókea

Bypassing the eyesore of Néa Potídhea, at the northern tip of Kassandra, some 6km beyond Néa Moudhaniá and across the ancient canal, the first place you might consider stopping at is **NÉA FÓKEA**, a modest place consisting mostly of holiday apartments for Greeks, rendered picturesque by a Byzantine watchtower on a grassy headland. From the harbour, a long beach heads north under cliffs; it improves as you distance yourself from the tower.

Sáni

Just north of Néa Fókea, an 8km paved side road takes you westwards through bucolic countryside to **SÁNI** on the west coast, which has a British-operated manicured marina full of boutiques and chic restaurants. Sáni is also noted for its summer **festival**, which boasts a cosmopolitan billing of world music, salsa, jazz and cutting-edge Greek stars. This takes place up by another quaint Byzantine watchtower on the headland.

Áfytos

Some 5km south of Néa Fókea, you reach the turning east for **ÁFYTOS** (or Áthytos), by far the most attractive spot on Kassándha. This large village of tile-roofed traditional houses spreads over a series of ravines that punctuate the bluff here, which ends in a sharp drop to the sea. Near the cliff bottom, a series of **springs** bubbles from a rock overhang, nurturing a little oasis – doubtless a spur in the founding of Aphytis, the village's ancient predecessor. Both **beaches** (turn left for Paralía Várkes, right for Paralía Moudhoúnou) are marred by rock sills with lots of sea urchins. On the **square**, the focus of a mesh of slightly twee cobbled lanes closed to traffic for the nightly promenade, stands the handsome **Church of St Demetrius** in post-Byzantine style; it dates only from 1850 but seems much older.

The southeastern shore

The modern and rather ugly resort of **KALLITHÉA** is useful only for its **ATMs** and **car, motorbike and windsurfer rental**. At **KRYOPIYÍ**, just under 6km further, most of the development is concentrated along the steep roads that cascade down to the water, where there's a beach, but Kryopiyí has managed to preserve its old village core up the hill, on the land side of the main road.

Beyond Kryopiyí, you head towards the "toe" of the Kassandhrian boot via a trio of tacky and missable coastal resorts – Polýkhrono, Haniótis and Pefkohóri – and the far more scenic and deserted bay of **Khroussoú**. From here, rather than continuing to the disappointing "toe"-cape at Kánistro, you're better off heading west and inland along the main road to the rambling ridgetop village of **PALIOÚRI**.

The southwestern shore

The southwestern shore of Kassándra is, in general, developed more for Greek weekenders than foreign holiday-makers. Some 6km beyond hilltop Palioúri lies **Ayía Paraskeví**, a delightful village with sea views, a little way beyond which you emerge on the coast at the **Loutrá Ayías Paraskevís**, where a popular **spa** complex (daily summer 9am–9pm, winter 10am–5pm; ☎23740 71810) contains a hot sulphurous pool and offers various treatments (€6–15). **NÉA SKIÓNI**, 4km northwest, can be a decent base, with its good clean beach and appealing seafront.

Tucked on the cape beyond Mála Kalýva is **POSÍDHI**, which covers a hill and spills down onto a harbour and fine stretch of beach. At the far end of the **beach**, the rock reef abates and you can skinny-dip from the tapering sand spit. On the opposite side of the promontory, the splendid beach of **Eyeopelayítiko** is one of the finest on the whole peninsula, with a single beach bar for refreshments. From here you can return to the main road and complete the clockwise coastal circuit, happily ignoring the unappealing resort of Síviri, although if time allows, you may choose to detour back to this coast for a peep at the yachting haven of **Sáni**.

ACCOMMODATION, EATING AND DRINKING   KASSÁNDHRA

You should have no trouble getting **accommodation** outside the busiest midsummer period, though places do start closing down in Sept, and few remain open between Oct and April. Large signs at the entrance to both peninsulas remind you that camping outside authorized sites is strictly prohibited. If you avoid the identikit tavernas at the most heavily touristic resorts, Kassándra has a decent sprinkling of reasonable **places to eat**. The liveliest nightlife is in Áfytos, where Greek musicians often play in the bars at summer weekends, sometimes under the aegis of the **Kassándra Festival** which Áfytos shares with Síviri: performances include blues, soul, classical and traditional Greek music.

NÉA FÓKEA

Seryiani Harbourside ☎ 23740 81677. This delightfully positioned seafood taverna is a rare year-round venue. Prices are low – fresh fish can cost only €40 per kilo. Good mezédhes and barrelled wine, too. Daily noon–1am.

Villa Madeleine On the hill behind the tower ☎ 23740 81441, ⊕ villa-madeleine.gr. These smart modern studios are comfortably furnished and have kitchenettes plus balconies overlooking the bay. Mid-June to mid-Sept. €50

SÁNI

Blue Dream Just north of the harbour ☎ 23740 31435, ⊕ campingbluedream.gr. Municipal campsite with adequate space, some shady spots and clean shared facilities. May–Sept. €25

Tomata On the marina ☎ 23740 99465, ⊕ sani-resort .com. The expensive but imaginative menu at this resort taverna is aimed at yachters who moor here, though some of the simpler meat dishes cost under €10. April–Oct noon–midnight.

ÁFYTOS

Hotel Afitis Paralía Várkes ☎ 23740 91233, ⊕ afitis-hotel.gr. Smart resort hotel with a vast pool and range of facilities. There's a huge difference in price between the modest rooms at the back and those with balconies facing the sea. April–Oct. €50

★**Ta Bakaliarakia tou Pirati** Centre of village ☎ 23740 91001. Slightly above-average prices but still a good place for quality fish and meat dishes (mainly around €8–10) and a convivial atmosphere. Daily noon–2am; Nov–April Fri–Sun only.

Ta Glarakia Paralía Várkes ☎ 23740 91211. Best of the seaside tavernas, this place has a range of daily specials for only €6–8 marked on the chalk board outside, such as baked swordfish. May–Oct daily 9am–1am.

Stratos Hotel Towards the main coast road ☎ 23740 91112, ⊕ stratoshotel.gr. The bright modern rooms in this sizeable complex are arranged around a fairly large pool. There is also a snack bar and leafy garden. May–Sept. €55

THE SOUTHEASTERN SHORE

ly Platia Tis Anthoulas Kryopiyí ☎ 23740 53001. Cosy traditional taverna serving delights such as stuffed chicken for €8 and artichokes in an egg-and-lemon sauce. Daily 10am–midnight; Nov–March Fri–Sun only.

Paliouri Camping Just above Khroussoú bay ☎ 23740 92169. This is an organized and shady spot with a mini-market and plenty of sites for your tent. May–Oct. €22

SOUTHWESTERN SHORE

★**Kyparissis** Posídhi ☎ 23740 42264. By far the friendliest and best of the half-dozen places along the front, here they serve mainly grilled meat and fish, plus some oven dishes. There are also a number of nicely decorated rooms behind (€40). Daily 10am–midnight; Nov–March Fri–Sun only.

★**Pansion Alexandros** Néa Skióni ☎ 23740 71386, ⊕ pansionalexandros.gr. With balconies overlooking the sea and a small rock jetty nearby, this homely place is basic but squeaky clean and one of the better deals on the peninsula. May–Sept. €45

O Kleon Néa Skióni ☎ 23740 71266. This inexpensive ouzerí-style restaurant a block back from the seafront is extremely popular with the locals for its wide range of mezédhes, such as vegetable fritters and small fish, all under €10. Daily noon–1am; Nov–April Fri–Sun only.

Possidi Paradise Posídhi ☎ 23740 42030, ⊕ possidiparadise.gr. Sparkling new upmarket hotel with a swimming pool and large rooms looking out onto the seafront. Breakfast included. May to mid-Oct. €80

Sithonía

As you move east across Halkidhikí and away from the frontline of tourism, the landscape becomes increasingly green and hilly, culminating in the isolated and spectacular scenery of **Mount Athos**, looming across the gulf. The **SITHONÍA** peninsula is more rugged but better cultivated than Kassándra, though here there are even fewer true villages, most of which date from the 1920s resettlement era. Pine forests cover many of the slopes, particularly in the south, and give way to olive groves on the coast. Small sandy inlets with relatively discreet pockets of campsites and tavernas make a welcome change. It's a good idea to follow the loop road clockwise around the east coast, so that the peak of Athos is always before you.

Ancient Olynthos

Tues–Sun 8am–3pm • €3 • ☎ 23730 22060

Some 6km beyond the last motorway exit at Néa Moudhaniá en route to Sithonía, it's worth making the slight detour to splendidly located **Ancient Olynthos**, atop a hill offering mountain and sea views. This is a rare example of an unmodified Classical town laid out to the geometric grid plan of **Hippodamus** – the fifth-century BC architect who designed Pireás and Rhodes. There's an initially off-putting walk of 700m, partly up a slope, from the ticket booth, but there are well-excavated streets, houses and even some **mosaics** to see once you arrive, most notably one of Bellerophon riding Pegasus and killing the Chimaira. Like the informative **museum** near the entrance, everything is clearly labelled in Greek and English. The modern village of Ólynthos, 1km west across the riverbed here, offers limited facilities.

Vourvouroú

VOURVOUROÚ, 8km down the coast from forgettable and built-up Órmos Panayías, is not a typical resort, since it stands on land expropriated from Vatopedhíou monastery on Athos. Islets astride the mouth of the bay make for a fine setting, but the beach, while sandy, is extremely narrow, and Vourvouroú is really more of a yachters' haven.

The central east shore

Some of Sithonía's best **beaches** lie off the 30km of corniche road between Vourvouroú and the busy tourist resort of **SÁRTI**: there are five signposted sandy coves, each with a **campsite** and little else. The names of the bays, such as Koutloumousíou or Zográfou, reflect the fact that most of the land here belonged to various Athonite monasteries until confiscated by the Greek government to resettle Anatolian refugees. A short way beyond **Armenistís**, a dirt track leads down to a pair of idyllic coves, almost tropical in appearance. Sárti itself may not ooze charm but does offer a good choice of facilities and one of the widest beaches in a major enclave.

Paralía Sykiás

PARALÍA SYKIÁS, 8km past Sárti, is a well-appointed beach, with just a few tavernas well back from the sea along 2km of coastal highway. The best strategy here is to follow the side road at the south end of the beach towards the more scenic coves and smattering of restaurants at **Pigadháki** or **Paleó Fánaro**. For a **post office** and shops head for **SYKIÁ**, 2km inland, hemmed in by a bowl of rocky hills.

Kalamítsi

KALAMÍTSI, another 8km south of Paralía Sykiás, consists of a beautiful double bay, now rather spoilt by development. The small strand at the sheltered north bay of Pórto can get cramped in summer, at which time you can easily swim out to the main islet for less company or head over the rocks to the north, where there's an informal nudist beach.

Pórto Koufó

The forest cover gets progressively thinner the further south you go from Sárti, until you reach the recently replanted tip of the peninsula, where the hills spill into the sea to create a handful of deep bays. **PÓRTO KOUFÓ**, just northwest of the cape, is the most dramatic of these, almost completely cut off from the open sea by high cliffs. The name Koufó ("deaf" in Greek) is said to come from one's inability to hear the sea within the confines of this inlet, which served as an Axis submarine shelter during World War II. There are a few fine **stretches of sand** around the bay, especially where the road drops down from the east. The north end of the inlet, 1km from the beach area, is a picturesque yacht and fishing **harbour**. Overall this area is one of the star attractions on the whole peninsula as a place to base oneself.

Toróni and Tristiníka

TORÓNI, 3km north of Pórto Koufó, is an exposed, 2km-long crescent of sand with wooded hills behind. It makes another plausible base and, for a little stimulation, there is a minimal **archeological site** on the southern cape, sporting the remains of a Byzantine fortress, while nearby is an early Christian basilica. Just 2km north is the turning for less-developed **TRISTINÍKA**, where there is another outstanding 2km beach.

Pórto Carrás and around

Beyond Tristiníka, you edge back into high-tech-resort territory, epitomized by Greece's largest planned holiday complex, **PÓRTO CARRÁS** (⊛portocarras.com), with four upmarket hotels that range from mock-Byzantine to futuristic and three-star to luxury. Established by the Carras wine and shipping dynasty, it features an in-house shopping centre, golf course and vineyards, while the expansive private beach in front hosts every imaginable watersport.

The nearest proper town to all this, with **banks** (ATMs) and a **post office**, is **Néos Marmarás**, a little fishing port with a small beach, popular with Greeks, who stay in a score of modest hotels and apartments.

Parthenónas

A detour inland to **PARTHENÓNAS**, the lone traditional village on Sithonía, will give you some idea of what Sithonía must have looked like before the developers moved in. Crouched at the base of 808m Mount Ítamos, it's 5km up from Néos Marmarás and reached via a good road lined with pine and olive groves. Parthenónas was abandoned in the 1960s in favour of the shore, and never even provided with mains electricity; its appealing houses have now largely been restored into chic residences.

Nikíti

The clockwise loop is completed back at the neck of the peninsula in the pleasant resort of **NIKÍTI**, which can also be used as a reasonable first base. Although there is nothing too spectacular about the seafront here, the old village on the inland side of the main road is full of venerable old stone houses and contains a few decent options for staying and dining.

GETTING AROUND — SITHONÍA

By bus Services are sparse: depending on the season, there are up to five buses daily around the west coast to Sárti, and up to three a day direct to Vourvouroú, but just a single daily KTEL connection, in Aug only, between these two end points. A complete circuit is only really feasible with your own transport.

ACCOMMODATION AND EATING

Finding somewhere to stay is only ever a problem during the short peak season in Aug, though locating an open hotel off-season can be a challenge. There is plenty of choice for campers. Sithonía presents Halkidhikí's best eating options of anywhere in.

VOURVOUROÚ

Diaporos On main village road ☎23750 91313, ⊛hotel-diaporos.com. A rather grand building with lush gardens and huge, well-appointed rooms, as well as its own rooftop restaurant. May–Sept. **€80**

Ekies All Senses Resort By the beach at the southern end of the village ☎23750 91000, ⊛ekies.gr. Ecologically minded, high-luxury resort, set in vast landscaped grounds, with designer rooms, an enticing pool and the gourmet *Bubo* restaurant. Minimum four-night stay in summer. **€60**

Gousto On main village road ☎23750 91379. This restaurant serves decent pasta, pizza and Greek standards for €7–12; there's also a fair-sized pool with chilled-out bar. May to early Oct 9am–late.

Mandala Alter Tavern Middle of main village road ☎23750 91151. Small homely place backing onto the seafront with a shady thatched roof. It serves simple, authentic Greek dishes such as oven-cooked lamb with potatoes for around €7–8. May–Oct 11am–1am.

THE CENTRAL EAST SHORE

★**Armenistis** Signposted off main coast road ☎ 23750 91487, ⓦ armenistis.com.gr. One of the best-developed campsites on the peninsula, with dorm beds too, and a major hangout for ravers from Thessaloníki. Often stages gigs and festivals. May–Sept. Dorm **€14**, camping **€19**

PÓRTO KOUFÓ

★**Boukadoura** On main road, 1km southeast of harbour ☎ 23750 51012, ⓦ boukadoura.gr. The menu contains over a hundred dishes, among which are some unusual creations like seafood *spetzofái* for €10–15 and a rich lobster *makaronádha* for €28. June–Aug daily noon–1am; Sept–May some weekends only.

★**Porto Koufo** On the beach ☎ 23750 51207, ⓦ portokoufohotel.gr. Attractive whitewashed complex of spacious rooms with subtle decoration, large bathtubs and bay-view balconies. Buffet breakfast included. May–Sept. **€60**

TORÓNI AND TRISTINÍKA

Barracuda Toróni. Lively beach bar towards the northern end of the seafront that serves a range of soft drinks, coffees, beers and snacks, while keeping everyone entertained with a fair selection of music, mostly in English. Late May to Oct daily 11am–1am.

Camping Isa Tristiníka ☎ 23750 51235. Campsite at the southern end of the beach. Besides tent space in well-landscaped olive groves, there are also wood chalets (€45) with all amenities. May–Sept. **€22**

Ethnik Tristiníka ☎ 694 435 6830. Imaginatively painted solid wooden beach bar, offering a range of drinks and snacks, as well as a laidback vibe, aided and abetted by the cool world sounds. June to early Sept 10am–2am.

★**Sakis Haus** Toróni ☎ 23750 51262, ⓦ haus-sakis.de.

Towards the northernmost end of the seafront, this place has comfortable, well-equipped kitchenettes and a warm welcome guaranteed, plus good food and German beer on tap in the restaurant below. Breakfast included. **€40**

★**Villa Sithonia** Tristiníka ☎ 23750 51118, ⓦ villasithonia.gr. Lovely, well-furnished and great-value rooms, plus more spacious apartments, spread across two buildings in lush gardens amid olive groves 500m from the beach. May–Oct. **€35**

PARTHENÓNAS

Pension Parthenon On high ground above the village centre ☎ 23750 72225, ⓦ parthenonas-chalkidiki.com. This beautifully decorated stone house offers some of the peninsula's most charming accommodation. All rooms have kitchens. Buffet breakfast included. **€70**

★**To Steki tou Meniou** Beside the village square ☎ 6945 414 052, ⓦ tavernaparthenonas.com. Friendly and very traditional restaurant that dishes up copious amounts of tasty oven recipes for €6–9, plus grills and occasionally even delicacies like quail. Daily 11am–midnight.

NIKÍTI

Danai Beach Resort 4km northwest of Nikíti ☎ 23750 20400, ⓦ danairesort.com. Occupying its own patch of beach, this is one of Greece's most exclusive resorts; the decor mixes shiny white marble with soft-coloured quality furnishings. There's a spa, three restaurants, a bar and sports facilities. Breakfast included. April–Oct. **€550**

Ta Tria Skalopatia In the centre village centre ☎ 6974 830 330. Family-run taverna which has partial sea views from its patio and offers traditional cuisine like shrimp *saganáki* and *papoutsáki* for around €7–9. May to mid-Oct 9am–midnight.

Secular Athos

From Sithonía, a road winds around the coast and up over a ridge to Halkidhikí's third peninsula, the upper part of which is **secular Athos**. The principal place where you're likely to stop for refreshment is **Pyrgadhíkia**, a ravine-set fishing village jutting out into the Sigitikós gulf. There's little beach to speak of, although there are some good ones dotted along the stretch leading towards it. From Pyrgadhíkia, the main road heads back inland, while a turn-off via Gomáti takes you through unspoilt moors to Ierissós at the neck of the Athos peninsula.

GETTING AROUND   SECULAR ATHOS

By public transport This route has no public transport links; to travel between Sithonía and Athos by bus you

will have to backtrack via Halkidhikí's inland capital, Políyros.

Ierissós and around

With its good, long beach and a vast, promontory-flanked gulf, **IERISSÓS** is the most Greek-patronized of the secular Athos resorts, although the sizeable town itself, built well back from the shore and with room to expand, is a sterile concrete grid dating from after a devastating earthquake in 1932. The only hint of its life pre-tourism is the vast boat-building area on the sand, at the back of the wide beach to the south.

The road beyond Ierissós passes through mundane **Néa Ródha** before veering inland to follow a boggy depression that is the remaining stretch of **Xerxes' canal**, cut by the Persian invader in 480 BC to spare his fleet the shipwreck at the tip of Athos that had befallen the previous expedition eleven years before.

Ammouliani

Apart from Thássos (see p.662), **AMMOULIANÍ** (Ⓦ visitammouliani.com) is Macedonia's only inhabited Aegean island, and after decades of eking out an existence from fishing, the island's population, originally refugees from the Sea of Marmara, has over the past couple of decades had to adjust to an influx of holiday-makers. Like anywhere else in Halkidhikí, it can get very busy in late July and August, but in early or late summer this low-lying, scrub- and olive-covered islet can make an idyllic hideaway.

The island is accessed from the ferry jetty at **Trypití**. The main village, where the ferries dock, is an unprepossessing grid of concrete slung over a ridge, with few pre-1960s buildings remaining; it is, however, chock-a-block with **rooms**, many self-catering, and a few tavernas.

Beaches

Two kilometres southwest of Ammouliani village is **Alykés**, the islet's most famous beach, named after the salt marsh just behind and home to Ammouliani's only campsite (see below). The island's best beaches, however, lie in the far southeast, facing the straits with the Athos peninsula. To reach them, bear left onto the paved road 1500m out of town and follow the signs some 2km along this to **Áyios Yeóryios**, whose tiny **chapel** overlooks the excellent beach. You can continue a final 500m to the even more enticing **Megáli Ámmos** beach. Still other, less accessible, beaches beckon in the northwest of the island, served in season by excursion boats from the town; a popular map-postcard on sale locally will give necessary hints on how to reach them on foot or by bicycle.

Ouranoúpoli

Cruises to Dhrénia 3hr; times vary · €20/person, depending on the season

Fifteen kilometres beyond Ierissós, **OURANOÚPOLI** is the last community before the restricted monastic domains, with a centre that's downright tatty, showing the effects of too much tourism. Somewhat mysteriously, it has become a major **resort**, as well as functioning as the main gateway to Mount Athos; local beaches, stretching intermittently for several kilometres to the north, are sandy enough but narrow and cramped. If you're compelled to stay here while waiting for passage to Athos, you can either take a cruise, or **rent a motorboat**, to the mini-archipelago of **Dhrénia** just opposite, which has almost tropical sandy bays and tavernas on the larger islets. Modern craft also offer **cruises**, which skim along the Athonite coast, keeping any female passengers 500m offshore as required by the monastic authorities.

ARRIVAL AND DEPARTURE   SECULAR ATHOS

By bus There are 4–6 daily buses between Thessaloníki and Ouranoúpoli via Ierissós and Trypití.

By ferry Ferries run from Ierissós and Ouranoúpoli to

Mount Athos (see p.306). Ferries to Ammouliani leave from Trypití (hourly in summer, 4 daily off season; €2.20, car €10.10; 15min).

ACCOMMODATION AND EATING

AMMOULIANÍ
Camping Alikes Alykés beach ☎ 23770 51379, Ⓦ alikescamping.gr. Set right behind the beach but with plenty of shade and good cooking and washing facilities:

it's also home to the *Metochi* restaurant and *Big Fish* beach bar. May–Sept. €21

★**Gripos** Áyios Yeóryios beach ☎ 23770 51049, Ⓦ gripos.gr. This hotel has rooms of considerable charm, with copper antiques, beamed ceilings, terracotta floor tiles, large balconies and a swimming pool in the garden, which is full of pheasants and other exotic fowl. You can get great meals and mezédhes at its ouzerí too (May–Oct 11am–midnight). €35

Hotel Gallery 150m from the port ☎ 23770 51405, ⓦ hotelgallery.gr. Modest-sized and simply furnished rooms, all with basic self-catering facilities: the best of them have balconies overlooking the harbour. €40

Megali Ammos Megáli Ámmos beach ☎ 23770 51183. The superb location is matched by the fresh fish served at this taverna: quality catches such as *barboúni* or *tsipoúra* should work out at around only €15 per portion. Mid-May to Sept daily 11am–1am.

Sun Rise Left from the harbour ☎ 23770 51273, ⓦ sunrise-ammouliani.gr. With its own swimming jetty and a surprisingly snazzy cocktail bar in the lobby, this is one of the island's largest hotels, yet it remains intimate. €55

Tzanis At the back of Limanáki port ☎ 23770 51322. Nearly 100 years old, this good all-round taverna serves the usual range of dips, salads, grills plus the odd oven dish at around €7–8. May–Oct daily 10am–late.

IERISSÓS

Camping Ierissos On the beach just north of town ☎ 23770 21125. Well-developed municipal beachside campsite, with reasonable shade, shared facilities and a minimarket. May–Sept. €20

Marcos 3 blocks back from the south end of the seafront ☎ 23770 22518, ⓦ hotelmarkos.gr. Overlooking its own garden and car park, this stylishly furnished two-storey hotel has medium-sized comfortable rooms. May–Oct. €40

To Kolatsi Behind the landscaped promenade ☎ 23770 22487. A cross between a grill house and fish taverna, *To Kolatsi* serves both succulent meats and fresh fish for €6–8. Daily noon–midnight.

OURANOÚPOLI

Efkalyptos On the south waterfront ☎ 23770 71240. Good all round taverna serving a mixture of starters, meat and fish favourites (most under €10), which can be washed down with the palatable house wine. Daily 9am–midnight.

Hotel Makedonia On a hill above the harbour ☎ 23770 71085, ⓦ hotel-makedonia.gr. Modest-sized hotel, with compact but comfortable rooms, some of which have balconies. Pleasant communal lounge and balcony. €45

Sorokadha Behind the main beach ☎ 23770 71332. Offers a wide range of meat dishes such as roast lamb, pork chops and beef *kokkinistó* from €6, plus plenty of vegetarian choices. Daily 9am–midnight.

Xenia Nearly 500m north along the beach ☎ 23770 71412, ⓦ xeniaouranoupolis.com. The area's swishest hotel, with good off-season deals. The main block houses 1960s-style rooms, and there are larger bungalows available too, plus a decent restaurant. €70

Mount Athos: the monks' republic

Known in Greek as the *Áyion Óros* (Holy Mountain), **MOUNT ATHOS** is an autonomous province of the country – a "**monks' republic**" – on whose slopes are gathered twenty monasteries populated exclusively by men. Women and even female farm animals have been banned here since an edict by the Byzantine emperor in 1060. Most of the **monasteries** were founded in the tenth and eleventh centuries; today, all survive in a state of comparative decline but they remain unsurpassed in their general and architectural interest and for the art treasures they contain.

If you are male, over 18 years old and have a genuine interest in monasticism or Greek Orthodoxy, sacred music or simply in Byzantine and medieval architecture, a visit is recommended; this requires a **permit** (see p.309) which can be easily arranged in Thessaloníki. In addition to the religious and architectural aspects of Athos, it should be added that the peninsula remains one of the most beautiful parts of Greece. For many visitors, this – as much as the experience of monasticism – is the highlight of time spent on the Holy Mountain.

Brief history

The **development of monasticism** on Athos is a matter of some controversy, and foundation legends abound. The most popular asserts that the **Virgin Mary** was blown ashore here on her way to Cyprus. The earliest historical reference to Athonite monks is to their attendance at a council of the Empress Theodora in 843; probably there were some monks here by the end of the seventh century. In 885, an edict of Emperor Basil I recognized Athos as the sole preserve of monks, and gradually hermits came

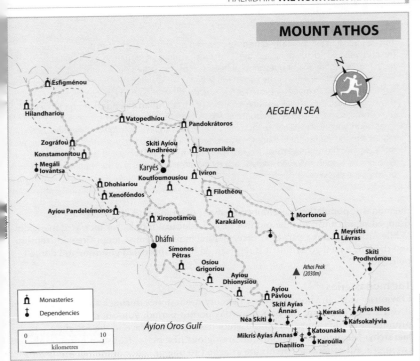

MOUNT ATHOS

AEGEAN SEA

Esfigménou

Hilandharíou

Vatopedhíou

Pandokrátoros

Zográfou

Skíti Ayíou
Andhréou

Stavronikíta

Konstamonítou

Megáli
Iovántsa

Karyés

Koutloumousíou

Iviron

Dhohiaríou

Xenofóndos

Filothéou

Ayíou Pandeleímonos

Xiropotámou

Karakálou

Morfonoú

Dháfni

Símonos
Pétras

Meyístis
Lávras

Osíou
Grigoríou

Skíti
Prodhrómou

Ayíou
Dhionysíou

Athos Peak
(2030m)

Ayíou
Pávlou

Skíti Ayías
Ánnas

Kerasiá

Ayios Nílos

Néa Skíti

Kafsokalývia

Áyion Óros Gulf

Mikrís Ayías Ánnas

Katounákia

Karoúlia

Dhanílion

| | Monasteries |
| | Dependencies |

0 ___ 10
kilometres

4

together to form communities known in church Greek as *koinobia* (literally "common life"). The year 963 is the traditional date for the **foundation of the first monastery**, Meyístis Lávras, by Athanasios the Athonite, largely financed by Emperor Nikiforos Fokas. Over the next two centuries foundations were frequent – the monasteries reached a total of forty – alongside many smaller communities.

Troubles for Athos began at the end of the eleventh century. The monasteries suffered sporadically from pirate raids and from the settlement of three hundred Vlach shepherd families on the mountain. After a reputedly scandalous episode between the monks and the shepherdesses, the Vlachs were ejected and a new imperial edict was issued, confirming that **no female** mammal, human or animal, be allowed to set foot on Athos. This edict, called the *ávaton*, remains in force today, excepting cats to control rodents.

During the twelfth century, the monasteries gained an international – or at least, a **pan-Orthodox** – aspect, as Romanian, Russian and Serbian monks flocked to the mountain in retreat from the turbulence of the age, although the peninsula itself was subject to raids by Franks and Catalans over the next two centuries. After the fall of the Byzantine Empire to the Ottomans, the fathers wisely declined to resist, maintaining good relations with the early sultans, one of whom paid a state visit.

The mountain's real decline came after the early nineteenth-century **War of Independence**, in which many of the monks fought alongside the Greek revolutionary forces but paid the price when Macedonia was easily subdued. This led to a permanent Turkish garrison and the first drastic reduction in the monastic population, which did not increase even when Macedonia returned to Greece in 1912. The Athonite fathers, however, resisted diluting the Greek nature of the Holy Mountain with too many foreign (mainly Russian) monks. By the early 1960s numbers were at their lowest, barely a thousand, compared to twenty thousand in Athos's heyday. Today, however,

MOUNT ATHOS TIME

The traditional Byzantine **daily schedule** observed on Athos is somewhat disorienting. On the northeast side of the peninsula the "12 o'clock" position on monastery clocks indicates neither noon nor midnight but sunrise, whereas on the opposite side of Athos it coincides with sunset. Yet Vatopedhíou, the largest monastery, keeps "worldly" time, as do most monks' wristwatches, and in many monasteries two wall clocks are mounted side by side, one showing secular, the other "Byzantine" time. However, the **Julian calendar**, a fortnight behind the outside world, is observed throughout Athos. Bedtime is shortly after sunset and in the small hours your hosts will awake for solitary meditation and study, followed by *órthros*, or matins. Around sunrise there is another quiet period, just before the *akolouthía*, or main liturgy, that precedes the morning meal. The rest of the day is devoted to manual labour until the *esperinós*, or vespers, followed immediately by the afternoon meal and the short *apódhipno*, or Compline service.

the **monastic population** has climbed to about two thousand, its average age has dropped significantly and the number of well-educated monks has increased markedly. While Athos remains a part of Greece, all foreign monks must adopt **Greek citizenship**, and the Greek civil government is represented by an appointed governor and a small police force.

The monasteries

Obviously you can't hope to visit all twenty monasteries during a short stay, though if you're able to extend the basic four-day permit period, you can see the most prominent foundations. Each monastery has a distinct place in the **Athonite hierarchy**: Meyístis Lávras holds the prestigious first place, Konstamonítou ranks twentieth. All other settlements are attached to one or other of the twenty "ruling" monasteries; the dependencies range from a *skíti*, or minor monastic community (either a group of houses, or a cloister-like compound scarcely distinguishable from a monastery), through a *kellí* (a sort of farmhouse) to an *isyhastírio* (a solitary hermitage, often a cave). Numerous laymen – including many Muslim Albanians – also live on Athos, mostly employed as agricultural or manual labourers by the monasteries.

For simplicity's sake, it is easiest to divide the monasteries according to which coast of the peninsula they belong to: **southwestern** or **northeastern**. Our listings (see p.309), which give brief descriptions of the main highlights, reflect this division. The institutions of each coast are described in geographical order, starting with those closest to the mainland. Apart from the four *skítes* that accept overnight visitors and thus merit their own entry, all other dependencies are mentioned in the account of their ruling monastery.

ARRIVAL AND DEPARTURE   MOUNT ATHOS

BY FERRY

All boats to Athos are run by Ayiorítikes Grammés (☎23770 71149, ⌨agioreitikes-grammes.com). Most visitors arrive at the main port of Dháfni on the southwest coast. From here, the small *Ayia Anna* sails round the southern tip of the peninsula as far as Kafsokalývia and stops at all the monastic communities en route; advance booking is advisable. Each monastery has a small harbour annexe (*arsanás*) which can be a considerable distance from the monastery itself.

From Ouranoúpoli The regular ferry sails at 9.45am as far as Dháfni (90min; €9), stopping at each harbour or coastal monastery en route. There are also faster boats at 8.45am and 10.40am (45min; €15) direct to Dháfni.

From Ierissós A single fast boat leaves Ierissós at 8.35am daily and travels along the northeast shore as far as the monastery of Megístis Lavras (2hr; €22); it may not stop at every harbour on the way but is guaranteed to halt at the Hilandharíou police post for the issue of permits.

From Thessaloníki To reach Athos from Thessaloníki, first take a Halkidhikí KTEL bus (see p.277) to Ouranoúpoli or Ierissós (see p.304).

INFORMATION

Permits Only ten permits per day are issued to non-Orthodox visitors to Athos (120 for baptized Greek Orthodox), so it is wise to apply as far in advance as possible (six months maximum), especially for summer or Easter visits. The first step is to contact the Holy Executive of the Holy Mount Pilgrims' Bureau in Thessaloníki (Mon–Fri 9am–2pm, Sat 10am–noon; ☎ 2310 252 578, ✉ athosreservation@gmail.com) at Egnatía 109. Staff speak English but walk-in visits are not encouraged. Once you have your booking, you must reconfirm two weeks before the intended date of entry. Last-minute permits can sometimes be obtained if there's a cancellation, though you won't have an accommodation reservation at any of the monasteries.

Fees and extensions You pay for and receive your permit (€30; students under 26 €10) on the day of entry itself, either from the pilgrims' bureau in Ouranoúpoli, if sailing from there, or at the police post at Hilandharíou, if sailing from Ierissós; make sure you have your passport with you. The permit entitles you to stay for three nights and four days, during which time board and meals at the monasteries are free. Many visitors apply for an extension. This can theoretically be done at the Ayía Epistasía (Holy Superintendency) in Karyés, the picturesque administrative capital; two or three extra days are normally granted, and your chances are much better out of season.

GETTING AROUND

By car Landrover minibuses meet the larger ferries at Dháfni and other harbours to carry people to Karyés and the more inland monasteries accessible by road; they can be expensive and, if they're driven by lay-workers, you should establish a price beforehand.

By foot Most foreign visitors choose to walk between monasteries, preferably armed with the excellent map by Road Editions (1:50,000), which includes an informative 48-page booklet. Even with that, it's wise to check the current condition of trails at each monastery.

MONASTERY ACCOMMODATION

Theoretically, all twenty major and four minor monasteries that receive guests require **advance reservations**, although several do not apply this rule strictly (see individual reviews below). Just about all the most interesting monasteries, however, do require booking, which can be done up to six months in advance. Where hours are shown, call during these times Monday–Saturday, though you may have to persevere for an answer – don't bother trying on Sunday or any major holy day. Alternatively, most monasteries have fax numbers and around a dozen have emails. Accommodation is typically in **dormitories**, and fairly spartan, but there's invariably a shower down the hall (often hot) and you're always given sheets and blankets. As long as you have a valid permit, accommodation is free.

THE SOUTHWESTERN COAST MONASTERIES

Zográfou ☎ 23770 23247, ✉ zograf.logos@gmail.com.

Almost an hour from its harbour, the most inland monastery is inhabited by Bulgarian and Macedonian monks. The name derives from a legend that the founders

---

ATHOS ETIQUETTE

Remember that the monks on Athos are expecting **religious pilgrims**, not tourists. Each monastery varies in its handling of visitors: some institutions forbid you from attending services or sharing meals with the monks; others put themselves at the disposal of visitors of whatever creed (though you may well find yourself being encouraged to switch to Greek Orthodoxy). Yet, wherever you stay, there's a certain amount of etiquette to observe.

You must reach the monastery where you will overnight **before dark**, since they all lock their front gates at sunset – which would leave you outside with the wild boars. Upon arrival, ask for the **guestmaster** (*arhondáris*), who will proffer the traditional welcome of a *tsípouro*, *loukoúmi* (Turkish delight) and often a Greek coffee, before showing you to your bed. Most guestmasters speak good English.

You should be **fully dressed** at all times, even when going from dormitory to bathroom; shorts should not be worn anywhere on the peninsula, nor hats inside monasteries. **Swimming** is officially prohibited, so if you are tempted, choose a cove where nobody can see you, and certainly don't skinny-dip. **Smoking** is forbidden, though it is often tolerated outside the monastery walls; it would be criminal to smoke on the trail, however, given the chronic fire danger. Singing, whistling and raised voices are taboo; as is standing with your hands behind your back or in your pockets. If you want to photograph the monks, always ask permission, though **photography** is forbidden altogether in many monasteries.

left out a wooden panel, upon which a painting of St George (known as St George the Zograf) appeared. Non-Orthodox and believers are segregated, but walk-in guests are usually accepted.

Konstamonítou ☎&✆23770 23228. Nearly 2hr from Zográfou and 45min from its own harbour. Set amid thick woodland, it's as humble, bare and poor as you'd expect from the last-ranking monastery. Non-Orthodox and believers are segregated but guests are happily taken on spec.

Dhohiaríou ☎&✆23770 23245. Nearly 2hr from Konstamonítou. Picturesque monastery with a lofty church nearly filling the courtyard. The best frescoes are in the long, narrow refectory, which has sea views.

Xenofóndos ☎23770 23633, ✉arhontariki @imxenophontos.gr. Only 30min from Dhohiaríou. The enormous, sloping, irregularly shaped court, expanded upwards in the nineteenth century, is unique in possessing two main churches. The small, older one, decorated with exterior frescoes of the Cretan school, was usurped during the 1830s by the huge upper one.

Ayíou Pandeleímonos ☎23770 23252, ✉rpm .palomnik@gmail.com; 10am–noon. Nearly 2hr from Dháfni and 1hr from Xenofóndos. Also known as "Róssiko", as many of its monks are Russian and it sports onion-shaped domes. The main attraction is the enormous bell over the refectory, the second largest ringer in the world.

Xiropotámou ☎23770 23251, ✆23770 23733; 10am–12.30pm. Under an hour from Dháfni. Most of its construction and church frescoes date from the eighteenth century. Non-Orthodox are kept segregated from the faithful at meal times.

Símonos Pétras ☎23770 23254, ✉hospitality @simonopetra.gr; 1–3pm. Best reached by boat. Though entirely rebuilt after an early twentieth-century fire, "Simópetra", as it is known, is perhaps the most visually striking monastery on Athos. With its multiple storeys, ringed by wooden balconies over-hanging sheer 300m drops, it resembles a Tibetan lamasery.

Osíou Grigoríou ☎23770 23668, ✆23770 23671; 11am–1pm. An hour and a half from Símonos Pétras. Hover-ing closely above the sea and renowned for the quality of its chanting, it has a fine common room/library with literature on Orthodoxy and an extra guest hostel outside the gate.

Dhionysíou ☎23770 23687, ✆23770 23686. Around an hour from Osíou Grigoríou, this fortified structure, perched spectacularly on a coastal cliff, is among the most richly endowed monasteries. The best icons are in the refectory rather than the dim church. Non-Orthodox must eat separately.

Ayíou Pávlou ☎23770 23741, ✆23770 23355; 10am–12.30pm. About an hour from Ayíou Dhionysíou, this edifice actually looks more imposing from afar; many Cypriot monks are in residence.

Néa Skíti ☎23770 23572, ✉iera.nea.skiti@gmail .com; 10am–noon. Under an hour from Ayíou Pávlou. There's nothing too special about this dependency, except that it serves as a handy base for Athos peak.

Skíti Ayías Ánnas ☎23770 23320. An hour and a half from Ayíou Pávlou, this monastery is in a pleasant location, with buildings tumbling down to the shore. It's used as the most common "base camp" for climbing Athos peak (2030m).

THE NORTHEASTERN COAST MONASTERIES

Hilandharíou ☎23770 23797, ✉pilgrims@hilandar .org. A beacon of Serbian culture since the thirteenth century, with monks on rotation from Serbia. The fourteenth-century church in the triangular courtyard has attractive frescoes – look out for the *Ouranóskala* or "Stairway to Heaven". The monastery also boasts the most salubrious guest quarters on the Mountain.

Esfigménou ☎23770 23653. This fortress-like monastery is right on the coast but little visited due to its reputation as the strictest institution on Athos. The monks refuse to accept Patriarch Bartholemew because of his ecumenical initiatives, and banners proclaim "Orthodoxy or death!"

Vatopedhíou ☎23778 88088, ✉monastery @vatopedi.gr; 9am–1pm. A great 3.5hr walk from Esfigménou, this is the largest and second most important monastery, home to over three hundred monks, many of them English-speaking. The cobbled, slanting courtyard with its free-standing belfry resembles a town plaza. The *katholikón* contains exceptional fourteenth-century frescoes and three exquisite mosaics.

Pandokrátoros ☎23770 23880, ✉pantokvisit @gmail.com. Nearly a 3hr walk from Vatopedhíou, its best features are the guest rooms overlooking its own picturesque fishing harbour and the citrus-laden courtyard. In a valley above looms its imposing dependency, Profítis Ilías.

Stavronikíta ☎&✆23770 23255; 10am–noon. An hour's walk from both Pandokrátoros and Ivíron, this monastery offers some of the best views of Athos peak and is the most distinct example of an Athonite coastal fortress-monastery. The narrow church occupies virtually all the gloomy courtyard. Orthodox and non-believer alike are roused for 3.30am matins.

Skíti Ayíou Andhréou ☎23770 23810. A former Russian dependency of the great Vatopedhíou monastery, erected in the nineteenth century. Almost deserted today but close to Karyés, and they may take walk-in overnighters.

Koutloumousíou ☎23770 23226, ✆23770 23731. Small and tidy monastery on the edge of Karyés. Its name is said to derive from a Seljuk chieftain who converted to Christianity.

víron ☎ 23770 23643, ✉ miviron@gmail.com; noon–2pm. Vast place housing around forty monks. Pilgrims flock to the miraculous icon of the *Portaítissa*, the Virgin Guarding the Gate, inside its own chapel. The huge main church has an elaborate mosaic floor dating from 1030 and interesting pagan touches such as ram's-head column capitals. There is also an immensely rich library and treasury-museum.

Filothéou ☎ 23770 23256, ✉ grammateia @philotheou.gr; noon–3pm. Around an hour's walk uphill from Ivíron, this is a lively place that was at the forefront of the monastic revival in the early 1980s, though it's not too attractive apart from the expansive lawn. Non-Orthodox visitors are barred from services and dining with the faithful.

Karakálou ☎ 23770 23225, 🖷 23770 23746. The lofty keep here, under an hour's walk downhill from Filothéou, is typical of the fortress-monasteries built to deter pirate attacks. Non-Orthodox are barred from services and dining with the faithful.

Meyístis Lávras ☎ 23770 23754, ✉ iera.moni .megistis.layras@gmail.com. The oldest and foremost of the ruling monasteries, as well as the most imposing complex on Athos, with fifteen chapels within its walls. At mealtimes you can enjoy the frescoes in the refectory, executed by Theophanes the Cretan in 1535. Among its many dependencies, just 10min away by marked path there's the hermitage-cave of Ayios Athanasios, watched over by five skulls.

Skíti Prodhrómou ☎ 23770 23294. A good 2hr walk from Meyístis Lávras, this large dependency is run by welcoming young Romanian monks, who often take guests in on spec. Other dependencies further along the southern tip include the *kellí* (farmhouse) of Áyios Nílos and the frescoed chapel of Kafsokalývia, from where boats depart to the southwestern coast.

EATING AND DRINKING

Athos grows much of its own **food** and the monastic diet is based on tomatoes, beans, olives, green vegetables, coarse bread, cheese and pasta, with occasional meat dishes or treats like *halvás* and fruit; a glass of **wine** is commonly served, and fish is standard after Sunday morning service. Only two meals are served daily in the *trápeza* (refectory or dining room): the first, more substantial one, any time between 8am and 11am, the latter about 1.5–2hr before sunset, depending on the time of year. Meals in the monasteries are free (with a valid permit). It's a good idea to bring supplementary provisions with you. There are a few shops in Karyés and Dháfni, but for a better selection you should stock up before coming to Athos.

Northeastern Macedonia

Few people ever venture into the arable plains of **northeastern Macedonia**, where attractions are sparsely spread among golden fields of corn and tobacco and incredible numbers of storks' nests. Up near the craggy mountains that form the frontier with Bulgaria, artificial **Lake Kerkíni** is home to masses of birds, some of which are extremely rare in Europe, which makes it as interesting to ornithologists as the Préspa lakes much further west. The tranquil setting and rich flora mean it is not only for avid twitchers.

An alternative route to the Egnatía Odhós for reaching Kavála is the scenic route that climbs northeast out of Thessaloníki, first taking you via Sérres before passing **Alistráti**, worth a visit for its memorable caves, and then heading towards Dhráma and ancient **Philippi** along a quieter road that offers majestic panoramas of Mount Meníkio (1963m), Mount Pangéo (1956m) and Mount Falakró (2230m). Regular **buses** from Thessaloníki and between Sérres and Dhráma ply this road.

The Kerkíni Wetlands

Artificial, marsh-fringed **Lake Kerkíni**, tucked up near the mountainous Bulgarian border some 80km northeast of Thessaloníki, enjoys international protected status, thanks to the 300-plus species of **birds** that spend at least part of the year here, some of them on the endangered species list. Huge expanses of water lilies stretch across the large anvil-shaped lake, out of which the River Strymónas flows to the northern Aegean near ancient Amphipolis, while a herd of water buffalo wallows and grazes the eastern banks, and local fishermen compete with every type of heron known to inhabit Europe. Other birds breeding in the Kerkíni wetlands include various species of grebes, terns, egrets, ducks, geese, ibis, spoonbills, avocets and pelicans, plus raptors such as the black kite, the short-toed eagle and the Levant sparrowhawk.

Kerkíni

Two kilometres from the lake's northern shore lies the village of **KERKÍNI**, where you will find the **Kerkíni Wetlands Information Centre** (see below). You can also negotiate **bird-watching** trips in a *pláva*, a traditional punt-like fishing boat. The surroundings reward exploration with their abundance of flora and fauna – there are huge numbers of wild flowers in the spring and early summer.

ARRIVAL AND INFORMATION   KERKÍNI

By bus Although you can get a bus or train from Thessaloníki or Sérres to Livadhiá, 7km north of the lake, you'll need your own vehicle, once here.

Information The Kerkíni Wetlands Information Centre is based in the centre of the village (Mon–Fri 8am–4pm, Sat & Sun 10am–2pm; ☎ 23270 28004, ⦿ kerkini.gr).

ACCOMMODATION AND EATING

★**Oikoperiigitis** Kerkíni village ☎ 23270 41450, ⦿ oikoperiigitis.gr. By far the best place to stay: in addition to comfortable rooms, a decent restaurant (try the buffalo meat) and camping facilities, the eco-friendly lodge offers local tours by boat, canoe, bike, jeep or on horseback. **€55**

0 Harisis Kerkíni village ☎ 23270 41232. Simple *psarotavérna* that serves fresh lake fish, such as trout for around €10, and a fair range of accompanying salads and vegetable dishes. Erratic hours.

4 Alistráti

Just over 20km before the dull market town of Dhráma, on the road from Sérres, you come to the large village of **ALISTRÁTI**, which is well placed for exploring the nearby mountains, although the main reason to stop here is to visit the impressive **caves** nearby.

Alistráti caves

Down a scenic side road 6km southeast of Alistráti village • Daily: June 9am–6pm; July 9am–7pm; Sept–May 9am–5pm • 1hr guided tours only €8 • ☎ 23240 82045, ⦿ alistraticave.gr • No photography

The **Alistráti caves** were first explored in the mid-1970s and surpass those at Pérama; indeed, some claim them to be the most extensive of their kind in Europe that do not require special equipment or training to visit. These gigantic **limestone** cavities are over two million years old, and bristle with a variety of wonderful formations, including the relatively rare eccentrites and helictites: respectively, stalactites sticking out at angles, rather than hanging vertically, and twisted forms resembling sticks of barley sugar. The entrance, a long tunnel bored into the hillside, takes you right into the caverns, and a winding path weaves its way through masses of stalagmites, many of them outstandingly beautiful, and some exceeding 15m in height.

ACCOMMODATION AND EATING   ALISTRÁTI

★**Archondiko Voziki** G. Stimenidi 11, signposted from main road ☎ 23240 20400. A delightfully restored tobacco factory-cum-mansion, painted a rich yellow, with beautifully furnished period rooms and a swimming pool. Breakfast included. **€40**

Ifiyenia On main road ☎ 23240 31886. The comfy cushioned chairs and gingham tablecloths are deceptive: this cheap local taverna does an interesting range of salads, seafood pasta and pork chops for a mere €5–6. Daily noon–1am.

Philippi

Daily 8am–7pm, Nov–May till 3pm; museum closed Mon • €6 • ☎ 2510 516 251 • Buses every 30min from Kavála or Dhráma

Just 14km short of Kavála on the busy road from Dhráma, you come to **PHILIPPI** (Filippoi on some maps and signs), a famous battlefield during the civil wars of ancient Rome and the subject of one of St Paul's Epistles. Apart from the scattered

Roman ruins, the principal remains of the site are several impressive, although derelict, **basilican churches**.

Brief history

Philippi was named after Philip II of Macedon, who wrested it from the Thracians in 356 BC for the sake of nearby gold mines on Mount Pangéo. However, it owed its later importance and prosperity to the Roman construction of the Via Egnatía. With Kavála/Neapolis as its port, Philippi was essentially the easternmost town of Roman-occupied Europe. Here, as at Actium (see p.260), the fate of the Roman Empire was decided, at the **Battle of Philippi** in 42 BC. After assassinating Julius Caesar, Brutus and Cassius had fled east of the Adriatic and, against their better judgement, were forced into confrontation on the Philippi plains with the pursuing armies of Antony and Octavian and were comprehensively beaten in two successive battles.

St Paul landed at Kavála and visited Philippi in 49 AD, and so began his religious mission in Europe. Despite being cast into prison, he retained a special affection for the Philippians, his first converts, and the congregation that he established was one of the earliest to flourish in Greece.

The site

The most conspicuous of the churches at the site is the **Direkler** (Turkish for "columns" or "piers"), to the south of the modern road which here follows the line of the Via Egnatía. Also known as Basilica B, this was an unsuccessful attempt by its sixth-century architect to improve the basilica design by adding a dome. The central arch of its west wall and a few pillars of reused antique drums stand amid remains of the Roman **forum**. A line of second-century porticoes spreads outwards in front of the church, and on their east side are the foundations of a colonnaded octagonal church, which was approached from the Via Egnatía by a great gate. Behind the Direkler and, perversely, the most interesting and best-preserved building of the site, is a huge monumental **public latrine** with nearly fifty of its original marble seats still intact.

Across the road on the northern side, stone steps climb up to a terrace. On the way up, on the right, you'll pass a Roman crypt, reputed to have been the **prison of St Paul** and appropriately frescoed. The terrace flattens out onto a huge paved atrium that extends to the foundations of another extremely large basilica, designated Basilica A. If you continue in the same direction around the base of a hill, you'll emerge above a **theatre** cut into its side. Though it dates from the same period as the original town, it was heavily remodelled as an amphitheatre by the Romans – the

---

THE TOMB OF AMPHIPOLIS

The most significant archeological find in Greece since the uncovering of the Royal Tombs at Vergina (see p.288) took place in 2012 with the discovery of the ancient tomb complex of **Amphipolis** on **Kasta Hill**, near the modern town of Néa Amfípoli. Although the site is not yet open to the public, excavations have unearthed three burial chambers within a huge tumulus surrounded by a 500m-long wall.

Among the stunning features that have come to light are sphinxes, Caryatids and colourful floor mosaics, while the hill is also believed to have been the original location of the ancient stone lion discovered by the Strymonas River in 1912. The greatest subject of debate, however, has been the identity of the **human remains** found inside, with some experts even claiming that one of the five skeletons was **Alexander the Great** himself. While that theory has been discredited, it is likely that it is the tomb of somebody closely connected to him.

Until the tomb opens to visitors, the closest you can get is the perimeter fence, a few kilometres north of the Egnatía Odhós motorway, just over halfway from Thessaloníki to Kavála. Meanwhile, check out two fascinating websites on the finds, ⓦtheamphipolistomb .com and ⓦamfipolis.com.

bas-reliefs of Nemesis, Mars and Victory all belong to this period. It is now used for performances during the annual summer Philippi-Thássos Festival. The best general impression of the site – which is extensive despite a lack of obviously notable buildings – and of the battlefield behind it can be gained from the **acropolis**, whose own remains are predominantly medieval. You can reach this via a steep climb along a path from the museum.

Kavála

Backing onto the easterly foothills of Mount Sýmvolo, **KAVÁLA** is Macedonia's second-largest city and the second port for northern Greece; it was an extremely wealthy place in the nineteenth century, when the region's **tobacco** crop was shipped from its docks to the rest of the world. Known in ancient times as **Neapolis**, the town was the first European port of call for merchants and travellers from the Middle East. It was here that **St Paul** landed en route to Philippi (see p.312), on his initial mission to Europe. In later years, the port and citadel were occupied in turn by the Byzantines, Normans, Franks, Venetians, Ottomans and (during both world wars) Bulgarians.

Although its attempt to style itself as the "Azure City", on account of its position at the head of a wide bay, is going a little overboard, it does have an interesting **historic centre**, focused on the harbour area and the few remaining tobacco warehouses. A picturesque **citadel** looks down from a rocky promontory to the east, and an elegant Ottoman aqueduct leaps over modern buildings into the old quarter on the bluff. Kavála is also one of the main departure points for Thássos (see p.662), as well as Límnos (see p.633) and other northeast Aegean islands.

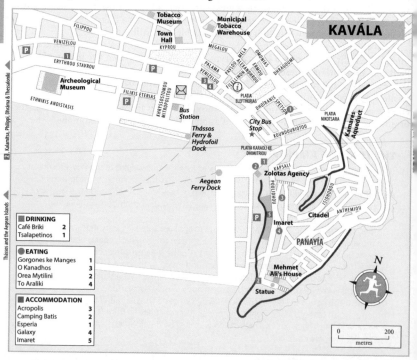

KAVÁLA

DRINKING

| Café Briki | 2 |
| Tsalapetinos | 1 |

EATING

Gorgones ke Manges	1
O Kanadhos	3
Orea Mytilini	2
To Araliki	4

ACCOMMODATION

Acropolis	3
Camping Batis	2
Esperia	1
Galaxy	4
Imaret	5

Panayía

Although the remnants of Kaválá's Ottoman past are mostly neglected, the wedge-shaped **Panayía** quarter to the east of the port preserves a scattering of eighteenth-and nineteenth-century buildings with atmospheric lanes wandering up towards the citadel. The most conspicuous and interesting of its buildings is the splendid **Imaret**, overlooking the harbour on Poulídhou. A long, multi-domed structure, it was built in 1817 as a hostel for theological students. Undoubtedly the best-preserved Islamic building on Greek territory, it was endowed to the city by **Mehmet (or Mohammed) Ali**, pasha of Egypt and founder of the dynasty which ended with King Farouk; it still officially belongs to the Egyptian government and today houses a luxury **hotel** (see p.316). Further up the promontory, near the corner of Poulídhou and Mohámet Alí, you can see the prestigious **Ottoman-style house** where Mehmet Ali was born to an Albanian family in 1769. Nearby rears an elegant equestrian bronze **statue** of the great man, one of the finest of its kind in Greece.

The citadel

Daily: April 8am–8pm; May–Sept 8am–9pm; Oct 8am–6pm; Nov–March 8am–4pm • €2.50 • ☎ 2510 231 011, ⓦ castle-kavala.gr

There are wonderful views from the Byzantine **citadel**, signposted "castle", where you can explore the ramparts, towers, dungeon and cistern. For three weeks in August, it co-hosts the Philippi-Thássos Festival (ⓦ philippifestival.gr) of drama and music in its main court.

Kamáres aqueduct

Sweeping imperiously across the traffic in Platía Nikotsára as it enters the centre below Panayía is the towering **Kamáres aqueduct**. The structure was built on a Roman model during the reign of Süleyman the Magnificent (1520–66), and it was still used to supply Kavála with drinking water until as recently as 1911.

Archeological Museum

Erythroú Stavroú 17 • Tues–Sun 8am–3pm • €2 • ☎ 2510 222 335

Kaválá's **Archeological Museum** contains a fine dolphin-and-lily mosaic upstairs in the Abdera room, plus painted sarcophagi in the adjacent section devoted to Thassian colonies. Downstairs, there are many terracotta figurines still decorated in their original paint and gold ornaments from tombs at Amphipolis (see p.313).

The Tobacco Museum

Paleológou 4 • Mon–Fri 8am–4pm, Sat 10am–2pm; June–Sept also Thurs 5–8pm & Sun 10am–2pm • €2 • ☎ 2510 223 344, ⓦ tobaccomuseum.gr

The potentially interesting **Tobacco Museum** falls down on its presentation and the lack of explanations in Greek, let alone English, though some of the exhibits, including historic photographs and antique cigarette packets, are worthwhile. A refurbishment is planned, however, which will incorporate displays from the now defunct Municipal Folklore Museum, so an all-round improvement can be expected. For a more impressive taste of the town's tobacco history, check out the fabulous facade of the **Municipal Tobacco Warehouse** (Dhimotikí Kapnapothíki), at Platía Kapnergáti.

ARRIVAL AND DEPARTURE   **KAVÁLA**

By plane Megas Alexandhros airport is about 25km east of Kavála and serves seasonal charter flights to and from Europe, plus regular flights to Athens (1–2 daily; 1hr 5min). An airport shuttle bus (€5) to Kavála meets Athens flights; taxis cost a fixed rate of €35.

By bus The main bus station (☎ 2510 222 294; ⓦ ktelkavalas.gr) is on the corner of Mitropolítou Khryssostómou and Filikís Eterías.

Destinations Alexandhroúpoli (4 daily; 3hr); Athens (2 daily; 9hr); Keramotí (hourly; 1hr); Komotiní (4 daily; 2hr); Philippi (Mon–Sat every 30min, Sun hourly; 20min); Thessaloníki (hourly; 2hr); Xánthi (hourly; 1hr).

By ferry Details for the services below are available from the port authority (☎ 2510 223 716) and tickets from agencies such as Zolotas (☎ 2510 835 671), around the harbourfront towards the terminal/customs house. Note that Keramotí, 46km southeast of Kaválla, offers a more frequent, shorter and marginally cheaper ferry crossing to Thássos (6–12 daily; 40min).

Destinations Híos (4 weekly; 10–12hr); Ikaría (3 weekly; 14–19hr); Lésvos (3 weekly; 7–9hr); Límnos (7 weekly; 4hr 30min–5hr); Sámos (3 weekly; 12–15hr); Thássos (Skála Prínou; 5 daily; 50min).

By car You can usually find parking spaces on the quay car park, near the Thássos dock, or in the one next to the Archeological Museum.

INFORMATION

Tourist office The City of Kaválla tourist office (Mon–Sat 8am–8.30pm, though sometimes shorter hours due to lack of staff; ☎ 2510 231 011, ⓦ kavalagreece.gr) in the main square, Platía Eleftherías, has a host of brochures and sells tickets for the summer Philippi-Thássos Festival.

ACCOMMODATION

Acropolis Venizélou 29 ☎ 2510 223 543, ⓔ hotel-acropolis@hotmail.com. This basic old-fashioned guesthouse is the cheapest place to stay in town. It has plain twins, two of which share a bathroom, while the en-suite rooms have had a bit of a makeover – one boasts a huge balcony with a harbour view. **€40**

Camping Batis On the shore, 4km west of the port ☎ 2510 245 918, ⓦ batis-sa.gr. The nearest campsite to town, with nicely landscaped grounds, a range of recreational facilities and some entertainment options. March–Oct. **€18**

Esperia Erythroú Stavroú 44 ☎ 2510 229 621, ⓦ esperiakavala.gr. This is a decent hotel with comfortable modern rooms – ask for the quieter side or ones at the back. Buffet breakfast, served on a terrace, is included. **€60**

Galaxy Venizélou 27 ☎ 2510 224 812, ⓦ airotel.gr. The most imposing building on the central harbourfront is run by the slick Airotel chain. The newly renovated rooms are a good deal most of the year, and there are great views from all the seafront rooms and the roof garden restaurant/bar. **€69**

★ **Imaret** Poulídhou 6 ☎ 2510 620 151, ⓦ imaret.gr. This unique and expertly refurbished Ottoman medrese (see p.315) has rooms and suites that have been faultlessly fashioned, while keeping the original building intact. Services include a traditional hammam with massage, a restaurant serving Ottoman dishes and a womb-like indoor pool. **€300**

EATING

As is often the case, many of Kaválla's **waterfront** establishments are somewhat overpriced, so head for the Panayía district, with its row of moderately priced tavernas and ouzerís.

★ **Gorgones ke Manges** Éllis 4 ☎ 2510 833 600. Tucked behind Áyios Nikólaos church, this friendly ouzerí serves great mezédes such as mackerel, chops, squid and prawns for as little as €4.50, plus excellent local *tsípouro*. Live music on Mon, Thurs & Sun. Daily 10am–1am.

★ **O Kanadhos** Poulídhou 27 ☎ 2510 835 172. Grilled meat and fish for around €6–9 are the forte at this friendly place run by returnees from Toronto – hence the name and the English-speaking management. They also do very cheap bulk wine and set meals for two. Daily 11am–1am.

Orea Mytilini Karaolí Dhimitríou 36 ☎ 2510 224 749. The most reliable of the waterfront restaurants, with most items on the menu under €10, as long as you avoid the top-quality fish, which costs €40–65/kg. Daily 11am–2am.

To Araliki Poulídhou 33 ☎ 6972 339 033. Just about all the main dishes are meaty ones from the grill and cost under €10. There is also a fair range of salads and dips, plus fine Limniot wine. Daily 10am–late; closed Sun.

DRINKING AND NIGHTLIFE

As a student town, Kaválla has plenty of lively bars and nightspots, especially around pedestrianized **Ayíou Nikoláou**, behind the eponymous church. A string of trendy café-bars also lurks on pedestrianized **Palamá**, parallel to Venizélou.

Café Briki Poulídhou 76 ☎ 694 43 33 220. This popular café-bar is converted from a large stone mansion beside the citadel and provides a chic venue for admiring the splendid bay view over a coffee or cocktail. Daily 8.30am–2am.

Tsalapetinos Platía Karaóli ke Dhimitríou 36 ☎ 2511 111 073. This popular spot in the corner of the harbour has a huge stone interior and an outdoor terrace. There are plenty of cocktails and musical styles ranging from swing to rock. Daily 9am–2am.

Thrace

The ethnically diverse Greek province of **THRACE** (Thráki) was once part of a much larger region now split between the modern states of Greece, Turkey and Bulgaria. Once across the Néstos River (the border with Macedonia), the change in population is obvious: Turkish settlements with their tiled, whitewashed houses and pencil-thin minarets contrast sharply with modern Greek villages built for the refugees of the 1920s (see box, below). The same features are combined in the region's most appealing urban centre, the attractive market town of **Xánthi**. Of the mountain villages north of Xánthi, **Stavroúpoli** stands out, while to the south and east a trio of **archeological sites** is to be found along the coast near **Komotiní**. Beyond the service town of **Alexandhroúpoli** lies the Évros River, which forms the heavily guarded land border with Turkey.

Xánthi

XÁNTHI is the most interesting point to break a journey in Thrace. There is a busy market area, good food and, up the hill to the north of the **Kendrikí Platía** (the main café-lined square), a very attractive old **Ottoman quarter**. Notable for its distinguished clocktower, Kendrikí Platía sits at the end of the main south–north thoroughfare, 28-Oktovríou, lined with fast-food outlets and sundry shops. The town is also home to the **University of Thrace**, which lends a lively air to the place, particularly in the area between the bazaar and the campus, where bars, cinemas and bistros are busy in term time.

Try to visit during Xánthi's huge **street fair** (Saturdays 7am–4pm): attended equally by Greeks, Pomaks and ethnic Turks, it takes place in an open space near the fire station on the eastern side of the town.

The old town

The narrow cobbled streets of the **old town** are home to a number of very fine mansions – some restored, some derelict – with colourful exteriors, bay windows and wrought-iron balconies; most date from the mid-nineteenth century, when Xánthi's tobacco merchants made their fortunes.

Further up, the roads become increasingly narrow and steep, and the Turkish presence (about fifteen percent of the total urban population) is more noticeable: many of the women have their heads covered, and the more religious ones wear full-length cloaks. Churches and mosques hide behind whitewashed houses with tiled roofs and

---

1923 AND ALL THAT

Separated from the Turkish territory of eastern Thrace by the Évros River and its delta, western Thrace is the Greek state's most recent acquisition, under effective Greek control only since 1920. While Muslims throughout the rest of the country were evacuated by force under the **Treaty of Lausanne in 1923** (see p.781), the Muslims of western Thrace were exempted and continue to live in the region in return for a continued Greek presence in and around Constantinople (Istanbul).

Nowadays, out of a total population of around 370,000, there are officially around 120,000 **Muslims**, about half of them Turkish-speakers, while the rest are **Pomaks** and Roma. Although there are dozens of functioning mosques, some Turkish-language newspapers and a Turkish-language radio station in Komotiní, only graduates from a special Academy in Thessaloníki have been allowed to teach in the Turkish-language schools here – thus isolating Thracian Turks from mainstream Turkish culture. Local Turks and Pomaks claim that they are the victims of discrimination, but despite violence in the past, relationships have improved with each decade, and as an outsider you will probably not notice the tensions. In mixed villages, Muslims and Greeks appear to coexist quite amicably, and this harmony reaches its zenith in Xánthi. All Thracians, both Muslim and Orthodox, have a deserved reputation for hospitality.

orange-brown tobacco leaves are strung along drying frames. Most of the houses, no matter how modest, sport a dish for tuning in to Turkish satellite television.

Folklore & Historical Museum of Xanthi

Antíka 7 • Tues–Sun 9am–2.30pm • €2 including tour • ☎ 25410 25421, ⓦ fex.org.gr

Two adjacent mansions at the bottom of the hill up into the right-bank quarter of the old town, originally built for two tobacco magnate brothers, have been turned into the excellent **Folklore & Historical Museum of Xanthi**. Worth seeing for the imposing exterior alone, some years ago the interior was lovingly restored with painted wooden panels, decorated plaster and floral designs on the walls and ceilings. The interesting displays include Thracian clothes and jewellery, numerous household objects and historical displays on the tobacco industry and society in general; entry includes an enthusiastic guided tour if requested.

ARRIVAL AND DEPARTURE   XÁNTHI

By train The train station lies just off the Kavála road, 2km south of the centre. At the time of writing, however, this section of rail line is closed, with replacement buses running between Dhráma and Alexandhroúpoli (see p.322). Destinations Alexandhroúpoli (2 daily; 1hr 20min–1hr 35min); Thessaloníki (2 daily; 4hr 40min–5hr 25min).

By bus The KTEL station (☎ 25410 22684, ⓦ ktelxanthis.gr)

is at Dhimokrítou 6, about 300m south of the main square. Destinations Alexandhroúpoli (4–6 daily; 2hr); Kavála (hourly; 1hr); Komotiní (8–11 daily; 1hr); Thessaloníki (9–10 daily; 2hr 30min).

By car Xánthi's pay-and-display parking scheme is pretty comprehensive, and fees are payable in the centre Mon–Sat 8.30am–3pm; Tues & Thurs also 5–8.30pm.

ACCOMMODATION

Town-centre hotel choices are limited and rather overpriced, and, disappointingly, there's no official accommodation in the atmospheric old town.

Elisso Vasilíssis Sofías 9 ☎ 25410 84400, ⓦ hotelelisso .gr. Conveniently placed for the university, the town's newest and smartest hotel contains slick, well-furnished rooms with state-of-the-art facilities, plus a smart wine bar cum bistro. Lavish breakfast included. **€85**

★Orfeas Mihaïl Karaolí 40 ☎ 25410 20121, ⓦ orfeashotel.gr. A short stroll south of Kendrikí Platía, the spacious, bright, en-suite rooms here constitute the best value in town. The atmosphere is also warmer than the average business hotel. Breakfast included. **€40**

EATING

Myrovolos P Khristídhi 7 ☎ 25410 72720. In the lower reaches of the old town, this spacious place behind a wooden façade serves a wide range of starters and some fish, while tasty grills and roasted meats go for €7–8. It stays open late for live music on Fri & Sat. Daily noon–midnight; open til later on Fri & Sat

★Palea Polis Hasirtsoglou 7 ☎ 25410 68685. The menu at this attractive stone and wood taverna includes

some Turkish recipes and ethnic dishes, like spicy Mexican pork, as well as game such as deer and wild boar; all main courses €8–13. Daily noon–1am.

Ta Fanarakia Yeoryíou Stavroú 18 ☎ 25410 73606. A good all-round taverna, just north of Kendrikí Platía, where you can tuck into succulent grilled meat or fish (€7–9) on its pavement seating. Daily 11am–2am.

DRINKING AND NIGHTLIFE

Xánthi's **nightlife** is focused on Vasilíssis Sofías, around the Kendrikí Platía, plus a few places up in the old town. There's a multiplex **cinema** in the Cosmos Centre on M Karaolí, 200m down from the square.

Kyverneio Vasilíssis Sofías 7A ☎ 25411 06030. Huge bar, perennially popular with students and local

youngsters. Fairly sedate by day, it comes into its own at night, pumping out the latest sounds. Daily 9am–late.

North of Xánthi

Much of the countryside **north of Xánthi**, towards the Bulgarian border, is a military controlled area, dotted with signs denoting the fact. If you venture up into the western Rodhópi range here, the main reward is some magnificent scenery around **Stavroúpoli**. There's not much arable land amid the wild, forested hills, and what there is – down in the river valleys – is devoted entirely to tobacco, hand-tilled by the **Pomaks**, who tend to keep themselves to themselves. Owing to the modest increase in material prosperity since the 1980s, the Pomak villages have mostly lost their traditional architecture to concrete multistorey apartments, although the mosque at rambling **Smínthi**, 14km due north of Xánthi, is still blessed with a tall, graceful minaret. **Oréo**, 6km up a side road northwest of Smínthi, is dramatically set on a steep hillside with cloud-covered peaks behind and terraces falling away to the riverbed.

Stavroúpoli

Set among some of the region's most inviting scenery – deep gorges, fir-draped crags and high waterfalls, more like the French Jura than a typically Greek landscape – neat little **STAVROÚPOLI**, 27km northwest of Xánthi, is doing its very best to attract tourists, so far mainly Greeks. Having suffered a major population drain during the decades of mass emigration, the village, with its immaculate cobbled streets, shady central platía, complete with traditional café, and well-restored Thracian-style houses, is showing signs of a revival. The town is conveniently placed for visiting the most spectacular stretch of the **Néstos River**, where the meanders and rapids lend themselves to safe rafting and canoeing.

Folklore Museum

Info and access from the KEP office in the small town hall • Mon–Fri 8am–2.30pm • Free • T 25423 50118

Signposted from the town centre is a delightful little **Folklore Museum** in a restored house. Its proudly displayed collection consists of local memorabilia donated by residents – everything from embroidered bodices to an ancient record player.

4

ARRIVAL AND ACTIVITIES — STAVROÚPOLI

By bus There are regular buses from Xánthi (Mon–Sat 6 daily, Sun 4 daily; 35min).

Activities The best source of information about kayaking, mountain bikes and horseriding in the region is the KEP office (see above).

ACCOMMODATION

Filidhimos In the upper town past the church T&F 25420 22444. This is a modern place, but built of stone in a traditional style. The comfortably furnished rooms have fine views. **€40**

Nemesis 4km south of Stavroúpoli T 25420 21005, W hotelnemesis.gr. Oddly resembling a medieval castle, this hotel has simple but comfortable rooms and a swimming pool. Breakfast included. **€50**

EATING AND DRINKING

To Steki 150m from the main square T 25420 22340, W tosteki.gr. Spacious modern taverna with wood fires and an outdoor terrace in summer. Does plenty of grills, starters and salads (mostly under €10), as well as oven dishes at weekends. Daily 11am–midnight.

South of Xánthi

South of Xánthi, the coastal plain, bright with fields of cotton, tobacco and cereals, stretches to the sea. If you head towards modern **Ávdhira**, 31km away, you'll pass through **Yenisséa**, an unspectacular farming village with one of the oldest **mosques** in Thrace, which dates from the sixteenth century. Now derelict, it's a low whitewashed building with a tiled roof, crumbled wooden portico and truncated minaret.

Ancient Abdera

Site and museum daily: June–Sept 8am–7.30pm, Oct–May 8.30am–3pm • Free • T 25310 21517 • 2–5 daily buses serve the village of Ávdhira, 3km west of the site, and, in summer, pass it en route to the beach of Paralía Avdhíron

Ancient Abdera was founded in the seventh century BC by Clazomenians from Asia

Minor. The walls of the ancient acropolis are visible on a low headland above the sea, and there are fragmentary traces of Roman baths, a theatre and an ancient acropolis. The remains are unspectacular, and the setting not particularly attractive, but the **archeological museum**, located in the village, puts it all into context with a beautifully presented exhibition, accompanied by extensive English texts. A rich collection of ceramics, coins, oil lamps, mosaics and jewellery is dominated by a moving section devoted to burial customs, including some spectacular reconstructions of graves dating from the seventh to fifth centuries BC.

East of Xánthi

The fertile central plains of Thrace, with their large ethnic Turkish population, are one of the least visited areas of the country, but are not without some appeal. Though outwardly unattractive, the market town of **Komotiní** rewards a brief visit, with its two well-presented museums, one folk, the other archeological. The contents of the latter are complemented by the delightful ancient site of **Maroneia**, on the coast, and **Mesembria**, further east.

Komotiní

Lying 48km east of Xánthi along the direct road skirting the Rodhópi foothills, **KOMOTINÍ** is larger and parts of the centre are markedly more Turkish than Xánthi, but overall it lacks its charm. Unlike Xánthi, social mixing between the different ethnic groups – roughly equal population-wise – is almost nonexistent, although Orthodox and Muslims live in the same neighbourhoods. Since the 1990s, the town has become even more polyglot, with an influx of Greek, Armenian and Georgian Christians from the Caucasus.

Bazaar

The old **bazaar**, to the north of Platía Irínis, is a little bit of Istanbul, lodged between fine mosques and an elegant Ottoman-era **clocktower**. Alongside shady cafés, tiny shops sell everything from dried apricots to iron buckets; it's especially busy on Tuesdays when the villagers from the surrounding area come into town to sell their wares. Behind this old quarter, you can see the remains of Komotiní's **Byzantine walls**.

Museum of Folk Life and History

Ayíou Yeoryíou 13 • Mon–Sat 10am–1pm • Free

Greek influence has been in the ascendant since the waning years of the Ottoman Empire, when rich Greeks funded schools in the city. Some of these educational foundations still survive: one, a handsome half-timbered building on Ayíou Yeoryíou has become the **Museum of Folk Life and History**, which displays examples of Thracian embroidery, traditional Thracian dress, silverware, copperware and a collection of religious seals, but avoids any mention of the ethnic Turkish community.

Archeological Museum of Komotini

Simeonídhi 4 • Tues–Sun 8am–3pm • €2 • ☎ 25310 22411

Worth a visit, the **Archeological Museum of Komotini** gives a lucid overview of Thracian history, by means of plans and finds from local sites, from its beginnings in the Neolithic period up to the Byzantine era. Look out for the impressive golden bust of Roman Emperor Septimius Severus (193–211 AD).

ARRIVAL AND DEPARTURE

KOMOTINÍ

By train The train station is just over 1km southwest of the centre, via P Tsaldári. This section of rail line is currently closed, however, with replacement buses running between Dhráma and Alexandhroúpoli (see p.322).

Destinations Alexandhroúpoli (2 daily; 55min–1hr); Thessaloníki (2 daily; 5hr–5hr 40min); Xánthi (2 daily; 30–35min).
By bus The KTEL bus station (☎25310 22912,

ⓦktelrodopis.gr) is around 400m to the south of central Platía Irínis, via Énou.
Destinations Alexandhroúpoli (5–9 daily; 1hr); Thessaloníki (8 daily; 4hr); Xánthi (4–6 daily; 45min–1hr).

ACCOMMODATION

Chris & Eve Mansion 3km from the centre, on Alexandhroúpoli ☎25310 33560, ⓦchris-eve.com. The best hotel in the area (though that's not saying much), this place has spacious, well-equipped rooms, a swimming pool and a reasonable restaurant. **€55**

Hellas Dhimokrítou 31, 250m from main square ☎25310 22055. This 1950s hotel has been fully refurbished but remains on the basic side, and most rooms are pretty cramped. Can suffer from traffic noise too. **€30**

EATING AND DRINKING

To Kouti Orféas 45 ☎25310 25774. Bright modern place with imaginative wall hangings and lampshades. It serves a variety of dips, salads and mostly grilled main dishes for €6–8, plus good local wine. Daily noon–1am.

To Petrino Bizaníou 4 ☎25310 73650. Tucked in the lanes of the bazaar, this traditional ouzerí offers a limited range of carefully prepared mezédhes and meat dishes for as little as €5.50, plus fine ouzo and *tsípouro*, naturally. Daily noon–2am.

Marónia

Not far off the E90 motorway, southeast of Komotiní, lie two archeological sites that make an excellent break in the journey to Alexandhroúpoli or a refreshingly rural alternative base for the area. Clearly indicated from the Sápes turn-off is **ancient Maroneia**, a set of Byzantine and earlier ruins scattered among seaside olive groves. It's just below the modern village of **MARÓNIA**, which has held onto a few surviving old Thracian mansions with balconies.

Ancient Maroneia

Follow the signs to Marónia's harbour of Áyios Harálambos, taking care not to enter the air-force camp nearby

The ruins of **ancient Maroneia** are attractively situated at the foot of Mount Ísmaros. Founded by Maron, the son of the god of wine, Dionysos, the city became one of the most powerful in all of ancient Thrace. Mostly **unexcavated**, the remains can be explored at will but are badly signposted. Even so, you should be able to track down traces of a theatre, a sanctuary of Dionysos and various buildings including a house with a well-preserved mosaic floor. The land walls of the city are preserved to a height of 2m, together with a Roman tower above the harbour. Over time, the sea has done its own excavation, eroding the crumbling cliffs and revealing shards of pottery and ancient walls.

ARRIVAL AND DEPARTURE   MARÓNIA

By bus Marónia is served by 7 daily buses (30min) from   Komotiní via the old road.

ACCOMMODATION AND EATING

Iy Lola ☎25330 41484. Under the thick shade of plane trees in the village square, this wonderful traditional taverna serves up succulent grills for €6–8, some oven dishes such as beef with quince and plum, plus excellent barrelled wine. Daily noon–1am.

Pension Petran ☎25330 41564. Good year-round fallback when *Roxani* (see below) is closed, this old-fashioned place, run by a friendly non-English-speaking

couple, has simple rooms with distant sea views from the balconies. **€30**

★**Roxani** ☎25330 21501, ⓦroxanihotel.gr. Large complex on the edge of the village with spacious and brightly coloured rooms looking out over fabulous views. They can arrange all manner of activities, from bird-watching and astronomy to sea canoeing and archery. Breakfast included and other meals available. June to mid-Sept. **€60**

Mesimvría

Daily 8am–7.30pm, winter till 3pm • €2

Ancient Mesembria, or **Mesimvría** in modern Greek, is clearly signposted from the motorway and is reached via the nondescript village of Dhíkela. Thanks to its unspoilt seaside location, fruitful recent excavations and a well-thought-out display, it easily qualifies as the most appealing of the three ancient sites on the Thracian coastline.

Alexandhroúpoli

Some 120km southeast of Xánthi, the modern city of **ALEXANDHROÚPOLI** (Dedeagaç in Turkish) was designed by Russian military architects during the Russo-Turkish war of 1878. The town only became Greek in 1920, when it was renamed after a visit from Greece's King Alexander. It does not, on first acquaintance, have much to recommend it: a border town and military garrison with Greek holiday-makers competing in summer for limited space in the few hotels and the campsite. There is, however, an excellent **museum** and a lively seafront promenade. The town also provides access to two excellent **bird-watching** sites, the nearby **Évros Delta** and, further north, the **Dhadhiá Forest Reserve**. No village nearby is complete without its stork's nest, dominating the landscape like a watchtower.

Ethnological Museum of Thrace

14-Maïoú 63, around ten blocks north of the ferry terminal • March–Sept Tues & Wed 9am–3pm, Thurs & Fri 9am–3pm & 6–9pm, Sat & Sun 10am–3pm; Oct–Feb Tues–Sat 9am–3pm, Sun 10am–3pm • €3 • ☎ 25510 36663, ⓦ emthrace.org

The excellent **Ethnological Museum of Thrace** is one of the best of its kind in the country and can easily fill an hour or so. Housed in a tastefully restored Neoclassical mansion, its eye-catching modern displays cover almost every aspect of **traditional life** in Thrace. For once, every ethnic group is covered: Pomaks, Turks, Armenians, Jews and Roma as well as Greeks. Professionally produced videos, with commentaries in Greek only, complement the beautifully lit cabinets. A delightful café, serving local specialities, and a good museum shop complete the picture.

Seafront

Alexandhroúpoli's **seafront** is dominated by the 1880 **lighthouse**, the town's symbol; it comes alive at dusk when the locals begin their evening promenade. In summer, café tables spill out onto the road and around the lighthouse; makeshift stalls on the pavements sell pumpkin seeds and grilled sweetcorn as well as pirate DVDs and the like. If you face south, you can usually see the dramatic silhouette of the island of Samothráki, over 40km off the coast.

ARRIVAL AND DEPARTURE

By plane The airport is 5km east of town. There is no dedicated airport bus, but the terminal is just off the main road where frequent buses from local villages stop en route to town.

Destinations Athens (3 daily; 1hr); Sitía, Crete (2 weekly; 1hr 45min).

By train The train station is next to the port.

Destinations Komotiní (2 daily; 1hr); Thessaloníki (2 daily; 6hr–6hr 40min); Xánthi (2 daily; 1hr 35min).

By bus The KTEL station is at Venizélou 36 (☎ 25510 26479, ⓦ ktelevrou.gr), four blocks inland from the port.

Destinations Dhadhiá (2 daily; 1hr); Dhidhymótiho (12 daily; 1hr 30min); Komotiní (5–9 daily; 1hr); Thessaloníki (6 daily; 4hr); Xanthi (4–5 daily; 2hr).

By ferry Alexandhroúpoli is the only access port for ferries to Samothráki (1–3 daily, 2hr 30min; ☎ 25510 38503, ⓦ saos.gr).

By car The best route into town is from the west along coastal Megálou Alexándhrou, then park in the huge car park beside the port (all day €3): pedestrianization and one-way systems effectively block movement further inland.

ACCOMMODATION

Booking ahead is wise in high summer, even though there are a number of choices, ranging from a campsite and no-frills hotels to a string of luxurious resort-cum-conference hotels, well west of town.

Astir Egnatia Egnatia Park, western edge of centre ☎ 25510 38000, ⓦ astiregnatia.com. Right behind the town beach, this vast 1960s' complex of rooms, suites and maisonettes is upmarket but rather institutionalized. Breakfast included. €100

Erika K Dhimitríou 110, just east of the port entrance ☎ 25510 34115, ⓦ hotel-erika.gr. Smart seafront hotel, recently upgraded, with comfortable rooms: the breakfast is hearty, but costs extra. €80

Municipal Campsite On main road 2km west of port ☎ 25510 28735, ⓔ ditea.gr. Large campsite with spacious, shady spots but fairly basic shared facilities. €16

Okeanis K Paleológou 20, five blocks northwest of the port ☎ 25510 28830, ⓦ hotelokeanis.gr. Renovated hotel, stylishly furnished in dark wood and fabrics, with comfortable, average-sized rooms. Breakfast included. €55

Vergina K Dhimitríou 74, opposite train station ☎ 25510 27583, ⓔ 25510 27580. By far the cheapest place in town, this very old-fashioned hotel has simple, plainly decorated rooms, some with sea-view balconies. €45

EATING AND DRINKING

The standard of restaurants in town is pretty good, especially in the streets just behind the seafront and near the train station. The trendiest and priciest restaurants, bars and cafés are, unsurprisingly, strung along the seafront.

Arhipelagos Apolloniádhos 20 ☎ 25510 32418. Towards the western end of the seafront, this breezy *psarotaverna* serves starters such as stuffed mushrooms, plus heaps of seafood: most dishes are €8–15, though there are also some pricier fish. Daily 10am–1am.

Nea Klimataria Platía Polytekhníou 18 ☎ 25510 26288. One block behind the seafront just west of the port, this *estiatório* serves an appealing variety of dishes from soups and starters like *saganáki* to oven-baked and grilled meat and fish for €6–7. Daily 8am–7pm.

To Diethnes (Kyra Dimitra) Kounouriotou 2 ☎ 25510 34434. A welcoming local favourite near the train station, where you can choose from a wide range of vegetable dishes or fried fish for around €5–8. Daily noon–1am.

★ **Sto Ftero** Miaoúli 3 ☎ 25511 10383. Just back from the seafront near the lighthouse, this small and welcoming *tsipourádhiko* has a relaxed atmosphere, pleasant music and great food. Fish such as sardines and gávros only cost €5.50, and there are plenty of meat options. Tues–Sun 11am–late.

Évros Delta

One of Europe's most important wetland areas for **birds** – and one of Greece's most sensitive military areas – the **Évros Delta** is home to more than 250 different bird species, including sea eagles, pygmy cormorants and the lesser white-fronted goose. The delta is crisscrossed with tracks along the dykes used by farmers who take advantage of the plentiful water supply for growing sweet corn and cotton. The **south** is the most inspiring part, well away from the army installations to the north; as you go further into the wetlands, the landscape becomes utterly desolate, with decrepit clusters of fishing huts among the sandbars and inlets. At the mouth of the delta sprawls a huge saltwater lake called **Límni Dhrakónda**. What you see depends heavily on the time of year, but even if birdlife is a bit thin on the ground, the atmosphere of the place is worth experiencing.

ARRIVAL AND INFORMATION ÉVROS DELTA

By car Leave Alexandhroúpoli on the main road towards Turkey and Bulgaria; some 10km after the airport, you'll reach the turn-off to Loutrá Traianoupóleos, the site of an ancient Roman spa and its modern continuation, Loutrós. The delta is best approached by turning right off the main road, opposite the side road to the hotels; the lane is paved only as far as the level crossing but remains good thereafter.

Information The helpful Management Authority of Evros Delta in Loutrá Treanoupóleos (daily 8am–8pm, winter 8am–4pm; ☎ 25510 61000, ⓦ evros-delta.gr) has a wealth of info on local wildlife and activities.

ACCOMMODATION

Athina Loutrá Treanoupóleos ☎ 25510 61208. This basic medium-sized hotel is the best of the bunch in the village. It offers pleasant rooms and is a decent base for exploring the delta. Breakfast included. €45

Dhadhiá National Park

Daily 8am–4pm, sometimes later in summer · Free · ☎ 25540 32202, ⓦ dadia-np.gr

A little under 40km northeast of Alexandhroúpoli, the **Dhadhiá National Park** stretches over 352 square kilometres of protected oak-and-pine forest which cover a succession of volcanic ridges in the Évros Valley. The diversity of landscape and vegetation and the proximity of important migration routes make for an extremely diverse flora and fauna, but **raptors** are the star attraction and the main impetus for this WWF-backed project. In all, 36 of Europe's 38 species of diurnal birds of prey, including eagles, falcons, hawks and buzzards, can be sighted at least part of the year. The region is also one of two remaining European homes of the majestic **black vulture** – the other is the Extremadura region of Spain.

ARRIVAL AND INFORMATION   DHADHIÁ NATIONAL PARK

By car The reserve is reached by a clearly marked road off to the left, 1km after passing the second right-hand turn-off to Likófi (Likófos). After a drive of 7km through the forested hills, you reach the reserve complex, where you can park. Cars aren't allowed into the core area of the park, but a tour van makes sorties into it several times a day (10–15min; €5).

On foot The core areas cover a total of 72 square kilometres, and foot access is restricted to two marked trails: a two-hour route up to the reserve's highest point, 520m Gíbrena with its ruined Byzantine castle; and a 90min loop-route to an observation hide overlooking Mavrórema canyon, where griffon vultures and other raptors make up the bulk of sightings.

Information The reserve complex has an information centre (daily 8am–4pm; ☎ 25540 32209) and exhibition about the region's wildlife.

ACCOMMODATION AND EATING

It's a good idea to stay the night, as the best raptor viewing is in the early morning or evening in summer (but virtually all day Oct–March).

Forest Inn Dhadhiá village ☎ 25540 32263, ⓦ forestinn.eu. A comfortable but affordable guesthouse that has been thoroughly refurbished: the rooms vary in size, but all have furnished verandahs and most enjoy lovely mountain views. The café serves breakfast (included in the price) plus light snacks in the evening. €65

Pelargos Dhadhiá village square ☎ 25540 32481. Simple *psistariá* (grill house) that churns out cheap and tasty meats for €6–7 plus a few salad and vegetable items for hungry twitchers. Daily 11am–11pm.

Souflí

The nearest town to Dhadhiá, 7km north of the side turning to Dhadhiá National Park, is **SOUFLÍ**, set among lush mulberry groves and renowned for its former silk industry. There are a number of surviving vernacular **houses** here, including semi-ruined *bitziklíkia*, or *koukoulóspita* in Greek (cocoon-houses), which lend Souflí some distinction.

Art of Silk Museum

Vassiléos Yeoryíou 199 · Daily except Tues: Easter to mid-Oct 10am–2pm & 5–7pm; rest of year 10am–4pm · €2 · ☎ 25540 24168

A little way uphill and west of the main road through Souflí, the **Art of Silk Museum** is lodged in a fine old yellow mansion. Inside, exhibits explain Dhadhiá's history as Greece's silk centre in Byzantine and Ottoman times, with a fascinating account of the whole silk-making process (with English text).

ACCOMMODATION AND EATING   SOUFLÍ

Egnatia Egnatía 225 ☎ 25540 24124. This small, simple hotel offers rudimentary comforts and gets some noise from the main road outside but is still the best-value option in town. €35

Lagotrofio Yiannoúli village, 4km from Souflí ☎ 25540 22001. Excellent taverna serving wild boar and other game for under €10, plus *mayireftá* standards, at a wonderful shady hilltop location with panoramic views. Daily noon–midnight; Oct–May from 8pm.

Dhidhymótiho

DHIDHYMÓTIHO, 30km northeast of Souflí, is the last place of any interest on the trunk route into Turkey. The old part of town is still partially enclosed by the remains of double **Byzantine fortifications**, and some old houses and churches survive, but the area has a feeling of decay despite continuing efforts at restoration.

Bayezid Mosque
Theotokopoulou • Closed for restoration

Below Dhidhymótiho's fortified hill, on the central platía, stands an important surviving monument, the fourteenth-century **Bayezid Mosque** – the oldest and second largest in the Balkans. A great square box of a building, its design harks back to Seljuk and other pre-Ottoman prototypes in central Anatolia, and you'll see nothing else like it between here and Divriui or Erzurum in Turkey. Unfortunately, the interior is closed indefinitely for restoration, and its unique pyramidal metal roof was destroyed by a fire in March 2017, though you can still admire the ornate west portal.

ACCOMMODATION AND EATING	DHIDHYMÓTIHO

Plotini 1km south of town ☎ 25530 23400, ⓦ hotelplotini.gr. A gaudy labyrinthine building set back from the main road. Rooms have slightly anachronistic decor but are generously sized, and there's an outdoor pool in summer. **€40**

Zythestiatorio Kypselaki Central market hall ☎ 25530 22688. This small restaurant in the market, just above the mosque, is the best choice in town for home-cooked favourites (€5–7) like baked beef and potatoes or fried aubergines. Daily 11am–6pm.

4

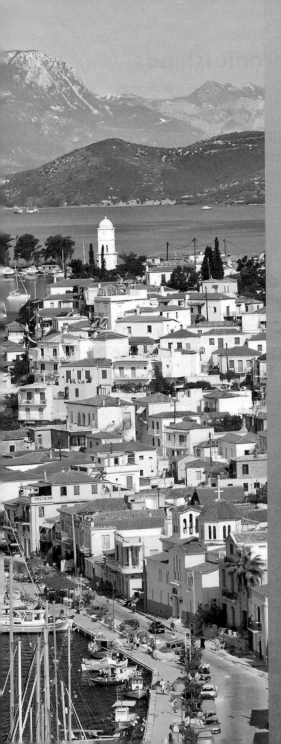

The Argo-Saronic Islands

PÓROS TOWN

5

The Argo-Saronic Islands

Given their proximity to Athens and their beauty, the Argo-Saronic islands are hugely popular destinations – Égina (Aegina) almost becomes a city suburb at weekends, while Póros, Ýdhra (Hydra) and Spétses are barely less busy, though their visitors include a higher proportion of foreign tourists. More than any other group, these islands are best out of season and midweek, when visitor numbers (and prices) fall dramatically and the ports return to a quieter, more provincial pace. You'll also notice a significant difference between Ýdhra and Spétses, the furthest of the islands, and those closer to Athens: because of the distance, and because they're accessible only by hydrofoil and catamaran rather than the cheaper conventional ferries, they're markedly more expensive and exclusive, with significant expat populations.

Rocky, partly volcanic and often barely an olive's throw from the mainland, the Argo-Saronics differ to a surprising extent not just from the land they face but also from one another. The northernmost, **Salamína**, is effectively a suburb of Pireás, with its narrow strait, barely a kilometre across, crossed by a constant stream of ferries. Ancient history apart, there's little to attract you, however, and the island is covered only briefly in this Guide. **Égina**, important in antiquity and more or less continually inhabited since then, is infinitely preferable: the most fertile of the group, it is famous for its pistachio nuts and home to one of the finest ancient temples in Greece. Tiny **Angístri** is often treated as little more than an adjunct of Égina, but it's a lovely place in its own right, ideal for a few days' complete relaxation. The three southerly islands, green **Póros**, chic, car-free **Ýdhra** and upmarket **Spétses**, each have their own unique character. With little water – they rely on supplies piped or brought by rusty tanker from the mainland – they were not extensively settled until medieval times, when refugees from the mainland established themselves here and adopted seagoing commerce (and piracy) as livelihoods. Their trading fleets became the navy of the Greek revolution, when the Argo-Saronics were at the heart of the battle for independence. Today, foreigners and Athenians have largely replaced locals in the depopulated harbour towns; hydrofoils, water-taxis and yachts are faint echoes of the massed warships, schooners and *kaïkia* (traditional wooden boats) once at anchor.

GETTING THERE

BY FERRY, HYDROFOIL AND CATAMARAN Virtually all services from Pireás to the Argo-Saronic islands leave from between gates E8 and E9, where there are ticket booths. For all these islands, hydrofoil or catamaran services are faster and more frequent than ferries, though they cost around twice as much. Fri evening and Sat morning sailings, as well as the returns on Sun night, can be very busy; for these, or if you hope to bring a vehicle for the weekend on a regular ferry, reserve your trip well in advance.

Tickets and agencies Contact details for Pireás are as follows (local island agencies are given in the individual island accounts): Aegean Flying Dolphins (to Égina and Angístri) ☎210 422 1766, ⏺aegeanflyingdolphins.gr; ANES (ferry to Égina Town, passenger boats to Souvála and Ayía Marína, Égina) ☎210 422 5625, ⏺anes.gr;

The Battle of Salamis p.331
Excursions to the Peloponnese p.341

Ýdhra's festivals p.348
Hiking on Ýdhra p.349

Highlights

❶ Temple of Aphaea, Égina The best-preserved ancient temple on any Greek island enjoys an evocative setting on a wooded hill, with magnificent views towards the mainland and Athens. **See p.336**

❷ Angístri Island Little known to outsiders, this dot of land is less than an hour from Athens by hydrofoil yet preserves the feel of an unspoilt hideaway. **See p.337**

❸ The Póros channel An ever-changing spectacle of small and not-so-small craft, the busy, narrow channel between Póros and the mainland is quite an experience – whether you're navigating your own yacht or arriving by hydrofoil. **See p.340**

❹ Ýdhra Town Ýdhra's perfect, horseshoe-shaped harbour, surrounded by grand eighteenth-century mansions and genuinely traffic-free streets, is one of the most evocative in all of Greece. **See p.345**

❺ Old Harbour, Spétses The food and nightlife hub of Spétses, with restaurants on pontoons over the water and bars oozing upmarket Athenian glitz. **See p.351**

HIGHLIGHTS ARE MARKED ON THE MAP ON P.330

5

Evoikos (passenger boat to Souvála, Égina) ☎210 482 1002, ⓦevoikoslines.gr; Hellenic Seaways (hydrofoils and Flying Cat to all points) ☎210 419 9000, ⓦhsw.gr; Leve Ferries (ferry to Égina) ☎210 431 1915, ⓦleveferries.gr; Saronic Ferries (all other ferries to Égina, Angístri and Póros, including Hellenic Seaways ones) ☎210 411 7341, ⓦsaronicferries.gr.

BY CAR OR BUS

Eventually you will have to take a boat, of course, but for Póros, and even more so Ýdhra and Spétses, it's substantially cheaper, if slower, to drive as far as you can before crossing; this is what most Athenians do. From Galatás there are passenger and car ferries to Póros; and there are passenger crossings from Metóhi (extensive parking) to Ýdhra, Ermióni to Ýdhra or Spétses, and Kósta or Pórto Héli to Spétses. Buses (2–3 daily) run from Athens' Kiffisoú bus station to Galatás, Ermióni, Kósta and Pórto Héli.

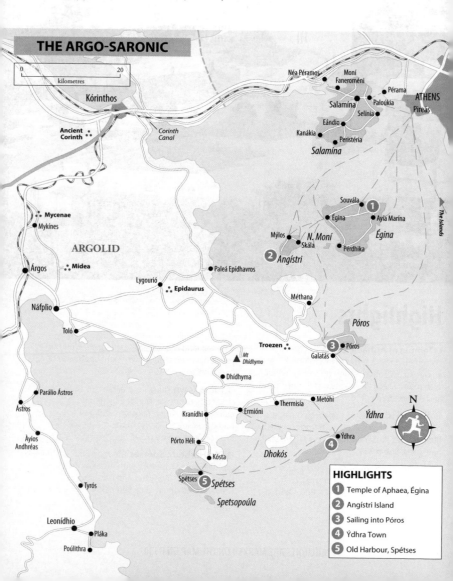

THE ARGO-SARONIC

HIGHLIGHTS

1. Temple of Aphaea, Égina
2. Angístri Island
3. Sailing into Póros
4. Ýdhra Town
5. Old Harbour, Spétses

Salamína

SALAMÍNA is the quickest possible island-hop from Pireás, and indeed much of its population commutes to the city to work. The island itself, however, is highly developed, has few tourist facilities, and is close enough to the Athenian dockyards to make swimming unappealing. The island's port is at **Paloúkia**, facing the mainland, just a short hop across a narrow, built-up isthmus to **Salamína Town** on the west coast. Five kilometres or so beyond Salamína Town, **Eándio** has the island's cleanest and most attractive beaches. A similar distance from Salamína Town to the north is the **monastery of Faneroméni** (daily 8.30am–12.30pm & 4pm–sunset), a working nunnery with impressive frescoes, beautifully sited amid pine woods overlooking the mainland.

ARRIVAL AND DEPARTURE SALAMÍNA

By boat There are small passenger boats every 30min from Pireás throughout the day (Gate E8; 45min), and a constant stream of small boats and roll-on, roll-off car ferries, day and night, from Pérama, on the mainland directly opposite (5min). Pérama is easily reached by bus: #843 from Pireás, G18 or B18 from Omónia in central Athens. There are also ferries every 20min or so between Faneroméni and Néa Péramos (aka Megára) on the mainland.

GETTING AROUND

By bus Salamína has a pretty impressive bus system, with departures from the ferry dock in Paloúkia to Salamína Town every 15min. Buses also run hourly to numerous other destinations on the island, including Eándio and Faneroméni.

Égina

A substantial and attractive island with a proud history, less than an hour from Pireás, **ÉGINA** (Aegina) is not surprisingly a popular weekend escape from Athens. Despite the holiday homes, though, it retains a laidback, island atmosphere, especially if you visit midweek or out of season. Famous for its **pistachio orchards** – the nuts are hawked from stalls all around the harbour – the island can also boast substantial ancient remains, the finest of which is the beautiful fifth-century BC **Temple of Aphaea**, which commands superb views towards Athens from high above the northeast coast.

THE BATTLE OF SALAMIS

Perhaps the main reason to head to Salamína is for the **boat trip** itself, through an extraordinary industrial seascape of docks and shipworks. The waters you cross were the site of one of the most significant **sea battles** of ancient times; some would say of all time, given that this was a decisive blow in preventing a Persian invasion, thus allowing the development of Classical Athens and with it modern Western culture.

In 480 BC, the Greeks were in full retreat from the vast **Persian army** under Xerxes following the defeat of the Spartans at Thermopylae. Many Greek cities, including Athens, had been sacked and burned by the invaders – indeed, smoke from the ruins on the Acropolis probably formed a backdrop to the **Battle of Salamis**. The Greeks had roughly twenty cities, the bulk from Athens, Corinth and Aegina; the Persian fleet was twice the size, with heavier ships that were even more diverse, with many from subject nations whose loyalty was questionable.

Through false information and strategic retreats, the Greeks managed first to tire many of the Persian crews – who rowed all night to cut off a nonexistent escape attempt – and then to lure them into the narrow strait off Salamína. Crowded in and unable to manoeuvre, and with the wind in the wrong direction, the Persians found themselves at the mercy of the more nimble Greek triremes, and the battle eventually became a rout. Some two hundred Persian ships were sunk, against forty-odd on the Greek side, and few of their heavily armoured crews or marines survived.

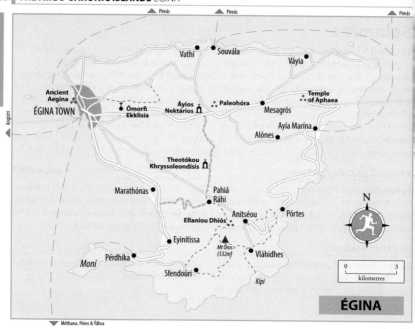

ARRIVAL AND DEPARTURE

BY FERRY AND HYDROFOIL

In Égina Town, ferries dock on the outer wall of the harbour and hydrofoils inside it, very close to each other and pretty much at the heart of things. The *Angístri Express* (see below) can be found among the pleasure and fishing boats a short distance to the south. The schedule summaries below are for summer weekday services; sailings are more frequent and significantly busier at weekends (Fri–Sun) and less regular from mid-Sept to June. Ayía Marína and Souvála are linked to Pireás two or three times daily in high season.

Tickets and agencies Immediately in front of the docks in Égina Town is a row of cabins displaying timetables and selling tickets for Aegean Flying Dolphins (to Pireás and Angístri ☎ 22970 25800, ⓦ aegeanflyingdolphins.gr), ANES (ferry to Pireás ☎ 22970 25625, ⓦ anes.gr), Hellenic Seaways (hydrofoils and Flying Cat to Pireás and Angístri

☎ 22970 22945, ⓦ hsw.gr), Leve Ferries (ferry to Pireás ☎ 22970 22217, ⓦ leveferries.gr) and Saronic Ferries (ferries to Pireás, Angístri, Méthana and Póros ☎ 22970 24200, ⓦ saronicferries.gr). They're open through the day, and the relevant ones will also open 30min or more before early-morning or late-night departures. ANES and Evoikos (ⓦ evoikoslines.gr) operate the Souvála and Ayía Marína routes; quayside booths open an hour or so before departure (Souvála T22970 52210, Ayía Marína T22970 32234). For the *Angístri Express* (☎ 6938 732 966), buy tickets on the boat.

Destinations Angístri (6 hydrofoils and 1 or 2 ferries daily, plus *Angístri Express* 2–3 daily except Sun; 15min); Pireás (from Égina Town 12 hydrofoils and 11 ferries daily, 40min–1hr 30min; from Ayía Marína 1–2 ferries daily, 1hr 15min; from Souvála 2–4 daily, 50min); Póros (via Méthana 2 ferries daily; 1hr 15min).

INFORMATION

Information There's no tourist office, but ⓦ aeginagreece.com is a useful resource.

Services There are numerous banks around Égina Town

harbour, many with ATMs. The post office is at the rear of Platía Ethneyersías, where the buses stop.

GETTING AROUND

By bus The bus station is on Platía Ethneyersías, immediately north of the dock; buy your tickets at the little booth, in summer located on the waterfront, the rest of the

year in the square by the bus stop. Three to five buses a day head to Souvála, to Ayía Marína, and along the coast to Pérdhika; on arrival, they turn round and head straight back. All buses towards Ayía Marína stop at Áyios Nektários and the Temple of Aphaea.

By car and motorcycle Several places on and behind Égina Town's main waterfront rent scooters, cars, motorbikes and mountain bikes – Égina is large and hilly enough to make a motor worthwhile for anything other than a pedal to the local beaches: Trust (📞 6942 022 274), in a narrow alley off the harbour behind Alpha Bank, has the best prices, though some of their mopeds are fairly battered. There are also hire places in Ayía Marína.

By taxi The taxi rank (📞 22970 22010) is at the base of the ferry jetty, opposite the ticket cabins; taxis meet ferry arrivals in Ayía Marína and Souvála too.

Brief history

Inhabited from the earliest times, ancient **Aegina** was a significant regional power as far back as the Bronze Age. It traded to the limits of the known world, maintained a sophisticated silver coinage system (the first in Greece) and fostered prominent athletes and craftsmen. The Aeginian fleet played a major role in the Battle of Salamis (see p.331).

Subsequent history was less distinguished, with a familiar pattern of occupation – by Romans, Franks, Venetians, Catalans and Ottomans – before the War of Independence brought a brief period of glory as seat of government for the fledgling Greek nation, from 1826 to 1828. For many decades afterwards, Égina was a penal island, and you can still see the enormous **jail** undergoing an apparently endless restoration on the edge of town; the building was originally an **orphanage** for victims of the independence struggle, founded by first president Kapodhístrias in 1828.

Égina Town

ÉGINA TOWN, the island's capital, makes an attractive base, with some grand old buildings around a large, busy harbour. The Neoclassical architecture is matched by a sophisticated ethos: by island standards this is a large town, with plenty of shopping and no shortage of tempting places to eat and drink. Life revolves around the **waterfront**, where ferries come and go, yachts moor, fishermen tend their nets and *kaïkia* (traditional wooden boats) tie up to sell produce from the mainland.

Markellos Tower

Thomaïdhou, inland from the harbour • No admission except during the occasional special exhibition

The restored Pýrgos Markéllou, or **Markellos Tower**, is an extraordinary miniature castle that was the seat of the first Greek government after independence. Despite appearances, it was built only around 1800 by members of the Friendly Society (see p.779) and the local politician Spýros Márkellos. You can't usually go inside, but walking here, through the cramped inland streets, is enjoyable in itself.

Folklore Museum

Spýrou Ródhi 16 • Fri 5.30–8.30pm, Sat 10am–1pm & 5.30–8.30pm, Sun 10am–1pm • Free • 📞 22970 26401

Égina's **Folklore Museum** is a lovely example of its type, housed in a nineteenth-century mansion. Its upper rooms are packed with fine old furniture, traditional costumes, and many of the trappings of island life a century ago, along with a small local historical archive. Downstairs are rooms devoted to fishing, with model boats and fishing gear, and to agriculture, with a collection of the basics of village life.

Ancient Aegina

Beyond the town beach, 600m north of the harbour • Tues–Sun 10am–5.30pm • €3 • 📞 22970 22248

The site of **Ancient Aegina** lies north of the centre on a promontory known as **Kolóna**, after the lone column that stands there. The extensive remains, centring on a Temple of Apollo at the highest point, are well signed, and some reconstruction makes it easier to make out the various layers of settlement from different eras. Near the entrance, a small but worthwhile **archeological museum** houses finds from the site, along with

5

information on the island's ancient history. Highlights of the display include a room of Minoan-influenced Middle Bronze Age pottery, rescued from a nearby building site.

The beaches

On the north edge of town, between the port and Kolóna, there's a tiny but popular **beach** with remarkably shallow water. This was the site of the ancient city's harbour, of which various underwater remains are clearly visible. You can swim south of town, too, but there are more enticing spots further north – immediately beyond Kolóna there's an attractive bay with a small, sandy beach, while other small coves lie off the road which heads further out of town in that direction. Only a couple have any facilities, with loungers and beach bars.

ACCOMMODATION   ÉGINA TOWN

Aeginitiko Archontiko Cnr Thomaïdhou and Ayíou Nikólaou ☎ 22970 24968, ⓦ aeginitikoarchontiko.gr. Brick-red Neoclassical mansion opposite the Markellos Tower, lovingly restored with period furnishings and a conscious attempt to preserve traditional island culture. About as far from a bland business hotel as you can get – there's lots of lace, old pictures on the walls, creaking, springy beds and a wonderful breakfast (included) with home-made preserves, cakes and pastries. The suite has painted ceilings; other rooms can be pretty basic, though all have a/c, TV and fridge. €65

Elektra Leonándrou Ladhá 25 ☎ 22970 26715, ⓦ aegina-electra.gr. Friendly, quiet establishment, directly inland from the ferry quay, past the police station, whose compact but comfortable rooms come with small balconies and free wi-fi. €45

★**Fistikies** Logiotatídhou 1 ☎ 22970 23783, ⓦ fistikies.gr. Lovely modern apartments around a small pool, slightly inland on the southern edge of town, near the

football stadium. The well-equipped apartments typically have a small bedroom, large living room and kitchen, all classily furnished and with cable TV. €90

Hotel Brown Waterfront ☎ 22970 22271, ⓦ hotelbrown.gr. Housed in a former sponge factory dating from 1886 and facing the southern part of the harbour, the *Hotel Brown* has a fabulous position and an excellent modern café-restaurant. The rooms, though, are a little dated: those at the front have great views of the harbour activity, but the garden bungalows are quieter; a galleried family suite sleeps four. Breakfast included. June–Oct. €65

Plaza Kazantzáki 4 ☎ 22970 25600, ⓦ plaza-aegina .com. One of a series of small waterfront hotels close to the town beach, the Plaza has refurbished rooms with quality bathrooms and elegant dark-wood decor, plus double-glazing, a/c and TV. The marginally more expensive rooms at the front have little balconies with great sea views. €55

EATING AND DRINKING

There are plenty of good places to eat and drink in Égina, where fussy Athenian patronage keeps the standards high. A couple of wonderfully old-fashioned *kafenía* can be found on the seafront by the fish market, while the backstreets boast an extraordinary number of bakeries and cake shops.

★**Agora** Panayióti Irióti ☎ 22970 27308. Also known as *Yeladhakis*, this is the best of the rival seafood ouzerís behind the fish market (though the others are very good too). Not the most attractive location with rickety no-frills tables in the alley, but it serves wonderful, inexpensive, authentic Greek food (around €8 per fish plate): accordingly, it's usually mobbed, and you may have to wait for a table. Daily Mon–Thurs 6pm–11.30pm, Fri–Sun noon–11.30pm.

Babis Aktí Tóti Hatzí 7 ☎ 22970 23594. The last restaurant at the southern end of the waterfront, *Babis* is a design-conscious modern taverna that also has tables on the seafront over the road, where it's candlelit at night. The menu is modern Greek, with plenty of well-cooked standards – moussaka €8, *soutzoukákia* €7.50 – plus daily fish and seafood specials. Daily 10am–1am.

Kappos Etsi Panayióti Irióti 9 ☎ 22970 27219. Dimitris Kappos is something of a celebrity chef on Égina, and his elegant restaurant looks a cut above, though the prices are barely any higher than elsewhere. From a simple pork steak flavoured with lime and rosemary (€8) to more complex creations like a whole grilled squid with bulgur salad, tomato, parsley and olive oil lemon dressing (€12), it all tastes great. Daily noon–1am.

Flisvos Kazantzáki 8 ☎ 22970 26459. An excellent spot for grilled fresh fish and traditional dishes at fair prices (*yemistá* €7, pork *souvláki* €8, grilled octopus €10), towards the end of a line of similar establishments behind the town beach. Good-value lunchtime specials. Daily noon–midnight.

Melenio Mitropóleos 4 ☎ 22970 26133. Close to the Markellos Tower, this is an exceptional modern *zaharoplastío* with fine ice cream and beautiful displays of cakes and sweets. Daily 8.30am–11.30pm.

Skotadis Dimokratías 46 ☎ 22970 24014. Popular with locals, this is the best of a cluster of harbourfront taverna-ouzerís just south of the market. It has a small menu, with meze at €6–7 a dish, along with fresh fish (priced by weight) and daily specials. At €16 the fish *souvláki* is pricey, but it could probably feed two and is made with the freshest of fish. Daily 11am–1am.

NIGHTLIFE

Caps Love Ahilléos 4 ☎ 22970 29418. A very cool little bar/café, just off the waterfront beyond the church, with chill-out music downstairs and dance sounds on the first floor. They also serve a mean brunch as well as burgers, pancakes and the like. Daily 1pm–1am.

Ellinikon Seaside Aktí Tóti Hatzí 10 ☎ 6936 111 213, ⓦ ellinikon.net. A big, enjoyable, somewhat touristy club on the seafront at the southern fringe of town, with mainstream and Greek dance music. It has a sister club in town, *Ellinikon Vintage* (Kapodístria Ioánni 7). July & Aug Wed–Sun 10.30pm–late.

Remvi Dhimokratías 51 ☎ 22970 28605. All-day café-bar on the harbourfront that becomes more raucous the later it gets; there's dancing and DJs most evenings, live music at weekends. Daily 8am–late.

ENTERTAINMENT

Cinemas There are three summer open-air cinemas – Anesis on Eákou close to the Pýrgos Markéllou; Olympia on Faneroménis opposite the football ground; and Akroyiali out beyond this on the Pérdhika road. Indoor Titina, opposite the Pýrgos Markéllou, is open year-round.

Across the island

Two main routes lead east towards Ayía Marína and the Temple of Aphaea: you can head directly **inland** from Égina Town across the centre of the island or follow the **north coast** road via Souvála. Along this north coast there are plenty of scruffy beaches and clusters of second-home developments, between which is a surprisingly industrial landscape, with boatyards and working ports. Souvála itself is something of an Athenian resort, with a couple of direct daily ferries to Pireás but little other reason to stop.

Áyios Nektários

Halfway between Égina Town and Ayía Marína, passed by 3–5 buses daily between the two • Daily, hours dependent on church routine and coach tours, but should be at least 9am–1pm & 4–6pm • Free • ☎ 22970 53800

On the inland route you'll pass the modern convent of **Áyios Nektários**, a site of Orthodox pilgrimage whose vast church is said to be the largest in Greece. The convent was founded by **Saint Nektarios**, who died in 1920 and was canonized in 1961. His tomb lies in the chapel of the original monastery, Ayía Triádha. Miracles surrounded Nektarios from the moment of his death, when nurses put some of his clothing on an adjacent bed, occupied by a man who was paralysed; the patient promptly leapt up, praising God.

Paleohóra

Unrestricted • Free

On the hillside opposite Áyios Nektários is the ghost town of **PALEOHÓRA**, the island capital through the Middle Ages. Established in early Christian times as a refuge against piracy, it thrived under the Venetians (1451–1540) but was destroyed by Barbarossa in 1537. The Turks took over and rebuilt the town, but it was again destroyed, this time by the Venetians, in 1654, and finally **abandoned** altogether in the early nineteenth century. The place now consists of some **thirty stone chapels** dotted across a rocky outcrop, an extraordinary sight from a distance. Little remains of the town itself – when the islanders left, they simply dismantled their houses and moved the masonry to newly founded Égina Town. At the entrance, a helpful map shows the churches and the paths that lead up the hill between them; many are semi-derelict or locked, but plenty are open too, and several preserve remains of frescoes. Despite their

5

apparent abandonment, many chapels have candles burning inside, and prayers left alongside the icons.

If you climb right to the top, you're rewarded with wonderful **views** in all directions – you can also appreciate the defensive qualities of the site, from which both coasts can be watched, yet which is almost invisible from the sea.

Temple of Aphaea

12km east of Égina Town • Daily 8am–8pm; museum Tues–Sun 9am–4pm • €6 • ☎ 22970 32398

The Doric **Temple of Aphaea** stands on a pine-covered hill, with stunning views all around: Athens, Cape Soúnio, the Peloponnese and Ýdhra are all easily made out. Built between 500 and 480 BC, it slightly predates the Parthenon, and is one of the most complete and visually complex ancient buildings in Greece, its superimposed arrays of columns and lintels evocative of an Escher drawing. Aphaea was a Cretan nymph who, fleeing from the lust of King Minos, fell into the sea, was caught by some fishermen and brought to ancient Aegina; her cult, virtually unknown anywhere else, was established on the island as early as 1300 BC. Little over two hundred years ago, the temple's pediments were intact and essentially in perfect condition. However, like the Elgin marbles, they were "purchased" from the Turks – this time by Ludwig I of Bavaria – and they currently reside in Munich's Glyptothek museum. The small **museum** on site offers a great deal of information about the history and architecture of the building. A well-signed path leads from the temple to Ayía Marína; an easy walk down, slightly tougher coming up.

Ayía Marína and around

The island's major beach resort, **AYÍA MARÍNA**, lies steeply below the Temple of Aphaea on the east coast. There's a good, clean, sandy **beach** that shelves very gently, plus there are rentable pedaloes and plenty of places to eat, many of them catering to day-trippers – direct boats arrive from Pireás daily. The place has clearly seen better days, as the number of empty premises and the ugly, half-built hotel overshadowing the beach attest, but package tourism seems to be on the up, and it can be lively and enjoyable in a bucket-and-spade sort of way, with plenty of hotels and rooms, and a main street lined with shops, bars and pubs; the occasional summer beach party sees an overnight invasion of young Athenians.

Pórtes

PÓRTES, 8km south of Ayía Marína, is a hamlet with a distinctly end-of-the-road feel, a partly sandy beach with decent snorkelling, and a couple of good tavernas. From here, the road climbs steeply inland, beneath the island's highest peak, and heads back towards Égina Town via the villages of **Anitséou** and **Pahiá Ráhi**. The latter, with fine views eastwards, has been almost entirely rebuilt in traditional style by foreign and Athenian owners.

ACCOMMODATION AND EATING

AYÍA MARÍNA AND AROUND

AYÍA MARÍNA

Argo Spa Hotel ☎ 22970 32266, ⊛ argohotel.com. In a great position directly above the bay as you come into town, the *Argo* has seafront decks and swimming area as well as a pool and small "spa" (sauna and hot tub). Refurbished, modern rooms mostly have sea views. Breakfast included. €65

Michalia's Studios ☎ 22970 32088, ⊛ aeginarooms. com/michalias. Set back behind the beach, these simple, slightly old-fashioned marble-floored rooms with TV, a/c and kitchenette, offer great value and a warm welcome. All

have balconies catching the morning sun, and with views towards the beach. €35

Hotel Liberty 2 ☎ 22970 32105, ⊛ hotelliberty2.gr. An ochre-coloured building overlooking the end of the beach; it's simple and old-fashioned, but all rooms have sea-view balconies as well as a/c, fridge and TV. €40

Paradisos ☎ 22970 32142. Lovely spot with tables on the beach and on a shady terrace behind. Tasty Greek dishes include squid stuffed with feta and tomato (€9), pork fillet with garlic and mushrooms (€8.50) or a fish menu for two at €20. They have loungers on the beach, free for customers. May–Oct daily 10am–11pm.

PÓRTES

Thanasis ☎ 22970 31348. A fine taverna that attracts visitors from around the island at weekends; a few tables

perch above the water beneath a pine tree, others are on a terrace behind. There's a menu, but it's barely relevant – instead check out the day's fish and other specials on the blackboard, mainly for around €8–10. May–Sept lunch and dinner daily; winter weekends only.

The west coast

The road south of Égina Town, along the **west coast** of the island, is flat and easy. Sprawling **Marathónas**, 5km from Égina, has the biggest if not the prettiest of the west coast's sandy beaches, which offers fine views and loungers, along with a scattering of rooms, tavernas and cafés. The next settlement, **Eyinítissa**, has a popular, sheltered cove backed by eucalypts and a beach bar.

Pérdhika

Scenically set on a little bay packed with yachts at the end of the coastal road, **PÉRDHIKA** is Égina's most picturesque village. The pedestrianized **waterfront** esplanade at the southern edge of the village, overlooking Moní islet and the Peloponnese, is the heart of tourist life. From the harbour, you can take a boat to **Moní** (10min; €5 return), most of which is fenced off as a nature conservation area but is worth the trip for a swim in wonderfully clear water. Pérdhika Bay itself is shallow and yacht-tainted, though you can swim from the rocky shore further round. If you have your own transport, a couple more **cove beaches** are accessible beyond Pérdhika, where new holiday homes are reached by steep concrete tracks.

ACCOMMODATION AND EATING   **THE WEST COAST**

MARATHÓNAS

Ostria ☎ 22970 27677. This place has an idyllic setting, with tables set out under the trees and the water lapping almost to your feet. The food is great too, especially the fresh kalamári (€6.40) and the cheese pies (€4.40), while the fresh fish (priced by kilo) is cheaper than usual. Daily lunch and dinner.

PÉRDHIKA

Antonis ☎ 22970 61443. One of a long line of tavernas along the waterfront, this is the best of the bunch for fish (priced by the kilo), with a big outdoor charcoal grill; check out what is fresh in the kitchen. Also fairly priced standards like soutzoukákia or pastítsio for €7. Daily lunch and dinner.

Antzi Studios ☎ 22970 61446, ⓦ antzistudios.gr. Large studio complex with a good-sized pool. All the units

are newly refurbished, comfortable and well equipped with TV, a/c and cooking facilities; those in the "Stone Building" are larger and more elegant, set on two levels. **€50**, Stone Building **€90**

Hermes ☎ 22970 61200. Bars and cafés are concentrated towards the end of the esplanade, where they can afford to turn the music up louder: *Hermes* is usually the busiest late-night spot, but there are plenty of other choices nearby. Daily 10am–late.

Hotel Hippocampus ☎ 22970 61363, ⓦ hippocampus-hotel-greece.com. Sweet little hotel built around a leafy garden courtyard, complete with private chapel. All rooms have balconies (some with fabulous views), a/c and TV, though some are tiny, and there's a roof terrace from which anyone can enjoy the views. **€50**

Angístri

ANGÍSTRI, fifteen minutes by fast boat from Égina, is a tiny island, obscure enough to be overlooked by most island-hoppers, though the visitors it attracts are a diverse mix: Athenian weekenders, retirees who bought and restored property here years ago, plus a few predominantly British and Scandinavian package holiday-makers. There's a small, not terribly attractive strip of development on the north coast facing Égina, but the rest of the island is pine-covered, timeless and beautiful – albeit with very few beaches. It's also strangely contradictory: holiday weekends can see hordes of young Greeks

5

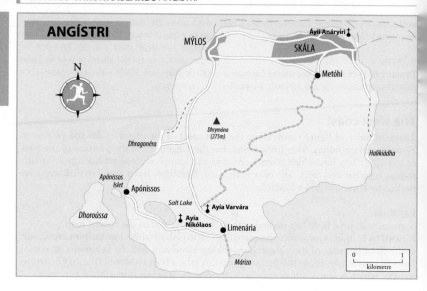

camping out on otherwise empty beaches, while in Skála a few small, classy hotels are juxtaposed with cafés serving English breakfasts to the package-trippers.

ARRIVAL AND DEPARTURE   ANGÍSTRI

BY FERRY
There are ferries and hydrofoils to and from Pireás via Égina; ferries dock at Skála, hydrofoils at Mýlos. The *Angístri Express* (☎ 6947 118 863) calls at both en route to and from Égina.
Agencies Hellenic Seaways (ferry and hydrofoil; ☎ 22970 91171, ⓦ hsw.gr or ⓦ saronicferries.gr) and

Aegean Flying Dolphins (hydrofoils; ☎ 22970 91221, ⓦ aegeanflyingdolphins.gr).
Destinations Égina (*Angístri Express* 2–3 daily; 15min); Pireás via Égina (ferries 1 or 2 daily; 25min/1hr 30min; hydrofoils 6–8 daily; 10min/1hr).

GETTING AROUND

By bus The island bus (☎ 22970 91224) connects Skála and Mýlos several times a day, timed to match ferry and hydrofoil arrivals; in summer it also runs regularly across the island, to Dhragonéra, Limenária and Apónissos. The day's timetable is chalked up at its starting point, outside the church in Skála.
By scooter and bike Scooters and mountain bikes are available for rent from several outlets in Skála and Mýlos; Kostas Motorent in Skála (☎ 6934 707 958) is

particularly helpful. It is less than 10km to the furthest point of the island, so in cooler weather you can comfortably cross Angístri by pedal power – albeit with a couple of steep climbs.
On foot The island is small enough to cross on foot, via Metóhi along a winding dirt track through the pines.
By water-taxi Water-taxis (☎ 6972 229 720 or 6944 535 659) serve the beaches and Égina: you'll pay about €30/boat from Skála to Dhragonéra, for example.

Skála and around
SKÁLA is Angístri's main tourist centre, its sandy beach backed by a straggle of modern development. Thanks to the weekending Athenian youth, there are lively bars and cafés here, and an unexpectedly busy nightlife; in summer, there's even an open-air cinema. The beach, and most of the new development, lies to the right (west) from the jetty, beyond the big church, but there are some far more attractive places to stay, which look out over a rocky coastline, left of the dock.

From the paved road's end in this direction, beyond the *Alkyoni Hotel* (see opposite), a path leads along the clifftop to secluded **Halikiádha**. This pebble beach,

5

backed by crumbling cliffs, is predominantly nudist; at busy weekends there may be crowds of young Greeks camping nearby, but the rest of the time it's almost deserted. The scary scramble down is rewarded by the island's best swimming in crystalline water. On the main town beach, you can rent sun-loungers, pedaloes and kayaks.

METÓHI, the hillside hamlet just above Skála, was once the island's main village, but now consists chiefly of holiday homes. If you can face the steep climb, you'll get the chance to take in some wonderful views out towards Égina.

ACCOMMODATION   SKÁLA AND AROUND

Aktaion Hotel Immediately right from the jetty ☎22970 91222, ⓦstayinagistri.gr. The best option in the main part of town, this hotel has a small swimming pool, and many of the recently refurbished rooms have big balconies and/or sea views. All rooms also have TV, fridge and kitchenette. They also rent out larger apartments. **€45**

★**Alkyoni Hotel** Left of the jetty ☎22970 91377, ⓦalkyoni-agistri.gr. All the excellent value stone-floored rooms at this hotel, southeast of the jetty, have been newly done up; those on the seafront side (€10 extra) have balconies directly above the water with stunning views.

Best of all are the duplex rooms on the upper floor, big enough for a family, with a raised sleeping area and kitchenette below. There's also a friendly coffee/breakfast bar. Room **€40** , family room **€60**

★**Rosy's Little Village** Left of the jetty ☎22970 91610, ⓦrosyslittlevillage.com. Delightful spot on the rocks southeast of the jetty, with a variety of rooms, most with sea views. *Rosy's* has direct access to its own rocky swimming spot, free kayaks for guests, and regular workshops and activities, from yoga to fishing trips. There's also a good restaurant, with plenty of healthy and gluten-free options. **€68**

EATING, DRINKING AND NIGHTLIFE

Moskhos Opposite the church, beneath *Saronis Hotel* ☎22970 91644. Long-established taverna, which offers a more interesting and authentic menu than many of the restaurants along the seafront. Fresh fish (priced by wieght) features strongly, along with the likes of grilled octopus (€9) or oven-baked lamb (€9.50). Daily lunch and dinner.

Parnassos Metóhi ☎22970 91339. The roof terrace at Parnassos, high above Skála, has some of the best views on the whole island – and there's excellent food too. Much of the produce comes from the owner's garden, so the menu

consists of what's available that day (mains around €7–9); check it out in the kitchen. May–Oct daily lunch and dinner.

Taboo Main road on the western edge of town ☎22970 91480, ⓦtabooclub-agistri.gr. The one real club on the island, which can be packed, sweaty and thumping or deserted, depending on the visiting crowds – watch out for posters advertising special events like beach parties and funk and soul nights. Summer Fri–Sun from 11pm, plus special events year-round.

Mýlos (Megalohóri)

The least attractive aspect of Angístri is the windblown road along the coast between Skála and **MÝLOS**. Mýlos itself, also known as Megalohóri, has an attractive, traditional village centre with a church and platía, but there's only a tiny beach, so relatively few people stay here. Access to the rest of the island is easy, however, and there are plenty of rooms and tavernas.

ACCOMMODATION AND EATING   MÝLOS

Fotis On the main street, village centre ☎22970 91325. This centrally located year-round taverna used to double as the local butcher, so the meat here is particularly good. It's worth checking out the day's specials in the kitchen – mains from €7–8. Daily lunch and dinner.

Kouros Harbourside ☎22970 91357. This café is in a lovely position looking out over the goings-on at the harbour, so it's a popular place to wait for the hydrofoil. They serve breakfasts, ice cream and waffles as well as

salads and full meals, and there's even live music some evenings. Daily 10am–11pm; kitchen closed 4.30–7.30pm.

Meltemi Studios Above the harbour ☎22970 91057, ⓦmeltemistudios.gr. Attractive purpose-built studios in a prime position, with views back along the coast towards Skála as well as over the harbour. Rooms are clean and cheerful, with a/c, TV, fridge and balcony, and there's a tiny deep pool that operates as a pool bar in high season. **€50**

5

Rest of the island

There's basically just one road on Angístri, and it runs from Skála and Mýlos round the west coast to the bottom of the island. Midway around, **Dhragonéra** is a beautiful but rocky pine-fringed beach with a dramatic panorama across to the mainland and a seasonal *kantína*; other small coves are accessible across the rocks. Despite the warning signs, many people camp in the woods around these beaches. **LIMENÁRIA**, a small farming community at the edge of a fertile plateau in the southern corner of the island, is largely unaffected by tourism. The closest swimming is a few hundred metres east down a cement drive, then steps, at **Máriza**, where a diminutive concrete lido gives access to deep, ice-clear water. The little anchorage of **Apónissos** lies 2km west, past a shallow salt marsh; there's swimming off the rocks or, in summer, you can cross the bridge to the private islet offshore, rent a sunbed and watch the peacocks.

EATING AND DRINKING   REST OF THE ISLAND

Aponisos Taverna Apónissos. This simple ouzerí has a matchless beachside setting, where wooden chairs are set on a terrace above the water. Simple meze dishes (€3.50–6) plus fish, seafood (octopus €9.50) and salads. June–Sept lunch and dinner daily.

O Tasos Limenária ☎ 22970 91362. Hugely popular with visiting mainlanders – and hence packed at weekend lunchtimes – *O Tasos* produces traditional cooking using local produce. Check out the blackboard for the day's dishes, typically the likes of goat in red sauce, meatballs and moussaka for around €8–10. June–Sept lunch and dinner daily; Oct–May Sat & Sun only.

Póros

Separated from the mainland by a 350m strait, **PÓROS** ("the ford") barely qualifies as an island at all. Popular with Brits and Scandinavians – more than any other Argo-Saronic island, Póros attracts package-holiday operators – it is also busy with weekending Athenians, who can get here by road (via Galatás) or on cheap ferries from Pireás, and with yachties taking advantage of the extensive mooring. There are in fact two islands, **Sferiá** (Póros Town) and the far larger **Kalávria**, separated from each other by a miniature

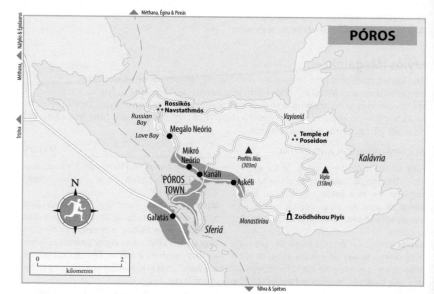

EXCURSIONS TO THE PELOPONNESE

You can easily get to mainland Peloponnese from Póros – boats shuttle constantly between Póros Town and **Galatás**, from where there are numerous potential excursions. Local travel agents run a variety of **tours**, or you'll see hire cars on offer in Galatás from around €25 a day.

TROEZEN

Ancient Troezen is an unenclosed site near the modern village of Trizína, barely 10km from Galatás. Legendary birthplace of Theseus, the scattered site is most easily understood if you purchase a map in the village – this also recounts the stories of Theseus' life. A short walk up a gorge from the site takes you to the spectacular natural rock arch of the Dhiavoloyéfyro, the Devil's Bridge.

EPIDAURUS / EPÍDHAVROS

Most famous for its fourth-century BC theatre, one of the finest ancient monuments in Greece, **Epidaurus** (see p.144) is also an extensive sanctuary to Asklepios, god of healing. The theatre is used for productions of Classical Greek drama on Friday and Saturday nights from June to August, as part of the annual Athens & Epidaurus Festival (ⓦ greekfestival.gr; organized excursions from many island travel agents).

NÁFPLIO

A long day-trip, but arguably the most rewarding destination in the Peloponnese, **Náfplio** (see p.140) is a gorgeous nineteenth-century town in a stunning coastal setting protected by forbidding fortresses. The town has plenty of excellent restaurants and cafés.

---

canal spanned by a bridge. The town is a busy place, with constant traffic of shipping and people: if your stay is longer than a couple of nights, you may want to base yourself on Kalávria for a little more peace, and come into town for the food, nightlife and shopping.

ARRIVAL AND DEPARTURE   PÓROS

BY FERRY

In addition to regular ferry and hydrofoil connections with Pireás and the other Argo-Saronics, Póros has frequent, almost round-the-clock passenger boats shuttling across from the mainland port of Galatás to Póros Town (5min; €1), plus a car ferry every 30min. Small passenger boats tie up among the yachts and other small vessels on the southerly side facing Galatás, hydrofoils next to them near the western end of the waterfront opposite Galatás, and ferries further round at the northern end of town.

Destinations Pireás via Méthana and Égina (1–2 ferries daily, 2hr 45min; 4–6 hydrofoils and Flying Cats, 1hr

15min); Spétses (4–6 hydrofoils and Flying Cats; 1hr 30min); Ýdhra (4–6 hydrofoils and Flying Cats, 30min).

Tickets and agents The island is served by hydrofoils and catamarans run by Hellenic Seaways (ⓦ hsw.gr), whose local agent is Marinos Tours (ⓣ 22980 23423, ⓦ marinostours.gr), and ferries by Saronic Ferries (ⓦ saronicferries.gr), represented by Family Tours (ⓣ 22980 25900, ⓦ familytours.gr). Both agents are directly opposite where their respective boats dock, and there are other travel and accommodation agencies are on the waterfront between the two.

INFORMATION

Tourist information Check ⓦ poros.com.gr for information on the island and for accommodation listings.

Services A couple of banks (with ATMs) and the post office are on Platía Iroön in the centre of Póros Town.

GETTING AROUND

By bus A bus runs from Póros Town east along the coast via Askéli to the monastery, hourly on the hour from the road across from Platía Iroön (June–Sept; €1.70).

By taxi The taxi rank (ⓣ 22980 23003) is close to Platía Iroön; a taxi to most beaches costs less than €6; €10 will take you right across the island to Vayioniá.

By car or bike Travel agents in town can rent you a car, mountain bike, e-bike, quad bike or scooter, though for

bikes of all kinds the best service and prices are from Fotis (ⓣ 22980 25873, ⓦ motofotis-poros.gr); their office is over the bridge, on the road towards Askéli, but they can deliver bike to your accommodation.

By boat Small boats head from the Póros Town waterfront to nearby beaches – west to Neório, Love Bay and Russian Bay, east to Askéli and Monastírou; timetables are seasonal and dependent on demand.

5

Póros Town

PÓROS TOWN rises steeply across the western half of tiny volcanic Sferiá, a landmark clocktower at its summit. There's a lovely little **Archeological Museum** on the waterfront (Korizi square; Tues–Sun 8am–3pm; €2; ☎ 22980 23276) whose local finds will fill a spare half hour, but otherwise there are few sights here. This is a place to eat, drink, shop and watch the world go by. Away from the waterfront, you'll quickly get lost in the labyrinth of steep, narrow streets, but nowhere is far away and most of the restaurants are reasonably well signed. For tremendous views over the rooftops and the strait, climb up to the restored **clocktower** (signed "Roloï"), whose mechanism can be admired behind glass – watch out for unprotected drops.

ACCOMMODATION

Rooms in **Póros Town** can be in very short supply at weekends and during holiday periods, when prices are inevitably high (they can be dramatically lower out of season); some noise is always likely too. Over on **Kalávria** (see opposite) there's considerably more choice, with plenty of apartments and small hotels in the touristy enclaves of Askéli – close to good beaches – or less attractive Mikró Neório. Travel agencies all along the waterfront act as representatives for many of these.

7 Brothers Platía Iroön ☎ 22980 23412, ⊛ 7brothers .gr. Painted a dusky pink, and with a great position set back from the main waterfront square, *7 Brothers* is arguably the town's premier hotel. Comfortably furnished rooms feature all amenities including central heating for winter; all have balconies, though only a few offer much of a view. **€50**

★ **Hotel Dionysos** Waterfront, opposite the ferry dock ☎ 22980 23511, ⊛ hoteldionysos.eu. Set in an imposing mansion, this hotel has large, classily decorated rooms, most of which have bare stone walls, and some with four-poster beds and wonderful old baths. Great value. **€45**

Manessi Waterfront, under the clocktower ☎ 22980 22273, ⊛ manessi.gr. Classy place in the centre of town, with lots of dark wood and designer touches. Some of the cheaper rooms can be a bit small and dark, but the larger ones have impressive power showers, while those at the front have fabulous views. **€45**

Villa Tryfon High up on the clocktower side of the hill ☎ 22980 25854, ⊛ poros.com.gr/tryfon-villa. Undeniably basic and overdue a refurb, the cheerful blue-and-white studio rooms at Villa Tryfon, with kitchenettes and a/c, make up for it with low prices, stunning views and an exceptionally friendly welcome. **€30**

EATING, DRINKING AND NIGHTLIFE

The central waterfront is mostly given over to competing **cafés**, all of which are open from breakfast till late, as well as bars and souvenir shops: the better tavernas lie towards the southeastern end of the waterfront or up in the steep streets of the hilltop town. The southeastern end of the waterfront is also the place for good-value cafés – on Platía Dhimarhíou, for example, or next to the archeological museum – and **bars and clubs**, though nightlife is highly seasonal. The open-air, rooftop Cine Diana (summer only) is on the northern waterfront towards the ferry dock.

★ **Apagio** Southeastern waterfront ☎ 6958 410 550. Excellent taverna run by an Anglo-Greek couple, with some interesting twists on traditional Greek dishes. There are good salads and excellent home-made cheese pies (€4) plus more unusual starters such as fresh tuna paté (€7). Mains include a delicious Beef Apagio (in lemon oregano sauce with carrots; €9) or lamb parcels with honey, veg and cheese (€13). There's often live Greek music too. Daily 10am–12.30am.

Karavolos Inland from northern waterfront, directly behind Cine Diana ☎ 22980 26158. Rightly popular with locals and expats, friendly *Karavolos* serves excellent traditional cuisine (meze around €4) as well as slightly more exotic dishes such as exohikó (pork roasted with garlic; €7.50). The name means snail, and you'll also find these on the menu (with tomato, garlic and onion sauce; €6). Daily 7pm–11.30pm.

Malibu Southeastern waterfront ☎ 22980 22491. One of

the first of the bars you come to at this end of the harbourfront, and the most reliably open year-round. Popular with expats, yachties and tourists alike, and a good place to start your evening – though many never leave. Daily 9pm–late.

Oasis Central waterfront ☎ 22980 22955. Despite being right in the centre and one of the most heavily touted spots on the waterfront, *Oasis* is actually pretty good. Plenty of locals eat here, and the simple, charcoal-grilled meats (lamb chops €12), fish (by the kilo, or a portion €13–15) and octopus (€9) are excellent. Daily 10am–1am.

Platanos On the main square of the upper town ☎ 22980 25409. *Platanos* serves earthy, rural food on a vine-covered terrace, washed down with powerful retsina. The owners have a butcher's shop over the road, so charcoal-grilled meat is the speciality – *try the* spit-roast chicken (€6.50) or suckling pig (€8) – and there are salads and seafood Daily 9am–1am.

Kalávria

KALÁVRIA, Póros's "mainland", is covered in pine forest and barely inhabited, though there are a couple of fertile plateaus on the northern side with olive terraces, vineyards and magnificent panoramic views.

Western Kalávria

Kanáli and **Míkro Neório**, immediately across the canal from Póros Town, are overdeveloped, though they do have some good seafront restaurants looking back toward town. The first place worth a stop in its own right, though, is **MEGÁLO NEÓRIO**, arguably the island's most pleasant resort: small-scale, with a sandy beach, an excellent waterski centre with courses to professional level (☎22980 42540, ⓦpassage.gr), and some fine beachside tavernas.

Love Bay, immediately west, has a lovely sandy beach, but is tiny and always packed; there's a friendly seasonal *kantína*, and kayaks and snorkel gear can be hired here. The **Rossikós Navstathmós** on Russian Bay, a crumbling early nineteenth-century Russian naval base, marks the point where the road turns inland; it's a popular yacht anchorage and there's a busy, mostly shadeless beach. Beyond, a couple of quieter beaches are accessible on foot.

Askéli

ASKÉLI, with its strip of hotels and villas, is the first place you reach as you head east on Kalávria. There are plenty of cafés and places to eat, many of which overlook the narrow, crowded beach. A good watersports centre (☎6978 016 500) has several boats for parascending, waterskiing, ringo rides and the like.

Monastiríou

The eighteenth-century **monastery of Zoödhóhou Piyís** (daily 7am–1pm & 5pm–sunset), next to the island's only spring, is the terminus of Póros's eastward bus. Below, the sandy beach of **Monastiríou**, overlooked by pine-covered slopes, is usually one of the island's less crowded strands: it's somewhat sad and neglected out of season, though in mid-summer a taverna and *kantína* liven things up.

Temple of Poseidon

Daily 8am–5pm • Free • ⓦ kalaureia.org

The remains of the **Temple of Poseidon** overlook the island's northern and western coasts, with great views towards Égina. The temple lay at the heart of **ancient Kalaureia**, whose heyday was in the fourth century BC, and it's an extensive site. Despite plenty of signage and an ongoing Swedish excavation, there's not a great deal to see above ground level – many of the stones were carted off to be used as building materials in the seventeenth and eighteenth centuries (much of it ended up on Ýdhra), and some of the more interesting sections are roped off while they are excavated. It was here that Demosthenes, fleeing from the Macedonians after encouraging the Athenians to resist their rule, took poison rather than surrender.

Vayioniá

Vayioniá, just about the only accessible beach on the island's north shore, was the port of ancient Kalaureia. The bay is beautiful when viewed from above; close up the pebbly beach is narrow and can be windy, but it's still a very pleasant spot, with a seasonal beach bar/café, and loungers to rent.

ACCOMMODATION AND EATING   **KALÁVRIA**

MEGÁLO NEÓRIO

★**Pavlou** ☎22980 22734, ⓦpavlouhotel.gr. Family-run hotel with pool and tennis court, right on one of the island's best beaches (where they also have a waterfront restaurant). Rooms are simple, with no frills, but spacious, with big balconies, half of which have great sea views. Breakfast included. **€60**

5

MIKRÓ NEÓRIO

Aspros Gatos Labráki 49, Waterfront ☎22980 25650. Friendly taverna serving good seafood dishes, such as rice pilaf with mussels and pine nuts (€9.50), on a waterfront terrace with lovely views over Póros Town and the bay. Only about 20min walk from town, or you can take the free water-taxi service for groups of five or more. Daily lunch and dinner.

MONASTIRÍOU

Sirene ☎22980 22741, ⓦsireneblueresort.gr. Large, modern hotel with pool and tennis courts, spectacularly sited on seven floors built into a steep slope above the sea,

with a small private beach below. The stunning location ensures fabulous views from the balconies, though some of the rooms are small. Good off-peak deals. **€120**

VAYIONIÁ

★**Paradisos** ☎22980 23419. Well signed on the main road just east of the turning down to Vayioniá, this rural taverna serves delicious, simple meals on a vine-shaded terrace, overlooking the vegetable and herb gardens where much of the produce is grown. Try their excellent local sausages (€4.50), yemistá (€5) or rabbit *stifádho* (€8.50), washed down with local retsina and home-made bread. Live Greek music on Sun. Daily noon–midnight.

Ýdhra

The island of **ÝDHRA (Hydra)** is one of the most atmospheric destinations in Greece. With its harbour and main town preserved as a **national monument**, it feels like a Greek island should, entirely **traffic-free** (even bicycles are banned) with a bustling harbour and narrow stone streets climbing steeply above it. Away from the main settlement the rest of the island is roadless, rugged and barely inhabited. The charm hasn't gone unnoticed – Ýdhra became fashionable as early as the 1950s, and in the 1960s characters ranging from Greek painter Nikos Hatzikyriakos-Ghikas to Canadian songster Leonard Cohen bought and restored grand old houses here. There's still a sizeable expat community, which contributes to a relatively sophisticated atmosphere and noticeably **high prices**. But even the seasonal and weekend crowds, and a very limited number of beaches, can't seriously detract from the appeal. The **interior** is mountainous and little-visited, so with a little walking you can find a dramatically different kind of island – one of rural cottages, terraces of grain to feed the donkeys, hilltop monasteries and pine forest.

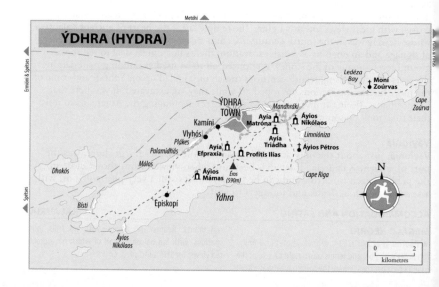

ARRIVAL AND DEPARTURE

BY FERRY

Hellenic Seaways hydrofoils and Flying Cats connect Ýdhra to Pireás via Póros. In the other direction they continue to Spétses, some via Ermióni or on to Pórto Héli on the mainland. Small passenger boats also cross to Metóhi and to Ermióni on the nearby mainland.

Tickets and agencies The local agent for Hellenic Seaways (w hsw.gr) is Hydreoniki Travel (☎ 22980 54007, w hydreoniki.gr), located in an alley at the eastern end of the harbour. Metóhi boats are operated by Hydra Lines (☎ 6947 325 263, w hydralines.gr) and Metohi Express (☎ 6981 222 550, w hydracelebrity.gr); small boats to Ermióni by Hydra Tours Travel (T6977 248 369, w hydratourstravel.gr).

Destinations Ermióni (April–Sept 3 hydrofoils and 3–4 small boats daily; 20min); Metóhi (June–Sept more than 20 daily; 15min); Pireás (6 daily 1hr 40min); Póros (6 daily; 30min); Pórto Héli (3 daily; 1hr); Spétses (4 daily; 45min).

INFORMATION

Tourist information The local municipality's website, w hydra.gr, is an excellent resource.

Services Several banks with ATMs can be found round the waterfront, while the post office is on the market square just inland.

GETTING AROUND

On foot There's only one paved road on Ýdhra, and it leads east from the harbour to Mandhráki, a couple of kilometres away, so to explore the island you either walk or take a boat (see above). The largely shadeless trails mean that in mid-summer walking can be a mercilessly hot experience. There are excellent, cobbled tracks which lead west of town to the beaches at Kamíni (about 20min), Vlyhós (30min) and Plákes (40min). Steeper, rougher paths lead into the interior and towards the south coast (see box, p.349).

By boat Small boats shuttle constantly in season from the harbour to the beaches, at prices ranging from about €6 per person one way to Vlyhós to €15 return to Bísti. You can also hire private water-taxis – good value for groups, at around €17 per boat to Vlyhós or €60 to Bísti.

By mule If you are carrying luggage or might struggle on the sometimes steep cobbles in Ýdhra Town, you can hire a mule at the harbour; fixed prices for various destinations are posted. The fancier hotels may provide a mule if they know when you are arriving – or more likely a porter with a handcart for your luggage.

Ýdhra Town

ÝDHRA TOWN, with tiers of grey-stone mansions and humbler white-walled, red-tiled houses rising from a perfect horseshoe harbour, makes a beautiful spectacle. Around the **harbour**, trippers flock to cafés and chic boutiques, but it's also worth spending time wandering the backstreets and narrow alleys.

The magnificent houses you'll encounter everywhere were mostly built during the eighteenth century on the accumulated wealth of a remarkable merchant fleet, which traded as far afield as America and – during the Napoleonic Wars – broke the British blockade to sell grain to France. In the 1820s, the town's population was nearly twenty thousand – an incredible figure when you reflect that today it is under three thousand – and Ýdhra's merchants provided many of the ships for the Greek forces during the War of Independence, and consequently many of the commanders. At each side of the harbour, cannons facing out to sea and statues of the heroes of independence remind you of the island's place in history.

The Koundouriótis mansions

The mansions of the wealthy eighteenth-century merchant families are still the great monuments of the town; some labelled at the entrance with "*Oikía*" ("Residence of …") followed by the family name. Among the finest are the **Koundouriótis mansions**, built by two brothers: Lázaros (see p.346) and **Yíoryios**. The latter was a leading politician of the fledgling Greek nation and grandfather of Pávlos, president of Republican Greece in the 1920s – consequently, the house, periodically open for art exhibitions, is usually known as the **Pávlos Koundouriótis Mansion**.

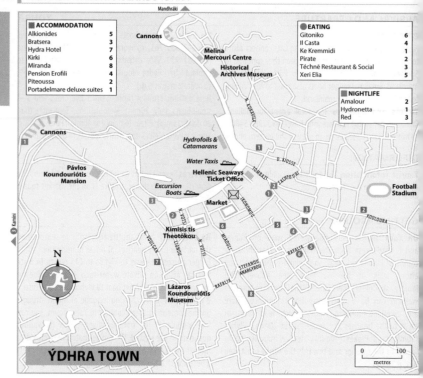

ÝDHRA TOWN

0   100
metres

Lázaros Koundouriótis Museum

High above the western side of town • March–Oct daily 10am–2pm; July & Aug also 6–9pm • €4 • ☎ 22980 52421

The hot climb up stepped alleyways to the **Lázaros Koundouriótis Museum** is rewarded with great views down over the town and port. The ochre-coloured landmark building, whose eponymous original owner played a prominent role in the struggle for Greek independence, boasts a lovingly restored interior that looks ready to move into. The red-tiled floors, panelled wooden ceilings and period furnishings outshine the contents of the museum, which includes paintings, folk costume and independence paraphernalia.

Historical Archives Museum

Eastern waterfront • Daily 9am–4pm, July & Aug also 7.30–9.30pm • €5 • ☎ 22980 52355, ⓦ iamy.gr

The **Historical Archives Museum** occupies one of Ýdhra's great houses, looking out across the harbour. It's a small, crowded and enjoyable display mostly of naval memorabilia – ships' prows and sidearms from the independence struggle and later conflicts – as well as clothing and period engravings; a particularly prized exhibit is the silver chalice containing the embalmed heart of Andreas Miaoulis, commander of the Greek navy during the War of Independence. The **Melina Mercouri Centre**, next door, often has interesting temporary art exhibitions (look out for posters around town).

Kímisis tís Theotókou

Harbour • Museum April–Nov Tues–Sun 10am–5pm • €2 • ☎ 22980 54071

The most obvious and important of Ýdhra's many churches is **Kímisis tís Theotókou** by the port, with its distinctive clocktower. The cloistered courtyard houses the small but rich collection of the **ecclesiastical museum** – silver-bound books, icons, vestments, bejewelled crosses and the like.

ACCOMMODATION ÝDHRA TOWN

Most accommodation in Ýdhra Town is high quality, though prices tend to be equally elevated. Midweek or out of season you should be able to negotiate significant reductions. Old buildings and the closely packed streets mean that some noise is inevitable, especially near the waterfront. Ask for directions when you book, as street signs are nonexistent.

★**Alkionides** ☎ 22980 54055, ⓦ alkionidespension .com. Lovely pension, quietly tucked away yet central, with an attractive courtyard and helpful management; the rooms are extremely comfortable and well equipped, and there's a wonderful studio apartment with its own roof terrace. Room €70, studio €85

Bratsera ☎ 22980 53971, ⓦ bratserahotel.com. This classy four-star hotel occupies a stylishly renovated former sponge factory; the extensive common areas (including bar, restaurant and courtyard pool) serve as a museum of the industry, displaying photos and artefacts. The lovely rooms have flagstone floors and beamed ceilings, though only superior and above have balconies. €170

★**Hydra Hotel** ☎ 22980 53420, ⓦ hydra-hotel.gr. Set in a mansion high above the harbour, this stunning boutique hotel offers glorious views from many of its rooms. Each room is different, from simple doubles up to a split-level family apartment. €125

Kirki ☎ 22980 53181, ⓦ kirkihotel.com. *Kirki's* unprepossessing entrance leads to a delightful old house, with a small courtyard garden and rather fussily decorated rooms; all have a/c, TV and balcony, though the attractive large terraces at the back do get some early-morning noise from the market. €55

Miranda ☎ 22980 52230, ⓦ mirandahotel.gr. A bougainvillea-draped 1810 mansion converted into a popular hotel, with highly individual rooms; best are nos. 2 and 3, both with painted, coffered ceilings and large sea-view terraces. Generous breakfasts in the shaded courtyard are included and there's a basement bar for winter. €120

Pension Erofili ☎ 22980 54049, ⓦ pensionerofili.gr. The simple but spacious rooms at this quiet, friendly and relatively inexpensive pension are set around a courtyard; all have a/c, fridge and television. A small apartment upstairs comes with its own kitchen. €45

★**Piteoussa** ☎ 22980 52810, ⓦ piteoussa.com. Named after the three giant pines at the front, this small, friendly inn is exceptional value, its units equipped with iPod speakers, CD and DVD players and Korres toiletries in the marble-floored bathrooms. Downstairs rooms are larger, but all have balconies and designer touches. €60

Portadelmare deluxe suites ☎ 22980 54105, ⓦ portadelmare.gr. Four luxurious studio/apartments, tucked away very close to the harbour, each individual in layout and decor, with a well-equipped kitchen, TV and DVD player. In the steeply stepped courtyard out back are seating areas and a hot tub (kept cool in summer). €130

EATING AND DRINKING

Brace yourself for some of the steepest food and drink prices in the Greek islands outside Mýkonos and Rhodes. The permanently busy quayside cafés and bars offer an incomparable people-watching experience, while the excellent bakery, that's tucked into the western corner of the harbour by the *Pirate* bar, sells *tyrópittes* (cheese pies) and cakes to take down to the beach.

Gitoniko (Manolis & Christina's) ☎ 22980 53615. Hidden away inland, near Áyios Konstandínos church, this traditional taverna with a big roof terrace serves excellent, well-priced *mayireftá* at lunch – check what's on offer in the kitchen, (most €7 or €8). This usually runs out early, but there's a regular menu in the evening, with plenty of fish, and dishes such as lamb casserole (€12.50), stuffed squid (€13) or chicken in the oven (€9). May–Sept daily noon–4pm & 6pm–midnight.

Il Casta ☎ 22980 52967. Neapolitan restaurant serving up tasty Italian specialities, including excellent antipasti (carpaccio di pulpo €13) and wonderful home-made pasta (fettucine with rabbit €13, spaghetti vongole €17), elegantly presented in a lovely courtyard that's candle-lit at night. Daily 6pm–1am.

Ke Kremmidi ☎ 22980 53099. A *souvláki* joint with

style, where they serve inexpensive *yíros* pita (€2.50) as well as more inventive and interesting stuff including good cheese and meat pies and a variety of Turkish-style dishes (€7.50–10). Daily 10am–2am.

Pirate ☎ 22980 52711. Café by day and an increasingly lively bar as the evening wears on, *Pirate* attracts a young crowd and plays Western music, often with DJs inside. Among the lowest prices on the waterfront for coffee, breakfast and sandwiches. Daily 9am–3am; food served 9am–5pm.

Téchnē Restaurant & Social ☎ 22980 52500. Beautiful modern restaurant/café/bar on the coastal path as it heads west out of town, with fine views. There are good breakfasts and coffees by day, while later they serve cocktails and upmarket modern Greek cuisine. Expect small plates and starters such as courgette and haloumi fritters,

5

ÝDHRA'S FESTIVALS

Over the weekend closest to June 21, Ýdhra Town celebrates the **Miaoulia**, in honour of Admiral Andreas Miaoulis whose fire boats, packed with explosives, were set adrift downwind of the Turkish fleet during the War of Independence. The highlight of the celebrations is the burning of a boat at sea as a tribute to the sailors who risked their lives in this dangerous enterprise.

Orthodox Easter is also a colourful and moving experience, especially on the evening of Good Friday when the fishermen's parish of Áyios Ioánnis at Kamíni carries its *Epitáfios*, or symbolic bier of Christ, into the shallows to bless the boats and ensure calm seas.

with yoghurt & turmeric (€8) or grilled octopus with fava bean purée (€13); mains include sea bream fillet, with wild greens, tomato and black pepper broth, mussels and cured fennel (€22). Daily noon–midnight.

★**Xeri Elia** ☎ 22980 52886. An excellent, busy, traditional taverna with a lovely setting in a vine-shaded inland platía. It serves all the Greek standards (soutzoukákia €8, lamb chops €12), along with good seafood (fish by the kilo; seafood spaghetti €16), and there's often live music in the evenings. Daily noon–4pm & 6pm–midnight.

NIGHTLIFE

Nightlife in Ýdhra Town is tame on the whole, though a number of bars do play music into the early hours; there's also an open-air cinema in summer, on Ikonómou, inland from the market.

Amalour ☎ 22980 29680. Laidback cocktail bar with an eclectic playlist – plenty of Latin and jazz – and 30-to-40-something crowd, plus DJs and dancing inside from 11pm. Almost always the busiest place in town in the early evening; sometimes hosts special events or theme nights. Daily 8pm–3am.

Hydronetta ☎ 22980 54160. The classic sunset-watching bar, where the music carries on into the small hours. Limited seating gives it an exclusive, chill-out vibe. It's also open during the day for food, drinks and swimming, with steps down the rocks into the water. Daily 10am–2am.

Red ☎ 6988 234 962. The closest thing you'll find to a dance club in town, *Red* is a late-night joint right on the waterfront, where they play 1960s and 1970s rock plus a few dance tunes and the odd Greek number. Fri–Sun 10pm–3am, plus some weekdays in summer.

Beaches

There's no big sandy beach on Ýdhra, just a series of small, mainly shingly, coves. Walk west from Ýdhra Town and you'll find several spots where you can clamber down to swim from the rocks in crystal-clear water, but the first tiny pebble beach lies just beyond the picturesque village of **Kamíni**. Next up is a popular swimming cove at **Kastéllo**, part taken over by a new beach bar, and then **Vlyhós**, a small hamlet with a rebuilt nineteenth-century bridge and a shingle beach with loungers and umbrellas; there's pleasant swimming in the lee of an offshore islet here. **Plákes**, a long, pebbly stretch with loungers, *palapa* shelters and a small resort hotel, is followed by the rather scruffy cove of **Palamidhás**, with the island's only surviving shipyard. This marks the end of the easy path; **Mólos**, just beyond, is not accessible on foot. At the western tip of the island, a very tough walk or easy journey by boat, are two coves sheltering perhaps the island's best beaches: **Bísti** has a smallish, white-pebbled beach surrounded by pine trees that offer shade; **Áyios Nikólaos** is larger and sandier, but with less shade and fewer boats. Both have seasonal snack-bars as well as loungers and kayaks to rent.

East of town, **Mandhráki** is the closest beach of all, but is currently somewhat blighted by a major rebuild of the *Miramare Hotel*, which dominates the bay. Normally, in season there's windsurfing and waterskiing here, along with pedaloes to hire and floating trampolines.

ACCOMMODATION, EATING AND DRINKING   BEACHES

KAMÍNI

Pension Petroleka ☎ 22980 52701, ⓦ petroleka pension.gr. There are just a couple of well-equipped apartments here, simply furnished but with a/c and sea views. The larger and more expensive one has two rooms with separate bathroom and kitchen and a huge balcony. **€60**

HIKING ON ÝDHRA

Many of the **paths** that track across the island's interior are signed, at least at their starting points, and a **map** of them is displayed on the harbour waterfront. Don't be misled into assuming that these walks are easy, however; once off the main coastal track, the terrain is rocky and unforgiving, there's little shade, and the trails are in places very hard to follow. These are the main routes:

WESTERN BEACHES

Very easy walking as far as **Palamidhás** (see opposite) where the track runs out and a path heads uphill towards the hamlet of **Episkopí**. The route avoids the village and eventually there's a fork: left to **Áyios Nikólaos** or straight on along the main path to **Bísti**. From either of the beaches you should be able to get a boat back. It's at least four hours to Bísti.

PROFÍTIS ILÍAS AND MOUNT ÉROS

The monastery of **Profítis Ilías** and nearby convent of **Ayía Efpraxía** are about an hour-and-a-half's climb above Ýdhra Town. What must be the longest stairway in Greece (or alternatively a zigzag path) constitutes the final approach to Profítis Ilías; it's closed from noon–4pm, but water and *loukoúm* (Turkish delight) are hospitably left at the gate. If you want to go further, take the rather tougher, harder-to-follow trail which continues south before splitting: left will take you to the 590m summit of **Mount Éros**, the Argo-Saronic islands' highest point (another 30min); right to the chapel of **Áyios Mámas** and eventually on to **Episkopí** (another 2hr), from where you can head on to Bísti or circle back round via Palamidhás.

ÁYIOS NIKÓLAOS

The path from Ýdhra Town towards deserted **Áyios Nikólaos** monastery offers spectacular views back down over the harbour before reaching, at the top, a broad, easy dirt track heading straight across a high plateau towards the monastery. Just beyond Áyios Nikólaos is a small settlement, from where you can in theory head down to **Limnióniza**, a scenic cove on the south coast an hour and a quarter from Ýdhra Town. However, it's a steep scramble on a path which is hard to find and there are no boats back unless you arrange to be picked up by water-taxi. A far easier alternative is to follow the broad track down from Áyios Nikólaos to **Mandhráki** (see opposite), where you can have a swim before heading back to town.

CAPE ZOÚRVA

This is Ýdhra's eastern tip and is over four hours' walk from town, on a path that heads east from Áyios Nikólaos. There are several small chapels along the way, along with the substantial **Moní Zoúrvas** (three hours). Water-taxis can drop off and pick up at the bay below the monastery, and perhaps the best way to do this trip is to take an early-morning water-taxi to **Ledéza Bay**, hike to the cape, and then back to town: with the return from the cape to the monastery, this will take over five hours.

Taverna Kodylenia ☎ 22980 53520. With a beautiful terrace overlooking the little harbour, *Kodylenia* is famous for its seafood (fish priced by weight) and wonderful sunset views. Crowds of weekend trippers mean slightly higher-than-average prices: shrimp *saganáki* €15, lamb €12. March–Oct daily 10am–10pm.

VLYHÓS

Antigone's Apartments ☎ 22980 53228, ✉ antigone@freemail.gr. Just above the jetty where the boats drop you, *Antigone's* has recently refurbished apartments overlooking the water; the small ones have a bedroom and living room/kitchenette, while a larger two-bedroom apartment occupies the entire top floor. June–Oct. **€80**

PLÁKES

Four Seasons ☎ 22980 53698, ⊛ fourseasonshydra.gr. Lovely beachfront restaurant with excellent fresh fish and seafood, plus a blackboard of daily specials. As ever, fish is pricey – gilthead bream with steamed veg €17.50; octopus €13 – but the meat and veggie dishes are more affordable (home-made cheese or spinach pies €8; pork chops or burger €8). Behind is a luxurious small suite-hotel with spacious modern suites and studio apartments. April–Oct daily 9am–midnight. **€190**

MANDHRÁKI

Mandraki 1800 ☎ 22980 52112. Above a tiny cove as you enter Mandhráki, this café/ouzeri has loungers and umbrellas, free for customers, and serves good fresh fish as well as a short menu of daily specials (€8–10). April–Oct daily noon–1am.

5

Spétses

A popular, upmarket escape for Athenians, **SPÉTSES** had brief fame and a vogue as a package destination, largely thanks to John Fowles, who lived here in the early 1950s and used the place, thinly disguised, as the setting for his cult novel *The Magus*. But the island never developed the mass infrastructure – or the convenient beaches – to match. Today, the town is much the biggest in the Saronic Islands, with **apartments and villas** spreading along the northeast coast, while the rest of the island remains almost entirely uninhabited, with **pine forest** inland and excellent **small beaches** around the coast.

ARRIVAL AND DEPARTURE

BY FERRY

At least five daily Hellenic Seaways hydrofoils and Flying Cats connect Spétses with Pireás (2hr 20min) via Ýdhra (45min) and Póros (1hr 25min). Around three a day call at mainland Ermióni en route, and in the other direction continue to Pórto Héli. A car ferry and seasonal passenger boats also run several times daily to Kósta on the nearby mainland (though you can't bring a car to the island). All of them dock pretty much in the heart of town at the cannon-studded main harbour known as the Dápia.

Tickets and agencies The local agent for Hellenic Seaways is Bardakos (☎22980 73141, ⓦhsw.gr), on the east side of the Dápia.

INFORMATION

Tourist information Mimoza Travel (☎22980 75270) and Alasia Travel (☎22980 74098, ⓦalasiatravel.gr), both on the waterfront immediately east of the Dápia, can help with accommodation and local information. A useful website is ⓦspetsesdirect.com.

Services There are banks with ATMs all around the Dápia.

GETTING AROUND

By bus There are two bus services to the beaches in high season: west to Kounoupítsa, Ligonéri and Vréllos from the waterfront by the *Hotel Poseidonion* (roughly hourly during the day); east and then around the island to Áyii Anáryiri and Ayía Paraskéví from behind the town beach (4–5 daily).

By boat Seasonal *kaïkia* (traditional wooden boats) offer shuttles to the beaches (€10 return to Áyii Anáryiri, for example) or round-the-island trips, and there are plentiful water-taxis (€20–85 per boatload depending on destination; ☎22980 72072).

By bike Bike Center (daily 10am–3.30pm & 5.30–10pm; ☎22980 72209), about halfway along the

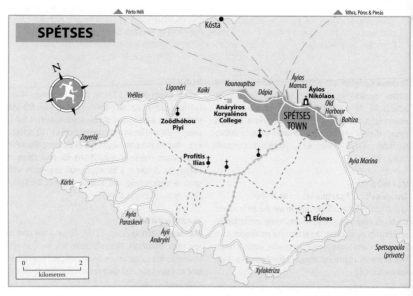

shopping street behind the seafront hotels, has good mountain bikes for €6 a day, plus maps and suggested routes; there are a few stiff slopes, but you could easily circle the island in a couple of hours.

By horse and carriage Horse-drawn carriages wait for passengers just off the Dápia; they charge around €10 to the old harbour, €20 for a tour of the town.

By scooter and motorbike Several rental places can be found behind the town beach. Try Bratopoulos (☎ 6932 333 014), often the cheapest if you bargain (from €15/day), or Nautilus (☎ 22980 77068); Stanathiotis (☎ 22980 75364) on Bótasi, the main street inland, generally has the newest bikes.

Spétses Town

SPÉTSES TOWN shares with Ýdhra a history of late eighteenth-century mercantile adventure and prosperity, and a leading role in the War of Independence, which made its foremost citizens the aristocrats of the new Greek state. Plenty of fine old homes and public buildings survive, but here there's been little restriction on new building, which spreads along the shore in both directions. And although most cars are banned in town, you won't notice it, as they're replaced by thousands of **mopeds and scooters** that pay little attention to whether a street is pedestrianized or not. In short, it's much less pretty than Ýdhra Town, but also a great deal more lively and earthy, and full of pricey shops, bars and restaurants.

For most visitors, shopping, eating and drinking are the principal attractions of Spétses, but it's a very enjoyable place to wander, with majestic old houses and gardens scattered through the narrow streets. The harbour, the **Dápia**, marks pretty much the centre of town, with the main square tucked in behind. To the east lies the **town beach** of Áyios Mámas, with the older part of town behind it. Beyond, via a lovely walk around the point, lies the **Old Harbour**, upmarket focus of the island's nightlife, where private yachts moor up. West of the Dápia is **Kounoupítsa** – much of the simpler accommodation is here, and there are small beaches and waterfront tavernas. It's a big place; to walk from Kounoupítsa to the far end of the Old Harbour will take at least forty minutes.

Bouboulína's Mansion

100m behind the Dapia • Guided tours (30min) up to a dozen times daily; times are posted outside, on boards around town and online • €6 • ☎ 22980 72416, ⓦ bouboulinamuseum-spetses.gr

Local heroine **Laskarína Bouboulína** was a wealthy widow who commanded her own small fleet in the War of Independence, reputedly seduced her lovers at gunpoint and was shot in 1825 by the father of a girl her son had eloped with. Her former home – **Bouboulína's Mansion** – signposted not far behind the Dápia, is now a private museum. On the entertaining tour, you'll hear the story of how she spent much of her fortune on ships and men for the independence struggle, while highlights among the arms, furniture, pictures and correspondence are a gorgeous wooden ceiling in the main room and a model of Bouboulína's flagship, the *Agamemnon*.

Spétses Museum

On the hill above the town beach • Tues–Sun 8.30am–2.45pm • €3 • ☎ 22980 72994

Spétses' enjoyable local **museum** is housed in one of the town's grandest mansions, the Hatziyánnis Méxis family home, perched high up in the eastern half of town. Apart from the house itself, highlights include magnificent polychrome wooden ships' prows from the revolutionary fleet, as well as its flag, plus (out of sight in a plain wooden ossuary) the bones of Laskarína Bouboulína (see above).

ACCOMMODATION	SPÉTSES TOWN

Athina Apartments Just behind the town beach ☎ 22980 74089, ⓦ athina-spetses.com. Comfortable, well-equipped self-catering apartments in a quiet spot near the beach, with a friendly and helpful English proprietor. **€60**

Kastro Hotel Towards Kounoupítsa, behind *Nissia* hotel ☎ 22980 75152, ⓦ kastrohotel-spetses.gr. An attractive complex of comfy studios and duplex apartments, arranged around a small pool and bar, that come with kitchen, a/c, TV and balcony. **€85**

Klimis 200m east of the Dápia ☎ 22980 73725, ⓦ klimishotel.gr. Newly renovated seafront hotel, boutique-style, with lovely modern bathrooms. There are

5

wonderful views from the balconied rooms at the front and some kind of sea view from most rooms. Downstairs there's a superb, old-fashioned *zaharoplastío* (cake shop), where breakfast (included) is served. **€115**

Poseidonion Immediately west of the Dápia ☎ 22980 74553, ⊛ poseidonion.com. Vast, imposing, *fin-de-siècle* edifice which reopened in 2009 after years of meticulous refurbishment. Grand, high-ceilinged rooms in the main building, many with freestanding claw-foot baths. There are larger but less characterful garden rooms at the back, behind the outdoor pool (there's also an indoor pool, gym and spa), and an amazing cupola suite in the tower. **€240**

Roumani Dápia ☎ 22980 72244. Prime location right on the Dápia, which means rooms at the front have stunning views, though they can also be noisy. All the rooms are simple and rather old-fashioned, but comfy enough and with some kind of sea view – they're great value for the position. Cool modern café downstairs where breakfast (included) is served. **€65**

Villa Christina 200m inland from the Dápia, just off Bótasi ☎ 22980 72218, ⊛ villachristinahotel.com. Friendly, restored inn occupying a rambling old building with two courtyards, set in a peaceful location. Rooms with a/c and TV, plus one studio (with kitchen) – all showing their age somewhat. Breakfast in the courtyard usually included. **€50**

Villa Orizontes 500m directly uphill from the back of Platía Oroloyíou ☎ 22980 72509, ⊛ villaorizontes.gr. Simple, no-frills place in a quiet spot, high up – look for the large veranda and blue shutters – with a variety of different-sized rooms and studios with fridge, a/c and TV, many have knockout views across town and out to sea. **€45**

★ Zoe's Club Signed inland, 200m east of the Dápia ☎ 22980 74447, ⊛ zoesclub.gr. Lovely, spacious, designer-decorated rooms, apartments and maisonettes on a quiet inland corner, set around a large pool. All have cool modern decor and cable TV, and many have great sea views. Expect it to be fully booked for Aug and summer weekends and almost empty the rest of the time, though there are few bargains even then. **€190**

EATING AND DRINKING

Spétses is almost as pricey as Ýdhra, especially in the cafés around the Dápia and romantic spots on the old harbour.

Exedra Old Harbour ☎ 22980 73497. A smarter, older crowd tends to come here to enjoy standard dishes like moussaka, *angináres ala políta* (artichokes with dill sauce, both €8) and fresh fish (priced by kilo), served in a lovely waterside setting. Daily noon–4pm & 7pm–midnight.

Kafeneion Dápia ☎ 22980 72202. Pebble mosaics underfoot and sepia photos indicate that this was the island's first watering hole. A prime people-watching spot, open all day for coffee and snacks, progressing later to a full range of mezédhes; or just have a drink while waiting for a hydrofoil. Daily 10am–1am.

Patralis Kounoupítsa ☎ 22980 75380. Old-fashioned, bourgeois *psarotavérna* (fish restaurant), very popular with Greek visitors, which can mean slow service and a wait for a table. The fish is excellent, though, and there are plenty of less expensive meaty alternatives (such as moussaka or roast lamb for €9) plus good barrelled wine. Daily 11am–midnight.

★ Mourayo Old Harbour ☎ 22980 73700. In a glorious setting on a pontoon at the base of the old harbour (alongside *To Liotrivi*), Mourayo serves delicious modern Greek food. The fish-heavy menu includes the likes of octopus with mushrooms and a balsamic sauce (€16), sea bass with fish soup (€18.50) and plenty of whole fish, as well as some interesting salads; there's also a daily changing, 3-course menu for €20. They serve good bottled house wine from family vineyards on the nearby mainland, and there's also a bar if you fancy a cocktail while enjoying the view. Daily 7pm–2am.

To Liotrivi Old Harbour ☎ 22980 72269. The "old olive oil press" offers an upmarket, Greek-Mediterranean menu – starters like sea bass ceviche (€14) or crispy shrimp tempura (€14.50), followed by Spetsiot fish (€17.40), steaks (from €27), pastas and risottos – to a Latin and jazz soundtrack, with occasional live music. Some tables enjoy a stunning position on a jetty that extends out into the harbour. Daily 7pm–1.30am.

To Nero tis Agapis Kounoupítsa ☎ 22980 74009. Virtually adjacent to *Patralis* (see above) and with a similar seafood-based menu, "The Water of Love" could hardly be a greater contrast in style and decor – self-consciously modern, island-style, with decent music and enthusiastic young staff. Mains include the likes of fettuccine with crayfish (€22) and red mullet fillet in fennel sauce (€16.80). Daily noon–12.30am.

NIGHTLIFE AND ENTERTAINMENT

Late-night nightlife is mostly centred on **Baltíza**, the furthest of the inlets at the old harbour. Closer to town, **Áyios Mámas** beach also has a couple of lively music bars. Two **cinemas** operate in summer, close to the main square – Titania (with a roof for shelter, but open sides; ☎ 22980 72434) and open-air, rooftop Marina (☎ 22980 72110).

Balkoni East of the Dápia ☎ 22980 77153. Elegant bar/café on the main shopping street with a balcony terrace overlooking the waterfront; wine, music and cocktails at night, coffee and snacks by day. Daily 9am–3am.

Bar Spetsa Áyios Mámas ☎ 22980 74131, ⓦ barspetsa. org. Chilled-out bar playing decent retro rock, mainly 1960s and 1970s. Keenly priced drinks and a great atmosphere most nights. March–Oct nightly 8pm–3am.

La Luz Old harbour ☎ 22980 75024, ⓦ laluzspetses.gr. Classy music bar spread over two upstairs floors in a beautifully restored mansion with plenty of exposed brickwork. Open from 4pm for coffee and drinks, but the main action is late at night – live music or DJs most weekends from 11.30pm; weekdays too in July and August. Daily 4pm–4am.

Mama's Beach Café Áyios Mámas beach ☎ 69740 61488. Lively café and lunch spot by day, with sandwiches, milk-shakes and waffles, plus free loungers on the beach for customers, while at night the upstairs music bar (playing summer party stuff) takes over. Daily 10.30am–2am.

Beaches

A single paved road circles Spétses, mostly high above a rocky coast but with access to beaches at various points. In season you can get to most of them by bus or excursion boat, and none is too far to cycle, or even walk.

Kaïki and Vréllos

Kaïki, or College Beach, is just twenty minutes' walk west of town, with a frequent bus service and extensive facilities including loungers, bars and a waterski outfit that also rents jet skis. **Vréllos**, a small, pebbly cove in a pretty, wooded bay, is the end of the line for buses heading west out of Spétses. Thanks to paved access and a beach cocktail bar pumping out loud Greek rock, it's almost always packed at weekends.

Zoyeriá

At the western extremity of the island, **Zoyeriá** is reached down a track that soon degenerates into a path (which doesn't stop locals riding their scooters) past a series of rocky coves. If you follow this, you'll eventually climb over a small headland to arrive at a sandy beach with a large and popular summer-only taverna, *Loula*. Many of the patrons here arrive the easy way, by boat.

Ayía Paraskeví

The bay of **Ayía Paraskeví**, on the southwest coast, shelters a part-sand beach that is almost always quieter than its near neighbour, Áyii Anáryiri (see below). The end of the eastern bus route, it has a seasonal café-bar, but no other development at all.

Áyii Anáryiri

Áyii Anáryiri is the largest and most popular beach on Spétses: a long, sheltered, partly sandy bay, with a good taverna, offshore swimming pontoon and a watersports centre offering kayaks, pedaloes, windsurfers and catamarans to rent, as well as a waterski boat. At the end of the beach concrete steps lead round to the **Bekiris Cave**, a low-ceilinged, shallow cavern; you can clamber in through a narrow entrance at the back and then swim out, though best to have something on your feet for the sharp rocks.

Xylokériza

Almost at the southern tip of the island a long, steep concrete track leads down to a cove of pale-coloured pebbles at **Xylokériza**. There's no sand at all here, but it's a beautiful spot, surrounded by pines and phoenix palms, and rarely crowded. There's a café and volleyball court.

Ayía Marína

Ayía Marína, or Paradise Beach, is a busy, almost suburban, pebble beach, within walking distance of the eastern edge of Spétses Town. Packed with loungers, it also has a popular bar-restaurant and a watersports operation offering kayaks and waterski and ringo rides. There are views offshore towards the tempting but off-limits islet of **Spetsopoúla**, the private property of the heirs of shipping magnate Stavros Niarchos.

The Cyclades

MYKONOS TOWN

The Cyclades

Named for the circle they form around the sacred island of Delos, the Cyclades (Kykládhes) offer Greece's best island-hopping. Each island has a strong, distinct character based on traditions, customs, topography and its historical development. Most are compact enough for a few days' exploration to show you a major part of their scenery and personality in a way that is impossible in Crete, Rhodes or most of the Ionian islands.

The islands do have some features in common. The majority are arid and rocky, and share the "Cycladic" style of brilliant-white cuboid architecture, a feature of which is the central **kástro** of the old island capitals. The typical kástro has just one or two entrances, and a continuous outer ring of houses with all their doors and windows on the inner side, so forming a single protective perimeter wall.

The impact of mass tourism has been felt more severely in the Cyclades than anywhere else in Greece; yet whatever the level of development, there are only three islands where it completely dominates their character in season: **Íos**, the original hippie island and still a paradise for hard-drinking backpackers; the volcanic cluster of **Santoríni**, a dramatic natural backdrop for luxury cruise liners; and **Mýkonos**, by far the most popular of the group, with its teeming old town, selection of gay, nudist and gay-nudist beaches, and sophisticated restaurants, clubs and hotels. After these, **Páros**, **Náxos** and **Mílos** are the most popular, their beaches and main towns packed at the height of the season. The once-tranquil **Lesser Cyclades** southeast of Náxos have become fashionable destinations in recent years, as have nearby **Amorgós**, and **Folégandhros** to the west. To avoid the hordes altogether the most promising islands are **Kýthnos** or **Sérifos** and for an even more remote experience **Síkinos**, **Kímolos** or **Anáfi**. For a completely different picture of the Cyclades, try the island of **Tínos** with its imposing pilgrimage church, or **Sýros** with its elegant Italianate townscape. Due to their proximity to Attica, **Ándhros** and **Kéa** are predictably popular weekend havens for Athenian families, while **Sífnos** remains a chic destination for tourists of all nationalities. The UNESCO site of **Delos** is certainly worth making time for, visited easily on a day-trip from Mýkonos. Note that the Cyclades is the group worst affected by the *meltémi*, which scatters sand and tablecloths with ease in July and August. Delayed or cancelled ferries are common, so if you're heading back to Athens to catch a flight, leave yourself a day's leeway.

ARRIVAL AND DEPARTURE   THE CYCLADES

BY PLANE
There are airports on Páros, Mýkonos, Santoríni, Sýros, Mílos and Náxos. In season, or during storms when ferries are idle, you have little chance of getting a seat on any flight at less than three days' notice, and tickets are predictably expensive. Expect off-season (Nov–April) frequencies to drop dramatically, sometimes to zero.

BY FERRY
Most of the Cyclades are served by main-line ferries from Pireás. Boats for Kéa, and seasonally elsewhere, depart from Lávrio. There are regular services from Rafína to Ándhros, Tínos and Mýkonos, with seasonal sailings elsewhere. Between June and Sept there are also a few weekly sailings to the most popular islands to and from

FYRIPLAKA BEACH, MÍLOS

Highlights

❶ **Beaches of Mílos** Spectacular shorelines characterized by multicoloured rocks and volcanically heated sand. **See p.373**

❷ **Mýkonos Town** Labyrinthine lanes crammed with restaurants, boutiques and nightlife. **See p.391**

❸ **Delos** The Cyclades' sacred centre, birthplace of Apollo and Artemis. **See p.396**

❹ **Ermoúpolis, Sýros** The elegant capital of the Cyclades, an Italianate architectural jewel and once Greece's busiest port. **See p.399**

❺ **Church of Ekatondapylianí, Parikiá** An imposing and ornate Paleochristian church on

Páros, incorporating a number of impressive architectural styles. **See p.404**

❻ **Mount Zas, Náxos** The must-do trek in the Cyclades: climb the archipelago's highest mountain. **See p.418**

❼ **Hóra, Folégandhros** The "town of five squares", free of traffic and sitting atop a spectacular cliff, is arguably the most beautiful island capital. **See p.433**

❽ **Caldera of Santoríni** The geological wonder of a crater left by a colossal volcanic explosion, offering unforgettable sunset views. **See p.437**

HIGHLIGHTS ARE MARKED ON THE MAP ON P.358

6

Crete and the eastern Aegean. The best website for Greek ferry routes is ⓦ gtp.gr.

Agents and tickets In high season (particularly Easter, Aug and during elections), popular routes may be booked up, so it's important to check availability upon arrival in Greece and book your outward and inbound pre-flight ferry tickets well ahead (particularly those returning to Pireás from the most popular islands). That said, agents have little advance information on ferry schedules, and purchasing a ticket too far in advance may prevent you getting a faster boat added later.

Timetables The frequency of Pireás, Lávrio and Rafína sailings given in the chapter is from June to Sept when most visitors tour the islands. During other months, expect schedules to be well below the minimum level listed, with some ferry routes cancelled entirely.

Catamaran services These run on some routes in summer from Pireás and Rafína, in addition to ferries. Catamaran travel is very expensive and has become more so recently with the doubling of Greek VAT to 24 percent, but when time is an issue these high-speed craft are a welcome addition to the conventional fleet.

Brief history

The Cyclades are the most quintessentially Greek of all the islands and their long history reflects that. The mining of **obsidian**, the black, sharp-edged volcanic glass used for making implements, originated on Mílos; shards dating to 11,000 BC have been found deep in the Peloponnese, demonstrating early seaborne Paleolithic trade. The

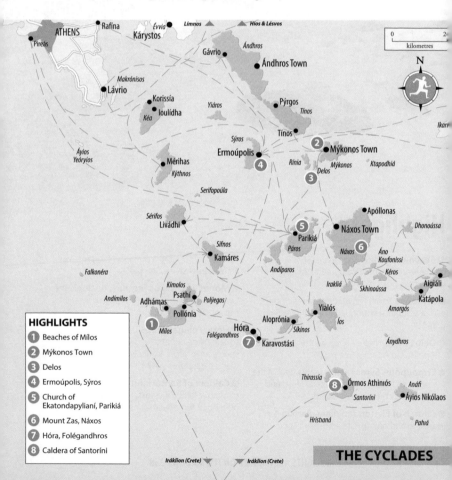

HIGHLIGHTS

1. Beaches of Mílos
2. Mýkonos Town
3. Delos
4. Ermoúpolis, Sýros
5. Church of Ekatondapylianí, Parikiá
6. Mount Zas, Náxos
7. Hóra, Folégandhros
8. Caldera of Santoríni

THE CYCLADES

Bronze Age started here around 2800 BC and with it came the **Cycladic civilization**, notable for its sought-after geometric, minimalist figurines made of marble from **Páros** or **Náxos**. **Mining** for copper, silver and gold, combined with the islands' strategic position, turned them into trading centres.

By 2000 BC the Cretan Minoans had become influential in the area, particularly on **Santoríni**. Such influence, however, came to an end with a catastrophic volcanic eruption around 1600 BC. The Ionian Greeks arrived around 1000 BC and within two hundred years the first cities had appeared. **Delos** became a great religious centre in antiquity.

During and after the Persian wars, **Athens** gradually stripped away the wealth and influence of the **Delian Confederacy**. The Cyclades only regained prosperity during the Hellenistic period, as demonstrated by the construction of numerous large, impressive watchtowers, most notably on Náxos. The subsequent Roman occupation converted Delos back into a successful commercial centre, until a series of raids from the east eventually destroyed it. Under **Byzantine** rule, with little control or support from distant Constantinople, the islands were vulnerable to **pirates**, and settlements moved from the coast to inland, defensive **kástros**, where you find them today.

With the fall of Constantinople to the Crusaders in 1204, the Cyclades came under **Venetian** control and were divided up by adventurers under **Marco Sanudo** who set up the Náxos-based Duchy of the Aegean. Catholicism prospered, some vestiges of which are still found today on **Sýros** and **Tínos**. Most of the islands were taken by the **Ottomans** from the 1530s onwards, though Tínos held out until 1715. As they rightly considered the West a bigger threat, the Turks encouraged the Orthodox Church to fight a resurgence against the former Catholic majority.

After the revolution against the Ottoman Empire in 1821, the Cyclades became part of the Greek state in 1832 and **Sýros**, in particular, prospered, as the new state's largest port and a major industrial base. However, the development of **Pireás** and the 1893 opening of the **Corinth Canal** led to a sharp industrial and commercial decline. This was only reversed in the 1960s when the discovery of the pleasures of **Mýkonos** kick-started the tourism boom that continues unabated today.

Kéa

KÉA (Tziá), the nearest of the Cyclades to the mainland, is extremely popular with Athenian families in August and at weekends year-round; their impact has spread beyond the small resorts, and much of the coastline is peppered with holiday homes built with the locally quarried green-brown stone. Because so many visitors self-cater, there is a preponderance of villa accommodation and not as many tavernas as you might expect. However, outside August or weekends, the island, with its rocky, forbidding perimeter and inland oak and almond groves, is an enticing destination for those who enjoy a rural ramble: ten separate walking paths have been earmarked and are well signposted.

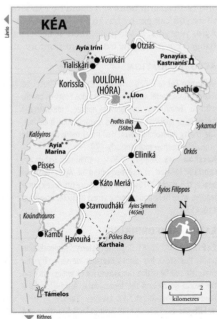

ANCIENT KARTHAIA

The only remains of any real significance from Kéa's past are fragments of temples of Apollo and Athena at **ancient Karthaia**, tucked away on the southeastern edge of the island above Póles Bay, with an excellent deserted twin beach. It is a good ninety-minute round-trip walk from the hamlet of Stavroudháki (on the paved road linking Ioulídha and Havouná), and the inland paved road is worth following along the island's summit from Ioulídha, as it affords fine views over the thousands of magnificent oaks, Kéa's most distinctive feature.

6

ARRIVAL AND GETTING AROUND   KÉA

By ferry Ferries dock at Korissía, on the northwest coast. You can buy ferry tickets from Kea Travel in Korissía (☎ 22880 21920, ⓦ keatravel.gr).

Destinations Ándhros (1 weekly; 6hr); Folégandhros (1 weekly; 12hr); Íos (1 weekly; 11hr); Kýthnos (3 weekly; 1hr 10min); Lávrio (3–5 daily; 1hr); Mílos/Kímolos (2 weekly; 11–14hr); Mýkonos (1 weekly; 5hr 20min); Náxos (1 weekly; 8hr 20min); Páros (3 weekly; 7hr 20min–10hr); Síkinos (1 weekly; 11hr); Sýros (3 weekly; 3–4hr); Tínos (1 weekly; 8hr).

By bus Most visitors bring their cars along from Athens,

so there are no extensive bus services. You may need one of the six taxis available that meet boat arrivals. In July and August, there are buses on the routes Ioulídha-Korissía-Vourkári-Otziás and Korissía-Ioulídha-Písses (1–2 daily; 45min).

By car or motorbike There is only one, expensive, rental outlet, so it's best to rent a car or motorbike in Athens (see p.115) – or at Athens International Airport, which is very close to Lávrio – and take it to Kéa, like Athenians do. The island has three petrol stations, all on the road to the port.

INFORMATION

Tourist office At the seafront in Korissía (daily 8am–2pm & 5pm to last boat arrival; ☎ 22880 21500).
Services There are two banks and one ATM in Korissía.

Ioulídha has one bank and one ATM. The island's only post office is opposite the archeological museum in Ioulídha.

Korissía

The small port of **KORISSÍA** is unlike any other in the Cyclades; with its red-tiled roofs and Neoclassical houses, it could be Pláka-by-the-Sea. It makes a convenient base; from there you can get by bus to Otziás (6km) or Ioulídha (6km). Although the port beach, **Áyios Yeóryios**, is adequate, there is better swimming at **Yialiskári**, a small, eucalyptus-fringed cove after the eastern promontory on the road to Vourkári.

ACCOMMODATION   KORISSÍA

Brillante Zoi ☎ 22880 22685/86, ⓦ brillante-hotel.gr. A comfortable hotel on the middle of Áyios Yeóryios beach, with a beautifully overgrown garden, idiosyncratic furnishings, spacious rooms and a sumptuous breakfast. The chatty, welcoming owner will feel more like an old acquaintance than your landlady. **€70**

Karthea ☎ 22880 21204, ⓦ hotelkarthea.gr. Centrally located at the beginning of Áyios Yeóryios beach, this dated 1970s hotel was where the Greek junta leaders were held under house arrest in 1974. Breakfast €10. **€55**

★ Keos Katoikies ☎ 22880 21661, ⓦ keos.gr. Cool, contemporary minimalist studios, each with its own large balcony in a dramatic setting overlooking Korissía bay – don't miss the sunset from the adjoining café. The room price includes an excellent English buffet breakfast. Free wi-fi at reception. Easter–Oct. **€100**

Porto Kea ☎ 22880 22870, ⓦ portokea-suites.com. Luxurious hotel behind the main road and by the church of Áyios Yeóryios, with a large swimming pool and spa. Its trendy bar, *Ammos*, on the beach in front offers free chairs for hotel clients. Breakfast included. Easter–Oct. **€130**

EATING AND DRINKING

En Plo ☎ 22880 22081. Opposite the ferry disembarkation point, this snack-bar serves delicious desserts. Try the chocolate soufflé with a cappuccino for €5 while watching the world go by and the ferries dock. April–Oct daily 8am–1am; Nov–March Fri & Sat 8am–1am.

★ Fillipas ☎ 22880 21690. Built in local Kéa stone and

sitting on the hill above Keos Katoikies, this is the best grill restaurant on the island. Although it's often booked for functions, they will always find you a table and serve you promptly. Try the giant steaks or its signature beefburger filled with local cheese (€8). April–Oct daily 6pm–1am; Nov–March Fri & Sat 6pm–1am.

Magazés ☎ 22880 21104, ⓦ kearestaurant.gr. The best in the cluster of the harbour restaurants, this traditional taverna with a small but tasty range of Greek dishes also offers fresh fish, often caught by the owner. If you crave meat instead, try the baked pork with potatoes for €12. April–Oct daily 9am–midnight.

Ioulídha

Kéa's capital, **IOULÍDHA** (Hóra), with its winding flagstoned paths, is beautifully situated in an amphitheatric fold in the hills. It is by no means a typical Cycladic town, but is architecturally the most interesting settlement on the island. Accordingly it has numerous bars and bistros, much patronized in August and at weekends, but at other times the town is quiet, its atmospheric, labyrinthine lanes excluding vehicles.

6

The lower reaches of the town stretch across a spur to the **kástro**, a tumbledown Venetian fortress incorporating stones from an ancient temple of Apollo. Ioulídha's **Archeological Museum** (Tue–Sun 8am–3pm; €2; ☎ 22880 22079) displays extensive finds from the four ancient city-states of Kéa, its highlight being thirteen female Minoan-style statues. Fifteen-minutes' walk northeast of Ioulídha on the path toward Otziás, you pass the **Lion of Kéa**, a sixth-century BC sculpture carved out of an outcrop of rock, 6m long and 3m high.

ACCOMMODATION AND EATING   IOULÍDHA

En Lefko ☎ 22880 21262. On the street between Hóra's two squares, this coffee shop has one of the most romantic gardens, suspended over the cliffs and overlooking the port and beyond. Dimly lit, this is the perfect place to snuggle up with a cappuccino (€4). April–Oct daily 8am–2am.
Hotel Serie ☎ 22880 22355, ⓦ serie.com.gr. Only 100m from the Ioulídha bus stop and employing a tasteful colour combination of blue and orange throughout – from the stone building itself to the furnishings – this is maybe the best-situated boutique hotel on the island with views both of Ioulídha and the valley below. Easter–Oct. **€70**
★ **Rolandos** Main square ☎ 22880 22224. The chef, Rolandos, comes from Corfu and serves a traditional Greek menu with an Ionian flavour. His moussaka (€8) – using courgettes instead of potatoes – is as famed as the house wine. Easter–Oct daily 10am–2am.

The north coast

Kéa's **north coast** attracts the most visitors. **VOURKÁRI**, strung out around the next bay, a couple of kilometres northeast of Korissía, is a fishing village, arguably more attractive than Korissía, serving as a hangout for the yachting set. Another 4km further, **OTZIÁS** has the biggest and best beach on the northern shore though it's more exposed to prevailing *meltémi* winds.

The eighteenth-century monastery of **Panayías Kastrianís** (June–Sept sunrise–sunset) is 7km east along a surfaced road from Otziás. From here you can take the pleasant walk on dirt tracks and occasional paths to Ioulídha in another two hours. Further on, **Spathí**, 3km south of the monastery on a dirt road, is by far the island's finest beach.

ACCOMMODATION AND EATING   THE NORTH COAST

Anemousa Otziás ☎ 22880 21335, ⓦ anemousa.gr. A modern cluster of villas alternating the brown-gold Kéa stone with whitewashed walls. The colour scheme extends to the tasteful furnishings inside the spacious studios which sleep up to four adults. April–Oct. **€70**
Aristos Vourkári ☎ 22880 21475. Don't be fooled by the look of this sleepy fish taverna at the entrance to the village; it is renowned for its crayfish spaghetti (€20–30), drawing customers from all over the island. April–Oct daily 10am–midnight; Nov–March Fri & Sat noon–midnight.
Strofi tou Mimi Vourkári ☎ 22880 21480, ⓦ istrofitoumimi.com. The locals are almost equally divided on whether this place, on the corner of the road towards Otziás, or *Aristos* (see above) is the best fish taverna on the island – you can make up your own mind by dining in both. *Strofi tou Mimi* is slightly cheaper. April–Oct daily 7pm–midnight.

Tis Annas Otziás ☎ 22887 21137. Located at the end of the beach, this is a small but popular taverna with a traditional island interior. Anna is long gone but the family cooks on: specialities include pork stew with haloumi cheese and a variation of coq au vin with pasta (€8). Decent house wine, too. Daily noon–midnight.

The south

The road southwest of Ioulídha twists around a scenic agricultural valley and emerges at a large sandy beach at **Písses**. Beyond here, the asphalt peters out at the end of the 5km road south to **Koúndhouros beach**, which consists of two sheltered coves popular with yachters. A further 2km south, at **Kambí**, there's a nice little beach and a good taverna of the same name.

Kýthnos

One of the lesser known and most low-key of the larger Cyclades, **KÝTHNOS** is an antidote to the overdevelopment you may encounter elsewhere, so much so that credit cards are still not accepted in many places. Few foreigners visit, and the island – known also as Thermiá, after its renowned hot springs – is even quieter than Kéa or Sérifos, particularly in the south where drives or long hikes from **Dhryopídha** to its coastal coves are the primary diversion. A bridge between Kea's Athenian neoclassical and Serifos' fully-fledged Cycladic architecture, it's a place to sprawl on sunbed-free beaches without having to jostle for space.

ARRIVAL AND GETTING AROUND

KÝTHNOS

By ferry Boats dock in Mérihas on the west coast.
Destinations Folégandhros (1–2 weekly; 6hr–8hr 30min); Íos (1 daily; 9hr 20min); Kéa (2–3 weekly; 1hr 10min); Kímolos (3–4 weekly; 10hr); Lávrio (1–3 daily; 1hr 40min–2hr 45min); Mílos/Kímolos (1–2 daily; 4hr); Náxos (1 weekly; 7hr); Mýkonos (1 weekly; 4hr); Páros (1 weekly; 5hr 30min); Pireás (4–6 weekly; 3hr); Sérifos (3–5 weekly; 1hr 30min); Sífnos (3–5 weekly; 2hr 30min); Síkinos (1 weekly; 7hr 30min); Sýros (2–5 weekly; 2hr 40min); Tínos (1–2 weekly; 6hr 50min).

By bus Two buses run from Mérihas port from June to Sept, one serving Hóra and Loutrá (4–5 daily; 30min) and another to Dhryopídha and Kanála (3 daily; 30min).

By boat There's a *kaïki* from Mérihas to Kolóna beach (July & Aug, 8 daily; ☎ 22810 32104; €10 return).

By car Larentzakis by the port steps has the better cars (☎ 22810 32104, ⌨ rentacarkythnos.gr).

INFORMATION AND ACTIVITIES

Tourist office A helpful information office is usually open by the jetty during ferry arrivals (July to mid-Sept ☎ 22810 32250).

Services There's one bank and two ATMs in Mérihas: one up the steps near the disembarkation point, and a second on the harbour road. Hotels and restaurants do not as a rule accept credit cards. Hóra has the only post office (Mon–Fri 9.30am–2pm).

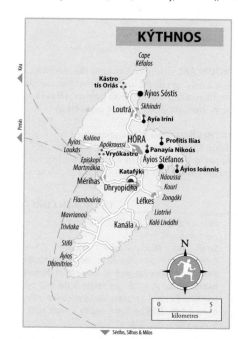

KÝTHNOS

Kéa

Pireás

Cape Kéfalos

Kástro tís Oriás

Áyios Sóstis

Loutrá Skhinári

Ayía Iríni

Áyios Loukás Kolóna Apókroussi HÓRA Profítis Ilías

Vryókastro Panayía Nikoús

Episkopí Áyios Stéfanos

Martinákia Katafýki Áyios Ioánnis

Mérihas Náoussa

Dhryopídha Kourí

Flamboúria Léfkes Zongáki

Mavrianoú Liotriví

Trívlaka Kanála Kaló Livádhi

Stifó

Áyios Dhimítrios

N

0   5
kilometres

Sérifos, Sífnos & Milos

Activities Aqua Team (☎ 22810 31333, ⓦ aquakythnos .com), opposite the spa in Loutrá, offers PADI, ANDI and DDI diving courses, plus diving excursions to the historic Nikki wreck off Áyios Stéfanos beach; it also arranges guided kayak tours from Apókroussi beach, plus walking tours and package deals including accommodation.

Mérihas and around

MÉRIHAS is an attractive ferry and fishing port – but not really the place to base your stay. The closest beach of any repute is the fine sandy cove of **Martinákia**, a ten-minute stroll north of the port, with **Episkopí**, a 500m stretch of clean grey sand, 3km further north. About 2km beyond Episkopí is the larger, shaded beach of **Apókroussi** with two good tavernas. Some 2km west of Apókroussi on a dirt road, the picturesque sandy spit **Kolóna** is one of Greece's most spectacular beaches, a joining Kýthnos to the islet of **Áyios Loukás**.

ACCOMMODATION AND EATING | MÉRIHAS AND AROUND

Martinos Studios Mérihas ☎ 22810 32469, ⓦ www .martinos-kythnos.gr. Just 30m from the sea, these studios have local furnishings, stone floors, fridge, TV, kitchenette and parking spaces. Room sizes vary and so do the views; it's worth paying more for those at the very top. Reception is closed in the afternoon. €40

To Kandouni Mérihas ☎ 22810 32220. For those who fancy meat in a sea of fish tavernas: this excellent grill – situated at the far end of the port – has many different starters and salads as well as specialities such as *sfougáto*

(local cheese croquettes) for €4.50. April–Oct daily 7pm–1am.

★**Villa Elena** Martinákia ☎ 22810 32275, ⓦ villa-elena.gr. Two-storey self-catering maisonettes situated on a slope with superb sea views over the Aegean: they have fully equipped kitchenettes, TV and parking with port transfers available. It's a stone's throw from Martinákia beach, where they run a café/bar serving breakfasts and traditional dishes (daily 8am–late). April–Sept. €60

Hóra

HÓRA lies 7.5km northeast of Mérihas, in the middle of the island. Though the town looks unpromising at first sight, wander into the narrow streets beyond the initial square and you'll find a wonderful network of alleyways, weaving their way past shops, churches and through tiny squares with colourful cafés. The early nineteenth-century church of **Áyios Ioánnis Theológos** is worth a visit for its elaborate wooden iconostasis. However, its most valuable possession is a miraculous seventeenth-century icon of the three matriarchs (Elisabeth, Anne and Virgin Mary), said to have been found floating in the sea by local fishermen.

ACCOMMODATION AND EATING | HÓRA

Apocalypsis ☎ 22810 31272. Relatively cheap café-bar (beer €3, cocktails €8), opposite the main church of St John, playing anything from trance to Greek popular tunes. It shares the seats on the square (and alternates the music) with the *Gazoza* indie lounge opposite. Both daily 7am–midnight.

Filoxenia ☎ 22810 31644, ⓦ filoxenia-kythnos.gr. Welcoming *pension* next to the main square, with clean,

basic rooms with balconies and kitchenettes arranged around a flowery courtyard. It's a convenient base if you want to travel by bus around the island. €50

Messaria ☎ 22810 31620. Large restaurant by the main village square that serves the Hóra speciality of local coq au vin for €9. Unlike other establishments in Hóra that close during the day, this stays open all day. Daily 1pm–midnight.

Loutrá and around

The resort of **LOUTRÁ**, 4.5km north of Hóra, is named after its mineral thermal baths, which became well-known when Greece's King Otto and Queen Amalia took the waters from 1847 onwards. Its nineteenth-century **spa** (summer daily 10am–6pm; day pass €6, plus a one-off charge of €3.50) was designed by Ernst Ziller, the architect of many of Greece's finest Neoclassical buildings. You can enjoy the hot springs for free on the right-hand side of Loutrá's small beach, where they run into the sea. A nicer spot for a dip, though, is the bay of **Ayía Iríni**, 1km east.

Just north of Loutrá, at **Maroúla**, Mesolithic graves dating to about the eighth millennium BC suggest Kýthnos may have been one of the earliest inhabited Cycladic islands; other sites indicate copper mining and smelting. About a ninety-minute walk from Loutrá, on Cape Kéfalos, lie the picturesque ruins of the medieval capital **Kástro tís Oriás**, once home to around five thousand people, but now abandoned.

ACCOMMODATION
LOUTRÁ AND AROUND

Meltemi ☎ 22810 31271, ⓦ meltemihotel-kythnos.gr. On the road out of Loutrá this hotel has dependable studios and apartments renovated in 2017, with beautifully tiled walls and a landscaped garden. Breakfast €6; half board €20. April–Oct. **€55**

★**Porto Klaras** ☎ 22810 31276, ⓦ porto-klaras.gr. It's worth the trip to Loutrá just to stay at this hotel, where

the huge self-catering rooms have decorated carved recesses, a large, sculpted bed and ceiling fans, while the balconies – some of which come with sofas – have great port views. Ferry and airport pickups from Athens can be arranged, as well as ferry tickets from Lávrio or Pireás. Breakfast (€5 extra) at *Stella* next door (see below). April–Oct. **€70**

EATING

Stella ☎ 22810 31082 For well-priced kalamári, octopus, crayfish or lobster, head for this fish taverna in the middle of the quay, which also serves à la carte breakfasts in the morning (mains €10–15). May–Oct daily 8am–1am.

★**Sofrano** ☎ 22810 31436. A waterfront fine-dining restaurant for the yachting jet-set, run by Greek celebrity

chef Nikolas Sakellariou, with arguably the best food in the Cyclades outside Mýkonos and Santoríni. There is immense creativity on show in the dishes, such as veal fillet in chocolate sauce (€19) or a stunningly presented octopus carpaccio (€15), though the inventiveness does not detract from the taste or the portion size. Daily 9am–midnight.

Dhryopídha and the south

From Hóra you can drive south to **DHRYOPÍDHA**; more visually appealing than Hóra by virtue of spanning a well-watered valley, its red-tiled roofs are reminiscent of Spain or Tuscany. It was once the island's capital, built around one of Greece's largest **caves**, the **Katafýki** (summer daily 10am–2pm & 6–8pm; free), that served as a hiding place from corsairs. South of Dhryopídha, **KANÁLA** is a relaxed alternative to Loutrá, with its **Panayía Kanála** church set in a tiny but pleasant pine woodland and home to a miracle-working icon by the seventeenth-century Cretan master, Skordhilis.

ACCOMMODATION AND EATING
DHRYOPÍDHA AND THE SOUTH

Akroyali Áyios Dhimítrios ☎ 22810 32208. Modern apartment complex at the end of Áyios Dhimítrios beach decorated in lime-washed white and comprising large suites with sea views and fully equipped kitchens. There's an on-site restaurant too. May–Sept. **€40**

Megali Ammos Kanála ☎ 22810 32052. Roomy self-catering apartments and studios on Megáli Ammos beach, all with a kitchenette, balcony or veranda and sea views. There's parking and a good on-site restaurant (daily 8am–2am). Easter–Oct. **€35**

Sérifos

SÉRIFOS has long languished outside the mainstream of history and modern tourism. Little has happened here since Perseus returned with Medusa's head in time to save his mother, Danaë, from being ravished by the local king Polydectes – turning him, his court and the green island into stone. Many would-be visitors are deterred by the apparently barren, hilly interior, which, with the stark, rocky coastline, makes Sérifos appear uninhabited until the ferry turns into postcard-picturesque Livádhi Bay. This element of surprise continues as you slowly discover a number of lovely **beaches** around the island. Sadly, there are still scars from a 2013 forest fire that reached the port; thankfully, the businesses and locals survived intact. Still, because of a tourism

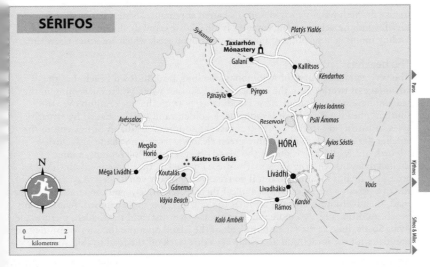

downturn after this event, this may well be the best-value Greek island at the moment, with prices stable or inching downwards.

Sérifos is also great for serious **walkers**, who can head for several small villages in the under-explored interior, plus some isolated coves for swimming. Many people still keep livestock and produce their own cognac-red wines, which are an acquired taste.

ARRIVAL AND GETTING AROUND

SÉRIFOS

By ferry The port is at the Livádhi promontory, with a regular fast catamaran service from Pireás (2hr), plus good connections in the summer from many other islands. Kondilis Shipping and Tourism (June–Oct daily 9am–10pm; ☎ 22810 52340, ⌨ kondilis.gr) sells ferry tickets

Destinations Folégandhros (1–3 daily; 2hr 30min); Íos (1–2 daily; 4hr 30min); Kéa/Lávrio (1 weekly; 6hr 30min/8hr); Kímolos (1–2 daily; 1hr 30min); Kýthnos (4–6 weekly; 1hr 40min); Mílos (2–4 daily; 1–2hr); Mýkonos (1 weekly; 7hr); Páros (2 weekly; 6–8hr); Pireás (2–3 daily; 2–4hr); Santoríni (1–3 daily; 3–8hr); Sífnos (2–4 daily; 25min-1-hr); Síkinos (1–3 weekly; 2hr–5hr 30min); Sýros

(1–2 weekly; 2hr 20min).

By bus The bus stop, with services to Hóra (hourly; 15min; €1.80), is at the base of the fishing-boat jetty. In summer, Kondilis (see above) runs buses to Psili Ammos and Ayios Ioannis (2–3 daily; €2) and Váyia/Gánema (2 daily; €3)

By car or motorbike For car and motorbike rental try Blue Bird, next to the petrol station in Livádhi (☎ 22810 51511, ⌨ rentacar-bluebird.gr), or Kartsonaki Bros, on the hill towards Livadhákia (March–Nov daily 9am–2pm & 5pm–9pm, ☎ 22810 51534, ⌨ kartsonakis.gr) who will deliver to your hotel if in Livádhi or Livadhákia.

By taxi There's a list of taxis with phone numbers on the bus stop: Livádhi–Hóra €8; Livádhi–Psilí Ámmos €8.

INFORMATION AND ACTIVITIES

Tourist information The information office opposite the disembarkation point (June–Aug daily 9.30am–1.30pm & 5.30pm–9.30pm; ☎ 22810 52606) can help with maps, buses and accommodation.

Services There's one ATM along the seafront in Livádhi. The island's post office is also in Livádhi, in the street

parallel to the western waterfront.

Diving, snorkelling and boat trips Avlómonas beach (see p.366) is the headquarters of Sérifos Scuba Divers (☎ 6932 570 552, ⌨ serifosscubadivers.gr), who operate scuba-diving and snorkelling trips plus day-long boat excursions during July and August.

Livádhi and around

Most visitors stay in the port, **LIVÁDHI**, which is set in a wide greenery-fringed bay and handy for most of the island's beaches. The usually calm bay is a magnet for yachts, here to take on fresh water which, despite its barren appearance, Sérifos has in abundance. Livádhi and the neighbouring cove of Livadhákia are certainly the easiest places for finding rooms, along with any amenities you might need, which are scarce elsewhere.

The beaches

The very attractive curve of **Avlómonas**, the long Livádhi town beach, has the advantage of overlooking the inland capital, so that when you're swimming in the sea you have a great inland view. Heading away from the dock, climb over the southerly headland to reach **Livadhákia**, a golden-sand beach, shaded by tamarisk trees. A further ten-minutes' stroll across the southern headland brings you to the smaller **Karávi** beach, with its blue-green clear waters but no shade or facilities.

North of Livádhi Bay is one of the island's best beaches **Psilí Ámmos**, a long, sheltered, award-winning stretch of white sand, backed by a large reservoir. It's accessible by bus in summer, but if you're coming by car you'll need to park in one of the two private taverna car parks and eat there. Alternatively, you can continue on the road, then by footpath for ten minutes to the larger, but more exposed, **Áyios Ioánnis** beach. Additionally, two more sandy coves, **Liá** (naturist) and the shaded, picturesque **Áyios Sóstis**, hide at the far eastern flank of the island opposite the islet Voús; they are popular with the locals, and accessible via a dirt track off the road to Psilí Ámmos.

ACCOMMODATION   LIVÁDHI AND AROUND

There are plenty of excellent value rooms advertised rooms around the port and Livadhákia.

★**Coralli Camping** Livadhákia Beach ☎22810 51500, ⓦcoralli.gr. Superbly located and managed campsite with a communal pool, self-service restaurant and bar (cocktails €6). The free wi-fi is slow and limited so opt for the €1/day faster version. They also run the more modern four-person *Coralli Studios*, closer to town. May–Oct. Camping **€19**, studio **€140**

Maïstrali Beginning of Livádhi beach ☎22810 51220, ⓦhotelmaistrali.com. Seventies-built and furnished hotel but, being the tallest building in town, it has balconies (many frequented by nesting birds) with the best views. It's at the start of the beach, so is situated conveniently for everything: nightlife, beach and restaurants. Ferry transfers included; continental

breakfast €5. April–Oct. **€55**

Naïas Between Livádhi and Livadhákia ☎22810 51749, ⓦnaiasserifos.com. A slightly dated, but comfortable, good-value hotel on the headland between Livádhi and Livadhákia, with a sociable owner; come here to make friends, not just pass through. All rooms with balconies, some with sea views. Twenty percent deposit for reservations required. Breakfast included. **€55**

Vasso Road to Livadhákia ☎6971898 986. Very basic but spacious and spotless rooms – some with kitchens – looking inwards into a common courtyard. If airiness and roominess are your thing, look no further – these are exceptional value. **€40**

EATING, DRINKING AND NIGHTLIFE

★**Bakakaki** Livádhi ☎22810 51010. Specializing in meat dishes – though its starter pies are large enough for a vegetarian main course (€4–5) – this place is a carnivore's dream serving 600g juicy steaks for €10–12. April–Oct daily noon–1am; Nov–March 5pm–midnight.

Metalleio Livádhi ☎22810 51755. Hidden behind the coastal road, this is one of the few restaurants on the island where you may have to book. Great service and food without breaking the bank; the portions are huge, with main courses such as veal in island wine sauce (€12). After midnight it becomes a club with occasional live DJs. Easter–Oct daily 7.30pm–1am.

Shark Livádhi ☎6932 411 657. Set in a conspicuous roof garden above the seafront mini-mall, this is an island

institution and plays mostly Top 10 hits. It serves a good selection of bottled beers for €5 and some strong cocktails from €9. May–Sept daily 9pm–late.

Tis Kalis Waterfront ☎22810 52301. One of the most popular ouzerís in town, where you may have to queue to get a table; you can simply stuff yourself with its excellent mezédhes, but it's worth leaving space for the delicious shrimp spaghetti (€18). April–Oct daily noon–midnight.

Yacht club Livádhi Beach ☎22810 51888. Hard to imagine that this was the first and only taverna in Livádhi back in 1938. It seems that every person under 30 on the island will come here to be seen at some point during the night, every night. Cocktails €9. Easter–Oct daily 8am–late.

Hóra

Quiet and atmospheric, **HÓRA** – only 2km from Livádhi – is one of the most unspoilt villages of the Cyclades. The best sights are in the **upper town**: follow signs to the kástro to reach the top via steep and occasionally overgrown stairways. The central square, Ayíou Athanasíou, just northwest of the summit, has an attractive church and a small but colourful Neoclassical town hall. From the main bus stop, starting from the *Vatrahos Bar* (see below), a steep staircase takes you to a path through the town and up to the church of Áyios Konstandínos at the top, where on a clear day you can see as far as Sífnos.

6

EATING AND DRINKING   HÓRA

Aloni ☎ 22810 52603. A restaurant 100m below the bus stop with superb westerly views over Livádhi, that offers tasty Mediterranean specialities (including rabbit in lemon sauce for €11). Many locals frequent it at weekends because of its occasional live Greek music evenings. Definitely book ahead. Daily 7pm–1am.

Stou Stratou ☎ 22810 52566, ⊕ stoustratou.com. An atmospheric café taking up half the main square with a poetry-strewn menu which offers a nice alternative to

eating on the busy seafront in Livádhi below. Its chocolate soufflé with ice cream (€6.50) is renowned throughout the island. April–Sept daily 9am–2am.

Vatrahos Bar ☎ 22810 52687. Just up from the final bus stop, this is a cosy hipster bar for people who just want to drink cold beer, sit at the bar and listen to the bass bouncing off the walls. "*Vatrahos*" means "frog", which are endemic on the island. April–Oct daily 10am–3am.

Northern Serifos

North of Psilí Ámmos (see opposite) your best bet for a swim is the sheltered cove of **Platýs Yialós** at the extreme northeastern tip of the island, reached easily by a partly paved road. Immediately after the Platýs Yialós turning is the fortified fifteenth-century monastery of **Taxiarhón**, once home to sixty monks but currently inhabited by only one. Treasures of the monastic **katholicón** include an ivory-inlaid bishop's throne, silver lamps from Egypt (to where many Serifiots emigrated during the nineteenth century) and the finely carved **iconostasis**. Call before you arrive (☎ 22810 51027) to arrange a visit; donations are expected.

Western Sérifos

Some 6km west of Livadhákia, along a newly tarmaced road, lies the most stunning beach in this part of the island, **Váyia**, overlooked by the exclusive *Coco-Mat* resort higher up. Beyond here, the road winds north for 2km to **Gánema**, another wide sandy beach, from where you can see **Koutalás**, 2km further west, with its fantastic semicircular shaded beach. A further 6km west is the lovely, remote fishing village of **Méga Livádhi**, with a beautiful beach and three tavernas. Iron and copper ores were once exported from here, via a loading bridge that still hangs over the water. From here, you can loop back to Livádhi via Hóra, 10km northeast of Méga Livádhi.

ACCOMMODATION AND EATING   WESTERN SÉRIFOS

Coco-Mat Váyia beach ☎ 22810 52603, ⊕ serifos .coco-mat-hotels.com. The company behind the upmarket Greek mattresses has opened its first hotel outside Athens on the slopes of Váya beach – and it's an exclusive, luxury affair frequented by Greek VIPs. The stylish rooms built of local stone are converted from former miners' cottages who worked in the island's iron

ore mines. Ferry transfers and a massive buffet breakfast are included. May–Sept **€270**

Marditsa Méga Livádhi ☎ 22810 51003. A great taverna shaded by beach tamarisks serving cheap, unfussy Greek food fresh from the family's own farm with a smile. Moussaka €6; salads €5. May–Oct daily noon–11pm.

6

Sífnos

SÍFNOS is prettier, tidier, greener and more cultivated than its northern neighbours. The island's modest size makes it eminently explorable, and there's a vast network of paths that are mostly easy to follow. The areas to head for are the port, **Kamáres**, the island's capital **Apollonía** – the handiest base for exploring the whole island – as well as the east and south coasts, and the beautiful scenery around **Vathý** in the far southwest. There's little to attract you to the island's north coast save the small fishing village of **Herrónisos**, with its beautiful, round shallow beach popular with families and children. Sífnos has a strong tradition of **pottery** (going back as early as the third century BC) and has long been esteemed for its distinctive cuisine, with sophisticated casseroles baked in the clay-fired *gástres* (pots), from where the word gastronomy derives.

The island is perhaps best appreciated today for its two blue flag **beaches** at Kamáres and Platýs Yialós and its network of **treks and trails** leading to some interesting churches and monasteries: indeed, hiking plays a significant role in Sífnos' tourism industry during the low and shoulder seasons, though camping rough is forbidden. As the island used to rely almost exclusively on domestic tourism, it has been badly affected by the economic crisis, so prices have remained static leading to considerable bargains for foreign visitors.

ARRIVAL AND GETTING AROUND   SÍFNOS

By ferry Ferries dock at the port in Kamáres on the east coast.
Destinations Amorgós, Katápola (1 daily; 6hr 20min); Ano Koufonísssi (1 daily; 5hr); Folégandhros (2–3 daily; 1hr 40min); Íos (2–3 daily; 2hr 20min); (Kéa/Lávrio (1 weekly; 8hr); Kímolos (1–2 daily; 2hr 40min); Kýthnos (3–5 weekly; 2hr 30min); Mílos (2–5 daily; 35min–1hr 20min);

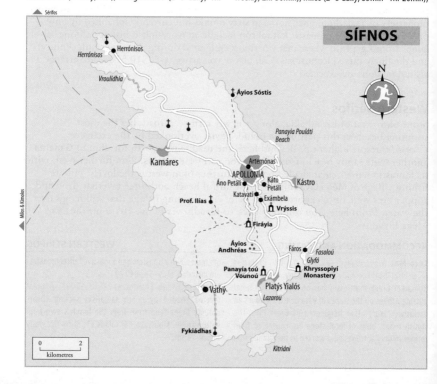

Mýkonos (1 daily; 6hr 40min); Páros (3 weekly; 5hr 35min); Náxos (1 daily; 4hr 45min); Pireás (3–5 daily; 2–3hr); Santoríni (3 daily; 2hr 30min); Sérifos (1–4 daily; 25min–1hr); Síkinos (2–3 weekly; 2–5hr); Sýros (3 weekly; 3hr).

By bus The bus service is excellent, and most of the roads are good. Buses run regularly from Kamáres to Apollonía/Artemónas (8–10 daily; every 30min in high season; 20min; €2.30); for all other destinations you have to change at Apollonía. Buses for Kamáres leave from Apollonía's central square, Platía Iróon. There is a second station by the *Anthoussa* hotel (see p.370) for Platys Yialós (6–8 daily; 30min), Fáros (5–6 daily; 30min), Kástro (5–6 daily; 10min), Vathý (3–4 daily; 50min) and Herrónisos (3 daily; 50min).

By car or motorbike Rentals at Kamares tend to be expensive: try the very competitive Apollo in Apollonia (daily 8am–8pm; ☎ 22840 33333; ⓦ automotoapollo.gr).

6

INFORMATION AND ACTIVITIES

Tourist office There's a helpful information centre opposite the ferry disembarkation point (daily 8am–3pm), next to the Room Owners' Association kiosk (open for ferry arrivals).

Services There are two ATMS in Kamares, three in Apollonía and one in Platys Yialós; the post office is beside the central square in Apollonía.

Travel agents Katsoulakis Travel (☎ 22840 31004) can help find accommodation, tours and ferry tickets, while Aegean Thesaurus (☎ 22840 33151/33527) can arrange

accommodation across the island: both have offices at the Kamáres waterfront and in Apollonía.

Hiking and tours Trekking is big on Sífnos with many kilometres of well-signposted routes: free detailed maps are available from the information centre (see above). Agency Miles Away in Platys Yialós (May–Sept 10m–2pm & 5.30–9.30pm; ☎ 22840 71373, ⓦ milesaway.gr) can organize hiking excursions and runs a six-hour guided bus tour of the island every Wednesday (or whenever there is enough demand) for €25pp.

Kamáres

KAMÁRES, the island's port, with its gorgeous, clean, sheltered beach stretching to the headland of **Ayía Marína** opposite the port, is tucked away in a long, steep-sided valley that cuts into the cliffs of the island's western side. A compact resort, though with concrete blocks of accommodations edging up to the base of the hill-slopes, Kamáres' seafront road is crammed with bars, travel agencies, ice-cream shops and restaurants. For more peace and quiet, base yourself in Ayía Marína where you'll get the best views in the bay – and most of the sun.

ACCOMMODATION   KAMÁRES

Boulis ☎ 22840 32122, ⓦ hotelboulis.gr. If you want to wake up and head straight for a swim, this hotel – arranged around a hedged and vine-covered courtyard in the middle of Kamáres beach – is the place for you. Optional breakfast (€6) is served in the good on-site restaurant. May–Oct. **€60**

Dina's rooms Ayía Marína ☎ 22840 32364. On the furthest side of the beach, these spotless rooms have the best views in Kamáres and are best suited to those who prefer quieter, more secluded accommodation. "Rooms" here is a misnomer – there are hotels that offer much less. May–Sept. **€45**

Makis Camping ☎ 22840 32366 or ☎ 6945 946 339,

ⓦ makiscamping.gr. A campsite on Kamáres beach with excellent facilities including a café-bar, free wi-fi, minimarket and a laundry open to non-guests. The obliging, friendly owner is a mine of information about the island. There are also on-site double studios. April–Nov. Camping **€18**, studio **€30**

★**Stavros** ☎ 22840 33383, ⓦ sifnostravel.com. A first-class, extremely helpful and reasonably priced hotel on the harbourfront with spacious self-catering rooms with kitchenette. It has a wide range of services including an information and booking centre for trips and the like – it also sells stamps. **€60**

EATING AND DRINKING

Follie Ayía Marína ☎ 22840 31183, ⓦ cafefolie.gr. Is it a bar? Is it a beach club? Is it a nightspot? A bit of everything, really; Athenian-owned and run, it's full for breakfast, rather muted in the afternoon, but packs them in again for evening drinks and dinner (€10). Don't let all this multi-functioning confuse you, though; the food in the restaurant is very good. Easter–Sept daily 9am–3am.

Ísalos Ayía Marina ☎ 22840 33716. Café-bar and restaurant with a shaded terrace serving more classy cuisine than anywhere else on the island, with pasta dishes from €8 and meat dishes from €10. Easter–Sept daily 10am–11pm.

The Old Captain Bar Kamáres ☎ 22840 31990. An institution in Kamares – they even sell their own T-shirts – this beach bar has deckchairs during the day, but it really comes alive after sunset with rock/jazz/reggae music and cocktails (€8). Easter–Oct daily 10am–3am.

★**Simos** ☎ 22840 32353. Family-run, popular taverna on the Kamáres main street with a reputation

second-to-none among the islanders, serving meat and vegetables from the owner's farm. Their casseroles (€8) are as traditional as they are tasty and an absolute must. Daily noon–midnight.

Apollonía and around

A steep bus ride from Kamáres takes you 5.5km up to **APOLLONÍA**, the centre of an amalgam of five hilltop villages that have merged over the years into one continuous community: immediately north is **Áno Petáli**, which then runs into **Artemónas**, about fifteen minutes away on foot. With white buildings, stepped paths, belfries and flower-draped balconies, it is very scenic, though not self-consciously so.

Sights in Apollonía include numerous churches and the rather overpriced **folk museum** on the central square (April–Oct daily 9.30am–2pm & 6–10pm; €3), with its collection of textiles, photos, costumes and weaponry. Behind and parallel to the square runs a pedestrian street, **To Stenó**, lined with restaurants, bars and boutiques, and the nightlife centre for the whole of Sífnos. The main pedestrian street north from the square leads via Áno Petáli to Artemónas, past the eighteenth-century church of **Panayía Ouranofóra**, which incorporates fragments of a seventh-century BC temple of Apollo and a relief of St George over the door.

Taking the road south to **Katavatí** you'll pass, after a few minutes, the beautiful empty monastery of Firáyia; fifteen minutes further along there's a turning to a vast Mycenaean **archeological site** (Tues–Sun 8.30am–3pm; €2, including museum). Next to it stands the church of **Áyios Andhréas**, from where there are tremendous views over the neighbouring islands.

ACCOMMODATION   APOLLONÍA AND AROUND

Anthoussa Hotel Apollonía ☎ 22840 31431, ⓦ hotelanthousa-sifnos.gr. A good, solid hotel with comfortable rooms, balconies with views and tasteful light-blue decor, plus a terrific patisserie below: try its home-made cakes, chocolates and ice cream for breakfast, if you dare. Free wi-fi. Breakfast €7.50. Easter–Nov. €50

★**Petali Village** Áno Petáli ☎ 22840 33024, ⓦ hotelpetali.gr. A boutique hotel in a quiet position, 300m from the centre of Apollonía. Easy to fall in love with, it has a shaded heated pool, nautical decoration and relaxing verandas overlooking the east of the island. It also rents electric bicycles (€25/day) for exploration and has parking and free ferry transfers. Wonderful home-made breakfast included. €130

EATING

Cayenne Stenó, Apollonía ☎ 22840 31080. This pricey restaurant (starters €10; mains €15; wine €10/0.5lt) is the current in-place for dinner on Sífnos, with tables in a large courtyard beneath drooping bougainvilleas and a large fig tree. Service gets overwhelmed after 9.30pm. April–Oct daily 12.45pm–late.

★**Drimóni** Apollonía ☎ 22840 31434, ⓦ drimoni.gr. On the southern road, 800m from Apollonía, this is an excellent value restaurant with a western-facing veranda where you can watch the sunset while feasting

on dishes such as pork with figs (€11) and a selection of mezédhes (€7). Excellent service, too. Easter–Oct daily 6pm–midnight, Nov–March Thurs–Sun 6pm–11pm.

Mamma Mia Apollonía ☎ 22840 33086. At the north-south highway crossroads of Apolloniá, this is a proper Italian restaurant run by a Milanese family who serve large wood-fired pizzas (€10) and delicacies such as swordfish carpaccio (€13). There's a second branch on Platys Yialós. March–Oct daily 7pm–2am.

DRINKING AND NIGHTLIFE

Argo Stenó, Apollonía ☎ 22840 31114, ⓦ argobar.gr. Long-standing island club playing everything from classical music to modern rock with a well-behaved, mixed-age clientele. Try their signature cocktail, Sífnos Mule, based on tsipouro and ginger beer. (€10). April–Oct daily 7pm–3.30am.

Cosí Stenó, Apollonía ☎ 6972 558 857. Sporting a large courtyard with armchairs and a dancefloor inside, this is a magnet for the young who flock here in droves to listen to lounge music early on and dance hits later from a live DJ. Cocktails €10. June to mid-Sept daily 8pm–3am.

The east coast

Most of Sífnos' coastal settlements are along the less precipitous **east coast**, within a modest distance of Apollonía and its surrounding cultivated plateau. **Kástro** may be more appealing than the resorts of **Fáros** and **Platýs Yialós**, which can get very overcrowded.

Kástro

KÁSTRO, the ancient capital of the island, retains much of its medieval character. It's essentially a sinuous main street along the ridge of a hilltop, the houses on either side, all of the same height, forming the outer defence wall. Their roofs slope inwards in order to collect rainwater inside in case of siege. There are some fine sixteenth- and seventeenth-century churches with ornamental floors; Venetian coats of arms, ancient wall fragments and cunningly recycled Classical columns are still on some of the older dwellings, while the occasional ancient sarcophagus lies incongruously on the pavement. In addition, there are the remains of the ancient acropolis, as well as a small **Archeological Museum** (Tues–Sun 9am–3pm; €2) operating in a former Catholic church in the higher part of the village.

You can walk along Kástro's northeastern peripheral path overlooking the picture-postcard church of the **Eptá Mártyres** (Seven Martyrs), which juts out into the sea. There's nothing approximating a **beach** near Kástro, as defence and not easy access was the aim of the inhabitants. For a swim you can use the Eptá Mártyres rocks, or possibly the rocky cove of **Serália** just south of Kástro, and the small shore at **Panayía Pouláti**, 1.3km to the northwest; both have facilities.

The fantastic views over the valley below might inspire you to tackle two well-signposted **walks** to Fáros (1hr 30min) and to Vrýsis monastery (50min) that start from the *Konáki* snack-bar. If you're driving, best park along the ridge and walk up as the car park at the end is small with little room to manoeuvre.

6

ACCOMMODATION AND EATING — KÁSTRO

Aris & Maria ☎ 22840 31161, ⓦ arismaria-traditional .com. Rooms and studios in six century-old, beautifully furnished houses around Kástro retain traditional Cycladic features such as wooden ceilings and stone floors, and all come with kitchenettes. No cars are allowed inside Kástro, so you'll need to carry your luggage for about 100m uphill to the reception following the signs to "Ancient Wall". **€60**

★**Dolci** ☎ 22840 32311. Shaded and with comfortable seats, this cafe/restaurant/cocktail bar is the perfect place to laze about, over an aperitif or mojito (€11), and gaze across to Apollonía beyond the valley below. Easter–Nov daily 9am–late.

Fáros

To the south of Kástro, the small fishing village of **FÁROS** is a possible fallback base, though the beaches are relatively small. The main beach is partly shaded and crowded in season while **Fasoloú**, a 400m walk to the southeast past the headland, is better and shaded by tamarisk trees. Head off west through the older part of the village to find the picturesque **Glyfó** beach, arguably the best of the three.

ACCOMMODATION AND EATING — FÁROS

Gorgona Fáros ☎ 22840 71460/1. A lively hippy and alternative commune on the main street that also offers rooms. Don't be put off by the tattooed arms on display, or the rock music blasting out of the speaker; this is the hangout of mellow souls who welcome strangers. Draught beer €4/0.5lt. May–Sept daily noon–late. **€40**

Sifneíko Arhontikó Fáros ☎ 22840 71422/71454, ⓦ sifneiko-arxontiko.gr. Don't be taken in by its Greek name ("Sifnos Manor"); this modern hotel is not housed in an old mansion, but was built in 1992 in typical Cycladic style. Hard to find because it's not signposted, it's worth tracking down, as it's the most comfortable option in Fáros – and convenient both for the buses and the beach. April–Sept. **€50**

Thalatta Glyfó ☎ 22840 71513 ⓦ sifnosthalatta.gr. Built on a slope and inaccessible to vehicles, this apartment complex overlooking Glyfó beach is ideal for those who want to leave it all behind, though there is access to a minimarket, bars and several tavernas within 200m. Four-night minimum stay. May–Sept. **€65**

Yórgos-Dimítris Fasoloú beach ☎ 22840 71493. An excellent and well-priced taverna offering only produce from its own farm and good house wine. The shady location

6

THE MONASTERY OF KHRYSSOPIYÍ

From the beach at Glyfó (see p.371), a hillside path leads in fifteen minutes to the longer beach of **Apokoftó**, where there are a couple of good grill tavernas. Flanking Apokoftó to the south, marooned on a sea-washed promontory, is the seventeenth-century **Khryssopiyí Monastery**, which features on every poster of the island. According to legend, the cleft in the rock (under the entrance bridge) appeared when two village girls, fleeing to the spit to escape the attentions of menacing pirates, prayed to the Virgin to defend their virtue. To celebrate the story, a large festival takes place forty days after Easter and involves the spectacular arrival of a holy icon on a large high-speed ferry, and its – often dramatic – transfer to a small boat to be brought ashore.

under the tamarisk trees and the nearby parking facilities make it the best beach eating option in this part of the island (mains start from €9). Easter–Sept daily noon–midnight.

Platýs Yialós

PLATÝS YIALÓS is 12km from Apollonía, near the southern tip of the island, and has a long stretch of beach that takes four bus stops to cross in its entirety. Buffeted by occasional strong winds, a continuous row of buildings – many of them pottery workshops – lines the entire stretch of beach, with a marina at the north end. A five-minute walk from the last bus stop over the southwestern headland brings you to **Lazárou Beach**, a tiny pebble bay entirely occupied by the eponymous beach bar and restaurant behind the water's edge.

ACCOMMODATION AND EATING
PLATÝS YIALÓS

★**Alexandros** ☎ 22840 71300, �🌐 hotelalexandros.gr. Getting off at the first bus stop at Platýs Yialós, you encounter this luxurious – as the large swimming pool demonstrates – but surprisingly affordable hotel where the focus is on room size rather than elaborate reception areas. Large, home-made buffet breakfast included. Mid-May to Sept. **€83**

Cyclades Beach ☎ 22840 71220/71320, �🌐 cycladesbeach.gr. Reputable hotel by the third bus stop

that's been operating since 1979 and offers the best-priced rooms on the island. Its restaurant, open to non-residents, has a good buffet breakfast (€5) and, later, traditional Greek food. Daily noon–10pm. **€45**

Omega3 ☎ 22840 72014. An excellent restaurant at the second bus stop, rather squeezed in by its neighbours. It serves innovative international seafood dishes – octopus shots anyone? – excelling in Brazilian *bolinhos* of cod (€9) and tuna sashimi (€13): reserve for dinner. May–Oct daily 1–11pm.

Vathý

A fishing village on the shore of an almost circular, almost enclosed bay, **VATHÝ** is the most attractive base on the island, with little to do but relax on the beach or in a waterfront taverna. A surfaced road and the luxury *Elies* resort (see below) haven't destroyed the character of this previously remote spot, which is accentuated by the poster-pretty all-white monastery of **Taxiárhis** on the promontory bisecting the beach.

ACCOMMODATION
VATHÝ

Elies Resort ☎ 22840 34000, �🌐 eliesresorts.com. This gated top-class resort on the slopes outside Vathý – where employees are dressed in white clothes, making it feel rather like the village in the *Prisoner* TV series – offers luxurious surroundings and claims to have the largest pool in the Cyclades. Drop in to play spot-the-VIP, as it is frequented by celebrities, politicians and industrialists. May–Oct. **€210**

Studios Nikos ☎ 22840 71512, �🌐 sifnosrooms.com. A villa compound right on the beach, with attractive, comfortable studios sharing a front grass garden with uninterrupted views to the sea. The studios have large balconies and verandas, separate kitchens and a lot of room inside for three or four people – great value for a family self-catering stay. April–Nov. **€50**

EATING

★**To Tsikali** ☎ 22840 71177. One of the better-known family tavernas on Sífnos. Most ingredients come from

their own farm, including three homemade cheeses, mezédhes, falafel balls made with potatoes rather than flour (€5), mastellos and rabbit stew (€11). Easter–Oct daily 8am–midnight.

Tou Koutsouna ☎ 22840 71156. Signposted just before the hairpin that descends to the village, this restaurant claims,

with good reason, to have the best views over Vathý. Its imaginative croquettes based on courgettes, tomatoes and chickpeas (€6) are worth sampling, but take it easy and don't rush the old couple who own it. Daily noon–midnight.

Mílos

6

Volcanic **MÍLOS** is a geologically diverse island with weird rock formations, hot springs and odd outcrops off the coast. Minoan settlers were attracted by obsidian; this and other products of its volcanic soil made it one of the most important of the Cyclades in the ancient world. Today, the quarrying of many rare minerals has left huge scars on the landscape but has given the island a relative prosperity which today translates into several gourmet restaurants with better wine lists than many of its neighbours. With some 75-odd **beaches** and sensational views, Mílos hasn't had to court tourism – indeed, the wealthy mining companies that employ a quarter of the population are happy to see tourism stay at low levels. It helps that the western half of Mílos, as well as the other islands around it, including **Kímolos**, is a nature reserve protecting three endemic species: the extremely rare **Mediterranean seal**, the **Mílos viper**, and the one you are most likely to encounter, the long, crocodile-shaped **Mílos wall lizard**. Note that the importance of the **archeological finds**, museums and sites here is surpassed only by Delos and Santoríni.

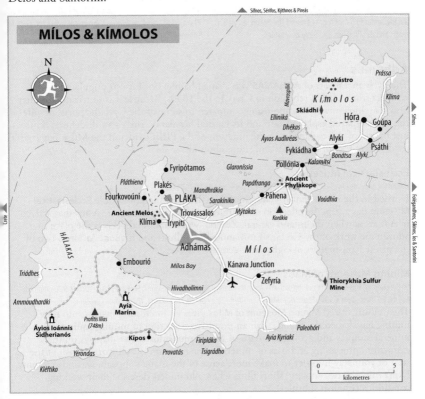

ARRIVAL AND GETTING AROUND

By plane The island's tiny airport (☎ 22870 22831), 5km southeast of the port, is served by Olympic and Sky Express with flights from/to Athens (2–4 daily; 45min).

By ferry Mílos is well-connected and ferries dock at the main port of Adhámas. In addition, a small car ferry to the neighbouring island of Kímolos leaves regularly from Pollónia on Mílos' north-western tip – a quicker and cheaper option than the larger ferries.

Destinations Amorgós, Katápola (1 daily; 4–7hr); Áno Koufoníssi (1 daily; 4hr 30min); Anáfi (1–2 weekly; 6hr 30min); Iráklio /Sitía Crete (1 weekly; 10hr 20min–14hr); Folégandhros (2–3 daily; 2hr 30min); Íos (1–2 daily; 1hr 30min–4hr); Kéa/Lávrio (1 weekly; 10hr); Kárpathos and Kássos (1 weekly; 20hr–23hr); Kímolos, from Adhámas (2–3 daily; 1hr); Kímolos from Pollónia (5–7 daily; 20min); Kýthnos (5 weekly; 4–10hr); Mýkonos (1–2 daily; 5–6hr); Náxos (1–3 daily; 4–6hr); Páros (3–4 weekly; 3hr 15min–7hr); Pireás (3–4 daily; 3hr 10min–7hr); Rhodes and Hálki (1–2 weekly;

26hr–28hr); Santoríni (2–3 daily; 2hr 25min–6hr) Sérifos (2–5 daily; 3hr); Sífnos (2–5 daily; 50min–2hr), Síkinos (4 weekly; 3hr 50min); Sýros (2–4 weekly 7hr–8hr).

By bus Services start from the main square of Adhámas by *Hotel Portiani* and are sometimes inconveniently timed in the shoulder season: Pláka/Tripití (every 30min; 20min), Pollónia (4–10 daily; 30min), Paleohóri via Zefyría (3–7 daily; 40min), Hivadholímni (8–10 daily; 15min), Sarakíniko (2–4 daily; 30min).

By taxi Taxis are used on Mílos more than on other islands with complicated fixed fares, rising almost weekly in high season, and displayed at the taxi rank by the Adhámas bus stop (☎ 22870 22219). Callouts cost €5 plus the fare.

By car or motorbike Rental is available on the Adhámas waterfront near the jetty from many places including Sea, Sun, Sophia (☎ 22870 21994) and RAC (☎ 22870 28036, ⓦ rac-sa.gr).

INFORMATION

Tourist office Situated opposite the ferry dock (daily 9am–5pm & 7–11pm; ☎ 22870 22445, ⓦ milos.gr), with a daily updated list of rooms around the island, as well as maps and detailed bus and ferry timetables.

Services There are several banks and ATMs in the main Adhámas square; there's also an ATM at Pollónia and one at Pláka. The post office is inconveniently located in Triovassalos, 3km from Adhámas.

Adhámas

The lively main port of **ADHÁMAS** was a small hamlet until it was populated by refugees from a failed rebellion in Crete in the 1840s. Because it is so recent, you may find it architecturally disappointing compared to some of the Cycladic ports, despite the marble-paved esplanade around its natural headland. There's an ill-defined centre just inland of the esplanade, at the junction of the Pláka road and the Mílos Bay coastal road, where restaurants, cafés and shops abound.

Ecclesiastical Museum

Behind the quayside • April–Oct Mon–Sat 9.15am–1.15pm • Free • ☎ 22870 23956

Housed in the ninth-century church of Ayía Triádha, the unmissable **Ecclesiastical Museum** has a superb collection of liturgical paraphernalia and rare icons that arrived in Adhámas when the inland capital, Zefyría, was abandoned. This is the place to admire the work of the Cretans Emmanouel Skordhílis and his son, Antonis, two of the prime icon-makers in eighteenth-century Greece.

Mining Museum of Mílos

On the seafront, 500m east of the centre of town • April, May & Oct daily 10am–2pm; June & Sept daily 10am–2pm & 5.30–9pm; July–Aug daily 9.30am–2pm & 5.30–10pm; Nov–March Sun 10am–2pm • €4 • ☎ 22870 22481, ⓦ milosminingmuseum.com

The well-organized **Mining Museum of Mílos** gives an interesting insight into how mining has shaped the island, with an extensive collection of mining equipment, mineral samples and geological maps of Mílos, plus informative displays on the extraction, processing and uses of minerals. The museum is well worth a visit at the start of your stay in order to make more sense of the island's appearance and economy. Don't miss the two moving short films where old miners describe their working conditions (English subtitles).

MÍLOS BOAT TOURS

One of the absolute must-dos on Mílos is a **boat tour**, either down the bizarre western coastline, making several stops at otherwise inaccessible swimming spots like the magnificent **Kléftiko**, or to **Kímolos** and **Polýaigos** to spot the rare Mediterranean seal. Weather permitting, the boats normally leave at 10am from the **Adhámas quayside** and return at 6–7pm: they cost around €50–60 including lunch and drinks.

Excellent Yachting ☎ 22870 41292, ⓦ e-y.gr. Runs boat tours, kayaking and alternative "snorkel safaris" from Pollónia or Adhámas, aimed at younger travellers.

★**Horizon Yachts** ☎ 22870 24083, ⓦ horizon yachts.gr. Operated by a real Milos seawolf, Horizon runs trips to a selection of sheltered coves whatever the weather and wind direction.

6

ACCOMMODATION
ADHÁMAS

Aeolis ☎ 22870 23985, ⓦ aeolis-hotel.com. Great-value hotel with large rooms and designer furniture, plus two rooms specially adapted for disabled travellers. It's a bit difficult to find, behind the main square, in the street by the dry rivulet. Two-night minimum stay. Breakfast included. €65

Portiani ☎ 22870 22940, ⓦ hotelportiani.gr. In the main square, this is Adhámas' most central hotel, with a spectacular port-view terrace and an excellent buffet breakfast included. Despite the double-glazing, it can be a bit noisy. It's worth paying extra for the larger top-floor rooms, which have their own balconies with sweeping views. €70

★**White Suites** ☎ 22870 22612 ⓦ whitesuites.gr. Up a short, steep set of stairs, this beautifully designed hotel complex has palatial, modern rooms in white and gold with comfortable beds and power showers – the wedding suite with a balcony and exceptional views is booked months in advance. Continental breakfast included. May–Sept. €108

EATING AND DRINKING

★**Aragosta** ☎ 22870 22292, ⓦ aragosta.gr. A gourmet restaurant until 11pm, it then morphs into a cocktail bar that takes its mixology very seriously with champagne cocktails from €10. With live DJs, two terraces and a good crowd, this may be the best reason to stay in Adhámas. May–Oct daily 6.30pm–late.

Flisvos Limani ☎ 22870 22275. An award-winning waterfront restaurant run by the same family for three generations. The menu includes everything from fried kalamári to grilled meats (€10) plus a variety of savoury filo pastries accompanied by a good wine list of Santoríni vintages. April–Oct daily noon–midnight.

Kinigos Limani ☎ 22870 22349. A popular waterfront place to eat, with a varied menu and excellent people-watching potential. Specialities include meatballs made to a secret house recipe and its famed moussaka (both €9). Come early to get a table. April–Oct daily noon–midnight.

Navagio Papikinou ☎ 22870 24124 In a pergola towards the Mining Museum, this is Adhámas' best fish taverna with a good wine list (glasses €4) and dishes such as octopus carpaccio (€13) and grilled shrimp with pasta (€17). Come early, as staff get overwhelmed after 9.30pm. April–Oct daily 1pm–midnight.

Pláka and around

PLÁKA, the capital of the island, is the largest of a cluster of traditional villages that huddle beneath a small crag on the road northwest of Adhámas. Steps beginning near the *Fóras* taverna lead up to the **kástro**, its upper slopes clad in stone and cement to channel precious rainwater into cisterns. The **Folk Museum** (Tues–Sat 11am–1pm & 7–10pm; €4; ☎ 22870 21292) has a well-presented array of artefacts related to the history of arts, crafts and daily life on Mílos. The small church of the **Dormition** nearby offers one of the best views in the Aegean, particularly at sunset.

On a long ridge 1km south of Pláka, the narrow, attractive village of **Trypití** ("perforated"), which takes its name from the cliff-side catacombs nearby, is less busy with traffic than Pláka. At the very bottom of the cliff edge and accessed via a road from the southern end of Trypití or steps down from the catacombs, **Klíma** is the most photogenic of the island's fishing hamlets, with its picturesque boathouses tucked underneath the colourful village dwellings.

Archeological Museum

Behind the lower car park • Tues–Sun 9am–4pm – it doesn't always look open, even when it is • €2 • ☎ 22870 21620

This Neoclassical jewel of a building, built by Ernst Ziller (see p.363) in the 1840s, contains numerous Neolithic obsidian implements, plus finds from ancient Phylakope (see opposite); highlights include a votive lamp in the form of a bull and a Minoan-looking terracotta idol, the **Lady of Phylakope**. You'll also recognize the plaster-cast copy of the **Venus de Milo**, the original of which was found on the island in 1820. It's not clear whether it was discovered with the arms already separated from the torso, or if they were broken off in a skirmish between French sailors and locals.

Catacombs

1km south of Pláka and 400m from Trypití • Tues–Sun: summer 9am–7pm; winter 8am–3pm • €4 • ☎ 22870 21625 • Groups of ten allowed in at a time

From Pláka's archeological museum, signs point you towards the early **Christian catacombs**, a fifteen-minute walk south of town; once there, steps lead down from the road to the inconspicuous entrance. Some five thousand bodies lie buried in three tomb-lined corridors with side galleries, stretching 200m into the soft volcanic rock, making these the largest catacombs in Greece. Bear in mind that only the first 50m are illuminated and accessible by boardwalk and the guided tour lasts only about fifteen minutes.

Ancient Melos

1km south of Pláka, near the catacombs

Just above the catacombs are the ruins of **Ancient Melos** whose focal point is a well-preserved Roman **amphitheatre**. En route to the theatre from the surfaced road is the signposted spot where the *Venus de Milo* was found in what may have been the compound's gymnasium.

ACCOMMODATION

PLÁKA AND AROUND

★**Eiriana** Tripití ☎ 22870 22730, ⊕ eiriana.com. Half a dozen luxury rooms on the eastern side of the village with a fantastic view of Mílos Bay. There's a pool, garden and parking while the designer rooms come with a Nespresso machine, satellite TV, Bluetooth speakers and an iPad with an app to order breakfast in your room (included). **€130**

Spiti tis Makhis Pláka ☎ 22870 22129. In the house where the *Venus de Milo* was hidden following its discovery, this stone hotel has self-catering studios furnished in bright colours. It's conveniently located for the bus, but set back from the main road, with plenty of parking space. June–Oct. **€75**

EATING

Arhontoula Pláka ☎ 22870 21384, ✉ arhontoula3 @yahoo.gr. One of the oldest and more reputable family restaurants in Pláka occupying the same spot in the main street for over a hundred years, offering Greek and international cuisine, plus a carefully selected wine list. Mains start from €9. April–Nov daily noon–midnight.

En Plo Pláka ☎ 22870 23124. An old-style *mezedhopolío* on the main road into Pláka. Expect Greek coffee, ouzo, a variety of local dishes (€8) and a loyal local clientele that's been coming here for decades to enjoy the food. Daily 10am–late.

The south

The main road to **southern Mílos** splits at Kánava junction, near the large power station. The sea there contains underwater hot vents resulting in fizzy hotspots that locals use for jacuzzi-like baths. The eastern fork leads to **Zefyría**, which was briefly the capital until an eighteenth-century earthquake (and subsequent plague) drove out the population. There's little to see in the old town but a magnificent seventeenth-century church with beautifully painted walls and ceilings. The original iconostasis was transferred to the church of the Dormition in Adhámas, while the icons are displayed in the Ecclesiastical museum.

South of Zefyría, it's a further 8km down a winding, surfaced road to the coarse sand of **Paleohóri**, one of the island's best beaches, warmed by underground volcanism. A little rock tunnel leads west to a second beach, which is backed by extraordinarily coloured cliffs and where steam vents heat the shallow water. **Ayía Kyriakí**, further to the west of Paleohóri, is a pebble beach under imposing sulphurous and red oxide cliffs.

ACCOMMODATION AND EATING   **THE SOUTH**

Artemis Paleohóri ☎ 22870 31222, ⊚ artemismilos.gr. A luxury apartment complex built with attention to detail: there are ceiling fans plus a/c, walk-in caves for showers, original art in every room and subdued lighting, plus an infinity pool with a bar and a rich breakfast buffet (included). May–Oct. **€150**

★ **Sirocco** Paleohóri ☎ 22870 31201, ⊚ restaurantsirocco.gr. An island institution, which uses the hot volcanic sand – that reaches a constant temperature of 100°C only 30cm below the surface – to bake casseroles of lamb, veal, pork and fish (€15) in clay pots overnight. April–Oct daily noon–midnight.

Hivadholímni and the west

The westerly road from the Kánava junction leads past the airport entrance to **Hivadholímni**, the best beach on Mílos Bay itself. Behind the beach is a salty lagoon where in May and September you can observe migrating birdlife. Just before Hivadholímni, you can fork south to **Provatás**, a short beach closed off by multicoloured cliffs to the east. It's easy to get to so it hasn't escaped development.

Forking to the east before Provatás, the road leads to the trendy and very popular south coast beach of **Firipláka**. Further east, on a dirt road, is sandy **Tsigrádho**, excellent for swimming and usually uncrowded. Going west from the Kanava junction the surfaced road ends at **Ayía Marína**, although a dirt road continues into **Hálakas** and the small fishing village of **Embourió**, where there's a perfectly acceptable beach.

For the most part, the southwestern peninsula of Hálakas, centred on the wilderness of Mount Profítis Ilías (748m), is an uninhabited nature reserve with unsurfaced dirt tracks, two of which lead to the fine, unspoilt beaches of **Triádhes** and **Ammoudharáki**. **Kléftiko**, in the southwest corner, is only reachable by boat, but repays the effort to get there with its stunning rock formations and semi-submerged tunnels.

ACCOMMODATION   **HIVADHOLÍMNI**

Milos Camping ☎ 22870 31410/11, ⊚ miloscamping .gr. Large campsite above Hivadholímni beach; its minibus meets ferries, and in the summer there are buses to and from Adhámas. It has a decent restaurant (mains €7) with a swimming pool plus bar and a well-stocked mini-market. Mid-May to Sept. Camping **€21**, bungalow **€40**

The north coast

From either Adhámas or the Pláka area, good roads run roughly parallel to the **north coast** which, despite being windswept and sparsely inhabited, is not devoid of geological interest. **Sarakíniko**, in particular, is an astonishing sculpted inlet, with a sandy seabed and gleaming white rocks popular with sunbathing local youth. Nearby **Mýtakas** is another good beach, accessible via a 500m dirt road, with dramatic views west along the rocky coastline.

Eastwards you reach another of Mílos' coastal wonders, **Papáfranga**, a short ravine into which the sea flows under a rock arch – the tiny beach at its inland end is accessed by rock-carved steps. To the right of the Papáfranga car park, the remains of three superimposed Neolithic settlements crown a small knoll at **Phylakope** (Sat–Mon 8am–3pm; €4).

At the end of the road 12km northeast of Adhámas, **Pollónia** is a former fishing village within a semicircular bay with a long, curved, tamarisk-lined beach. Smaller and more sophisticated than Adhámas, it has a string of excellent restaurants and cafés strung along the harbourfront, as well as several very good value hotels and villas, which fill up fast in season. It's also where you get the small ferry to Kímolos (see below) opposite – a cheap and interesting daytrip.

ACCOMODATION
THE NORTH COAST

Andreas Pollónia ☎22870 41262, ⓦandreas-rooms.gr. Villa complex at the western edge of Pollónia with self-catering studios and easy access to the quiet neighbouring bay. It has its own boat, *Perseas*, bookable for trips and fishing expeditions, and you can help yourself to vegetables from the garden. **€65**

★**Breeze** Pollónia ☎22870 41084, ⓦmilosbreeze.gr. Opened in 2016 on top of a hill with an incredible panorama of Pollónia bay and Kímolos from its grand infinity pool,

this boutique hotel has spacious rooms with sea views: al come with either a garden or a balcony, some with jacuzzis and others with private pools. Buffet breakfast included May–Oct. **€245**

Kapetan Tasos Pollónia ☎22870 41287, ⓦkapetantasos.gr. One of the more luxurious options in the quay area with "superior" suites as big as a two-bedroom flat. Organizes ferry transfers, and has a mini-gym and optional breakfast until 1pm. Mid-April–Oct. **€139**

EATING AND DRINKING

★**Armenaki** Pollónia ☎22870 41061, ⓦarmenaki.gr. Claiming never to use anything frozen and nothing but olive oil, this is one of the best restaurants on Mílos, packed day and night, so it's wise to make a reservation. Its fish stew (which you order by weight; €46/kg) and seafood pasta (€14) go down well with the diligently chosen white wines, which are served by a proper sommelier. April–Oct daily noon–1am.

★**Yialos** Pollónia ☎22870 41208, ⓦgialos-pollonia.gr. Small but stylish restaurant with a well-thought-out menu and a wide range of seafood and fish dishes. Try the prawn tartare or sea bream carpaccio (both pricey starters at €17 each), followed by an imaginative main course such as kalamári stuffed with seafood (€19). April–Oct daily noon–midnight.

Kímolos

Of the three islands off the coast of Mílos, only rugged, scenic **KÍMOLOS** is inhabited. Volcanic like Mílos, it profits from its geology and used to export chalk (*kimolía* in Greek) until the supply was exhausted. Bentonite is still extracted locally, and the fine dust of this clay is a familiar sight on the northeastern corner of the island. Apart from the inhabited southeast, the rest of the island is a nature reserve, which explains the lack of surfaced roads.

Even in August Kímolos isn't swamped by visitors. Just as well, since, although there are around 450-odd beds on the whole island, there is little in the way of other amenities. There's only one bus, no car or motorbike rental (rent your vehicle from Mílos) and few restaurants. Those visitors who venture here come for the tranquillity and for trekking in pristine nature.

ARRIVAL AND DEPARTURE
KÍMOLOS

By ferry Ferries dock at the tiny port of Psáthi on the southeast coast. Larger ferries call briefly on their way to and from Adhámas on Mílos, though the *Panagia Faneromeni* ferry (☎6948 308 758, ⓦkimolos-link.gr) from Pollónia on Mílos (€2) is shorter and more frequent. Ferry tickets for onward journeys – unless bought in advance up in Hóra (see below) – are only sold an hour or so before the arrival of the boat.

Destinations Folégandhros (3–4 weekly; 1hr 30 min); Íos (4–6 weekly; 2hr 50min); Kéa/Lávrio (1 weekly; 9hr); Kýthnos (5–6 weekly; 3hr 30min–7hr); Mílos, Adhámas

(2–3 daily; 1hr); Mílos, Pollónia (5–7 daily; 20min); Mýkonos (1 weekly; 7hr 30min); Páros (2–3 weekly; 4hr 30min); Pireás (1–2 daily; 3hr 50min–8hr); Náxos (1 weekly; 4hr 45min); Santoríni (4–6 weekly; 1hr 30min–4hr 30min); Sérifos (1–2 daily; 1hr 30min); Sífnos (1–2 daily; 1hr 20 min–2hr 40min); Síkinos (1–3 weekly; 1hr 30min); Syros (1–3 weekly; 6–9hr).

Travel agents There are two reputable shipping agencies: Kimolos Travel (☎22870 51219) and Maganiotis (☎22870 51000, ✉smagan@otenet.gr).

WINDMILL, SANTORÍNI (P.434) >

GETTING AROUND AND INFORMATION

By bus There are regular buses in high season from Psáthi to the capital, Hóra (8–10 daily; 10min). Some continue to the western beaches all the way to Prássa (4 daily; 20min), and others to the eastern beaches of Alykí, Bonátsa and Kalamítsi (4 daily; 30min).

By taxi There's only one taxi on the island (☏ 22870 5155? or ☏ 6945 464 093).

Services There is one ATM in Psáthi, and one bank and one ATM in Hóra; the island's post office is in the west of the village.

6 Hóra

Dazzlingly white **HÓRA** (known locally as Horió) is perched on the ridge above Psáthi behind a few old windmills overlooking the bay. The magnificent, two-gated, sixteenth-century **kástro** was built against marauding pirates. The perimeter houses are still intact and inhabited, though its heart is a jumble of ruins except for the small church of **Christós** (1592) and the chapel of the island's own saint **Ayía Methodhía**, beatified in 1991. Just outside the kástro to the north stands the conspicuously unwhitewashed, late seventeenth-century church of **Khryssóstomos**, the most beautiful on the island. Near the church is the **Archeological Museum** (July–Sept Tues–Sun 8.30am–3pm; free), displaying pottery from the Geometric to the Roman period. In a restored house near the eastern gateway is the privately run **Folk and Maritime Museum** (July–Sept daily 9am–1.30pm; €1).

ACCOMMODATION HÓRA

★**Meltemi** ☏ 22870 51360/86, ⊛ kimolos-meltemi .gr. A superlative option in the west of the village, with modern, simple, well-furnished rooms, airy balconies, terrific views and an excellent restaurant below. The owner works on the *Panagia Faneromeni* and can arrange for your pick-up at Psáthi. **€50**

Villa Maria ☏ 22870 51392. Central hotel, right by the entrance to Hóra, with rooms and studios that are up there with the most comfortable in the Cyclades; however, check carefully (and then reconfirm) whether it is block-booked, something that happens often. No breakfast served. **€50**

EATING

Panorama ☏ 22870 51531. Near the northeastern gate of the kástro, this is the best place to eat in Hóra, with a tasteful marine decor and a pretty veranda. It serves well-cooked dishes (mains €8) made with fresh ingredients. Most importantly in an island as sleepy as this, the place is almost constantly open. Daily 9am–midnight.

To Kyma Psáthi ☏ 22870 51001. An excellent taverna midway along the beach, specializing in fresh seafood (€10) and vegetarian dishes that come directly from their own farm. This is the place to try fried rather than the normally grilled octopus – flavoured with oregano. March–Oct daily noon–late.

Rest of the island

The hamlet of **Alykí** on the south coast is about thirty minutes' walk on the paved road that forks left from Psáthi; it's named after the saltpan that sprawls behind a pebbly beach. Here you can indulge in some serious bird-watching or try to spot the rare, endemic Mílos wall lizard. If you stroll west one cove, you arrive at **Bonátsa**, which has better sand and shallower water. Passing another cove you come to the even more attractive beach of **Kalamítsi**, with decent shade.

There are three signposted beaches next to each other starting from the dirt track at the end of the asphalted road off **Fykiádha**, a 45-minute walk west of Alykí. The first one, dotted with caves and ancient tombs, is **Dhékas**. It's divided by a low bluff from the long coarse-sand beach of **Elliniká**, itself separated by a rocky promontory from **Mavrospiliá**, the best spot to watch the sunset. There are no facilities on any beach.

Some 7km northeast from Hóra is **Prássa**, arguably the best easily accessible beach on the island, with crystal-clear water, fine sand and radioactive thermal springs. The route takes in impressive views across the straits to the island of **Políaigos**, and there are several peaceful coves where it's possible to swim in solitude. In the northwest, on

Kímolos's 361m summit, are the scant ruins of a Venetian fortress known as **Paleókastro** which can be reached after a reasonable trek (2hr 30min) from the dirt road off Prása. The road forks by the peak to Sklavos, with one branch leading to **Skiadhi**, an odd rock formation like a mushroom which has been adopted as the island landmark.

ACCOMMODATION AND EATING

REST OF THE ISLAND

Bonatsa Beach House Bonátsa ☎ 22870 51429, ⚲ bonatsa.gr. Right behind a line of salt cedars, this apartment complex has studios of exceptional quality in bright red and yellow colours. The owner also runs a good restaurant next door (7pm–midnight). Breakfast included. June–Sept. **€90**

Kimolia Yi Prássa ☎ 22870 51192, ⚲ kimoliagi.gr. Some 200m from the beach, this villa complex is eye-catchingly decorated, with much ornamental bric-à-brac on show. Ferry transfers can be arranged and breakfast is included: minimum 2 nights stay. Its restaurant *Kouzinaki* (daily noon–midnight) is rated highly by the locals. April–Sept. **€108**

6

Ándhros

ÁNDHROS, the second largest and northernmost of the Cyclades, is also one of the most verdant, its fertile, well-watered valleys and hillsides sprouting scores of holiday villas. With an attractive capital, three Blue Flag beaches, plus some idiosyncratic reminders of the Venetian period – such as the *peristereónes* (dovecote towers) and the *frákhtes* (dry-stone walls) – Ándhros has a special charm. Due to its size and proximity to Athens, the island is a popular **watersports** destination, particularly for windsurfing and diving, as well as boasting a well-signposted 100km-long network of **hiking trails**, some of the best in Greece (⚲ androsroutes.gr). **Driving** is also a joy, with precipitous coastal roads offering panoramic views over the Aegean.

ARRIVAL AND GETTING AROUND

ÁNDHROS

By ferry Ándhros has limited connections to the rest of the islands. All ferries and catamarans arrive at the main port, Gávrio, on the east coast.

Destinations Mýkonos (4–6 daily; 2hr 30min); Náxos (June-Sept 1 daily; 4hr); Rafína (up to 4 daily; 2hr); Sýros (1–2 weekly; 2hr 45min); Tínos (4–6 daily; 1hr 40min).

By bus Buses (☎ 22820 22316, ⚲ ktelandrou.webnode.gr) run from the port's waterfront to Batsí (6–8 daily; 20min), Hóra (4–8 daily; 50min) and Kórthi (2–5 daily; 1hr).

By car or motorbike As the island is large, tricky to explore and bus services are limited, you are advised to book your transport before arriving. Gávrio is the easiest place for car rental: try the reliable and friendly Euro Car (☎ 22820 72440, ⚲ rentacareuro.com) in front of the disembarkation point.

Travel agents Batis (☎ 22820 71489) and Kyklades Travel (☎ 22820 72363/71750) operate near the centre of the port.

INFORMATION

Tourist offices A tiny converted dovecote by the disembarkation point in Gávrio houses an information booth manned during ferry arrivals in July–August. There's also an unmanned but signed information kiosk by the jewellers' in Batsí. For online information check ⚲ andros.gr.

Services There is one bank and three ATMs on the waterfront in Gávrio, and the post office is in the centre of the port. Batsí has an ATM behind the *Dodóni* café-bar. There are several banks and four ATMs in Hóra, and the post office is on the main street. There is one ATM in Ormos Korthíou, on Yeoryíou Psálti, parallel to the esplanade.

Gávrio and around

GÁVRIO is a pleasant enough small port set in an oval bay, with several good places to eat, though the better hotels are out of town. There's an adjacent beach, but there are more attractive alternatives 5km northwest of the port: beautiful **Fellós** is very popular with self-catering Brits, while **Kourtáli**, hidden beyond the headland, is as popular but with fewer facilities.

6

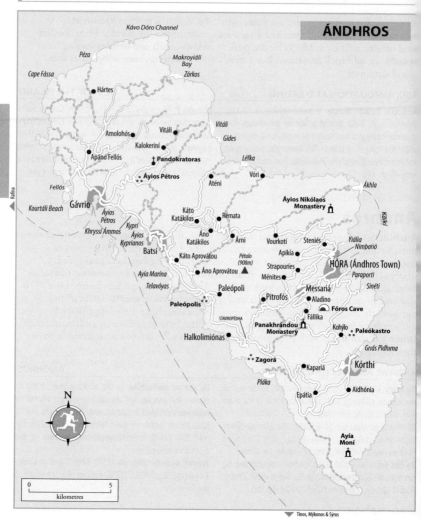

ÁNDHROS

Kávo Dóro Channel

Péza
Cape Fássa
Makroyiáli Bay
Zórkos
Hártes
Amolohós
Vitáli
Vitáli
Gídes
Kalokeriní
Apáno Fellós
† Pandokratoras
Léfka
Fellós
† Áyios Pétros
Aténi
Vóri
Ákhla
Áyios Nikólaos Monastery †
Gávrio
Áyios Pétros
Káto Katákilos
Rémata
Kourtáli Beach
Kyprí
Khryssí Ámmos
Áyios Kyprianos
Áno Katákilos
Árni
Vourkotí
Steniés
Yiália Nimborió
Batsí
Káto Aprovátou
Pétalo (908m) ▲
Apikía
Strapouriés
HÓRA (Ándhros Town)
Ayía Marína
Áno Aprovátou
Ménites
Paraporti
Telavóyas
Paleópoli
Pitrofós
Messariá
Sinéti
Paleópolis
Aladino
STAVROPÉDHA
Fóros Cave
Panakhrándou Monastery †
Fállika
Kohýlo
Paleókastro
Halkolimiónas
Griás Pídhima
Zagorá
Kapariá
Kórthi
Pláka
Epátia
Aïdhónia
Ayía Moní †

N

0   5
kilometres

Rafína

Kafkí

Tínos, Mýkonos & Sýros

Head inland and south from Gávrio, and you reach the best beaches on the island in a row: **Áyios Pétros** attracts the young because of the lively beach bars; **Khryssí Ámmos** is long, sandy and very popular with families; **Kyprí** is a long stretch of fine sand; and **Áyios Kyprianos**, just before you reach the major resort of **Batsí**, is located in a small sheltered cove of the same name.

ACCOMMODATION

GÁVRIO AND AROUND

Andros Gávrio ☎ 22820 71444, ⓦ campingandros.gr. A very pleasant campsite, 300m behind the centre of town, with a minimarket, café and good communal kitchen facilities. The massive swimming pool partly compensates for the fact that it is not near the sea. Free pickups to and from the port. As the reception is not always open, make

sure they're waiting for you. May–Oct. **€17.50**

★**Andros Holidays** 400m south of Gávrio ☎ 22820 71443, ⓦ androsholidayhotel.com. Luxury hotel on the headland side road south of town with lovely sea views from its garden terraces and arched verandas. With a large pool, designer bamboo furniture, a bar/

...staurant, and a private cove in front, its rooms are ...xceptional value. Breakfast included. Good online ...eals. April–Oct. €80 ...errakis Kyprí ☎ 22820 71456, ☻ hotelperrakis.com.

Top hotel built in local stone, that offers great views from even its standard-rate rooms. It houses the headquarters of Andros Surf Club as well as the most creative restaurant on the island with mains around €15. April–Oct. €100

EATING

...aliva Beach Bar Áyios Pétros ☎ 6977 352 662. The ...est of the four beach bars at Áyios Pétros: friendly, ...outhful with lively, chatty international staff and a ...tudenty atmosphere. It rents deckchairs and beach ...mbrellas for €6 and serves beer and cocktails while lulling ...ou with lounge music. June–Sept daily 10am–8pm.

Sails Gávrio ☎ 22820 71333. An excellent fish taverna at the northern end of Gávrio offering the daily catch from its own fishing boat (€12). Highly recommended by all the locals and, as you will soon find out, by a clowder of local stray cats. Daily noon–midnight.

6

Batsí and around

Most visitors head 8km south to **BATSÍ**, the island's main resort with its hotels, rooms and bars set around a fine natural harbour. The beautiful though often crowded beach curves twice around the bay, and the sea is cold, calm and clean. South of town, a coastal road leads to the small, picturesque sandy cove of **Ayía Marína** and, further on, the gorgeous beach of **Telavóyas**.

Some 8km south of Batsí on the highway to Hóra, a tiny but interesting **Archeological Museum** (summer: Tues–Sun 9am–4am; free) displays finds from the nearby ancient city of Paleópolis, which flourished from the sixth century BC to the end of the eighth century AD, when it was the island's capital. In the museum, check out the fifth-century BC clay puppet with moving limbs, found on a child's grave, and the large inscription containing a hymn to Isis, proving that Greeks did worship Egyptian gods. The site of **Paleópolis** (free access) is reached via a shady, signposted path leading from the modern-day village of Paleópoli to the eponymous beach.

ACCOMMODATION   BATSÍ AND AROUND

★**Chryssí Akti** Batsí ☎ 22820 41236, ☻ hotel -chryssiakti.gr. Right on the main beach, this hotel, which depends mainly on package tours, is solid, central, efficient and comfortable. Good swimming pool, and even better interior café-bar with a first-class range of snacks. Free parking next to the hotel. Breakfast included. Book early to get the best price. April–Oct. €60

Villa Rena Batsí ☎ 22820 41024, ☻ villarena.gr. Reached both by car from the ring road (limited parking) and via a five-minute climb from the beach, this hotel has a super collection of tastefully decorated apartments around a sloping shady garden and a surprisingly deep swimming pool. April–Oct. €50

EATING AND DRINKING

Balkoni tou Aigaiou Áno Aprovátou ☎ 22820 41020. Accessed via a narrow, winding hill road to the village of Áno Aprovátou, 3km from the highway south of Batsí, the "Balcony of the Aegean", set high above the coast, has superior, well-priced rural food; try its home-made Ándhros sausage (€9). The panoramic views are legendary. Easter–Oct daily noon–4pm & 6–11pm.

Café Scala Batsí ☎ 22820 41656. The largest and coolest hangout in the village with a DJ playing easy-listening

music after sunset, and an eclectic selection of beers from €5. Check out the Bahama-Mama signature cocktail made with two kinds of rum, malibu and pineapple (€10). Easter–Oct daily 9am–late.

★**Stamatis** Batsí ☎ 22820 41283. An old-style family taverna – the locals' choice – with a balcony for balmy nights and a large indoor area for when the *meltémi* hits. Try the Batsí speciality, chicken roll stuffed with local cheese for €10. Daily noon–midnight.

Hóra and around

Stretched along a rocky spur that divides a huge bay 32km from Gávrio, the capital **HÓRA** (also known as **Ándhros Town**) is the most attractive town on the island. Paved in marble and schist from the still-active local quarries, the buildings near the bus station are grand nineteenth-century edifices, and the squares with their ornate wall fountains and gateways are equally elegant. The old port, **Plakoúra**, on the west side of the headland, has a yacht supply station and a former ferry landing from where occasional boats run to the isolated but superbly idyllic **Ákhla** beach in summer. More locally, there are beaches on both sides of the town headland: **Nimborió** to the north and the less developed **Parapórti** to the southeast, though both are exposed to the *meltémi* winds in summer – the reason Gávrio (see p.381), on the other side of the island, became the main port instead.

From Platía Kaïri, at the end of Hóra's main pedestrianized street, **Embiríkou**, you pass through an archway and down through the charming residential area of Kamára past the town theatre to **Ríva Square**, with its Soviet-looking statue of *The Unknown Sailor* by Michalis Tombros (see below).

Archeological Museum

Platía Kaïri • Tues–Sat 9am–4pm • €4 • ☎ 22820 23664/29134

The **Archeological Museum** has well laid-out and clearly labelled displays, mostly from Paleópolis (see p.383) and Zagora. There are funerary stelae, amphorae and a torso of Artemis, but its prize item is the fourth-century *Hermes of Ándhros*, reclaimed from the Athens' National Archeological Museum (see p.85) in 1981. This is a remarkably preserved Roman copy of a Hermes by Praxiteles, one of antiquity's greatest sculptors.

Goulandhrís Museum of Contemporary Art

Below Platía Kaïri • Winter Tues–Sat 10am–2pm €3; summer Wed–Mon 11am–3pm & 6–9pm, though opening hours change yearly, so call to be sure.• €5 • ☎ 22820 22444; ⊛ moca-andros.gr

The surprisingly good **Goulandhrís Museum of Contemporary Art** is housed in two four-storey mansions opposite each other. One house displays a permanent collection of works by prominent Greek artists, including local sculptor Michalis Tombros; the other building houses annual temporary exhibitions in the summer.

Around Hóra

The **Fóros Cave** (signposted as Aladinos cave), 4km west of Hóra on the road to Gávrio, was one of the first caves to be explored in Greece, but only recently opened to the public (July to mid-Sept Mon, Tues & Thurs–Sat 10am–8pm, Wed & Sun 11am–3pm; guided tours only; €5; ☎69396 96835, ✉caveforos@hotmail.com). Its name comes from the fact that wild animals used to fall into the cave's concealed entrance and were considered by the superstitious locals as a kind of blood tax (fóros) for the resident evil spirits.

The tidy village of **Apikía**, 6km north of Hóra, is the source of the Sáriza spring, Greece's best-known brand of mineral water. An uphill turn at the southwestern end of the village leads, via a signed fifteen-minute path, to the **Rematiá Pytháras**, a pretty wooded stream with small waterfalls. The road continues to **Vourkotí** and, after a turn-off to Ákhla (a dirt track continuing for 8km), it then becomes a broad, mostly unused highway, via Árni, to the west coast. In July and August, a regular *kaïki* runs from Hóra to Ákhla (4–5 daily; €12; ☎69765 50224, or ask at your hotel).

> ### PANAYÍA PANAKHRÁNDOU
>
> Two hours' pleasant walk from Hóra via the village of Fállika, or via a signposted turn-off on the road to Kórthi by car, is the finest monastery on the island, **Panayía Panakhrándou** (sunrise–1pm & 4.30pm–sunset). Founded around 961 and with an icon said to be by St Luke, it's still defended by massive walls but is occupied these days by just a few monks. From the entrance door, a long passageway leads in past gushing springs to the atmospheric *katholicón* dedicated to the Dormition of the Virgin with its impressive and colourful iconostasis. Its lower decoration with **Ottoman Iznik tiles** is unique in the Aegean and it represents a gift to the monastery by Patriarch Dionysius III in the 1660s.

Andria Studios Nimborió beach ☎ 22820 22905, ⓦ andriastudios.com. Just one block away from the main road, behind Nimborió beach, you can hear a pin drop in these huge, well-furnished studios with their own kitchenette – the best priced in Hóra. Easter–Oct. €50

Niki Embirikou, Hóra ☎ 22820 29155, ⓦ androshotelniki.com. Centrally located, this small four-star hotel occupies a beautiful neoclassical mansion over 150 years old, and has been renovated with great respect to the building's past. High ceilings, cast iron beds, designer tiles, balconies with views, and a café below to watch the world go by. Breakfast included. €65

Onar Residence Ákhla beach ☎ 6932 563 707, ⓦ onar-andros.gr. Extremely difficult to reach – it's 40km from Gávrio, including 8km on a dirt road – but worth it. This ecolodge lies in the middle of one of the best beaches on Ándhros, with self-catering bungalows built of stone, wood and reeds, but with all modern facilities; it's as close

to feeling stranded on a desert island as you could dream of. May–Oct. €170

★Paradise Art Hotel Entrance to Hóra ☎ 22820 22187/8/9, ⓦ paradiseandros.gr. If you have your own transport, this hotel, though some distance from the town centre, makes an appealing holiday sanctuary, with modern art paintings in the common areas, a striking swimming pool, a tennis court and regal furnishings. Breakfast included. Easter–Sept. €90

★Yacht Club Nimborió beach ☎ 22820 29072. Rub shoulders with some of the wealthiest families in Greece who come to this members' club to swim and relax during the day. The restaurant – the best on the island – serves creative Greek cuisine and is open to non-members after 8pm for dinner (mains €15). There are also music nights in August (free entry). Reservation recommended. June–Sept daily 8pm–midnight.

The south

If you're exploring **the south** from Hóra, take the road that runs through the dramatic **Dipotámata** valley; at the seaward end, the fine, sheltered cove of **Sinéti** is worth a detour, though the access road is somewhat steep.

Paleókastro

Two kilometres south of Sinéti, the entry road to Kohýlo village forks: the left goes 2km (partly surfaced) to **Paleókastro** (aka Kástro Faneroménis), a ruined Venetian castle perched on a rocky crest at 586m, with amazing views overlooking Kórthi Bay.

Kórthi

A short distance south of Paleókastro is the pleasant resort of **Kórthi** (or Órmos Korthíou or simply Órmos), a small town, with a new seafront esplanade. Set on a large bay, isolated from the rest of the island by the high ridge and relatively unspoilt, it's popular with windsurfers; this is where the Greek Olympic team practises. **Kandoúni** beach covers the southern half of the main bay, while from the northern end of the esplanade a signed road and dirt track leads to the lovely **Griás Pídhima** beach, whose name in Greek means "Granny's jump". Legend has it that an old woman, who betrayed the nearby fortified village of Kohilos to the Turks, jumped from the top of the surrounding cliffs in remorse, and remains where she landed in the sea as a distinct column of rock that's still visible today.

★Lithodomi Kórthi ☎ 22820 61093/61130. One of those surprise finds that make your heart beat faster with excitement: a restaurant in the middle of the Kórthi esplanade with great rustic stone decor, an inventive

menu offering many vegetarian options (€10), good service, fresh ingredients and a great wine list. A must if you've come all this way. Daily noon–1am.

Tínos

TÍNOS still feels like one of the most Greek of the larger islands in the Cyclades. A few foreigners have discovered its beaches and unspoilt villages, but the majority of visitors are Greek, here to see the church of **Panayía Evangelístria**, a grandiose shrine erected on

6

the spot where a miraculous icon with healing powers was found in 1823. A local nun, now canonized as Ayía Pelayía, was directed in a vision to unearth the relic just as the War of Independence was getting under way, a timely coincidence that served to underscore the links between the Orthodox Church and Greek nationalism: since all Greek warlords prayed at the icon and the dream of independence came true, the icon was deemed to have with miraculous powers. Today, there are two major annual pilgrimages, on March 25 and August 15, when Tínos is inundated by the faithful.

The Ottoman tenure here, and on adjoining Sýros, was the most fleeting in the Aegean. **Exóbourgo**, the craggy mount dominating southern Tínos and surrounded by most of the island's sixty-odd villages, is studded with the ruins of a Venetian citadel that defied the Turks until 1715, long after the rest of Greece had fallen; an enduring legacy of the long Venetian rule is a **Catholic minority**, which accounts for almost half the population. Hills are dotted with distinctive and ornate **dovecotes**, even more in evidence here than on Ándhros. Aside from all this, the inland village architecture is striking, with the geometric dovecoat motif much in evidence, and there's a flourishing **marble-sculpting** tradition, with one of Europe's top marble art schools at **Pýrgos**.

ARRIVAL AND DEPARTURE TÍNOS

By ferry All ferries dock at Tínos Town. There are two harbours next to each other: one for catamarans (Old Port) and one for ferries (New Port), while the yacht marina is in the centre of town.

Destinations Ándhros (4–6 daily; 1hr 40min); Mýkonos (3–7 daily; 15–30min); Náxos (1 daily; 1hr 50min); Páros (1–2 daily; 1hr); Pireás (1 daily; 5hr); Rafína (up to 4 daily; 1hr 40min–3hr 50min); Santoríni (1 daily; 4hr); Sýros (1 daily; 1hr).

GETTING AROUND

By bus Buses leave from a small parking area in the Tínos Town Old Port. Bus information is available at ☎ 22830 22440, ⓦ kteltinou.gr.

Destinations Áyios Fokás (8–9 daily; 15min); Falatádos/ Steni (4–6 daily; 20min); Kalloní via Xinára (3 daily; 20min); Kiónia (2 hourly; 10min); Pánormos via Pýrgos

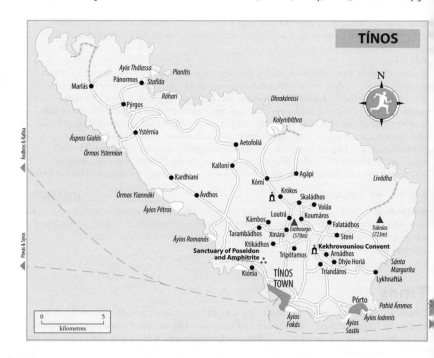

TÍNOS

(2–4 daily; 50min); Kalloní (2–3 daily; 45min); Pórto (1 hourly; 20min).

By car or motorbike Renting your own transport is a more reliable means of exploring than by bus, especially in shoulder season, and the only way to reach some of the beaches. Vidalis has four rental outlets in Tínos Town (☎ 22830 23400, ⓦ vidalis-rentacar.gr), though the smaller Jason Rental at the port (☎ 22830 24283, ⓦ jason-rentacar.gr) is cheaper.

INFORMATION AND SERVICES

Information There's an information and accommodation kiosk at Platía Pandanássis in Tínos Town (June–Aug open when the ferries dock; ☎ 22830 22210, ⓦ traveltotinos.gr).

Banks There is no shortage of banks or ATMs in Tínos Town, plus an ATM at Pýrgos.

Festivals Tínos has almost as many festivals as there are weekends, and you will almost certainly stumble into one in the summer. They range from the wacky artichoke festival (mid-June) and the wobbly Rakí festival (early Sept) to the wonderful half-Marathon, with medals in so many categories that you are likely to win one just by taking part (early June; ⓦ tinosrunningexperience.gr/en).

6

Tínos Town and around

TÍNOS TOWN is large and commercial, possessing a unique mixture of religion and commerce: trafficking in devotional articles certainly dominates the streets leading from the busy waterfront up to the church of Panayía Evangelístria towering above. On the way, check out the **Archeological Museum** (Tues–Sun 8.30am–3pm; €2) whose collection includes a fascinating sundial from the local Roman sanctuary of Poseidon and Amphitrite (see p.85). If you have a sweet tooth, try the highly calorific Tiniot specialities: *amygdalotó*, a marzipan-style sweet, and *loukoúmia* (Turkish delight), sold by street vendors or patisseries.

Panayía Evangelístria

Leofóros Megalóharis • Daily 8am–8pm • Free

The striking Neoclassical church of **Panayía Evangelístria** is approached via a massive marble staircase; inside, the church's famous **icon** is completely buried under a dazzling array of jewels. Below is the crypt (where the icon was discovered) and a mausoleum for the sailors drowned when the Greek warship, *Elli*, at anchor off Tínos, was torpedoed by an Italian submarine on August 15, 1940.

Kiónia

Kiónia, 3km northwest of the capital, is the site of the **Sanctuary of Poseidon and Amphitrite** (Tues–Sun 8.30am–3pm; free). The excavations yielded many columns (*kiónia* in Greek), but also a temple, baths, a fountain and hostels for the ancient pilgrims. The **beach** is a long thin strip, lined with rooms to rent and snack-bars, but west of the *Tinos Beach* hotel you can follow an unpaved road to a series of isolated sandy coves.

The southern beaches

There are several first-class but mostly unshaded beaches at the southern tip of the island. In order of proximity to Tínos Town they are: **Áyios Fokás**, just beyond the eastern headland, which is a good, fine-sand beach after a pebbly start, the fishing village beach of **Áyios Sóstis**, shallow **Áyios Ioánnis** (served by six daily buses), and beyond that the idyllic **Pahiá Ámmos**, with a view of Mýkonos.

ACCOMMODATION   TÍNOS TOWN AND AROUND

Avra Konstandínou 4–6, Tinos Town ☎ 22830 22242. Charming Neoclassical building on the waterfront with spacious renovated rooms, some with balconies, plus an attractive plant-filled communal atrium area. Port transfers and breakfast included. May–Oct. **€50**

Cavos Áyios Sóstis ☎ 22830 24224, ⓦ cavos-tinos.com. Well located for the beach and adorned with flowers and palm trees, these large apartments and suites can sleep up to four people and are ideal for families. Two nights minimum, three nights gets a discount. Breakfast included. April–Nov. **€95**

★**Prasino Oneiro** Louisas Sohou 5, Tinos Town ☎ 22830 22344 ⓦ prasinooniro.gr. An upgraded former campsite with a series of simple, but roomy, en-suite bungalows with cooking facilities and parking spaces. Set among lemon trees and cypresses, 300m from the centre of town and Áyios Fokás beach, this is one of the island's most attractive options. Easter–Oct. **€35**

Tinion Hotel Alavánou 1, Tinos Town ☎ 22830 22261, ⓦ tinionhotel.gr. A 1920s Neoclassical hotel just back from the waterfront, resonating with history; a Greek prime minister once resigned in the dining room in a fit of pique. Its grandeur recently restored, it has spacious

elegant rooms, some with balconies: port transfers and a good breakfast are included. March–Nov. **€60**

Tinos Beach Kiónia ☎ 22830 22626, ⓦ tinosbeach.gr. Modernist 1970s hotel that dominates the beach: however, its recently renovated rooms with verandas, good swimming pool, large breakfast (included), range of facilities and regular shuttle into town makes this rather anonymous resort a more attractive option than expected. Two nights minimum May–Oct. **€104**

EATING

★**Metaxy Mas** Aktí Názou, Tínos Town ☎ 22830 24137, ⓦ metaximastinos.gr. One of a new breed of restaurants offering an imaginative menu that includes excellent Tiniot meats and a wealth of unusual appetisers such as wild artichokes (€7.50) and aubergine soufflé (€9.50): there's a well chosen wine list, too. March–Nov daily noon–midnight.

Symposion Evangelistrias 13, Tínos Town ☎ 22830 24368, ⓦ symposion.gr. Sophisticated restaurant at the top of a converted Neoclassical house, which succeeds in

marrying Greek and international cuisine. It's worth trying the American brunch (€14) at least once during your stay. April–Oct daily 9am–midnight.

★**To Koutouki tis Elenis** G. Gafou 5, Tínos Town ☎ 22830 24857, ⓦ koutouki-elenis.gr. In a building dating from 1812, this gem of a restaurant has a creative chef who mixes international and traditional cooking with superb results. Try the baked cheese starter (€6), pork with fetafor a main course (€10), then finish up with the irresistible walnut pie. Daily noon–midnight.

The north

A good beginning to a foray into **northern Tínos** is to drive the so-called **Dovecote Trail** (see box, below), or take one of several daily buses along the route from Tínos Town to Pýrgos. The ornate dovecotes are mostly found in the villages off the main road between **Tínos Town** and **Ystérnia**.

Pýrgos

A few kilometres beyond Ystérnia, **PÝRGOS** lies in the middle of the island's marble-quarrying district – even its bus stop is magnificently crafted from marble. The town is home to a School of Fine Arts, whose graduates are renowned throughout Greece for their skill in producing marble ornamentation; flamboyant fanlights and bas-relief plaques fashioned here adorn houses throughout Tínos, while Pýrgos' small **cemetery** up and left from the main square, is a great showcase for their talent.

THE DOVECOTE TRAIL

From the port of Tínos drive up Evangelistrías, turn right and follow the signs to **Tripótamos** where you can visit the only still-functioning clay pot workshop on the island. Nearby **Ktikádhos** is a fine village with two superb churches. Heading northwest from the main road junction beyond Ktikádhos, you can see several beautifully restored **dovecote houses** at the turn-off to **Tarambádhos** – it's worth stopping there and following an hour-long signed path through the village, to get as close to these dovecotes as possible, as they are the most photogenic in the Cyclades. Heading further north from the Tarambádhos turn-off, you can break your trip by turning off at Ystérnia to **Órmos Ysterníon**, a pretty, compact beach with an unmissable fish taverna: the even prettier Skhináki beach lies at the far end.

★**To Thalassaki** Órmos Ysterníon ☎ 22830 31366, ✉ tothalassaki@gmail.com. Award-winning, if pricey, fish taverna right on the beach serving an exceptional range and quality of food for something so out of the

way – try the seafood spaghetti for €22. It's popular with Mykoniots (high praise indeed) and worth making a detour for the sunset views and extensive ouzo selection, alone. April–Oct daily noon–midnight.

The village is home to three museums, including one of the Cyclades' most interesting, the private **Museum Of Marble Crafts** (March to mid-Oct Wed–Mon 10am–6pm; mid-Oct to Feb Wed–Mon 10am–5pm; €3; ☎22830 31290, ⓦpiop gr), its modernist silhouette hidden from view at the edge of Pýrgos. The museum showcases the hard manual work of extracting the marble from the quarries and the specialized skills exhibited in the artists' ateliers. At the entrance to the village, the **Museum Of Tinian Artists** (April–Oct daily 11am–3pm & 6pm–8pm; €3, including entry to the Yiannoúlis Halepás Musuem) contains works from some of Tínos' finest artists, while the **Yiannoúlis Halepás Museum** next door (same hours) is devoted exclusively to the work of Greece's most important modern sculptor. Although his masterpiece, Koimoméni (fashioned when he was 25) is not on display here – it's in the Athens' First Cemetery – plenty of his other works are and the enthusiastic curator is a mine of information about Halepás' tortured life (his parents, who didn't want him to be an artist, broke his sculptures and confined him to a psychiatric institution).

6

Pánormos

Pýrgos' marble products were once exported from **Pánormos** harbour, 4km northeast, with its small, shaded **Stafídha** beach. The village itself gives access to a number of good beaches reachable on foot: **Róhari** is to the southeast, facing north, and with deep clear waters and massive waves, while **Ayía Thálassa** and **Kaválargos** are much more sheltered on the northwest side of the bay.

EATING AND DRINKING	**THE NORTH**

Marina Pánormos ☎22830 31314. A seaside ouzerí with a great ouzo and mezédhes selection; spoilt for choice, you may want to order a starters platter (€10) but, unless there are two of you, wait until you've finished before you venture into a main; the portions are quite large. May–Sept daily noon–midnight.

Myronia Pýrgos ☎22830 31229, ✉iliasofi@otenet.gr. The best of the tavernas and patisseries on the attractive main village square, with seats around the 150-year-old plane tree. It serves baked pigeon with pasta (€15) if you pre-order 24hrs in advance. Easter–Oct daily noon–midnight.

Around Exóbourgo

The ring of villages around the mountain of **EXÓBOURGO** is worth visiting if you have a car. The fortified pinnacle itself (570m), with the ruins of three Venetian churches and a fountain, is reached by steep steps from **Xinára** (near the island's major road junction), the old seat of the island's Roman Catholic bishop. Most villages in north-central Tínos have mixed populations, but Xinára and its immediate neighbours are purely Catholic; the inland villages also tend to have a more sheltered position, with better farmland nearby – the Venetians' way of rewarding converts and their descendants.

At **Loutrá**, an almost deserted village north of Xinára, there's an Ursuline convent with just one remaining nun and a small **Folk Art Museum** (daily 9.30am–2.30pm; free) in the seventeenth-century Jesuit monastery. From Krókos, 1km northwest of Loutrá, it's 4km to tiny **Volax**, the most spectacular village on the island: a windswept oasis surrounded by hundreds of giant granite boulders, as far from a typical Greek landscape as you can get in the Cyclades. Some 5km north of Krókos, at **Kolymbíthra**, is a magnificent double beach, the best on the island.

Falatádhos

Some 5km southeast of Volax, the village of **FALATÁDHOS** is home to the museum of **Spíti tou Skítsou** (daily 10am–10pm, or ask at taverna *Léfkes* next door to open it; free), displaying cartoons by Vassílis and Kóstas Mitrópoulos, Greece's best known cartoonists: natives of the village, they donate original designs to the museum every summer. The village church, **Áyios Ioánnis**, has an attractive bust of Dimítris Vlássis who found the miraculous icon of the Virgin, and a marble relief of the scene of its discovery.

Léfkes Falatádhos ☎ 22830 41335. An almost perfect Greek taverna, where traditional home-made cooking (mains €6) is served with a smile: sit on the terrace beneath the shade of a huge poplar with a view over well-tended fields. March–Oct daily 7.30am–late.

Mýkonos

MÝKONOS has become the most popular, the most high-profile and the most expensive of the Cyclades. Boosted by direct air links with Europe, it sees several million tourists a year pass through, producing some spectacular August overcrowding on the island's 85 square kilometres. But if you don't mind the tourist hordes, or you come in the shoulder season, its striking capital is still one of the most photogenic Cycladic towns, with whitewashed houses concealing a dozen little churches, shrines and chapels.

The sophisticated nightlife is hectic, amply stimulated by Mýkonos's former reputation as *the* gay resort of the Mediterranean, although today gay tourists are well in the minority. While everywhere on the island is at least gay-friendly, gay tourists prefer to congregate in Mýkonos Town itself or the beaches of Super Paradise and Eliá. The locals take it all in their stride, ever conscious of the important revenue generated by their laissez-faire attitude. When they first opened up to the hippy tourists who began appearing on Mýkonos in the 1960s, they assumed their eccentric visitors were sharing cigarettes due to lack of funds. Since then, a lot of the innocence has evaporated, and you shouldn't come for scenery, solitude or tradition, but Mýkonos offers lovely and lively beaches and a party lifestyle second to none.

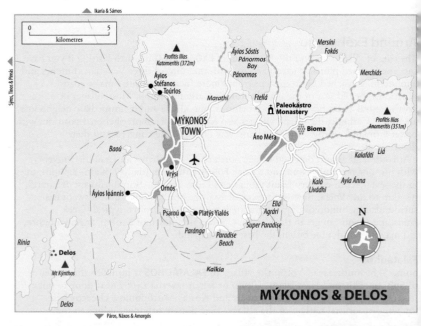

ARRIVAL AND DEPARTURE

By plane The airport is 3km outside Mýkonos Town in the centre of the island. Taxis to the centre cost €10, buses €2.

Destinations Athens (2–7 daily with Aegean and Olympic; 35min); London (2 daily each with EasyJet/BA; 4hr); Thessaloníki (5 weekly with Aegean; 1hr).

By ferry Most ferries at the Old Port at the north end of Mýkonos Town. Cruise ships and any overflow anchor at the New Port, 1km further north: check your ticket to make sure you know which port you're leaving from. Boats for Delos leave from the west end of the waterfront in town.

Destinations Áno Koufoníssi (1 weekly; 5hr 45min); Amorgós, Aigiáli (1–4 weekly; 2hr-); Ándhros (4–6 daily; 2hr 30min); Dhonoússa (1 weekly; 9hr); Folégandhros (1–2 daily; 4hr–6hr 30min); Irakliá (1 weekly; 4hr 15min); Iráklio Crete (1 daily; 5hr); Ikaría (5–6 weekly; 2hr); Íos (3–5 daily; 1hr 15min); Kímolos (1–2 weekly; 8hr); Kýthnos (1 weekly; 4hr 50min); Mílos (1–2 daily; 5hr 30min–9hr); Náxos (2–3 daily; 45min–1hr 30min); Páros (4–5 daily; 50min–1hr 30min); Pireás (3–4 daily; 2h 30min–4h 30min); Rafína (up to 7 daily; 2hr–4hr 40min); Sámos (5–6 weekly; 3hr 30min); Santoríni (1–4 daily; 2hr 15 min–3hr 30min); Skhinoússa (1 weekly; 10hr); Sérifos (1–3 weekly; 6hr 30min); Sífnos (1–3 weekly; 5hr 30min–7hr); Síkinos (1 weekly; 5hr 30min); Sýros (1–2 daily; 50min); Tínos ((3–7 daily; 15–30min).

GETTING AROUND

By bus The north bus station for Toúrlos, Áyios Stéfanos, Kalafáti, Eliá and Áno Méra is by the old port; the south bus station for all western and the popular southern beaches is just outside the pedestrianized area at the other end of town. If you use public transport to the beaches from Paránga to Paradise, you won't be alone – on a sunny day in season the beaches and transport range from busy to overcrowded. Buses to Paradise run hourly through the night in high season. Chartered buses to Super Paradise leave from near the Old Port every 30min in season (11am–11pm). All timetables are online at ⓦ mykonosbus.com.

By car or motorbike Rental agencies are concentrated around the two bus stops. The only free parking near the town is by the north bus station. Parking spaces at most beaches are inadequate and signposting poor.

By taxi Taxis run from Mantó square on the main seafront and from the south bus station; rates are fixed but if there's more than one passenger and it's late at night, you may be asked each to pay the full fare. Try Mykonos Radio Taxi (☎ 22890 22400).

By boat *Kaïkia* head from town and Orkós to all of the southern beaches in June–September.

INFORMATION AND ACTIVITIES

Services There is no shortage of banks or ATMs in Mýkonos Town. The island post office is near the south bus station.

Diving and watersports Kalafáti beach (see p.395) is the island's activity hub between late May and early Oct: operators here include W-Diving (☎ 694 524 3928, ⓦ mykonos-diving.com) for scuba diving and Pezi-Huber (☎ 22890 72345, ⓦ pezi-huber.com) for wind-surfing. Alternatively, Dive Adventures, behind Paradise beach (☎ 22890 24808, ⓦ www.diveadventures.gr), runs introductory scuba and a full range of PADI courses.

Mýkonos Town

Don't let the crowds put you off exploring **MÝKONOS TOWN**, the quintessential image of the Cyclades. In summer most people head out to the beaches during the day, so early morning or late afternoon are the best times to wander the maze of narrow streets. The labyrinthine design was supposed to confuse the pirates who plagued Mýkonos in the eighteenth and early nineteenth centuries, and it has the same effect on today's visitors.

Getting lost in the convoluted streets and alleys is half the fun of Mýkonos, although there are a few places worth seeking out. Coming from the ferry quay you'll pass the **Archeological Museum** (Tues–Sun 9am–4pm; €4; ☎ 22890 22325) on your way into town, which was built in 1905 to exhibit artefacts from the cemeteries on Rínia island, opposite Delos (see p.396). The town also boasts a **Maritime Museum** displaying various nautical artefacts and model ships as well as an 1890 lighthouse lantern re-erected in the back garden (April–Oct Tues–Sun 10.30am–1pm & 6.30–9pm; €4; ☎ 22890 22700). Next door is **Lena's House** (Mon–Sat 6.30–9.30pm; ☎ 22890 22591), a restored and furnished merchant's home from the turn of the twentieth century. Near the base of the Delos jetty, the **Folklore Museum** (Mon–Sat 4.30–8.30pm; free; ☎ 22890 22591), housed in an eighteenth-century mansion, crams in a

6

MÝKONOS TOWN

■ ACCOMMODATION

Elysium	5
K Group	6
Leto	2
Manto	3
Matogianni	4
Stelios	1

● EATING

Kostas	5
Kounelas	4
Nikos	3
Olla	6
Kalamaki Mykonos	2
Salparo	1

■ DRINKING

Bao's	6
Jackie O'	1
Katerina's	2
Lola's	5
Montparnasse	3
Skandinavian Bar	4

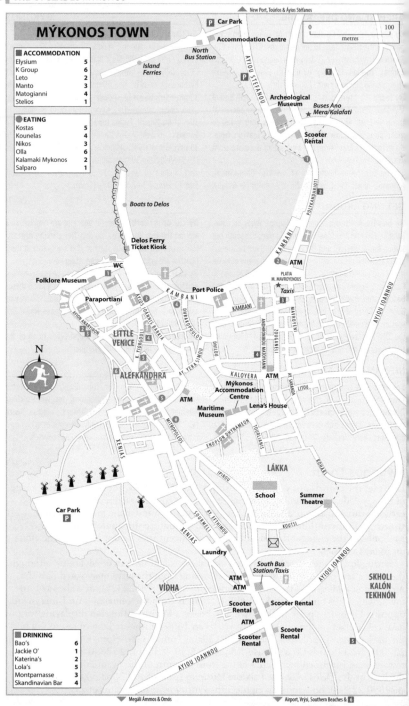

New Port, Toúrlos & Áyios Stéfanos

Buses Ano Mera/Kalafati

Megáli Ámmos & Ornós

Airport, Vrýsi, Southern Beaches & 6

larger-than-usual collection of bric-à-brac, including a basement dedicated to Mýkonos' maritime past. The museum shares the promontory with Mýkonos' oldest and best-known church, **Paraportianí**, a fascinating asymmetrical hotchpotch of four chapels amalgamated into one.

Beyond the church, the shoreline leads to the area known as **Little Venice** because of the high, arcaded Venetian houses built right up to the water's edge on its southwest side. Together with the adjoining **Alefkándhra** district, this is a dense area packed with art galleries, trendy bars, shops and clubs. Beyond Little Venice, the famous **windmills** look over the area, renovated and ripe for photo opportunities.

6

ACCOMMODATION   MÝKONOS TOWN

There are two accommodation offices 100m south from the Old Port jetty; one deals with **hotels** (☎ 22890 24540, ⓦ mha .gr), the other with **rented rooms** (☎ 22890 24860) – both open during ferry arrivals. A private agency by the southern bus stop at the lower end of town (daily 9am–9pm; ☎ 22890 23160; ⓦ mykonos-accommodation.com) also rents accommodation around the island. Note that in July and August accommodation prices can be up to fifty percent more expensive than quoted below.

Elysium By the School of Fine Arts ☎ 22890 23952, ⓦ elysiumhotel.com. Exclusively gay hotel with beautiful views, boasting a poolside bar open to non-residents, a popular setting for an early-evening party complete with go-go dancers and drag shows. Occasional all-night parties with international DJs. Breakfast included. May–Oct. **€300**

K Group Vrýsi ☎ 22890 23415, ⓦ myconiancollection .gr. A cluster of hotels, *Kalypso*, *Kochyli*, *Korali* and *Kyma*, about 1km south of town. Many of the comfortable rooms have wonderful views and there's also a pool and restaurant. Often available when smaller places are fully booked. Breakfast included. Easter–Oct. **€220**

★**Leto** Old Port ☎ 22890 22207/22918, ⓦ letohotel .com. The best of the luxury town hotels, slightly raised above the small town beach, with a large swimming pool that becomes the focus both in the daytime and, fully lit, at night when the hotel restaurant – one of the best on the island – lays its tables around it. Breakfast included. **€330**

Manto Evangelistrías 1 ☎ 22890 22330, ⓦ manto -mykonos.gr. Situated in a small side street, the hotel's exterior belies its Tardis-like interior expanse. Good, simple rooms with a/c and fridge for those who just want a comfortable bed to crash in. Breakfast included. March–Nov. **€120**

Matogianni Matogianni Str ☎ 22890 22217, ⓦ matogianni.gr. Living proof that it's possible to stay in Mýkonos Town without mortgaging your home, this is a comfortable hotel with classically minimalist decor and as peaceful as can be in the buzz of the backstreets. **€160**

Stelios View Enoplon Dhinameon 10 ☎ 22890 24641, ⓔ pensionstellios@mykonos-accommodation.com. This white-washed Mykoniot-style building is an excellent-value pension, newly renovated, in a prime location overlooking the old port. The only hitch may be hauling your luggage up the fifty steep steps from the waterfront. No breakfast. April–Oct. **€90**

EATING

Kostas Mitropoléos 5 ☎ 22890 23326. Buried deep within Alefkándhra, this restaurant founded in 1963 serves everything from seafood to grills with a good wine list including wine straight from the barrel (€10/ half litre). Prices for mains start at €14. Daily noon–2am.

Kounelas Svorónou ☎ 22890 28220. Seafood taverna set in an appealing garden, with a reputation for offering the freshest fish on the island and dishes from €15. Very popular with the gay crowd, it is tucked away in a narrow street but signposted. May–Oct daily 6.30pm–2am.

Nikos Ayías Monís square ☎ 22890 24320. One of the most famous tavernas on the island, strong on the catch of the day but also serving traditional Greek cuisine (€15). Every centimetre of its side of the square is packed with customers after 10pm, which sometimes has a

detrimental effect on service. April–Oct daily noon–2am.

Olla Mitropoléos 11 ☎ 22890 77177, ⓦ olla -mykonos.gr. Inspired Mediterranean cuisine in cheerful designer surroundings in a cul-de-sac off Mitropóleos. Salads €10, mains €14–20. April–Oct daily 10am–1am.

Kalamaki Mykonos Platía Mantó. Central and open all hours, this is an essential pit stop for clubbers; the only 24hr fast food in town to quench the clubbers' munchies – and it's not bad. Chicken skewers €2.50, salads €6, kebab plate €12. April–Oct 24hr.

★**Salparo** Kaminaki Waterfront ☎ 22890 78950. Formerly *Baboulas*, this serves the best coal-grilled seafood mezédhes on Mýkonos, supervised by Petroúla, the owner and chef – try the mussels cooked in seawater (€15) and marvel. April–Nov daily noon–midnight.

DRINKING AND NIGHTLIFE

Bao's Alefkándhra ☎ 22890 26505, ⓦ baosmykonos .com. The latest trendy, yet informal, hideaway with a reputation for imaginative cocktails (€12–16) and a thirty-something crowd that's better behaved than many. Come straight from the beach at sunset for the best views of Little Venice. May–Sept daily 6pm–5am.

Jackie O' Paraportianí ☎ 22890 77168, ⓦ jackieomykonos.com. The busiest gay club in town, it attracts a mixed crowd of all sexual persuasions who like to dance to relentless funky house mixed with the occasional disco hit. It's on two floors, though reaching the top bar through the crowd is sometimes impossible. Easter–Oct daily 10pm–6am.

Katerina's Little Venice ☎ 22890 23084. Owned by the first female captain in the Greek navy, Katerina, this low-key bar-restaurant with sea and sunset views from the balcony, is one of the most laidback places for a drink (cocktails €10). April–Oct daily noon–late.

Lola's Pittaraki St ☎ 22890 78391. Chic gay bar owned by long-standing Mýkonos residents Dimitris and Gilles, with gay icons on the wall, camp decor and torch songs on the radio. Try the kick of their espresso martini (€15) and you'll never touch a vodka Red Bull again. April–Oct 8pm–3am.

Montparnasse Ayíon Anargýron 24, Little Venice ☎ 22890 23719, ⓦ thepianobar.com. With great cocktails (€12) and a balcony over the sea, this gay piano bar is a very good place to warm up for the night ahead. Sunset views followed by cabaret and live music. May–Oct daily 7pm–3am.

Skandinavian Bar Áyios Ioánnis Barkiá ☎ 22890 22669, ⓦ skandinavianbar.com. For serious drinking, head to the *Skandinavian*, which has been thumping out dance music, beer (€6–8) and cocktails (€10–15) until the early hours since 1978. May–Sept daily 8pm–late.

Around Mýkonos Town

The closest **beaches** around Mýkonos Town are those to the north, at **Toúrlos** (only 2km away but not up to the usual standard) and **Áyios Stéfanos** (3km away, much better), both developed resorts and connected by a very regular bus service to Mýkonos Town. There are tavernas, rooms and package hotels at Áyios Stéfanos. You'll need your own transport, a bus or *kaïki*, to get to most of them.

The undistinguished but popular beaches southwest of the town are tucked into pretty bays. The nearest, 1km away, is **Megáli Ámmos**, a good but often windy beach backed by flat rocks and pricey rooms, but nearby Kórfos Bay is unpleasant, thanks to the town dump and machine noise. Buses serve **Ornós**, a package resort on a low-lying area between the rest of the island and the Áyios Ioánnis peninsula. The south side has a reasonable beach, plus *kaïkia* to other beaches, a handful of tavernas, and numerous accommodation options.

Two kilometres west is **Áyios Ioánnis**, the island's westernmost bay and small, namesake church, overlooking Delos – the tiny public beach achieved a moment of fame as a location for the film *Shirley Valentine*. Accessed by a 500m dirt track northwest from Áyios Ioánnis is the small but popular beach at **Kápari**, with good views of Delos and the sunset.

ACCOMMODATION   AROUND MÝKONOS TOWN

Dionysos Ornós ☎ 22890 23313, ⓦ dionysoshotel.gr. Easily the most comfortable hotel in the area with a pool and adjoining bar, satellite TV, children's area and a fitness room, as well as parking space – mission impossible in Ornós. Two nights minimum. Breakfast included. May–Oct. **€150**

Manoulas Beach Áyios Ioánnis ☎ 22890 22900, ⓦ hotelmanoulas.gr. A surprisingly affordable high-class hotel, blindingly white set against the background of the deep blue of the Aegean. The panoramic view from its restaurant (mains from €15) across to Delos is breathtaking. Breakfast included. May–Oct. **€150**

The south coast

The western half of the **south coast** is the busiest part of the island. *Kaïkia* and buses head from town to all of its beaches. Drivers will find that parking spaces at most beaches are inadequate and signposting poor.

The southern beaches

Platýs Yialós, 4km south of town, is one of the longest-established resorts on the island, where the sand is monopolized by end-to-end hotels. **Psaroú**, just a steep hairpin road away to the west, is much prettier – 150m of white sand backed by foliage and reeds.

Just over the headland to the east of Platýs Yialós lies **Paránga**, actually two beaches separated by a smaller headland, the first of which is quieter than its neighbour. Next is the golden crescent of **Paradise beach**. Here, as on many of Mýkonos' most popular beaches, it can be packed in high season, and any space clear of people is likely to be taken up by straw umbrellas, rentable (usually along with two accompanying loungers) for about €16 per day.

The next bay east contains **Super Paradise beach**, accessible by *kaïki*, or by a surfaced but extremely steep access road. It is one of the most fun spots on the island, with its main beach bar staging a party every evening at 6pm. The western part is dominated by the *Jackie O'* gay complex (daily 9am–9pm; ☎ 22890 77298) which has a separate signposted entrance for cars. The more secluded **Agrári** beach is 300m to the east.

One of the more attractive beaches on Mýkonos, **Eliá** is a broad, sandy stretch, with a mountainous backdrop at its eastern end: it's also the longest beach on the island and almost exclusively gay.

The eastern beaches

East from the Eliá road, **Kaló Livádhi** is long and sandy, fronting an agricultural valley scattered with little farmhouses. Both beaches are served by a seasonal bus service and kaïkia.

The main road east via the unexciting village of Áno Méra leads to **Ayía Ánna**, on a double-headed headland with a shingle beach and taverna, just before the larger, more attractive **Kalafáti**: the island's cleanest beach, and its main hub for activities and watersports, it's also one of Greece's top windsurfing destinations. **Liá**, roughly 4.6km east by road from Áno Méra, is smaller than Kalafáti, but as pleasant and with as clear water.

ACCOMMODATION AND EATING   THE SOUTH COAST

★Aphrodite Beach Kalafáti beach ☎ 22890 71367, ⓦ aphrodite-mykonos.gr. A four-star hotel 18km from Mýkonos Town, on the island's main activities beach, and completely self-sufficient should you want to sample Mýkonos without the crowds. Taxi to town €20. April–Nov. **€180**

Liasti Liá ☎ 22890 72150, ⓦ liasti.com. The island's most easterly restaurant, but don't let that deter you if you have your own transport. You may be surprised by how busy it is, but once you sample the Italian-Greek menu (€12) you'll understand. April–Sept daily 10am–9pm.

★ Paránga Beach Hostel ☎ 22890 25915, ⓦ mycamp.gr. This Paránga beach campsite and hostel has one of the most attractive settings on the island. It has a pool with adjoining cocktail bar, restaurant and minimarket, as well as relative peace and quiet from the relentless Mykoniot buzz. May–Oct. Camping €25, dorm €13, bungalow €35

Paradise Beach Resort Paradise beach ☎ 22890 22852, ⓦ paradise-greece.com. An industrial-size (and feel) campsite operating since 1969, with a huge choice of accommodation including cabins and bungalows. Totally self-sufficient with a restaurant, various bars, a clothes shop and its own club with resident DJs. April–Oct. Camping €13.50, cabin €40, bungalow €45

Thalassa Kalafáti beach ☎ 22890 72081. Happening beach bar during the day and one of the best places to eat on Mýkonos for dinner. Its pork in cheese and mushroom sauce (€17) is one of the top gastronomic experiences on the island. May–Sept daily noon–midnight.

NIGHTLIFE

★Cavo Paradiso Paradise beach ☎ 22890 27205, ⓦ cavoparadiso.gr. *The* after-hours club in the Cyclades, regularly voted by DJ magazine as one of the world's top twenty, where party animals of all persuasions come together, united by world-famous DJs. The €20–25 entrance fee includes the first drink, but ask for a discount flyer at the Lakka boutique in Mýkonos Town. Mid-June to mid-Sept 2–3 times a week on varying days (daily in July & Aug) 11.30pm–7am.

★Scorpios Paránga beach ☎ 22890 29250, ⓦ scorpiosmykonos.com. A beach bar/restaurant on a headland in Paránga with its own sandy cove – come for the parties starting at 5pm on Tues, Thurs and, most of all, Sun. Cocktails €17–19. Mid-May to Sept daily 11am–1am.

The north coast

The **north coast** suffers persistent battering from the *meltémi* and for the most part is bare, brown and exposed. The deep inlet of **Pánormos Bay** is the exception to this, with the lovely, relatively sheltered beaches of **Pánormos** and **Áyios Sóstis**; although not served by buses, they are becoming increasingly popular, but still remain among the least crowded on the island. At the southern, inner end of the bay, **Fteliá** is a good windsurfers' beach and legendary burial site of Ajax, one of *The Iliad*'s mythical heroes. If you are driving there, stop by at the only – but excellent – vineyard on the island, **Bíoma** (☎22890 71883), for some wine tasting.

Delos

The remains of **ANCIENT DELOS (Dhílos)**, the Cyclades' sole UNESCO Heritage Site, manage to convey the past grandeur of this small, sacred isle a few kilometres west of Mýkonos. The ancient town lies on the west coast on flat, sometimes marshy ground that rises in the south to **Mount Kýnthos**.

ARRIVAL AND DEPARTURE DELOS

By boat In season, excursion boats to Delos leave from the west end of Mýkonos harbour (Tues–Sun at 9am, 11am, 1pm and 5pm, returning from the site at 12.15pm, 1.30pm, 3pm & 7.30pm; €18 return from a kiosk at the front). Allow 4hr to walk the site and see the museum. Guided day-trips are also possible from Mýkonos and Tínos (see p.385). Note that it is illegal to remove anything from Delos as well as anchor, swim or dive at or near the island.

The site

Daily 8am–8pm • €12 • ☎22890 22259

As you disembark from the boat, the Sacred Harbour is on your left, the Commercial Harbour on your right and straight ahead lies the **Agora of the Competaliasts**. The Competaliasts were Roman merchants who worshipped the Lares Competales, the guardian spirits of crossroads; offerings to Hermes would once have been placed in the middle of the agora (market square), their positions now marked by one round and one square base.

OLD DELOS DAYS

Delos's ancient fame arose because **Leto** gave birth to the divine twins **Artemis** and **Apollo** here, although the island's fine, sheltered harbour and central position in the Aegean did nothing to hamper development from around 2500 BC. When the Ionians colonized the island about 1000 BC it was already a cult centre, and by the seventh century BC it had also become a major commercial and religious port. Unfortunately Delos attracted the attention of Athens, which sought dominion over this prestigious island; the wealth of the **Delian Confederacy**, founded after the Persian Wars to protect the Aegean cities, was harnessed to Athenian ends, and for a while Athens controlled the Sanctuary of Apollo. Athenian attempts to "purify" the island began with a decree (426 BC) that no one could die or give birth on Delos – the sick and the pregnant were shipped to the neighbouring island of **Rínia** – and culminated in the simple expedient of banishing the native population.

Delos recovered in Roman times and reached its peak of prosperity in the third and second centuries BC, after being declared a free port by its Roman overlords; by the start of the first century BC, its population was around 25,000. In the end, though, its undefended wealth brought ruin: first **Mithridates** of Pontus (88 BC), then the pirate **Athenodorus** (69 BC) plundered the treasures, and the island never recovered.

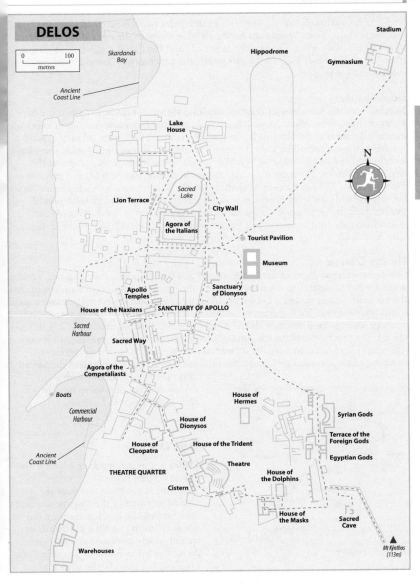

Sacred Way and Sanctuary of Apollo

The **Sacred Way** leads north from the far left corner of the Agora of the Competaliasts and was formerly lined with statues and the grandiose monuments of rival kings; walk up it to reach the three marble steps of the **Propýlaia** leading into the **Sanctuary of Apollo**. On your left is the Stoá of the Naxians, while against the north wall of the House of the Naxians, to the right, is the spot where a huge statue of Apollo (c.600 BC) stood in ancient times; parts of it can be seen behind the **Temple of Artemis** to the left. In 417 BC the Athenian general Nikias led a procession of priests across a

6

bridge of boats from Rínia to dedicate a bronze palm tree whose circular granite base you can still see. Three **Temples to Apollo** stand in a row to the right along the Sacred Way: the massive Delian Temple, the Athenian, and the Porinos, the earliest, dating from the sixth century BC. To the east stands the **Sanctuary of Dionysus** with its colossal marble phallus.

Lions' Quarter

Northwest of the Sanctuary of Dionysus, behind the small **Letóön** temple, is the huge **Agora of the Italians**, while on the left are replicas of the famous **lions**, their lean bodies masterfully executed by Naxians in the seventh century BC to ward off intruders who would have been unfamiliar with the fearful creatures. Of the original lions, three have disappeared and one – looted by Venetians in the seventeenth century– adorns the Arsenale in Venice. The remaining originals are in the site **museum** (Tues–Fri & Sun 8am–7pm, Sat & Mon 8am–3pm; included in the site entrance fee), whose nine rooms include a marble statue of Apollo, mosaic fragments and an extensive collection of phallic artefacts. Opposite the lions, tamarisk trees ring the site of the **Sacred Lake**, where Leto gave birth, clinging to a palm tree. On the other side of the lake is the City Wall, built – in 69 BC – too late to protect the treasures.

Theatre Quarter

Bear right from the Agora of the Competalists and you enter the residential area, known as the **Theatre Quarter**. The remnants of impressive private mansions are now named after their colourful main **mosaic** – Dionysus, Trident, Masks and Dolphins. The **theatre** itself seated no fewer than 5500 spectators; just below it and structurally almost as spectacular is a huge underground cistern with arched roof supports. Behind the theatre, a path leads towards the **Sanctuaries of the Foreign Gods**, serving the immigrant population. It then rises steeply up Mount Kýnthos for a **Sanctuary of Zeus and Athena** with spectacular views out to the surrounding islands. Near its base, a small side path leads to the **Sacred Cave**, a rock cleft covered with a remarkable roof of giant stone slabs – a Hellenistic shrine to Hercules.

SÝROS

Sýros

SÝROS is a living, working island with only a fleeting history of tourism, rendering it the most Greek of the Cyclades. There's a thriving, permanent community, the beaches are busy but not overflowing and the villages don't sprawl widely with new developments. As well as being home to a number of excellent restaurants, the island is known for its numerous shops selling *loukoúmia* (Turkish delight), *mandoláta* (nougat) and *halvadhópita* (soft nougat between disc-shaped wafers). In addition Sýros still honours its contribution to the development of **rembétika** music: Markos Vamvakaris, one of its prime proponents, hailed from Áno Sýros where a square has been named after him.

The island's sights – including the best beaches – are concentrated in the south and west; the north is unpopulated and barren, offering little interest. Most people tend to stay in **Ermoúpolis**, the island's and the Cyclades' capital, which offers better connections to a variety of beaches, none further than 15km away.

ARRIVAL AND GETTING AROUND

By plane The island is served by Olympic (Athens, 6 weekly; 35min; Thessaloniki 3 weekly; 1hr). There's no bus service from the airport, so you'll need to arrange a pick-up or take a taxi (around €8).

By ferry All ferries dock at Ermoúpolis, on the east coast.

Destinations Amorgós, Aigiáli (1 weekly; 6hr 30min); Anáfi (1–3 weekly; 11hr); Astypálea (1 weekly; 6hr 30min); Dhonoússa (1 weekly; 3hr 30min); Folégandhros (3 weekly; 5hr 30min); Ikaría (5–6 weekly; 3hr); Íos (1–2 weekly; 5–7hr); Lávrio via Kéa/Kýthnos (2–3 weekly; 5hr); Mílos/Kímolos (3–4 weekly; 6hr); Mýkonos (1–2 daily; 50min); Náxos (2–5 weekly; 2–3hr); Páros (2–5 weekly; 1hr 10min–6hr); Pátmos (1 weekly; 4hr); Pireás (2–3 daily; 3–4hr); Sámos (1 weekly; 5hr 30min); Santoríni (2–4 weekly; 5–8hr); Sérifos (3 weekly; 4hr); Sífnos (3 weekly; 5hr); Síkinos (1–2 weekly; 6hr 40min); Tínos (1 daily; 1hr).

By bus The bus station is south of the ferry docks on Akti Papagou in Ermoúpolis (☎ 22810 82575). Buses inside the city are free, but there are moves to start charging soon. Two hourly route loops run in opposite directions: Ermoúpoli to Galissás (20min), Fínikas (25min), Posidonía (30min), Mega Yialos (35min), Vari, Azólimnos then back to Ermoúpoli; and vice versa, from Ermoúpoli to Azólimnos (15min), Vari (20min), Mega Yialos (25min), Posidonía (30min), Fínikas and Galissas. There is also a seasonal route from Ermoúpoli to Kini (4–5 daily; 20min).

By taxi Sýros taxi drivers tend not to use the meter, so insist. Minimum fare (i.e. inside the city) should cost around €3.60 and from the port to Áno Sýros €5 (☎ 22810 84222). Taxis from the port add €3 extra.

By car or motorbike There are many car and motorbike rental agencies on the Ermoúpolis waterfront, including the reliable Gaviotis, Akti Papagou 20 (☎ 22810 86610).

INFORMATION AND TOURS

Information and tours TeamWork at Aktí Papágou 18 on the Ermoúpolis waterfront (daily 9am–9pm; ☎ 22810 83400, ⊗ teamwork.gr) is a great source of information and can help with accommodation, excursions and tickets. They also run a selection of tours, including to Ano Syros, a 3hr walking tour of Ermoúpolis (recommended) and a round-island tour.

Services There are several banks and half a dozen ATMs in Ermoúpolis, mostly around the waterfront. The post office is on Protopapadháki.

Ermoúpolis

Possessing an elegant collection of grand townhouses that rise majestically from the bustling, café-lined waterfront, **ERMOÚPOLIS** – once Greece's chief port – is one of the most striking towns in the Cyclades, and is certainly worth at least a night's stay.

Medieval Sýros was largely Catholic, but the influx of refugees from Psará and Híos during the nineteenth century created two distinct communities. Today, the Orthodox community accounts for two-thirds of the population; Lower Ermoúpolis is mostly Orthodox while the Catholics live in the Upper Town and in the majority of the villages. They do, however, commonly celebrate each other's festivals (including Easter on the Orthodox dates only), resulting in a vibrant mix of cultures that gives the island its colour.

Platía Miaoúli and around

The long, central square, **Platía Miaoúli**, is named after an admiral of the War of Independence whose statue stands there, and in the evenings the population parades in front of its arcades. Facing the platía, the Neoclassical **Town Hall** is one of the most beautiful in Greece, on a par with Athens' parliament building. Southeast of Platía Miaoúli, the partly pedestrianized street of Roïdi and its side streets are home to most of the town's better eating options.

Up the stepped street (Benáki) to the left of the town hall is a small **Archeological Museum** (summer: Tues–Thurs 9am–4pm, Fri–Sun 9am–9pm; winter Tues, Wed, Fri & Sun 8am–3pm; €2; ☎ 22810 88487) with three rooms of finds from Sýros, Páros

6

and Amorgós. To the left of the clocktower more steps climb up to **Vrondádho**, the hill that hosts the Orthodox quarter. The wonderful church of the **Anástasis** stands atop the hill, with its domed roof and panoramic views over Tínos and Mýkonos.

Below Platía Miaoúli, on Proïou, are the once-stylish but now rather scruffy **Casino** (daily noon–4am; ☎22810 84400, ⊛www.casinosyros.gr; €5 day membership) and the **Church of the Dormition** (daily: April–Aug 8am–6.30pm; Sept–March 7.30am–12.30pm & 4.30–5.30pm; free), which contains the town's top art treasure: a painting of the Assumption by **El Greco**, executed while he was around 20 years old.

North to Vapória

North of Platía Miaoúli is the **Apollon Theatre**, built like an Italian provincial opera house, which occasionally hosts performances: if there are no rehearsals you can visit the interior and its small museum (daily 10am–3pm; ☎ 22810 85192; €2). Further on up is the handsome Neoclassical Orthodox church of **Áyios Nikólaos**, built in 1848–70 with an impressive marble iconostasis (daily 8am–8pm; free). Beyond it lies the **Vapória** district, where the island's wealthiest shipowners, merchants and bankers built their mansions. Below Vapória are the Áyios Nikólaos **swimming platforms.**

6

Áno Sýros

On the taller hill 2km northwest of Platía Miaoúli is the intricate medieval quarter of **Áno Sýros**, with a clutch of Catholic churches below the cathedral of St George. Just below it lies the **Capuchin monastery of St Jean**, founded in 1535 as a poorhouse. Once up here it's worth visiting the local art and rembétika exhibitions, as well as personal items of the man himself at the **Markos Vamvakaris museum** (Sat & Sun 12.30–6pm; €1.50).

ACCOMMODATION   ERMOÚPOLIS

Hermes Platía Kanári ☎ 22810 83011/88011, ⓦ hermes-syros.com. Modernist 1960s hotel in a prime location, overlooking the port and home to a very popular seafront restaurant (mains €12). Ask for a room with waterfront views; the hotel is slightly away from the harbour hubbub and unaffected by noise. Breakfast included. **€75**

Palladion Proïou 60 ☎ 22810 86400, ⓦ palladion -hotel.com. Not far from the casino and one block from the port yet quiet, spotlessly clean, with attentive staff and reasonably sized rooms overlooking a garden – overall excellent value. Buffet breakfast €5pp. **€65**

Paradise Omírou 3 ☎ 22810 83204, ⓦ paradiserooms. gr. Modern, stylish rooms in a quiet part of town yet close

to the centre. All rooms have access to a pleasant shaded courtyard, while the top-floor rooms have good views. **€40**

Sea Colours Apartments Athinás 10 ☎ 22810 81181, ⓦ seacolours.gr. Traditionally decorated self-catering apartments with sea views (sleeping up to six people). They are just above the Áyios Nikólaos swimming platforms, a 5min walk from Platía Miaoúli. April–Nov. **€40**

★**Sýrou Mélathron** Babayiótou 5 ☎ 22810 85963, ⓦ syroumelathron.gr. Regal hotel in a restored 1856 mansion in the Vapória district, with elaborate ceilings, walnut furniture and a grand staircase. It has suites as well as spacious rooms, some with sea views (about €10 extra). Breakfast included. **€82**

EATING

Amvix Aktí Papágou 26 ☎ 22810 83989. Owned by Roberto, an Italian chef from Padua, since 1995, this trattoria offers a taste of real Italy. Best pizza and pasta on the island (mains €15). Daily noon–midnight.

Archontariki tis Maritsas Roïdi 8 ☎ 22810 86771. Very popular rustic taverna that serves island specialities, including its signature dish of mushroom and spicy local sausage casserole with peppers (€10). Daily noon–midnight.

Lilis Piazza, Áno Syros ☎ 22810 88087. An institution in the old town, with an unmatched view by the Kamares entrance, this is the taverna where Vamvakaris (see above) played his rembétika. It's been going since 1953, serving

Greek specialities from Asia Minor (€9) – expect the likes of *soutzoukakia Smyrna-style* (spicy meatballs). Daily noon–midnight.

Stin Ithaki tou Aï Klonos, corner with Ayíou Stefánou 1 ☎ 22810 82060, ⓦ estiatorio-ithakitouai.gr. Welcoming taverna serving traditional *ladherá* dishes (vegetables cooked in oil), as well as a good, cheap *souvláki* (€10). Daily noon–midnight.

Yiannena Platía Kanári ☎ 22810 82994. Popular, friendly spot, seemingly unchanged since the 1950s, serving great *souvláki* and other Greek standards (€8–9). Tues–Sun 11am–1am.

DRINKING AND NIGHTLIFE

Severo Pétrou Rálli ☎ 22810 88243. Busy, hipster space with neon décor: it starts as a café, becomes a snack bar at lunchtime then continues as a club after 10.30pm with a DJ playing lounge music until early in the morning when it starts serving coffees again. Draught beer €5. Daily 8am–7am.

Severo+ Lazareta ☎ 693 619 1872. The only clubbing option in town and it's not at all bad, playing mainstream dance music till 4am and then turning to Greek pop hits. The hangar-like interior holds 500 people, with the exterior terrace housing a further 800. Cocktails €9. Entrance is free, but there's a €10 fee for live gigs. Fri & Sat midnight–8am.

The beaches

Syros offers a small, but decent choice of **beaches**, which rarely become overwhelmingly crowded, even in high season. The best are located on the south and west coasts, within easy reach of Ermoúpolis, served by the circular bus route around the island (see p.399).

The southwest and south coasts

The first stop on the (anticlockwise) bus round-trip from Ermoúpolis is well-developed **Galissás**, the largest beach on the island. If you feel the urge to escape the crowds, walk ten minutes around the *Dolphin Bay Hotel* to reach the nudist beach of **Armeós**. You can also drive southwest to the end of the dirt road over the ridge of Charassónas and walk down (30min) to the **sea cave** of Áyios Stéfanos (signposted), with a remarkable chapel built inside.

A ten-minute bus ride south of Galissás, the colourful fishing village of **Fínikas** has a long and narrow beach protected from the road by a row of tamarisk trees. It's separated by a small headland from neighbouring **Agathopés**, Syros' best sandy beach, that faces a little offshore islet, Skhinonísi: be careful about taking photos here, as the Greek navy has a base next door. At the end of the road leading south 500m from Agathopés, **Kómito** is a small, quiet sandy bay below a private olive grove.

From Fínikas the road swings inland to **Poseidonía** (also known as Dellagrazia due to its Catholic church) and then southeast to **Mégas Yialós**, a diffuse resort with two beaches: Mégas Yialós, lined with shady tamarisks, and Ambéla, small and quiet with one taverna. Beyond here, the road passes the tiny, sheltered, family-friendly cove of **Akhládhi** to reach **Vári**, the most sheltered of the island's bays – something to remember when the *meltémi* is up. Its volleyball and racquetball facilities and the *Loco Verano* beach bar (see below) attract a younger, studenty crowd. The final resort on the circular tour is **Azólimnos**, accessed by a narrow road from Vári, or a wider one from Ermoúpolis.

Kíni

A separate bus runs to **Kíni** on the west coast, 7km from Ermoúpolis. It has umbrellas, sunbeds and tamarisk trees for shade, with several seasonal beachside tavernas. At the end of the beach, there's a rather tired-looking **aquarium** with fifteen displays of fish native to these waters (Tues–Sat 10am–2pm & 6–10pm; €2).

ACCOMMODATION
THE BEACHES

Akrothalasia Azólimnos ☎ 22810 61653. Astonishingly good value hotel, with self-catering studios next to the beach, a pool and children's pool, parking and a cafeteria on the premises. May–Sept. **€40**

Brazzera Fínikas ☎ 22810 79173, ⓦ brazzera.gr. Modern, well-situated hotel close to the beach, whose green furnishings tastefully match the green of the salt cedars in front. Large rooms with tiled floors adorned with flowers make this one of the best stays outside Ermoúpolis. Breakfast included. April–Oct. **€55**

Dolphin Bay Galissás ☎ 22810 42924, ⓦ dolphin-bay.gr. Luxurious hotel, with impressive views over the bay from its large swimming pool and bar. Most rooms suit families (two adults plus one or two children) and the complex includes an excellent restaurant (mains €15). Breakfast included. May–Sept. **€75**

EATING AND NIGHTLIFE

Loco Verano Vári ☎ 22810 62149, ⓔ locoveranosyros @gmail.com. With groove music playing on the sound system at a reasonable volume, this beach bar-cum-club attracts the youth of Syros during school and university holidays: cocktails €8. June–Sept daily 10am–late.

Niriídhes Akhládhi ☎ 6978 830 332. This fish taverna, the beach offshoot of the *Archontariki tis Maritsas* (see p.401) in Ermoúpolis, specializes in imaginative seafood dishes such as shrimp omelette, yet still has a place for time-honoured platters like grilled octopus (€13). May–Oct noon–midnight.

To Iliovasilema Galissás ☎ 22810 43325. A fine-dining seaside restaurant with an inventive menu and an excellent reputation: try the tuna carpaccio (€15) or moussaka baked in a clay pot (€10). Daily March–Nov noon–midnight.

Páros

With a gentle and undramatic landscape arranged around the central peak of Profítis Ilías, **PÁROS** has a little of everything one expects from a Greek island: old villages, monasteries, fishing harbours, nice beaches and varied nightlife. However, **Parikiá**, the capital, can be touristy and expensive, and it is very difficult finding rooms and beach space here in August, during which the port of **Náoussa** and the satellite island of Andíparos (see p.410), handle most of the overflow. Drinking and carousing is most people's idea of a holiday on Páros, so it's not surprising that both Parikiá and Náoussa have a wealth of pubs, bars and discos, with staggered happy hours. Happily, culture is also available, in the form of the Paleochristian church of **Ekatondapyliani** and an interesting **archeological museum**.

6

ARRIVAL AND GETTING AROUND   PÁROS

By plane Páros' new airport is 12km south of Parikiá, with regular Olympic flights from Athens (2–4 daily; 35min): buses meet flight arrivals in summer.

By ferry Parikiá is a major hub for inter-island ferry services and serves almost all islands in the Cyclades. There are two ferries from Páros to Andíparos: the first is a passenger ferry from Parikiá (see p.404) and the second is a car ferry from Poúnda, 7km south of Parikiá (every 30–45min in summer 7.15am–1.30am; less frequently out of season). For more information on ferries, call ☎ 22840 21240.

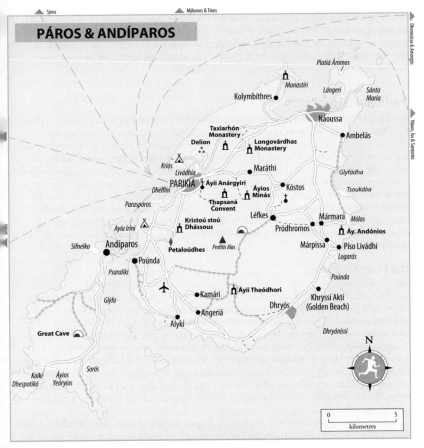

6

Destinations Amorgós, Aigiali and Katápola(1 weekly; 6hr); Áno Koufoníssi (1 weekly; 6hr 40min); Anáfi (1–2 weekly; 8–9hr); Andíparos (hourly in season; 40min); Astypálea (1–2 weekly; 5hr); Dhonoússa (1 weekly; 2hr 50min); Irakliá (1 weekly; 2hr 30min); Iráklio Crete (1–2 daily; 3hr 40min); Folégandhros (3 weekly; 3hr 30min); Íos (3–4 daily; 1hr–2hr 20min); Kálymnos (1–2 weekly; 6hr 30min); Kímolos (2 weekly; 4hr 30min); Kós (1–2 weekly; 5hr 30min); Lávrio via Kéa/Kýthnos (1–3 weekly; 8–13hr); Mílos (4–5 weekly; 5hr 45min–7hr); Mýkonos (4–5 daily; 30min–1hr 30min); Náxos (3–6 daily; 35min–1hr 30min); Pireás (3–5 daily; 3–6hr); Rhodes/Tílos (July & Aug 1–2 weekly; 15–24hr); Samos (1 weekly; 7hr 50min); Santoríni (3–6 daily; 2–3hr); Sérifos (2–4 weekly; 6hr 30min); Sífnos (2–4 weekly; 5hr 35min); Síkinos (3 weekly; 3hr 40min); Skhinoússa (1 weekly; 3hr 15min); Sýros (1 daily; 1hr 35min); Tínos (2–4 daily; 1hr–1hr 30min).

Travel agents Polos Tours (☎ 22840 22333, ⓦ polostours.gr) in Parikiá is one of the better travel agencies, offering boat trips, bus tours and ferry pick-ups.

By bus The bus station is 100m or so west of the ferry dock. Note that there are two places called Poúnda on Páros, one being the west-coast port, the other a beach on the east coast (see p.410).

Destinations Dhryós (3–5 daily; 1hr); Náoussa (hourly through the night in high season; 20min); Poúnda for Andíparos (1–2 hourly; 20min).

By car or motorbike There are many rental outfits near the ferry docks in Parikiá but walk a few hundred metres further on to Paros European (☎ 22840 21771, ⓦ parosrentcar.com) or Karent (☎ 22840 22303, ⓦ karent.gr), for better deals and newer cars. Traffic rules are strictly enforced and many streets are one way. Parking is only allowed in designated areas and parts of the Parikiá seafront are closed to traffic on summer evenings.

INFORMATION

Tourist information There is a tourist office inside the windmill by the ferry docks in Parikiá, but, because it's manned by volunteers, the hours are erratic (officially daily 9am–9pm). Bus timetables are posted by Parikiá's main bus station.

Services There is no shortage of banks or ATMs in Parikiá. The island's only post office is west of the windmill, past the ancient cemetery. Luggage can be left at various travel agents (look for signs) along Parikiá's waterfront.

Parikiá and around

Bustling **PARIKIÁ** sets the tone architecturally for the rest of Páros, its ranks of typically Cycladic white houses punctuated by the occasional Venetian-style building and church domes. The town's sights apart, the real attraction of Parikiá is simply to wander the town itself, especially along the meandering **old market street** (Agorá) and adjoining Grávari. Arcaded lanes lead past Venetian-influenced villas, traditional island dwellings, ornate wall-fountains and trendy shops. The market street culminates in a formidable **kástro** (1260), whose surviving east wall incorporates a fifth-century BC round tower and is constructed using masonry pillaged from a nearby temple of Athena which is still highly visible. On the seafront behind the port police are the exposed, excavated ruins of an **ancient cemetery** used from the eighth century BC until the third century AD.

The Ekatondapyliani

Daily 7am–9pm • Free

Just beyond the central clutter of the ferry port, Parikiá has the most architecturally important church in the Aegean – the **Katopoliani** ("facing the town"). Later Greek scholars purified the name and connected it with past glories, so they changed it to **Ekatondapyliani** ("The One Hundred Gated"), a name that baffles today's visitors. Tradition, supported by recent excavations, claims that it was originally founded in 326 AD by St Helena, mother of Emperor Constantine, but what's visible today stems from a sixth-century Justinian reconstruction. Look through the iconostasis (which still retains its ancient marble frame) to see two unique features: a set of amphitheatric steps, the **synthronon**, where the priests used to chant, and the **ciborium**, a marble canopy over the altar.

Enclosed by a great front wall, sign of an Imperial-built church, the church is in fact three interlocking buildings. The oldest, the chapel of **Áyios Nikólaos** to the left of the

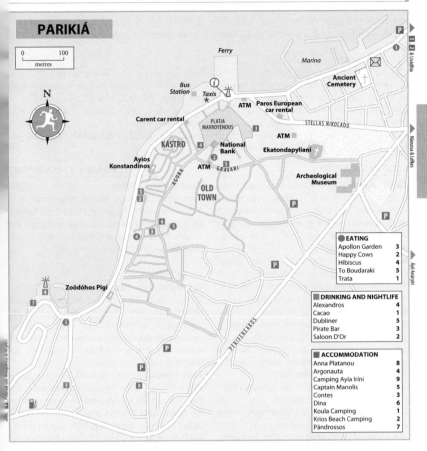

apse, is an adaptation of a pagan building dating from the early fourth century BC. On the right, there is another building attached, housing a Paleochristian **baptistry**, where the initiate used to dip in a cross-shaped pool. Inside the church courtyard is a small **Byzantine museum** displaying a collection of icons (€2; ☎ 22840 21243).

Archeological Museum

Behind the Ekatondapyliani • Tues–Sun 8am–3pm • €2 • ☎ 22840 21231

Parikiá's **Archeological Museum** has a good collection and is definitely worth a visit. Its prize exhibits are a large Gorgon, a fifth-century winged Nike by **Skopas** and – hidden at the back of the main room – a piece of the **Parian Chronicle**, a social and cultural history of Greece up to 264 BC engraved in marble.

Beaches near Parikiá

Less than 1km north of the harbour lies the twin crescent of **Livádhia** beach, with shallow waters and shaded by salt cedars; further on lies **Kriós** beach, much better, served by *kaïki* from just to the right of the ferry terminal (€4). The beaches south along the asphalt road are even better: the first unsurfaced side track leads to the small, sheltered **Dhelfíni**; fifteen minutes further on is **Paraspóros** near the remains of an ancient temple to Asklepios, the god of healing. Continuing for 45 minutes (or a short hop by bus) brings you to arguably the best of the bunch, **Ayía Iríni**, a palm-fringed beach with fine sand, a taverna and a beautiful **campsite** (see below).

Petaloúdhes

Not far from the turning to Ayía Iríni, 7km from Parikiá, is the "**Valley of the Butterflies**"(Petaloúdhes), a walled-in private oasis where millions of Jersey tiger moths perch on the foliage in summer (June–Sept 9am–8pm; €2; ☎ 22840 91211/91554). The trip can be combined with a visit to the eighteenth-century nunnery of **Áyios Arsénios**, at the crest of a ridge 1km to the north. Only women are allowed in the sanctuary, although men can wait in the courtyard. Petaloúdhes can also be reached from Parikiá by bus during the summer months.

ACCOMMODATION   PARIKIÁ AND AROUND

Anna Platanou 600m southwest of the port, Parikiá ☎ 22840 21751, ⓦ annaplatanou.gr. This boutique family-run three-star hotel has clean, refurbished rooms in a peaceful location overlooking an enticing swimming pool with bar. Continental breakfast €7pp. Port transfers available. May–Sept. **€75**

Argonauta Parikiá Waterfront ☎ 22840 21440, ⓦ argonauta.gr. Stylish hotel in the white-and-blue Cycladic fashion with smart rooms arranged around a beautiful stone courtyard. There's a good restaurant below. April–Oct. **€85**

★ **Captain Manolis** Platía Mavrogenous, Parikiá ☎ 22840 21244, ⓦ paroswelcome.com. Central – behind the National Bank – but unbelievably quiet; the basic, spotlessly clean rooms have a/c and a fridge, plus ivy-covered balconies or verandas facing a beautiful communal garden with fruit trees. **€58**

Contes Opposite the ferry dock, Parikiá ☎ 22840 25001, ⓦ hotelkontes.gr. Opened in 2017 on the waterfront, this hotel has large designer rooms in beige and lime green with double-glazed and mosquito-netted windows. One of the few hotels with facilities for mobility-impaired guests. Breakfast included **€100**

Dina Agorá, Parikiá ☎ 22840 21325, ⓦ hoteldina.com. Small family pension, right in the middle of the Agorá action by the Ayía Triádha church. Rooms at the front are high-ceilinged and have balconies that look down on the continuous stream of people: they're double-glazed, but if you're sensitive to the noise, either come home when the bars close or ask for a room at the back. May–Oct. **€50**

Pandrossos Parikiá ☎ 22840 22903, ⓦ pandrossosparos.com. Perched magnificently on a high hill over-looking the port and beyond, this four-star hotel has a good restaurant, a deep swimming pool and colourful rooms with balconies offering exceptional sunset views. Breakfast included. March–Nov. **€80**

CAMPSITES

★ **Camping Ayia Irini** Ayía Iríni ☎ 22840 91496, ⓦ campingai.gr. One of the most atmospheric campsites in the Cyclades: you're right on the beach, but it feels like you're camping in someone's overgrown garden. It has its own cheap taverna, although the olive, citrus and summer-ripening fruit trees also provide free sustenance. Bus transfers organized. June to mid-Sept. **€16**

Koula Camping Parikiá, 900m east of the bus station ☎ 22840 22081, ⓦ campingkoula.gr. Very close to the town, this campsite is a reasonable choice for a night or two a wide range of cabins or bungalows, and even a covered area for just sleeping bags (tents available for rent; €4). The owners also run a cheap but good restaurant next door – go there if reception is closed. April–Oct. **€12**

★ **Krios Beach Camping** Krios ☎ 22840 21705, ⓦ krios-camping.gr. Excellent facilities, including a pool and wi-fi, in a shady, flat site, 2km east of Parikiá, supplemented by a cool beach bar next door. Frequent Greek parties, which include plate smashing, see crowds specially bussed in from Parikiá; they finish early enough so that you can enjoy your sleep. Free pick-ups from port. June–Sept. **€18.50**

EATING

★ **Apollon Garden** Off Agorá, Parikiá ☎ 22840 21875, ⓦ apollongarden.gr. Housed in a converted 1920s olive press with a large garden near the market, this is one of the island's classiest restaurants. Despite high prices, its popularity never wanes – the pork with prunes and apricots (€19) is highly recommended. April–Oct daily 7pm–late.

Happy Cows Off Gravari, Parikiá ☎ 6981053607. Eclectic former vegetarian restaurant in a side street

behind the National Bank that now makes several concessions to carnivores (chicken and duck). Reasonably priced, yet imaginative, dishes (mains around €12), sourced fully with local ingredients. Reserve if eating after 9pm. April–Oct daily 6pm–midnight.

Hibiscus Waterfront, Parikiá ☎ 22840 21849. Páros' oldest Greek restaurant, in a great, central spot on the waterfront south of the windmill, overlooking the sea; it serves up the usual Greek dishes, but is best known for its

6

generous-sized pizzas baked in a wood-fired oven (€12). April–Oct daily noon–midnight.

To Boudaraki Southwest of the old town, by the bridge, Parikiá ☎ 22840 22297. This ouzerí is highly rated by locals and provides good service even when it's packed – you can expect an excellent selection of mezédhes

and mains (€12), as well as home-made *baklavá* to finish. May to mid-Oct daily noon–4pm & 6pm–midnight.

Trata Parikiá ☎ 22840 24651. This popular, family-run taverna specializes in serving large plates of tasty seafood (€12) in the quieter, eastern edge of the waterfront. April–Oct daily noon–midnight.

DRINKING AND NIGHTLIFE

Alexandros Parikiá ☎ 6930 671 269, ⊛ alexandros-cafe.gr. The best location for a sophisticated evening drink in a romantic spot around a real windmill. Set apart from the town, on an elevated promontory at the southern end of the promenade, it has wonderful sunset views which you can enjoy while listening to classical music. Cocktails €10-12. June–Sept daily 6.30pm–3am.

Cacao Parikiá. Upstairs bar at the seafront, east of the windmill and up the steps from the kiosk, playing jazz and lounge music, with good sunset views and excellent cocktails (€7). It opens early for breakfast, but the crowds start coming to watch the sunset around 8pm and then return after midnight. April–Oct daily 8.30am–late.

Dubliner Parikiá ☎ 22840 21113, ⊛ dubliner.gr. Large, brash and youthful dance complex set back from the main

drag just off the seafront bridge. It comprises three loud bars – opening gradually as the summer hots up – a main club and an outdoors chill-out area. Entrance with first drink €5. June–Sept daily 11pm–6am.

Pirate Bar Parikiá ☎ 22840 21224. Popular, established jazz and swing bar near the town hall, opposite *Dina*. It's rather small, so most of its clientele tend to stand outside. Cocktails from €8.50. April–Oct daily 10am–2pm & 6.30pm–3am.

Saloon D'Or Parikiá ☎ 22840 22176. Rowdy but fun spot on the seafront south of the windmill, with cheap drinks and reggae music. It has hookahs in various flavours, as well as comfortable oriental divans and settees to sink in and enjoy them. Cocktails €7. May–Sept daily 8.30pm–5am.

Alykí

There's little to stop for southwest of Parikiá until **Poúnda**, 6km away, the island's watersports centre. A further 6km south, past the airport, you reach **ALYKÍ**, a pretty resort on a picturesque bay with two beach sections: one pebbly and bare and the other sandy and shaded.

Skorpios Cycladic Folk Museum

Entrance to Alykí • Daily May–Sept 9.30am–2pm • Free • ☎ 22840 91129

The idiosyncratic **Skorpios Cycladic Folk Museum** houses a collection of model boats and miniatures of various typical buildings from the Cyclades. You can find here painstakingly reconstructed examples, from the dovecotes of Tínos to Náxos cereal grinding mills, and from the Lion Avenue of Delos to the windmills of Mýkonos. It's all a bit kitsch, but fascinating nevertheless.

ACCOMMODATION AND EATING ALYKÍ

Galatis Alykí ☎ 22840 91355, ⊛ galatishotel.gr. The best hotel outside Parikiá and Náoussa, several notches up from merely comfortable, with a pool, a restaurant

and (mostly) sea-view rooms including some which are wheelchair-accessible. Breakfast included. April–Oct. €50

Náoussa and around

The more fashionable alternative to Parikiá, **NÁOUSSA** is a major resort town, with modern hotels and attendant trappings, which developed around a charming little port whose layout has not been adversely affected. The local festivals are still celebrated with enthusiasm, especially the re-enactment on August 23 of a naval victory over the pirates, followed by a fireworks display.

Despite a 3am music curfew, the nightlife here is on a par with Parikiá, though most people come for the local beaches. **Áyii Anáryiri** is just off the path that goes east of Náoussa's harbour, while **Pipéri** is a couple of minutes' walk west. To the northwest,

4km on the road around the bay brings you to **Kolymbíthres**, with its wind- and sea-sculpted rock formations. Beyond that, **Monastíri beach**, below the abandoned Pródhromos monastery, is similarly attractive for diving and snorkelling. A regular summer *kaïki* service connects both to Náoussa (€6 return).

Northeast of town the sands are better still: after the glorious sandbank of **Xínari** you reach the barren **Viglákia** headland, also accessible by *kaïki*. It is dotted with good surfing beaches such as **Platiá Ámmos**, on the northeastern tip of the island, and **Lángeri** which is backed by dunes; a walk ten minutes south of the main beach brings you to the mostly gay section. The best surfing beach, however, is at **Sánta María**, an expanse of sand 6km by road from Náoussa.

Ambelás, 3km southeast of Náoussa, has a safe, sheltered beach, as you might guess from the number of fishing boats moored here. It's also the start of a 6km-long, partly-paved coast road that leads south, passing several undeveloped shady coves on the way such as **Glyfádha** and the almost deserted **Tsoukália**, until you reach the impressive spread of **Mólos beach**, never particularly crowded. From here you can pick up the asphalted road straight back to Náoussa or through the **inland villages** back to Parikiá.

ACCOMMODATION
NÁOUSSA AND AROUND

Astir of Paros Kolymbíthres ☎ 22840 51976, ⊛ astirofparos.gr. Superb, lavish five-star resort on the road to Kolymbíthres with marble baths, huge balconies and excellent service. Its eighteen-acre site includes two restaurants, a large pool, children's pool, sushi bar, tennis court, three-hole golf course and even a wedding chapel. April–Oct. **€260**

Christiana Ambelás ☎ 22840 51573, ⊛ christianahotel.gr. Ever-improving, good-value hotel, 3km from Náoussa, with a cool pool and friendly proprietors; they have rooms and fully-equipped apartments, most with seaview balconies. The in-house restaurant is the best in the area for fresh fish. Breakfast included. Easter–Oct. **€50**

Mr & Mrs White House on the ring road around Náoussa ☎ 22840 55207 ⊛ mrandmrswhitehotel.

com. Opened in June 2017, this boutique hotel with grey-and-white minimalist decor is the perfect hideaway for couples: it has two great pools, a snack bar and car park. May–Sept. **€150**

Stella Náoussa ☎ 22840 21367, ⊛ hotelstella.gr. Out of season, you should be able to haggle for reduced prices at this basic but well-located hotel with rooms arranged around its own garden, several blocks inland from the old harbour. In high season, prices can triple. **€55**

Surfing Beach Village Sánta María ☎ 22840 52492/3, ⊛ surfbeach.gr. A well-organized resort-campsite where surfers rub shoulders with families. The range of watersports on offer is staggering, with a great, long pool, two restaurants, a café, beach huts and en-suite bungalows with a/c. Courtesy minibus to and from Parikiá. June–Sept. Camping **€10**, bungalow **€50**

EATING

Fitzadakis Náoussa ☎ 22840 51205. Sensible prices, good portions and high quality food, this excellent grill restaurant is the locals' choice, with people even travelling here from Parikiá for dinner. It serves the freshest seafood in Naoussa – try the shrimps in ouzo and saffron (€15) or crayfish sporzetto (€16). Easter–Oct daily noon–midnight.

Ouzerí ton Naftikon Náoussa ☎ 22840 51662. Probably the best *mezedhopolío* in the harbour area. Offers

fresh fish and a rather standard Greek menu (mains €8), but has a reputation second to none. Come before 9pm or you won't find a seat. April–Oct daily 6.30pm–1am.

Yemeni Náoussa ☎ 22840 51445, ⊛ yemeni.gr. Popular family restaurant in the winding streets of central Náoussa, offering traditional Greek dishes for around €14–16. Everything comes from the family farm – from the greens and the chicken to the oil you pour on your salad. Easter–Oct daily 6pm–midnight.

DRINKING AND NIGHTLIFE

Akanthus Potami district, Naoussa. Classic club playing pop hits and frequented mainly by the under-30s. The script is predictable enough – beer will flow, patrons will dance on the tables and holiday romances will blossom – but it's still great fun. Entrance fee €5. Mid-July to mid-Sept (days vary) 11pm–6am.

Barbarossa Náoussa ☎ 22840 51391. Chic bar bathed in candle-light at the far end of the harbour (not to be confused with the expensive restaurant at the opposite end). Frequented mostly by twenty-something Greeks, this may be the place to try your language skills. Cocktails from €8. June–Sept daily 7pm–3.30am.

6

THE INLAND VILLAGES

Most people bypass Páros interior, but on a cooler day try walking the **medieval flagstoned path** that once linked both sides of the island. Start from the main square of the village of **Mármara** and go west. First up is **Pródhromos**, an old fortified farming settlement with defensive walls girding its nearby monastery. **Léfkes** itself, 5km from Pródhromos, is perhaps the most unspoilt settlement on Páros. The town flourished from the seventeenth century on, its population swollen by refugees fleeing from coastal piracy; indeed it was the island's capital during most of the Ottoman period. Léfkes' marbled alleyways and amphitheatrical setting are unparalleled – and undisturbed by motor vehicles, which are banned from the town centre. Another 5km towards Parikiá and you hit **Maráthi**, from where Parian marble was supplied to much of Europe. Considered second only to Carrara marble, the last slabs were mined here by the French in 1844 for **Napoleon's tomb** in Les Invalides. Just east of the village, marked paths lead to two huge entrances of ancient marble mines which can be visited with an organized tour only. From Maráthi, it's easy enough to pick up the bus on to Parikiá.

Sommaripa Náoussa ☎ 22840 55233. On a first-floor balcony overlooking the harbour, this popular bar is open all year; Manolis, the friendly owner, inherited the building from his grandfather whom you can see featured in the "Kalimera Griechenland" German poster over the door. Elaborate cocktails for every mood from €8. Daily 9.30pm–3.30am.

The southeast coast

The coast southeast of the inland junction at **Marpíssa** – itself a maze of winding alleys and ageing archways overhung by floral balconies – is comparatively off the tourist radar, yet it is easily reachable by regular buses during the summer and boasts some magnificent beaches.

The first resort you reach, **Píso Livádhi**, was once a quiet fishing village, but it is now dominated by open-air car parks and relatively indifferent tavernas. However, between here and **Dhryós** to the south there are no fewer than four excellent beaches. **Logarás** just over the promontory from Píso Livádhi has a superb stretch of sand, while the next beach, **Poúnda** (not to be confused with the port of the same name on the west coast), is home to a beach club with parties that go on well into the night. The final two are the twin windsurfing beaches of **New** and **Old Khrissí Akti** (Golden Beach), the main resorts in the southeast.

Dhryós, the end of the bus routes, is the only settlement of any size in this part of Páros. Although the village is mostly modern and characterless, it has an attractive, quiet beach.

ACCOMMODATION AND EATING   **THE SOUTHEAST COAST**

Fisilanis Logarás ☎ 22840 41734. In operation since 1964, this is an outstanding-value family hotel and taverna (mains €8) on the beach worth experiencing if only for a few days. Well-stocked self-catering rooms with sea views, friendly service and unbeatable prices. Breakfast included. April–Oct. **€52**

Golden Beach Khrissí Akti ☎ 22840 41366, ⓦ goldenbeach.gr. The dominant hotel on the Old Golden Beach refurbished and expanded in 2017: there are windsurfing facilities next door, a fashion shop, a good adjoining restaurant open for breakfast through to dinner (mains €8–10) and a pool with a beach bar (open until 2am; cocktails from €8). Breakfast included. April–Oct. **€85**

Andíparos

ANDÍPAROS is no longer a secret destination: the waterfront is lined with hotels and apartments, and in high season it can be full, though in recent years families have displaced the former young, international crowd. However, the island has retained its friendly backwoods atmosphere and has a lot going for it, including good sandy beaches and a remarkable cave. Furthermore, rooms and hotels here are much less expensive than on Páros.

ARRIVAL AND GETTING AROUND

By ferry There are ferries to Andíparos Town from two different ports on Páros: the passenger-only ferry comes from Parikiá (see p.403), while the car ferry leaves from Poúnda, 7km south of Parikiá (see p.403).

By bus The bus stop is by the ferry disembarkation point;

from here you can get to the Great Cave (30min) and Áyios Yeóryios (50min).

By car or motorbike Antiparos Europcar (☎22840 61346, ⓦantiparos-cars.com) is a good rental outlet near the ferry dock.

6

INFORMATION AND ACTIVITIES

Services There's a bank on the waterfront in Andíparos Town, as well as a small post office.

Travel agents Oliaros Tours (☎22840 61231, ⓦantiparostravel.gr) on the main shopping street in Andíparos Town can help with accommodation, boat and

plane tickets, excursions and car rental. They also operate a currency exchange and a postal courier service.

Diving Blue Island Divers (☎22840 61767, ⓦblueisland-divers.gr) on Andíparos Town waterfront offers several PADI diving courses starting from €240.

Andíparos Town

Most of the population lives in the large low-lying **ANDÍPAROS TOWN**, across the narrow straits from Páros, the new development on the outskirts concealing an attractive traditional settlement. A long, flagstoned pedestrian street forms its backbone, leading from the jetty to the Cycladic houses around the outer wall of the **kástro**. It was built by Leonardo Loredano in the 1440s as a fortified settlement safe from pirate raids – his family coat of arms can still be seen on a house in the courtyard. The only way in is through a pointed archway from the main square, where several cafés are shaded by a giant eucalyptus. Inside, more whitewashed houses surround two churches and a cistern built into the surviving base of the central tower. The town has also developed into a prime **diving** centre.

ACCOMMODATION

Camping Antiparos ☎22840 61221, ⓦcamping-antiparos.gr. This fully equipped campsite is a 10min walk northeast of town along a track, next to its own nudist beach; the water here is shallow enough for campers to wade across to the neighbouring islet of Dhipló. May–Sept. **€17**

Kouros Village ☎22840 61084/5, ⓦkouros-village.gr. If proof were needed that Andíparos is value for money you need only visit this extensive resort. It has a large, clean pool, a restaurant with panoramic views (mains €6), an

open-air dancefloor and apartment-sized rooms. May–Oct. **€70**

Mantalena ☎22840 61206, ⓦhotelmantalena.gr. In 1960 a Greek film, *Mantalena*, was shot on Andíparos by director George Roussos. Three years later his brother built this hotel north of the jetty, which is still run by his family. This is one of the more fashionable places on Andíparos and has large rooms with balconies and satellite TV – plus some apartments in the old town. Breakfast €7. May–Oct. **€55**

EATING AND DRINKING

Anargyros ☎22840 61204. The most central taverna in the port, where you can rest assured that the daily special (around €8) will be also be consumed later by the owner's family. June–Sept daily 10am–midnight.

Boogaloo ☎69782 30103, ⓦboogaloo.gr. An innovative cocktail bar (cocktails €9) that mutates into a laidback late-night club. This is a place for the very young that will make you feel nostalgic for your salad days, if you're over 30. June–Sept daily 6pm–6am.

The beaches

Andíparos' **beaches** begin right outside town: **Psaralíki**, just to the south with golden sand and tamarisks for shade, is much better than **Sifnéïko** on the opposite side of the island. Villa development is starting to follow the surfaced road down the east coast, but has yet to get out of hand. **Glýfa**, 4km down, is another good beach, while, in the southeast of the island, **Sorós** is by far the most bewitching beach on the island. On the southwest coast there are some fine sand dunes at **Áyios Yeóryios**, the end of the surfaced road. From there, a *kaïki* makes a daily trip (at 11am) to the uninhabited, but archeologically rich, island of **Dhespotikó**, opposite.

ACCOMMODATION AND EATING | **THE BEACHES**

Dolphin San Giorgio Áyios Yeóryios ☎ 22840 24506, ⓦ dolphinantiparos.gr. Modern studios sleeping up to four people, with large verandas right on the beach. There's a café-bar for breakfast and lunch as well as a grill for dinner. Although off the beaten track, this is a lively hotel, offering a range of excursions and activities. Four nights minimum. Breakfast included. May–Sept. **€95**

The Great Cave

Áyios Ioánnis Hill • Summer daily 10am–3.30pm • €5 • Buses from Andíparos Town (30min)

The **Great Cave** in the centre of the island is the chief attraction for day-trippers. In these eerie chambers the Marquis de Nointel, Louis XIV's ambassador to Constantinople, celebrated Christmas Mass in 1673 while a retinue of five hundred, including painters, pirates, Jesuits and Turks, looked on; at the exact moment of midnight explosives were detonated to emphasize the enormity of the event. Although electric lights and cement steps have diminished its mystery and grandeur, the cave remains impressive. Check out the historical graffiti carved over the centuries.

Náxos

NÁXOS is the largest and most fertile of all the Cyclades islands and with its green and mountainous highland scenery it appears immediately dissimilar to its neighbours. The difference is accentuated by the **unique architecture** of many of the interior villages: the Venetian Duchy of the Aegean, headquartered here from 1204 to 1537, left towers and fortified mansions scattered throughout the island, while medieval Cretan refugees bestowed a singular character upon Náxos' eastern settlements.

Today Náxos could easily support itself without visitors by relying on its production of potatoes, olives, grapes and lemons, but it has thrown in its lot with mass tourism, so that parts of the island are now almost as busy as Páros (see p.403) in season. The island has plenty to see if you know where to look: the highest mountains in the Cyclades, intriguing central valleys, a spectacular north coast and long, marvellously sandy beaches in the southwest. It is also renowned for its wines, cheese and *kítron*, a sweet liqueur distilled from the leaves of this citrus tree and available in green, yellow or clear varieties depending on strength and sugar level.

ARRIVAL AND GETTING AROUND | **NÁXOS**

By plane Náxos is served by regular Olympic flights from Athens (1–3 daily; 45min). From the airport it's a 10min bus ride to Náxos Town (€12).

By ferry Ferries dock in the northern harbour quay of Náxos Town.

Destinations Amorgós, Aigiáli (3–4 weekly; 3hr–5hr 20min); Amorgós, Katápola (1–2 daily; 4hr); Anáfi (1–3 weekly; 3hr 45min–8hr); Áno Koufoníssi (1–3 daily; 1hr–2hr 30min); Ándhros (1 daily; 4hr); Astypálea (2–4 weekly; 3hr 45min); Dhonoússa (3–4 weekly; 4hr); Folégandhros (1–2 daily; 2hr–3hr 40min); Íos (1–2 daily; 1hr–1hr 30min); Iráklio Crete (4–5 weekly; 3hr 40min); Irakliá (1–2 daily; 1hr 30min); Kálymnos (1–2 weekly; 6hr); Lávrio via Kéa-Kýthnos (1 weekly; 8hr); Mílos (1–2 weekly; 6hr); Mýkonos (3–6 daily; 1hr 10min–2hr); Nísyros (1–2 weekly; 9hr 30min); Páros (3–6 daily; 25–45min); Pireás (4–6 daily; 4–6hr); Rafína (1 daily; 6hr); Rhodes/ Tílos (1 weekly; 12hr); Sámos (1 weekly; 7hr 30min); Santoríni (4–6 daily; 2hr); Skhinoússa (1–2 daily; 2hr); Sérifos (1–3 weekly; 5hr 30min–8hr); Sífnos (1–3 weekly; 4hr 30min); Síkinos (1–2 weekly; 3hr 15min); Sýros (2–3 weekly; 2hr 40min–4hr); Tínos (3–4 daily; 1hr 50min).

By bus The bus station (☎ 22850 22291, ⓦ naxosdestinations.com) is opposite the main dock.

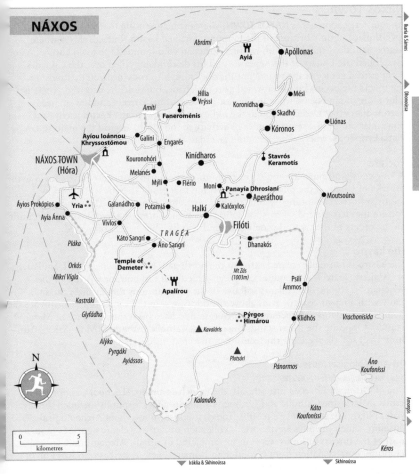

NÁXOS

Printed timetables are available and change monthly. The travel agents in the KTEL office at the bus station runs a daily bus excursion around the island (8hr; €25).

Destinations Aperáthou (6 daily; 1hr); Apóllonas (4 daily; 1hr; 2hr via scenic coastal route); Áyios Prokópios/Ayía Ánna/Pláka (10 daily; mid-June to Aug every 30min; 15min); Engarés (2 daily; 15min); Filotí/Hálki (7–8 daily; 45min); Kastráki-Pyrgáki (4 daily; 45min); Pláka (10 daily; July & Aug every 30min; 30min).

By car or motorbike The best one-day drive is Halkí–Filotí–Aperáthou–Apóllonas returning via the northern coastal route. Auto Tour Rent-a-Car by the bus station in Náxos Town (☎ 22850 25480, ⓦ www.naxosrentacar.com) rents cars and offers a wealth of information.

By taxi 24hr taxis at ☎ 22850 22444.

INFORMATION AND ACTIVITIES

Services The post office is north of the Town Hall square in Náxos Town.

Travel agents Excursions around Náxos and to other islands can be booked at Zas Travel (☎ 22850 23330) on the seafront near the jetty. Proto Tourism (☎ 22850 24949, ⓦ proto-tourism.com) opposite the bus station has left luggage facilities (lockers €6/day or bags €1.50 each) and can help with private room accommodation.

Watersports Flisvos Sportsclub (☎ 22850 22935, ⓦ flisvos-sportclub.com) at Áyios Yeóryios beach runs windsurfing courses, while Blue Fin Divers (☎ 22850 42629, ⓦ bluefindivers.gr) on Áyios Prokópios beach is a PADI diving centre that runs children's programmes (over 8s).

Náxos Town

As your ferry approaches **NÁXOS TOWN**, you can't help sensing that this is a really special place, if only because of the looming, fortified **kástro**. Indeed, this is where Marco Sanudo – the thirteenth-century Venetian who founded the town and established the Duchy of the Aegean – and his descendants ruled over the Cyclades. A superficial glance at the waterfront may be enough to convince you that most of the town's life occurs by the crowded port esplanade, but don't be deceived. There is a lot more life in Náxos Town in the vast network of backstreets and low-arched narrow alleys that lead up through the old town, **Boúrgo**, to the **kástro** itself. And don't miss out on the second centre of activity to the south, around the main square, **Platía Evripéous**, where there are more tavernas, shops and cafés.

Portára

A long causeway, built to protect the harbour to the north, connects Náxos Town with the islet of Palátia – the place where, according to legend, Theseus was duped by Dionysos into abandoning Ariadne on his way home from Crete. The famous stone **Portára** that has greeted visitors for 2500 years is the portal of a temple of Apollo, built on the orders of the tyrant Lygdamis around 530 BC, but never completed.

The kástro

The **kástro** is normally entered through the **north gate** (also known as the Traní Pórta or "Majestic Gate"), a splendid example of a medieval fort entrance. A few of the Venetians' Catholic descendants still live in the old mansions that encircle the site, many with ancient coats of arms above the doorways. In the centre of the kástro are the plain stone remains of a **rectangular tower**, said to have been the residence of Marco Sanudo. Opposite the tower stands the restored **Catholic Cathedral** (Mon–Sat 9.30am–3pm; free) still displaying a thirteenth-century crest inside.

The Archeological Museum

Kástro • Tues–Sun 8am–3pm • €2 • ☎ 22850 22725

One of Ottoman Greece's first schools, the **French Commercial School** was opened by Jesuits in 1627 for Catholic and Orthodox students alike: its pupils included, briefly, writer Nikos Kazantzakis (see p.808). Today, it houses an excellent **Archeological Museum**, which includes an important collection of Early Cycladic figurines (note how most of the throats or limbs were cut in some kind of ritual), Archaic and Classical sculpture, pottery dating from Neolithic to Roman times, as well as obsidian knives and spectacular gold rosettes. On the terrace, a Hellenistic-period mosaic floor shows a Nereid (sea nymph) astride a bull surrounded by deer and peacocks.

Town beaches

Grótta, just to the northeast of the town, is the easiest **beach** to reach. It's not ideal for swimming but snorkellers can spot the remains of submerged Mycenaean buildings. The other town beach, **Áyios Yeóryios**, is an improvement: a long sandy bay fringed by the town's southern accommodation area, it's within ten minutes' walking distance from Platía Evripéous.

ACCOMMODATION NÁXOS TOWN

Apollon Fontana ☎ 22850 22468, ⊚ apollonhotel-naxos.gr. Its reception dwarfed by the church outside, this is a family-run hotel with comfortable doubles in a quiet spot convenient for the port and Grótta beach. Breakfast is included and served in a beautiful courtyard. **€60**

Despina's Rooms Boúrgo ☎ 22850 22356. Hidden (but well signposted) beneath the castle; you'll need to climb some distance to reach it. The rooms are small but clean and airy, some en suite but three have a shared bathroom; most have balconies with sea views. The owner organizes boat trips to the Lesser Cyclades. **€35**

★**Grotta** Grótta ☎ 22850 22215, ⊚ hotelgrotta.gr. Everyone's favourite Naxos hotel in a good location, with fabulous sunset views. It has comfortable moden rooms, an

6

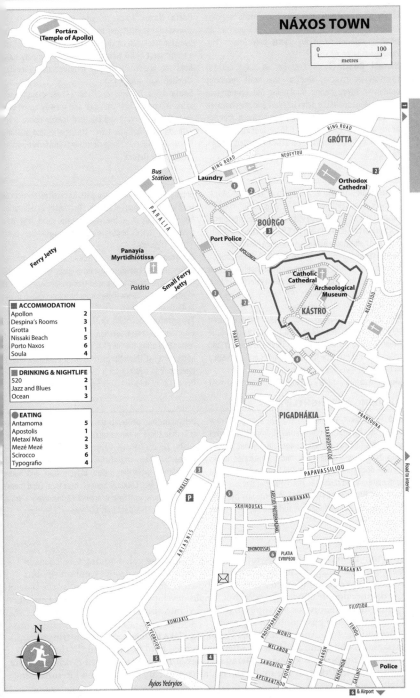

NÁXOS TOWN

0   100
metres

Portára
(Temple of Apollo)

GRÓTTA

RING ROAD

NEOFYTOU

RING ROAD

Bus
Station

Laundry

Orthodox
Cathedral

BOÚRGO

Port Police

APOLLONOS

Ferry Jetty

Panayía
Myrtidhiótissa

Palátia

Small Ferry
Jetty

Catholic
Cathedral

Archeological
Museum

KÁSTRO

PARALIA

PARALIA

■ ACCOMMODATION

Apollon	2
Despina's Rooms	3
Grotta	1
Nissaki Beach	5
Porto Naxos	6
Soula	4

■ DRINKING & NIGHTLIFE

520	2
Jazz and Blues	1
Ocean	3

● EATING

Antamoma	5
Apostolis	1
Metaxí Mas	2
Mezé Mezé	3
Scirocco	6
Typografio	4

PIGADHÁKIA

PRANTOUNA

EXANROPOULIOU

PAPAVASSILIOU

PARALIA

P

SKHINOUSSAS

ARISTIDI PROTOPAPADAKI

DAMBANAKI

ARIADNIS

DHONOUSSAS

PLATIA
EVRIPEOU

TRAGANAS

KOMIAKIS

FILOTIOU

AY. YEORYIOU

PROTOPAPADAKI

MONIS

MELANON

SANGRIOU

APEIRANTHOU

POTAMIAS

ENGARON

TRIPODHON

GALLINIS

FENDU

Police

Áyios Yeóryios

& Airport

N

Road to interior

indoor jacuzzi and pool, a fantastic home-made breakfast (included) cooked fresh daily, free port pick-ups plus an excellent cafe-restaurant for guests only (mains €9). Parking available. **€75**

Nissaki Beach Áyios Yeóryios ☎ 22850 25710, ⓦ nissaki-beach.com. One of the most luxurious options in town, oozing minimalist but comfortable Cycladic elegance. If the palm trees around the pool area don't tempt you, then the views over Ayios Yeóryios beach will. Its excellent seaside restaurant has one of the island's best menus. Breakfast included. April–Oct. **€210**

Porto Naxos Áyios Yeóryios ☎ 22850 23970/1/. ⓦ portonaxos.gr. If you have your own transport, th five-star hotel with parking spaces, a swimming pool ar a tennis court by the Náxos circular road – but only 200 from the beach – is highly recommended. Breakfa included. April–Oct. **€150**

Soula Áyios Yeóryios ☎ 22850 23196, ⓦ soulahote .com. A modern, well-equipped and friendly hostel wit six-bed mixed dorms and four-bed female dorms, eac with its own bathroom/WC, kitchenette and balcony Private rooms also available. Free sheets and ferry transfers Breakfast €6. Dorm **€15**

EATING

Antamoma southern end of seafront ☎ 22850 24324. Laidback minimalist restaurant serving Naxiot nouvelle cuisine (mains €9–14) made with organic local ingredients – try the *torta* (vegetable pie) for €8, or the cheese pie with leeks and hand-made filo (€6). Daily 1pm–midnight.

★ **Apostolis** Old Market ☎ 22850 26777. Always busy, a sign of its regard in the town, with invariably excellent family dishes and grills (€10) plus a good selection of local wines. Beware its side salads (€7) – they are a meal in themselves. Daily noon–midnight.

Metaxi Mas Boúrgo ☎ 22850 26425. Friendly ouzerí serving excellent, well-priced food (mains €9) on a little street heading up to the kástro. Service is friendly and unhurried, and even the fussiest demands are met with a smile. March–Nov daily noon–midnight.

Mezé Mezé Seafront ☎ 22850 26401. The best and most

popular of the seafront restaurants. Its excellent service ca cope with the throngs of tourists attracted by its reputatio for fresh seafood – the warm skate salad (€9) is a revelation. Good house wine, too. April–Oct dail 11am–midnight.

Scirocco Platía Evripéous ☎ 22850 25931, ⓦ scirocco naxos.gr. Well-known restaurant popular with locals anc tourists alike for its well-priced traditional dishes such as *kleftiko* (€10) – hence there might be a long queue to get in. Daily noon–midnight.

Typografio Pigadhákia ☎ 22850 22375, ⓦ typografio. com. Superb central location, delicious local cuisine and reasonable prices (mains €12) with a menu as imaginative as the wine list. This is the place to go for a romantic tête-à-tête: book in advance for a table with the best views in front. May to mid-Oct daily 6pm–midnight.

DRINKING AND NIGHTLIFE

520 Old Market ☎ 22850 27271. On a huge balcony above the harbourfront but entered from Old Market street, this café-bar attracts all ages throughout the day with its mellow lounge music and sophisticated drinks menu – don't miss the delicious Old Town cocktail (tequila with mate tea and chilli €10). Daily 10am–late.

Jazz and Blues ☎ 6944 701 215. A petite jazz bar, with the occasional live performance, tucked away on a street

behind the port police. Its classy drinks are much cheaper (€5) than those in the surrounding bars. April–Oct daily 10am–2pm & 7.30pm–3am.

Ocean Southern end of the seafront ☎ 69848 55986. The island's main dance club, playing funk and house mainstream hits. Cocktails from €7, beer from €6; if there's a special show, entrance is around €8 including a drink. Easter–Sept Fri & Sat (daily in season) 7pm–6am.

The beaches

Just 4km from Náxos Town, **Áyios Prokópios** is regularly voted among Greece's top **beaches**. The village itself lies in the southern part of the main road and on the bus route, but the best and quieter part of the beach is closer to Náxos Town, at the base of the distinct double cone of Stelídha hill. Rapid development along the southwestern stretch means that Áyios Prokópios has blended into the next village, **Ayía Ánna**, further along the busy southern highway.

Beyond the Ayía Ánna headland is 5km-long **Pláka beach**, a vegetation-fringed expanse of white sand accessed by a flat, unsurfaced road from the north: the top section of the beach is known as **Marágas**. Parts of Pláka (by the *Plaza Beach* hotel) are naturist, while **Orkós**, at the southern end, attracts plenty of wind- and kitesurfers in high season.

You'll find more windsurfers along the coastal stretch south from Pláka through remote **Glyfádha** down to **Alykó** and nearby **Pyrgáki**, where the coastal road ends and the asphalted highway to Náxos begins. On the juniper-covered promontory by Alykó is a beach known locally as **Hawaii** for the vibrant blue colour of its waters, while 4km beyond by unsurfaced road is **Ayiassós** beach – this is where Marco Sanudo landed in 1207 to conquer the island from the Byzantines and promptly burned his ships so that there could be no way back.

ACCOMMODATION
THE BEACHES

Finikas Pyrgáki ☎ 22850 75230, ⓦ finikashotel.gr. At the end of the coastal dirt road away from it all, this is a self-sufficient hotel, offering everything from a good traditional restaurant to a sauna and gym. It also organizes its own watersports. Breakfast included. May–Sept. €**150**

Naxos Imperial Resort and Spa Stelídha ☎ 22850 26620, ⓦ naxosimperial.com. The best deluxe hotel of many on the Stelídha peninsula, it is also close to the best section of Áyios Prokópios beach. There's volleyball, gym, spa, restaurant, bar and a pool. Breakfast included. May–Sept. €**100**

Orkos Beach Mikrí Vígla ☎ 22850 75194, ⓦ orkosbeach.eu. Next to the Flivsos Kite Center, with a cool pool where families rub shoulders with surfers. Its garden is perfect to laze in, there's a small wedding chapel and the massive new spa is a great place to relax. Parking and breakfast included. May–Oct. €**105**

Stella Ayía Anna ☎ 22850 42526, ⓦ stella-apartments -naxos.gr. Close to the sea, this Rough Guides' favourite

started with some spotless studios with kitchenette and bougainvillea-bursting balconies, and is now a full-blown hotel with a pool and a bar. Possibly the best option south of Náxos Town, though wi-fi reception is a problem in some areas. April–Oct. €**60**

CAMPSITES

Maragas Ayía Anna ☎ 22850 42552, ⓦ maragascamping.gr. A suitably laidback shaded campsite with a beach bar, watersports facilities, en-suite studios and a good restaurant (€7 for a main plus a beer). There's a regular bus service to Náxos Town. April–Oct. Camping €**14**, studio €**40**

Plaka Pláka ☎ 22850 42700, ⓦ plakacamping.gr. Near the beginning of the Cyclades' longest beach, this is a fabulous campsite with a pool, restaurant and café. It's flanked by the imaginatively named *Plaka I* and *Plaka II* sister hotels (€45–60); the latter has its own private pool. Bus service to Náxos Town every 20min in season. April–Oct. €**14**

EATING AND DRINKING

Gorgóna Ayía Anna ☎ 22850 41007. Cool, large, shaded, family-run beach bar that becomes a fish restaurant with reasonable prices (€10) in the evening then continues as a late-night bar until the morning. Known locally for its delicious home-made *rizógalo*, a spiced rice pudding. Daily 8am–3am.

Molos Áyios Prokópios ☎ 22850 26980. Fish taverna serving only fresh fish caught on the day and assorted seafood, which tends to be fried rather than grilled. Occupying the best spot on the beach, it is unsurprisingly popular. May–Oct daily 9am–1am.

Central Náxos

After its beaches, **Central Náxos** is the island's second unique selling point, with its lush green valleys, mountains, picturesque villages, historic churches, old forts and Classical sites. Because of the sheer size of the island these are best enjoyed via two day-long drives: one short and one much longer. The short drive is Náxos–Galanádho–Sangrí–Halkí–Moní–Kinídharos–Flério–Náxos, while the longer drive is Náxos–Galanádho–Sangrí–Halkí–Filóti–Aperáthou–Apóllonas–Náxos via the northern coastal road.

Galanádho and Sangrí

From Náxos Town, head for the market village of **Galanádho** to reach the twin villages of **SANGRÍ**, on a vast plateau at the head of a long valley. On the way have a look at the domed eighth-century church of **Áyios Mámas**, neglected since the Ottoman conquest. Káto Sangrí has the ruins of a Venetian castle, while Áno Sangrí is an attractive little place, all cobbled streets and fragrant courtyards. From there, it's about ninety minutes' walk to the Byzantine castle of **Apalírou**, at 474m, which held out for two months against the besieging Marco Sanudo. Its fortifications are relatively intact and the views

6

magnificent. Some 3km south of Áno Sangrí on a paved road, are the partially rebuilt remains of a **Classical temple of Demeter** (Tues–Sun 8.30am–3pm; free): dating from 530 BC, it was the first Greek temple to be wholly constructed from marble, including the roof.

The Tragéa and Halkí

From Sangrí, the road twists northeast into the **Tragéa** region, scattered with olive trees and occupying a vast highland valley. The area is the only part of the Cyclades to have a regular winter snowfall, and the only part with traditional songs about snow. It's a good jumping-off point for all sorts of exploratory rambling. **HALKÍ**, 16km from Náxos Town, is a fine introduction of what is to come; set high up, it's a quiet town with some lovely churches, including the **Panayía Protóthronis** church (daily 10am–1pm; free), with its eleventh- to thirteenth-century frescoes. Just behind is the restored seventeenth-century Venetian **Grazia-Barozzi Tower**, and nearby is the distillery (1896) and shop of **Vallindras Naxos Citron**, whose charming proprietors explain the process of producing *kítron* followed by a little tasting session (April–Oct 10am–5pm; July & Aug open til 8 or 9pm; free).

Moní

Driving from Halkí to Moní you pass the sixth-century church of **Panayía Dhrosianí** (daily 11am–5pm; donation expected), historically the most important church on the island with some of the oldest frescoes in Greece. **MONÍ** itself, at an altitude of 550m, enjoys an outstanding view of the Tragéa and Mount Zas, and has numerous woodcarving workshops.

Kinídharos and Flério

From Moní you can loop back to Náxos Town, via the village of **KINÍDHAROS**, with its marble quarries and daily folk evenings; it has a reputation of staging one of the best carnivals in the Cyclades. Five kilometres beyond is the village of **FLÉRIO**. Nearby is the most interesting of the ancient marble quarries of the seventh- to sixth-century BC on Náxos, home to two famous **koúroi**, left recumbent and unfinished; even so, they're finely detailed figures, over 5m in length. The Koúros Fleriou (Koúros Melánon), from around 570 BC, is a short walk along the stream valley; the Koúros Farangiou (Koúros Potamiás) is a steeper walk up the hillside. Both are well signposted.

Filóti and Aperáthou

At the far side of the gorgeous Tragéa valley, **FILÓTI**, the largest village in the region, lies on the northwestern slopes of **Mount Zas**, which at 1001m is the highest point in the Cyclades. **APERÁTHOU** (officially Apíranthos), 8km beyond Filóti, is hilly, winding and highly picturesque; it shows the most Cretan influence of all interior villages and gave Greece one of its prime ministers, **Petros Protopapadakis** (it's unfortunate that he was executed for high treason in 1922). Its location high in the mountains means it is

---

CLIMBING MOUNT ZAS

If you're arriving by bus and intend to climb **Mount Zas** you should start from the steps opposite the taverna *Baboulas* on Filóti's main square. This is a round-trip walk of three to four hours on partly marked trails to the summit, a climb that rewards you with an astounding panorama of virtually the whole of Náxos and its Cycladic neighbours. The initial path out of the village climbs up to rejoin the road to Apóllonas. The final approach trail begins beside the small **Ayía Marína chapel**. You can return to Filóti via the trail to the 150m-deep **Zas Cave**, which is also accessed by a separate route through **Ariés**, ten minutes' drive from Filóti.

If you have your own transport, you can drive all the way to the trailhead at Ayía Marína and continue on from there.

noticeably cooler and greener than the coast. There are two Venetian **fortified mansions**, Bardáni and Zevgóli, a state **Archeological Museum** (Tues–Sun 8.30am–3pm; €2; ☎ 22850 61725) and, amazingly, four small private **museums**: Natural History, Geological, Fine Arts and a Folklore Museum (all daily: May & Oct 11am–2pm; June & Sept 11am–3pm; July 11am–4pm; Aug 11am–5.30pm; €3 combined entry for Natural History & Fine Arts; Geological and Folklore museums are free; ☎ 697 3865 158). There's some good **shopping** in Aperáthou, as well: **Epilekton** in the main street is an excellent delicatessen with a selection of local cheeses, hot peppers and sun-dried aubergines (Easter–Oct daily 9.30am–9pm).

6

Pýrgos Himárrou and Kalandós

A turning at the southern end of Filóti is signposted to the **Pýrgos Himárrou** (12.5km), a remote 20m-high Hellenistic watchtower – one of the tourist landmarks of the island – and onward (another 12km) to the deserted but excellent in all respects **Kalandós** beach on the south coast. Bring your own water and food supplies if you're planning to stop here.

EATING   **CENTRAL NÁXOS**

Amorginos Aperáthou ☎ 22850 61233. Mountain decor, good balcony views over the Tragea and food to rival *Lefteris* (see below). It specializes in barbecued meat, all sourced from the village except the chicken – try the *rósto*, an Aperathou staple of pork casserole with garlic (€8), then ask for the yoghurt-and-lime they offer free as a digestive. Daily 10am–11pm.

Lefteris Aperáthou ☎ 22850 61333. A restaurant with an unmatched reputation on Náxos and not as full as others closer to the main road, which are always busy. At the end of your meal (mains €8) ask if they have their homemade *glyká koutalioú*, stewed syrupy fruit which are so sweet that a few teaspoonfuls constitute a serving. June–Sept daily 10am–midnight.

Panorama Moní ☎ 22850 31070. Small family restaurant with exceptional views. Whatever the dish of the day is (€8), order it; it will most likely involve some kind of meat, as this part of Náxos is famous for its tender beef and veal. Daily 11am–11pm.

Northern Náxos

The route to **Northern Náxos** through the mountains from Aperáthou to Apóllonas is very scenic, and the road surface is in reasonable condition all the way. Jagged ranges and hairpin bends confront you after **Kóronos**, past **Skadhó**, to the remote emery-miners' village of **Koronídha** – the highest village on the island. **Apóllonas** is a small resort with two good beaches: a tiny and crowded stretch of sand backed by a line of cafés and restaurants, and a longer and quieter stretch of shingle, where *Kouros* hotel lies. The major attraction in Apóllonas is a 12m-long **koúros**, approached by a path from the main road just above the village. Lying *in situ* at a former marble quarry, this is the largest of Náxos' abandoned stone figures, but less detailed than those at Flério. The return to Náxos Town is via the northern coastal road, which is spectacular, set high above the sea. Stop for a break at the village of **Engarés** to visit a 200-year-old **olive press** that houses an olive and folklore museum (May–Sept daily 11am–6pm; free; ☎ 22850 62021, ⦿ olivemuseum.com).

ACCOMMODATION   **NORTHERN NÁXOS**

Kouros Apóllonas ☎ 22850 67000, ⦿ hotelkouros .blogspot.com. Relaxing, dreamy hotel standing alone in the middle of the shingle beach with spacious, quiet rooms and a well-stocked beach bar. Despite it being out of the way, it attracts a young clientele. Breakfast included May–Sept. **€50**

Lesser Cyclades

Four of the six small islands in the patch of the Aegean between Náxos and Amorgós have slid from obscurity into fashion in recent years. Inhabited since prehistoric

6

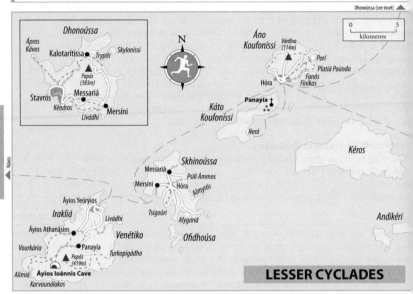

LESSER CYCLADES

times, the group is known commonly as the **Lesser Cyclades** and includes **Irakliá**, **Skhinoússa**, **Áno Koufoníssi** and **Dhonoússa**. The islands' popularity has hastened the development of better facilities and higher prices, but since only Áno Koufoníssi is on the large ferry and catamaran routes (mid-June to early September), they've avoided mass tourism so far

ARRIVAL AND INFORMATION   LESSER CYCLADES

By ferry Regular ferries always call at Náxos before continuing on to the lesser Cyclades (see individual island accounts for ferry frequencies). Speedboats and ferries run from Pireás in high season, most stopping only at Áno Koufoníssi.

Day-trips from Náxos Boat trips from Náxos take in Irakliá and Skhinoússa, but rarely Áno Koufoníssi.

Island transport Apart from a seasonal bus on Áno Koufoníssi, there are no buses or taxis on the islands; hotels will organize your transport to and from the port. There is no car or scooter rental.

Health There are no pharmacies on any of the islands, but some drugs are dispensed from the rural GP practices. In case of emergency there are speedboats on call 24/7, so make sure you have good travel insurance.

Irakliá

IRAKLIÁ, the westernmost of the Lesser Cyclades, and with the least spoilt scenery, has just over 150 permanent residents. As the first stop on the ferry service from Náxos, the island is hardly undiscovered by tourists, but with fewer amenities than some of its neighbours, it retains the feel of a more secluded retreat.

The port of **Áyios Yeóryios** is a small but sprawling settlement behind a sandy tamarisk-backed beach that gets quite crowded in August. **Livádhi**, a big, shallow beach, is 2km southeast of the port and its crystal-clear waters are the main tourist attraction of the island. The asphalted road continues 3km on to the tiny capital **Panayía (Hóra)**. In season, a local boat sails from the port to make a tour of the island, stopping at the small sandy beach at **Alimiá** and the nearby pebble beach of **Karvounólakos**, which is surrounded by coloured rock formations.

On August 28, the feast of St John the Baptist, a 4pm service is held inside the large cave where his miraculous icon is said to have been found.

By ferry Ferries dock at Áyios Yeóryios.
Destinations Amorgós, Aigiáli and Katápola (3–6 weekly; 2–3hr); Áno Koufoníssi (1–2 daily; 1hr); Dhonoússa (3–4 weekly; 1hr 15min–4hr); Náxos (1–2 daily; 1hr 30min); Páros (2–4 weekly; 2hr 30min); Pireás (1–4 weekly; 7hr);

Skhinoússa (1–2 daily; 15min); Sýros (1 weekly; 9hr).
Services There's an ATM at Áyios Yeóryios, and a doctor with a dispensary.
Travel agents Gavalas agency (☏ 22850 71539) can take care of all your travel and ticket needs.

ACCOMMODATION AND EATING

Anna's Place Áyios Yeóryios ☏ 22850 74234, ✆ annasplace.gr. Eight double rooms with a communal kitchen, plus six studios with kitchenette in a palm-fringed complex on the slope at the back of the village with great views. All rooms have private bathrooms. **€60**
Maïstrali Áyios Yeóryios ☏ 22850 71807, ✆ maistraliclub.com. The best place to eat on the island, with a menu of seafood, especially crustaceans, as well as

standards like moussaka (€8). The veranda has a good view of the port below and there are two family rooms above for rent. June–Sept daily 6pm–midnight.
Sunset Áyios Yeóryios ☏ 22850 71569, ✆ sunset -iraklia.gr. Four large apartments (sleeping 2–4) on a small hill 500m from the port with sweeping sunset views: the apartments have a/c, TV, fridge and limited cooking facilities such as stovetops. May–Sept. **€75**

Skhinoússa

A little to the northeast of Irakliá, the island of **SKHINOÚSSA** is just beginning to awaken to its tourist potential. Its indented outline, sweeping valleys and partly submerged headlands – such as the sinuous, snake-like islet Ofidhoúsa (Fidoú) – provide some of the most dramatic views in the group.

An asphalted road leads up from the port of **Mersíni** to the capital, **Hóra** (also called **Panayía**). From Hóra you can reach no fewer than sixteen beaches dotted around the island, accessible by a network of dirt tracks. **Tsigoúri**, the most developed, is a ten-minute steep walk downhill from Hóra. The locals' preferred choice of beaches are **Alygariá** to the south, **Psilí Ámmos** to the northeast, and **Almyrós**, half an hour southeast. All have beach bars during high season.

By ferry Boats dock at the small port of Mersíni.
Destinations Amorgós, Aigiáli and Katápola (1–2 daily; 1hr 30min–2hr); Áno Koufoníssi (1–2 daily; 30min); Dhonoússa (3–4 weekly; 3hr 40min); Irakliá (1–2 daily; 15min); Náxos (1–2 daily; 2hr); Pireás (1–4 weekly; 7hr 30min).

Travel agents Grispos Tours (☏ 22850 29329) can help with tickets and information.
Services There's an ATM at Hóra, as well as several mini-markets, bars and tourist shops plus a sub-post office.

ACCOMMODATION AND EATING

Grispos Villas Tsigoúri ☏ 22850 71930, ✆ grisposvillas .com. Perched above Tsigoúri beach at the northwest end, this complex has studios, apartments and large suites with cooking facilities, plus a mini-market and restaurant on the premises; they also sell ferry tickets in season. Continental breakfast €5pp. **€60**

Iliovasilema Hóra ☏ 22850 71948/71161, ✆ iliovasilemahotel.gr. Well-priced friendly hotel, which is comfortable rather than luxurious: all rooms have private balconies with spectacular views of the harbour. They run a free shuttle to and from every beach on the island for guests. June–Sept. **€60**

Áno Koufoníssi

ÁNO KOUFONÍSSI (usually referred to simply as Koufoníssi) is the flattest, most developed and most densely inhabited island of the group. With some of the least-spoilt beaches in the Cyclades, the island is attracts increasing numbers of Greek and foreign holiday-makers. Since it's small enough to walk round in a day, it feels overcrowded in July and August.

Hóra, on a low hill behind the ferry harbour, has been engulfed by new room and hotel development, but the town, with great views across the water to

6

mountainous Keros island, still retains an affable, small-island atmosphere. All the good **beaches** are in the east and southeast of the island, improving as you go east along a road that skirts the gradually developing coastline along the edge of low cliffs. **Fínikas** (or **Harokópou**), a fifteen-minute walk from town, is the first of four wide coves with gently shelving golden sand. The next beach, **Fanós**, is the youngsters' favourite, because of the beach bar that dominates the stretch of sand in season. Next is **Platiá Poúnda** (or **Italídha**), which is a small, pretty and clothing-optional beach. From here, the path rounds a rocky headland to **Porí**, a much longer and wilder beach, backed by dunes and set in a deep bay. It can be reached more easily from the town by following the asphalt road heading inland through the scrub-covered hills.

You can also travel by pleasure boat for a swim to the beaches of **Káto Koufoníssi**, but not to **Kéros** which is out of bounds; the whole island and its waters are an archeological area (much like Delos), which is still being excavated.

ARRIVAL AND INFORMATION

By ferry Boats dock at the jetty below Hóra.
Destinations Amorgós, Aigiáli and Katápola (1–2 daily; 30min–1hr 45min); Dhonoússa (3–4 weekly; 3hr); Folégandros (1–2 daily; 3–5hr); Irakliá (1–2 daily; 1hr); Mýkonos (1 daily; 1hr 30min); Náxos (1–3 daily; 30min–2hr 20min); Páros (2–3 weekly; 3hr 20min); Pireás (1–2 daily; 5–7hr); Santoríni (1–2 daily; 1hr 45min–4hr); Sérifos (2 weekly; 6hr); Sífnos (2 weekly; 7hr); Skhinoússa (1–2 daily; 30min); Sýros (1 weekly; 5hr 15min);

ÁNO KOUFONÍSSI

By bus In July & Aug, an hourly bus (10am–8pm) makes the trip from Hóra to Porí, stopping at Fínikas.
Travel agents Koufonissia Tours (☎ 22850 74435/74091, ⓦ koufonissiatours.gr; open during ferry arrivals) deals with accommodation, while Prásinos Tours (☎ 22850 71438; daily 7am–10pm) sells ferry tickets.
Services There's a sub-post office with an ATM behind the Myrtó hotel.

ACCOMMODATION

Aeolos Hóra ☎ 22850 74296, ⓦ aeoloshotel.com. Modern, well-designed hotel with a landscaped garden, stone pool and bar overlooked by bougainvillea-draped balconies: the large rooms have minimalist four-poster beds. Big breakfast buffet included. June–Sept. **€110**
Koufonissia Hotel & Resort On the road from Hóra to Porí ☎ 22850 74067, ⓦ hotelkoufonisia.gr. This good-value spa resort was renovated in 2017, with landscaped

gardens and a 25-metre pool: its range of massages includes a chocolate therapy treatment. Breakfast included. Mid-May to Sept. **€80**
★**Myrto** Hóra ☎ 22850 74400, ⓦ myrto-hotel.com. Inaugurated in 2014, this hotel is a winner: it's just 50m from the beach, with smiling service. The rooms have high ceilings, marble bathrooms and balconies with smashing views of Keros opposite. Breakfast included. Two nights minimum. June–Sept. **€120**

EATING

Capetan Nicolas Hóra ☎ 22850 71690. After many decades, this is still the best place to eat seafood on the island. At the west end of the village, it serves a fine array of grilled seafood fresh from the owner's fishing boat. Try the shrimp risotto for €14 and home-made *taramosaláta* (€5) that bears no resemblance to supermarket varieties. May–Oct daily 12.30pm–late.

Gastronautis Hóra ☎ 22850 71468. Chef Petros acquired a cosmopolitan view of Mediterranean food in Berlin, bringing gourmet food at reasonable prices to the island. Try his slowly cooked veal, chicken or lamb stews (€12) complemented by an eclectic choice of wines. Mid-April to mid-Oct daily 9am–noon & 4pm–1am.

Dhonoússa

DHONOÚSSA is a little out on a limb compared with the other Lesser Cyclades, and ferries call less frequently. Island life centres on the pleasant port settlement of **Stavrós**, spread out behind the harbour and its first-rate beach. Most sunbathers head for **Kéndros**, a long and sheltered stretch of shadeless sand twenty minutes over the ridge to the east; a World War II German wreck can be easily spotted by snorkellers. The village of **Mersíni** is an hour's walk from Stavrós, while a nearby path leads down to **Livádhi**,

...n idyllic nudist beach with tamarisks for shade. In high season a beach-boat runs from ...he port to all beaches.

ARRIVAL AND DEPARTURE

By ferry Ferries dock at Stavrós.

Destinations Amorgós, Aigiáli and Katápola (2 weekly; 2hr 15min); Áno Koufoníssi (3–4 weekly; 1–3hr); Astypálea (3 weekly; 2hr 20min); Irakliá (3–4 weekly; 2hr–4hr

DHONOÚSSA

15min); Náxos (1–2 daily; 1hr 10min–5hr); Páros (3–4 weekly; 2hr 30min–7hr); Pireás (2–4 weekly; 7hr); Skhinoússa (3–4 weekly; 1hr 40min–4hr 30min); Sýros (1 weekly; 8hr 30min).

ACCOMMODATION AND EATING

Chryssa Stavrós ☎ 22850 51575, ⓦ donoussarooms.gr. Set back from the village, this pension has basic but large studios and apartments some with private balconies, others opening onto a communal veranda overlooking the port. Most rooms have their own kitchenette with cooking implements. May–Oct. **€60**

Corona Borealis Stavrós Café-restaurant that slowly becomes the life and soul of the party, playing alternative indie rock until the early hours. Young clientele, because, well, there's nowhere else to go. June–Sept daily 10am–3am.

Amorgós

AMORGÓS, with its dramatic mountain scenery and laidback atmosphere, is attracting visitors in increasing numbers. The island can get extremely crowded in midsummer, the numbers swollen by film buffs paying their respects to the film location of Luc Besson's *The Big Blue*, although few venture out to **Líveros** at the island's western end to see the wreck of the *Olympia* which figures prominently in the film. In general it's a low-key, escapist clientele, happy to have found a relatively large, interesting, uncommercialized and hospitable island with excellent walking possibilities. Families tend to herd around **Katápola**, while younger tourists prefer **Aigiáli**. However, if you rent a car, **Hóra**, the island capital, is the best base from which to explore the island.

Almost every hotel will offer you a glass of *rakómelo* as a welcome drink. It's a kind of fermented grappa with honey, herbs and spices, drunk in shots as an aperitif.

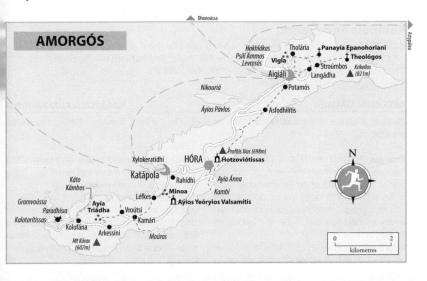

ARRIVAL AND DEPARTURE

AMORGÓS

Ferries and catamarans call at **Katápola** in the southwest or **Aigiáli** in the north, while some dock at both. Be aware that it is those destinations, rather than "Amorgós", that are named on **ferry schedules**. There are more onward connections from Katápola than Aigiáli.

AIGIÁLI

By ferry The ferries stop at the town jetty; some continue on to Katápola (15–30min).

Destinations Áno Koufoníssi (3–4 weekly; 1hr 40min); Astypálea (1–3 weekly; 1hr 30min); Dhonoússa (2–4 weekly; 40min); Irakliá (3–4 weekly; 3hr); Náxos (3–4 weekly; 2hr); Páros (3–4 weekly; 3hr 20min); Pireás (3–4 weekly; 8hr); Skhinoússa (3–4 weekly; 3hr 15min); Sýros (1 weekly; 7hr 20min).

KATÁPOLA

By ferry The ferries stop at the town jetty; some continue on to Aigiáli.

Destinations Áno Koufoníssi (1–2 daily; 30min); Dhonoússa (2–4 weekly; 2hr 15min); Irakliá (1–2 daily; 1hr 50min–3hr); Íos (1 weekly; 5hr 20min); Kos (1 weekly; 5hr); Léros (1 weekly; 3hr 20min); Mýkonos (1–2 daily; 2hr); Milos (1–2 daily; 7hr); Náxos (1–3 daily; 1–4hr); Páros (1–2 daily; 2hr 30min–4hr 15min); Pátmos (1 weekly; 2hr); Pireás (1–2 daily; 6–9hr); Rhodes (1 weekly; 8hr); Santoríni (1–2 daily; 1hr–4hr 40min); Skhinoússa (1–2 daily; 1hr 25min –3hr); Sýros (1 weekly; 6hr 30min).

GETTING AROUND

By bus In season, a bus shuttles between Katápola and Hóra (3–8 daily; 15min) then continues to Hotzoviótissas monastery and Ayía Ánna. There is a bus from Katápola to Aigiáli via Hóra (4–8 hourly; 1hr) and another (3–7 weekly; 45min) out to the southern beaches returning the same day. From Aigiáli, a bus runs up to Langádha and Tholária, the two villages east of and 200m above Aigiáli bay (5–6 return daily; ⓦ amorgosbuscompany.com).

By boat From Katápola there's a *kaïki* service to the nearby beaches at Maltézi and Plákes (€3 return) and a daily excursion *kaïki* to the islet of Gramvoússa off the western end of Amorgós (€8 return).

By car or motorbike There are several car/bike-rental outfits; the longest-established is Thomas Rental (ⓣ 22850 71777, ⓦ thomas-rental.gr) with offices at Katápola, Hóra and Aigiáli.

INFORMATION

Services The island's main post office is in the upper square in Hóra. There's an ATM in Katápola, Aigiáli and Hóra.
Travel agents Aegialis Tours (ⓣ 22850 73393, ⓦ aegialistours.com) in Aigiáli can book tickets,

transfers, car rental and accommodation. Prekas (ⓣ 22850 71256) in Katápola, just along from the ferry dock, is a boat-ticket agency.

Katápola and around

KATÁPOLA, set at the head of a deep inlet, is actually three separate villages: **Katápola** on the south side, **Xylokeratídhi** on the north shore, and **Rahídhi** on the central ridge. The beach of Káto Krotíri to the west of the ferry dock is where you should aim for, though.

ACCOMMODATION

KATÁPOLA AND AROUND

There's an on-off free municipal **campsite** behind the beach in front of Rahídhi; enquire whether it's open when you arrive.

Amorgos Katápola ⓣ 22850 71013, ⓦ pension -amorgos.com. No communal areas as such, but good-sized rooms (with small bathrooms) in the centre of Katápola, all with coffee-making facilities, some with kitchenettes. Completely refurbished in 2014, they are soundproofed from street noise. Wi-fi and satellite TV. **€50**
Anna Studios Katápola ⓣ 22850 71218, ⓦ studioanna -amorgos.com. Well-signed and difficult to miss because

of its height, this hospitable *pension* with a garden setting has very good views to the sea from the top floors. It also has a cheap laundry and ironing service. **€45**
Eleni Kato Krotiri ⓣ 22850 71628, ⓦ roomseleni.gr. Great location for this basic but good-value rooms complex above the Káto Krotíri beach. All rooms have a kitchenette, and from some you can see the three Roman tombs adjacent to the property. No breakfast. Easter– Nov. **€40**

EATING

Mourayio Katápola ☎ 22850 71011. The most popular taverna in town, cooking a wide range of seafood since 1980, including a good fish soup, lobster spaghetti (around €25–35) and marinated octopus (€10), all worth the wait while you enjoy the waterfront views. April–Oct daily noon–midnight; Nov–March daily 5pm–midnight.

Vitzentzos Xylokeratídhi ☎ 22850 71518. Serves traditional Amorgós dishes that include island slow-roasted goat with potatoes, crawfish spaghetti and a range of vegetable dishes cooked in oil and tomato sauce (€8). Easter to early Oct daily noon–3pm & 6pm–midnight.

6

Hóra and around

HÓRA is one of the better-preserved settlements in the Cyclades, with a scattering of tourist shops, cafés, tavernas and rooms. Dominated by an upright volcanic rock plug, wrapped with a chapel or two, the thirteenth-century **Venetian fortifications** look down on nearly thirty other **churches**, some domed, and a line of decapitated windmills beyond.

Monastery of Hotzoviótissas

Above Ayía Anna beach. Daily 9am–1pm & 5–7pm • Donation expected

The spectacular **Monastery of Hotzoviótissas**, gleaming white at the base of a towering, vertical cliff, can be reached on foot via a steep, cobbled path starting from a car park 150m below. Modest dress is required: no shorts for men while women must be fully covered. Only three monks occupy the fifty rooms now, but they are quite welcoming considering the crowds who file through. The main church is dominated by the miraculous **icon** around which the monastery was founded, along with other treasures. Tradition, supported by evidence, has it that in the ninth century AD, a precious icon of the Virgin was brought here by beleaguered monks from the monastery of **Khotziba** in Palestine, who settled here to escape Arab raids. Sitting and admiring the view from the terrace, while being treated to a shot of *rakómelo* and a sweet by the monks, is one of the highlights of visiting Amorgós.

Monastery of Áyios Yeóryios Valsamítis

5km south of Hóra on the way to Mouros Beach • Daily 9am–1pm & 5–7pm • Donation expected • ☎ 22857 70199

After a hiatus of 250 years during which the monastery was simply a church, a nun now lives again in the **Monastery of Áyios Yeóryios Valsamítis**. The *katholikón* is built in the old hydromanteion (water oracle) of Apollo where the priests predicted the future by divining the waters of a sacred fountain. This custom of "consulting the waters" continued until the 1950s on Amorgós, until the Orthodox Church cemented the fountain. You can still see the fountain enclosure, and also the (stagnant) waters of the now defunct spring.

Beaches

The nearest **beach** to Hóra, at **Ayía Ánna**, is small but more than adequate. If you skip the first tiny coves, the path will take you to the nudist bay of **Kambí**; bring food and water for the day. An alternative is **Moúros**, 5km west, with clean, crystal-clear waters and a seasonal taverna.

The best beach, however, is at the end of the road west, about 20km from Hóra, at spectacular **Kalotarítissas Bay**, its tiny fishing jetty and small sand and pebble beach partly enclosed and sheltered by a rocky headland. A beach hut selling snacks and drinks operates in season, and in July and August there are **boat trips** (€4) from here to the uninhabited but picturesque islet of **Gramvoússa**, opposite; boats leave at 11am, returning at 7pm. About 1.8km before Kalotarítissas, the **wreck of the Olympia** is visible down to the right, in **Líveros Bay**.

ACCOMMODATION

★**Emprostiada** Hóra ☎ 22850 71814, ⓦ emprostiada .gr. A guesthouse built and decorated in the style of a Cycladic manor, in the middle of a spacious landscaped garden. The idiosyncratic furnishings include several traditional hole-in-the-wall double beds. Free wi-fi and coffee facilities in all rooms. **€50**

Panorama Hóra ☎ 22850 74016/71606 ⓦ panorama-amorgos.gr. In two different sites in Hóra, these rooms and studios are large and comfortable with fitted kitchens; some have balconies with western views towards the kástro. Wi-fi and parking available. **€55**

EATING AND DRINKING

Liotrivi Hóra ☎ 22850 71700. With a roof terrace facing the kástro, this taverna, down the steps from the bus stop, is where you should try the local casseroles such as veal with aubergines (€10) or goat stew. Its home-made wine straight from the barrel is also excellent (€5/half litre). Mid-May to mid-Oct daily noon–1am.

Jazzmin Hóra ☎ 22850 74017, ✉ jazzminamorgos @yahoo.com. Bars rise and disappear like shooting stars but *Jazzmin* has been quietly going since 2004, and is still popular both for its breakfasts and for its late-night cocktails (€10) and occasional live music. Daily 9am–4am.

Aigiáli and around

The road from Hóra to **AIGIÁLI** (Eyiáli), 15km away, is one of the most impressive in the Cyclades, overlooking several beautiful small coves. The town itself is smaller and more picturesque than Katápola, and so tends to be more popular. The main Aigiáli **beach** is more than satisfactory, getting better and better as you stroll further north. A trail here leads over various headlands to three bays: sandy **Levrósos** (a 20min walk), the most popular, with a taverna; **Psilí Ámmos** (30min walk), which is mixed sand and gravel; and **Hókhlakas** (20min), where naturism is tolerated; there are no facilities in the last two so bring what you need. The best of all the northern beaches is **Áyios Pávlos**, 5km south of Aigiáli, from where seasonal boats also leave for the beaches on the island of **Nikouriá** opposite.

ACCOMMODATION

★**Aegialis** Aigiáli ☎ 22850 73393, ⓦ amorgos -aegialis.com. High on the hillside on the far side of the bay, this is the island's largest hotel, and has superb views, an infinity pool, spa with thalassotherapy treatments, sauna, jacuzzi, gym and a good restaurant (mains €15). Because of its size, rooms and their views vary, so check when you book. **€200**

Aegiali Camping Aigiáli ☎ 22850 73500, ⓦ aegialicamping.gr. Usually busier than the one in Katápola but not necessarily better, this is a tree-covered, cheerful campsite 100m from the middle of the beach. Free wi-fi at reception and in the site's restaurant. May–Oct. **€15**

Karkisia Aigiáli ☎ 22850 73180, ⓦ karkisia-hotel.gr.

Well-priced option that's very comfortable and easy on the eye, near Aigiáli beach over which the top-floor balconies have views. Every double room has a sofabed that can be used to sleep a third person at no extra cost. All rooms have kitchenette and cooking facilities. Mid-May to mid-Oct. **€55**

★**Lakki Village** Aigiáli ☎ 22850 73253/73505, ⓦ lakkivillage.com. Literally a village with well-equipped studios and rooms in labyrinthine pebbled alleys. Don't just stop by the pool; this huge site extends all the way from the Tholária road to the beach. There's a good restaurant and children's club on the premises, too. Breakfast included. April–Oct. **€65**

EATING AND DRINKING

Embassa Aigiáli ☎ 22850 73277. The coolest café-bar to lounge about and chill at while watching the sunset, favourite of backpackers and the itinerant European youth. Very strong cocktails for €8 and harder rock music as the night goes on. Easter to mid-Oct daily 9am–late.

Limani Aigiáli ☎ 22850 73269, ⓦ limani.amorgos.net. Also known as *Kyra-Katinas* after the taverna's former matriarch who sadly is no more: her two sons carry on the taverna tradition. One of them has married a Thai lady who cooks authentic Thai dishes on Fridays. Otherwise, it's the usual Greek staples (mains €8). Easter to mid-Oct daily 9am–1am.

Íos

Though not terribly different –
geographically or architecturally – from
its immediate neighbours, no other
Greek island attracts such vast crowds of
young people as **ÍOS**. Although it has
worked hard to shake off its late-
twentieth-century reputation for
alcoholic excesses and to move the
island's tourism up a class, with some
success, Íos is still extremely popular with
the student backpacker set, who take over
the island in July and August.

The only real villages – **Yialós** (for
families), **Hóra** and **Mylopótas** (for the
18–25s) – are clustered in a western
corner of the island, with development
elsewhere restricted by poor roads. Most
visitors stay along the arc delineated by
the port – at Yialós, where you'll arrive,
in Hóra above it, or by the beach at
Mylopótas. Despite its past popularity,
sleeping on the beach on Íos is strictly banned these days and so is nudism.

6

ARRIVAL AND GETTING AROUND

ÍOS

By ferry Ferries dock in Yialós, an easy 20min trek from the capital, Hóra, or a short hop by bus.
Destinations Amorgós, Katápola (1–3 weekly; 2hr); Anáfi (1–3 weekly; 3hr 15min); Folégandhros (2–4 daily; 30min–1hr 40min); Iráklio (1–2 daily; 3hr); Kímolos (4–6 weekly; 2hr 50min); Lávrio via Kéa/Kýthnos (1 weekly; 12hr); Mílos (4–6 weekly; 4hr); Mýkonos (3–5 daily; 1hr 15min); Náxos (1–2 daily; 1hr–1hr 30min); Páros (3–4 daily; 1hr –2hr 20min); Pireás (3–5 daily; 3hr 30min–5hr 30min); Santoríni (6–9 daily; 45min–1hr 30min); Sérifos (1–2 daily; 4hr 30min); Sífnos (1–2 daily; 2hr 45min–3hr 15min); Síkinos (1 daily; 25min); Sýros (1–3 weekly; 6hr).
By bus Buses shuttle between Yialós, Hóra and Mylopótas (every 15–30min; 8am–midnight) and between Yialós

and Koumbára beach (every 30min). In season, there are daily buses to and from the beaches at Manganári, Psáthi and Ayía Theodhóti; they sell return tickets only and are quite pricey (€6); timetables at ☎ 22860 92015, ⓦ ktel-ios. gr.
By boat Daily boats depart from Yialós at around 10am for the beaches on the south coast, returning in the late afternoon (€12 return).
By car or motorbike Hiring a car is not really necessary; the main strip, Yialós to Hora and Mylopótas, is walkable and a very nice hike. To rent your own transport, try Vangelis Rentals (☎ 22860 91919, ⓦ vangelis-rental.com) in Hóra or Jacob's Car & Bike Rental (☎ 22860 91047, ⓦ jacobs-los.gr) in Yialós.

INFORMATION AND ACTIVITIES

Travel agents Akteon Travel (☎ 22860 91343, ⓦ acteon.gr) has branches in the main church square at Hóra and in the middle of the port (both daily 9am–2pm & 5–9pm); it acts as the unofficial tourist information office.
Services There are two ATMs at the port and two in Hóra. The post office is in the new town of Hóra, a block

behind the town hall.
Watersports Meltemi Watersports (☎ 6932 153 912, ⓦ meltemiwatersports.com) is a British-owned outlet on Mylopótas and Manganári beaches, offering waterskiing, windsurfing and wakeboarding lessons. They also hire out canoes, pedaloes, snorkelling equipment and sailing boats (April–Oct).

Hóra and around

HÓRA (also called Íos Town) is a twenty-minute walk up behind Yialós port, and is one of the more accessible picturesque towns in the Cyclades, filled with meandering arcaded lanes and whitewashed chapels. Still, it gets pretty raunchy when the younger crowd moves in for the high season, and the laddish logos and inscriptions available on T-shirts and at tattoo parlours clash with its superior aspirations. The main road divides it naturally into two parts: the **Old Town** climbing the hillside to the left as you arrive, and the **New Town** to the right. The **Archeological Museum** in the new town (Tues–Sun 8am–3pm; €2) is part of an attempt to attract a more diverse range of visitors to the island, containing finds from ancient **Skárkos**, a few kilometres inland from Yialós.

Yialós – with its surprisingly peaceful and uncrowded beach – isn't as attractive as Hóra above but provides a refreshing, breezy escape from the hot, noisy capital. Twenty minutes' walk on the other side of Hóra there's the popular **Mylopótas**, the site of a magnificent beach, lots of watersports outlets but surprisingly little nightlife outside the campsites.

ACCOMMODATION

HÓRA

★**Francesco's** Old Town ☎ 22860 91223, ⓦ francescos .net. An excellent hostel with mostly of super-clean doubles and relatively few dorm beds. With free pick-ups, a bar, pool and jacuzzi plus spectacular views over the port, it offers the best value for money on the island. May–Sept. Dorm €12, double €34

Lofos New Town ☎ 22860 91481. Right by the archeological site, this family-owned, shaded complex, with simple but well-furnished rooms, is very convenient for access to the bus stop and to Hóra's nightlife opposite. Best of all, for something so close to the action, it's quiet. May–Oct. €50

Lofos Village New Town ☎ 22860 92481, ⓦ lofosvillage.com. A luxurious set of modern villas up the hill with panoramic views over Hóra from the designer pool. Facilities include currency exchange, port transfers, jacuzzi and parking. Check for online deals. May–Oct. €75

YIALÓS

Galini Pension ☎ 22860 91115, ⓦ galini-ios.com. A good-value, quiet choice in a rural setting just over 200m down the lane by the centre of the beach; relaxing in the well-tended large garden is as big a delight as lying on the beach. Free port pick-ups. April–Oct. €30

★**Golden Sun** ☎ 22860 91110, ⓦ iosgoldensun.com. Cheap-for-its-class hotel about 300m up the road to Hóra, with meticulously clean, brightly painted rooms offering views over the bay: the large, well thought-out common areas are arranged around the pool. Mid-May to Sept. €40

HÓRA AND AROUND

Yialos Beach ☎ 22860 91421, ⓦ yialosbeach.gr. Stylish hotel, just behind the hospital, offering smart doubles and studios with their own private gardens, built around a large pool with a children's pool nearby. Two-night minimum stay in high season. Breakfast included. May–Oct. €80

MYLOPÓTAS

Dionysos ☎ 22860 91215, ⓦ dionysos-ios.gr. Both attractive and luxurious, with buildings arranged around a swimming pool, this complex comes up trumps on location and services offered including free wi-fi, children's pool, a fitness studio and tennis courts. Breakfast included. May–Oct. €130

Far Out Beach Club ☎ 22860 91468, ⓦ faroutclub .com. Large party campsite with well-organized facilities, including a pool, laundry, bungalows and a cafeteria. However, it can get very noisy and crowded in Aug. Student discounts offered. May–Sept. Camping €12, bungalow €20

Íos Palace ☎ 22860 92000, ⓦ iospalacehotel.com. Stylish luxury hotel with three pools, a spa, jacuzzi, Turkish bath, pool bar and gym, plus deckchairs on the beach in front (free to residents). Breakfast included. May–Oct. €280

Purple Pig/Stars Camping ☎ 22860 91302, ⓦ purplepigstars.gr. A party hostel by the road up to Hóra, with a range of facilities, including its own club, minimarket, pool and poolside bar. It runs film shows and late-night barbecues with live Djs. Dorm €13, en-suite bungalow €35

EATING

HÓRA

Lord Byron Old Town ☎ 22860 92125, ⓦ lordbyronios .gr. A *mezedhopolio* off the main square that tries hard to re-create a traditional atmosphere, with occasional rembétika music and a good Greek menu (mains €12). Extremely popular, so make a booking or come early. Daily 7pm–late.

The Nest Old Town ☎ 22860 91778. Signposted from everywhere in Hóra, this is where the locals go to eat and

you'll soon find out why: from the moment you sit down the service, presentation and taste are exceptional. Try the *yiuvétsi* (veal baked in pasta), a snip at €10. April–Oct daily noon–1am.

YIALÓS

Octopus Tree ☎ 6972 754 365. A warm, intimate space a bit out of the way by the fishing boats on the Yialós waterfront, which serves fresh seafood caught by the owner. With mains starting at €15 it's not exactly cheap but you pay for the freshness. Daily 9am–3pm & 7pm–1am.

MYLOPÓTAS

Drakos ☎ 22860 91281. Right at the water's edge, this is the best fish taverna in Mylopótas offering mostly fried seafood dishes (€12) since the 1960s. If you want to challenge your tastebuds, try its cod the garlic sauce, which is thankfully based mostly on mashed potato. May–Sept daily noon–2am.

DRINKING AND NIGHTLIFE

Every evening during the summer, Hóra is the centre of the island's **nightlife**, its streets throbbing with music from ranks of competing discos and clubs – mostly free, or with a nominal entrance charge, and inexpensive drinks. Most of the smaller **bars** and **pubs** are tucked into the narrow streets of the old village on the hill, offering something for everyone, and you'll have no trouble finding them.

6

Fun Pub Ios Hóra, Old Town ☎ 22860 92022. An early starter and late finisher, this is a lively sports bar in the narrow backstreets of Hóra. From karaoke and quiz nights to Sunday roast and a pool table, you can come here seven nights a week and still be entertained. April–Oct daily 6pm–3am.

Íos Club Entrance to Hóra ☎ 69857 20049, ⊛ iosclub .gr. Established in 1969, this café-bar at the top of the stairs leading to Yialós starts off the evening with classical music while the guests sit back and enjoy the sweeping sunset views over Yialós. Cocktails €9. June–Sept daily 7pm–3am.

Skorpion 200m on the road to Mylopótas ☎ 69815 40703. Cavernous club with an excellent sound and lighting system; its frenetic atmosphere is up there with the best on Mýkonos. This is where everyone ends up when the clubs in Hóra close, so large queues start forming around 2am. Entrance €15 with first drink free. June–Sept nights very from week to week 1am–early.

The beaches

The best **beach** on the Yialós side is **Koumbára**, a twenty-minute stroll from Yialós over the headland, where the scenery is rockier and more remote. There is also a smaller beach further on with a cove backed by extraordinary green cliffs and a rocky islet to explore. Its western-facing setting and string of palm trees makes it ideal to watch the sunset, and attracts many amateur photographers. However, a luxury mega-resort is currently being built here which may well change the face of the beach.

On the south coast, there's a superb beach at **Manganári** easily reached from Yialós by boat or bus (see p.427). Another decent beach is at **Kálamos**: get off the Manganári bus at the turning for Kálamos, which leaves you with a 4km walk, or else take a *kaïki* from Yialós. There's more to see, and a better atmosphere, at **Ayía Theodhóti** up on the east coast. You can get there on a paved road across the island – the daily excursion bus costs €6 return. A couple of kilometres south of Ayía Theodhóti is **Paleókastro**, a ruined Venetian castle which encompasses the remains of a marble-finished town and a Byzantine church.

In the unlikely event that the beach at Ayía Theodhóti is too crowded, try the one at **Psáthi**, 4km to the southeast, although you may need your own transport to get there: taxis don't like coming to this side of the island and will charge you €30 each way.

ACCOMMODATION AND EATING   THE BEACHES

Koukos Ayía Theodhóti ☎ 22860 92420. A very good family restaurant, highly regarded by the locals, because it serves produce from its own farm next door (mains €8). It also offers basic but decent en-suite rooms above the

---

HOMER'S TOMB

Homer's tomb can be reached by car or motorbike (signposted from the road to Ayía Theodhóti, 4.5km from Hóra). An ancient town has long since slipped down the side of the cliff, but the rocky ruins of the entrance to a tomb remain, as well as some graves. There is certainly an ancient tradition, from Pausanias and Pliny, that Homer was buried on the island; furthermore, Hellenistic coins from Íos bear his name and his head. However, it was Dutch archeologist Pasch van Krienen who first discovered these tombs in 1771 and immediately claimed one of them as Homer's – in reality, though, it probably dates only to the Byzantine era.

restaurant for those who want to escape the Íos buzz. May–Sept daily noon–8pm. **€40**
Polydoros Koumbára ☎22860 91132. This grill taverna is one of the better places to eat on Íos, serving

coal-grilled meats and local specialities such as pork with celery casserole (€12) and stuffed courgette flowers on a shaded patio. Mid-June to mid-Sept daily noon–11.30pm.

Síkinos

6

SÍKINOS has so small a population – around 240 – that the mule ride or walk from the port up to the capital was only replaced by a bus in the late 1980s. At roughly the same time the new jetty was completed; until then Síkinos was the last major Greek island where ferry passengers were still taken ashore in launches. With no dramatic characteristics and no nightlife to speak of, few foreigners make the short trip over here from neighbouring Folégandhros or Íos. The end result, however, is the most unspoilt countryside in the Cyclades where the clichéd image of a priest riding a donkey can suddenly materialize from over a hill.

ARRIVAL AND DEPARTURE
SÍKINOS

By ferry Ferries dock at the far end of the port of Aloprónia, on the east coast.
Destinations Anáfi (1–2 weekly; 4hr 15min); Folégandhros (2–5 weekly; 45min); Íos (4–5 weekly; 30min); Kímolos (1–3 weekly; 2hr 15min); Lávrio via Kéa/Kýthnos (1 weekly; 12hr); Mílos (3 weekly; 3hr

45min); Mýkonos (1 weekly; 5hr 30min); Náxos (3 weekly; 3hr); Páros (3 weekly; 4hr 30min); Pireás (5–6 weekly; 4hr 30min–10hr); Santoríni (3–4 weekly; 2–3hr); Sérifos (1–3 weekly; 2hr–5hr 30min); Sífnos (1–3 weekly; 2–5hr); Sýros (1–2 weekly; 6hr 40min).

GETTING AROUND AND INFORMATION

By bus There's a single island bus, which in high season shuttles regularly between the harbour and Hóra (4–8 daily; 7.15am–11.45pm). Note that the bus is replaced by a four-seater car out of season.
By car or motorbike The island's only rental office,

Rent a Car Sikinos (☎22361 00001, ✉info@rac-rentals .gr) is at the Eko petrol station 50m back from the port.
Services There's a bank with an ATM in Kástro, while the post office is at the entrance to Kástro.

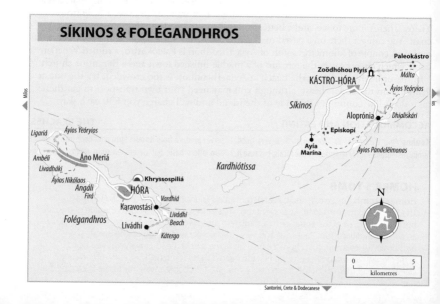

Santorini, Crete & Dodecanese ▼

Aloprónia

Such tourist facilities that exist are concentrated in the little harbour of **ALOPRÓNIA**, with its crystal-clear water, sandy beach, breakwaters and jetty. Many of the few dozen houses around the bay are summer holiday homes owned by expat Sikiniots now resident in Athens or beyond.

ACCOMMODATION AND EATING   ALOPRÓNIA

Lucas ☎ 22860 51075, ⓦ sikinoslucas.gr. Family studios at the water's edge on the opposite side of the dock, plus rooms and studios with kitchenette at the back of the village, 700m from the harbour along the road to Hóra. The family also run a taverna which in May and June is your only eating option in the port (mains €10). April–Oct. **€40**

Maïstrali ☎ 69775 07234, ⓦ maistrali-sikinos.gr. Modern hotel behind the lighthouse, unimaginatively built like a square, urban two-storey house, but offering large, well-furnished rooms with the best views over the port (€10 extra for seaviews). Free shuttle service. April–Oct. **€55**

★**Porto Sikinos** ☎ 22860 51220, ⓦ portosikinos.gr. The place to stay in Aloprónia, a pricey option but on the swish side: the rooms have a fridge, TV, a/c, island furnishings and everything else you might require for a restful stay. Breakfast included. May–Sept. **€100**

Hóra

HÓRA consists of the double village of **Kástro** and **Horió**. As you drive or walk up from Aloprónia, the scenery turns out to be less desolate than initial views from the ferry suggest, while the village itself, draped across a ridge overlooking the sea, is a delightfully unspoilt settlement. Most of the facilities are in the larger, northeastern Kástro, whereas Horió is purely residential. The fortress-monastery of **Zoödhóhou Piyís** ("Life-giving Fountain") crowns the cliff-edged hill above, and is accessed by a stepped path out of the top of Kástro. The architectural highlight of the village is the **kástro** itself, a quadrangle of eighteenth-century mansions arrayed defensively around the blue-domed church of **Panayía Pantánassa**, which opens for evensong at around 6pm. Although tourists don't tend to stay here, eating options cater for the locals and are surprisingly varied and better than in Aloprónia.

EATING AND DRINKING   HÓRA

★**Anemelo** ☎ 22860 51216. A friendly café-bar with the only shade in town; it has just a few tables outside, but you can share a table with strangers. Good cup of coffee and a snack menu ranging from omelettes (€5) to home-made syrupy desserts. May–Oct daily 10am–midnight.

To Steki tou Garbi ☎ 22860 51215. Unpretentious and cheap with a first-class selection of traditional Greek island cooking (€8–12), sourced from its own farm and served with its own barrel wine, which has been made in the same traditional way for generations. March–Nov daily noon–midnight.

Around the island

Ninety minutes' walk northeast from Hóra lies **Paleókastro**, the patchy remains of an ancient fortress. In the opposite direction, another ninety-minute walk takes you by an old path or higher road through a steeply terraced landscape to **Episkopí**, where elements of an ancient temple-tomb have been incorporated into a seventh-century church – the structure is known formally as the Herőön, though it is now thought to have been a Roman mausoleum rather than a temple of Hera. Note the weathered wooden door, and the cistern under long stone slabs in the courtyard.

The beaches of **Dhialiskári** and **Áyios Yeóryios** are reachable by road – though only the latter is asphalted – while **Málta** is only reachable by *kaïki* from Aloprónia. A more feasible journey by foot is to the pebble beach at **Áyios Pandeleïmonas**: just under an hour's trail walk southwest of Aloprónia, it's the most sheltered on the island, and also served by *kaïki* in season.

6

Folégandhros

The sheer cliffs of **FOLÉGANDHROS** rise 300m from the sea in places, and until the early 1980s they were as effective a deterrent to tourists as they had historically been to pirates. Folégandhros was used now and then as an island of political exile from Roman times right up until 1969, and life in the high, barren interior was only eased in 1974 by the arrival of electricity and the subsequent construction of a road running from the harbour to Hóra and beyond. Development has been given further impetus by the recent increase in tourism and the ensuing commercialization. The island is becoming so trendy that Greek journalists speak of a new Mýkonos in the making, a fact that is reflected in its swish jewellery and clothes shops. Yet away from showcase Hóra and the beaches, the countryside remains mostly pristine. Donkeys are also still very much in evidence, since the terrain on much of the island is too steep for vehicles, and goats – domestic and wild – are a guaranteed sight.

ARRIVAL AND GETTING AROUND
FOLÉGANDHROS

By ferry Ferries dock at Karavostási on the southeast coast. Destinations Anáfi (1 weekly; 5hr 30min); Áno Koufoníssi (1 weekly; 3hr 30min); Amorgós, Katápola (1 weekly; 3hr); Íos (2–4 daily; 30min–1hr 20min); Kéa/Lávrio (1 weekly; 10–11hr); Kímolos (2–3 daily; 1hr 30min); Kýthnos (2–4 weekly; 6–8hr 30min); Mílos (2–3 daily; 2hr 30min); Mýkonos (1–2 daily; 4hr); Náxos (1–2 weekly; 4hr); Páros (3 weekly; 3hr 40min); Pireás (2–3 daily; 5–10hr); Santoríni (2–3 daily; 45min–3hr); Sérifos (2–3 daily; 2hr 30min); Sífnos (2–3 daily; 1hr 45min); Síkinos (1–2 daily;

45min); Sýros (2 weekly; 5hr).

By bus The bus station is just outside Hóra by the Town Hall.
Destinations from Hóra Angáli beach (4 daily; 30min); Áno Meriá (5 daily; 30min); Karavostási (every 50min–1hr; 10min).

By car or motorbike It may be worth renting a car for a day – Spyros' Motorbike Rental in Karavostási (☎ 22860 41448) is cheaper than its counterparts in Hóra – but generally the buses go to most places you'll want to go.

INFORMATION AND TOURS

Services The island's post office is at the entrance to the city by the bus station. There are three ATMs: at Dhoúnavi square; at the post office; and at the port.
Travel agent Diaplous (☎ 22860 41158, ⊚ diaploustravel .gr) is the main source of information on the island. It has three offices: one in Karavostási; and two in Hóra between platías Dhoúnavi and Poúnda, and between platías Piátsa and Maráki (all daily 9am–2.30pm & 6pm–midnight). It also operates a popular round-the-island boat trip stopping at five beaches for swimming (5hr; €40).

Karavostási and around

KARAVOSTÁSI, the port, serves really as a last-resort base. There are several hotels and plenty of rooms but compared to the beauty of Hóra, just above, little atmosphere. The closest **beach**, other than the narrow main shingle strip, is the cosy sand-and-pebble **Várdhia**, signposted just north over the tiny headland. Some fifteen minutes' walk south lies **Livádhi**, a family beach with tamarisk trees. Just before Livádhi are the much smaller but more romantic beaches of **Vitséntzou** and **Poundáki**, reached by steep paths.

Touted as the island's most scenic beach, **Kátergo** is a 300m stretch of pea-gravel with two offshore islets, on the southeastern tip of the island. Most visitors come by boat from Karavostási (4–6 daily; 15min), but you can also get there on foot (20min) from the hamlet of Livádhi, itself a fifteen-minute dirt-road walk inland from Livádhi beach. It's a rather arduous and stony trek, with the final 80m descent on loose-surfaced paths, and there's no shade on the walk or the beach. The narrow sea passage between the beach's southern cliffs and the right-hand islet, **Makrí**, has very strong currents and swimming through is not recommended.

ACCOMMODATION AND EATING
KARAVOSTÁSI AND AROUND

Kalymnios Karavostási ☎ 22860 41146. Fish taverna said to have the freshest seafood on the island, though it's rather pricey and service can get overwhelmed in high season. Whether you order crab claws, fried kalamári (€15) or lobster spaghetti, it's guaranteed to have been caught on the day. April–Oct daily 7am–1am.

Livadhi Camping Livádhi ☎ 22860 41204, ⓦ folegandros.org. A friendly and more than adequate campsite with a café-restaurant, bar and minimarket, free port transfers, but somewhat lacking in shade. They also rent apartments for two people in Karavostasi

(€50). June–Sept. **€14**

Vardia Bay Várdhia ☎ 22860 41277, ⓦ vardiabay.com. Grand, recently refurnished hotel with luxurious rooms and studios in a great location above the jetty, facing the eponymous beach. Everything here is on the large side – from the rooms and the verandas with their stupendous sea views to the breakfast buffet (included). **€100**

6

Hóra

The island's real character and appeal are rooted in the spectacular **HÓRA**, perched on a cliff-edge plateau, a steep 3km from the port. Locals and foreigners mingle at the cafés and tavernas beneath the trees of its five adjacent squares (Poúnda, Dhoúnavi, Kondaríni, Piátsa and Maráki) passing the time undisturbed by traffic, which is banned from the village centre. Towards the northern cliff-edge and entered through two arcades, the defensive core of the medieval **kástro** neighbourhood is marked by ranks of two-storey residential houses, with almost identical stairways and slightly recessed doors.

Kímisis tis Theotókou

From the cliff-edge Platía Poúnda, where the bus stops, a path zigzags up – with views along the northern coastline – to the wedding-cake church of **Kímisis tis Theotókou**, whose unusual design includes two little fake chapels mounted astride the roof. The church, formerly part of a nunnery, is on the gentlest slope of a pyramidal hill with 360m cliffs dropping to the sea on the northwest side and is a favourite spot for watching some of the Aegean's most spectacular sunsets.

The Khryssospiliá

Beyond and below Kímisis tis Theotókou hides the **Khryssospiliá**, a large **cave** with stalactites and ancient inscriptions, centre of an ancient Greek male youth cult, but closed to the public for archeological excavations. However, a minor, lower grotto can still be visited by excursion boat from the port.

ACCOMMODATION   HÓRA

Anemomilos Apartments ☎ 22860 41309, ⓦ anemomilosapartments.com. Wonderfully appointed at the cliff's edge with dramatic vistas, these are super-luxurious apartments from which watching the sunset becomes an artistic experience. "Blue" coded rooms have better views and are more expensive than "green" ones. There's also a pool and in-house restaurant. April–Sept. **€200**

Chora Resort & Spa ☎ 22860 41590/4, ⓦ choraresort. com. Grand luxury resort at the northern end of town, spanning a couple of acres, with a large pool, fitness centre, designer rooms, mini-golf and even its own wedding chapel. Larger rooms have their own jacuzzi. Breakfast included. April–Sept. **€180**

Meltemi ☎ 22860 41328, ⓦ meltemifolegandros.gr. A reasonably priced hotel just before Platía Poúnda, with basic, but charming rooms, which get booked up quickly. The same family manages a more basic (but immaculately clean) option, *Evgenía* rooms (☎ 22860 41006) next door. April–Oct. **€40**

★**Polikandia** ☎ 22860 41322, ⓦ polikandia-folegandros.gr. Centred around a large swimming pool flanked by palm trees, this is a superbly designed boutique hotel before Platía Poúnda; great attention is paid to detail, with a communal jacuzzi and impressive individual massage showers. The large breakfast spread (€9) is recommended. April–Sept. **€70**

EATING

Asigrito ☎ 22860 41467. On Platía Maráki (the last square), so filling up later than the others, this is the best restaurant to eat the local *matsáta* (hand-made tagliatelle with veal, chicken or meatballs) for €12. Easter–Oct daily 1pm–midnight.

★**Eva's Garden** ☎ 22860 41110. If proof be needed that Folégandhros is sophisticated, this elegant fine-dining restaurant beyond Platía Maráki has an inventive menu (mains €12–15), a great wine list and a romantic atmosphere punctuated by the smell of jasmine. Book if

eating after 9pm. May–Oct daily 6.30pm–midnight.
Kritikos ☎ 22860 41219. A Cretan grill on Platía Piátsa with the best *dakos* (feta, crispy roll and tomato salad) in the Cyclades and some good Cretan wines. Excellent barbecued and grilled steaks from €8. April–Oct daily noon–1am, though opening months can vary.

DRINKING AND NIGHTLIFE

The town's burgeoning **nightlife** – a few dance bars along with a number of music pubs and ouzerís – is on a side street off Platía Kondaríni, where you'll find all our recommendations below.

Astarti ☎ 22860 41091 A very popular bar just off Platía Kondaríni with an alternative feel, elegant furnishings, wooden decor and large cocktails from €8.50. Night owls congregate here to listen to "quality Greek contemporary music" then continue to *Patitiri*, a few doors down, which stays open after everything else has closed. May–Oct daily 7pm–3am.

BaRaki ☎ 69485 73214. One block from *Beez* (see below), this is a cosy, friendly bar with a good selection of cocktails for €9. Indie music with a DJ whose booth takes up almost half the space inside, but who cares when you'd rather be outside anyway? June–Sept daily 10pm–3am.

★ **Beez** ☎ 69458 06652. This is the best cocktail bar on Folégandros with a reputation that goes beyond the island confines. Try its Coconut Painkiller, a five-rum cocktail served in a pineapple. Music is mostly jazz-funk with an Athenian DJ in July–August. May–Sept daily 7pm–3am.

Áno Meriá and around

West of Hóra, a paved road threads its way along the spine of the island towards sprawling **ÁNO MERIÁ** – in fact a multitude of tiny hamlets. In the middle of the settlement stands the large parish church of Áyios Yeóryios (1905), with an unusual white, carved iconostasis. Ask the bus driver to drop you off at the long footpaths down to the beaches on the western half of the island. Dirt roads lead to the beaches at **Ambéli**, **Ligariá** and **Áyios Yeóryios**; the first two are small and can get crowded, the last is a much better beach but faces north and is only comfortable when the wind blows from the south. **Livadháki beach**, accessed by signed path from just beyond Taxiárhis, is much larger, pebbly and more comfortable.

The best swimming in this part of the island is at the attractive and popular sheltered south-coast beach of **Angáli**, where there are several tavernas. Naturists should take the paths which lead twenty minutes east to **Firá** or west to **Áyios Nikólaos** beaches respectively. The latter is particularly fine, with many tamarisks, coarse sand and views back over the island. There are two tavernas (one cheap, one very expensive) at Áyios Nikólaos, while Firá has no facilities.

ACCOMMODATION AND EATING

ÁNO MERIÁ AND AROUND

Blue Sand Angáli ☎ 22860 41042, ⓦ bluesand.gr. A three-star boutique option on this well-connected beach with white, minimalist undulating staircases and rooms with verandas offering mesmerizing sea views. Port transfers and breakfast included. Two nights minimum. May–Sept **€240**

Synantisi Áno Meriá ☎ 22860 41208. A taverna at the last but one bus stop in Áno Meriá serving up a bit of everything: fresh fish, home-grown vegetables and hotpots of local meat such as rabbit, goat or chicken. This is a good place to try the local *kalasoúna* pies as well as *matsata* (€12) June–Sept 11am–midnight.

Santoríni

As the ferry manoeuvres into the great caldera of **SANTORÍNI (Thíra)**, the land seems to rise up and clamp around it. Gaunt, sheer cliffs loom hundreds of metres above the deep blue sea, nothing grows or grazes to soften the awesome view, and the only colours are the reddish-brown, black and grey pumice layers on the cliff face of Santoríni, the largest island in this mini-archipelago. The landscape tells of a history so dramatic and turbulent that legend hangs as fact upon it.

FROM TOP RESTAURANT AT IMEROVÍGLI (P.437); CHURCH OF EKATONDAPYLIANI, PARIKIA(P.404) >

These apocalyptic events, though, scarcely concern modern tourists, who come here to take in the spectacular views, stretch out on the island's dark-sand beaches and absorb the peculiar, infernal geographic features. The tourism industry has changed traditional island life, creating a rather expensive playground. There is one time-honoured local industry, however, that has benefited from all the outside attention: **wine**. Santoríni is one of Greece's most important producers, and the fresh, dry white wines it is known for (most from the *assýrtiko* grape for which the region is known) are the perfect accompaniment to the seafood served in the many restaurants and tavernas that hug the island's cliffs.

Brief history

From as early as 3000 BC, Ancient Thíra developed as a sophisticated outpost of Minoan civilization, until some time between 1650–1600 BC when catastrophe struck: the volcano-island erupted some 60 cubic kilometres of magma over a period of months. The island's heart sank below the sea, leaving a caldera 10km in

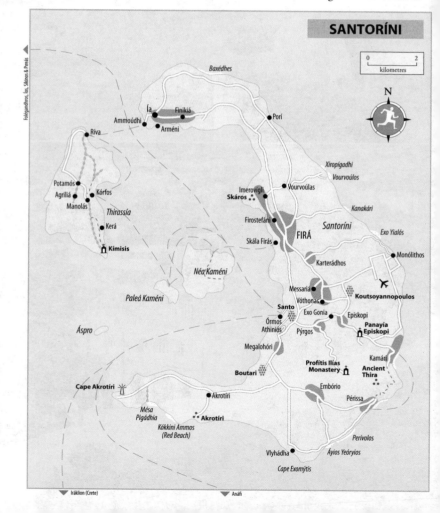

diameter. Earthquakes and tsunami reverberated across the Aegean (one full metre of ash was discovered on Rhodes), Thíra was destroyed, and the great Minoan civilization on Crete was dealt a severe blow by the ensuing ash fallout and tsunami. The island's history has become linked with the legend of Atlantis, all because of Plato. Although he dated the cataclysm to approximately 9500 BC, he was perhaps inspired by folk memories.

ARRIVAL AND DEPARTURE

By plane The airport is on the east side of the island, near Monólithos, and is served by several airlines with direct flights from the UK, including Easyjet and BA. Buses run from the airport to Firá infrequently (€2.30) and taxis are expensive (€40), so make sure you've arranged a pick-up.
Domestic destinations Athens (Aegean, 3–4 daily; 45min); Iráklio, Crete (Aegean, 1 daily; 30min); Rhodes (2 weekly; 50min); Thessaloníki (Aegean, 2–4 daily; 1hr 5min).
By ferry All ferries dock at the port of Órmos Athiniós on the west coast, 10km south of the island's main town, Firá. The old ports of Skála Firás (just below Firá) and Ammoúdhi (near Ía, in the north of the island) are used only by local excursion boats and cruise ships. Note that the old, traditional route of 580 steps from Skála Firás up to Firá is a strenuous 45min walk; you can also go by mule (€5) or

cable car (daily: April–Oct 6.30am–11pm; Nov–March 7.30–10.30am & 2.30–4.30pm; €5, luggage €2.50; ☎22860 22977).
Destinations Amorgós, Katápola (5–6 weekly; 1hr 5min); Anáfi (3 weekly; 1hr 35min); Áno Koufoníssi (5–6 weekly; 2hr 10min); Hálki (1–2 weekly, 13hr); Iráklio Crete (1–2 weekly; 1hr 30min–6hr); Folégandhros (2–3 daily; 45min–3hr); Íos (1–3 daily; 30min–1hr); Kárpathos/ Kássos (1–2 weekly; 6–11hr); Kímolos (1–2 daily; 1hr 30min); Lávrio via Kéa/Kýthnos (1 weekly; 12hr); Mílos (2–3 daily; 2–6hr); Mýkonos (1–4 daily; 2hr 15min–3hr 30min); Náxos (4–6 daily; 2hr 15min); Páros (5–7 daily; 2hr 30min); Pireás (3–5 daily; 4hr 30min–8hr); Rhodes/ Hálki (1–2 weekly; 8–14hr); Sérifos (3 daily; 4hr); Sífnos (3 daily; 3hr); Síkinos (6–8 weekly; 2hr); Sitía Crete (1–2 weekly; 10hr); Sýros (2 weekly; 8hr 20min); Thirassiá (2–3 daily from Ammoúdhi; 15min);

GETTING AROUND AND INFORMATION

By bus Buses leave Firá, the island's capital, from just south of Platía Theotokopoúlou to Oia, Períssa, Perívolos, Kamári, Monólithos (via the airport), Voúrvoulos, Órmos Athiniós and Vliháda. The timetables vary wildly from month to month, so check on ☎22860 25404, ⓦktel-santorini.gr.
By taxi The island's taxi base (☎22860 22555) is near the Firá bus station, 50m from Platía Theotokopoúlou. There are fewer than forty in the whole island, so make sure you have your onward transport arranged well in advance.
By car or motorbike If you want to see the whole island, a rented motorbike or car is essential. Nomikos Travel in Firá (☎22860 24940, ⓦnomikoscarrental.com) and Loïzos in

Kamári (☎22860 31749, ⓦloizos-santorini.com) are good, reliable agencies.
Day-trips and tours There are many travel agents clustered around Firá's main square, Platía Theotokopoúlou: Dakoutros Travel (☎22860 22958, ⓦsantorini-excursions .com) has the biggest variety of tours for all budgets, including day-trip to the Inner Archipelago (see p.440), while Ancient Thira Tours in Kamári (☎22860 32474, ⓦancient-thira.gr) runs guided tours of the ruins of Ancient Thíra.
Services There are many banks and ATMs on the island. The post office is opposite and up from the museum of Prehistoric Thira.

Firá and around

Half-rebuilt after a devastating earthquake in 1956, **FIRÁ** (also known as Hóra) clings precariously to the edge of the enormous **caldera**. The rising and setting of the sun are especially beautiful when seen here against the Cycladic buildings lining the clifftop, and are even enough to make battling through the high-season crowds worthwhile. Although Firá's restaurants are primarily aimed at the tourist market, the food can be very good; views of the crater add considerably to the price. Similarly, accommodation isn't cheap and rooms facing the caldera tend to be particularly expensive.

Using a spectacular two-hour footpath along the lip of the caldera you reach the village of **Firostefáni** and further to the north, **Imerovígli**, both of which have equally stunning views and prices. The only alternative location, where you don't

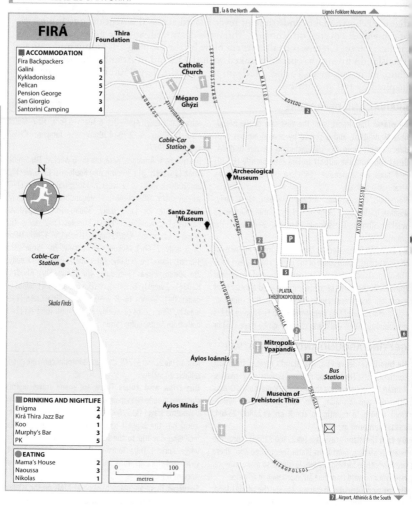

FIRÁ

Thira Foundation

■ ACCOMMODATION

Fira Backpackers	6
Galini	1
Kykladonissia	2
Pelican	5
Pension George	7
San Giorgio	3
Santorini Camping	4

Catholic Church

Mégaro Ghýzi

Cable-Car Station

N

Archeological Museum

Santo Zeum Museum

Cable-Car Station

Skala Firás

PLATIA. THEOTOKOPOULOU

Mitropolis Ypapandís

Áyios Ioánnis

Bus Station

Museum of Prehistoric Thira

Áyios Minás

■ DRINKING AND NIGHTLIFE

Enigma	2
Kirá Thira Jazz Bar	4
Koo	1
Murphy's Bar	3
PK	5

● EATING

Mama's House	2
Naoussa	3
Nikolas	1

0   100
metres

have to pay as much for the view, is **Karterádhos**, a small village about twenty minutes' walk southeast of Firá.

Museum of Prehistoric Thira

Between the cathedral and bus station • Wed–Mon 8am–3pm • €3 • ☏ 22860 23217

Firá's **Museum of Prehistoric Thira** has informative displays of fossils, Cycladic art and astonishing finds from submerged Akrotíri (see p.443) that include plaster casts of prehistoric furniture such as tables, lamps and a portable oven.

The Archeological Museum

Near the cable car to the north of town • Tues–Sun 8am–3pm • €2 • ☏ 22860 22217

The **Archeological Museum** is well presented, and has a collection from the later Homeric Classical and Hellenistic eras, much of which came from the excavations of Ancient Thira. The highlight is a mourning woman from the seventh century BC whose coloration has been remarkably preserved.

SANTORÍNI SITES JOINT TICKET

If you're planning on visiting several of Santoríni's ancient sites and museums, it may be worth buying the **joint ticket** (€14) that includes entry to the sites of Ancient Thira (see p.442) and Akrotíri (see p.443), Firá's Archeological Museum (see p.438) and Museum of Prehistoric Thira (see p.438), plus the not-so-interesting Collection of Icons and Ecclesiastical Artefacts at Pýrgos.

Mégaro Ghýzi

Just north of the Archeological Museum • May–June & Sept–Oct Mon–Sat 10am–4.30pm; July & Aug Mon–Sat 10am–8pm, Sun 10.30am–4.30pm • €3 • ☎ 22860 23077, ⓦ gyzimegaron.gr

The handsome **Mégaro Ghýzi**, housed in an old mansion owned by the Catholic diocese of Santoríni, has been restored as a cultural centre hosting special exhibitions. It also has a good collection of old prints and maps as well as photographs of the town before and after the 1956 earthquake.

Santo Zeum

Ayíou Miná, just south of the Archeological Museum • May–Oct daily 10am–6pm • €5 • ⓦ santozeum.com

Opened in 2011, **Santo Zeum** is a one-trick museum – but what a trick it is: it contains fantastic photographic reproductions (using a technique specially invented by Kodak) of the Akrotíri murals, which can be reasonably assumed to mark the beginning of the art of painting per se.

ACCOMMODATION   FIRÁ AND AROUND

Accommodation prices in Santorini prices are astronomical from June to August, so consider going in April/May or September/October. The prices below are for the shoulder season.

Fira Backpackers Place Firá ☎ 22860 31626, ⓦ firabackpackers.com. Modern well-organized hostel with 24hr reception, late check-out, cooking facilities, free laundry and female-only dorms. The bright, yellow-and-green lounge with comfortable sofas and a digital jukebox is a great place to chill out. No breakfast. Dorm **€28.50**

Galini Firostefáni ☎ 22860 22095, ⓦ hotelgalini.gr. Possibly the cheapest hotel with decent-sized rooms having a balcony and caldera view, situated in a relatively quiet spot a 10min walk from Firá. Great café terrace, too. Breakfast included. March–Nov. **€215**

Kykladonisia Firá ☎ 22860 22458, ⓦ santorinihostel .com. Sleek, upmarket hostel with a swimming pool carved out of a lava bed and single-sex dorms (maximum six people), plus a few en-suite doubles: ask for a room with a sunset view. Dorm **€28**, double **€70**

Pelican Firá ☎ 22860 23114, ⓦ pelicanhotel.gr. Large hotel on Platía Theotokopoúlou with spacious rooms but no views; it's owned by a travel agency a few blocks away, who can organize all aspects of your stay. There's satellite TV, 24hr reception and parking nearby. Breakfast included. **€125**

Pension George Karterádhos ☎ 22860 22351, ⓦ pensiongeorge.com. Comfortable rooms and studios (some with a/c, but no views), just a 15min walk from Firá. It also has a well-tended garden and pool where you can relax among the palm trees. Free port transfers. Limited number of budget rooms at this price. **€80**

San Giorgio Firá ☎ 22860 23516, ⓦ sangiorgiovilla .gr. Tucked away to the left of Firá Town Parking, this hospitable, clean hotel has simple rooms, some en-suite; it's excellent value for budget travellers. April–Nov. **€85**

Santorini Camping Firá, 300m east of the centre ☎ 22860 22944, ⓦ santorinicamping.gr. A shady campsite with a pool, restaurant, games room, 24hr reception and free internet access. Double bungalows with shower/WC also available. Breakfast €5. March–Nov. Camping **€20**, dorm **€20**, bungalow **€45**

EATING

Mama's House Firá Right below Platía Theotokopoúlou, this is a cheap, backpacker-friendly spot with hearty continental and English breakfasts, filling pasta dishes (€8) and a shaggy dog, but sadly without the chatty presence of Mama herself, who has now retired passing the baton to her daughter. March–Nov daily 8am–midnight.

Naoussa Firá ☎ 22860 24869/21277. Good traditional Greek cuisine and the cheapest place to eat and watch the sunset at Firá. Dishes as close to home-made as you'll get anywhere in town – try the celebrated moussaka for €10 – and the wine at €7/half litre is a steal. Daily noon–midnight.

6

6

Nikolas Erythroú Stavroú, Firá ☎ 22860 24550. An old and defiantly traditional taverna, insisting on using nothing frozen or not in season; the locals know this, so it can be very hard to get a table. Mains around €10 Daily noon–midnight.

DRINKING AND NIGHTLIFE

Most of the first-rate **nightlife** is northwest of the Platía Theotokopoúlou, on Erythroú Stavroú, often not starting long before midnight and busiest between 1am and 4am.

Enigma Erythroú Stavroú, Firá ☎ 22860 22466, ⓦ enigmaclub.gr. Long-established, upmarket club with three large barrel-roofed arches and an outdoor area with a palm-tree bar. Its VIP room has seen some of the world's most famous celebrities and still attracts the island's *beau monde*. June–Sept daily midnight–late.

Kira Thíra Jazz Bar Erythroú Stavroú, Firá ☎ 22860 22770. Going back more than three decades, this small, laidback venue with live DJs and music has fanatic followers who pack the place to the rafters year after year for its famous sangria (€8), despite its less-than-ideal acoustics. May–Oct daily 8pm–late.

Koo Erythroú Stavroú, Firá ☎ 22860 22025, ⓦ kooclub .gr. In direct competition with *Enigma* (see above), it offers less frenetic chill-out and trance music, with candles and cocktails, three bars, and a reservation service if you want to book a table in the VIP room. June–Sept Mon 8am–11pm, Tues 8pm–6am, Thurs noon–midnight, Fri 11pm–late, Sat, Sun 8pm–late.

Murphy's Bar Erythroú Stavroú, Firá ☎ 22860 23447, ⓦ murphysbarsantorini.eu. Reasonably priced Irish pub (beer €6) with all the obligatory hilarity. Established in 1999 it hasn't looked back since; in 2014 it took over another floor and expanded to twice its size. The wall of drinks behind the bar reaches to the ceiling and this is a rather tall venue. March–Oct daily noon–late.

PK Ayíou Miná, Firá ☎ 22860 22430, ⓦ paliakameni .com. Home of the gate-to-nowhere that you may have

---

THE INNER ARCHIPELAGO

The best and most popular **day-trip** from Firá is to the three islands of the **Inner Archipelago**: see p.437 for details of companies who run the trips. Most people stick to the still volcanically active Paleá and Néa Kaméni, while Thirassía provides a glimpse of what Santoríni used to feel like before the cruise ships arrived.

PALEÁ AND NÉA KAMÉNI

Local ferries from either Skála Firás or Ía (Ammoúdhi), venture to the charred volcanic islets of **Paleá Kaméni (**active 46–1458 AD) and **Néa Kaméni** (active 1707–1950). At Paleá Kaméni you can swim from the boat to warm mineral-laden springs, while Néa Kaméni with its own mud-clouded hot springs, features a demanding hike to a smouldering, volcanically active crater.

THIRASSÍA

The boat excursions continue to the relatively unspoilt islet of **Thirassíá** (ⓦ thirasia.gr), once part of Santoríni until sliced off by an eruption in the third century BC. It's an excellent destination, except during the tour-boat lunch hour rush. At other times, the island is possibly the quietest in the Cyclades, with views as dramatic as any on Santoríni. The downside is that there's no proper beach and the tavernas in Kórfos close early. There's an ATM at the Citizen's Service office (KEP) and credit cards are normally not accepted on the island.

Tour boats head for the village of **Kórfos**, a stretch of shingle backed by fishermen's houses and high cliffs, while a few ferries dock at **Ríva**. From Kórfos a steep, stepped path climbs up to **Manolás**, nearly 200m above, where donkeys are still used for transport (€5). Manolás straggles along the edge of the caldera, an attractive small village that gives an idea of what Santoríni was like before tourism arrived there.

EATING   THE ARCHIPELAGO

Panorama Manolás, Thirassía ☎ 697 857 5646. Just when you thought there was no more enthralling vista to be had in the archipelago, here comes Panorama, a steep climb from Kórfos, with a terrace looking over the Santorini crescent opposite. The food may be simple, of the moussaka and meatball variety, but it's filling and cheap (mains €8). Easter–Oct daily noon–10pm.

seen on island posters, this cocktail bar has steeply set terraces on three different levels and is perfect for sunset-watchers – in fact, if you book online, you can see how the sunset looks exactly from your table. Cocktails €12. Easter–Oct daily 6pm–late.

Ía

ÍA (Oía), the most photographed town on the island, was once a major commercial centre in the Aegean, but it has declined in the wake of economic depression, wars, earthquakes and depleted fish stocks. Partly destroyed in the 1956 earthquake, the town has been sympathetically reconstructed, its white and cyan houses clinging to the cliff face. Apart from the **caldera** and the town itself, there are a couple of things to see, including the **Naval Museum** (Mon & Wed–Sun 10am–2pm & 5–8pm; €3; ☎22860 71156) and the very modest remains of a Venetian castle. It is a quieter, though still touristy, alternative to Firá except during sunset, for which people are coached in from all over the island, creating traffic chaos and driving up prices. Public buses are extremely full around this time (after 6pm, although in the summer the sunset occurs around 8.30pm).

Below the town, two sets of 220-odd steps lead to two small harbours: one to **Arméni** for the fishermen, and the other to **Ammoúdhi**, where the excursion boats dock.

ACCOMMODATION   ÍA

Much of the town's accommodation is in restored **cave houses**, and rooms here are even more expensive than Firá.

Alexander's ☎22860 71818, ⓦalexandershotel.gr. Believe it or not, this is one of the best value cave hotels in Ía sporting rooms with antique furniture, four-poster beds and leafy, shaded terraces. Free parking (a rarity in Ía) is available nearby and airport transfers are offered for €35. Breakfast included. April–Oct. **€300**

Delfini Villas ☎22860 71600, ⓦdelfinihotel.net. Unlike other Ía lodgings this small boutique hotel has rooms with jacuzzis and private balconies with caldera views that are hidden away from the cameras of the tourists above. Breakfast included. **€260**

EATING

At the older, western end of town, **restaurant** prices can be as steep as the cliffs. In general the further east you go along the central ridge the better the price.

1800-Floga ☎22860 71485, ⓦoia-1800.com. One of the best restaurants on the island, serving French-inspired, though still Greek, cuisine, the interiors here have a fin-de-siècle feel and the roof garden offers unique unhindered views over the caldera. Its wines are excellent and, like the food (mains around €30), expensive. May–Oct daily 6.30pm–midnight.

Neptune ☎22860 71294, ⓦneptune-restaurant.gr. With a rooftop bar to rival the best for views and dishes for €15 that don't break the bank, this is the best-value combination of good food, view and atmosphere in Ía. Come early for dinner before the sunset buses invade, get a front-row table and chill. April–Nov daily noon–midnight.

The east coast

Santoríni's **beaches**, on the island's **east coast**, are long black stretches of volcanic sand that get blisteringly hot in the afternoon sun. They're no secret, and in the summer the crowds can be overpowering. Among the resorts lie the substantial and beautifully sited remains of **ancient Thira**.

In the southeast, the family resort of **Kamári** is popular with package-tour operators, and hence more touristy. Nonetheless it's quieter and cleaner than most, with a well-maintained seafront promenade.

Things are considerably scruffier at **Paríssa**, around the cape. Because of the abundance of cheap rooms, it's crowded with backpackers. Its beach extends several kilometres to the west, through Perívolos to Áyios Yeóryios, sheltered by the

6

occasional tamarisk tree and with beach bars dotted along at intervals. Teríssa is also home to the interesting **Museum of Minerals and Fossils** (summer daily 10am–2pm; winter Sun 10am–2pm; free), with exhibits that include rare palm-tree fossils from pre-eruption Santoríni.

Ancient Thira

Between Kamári and Teríssa • Tues–Sun 8am–3pm • €4 • Excursion minibuses depart from Kamári (see p.441); alternatively, it's a steep 2hr climb along a looping cobbled road – Archaías Thiras – starting from Ancient Thira Tours in Kamári

Kamári and Teríssa are separated by the Mésa Vounó headland, on which stood **ancient Thira**, the post-eruption settlement, dating from 915 BC through to the Venetian period. Starting from Teríssa, a stony shadeless path to the site passes a chapel dating back to the fourth century AD before skirting round to the **temple of Artemidoros** with bas-relief carvings of a dolphin, eagle and lion representing Poseidon, Zeus and Apollo. Next, the trail follows the sacred way of the ancient city through the remains of the **agora** and past the **theatre**. The path meets the paved road to Kamári at a saddle between Mésa Vounó and Profítis Ilías, the only remaining visible components of the pre-eruption landscape.

ACTIVITIES
THE EAST COAST

Diving Kamári is the base of Navy's Waterworld (☎ 22860 28190, ⓦ navyswaterworld.gr), which offers PADI courses for beginners, volcanic reef diving for certified divers, plus simple snorkelling trips.

ACCOMMODATION

Anny Studios Teríssa ☎ 22860 82669, ⓦ annystudios .com. Formerly a hostel, *Anny's* is now a collection of studios sleeping 1–6 people, and is still pretty good value. It has a range of modern, well-equipped rooms with balconies set around a central pool and bar in a quiet cul-de-sac close to the beach. Double **€35**

★ **Chez Sophie** Kamári ☎ 22860 32912, ⓦ chezsophie .gr. A stunningly designed boutique hotel with large rooms set around a swimming pool towards the southern end of the beach. There's superb and friendly service, parking, plus a delicious home-made buffet breakfast (included). They also run a second site opposite. May–Oct. **€90**

Rose Bay Hotel Kamári ☎ 22860 33650, ⓦ rosebay .gr. Less pricey than other luxurious hotels in the north part of town, with a pleasant pool setting beneath several palm trees, this four-star hotel has a gym, free parking and a good restaurant. Breakfast included. April–Oct. **€150**

EATING AND DRINKING

Teríssa's young crowds aren't so choosy when it comes to food, so the **restaurants** at Kamári catering to over-35s are much better. The best of the **bars** at Kamári are towards the southern end of the beach, offering staggered happy hours 8pm–midnight, and there's a licensed open-air **cinema** at the north end of the town.

Kritikos North of Kamári ☎ 22460 44277. A taverna much frequented by locals, this is one of the better grill places to eat on the island (mains €15). It's a long way out of Kamári on the road up to Messariá, and too far to walk, but the bus stops outside. April–Nov daily noon–midnight.

★ **Metaxy Mas** Exo Gonia ☎ 22860 31323, ⓦ santorini-metaximas.gr. On terraces overlooking the eastern side of the island, a 15min drive from Firá, brothers Dimitris and Kostas offer several Cretan dishes (mains €15) with an international twist. Feb–June & Sept–Dec daily 2.30pm–midnight; July & Aug daily 12.30pm–midnight.

★ **Meli & Thymari** Kamári ☎ 22860 31835, ⓦ melithymari-santorini.com. Old restaurant with new management and a female chef who has taken Kamári by storm. Tasty variations on traditional dishes such as beef fillet in vinsanto sauce (€14) and chicken in a clay pot with cheese and vegetables (€10). They also bottle their own Syrah /Merlot which you can drink on the premises. Easter–Oct daily noon–midnight.

West to Pýrgos

As you drive west of Kamári towards Pýrgos you can't miss the sight of **Panayía Episkopí**, the most important Byzantine monument on the island. Built in the eleventh century, it was the setting of centuries of conflict between Orthodox Greeks and

Catholics, but is most notable today for its carved iconostasis of light blue marble with a white grain.

Further west is **PÝRGOS**, one of the oldest settlements on the island, a jumble of weather-beaten houses and alleys that form several concentric circles around the village kástro. It climbs to another Venetian fortress crowned by the seventeenth-century church of the **Presentation of the Virgin**. You can clamber around the battlements for sweeping views over the entire island and its Aegean neighbours.

Nearby **MEGALOHÓRI**, 2.5km southwest of Pýrgos , is home to one of the Cyclades' most intriguing cultural centres, **Symposion** (April–Nov Tues–Sun 10am–10pm; free; ☎ 22860 85374, ⓦ thesymposion.com) with an exhibition of ancient and traditional Greek instruments, as well as daily musical presentations, instrument-making workshops and evening concerts.

6

EATING

PÝRGOS

★**Selene** ☎ 22860 22249, ⓦ selene.gr. Santoríni's most famous restaurant, awarded Greece's top gastronomic accolade in 2011 and 2014 and still serving delicious, inventive food, is the main reason to come to Pýrgos. Choose from dishes such as lamb with aubergine purée and caper chutney (around €30) or the taster menu from €90/person. Downstairs, they run the new, cheaper *Meze and Wine* bistro where more mainstream mains cost only €12–15. Booking essential. April–Oct daily noon–11pm.

Akrotíri and the south coast

Evidence of the Minoan colony that once thrived here has been uncovered at the ancient site of **AKROTÍRI** (summer 8am–8pm; winter 8am–3pm; €12; ☎ 22860 81366) at the southwestern tip of the island; the site was inhabited from the Late Neolithic period through to the seventeenth century BC. Allow at least an hour to visit the site.

The spectacular **Kókkini Ámmos** (Red Beach) is about 500m west of the site, with high reddish-brown cliffs above sand of the same colour: it's currently off-limits due to falling rocks, but is still worth viewing from afar – just don't go beyond the warning signs. More secluded black-sand beaches lie under the surreal, pockmarked pumice stone that dominates the lunar-looking coast around **Cape Exomýtis** at the island's southern extremity. Both **Vlyhádha** to the west and **Áyios Yeóryios** to the east of the cape are accessed by decent roads branching off from the main one to Embório, though no buses run here and there are no amenities to speak of. An hour's walk west of ancient Akrotíri, a lighthouse marks the tip of **Cape Akrotíri**, which offers better sunset views of the caldera than Ía.

THE WINERIES

Some of Santoríni's most important **wineries** are scattered around Pýrgos and the south, and offer **tours**. Whichever tour you go on, none is complete without a taste of Santoríni's dry white assýrtiko that's creating a buzz in sommelier circles and its prized dessert wine, **vinsánto**, which is used by the Orthodox Church in Holy Communion. Tour prices at the smaller wineries usually include tastings, while samples are available from the larger wineries for a nominal fee.

Boutari Megalohóri ☎ 22860 81011, ⓦ boutari.gr. This is the Santoríni branch of one of the largest wineries of Greece with an exceptional Vinsanto. Easter–Oct daily 10am–6pm.

★**Koutsoyannopoulos** Kamári ☎ 22860 31322, ⓦ santoriniwinemuseum.com. Santoríni's best-known winery; it has a 300m-long cellar that's home to an extensive and informative wine museum (€9.50) offering a more intimate glimpse of the winemaking process. April–May daily 10am–5pm; June–Oct daily 10am–6pm; Nov–March Mon–Sat 9am–4.30pm.

Santo Wines Pýrgos ☎ 22860 28058, ⓦ santowines .gr. Santo Wines is the island's co-operative uniting smaller producers since 1947: its showroom, complete with multimedia presentations, is easy to find, just over 1km south of Firá. Daily: Sept–June 10am–6pm; July & Aug 9am–11pm.

6

Avant Garde Suites Akrotíri ☎22860 82986, Ⓦavantgarde-suites.com. Situated 3km from Firá on the caldera rim, this stylish villa complex with an infinity pool to-kill-for has better sunset and caldera views than other pricier options on the island. It also lies above the only caldera beach in Santoríni. You'll need your own wheels to stay here, though. Breakfast included. June–Sept. **€280**

To Psaráki Vlyhádha ☎22860 82783. Beautifully perched above the fishing port, this is a seafood taverna where the waiters inform you obsessively where and how your fish was caught. A bit out of the way for tourists, it's where the locals come to eat. Mains €15. Daily noon–midnight.

Anáfi

A ninety-minute boat ride to the east of Santoríni, **ANÁFI** is the last stop for ferries and is something of a travellers' dead end. It was so for the Argonauts who prayed to Apollo for some land at which to rest; he let the island emerge from the sea for their repose. If rest is what you crave, you'll have it here in abundance. Not that this is likely to bother most of the visitors, who come here for weeks in midsummer to enjoy exactly that: its seclusion. Although idyllic geographically, Anáfi is a harsh place, its mixed granite and limestone core overlaid by volcanic rock spewed out by Santoríni's eruptions. Apart from the few olive trees and vines grown in the valleys, the only plants that seem to thrive are prickly pears. The quiet, unassuming capital, **Hóra**, provides a daring dash of white in a treeless, shrub-strewn hillock, its narrow, winding streets offering protection from the occasionally squally *gharbís* wind that comes unencumbered from the southwest.

The beaches

The glory of Anáfi is a string of south-facing beaches starting under the cliffs at **Áyios Nikólaos**. These – along with two nearby monasteries – are accessible by bus, although walking is still an option. The nearest beach is **Klisídhi**, east of the harbour, which has 200m of gently shelving sand. The next big beach is **Roúkounas** with some 500m of broad sand rising to tamarisk-stabilized dunes where free camping is allowed. Beyond Roúkounas, it's another half-hour on foot to the first of the exquisite half-dozen coves of **Katalymátsa**, the ancient port. On the craggy hill of **Kastélli**, an hour's scramble above the beach, is the site of **ancient Anáfi**; a further forty-five minutes takes you to **Monastíri**, where the bus stops.

The monasteries

Monastíri in Anáfi means the **monastery of Zoödhóhou Piyís**. The bus stops only a few hundred metres before the building. A ruined temple of Apollo, supposedly built by the grateful Argonauts, is incorporated into the monastery, while the courtyard, with a welcome cistern, is the venue for the island's main festival, celebrated on September 7–8. Go left immediately before the monastery to join the spectacular onward path to **Kalamiótissa**, another monastery perched atop the abrupt limestone pinnacle at the extreme southeast of the island. It takes another hour to reach, but is eminently worthwhile for the

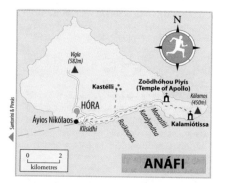

tunning scenery and views over the entire south coast – there is no accessible water up here, so bring enough with you.

ARRIVAL AND DEPARTURE

By ferry All ferries dock at the small port of Áyios Nikólaos, on the south coast. Buses usually wait for ferries to take arriving passengers to Hóra (10min).

Destinations Iráklio Crete (1 weekly; 4hr); Folégandhros (2 weekly; 5hr); Íos (2–3 weekly; 3hr 30min); Kárpathos/Kássos/Háлки (2 weekly; 5–10hr); Lávrio via Kéa/Kýthnos (1 weekly; 16hr); Mílos (1 weekly; 6hr 40min); Náxos (2–3 weekly; 5–7hr); Páros (2–3 weekly; 6–8hr); Pireás (2–4 weekly; 10–12hr); Rhodes (1–2 weekly; 13hr); Santoríni (3 weekly; 1hr 35min); Síkinos (1 weekly; 4hr 15min); Sitía Crete (1 weekly; 8hr); Sýros (2 weekly; 11hr);

Travel agents Anafi Travel (☎ 22860 61220) sells boat tickets, but it's best to organize everything in advance.

GETTING AROUND AND INFORMATION

By bus There are buses from Hóra to Áyios Nikólaos (6–7 daily; 10min) and Monastíri (3–4 daily; 25min), via the beaches.

By car or motorbike You can rent cars and motorbikes at Moto Manos (☎ 22860 61430, ⌨ rentacarmanos.com).

Services There's an ATM in Áyios Nikólaos and the island's sub-post office in Hóra. There's no pharmacy on the island (some drugs are dispensed from the GP practice).

ACCOMMODATION

Apollon Village Klisídhi ☎ 22860 28739, ⌨ apollonvillage.gr. This complex, 1km from the port, has twelve elegant maisonettes on the hillside overlooking Klisídhi beach, each named after Muses or Olympian gods and every one designed accordingly. Breakfast included. May–Sept. **€90**

Ostria Hóra ☎ 22860 61375. Self-catering studios in Cycladic blue-and-white with kitchenette and dining table, each with a balcony facing the Aegean: it's conveniently located below the centre of Hóra, with parking facilities. May–Sept. **€55**

EATING

Liotrivi Hóra ☎ 22860 61209. A popular taverna where you're invited into the kitchen to choose from the prepared dishes (€9) made using vegetables from their own garden, eggs from their own chickens and fish from their own boat. May–Sept daily noon–midnight.

★**Roukounas** Roukounas beach ☎ 22860 61206. Popular family taverna 150m from Roukounas beach serving breakfast, lunch and dinner – try the Anafiot dishes, such as the local *balófia* hand-made pasta (€8) or *meliterá* (sweet egg-and-cheese filo pastries) baked a wood-fired oven. May–Oct 10am–midnight.

Crete

CHANIA HARBOUR

Crete

Crete (Kríti) is a great deal more than just another Greek island. In many places, especially in the cities or along the developed north coast, it doesn't feel like an island at all, but rather a substantial land in its own right. Which of course it is – a mountainous, wealthy and at times surprisingly cosmopolitan one with a tremendous and unique history. At the same time, it has everything you could want of a Greek island and more: great beaches, remote hinterlands and hospitable people.

With a thriving agricultural economy (and some unexpectedly good vineyards), Crete is one of the few Greek islands that could probably support itself without visitors. Nevertheless, tourism is an important part of the economy, particularly along the **north coast**, where many resorts cater to rowdy young revellers lured by thumping bars and cheap booze. The quieter, less commercialized resorts and villages lie at either end of the island – west, towards **Haniá** and the smaller, less well-connected places along the south and west coasts, or east around Sitía. The **high mountains** of the interior are still barely touched by tourism.

Of the cities, sprawling **Iráklio** (Heraklion) can give a poor first impression, but it's a place that grows on you. The wonderful archeological museum here is an essential visit, Minoan **Knossós** is a short bus ride away, and there are more Minoan sites at **Festós** and **Ayía Triádha** to the south, with Roman **Górtys** to provide contrast. Further east, the upmarket resort of **Áyios Nikólaos** provides sophisticated restaurants and hotels, while laidback **Sitía** is a perfect base for exploring the eastern coastline. In the west, **Réthymno** boasts a pretty old town and an excellent beach, though **Haniá** (Chania) in the extreme west arguably beats it in terms of style and atmosphere. South of here is the **Samariá Gorge**, one of the best hikes in Greece.

In terms of **climate**, Crete has the longest summers in Greece, and you can get a decent tan here right into October and swim at least from May until early November. The one seasonal blight is the *meltémi*, a northerly wind, which regularly blows harder and more continuously here than anywhere else – the locals may welcome its cooling effects, but it's another reason (along with crowds and heat) to avoid an August visit if you can.

Brief history

Crete's strategic position between east and west has ensured a history far richer than many a full-grown nation. The island is distinguished above all as the home of Europe's earliest civilization, the **Minoans**, whose remarkably advanced society lay at the centre of a far-reaching maritime trading empire as early as 2000 BC. Control of the island subsequently passed from **Greeks** to **Romans** to **Saracens**, through the **Byzantine empire** to **Venice**, and finally to Turkey for more than two centuries. During **World War II**,

SAMARIÁ GORGE

Highlights

❶ Archeological Museum, **Iráklio** The finest collection of Minoan artefacts in the world, gloriously displayed. **See p.454**

❷ Knossós Even with the crowds, the Minoan palace of Knossós is the standout archeological site on the island. **See p.459**

❸ Lasíthi Plateau This fertile high mountain plateau is a taste of traditional Crete, with a cave that's the mythological birthplace of Zeus. **See p.467**

❹ Palékastro Great beaches and simple accommodation in the far east, plus access to gorge walks and ancient sites. **See p.479**

❺ Amári Valley Wonderfully scenic mountain drives, white-walled villages and olive groves, plus some lovely hiking country. **See p.488**

❻ Haniá old town Atmospheric city centre where vibrant modern life coexists with the beautiful architectural legacies of Venetian and Turkish history. **See p.494**

❼ Samariá Gorge A magnificent gorge, offering a chance to see brilliant wild flowers, golden eagles and perhaps a Cretan ibex. **See p.501**

❽ Sfakiá coast Having made it through the Samariá Gorge, you'll find some of Crete's least-visited coastline. **See p.503**

HIGHLIGHTS ARE MARKED ON THE MAP ON PP.450–451

Crete was occupied by the Germans and attained the dubious distinction of being the first place to be successfully invaded by paratroops.

ARRIVAL AND DEPARTURE CRETE

By plane Crete has two international airports, Iráklio (Heraklion) and Haniá (Chania), both served by direct flights from the UK and Europe between April and Oct; Sitía also sees the occasional summer international charter. Domestic flights include daily year-round services from Athens and Thessaloníki to Iráklio (see p.455) and Haniá (see p.497), plus several flights a week from Athens to Sitía (see p.477); in addition, there are flights from a number of other islands and mainland cities to Iráklio and Sitía.

By ferry There are daily year-round ferry connections from Pireás to both Iráklio and Haniá, and there's also a ferry linking Sitía in the east with the islands of the Dodecanese. Fast cats run from Iráklio and Réthymno to Santoríni and other Cycladic islands.

GETTING AROUND

By bus There are excellent, inexpensive bus connections across most of Crete. Fast buses run constantly along the north-coast highway, linking the major towns, while less frequent connections from the main hubs of Iráklio, Áyios Nikólaos, Réthymno and Haniá head inland and to the south coast. Current timetables and online booking are available on Ⓦ ktelherlas.gr for Iráklio and the east, Ⓦ e-ktel.com for the west.

By car or motorbike The main routes across the island and to the south are generally well surfaced and fairly well signposted. Beware of heading off on unsurfaced roads though, particularly on mountain tracks, which often just peter out before coming to a dead end. Local car rental outlets can be found in every town and resort; to pick up from the airport or arrange delivery to a hotel try Blue Sea, based in Iráklio (Ⓣ 2810 241 097, Ⓦ bluesearentals.com), or Alianthos, with offices at both airports and across the west (Ⓣ 28320 32033, Ⓦ alianthos-group.com).

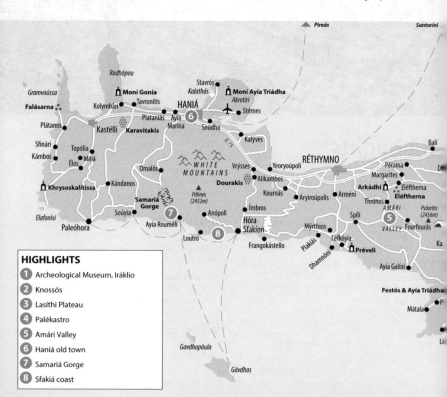

HIGHLIGHTS

1. Archeological Museum, Iráklio
2. Knossós
3. Lasíthi Plateau
4. Palékastro
5. Amári Valley
6. Haniá old town
7. Samariá Gorge
8. Sfakiá coast

Central Crete

Crete's heartland, centred on the island capital, **Iráklio**, is busier with tourists than anywhere else on the island. They come for two simple reasons: the string of big resorts to the east of the city, just an hour or so from the airport, and the great Minoan sites, almost all of which are concentrated in the centre of the island. The **resorts**, especially those closest to the capital, are dominated by package tours and are not the island's most attractive, but they're well-connected and in easy reach of the capital, with its magnificent **Archeological Museum**, and of the sites of **Knossós** and **Mália**. West of Iráklio mountains drop straight into the sea virtually all the way to Réthymno, with just two significant coastal settlements, at **Ayía Pelayía** and **Balí**. **Inland** lies agricultural country, some of the richest on the island, including a cluster of Crete's better vineyards and a series of wealthy villages; the **Lasíthi Plateau** makes a particularly striking contrast to the coastal development just a few kilometres away. To the south lie more ancient sites, at **Górtys**, **Festós** and **Ayía Triádha**, all of which could potentially be visited in a full day, with a lunchtime or evening swim on the south coast at **Mátala** or **Léndas**.

7

Iráklio

IRÁKLIO (Heraklion) is a big, boisterous city – the fourth largest in Greece. Strident and modern, it's a maelstrom of crowded thoroughfares, and, in high summer, its great sites are packed. Penetrate behind this facade, however, and you can discover a vibrant working city with a myriad of attractive features that do much to temper initial

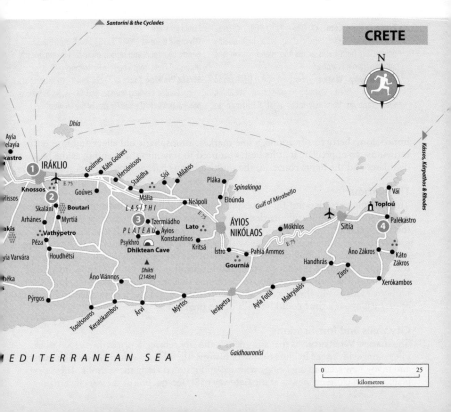

7

ADVENTURE SPORTS

Crete is a great place for **adventure holidays**, and there are numerous companies across the island offering everything from mountain biking and canyoning to trekking and horseriding. Watersports and diving operators are also listed throughout the chapter.

CLIMBING/ADRENALINE SPORTS

Cretan Outdoor Adventures ☎ 6909 008 502, ⓦ cretan-outdoor-adventures.com. Climbing, canyoning, Via Ferrata and more, from a base near Léndas on the central south coast.
Liquid Bungy ☎ 6937 615 191, ⓦ bungy.gr.

White-knuckle bungee jumping (Europe's second highest) at the Arádhena Gorge, Haniá.
Trekking Plan ☎ 6932 417 040, ⓦ cycling.gr. Rock climbing, mountaineering, canyoning, rapelling, kayaking and mountain biking in Haniá province.

HORSERIDING

Horse Riding Center ☎ 28320 31196, ⓦ cretehorseriding.com. Horse and donkey rides and instruction outside Plakiás.
Melanouri ☎ 28920 45040, ⓦ melanouri.com. Horseriding and instruction, from an hour-long jaunt to a week's riding holiday, at a stable near Mátala.

Odysseia ☎ 28970 51080, ⓦ horseriding.gr. One- to six-day guided and unguided horse treks from their base at Avdhoú near the Lasíthi Plateau.
Zoraïda's Horseriding ☎ 28250 61745, ⓦ zoraidas-horseriding.com. Horseriding holidays and treks from their stables in Yeoryioúpoli, Haniá.

WALKING, CYCLING AND KAYAKING

Cretan Adventures ☎ 28103 32772, ⓦ cretanadventures.gr. Kayaking, hiking, cycling and a huge variety of other adventure and family activities throughout Crete.
Crete-Cycling.Com ☎ 6986 927 706, ⓦ crete-cycling.com. Hard-core cycling with high-quality equipment from bases across the island; spring and autumn training camps.
The Happy Walker Tombázi 56, Réthymno ☎ 28310 52920, ⓦ happywalker.com. Walking tours ranging from day-hikes near Réthymno to

ten-day mountain hikes.
Hellas Bike ☎ 28210 60858, ⓦ hellasbike.net. One- to seven-day bike tours ranging from family to committed mountain-biker level, from Ayía Marína in Haniá province.
Olympic Bike ☎ 28310 72383, ⓦ olympicbike.com. Gentle bike tours and serious mountain biking, mostly in central Crete from a base in Réthymno.
Strata Walking Tours ☎ 28220 24249, ⓦ stratatours.com. Guided trekking holidays and day-walks as well as other activities in the Kastélli area of the far west.

---

impressions: hefty fortifications, a fine market, atmospheric old alleys and interesting museums. To appreciate it at its best, you need to stay into the evening; as the heat dissipates and the lights come on, the multitudinous bars and restaurants start to buzz.

The harbour

The obvious starting point for any exploration of Iráklio is the **harbour**, now home only to small craft but still guarded by an impressive sixteenth-century **Venetian fortress**, generally known by its Turkish name of **Koúles**. Though it withstood a 22-year Ottoman siege, time has caught up with its underwater foundations and the building is closed to visitors pending restoration; nonetheless the causeway leading to and around the fort is a favourite place for a stroll and for locals to fish. On the landward side of the harbour, the vaulted **Arsenali** are marooned in a sea of traffic scooting along the harbour road, but in their heyday these shipyards were at the water's edge and as many as fifty galleys at a time could be built or repaired here.

City walls and fortifications

The massive **Venetian walls** that still encircle the city centre, in places up to 15m thick, offer more evidence of Iráklio's turbulent history. Their fabric is incredibly well preserved, and many new sections are being excavated and restored along the seafront. The easiest place to get a close-up view is at the **Gateway of St George**, one of the old city's main

IRÁKLIO CITY

gateways whose restored subterranean vaults now house temporary exhibitions – it's approached down steps from the middle of Platía Eleftherías. Nearby, if you follow Odhós Pedhiádhos south from Platía Eleftherías you can climb to the dusty track that runs around the top of the ramparts all the way to the Áyios Andhréas Bastion, over the sea in the west. You can't actually see much of the walls from up here, but at the major gates you pass there are stairs down to the road. The only real sight, on the Martinengo Bastion at the southernmost point, is the **tomb of Nikos Kazantzakis**, Cretan author of *Zorba the Greek*, whose epitaph reads: "I believe in nothing, I hope for nothing, I am free."

25-Avgoústou Street and around

Pedestrianized **Odhós 25-Avgoústou**, lined with shipping and travel agencies, banks and stores, heads up from the harbour. On the left as you climb is the much-revered church of **Áyios Títos** (the island's patron saint), which commands a lovely little plaza, while just beyond are the **Venetian City Hall** with its famous **loggia**, and **San Marco**, the cathedral in the Venetian era, later converted to a mosque. The last two are not always open, but often host temporary exhibitions.

Platía Venizélou

Platía Venizélou (aka Fountain Square or Lion Square) is crowded most of the day with locals and tourists sitting outside its many cafés. Its focal point is the **Morosini Fountain**, which dates from the final years of Venetian rule and was once the city's main source of fresh water. Originally the whole thing was topped by a giant statue of Poseidon, but even without him it's impressive: the lions on guard are two to three hundred years older than the rest of the structure, while the eight basins are decorated with marine themes including dolphins and Tritons.

Platía Eleftherías

Platía Eleftherías, with seats shaded by palms and eucalyptuses, is the traditional heart of the city, though rarely very peaceful; traffic swirls around it constantly, on summer evenings crowds of strolling locals come to fill its café terraces. The streets leading off here are home to most of Iráklio's more expensive shops.

The Archeological Museum

Xanthoudhídhou 2 • mid-April to Oct daily 8am–8pm; Nov to mid-April Mon 11am–5pm, Tues–Sun 8am–3pm • €10, joint ticket with Knossós €16 • ☎ 2810 279 000, ⓦ heraklionmuseum.gr

Iráklio's revamped **Archeological Museum** can seem underwhelming at first – there's nothing remotely spectacular or flashy about the displays. Spend a little time here, however, and you realize just how clever it is; the superb artefacts are displayed with sparkling clarity and allowed to speak for themselves.

Ground floor

You go straight into the museum's most important section – the finest collection of **Minoan artefacts** in the world – arrayed in a series of thematic and chronologically arranged rooms on the ground floor. The sheer quantity of high-quality objects, most of them around 4000 years old, is staggering: there are entire walls covered in arrowheads, for example, or bronze ingots, or Minoan double-axe symbols. There's so much that it's hard to pick out **highlights** (and if there's one criticism to be made, it would be that individual objects are not always labelled). Nonetheless, exhibits to look out for in particular include the extensive collection of **Kamares ware** pottery, whose polychrome decoration seems extraordinarily modern; gold jewellery including the famous **bee pendant** from the Palace of Mália; a beautiful **axe head** shaped like a leopard; a clay **model house**, complete with balcony; the **Town Mosaic**, a series of painted plaques depicting buildings, probably once attached to a piece of wooden furniture; the enigmatic and still-undeciphered **Festós disc**; and the intricately decorated black stone **Harvesters Vase** from Ayía Triádha.

irst floor

Jpstairs in the **fresco gallery**, the most famous frescoes from Knossós are displayed. Only tiny fragments of the originals survived, but they have been almost miraculously reconstituted to give an impression of the entire fresco; the displays also show alternative interpretations of some of them. Beyond, the **Classical, Hellenistic and Roman era** galleries are perhaps most interesting in showing the continuity of art and ideas. Giant *píthoi* (clay storage jars), for example, are identical in shape and function to those made almost two thousand years earlier, but with very different decoration.

Odhós 1866: the market

Daily 8am–8pm (individual stalls vary; some close on Sun, while many take a siesta around 2–5pm)

Odhós 1866 is packed throughout the day with the stalls and customers of Iráklio's **market**. This is one of the few living reminders of an older city, with an atmosphere reminiscent of an eastern bazaar. There are luscious fruit and vegetables, as well as butchers' and fishmongers' stalls and others selling a bewildering variety of herbs and spices, cheese and yoghurt, leather and plastic goods, CDs, tacky souvenirs, an amazing array of cheap kitchen utensils, pocket knives and more.

Historical Museum

Sófokli Venizélou 27 • April–Oct Mon–Sat 9am–5pm; Nov–March Mon–Sat 9am–3.30pm • €5 • ☎ 2810 283 219, ⓦ historical-museum.gr

The **Historical Museum** offers a comprehensive overview of Cretan history. There are sculptures and architectural pieces from the Byzantine, Venetian and Turkish periods as well as documents and photos recalling the German invasion of Crete, plus exhibits on island folklore. Local memorabilia include the reconstructed studies of the writer Nikos Kazantzakis and of Cretan statesman (and Greek prime minister) Emanuel Tsouderos. There's enough variety and interactivity to satisfy just about anyone, plus the only **El Greco** paintings on the island of his birth, the small *View of Mount Sinai and the Monastery of St Catherine* (painted around 1570) and the even smaller *Baptism of Christ* (1567).

Natural History Museum

Sófokli Venizélou • Mon–Fri 9am–9pm, Sat & Sun 10am–9pm • €7.50 • ☎ 2810 282 740, ⓦ nhmc.uoc.gr

Spectacularly housed in a converted seafront power plant, the **Natural History Museum** examines the ecosystems of the eastern Mediterranean along with Crete's geological evolution, the arrival of man, and the environment as it would have appeared to the Minoans. There's also an **earthquake simulator**, a planetarium and, for kids, the interactive **Discovery Centre**, with plenty of dinosaurs.

The beaches

If cultural pursuits become overwhelming, it's easy to escape the city for a few hours to lie on the **beach**. The simplest course is to head east, beyond the airport, to the municipal beach at **Amnísos** or marginally quieter **Tobróuk**. Beaches to the west, around **Amoudhára**, are less prone to aircraft noise but also more commercialized and more exposed; getting to the sand can be tricky too, with few access roads penetrating the line of hotels. You'll find food, drink and other facilities at all of them; bus details are given in "Getting Around" (see p.450).

| **ARRIVAL AND DEPARTURE** | **IRÁKLIO** |

BY PLANE

Iráklio Airport The airport (Heraklion; ☎ 2810 397 800) is right on the coast, 4km east of the city. Plans for a new airport seem indefinitely on hold; in the meantime, the old one barely copes at peak times. Bus #1 leaves for Platía Eleftherías from outside the terminal (every 10min 6am–11.45pm; €1.20); buy your ticket at the booth before boarding. Virtually all long-distance buses heading east also stop at the airport, with departures towards Mália and Áyios Nikólaos every 15 minutes for most of the day. There are also plenty of taxis, with prices to major destinations posted – it's €10–12 to the centre of town; agree the fare before taking the cab.

7

Airlines and domestic destinations Aegean (waegeanair.com) operates scheduled flights to Athens (at least 7 daily; 50min), Thessaloníki (at least 1 daily; 1hr 15min) and Rhodes (at least 1 daily; 1hr); Ellinair (wellinair.com) also flies to Athens and Thessaloníki, Blue Air (wblueairweb.com) to Athens, and Astra (wastra-airlines.gr) to Thessaloníki. Sky Express (wskyexpress.gr) runs small planes to Athens and seasonal services to a number of islands including Ikaría, Kós, Kýthira, Mytilíni (Lésvos), Páros and Santoríni.

BY FERRY

From the port, cut straight up the stepped alleys behind the bus station (from where city buses depart to all areas) towards Platía Eleftherías (about a 15min walk) or follow the main road west along the coast, past the bus station and the Venetian harbour, then cut up towards the centre along 25-Avgoústou.

Operators and destinations Minoan Lines (wminoan. gr) and ANEK/Superfast (wanek.gr) have nightly ferries to Athens (9/9.30pm; 9hr); ANEK also operates the *Prevelis*, departing Sat (and Wed in summer) to Sitía, Kássos (6hr), Kárpathos (8hr), Hálki (10hr) and Rhodes (12hr), Sun to Santoríni (6hr) and Mílos (11hr). Hellenic Seaways (whsw. gr; April–Sept) and Seajets (wseajets.gr; June–Sept) between them operate daily fast catamarans to Santoríni (2hr), Íos (2hr 30min), Náxos (Seajets only, 3hr 30min), Páros (4hr) and Mýkonos (4hr 30min).

Agents The biggest local ferry agent, Paleologos Travel, 25-Avgoústou 5 (2810 346 185, wferries.gr), displays

current timetables and can sell tickets for all ferries; the also have a booth at the port.

BY BUS

Timetables, booking and info 2810 246 530 wktelherlas.gr. Timetables are seasonal and there are fewer buses to most places on Sunday.

Bus Station A On the main road between the ferry dock and the Venetian harbour, Bus Station A serves all the main north coast routes – west to Réthymno and Haniá, east to Hersónisos, Mália, Áyios Nikólaos and Sitía – as well as southeast to Ierápetra and points en route.

Destinations Ay. Nikólaos (18 daily; 1hr 30min); Haniá (18 daily; 3hr); Hersónisos (every 15min; 45min); Ierápetra (7 daily; 2hr 30min); Mália (every 15min; 1hr); Réthymno (18 daily; 1hr 30min); Sitía (6 daily; 3hr 15min).

Bus Station B Buses for the southwest (Festós, Mátala and Ayía Galíni) and along the inland roads west (Týlissos and Anóyia) operate out of Bus Station B just outside Pórta Hanión, a 15min walk from the centre down Kalokerinoú (or jump on any city bus heading along this street).

Destinations Anóyia (3 daily; 1hr); Ay. Galíni (5 daily; 2hr); Festós (3 daily; 1hr 30min); Mátala (3 daily; 2hr); Míres (11 daily; 1hr 15min).

BY CAR

Arriving in town by car, head for one of the signposted city-centre car parks (€3–6/day depending on location). One of the best is the shady museum car park on Doúkos Bófor, 70m downhill from the Archeological Museum.

GETTING AROUND

By bus Only the further-flung sites and beaches really justify taking a bus. For the beaches, head for Platía Eleftherías; westbound bus #6 stops outside the *Capsis Hotel* (every 15min); eastbound #7 departs from the tree-shaded stop opposite (every 20min). Knossós buses start from the city bus stands alongside Bus Station A (#2; every 15min) and pass through Platía Eleftherías; airport buses also pass through the

square. Buy tickets before you board, from machines in Platía Eleftherías and elsewhere, or from many kiosks (€1.20 for city and airport, €1.70 to the beach or Knossós; day pass €5).

By taxi Major taxi stands are in Platía Eleftherías, Platía Kornarou, opposite the harbour and at the bus stations; or call 2810 210 102/168. Prices should be displayed on boards at the taxi stands.

INFORMATION AND TOURS

Tourist office There's an "info-point" (Mon–Fri 8.30am–2.30pm; 2813 409 777, wheraklion.gr) in a booth on the east side of Platía Venizélou.

City tours Two rival companies (wher-openbus.gr and wcretecitytour.com) run hop-on, hop-off bus tours with

stops at all the major sights and museums outside the walls; the route doesn't include the city centre, but does go out as far as Knossós. In high season, buses run every 40min or so; a 24hr ticket costs €20, though if you hesitate their ubiquitous touts may offer you a better deal.

ACCOMMODATION

Finding a room can be difficult in high season and noise can be a problem wherever you stay. **Inexpensive places** tend to be concentrated in the streets above the Venetian harbour to the west of Odhós 25-Avgoústou, while more **luxurious hotels** mostly lie closer to Platía Eleftherías and near the eastbound bus station.

Atrion Hronáki 9 2810 246 000, watrion.gr. This attractive, modern, business-style hotel, with all the

comforts that implies – marble bathrooms, minibar, silent a/c – combines luxury with a personal touch and friendly welcome. Top-floor suites have stunning views. Breakfast included. **€85**

Heraklio Youth Hostel Výronos 5 ☎ 2810 286 281, ✉ heraklioyouthhostel@yahoo.gr. The youth hostel occupies a fine old building with high ceilings and tiled or wood floors and you certainly can't complain about the price, though the dorms – single sex, with eight to ten bunks – and bathrooms are very basic indeed. Simple private rooms too. Dorm **€12.50**, room **€27**

Iraklion Hotel Kalokerinoú 128 ☎ 2810 281 881, 🌐 iraklionhotel.gr. Not in the most attractive part of town, but this comfortable, good-value well-run place is close to Platía Ekaterínis (Cathedral Square) and handy for Bus Station B. Rooms come equipped with a/c, fridge and satellite TV, and many of those on the third and fourth floors have fine views out to sea. Cheap parking (€5/day) on site. **€55**

Kronos Agárthou 2 ☎ 2810 282 240, 🌐 kronoshotel.gr. This two-star hotel has a fabulous location by the central seafront, though the busy surrounding streets can mean some traffic noise. The en-suite rooms have a/c, TV, fridge and balcony, some with wonderful sea views (at extra cost). **€60**

★**Lato** Epimenídhou 15 ☎ 2810 228 103, 🌐 lato.gr. Stylish boutique hotel in a great central location, with luxurious rooms sporting a/c, minibar, TV and fine balcony views over the port (higher floors have better views; some cheaper rooms in a new extension across the road). Excellent rooftop bar and restaurant in summer. Breakfast included. **€90**

Mirabello Theotokopoúlou 20 ☎ 2810 285 052, 🌐 mirabello-hotel.gr. Welcoming, family-run hotel; the recently refurbished balcony rooms have a kettle, fridge, a/c and TV, while a couple of "economy" rooms have (private) baths across the hall. Economy **€45**, standard **€55**

★**Olive Green** Idhomonéos 22 ☎ 2810 302 900, 🌐 olivegreenhotel.com. Classy, modern hotel that claims to be both eco-friendly and high-tech (every room has a tablet to control lighting, a/c, etc). The beautifully designed rooms have powerful showers separate from the sink and loo. Impressive buffet breakfast included. **€100**

★**Rea** Kalimeráki 1 ☎ 2810 223 638, 🌐 hotelrea.gr. A great budget option, this friendly, comfortable and clean *pension* enjoys a quiet but central position. Some of the newly done-up rooms are en suite, others share a bathroom. Shared bath **€35**, en suite **€45**

EATING

There's no shortage of excellent places to **eat** in Iráklio, though prices are generally slightly higher than elsewhere on the island. For good quality and reasonably priced food, you need to get away from the more obvious tourist haunts, above all the main squares of Venizélou and Eleftherías (though the former is a great coffee stop).

CAFÉS

Kirkor Platía Venizélou 29 ☎ 2810 242 705. The cafés on Platía Venizélou that specialize in luscious pastries to accompany a mid-morning coffee are an essential visit. *Kirkor* is *the* place to sample authentic *bougátsa* (creamy cheese pie served warm and sprinkled with sugar and cinnamon; €3 a portion); also excellent *loukoumádhes* (dough fritters in honey) and *tyrópita*. Daily 6am–10pm.

Mare Sófokli Venizélou, opposite the Historical Museum ☎ 2810 241 946. Stylish coffee and drinks bar with a wonderful setting and spectacular glass seafront terrace. Serves a range of snacks and light lunches (burgers, sandwiches, pasta and risotto; €6.50–8), and good cocktails (€8) at night. Daily 8am–2am.

Utopia Hándhakos 51 ☎ 2810 341 321. Locals flock here for cakes and biscuits, served on fancy cake stands, and above all for the chocolate fondue and chocolate fountains – not cheap at €7.50 per person, but irresistibly indulgent. At night they also serve more than sixty different beers from all over the world, along with "beer meze" (sausages, mainly), but even then, most people are here for the chocolate and cake. Daily 9am–2am.

Veneris Bakery Cafe Yiannitsón 12 at Smyrnis ☎ 2810 280 161. Simple, self-service place with tables in a courtyard alongside an excellent bakery, serving inexpensive coffee, bread and cakes hot from the oven, fresh juices and tasty sandwiches. Mon–Fri 6.30am–9pm, Sat 6.30am–6pm.

RESTAURANTS

Giakoumis Fotíou Theodosáki 5 ☎ 2810 284 039. The little alley connecting the market with Odhós Evans boasts several tavernas catering for market traders and their customers as well as tourists. Established in 1935, *Giakoumis* claims to be the city's oldest taverna: although it's very touristy, locals reckon it still serves up some of the best *païdhákia* (lamb chops; €10) on the island – some tribute, given the competition. Also traditional *mayiréfta* (€6–8). Tues–Sun 10am–late.

I Avli tou Defkaliona L. Kalokerinoú 8 ☎ 2810 244 215. Very popular taverna-ouzerí behind the Historical Museum, serving up excellent meat and fish dishes (mains €8–12). In high summer, you may need to book to ensure an outdoor table; if you despair of getting one, there are a couple of excellent modern ouzerís on the square opposite. Daily 5pm–1am.

★**Ippokampos** Sófokli Venizélou 3 ☎ 2810 280 240. The first of a row of places with glassed-in, sea-view terraces immediately west of the harbour, *Ippokampos* serves excellent fish at competitive prices (sardines €6.50,

7

7

red mullet €12). Highly popular with locals, it's often crowded late into the evening, and you may have to queue or turn up earlier than the Greeks. Mon–Sat 1pm–midnight.

★**Katsinas** Marinéli 12, Platía Pireós ☎ 2810 221 027. A simple, economical and friendly ouzerí/grill serving tasty mezédhes (€3–5) and traditional dishes at outdoor tables. Authentic homemade food, with hand-cut chips, good seafood (sardines €7, kalamári or cuttle-fish €9.50) and meat dishes (pork chops €7.50). Tues–Sun 11.30am–1am.

Ligo Krasí, Ligo Thálassa Marinéli at Mitsotáki ☎ 2810 300 501. Ouzerí that's very popular with locals and serves up a good selection of seafood mezédhes (seafood feast for two €39.80; individual dishes around €4), as well as simple grilled meat, on a small terrace on a busy corner facing the harbour. At the end of the meal there's often a complimentary loukoumádhes dessert

and rakí on the house. Daily noon–1am.

Loukoulos Koraí 5 ☎ 2810 224 435. With a leafy courtyard terrace and an Italian slant to its international menu, this is one of the more elegant tavernas in Iráklio. Not as pricey as it looks (wood oven pizza from €6; grilled meats €7–12; fish €10–15), though the wine list can bump prices up. Also lunchtime menus for €10 (meat) and €12 (fish). Daily 1pm–midnight.

★**Peskesi** Kapetán Haralábi 3 ☎ 2810 288 887. Traditional Cretan dishes with a creative twist served in a lovingly restored mansion with hidden nooks and secluded patios. Everything is locally sourced, including veg from the restaurant's own farm and an exclusively Cretan wine list. Starters cost €6–8, mains such as chicken with chestnuts or kreokákavos (claimed to be an ancient Minoan dish of pork roasted with honey and thyme) are €10–14. Daily noon–1am.

DRINKING AND NIGHTLIFE

As a university town, Iráklio has plenty of late-night spots, though young Cretans tend to be more into sitting and chatting over background music than energetic dancing; consequently large areas of **Koraï** and the surrounding pedestrianized streets are packed with alfresco cafés which transform into **bars** as the lights dim and the volume ramps up. The bigger **clubs** are generally away from the central zone; most don't open their doors before 11pm, with the crowds drifting in after 1am and dancing until dawn. For livelier, and earlier, partying head to one of the nearby resorts or look out for posters advertising beach parties in summer. There are good events listings online at ⊕ nowheraklion.com.

Halavro Koraí 9 ☎ 2810 223 153. Beautiful, busy bar/café in a mostly derelict building with entrances on both Koraí and Milátou. The main area is in a roofless courtyard lit with fairy lights where they serve cocktails (and food, though few order it) and DJs set up as the evening wears on. Daily 10am–4am.

Jailhouse Ayiostefanitón 19 ☎ 6978 090 547. Friendly rock bar in an ancient stone building on two levels; a gathering place for Iráklio's alternative crowd who hang out here until the live music starts next door at the Rolling Stone. Daily 5pm–4am.

Kafenion Fix Aretoúsas 2 ☎ 2810 289 023. Traditional café and bar, busiest in the evenings, with tables beneath the trees of an attractive platía. There's no music, so it's a popular place to chill out over a quiet, early drink. Daily 9am–1am.

Opus Kapetán Haralábi 3 ☎ 2810 225 151. In a

superbly restored Venetian-Turkish structure, part of which was once a prison – hence the sturdy walls – this atmospheric wine bar offers dozens of Greek wines (most €20–36 per bottle, many available by the glass for €5–7). They also serve cocktails and some interesting food. Daily 10am–2am.

Senses Club Papandréou 277, Amoudhára ☎ 6944 269 733. A lively, summer-only club with a party atmosphere, 5km west of the city by Amoudhára beach, playing various types of international music including dance and R&B. Good theme nights and special events. Summer daily 6pm–late.

Take Five Arkoléondos 7, El Greco Park ☎ 2810 226 564. One of the oldest bars in Iráklio, Take Five began as a rock bar in the 1980s and is now a slick pavement café with an indoor bar, playing jazzy music; a favourite late-night hangout for a slightly older crowd. Daily 9am–4am.

SHOPPING

In addition to Iráklio's **central market** (see p.455) there's a farmers' market selling wonderful produce every Mon, Wed & Fri (10am–2pm) in Yeoryiádhi park, which is adjacent to the Public Gardens, southeast of Platía Eleftherías, and a huge **street market** every Sat morning in an open area off Leonídhou, a little further out in the same direction. Upmarket **shops**, especially those selling jewellery, clothes and fabrics, cluster around Dedhálou, Odhós 1821 and Odhós Evans (east and west of the market respectively) and along Kalokerinoú heading west from here.

Planet International Bookstore Hándhakos 73 ☎ 2810 289 605. This excellent bookshop has the island's

biggest stock of English-language titles. Mon, Wed & Sat 8am–2pm, Tues, Thurs & Fri 9am–2pm & 5.30–8pm.

DIRECTORY

Banks There are ATMs all over town, but the main bank branches are on 25-Avgoústou.

Car rental 25-Avgoústou is lined with companies offering car and motorbike rental, but you'll often find better deals on the backstreets nearby; Blue Sea, Kosmá Zótou 7 (📞 2810 241 097, 🌐 bluesearentals.com) are good for cars and bikes.

Hospital The closest is the Venizélou Hospital, on the Knossós road south out of town (📞 2810 368 000).

Laundry Washsalon, cnr Evgenikoú and Ayiostefanitón (Mon & Wed 9am–6pm, Tues, Thurs & Fri 9am–9pm, Sat 9am–3pm), and Wash Center, Epimenídhou 38, near the *Lato* hotel (📞 6944 758 511, Mon–Sat 10am–9.30pm, Sun 6.30–9pm); both do good service washes.

Pharmacies Plentiful on the main shopping streets – at least one is open 24hr on a rota basis; check the list on the door of any pharmacy. There are also traditional herbalists in the market.

Knossós

5km southeast of Iráklio • Daily: April–Oct 8am–8pm; Nov–March 8am–5pm • €10, or €16 joint ticket with Iráklio Archeological Museum • 📞 2810 231 940

KNOSSÓS is the largest and most important of the **Minoan palaces**, and the most visited. The mythological home of King Minos and the Minotaur (see below), it dates from the second millennium BC, and its labyrinthine interconnected rooms and corridors provide a fitting backdrop to the legend.

The discovery of the palace is among the most extraordinary tales of modern archeology. **Heinrich Schliemann**, the German excavator of Troy, suspected that a major Minoan palace lay under the various tumuli here, but was denied permission to dig by the local Ottoman authorities. His loss was Englishman **Sir Arthur Evans's** gain. Evans excavated and liberally "restored" the palace from 1900 onwards, and though his restorations have been the source of furious controversy among archeologists ever since, his guess as to what the palace might have looked like is arguably as good as anyone's. It makes Crete's other Minoan sites infinitely more meaningful if you have seen Knossós first.

To avoid the hordes, try get to the site early, before the coach tours arrive, or in the evening when they've left.

The site

As soon as you enter the **Palace of Knossós** through the West Court, the ancient ceremonial entrance, it is clear how the legends of the labyrinth grew up around it. Even with a map and description, it can be very hard to work out where you are. If you are worried about missing the highlights, you can always tag along with a group for a while, catching the patter and then backtracking to absorb the detail when the crowd has moved on. You won't get the place to yourself, whenever you come, but exploring on your own does give you the opportunity to appreciate individual parts of the palace in the brief lulls between groups, though the **walkways** that channel visitors around the site severely restrict the scope for independent exploration.

7

> ## THE LEGEND OF THE MINOTAUR
>
> Knossós was the court of the legendary **King Minos** whose wife Pasiphae, cursed by Poseidon, bore the **Minotaur**, a creature half-bull, half-man. The **labyrinth** was constructed by Daedalus to contain the monster, and every nine years (some say every year) seven youths and seven maidens were brought from Athens as human sacrifice, to be devoured by the beast. Finally **Theseus**, son of the king of Athens, volunteered as one of the youths, vowing to slay the Minotaur. In Crete, Minos' daughter **Ariadne** fell in love with Theseus and showed him how to escape the labyrinth using a ball of thread. It ended well for nobody: Ariadne left with Theseus, but was abandoned on Naxos; Daedalus, imprisoned in his own maze by a furious king, constructed the wings that bore him away to safety – and his son **Icarus** to his untimely death; and Theseus' father killed himself, believing that his son's mission had failed.

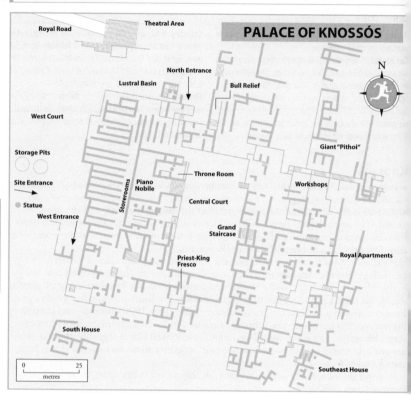

PALACE OF KNOSSÓS

Royal Road — Theatral Area — North Entrance — Lustral Basin — Bull Relief — West Court — Storage Pits — Giant "Pithoi" — Site Entrance — Piano Nobile — Throne Room — Workshops — Statue — Storerooms — Central Court — West Entrance — Grand Staircase — Royal Apartments — Priest-King Fresco — South House — Southeast House

0   25
metres

7

For some idea of the size and complexity of the palace in its original state, take a look at the cutaway drawings (wholly imaginary but probably not too far off) on sale outside.

Royal Apartments

The superb **Royal Apartments** around the central staircase are plainly the finest of the rooms at Knossós. The **Grand Stairway** is a masterpiece of design, its large well bringing light into the lower storeys. At the bottom is the **Queen's Suite**, decorated with the celebrated **dolphin fresco** and with running friezes of flowers and abstract spirals. Remember, though, that all this is speculation; the dolphin fresco, for example, was found on the courtyard floor, not in the room itself, and would have been viewed from an upper balcony as a sort of trompe l'oeil, like looking through a glass-bottomed boat. A dark passage leads around to the queen's **bathroom** and a clay tub, the famous "flushing" toilet (a hole in the ground with drains to take the waste away – it was flushed by throwing a bucket of water down).

Above the queen's domain are the **King's Quarters**, where the staircase opens into a grandiose reception chamber known as the **Hall of the Royal Guard**, its walls decorated in repeated shield patterns. Immediately off here is the **Hall of the Double Axes** (or the King's Room); believed to have been the ruler's personal chamber, its name comes from the double-axe symbol carved into every block of masonry.

The Central Court and Throne Room

The paved **Central Court** at the heart of the palace covers the oldest remains found on the site, dating back to the Neolithic era. In Minoan times high walls would have hemmed the courtyard in on every side, and the atmosphere would have been very different from the open, shadeless space which survives. Off the northwestern corner is the entrance to the **Throne Room**. Here, a worn stone throne sits against the wall of a surprisingly small chamber; along the walls around it are ranged stone benches, suggesting a king ruling in council, and behind there's a reconstructed fresco of two griffins.

The rest of the palace

Don't miss the giant *pithoi*, the storage chambers (which you see from behind the Throne Room), or the many other frescoes (all reproductions) including the Priest-King looking down on the south side of the central court, or the relief of a charging bull on its north side. The celebrated **drainage system**, evident in various locations, was a series of interconnecting terracotta pipes running underneath most of the palace. Guides to the site never fail to point these out as evidence of the advanced state of Minoan civilization.

Just outside the North Entrance is the **theatral area**, an open space a little like a stepped amphitheatre, which may have been used for ritual performances or dances. From here the **Royal Road**, claimed as the oldest road in Europe, sets out. Circling back around the outside of the palace, you can get an idea of its scale by looking up at it; on the south side are a couple of small reconstructed Minoan houses which are worth exploring.

7

ARRIVAL AND DEPARTURE   **KNOSSÓS**

By bus Local bus #2 (every 15min) starts from the city bus stands alongside Bus Station A, passes through Platía Eleftherías, and leaves town along Odhós-1821 and Evans.
By taxi A taxi from the centre of Iráklio will cost around €12.
By car From the centre of Iráklio head out through Evans

gate; from anywhere else on the island turn directly off the bypass onto the badly signed Knossós road. There's a free car park immediately before the site entrance; avoid paying exorbitant rates for the private car parks, whose touts will attempt to wave you in.

Inland from Iráklio: wine country

Heading south from Knossós you immediately leave any crowds behind as you enter the rich agricultural countryside dominated by **Mount Yioúhtas** (811m), said by ancient Cretans to be the final resting place of Zeus. Seen from the northwest, the mountain has an unmistakeably human profile. This is one of Crete's major **wine-producing** areas (see box, p.462), with a particular concentration of wineries around the village of **Péza**, and there are also some fascinating Minoan s ites near **Arhánes**.

Arhánes

ARHÁNES, at the foot of Mount Yioúhtas, is a sizeable, wealthy farming town, as it was in Minoan times. The main square has several tavernas, cafés and bars, while 100m to the north is an excellent **Archeological Museum** (daily except Tues 8.30am–2.30pm; free; ☎2810 752 712), which displays a series of exceptional finds from the town and surrounding sites. Check here for details of the nearby sites, and their current opening status. These include the burial ground at **Foúrni** (July & Aug Tues–Sun 8am–3pm; at other times check at the museum), immediately west of town, and **Anemospiliá** (not normally open, but viewable through fence), 2km northwest of town. The latter has caused huge controversy since its excavation in the 1980s: many traditional views of the Minoans have had to be rethought in the light of the discovery of an apparent human sacrifice. From Arhánes you can also drive (or walk, with a couple of hours to spare) to the summit of Mount Yioúhtas to see the imposing remains of a Minoan **peak sanctuary** and enjoy spectacular panoramic **views**.

7

WINE TASTING IN CRETE

The Péza region is traditionally Crete's major wine-producing area, but there are also **vineyards** all across the island, many of which welcome visitors. Wine has been made in this area for four thousand years (see p.461), while in recent years the Cretan wine "revolution" has seen the emergence of many prize-winning vineyards. These are just a few of the biggest and best; pre-booking is always advisable. For more, see ⓦ winesofcrete.gr.

Boutari Skaláni, Iráklio ☎ 2810 731 617, ⓦ www .boutari.gr. Not far south of Knossós lies the spectacular modern Fantaxometocho estate, owned by one of Greece's biggest winemakers. Specializing in organic production methods, they make excellent wines. Mon–Fri 9am–5pm.

Douloufakis Dáfnes, southwest of Iráklio ☎ 2810 792 017, ⓦ cretanwines.gr. Award-winning family winery which organizes a particularly good tour of the whole process, from vine to bottle. Mon–Fri 10am–3.30pm.

Dourakis Between Alíkambos and Vrýsses, near Haniá ☎ 28250 51761, ⓦ dourakiswinery.gr. Founded in the 1980s, this small, family-owned winery offers tasting and tours (from €6), often guided by amiable owner Andreas Dourakis, or by the next

generation of the family. Mon–Sat 11am–5pm.

Karavitakis Near Áno Voúves, Haniá ☎ 28240 23381, ⓦ karavitakiswines.com. An exemplar of the new wave of Cretan winemaking, a serious small boutique operation with 150 acres of vineyards. The informative short tour (€4) is followed by a tasting of some of their award-winning wines. April–Oct daily 10am–6.30pm.

Peza Union Pezá, on the Kastélli road at the eastern edge of town ☎ 2810 741 945, ⓦ pezaunion.gr. The union of agricultural cooperatives of Pezá produces olive oil as well as wine, from the vines and trees of many small producers. Free tours of their exhibition centre are followed by wine tasting and a small meze. May–Oct Mon–Sat 9am–5pm.

Vathýpetro

3km south of Arhánes • Tues–Sun 8am–3pm • Free

At the rather neglected site of **Vathýpetro** the remains of a large **Minoan villa** are surrounded by a vineyard with a valid claim to be the oldest in the world – winemaking has apparently been carried on here almost continuously since the second millennium BC. The house was originally a substantial building of several storeys, and inside was discovered a wonderful collection of everyday agricultural items, many of them in the basement workrooms. Most remarkable is an exceptionally well-preserved **winepress**, which can still be seen *in situ*.

GETTING AROUND	INLAND FROM IRÁKLIO: WINE COUNTRY
By bus Buses from Iráklio (Bus Station A) serve many of the villages in this region. Destinations Arhánes (14 daily, fewer at weekends; 30min); Péza (12 daily, fewer at weekends; 35min).	**By car** The old road out via Knossós is the most pleasant route, but directions can be confused by the presence of the new road, which cuts across the island via Peza and Houdhétsi, often extremely close to the older road.

The Messára and the south coast

The route southwest from Iráklio climbs through the mountains before winding down to **Áyii Dhéka** and the Messará plain. Here on the fertile Messará lie three major archeological sites – Roman **Górtys** and Minoan **Festós** and **Ayía Triádha** – while beyond them it's an easy drive to the south-coast resort of **Mátala**, or a rather longer, hillier one to **Léndas**.

Áyii Dhéka

For religious Cretans, **ÁYII DHÉKA** is a place of pilgrimage, named for "The Ten Saints", early Christians martyred here under the Romans. The fine Byzantine church in the centre of the village preserves the stone block on which they are supposed to have been decapitated, and in a crypt below the modern church on the village's western edge you can see the martyrs' (now empty) tombs. It's an attractive village to wander around, with several places to eat.

Górtys

600m west of Áyii Dhéka · Daily: April–Oct 8am–8pm; Nov–March 8am–5pm · €6 · ☎ 28920 31144

The remnants of the ancient city of **GÓRTYS**, once capital of a Roman province that included not only Crete but also much of North Africa, are scattered across a large area, covering a great deal more than the fenced site beside the road that most people see. The best way to get some idea of the scale is to follow the path through the fields on the south side of the main road from Áyii Dhéka, an easy walk of less than 1km. Along the way you'll skirt most of the major remains.

In the **fenced site**, to the north of the road, are the ruins of the still impressive sixth-century **basilica of Áyios Títos**, and beyond this the **Odeion**, which houses the most important discovery on the site, the **Law Code**. Written in an obscure early Doric-Cretan dialect, this is, at 9m by 3m, the largest Greek inscription ever found. The laws set forth reflect a strictly hierarchical society: five witnesses were needed to convict a free man of a crime, only one for a slave; raping a free man or woman carried a fine of a hundred *staters*, a serf only five. A small **museum** holds a number of large and finely worked sculptures found at Górtys, more evidence of the city's importance.

Festós

15km west of Míres · Daily: April–Oct 8am–8pm; Nov–March 8am–5pm · €8 · ☎ 28920 42315

In a wonderfully scenic location on a ridge at the eastern end of the Messará plain, the **palace of Festós** enjoys a stunning setting, overlooked by the snowcapped peaks of Psilorítis and with magnificent views east across the plain. While no traces of frescoes were found here, and few other artworks, this doesn't imply that the palace wasn't luxurious: the materials were of the highest quality, there were sophisticated drainage and bathing facilities, and remains suggest a large and airy dining hall on the upper floors overlooking the court.

Excavated by the Italian Federico Halbherr (also responsible for the early work at Górtys) at almost exactly the same time as Evans was working at Knossós, Festós is a huge contrast. Here, to the approval of most traditional archeologists, reconstruction was kept to an absolute minimum – it's all bare foundations, and walls which rise at most 1m above ground level. It's interesting to speculate why the palace was built halfway up a hill rather than on the plain below – certainly not for defence, for this is in no way a good defensive position. Psychological superiority over the peasants or reasons of health are both possible, but it seems quite likely that it was simply the magnificent **view** that finally swayed the decision.

Once you start to explore, the strong similarities between Festós and the other palaces are unavoidable: the same huge rows of storage jars, the great courtyard with its monumental stairway, and the theatral area. Unique to Festós, however, is a third courtyard, in the middle of which are the remains of a **furnace** used for metalworking.

Ayía Triádha

4km west of Festós, on the far side of the hill · Daily: April–Oct 10am–4pm; Nov–March 8.30am–3pm · €4

Some of the finest artworks in the museum at Iráklio came from **Ayía Triádha**, 4km west of Festós. No one is quite sure what this site is, but the most common theory has it as some kind of royal summer villa. It's smaller than the palaces but, if anything, even more lavishly appointed and beautifully situated. In any event, it's an attractive place to visit, far less crowded than Festós, with a wealth of interesting little details. Look out in particular for the row of **stores** in front of what was apparently a marketplace, and the remains of a **paved road** that probably led down to a harbour on the Gulf of Messará. There's a fourteenth-century **chapel** – dedicated to Áyios Yeóryios – at the site, worth visiting in its own right for the remains of ancient frescoes.

7

7

Mátala

MÁTALA is famed above all for the **caves** cut into the cliffs above its beautiful sands. These are ancient tombs first used by Romans or early Christians, but more recently inhabited by a sizeable hippy community in the 1960s and 1970s (including some famous names such as Bob Dylan and Joni Mitchell). The caves have long since been cleared and cleaned up, and these days they are an archeological site (April–Sept daily 10am–7pm; €2), open by day to visitors but searched by the police – and floodlit – every night.

Out of season the resort can still have an agreeably laidback feel, but summer sees the **beach** packed to overflowing, above all in the early afternoon when the tour buses pull in for their swimming stop. The main beach beneath the caves is beautiful, though, and if the crowds get excessive you can climb over the hill behind town in about twenty minutes to another excellent stretch of sand, known locally as "Red Beach". Stay the night and you can start to experience the real Mátala, and enjoy the waterside bars and restaurants in relative peace.

Léndas

The reputation of **LÉNDAS** as a hippy resort, a fishing village where you can hang out by the beach and camp for free, is somewhat outdated: the hippies grew up and now they come back with their families to stay in comfortable rooms and eat at excellent restaurants. For a quiet break, though, you could hardly choose better: it's small, low-key (though busy with locals at the weekend) and a little alternative, but it's no longer especially cheap, nor the sort of place where campers are welcomed on the beach. Something of the old ethos survives, however, at the slightly harder-to-reach beaches of **Dytikós**, to the west, and **Petrákis**, eastwards; there are rooms and places to eat at both.

GETTING AROUND

By bus The area is served by Iráklio's Bus Station B; there are fewer buses out of season and on Sundays. There is no bus to Lendás, so without transport of your own you'll need a taxi transfer from Míres.

Destinations from Iráklio Áyii Dhéka (11 daily; 1hr); Festós (4 daily; 1hr 40min); Górtys (11 daily; 1hr 5min); Mátala (4 daily; 2hr); Míres (11 daily; 1hr 15min).

THE MESSÁRA AND THE SOUTH COAST

By boat From both Léndas and Mátala, boat trips run to nearby beaches.

By car The main road south is the fast route via Veneráto and Ayía Varvára, but you can also follow a scenic detour via Voutés, Áyios Míronas and Pírgou, an undulating ride through some lovely out-of-the-way villages.

ACCOMMODATION

MÁTALA

Much of the better accommodation in Mátala is on "Hotel Street", off to the left as you enter town, behind the *Hotel Zafiria*. This is entirely lined with similar purpose-built rooms and apartments, all of them with parking, wi-fi and a/c.

Fantastic Hotel St ☏ 28920 45362, ⍵ fantastic -matala.com. There may be a touch of hyperbole in the name, but these recently refurbished studios, rooms and apartments are among the best in the street. On the town side of the street, with a private entrance at the back directly onto the town square. April–Nov. **€50**

Matala Camping Above the car park, close to the beach ☏ 28920 45720. Campsite with shady tamarisk trees; fine if you don't mind camping on sand. There's a busy bar, and Aug can bring a rowdy party atmosphere. May–Oct. **€10.50**

Matala View Hotel St ☏ 28920 45114, ⍵ matala -apartments.com. Simple rooms, mostly with small balconies, as well as some larger studios and apartments, on the quiet side of Hotel St. Breakfast available at extra cost. March–Nov. **€40**

Sunshine Matala Hotel St ☏ 28920 45110, ⍵ matala -holidays.com. Friendly, comfortable *pension* offering classily renovated rooms with fridge, and one- and two-room apartments with kitchens, on the quieter side of the street. May–Oct. **€50**

LÉNDAS

Nikis Rooms Centre of the village, behind *El Greco* ☏ 28920 95246, ⍵ nikisrooms-lentas.gr. Super-friendly place with inexpensive rooms equipped with kettle and fridge, around a lovely flower-filled courtyard; a couple of upper-floor rooms have views (at extra cost),

...ut there's a shared roof terrace for those who don't. ...iki's daughters run several other rooms places around ...wn. April–Oct. **€30**

'etrakis Beach Petrákis Beach, 2km east of the ...illage ☎ 28920 95345, Ⓦ petrakisbeach.com.

Welcoming, excellent-value taverna-rooms all with sea views, terrace and fridge; there are also two rooms in the round tower alongside the main building. Free beach loungers, and Aris, the proprietor, also organizes boat trips along the coast. **€30**

...ATING AND DRINKING

...YIOS IOÁNNIS

...averna Ayios Ioannis On the main road just south of ...estós ☎ 28920 42006. Picturesque roadside taverna ...erving excellent food at tables set under a shady vine trellis; ...he house speciality of charcoal-grilled rabbit (€8.50) is ...ecommended, and the lamb is tasty, too. Service can be slow ...t busy times. April–Sept daily 11.30am–11pm.

...ÉNDAS

★Taverna El Greco ☎ 28920 95322. A particularly ...jood restaurant with a large leafy terrace above the beach. ...he food is mostly traditional Greek – the day's baked ...dishes (generally €7–9) are on display in the kitchen – but ...cooked with exceptional care using the best local ...ingredients. There's an unusually good wine list, too, and ...they also have rooms. May–Oct daily 11am–midnight.

...MÁTALA

...Hakuna Matata Main street at far end of town ☎ 6947 343 688. A bar/café/taverna that's open all day, ...distinguished by the pirate ship's prow hanging out over the water, and the fact that you have to walk through to reach the far end of town. There's plenty of choice of food,

but that's not really the point; the place really comes alive at night, serving cocktails (around €7) and with dancing and frequent live bands. April–Oct daily 11am til the early hours.

La Scala Far end of town above the harbour ☎ 28920 45489. Big Greek/Italian place with a wonderful terrace overlooking the bay; more elegant than most and only marginally more expensive. Extensive fish menu (fish for two €35), *kakaviá* (traditional fish soup) €8, seafood spaghetti €13. May–Oct daily noon–midnight.

Petra and Votsalo Seafront beyond the market ☎ 28920 45361. Attractive taverna above the beach with a good reputation for fresh fish and a loyal clientele. Slightly pricier than nearby places, but worth the extra and has a nice line in creative salads with pasta and seafood. Meze €2.50–8; main dishes €6–17. Daily 11am–11pm; Nov–March Fri–Sun only.

Skourvoulianos Just off the main street towards the square ☎ 6985 739 869. One of the newer places in town, with a simple but authentic menu, and the day's specials listed on a blackboard. Go for the likes of *yemistá* (stuffed veg €7.50), soutzoukákia (meat balls €8) or sea bream (€12). May–Oct daily noon–midnight.

7

East of Iráklio: the package-tour coast

East of Iráklio, the main package-tour resorts are at least 30km away, at **Hersónissos** and **Mália**, although there is a string of mostly unattractive development all the way there. Worth stopping for along the way are the impressive **Cretaquarium** at Goúrnes, the **old villages** in the hills behind Hersónissos, a couple of **water parks**, and, beyond the clubbing resort of Mália, a fine **Minoan palace** that will transport you back three and a half millennia.

Cretaquarium

Goúrnes • Daily: May–Sept 9am–9pm; Oct–April 9.30am–5pm • €9, children 5–17 €6; audio-guide €3 • ☎ 2810 337 788, Ⓦ cretaquarium.gr

A former NATO air base is home to the **Cretaquarium**, a spectacular marine aquarium boasting vast tanks that house everything from menacing sharks to dazzling jellyfish. It's an excellent display that includes most of the island's native fish and crustaceans among the 250 species and over 2500 specimens on display, and it has serious scientific and educational credentials as well as being great fun. Unless you're a marine biologist the audio-guide (easily shared between two or three) is pretty well indispensable and gives loads of fascinating background information on the creatures you're looking at.

Hersónissos

The first of the really big resorts, **HERSÓNISSOS** – or more accurately **Límin Hersonísou**, the Port of Hersónisos – is a sprawling and rather seedy place overrun

7

CRETE'S WATER PARKS

Crete boasts three major **water parks** as well as a number of smaller ones, two of them in the resort strip east of Iráklio. All offer online and advance booking discounts.

Acqua Plus 3km inland from Hersónissos ☎ 6944 000 044, ⓦ acquaplus.gr. A big water park that comes close to rivalling Water City, but doesn't quite match up in terms of size or number of slides. It's a good day out nonetheless, with an attractive setting in a natural bowl of hills and a fair amount of natural shade. Admission is €27/person (children 5–12 €17) but there cut-price late-entry deals. May, June, Sept & Oct daily 10am–6pm, July & Aug 10am–7pm.

Limnoupolis Varýpetro, 8km southwest of Haniá ☎ 28210 33246, ⓦ limnoupolis.gr. Not quite as fancy as its eastern rivals, but still with plenty of big slides

and an attractive setting in the foothills of the White Mountains; entry is €25/person (children 4–12 €18), with cut-price late-entry deals. June–Sept daily 10am–7pm; limited opening May & Oct.

Water City Anópoli, 4km inland from Goúrnes, 15km from Iráklio ☎ 2810 781 317, ⓦ watercity.gr. The largest and probably the most impressive on the island, with many of the rides taking advantage of the natural hillside over which the place is built. There's the usual array of slides, pools, snack-bars and fast-food outlets. Admission is €27/person (children 90–140cm €18.50).

with bars, touristy tavernas and nightclubs. Beach and clubs excepted, the main attractions are the **Lychnostatis Open-air Museum of Folklore** (April–Oct Sun–Fri 9am–2pm; €5; ⓦ lychnostatis.gr), an unexpectedly rewarding museum of traditional Crete with imaginative reconstructions of island life past and present, and, a short distance inland, the three pretty **hill villages** of Koutoulafári, Piskopianó and "old" Hersónissos. A glimpse of more traditional Crete, they offer some attractive rooms and good tavernas; Piskopianó also boasts an impressive **Museum of Rural Life** (June–Oct Mon, Wed & Sat 10am–6pm; €4; ⓦ historical-museum.gr), one of the best of its kind on the island.

Mália

MÁLIA is, perhaps, the most notorious resort in Crete: brash, commercial, with a reputation for wild nightlife. The **beach**, long and sandy as it is, becomes grotesquely crowded at times. That said, it can be a great place to stay if you're prepared to enter into the spirit of things – party all night and sleep all day – with the bonus of a genuine town that existed before the tourists came, and a fabulous **Minoan palace** just down the road.

The Palace of Malia

3km east of Mália, just off the old highway • June–Sept Tues–Sun 8am–5pm; Oct–May Tues–Sun 8.30am–3pm • €6 • ☎ 28970 31957 • Any bus passing along the main highway should stop at the turn-off for the site

Much less imposing than either Knossós or Festós, the **Palace of Malia** in some ways surpasses both. For a start, it's a great deal emptier and you can wander among the remains in relative peace. While no reconstruction has been attempted, the palace was never reoccupied after its second destruction in the fifteenth century BC, so the ground plan is virtually intact.

From this site came the famous **gold pendant** of two bees and the beautiful **leopard-head axe**, both of which are displayed in Iráklio's Archeological Museum. Look out for the strange indented stone in the central court (which probably held ritual offerings), for the remains of ceremonial stairways and for the giant *píthoi*, which stand like sentinels around the palace. To the north and west of the main site, archeological digs are still going on as the large town which surrounded the palace comes slowly to light.

Leaving the archeological zone, you can follow the road down to a lovely stretch of clean and relatively peaceful **beach**.

GETTING AROUND   **EAST OF IRÁKLIO: THE PACKAGE-TOUR COAST**

By bus Buses from Iráklio (Bus Station A) serve the coastal resorts, running at least every 30min until 11pm to Hersónissos and Mália, with stops near all the main hotels in route. Major attractions like Cretaquarium and Water

City also feature on tours from all the resorts.
By car The E75 Highway runs a short way inland, bypassing all the major attractions and resorts; you'll need to turn off onto the old road to access any of them.

The Lasíthi Plateau

Every day, scores of bus tours toil up to the **LASÍTHI PLATEAU** to view the "thousands of white-cloth-sailed windmills" which irrigate the high plain. In reality there are very few working windmills left, although many roadside tavernas have adopted them as marketing features. The drive alone is worthwhile, however, and the plain is a fine example of rural Crete at work, every inch devoted to the cultivation of potatoes, apples, figs, olives and a host of other crops; stay in one of the **villages** for a night or two (bring some warm clothing, as the nights can get cold) and you'll see real life return as the tourists leave. Good targets include **Tzermiádho**, **Áyios Konstantínos**, **Áyios Yeóryios** and **Psykhró**

7

The Dhiktean Cave

1km southwest of Psykhró • Daily: April–Oct 8am–8pm; Nov–March 8.30am–3pm • €6 • From Psykhró a signed side road takes you up to a car park (€2 parking fee) from where the cave is a 10min climb on a steep, rocky path, or a longer but easier walk up a paved track; you can also go up by mule (€10 one-way, €15 return)

According to legend, it was in the **Dhiktean Cave** that Zeus was born to Rhea. Zeus's father, Kronos, had been warned that he would be overthrown by a son, and accordingly ate all his offspring. On this occasion, however, Rhea gave Kronos a stone to eat instead and left the baby Zeus concealed within the cave, protected by the Kouretes, who beat their shields outside to disguise his cries. The cave was a cult centre from the Minoan period onwards, and offerings to the Mother Goddess and to Zeus dating through to Classical Greek times have been found here.

Concrete steps and electric lighting have made the cave an easy place to visit, although some of the magic and mystery has inevitably been lost. The steps lead you on a circular tour, passing the bottom of the cave where you are confronted with an artificial **lake**. The one experience that has survived the alterations is the view back from the depths of the cave towards the peephole of light at the entrance. It's not hard to believe the tales that this was the infant Zeus' first sight of the world destined to become his kingdom. To avoid the crowds, try to arrive early (coaches start to arrive around 11.30am) or after 5pm.

MOUNTAIN DRIVES

Crete's mountains offer many spectacular and scenic driving routes – here are our five favourite:
Lasíthi plateau Beautiful, however you approach it: try a complete circuit, climbing up from the north coast and back through Neápoli. See p.467

Amári Valley and Psilorítis Heading southeast from Réthymno, the Arkádhi monastery marks the entry to the Amári valley, whose east side, especially, offers glorious mountain scenery; combine this with the drive through Anóyia for a complete circumnavigation of the mountain. See p.488

The far east Barren and lonely: from Sitía, head east to Vái beach, south through Zákros and Xerókambos, then back on the inland road via Zíros. See p.477

North to South West of Réthymno, a choice of roads crosses the island towards Frangokástello and Plakiás, each more spectacular than the next. See p.489

The far west A circuit from Kastélli Kissámou, down the west coast and back on the inland roads via Élos offers a bit of everything; stunning coastal vistas, traditional villages, mountains and gorges. See p.505

ARRIVAL AND GETTING AROUND

By bus There are no public buses to the plateau, though tours run from all parts of the island.

By car The quickest and easiest routes up to the plateau are from the north and northwest, from Mália and Hersónissos (see p.465). The approach from Áyios Nikólaos via Neápoli is slower – a tortuous 30km climb.

On foot On the plateau you can easily walk through the fields from one village to another – the paths between

THE LASÍTHI PLATEAU

Áyios Yeóryios and Káto Metóhi via Psykhró even form part of the E4 Pan-European walking route: crossing the whole plain, from Psykhró to Tzermiádho, takes 1hr 30min or less. More ambitiously, you can also hike up to the plateau, most directly from Kritsá in the east, or on the E4 path from Kastélli in the west. A good time to take a walk here is the early evening, when you'll encounter the villagers on their carts, donkeys and pick-ups making their way back home.

ACCOMMODATION AND EATING

TZERMIÁDHO

Kronio Village centre ☎ 28440 22375. Traditional Cretan dishes with a French twist thanks to the proprietor's Gallic wife. It's terrific value and excellent cooking – if you're hungry and in no hurry, try the meze menu, with eighteen meze dishes, main course, wine and dessert at €28 for two. The eighteen meze alone cost €9.40, or there's a more modest menu of the day for around €8. Watch out for the occasional coach party, though. April–Oct daily 11am–10pm.

ÁYIOS KONSTANTÍNOS

★ **Taverna Vilaeti** On the main street ☎ 28440 31983, ⓦ vilaeti.gr. A beautifully restored old stone building, much more elegant than you'd expect in this setting, serving exceptionally good traditional food (most of it local and organic) at standard prices (mains €10–14). April–Oct daily 9am–late, Nov–March Sat & Sun only.

Vilaeti Traditional Guesthouses Info at *Taverna Vilaeti* ☎ 28440 31983, ⓦ vilaeti.gr. Lovely, fully equipped restored village apartments and stone-built cottages, all with fireplaces for winter and full kitchen with the basics supplied, sleeping up to seven. Two-night minimum stay; superb breakfast included. **€65**

ÁYIOS YEÓRYIOS

Hotel Maria Hidden away in the backstreets ☎ 28440 31774. Sweet, old-fashioned place with framed embroidery on the walls and tiny bathrooms. Some of the double beds are exceptionally small too – they also have three- and four-bed rooms. April–Sept. **€35**

PSYKHRÓ

Taverna Dionysos Magoulás, around 1km east of Psykhró ☎ 28440 31672. Roadside taverna with quiet en-suite rooms with balconies (a couple at the back have a great view over the plain) and good traditional food using local produce (mains €6–9). April–Oct daily 8am–11pm. **€30**

West of Iráklio

Heading west from Iráklio the **E75 highway**, cut into the cliffs, is fast and efficient. It's a spectacular drive, but with very little in the way of habitation; there are just a couple of developed beach resorts, at **Ayía Pelayía** and **Balí**, until the final, flat stretch towards Réthymno. If you're in no hurry, take the **older roads west**; these curl up amid stunning mountain scenery and archetypal rural Crete, with tracks tramped by herds of sheep and goats, isolated chapels or farmsteads beside the road, and occasionally a village beneath the heights of the **Psilorítis** range.

Ayía Pelayía

AYÍA PELAYÍA, some 15km from Iráklio, appears irresistibly inviting from the highway far above, a sprinkling of white cubes set around a deep blue bay. Closer up, you're likely to find the narrow, taverna-lined beach packed to capacity, especially at weekends and on summer afternoons when it's popular with local families. However, the water is clear and calm, the **swimming** excellent and there's a superb view, at night, of the brightly lit ferries heading out of Iráklio.

Balí

BALÍ, about halfway between Iráklio and Réthymno, is a resort set around a series of little coves. The place is much bigger than it first appears, especially as the streets are winding and hilly – it's a couple of kilometres from the main road to the village, more to the best beach. Sadly, although the beaches are spectacular, they're very much overrun, and Balí has become a package resort too popular for its own good. It's lively and friendly, but only really tempting well out of season, when there are bound to be bargains given the number of rooms.

Anóyia

ANÓYIA, a small, exceptionally friendly town perched beneath the highest peaks of the Psilorítis range, is the obvious place from which to approach the **Idean Cave** and the **summit of Psilorítis** (see below). The weather, refreshingly cool when the summer heat lower down becomes oppressive, is one good reason to come, but most people are drawn by the proximity of the mountains and the town's (slightly exaggerated) reputation for some of the best woven and embroidered **handicrafts** in Crete. Anóyia is also known as a centre of **lyra** playing and has a buoyant sheep-farming sector; don't miss the **spit-roast lamb** if you're carnivorously inclined.

Mount Psilorítis and the Idean cave

Above Anóyia, a smooth road ascends 21km to the **Nídha Plateau** at the base of Mount Psilorítis. Here, at the end of the road, is the path up to the celebrated Idean cave (about a 15min walk) and the start of the trail to the summit of **Mount Psilorítis** (2456m), Crete's highest mountain. The **Idean cave** (Idhéon Ándhron) is a rival of that on Mount Dhíkti for the title of Zeus' birthplace. It was certainly associated from the earliest times with the cult of Zeus, and at times ranked among the most important centres of pilgrimage in the Greek world: Pythagoras visited; Plato set *The Laws* as a dialogue along the pilgrimage route here; and the finds within indicate offerings brought from all over the eastern Mediterranean. Visiting today, though, is something of a letdown – it's not an impressive cavern, and there's little to see.

| GETTING AROUND | WEST OF IRÁKLIO |

By bus Buses between Iráklio (Bus Station A) and Réthymno along the main coastal highway run at least hourly, and stop at the exit roads to Ayía Pelayía and Balí; you'll then have a 2–3km walk to each village, though in Balí the local road train meets most arrivals. In midsummer, Ayía Pelayía also has four direct buses a day from Iráklio. Three buses a day head for Anóyia (1hr) from Iráklio's Bus Station B.

ACCOMMODATION AND EATING

AYÍA PELAYÍA
Creta Sun Hotel On the road behind the village ☎2810 811 626, ⓦcretasunhotel.gr. Flower-decked studio complex with exceptionally helpful proprietors, a pool and well-kept a/c rooms with fridge and balcony, most with fine views; a four-night minimum at peak times. June–Sept. **€41**
Out of the Blue ☎2810 811 112, ⓦcapsis.com. This five-star luxury resort complex sits on a private peninsula, comprising five hotels, seven pools, luxury villas with private pools and three private beaches. It even has its own zoo. April–Oct. **€300**
Zorba's Beach Road ☎2810 811 074, ⓦzorbas.gr. Recently refurbished apartments and studios with balconies – many offer a sea view – above a shop just seconds from the beach. Facilities include a/c plus kitchen (apartments) or kitchenette (studios). Studio **€55**, apartment **€70**

CLIMBING MOUNT PSILORÍTIS

For experienced and properly equipped hikers, climbing **Mount Psilorítis** is not especially arduous. The **route**, which diverts from the path to the Idean Cave just beyond a small chapel, forms a stretch of the E4 Pan-European footpath and is marked with red arrows and E4 waymarkers. It should be a 6–8hr return journey to the summit, although in spring, thick snow may slow you down. Don't attempt the walk alone as you could face a very long wait should you run into trouble.

If you're prepared to camp on the Nídha plateau (it can be very cold), you could continue on foot the next day down to the southern slopes of the range. It's a beautiful, relatively easy hike, five hours or so down a fairly clear path to **Vorízia** or **Kamáres**. There are also routes, and guided hikes, up Psilorítis from the Amári Valley in the west (see p.488).

7

BALÍ

Bali Blue Bay Hotel On the ridge between Varkótopos cove and Limáni ☎28340 20111, ⓦbalibluebay.gr. Friendly, family-run, modern hotel with great views from most rooms and even better ones from the rooftop pool. Buffet breakfast included. April–Oct. €65

Mira Mare Above Varkótopos cove ☎28340 94256, ⓔmiramare_bali@yahoo.gr. Handily located above a supermarket, these traditional rooms with a/c, fridge and sea views from the balcony are basic but excellent value. May–Oct. €35

ANÓYIA

Aetos Main street, upper village ☎28340 31262. Excellent local taverna with a wood-fired grill and spacious terrace. Specialities include *souvláki* and goat dishes as

well as rotisserie chicken (€6.50) and a mouth-watering *ofto* (wood-fire-roasted lamb; €9 a portion). Daily 11am–11pm.

★**Aristea** Ring road, upper village ☎28340 31584, ⓦhotelaristea.gr. Lovely room and apartment complex run by the irrepressible Aristea, her daughter and granddaughter (both also called Aristea). There's a beautiful maisonette for up to six people, as well as family duplex apartments and simpler rooms, all with sensational views. Good-value breakfasts available. Double €35, apartment €50

Mihalos Platía Livádhi T28340 31396. Tavernas in the lower town are not great value on the whole, but this retro *kafenío* right on the square is a perfect people-watching spot serving breakfast, drinks, snacks and delicious *galaktoboúreko* (traditional custard pie, here made with fresh ewes' milk; €2.50). Daily 8am–midnight.

Eastern Crete

Eastern Crete is dominated by the resort of **Áyios Nikólaos** and the upmarket tourism it attracts. Nearby **Eloúnda** is the home of many of the island's most luxurious hotels, as well as the gateway to the forbidding islet of **Spinalónga**. Inland, **Kritsá**, with its famous frescoed church and textile sellers, and the imposing ruins of **ancient Lató**, make for good excursions. Far fewer people venture further: **Sitía**, an attractive, traditional town where tourism has had little visible effect, is the gateway to the far east and some of Crete's finest **beaches**, as well as a dramatic Minoan palace at **Káto Zákros**; while the south coast offers attractive small resorts at **Mírtos** and **Makriyialós**.

Áyios Nikólaos

Set on a hilly peninsula around a supposedly bottomless **lake**, in a lovely setting overlooking the **Gulf of Mirabéllo** ("Beautiful View"), **ÁYIOS NIKÓLAOS** is wonderfully picturesque, with dozens of excellent cafés, restaurants and bars around the lake, the harbour and the nearby coast. Curiously, what it doesn't have is a beach of any significance, so the five-star hotels are all some way out – mostly to the north, around Eloúnda – where they have private access to the coast.

By day, things to do in town are pretty limited – most people stroll the area around **Lake Voulisméni**, nose around the shops, walk to one of the municipal **beaches**, all of which have Blue Flag status, or visit the interesting **Folk Museum** (officially May–Oct Tues–Sat 10am–2pm & 5–7pm, but hours are unreliable; €3; ☎28410 25093), near the tourist office. There's also a wide choice of **boat trips** around the bay (see below).

ARRIVAL AND DEPARTURE
ÁYIOS NIKÓLAOS

By bus The bus station is north of the centre in the new town. There are local buses to the centre hourly, or it's a steep up-and-down walk. For timetables, see ⓦktelherlas.gr. There are generally fewer services at weekends.

Destinations Eloúnda (hourly 9am–8pm; 20min); Ierápetra (7 daily; 1hr); Iráklio (18 daily; 1hr 30min); Kritsá (9 daily; 20min); Pláka (every 2hr 9am–7pm; 30min); Sitía (7 daily; 1hr 45min).

INFORMATION AND ACTIVITIES

Tourist information The tourist office (April–June & Oct daily 9am–5pm; July–Sept 8am–9pm; ☎28410 22357, ⓦaghiosnikolaos.gr), by the bridge, is particularly helpful, if often busy. They have lots of maps and brochures,

as well as currency exchange at good rates.

Boat trips Daily trips to Spinalónga (€25 with lunch, €15 without), plus various fishing, barbecue, beach and sunset tours, often with meals included, leave from around the harbour.

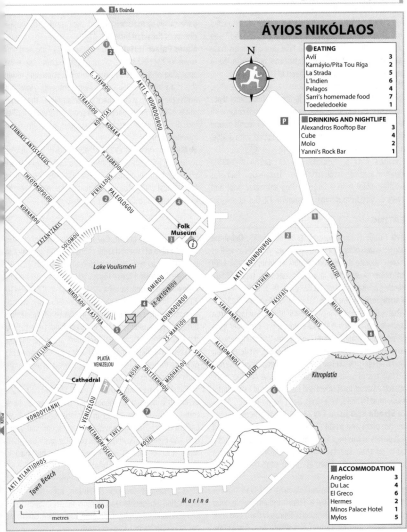

ÁYIOS NIKÓLAOS

●EATING	
Avlí	3
Karnáyio/Píta Tou Ríga	2
La Strada	5
L'Indien	6
Pelagos	4
Sarri's homemade food	7
Toedeledoekie	1

■DRINKING AND NIGHTLIFE	
Alexandros Rooftop Bar	3
Cube	4
Molo	2
Yanni's Rock Bar	1

■ACCOMMODATION	
Angelos	3
Du Lac	4
El Greco	6
Hermes	2
Minos Palace Hotel	1
Mylos	5

Car and bike rental For cars, try Clubcars, 28-Oktovríou 24 (☎28410 25868, ⓦclubcars.net), and for scooters Manolis, Aktí S. Koundoúrou 16 (☎28410 24940). Martinbike at the *Sunlight Hotel* (☎28410 26622, ⓦmartinbike.com), on the coast road towards Eloúnda, rents quality mountain and road bikes, and organizes tours.

Diving and watersports Pelagos Dive Centre, based at the *Minos Beach Hotel* (☎28410 24376, ⓦdivecrete.com), is a quality operation that also rents out motorboats and sailing dinghies by the hour, and can arrange private sailing excursions.

ACCOMMODATION

★**Angelos** Aktí S. Koundoúrou 16 ☎28410 23501. Welcoming small hotel on the seafront, offering super value balconied a/c rooms with TV and fridge plus fine views over the Gulf. No breakfast, but there's a supermarket,

owned by the same people, directly beneath; ask here for information if there's no one around. **€35**

★**Du Lac** 28 Oktovríou 17 ☎28410 22711, ⓦdulachotel.gr. Perhaps the most unexpected bargain in

7

Áyios Nikólaos. The rooms and studios are classily renovated in designer style, exceptionally well-equipped, and in an prime location overlooking the lake. Not all rooms have lake views, however, and night-time noise can be a problem, as you're right in the heart of things. €45

El Greco Aktí Themistokléous 1 ☎28410 28894, ⓦhotelelgreco.eu. Fabulously located seafront hotel that's not as fancy as it first appears. Rooms at the front come with fantastic sea views from their balconies (well worth paying the approx €10 extra) and all are equipped with fridge, minibar and tea-making facilities. April–Oct. €55

Hermes Aktí S. Koundoúrou 21 ☎28410 28253, ⓦwww.avrahotelscollection.gr. Luxurious four-star seafront hotel with a large rooftop saltwater pool and every facility from minibar to satellite TV. Out of season,

prices fall by up to 50 percent and there are often big online discounts. Breakfast included. €100

Minos Palace Hotel On the promontory 1km north of town ☎28410 23801, ⓦminospalace.com. The most appealing of a clutch of luxury hotels just outside town, this is a veritable village in its own right, with views out across the Gulf as well as back towards town – the pricier suites have a private pool. Lovely rooms and every facility including private beach with watersports. Breakfast included. €200

★**Mylos** Sarolídi 24 ☎28411 00839, ⓦpensionmylos .com. Exceptionally welcoming pension where guests are often plied with homemade cakes and sweets. The spotless rooms, most with balconies and spectacular views over the Gulf, all have TV, fridge and a/c. April–Oct. €49

EATING

Avlí Odhós P. Georgíou 12 ☎28410 82479. Delightful garden ouzerí offering a wide mezédhes selection as well as more elaborate dishes such as pork in wine, or lamb with artichokes slow-cooked in a traditional oven (both €9.50). Booking advisable. May–Oct daily 12.30–3pm & 7–11pm.

Karnáyio/Píta Tou Ríga Paleológou 24 ☎28410 25968. What appear to be two separate establishments in fact share a colourful terrace above the lake, where you can order from either menu. *Karnáyio* is a modern incarnation of a traditional ouzerí serving tasty mezédhes (€4–8 each), while *Píta tou Ríga* is an upmarket kebab joint – their speciality *píta tou ríga* (€3.80) comes with added bacon and cheese. The place attracts a young, local crowd and there's *lýra* and *laoúto* (lute) music most Fri and Sat evenings. Daily noon–1am.

La Strada N. Plastíra 5 ☎28410 25841. There's decent risotto, pizza and pasta (€7–11) plus reasonably priced fish dishes at this popular, Greek-Italian restaurant; get a table on their spectacular terrace above the lake for some of the best views in town. March–Dec daily 11am–11pm.

★**L'Indien** N. Aktí Papanikoláou 4 ☎28413 00876. Indian restaurant run by a French-Indian couple who moved here from Paris. The food is delicately flavoured with fresh spices and rarely hot; the whole fish curries are

amazing (€18 for bream, €20 for seabass) and they also have the likes of tandoori lamb chops (€12.50) and chicken biryani (€9) as well as interesting Indian salads (€5–9). March–Dec daily 11am–11pm.

Pelagos Stratígou Kóraka and Kateháki 10 ☎28410 25737. Housed in an elegant mansion, this stylish, upmarket fish taverna has an attractive leafy garden terrace that complements the excellent food: fresh fish by the kilo is pricier than usual, but there are more modest options like grilled octopus (€11), rice with seafood (€13) or pasta dishes (€11–14). Booking advisable. April–Oct daily noon–3pm & 7pm–1am.

★**Sarri's homemade food** Kýprou 15 ☎28410 28059. Great little budget neighbourhood taverna in a quiet corner, with outdoor tables in a platía overlooking an ancient church. The meze with wine is exceptional value (€9) and they also have daily specials like lamb in lemon sauce (€10) or chicken in the oven (€7.50): breakfast is served, too. Daily 9am–midnight.

Toedeledoekie Aktí S. Koundoúrou 19 ☎28410 25537. Friendly, low-key Dutch-run café that offers international papers to read, yummy toasties, sandwiches and milkshakes; at night, it morphs into a chilled, candle-lit bar. May–Oct daily 10.30am–2am.

DRINKING AND NIGHTLIFE

A string of **bars** along Aktí I. Koundoúrou on the east side of the harbour play cool sounds on their waterside terraces, and many have dancefloors inside that fill as the night wears on. Late-night music venues and **clubs** line the bottom of 25-Martíou as it heads up the hill – though few seem to survive in the same incarnation for long.

Alexandros Rooftop Bar Kondhiláki ☎28410 24309. The name says it all; a great eyrie for a relaxed drink overlooking the lake, becoming increasingly rowdy as the cocktails take effect and the small dancefloor fills. The playlist ranges from the 1960s to the present day but is mostly oldies. Happy hour till 10.30pm. Daily 8pm til the early hours.

Cube 25-Martíou 9. One of the longest-established of the clubs on 25-Martíou, *Cube* boasts theme nights, local DJs and a broad sweep of music. June–Sept Thurs–Sat midnight–8am.

Molo Aktí I. Koundoúrou 6 ☎28410 26250. One of a string of harbourside cafés with waterside terraces, *Molo*

CLOCKWISE FROM TOP LEFT STAVRÓS BEACH (P.501); AYÍA TRÍADHA (P.500); MOUNT PSILORÍTIS (P.469) >

rarely closes; it's a café and local hangout by day and a cocktail bar in the evening; later on the action moves inside for dancing, club nights and occasional live music. Daily 8am til the early hours.

Yanni's Rock Bar Akti I. Koundoúrou 1 ☎ 28410 23581 Long-running classic rock music bar, with a party atmosphere and a soundtrack of 1970s and '80s music, blues, hard rock and heavy metal. Daily 10pm–4am.

Eloúnda and around

The busy little resort of **ELOÚNDA** has a strangely split personality: surrounded by the most expensive hotels in Crete and boasting plenty of jewellery and fashion stores and pricey seafront restaurants, it also has a much more earthy side, with plenty of inexpensive rooms and cafés that compete to provide the biggest, cheapest English breakfast. There are small beaches all around, though many of the best are monopolized by the big hotels; a good, sandy **municipal beach** stretches out north from the centre, and there are numerous popular swimming spots further out in this direction. Just before the centre of the village, a road (signposted) leads downhill to a natural causeway leading to the ancient "sunken city" of **Olous**. Here you'll find restored windmills, a short length of canal, Venetian saltpans and a well-preserved Roman dolphin **mosaic**, but nothing of the sunken city itself beyond a couple of walls in about 70cm of water.

Pláka

PLÁKA, some 5km north of Eloúnda, lies directly opposite the islet of Spinalónga and was once the mainland supply centre for the leper colony there. Boats still make the short trip across, nowadays carrying tourists, and the formerly decaying hamlet has become quite chichi; it's overlooked by a vast luxury hotel and many of its houses have been done up by foreign owners or villa companies. It's still an attractive, tranquil place, with a couple of excellent tavernas and crystal-clear water – though the beach is made up of large, uncomfortable pebbles.

Spinalónga

April, May & Oct daily 9.30am–3.30pm; June–Sept daily 9am–7pm; Nov–March Sat & Sun 9am–3pm • €2 • Boats run every 30min in season from both Eloúnda (€10 return) and Pláka (€8); most give you 1hr on the island, though you can take a later boat if there's room; it's also included on many day-trips from Áyios Nikólaos

As a bastion of the Venetian defence, the fortress-rock of **Spinalónga** withstood the power of the Ottoman Empire for 45 years after the mainland had fallen. The most infamous part of the islet's history, however, is more recent; it served as a **leper colony** for five decades until 1957. Even today, despite the crowds of visitors, there's a real sense of the desolation of those years as you walk through the gated tunnel entrance and emerge on a narrow street below the castle, with the roofless shells of houses once inhabited by the unfortunate lepers all around. Although everything is crumbling, you can still pick out a row of stores and some houses that must once have been quite grand. A couple have been restored to make a small **museum**.

ARRIVAL AND INFORMATION

ELOÚNDA AND AROUND

By bus Frequent buses run between Áyios Nikólaos and Eloúnda (hourly 9am–8pm; 20min) and some continue to Pláka (every 2hr 9am–7pm; 30min).

Information Olous Travel (☎ 28410 41324, ⓦ olous-travel.gr), on the main square in Eloúnda, can provide information and assist with finding accommodation, changing money and arranging tours and car rental.

ACTIVITIES

Boat trips From Eloúnda harbour boats leave every 30min from 9am for the trip to Spinalónga (€10 return; ☎ 6974 385 854, ⓦ eloundaboat.gr); longer day-trips taking in local beaches are also available. In Pláka boats depart from quays at each end of the village (April–Oct daily 9am–6pm every 30min; €8 return; ☎ 6977 446 229, ⓦ plakaboat.gr); the far end, by the *Spinalonga* taverna, is generally quieter, and the *Spinalonga*'s boat also offers fishing trips (€80/hr; up to four people) with the catch cooked up at the taverna on your return.

ACCOMMODATION

Akti Olous On the road to the causeway, Eloúnda ☏ 28410 41270, ⓦ eloundaaktiolous.gr. Newly refurbished four-star seafront hotel where comfortable balcony rooms come with a/c, TV and fridge; many have a sea view. There's a bar and pool on the roof, with great views, and a seafront café flanked by a small beach. Breakfast included. May–Oct. €90

Athina Villas In the centre of Pláka ☏ 28410 41342, ⓦ spinalonga.com. A modern complex of comfortable a/c studios and apartments, many with sea views, right in the heart of the village. Studio €45, apartment €70

Corali Studios Behind the far end of Eloúnda town beach ☏ 28410 41712, ⓦ coralistudios.com. A sizeable complex, *Corali* (together with neighbouring *Portobello Apartments*, under the same management) has good modern a/c studios and apartments with cooking facilities, most with a sea view, and a pool and bar in the garden area behind. May–Oct. €65

Elounda Peninsula 2km south of Eloúnda ☏ 28410 68250, ⓦ eloundapeninsula.com. Spectacular hotel draped across its own private peninsula. Accommodation is in duplex suites or larger villas, all with private pools, and there's virtually every facility you could wish for, from an elegant spa to tennis courts, nine-hole golf course, sandy beach and kids' clubs and activities. Part of a complex with the *Elounda Mare* and *Porto Elounda* hotels, which share the same beaches and facilities, but offer some more standard hotel rooms. May–Oct. €500

Milos Rooms Upper part of Eloúnda ☏ 28410 41641, ⓦ pediaditis.gr. This small complex of rooms, studios and apartments is set around a pool and bar: all are a/c and larger units have kitchens; they also have simpler seafront places for the same price. Info at the family's bookshop on the main square. May–Oct. Double €45, apartment €60

EATING AND DRINKING

Eloúnda has a huge choice of **restaurants**, mostly strung out along the waterfront or around the harbour; you'll probably need to book to get into any of those below. There are plenty of all-day **café-bars** interspersed between them, a couple of which have dancefloors inside and stay open to the early hours. Pláka is far quieter, and there's nowhere to eat at all on Spinalónga.

Ergospasio At the start of the causeway, Eloúnda ☏ 28410 42082. Elegant ouzéri-taverna inside an old stone-built carob factory. The interior is bright and stylish and there's a seafront terrace plus another on the first floor. The menu is short, with a mixture of Italian and Greek dishes such as saffron, prawn and mussel risotto, or stuffed lamb roll with feta; the roasted lamb is superb. Mains €16–22, mezédhes €3–6 per plate. May–Oct daily 11am–11pm.

Ferryman Eloúnda waterfront, south of the harbour ☏ 28410 41230. Glitzy place named for the 1970s BBC TV series *Who Pays the Ferryman?* in which it featured. Justly popular for the candlelit tables right above the water and short menu of interesting variations on traditional Greek recipes, many cooked in the hi-tech wood oven or giant barbecue – pork belly *yíros*-style €13.80, mussels steamed

in ouzo €12.40, vegetarian special €8.80. April–Oct daily noon–4pm & 7pm–midnight.

★ **Paradisos** Edge of Eloúnda, poorly signed down a dirt track off the Áyios Nikólaos road ☏ 28410 41631. An idyllic taverna with rooms on the landward side of the causeway. Prices for fish and meat are very reasonable, with *tsipoúra* (bream) for €15, and dishes like *kontosoúvli* (spit-roast pork0 for €10. The day's specials are chalked up on the blackboard. April–Oct daily noon–10pm.

Taverna Spinalonga Pláka ☏ 28410 41804. With a lovely seafront terrace looking across to Spinalónga, this big, welcoming taverna at the far end of the village has some of the lowest prices locally (moussaka or grilled octopus €9), especially for fish (priced per kilo), fresh from the day's catch. Daily lunch and dinner.

SHOPPING

Eklektos A. Papandreou 13, Eloúnda ☏ 28410 42086. Great little English bookshop 50m uphill from the square in the direction of Áyios Nikólaos, on the steps down to the water. Mon–Sat 9.30am–9.30pm, Sun 10.30am–9.30pm.

Kritsá

The "traditional" village of **KRITSÁ**, 9km inland of Áyios Nikólaos, is a popular destination for tour buses and day-trippers. Despite some commercialization, a visit here makes a welcome break from the frenetic pace of the coast. Kritsá is known for its **crafts**, and the main street is lined with stores selling local weaving, ceramics, carved olive wood, leather goods and embroidery. Once you get past the touristy shops and explore the maze of streets winding up the hillside, with their wonderful valley views, you get a real sense of a genuine Cretan village. Easily included in a trip up here, too, is a remarkable church, the **Panayía Kerá**, and an atmospheric ancient site, **Lató**.

Church of Panayía Kerá

About 1km before Kritsá on the Áyios Nikólaos road • Tues–Sun 8am–3pm • €2

Inside the lovely Byzantine **church of Panayía Kerá** is preserved perhaps the most complete and certainly the most famous set of **Byzantine frescoes** in Crete. The biblical scenes were originally created in the fourteenth and early fifteenth centuries, though all have been retouched and restored to such an extent that they're impossible to date accurately.

Lató

4km north of Kritsá • Tues–Sun 8.30am–3pm • €2 • ☎ 28410 22462

On the outskirts of Kritsá a lovely rural drive takes you to the archeological site of **Lató**, where the substantial remains of a **Doric city** are coupled with a grand hilltop setting. The city itself is extensive, but largely neglected, presumably because visitors and archeologists on Crete are more concerned with the Minoan era. Ruins aside, there are spectacular **views** west over Áyios Nikólaos and beyond to the bay and Olous (which was Lató's port), and inland to the Lasíthi mountains.

ARRIVAL AND DEPARTURE   KRITSÁ

By bus A regular service runs from Áyios Nikólaos to Kritsá (9 daily; 20min).

ACCOMMODATION

Argyro Main road as you enter Kritsá ☎ 28410 51174, ⓦ argyrorentrooms.gr. Clean, pleasant and economical a/c rooms with balconies, many with views across the olive-tree-lined valley. The small courtyard café serves an excellent breakfast (extra). €35

East to Sitía

From Áyios Nikólaos the main road heads south and then east, above the occasional sandy cove, through barren hills sprinkled with new developments and villas. In places the engineering of the new road (an ongoing process still years from completion) is breathtaking. Just past the remarkable Minoan site of **Gourniá** is the turn-off to Ierápetra and the south coast: from here on the road to **Sitía** is one of the most exhilarating in Crete. Carved into cliffs and mountainsides, the road teeters high above the coast much of the way. Of the beaches you see below, only the one at **Mókhlos** is easily accessible, some 5km below the main road.

Gourniá

20km east of Áyios Nikólaos; a hazardous turning off the E75 onto a dirt track • Tues–Sun 8am–3pm • €2 • ☎ 28420 93028

Gourniá, slumped in the saddle between two low peaks, is the most completely preserved **Minoan town**. Its narrow alleys and stairways intersect a throng of one-roomed houses centred on a main square, and the rather grand house of what may have been a local ruler or governor. Although less impressive than the great palaces, the site is strong on revelations about the lives of the ordinary people – many of the dwellings housed craftsmen, who left behind their tools and materials to be found by the excavators. Its desolation today only serves to heighten the contrast with what must have been a cramped and raucous community 3500 years ago, though bear in mind that the site occupies only part of the original town, which would have stretched all the way to the sea and a small harbour.

Mókhlos

In a sleepy way, **MÓKHLOS** is a surprisingly developed place. Small as it is, almost every house seems to advertise rooms for rent, and there are several good tavernas around the little harbour. The village beach is very small and pebbly, but there's a slightly larger beach (also pebble) to the west. There's not a great deal to do here – hang out in the harbour taverna-cafés or swim out to the **islet of Mókhlos** just offshore, where there are remains of Minoan houses – but it's very easy to do nothing in this laidback place.

ETTING AROUND

bus There are 7 buses daily from Áyios Nikólaos to both
tía and Ierápetra; any of them can drop you very close to
urniá, but only the Sitía buses pass Mókhlos: be warned

that you'll be dropped on the main road, a full hour's walk
above the village (and a sweaty slog back up).

CCOMMODATION AND EATING

Limenaria Overlooking the new harbour, 600m
est of Mókhlos ☎28420 27837, ⓦmochlos-crete.gr.
tranquil hideaway in flower-filled gardens with
tractive, fully equipped sea-view terrace apartments
eeping up to four; big balconies front and back allow you
appreciate the view. **€60**

★Mesostrati On Mókhlos harbour ☎28430 94170.
Traditional Cretan cuisine from family recipes, as well as
fresh fish, served on a pretty seaside terrace; also good
breakfasts and a weekly Cretan cooking demonstration
Wed at 5pm. Delicious daily specials €7–10, mixed meze
€11. April–Oct daily 9am–late.

Sitía

After the excesses of Mália or Áyios Nikólaos, arriving in **SITÍA** can seem something
f an anticlimax. But don't be fooled: the town's charms are subtle. Allow yourself to
djust to the more leisurely pace of life here and you may, like many other visitors
efore you, end up staying much longer than intended. An ideal base from which to
isit the local attractions, Sitía hasn't entirely escaped the tourist boom; many of the
isitors are French or Italian. Things to do include a sandy **town beach**, stretching
ar into the distance south of town; an excellent **Archeological Museum** (Tues–Sun
3am–3pm; €2; ☎28430 23917); a Venetian **fortress** (Tues–Sun 9am–4pm; free);
ind a small **Folklore Museum** (Mon–Sat 10am–2pm; €2). A colourful weekly **market**
akes place on Tuesdays between 7am and 2pm along Odhós Itanou near the
Archeological Museum.

7

ARRIVAL AND DEPARTURE
SITÍA

By bus The bus station (☎28430 22272) is on the
outhwest fringe of the centre; head north along Odhós
Venizélou to get into town. Info is available at
ⓦktelherlas.gr. There are generally fewer services at the
weekends.

Destinations Ay. Nikólaos (7 daily; 1hr 45min); Ierápetra
4 daily; 1hr 30min); Iráklio (7 daily; 3hr 15min); Káto
Zákros (Mon, Tues & Fri 10.15am & 2.15pm; 1hr);
Makriyialós (4 daily; 1hr); Palékastro (5 daily; 30min); Vái
4 daily; 30min).

By ferry The ferry dock is 500m northeast of the
centre. Just one ferry currently calls at Sitía, the
Prevelis (☎28430 28555, ⓦwww.anek.gr). It departs
Sat (and Wed in summer) to Kássos (3hr),
Kárpathos (5hr), Hálki (7hr) and Rhodes (9hr); and Sun
to Iráklio (3hr), Santoríni (10hr), Mílos (14hr) and
Pireás (19hr).

By plane Sitía Airport (☎28430 24424) lies
immediately north of town. There's no public
transport, but it's a taxi ride of just 5min (less than
€10). Although it can cater for international flights,
there's only a very occasional charter. Olympic
(ⓦolympicair.com) flies to Athens (4–5 weekly); Sky
Express (ⓦskyexpress.gr) to Alexandhroúpoli, Iráklio,
Kárpathos, Kássos, Préveza and Rhodes (1–2 weekly).

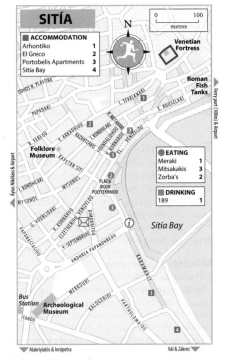

SITÍA

N

0   100
metres

■ ACCOMMODATION
Arhontiko	1
El Greco	2
Portobelis Apartments	3
Sitia Bay	4

Venetian
Fortress

Roman
Fish
Tanks

Ferry port (100m) & Airport

Áyios Nikólaos & Airport

Folklore
Museum

● EATING
Meraki	1
Mitsakakis	3
Zorba's	2

■ DRINKING
| 189 | 1 |

Sitía Bay

ⓘ

Bus
Station   Archeological
Museum

▼ Makriyialós & Ierápetra

Vái & Zákros ▼

7

INFORMATION

Tourist office The municipal tourist office, on the seafront along the Beach Rd (May–Aug Mon–Fri 10am–2pm & 6–8pm, though in practice often closed; ☏ 28430 28300, ⓦ sitia.gr) can supply accommodation lists, town ma and a free guide to the region that also describes son walking routes.

ACCOMMODATION

★**Arhontiko** Kondhiláki 16 ☏ 28430 28172. The pick of the budget places, in a lovely, little-modernized traditional house with a shady garden. Only one of the rooms is en suite, but they're spotless and attractive. €35

El Greco G. Arkadhíou 13 ☏ 28430 23133, ⓦ elgreco -sitia.gr. Charming small hotel in the upper town with an old-fashioned feel; simple a/c balcony rooms have fridge and TV, and a couple have sea views. April–Nov. €40

Portobelis Apartments Karamánli 34 ☏ 28430 22370, ⓦ portobelis-crete.gr. Studios and two-room apartments with kitchens for up to four people, pl some rooms. All are modern and well-equipped, ar some have sea-view balconies, though most overlook small garden. Room/studio €48, apartment €68

★**Sitia Bay** Trítis Septemvríou 8 ☏ 28430 2480 ⓦ sitiabay.com. Purpose-built apartment comple overlooking the town beach, with a large pool. Love modern studios and two-room apartments, all with sea view balconies and fully equipped kitchens, plus a ver warm welcome. Substantial discounts out of season. Stud €70, apartment €100

EATING AND DRINKING

A line of enticing outdoor **tavernas** crowds the harbourfront, while Sitía's **nightlife**, mostly conducted at an easy pace centres on the music bars and cafés at the northern end of Venizélou.

189 Venizélou 189 ☏ 28430 20660. Big café-bar that's a favourite local hangoout, open most of the day and night. By day there's coffee, snacks – burgers, sandwiches – and sofas for lounging, and at night you can enjoy cocktails and music, plus occasional special events. Daily 9am til the early hours.

Meraki Venizélou 151 ☏ 28430 23460. One of a group of fashionable *rakádhika* (like an ouzerí, but serving *raki*) on the seafront. You can order (by ticking items off on a sheet) from a substantial menu combining modern and traditional dishes (€3–8), but the best deal is to go for a drink with meze (around €7); it's not quite a meal, but you'll probably want another drink anyway, or you can order a few extras. The wine from Toploú monastery is also excellent. Daily 9am–late.

Mitsakakis Karamánli 6 ☏ 28430 20200. Wonderfu traditional *zaharoplastío* with a terrace facing the harbour always busy with locals. Try their delicious *loukoumádhe* (dough fritters) with honey (€2.90) or ice cream (€3.70) they also have sandwiches and crêpes. Daily 8am–midnight.

Zorba's Venizélou 56 ☏ 28430 22689. Occupying the prime position in the corner of the harbour, this is the biggest and busiest place on the seafront, with far more authentic food than you might expect from its tourist appearance. Generous portions of simple home-cooking (lamb in the oven €8.50, moussaka €6.50) as well as fresh fish and exceptional value set menus, from around €10 a head. Daily 11am–midnight.

The far east

Crete's eastern edge is among its most tempting destinations, at least if it's beaches and isolation you're after. You won't find much solitude at **Vái beach**, which features on almost every Cretan travel agent's list of excursions, but it's a beautiful spot, and there are plenty of escapes roundabout. Nearby **Palékastro** is a lovely small town within easy reach of many less well-known beaches, as well as some of Crete's best windsurfing. From here a road winds south to still less-visited country at **Zákros**, site of the fourth great Minoan palace, and little-known **Xerókambos**.

Monastery of Toploú

15km east of Sitía • Daily 9am–1pm & 2–6pm; Oct–March closes at 4pm • €3

The **Monasterty of Toploú**'s forbidding exterior reflects a history of resistance to invaders, and doesn't prepare you for the gorgeous flower-decked cloister within. The blue-robed monks keep out of the way as far as possible, but in quieter periods their cells and refectory are left discreetly on view. In the church is one of the masterpieces of Cretan art, the **eighteenth-century icon** *Lord Thou Art Great* by Ioannis Kornaros. This

arvellously intricate work incorporates 61 tiny scenes, each illustrating a phrase from
e Orthodox prayer that begins with this phrase. In the monastery's shop you can buy
pensive reproductions of the work as well as olive oil and wine made by the monks (a
ack opposite the monastery leads to their **winery**, open for visits Mon–Fri 10am–6pm
summer).

ái

he beach at **Vái** is famous above all for its **palm trees**. The sudden appearance of what
claimed to be Europe's only indigenous wild date-palm grove is indeed an exotic
urprise, and dreams of Caribbean beaches are easy to indulge. Rarely for long,
owever, since throughout summer the beach fills to overflowing as buses pour in and
ars, unable to squeeze into the car park (€2.50), line the access road for hundreds of
etres. On the sand, only the boardwalks guarantee a route through the mass of
aking bodies. Pricey sun loungers are available and a watersports centre offers
aterskiing, ringos and other high-speed rides. There's a café and expensive taverna,
nd you'll pay again to have a shower or use the toilet. Out of season, however, or for a
ouple of hours at each end of the day, you can still enjoy Vái as it ought to be – for
ore solitude, try climbing the rocks or swimming to one of the smaller beaches on
ither side. **Ítanos**, twenty minutes' walk north by an obvious trail, has a couple of tiny
eaches and some modest ruins from the Classical era.

alékastro

substantial village with easy access to numerous excellent beaches, and with plenty of
ccommodation both in town and in the surrounding area, **PALÉKASTRO** makes an
njoyable, quiet base. There are several good tavernas and just about every other facility
ou might need.

ncient Palékastro

ose to Hióna beach, about a 20min walk from Palékastro village • Tues–Sun 8am–3pm; in practice, it's rarely locked • €2, if there's
nyone to collect it

or archeologists the Minoan site of **Palékastro** is a very significant excavation, the
argest Minoan town yet discovered and a rich source of information about everyday
Minoan life. For an amateur it's less enthralling, but there's plenty to see (though
ignage could be improved), and continuing excavation means that new finds are still
oming to light. Recent explorations on the site's northern side, for example, have
evealed a road leading from the town to a nearby harbour (no trace of which has yet
een found), while beneath the olive groves to the south and west more of the Minoan
own lies waiting to be revealed.

Hióna beach

2km east of Palékastro

Hióna beach, a good stretch of blue-flagged pebble and sand, lies to the south of a
flat-topped hill named Kastrí which dominates the coastal landscape. The closest beach
to Palékastro, it's less than twenty minutes' walk via the hamlet of **Angathiá**. Though
far from crowded, it is probably the most popular beach hereabouts: you can walk to
still quieter coves around the bay to the south.

Koureménos beach

2.5km northeast of Palékastro

Koureménos beach, to the north of the Kastrí bluff, is Crete's top **windsurfing** spot.
Not surprisingly, it can be windy (a funnel effect creates ideal windsurfing conditions),
but it's a fine, long sand-and-pebble beach, with several tavernas and rooms places
– even a bar – directly behind. There's also quite a community of camper vans in
summer, and a couple of excellent windsurf centres, too.

7

Káto Zákros

From the first spectacular view as you approach along the clifftop road, **KÁTO ZÁKROS** – "Lower" Zákros – is a delight. There's a pebbly beach, half a dozen waterfront tavernas and café-bars, and a few places offering rooms and apartments; along with a tiny harbour with a few fishing boats, this is about all the place amounts to. It's best to bring cash and anything else you might need: there's no shop, or anything else much. But if it's laidback tranquillity you're after, you've come to the right place.

Palace of Zákros

50m inland from Káto Zákros • Daily: June–Oct 8am–8pm; Nov–May 8am–3pm • €6 • ☎ 28430 26897

Though the **Palace of Zákros** is small, it is full of interest, and can match any of the more important Minoan centres for quality of construction and materials. It's also much easier to understand than many of the other Minoan sites: here, the remains are of one palace only, dating from between 1600 and 1450 BC. Although there is an earlier settlement at a lower level, it is unlikely ever to be excavated – mainly because this end of the island is gradually sinking. Even the exposed parts of the palace are marshy and often waterlogged: there are terrapins living in the green water in the cistern. When it's really wet, you can keep your feet dry and get an excellent view of the overall plan of the palace by climbing the streets of one of Zákros's unique features, the **town** – a place very like Gourniá (see p.476) – that occupied the hill above it.

Xerókambos

Straggling across a little coastal plain in the lee of the Sitían mountains, the tiny hamlet of **XERÓKAMBOS** is not especially attractive, but it's as isolated and peaceful as you could wish for. There's no real centre, just a street along which, between fields of olive groves, are spaced some houses, a few tavernas and a couple of basic minimarkets, with rooms and apartment places scattered along the road and down by the beach. Despite the stirrings of development, this **main beach** is more than long enough to find seclusion if you want it, and there are isolated coves either side where you might never see another soul. The crystal-clear waters here are great for **snorkelling** too.

GETTING AROUND AND INFORMATION

By bus There are services from Sitía to Káto Zákros (Mon, Tues & Fri 10.15am & 2.15pm; 1hr), Palékastro (5 daily; 30min) and Vái (4 daily; 30min). There is no public transport south of Zákros.

Tourist information There's no tourist office, but a couple of locally run websites have details of attractions and comprehensive accommodation listings: check out ⓦ eastcrete-holidays.gr and ⓦ palaikastro.com.

ACTIVITIES

Cycling Freak Mountain Bike Centre (ⓦ freak -mountainbike.com), at the edge of Palékastro on the Vái road, offers bike rental, guided day-trips and cycle holiday packages.

Windsurfing There are two rival operations at Koureménos, both offering lessons and quality gear rental; Freak (☎ 6979 253 861, ⓦ www.freak-surf.com) and Gone Surfing (☎ 6941 427 787, ⓦ gonesurfing.gr).

WALKS AROUND ZÁKROS

The most obvious and best-known of the **walks** around Zákros is the 6km **Gorge of the Dead**, a beautiful ravine that leads from the larger village of Áno ("Upper") Zákros, on the main road, to Káto Zákros, passing the palace en route. It makes up the final stage of the E4 trans-European footpath, so it's pretty well marked. In addition, there are several other well-signed and waymarked walks in the surrounding hills (mostly 3–4hr). Best of them is perhaps the **Hokhlakiés Gorge**, halfway between Palékastro and Áno Zákros, a well-signed 3km route to a deserted beach. From the bottom you can either return up the gorge (1hr 10min) or strike out along the coast in either direction; north to Palékastro, south to Káto Zákros, each about 6km further.

ACCOMMODATION AND EATING

PALÉKASTRO

Hellas On the main square ☎ 28430 61240, ⓦ palaikastro
com/hotelhellas. Simple a/c rooms come with balcony, TV
and fridge; a little impersonal, but could hardly be closer to
the action. There's a good traditional taverna, serving dishes
such as lamb with lemon sauce (€8.50) and *soutzoukákia*
(meat balls; €6.50) on the terrace beneath the hotel,
facing the square. Daily 10am–late. **€35**

Hiona Hióna beach ☎ 28430 61228. Stunningly
beautiful seafood restaurant on a promontory at the
northern end of the beach – it's a touch more formal than
others in the area and a little pricier, but worth it. Try the
kakaviá traditional fish stew (€25 for two). Often booked
up in season. May–Oct daily noon–midnight.

Kouremenos Beach Apartments Kouremėnos beach
☎ 6932 356 825, ⓦ kouremenosbeach.gr. A couple of
small studios for two in the olive groves immediately behind
the beach, as well as some larger apartments for up to six
people, all with a/c, TV and fridge; the larger ones have a
separate kitchen. April–Oct. Studio **€45**, apartment **€65**

★ **Kouremenos Villas/Panorama Apartments** On
the hillside beyond Kouremėnos beach ☎ 28430 61370,
ⓦ palaikastro.com/kouremenos_apts. A glorious
setting with great views over beach and countryside and
an exceptionally friendly welcome, make this place special;
very comfortable apartments with modern kitchen, a/c,
satellite TV, and a pool. April–Oct. **€55**

Marina Village Off the Hióna Beach road, about 600m
from Hióna, 800m from Kouremėnos ☎ 28430 61284,
ⓦ marinavillage.gr. A peaceful haven with well-furnished
a/c balcony rooms, surrounded by olive groves and a
garden of bougainvillea and banana plants, plus pool and
tennis court. They also have a tiny house (for up to four
people) right by Hióna beach. Buffet breakfast included.
April–Oct. **€58**

KÁTO ZÁKROS

★ **Akrogiali** End of the beach road ☎ 28431 10710,
ⓦ kato-zakros.gr. The last of the places on the waterfront,

with a particularly attractive terrace away from the road.
Excellent, simple Greek food (mains €6–10) and the
friendly owner, Nikos, is a fount of information; he also acts
as an agent for several room options nearby. March–Nov
daily 9am–late.

Coral & Athina On the rise immediately beyond
Taverna Akrogiali ☎ 28430 26893, ⓦ kato-zakros.gr.
Rooms directly above the beach, with great sea views from
large communal terraces; clean and simply furnished, with
a/c, fridge and TV. Information at *Akrogiali*; breakfast
included. March–Nov. **€50**

Stella's Traditional Apartments About 500m inland,
beyond the palace ☎ 28430 23739, ⓦ stelapts.com.
Large, elegantly decorated, stone-built a/c apartments,
with hammocks and lovely views in the verdant gardens,
and some slightly simpler studios. Exceptionally well
equipped and well run. March–Nov. Studio **€60**,
apartment **€80**

★ **Zakros Palace Apartments** On the entry road
above the village ☎ 28430 29550, ⓦ katozakros-apts.
gr. Perched high above the coast with spectacular views of
the gorge, palace and beach; a/c rooms and studios with
TV, fridge, kitchen (in studios) or kettle, plus communal
library and laundry. Expect an exuberant welcome and
gifts of fresh produce grown right outside. **€50**

XERÓKAMBOS

Asteras Just above the main road ☎ 28430 26787,
ⓦ asterasapartments.gr. Set in their own garden, above
the olive groves, these modern a/c studio rooms and two-
room apartments all come with kitchenette, fridge and
good sea views. May–Oct. **€45**

Lithos Main road towards the south end of Xerókambos
☎ 28430 26729, ⓦ lithoshouses.gr. The village's most
luxurious option, with elegantly furnished stone-built sea-
view apartments (bedroom upstairs, living quarters below)
– all come with kitchen, satellite TV, sound system and
woodburner for winter. Free olive oil, wine and *rakí* are
provided. **€75**

Ierápetra and the southeast coast

There are three main approaches to Crete's southeastern corner: the long haul across the
centre of the island from Iráklio via Áno Viánnos in order to approach from the west;
the road south from Sitía that emerges on the coast close to **Markryialós**; or the short
cut across the isthmus from Pahiá Ámmos to Ierápetra.

IERÁPETRA itself has various claims to fame – the southernmost town in Europe, the
most hours of sunshine, the largest town on the south coast of Crete – but charm is not
really one of them. Though there's an excellent **beach**, it's a sprawling place and a major
supply centre for the farmers who have grown rich from the plastic greenhouses that
scar much of the surrounding coast. In recent years some resources have been devoted
to smartening the town up, and on the **seafront**, where a string of restaurants and bars
stretches out in either direction, Ierápetra can be genuinely picturesque. However

7

ISLAND ESCAPE: GAIDHOURONÍSI

The most popular way to escape Ierápetra's often stifling summer temperatures is to take a boat trip to **Gaidhouronísi** (aka Donkey Island or Chrissi Island) some 10km offshore. A real desert island a little over 4km in length, with a cedar forest and a couple of tavernas, Gaidhouronísi has some excellent sandy **beaches** and plenty of room to escape – although you wouldn't want to miss the boat back. There's a waymarked **walking route** around the island, passing the fabulous "**Shell Beach**" covered with millions of multicoloured mollusc shells. Two competing companies, Chrysi Cruises (☎ 28420 20008, ⓦ chrysicruises.com) and Zanadu (☎ 28420 26649) run **daily trips** to Gaidhouronísi, on large boats with on-board bars, from the jetty on the seafront (May–Oct; peak-season departures 10.30am, 11am & 12.30pm, returning 4pm, 5pm & 6pm; 55min). Tickets are sold by agents throughout town, or at the boat; officially they cost €25 but off season, or if you bargain, you may get them for much less. There are also various small-boat trips on offer from the harbour by the fortress.

tourism seems very much an afterthought, and things to do by day – apart from lie on the beach – are limited to a decent **Archeological Museum** (Tues–Sun 9am–3pm; €2; ☎ 28420 28721) and a visit to the **Venetian fort** (usually open in daylight hours; free) that guards the harbour.

Makryialós

MAKRYIALÓS, some 27km east of Ierápetra, is strung out along the coastal road and at first sight not at all attractive. Turn off the road, though, and there are plenty of quiet corners, plus one of the best **beaches** at this end of Crete, with fine sand that shelves so gently you almost feel you could walk the two hundred nautical miles to Africa. There's an attractive little harbour too, plenty of other beaches nearby, and some interesting walks into the hills behind.

Mýrtos

MÝRTOS, just off the main road 15km west of Ierápetra, is an unexpected pleasure: a charming, white-walled village with a long shingle beach. Even in August, when the place can get pretty full, the pace of life remains slow. A one-room village **museum** (Mon & Fri 10am–2pm, Wed 5–8pm; free) houses some of the finds from a couple of nearby **Minoan sites**, a villa at Pýrgos and a small settlement at Fournoú Korifí; both are immediately west of Mýrtos, signed off the main road, and generally left unlocked in daylight hours.

ARRIVAL AND DEPARTURE	IERÁPETRA AND THE SOUTHEAST COAST

By bus Ierápetra bus station (☎ 28420 28237) is on Lasthénous, the Áyios Nikólaos road, a 5min walk from the centre.

Destinations Áyios Nikólaos (7 daily; 1hr), Iráklio (9 daily; 2hr 30min), Makriyialós (9 daily; 30min), Mýrtos (6 daily; 30min), Sitía (4 daily; 1hr 30min).

ACCOMMODATION

IERÁPETRA

Camping Koutsounari 7km east of Ierápetra on the Makryialós road ☎ 28420 61213, ⓦ camping-koutsounari.gr. The only campsite on this stretch of the south coast, with a taverna, store and pool, and although the ground is a bit gritty there's a good beach and plenty of shade. May–Oct. €18

Cretan Villa Lakérdha 16 ☎ 28420 28522, ⓦ cretan-villa.com. Sparkling a/c rooms with TV and fridge overlook the flower-bedecked patio of a beautifully restored

eighteenth-century stone house, close to the bus station. They also rent out some equally attractive apartments nearby. Room €45, apartment €60

Coral Boutique Hotel Platía Eleftherías 19 ☎ 28420 20444, ⓦ coralhotelcrete.gr. Swish new small hotel with luxuriously decorated balcony rooms and suites (the higher ones come with sea views), kitted out with fridge, satellite TV and tea-making facilities. They also have modern apartments, some with sea views, nearby. Room €50, apartment €60

MAKRYIALÓS

★ **Aspros Potamos Traditional Houses** Signed off the Pefkí road ☎ 28430 51694, ⓦ asprospotamos. com. A group of tiny stone houses has been delightfully converted into studios and apartments at this back-to-nature accommodation, slightly further up the valley from the *White River Cottages* (see below): you can walk down the valley to town in about 20min. There's only solar power here; rooms have a fridge, single bathroom light and LED reading lamp (plus solar hot water), and in reception there's wi-fi and power for chargers, otherwise you are reliant on oil lamps and candles for lighting, and a fireplace to warm you in winter (extra charge for firewood). **€55**

Maria Tsankalioti Apartments Seaward side of the main road, halfway through town ☎ 28430 51557, ⓦ makrigialos-crete.com. In an unbeatable beachfront position and run by a super-friendly family, these slightly old-fashioned but immaculate studios and apartments have kitchenette, a/c and TV; some also have big balconies overlooking the sea. **€40**

★ **White House** On the harbour ☎ 28430 29183, ⓦ makrigialos.com. Three houses and two apartments in beautifully restored harbour buildings, each one architect-designed and unique. Equipment includes everything from washing machine to champagne glasses. Closed Dec. **€110**

White River Cottages 500m up a signed track at the eastern end of town ☎ 28430 51120, ⓦ whiterivercottages.com. An abandoned hamlet of traditional stone dwellings has been restored as a warren of studios and apartments (for up to four people) around a small pool. Built partly into the rocks, with the original stone floors and whitewashed walls, they come with kitchens, a/c and private terraces. Minimum three-night stay. **€90**

MÝRTOS

Big Blue Apartments West side of village ☎ 28420 51094, ⓦ big-blue.gr. Lovely rooms with fridge, studios with kitchenette, and larger two-bedroom apartments, all with a/c and sea-view balconies in a stunning position high above the beach. Room **€45**, studio **€65**, apartment **€75**

Nikos House In the heart of the village ☎ 28420 51116. Very simple studios or two-room apartments with a/c and kitchenette; the upstairs studio, especially, is lovely, and you feel very much part of village life here. **€40**

EATING AND DRINKING

MAKRYIALÓS

Faros Overlooking the beach beside the harbour ☎ 28430 52456. Big taverna in a great position, with everything from pizza and pasta to octopus and kalamári; good fish from their own boat too (lamb chops €9.50; fish dishes €10–12). Daily noon–late.

Helios Overlooking the beach beside the harbour ☎ 28430 51280. Housed in a refurbished carob warehouse, this bar-café serves breakfast, but is better later on, when it's the perfect place for a sundowner. Daily 9am–2am.

★ **Kalliotzina** Koutsourás, 3km west of Makriyialós ☎ 28430 51207. A classic old-fashioned taverna, serving home-cooked food and excellent fish on a tree-shaded terrace right by the sea. There's no written menu, so check out what's on offer in the kitchen or listen carefully as the day's dishes are reeled off at speed; mains are around €7, or less for the veggie options. There's often music on summer weekends. Daily 11am–late.

★ **Piperia** Pefkí, 5km inland from Makriyialós ☎ 28430 52471. A lovely spot under a spreading pepper tree, with authentic, traditional food and great views over the coast. Mains like okra with lamb or rabbit in wine sauce go for around €8; they also have live Greek music some summer evenings (with a set menu), and sell their own jams, olives and liqueurs. Daily noon–midnight.

MÝRTOS

Votsalo Seafront, in the middle of the beach ☎ 28420 51457. A likeable place with a great position at the centre of the beachfront promenade; hand-painted menus detail a good traditional set of dishes (meze €3–5; mains €7–10), washed down with home-produced wine. They also do breakfast, and coffee and drinks throughout the day. April–Oct daily 9am–midnight.

Réthymno and around

The province of **Réthymno** has something for everyone. Réthymno Town itself is a relaxed university town overlooked by one of the most imposing Venetian fortresses on the island. It also retains a picturesque old quarter, redolent of traditional urban life, plus a fine beach. Inland, the countryside is dominated by mountains, with Psilorítis in the east and the White Mountains in the west. Between them the **Amari Valley** offers pretty villages and magnificent hiking, while on the south coast, in particular around **Plakiás**, are more excellent beaches.

Réthymno Town

Although it's the third largest town in Crete, **RÉTHYMNO TOWN** never feels like a city, as Haniá and Iráklio do. Instead, it has an easy-going provincial air; it's a place that moves slowly and, for all the myriad bars springing up along the seafront, the **old town** still preserves much of its Venetian and Turkish appearance. There are hundreds of tavernas, bars, cafés and clubs, but the big hotels are all out of town, stretching away along the shore to the east. Dominating everything from the west is the superbly preserved outline of the **fortress**.

The harbour and old town

The Venetian or inner **harbour** is the most attractive part of Réthymno's waterfront, although these days its elegant sixteenth-century lighthouse looks down on a line of bars and tavernas, rather than the sailing ships and barges of bygone eras. Immediately behind spreads the atmospheric **old town**, a warren of ancient buildings with ornate wooden doors and balconies, of fountains and rickety old stores, some still with traditionally dressed craftsmen sitting out front. Look out for the **Venetian loggia** which houses a shop selling Classical art reproductions; the **Rimóndi Fountain**, another of the more elegant Venetian survivals; and the **Neratsés mosque** with its **minaret**, currently serving as a music school. Ethnikís Andístasis, the street leading straight up from the fountain, is the town's **market** area.

The Venetian fortress

Daily: May–Sept 8am–8pm; Oct–April 8.30am–6pm • €4 • ☎ 28310 28101

Overlooking the old town from a rise at the western end of the seafront stands the massive **Fortezza** or **Venetian fortress**. Said to be the largest Venetian castle ever built, this was a response, in the last quarter of the sixteenth century, to a series of **pirate raids** (by Barbarossa among others) that had devastated the town. Inside now is a vast open space dotted with the remains of all sorts of barracks, arsenals, officers' houses, earthworks and deep shafts, and at the centre a large domed **mosque** complete with surviving *mihrab* (a niche indicating the direction of Mecca). The fortress was designed to be large enough for the entire population to take shelter within the walls. Although much is ruined, it remains thoroughly atmospheric, and you can look out over the town and harbour, and along the coast to the west.

Historical and Folk Art Museum

Vernádhou 28, near the Neratsés mosque • Mon–Sat 10am–3pm • €4 • ☎ 28310 23398

A beautifully restored seventeenth-century Venetian mansion is home to the small but enjoyable **Historical and Folk Art Museum**. On display inside are musical instruments, old photos, farm implements, traditional costumes and jewellery, weaving and embroidery, as well as a reconstructed sitting-room with all its furnishings, plus a recreation of a typical city street including a kafenío, pharmacy, etc. It makes for a fascinating insight into local lifestyles which survived virtually unchanged from Venetian times to the 1960s.

Archeological Museum

Ayíou Frangískou, off Ethnikís Andístasis • Tues–Sun 10am–6pm • €2

Rethymno's **Archeological Museum** occupies the church of St Francis, a beautiful building that was once part of a Venetian monastery. Later incorporated into the Nerátses mosque complex – a gorgeous archway beyond the museum opens into Platía Mikrasiatón, behind the mosque – it is supposed to be a temporary home for the museum, though seems likely to stay here for the foreseeable future. The collection, all of it from Rethymno province, is exceptionally rich, ranging from stone axe-heads over 100,000 years old, through fine Minoan pottery and jewellery and Roman-era statuary and glass, to Byzantine and Arab items including rescued frescoes and mosaic floors.

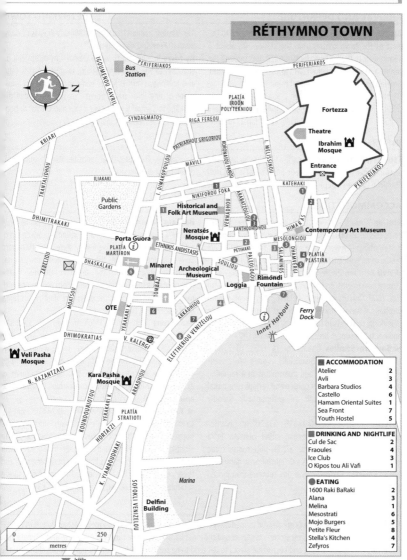

RÉTHYMNO TOWN

■ ACCOMMODATION	
Atelier	2
Avli	3
Barbara Studios	4
Castello	6
Hamam Oriental Suites	1
Sea Front	7
Youth Hostel	5

■ DRINKING AND NIGHTLIFE	
Cul de Sac	2
Fraoules	4
Ice Club	3
O Kipos tou Ali Vafi	1

● EATING	
1600 Raki BaRaki	2
Alana	3
Melina	1
Mesostrati	6
Mojo Burgers	5
Petite Fleur	8
Stella's Kitchen	4
Zefyros	7

The beach

Réthymno's **beach** is an invitingly broad swathe of tawny sand, right alongside the old town. There are showers and cafés, and the waters protected by the breakwaters are dead calm (and ideal for kids). Sadly, they're also crowded and often none too clean. Outside the harbour, less sheltered sands stretch for kilometres, only marginally less crowded but with much cleaner water. There's a big watersport centre right at the beginning of this stretch, and interspersed among the hotels along here is every facility you could need –travel agents, bike rental, bars and restaurants.

ARRIVAL AND DEPARTURE

By bus The bus station in Réthymno is by the sea to the west of the town centre; from the station, it's about a 10min walk to the harbour; local bus #20 runs through the centre and east along the coast to the hotel zone. Info, timetables and tickets at ⓦe-ktel.com.

Destinations Amári (Mon–Fri 2.30pm; 1hr); Anóyia (Mon–Fri 5.30am & 2pm; 1hr 30min); Arkádhi monastery (3 daily; 30min); Ayía Galíni (5 daily; 1hr); Haniá (19 daily;

1hr 30min); Iráklio (18 daily; 1hr 30min); Plakiás (5 daily; 50min); Préveli (2 daily; 50min).

By ferry In summer, there's a weekly fast catamaran on Tuesdays to Santoríni (2hr 15min), Íos (3hr), Náxos (4hr) and Mýkonos (5hr). It leaves early and returns the same evening: any local travel agent can sell you a day-trip package to Santoríni (including a tour and meals) or book direct with SeaJets (ⓦseajets.gr)

INFORMATION

Tourist information Information booths can be found at the corner of the old harbour and in Platía Tessáron Martíron (June–Sept Mon–Fri 9am–2pm, but

unreliable). The municipal website, ⓦrethymno.gr, is dated but has good maps.

ACCOMMODATION

Atelier Himáras 25 ☎28310 24440, ⓦfrosso-bora. com. This small place near the fortress is run by a talented potter, above her workspace and shop. The attractive a/c rooms come with kitchenette and satellite TV. **€45**

★**Avli** Xanthoudhídhou 22 ☎28310 58250, ⓦavli.gr. Luxury apartments and suites from the people who also run *1600 Raki BaRaki* (see below). They have several locations at various prices, but the best are within a couple of lovingly restored old townhouses, with a rooftop terrace and hot tub; a superb breakfast is included. **€100**

★**Barbara Studios** Dhamvérgi 14 ☎28310 22607, ⓦbarbarastudios.gr. Beautifully done-up, well-equipped rooms, studios and apartments in a rambling old building, sharing a roof garden and various communal areas. Great location and an exceptionally friendly welcome. April–Oct. **€50**

Castello Karaolí 10 ☎28310 23570, ⓦcastello-rethymno.gr. A very congenial small pension in a 300-year-old Turkish mansion; a/c en-suite rooms come with fridge and TV and there's a delightful patio garden for taking breakfast (extra), plus a tiny subterranean jacuzzi pool. **€60**

Hamam Oriental Suites Nikifórou Foká 86 ☎6984 122 344, ⓦhamamsuites.com. A stunning conversion of a Turkish hammam into five luxury suites. The Hamman Suite (Cyclamen) occupies the main, domed room and has a private steam bath; the top-floor Ottoman Suite (Hyacinth) is a fully-equippped two-room apartment with mini sauna and tiny pool; the others are slightly less fancy (and cost less). **€100**

Sea Front Arkadhíou 159/Venizélou 45 ☎28310 24533, ⓦrethymnoatcrete.com. Attractive a/c rooms and studios in a waterfront house, some with sea-view balconies (well worth the extra €10), and all with fridge and TV. The welcoming owners also have a number of excellent sea-view apartments nearby. Double **€45**, apartment **€50**

★**Youth Hostel** Tombázi 41 ☎28310 22848, ⓦyhrethymno.com. Long-established, friendly and popular hostel with the cheapest beds in town, in six- to eight-bed newly refurbished dorms. Each bed has power and a locker, the bathrooms have also been renewed, and there's a communal kitchen and washing machines, plus a sociable café for breakfast, juices and drinks. **€14**

EATING

The most touristy **restaurants** are arrayed immediately behind the town beach and have menu picture boards outside – many of them overpriced and mediocre – while around the inner harbour there's a cluster of expensive and intimate **fish tavernas**. The most inviting and best-value places to eat tend to be scattered in less obvious parts of the old town; the stretch of Vernádhou near the Nerátses mosque, for example, is crowded with new meze places, extremely popular with locals late in the evening.

1600 Raki BaRaki Arabatsóglou 17 ☎28310 58250. Big, modern meze place from the people who run *Avli* (the hotel and very fancy restaurant next door). It's pricier than some, but the food is very good, the ambience welcoming, it's open all day and there's a huge amount to choose from, whether its cheese pie with *apáki* (smoked pork; €6.90), aubergine and filo rolls with goat cheese (€6.80), grilled sardines (€7.90) or moussaka (€8.70). Daily noon–midnight.

Alana Salamínos 15 ☎28310 27737, ⓦalana-restaurant.gr. An attractive, tree-filled courtyard provides the setting for an elegant restaurant serving both traditional and updated Cretan dishes. Among the former, try lamb *tsigariasto* (a traditional, slow-cooked stew; €15.50), the latter includes the likes of sea bass cooked sous-vide with citrus sauce (€19.50). Also good house wine and a range of bottles. Daily noon–midnight.

Melina Himáras 22 ☎ 28310 21580, ☺ melinarestaurant.gr. Traditional café/taverna handy for the Fortezza, specializing in meat cooked on the outdoor barbecue (chicken €14; lamb €19.50) – give them an hour or so's notice and they'll barbecue an entire joint for you. There are great views over the town from the terrace. Daily 10am–1am.

★ **Mesostrati** Yerakári 1 ☎ 28310 29375. An economical little neighbourhood taverna-ouzerí serving well-prepared country dishes on a shady small terrace; salads are all €5, Greek oven dishes €6, grills €7. The main reason to come, though, is for the excellent live Cretan lyra and laoúto (lute) music (Wed–Sat from 9pm). Mon–Sat 11am–3pm & 6pm–2am, Sun 6pm–2am.

Mojo Burgers Dhamvérgi 38 ☎ 28310 50550. If you need a break from Greek food, *Mojo* serves up excellent burgers (from €3.50 to €7.40 for an "Elvis" with cheese, bacon and syrup) and hot dogs (around €2.50) in a diner-style space. Daily noon–1am.

Petite Fleur Venizélou 36 ☎ 28313 306868, ☺ petitefleur.gr. Very different from the bulk of seafront places, with a modern Greek-Mediterranean menu and bistro atmosphere. They have delicious salads (fig & pomegranate, for example, €7.50), snacks or starters like stuffed mini-pitas (€5.50), and mains ranging from their house burger (€10.50) to a huge beer-marinated pork shank served with home-made spätzle (€16.50), plus plenty of pasta and fish dishes. Tues–Sun noon–1am.

Stella's Kitchen Soulíou 55 ☎ 28310 54896. A great-value and welcoming little diner run by the eponymous and ebullient proprietor. Stella serves up half-a-dozen fresh, home-made daily specials (€6–8; at least two are vegetarian); it's also a good spot for breakfast. Mon–Sat 8am–8pm.

Zefyros Inner harbour ☎ 28310 28206. If you're determined to eat by the water, *Zefyros* is one of the more reliable of the harbourside fish tavernas, offering reasonably priced (for this location) fish and seafood such as sole fillet stuffed with prawns (€18.50) or fisherman's spaghetti (€17.50). March–Oct daily 10am–midnight.

DRINKING AND NIGHTLIFE

Cul de Sac Platía Petiháki ☎ 28310 26914. Prime people-watching spot on the busy corner by the Rimóndi Fountain. They serve brunch, sandwiches and burgers but mostly it's a place to drink – coffees by day, pitchers of beer and cocktails later, when there's sometimes a DJ or live band. Daily 8am–2am.

Fraoules Venizélou 62 ☎ 28310 24525. One of several lively all-day bar-cafés on this stretch that are especially busy late in the evening with a pre-club local crowd. Occasional events or live music, and good cocktails. Daily 9am–2am.

Ice Club Salamínos 22 ☎ 6949 986 294. One of half a dozen clubs around the junction of Salamínos, Mesolongíou and Melissinoú, *Ice* is popular with young locals and open year-round; mixed Greek and international playlist. Tues–Sun midnight–dawn.

0 Kipos tou Ali Vafi Vounialí 65 ☎ 28310 23238. A vaulted tunnel off the street leads to a hidden garden and a cool café-bar with shisha pipes, board games, and events including live Cretan music on Sunday afternoons. They also serve good food. Daily 10am–2am.

Into the mountains

The main road south from Réthymno offers a fairly easy, flat drive towards Plakiás and the south coast (see p.489). There's far more of interest to be found by heading further east, into the foothills of the **Psilorítis range**. Here the **monastery of Arkádhi** is a popular and easy short trip. Beyond the monastery you can either head east via the ancient sites of **Eléftherna** and the potters' village of **Margarítes** (p.488) towards Anóyia, a spectacular mountain drive, or south into the beautiful **Amári Valley**.

Monastery of Arkádhi

25km southeast of Réthymno • Daily: April–Oct 9am–7pm; Nov–March 9am–4pm • €3 • ☎ 28310 83135

The **Monastery of Arkádhi** is, for Cretans, a shrine to the struggle for independence. During the 1866 rebellion against the Turks, the monastery became a rebel strongpoint in which, as the Turks gained the upper hand, hundreds of Cretan independence fighters and their families took refuge. Surrounded and on the point of defeat, the defenders ignited a powder magazine just as the Turks entered the compound. Hundreds were killed, Cretan and Turk alike, and the tragedy did much to promote international sympathy for the cause of Cretan independence. Nowadays, you can peer into the roofless vault where the explosion occurred and wander about the rest of the well-restored grounds. The sixteenth-century **church** survived, and is one of the finest Venetian structures left on Crete.

Eléftherna

From Arkádhi a lovely, lonely road winds through the village of Néa Eléftherna to the far more interesting hamlet of **ARHÉA ELÉFTHERNA** and the spectacular remains of ancient Eléftherna. This was one of the most important cities in eighth- and seventh-century BC Dorian Crete; when the Romans came in 67 BC it put up a stiff resistance, and later flourished as the seat of a Christian bishop. The Saracen invasions finished it off, however. Reminders of the city surround the village, above all the **acropolis** (daily: April–Oct 8am–6pm; Nov–March 8.30am–3pm; free), which enjoys a magnificent defensive position on a steep-sided spur of rock surrounded by narrow ravines. In the valley below you can see both the **main site of ancient Eléftherna**, to the east, and, to the northwest, its **necropolis** (both have the same hours as the acropolis) while, just outside Néa Elefthérna, a new futuristic-looking **museum** (Tues–Sun 10am–6pm, €4; ⓦen.mae.com.gr) displays finds from the site.

Margarítes

MARGARÍTES, a very pretty place on the edge of a ravine, some 3km north of Eléftherna, with views back towards the coast, has a long tradition of making **pottery**. A hundred years ago there were as many as eighty sizeable workshops here, producing all sorts of items for everyday and agricultural use. Today, smaller artisan producers are scattered throughout the village, and you can buy their work in a dozen or more outlets along the steep main street.

The Amári Valley

The little-travelled route south via the **Amári Valley** is a delight. Although there's not a great deal specifically to see or do (a number of frescoed Byzantine churches are hidden away en route), it's an impressive drive under the flanks of the mountains and a reminder of how, in places, rural Crete continues to exist regardless of visitors. The countryside here is delightfully green even in summer, with rich groves of olive and assorted fruit trees, and if you **stay** you'll find that the nights are cool and quiet. It may seem odd that many of the villages along the way are modern: they were systematically destroyed by the German army in reprisal for the 1944 kidnapping of General Kreipe, and many have poignant roadside monuments commemorating those tragic events.

Spíli

The pleasant country town of **SPÍLI** is tucked beneath the mountains about 30km south of Réthymno. A popular lunch break for drivers and coach tours passing this way, it doesn't look much as you drive through. If you get off the main road, however, narrow alleys of ancient houses wind upwards from an attractive platía with a prodigious 25-spouted **fountain**. It's good hiking country too, and a peacefully rural place to stay once the day-trippers have moved on.

HIKING IN THE AMÁRI VALLEY AND AROUND SPÍLI

Both the **Amári Valley** and **Spíli** offer plentiful opportunities for walking, from gentle rural strolls between villages to challenging mountain ascents. Expert advice is available at *Aravanes* (see oppposite) in Thrónos, a sizeable village at the Amári Valley's northern end, or at *Heracles* (see oppposite) in Spíli. The proprietor of *Aravanes* – Lambros Papoutsakis – is a keen if ageing walker and conducts guided treks (€20/hr) around the valley, plus moonlit, full-moon ascents to the peak of **Mount Psilorítis** (see p.469; €70, including meals). Other hikes from Thrónos include a relatively easy path leading north through the foothills in a couple of hours to the monastery of Arkádhi (see p.487), or a variety of routes south into the valley. From Spíli there are plenty of marked circular hikes, while the E4 path passes through, heading up towards the valley – it's a tough, all-day, 19km trek with plenty of climbing.

GETTING AROUND

By bus From Réthymno, there are 3 daily buses (Sat & Sun 2 daily) to Arkádhi (30min), as well as countless bus tours; the 10am bus continues to Eléftherna (45min) and Margarítes (50min); there's also 1 weekday service to the village of Amári (2.30pm; 1hr); and 5 daily to Ayía Galíni that will drop you in Spíli (40min).

By car Head east out of Réthymno before turning inland

INTO THE MOUNTAINS

for Arkádhi and Amári. Watch out for the road layout around the monastery: the Amári road passes the monastery on one side, the route east towards Anóyia on the other; they're connected only by the track through the monastery's car park. Spíli lies on the main road south of Réthymno; you can also reach it on a good new road that cuts across from the western edge of the Amári Valley.

ACCOMMODATION AND EATING

MARGARÍTES

Taverna Mantalos Main square ☎ 28340 92294. On the village's attractive upper platía, this great little taverna has a shady terrace offering fine views over the valley. The friendly proprietors cook up tasty traditional Cretan food including delicious *kolokithoánthi yemistá* (stuffed courgette flowers, €5); daily specials are €7–9. Daily 9am–10.30pm.

THRÓNOS

Aravanes Thrónos ☎ 28330 22760, ⓦ aravanes.com. The stone-built *Aravanes* has stunning panoramic views across the valley to Mount Psilorítis. Some of the rooms are newly refurbished with a wood-burner (and central heating for winter), a/c, flat-screen TV and fridge; there's also a family

apartment and a couple of slightly older rooms. The family run the attractive taverna below (mains €6–8), together with a small shop selling mountain herbs and homemade honey; if you wish you can get involved in the daily life of the farm. €40

SPÍLI

Heracles Just off the main road ☎ 28320 22111, ⓦ heracles-hotel.eu. Friendly *pension* with spotless a/c balcony rooms with TV and fridge; excellent breakfast (extra). The genial proprietor can advise on some superb walks in the surrounding hills, and rents out mountain bikes. He also has exceptionally well-equipped apartments, sleeping up to four, in his grandparents' converted house in the old part of town. Double €40, apartment €70

7

The south coast

The main road south from Réthymno heads straight out from the centre of town, an initially featureless drive across the middle of the island. About 20km out, two smaller roads cut off to the right for **Plakiás** and **Mýrthios**; the first via the **Kotsifóu gorge**, the second, slightly more direct route, following the course of the even more spectacular **Kourtaliótiko ravine**. The main road continues towards **Ayía Galíni** via Spíli (see opposite).

Plakiás

PLAKIÁS is the biggest attraction on Réthymno's south coast. A well-established resort, it's still a long way from the big league, with plenty of simple accommodation, few big hotels and a relatively young crowd. Don't come for sophisticated nightlife or for a picturesque white Greek island village: what you'll find is a lively, friendly place that makes a good base for **walks** in the beautiful countryside and is in easy reach of some great **beaches**. Among the best of these are three splashes of yellow sand, divided by rocky promontories, that together go by the name **Dhamnóni**, a thirty- to forty-minute walk away.

Mýrthios

The village of **MÝRTHIOS** hangs high above Plakiás, with wonderful views over the bay. There are few facilities beyond a couple of small shops and a post office, so you really need transport. You can, however, walk down to Plakiás, about twenty minutes steeply downhill, or to several of the nearby beaches – the walk back up is considerably tougher, though.

Préveli Monastery

11km east of Plakiás • April & May daily 9am–6pm; June–Oct Mon–Sat 9am–1.30pm & 3.30–9pm, Sun 8am–7pm; in winter, knock for admission • €3 • In summer 2 buses a day run from Réthymno, and 4 from Plakiás; you can also get here by taking a boat to Palm Beach from Plakiás or Ayía Galíni and climbing up – a strenuous 30min or so • ⓦ www.preveli.org

The celebrated **Moní Préveli**, perched high above the sea, is justifiably proud of its role in centuries of Cretan resistance, and famed above all for the shelter provided to Allied troops, many of them Australian, stranded on the island after the Battle of Crete in World War II. The monks supported and fed many soldiers and helped organize them into groups to be taken off nearby beaches by submarine. Today there's a monument to these events, a small museum, and scintillating sea views.

Palm Beach

Below Préveli Monastery • Constant boat tours from Plakiás and Ayía Galíni, or take the bus to Préveli and climb down; drivers can park in the Prevéli car park or in the valley 2km away, and walk down

A sand-filled cove at the mouth of the Kourtaliótiko gorge, where a stream feeds a little oasis complete with palm grove and cluster of oleanders, **Palm Beach** certainly looks beautiful – though for much of the year it's overwhelmed by visitors. Behind the beach, you can escape up the palm-lined riverbanks on foot or take a pedalo through the icy water. Further upstream, before the gorge becomes too steep to follow, are a couple of deep **pools** to swim in. On the beach, a small **bar-taverna** provides basic food and sells drinks, snacks and a few provisions. It's strange to think, as you bask on the crowded sands, that from here, in 1941, many of the Allied soldiers who sought refuge at Moní Préveli (see above) were evacuated by submarine.

Ayía Galíni

AYÍA GALÍNI is a picturesque place nestling in a fold in the mountains. Once an idyllic, isolated spot, it now swarms with package tourists throughout the season; the beach, a short walk to the east of town, can barely cope. Nonetheless there's something about Ayía Galíni that attracts a loyal following, and there are certainly plenty of excellent restaurants and bars, a lively nightlife scene, well-priced rooms and a friendly atmosphere that survives and even thrives on all the visitors.

GETTING AROUND   THE SOUTH COAST

By bus 5 buses a day connect Réthymno with Mýrthios and Plakiás (50min). From May–Oct, there are also 2 buses a day from Réthymno to Préveli (50min) and 4 between Plakiás and Préveli (20min). Ayía Galíni has connections with both Réthymno (5 daily; 1hr) and Iráklio (bus station B; 5 daily; 2hr).

ACTIVITIES

Boat trips Both Plakiás and Ayía Galíni have a wide choice of daily boat trips from their harbours, not just to Palm Beach but to a variety of other beaches and islets, as well as fishing and occasional dolphin-spotting trips.
Diving There's good diving around Plakiás; try Dive2gether (☎28320 32313, ⓦdive2gether.com) or Kalypso Rocks Dive Centre (☎28310 74687, ⓦkalypsodivecenter.com).
Horseriding Treks and lessons near Plakiás are offered by the Horse Riding Center (☎28320 31196, ⓦcretehorseriding .com; info at the large *Alianthos Beach Hotel*, on the seafront as you enter town).

ACCOMMODATION

PLAKIÁS

Anna Plakias Apartments Inland, towards the youth hostel ☎6974 078 308, ⓦanna-plakias.gr. Classy modern apartments and studios with a/c and kitchenettes, plus a suite with a tiny swimming pool, in a quiet spot shaded by palm trees. **€55**
Gio-ma Western end of the seafront ☎28320 31942, ⓦgioma.gr. In a prime position overlooking the harbour, these simple but fabulously located, newly renovated rooms (with fridge, flatscreen TV and a/c) sit above the taverna of the same name, right on the water. Over the road are studios and two-room apartments, also recently refurbished, also with sea views. Great value. April–Oct. Double **€35**, apartment **€45**
Morpheas Apartments On the seafront, above Plakiás Market ☎28320 31583, ⓦmorpheas -apartments-plakias-crete-greece.com. Fine modern rooms, studios and duplex apartments with balconies overlooking the beach (although not all have sea view). They're double-glazed against the potentially noisy location, with a/c, TV, fridge and, in the larger apartments, even a washing machine. Room **€40**, apartment **€65**
★**Youth Hostel** 500m inland, signed from the seafront ☎28320 32118, ⓦyhplakias.com. The best hostel on Crete – friendly, relaxed and well run, in an attractively rural setting, with a terrace for breakfast and

evening drinks and a busy social scene. Hot showers and wi-fi included. March–Nov. Dorm **€10**

MÝRTHIOS

★Anna Apartments Mýrthios ☎6973 324 775, ⓦannaview.com. These classy apartments, built with traditional stone and wood, are beautifully furnished and have fantastic views over Plakiás Bay. All come with kitchenette, balcony, a/c and satellite TV. March–Nov. **€55**

AYÍA GALÍNI

Camping No Problem Behind the beach ☎28320 91386. Big campsite with a pool, shop and restaurant, with sandy, tree-shaded pitches. April–Oct. **€16**

Hariklia On entry road from Réthymno just before the descent ☎28320 91257, ⓦhotelhariklia.gr. Delightful, spotless pension with refurbished en-suite a/c rooms with fridge. The communal balconies have fine

views and guests can also use the kitchen to prepare breakfasts and snacks. **€35**

★Minos Entry road from Réthymno on left ☎28320 91292, ⓦminoshotel.gr. Welcoming hotel with comfortable, modern a/c rooms with fridge and TV; there's also a small family apartment and studio – other rooms have use of a shared kitchen. Many of the rooms enjoy the best sea views in town (well worth the extra €10). Superb breakfast €10 extra. **€40**

Tropica Club Behind the beach, on the far side of the river ☎28320 91351, ⓔtropica@otenet.gr. Run by an Anglo-Greek couple, these studios and apartments right behind the beach have the added attraction of a big seawater pool. Studios have a/c, TV and fridge, while the more spacious apartments also have a kitchen; the newer units come with sea views and handmade wooden furnishings. Beachfront bar/taverna (breakfast available) and poolside yoga sessions, too. Double **€50**, apartment **€60**

EATING AND DRINKING

PLAKIÁS

Medousa Inland, near the back of the *Alianthos Garden* hotel ☎6937 133 234, ⓦmedousa-plakias.com. The fanciest place in town, in both appearance and menu. A beautiful room and great service, though the more inventive dishes can be a bit hit and miss; choose from standard Greek fare such as cumin-spiced meatballs (€9) and lamb with beans and tomato sauce (€10.50), or more ambitious creations like kalamári stuffed with chickpeas, citron, rose, geranium, herbs and feta (€11). There's a decent wine list, too, and good rooms above. Daily noon–3pm & 6.30–10.30pm.

Ostraco On the waterfront, close to the harbour. Long-established music bar set over two storeys and an upstairs terrace, with a rock-based playlist and fun atmosphere. Daily 9am–3am.

★Tassomanolis Facing west along the shore beyond the harbour ☎28320 31229. Seafood is king here, most of it caught by the proprietor from his own boat and competitively priced by the kilo. Dishes include snapper for €13.50, sardines at €7.50 and mixed fish for 2 at €23. Daily noon–midnight.

Throubi On the street heading inland by the end of the beach ☎28320 31915. Family-run traditional taverna serving excellent, simple, good-value food. Daily specials such as rabbit stew or moussaka for around €8, grilled meats for €7–8. Daily noon–3pm & 6.30–10.30pm.

MÝRTHIOS

Taverna Plateia ☎28320 31560. This long-established taverna with arguably the most spectacular terrace view on the island serves up tasty Cretan cuisine with the odd creative twist – dishes include red lamb (€9.40), rabbit in lemon sauce (€8.90) and vegetarian lasagne (€7.80). It can get busy, especially at Sun lunchtimes, so turn up early if you don't want to wait; they don't accept bookings. Daily noon–11pm.

AYÍA GALÍNI

Faros Just inland from the harbour ☎28930 91346. The resort's best and most unpretentious fish restaurant, with a small street terrace, where the friendly family who run it serve up what they catch themselves. The catch of the day is chalked up on a blackboard – it's priced per kilo, with a portion of fish typically around €12; they also specialize in *astakomakaronada* (lobster with spaghetti). Daily 6pm–midnight.

To Petrino Just off the bus stop platía ☎28320 91504. Tiny little gem of an ouzerí whose proprietor is an ex-sea captain. Serves breakfast and coffee plus excellent mezédhes later in the day (small selection €7, large €14), and retains some of the flavour of the pre-tourist days. Daily 9am–2pm & 4.30pm–midnight.

Yeoryioúpoli

To the west of Réthymno, the main road climbs for a while above a rocky coastline before descending to the sea, where it runs alongside sandy **beaches** for perhaps 14km. About 7km before Yeoryioúpoli, the beach widens and scattered hotel development appears along the coast. If you have your own vehicle, you'll come across plenty of places to stop for a swim, some with hardly anyone else around – but beware of some very strong currents.

On arriving in **YEORYOÚPOLI** (Georgioupolis) you'll find a place with a distinctly split personality: on the one hand it's a pretty **old town** by the river, its approaches shaded by ancient eucalyptus trees; on the other it's a lively **package resort**, with development spreading further every year along the beach to the east of town. As long as you don't expect to find too many vestiges of traditional Crete, it's a very pleasant spot to spend a few days. Yeoryioúpoli's central beach is narrow and busy; walk east a few hundred metres for the quieter and wider sands.

Lake Kournás

Crete's only freshwater lake, **Lake Kournás**, shelters in a bowl of hills 4km inland from Yeoryioúpoli, 4km below the hilltop village of **Kournás**. As lakes go, it's small and shallow, but it nevertheless makes for an interesting excursion; for hikers there's a beautifully scenic route via the hamlet of **Mathés**. Spring, when the mountain views and profusion of wild flowers are stunning, is the best time to visit the lake; in high summer you could be in a completely different place, as the winter waters recede and the lake-shore "beach" is packed with umbrellas and sunloungers.

7

ARRIVAL AND DEPARTURE	**YEORYIOÚPOLI**

By bus Buses running along the main highway between Réthymno (40min) and Haniá (50min) stop at Yeoryioúpoli (virtually hourly until midnight).

ACCOMMODATION AND EATING

Andy's Rooms Near the church, on the road towards the beach from the south end of the square by the supermarket ☏ 28250 61394, ⊚ andys.georgioupoli. net. This friendly place shaded by trees has good-value a/c rooms, simple but spotless, with big balconies and fridge, plus a couple of well-equipped apartments. Double **€30**, apartment **€50**

Anna's House Just across the river from town, on the Exópoli road ☏ 28250 61556, ⊚ annashouse.gr. Lovely, newly-built studios and apartments with well-equipped kitchens and modern decor, based around a full-size pool; a short walk to town or Kaliváki beach. Studio **€80**, apartment **€120**

Babis On the cross street between the square and the

beach ☏ 28250 61760. Traditional taverna with good-value, simple Cretan food; try their excellent rabbit *stifádho* (€7.50). Daily 11am–midnight.

Eligas On the first cross street below the square, heading towards the beach ☏ 28250 61541, ⊚ eligas. gr. Simply furnished but well-maintained a/c studios, plus one apartment, in a bougainvillea-draped building; upper floors have good views from the back. **€35**

Sirtaki Main street near the bridge ☏ 28250 61382. Excellent taverna-ouzerí with a raised terrace serving well-prepared mezédhes (mixed plate for 2, €19), traditional dishes (yemistá €6.50) and delicious grilled meat and fish; lamb chops €12, mixed fish for 2 €30. April–Oct daily noon–midnight.

Western Crete

Although tourist development is spreading fast, and has already engulfed much of the coast around the city of Haniá, Crete's westernmost quarter is still one of the emptier parts of the island, partly because there are few beaches suited to large resort hotels, and partly because the great archeological sites are a long way from here. In their place are some of the classic elements of the island: scattered coves, unexploited rural villages, and a spectacular vista of mountains.

Haniá (Chania) itself is the most enjoyable of Crete's larger towns, littered with oddments from its Venetian and Turkish past, and bustling with harbourside life. The coast around the city is not particularly exciting; if you want beaches head for the south coast or the far west. Here, **Paleóhora** is the only place which could really be described as a resort, and even this is on a thoroughly human scale; others are smaller still. Elsewhere on the south coast, **Ayía Rouméli** and **Loutró** can be reached only on foot or by boat; **Hóra Sfakíon** sees hordes passing through but few who stay; **Frangokástello**, nearby, has a beautiful castle and the first stirrings of development.

Behind these lie the **White Mountains** (Lefká Óri) and the famed walk through the **Samariá Gorge**. In the far west, great beaches at **Falásarna** and **Elafonísi** are mostly visited only as day-trips.

Haniá

HANIÁ, as any of its residents will tell you, is spiritually the capital of Crete, even if the political title was long ago passed back to Iráklio. It is also the island's most attractive city, especially if you can catch it in spring, when the White Mountains' snowcapped peaks seem to hover above the roofs. Although it is for the most part a modern place, you might never know it as a tourist. Surrounding the harbour is a wonderful jumble of **Venetian streets**, a maze-like old town contained by ancient city walls and littered with Ottoman, Byzantine and Minoan ruins.

The harbour

7

The **harbour** area is at its busiest and most attractive at night, when the lights from bars and restaurants reflect in the water and crowds of visitors and locals turn out to promenade. By day, things are quieter. Straight ahead from Platía Sindriváni ("Harbour Square") lies the curious domed shape of the Küçük Hasan Pasha Mosque – also known as the Seaside Mosque. Built in 1645, though heavily restored since, it is the oldest Ottoman building on the island: it's usually open for temporary exhibitions. Further east, on the inner harbour, the arches of sixteenth-century **Venetian arsenals**, a couple of them beautifully restored, survive alongside remains of the outer walls.

The Naval Museum

Aktí Koundouriótou • May–Oct Mon–Sat 9am–5pm, Sun 10am–6pm; Nov–April Mon–Sat 9am–3.30pm • €3, joint ticket with Exhibition of Naval Architecture €4 • ⓦ www.mar-mus-crete.gr

A hefty bastion at the western end of the harbour houses Crete's **Naval Museum**. Inside, you'll see displays of model ships and other naval ephemera tracing the history of Greek navigation, plus a section on the 1941 Battle of Crete which has fascinating artefacts and poignant photos depicting the suffering here under the Nazis. The modern Greek flag was first flown on Crete in 1913 from the **Fírkás**, the fortress behind the museum; today, you can climb the Fírkás' ramparts for great harbour views.

Exhibition of Traditional Naval Architecture

Aktí Enóseos • May–Oct Mon–Sat 9am–5pm, Sun 10am–6pm • €2, joint ticket with Naval Museum €4 • ⓦ www.mar-mus-crete.gr

A restored Venetian arsenal facing the far end of the inner harbour is home to the naval museum's **Exhibition of Traditional Naval Architecture**. The outstanding highlight here, along with the vast boat shed itself, is a reconstruction of a fifteenth-century BC **Minoan ship**, which was rowed to Athens for the start of the 2004 Olympics.

Byzantine Museum

Theotokopóulou 78 • Tues–Sun 8am–3pm • €3, combined ticket with Archeological Museum, Kastélli Museum and Aptéra site €6 • ⓣ 28210 96046

The **Byzantine Museum**, in the Venetian chapel of San Salvatore, has a tiny but beautifully displayed collection of mosaics, icons, jewellery, coins, sculpture and everyday objects, giving a fascinating insight into an era that's largely overlooked.

City walls and backstreets

From the waterfront west of the Byzantine Museum, Odhós Pireós cuts inland outside the best-preserved stretch of the **city walls**, which are impressive, weighty and threatening. Following them on the inside is rather trickier, but far more enjoyable. This is where you'll stumble on some of the most picturesque little alleyways and finest Venetian houses in Haniá, and also where the pace of renovation and gentrification is

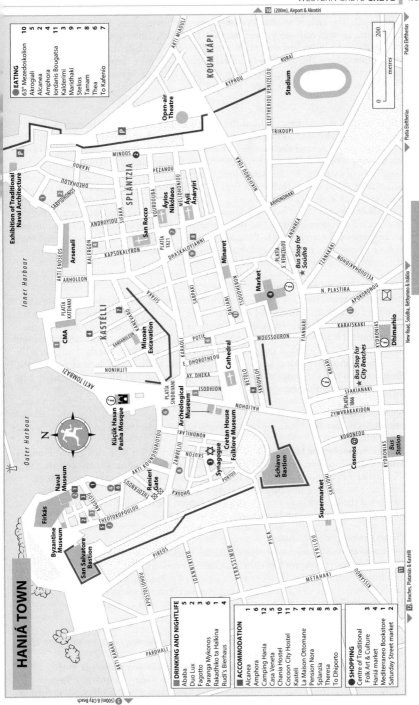

HANIÁ TOWN

EATING
63° Mezedoskolion	10
Akrogiali	5
Alcanea	2
Amphora	4
Iordanis Bougatsa	11
Kalderimi	3
Maridhaki	9
Stelios	1
Tamam	8
Thea	6
To Kafenío	7

DRINKING AND NIGHTLIFE
Ababa	5
Duo Lux	2
Fagotto	3
Paranga Mykonos	6
Rakadhiko ta Halkína	1
Rudi's Bierhaus	4

ACCOMMODATION
Alcanea	1
Amphora	6
Camping Hania	12
Casa Veneta	5
Chania Hostel	10
Cocoon City Hostel	11
Kasteli	7
La Maison Ottomane	4
Pension Nora	2
Splanzia	8
Theresa	3
To Dhiporto	9

SHOPPING
Centre of Traditional Folk Art & Culture	3
Haniá market	4
Mediterraneo Bookstore	1
Saturday Street market	2

KOUM KÁPI

SPLANTZIA

KASTELLI

Inner Harbour

Outer Harbour

Exhibition of Traditional Naval Architecture

Open-air Theatre

Stadium

Arsenali

Áyios Nikólaos

San Rocco

Minaret

Market

CMA

Minoan Excavation

Cathedral

Archeological Museum

Küçük Hasan Pasha Mosque

Naval Museum

Byzantine Museum

Firkás

San Salvatore Bastion

Renieri Gate

Synagogue

Cretan House Folklore Museum

Schiavo Bastion

Supermarket

Dhimarhío

Cosmos @

Bus Station

Bus Stop for Soudha

Bus Stop for City Beaches

Platía 1821

Platía Katehaki

Platía Sindriváni

Platía 1866

Platía S. Venizélou

7

0 — 200 metres

N

Airport & Akrotíri

New Road, Soudha, Réthymno & Iráklio

Platía Eleftherías

Beaches, Platanias & Kastélli

500m & City Beach

most rapid. The arch of the **Renieri Gate** is particularly elegant. There are also interesting art and craft stores here, around Theotokopóulou and in the many alleys that lead off the outer harbour. Haniá's renovated fifteenth-century **Etz Hayyim synagogue** (Mon–Thurs 10am–6pm, Fri 10am–3pm; June–Sept also Sun 11am–4pm; free; ⓦetz-hayyim-hania.org) lies down one such alley, a poignant reminder of a Jewish population that was entirely wiped out in 1944.

Kastélli and Splántzia

The section of the old town behind the inner harbour is far less touristy, though it's rapidly being colonized by boutique hotels, chic restaurants and alternative bars. The little bluff rising behind the mosque is **Kastélli**, site of the earliest habitation in Haniá. Archeologists believe that they may have found the remains of a Minoan palace, the "lost" city of **Kydonia**, in the excavations being carried out – and open to view – along Kanevárou. It's also here that you'll find traces of the oldest **walls**; there were two rings, one defending Kastélli alone, a later set encompassing the whole of the medieval city. The adjoining area to the east, still known by its Turkish name of **Splántzia**, is full of unexpected architectural delights, with minarets, carved wooden balconies and houses arching across the street at first-floor level. Many of the streets between here and the inner harbour have been re-cobbled and refurbished, and they're among the most atmospheric and tranquil in the old town.

Odhós Hálidhon and around

Odhós Hálidhon is perhaps the most touristy street in Haniá, and the major junction at its inland end (Platía 1866) marks the centre of town. From here, **Odhós Yiánnari** leads east past the **market** and eventually out towards the Akrotíri peninsula, while to the west, **Skalídhi** leads out of town towards Kastélli Kissámou. North, Hálidhon descends to the harbour and into the heart of the old town; some 70m from the junction is the animated **Odhós Skridhlóf** ("Leather Street"), where, traditionally, leather-makers plied their trade. While the shops are now geared to tourists, prices for leather sandals, bags and the like remain the best in Crete.

Archeological Museum

Odhós Hálidhon 28 • Mon 1–8pm; Tues–Sun 8am–8pm • €4, combined ticket with Byzantine Museum, Kastélli Museum and Aptéra site €6 • T28210 90334

Haniá's **Archeological Museum** is housed in the Venetian-built church of San Francesco. The building has been substantially restored and contains a fine display, covering the local area from Minoan through to Roman times. In the courtyard garden a huge fountain and the base of a minaret survive from the period when the Ottomans converted the church into a mosque; around them are scattered various other sculptures and architectural remnants.

Cretan House Folklore Museum

Odhós Hálidhon 46b • Mon, Tues, Thurs & Fri 9am–9pm, Wed & Sat 9am–5pm, Sun 11am–4pm • €2 • ☎ 28210 90816

The **Cretan House Folklore Museum** is a cluttered collection of artefacts, tapestries and traditional crafts equipment set out in a replica of a "traditional" house (though few can have been quite so packed). On your way out, take a look at Haniá's elegant **Roman Catholic church** in the same hidden courtyard.

The beaches

Áyii Apóstoli, Khrissi Akti and Kalamáki are accessible on city bus #21 from Platía 1866, departing every 20 mins (€1.20), while Áyia Marína, Kalathás and Stavrós are served by KTEL buses from the main station

Haniá's beaches lie to the west of the city and on the Akrotíri peninsula to the northeast. The **city beach** (Néa Hóra) is no more than a ten-minute walk west, following the seafront, but for more expansive sands you're better off heading further west along the coast to the beaches of **Áyii Apóstoli**, **Khrissi Akti** and **Kalamáki**. Further afield there are even better beaches at **Ayía Marína** (see p.501) to the west, or **Kalathás** and **Stavrós** (p.501) out on the Akrotíri peninsula.

ARRIVAL AND DEPARTURE HANIÁ

By plane Haniá Airport (Chania) lies 15km northeast of the city on the Akrotíri peninsula. As well as international scheduled and charter flights, there are domestic services from/to Athens (6 daily; 50min) and Thessaloníki (1–2 daily; 1hr 15min) with Aegean (ⓦaegeanair.com) and Ryanair (ⓦryanair.com). Buses run to Haniá (every 30min for most of the day, 6.30am–11.45pm; 30min; €2.50) and to Réthymno (6 daily; 1 hr 30min): a taxi to the city costs about €20. The driving route into Haniá is pretty clear: for all other destinations it's quicker and easier to take the left turn signed to Soúdha at the roundabout some 7km from the airport; this will take you down past the head of Soúdha Bay and out onto the main E75 highway, bypassing Haniá's congestion.

By ferry Arriving by ferry, you'll dock about 10km east of Haniá at the port of Soúdha: take a bus (every 20min; 20min; €1.70) or taxi (around €12) to the city; KTEL buses

to Réthymno and Kastélli also meet most ferries. If you're stuck in Soúdha you can find just about everything you need on the square right by the ferries, but it's not an attractive place. Ferry tickets are available from any travel agent or online (ⓦwww.anek.gr). There are departures to and from Pireás (9hr) every evening year-round, plus daytime sailings at peak summer periods.

By bus The bus station is on Kydhonías, an easy walk from the centre; info and online tickets at ⓦe-ktel.com.

Destinations Elafonísi (1 daily at 9am; 2hr 15min); Falásarna (3 daily; 1hr 30min); Hóra Sfakíon (2 daily 8.15am & 2pm; 1hr 40min); Iráklio via Réthymno (18 daily; 1hr 30min/3hr); Kastélli (15 daily; 45min); Kolymbári via Ayía Marína and the hotel zone (6.15am–11pm, at least every 30min; 15–40min); Omalós (Samariá Gorge; summer only 3 daily 6.15am–8.45am; 1hr 30min); Paleóhora (4–5 daily; 2hr); Soúyia (3 daily; 1hr 45min); Stavrós (5 daily; 25min).

7

GETTING AROUND AND INFORMATION

By bus Information on city buses at chaniabus.gr. The most useful services are #21, to the beaches, from Platía 1866, and #13, to Soúdha, from the market. Buy your ticket before boarding; fares are €1.20 within the city, €1.70 further afield. For the hotel zone, buses leave from the main bus station (see above).

By car, motorbike or bicycle For car rental, try Tellus, Hálidhon 108 (☎28210 91500, ⓦtellustravel.gr), one of many outlets around the top of Hálidhon. Alianthos is another reliable company (☎28320 32033, ⓦalianthos -group.com) with offices at the airport and in Ayía Marína. Summertime, Dhaskaloyiánni 7 and other local branches (☎28210 45797, ⓦstrentals.gr), has a huge range, including cars, motorbikes and mountain bikes.

By taxi The main taxi ranks are on Platía 1866, with smaller ones nearby at the bus station and on Venizélou near the market. For radio taxis call ☎18300 or 28210 98700, ⓦchaniataxi.gr.

Tourist office The helpful municipal tourist office is at Milonyiánni 53, at the side of the Dhimarhío (town hall; Mon–Fri 8.30am–3pm; ☎28213 41665, ⓦchaniatourism.com). They also run two seasonal booths – one at the Seaside Mosque, the other in front of the market (July–Sept daily 10am–2pm). The Greek National Tourist Office is nearby at Kriári 40, just off Platía 1866 (Mon–Fri 9am–2pm; ☎28210 92943), and there's also an office at the airport in summer (July–Sept Mon–Sat 9am–9pm).

TOURS AND ACTIVITIES

Boat trips A number of boats run trips from the harbour (around €15 for 2hr), mainly to the nearby islands of Áyii Theódori and Lazarétta, for swimming and *kri-kri* (ibex) spotting; other tours include sunset cruises and all-day

trips to the Rodhopoú peninsula.

Diving Chania Diving Center, Kaneváro 1 (☎28210 58939, ⓦchaniadiving.gr), runs daily diving and snorkelling trips.

Waterpark Limnoupolis ⓦlimnoupolis.gr.

ACCOMMODATION

There's a huge range of accommodation in and around Haniá, from simple rooms for rent to elegant boutique hotels. The popularity of the latter has led to anyone with a room near the harbour to tart it up, call it boutique, and attempt to rent it out at an inflated price. Perhaps the most desirable rooms are those overlooking the harbour, which are sometimes available at reasonable rates: this is because they're often noisy at night. Most are approached from the streets behind; those further back are likely to be more peaceful. Theotokopóulou and the alleys off it make a good starting point. The best of the more expensive places are here, too, equally set back but often with views from the upper storeys. In the addresses below, Párodhos means side street, so 2 Párodhos Theotokopóulou, for example, is the second alley off Theotokopóulo. Dozens of small rooms places can be found at ⓦchaniarooms.gr.

7

HARBOUR AREA

★**Alcanea** Angélou 2 ☎ 28210 75370, ⓦ ariahotels.gr. Gorgeous eight-room boutique hotel in a historic building beside the Naval Museum. Rooms come with all facilities including satellite TV and bluetooth speakers, with coffee machines and traditional teas in the communal areas. The pricier rooms (around twice the price of the most basic) have stunning views and balconies. Excellent breakfast included. March–Dec. **€120**

Amphora 2 Párodhos Theotokopóulou 20 ☎ 28210 93224, ⓦ amphora.gr. Hotel in a beautifully renovated fourteenth-century Venetian building, with spiral staircases, wooden floors and four-poster beds. Balcony rooms (such as Room 20) with harbour view are the best value; those without a view are cheaper. April–Oct. **€100**

Casa Veneta Theotokopoúlou 57 ☎ 28210 90007, ⓦ casa-veneta.gr. Very well-equipped, comfortable studios and apartments, with kitchenette, TV and (some) balcony sea views behind a Venetian facade; the large duplex apartment is particularly attractive. April–Oct. Studio **€55**, apartment **€60**

Pension Nora Theotokopoúlou 60 ☎ 28210 72265, ⓦ pension-nora.com. Charming, old-fashioned a/c rooms in a refurbished Ottoman house with wooden floors, rickety wooden staircase and a communal kitchen. Also appealing studios (same price) in a building nearby. **€40**

Theresa Angélou 8 ☎ 28210 92798, ⓦ pensiontheresa.gr. Beautiful old pension in a great position with stunning views from its roof terrace and some rooms; it has characterful traditional decor and a kitchen (with breakfast ingredients supplied) for guests' use. They also have a 3-bedroom house round the corner. Very popular, so book ahead. **€50**

THE OLD TOWN

★**Kasteli** Kaneváro 39 ☎ 28210 57057, ⓦ kastelistudios.gr. Comfortable, modern, reasonably priced *pension*, very quiet at the back. All en-suite rooms come with a/c and fridge. The proprietor is helpful and also has studios and a couple of beautiful apartments to rent nearby. Double **€65**, studio **€90**, apartment **€120**

★**La Maison Ottomane** Párodhos Kanenváro ☎ 28210 08796, ⓦ lamaisonottomane.com. Stunning boutique hotel with just three luxurious suites, opulently decorated in Ottoman pasha style, with objets d'art scoured from markets in Crete, London and the Middle East. Modern comforts include a/c, flatscreen TV and Nespresso machines, plus a superb breakfast. **€180**

Splanzia Dhaskaloyiánni 20 ☎ 28210 45313, ⓦ splanzia.com. Attractive and friendly boutique hotel in an elegantly refurbished Venetian mansion, with stylish rooms, some with four-posters, and extraordinary lighting. Breakfast (included) is served in a pretty courtyard. **€115**

To Dhiporto Betólo 41 ☎ 28210 40570, ⓦ todiporto.gr. The "Two Doors" runs between Betólo and pedestrian Skridhlóf: the balcony rooms over the latter, especially, are quiet. Friendly and good value, with a/c, TV, fridge and coffee machine in the rooms, which include singles and triples. **€45**

HOSTELS

Chania Hostel Venizélou 116 ☎ 28210 44955, ⓦ chaniahostel.gr. Exceptionally friendly backpacker-style hostel, run by Cretan-Australian Angeliki. Great atmosphere and plenty of activities, though facilities, from chunky home-made wooden bunks to lack of a/c, are fairly basic, and it's about a 15-minute walk from the harbour. Continental breakfast included. Dorms **€20**

Cocoon City Hostel Kydhonías 145 ☎ 28210 76100, ⓦ cocooncityhostel.com. New designer-style backpackers with classy, custom-furnished 4- and 6-bed dorms, with individual lockers and power points. Also two double rooms, 1 with private bath. It's about 3 blocks from the bus station, a 10-minute walk to the harbour. Dorm **€20**, double **€60**

CAMPING

Camping Hania Behind the beach in Áyii Apóstoli, 5km west of the city ☎ 28210 31138, ⓦ camping -chania.gr. A small site, hemmed in by new development, but with a pool and all the usual facilities, just a short walk from some of the better beaches, and with a regular local bus to town. They also have tents and trailers to rent. May–Oct. **€18**

EATING

The harbour is encircled by a succession of pricey **restaurants**, **tavernas** and **cafés** which are usually better for a drink than a meal. Away from the water, there are plenty of more interesting possibilities.

CAFÉS AND SNACKS

Alcanea Angélou 2 ☎ 28210 75377. Appealing terrace bar with great harbour view beneath the hotel of the same name; it's good for breakfast, coffee and mezédhes and, after sunset, cocktails and Cretan wines. Occasional live acoustic music at night. March–Dec daily 8am–2am.

Iordanis Bougatsa Apokorónou 24 ☎ 28210 88855. Serves only delicious traditional bougátsa (creamy cheese pie served warm and sprinkled with sugar and cinnamon), to eat in or take away. Mon–Sat 6am–2.30pm, Sun 6am–1.30pm.

Thea Platía Sindriváni ☎ 28210 73377. Café-bar over-looking the harbourside crowds from a first-floor terrace

– a great spot for people-watching in peace Daily 9am–3am.

To Kafenío Platía 1821 ☎ 28210 43755. Perhaps the best of the cafés on this great old square, and the closest thing to a traditional *kafenío* in central Haniá; good prices, too, and in the evening a great place for ouzo and meze. Daily 7.30am–3am.

RESTAURANTS

63° Mezedoskolion Daliáni 63 ☎ 28213 05080. The "School of Meze" is a fashionable modern *mezedhopolío* (meze €3–7) with a literal old-school theme – you sit at old school desks, chalky blackboards are everywhere, and you tick off your order on paper in the style of a multiple-choice exam. Packed with young locals late at night, as is this entire street. Thurs–Tues 7pm–1am.

★**Akrogiali** Aktí Papanikolí 19, Néa Hóra ☎ 28210 73110. Opposite the city beach, with a summer terrace, this excellent, reasonably priced fish and seafood taverna is well worth the 15min walk or short taxi ride. Whole fish are priced by the kilo, or there's seafood spaghetti (€12.80), cuttlefish in ink with rice (€11.80), sardines (€8.60) and even a few meat dishes. Always packed with locals, so may be worth booking – though there are plenty of alternatives along the same street. Daily lunch and dinner.

Amphora Aktí Koundouriótou 49, outer harbour ☎ 28210 71976. Excellent option among the touristy places on the outer harbour, with good, plain Greek food and no hard sell. Check the blackboard for the day's specials and fresh fish – or the lamb stamnagáthi (with local greens, €13.90) is always good. April–Oct daily noon–midnight.

Kalderimi Theotokopóulou 53 ☎ 28210 76741. A little gem of a place serving traditional Cretan dishes such as lamb *tsigariastó* with fried potatoes (€10.80), *bouréki* (cheese, potato and courgette pie, €7) or local pasta with shrimps (€9.50). Occasional live traditional music too. Mon–Sat noon–1am.

Maridhaki Dhaskaloyiánni 33 ☎ 28210 08880. Exceptional fish and seafood, keenly priced, at this on-trend place in the heart of a newly fashionable area, where young locals hang out at a series of bars, restaurants and ouzerís. Go for the catch of the day, and they also sell most fish by the portion (€9.90–16.50, depending on the type of fish) as well as the likes of octopus with fáva (€9.50) and some meat dishes. Mon–Sat noon–midnight.

Stelios Aktí Enóseos ☎ 28210 54240. Simple, old-fashioned seafood place towards the far end of the inner harbour. Very few frills, but excellent fish, squid and the like, especially if you order what's fresh that day. The stuffed kalamári is delicious (€11) as is the fish soup (€12), and fish priced by the kilo goes for less than anywhere else around the harbour. Daily noon–1am.

Tamam Zambelíou 49 ☎ 28210 96080. Popular place where the adventurous Greek menu has an eastern flavour, reflecting its location in an old Turkish hammam. Dishes include Smyrnian rabbit (€11.60) and Yiaourtlou (boneless lamb in tomato sauce with raisins and fresh mint; €7.60). There's a less atmospheric annexe opposite, and tables squeezed into the narrow alley between the two, where you're likely to be jostled by the passing crowds. Daily noon–12.30am.

DRINKING AND NIGHTLIFE

The harbour area contains dozens of beautifully set but touristy **bars**; locals tend to head to the fringe of the old town. In summer the action moves to the vibrant **club** scene in the resorts west of town.

Ababa Isodhíon 12. Funky bar with childishly colourful decor, open all day, offering snacks, books and board games; chilled sounds and cocktails in the evening through to the early hours. Daily 10am–late.

Duo Lux Sarpidhónos 8 ☎ 28210 52515. Comfy café-bar in a street full of similar places, just off the inner harbour; regular DJs and club nights inside after midnight, and occasional live bands. Daily 10am–late.

Fagotto Angélou 16 ☎ 28210 71877. Cosy, atmospheric backstreet jazz bar housed in an impressively restored Venetian mansion. Great cocktails, and high-quality live performances in season. Daily 8pm–late.

Paranga Mykonos Potié 32 ☎ 6947 003 848. Achingly trendy café-bar surrounded by similar places in a newly fashionable area. There's coffee and food by day, but it really comes into its own at night, with cocktails and chilled sounds. Daily 8.30am–late.

★**Rakadhiko ta Halkina** Aktí Tombázi 29–30 ☎ 28210 41570, ⊚ chalkina.com. Live Cretan music every evening, though the place doesn't really liven up till well after midnight, when the locals start to dance. There's also good food (meze plates €5–7; mains €7–9) and wine, but it's the traditional music everyone comes for. Hugely popular, but they can usually squeeze you in somewhere. Daily noon–late, music from 9pm.

Rudi's Bierhaus Kalergón 16 ☎ 28210 20319. Haniá's beer shrine: Austrian – and longtime Haniá resident – Rudi Riegler's bar stocks more than a hundred of Europe's finest brews, plus excellent mezédhes to accompany them. Other, more fashionable, bars crowd this street. Tues–Sat 7.30pm–3am.

7

SHOPPING

Stores aimed at tourists are mainly found in the old town, especially **jewellery** and **souvenirs** on Hálidho[.] and all around the harbour, plus **leather** goods on Skridhlóf; check out also the traditional **knife-makers** on Sífaka. Around the junction of Hálidhon and Yiánnari and down towards the market you'll find pharmacies, newspaper stores, photographic shops and banks, and there's a sizeable **supermarket** at the top of Pireós, close to the Schiavo Bastion.

Centre of Traditional Folk Art & Culture Skúfon 20 ☎ 28210 92677. A wonderful place that feels more like a museum than a shop, displaying the astonishing embroideries made by the owner, some of which fetch thousands of euros. April–Nov Mon–Sat 10.30am–9pm, Sun 2–7pm.

Haniá market Odhós Yiánnari, with another entrance on Tsoudherón. Haniá's market, an imposing and rather beautiful cross-shaped structure, has some interesting souvenirs and good places to eat among the stalls of meat, fish and veg. Mon–Sat 8am–2pm.

Mediterraneo Bookstore Aktí Koundouriótou 57, near the Naval Museum, ☎ 28210 86904. Impressively stocked bookshop, with lots of English-language titles. Daily 8am–11pm.

Street market Minóos. There's a fabulous weekly street market inside the eastern city wall, where local farmers sell their produce. Sat mornings.

DIRECTORY

Banks and exchange The main branch of the National Bank of Greece, with ATMs, is opposite the market. There's a cluster of banks with more ATMs around the top of Hálidhon, and lots of out-of-hours exchange places on Hálidhon, in the travel agencies.

Laundry Service washes at Old Town Laundromat, Karaóli 40 (Mon–Sat 9am–2pm; Tues, Thurs & Fri also 5.30–8.30pm); cheap self-service at easywash, Dhaskaloyiánni 8 (daily 7am–midnight).

Around Haniá

Northeast of Haniá, the **Akrotíri peninsula** loops around, protecting the magnificent anchorages of the Bay of Soúdha. On its northeast coast are a number of coves and **beaches**, above all sandy **Kalathás** and spectacular **Stavrós**. Inland you can visit the monasteries of **Ayía Triádha** and **Gouvernétou**.

West of Haniá, the E75 speeds you towards Kastélli with little to see along the way. The **old road**, meanwhile, follows the coastline through a string of small towns and resorts. Occasionally it runs right above the water, more often 100m or so inland, but never more than easy walking distance from the sea. There are hotels and apartments the whole way, but the first real resort area starts at **Káto Stalós**, which runs into **Ayía Marína** and then into **Plataniás** without a break, creating the most built-up, touristy strip in the west of the island.

The Akrotíri monasteries

Ayía Triádha is 2km north of the airport; 4km beyond is Gouvernétou, where you can park and continue on foot 1km to Katholikó • Ayía Triádha daily: summer 8am–7pm; winter 8am–2pm • €2.50 • Katholikó daily 7.30am–1pm & 4–7pm • free

The majestic three-domed **Ayía Triádha** monastery, established in the seventeenth century and built in Venetian style, is one of the few on Crete to preserve real monastic life to any degree. Its imposing ochre frontage is approached through carefully tended fields of vines and olive groves – all the property of the monastery, which now bottles and markets its own wine and organic olive oil. Inside, you can wander freely around the shady complex, and visit the church and a small museum.

Fortress-like **Gouvernétou**, one of the oldest monasteries on Crete, dating from around 1537, is a strict community, closed to visitors. Beyond it, a steep path heads down a craggy ravine towards the sea, passing the ruined **monastery of Katholikó**, the island's most ancient, abandoned long ago following repeated pirate raids. It's an exceptional place, surrounded by caves where there's evidence of still earlier Christian and pre-Christian worship.

FESTIVAL ISLAND

The Cretans love a *glendi* (party) and **festivals** are celebrated with plenty of eating, drinking, live music and dancing. Here are some of those which celebrate local harvests (check locally for specific dates):

Chestnut Festival Élos and Prásses, West Crete, end of Oct. The village squares are packed with tables and chairs as the villages celebrate the local chestnut harvest with eating, drinking, dancing, and roast chestnuts, of course.

Sardine Festival Néa Hóra, Haniá. The first week of Sept is the date for this annual festival at the small harbour by the town beach, with plentiful free fish and wine, and local musicians and dancers.

Sultana Festival Sitía, Aug. The region is well known for its sultana production, and the harvest is celebrated with traditional Cretan music and dance in the main square, accompanied by food and wine.

Tsikoudiá (Raki) Festival Haniá, Iráklio, Sitía and Voukoliés, mid-Oct and early Nov. At the end of the grape harvest the must-residue from the wine press is boiled and distilled to make *tsikoudiá*, the local fire water. Hot *tsikoudiá*, with an alcohol content as high as 60 percent, is scooped from the vats and proffered in shot glasses, and so the merriment begins.

7

Stavrós

Akrotíri peninsula, 15km northeast of Haniá • 5 daily buses from the city (25min)

Stavrós beach is superb if you like the calm, shallow water of an almost completely enclosed lagoon; this one sits right beneath the imposing "Zorbas" mountain (the cataclysmic climax of *Zorba the Greek* was filmed here). It's not very large, so it does get crowded, but rarely overpoweringly so. There's a makeshift café/*kantína* on the beach, and a couple of tavernas across the road.

Ayía Marína

AYÍA MARÍNA, 8km west of Haniá, is a developed resort of some size, known locally for its beach bars and clubs, which attract hordes of young locals and tourists late into the summer nights. The west end of the long sandy beach is quieter and there are good **watersports** facilities here, including jet skiing and paragliding. Just offshore is **Theodorou** island, said to be a sea monster petrified by Zeus before it could swallow Crete. Seen from the west, its "mouth" still gapes open.

Kolymbári

At the base of the Rodhopoú pensinsula, **KOLYMBÁRI** marks the end of the bus line to the western hotels. Beginning to develop, it still has far more appeal than anything that has preceded it along the north coast, with a long pebble beach looking back along the coast towards Haniá in the distance. There's every facility you might need, including boat trips and car rental, plus a couple of excellent tavernas. A short walk out of the village, the seventeenth-century monastery **Moní Goniá** (Daily: April–Sept 8am–2pm & 4–7.30pm; Nov–March M 8am–12.30pm & 3.30–5.30pm, €2) occupies a prime site, with stupendous views and a scramble down to a sandy cove – rumoured to be the monks' private beach.

The Samariá Gorge

May–Oct 7am–sunset, weather conditions permitting, last entry to hike through 3pm • €5 • ☎ 28210 67179, ⓦ samaria.gr

The 18km hike down the spectacular **SAMARIÁ GORGE**, which claims to be Europe's longest, is one of the most popular day-trips on the island; still better if you make it part of a longer excursion to the south. Although often crowded it's not a walk to be undertaken lightly, particularly in the heat of summer; it's strenuous – you'll know all about it next day – the path is rough, and walking boots or sturdy trainers are vital, as is plenty of water.

The **gorge** begins at the *xylóskalo*, or "wooden staircase", a stepped path plunging steeply down from the southern lip of the Omalós plain. The descent is at first through almost alpine scenery: pine forest, wild flowers and greenery – a verdant shock in the spring, when the stream is at its liveliest. About halfway down you pass the abandoned village of **Samariá**, now home to a wardens' station, with picnic facilities and toilets. Further down, the path levels out and the gorge walls close in until, at the narrowest point (the *sidherespórtes* or "iron gates"), you can practically touch both tortured rock faces at once and, looking up, see them rising sheer for well over 300m.

At an average pace, with regular stops, the walk down takes between five and seven hours (though you can do it quicker). Beware of the kilometre markers; these mark only distances within the **National Park** and it's a further 2km of hot walking before you finally reach the sea at **Ayía Rouméli** (see opposite). On the way down there is usually plenty of water from springs and streams, but nothing to eat. The park that surrounds the gorge is a refuge of the Cretan wild ibex, the *krí-krí*, but don't expect to see one; there are usually far too many people around.

7

Omalós

OMALÓS lies in the middle of the mountain plain from which the Samariá Gorge descends. The climate is cooler here all year round and the many paths into the hills surrounding the plateau are a welcome bonus; in spring a profusion of wild flowers and birdlife is to be seen. There are plenty of **tavernas** and some surprisingly fancy **rooms** should you want to stay overnight to get an early start into the gorge. Another reason to stay up here is to undertake some other **climbs** in the White Mountains; the **Kallérgi mountain hut** (April–Oct daily ☎6976 585 849; Nov–March Sat & Sun ☎6973 400 077; ⓦkallergi.co; €12) is about ninety minutes' hike (signed) from Omalós or the top of the gorge.

ARRIVAL AND DEPARTURE   THE SAMARIÁ GORGE

WITH A TOUR

Tours to the Samariá Gorge run from virtually everywhere on the island: they involve a very early bus to the top, walk down by early afternoon, boat from Ayía Rouméli to Hóra Sfakíon or Soúyia and bus from there back home.

BY PUBLIC TRANSPORT

Buses to the gorge You can take regular buses to the top of the gorge from Haniá (daily at 6.15am, 7.45am & 8.45am), or marginally less straightforwardly from Soúyia (daily at 7am) or Paleóhora (daily at 6.15am). Early-morning buses from Iráklio and Réthymno connect at Haniá. Be sure

to buy a return ticket if you're coming back the same day.

Ferries from Ayía Rouméli Once at Ayía Rouméli, at the bottom of the gorge, you'll see a kiosk selling boat tickets as you approach the beach; there are ferries (ⓦanendyk. gr) to Loutró/Hóra Sfakíon (May–Oct 3 daily; 40min/1hr) and Soúyia/Paleóhora (May–Oct daily at 5.30pm; 45min/1hr 20min). Alternatively you can walk to any of these on the coastal path.

Return buses Return bus journeys from Hóra Sfakíon (at 6.30pm) or Soúyia (at 6.15pm) are timed to coincide with the ferries and will wait for them – theoretically, no one gets left behind.

ACCOMMODATION AND EATING

Wardens ensure that no one remains in the gorge overnight, where camping is strictly forbidden. The nearest accommodation is at Omalós, where there are several options: those below offer lifts to the top of the gorge in the morning.

Hotel Exari Omalós village ☎28210 67180, ⓦexari. gr. Impressive looking, stone-built hotel with comfortable balcony rooms with TV and a decent restaurant; breakfast is included. April–Oct. Daily 6am–midnight. **€40**

Hotel Neos Omalos Omalós village ☎28210 67269, ⓦneos-omalos.gr. Perhaps the pick of the hotels in Omalós, and certainly with the busiest taverna, this has pleasant balcony rooms with central heating and satellite TV. Daily 7am–10pm. **€37**

The Sfakiá Coast

The ancient capital of the Sfakiá region, **Hóra Sfakíon**, lies 70km south of Haniá, reached via a spectacular twisting road over the mountains. It's the main terminus for

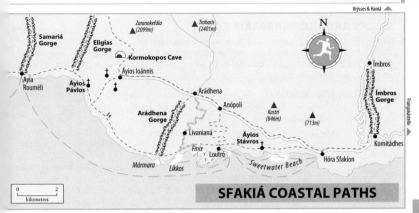

SFAKIÁ COASTAL PATHS

7

gorge walkers, with a regular boat service west along the coast to **Ayía Rouméli** and **Loutró**, both accessible only on foot or by boat. **Frangokástello**, with its castle and sandy **beaches**, lies a few kilometres east of Hóra Sfakíon.

Hóra Sfakíon

HÓRA SFAKÍON sees thousands of people passing through daily; those who have walked Samariá Gorge come striding, or staggering, off the boat from Ayía Rouméli to pile onto waiting coaches. Relatively few stay, although there are plenty of great-value **rooms** and some excellent waterfront **tavernas**. Aside from a couple of pebbly coves, Hóra Sfakíon lacks a decent **beach**; to get to one, you could walk (or for much of the year take an excursion boat) west to **Sweetwater**; there are also numerous opportunities for a dip along the coast road east towards Frangokástello and beyond.

Loutró

Of all the south coast villages, **LOUTRÓ** perhaps best sums up what this coast ought to be all about. It's a soporific place, where there's nothing to do but eat, drink and laze – and where you fast lose any desire to do anything else. The big excitements of the day are the occasional arrivals and departures of the ferries. Loutró itself has beautifully clear water but the small **beach** can get very crowded; if you're prepared to walk, however, there are plenty of lovely alternatives along the coast in each direction; these can also be reached by hired **canoe**, and some (particularly Sweetwater to the east and Mármara to the west) by regular excursion boats.

Ayía Rouméli

AYÍA ROUMÉLI, the small coastal settlement at the end of Samariá Gorge, is visited daily by hundreds of weary walkers for whom the sea is a welcome shimmering mirage after their long hike. After an iced drink, a plunge in the sea to cool the aching limbs, and lunch at one of the cluster of tavernas, most of them move straight on. Should you stay, you'll find that while it's far from the most attractive place on this coast, it is wonderfully peaceful at night, and locals are making strenuous efforts to develop alternative attractions – notably other **hikes**, boat trips and kayaks to rent.

Frangokástello

FRANGOKÁSTELLO, 14km east of Hóra Sfakíon, is named after a four-square, crenellated thirteenth-century **castle** (May–Oct daily 9am–7pm; €1.50) isolated below a chiselled wall of mountains. Though impressive from a distance, at close quarters the castle turns out to be a bare shell, with little to see inside. There's a lovely, fine-sand

7

WALKS AROUND THE SFAKIÁ COAST

Many people arrive at this part of Crete by walking down the Samariá Gorge, but that's just the start of the local hiking possibilities; there are other **gorges** with far fewer people and infinitely more sense of adventure, plus a **coastal path** linking all the settlements as far as Paleóhora and the island's western tip.

ARÁDHENA AND ÍMBROS

The two most accessible local gorges are Arádhena, west of Loutró, and Ímbros, east of Hóra Sfakíon. The classic **Arádhena** walk is to climb up from Loutró, back and forth across an intimidating-looking cliff face, to Anópoli, and from there by a broad track to the top of the gorge, where there's a spectacular bridge and bungee jump. The descent into the gorge is on an impressive, ancient stone path, but this soon runs out and it's quite a rugged descent to Mármara beach, where you should be able to pick up a boat back to Loutró. It's about 11km to Mármara, or at least 6 hours. **Ímbros Gorge** (April–Oct 8am–sunset; €2) is rather more straightforward. The walk starts from the village of Ímbros on the main Hóra Sfakíon road, easily reached by bus, car or taxi; it's a well-marked and relatively easy 3hr hike down to the village of Komitádhes, above the coast 5km from Hóra Sfakíon. You can either walk this last bit, hitch, or take a local taxi.

THE COASTAL PATH

The **coastal path** is well-marked and well-used, which is not to say it's easy: there's little shelter from a relentless summer sun, and in places it's intimidatingly narrow and uneven. The most travelled and most straightforward section is **between Loutró and Hóra Sfakíon** – about 8km (2hr) – with an inviting swimming spot halfway at Sweetwater beach. West from **Loutró to Ayía Rouméli** is twice as far and significantly tougher, though again there are potential swim stops, and seasonal tavernas, at Mármara beach and the chapel of Áyios Pávlos.

---

beach immediately below the castle, and marginally less attractive sands spreading in each direction. Behind them has sprung up a rather straggling resort, with no real centre but plenty of decent places to stay and to eat.

GETTING AROUND

THE SFAKIÁ COAST

By bus Buses between Hóra Sfakíon and Haniá (3 daily; 1hr 45min) are timed to coincide with ferries. There are also buses from Hóra Sfakíon to Frangokástello (3 daily; 15min) and Anópoli (2 daily; 15min), one of which continues to Arádhena (25min).

By boat There are ticket booths for the local ferries (ⓦanendyk.gr) close to the departure points in all the coastal villages. Boat trips run to local beaches from both

Loutró and Hóra Sfakíon, where you can also hire taxi-boats.

Destinations from Hóra Sfakíon Ayía Rouméli (May–Oct 3 daily; 1hr) Gávdhos (2–3 weekly; 3hr); Loutró (May–Oct 7 daily; 20min).

Destinations from Ayía Rouméli Gávdhos (2–3 weekly; 2hr 30min); Soúyia/Paleohóra (May–Oct daily at 5.30pm; 45min/1hr 20min).

ACCOMMODATION AND EATING

HÓRA SFAKÍON

There's little to choose between Hóra Sfakíon's excellent seafront tavernas, which also have a good array of vegetarian options; you'll find cheaper cafés and takeaway places on the east side of the bay, towards the ferry jetty.

Stavris ☎ 28250 91220, ⓦstavris.com. A variety of rooms and studios, all with balconies, increasing in price as you add a/c, kitchenette, or sea views. The Perrakis brothers, who own and run the place, have more rooms elsewhere in town, and at Frangokástello. **€35**

★**Xenia** ☎ 28250 91202, ⓦsfakia-xenia-hotel.gr.

This former state-owned hotel, now refurbished, has the best location in town with amazing views across the Libyan Sea. All rooms have a/c, fridge, satellite TV and balcony with sea view; some are huge, though rather sparsely furnished. Steps at the rear let you swim off the rocks, and the bar-taverna terrace is a great place to watch the harbour activity. There's a car park, and breakfast is included. **€55**

LOUTRÓ

★**Blue House** ☎ 28250 91035, ⓦthebluehouse.gr. One of the original places here, and still one of the riendliest and best. Good-value a/c, sea-view rooms with fridge and TV, plus superior rooms in a wonderful more expensive) top-floor extension. Also some of he best food in town at the taverna downstairs. April–ct. **€45**

★ **Nikolas** ☎ 28250 91352. Virtually the last building in .outró and probably the quietest you'll find; simple but comfortable a/c rooms all with fridge and most with great views. Top-floor rooms cost more but are bigger, with large balconies and even finer views. April–Oct. **€40**

AYÍA ROUMÉLI

Calypso Western side of the village, not far from the jetty ☎ 28250 91314, ⊚ calypso.agiaroumeli.gr. Friendly, family-run taverna with rooms. The taverna has good fresh seafood from its own boat (swordfish €11) as well as local goat and all the usuals (meat mains €6–8). They rent kayaks on the beach and have a wall map of local kayaking and walking routes. The comfortable a/c rooms have fridge, balcony and sea view. Daily 8am–11pm. **€35**

Kastélli and the far west

Apart from being Crete's most westerly town, and the end of the main coastal highway, **KASTÉLLI** (**Kíssamos**, or **Kastélli Kissámou**, as it's variously known) has little obvious appeal. It's a bustling place with a long seafront, a rather rocky strand to the east and a small sandy **beach** to the west. This very ordinariness, however, has real charm: life goes on pretty much regardless of outsiders, and there's every facility you might need. The town was important in antiquity, when the Greco-Roman city-state of **Kísamos** was a major regional power.

To the west of Kastélli lies some of Crete's loneliest and, for many visitors, finest coastline. On the far western tip, isolated **Bálos** is mainly visited on boat trips, **Falásarna** has beautiful beaches and ancient ruins, while **Elafonísi's** "pink" beaches and lagoon lie in the southwest corner; the spectacular coastal road connecting them has little development along the way, just a couple of villages high above rocky coves. The inland routes south over the mountains, to the small resort of **Paleóhora** and the laidback seaside village of **Soúyia**, are beautifully rural

Kastélli Archeological Museum

Platía Tzanakáki • Tues–Sun 8.30am–3pm • €2, combined ticket with Archeological and Byzantine museums in Haniá and Aptéra site €6 • ☎ 28220 83308

The highlight of Kastélli's superb **Archeological Museum** is its stunning Roman-era **mosaics**; mosaic production was a local speciality, and many more are still being excavated around town. In addition, the museum displays other Roman artefacts, as well as prehistoric and Minoan relics from excavations in the town and from nearby ancient Polyrínia.

Falásarna

The ruins of an ancient city and port are ignored by most visitors to **FALÁSARNA** in favour of some of the best beaches on Crete, wide and sandy with clean water, though far from undiscovered. There's a handful of **tavernas** and an increasing number of **rooms** for rent, and plenty of people **camp** out here too. Although the beach can occasionally be afflicted by washed-up tar and discarded rubbish, this

---

MILIÁ: AN ECOTOURIST VILLAGE

Off the inland route south from Kastélli towards Paleóhora lies **Miliá** (☎ 28210 46774, ⊚ milia.gr), an abandoned hamlet of stone houses that has been restored by a cooperative of local people and is now a wonderful eco-retreat. The cottages (€77, breakfast included) have only solar power and candles, while the taverna uses organic local ingredients. Visitors are welcome to get involved in the life of the farm, and there are cookery courses and other **activities** – you can even help make *raki* at the village's still. Otherwise you can walk in the nearby hills – the easier paths are signed – or simply contemplate the natural surroundings; nights up here are truly magical.

doesn't detract from the overall beauty of the place. You can always escape the crowds of locals on summer weekends if you're prepared to walk, and the beaches are worth it.

Moní Khrysoskalítissa

5km north of Elafonísi • Daily 7.30am–7pm • €2 • ☎ 28220 61261

Moní Khrysoskalítissa (the Monastery of the Virgin of the Golden Step), is a weathered white-walled nunnery beautifully sited on a rocky promontory with marvellous views along the coastline. There may have been a Minoan shrine on this spot, and the earliest church was built in a cave in the thirteenth century. Look out today for a much-venerated thousand-year-old icon of the Virgin, a small **museum**, and the **golden step** (*hrissí skála*), one of the ninety leading up to the monastery, which appears gold only to those who are pure of spirit.

Elafonísi

The tiny uninhabited islet of **Elafonísi** shelters an almost tropical lagoon, where white sand tinged pink by coral borders aquamarine waters. The water is incredibly warm, calm and shallow and the islet itself is a short wade across the sandbar.

At peak times Elafonísi can be unbearably crowded, with lines of loungers, but little else in the way of infrastructure: there are stalls selling cold drinks and basic food, along with portable toilets and an incongruous phone box. If you're here on a day-trip, bring your own picnic.

Paleóhora

The only real resort in the southwest, **PALEÓHORA** retains an enjoyably end-of-the-line feel, helped by extensive sands and the fact that there are no big hotels. Other than head for the beach, eat and drink, there's not a great deal to see or do here, which of course is a major part of its attraction. Built across the base of a narrow peninsula with a harbour and pebble beach on the eastern side, wide sands on the west, Paleóhora is overlooked by the ruins of its Venetian fortress. In the evening the narrow main street closes to traffic so diners can spill out of the restaurants and bars onto tables set out in the road.

Soúyia

A small village slowly on its way to becoming a resort, **SOÚYIA** is not a particularly attractive place at first sight, but it does grow on you. Its best feature is an enormous swathe of grey pebble beach with sparkling clear water. At the far end of this bay most summers there's something of a nudist and camping community – known locally as the Bay of Pigs. Otherwise, sights are few – the local church has a sixth-century Byzantine mosaic as the foundation, although most of it is in Haniá's archeological museum – but there are a couple of fabulous walks: down the beautiful **Ayía Iríni Gorge** or a wonderful hour-long hike, which can be combined with a boat back, to the nearby site of **Lissós**, with its temples and mosaics.

ARRIVAL AND DEPARTURE | KASTÉLLI AND THE FAR WEST

By bus Frequent buses ply the main road between Haniá and Kastélli, with onward connections from there to the far west; Paleóhora and Soúyia have direct connections with Haniá but not Kastélli. For more info, see ⓦ e-ktel.com.

Destinations from Kastélli Haniá (14 daily; 45min); Elafonísi (May–Sept 1 daily at 10am, returning 4pm; 1hr 20min); Falásarna (May–Sept 3 daily; 40min).

Destinations from Paleóhora Elafonísi (May–Sept 1 daily 10am, returning 4pm; 1hr 20min); Haniá (5 daily; 2hr); Soúyia (3 daily; 6.15am bus continues to Omalós; 1hr).

Destinations from Soúyia Haniá via Omalós (3 daily; 1hr/2hr); Paleóhora (May–Sept daily at 9am; 1hr).

By ferry There's a daily ferry at 8.30am (May–Oct, ⓦ anendyk.gr) from Paleóhora to Ayía Rouméli (1hr 20min) via Soúyia (30min); on Mon and Wed this continues to Gávdhos (6hr).

TOURS

Boat trips Daily boat trips (ⓦgramvousa.com) run from Kastélli port to the beautiful beaches at Gramvoússa and Bálos Bay, at the far northwestern tip of Crete; there are also a variety of boat trips from Paleóhora, including daily runs to Elafonísi and dolphin spotting.

Hiking Strata Tours in Kastélli (☎28220 24249; ⓦstratatours.com) runs walking and wildlife tours as well as other special-interest activities.

ACCOMMODATION AND EATING

KASTÉLLI

Argo Central seafront ☎28220 23563, ⓦpapadakisargo.gr. Given their great location, these refurbished, marble-floored a/c balcony rooms, with fridge and TV, are a real bargain. Buffet breakfast included. April–Oct. **€40**

Maria Beach On the western beach ☎28220 22610, ⓦmariabeach.gr. Right on the sandy beach, Maria's consists of two separate buildings housing some fairly plain rooms (some with fridge) as well as new, fully equipped sea-view studios (with kitchenette) and apartments (sleeping 5) with kitchen; breakfast is included in the room rates for, not for studios or apartments. April–Nov. Double **€60**, apartment **€65**

★ **Akrogiali** Korfalónas Beach, about 4km east of town ☎28220 31410. *Akrogiali* is the real deal, serving fresh seafood caught daily by the friendly proprietor from his own boat, accompanied by homemade bread, veg from their garden and wine from the family vineyards. It's not attractive as you approach (immediately east of a seafront soap factory whose chimney stacks are visible from some distance), but food is served on a terrace with the waves almost lapping the table legs. Apart from the fish (priced by weight), try the likes of fresh squid (€10.50), or *yemistá* (€6.50). They also have rooms. April–Oct daily 11am–midnight. **€40**

FALÁSARNA

Magnolia Apartments Overlooking Big Beach ☎28220 41407, ⓦmagnolia-apartments.gr. Modern studio and apartment complex with some of the area's finest views from the surrounding gardens and from many of the balconies; well-equipped and comfortable. Studio **€50**, apartment **€60**

PALEÓHORA

Anonymous Homestay In a backstreet off Venizélos ☎28230 42098, ⓦcityofpaleochora.gr. Among the least expensive places in town, and something of a travellers' meeting place. Simple rooms, with use of a communal kitchen, off a charming garden courtyard, plus two two-bedroom apartments. A/c €5 extra. Double **€28**, apartment **€50**

★ **Aris** Last place on the upper road at the south end of the peninsula ☎28230 41502, ⓦarishotel.gr. Charming, welcoming and peaceful hotel, newly and artistically renovated with lovely handmade wooden headboards. A/c rooms have balconies, many with sea views, others over the lush gardens, along with fridge and tea- and coffee-making facilities (but no TV), and there's an excellent breakfast available. **€60**

Caravella Seafront, just south of the ferry jetty ☎28230 41131, ⓦcaravella.gr. Paleóhora's best seafood restaurant, with a waterfront terrace. All the fish is caught locally (and sold by weight; typically around €12 a portion), and their house wines are excellent. They also serve some meat (mains €7.50–8.50), plus a daily selection of *mayireftá*. April–Nov daily 9am–11.30pm.

★ **Castello Rooms** Overlooking the southern end of Sandy Beach ☎28230 41143. Exceptionally friendly place, most of whose simple rooms come with a/c and fridge and have balconies overlooking the beach; a few rooms at the back without view are less expensive (singles available too), and you can still get the views from the terrace taverna. **€37**

Haris Studios On the seafront below the east side of the castle ☎28230 42438, ⓦpaleochora-holidays.com. A friendly Cretan-Scottish-run place with some simple a/c studios close to the water, most with great sea views, plus a new block (*Yiorgos Studios*) of excellent, well-equipped modern studios and apartments with a garden, roof terrace and small pool (which all guests can use) set further back. Their waterfront terrace café is a great place for breakfast and evening meals; the latter featuring fish caught by Haris and a great burger (€8.50). Studio **50**, apartment **€60**

Oriental Bay Northern end of Pebble Beach ☎28230 41322. With an inviting, tamarisk-shaded terrace fronting the sea, *Oriental Bay* serves some of the best traditional food in town, with daily specials such as arnáki kokkinistó (lamb stewed with tomatoes, onion and garlic, €7) stuffed courgette flowers (€5) or "granny's meatballs" €9. There's occasional live music and also fresh juices and breakfasts. Daily noon–11pm.

The Third Eye Inland from Sandy Beach ☎28230 41234, ⓦthethirdeye-paleochora.com. Excellent vegetarian restaurant with flavours rarely seen on Crete, from curries to *gado-gado*, as well as more conventional Greek dishes: interesting salads such as beetroot and walnut (€5.50), Thai curry (€9) and yemistá (€8.50). Daily noon–3pm & 6–11pm.

7

SOÚYIA

Pension El Greco To the west of the main street, near the top ☎28230 51186, ⓦsougia.info/hotels/elgreco. Set back from the road in a quiet, semi-rural setting, these simple upper-floor a/c rooms have a balcony, fridge and kettle; there are also a couple of ground-floor studios. April–Oct. Double €40, studio €50

Santa Irene Seafront ☎28230 51342, ⓦsanta-irene. gr. Smart, modern studios and apartments around a courtyard in a great waterfront location, all with a/c, TV, kitchenette and balcony (though only a few have sea views). March–Oct. €50

Rembetiko Halfway up the main street ☎2823? 51510. Served up on a shady garden terrace, the shortis? menu here features home-cooked traditional dishe including plenty of vegetarian options such as rice-stuffec tomatoes and peppers (€6.20), plus meat reared on thei own farm (lamb chops €8.50). Daily 1pm–midnight.

Villa Galini Main road, at the top of the hill ☎2823C 51488, ⓦgalinisougia.com. Run by a friendly proprietor *Villa Galini* has big, comfortable, good-value modern studios and apartments with balconies and satellite TV – one apartment has a hidden upper level, perfect for kids. March–Dec. Studio €60, apartment €80

Gávdhos

7

GÁVDHOS, some 50km of rough sea south of Crete, is the southernmost island in Greece (and Europe if you don't count Spain's Canary Islands). Gávdhos is small (about 10km by 7km) and barren, but it has one major attraction: the enduring **isolation** which its inaccessible position has helped preserve. If all you want is a beach and a taverna that will grill you some fish, this remains the place for you. There's a semi-permanent community of campers and would-be "Robinson Crusoes" on the island year-round, swelling to thousands in August – but just six indigenous families.

Most people choose to base themselves near to one of the three largest beaches; at the most popular of all, **Sarakíniko**, there are several beachfront tavernas and cafés and a few rooms places. **Áyios Ioánnis**, 2km to the northwest, boasts a thriving hippy-type community of nudist campers. The third, quieter choice is pebbly **Kórfos**, south of the port and capital at **Karabé**.

ARRIVAL AND DEPARTURE

By ferry In windy or bad weather the ferry won't run, so don't plan to leave the day before your flight home. Sometimes people are stranded here for days, even in mid-summer. There are high-season departures from Hóra Sfakíon (connecting with Haniá buses in both directions) on Fri, Sat & Sun at 10.30am (3hr), and from Paleóhora via Soúyia and Ayía Rouméli on Mon & Wed at 8.30am (4hr 30min); return sailing at 2pm same day; check the current timetable at ⓦanendyk.gr.

GETTING AROUND AND PRACTICALITIES

By bus There are two buses, one run by KTEL the other by Gavdos Tours (☎6942 480 815), at least one of which meets every ferry and makes the trip to Sarakíniko, Áyios Ioánnis and Kastrí (€2); there's a return trip from the beaches about 1hr before the ferry departs. Timetables are posted at Karavé, Sarakíniko and elsewhere; the schedule changes daily, but there's an evening round-island trip most days in summer (€5).

Services There's no bank or official exchange on the island, so bring plenty of cash with you. Minimarkets can be found at the port, Sarakíniko and Áyios Ioánnis, and there's an excellent bakery on the road below Kastrí. However, they're all pricey and not very well stocked, since almost everything is brought over on the ferry, and there's little in the way of fresh fruit or vegetables. Try and bring some supplies with you, especially if you plan to camp.

Vehicle rental Gavdos Travel (☎6940 813 613, ✉metoxigavdos@gmail.com; cash only) rents battered cars (around €35–40/day plus petrol) and elderly mopeds (around €15–20/day including petrol); Odyssey (☎6948 635 685, ✉nikoskaramarkos@gmail.com) has reasonably new mountain bikes for around €10 a day. Both deliver the vehicle to you, which is a great deal easier than seeking them out.

ACCOMMODATION AND EATING

you turn up in August without a booking you may well find yourself camping on the beach. Travel agents in Paleóhora or Hóra Sfakíon can arrange **rooms**. Water and power are in short supply, so most places are pretty basic, and few have effective air-conditioning, though plenty have a/c units they can't use because the promised mains electricity never materialized.

★**Vailakakis (aka Gerti & Manolis)** Sarakíniko ☎ 28230 41103, ⓦ gavdos-crete.com. Simple rooms (with 24hr generator power) and rather fancier stone-built houses, with full kitchen, for four to six people. It also has probably the best food on the beach, with excellent, good-value seafood caught daily by Manolis himself. **€40**

Sofia Áyios Ioánnis ☎ 28230 41418 ⓦ sofiaroomsgavdos.com. Lovely modern rooms with huge picture windows and spectacular terraces looking towards Crete. There's air-conditioning but only solar power, so it can only be used during the day. Also a friendly family bar-taverna. May–Oct. **€45**

Akroyiali Kórfos ☎ 28230 42384, ⓦ gavdoshotel.com. Plain but comfortable rooms directly above the beach, so you're lulled to sleep by the sound of the sea; 24hr power from the island's solar plant means effective a/c and hot water, and the taverna serves good food on a seafront terrace. There's a minibus to pick guests up from the ferry, and which also does occasional tours of the island. April–Sept; taverna daily 9am–10pm. **€25**

7

The Dodecanese

TRADITIONAL WINDMILLS OF ASTYPALEA ISLAND.

The Dodecanese

Curving tightly against the Turkish coast, almost within hailing distance of Anatolia, the Dodecanese (Dhodhekánisos) are the furthest island group from the Greek mainland. They're a diverse bunch. The two largest, Rhodes (Ródhos and Kos, are fertile giants where traditional agriculture has almost entirely been displaced by a tourist industry focused on beaches and nightlife. Kastellórizo, Sými, Hálki, Kássos and Kálymnos, on the other hand, are essentially dry limestone outcrops that grew rich enough from the sea – especially during the nineteenth century – to build attractive port towns. Níssyros is a real anomaly, created by a still-steaming volcano that cradles lush vegetation, while Kárpathos is more variegated, its forested north grafted onto a rocky limestone south. Tílos, despite its lack of trees, has ample water, Léros shelters soft contours and amenable terrain, and further-flung Pátmos and Astypálea offer architecture and landscapes more reminiscent of the Cyclades.

Major Dodecanese attractions include the beaches on **Rhodes** and **Kos**; the wonderful medieval enclave of **Rhodes Old Town**; the gorgeous ensemble of Neoclassical mansions that surrounds the harbour on **Sými**; the rugged landscapes of **Kálymnos**, **Kárpathos** and **Níssyros**; the cave and monastery on **Pátmos**, where St John had his vision of the Apocalypse; and the hilltop village of **Hóra** on **Astypálea**. Each island has its own subtler pleasures, however; every visitor seems to find one where the pace of life and friendly ambience strike a particular chord.

Thanks to their position en route to the Middle East, the Dodecanese – too rich and strategic to be ignored, but never powerful enough to rule themselves – have had a turbulent history. The scene of ferocious battles between German and British forces in 1943–44, they only joined the modern Greek state in 1948 after centuries of rule by Crusaders, Ottomans and Italians.

That historical legacy has given the islands a wonderful blend of **architectural styles** and **cultures**; almost all hold Classical remains, a Crusaders' castle, a clutch of vernacular villages and whimsical or grandiose public buildings. For these last, the Italians, who held the Dodecanese from 1912 to 1943, are responsible. Determined to turn them into a showplace for Fascism, they undertook ambitious public works, excavations and reconstruction.

GETTING AROUND   THE DODECANESE

The largest islands in the group are connected by regular ferries and catamarans, as well as flights; only Kastellórizo, Symi, Tílos and Astypálea have sporadic connections. Rhodes and Kos are the main transport hubs, with connections to Crete, the northeastern Aegean and the mainland too. The fastest, most useful connections are provided by twin catamarans, the *Dodekanisos Express* and the *Dodekanisos Pride*, which follow a busy schedule between Rhodes, Pátmos and other islands in the chain (see ⊕ 12ne.gr), while the slower Bluestar Ferries run services at least twice weekly around the region in high season (see ⊕ bluestarferries.com).

SÝMI HARBOUR

Highlights

❶ Rhodes Old Town One of Europe's most magnificently preserved medieval towns. **See p.517**

❷ Líndhos Acropolis, Rhodes Occupied for over 3000 years, this hilltop citadel enjoys great views over the town and coast. **See p.526**

❸ Northern Kárpathos Old walking trails thread through a spectacular mountainous landscape to reach isolated villages. **See p.544**

❹ Sými Graceful Neoclassical mansions soar to all sides of Sými's gorgeous harbour. **See p.545**

❺ Bros Thermá, Kos Relax in shoreline hot springs which flow into the sea, protected by a boulder ring. **See p.568**

❻ Hóra, Astypálea Wrapped around a beautiful *kástro*, the windswept island capital perches proudly above the sea. **See p.573**

❼ Télendhos islet, Kálymnos Whether admired at sunset from western Kálymnos, or visited via local ferries, beach-fringed little Télendhos should not be missed. **See p.580**

❽ Léros kástro Drive up past quaint windmills to the *kástro* with 360-degree views across the island. **See p.584**

❾ Hóra, Pátmos With its fortified monastery dedicated to St John of the Apocalypse, this is the Dodecanese's most atmospheric village. **See p.590**

HIGHLIGHTS ARE MARKED ON THE MAP ON P.514

Rhodes

Rhodes (**Ródhos**) is deservedly among the most visited of all Greek islands. Its star attraction is the beautiful **medieval Old Town** that lies at the heart of its capital, Rhodes Town – a legacy of the crusading Knights of St John, who used the island as their main base from 1309 until 1522. Elsewhere, the ravishing hillside village of **Líndhos**, topped

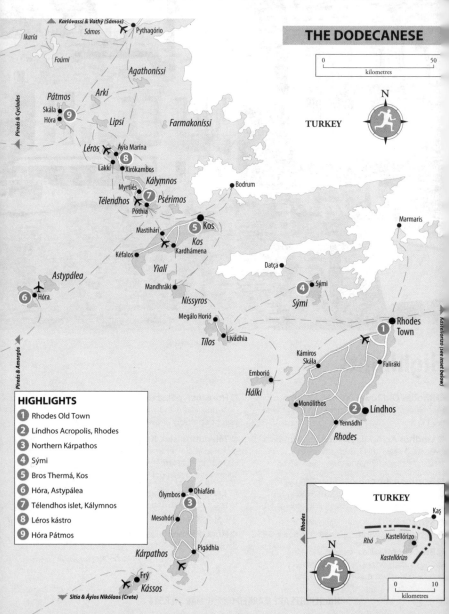

THE DODECANESE

0 _____ 50
kilometres

TURKEY

N

Karlóvassi & Vathý (Sámos)
Ikaría
Sámos
Pythagório
Foúrni
Agathoníssi
Arkí
Pátmos
Skála
Hóra ⑨
Lipsí
Farmakoníssi
Léros
Ayía Marína
⑧
Lakkí
Xirókambos
Kálymnos
Myrtiés
⑦
Psérimos
Télendhos
Póthia
Bodrum
Mastihári
⑤ Kos
Kéfalos
Kos
Kardhámena
Marmaris
Astypálea
⑥ Hóra
Yialí
Mandhráki
Níssyros
Megálo Horió
Tílos
Livádhia
Datça
④ Sými
Sými
Rhodes Town
①
Kámiros
Skála
Faliráki
Emborió
Hálki
Monólithos
② Líndhos
Yennádhi
Rhodes

Piréas & Cyclades
Piréas & Amorgós
Kastellórizo (see inset below)
Rhodes

HIGHLIGHTS
① Rhodes Old Town
② Líndhos Acropolis, Rhodes
③ Northern Kárpathos
④ Sými
⑤ Bros Thermá, Kos
⑥ Hóra, Astypálea
⑦ Télendhos islet, Kálymnos
⑧ Léros kástro
⑨ Hóra Pátmos

Ólymbos
Dhiafáni
③
Mesohóri
Kárpathos
Pigádhia
Frý
Kássos
Sitía & Áyios Nikólaos (Crete)

TURKEY
Kaş
Rhó
Kastellórizo
Kastellórizo
N
0 _____ 10
kilometres

·y an ancient acropolis, should not be missed. It marks the midpoint of the island's
·ong eastern shoreline, adorned with numerous sandy **beaches** that have attracted
·onsiderable resort development. At the southern cape, **Prassoníssi** is one of the best
·indsurfing spots in Europe. If you want to escape the summer crowds, take a road trip
·nto the island's craggy and partly forested interior: worthwhile targets include the
·astles near **Monólithos** and **Kritinía**, and the frescoed churches at **Thárri**, **Asklipió** and
·yios Yeóryios Várdhas.

Brief history

·lessed with an equable climate and strategic position, Rhodes, despite its lack of
·ood harbours, was important from the very earliest times. The finest natural port
·erved the ancient town of **Lindos** which, together with the other Dorian city-states
Kameiros and **Ialyssos**, united in 408 BC to found a new capital, **Rodos** (Rhodes), at
·he windswept northern tip of the island. The cities allied themselves with
·lexander, the Persians, Athenians or Spartans as conditions suited them, generally
·scaping retribution for backing the wrong side by a combination of seafaring
·udacity, sycophancy and burgeoning wealth as a trade centre. Following the failed
·iege of Macedonian general Demetrios Polyorketes in 305 BC, Rhodes prospered
·ven further, displacing Athens as the major venue for rhetoric and the arts in the
·ast Mediterranean.

Decline set in when the island became involved in the Roman civil wars and was
·acked by Cassius; by late imperial times, it was a backwater. The Byzantines ceded
·Rhodes to the Genoese, who in turn surrendered it to the Knights of St John. After
·he second great **siege** of Rhodes, in 1522–23, when Ottoman Sultan Süleyman the
·Magnificent ousted the stubborn knights, the island once again lapsed into relative
·bscurity, though heavily colonized and garrisoned, until its seizure by the Italians
·n 1912.

8

ARRIVAL AND DEPARTURE   RHODES

BY PLANE
·Rhodes' airport lies on the island's west coast, 14km
·southwest of Rhodes Town, alongside Paradhísi village.
·Buses to and from town stop between the two terminals –
·turn left out of arrivals (frequent services 6.30am–
·midnight; €2.50 from the ticket booth, €2.60 on the bus). A
·taxi ride into town should cost around €20.

·Destinations Astypálea (2–3 weekly via Kos and Kalymnos);
·Athens (5 daily); Iráklio (Heraklion), Crete (2 daily); Kárpathos
·(1–2 daily); Kássos (1 daily); Kos (3 weekly); Léros (2 weekly
·via Kalymnos); Mytilene (Lesvos); (3 weekly via Samos);
·Samos (3 weekly); Thessaloníki (1 daily); Sitía (3 weekly).

BY FERRY
·Ferries to Rhodes use three separate harbours in Rhodes Town.
·Large boats dock at Akándia, catamarans at Kolóna,
·immediately outside the Old Town, while smaller vessels and
·excursion craft use the yacht harbour of Mandhráki facing the
·New Town.

Ticket offices Triton Tours (Plastiria 9; ☎22410 21690,
✆tritondmc.gr), can book all ferry, hydrofoil and day-trip

tickets; Dodhekanisos Seaways have a kiosk at their departure
point in Kolóna Harbour (☎22410 70590, ✆12ne.gr);
Tsangaris (☎22410 36170) for GA boats; Skevos (111 Amerikis
St; ☎22410 22461, ✆bluestarferries.gr), for Blue Star;
Zorpidhis (☎22410 20625) for LANE; and Stefanakis, Alex
Diakou St, for Sea Star.

Destinations Anafi (1–2 weekly; 17hr); Astypálea
(1 weekly; 9hr 10min); Crete (3 weekly; 12hr 30min); Hálki
(3 weekly; 1hr 25min–2hr); Kálymnos (1–2 daily; 2hr
40min–8hr 15min); Kárpathos (5hr); Kássos (3
weekly; 6hr 30min); Kastellórizo (3 weekly; 2hr 20min–3hr
40min); Kos (2–3 daily; 2hr 10min–6hr 15min); Léros (1–2
daily; 4hr–5hr 15min); Lipsí (6 weekly; 5hr 10min–8hr
20min); Milos (1 weekly; 23hr); Níssyros (4 weekly; 3hr
10min–4hr 45min); Pátmos (1 daily; 4hr 45min–9hr
45min); Pireás (1–2 daily; 12hr 30min–17hr); Santoríni (3
weekly; 7–20hr); Sitía (3 weekly; 9hr 20min); Sými (2 daily;
50min–1hr 40min); Sýros (3 weekly; 9hr); Tílos (4 weekly;
1hr 20min–2hr 15min). The tiny port at Kámiros Skála,
45km southwest of Rhodes Town, is used only by regular
boats to Hálki (daily except Sun; 1hr 15min).

INFORMATION AND ACTIVITIES

Tourist offices The municipal tourist office is at Platía
Rimínis, just north of the Old Town (June–Sept Mon–Sat

7.30am–9.30pm; Sun 9am–3pm; Oct–May daily
7.30am–3pm). A short walk from here up Papágou, on the

RHODES

Kos, ◄

Tílos, Níssyros & Astypálea ◄

Kárpathos, Kássos & Crete ◄

Háki ◄

8

Ialyssos (Filérimos)

Rhodes Town

Triánda   Ixiá   Kritiká
Kremastí   Asgoúrou
   Réni Koskinoú
Paradhísi   Tris   **Piyés**
   Koskinoú   **Kallithéas**
Theológos   Dhamatriá   Pastídha
Soroní   Páno   Maritsá   Kallithéa Bay
   Kalamónas
Fánes   Kalythiés   Faliráki
Kalavárdha   Ladhikó
Petalóudhes   Traganoú
Kameiros   Psínthos   Afándou
Sálakos   Afándou Bay
Dhimyliá   Eleoússa   Cape Vayiá
Alimniá   Mt   Arhípoli
Paralía Kopriás   Kámiros   Profítis Ilias   Platánia   Kolýmbia
Kástro   Skála   (798m)   **Áyios**   Eptá   **Tsambíka**
Kritinías   Kápi   Apóllona   **Nikólaos**   Piyés
Kritinía   **Foundoúklí**   **Arhángelos**
Émbona   Malóna   Stegná
Glyfádha   Mt Atávyros   **Artamíti**   Mássari   Ayía Agathí
   (1215m)   **Féraklos**
Mt. Akramýtis   Láerma   Haráki
Cape   (825m)   Áyios
Armenistís   Siánna   Isídhoros   **Thárri**   Kálathos   Paralía Kaláthou
Monólithos   Pylónas   Vlyhá
Ístrios   Lárdhos
Foúrni   Profília   **Líndhos**
Áyios   Péfki   St. Paul
Yeóryios   Glýstra
Várdhas   Asklipió   Stafýlia
Apolakkiá   Arnítha   Váti   **Ayía**   Kiotári
   Anastasía
   Roméa   Yennádhi
Skiádhi   Mesanagrós
Kteniá   Laháa
   Áyios   Hokhlakás
   Pávlos   **Zoödhóhou Piyís**
Kattaviá   Cape   Plimýri
   Yermátá
   Áyios   Áyios Yeóryios
   Yeóryios
   Kórakas
Prassoníssi

N

0   10
kilometres

corner of Makaríou, the Greek National Tourist Office (Mon–Fri 8.30am–2.45pm) dispenses bus and ferry schedules.

Scuba diving For scuba diving, contact Waterhoppers (ⓦ waterhoppers.com) at Mandhráki quay; as well as running beginners' courses in the bay at Kallithéas beach, they offer more challenging deep-wall dives at Ladhikó, just south of Faliráki, and near Líndhos.

GETTING AROUND

By bus Buses from Rhodes Town to the west and east coasts leave from adjacent terminals on Avérof in the New Town, immediately north of the Old Town just outside the Italian-built New Market. The main local operator is KTEL

22410 27706, ⓦ ktelrodou.gr).

By taxi The main taxi rank is at Platía Rimínis, immediately north of Rhodes Old Town, across from the bus stops. A taxi to the airport officially costs €25; the fare to Líndhos is €55. Taxi drivers can't enter Rhodes Old Town – expect to walk to your hotel from the nearest gate, though some hotels may come and meet you.

By car Major car rental chains have outlets at the airport. In Rhodes Town, try Budget, Plastira 9 (ⓣ 22410 21690, ⓦ tritondmc.gr) or City Car Rental, Al. Diakou 84 (ⓣ 22410 23923, ⓦ cityrentacar.gr). Driving is not permitted in Rhodes Old Town, while parking outside can be hard to find; the best bet is along Filellínon on the south side, between the Ayíou Athanasíou and Koskinoú gates.

By bike and motorcycle Outlets that rent bikes, scooters and motorcycles include Kiriakos (Apodhímon Amerikís 16; ⓣ 22410 36047, ⓦ motorclubkiriakos.gr), who will deliver to Rhodes Old Town and shuttle you back once you've finished; Bicycle Centre (Griva 39; ⓣ 22410 28315); and Mike's Motor Club (Ioánni Kazoúli 23; ⓣ 22410 37420).

DIRECTORY

Hospital/clinic The state hospital, just northwest of town, is modern but understaffed and has a poor reputation; if you're insured, it's much better to head for the well-signed Euromedica clinic in Koskinoú, 6.5km south (24hr; English-speaking staff; ⓣ 22410 45055 ⓦ www .euromedica-rhodes.gr).

Rhodes Town

By far the largest town on the island, **Rhodes Town** straddles its northernmost headland, in full view of Turkey less than 20km north. The ancient city that occupied this site, laid out during the fifth century BC by Hippodamos of Miletos, was almost twice the size of its modern counterpart, and with over a hundred thousand residents, held more than double its population.

While the fortified enclave now known as the **Old Town** is of more recent construction, created by the Knights Hospitaller in the fourteenth century, it's one of the finest medieval walled cities you could ever hope to see. Yes, it gets hideously overcrowded with day-trippers in high season, but at night it's quite magical, and well worth an extended stay. It makes sense to think of it as an entirely separate destination to the **New Town**, or **Neohóri**, the mélange of unremarkable suburbs and dreary resort that sprawls out from it in three directions.

It was the entrance to **Mandhráki** harbour, incidentally, that was supposedly straddled by the **Colossus**, an ancient statue of Apollo erected to commemorate the 305 BC siege. In front of the New Town, the harbour is today used largely by yachts and excursion boats.

Rhodes Old Town

The Citadel of Rhodes was designated a UNESCO World Heritage Site in 1988 and is one of the best-preserved Old Towns in the world. It is an absolute gem, a superb medieval ensemble that's all but unique in retaining the feel of a genuine lived-in village – it neither grew to become a city nor became overly prettified for visitors. Still entirely enclosed within a double ring of mighty sandstone walls, it stands utterly aloof from the modern world.

Although the newly arrived Knights encircled the local population as well as their own castle within their fourteenth-century walls, they took the precaution of keeping whatever they needed for survival north of the straight-line street of **Sokrátous**, which could be sealed off in times of emergency. Broadly speaking, that distinction remains, with the monumental district, now also scattered with Ottoman mosques and minarets, set somewhat apart.

While it does hold some fascinating sights and museums, however, what makes the Old Town so special is the sheer vibrancy of the place as a whole. Its busiest commercial lanes, packed with restaurants, cafés, and souvenir stores selling anything from T-shirts to fur coats, and *gelati* to jewellery, can be overpoweringly congested in summer – Sokrátous itself is the worst culprit – but it's always possible

8

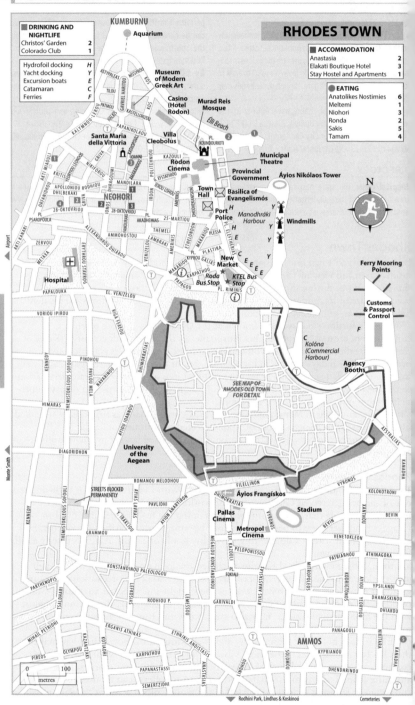

RHODES TOWN

DRINKING AND NIGHTLIFE

Christos' Garden	2
Colorado Club	1

Hydrofoil docking	H
Yacht docking	Y
Excursion boats	E
Catamaran	C
Ferries	F

ACCOMMODATION

Anastasia	2
Elakati Boutique Hotel	3
Stay Hostel and Apartments	1

EATING

Anatolikes Nostimies	6
Meltemi	1
Niohori	3
Ronda	2
Sakis	5
Tamam	4

KUMBURNU
Aquarium
Museum of Modern Greek Art
Casino (Hotel Rodon)
Murad Reis Mosque
Elli Beach
Santa Maria della Vittoria
Villa Cleobolus
Municipal Theatre
Rodon Cinema
Provincial Government
Áyios Nikólaos Tower
Town Hall
Basilica of Evangelismós
NEOHORI
Port Police
Manodhráki Harbour
Windmills
New Market
Hospital
Roda Bus Stop
KTEL Bus Stop
Ferry Mooring Points
Customs & Passport Control
Kolóna (Commercial Harbour)
Agency Booths
SEE MAP OF RHODES OLD TOWN FOR DETAIL
University of the Aegean
STREETS BLOCKED PERMANENTLY
Áyios Frangískos
Pallas Cinema
Stadium
Metropol Cinema
AMMOS
Airport
Monte Smith

0   100
metres

Rodhini Park, Lindhos & Koskinoú   Cemeteries

o escape into the time-forgotten tangle of **cobbled alleyways** that lie further south, and away from the sea. No map can do justice to what a labyrinth it all is; mysterious ruins lie half-buried, overrun with cats or wild flowers, while isolated Cyclopean arches suddenly rear into view, without a trace of the buildings they used to hold up.

Palace of the Grand Masters

ppoton, Platía Kleovoúlou • Tues–Sun: Summer 8am–4pm; winter 8am–2.40pm • €6, combined fee with Archaeological Museum €10; free Sun Nov–March • ☎ 22413 65270

The **Palace of the Grand Masters** dominates the northwestern corner of the Old Town's walls. Destroyed by an ammunition explosion in 1856, it was reconstructed by the Italians as a summer home for Mussolini and King Vittore Emmanuele III, although neither ever visited Rhodes. While its external appearance, based on medieval engravings and accounts, remains reasonably authentic, free rein was given in its interior to Fascist delusions of grandeur.

The two splendid ground-floor galleries jointly constitute the town's best **museums**. They often close due to staff shortages; check whether they're open before you pay for admission, because otherwise there's precious little to see. One covers ancient Rhodes, documenting everyday life around 250 BC; highlights include a Hellenistic floor mosaic of a comedic mask. The other, across the courtyard, covers the medieval era, stressing the importance of Christian Rhodes as a tradecentre. The Knights are represented with a display on their sugar-refining industry and a gravestone of a Grand Master; precious manuscripts and books precede a wing of post-Byzantine icons.

Street of the Knights

The Gothic, heavily restored **Street of the Knights** (Odhós Ippotón) leads east from Platía Kleovoúlou in front of the Palace of the Grand Masters. The various "Inns" along the way lodged the Knights of St John, according to linguistic and ethnic affiliation, until the Ottoman Turks forced them to leave for Malta in 1523. Today the Inns house government offices, foreign consulates or cultural institutions vaguely appropriate to their past. Several stage occasional exhibitions, but the overall effect of the Italian renovation is sterile and stagey.

Archeological Museum

Summer daily 8am–8pm; winter Tues–Sun 8am–3pm • €8, combined fee with Palace of the Grand Masters €10 • ☎ 22413 65256

At the foot of the Street of the Knights, the Knights' Hospital now houses the town's **Archeological Museum**. A very lovely complex in its own right, which takes at least an hour to explore, it consists of several galleries in the medieval hospital itself, plus a delightful raised and walled garden where extensions and outbuildings hold further displays. Rather too many rooms simply hold glass cases filled with small artefacts, displayed with little contextual information, but there's a lot of interesting stuff including votive offerings from Egypt and Cyprus found in the Kamiros acropolis, and an amazing array of ancient painted pottery. The grandest hall upstairs is lined with the tomb slabs of fourteenth- and fifteenth-century Knights, but the light-filled gallery of **Hellenistic statues** nearby is the true highlight. *Aphrodite Adioumene*, the so-called "Marine Venus" beloved of Lawrence Durrell, stands in a rear corner, lent a sinister aspect by her sea-dissolved face that makes a striking contrast to the friendlier *Aphrodite Bathing*.

Turkish Rhodes

Many of the mosques and *mescids* (the Islamic equivalent of a chapel) in which the old town abounds were converted from Byzantine churches after the Christians were expelled in 1522. The most conspicuous of all is the rust-coloured, candy-striped **Süleymaniye Mosque**, rebuilt during the nineteenth century on 300-year-old

8

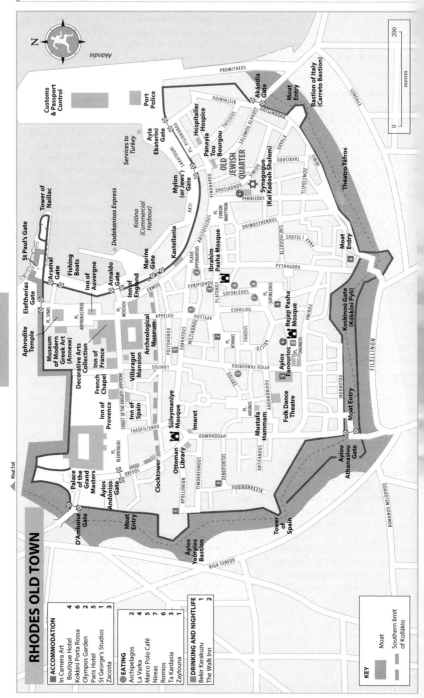

RHODES OLD TOWN

KEY
Moat
Southern limit of Kollákio

foundations. Like most local Ottoman monuments, it's not open to visitors, though the purpose-built (1531) **Ibrahim Pasha Mosque** on Plátonos, for example, is still used by the sizeable Turkish-speaking minority.

The Ottomans' most enduring civic contributions are the **Ottoman Library**, opposite the Süleymaniye (Mon–Sat 9.30am–4pm; tip custodian), which has a rich collection of early medieval manuscripts and Korans; the **imaret** (mess-hall) at Sokrátous 179, now a quaint café (*Palio Syssitio*); and the imposing 1558 **Mustafa Hammam** (Turkish bath) on Platía Aríonos (Mon–Fri 10am–5pm, Sat 8am–5pm, last admission 4pm; €5) – bring everything you need (soap, shampoo, towel, loofah) to enjoy separate, *au naturel* men's and women's sections.

Jewish Rhodes
Beyond the tiled central fountain in Platía Ippokrátous, Odhós Aristotélous leads to **Platía tón Evréon Martýron** ("Square of the Jewish Martyrs"), named in memory of the 2100 Jews of Rhodes and Kos who were sent to the concentration camps in 1944; a black granite column honours them. Of four **synagogues** that once graced the nearby Jewish quarter, only ornate, arcaded, pebble-floored **Kal Kadosh Shalom** (April–Oct Sun–Fri 10am–3pm; donation) on Odhós Simíou, just south, survives. To one side of the synagogue, a well-labelled, three-room **museum** thematically chronicles the Jewish community's life on Rhodes.

New Town (Neohóri)
What's now known as the **New Town** – in Greek, **Neohóri** – dates originally to the Ottoman era, when Orthodox Greeks excluded from the fortified city built their own residential districts outside the walls. Only **Kumburnú**, the area immediately north of the Old Town, at the tip of the headland, bears any relevance to visitors. On its eastern side, Mandhráki yacht harbour serves as the base for excursion boats and some ferry companies, while the streets immediately inland hold the workaday shops, offices and agencies that keep the town as a whole ticking along. The headland itself is surrounded by a continuous **beach** of gritty shingle (loungers, parasols and showers), particularly at **Élli**, the more sheltered east-facing section. Despite being so close to the city, the water offshore is exceptionally clean, which explains the many hotels and restaurants hereabouts.

Aquarium
Kos St • Daily: April–Oct 9am–8.30pm; Nov–March 9am–4.30pm • €5.50 • ⓦ rhodes-aquarium.hcmr.gr

Perched at the northernmost point of the island, Rhodes' **Aquarium** is as much a museum as a conventional aquarium. It does have tanks of live fish, not necessarily captioned correctly, but most of its space is taken up with displays on the history and function of the building itself, as well as a monk seal buried as an ancient family's pet, and a stuffed Cuvier's beaked whale.

Museum of Modern Greek Art
Pl. G. Haritou • Tues–Sat 8am–2pm • €3 (includes annexe) • ⓦ mgamuseum.gr

Near the northernmost tip of the New Town, on what's colloquially known as "100 Palms Square", is Rhodes' **Museum of Modern Greek Art**, which holds the most important collection of twentieth-century Greek painting outside Athens. All the heavy hitters – Hatzikyriakos-Ghikas, surrealist Nikos Engonopoulos, naive artist Theophilos, neo-Byzantinist Fotis Kontoglou – are amply represented. Some of Kontoglou's greatest frescoes, dating from 1951–61, are in the **Evangelismós basilica** at Mandhráki. The museum's former home, on Platía Sýmis 2 in the Old Town, is now an **annexe**, devoted to maps, prints and special exhibits. Both sites have excellent gift shops.

Hellenistic Rhodes

2km west of the Old Town

A half-hour uphill hike from the Old Town – a hike best undertaken just before sunset, both for the views and the temperature – leads to the unenclosed remains of the **acropolis of Hellenistic Rhodes**, atop Monte Smith. Formerly known as Áyios Stéfanos, this hill was renamed for a British admiral during the Napoleonic Wars. While the ruins cover an extensive area, there's not really all that much to see – a restored theatre and stadium, plus three columns of a temple to **Apollo Pythios**. It's striking to realize, however, that the ancient city stretched from here all the way down to the sea.

The cemeteries

While the vast **municipal cemeteries** at Korakónero, just inland from Zéfyros beach 2km southeast of the centre, might not sound like a hot tourist destination, they can be strangely compelling. This is one of the very few remaining spots in the Balkans where the dead of four faiths lie in proximity, albeit separated by high walls. The easterly **Greek Orthodox section**, the largest, holds the fewest surprises. The small **Catholic section** is not only the last home of various north European expatriates, but also demonstrates that a fair number of Italians elected to accept Greek nationality and stay on after the 1948 unification with Greece. The **Jewish section** (Mon–Fri 8am–1pm) has, understandably, seen little activity since 1944, and is full of memorials in French to those who were deported. Opposite its gate, across the busy road, a small **Allied War graves** plot holds 142 burials. Just south of the Jewish section, the "**Muslim**" **section** (ie Turkish) is the most heavily used and best maintained of the three minority cemeteries.

8

ACCOMMODATION RHODES TOWN

Since the 2008 financial crisis, Rhodes' Old Town has seen a growth in pricey, luxury and boutique hotel establishments: even so, bargains can still be found, especially if booked direct.

OLD TOWN

★**In Camera Art Boutique Hotel** Sofokleous St 35 ☎22410 77277, ⓦincamera.gr; map p.520. Superb conversion of an old Turkish mansion, this family-run hotel owned by a professional photographer is in one of the old town's most popular squares with a small jacuzzi in its courtyard. All the suites have king-sized beds and are furnished with the owner's photos; some can accommodate families, and one even has a bathroom converted from a hammam. Breakfast (included) is served on the terrace. April–Oct. **€225**

★**Kokkini Porta Rossa** Archiepiskopou Efthimiou 24 ☎22410 75114, ⓦkokkiniporta.com; map p.520. This outstanding and lovingly converted old Turkish mansion has six large suites. Luxuries such as a pillow menu, antiques scattered throughout, a grand piano and a sun-dappled courtyard, where free drinks are served nightly, add to the overall ambience. A three-course breakfast using locally sourced ingredients in included. Pricey, but well worth it and special deals often available direct from hotel. Late March to mid-Nov. **€240**

Olympos Garden Ayíou Fanouríou 56 ☎22410 33567, ⓦpension-olympos.gr; map p.520. Small tucked-away pension with seven rooms and one studio sleeping three

people (€90). The building is adorned with statues wearing traditional Greek costume and various trinkets, and there's a garden at the back, where you can eat the optional breakfast. **€65**

Paris Hotel Ayíou Fanouríou 88 ☎22410 26356, ⓦparis-hotel-rhodes.gr; map p.520. On the corner of Omirou, opposite Ag. Fanouris church, this Greek-run establishment has tastefully decorated doubles, studios and two luxury suites. The courtyard bar is open all day for snacks and drinks, and is a great location for breakfast (included) and to relax . **€85**

St. George's Studios Apollonion 35 ☎22410 33593, ⓦsaintgeorgeoldcityrhodes.gr; map p.520. Attractive and welcoming little place that has four large studios with kitchens decorated in bright, Mediterranean colours. It has a lovely courtyard with an olive tree at its centre, and its location in a cul-de-sac – opposite the Áyios Yeóryios Bastion – is central, yet very quiet. **€90**

Zacosta Villa Hotel Xenofontos 23 ☎22410 33450, ⓦzacosta.com; map p.5220. A stylishly renovated old house with four suites and one room, in a quiet location, hidden away among twisty alleyways. The bougainvillea-draped courtyard is a delightful place to eat breakfast (included), made from local produce: the owner also offers wine tasting sessions. **€120**

NEW TOWN

Anastasia 28-Oktovríou 46 ☎ 22410 28007, ⓦ anastasia-hotel.com; map p.518. Italian-era mansion with high ceilings and tiled floors that's been converted into a family-run guesthouse. The rooms are simple and can sleep up to four, there's a beautiful garden with bar, where the resident tortoises live. Breakfast is extra. **€60**

Elakati Boutique Hotel Lochagou Fanouraki 29 ☎ 22410 70688, ⓦ elakati.com; map p.518. This sleek boutique establishment is efficient, yet lacking a little warmth. The eleven double rooms – all with a balcony– have a contemporary feel with exposed stone, and the suite (€340) has a Jacuzzi and fireplace. Breakfast included. **€190**

Stay Hostel & Apartments Lochagou Fanouraki 19-21 ☎ 22410 24024, ⓦ stay-rhodes.com; map p.518. Trendy new hostel with fifteen rooms, including singles, doubles and dorms, over four floors. There's a communal basement kitchen and cinema room, plus a rooftop gym with yoga and pilates in the summer. Bar area in reception and friendly international staff. Dorm **€25**, double **€65**

EATING AND DRINKING

While the Old Town holds a quite staggering number of restaurants, prices can be high, and both value and quality tend to improve away from the main commercial lanes. Most places serve those with children from about 6.30pm, tourists until perhaps 10pm, and locals till midnight or later.

OLD TOWN

Archipelagos Platía Hippocratous 18 ☎ 22410 22322; map p.520. Good, reasonably priced home cooking in a friendly atmosphere – stifado (traditional Greek beef stew) is €14, while stuffed kalamári with feta and peppers will set you back €13. Eat at street-level tables or on the terrace overlooking a lively square – both are great for people-watching. Hearty breakfasts also served. April to mid-Nov daily 7am–midnight.

La Varka Sofokléous 5; map p.520. Indoor-outdoor ouzerí, with live Greek music and a table-filled terrace on a busy alleyway, plus a cosy interior for the cooler months. Good salads, cheapish ouzo and soúma by the carafe – seafood risotto (€7.50) and orange and lamb curry (€8) are favourite dishes. Daily 11.30am–1am.

★**Marco Polo Café** Ayíou Fanouríou 42 ☎ 22410 25562; map p.520. Lovely, deservedly popular restaurant in a garden courtyard behind a blue door; the lack of a street sign is to keep the crowds down. Traditional recipes blending subtle flavours include the popular sea bass marinated in lime and chilli (€12.50), and pork fillet with potato purée (€15). Excellent wine list and desserts of the day. Reservations essential. April–Oct daily 6pm–midnight.

Nireas Sofokléous 22 ☎ 22410 21703; map p.520. This long-standing, family-run fish specialist, on a quiet square away from the bustle, has earned its sky-high reputation thanks to the hard work and friendly professionalism of its owners and its atmospheric indoor/outdoor seating. Seafood dishes, like stuffed kalamári, cost around €10.50, with sea bream for €12. They offer a range of Italian desserts too. Daily lunch and dinner.

★**Romios** Sofokleous 15 ☎ 22410 25549; map p.520. Friendly restaurant with courtyard and indoor seating, serving traditional local dishes plus international fare such as curried chicken (€15). Fresh seafood and grilled meat (from €10) and homemade pastas (€12) plus desserts to-die-for ensure repeat clientele. Daily 1pm–late.

Ta Kardasia Platonos 4–8 ☎ 22410 27074; map p.520. Friendly restaurant in the small Platonos Square that is popular with locals and tourists alike – expect starters such as sausage with honey (€5.50), and grilled meat mains such as chicken à la crème (€10.50). May–Nov daily lunch and dinner, Sun till 6pm.

Zaytouna Sokrátous 42 & Apallou ☎ 22410 76932; map p.520. Small take-away with some tables on a busy street serving Mediterranean/Middle Eastern cuisine – it's great for dishes such as falafel platter (€9.50) and their hummus dip with two types of pitta bread (€5) is the best in the area. Also serves the usual pork and chicken gyros (€6.50). May–Nov daily 11am–11pm.

NEW TOWN

Anatolikes Nostimies Klavdhíou Pépper 109, Zéfyros Beach ☎ 22410 29516; map p.518. The name means "Anatolian Delicacies": Thracian Pomak/Middle Eastern dips and starters such as baba ghanoush (€5), plus chicken kebab platter (€9.50). It's friendly and popular with a beach-hut atmosphere. Post-meal hubble-bubble on request. Daily noon–midnight.

★**Meltemi** Platía Koundourióti 8, Élli beach ☎ 22410 30480; map p.518. Beachfront ouzerí, with a shaded beach-level patio, serving such delights as grilled kalamári stuffed with feta and peppers (€12.80) – the saganaki shrimps glazed with cream, courgette, onions and peppers is a favourite (€11). Daily 5pm–11pm .

Niohori Ioánni Kazoúli 29, Neohóri ☎ 22410 35116; map p.518. Alias "Kiki's" after the jolly proprietress, this homely, inexpensive local is tops for meat grills, sourced from their own butcher/farm – try the roast lamb (€6.50) or village sausage (€4). There's usually a cooked vegetable

8

dish, too, such as stuffed tomato (€6.50). Daily lunch and dinner.

Ronda Platía Koundourióti 6, Neohóri ☎ 22410 76944; map p.518. Built by the Italians as a waterfront spa complex, this large-domed room now houses a very spacious café. Enjoy views of the beach and harbour through its huge arched windows. Daily 9am–1am.

Sakis Kanadhá 95, at Apostólou Papaïoánnou, Zéfyros ☎ 22410 21537; map p.518. A friendly old favourite with patio and indoor seating, equally loved by locals and foreigners. Dishes like lamb ribs (€7.50) are popular, as is the kalamári (€8), which is often caught by Sakis himself,

along with the other fish dishes on the menu – try the limpets (€5.50). Mon–Sat 5pm–1am, Sun 12.30pm–midnight.

Tamam Yeoryíou Léondos 1, Neohóri ☎ 22410 73522; map p.518. This small, enormously popular restaurant serves good but expensive traditional cuisine with a wine list to match. Dishes such as prawns with ouzo and orange sauce (€9.50) or pork shank (€15) are popular. If you spend a lot, you'll have a real feast; show any reluctance, and the charming service will turn off like a tap. Reserve in advance, or expect to queue out the door. Daily 1pm–11pm.

NIGHTLIFE

In the Old Town, an entire alley (Miltiádhou) off Apellou is home to a score of loud music bars and clubs, extending towards Plátonos and Platía Dhamayítou, and frequented mostly by Greeks (in winter too).

Bekir Karakuzu Sokrátous 76, Old Town; map p.520. The last traditional Turkish *kafenío* in the Old Town, with an Oriental-fantasy interior, simply oozes atmosphere. Yoghurt, *loukoúmi*, sage tea and coffees are on the expensive side – consider it admission to an informal museum. Daily 11am–midnight.

Christos' Garden Dhilberáki 59, Neohóri; map p.518. This art gallery/bar/café occupies a carefully restored old house and courtyard with pebble-mosaic floors throughout. Daily 10pm–late.

Colorado Club Orfanídhou 57, at Aktí Miaoúli,

Neohóri ☎ 22410 75120, ⓦ coloradoclub-rhodes. com; map p.518. Triple venue, just back from the sea on the west side of the New Town, comprised of a "disco-house" dance club, a live music venue and "Heaven", the top-floor chill-out bar. Daily 9pm–late.

★**The Walk Inn** Platía Dhorieos, Old Town ☎ 22410 74293; map p.520. Where locals and English ex-pats hang out, with a great pub atmosphere in a Greek setting, plus outdoor seating in a lovely old square. It serves the usual beers, wines and soft drinks, plus large pizzas for €6 and burgers for €7.50. Live music on a Sunday from 4pm. Daily 10am–1am.

The east coast

From the capital as far south as Líndhos, the **east coast** of Rhodes has been built up with a succession of sprawling towns and resorts. Some, such as **Faliráki**, have long since lost any charm they may once have possessed, but there are still some traditional lower-key alternatives, including **Stegná** and **Haráki**.

Piyés Kallithéas

7km south of Rhodes Town • Daily 8am–8pm • €3 • ⓦ kallitheasprings.gr

A prize example of orientalized Art Deco from 1929, the former spa at **Piyés Kallithéas** was the work of a young Pietro Lombardi who, in his old age, designed Strasbourg's European Parliament building. Accessed via a short side road through pines, it's situated in a picturesque bay where many come to swim. The upmarket bar serves from inside artificial grottoes at the swimming lido, just below the dome of the **Mikrí Rotónda** in its clump of palms. The main **Megáli Rotónda** higher up is now a small showcase area, with changing modern art exhibits.

Faliráki

The overblown and unappealing resort of **Faliráki**, 10km south of the capital, is a town of two halves. The half-dozen high-rise family hotels in its northerly zone sit uneasily alongside the cheap-and-nasty southern zone, notorious for its drink-fuelled brawls, rapes and even murder. Since the island police forcefully curbed the local club-crawling culture, the place is now a shadow of its former self.

Faliráki's sandy sweep is closed off on the south by the cape of **Ladhikó**. For the best swimming, head for the main cove, south of the promontory. The scenic bay of

'**Anthony Quinn**", on its northern flank, is named after the late Mexican American actor, whom Greeks took to their hearts following his roles in *Zorba the Greek* and *The Guns of Navarone*. Quinn bought much of this area and constructed the first road to the beach, but during the 1980s the Greek government swindled him out of his claim; legal battles continue to this day.

Afándou Bay
South of Ladhikó, the coastline is adorned, all the way to Líndhos, by striking limestone turrets that punctuate long stretches of beach. The first is the pebble-and-sand expanse of **Afándou Bay**, the least developed large east-coast beach, with just a few showers and clusters of inexpensive sunbeds. Spare a moment, heading down the main access road to mid-beach, for the atmospheric sixteenth-century church of **Panayía Katholikí**, paved with a *votsalotó* floor and decorated with frescoes.

Kolýmbia
Immediately north of the Tsambíka headland, 25km south of Rhodes Town, is **Kolýmbia**, which was laid out by the Italians not long before World War II, as a model farming village. Its original little grid of streets now serves a fast-growing resort that's become a favourite with more upscale package travellers. Reasonable beaches lie to either side of the low hill at road's end; the northern one has more facilities.

Tsambíka
The enormous promontory of **Tsambíka**, 26km south of town, offers unrivalled views along some 50km of coastline. From the main highway, a steep, 1500m cement drive leads to a small car park from where steps mount to the summit. On its September 8 festival childless women climb up – on their hands and knees in the final stretches – to an otherwise unremarkable **monastery** to be cured of their barrenness. Shallow **Tsambíka Bay**, south of the headland (2km access road), has an excellent if packed beach.

Stegná
A kilometre or so south of Tsambíka Bay, a steep road drops for 3.5km down to the sea from the main highway, in huge sweeping curves. It ends at the scruffy but appealing semicircular bay of **Stegná**, where for once no large hotels lurk behind the fine-gravel shore, just some relatively tasteful apartment complexes.

Haráki and around
Haráki is a likeable little crescent bay, overlooked by the stubby ruins of **Feraklós castle**, the last Knights' citadel to fall to the Turks. There's no road along the shoreline, just a walkway beside a part pebble, part grey-sand **beach** that's backed by a solid row of small two- or three-storey studios, interspersed with the occasional café.

The long straight shoreline south of Haráki is lined with beaches of sand and fine gravel, such as **Paralía Kaláthou**. It ends after 8km, just short of Líndhos, at the little cove of **Vlyhá**, which holds a couple of enormous hotels.

ACCOMMODATION	THE EAST COAST

Atrium Palace Paralía Kaláthou ☎ 22440 31601, ⓦ atrium.gr. Surprisingly unobtrusive despite its 300-plus luxurious rooms, this upmarket hotel is one of the few developments on Kaláthou Beach, with expensively landscaped grounds and curved pools. The remoter villa wings, towards the spa, are best. Breakfast included. April–Oct. **€130**

Haraki Village Haráki ☎ 6946 350 401, ⓦ harakivillage.gr. Eight little pastel-coloured studios and apartments, all with balconies or outdoor space, at the north end of the beach below the castle. Breakfast included. **€130**

Blugreen Stegná Stegná ☎ 22440 22516, ⓦ stegna. gr. Laidback boutique B&B, with studios and rooms in a

8

peaceful setting a short walk back from Stegná beach: there's a breezy shared terrace and a hot tub. Breakfast included. **€60**

Lindos Blu Vlyhá ☎ 22440 32110, ⊛ lindosblu.gr. Very opulent, stylish, adult-only resort hotel, tumbling down the slopes of a pretty bay immediately north of Líndhos, with a spa, infinity pools, and on-site restaurants. All seventy units have sea views; villas/maisonettes have private pools. Delicious breakfast included. Minimum stay 4 nights in high season. **€380**

EATING AND DRINKING

Argo Restaurant Haráki ☎ 6946 351 410. Behind its weathered, custard-yellow exterior, this seafront restaurant, squeezed among the toothy rocks at the southern end of Haráki beach, is surprisingly smart and offers views of the castle and a good Greek menu, with mussels, chicken or shrimp main dishes (€8–12). Daily noon–10pm.

★ **To Periyiali** Stegná ☎ 22440 23444. The best taverna in Stegná, down by the fish anchorage. Greeks flock here for seafood, hand-cut round chips, home-made *yaprákia* and substantial salads washed down with good bulk wine (€15 or under per head); the travertine-clad toilets must be the wackiest, most charming, on the island. Daily lunch and dinner.

Líndhos

Set on a stark headland 50km south of Rhodes Town, **LÍNDHOS** is almost too good to be true. A classic Greek village of crazily stacked **whitewashed houses**, poised between a stupendous castle-topped acropolis above and sandy crescent beaches below, it's the island's number-two tourist attraction. Inevitably, it's so tightly packed with day-trippers in summer that you can barely move along its impossibly narrow lanes. Almost all its shining white homes have long since been bought up by foreigners; most of those along the ancient agora, or serpentine main alleyway, are now run as restaurants, cafés and souvenir stores, while rental properties lie to either side.

Arrive outside peak season, or at least in the early morning, and strolling through the village is still hugely atmospheric. The belfried, post-Byzantine **Panayía church** (Mon–Sat 9am–3pm & 6.30–8pm, Sun 9am–3pm) is covered inside with well-preserved eighteenth-century frescoes. The most imposing **medieval captains' residences** are built around *votsalotó* courtyards, their monumental doorways often fringed by intricate stone braids or cables supposedly corresponding in number to the fleet owned.

The acropolis
April–Oct daily 8am–8pm; Nov–March Tues–Sun 8am–3pm • €12

Although the dramatic battlements that circle the **acropolis** on the bluff directly above Líndhos belong to a **Knights' castle**, the precinct they enclose is much more ancient. A sanctuary dedicated to local deity Lindia was founded here in the ninth century BC, while the surviving structures were started by local ruler Kleoboulos three hundred years later.

A short climb up steep steps from the centre of the village, or a longer walk (or even donkey ride) up a gentler but more exposed pathway, brings you to the stairway to the castle itself. The relief sculpture of a ship's prow at its foot dates from the second century BC. Once you pass through the sole **gateway**, restrain the impulse to head straight for the summit, and explore the site from the bottom upwards instead. That way the **temple of Athena Lindia** at the top, set on a level platform that commands magnificent coastline views to both north and south, will appear in a stunning climax. Almost all the buildings are recent **reconstructions**, replacing older restoration work now deemed inaccurate, though some ancient stones have been incorporated.

Come early or late in the day, to avoid the crowds and enjoy the best light. And be warned that many of the stairways, parapets and platforms have precipitous, unrailed drop-offs.

8

Beaches

Líndhos's main **beach**, once the principal ancient harbour, tends to get very overcrowded; quieter options lie one cove beyond at **Pállas beach**. The small, perfectly sheltered **St Paul's harbour**, south of the acropolis and well away from town, has excellent swimming. According to legend, the Apostle landed here in 58 AD on a mission to evangelize the island.

ARRIVAL AND INFORMATION   LÍNDHOS

By car No cars are allowed in the village or to access the acropolis. Arriving drivers instead have to perform an elaborate U-turn at the tiny main square to reach car parks towards the beach, some of which are free.

ACCOMMODATION

★**Melenos** ☎22440 32222, ⓦmelenoslindos.com. The only hotel in Líndhos itself is a gem, exquisite and exclusive, discreetly sited on the second lane above the north beach, by the school. No expense has been spared in laying out the twelve luxurious suites with semi-private terraces and sophisticated furnishings; there's also a tasteful garden-bar and restaurant. Breakfast included. **€290**

EATING AND DRINKING

The lanes of Líndhos are crammed with run-of-the-mill restaurants, but there are still a few standouts. Almost all have roof terraces with castle views; most diners end up sitting on bare concrete patios in a parallel rooftop world.

Acropolis Roof Garden Trapeza 26 ☎22440 32160. The best option along the lanes, with a solid menu of Greek specialities such as rabbit *stifhádo* (€9.50) and a fine array of mezhédes, including tasty *dolmádhes* (€7), all served on a castle-view terrace. Daily lunch and dinner.

★**Mavrikos** Main Square ☎22440 31232. Prominent restaurant, on the fig-tree square where the traffic turns around. Starters such as *yígandes* in carob syrup (€7.50) or sweet marinated sardines (€4) are accomplished, as are superior traditional recipes and fish mains such as skate timbale with sweetened balsamic (€11), or *dolmádhes* and *tyrokafterí*. Daily noon–midnight.

Village Café ☎22440 31554, ⓦlindostreasures.com/village. Friendly café and snack-bar, set around a little pebbled courtyard, with a fine array of pastries from €5, juices, sandwiches and light bites such as cheese pies (€3). Daily 10am–5pm.

The southeast coast

Until recently, tourist development petered out south of Líndhos, but today Rhodes' **southeast coast** has plenty of facilities for travellers seeking to escape the hectic atmosphere of the northern resorts. **Péfki** and **Yennádhi** are the best overnight stops, while **Prassoníssi** at the southern tip is popular with windsurfers. Even if you're not staying down here, it's worth touring in your own vehicle, stopping off perhaps in the villages just inland, like **Asklipió**, with its wonderful church.

Péfki

A couple of kilometres around the headland beyond Líndhos, **PÉFKI** was originally the garden annexe of its illustrious neighbour, but has now become a resort in its own right. Its principal **beach**, a gorgeous little cove lined with sand and lapped by sparkling clear waters, inevitably gets very crowded in summer, but there are other, more secluded little beaches tucked at the base of the low cliffs to the west.

Lárdhos

Although the village of **LÁRDHOS** stands well in from the sea, it has lent its name to dense beachfront development a little further south. Its main beach, 2km south of the centre, is gravelly and heavily impinged upon by hotels; Glýstra cove, 3km south, is a small and more sheltered crescent, at its best in low season.

WINDSURFING AT PRASSONÍSSI

Situated at the very southern tip of Rhodes, **Prassoníssi** is regarded as one of the finest **windsurfing** sites in Europe. Strictly speaking, the name refers to "Leek Island", the sturdy little islet just offshore, which is connected to the mainland by a long, low and very narrow sandspit through which a small natural channel frequently opens.

Not only do the waters here belong to different seas – the **Aegean** to the west of the spit, and the **Mediterranean** to the east – but in season they usually offer dramatically contrasting conditions. Thanks to the prevailing **meltémi** wind, and the funnelling effect of the islet, the Aegean side is generally much rougher, with head-high waves. On summer days it therefore becomes the area for expert windsurfers and daredevil kitesurfers. The Mediterranean side, meanwhile, tends to be much calmer, almost lagoon-like, and its shallow sandbars make it especially ideal for beginners.

The **season** at Prassoníssi lasts from May until mid-October. Of the three **windsurfing schools** that operate here, the Polish-run Prasonisi Center (late April–Oct; ☎ 22440 91044, ⓦ prasonisicenter.com) is the keenest and friendliest.

Asklipió

Nine kilometres south of Lárdhos, close to the unexciting resort of Kiotári, a side road heads 3.5km inland to **ASKLIPIÓ**, a sleepy village enlivened by a crumbling Knights' castle and Byzantine **Kímisis Theotókou church**.

Kímisis Theotókou church

Daily: spring & autumn 9am–5pm; summer 9am–6pm • €1

Asklipió's central **Kímisis Theotókou church** dates from 1060, and has a pebble-floored ground plan, to which two apses were added during the eighteenth century. Thanks to the dry local climate, the **frescoes** inside remain in breathtaking condition. Didactic "cartoon strips" extend completely around the church and up onto the ceiling, featuring Old Testament stories alongside the more usual lives of Christ and the Virgin. Half of the adjacent **Asklipió Museum** (same hours and ticket) is devoted to ecclesiastical treasures; the other, housed in a former olive mill, holds a folklore gallery, full of craft tools and antiquated machinery.

Yennádhi and Lahaniá

The drab outskirts of **YENNÁDHI**, 13km south of Lárdhos and the only sizeable settlement on the southeast coast, mask the attractive older village core inland. Though the present, barrel-vaulted structure of the village cemetery and church, **Ayía Anastasía Roméa**, dates from the fifteenth century, it's built on sixth-century foundations, and covered inside with post-Byzantine **frescoes**. Yennádhi's dark-sand-and-gravel **beach**, clean and offering the usual amenities, extends for kilometres in either direction.

The tiny and picturesque village of **LAHANIÁ**, 10km south of Yennádhi, then 2km inland, was abandoned after a postwar earthquake, though since the 1980s its older houses have been mostly occupied and renovated by foreigners.

Prassoníssi

The main circular island highway doesn't run all the way down its southernmost tip. Branch south at Kattaviá, however, and a paved 8km spur road will bring you to **Prassoníssi**, a two-hour, 90km drive south of Rhodes Town. This gloriously desolate spot has become a major rendezvous for **windsurfers** (see box, above).

ACCOMMODATION   THE SOUTHEAST COAST

Effie's Dreams Yennádhi ☎ 22440 43437, ⓦ rodos -apartments.com. Surrounded by citrus groves and great walking paths, these six good-value studios overlook a fountain-fed oasis at the northern end of Yennádhi – they come with sea or mountain views, and there's also an on-site bar. **€45**

Lindian Village Lárdhos ☎22440 35900, ⓦlindianvillage.gr. This sumptuous beachfront resort, 5km south of Lárdhos, is an attractive complex of bungalows (suites have their own plunge pools), with several gourmet restaurants, a spa/gym and large pool plus private beach. Minimum stay 3 nights in high season. Includes breakfast. April–Oct. **€166**

Oasis Prassoníssi ☎22440 91031, ⓦoasis-prasonisi .com. The better of the two accommodation options at the island's southernmost tip, it has sixteen basic but clean rooms, all with balconies, some with sea views. Rates include breakfast and dinner in their downstairs taverna **€52**

Pefkos Blue Hotel Péfki ☎22440 48017. ⓦwww .pefkosbluehotel.com. Good-value studio hotel on the hillside above Péfki; the 35 clean, comfortable apartments sleep two to four, with kitchens and panoramic views. Minimum stay 3 nights. **€38**

EATING AND DRINKING

Kyma Beach Restaurant Péfki ☎22440 48213. High-class restaurant at the midpoint of Péfki beach, with lovely sunset views. They serve delicious Greek specialities with a creative twist; try the octopus carpaccio. It's a little pricey: starters and main (without drinks) will set you back about €30 – you pay for the view. Book ahead in summer. Daily noon–10pm.

★**Platanos** Lahaniá Prassoníssi ☎6944 199 991, ⓦlachaniaplatanostaverna.com. On the tiny little main platía at the lower, eastern end of Lahaniá village, this welcoming rural taverna has superb mezédhes platters like hummus and *dolmadhákia* (€10). Sit outside at the front, under the eponymous plane tree, or in the dining room, overlooking a deep wooded valley. Daily lunch and dinner.

The west coast

While Rhodes' windward **west coast** is damp, fertile and forested, its beaches are exposed and often rocky. None of this has deterred development and, as on the east coast, the first few kilometres of the busy main road have been surrendered entirely to tourism. From Rhodes Town to the airport, the shore is lined with generic hotels, though **Triánda**, **Kremastí** and **Paradhísi** are still nominally villages, with real centres.

Kameiros

Summer daily 8am–8pm; winter Tues–Sun 8am–3pm • €6 • ☎22413 65200

The site of ancient **KAMEIROS**, which united with Lindos and Ialyssos to found the city-state of Rhodes, stands above the coast 30km southwest of Rhodes Town. Soon eclipsed by the new capital, Kameiros was only rediscovered in 1859, leaving a well-preserved Doric townscape in a beautiful hillside setting. Visitors can make out the foundations of two small **temples**, the re-erected pillars of a Hellenistic **house**, a Classical **fountain**, and the **stoa** of the upper agora, complete with a water cistern. Kameiros had no fortifications, nor even an acropolis – partly owing to the gentle slope of the site, and also to the likely settlement here by peaceable Minoans.

Kámiros Skála

The tiny anchorage of **KÁMIROS SKÁLA** (aka Skála Kamírou), 45km southwest of Rhodes Town, is noteworthy only as the home port for a regular ferry service to the island of Hálki (see p.535). It does have a handful of restaurants, however, while the off-puttingly named **Paralía Kopriás** ("Manure Beach") is 400m southwest.

Kástro Kritinías

From afar, **Kástro Kritinías**, 2km south of Kámiros Skála, is the most impressive of the Knights' rural strongholds; the paved access road is too narrow and steep for tour buses. Close up, it proves to be no more than a shell, albeit a glorious one, with fine views west to Hálki, Alimniá, Tílos and Níssyros.

Monólithos

The tiered, flat-roofed houses of **MONÓLITHOS**, high atop the cliffs 22km south of Kámiros Skála, don't themselves justify the long trip out, but the view over the Aegean s striking. Local diversions include yet another **Knights' castle**, out of sight of town 2km west, which is photogenically perched on its own pinnacle but encloses very little, and the sand-and-gravel beaches at **Foúrni**, five paved but curvy kilometres below the castle.

ACCOMMODATION AND EATING	MONÓLITHOS
Hotel Thomas At the top of the village ☎ 22460 61264, ⓦ thomashotel.gr. Don't be fooled by its somewhat grim exterior, this welcoming hotel has ten plain but clean and fair-sized rooms with kitchen facilities and panoramic balconies. Breakfast included. **€40**	**Old Monolithos** Opposite Monólithos church ☎ 22460 61276. The best taverna in the village is known locally for its grilled meat, and starters like wild mushrooms (€6) and briam (€6.50) accompanied by bread made in the village; expect mains such as seafood risotto (€8) and mousakka (€7). Daily lunch and dinner; Sat & Sun only off season.

Inland Rhodes

You'll need a vehicle to get around **Inland Rhodes**, which is hilly and still part-forested (despite the ongoing efforts of arsonists), with soft-contoured, undulating scenery, and villages showing the last vestiges of agrarian life. Most people under retirement age are away working in the tourist industry, returning only at weekends and during winter.

Ialyssos

10km southwest of Rhodes Town • Summer daily 8am–8pm; winter Tues–Sun 8am–3pm • €6, grounds free

From the scanty acropolis of ancient **Ialyssos**, on Filérimos hill, Süleyman the Magnificent directed the 1522 siege of Rhodes. Filérimos means "lover of solitude", after tenth-century Byzantine hermits who dwelt here; **Filérimos monastery** is the most substantial structure. Directly in front of the church sprawl the foundations of third-century temples to Zeus and Athena, built atop a far older Phoenician shrine, with peacocks strutting around the grounds.

8

Petaloúdhes

Daily 9am–6pm • Mid-June to Oct €5; Nov to mid-June €3

Petaloúdhes ("Butterfly Valley"), reached by a 7km side road that bears inland between Paradhísi and Theológos, is a rest stop for **Jersey tiger moths**, who congregate here between mid-June and September, attracted by the abundant *Liquidambar orientalis* trees growing in this stream canyon. The moths, which roost in droves on the tree trunks and cannot eat during this final phase of their life cycle, rest to conserve energy, and die of starvation soon after mating. When stationary, the moths are a well-camouflaged black and yellow, but in flight they flash cherry-red overwings.

Eptá Piyés to Profítis Ilías

Eptá Piyés ("Seven Springs"), 4km inland from Kolýmbia junction on the main east-coast highway, is an oasis with a tiny irrigation dam created by the Italians. A trail and a rather claustrophobic Italian aqueduct-tunnel both lead from the vicinity of the springs to the reservoir. Continuing on the same road, you reach **ELEOÚSSA** after another 9km, in the shade of dense forest. Built as the planned agricultural colony of Campochiaro in the mid-1930s, it's now a bizarre **ghost town**, with a central square lined by eerily derelict Italian structures that visitors can wander through at will. From the vast, yellow-trimmed Art Deco fountain-cum-pool just west of the village, stocked with endangered *gizáni* fish, keep straight 3km further to the gorgeous little late Byzantine church of **Áyios Nikólaos Foundouklí** ("St Nicholas of the Hazelnuts").

Émbona

All tracks and roads west across Profítis Ilías converge on the road from Kalavárdha bound for **ÉMBONA**, a large but unremarkable village backed up against the north slope of 1215m **Mount Atávyros**. Émbona lies at the heart of the island's most important **wine-producing districts**.

Thárri monastery

Katholikón Daily, all day • Free

Accessible from Apóllona and Laerma to the north, or via a rough but passable road from Asklipió 11km south, the Byzantine **Thárri monastery** is the oldest religious foundation on Rhodes, re-established as a vital community in 1990 by charismatic abbot Amfilohios. In the striking *katholikón*, successive cleanings have restored damp-smudged **frescoes** dated 1300–1450 to a pale approximation of their original glory.

ACCOMMODATION AND EATING | INLAND RHODES

★**Elafos Hotel** Profítis Ilías ☎22410 44808, Ⓦelafoshotel.gr. Splendid, restored Italian, 1929-vintage chalet-hotel, in a village west of Áyios Nikólaos church: its 22 high-ceilinged rooms ooze retro charm, and the arcaded ground-floor common areas include a restaurant and a sauna. Breakfast included. **€60**

★**Pigi Fasouli** On the edge of Psínthos village, 6km southeast of Butterfly Valley ☎22410 50071. Excellent taverna serving fish and meat grills (from €5.50) plus the usual appetizers such as tzatziki dip (€3) and Greek salad (€4.50) at tables over-looking the namesake spring. Daily lunch and dinner.

8

Kastellórizo

Although **KASTELLÓRIZO**'s official name of Meyísti means "Biggest", it's actually among the smallest Dodecanese islands; it's just the biggest of a local archipelago of islets. It's also extremely remote, located more than 100km east of Rhodes and barely more than a nautical mile off mainland Asia. At night, its lights are outnumbered by those of the Turkish town of Kaş opposite, with which Kastellórizo has excellent relations.

The island's population has dwindled from around ten thousand a century ago to perhaps just three hundred today. An **Ottoman** possession from 1552, it was occupied by the **French** from 1915 until 1921, and then by the **Italians**. When Italy capitulated to the Allies in 1943, 1500 **Commonwealth** commandos occupied Kastellórizo. Most departed that November, after the Germans captured the other Dodecanese, which left the island vulnerable to looters, both Greek and British. By the time a fuel fire in 1944 triggered the explosion of an adjacent arsenal, demolishing half the houses on Kastellórizo, most islanders had already left. Those who remain are supported by remittances from more than thirty thousand emigrants, as well as subsidies from the Greek government to prevent the island reverting to Turkey.

Yet Kastellórizo has a future of sorts, thanks partly to "Kassies" returning each summer to renovate their crumbling ancestral houses as **second homes**. Visitors tend either to love Kastellórizo and stay a week, or crave escape after a day; detractors dismiss it as a human zoo maintained by the Greek government to placate nationalists, while devotees celebrate an atmospheric, little-commercialized outpost of Hellenism.

ARRIVAL AND DEPARTURE | KASTELLÓRIZO

By air Kastellórizo's airport, 1km above the harbour, is served by Olympic/Aegean Air flights from Rhodes (1 daily; 25min). The island's lone taxi serves the aiport (€5 per passenger).

By ferry Day-trips to Turkey leave regularly from the port in summer, for around €20.

Rhó ▲ ▲ Rhodes ▲ Kaş

MEDITERRANEAN
SEA

Áyios Stéfanos ♱ *Vathoryáki*

Plákes

Army
base

**Profítis
Ilías**

Psorádhia

Knights' Castle
**Lycian
House
Tomb**

**Áyias
Triádhos**

Horáfia

Cemetery

Paleókastro

**KASTELLÓRIZO
TOWN**

Mandhráki

**Power
plant**

*Cape
Nýftis*

▲ *Vigla (270m)*

AVLÓNIA

Wine press

**Ayíou Yeoryíou
toú Vounioú**

Wine press

Airstrip

N

8

Návlakas

Rubbish tip

**Perastá
(Galázio Spílio)**

KASTELLÓRIZO

Destinations Astypálea (1 weekly; 16hr); Kalymnós (2 weekly; 11hr 40min); Kos (2 weekly; 10hr); Níssyros (2 weekly; 8hr 30min); Pireás (2 weekly; 28hr); Rhodes (3 weekly; 2hr 20min–4hr); Sými (2 weekly; 3hr 50min–6hr 25min); Tílos (2 weekly; 7hr).

Travel agents Papoutsis, by the harbour, sells all sea and air tickets (☎ 22410 70630).

Kastellórizo Town

The island's population is concentrated in **KASTELLÓRIZO TOWN** on the north coast –around what's said to be the finest natural harbour between Beirut and Fethiye on the Turkish coast – and its "suburb" of Mandhráki, just over the fire-blasted hill and boasting a half-ruined Knights' castle. In summer, it's what Greeks call a *klouví* (bird cage) – the sort of place where, after two strolls up and down the pedestrianized quay, you'll have a nodding acquaintance with your fellow visitors and all the island's characters.

Most of the town's surviving original **mansions** are ranged along the waterfront, sporting tiled roofs, wooden balconies and blue or green shutters on long, narrow windows. Derelict houses in the backstreets are being renovated, and even the hillside is sprouting new constructions in unconventional colours, though the cumulative effect of World War I shelling, a 1926 earthquake, 1943 air raids and the 1944 explosions will never be reversed. The black-and-white posters and postcards depicting the town in its prime, on sale everywhere, are poignant evidence of its later decline.

ACCOMMODATION

Karnayo ☎ 22460 49266, ⓦ karnayo.gr. A good mid-range choice, off the platía at the west end of the south quay: it's spread over two quiet, sensitively restored buildings, with four double rooms and two studios, one of which sleeps four. **€70**

★ **Kastellorizo Hotel** ☎ 22460 49044, ⓦ kastellorizohotel.gr. Right in the thick of things in the middle of west quay, this boutique hotel has some of the best amenities on the island. Its fourteen individually styled suites have kitchenettes, four have balconies, and there's a Thalasso-spa-pool as well as waterfront lido. Breakfast included. March–Nov. **€130**

Megisti Hotel ☎ 22460 49219, ⓦ megistihotel.gr. Not the friendliest service, but in an unbeatable location at the northwest corner of the harbour, with fabulous views, this hotel has fifteen spotless, attractively decorated rooms plus

four large and very lavish suites (€153). There's great swimming immediately off the spacious patio. Buffet breakfast included. **€90**

Pension Mediterraneo ☎ 22460 4900, ⓦ mediterraneo-kastelorizo.com. Eight simple rooms at the end of the northwest quay, furnished with mosquito nets and wall art. The arcaded waterside basement suite is worth the extra cost for the privilege of being able to roll out the door and into the sea. Breakfast included. **€80**

Poseidon ☎ 22460 49257, ⓦ kastelorizo-poseidon.gr. Five houses converted in a traditional style, set back from the platía at the west end of the south quay, with a total of twenty well-appointed studios, some with balconies It's worth paying the extra €20 for a room with sea view. Includes basic buffet breakfast. **€70**

EATING AND DRINKING

Kastellórizo's harbour quayside is a wonderfully romantic spot to enjoy a leisurely meal, though taverna prices are significantly higher than elsewhere. The island has its own fish, goat meat and wild-fig preserves, and assorted produce is smuggled over from Kaş, but otherwise food and drinking water have to be shipped here from Rhodes. Note that the mains water is contaminated by goat droppings, and tap water on the island is not safe to drink.

★ **Alexandra's** ☎ 22460 49019. Along the waterfront, in a quiet location near the west end of the quay, this taverna serves up grills and salads with four different dishes of the day such as roast lamb (mains around €14.50), plus homemade taramasalata (€3) and hummus (€3). Feb–Nov daily 10am–late.

Radio Café ☎ 22460 49029. Café with great views, close to the ferry jetty, which serves breakfast and lunch dishes such as avocado toast (€5.80) and tuna sandwiches (€6.20). There's free wi-fi. Daily 9am–late.

Ta Platania ☎ 22460 49206. Set well back from the sea, up the hill on the Horáfia platía, this welcoming place is a good option for daily-changing *mayireftá* and desserts, though the prices no cheaper than down by the port – expect to pay around €14 for stifado. June–Sept daily lunch and dinner.

To Mikro Parisi (Little Paris) ☎ 22460 49282. Long-established seafood specialist alongside the port, with tables right on the harbour front – try the succulent soups and stews (€8), meat grills (€9) or kalamári (€12). Daily lunch and dinner.

The rest of the island

Kastellórizo's austere **hinterland** is predominantly bare rock, flecked with stunted vegetation; incredibly, until 1900 this was carefully tended, producing abundant wine of some quality. A rudimentary paved road system links points between Mandhráki and the airstrip, and a dirt track heads towards Áyios Stéfanos, but there are few specific attractions, and no scooters for rent. Karstic cliffs drop sheer to the sea, offering no anchorage except at the main town, Mandhráki and Návlakas fjord (see below).

The shoreline

Swimming on Kastellórizo is made difficult by the total lack of beaches, and the abundance of sea urchins and razor-sharp limestone reefs. Once clear of the **shoreline**, however, you're rewarded by clear waters with a rich variety of marine life, and amphora shards that testify to the ancient wine trade. Many visitors simply dive in from the lidos on the northwest quay; otherwise the safest bathing points near town lie beyond the graveyard at Mandhráki and the cement jetty below the power plant at road's end. **Taxi-boats**, such as Barbara & St. George Boats (☎69778 55756) or Paniniotis Antonis (☎69777 76927), can take you to otherwise inaccessible coves such as **Plákes**, along the western shoreline of the town bay, where

he flat surfaces of a former quarry are equally good for sunbathing on, or
wimming off.

Návlakas fjord and Perastá grotto

Halfway along Kastellórizo's southeastern coast, **Návlakas fjord** is a favourite mooring
spot for yachts and fishing boats. Uniquely for the island, Návlakas is free of sea
urchins. Freshwater seeps keep the temperature brisk, and there's superb snorkelling to
20m depths off the south wall. Another popular stop for boat excursions, a little
further south, is **Perastá grotto** (Galázio Spílio), which deserves a visit for its stalactites
and strange blue-light effects. The low entrance, negotiable only by inflatable raft, gives
little hint of the enormous chamber within, with monk seals occasionally sheltering in
an adjacent cave. Taxi-boats can arrange trips here.

Hálki

The little island of **Hálki**, a waterless limestone speck west of Rhodes, continues to
count as a fully fledged member of the Dodecanese, even if its population has
dwindled from three thousand to barely three hundred in the century since its Italian
rulers imposed restrictions on sponge fishing. Other than in the height of summer,
Hálki tends to be very quiet: that said, in the middle of the day in high season,
day-trippers from Rhodes can vastly outnumber locals in Emborió's broad
quayside-cum-square.

8

ARRIVAL AND DEPARTURE
HÁLKI

By ferry Hálki's port is in Emborió. Zifos Travel sell ferry
tickets (☎ 22460 45028).

Destinations Anáfi (2 weekly; 9hr 50min); Iráklio
(Heraklion), Crete (2 weekly; 7hr 20min); Kárpathos (2
weekly; 2hr 40min); Kássos (2 weekly; 5hr); Kos (2 weekly;

2hr 45min); Níssyros (2 weekly; 1hr 40min); Pireás (2
weekly; 20–24hr); Rhodes Kámiros Skála (daily; 1hr 15min);
Rhodes Town (4 weekly; 1hr 25min–2hr); Santoríni (2
weekly; 11hr 20min); Sítia, Crete (2 weekly; 4hr 10min);
Sými (2 weekly; 2hr 20min); Tílos (2 weekly; 35min).

GETTING AROUND

By bus A sixteen-seat bus shuttles between the
waterfront, Póndamos and Ftenáya (€2) and a

twice-weekly bus runs to the monasteries (€5).

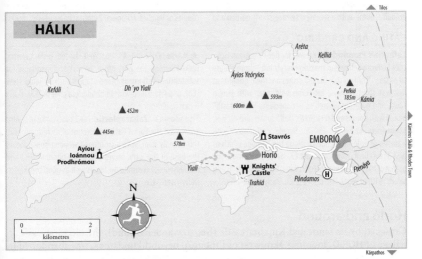

Emborió

With its photogenic ensemble of restored Italianate houses rising from the waterfront, **EMBORIÓ**, facing east towards Rhodes from the head of a large bay, is a sort of miniature version of Sými (see p.545). Hálki's port as well as the only inhabited town, its skyline is pierced by the tallest freestanding **clocktower** in the Dodecanese, as well as – a bit further north – the **belfry** of Áyios Nikólaos, which holds a fine *votsalotó* (pebble-mosaic) courtyard. The **waterfront** has been paved with fieldstones, generally prettified and declared off limits to vehicles in season.

Although there's no **beach** at Emborió, many visitors swim anyway, simply lowering themselves into the water from the quayside or shoreline rocks. If that doesn't suit you, you'll find two beaches within easy walking distance, both equipped with good seaside tavernas. The island's only sandy beach, long narrow **Póndamos**, a fifteen-minute walk west over the hilltop, along the grandly named Tarpon Springs Boulevard, fills with day-trippers in summer. The best alternative, the tiny pebble cove and the gravel sunbed-lido at **Ftenáya**, lies a few minutes south of Emborió, along a signposted path that starts at the end of the harbour; it too can get busy.

Hálki's remotest beaches can be reached either on **boat excursions** from Emborió quay – aboard the *Kristani* (☏69361 16229) – or via demanding **hiking trails**. Experienced walkers can hike from the main harbour to **Aréta fjord**, on the north coast, an impressive, cliff-girt place where seabirds roost and soar. There's some morning and afternoon shade at the small-pebble beach, but only a brackish well for inquisitive sheep, so bring plenty of water: the walk takes about ninety minutes.

8

ACCOMMODATION   EMBORIÓ

Book ahead for accommodation in high season. Some places perch right over the sea with access ladders for swimming.

Admiral's House ☏6937 181 225, ⊛admiralshouse. gr. Two one-bedroomed, adult-only villas, formerly belonging to an admiral, at the end of the harbour. Ladders give direct access into the sea and there's satellite TV; transfers can be arranged from Rhodes airport. Minimum 6 night stay. May–Oct. **€220**

Captain's House ☏6932 511 762. Two delightful en-suite rooms, with a sea-view terrace, shady garden and

the feel of an old French pension. The owner really makes her guests feel at home. April–Oct. **€40**

★**Halkis Muses** ☏6936 676 667, ⊛halkismuses.gr. A selection of seven traditional stone houses (one- and two-bedroomed) along the harbour, some spilling out right onto the water's edge. All are individually designed to a high standard and come with super fast wi-fi. A fantastic spot for couples or families. Minimum 2 night stay. April–Oct. **€90**

EATING AND DRINKING

Lefkosia's Paradosiako Known for her TV appearances, chef Lefkosia believes in making everything – from cheese to pasta – from scratch. Baked dishes are the highlights at her waterfont taverna, including wild goat with lemon sauce and potatoes as well as her speciality "Halki pasta", baked with onions and feta (€18). Daily lunch and dinner.

Magefseis ☏22460 45028. Simple grill house with a cluster of little tables outside along the harbour, which as well as excellent *gyros* for around €7, serves pretty much the gamut of tourist-favoured Greek cuisine; from mixed grills and salads (€10) to vegetarian dishes (€12). Daily noon–late.

★**Maria** ☏22460 45300. Well-shaded little taverna, tucked behind the post office, *Maria's* is dependable for substantial portions of island staples such as lamb stew (€8), or pasta baked with bubbling feta cheese (€7). Daily lunch and dinner.

Theodosia's Zaharoplastio ☏22460 45218. Also known as "The Parrot Café" on account of its resident bird, this friendly joint, with a cushioned wooden bench facing the base of the jetty, serves Greek rice pudding (€4) and homemade ice cream to die for, as well as good breakfasts. Daily 7am–late.

Horió and around

Crowned by its renovated Knights' castle (free to wander around), the old pirate-safe village of **HORIÓ**, looming 3km west of Emborió, beyond Pondamos, was abandoned in he 1950s. Across the valley, little **Stavrós monastery** hosts another big bash on September 14. **Trahiá**, directly below Horió's castle, and served by a very rough path from Yialí, consists of two coves to either side of an isthmus.

There's little else inland, though Tarpon Springs Boulevard continues across the island to the charming monastery of **Ayíou Ioánnou Prodhrómou** (festival Aug 28–29; *kantína* otherwise). The terrain en route is bleak, but gives views over half the Dodecanese and Turkey.

Kássos

The southernmost Dodecanese island, less than 48km northeast of Crete, **KÁSSOS** is very much off the beaten tourist track. Ever since 1824, when an Egyptian fleet punished Kássos for its active participation in the Greek revolution by slaughtering most of the 11,000 Kassiots, the island has remained **barren and depopulated**. Sheer gorges slash through lunar terrain relieved only by fenced smallholdings of midget olive trees; spring grain crops briefly soften usually fallow terraces, and livestock somehow survives on a thin furze of scrub. The remaining population occupies five villages facing Kárpathos, leaving most of the island uninhabited and uncultivated, with crumbling old houses poignantly recalling better days.

ARRIVAL AND INFORMATION

KÁSSOS

By air The island's airport is 1km west of Frý.
Destinations Kárpathos (1–2 daily; 15min); Rhodes, via Karpathos (1–2 daily; 1hr 15min); Sitía, Crete (1–2 daily; 25min).

By ferry The island's port is in Frý, where the main ferry tickets agent is Kasos Maritime & Travel Agency (☎ 22450 41495, ⓦ kassos-island.gr). In addition to the scheduled ferries, excursion boats also run to Frý from tiny Finíki on Kárpathos' west coast (in season; no fixed schedule): the *M/v Kasos Princess* sails roughly three times a week, or as a day-trip to Kárpathos every Wed in season (8.30am–5pm).

Destinations Anáfi (2 weekly; 4hr 30min–10hr 30min); Hálki (3 weekly; 5hr 20min); Iráklio (Heraklion), Crete (2 weekly; 6hr); Karpathós (7 weekly; 1hr 20min); Mílos (1 weekly; 17hr 15min); Pireás (2 weekly; 15–22hr); Rhodes (3 weekly; 7hr 40min); Santoríni (2 weekly; 7–15hr 30min); Sítia, Crete (2 weekly; 2hr 30min).

Tourist information The official island website is ⓦ kasos.gr.

8

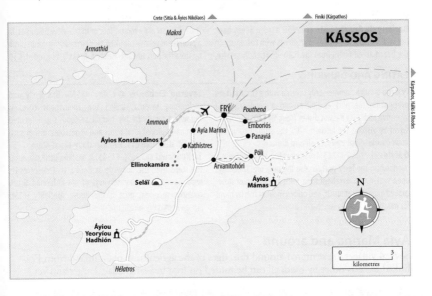

GETTING AROUND

By bus A Mercedes van connects all the island's villages several times daily in summer, for a flat fare of €0.80.

By car and scooter Oasis in Frý rents out cars an scooters (June–Sept; ☎ 22450 41746).

Frý

The capital of Kássos, **FRÝ** (pronounced "free"), is halfway along the island's north coast, with views towards northwest Kárpathos. It's a low-key little place, with most of its appea concentrated in the **Boúka** fishing port, protected by two crab-claws of breakwater and overlooked by Áyios Spyrídhon cathedral. Inland, Frý is engagingly unpretentious, even down-at-heel; there are few concessions to tourism, though some attempts have been made to prettify a scruffy little town that's quite desolate out of season.

There's no **beach** in Frý itself: what's generally regarded as the town beach is the sandy cove at **Ammouá**, a half-hour walk along the coastal track west, beyond the airstrip. The first section you reach is often caked with seaweed and tar, but keep going another five minutes and you'll find cleaner pea-gravel coves. Determined swimmers use the little patch of sand at **Emboriós**, fifteen minutes' walk east from Frý, where there's also a more private pebble stretch off to the right. Once you've got this far, however, it's worth continuing ten minutes along the shore to the base of the **Pouthená ravine**, which cradles another secluded pebble cove.

In high season, boat excursions head to far better beaches on two islets visible to the northwest, **Armáthia** and **Makrá**. Armáthia has five white-sand beaches to choose from, while Makrá has just one large cove. There are no amenities on either islet, so bring all you need.

ACCOMMODATION   FRÝ

Accommodation is very hard to find. Don't leave it until you arrive; be sure to book ahead.

Angelica's ☎ 22450 41268, ⓦ angelicas.gr. Four bright, roomy kitchenette apartments in a converted mansion 200m above Boúka harbour, with traditional furnishings, and some extraordinary floor-paintings by the owner's mother. All have outside space, but only two enjoy sea views. **€60**

Borianoula Apartments ☎ 22450 41495. Seven basic but well-equipped en-suite apartments with balconies, on the beach about 600m from the harbour. Friendly service,

and they offer airport or port pick-up. **€64**

★ **Evita Village** ☎ 22450 41731. Small family-run complex of five impeccable and very spacious modern studios, 200m uphill from Emboriós, with comfortable furnishings and plenty of room to spread out. **€70**

Fantasis Apartments ☎ 22450 41695, ⓦ fantasis -hotel.gr. Six plain rooms, four with sea-view balconies, in a prominent yellow-trimmed modern building, 5min climb up from the port towards Panayía. Breakfast included. **€30**

EATING AND DRINKING

Iy Orea Bouka Summer-only taverna with a small terrace overlooking the port at Boúka, and a good range of inventive and tasty Kassiot dishes (roughly €10) which you select by visiting the kitchen – try the stuffed courgette flower. June–Sept daily lunch and dinner.

O Mylos ☎ 22450 41825. Frý's finest full-service taverna, overlooking the ferry port, is also the only one that stays open year-round. Excellent food, with a selection of slow-cooked *mayireftá* at lunch, and grilled meat or fish by night for roughly €12. Daily lunch and dinner.

Taverna Emborios ☎ 22450 41586. This lively and welcoming taverna, facing the eponymous cove, is renowned for its freshly caught seafood, supplemented with hand-picked local herbs and vegetables: dishes such as lamb stew from €13. Summer daily 11am–2am.

To Koutouki ☎ 22450 41545. A bustling little place, up the steps from the quayside at Boúka, that deserves its reputation for sizeable servings of old-fashioned Greek cooking; succulent goat is the house speciality (€15). June–Sept daily lunch and dinner.

Ayía Marína and around

Several villages are scattered around the edges of the agricultural plain inland from Frý, linked to each other by road; all can be toured on foot in a single day. Larger and yet more rural than Frý, **AYÍA MARÍNA**, 1500m inland and uphill, is best admired from the south, arrayed above olive groves; its two belfried churches are the focus of lively **festivals**, on July 16–17 and September 13–14. Fifteen minutes beyond the hamlet of **Kathístres**, a further 500m southwest, is the cave of **Ellinokamára**, which has a late Classical, polygonal wall blocking the entrance; it may have been a cult shrine or tomb complex.

Ayíou Yeoryíou Hadhión

Between Ayía Marína and Arvanitohóri, a paved road veers southwest towards the rural monastery of **Ayíou Yeoryíou Hadhión**. The entire route is 12km, and best tackled by scooter. Once you've skirted the dramatic gorge early on, you're unlikely to see another living thing aside from goats, sheep or the occasional falcon. Soon the Mediterranean appears; when you reach a fork, take the upper, right-hand turning, following the phone lines. Cistern water is always available in the monastery grounds, which only come to life around the April 23 **festival** (see p.45).

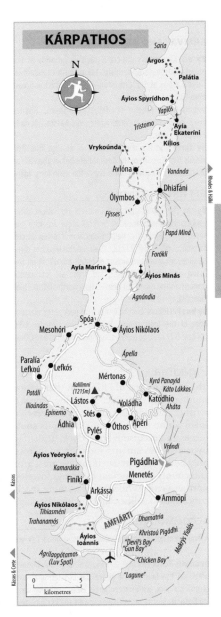

Kárpathos

Despite being the third-largest Dodecanese island, poised halfway between Rhodes and Crete, long, narrow **KÁRPATHOS** has always been a wild and underpopulated backwater. The island's usually cloud-capped mountainous spine, which rises to over 1200m, divides it into two very distinct sections – the low-lying **south**, with its pretty bays and long beaches, and the rugged **north**, where traditional villages nest atop towering cliffs. **Pigádhia**, on the east coast, is Kárpathos' capital and largest port, with a wide range of hotels and a good beach, though it caters mostly for the Scandinavian and German package-holiday crowd. Several smaller resorts, such as **Ammopí**, and isolated coves also hold lovely beachfront accommodation.

Touring Kárpathos' magnificent, windswept **coastline** is consistently superb, with its verdant meadows, high peaks, isolated promontories and secluded **beaches**, lapped by crystalline waters. The **interior**, however, isn't always as alluring: the central and northern forests have been scorched by repeated fires, while agriculture plays a minor role. The Karpathians are too well off to bother much with farming; emigration to North America and the resulting remittances have made this one of Greece's wealthiest islands.

Although the Minoans and Mycenaeans established trading posts on what they called Krapathos, the island's four Classical cities figure little in ancient **history**. Kárpathos was held by the Genoese and Venetians after the Byzantine collapse and so has no castle of the Knights of St John, nor any surviving medieval fortresses of note.

ARRIVAL AND DEPARTURE
KÁRPATHOS

By air Kárpathos's airport is on the flatlands at the island's extreme southern tip, 14km south of Pigádhia. There's a bus at 1.15pm (Mon–Fri), or a taxi will cost from €30 to Pigádhia.

Destinations Athens (1 daily; 1hr 5min); Rhodes (1–2 daily; 40min); Sitía, Crete, via Kássos (1 daily except Fri; 1hr).

By ferry The island's main port is at Pigádhia. One weekly ferry to each of the destinations below also calls at Dhiafáni on Kárpathos's north coast. The main ferry agent

in Pigádhia is Possi Travel (☎22450 22235, ✉possitv@hotmail.com), who also sell day-trips to Hálki by ferry (Tues), and Kássos by air and ferry (Sat).

Destinations Anáfi (2 weekly; 6hr 15min–12hr); Hálki (2 weekly; 2hr 40min); Iráklio (Heraklion), Crete (1 weekly; 7hr 20min); Kássos (2 weekly; 1hr 20min); Kos (1 weekly; 12hr); Mílos (2 weekly; 17hr 30min); Pireás (3 weekly; 21hr); Rhodes (3 weekly; 5hr); Santoríni (2 weekly; 12hr); Samos (1 weekly; 10hr); Sítia, Crete (1 weekly; 4hr 10min).

GETTING AROUND

By car The airport's car rental outlets are Budget/Drive (ⓦkarpathosrentacar.com). Several more agencies are based in Pigádhia; the helpful and competitively priced Euromoto (☎22450 23238, ⓦeuromotokarpathos.com) can deliver cars to the airport or hotels anywhere on the island, and rent quad bikes, too. There are four petrol stations on the island, all immediately north and south of Pigádhia.

By bus Pigádhia's "bus station" is a car park at the western edge of the town centre. Regular buses, run by KTEL (☎22450 22338), go to Pylés, via Apéri, Voládha and Óthos

(3–4 daily); Ammopí (2 daily). Less frequent services run to Menetés, Arkássa, Finíki and Lefkos, with some continuing to Mesohóri; and to Kyrá Panayía, Ápella and Spóa.

By taxi Set-rate, unmetered taxis congregate two blocks inland from the harbour. Typical fares range from €10 to Ammopí up to €42 to Lefkos.

Boat excursions Boat day-trips run regularly from Pigádhia to isolated east-coast beaches. In addition, *Chrisovalandou III* (☎02410 51292) sails to and from Dhiafáni every day, typically leaving Pigádhia at 8.30am and Dhiafáni around 4.30pm (€15 one-way).

Pigádhia

The island capital of **PIGÁDHIA (Kárpathos Town)** lies on the southeast coast, at the southern end of scenic, 3km-long **Vróndi Bay**. The town makes little of its spectacular setting, reaching just one or two streets back from its long curving **waterfront**. All the main action is concentrated along its **southernmost section**. From the jetty where ferries and excursion boats dock, at the far end, the quayside curls north, lined initially by seafood restaurants and then an increasing number of cafés and music bars. The only buildings that catch the eye are a group of stately but fading Italian-era port police and county-government buildings, overlooking the port from a low bluff at its northern end. While there's nothing special to see, Pigádhia does offer most conceivable facilities, albeit with a package-tourism slant.

ACCOMMODATION
PIGÁDHIA

A long line of hotels snakes northwards along Vróndi Bay; you're likely to enjoy Pigádhia more if you stay closer to the harbour.

Amarylis Hotel ☎22450 22375, ⓦamarylis.gr. Budget hotel, on the hillside just above the bus terminal and central car park, with sixteen large, clean, white-washed studios and apartments. All have showers and kitchenettes,

half have sea-view balconies. **€35**

Atlantis Hotel ☎22450 22777, ⓦatlantishotelkarpathos.gr. Welcoming little hotel, with helpful management and pleasant rooms, in a great entral location facing the Italian "palace" just up from the ort. Pay €8 extra for a sea view. **€42**

lectra Beach Hotel ☎ 22450 23256, ℮ electrabeachhotel.gr. Imposing modern hotel a 5min walk along the beach from the harbour. All the small but astefully modernized rooms have balconies with dazzling views of the bay, and there's also a good pool. Usually filled with Scandinavian groups in summer, but bargain low-season rates available. Buffet breakfast included. **€100**

Hotel Alex ☎ 22450 22004, ℮ alexhotel.gr. A traditional Karpathian family hotel with quiet gardens and a pool, 1.5km from the centre of Pigádhia; all 25 clean rooms on two floors have balconies with pool views. Buffet breakfast included. **€55**

EATING AND DRINKING

Mezedhopolio To Ellinikon ☎ 22450 23932. Serving Pigádhia's finest food, this cosy indoor dining room is a block inland from the middle of the harbour. Diners choose daily specials like fabulous stuffed aubergine (€5), or a substantial grilled bream (€12) from the raised kitchen; expect free trimmings such as a rich tapenade. Daily lunch and dinner.

★ **Orea Karpathos** ☎ 22450 22501. Running for over 25 years, the island's best-value restaurant is along the harbour front strip near the southern end – almost nothing costs more than €10. Try *Trahanádhes* soup for €4.50, spicy sausages for €7.50, or marinated artichokes, manouri cheese, great spinach pie and palatable local bulk wine. Locals use it as an ouzerí, ordering just *mezédhes*. April–Oct dinner only.

Sofia's Place ☎ 22450 23152. Sit and watch the life of the port from the terrace of this pretty, bustling and popular restaurant in the heart of the action. Very friendly service and good local seafood such as fried kalamári (€10) plus tasty grilled-meat specials (grilled chicken with choice of sauces) for around €13. Daily noon–late.

The south

Immediately south of Pigádhia, reached by a detour off the main road down the other side of a low headland, the purpose-built resort of **AMMOPÍ** (also known as "Amoopi") is not so much a town as a succession of sand-and-gravel, tree- or cliff-fringed coves. There's no commercial centre to it, but the hotels here make an appealing base for a beachside holiday. Keep going beyond them all to find some delightful little **turquoise bays**, usually deserted except at the height of summer.

Back on the main road, the further south you go, the flatter and more desolate Kárpathos becomes. The long windswept beach that leads all the way down to the airport has become popular with foreign **windsurfers**, who take advantage of the prevailing northwesterlies, especially during the annual summer European championships. As such, different segments are known these days by their windsurfing nicknames, such as Gun Bay. For non-surfers, the best beach here is **Chicken Bay**, a few metres from the airport runway, though it's too exposed to spend a whole day here.

ACTIVTITIES

THE SOUTH

Scuba diving Karpathos offers good scuba diving, with underwater visibility of over 20m and many underground caverns to explore: the best school is Kárpathos Diving Centre (☎ 22450 22860 or ☎ 697 875 3131, ℮ divingkarpathos.gr), who run beginners diving courses up to advanced dives, plus day trips to the tiny northern tip island of Sari.

Windsurfing and kitesurfing The most established windsurf and kitesurf school in southern Kárpathos is Pro Center Kárpathos (☎ 22450 91063 or ☎ 697 788 6289, ℮ chris-schill.com), which uses three separate bays and caters to different abilities. Kitesurfers need to be at expert level, due to the strong winds on this side of the island.

ACCOMMODATION AND EATING

★ **Althea Boutique Hotel** Ammopí ☎ 22450 81152, ℮ altheakarpathos.gr.gr. Ammopí's prime accommodation, these sixteen luxurious apartments have comfortable mattresses and magnificent sweeping sea views from private balconies. Breakfast (included) features local fruits and vegetables (used for omelettes) plus jams. **€120**

Esperida Ammopí ☎ 22450 81002, ℮ esperida.gr. Large, welcoming taverna, set back from the sea halfway down the approach road to Ammopí. Delicious local food, including island cheese, wine and sausage, roast aubergine and pickled wild vegetables. Main dishes around €8, mezes €4. They also have six clean, good-value rooms, and two apartments (€80). Daily breakfast, lunch and dinner. **€50**

Irini Beach Hotel Gun Bay ☎ 22450 91000, ℮ karpathos-windsurfing.gr. Upscale hotel complex on the island's prime windsurfing beach, with large comfortable rooms, a good sized pool and spa. Breakfast included. **€60**

8

The west

Although it's much less developed than the area around Pigádhia, the **western shoreline** of Kárpathos holds several of the island's most attractive **beaches**. Small resorts such as Finíki and Lefkós make great bases for low-key holiday relaxation, amid scintillating scenery.

Arkássa

The main road from Pigádhia reaches the west coast at the little town of **ARKÁSSA**. Hardly anything survives of the original village – the rocky coastal frontage now consists of unremarkable studios and tavernas. Head a few hundred metres south, and you'll come to the signposted side road that leads to the whitewashed chapel of **Ayía Sofía**. Remains of a much larger Byzantine basilica here feature several mosaic floors with geometric patterns.

The finest **beach** hereabouts is also located just south of Arkássa. The broad 100m stretch of good-quality sand known as **Áyios Nikólaos** still feels pleasantly rural, even though a newly built hotel has just joined its long-standing taverna.

Finíki

A couple of kilometres north of Arkássa, facing it from the northern end of a long bay, the even smaller resort of **FINÍKI** is still very recognizable as the fishing village it used to be. A brief detour down from the main road, the port is arrayed along the curve of a minuscule beach, and has several welcoming tavernas. In summer, excursion boats head across from here to Kássos.

Lefkós

To reach the attractive resort of **LEFKÓS** – also known as **Paralía Lefkoú** – take a side turning that drops back down from the main road as it climbs through the dense forest around 10km north of Finíki. While considerably more developed than Finíki, it started out as a fishing village. Its best tavernas are concentrated around the **harbour**, which also holds a great sheltered beach, and accommodation is plentiful too. Several more beaches lie nearby, separated by a striking topography of cliffs, islets and sand spits.

Mesohóri

The main road climbs northeast from Lefkos through the pine forest to the dramatically sited village of **MESOHÓRI**. Tumbling seaward along narrow, stepped alleys, Mesohóri comes to a halt at the edge of a bluff that's dotted with three tiny, ancient chapels, separated from the village proper by extensive orchards.

ACCOMMODATION   **THE WEST**

Arhontiko Studios Finíki ☎22450 61473, ⊛hotelarhontiko.gr. Simple, well-run hotel on the main coast road just above Finíki, where all seven comfortable studios and five larger apartments have sea-view balconies. **€35**

Hotel Krinos Lefkos ☎22450 71410, ⊛krinoshotelkarpathos.com. Low-rise complex, just before the road reaches the town centre, that's popular with returning German guests. All its rooms, studios and apartments are en-suite and have either balcony or terrace. Breakfast included. March–Oct. **€40**

★**Lefkorama Hotel** Lefkos ☎22450 71173, ⊛lefkorama.gr. Cute family-run hotel with ten simple, well-equipped rooms plus two apartments; it's in a peaceful location in the pine forest, but walking distance from the beach. Homemade breakfast with local produce included. **€45**

Pine Tree Ádhia ☎6977 369 948, ⊛pinetree-karpathos.gr. Simple rooms in a gorgeous rural location, with long-range sea views a short walk up the hillside from the *Pine Tree Restaurant* (see opposite). A little higher up is a lovely stand-alone studio, with traditional sleeping platform, and there's free camping. There's no wi-fi. Breakfast included (except for campers). **€35**

EATING AND DRINKING

★**Delfini** Finíki ☎22450 61060. Finíki's finest waterfront taverna, with a shady patio right by the beach. All vegetables are from the family's garden, cheese is made by the owner's mother and olive oil grown and harvested by the family. Seafood is the speciality, for example mixed seafood grill for €18.50 but also meat dishes such as curry hicken (€9.50). They also rent two small rooms above the averna (€30). Daily lunch and dinner.

hramoundana 1 Mesohóri ☎ 22450 71373. The est food in this hillside village, but fiendishly difficult o find; it's near the church of Panayía Vryssianí, low own at the far north end. A couple of outdoor tables njoy fabulous views, but the food is the main attraction – capers, sausages, home-made *dolmádhes* and marinated "sardines" cost around €15 per person. Daily unch and dinner.

ilaros Áyios Nikólaos, Arkássa ☎ 22450 61015, ⓦ glarosstudios-karpathos.com. Five tastefully furnished,

good-value studios beside one of Kárpathos' best beaches. The returned Karpathian-Virginian hosts also run the open-air *Glaros* beach taverna, with grilled meat dishes for €8.50, or Karpathos spaghetti for €6.50. Daily 8am–late. €70

Pine Tree Restaurant Ádhia ☎ 6977 369 948, ⓦ pinetree-karpathos.gr. Delightful, isolated restaurant, set amid orchards and lush gardens, just up from the sea, 7km north of Finíki. Relax on the flower-decked terrace and sample such delights as stifádo (€12) baked in the outside oven, washed down by sweet Óthos wine. Daily noon–8pm.

The centre

Central Kárpathos supports a group of villages blessed with commanding hillside settings, ample running water and a cool climate, even in August. Nearly everyone here has "done time" in North America before returning home with their nest eggs; the area is said to have the highest per capita income in Greece.

You're more likely to take a driving tour through the interior than to spend much time in any one place. Villages to look out for include **ÓTHOS**, which is the highest (around 400m) and the chilliest, on the flanks of 1215m Mount Kalilímni, and is noted for its bread, sausages and sweet, tawny-amber wine. **VOLÁDHA**, downhill to the east, cradles a tiny Venetian citadel, while the most attractive, **PYLÉS**, faces west atop a steeply switchbacking road that branches from the main west-coast road 6km north of Finíki.

The north

Despite the now fully asphalted road north from Spóa, the hairpin route remains a frightening prospect for all but the hardiest mountain drivers, and **Northern Kárpathos** still feels very much a world apart. Most visitors, therefore, still arrive by boat at the little port of **Dhiafáni**, and then take a bus up to the traditional hilltop village of **Ólymbos**. All the beaches in northern Kárpathos are pebbly, but don't let that put you off.

Spóa

The gateway to northern Kárpathos, where the road to Ólymbos branches off the main circle-island road, is the village of **SPÓA**, just east of the island's central spine. No road enters the village itself. If you're heading this way along the east coast, you might prefer to take a break at the best beach in these parts, down at **Ápella**, though from the taverna at the road's end you still have to walk a short pathway to reach the scenic 300m gravel strand.

Dhiafáni

The sleepy seafront village of **DHIAFÁNI** only springs to life twice a week, when its rare mainline ferries – one heading towards Rhodes, the other towards Crete – call in. Otherwise, the daily excursion boats from Pigádhia (see p.540) keep a low-key tourist industry – including several tavernas – ticking along.

Dhiafáni itself has a reasonable fringe of shingle beach, and there's a quieter alternative at **Vanánda** cove; follow the signposted path north through the pines for thirty minutes, short cutting the road. Naturist beach **Papá Miná**, with a few trees and cliff shade, lies an hour's walk south via the cairned trail which starts from the road by the ferry dock.

8

HIKING IN NORTHERN KÁRPATHOS

Northern Kárpathos is renowned for excellent **hiking**. The most popular walk follows the jeep track down from Ólympos to the superb west-coast beach at **Fýsses**, a sharp drop below the village, while most local trails head more gently north or east, on waymarked paths.

Ólymbos to Dhiafáni An easy ninety-minute walk leads down to Dhiafáni, starting just below the two working windmills. The way is well marked, with water twenty minutes along, and eventually drops to a ravine amid extensive forest.

Ólymbos to Vrykoúnda Heading north from Ólymbos, it takes around an hour and a half to reach sparsely inhabited Avlóna, set on a high upland devoted to grain. From there, less than an hour of descending first moderately, then steeply, along an ancient walled-in path, will bring you to the ruins and beach at Vrykoúnda. Once you've seen the Hellenistic/Roman masonry courses and rock-cut tombs here, and the remote cave-shrine of John the Baptist on the promontory (focus of a major Aug 28–29 festival), there's good swimming in the pebble coves to one side.

Avlóna to Trístomo Starting just above Avlóna, a magnificent cobbled path leads in two and a half hours, via the abandoned agricultural hamlets of Ahordhéa and Kílios, to Trístomo, a Byzantine anchorage in the far northeast of Kárpathos. The views en route, and the path itself, are the thing; Trístomo itself is dreary, with not even a beach.

Trístomo to Vanánda If you've hiked to Trístomo, and would prefer not to retrace your steps to Avlóna, you can hook up, via a shortish link trail east from Trístomo, with a spectacular coastal path back to Vanánda (3hr 30min). Once clear of abandoned agricultural valleys and over a pine-tufted pass, it's often a corniche route through the trees, with distant glimpses of Dhiafáni and no real challenge except at the steep rock-stairs known as Xylóskala.

8

Ólymbos

Founded in Byzantine times as a refuge from pirates, the windswept village of **ÓLYMBOS** straddles a long ridge below slopes studded with ruined windmills. Isolated for centuries, the villagers speak a unique dialect, with traces of its Doric and Phrygian origins. Their home has long attracted foreign and Greek ethnologists for **traditional dress**, **crafts**, **dialect and music** that have vanished elsewhere in Greece. Here too the traditions are dwindling by the year; only the older women, or those who work in the tourist shops, still wear the striking, colourful clothing. Live folk music is still played regularly, especially at festival times (Easter and Aug 15), when visitors have little hope of finding a bed.

Women still play a prominent role in daily life, however: tending gardens, carrying goods on their shoulders or herding goats. Nearly all Ólymbos men historically emigrated to Baltimore or work outside the village, sending money home and returning only on holidays.

ACCOMMODATION AND EATING

THE NORTH

DHIAFÁNI

★**Gorgona** ☎22450 51509. Behind the seafront fountain, this Italian-run place is a favourite local rendezvous, with dishes such as spaghetti seafood (€13), wonderful desserts such as tiramisu (€5), proper coffees and *limoncello* digestif. Daily 9am–late.

★**Hotel Studios Glaros** ☎22450 51501. Run by the welcoming George and Anna Niotis, these twenty top-of-the-range units, some of which sleep four and all with sea views, are ranged in tiers up the southern slope of the cliffs. Breakfast with local products included. **€40**

Maistrali Studios ☎22450 51020, ⓦmaistralikarpathos.gr. Centrally located above the *Gorgona* restaurant, these seven a/c and en-suite rooms,

plus one apartment, offer a simple yet comfortable place to stay, within short walking distance of Dhiafáni's beach. **€30**

ÓLYMBOS

Hotel Aphrodite ☎22450 51307, ⓦdiscoverolympos.com. Small hotel with just four spacious self-catering double rooms, one of which has a kitchen. All have phenomenal views to the windmills and the sea. **€40**

Hotel Astro ☎22450 51421. Smart rooms with traditional furnishings and a warm welcome from its owners – the two sisters who run *Café-Restaurant Zefiros* on the other side of the village, where breakfast (included) is taken. **€35**

ension Olymbos ☎ 22450 51009. This friendly little
lace, near the village entrance, has modern units with
aths, as well as ones with traditional furnishings such
s platform beds. It also has an excellent, inexpensive
estaurant, specializing in traditional home cooking and
with some unusual shellfish dishes (from €12). **€30**

ÁVLONA

Restaurant Avlona ☎ 22450 51046. This offshoot of
the restaurant at *Pension Olymbos* (see above) lies on a spur
road away from the Dhiafáni–Ólymbos road. The signature
dish is *makaroúnes*, home-made pasta with onions and
cheese (€12). **Daily lunch and dinner.**

Sými

For sheer breathtaking beauty, the Greek islands can offer nothing to beat arriving at
SÝMI. While the island as a whole is largely barren, its one significant population centre,
Sými Town is gorgeous, a magnificent steep-walled bay lined with Italian-era mansions.
  With its shortage of fresh water and relative lack of sandy beaches, Sými has never
developed a major tourist industry. Sými Town, however, is an upmarket destination,
with a range of small hotels and abundant delightful rental properties, while
day-trippers from Rhodes – and yachties lured by the enticing harbour – mean it can

8

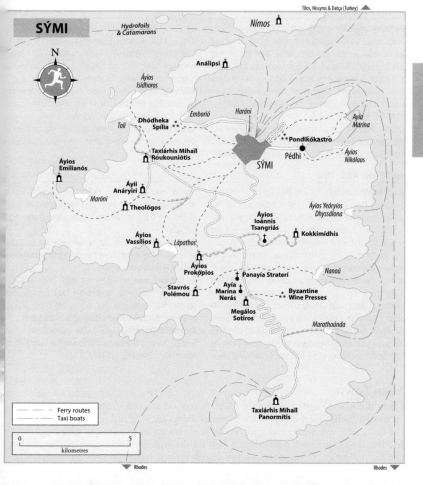

support some very good restaurants too. In the height of summer, it can get uncomfortably crowded, with a large influx of Italian visitors as well as mainland Greeks, but in **spring and autumn** it's wonderful, and even in winter a substantial expat community keeps many businesses open.

Visitors who venture beyond the inhabited areas find an attractive island that has retained some **forest** of junipers, valonea oaks and even a few pines – ideal walking country in the cooler months. Dozens of tiny, privately owned **monasteries** dot the landscape; though generally locked except on their patron saint's day, freshwater cisterns are usually accessible. Near the southern tip of the island, the much larger monastery of **Taxiárhis Mihaïl Panormítis** is an important pilgrimage destination.

Little more than a century ago, Sými Town was home to more people than Rhodes Town, thanks to the wealth generated by its twin ancient skills of **shipbuilding** and **sponge diving**. Many of the **mansions** built during that age of prosperity have long since tumbled into decay – a process hastened in September 1944, when an ammunition blast set off by the retreating Germans levelled hundreds of houses up in Horió. While restoration is gradually bringing them back to life, the scattered **ruins** lend the island an appealing sense of time-forgotten mystery.

ARRIVAL AND INFORMATION   SÝM

By ferry Larger ferries dock at the main harbour in Sými Town, while smaller ferries dock at the new harbour just out of town on the road to Emborió. Most ferries from Rhodes to Sými Town also call in at Panormítis monastery, at the island's southern tip; only the *Proteus* sails from Sými Town to Panormítis, three times weekly. Tickets can be bought from Sými Tours on the harbourfront (☎ 22460 71307, ⓦ symitours.com).

Destinations Astypálea (1 weekly; 9hr); Hálki (2 weekly; 2hr 20min); Kálymnos (9 weekly; 2hr 10min–6hr 20min); Kastellórizo (3 weekly; 3hr 20min–6hr); Kos (7 weekly;

1hr 30min–4hr 50min); Léros (6 weekly; 3hr 20min–5h 50min); Lipsí (6 weekly; 3hr 45min–7hr); Níssyros (weekly; 3–4hr); Pátmos (6 weekly; 5hr 10min–8hr 10min) Pireás (2 weekly; 17–21hr); Rhodes (3–4 daily; 50min–1h 40min); Tílos (3 weekly; 1hr 30min–3hr 10min).

Information Sými Visitor, based above *Pahos* café by th taxi-boat jetty, sells books and maps of local interest, an runs its own website, ⓦ symivisitor.com.

Tours Sými Tours (see above) operates regular trips i season to the Byzantine Wine Press and Panormíti monastery.

GETTING AROUND

Boat excursions Between late May and late Sept, taxi-boats from Yialós harbour run to the east-coast beaches (see p.549), and north to Emborió (see p.547). In August, with several boats a day it's possible to beach-hop; in lower season, pick a single day-trip destination. Fares range up to €14 for the round-trip to Marathoúnda. Larger boats offer round-island cruises in summer, with snorkelling and picnic stops, or day-trips to Turkey, for around €40. You can also take a day-trip to Kastellórizo aboard the *Dodekanisos Express* catamaran (Mon only; €36; ⓦ 12ne.gr). On Saturdays, the same catamaran makes a day-trip to Datca in Turkey; excursion boats also run there in summer (no fixed schedule).

By bus A year-round bus service operates from a tiny car park on the south side of the harbour. A coach shuttles at

regular intervals between Yialós and Pédhi via Horió while a minibus makes two or three round-trips daily all the way south to Panormítis monastery (both €1.5C flat fare).

By taxi Sými's six taxis, based alongside the bus stop serve the entire island. Expect to pay €8 to get between Yialós and Horió with baggage.

By car and scooter There's not much point renting a vehicle on Sými, with its minimal road network, but should you want one, try Glaros (☎ 22460 71926, ⓦ glarosrentacar.gr) or Sými Tours (ⓦ symitours.com).

By tourist train Every hour a little red tourist train runs from the harbour to Emborió (Nimborió) Bay (11am–4pm; 40min; €6; children €3; ☎ 6941 474 514).

Sými Town

SÝMI, the island's capital and only town, is arrayed around a superb natural harbour in an east-facing inlet on the island's north shore. Inter-island ferries arrive right in the heart of town, while excursion boats jostle for room in summer with mighty Mediterranean cruisers. Immediately behind the straight-line quaysides that enclose the main segment of the port, scattered with sponge stalls and souvenir stores, a row f **Italian-era mansions** clings to the foot of the hillsides. Each is painted in a palette of ochres, terracotta, cream or the occasional pastel blue, and topped by a neat triangular pediment and roof of ochre tiles. The hills are steep enough that the houses seem to stand one above the other, to create a gloriously harmonious ensemble.

The lower level of the town, known as **Yialós**, extends northwards to incorporate the smaller curving **Haráni Bay**. Traditionally this was the island's shipbuilding area, and you'll still see large wooden boats hauled out of the water. Yialós also stretches some way inland from the head of the harbour, beyond the main town square, which is used for classical and popular Greek performances during the summer-long **Sými Festival**.

On top of the high hill on the south side of the port, the old village of **Horió** stands aloof from the tourist bustle below. It's hard to say quite where Yialós ends and Horió begins, however; the massive **Kalí Stráta** stair-path, which climbs up from the harbour, is lined with grand mansions, even if some are no more than owl-haunted shells. Another similar stairway, the **Katarráktes**, climbs the west side of the hill, from further back in Yialós, but it's more exposed, and used largely by locals.

Horió

As the 350-plus steps of Kali Stráta deter most day-trippers from attempting to reach Horió, the old hilltop village makes a great refuge whenever Yialós is too hot or crowded. It too holds its fair share of Italianate splendours and impressive basilicas. Once you venture away from the main pedestrian lane, it can be quite a tangle to explore – the part you can see from the harbour is just a small portion of the village, which stretches a long way back above Pédhi Bay. At the very pinnacle of things, a **Knights' castle**, largely destroyed by the wartime explosion, occupies the site of Sými's ancient acropolis; you may glimpse a stretch of Classical polygonal wall on one side. The **church of the Assumption**, inside the fortifications, is a modern replacement. One of the bells in the new belfry is the nose cone of a thousand-pound bomb, hung as a memorial.

Folk Museum

Horió • Summer Tues–Sun 8.30am–2pm; winter closed • €2

A series of arrows leads deep into Horió to the excellent local **Folk Museum**. Housed in a fine old mansion, its collection highlights Byzantine and medieval Sými, particularly frescoes in isolated, often locked churches. Displays continue in the eighteenth-century **Hatziagapitos mansion** below, with superb carved wooden chests and allegorical wall paintings.

Beaches

There's no **beach** in Sými Town. Some visitors clamber into the sea from the harbour wall in Haráni Bay, but neither there nor at the tiny, man-made **Sými Paradise** "beach", around the headland beyond Haráni, is the water clean enough for swimming to be advisable.

Keep walking along the paved coast road from Haráni, however – there's no shade, but the stunning views more than compensate, and there's seldom any traffic – and in around half an hour you'll come to quiet **Emborió** (Nimborió) Bay. The beach is just a narrow strip of coarse shingle, but it's a great place to swim, snorkel and eat at the friendly taverna. In summer, the beach is served by regular taxi-boats and the tourist train (see opposite).

ACCOMMODATION

SÝMI TOWN

Albatros Marketplace, Yialós ☎ 22460 71707, ⓦ www .albatrosymi.gr. This classy little hotel has four rooms, an attractive second-floor breakfast salon and distant sea views. The website can also book a number of magnificent apartments in Neoclassical villas. April–Nov. Breakfast included. **€45**

8

★**Emporio Symi** Emborió ☎69573 02565, ⓦemporiosymi.com. A boutique B&B in Emborió, with five rooms and two suites in landscaped gardens with views to the sea. A shuttle bus runs the 2km to Symi Harbour and guests can use the amenities of its sister hotel, *The Old Markets* (see below). Breakfast included. **€175**

Fiona Near the top of the Kalí Stráta, Horió ☎22460 72088, ⓦfionahotel.com. The large, simply furnished but attractive and airy rooms upstairs at this village hotel enjoy stunning views and have small balconies. There are also three studios next door. Breakfast, on the terrace, is included. April to mid-Oct. **€50**

Hotel Chorio Horió ☎22460 71800, ⓦhotelchorio.gr. A short walk from *George & Maria's* taverna (see below), these five rooms all have balconies, some with lovely views over the harbour. Buffet breakfast included. April to mid-Oct. **€55**

Nireus Hotel Yialós ☎22460 72400, ⓦnireus-hotel.gr. Sými's most conspicuous hotel, in prime position near the clocktower at the harbour entrance, with a lovely waterfront bar and restaurant. The stunning sea views from the adequate but unexceptional seafront rooms just about justify the high prices; don't even consider the cheaper rear-facing ones. April to mid-Oct. **€120**

Niriides Apartments Emborió ☎22460 71784, ⓦniriideshotel.com. Ten simply furnished, spacious and quiet rental units, spread over five hillside buildings above the beach at Emborió, 2km north of Yialós. All sleep four and have a/c; friendly management and on-site

"lounge-café", with a good taverna immediately below. Breakfast included. **€115**

★**The Old Markets** Not far up the Kali Stráta, Yialó ☎22460 71440, ⓦtheoldmarkets.com. Boutique B& in an imposing and very elegant converted mansion, wit magnificent harbour views and an indoor plunge pool. Th seven rooms and three suites are luxuriously furnishe Includes breakfast made from local produce. May to mid Oct. **€190**

Opera House Yialós platía ☎22460 72034 ⓦsymioperahouse.gr. This large complex, a short wa inland from Yialós' main square, consists of severa separate houses, newly built in traditional style. They'r divided into apartments for two to six people; all hav balconies, though few have views. The rates are low fo the amount of space you get, especially off-seaso Includes breakfast. **€70**

★**Symi Thea** Yialós ☎22460 72559, ⓦsymi-thea.g These five traditional-style apartments, furnished wit local antiques, are housed in a renovated old family hous with great harbour views. The Mother-and-son owner ensure a real personal service, with a basic breakfas provided in-room. April–Nov. **€100**

Sými Visitor Accommodation ☎22460 71785 ⓦsymivisitor.com. Rents out restored private homes i Yialós and Horió, ranging from simple studios to famil mansions. They also offer a laundry service for an extr charge. Two-person property **€85**, four-person **€115**

EATING AND DRINKING

CAFÉ-BARS

Bar Tsati Haráni quay ☎22460 72498. You can't get any closer to the water than this friendly Italian-run little café-bar, a short walk from the clocktower around Haráni bay. A cluster of pastel-coloured tables and chairs in a harbourfront nook, plus cushions on the sea wall itself. Proper Italian espresso and tasty titbits, and a lively late-night scene. Daily 11am–1am or later.

Evoi Evan Yialós platía. Sprawling beneath the spreading ficus trees, with a cavernous interior that includes a pool table upstairs, *Evoi Evan* serves coffee, smoothies and juices first thing, and a full drinks menu later on. Daily 8am–late.

★**The Olive Tree** Horió ☎22460 72681. Friendly English-run café, across from the *Fiona* hotel (see above), with fantastic views over the harbour below. Enjoy free wi-fi, top-quality coffee and home-made cakes, excellently priced juices and smoothies, good sandwiches (hummus and roasted vegetables; €4.80) and healthy breakfasts. Daily 8.30am–3.30pm.

Pahos Yialós. Classic *kafenío*, little changed since it opened during World War II. Facing the west quay south of Yialós bridge, it's still the spot for an evening ouzo or coffee and people-watching. Pahos himself has retired but can sometimes be found sitting out front as a customer. Daily 8am–late.

Porte Cafe Yialós ☎6944 974 398. Popular little café bar in a great location right on the harbour – enjoy a frappe or beer with pizza (€10), as you watch the yachts come in Daily April–Nov 8am–late.

★**The Secret Garden** Pédhi ☎22460 72153. Michali and Katya run a lovely establishment, tucked away in a courtyard garden but well signposted on the road to Pédh beach. Breakfasts such as Katya's eggy-bread (€5), plu delicious aubergine and feta casserole (€6) in the evening guarantee a repeat clientele of both expats and locals Occasional music nights in the summer. Daily 9am–late.

Sunrise Café/Anatoli Iliou Horió ☎22460 72720 Cosy English/Austrian-run café, on the eastern edge of Horió. Well-priced drinks, breakfasts, good salads and light snack (home-made apple cake, €5), plus a courtyard with a boo swap. Daily mornings, plus afternoons after siesta–late.

RESTAURANTS

George & Maria's Top of Kalí Stráta, Horió. Jolly, much-loved Sými institution, with a pebble-mosaic courtyard. Expect to be invited to inspect the pots in the kitchen before choosing – perennial dishes include feta-stuffed peppers (€8), beans with sausage (€9) and lemon chicken (€10). Dinner daily, plus random lunchtimes in season.

ythos South quay, Yialós ☎ 22460 71488. This dinner-nly, harbour-view roof terrace near the bus stop serves me of the tastiest food on the island. Chef-owner Stavros' ecialities include *psaronéfri* with mushrooms and sweet ine sauce (€15), lamb *stifádho* and feta *saganáki* in fig uce (€12). Best is the phenomenal meze menu, with aring dishes such as scallops in cheese sauce (€16). Late ay to late Sept daily 7.30–11pm.

Pantelis Yialós ☎ 6977 261 710. Pantelis' father is a sherman so, unsurprisingly, *Pantelis* is predominantly a afood restaurant. Sit outside and watch the harbour ustle over dishes such as swordfish (€16) or garlic prawns €19). Daily Lunch and Dinner.

averna Zoi Top of Kalí Stráta, Horió. This delightful cal taverna is run by the lovely Zoi who serves up delicious home-made dishes such as chicken with orange and lemon sauce (€9) and "Granny's *dolmádhes*" (€7.50). Daily noon–3pm & 7–11pm.

Tholos Haráni quay ☎ 22460 70203. The last restaurant you come to as you walk around Haráni bay, with waterside tables laid out right on the headland. A fabulously romantic spot for a fine meal of grilled fresh fish (around €15 per head); the cheese-topped aubergine is pretty good too (€12.50). May–Oct daily lunch and dinner.

Trata Platía Trata, Yialós ☎ 22460 71411. This lively, very informal local hangout fills most of the small square at the foot of the Kalí Stráta. The fresh seafood is great, or simply see what delights – especially vegetable dishes such as briam (€8) – may be lurking in the kitchen. Daily 9am–late.

he rest of the island

Away from Sými Town, the only other settlements on the island are little **Pédhi**, on the horeline below Horió, and **Panormítis** down at the southern tip. The main attractions or visitors are isolated pebbly **beaches** that stand at the heads of the deeply indented ays along the eastern coast – accessible by taxi-boat in summer – and the tiny cattered **monasteries** that make great targets for hikers.

Pédhi

The indented bay lying south of Sými Town, on the far side of the ridge that stretches away from Horió, is home to the pretty little community of **PÉDHI**. Originally a fishing hamlet with a sideline in boatbuilding, Pédhi has slowly expanded over the past twenty ears. Much of the waterfront is now lined with new houses built in the standard talian-influenced Sými style, and there's a hotel and a couple of tavernas – but no beach. About a thirty-minute walk down the hillside from Horió, it's also served by regular buses.

Ayía Marína

A small indentation in the headland that separates Sými Town from Pédhi Bay, known as **Ayía Marína**, has been developed as a miniature beach. With wonderful turquoise vater, and a monastery-capped islet within easy swimming distance just offshore, it's an attractive spot, but in summer it tends to fill up (largely with Italians) the moment the ay's first taxi-boat arrives. The waterfront is an unbroken row of sunbeds, and the one averna does a brisk trade.

It's possible to beat the crowds by walking here, either along a paint-splodge-marked path from Pédhi or over the top of the ridge from the east end of Horió, but the best ime to hike is in low season, when the taxi-boats aren't running and you may have the place to yourself.

Áyios Nikólaos

An exposed fifteen-minute footpath along the south side of Pédhi Bay – simply push your way through the gate at the end of the quayside, then follow the cairns along the slope – leads to **Áyios Nikólaos**, the only all-sand cove on Sými. Also served by regular taxi-boats in season, this offers sheltered swimming, shady tamarisks, a bar, beach volleyball and a relaxing taverna.

Áyios Yeóryios Dhyssálona

The first significant bay to interrupt Sými's eastern coastline south of Pédhi is **Áyios Yeóryios Dhyssálona**. This spectacular fjord can only be accessed by boat, as no path

HIKING ON SÝMI

Sými is an extremely popular **hiking** destination. With midsummer temperatures high even by Greek-island standards, spring and autumn are much the best seasons to come. Most trails lead through depopulated and waterless areas, so you need good equipment and provisions, and ideally relevant experience. Lance Chilton's *Walks in Sými*, sold locally with his *Walker's Map of Sými*, is a very good investment for all hikers.

One excellent trail takes three hours (one way) to cross the island from Yialós to its westernmost tip, where the tiny monastery of **Áyios Emilianós** is tethered to the mainland by a slender causeway. Some of the route runs through forest. Along the way, you'll pass Sými's oldest monastery, **Taxiárhis Mihaïl Roukouniótis** (daily 9–11am & 5–6pm), which contains naive eighteenth-century frescoes. For a shorter walk, you can drop down a dirt track from the monastery to reach small, pebbly **Tolí Bay**, which has a summer-only taverna. An eastward trail over the hilltop from there drops down to **Emborió**, to complete a potential loop back to Yialós.

Another meaty hike crosses the island from Horió in ninety minutes to the scenic **Áyios Vassílios** gulf; for the final forty minutes, follow a paint-splodge-marked path from the road's end. Immediately above **Lápathos beach** is a little monastery, which has some interesting frescoes and accessible water.

The finest frescoes on the island are at the hilltop, **Kokkimídhis monastery** (usually open) dating from 1697, where a complete cycle shows the acts of the Archangel and the risen Christ; it's reached by a steep track off the Panormítis road

It's also possible to hike from Horió to **Nanoú beach** (see below) in around three hours. That leaves you with time for a meal and swim before catching the boat back to Yialós. Alternatively, as the route leads first to the chapel at **Panayía Stateri** on the main road, you could take a scooter that far then walk the final 45 minutes, through a scenic forested gorge, down to the beach.

8

could find a foothold in the smooth limestone that soars at its inland end. There's no taverna, and the whole place falls into shade in the early afternoon.

Nanoú

The largest east-coast bay, **Nanoú**, holds the most popular beach for boat-trippers. A 200m stretch of gravel, sand and small pebbles, with a scenic backdrop of pines, it offers good snorkelling, and has a decent, seafood-strong **taverna**. Nanoú isn't on a paved road, but it is possible to hike down here, from the main trans-island road (see box, above).

Marathoúnda

The southernmost taxi-boat stop, **Marathoúnda**, is a magnificent bay, fringed by a long beach of coarse pebbles and ideal for tranquil swimming. It's also accessible via a paved road, which branches off the main road just after it switchbacks down from the island's central spine towards the monastery at Panormítis. Just back from the beach, the valley floor is flat enough to support a few fields, as well as goats who regularly stroll along the waterfront in search of titbits.

Taxiárhis Mihaïl Panormítis monastery

Museums daily 8.30am–2pm & 3–4pm • €1.50 combined admission

In summer, at least one daily inter-island ferry, plus countless excursion boats from Rhodes, call in at the large **Taxiárhis Mihaïl Panormítis monastery**, located in a gorgeous (albeit beachless), almost entirely closed bay in the far south of Sými. You can also get here by road, on one of the daily buses that heads down from Yialós. A shop, bakery and simple taverna cater to the needs of day-trippers.

Built in honour of the Archangel Michael (*Taxiárhis* in Greek), patron saint of the island, the monastery was thoroughly pillaged during World War II, so – except for

ts lofty belfry – don't expect much of the building or its contents. Away from its
pruce main **courtyard**, which has an attractive pebble-mosaic floor, most of the
omplex is gently fading. Lit by an improbable number of oil lamps, the central
atholikón is also graced by a fine *témblon* and the cult icon, though the frescoes are
nremarkable.

The monastery courtyard contains two small **museums**. One, devoted to artefacts related
o the monastery's religious significance, contains a strange mix of precious antiques, exotic
unk, and votive offerings including bodybuilding and motocross trophies. A small boat is
iled with messages-in-bottles carried here by the Aegean currents – the idea is that if the
ottle or toy boat arrives, the sender's prayer is answered. In the opposite corner, a folklore
nuseum holds displays on costumes, weaving, and domestic activities.

ACCOMMODATION AND EATING
THE REST OF THE ISLAND

Symi Residences Pédhi ☎22460 72300, ⊕asymi
gr. Gorgeous boutique-style waterfront apartment
omplex with balconies and sea views; the fourteen
lean, sleek apartments sleep 2–4 people. Breakfast
ncluded. **€100**

Apostolis Pédhi ☎22460 72221. Great location on the
waterfront, this family-run taverna – popular with locals
– serves up simple fare such as pork or chicken kebabs

(€7.50) plus larger seafood dishes (kalamári €9). June to
end Oct daily 10am–late.
★**Taverna** Marathoúnda. Run by the Kalodoukas family
and supplied with fresh organic produce from their
adjoining fields, this excellent waterfront taverna offers
top-quality mezes such as stuffed peppers for around €8, or
beautifully prepared fish from around €12.50. Mid-May to
mid-Sept daily lunch and dinner.

Tílos

8

Stranded midway between Kos and Rhodes, the small, usually quiet island of **TÍLOS**
s among the least frequented and most unpredictably connected of the Dodecanese.
For visitors, however, it's a great place to relax on the beach, or hike in the
craggy hinterland.

Tílos shares the characteristics of its closest neighbours: limestone **mountains** like
hose of Hálki, plus volcanic lowlands, pumice beds and red-lava sand as on

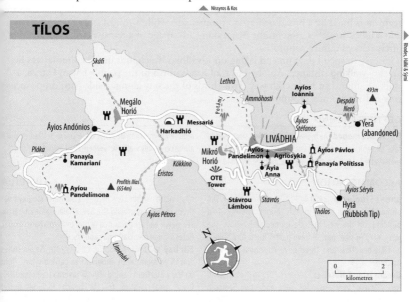

Níssyros. With ample groundwater and rich volcanic soil, the islanders could afford to turn their backs on the sea, and made Tílos the **breadbasket** of the Dodecanese. Until the 1970s, travellers were greeted by the sight of shimmering fields of grain bowing in the wind. Nowadays, the hillside terraces languish abandoned, and the population of five hundred dwindles to barely a hundred in winter.

While recent development has turned the port of **Livádhia** ever more towards tourism, Tílos remains low-key. This is still a place where you can get away from it all: **walkers** can explore several small Knights' **castles** studding the crags, or stumble on some of the inconspicuous, often frescoed **medieval chapels** that cling to the hillsides. Tílos also has a reputation as Greece's greenest island and plans to become the first Mediterranean island to run totally off renewable energy by 2018.

ARRIVAL AND INFORMATION

By ferry The island's port is at Livádhia; buy ferry tickets from Stefanakis, close to the jetty (☎ 22460 44310, ⓦ tilos-travel.com).

Destinations Astypálea (1 weekly; 7hr 15min); Hálki (2 weekly; 45min); Kálymnos (4 weekly; 5hr 30min); Kastellórizo (2 weekly; 6hr 35min–10hr); Kos (4 weekly; 2–3hr); Níssyros (4 weekly; 50min); Pireás (2 weekl; 14–19hr); Rhodes (7 weekly; 1hr 20min–2hr 15min); Sýn (2 weekly; 1hr 30min–3hr 10min).

Maps The best maps on Tílos are published by SKA Purchase from any supermarket.

GETTING AROUND

By bus A blue-and-white bus, charging €1.50, links Livádhia and Megálo Horió, to coincide with ferry arrivals. It also makes up to five runs daily between Livádhia and the beaches at Áyios Andónios and Éristos, plus a €4 round trip to Ayíou Pandelímona monastery o Sun mornings.

By car and scooter Iris Rent a Car (☎ 6972 842 665) an Drive (☎ 22460 44173) in Livádhia.

Livádhia

At its core, the port-cum-resort of **LIVÁDHIA**, at the head of a splendid bay on the island's north shore, is still recognizable as a traditional harbourfront village. The entire seafront is lined by a broad pedestrian promenade, while a row of little tavernas, hotels and studios stretches away to the east, taking advantage of a narrow strip of beach that offers relaxed family swimming.

It's easy to spend days on end lazing on Livádhia's beach, but quieter alternatives lie an easy **walking** distance. An obvious trail heads north to the pebble bay of **Lethrá**, a walk of around an hour each way. Two-thirds of the way along, a side path drops to the tiny red-sand beach of **Ammóhosti**.

GETTING AROUND

By car and moped The bypass road that was supposed to take all vehicles around the back of the village still hasn't materialized, so even the shortest journey by road can require labyrinthine detours. Once you're settled in you'l almost certainly walk everywhere local anyway.

ACCOMMODATION

Anna's Studios ☎ 22460 44334, ⓦ tilosrooms.gr. The immaculate nine units in this bright whitewashed building, on the west hillside immediately above the jetty, vary in size, but all have pastel-hued furnishings and kitchenettes, and three have enormous sea-view balconies. **€45**

Dream Island Hotel ☎ 22460 70707, ⓦ dreamisland .gr. Eleven very spacious one-and two-bedroom apartments, within a few metres of the water roughly two-thirds of the way around the bay. All have at least partia sea views, and are decorated in cool contemporary colours Rates include breakfast and sunbeds. **€80**

Elli Bay ☎ 22460 44435. ⓦ ellibay.com. Seven suites and three rooms with either sea or garden views: right on the waterfront behind *Mihalis* taverna (see opposite), it's a great location for the beach. Includes buffet reakfast. Early May to late Oct. €60

★**Faros Hotel** ☎22460 44068, Ⓦfarosroomstilos .om. Friendly, family-run, hotel-taverna, out on its own t the far east end of the bay, with quiet, well-cared-for ^hree-bedded rooms, plus what's effectively its own .ebbly beach. It's a good 30min walk from the main .estaurant strip, though the food and service here are .erfectly good – the peaceful location, plus dishes such as .aby goat with lemon sauce (€9), ensure repeat clientele, 'ear after year. April–Oct. €45

lidi Rock ☎22460 44293, Ⓦilidirock.gr. Tílos'largest ^otel, dropping in bright-white tiers to the water's edge .t the west end of the bay, a 5min walk from the ferry. It ^as state-of-the-art studios and apartments – one wing has disabled access –with two little private pocket beaches, plus gym facilities. Mainly caters to Scandinavian tour groups; a/c costs extra. €62

Marina Rooms ☎22460 44169, Ⓦmarinarooms.com. Not far from *Faros Hotel*, some 25min walk out of town, these ten rooms in quiet surroundings all have sea views – a perfect spot to get away from the crowds. Breakfast Included. May to mid-Oct. €45

Tilos Fantasy ☎22460 44425, Ⓦtilosfantasy.gr. Substantial modern complex of studios, with mainly Italian clientele, in a quiet hillside location 400m back from the sea. The rooms are perfectly presentable, though the furnishings look out of an IKEA catalogue, and there are two single beds in each room. €40

EATING AND DRINKING

CaféBar Georges ☎22460 44257. Traditional old kafenío on the main square, where the outdoor tables are filled nightly with locals watching the world go by. Daily 8am–late.

ly Omonoia ☎22460 44287. Enduringly popular traditional café, also known locally as *Tou Mihali*, stretching beneath trees strung with light bulbs beside the square, just up from the sea. A good venue for breakfast and delicious local specialities, such as grilled octopus (€11) or grilled pork (€8). Daily 8am–late.

Mediterranean Delights Mediterranean cuisine restaurant – with a twist – next to the bakery in the platía. Chef Anthony is American trained and dishes up excellent breakfast choices such as omelettes and eggs benedict for €8. Enjoy food such as stuffed chicken with prosciutto, peppers and mozzarella (€11) and drinks on the roof terrace, with a view of the harbour. June to mid-Oct daily 8am–3pm and 6pm–midnight.

★**Mihalis** ☎22460 44359. Welcoming taverna, set in attractive gardens a short walk back from the sea, 50m east of the central square. The food here is well-regarded, with dishes such as fish souvlaki (€10), roast goat in lemon sauce (€8.50) as well as good vegetable platters including stuffed tomatoes (€7.50). Early May to late Oct daily 10am–midnight.

Nautilos ☎22460 44168. Relaxed taverna with six basic, clean, sea-view rooms, on the promenade, just past the church. It serves great local dishes such as goat with chickpeas (€9) and vegetarian dishes including *briam* (€7). Daily 9am–late. €40

Oneiro/Dream Very popular "grill-and-fish house", open to the sea breezes near the centre of the beachfront promenade. Excellent grills and spit-roasts, typically costing €8 for meat and €12 for fish. Be prepared to wait for your food in high season. Daily lunch and dinner.

To Armenon ☎22460 44134. Professionally run and salubrious beach-taverna-cum-ouzerí, right by the sea in the middle of the bay, with large portions of octopus salad (€8.50), white beans, meaty mains and fish platters (typically €12.50), plus pasta and pizza, all washed down by Alfa beer on tap. Daily 10am–late.

To Mikro Kafé Pretty little shoreline cottage, nicely restored to create a buzzing, music-oriented bar and café. The rooftop terrace is a great spot for late-night stargazing. Daily: summer noon–late; winter 5pm–late.

South coast beaches

An hour-long hike south of Livádhia takes you to the secluded cove of **Stavrós**: the path starts between the *Tilos Mare Hotel* and the *Castellania Apartments*, then leads up to the saddle with its paved road, followed by a sharp drop to the beach. Ignore the cairns in the ravine bed; the true path is up on the right bank.

The trail (1hr) to the similar cove of **Thólos**, just east of Stavrós, begins by the cemetery and the chapel of **Áyios Pandelímon**, then curls beneath the seemingly impregnable castle of **Agriosykiá**. From the saddle on the paved road overlooking the descent to Thólos (25min; also red-marked), a cairned route leads northwest to the citadel in twenty minutes. Head east a couple of curves along the paved road to the trailhead for **Áyios Séryis Bay**, Tílos's most pristine beach but also the hardest to reach (30min from the road).

Mikró Horió

The ghost village of **Mikró Horió**, whose 1200 inhabitants left for Livádhia during the 1950s, is less than an hour's walk west of the port, with some surviving path sections short-cutting the road curves. Its only intact structures are churches (locked to protect their frescoes) and an old house restored as a small-hours **music bar** (July–Sept daily 9pm–late). Run by the owners of To Mikro Kafé (see p.553), it runs a free hourly shuttle bus to and from Livádhia in summer.

Megálo Horió

Tílos' capital, the village of **MEGÁLO HORIÓ**, lies 7km west of Livádhia along the main road. The only other significant settlement on the island, it enjoys sweeping views over the vast agricultural plain that stretches down to Éristos, and is overlooked in turn by a prominent **Knights' castle** (unrestricted access). Reaching the castle requires a stiff thirty-minute climb, which threads its way through a vast jumble of cisterns, house foundations and derelict chapels.

Museum

Main street • Sporadic opening times – your accommodation can call the caretaker to come and open it

A little **museum** in the town hall displays the bones of midget elephants, found in the **Harkadhió cave** not far east in 1971. Such remains have been found on a number of Mediterranean islands, but Tílos' group may have been the last to survive, until as recently as 4000 BC.

Éristos beach

3km south of Megálo Horió

Long, pink-grey-sand **Éristos beach**, ranks among the island's finest, though swimmers have to cross a reef to reach open sea. The far south end, where the reef recedes, is nudist, as are the two secluded all-naturist coves at **Kókkino** beyond the headland (accessible by path from the obvious military pillbox).

ACCOMMODATION AND EATING

Eristos Beach Hotel Éristos ☎ 22460 44025, ⓦ eristosbeachhotel.gr. Crisp modern complex, catering mainly to large package-tour groups, facing the large, barely developed beach at Éristos on the southwest, with lots of outdoor space, including a shady terrace and large pool. Studios sleeping two to four have large balconies, plus there are sizeable apartments suitable for four to six. Breakfast included. **€50**

Filoxenia 1200m north of Éristos beach ☎ 22460 44347. In the middle of the countryside, 1km south of Megálo Horió, these three large, very quiet apartments are located in lush gardens where the owners grow their own produce for the family-run taverna on the ground floor, which serves simple dishes such as aubergines in tomato sauce (€7.50) for guests and the odd passing local. It's a great area for nature lovers and walking distance to the beach, but a car is essential if you're staying here. **€45**

Kastro Megálo Horió ☎ 22460 44232. While the interior of Megálo's only taverna can be a little gloomy, its patio has lovely long-distance views, and the food is good, with meat and goat cheese from their own flock, and home-made *dishes such as mousakka for €8*. Daily lunch and dinner.

Milios Apartments Megálo Horió ☎ 22460 44204. Ten attractive rooms and apartments set in lush flowery gardens in the heart of Megálo Horió, on the road to Éristos beach. All have balconies offering (distant) sea views, and there's a free shuttle bus service to Éristos beach and Livádhia. Breakfast included. **€38**

The far northwest

The main road west of Megálo Horió hits the coast again at somewhat grim **ÁYIOS ANDÓNIOS**, which has an exposed, truncated beach and two tavernas. There's better, warm-water swimming at isolated, sandy **Pláka beach**, another 2km west, where people camp rough despite a total lack of facilities.

Ayíou Pandelímona monastery

Grounds daily 10am–7pm (Oct–April till 4pm), may close briefly at noon; monastery Sun only same hours • Free

The paved road ends 8km west of Megálo Horió at fortified **Ayíou Pandelímona monastery**, founded in the fifteenth century for the sake of its miraculous spring, still the best water on the island. A fitfully operating drinks café hosts the island's major **festival** of July 25–27. The monastery's tower-gate and oasis setting, high above the forbidding west coast, are its most memorable features, though a photogenic inner courtyard boasts a *votsalotó* surface, and the church a fine tesselated mosaic floor.

Níssyros

The volcanic island of **Níssyros** is unlike its neighbours in almost every respect. It's much lusher and greener than dry Tílos and Hálki to the south, blessed as it is with rich soil that nurtures a distinctive flora, and it supported a large agricultural population in ancient times. In contrast to long flat Kos to the north, Níssyros is round and tall, with the high walls of its central caldera rising abruptly from the shoreline around its entire perimeter. And Níssyros conceals a startling secret; behind those encircling hills, the interior of the island is **hollow**, centring on a huge crater floor that's dotted with still-steaming vents and cones.

For most visitors, the **volcano** is Níssyros' main attraction. It's easy enough to see it on a day-trip from Kos, so few bother to spend the night. That's a shame, because it's a genuinely lovely island, very short on beaches but abounding in spectacular scenery.

8

The port and sole large town, **Mandhráki** on the northwest coast, is an appealing tight-knit community with some fine ancient ruins, while two delightful villages, Emboriós and Nikiá, straddle the crater ridge.

These days, much of the island's income is derived from the offshore islet of **Yialí**, a vast lump of pumice, all too clearly visible just north of Mandhráki, that's slowly being quarried away. Substantial concession fees have given the islanders economic security.

Níssyros also offers good **walking**, on trails that lead through a countryside studded with oak and terebinth; pigs gorge themselves on the abundant acorns, and pork figure prominently on menus.

ARRIVAL AND DEPARTURE
NÍSSYROS

By ferry Ferries moor at a concrete jetty a few hundred metres east of Mandhráki, out of sight of town. Book tickets with either Dhiakomihalis (☎22420 31459) or Kendris (☎22420 31227).
Destinations Astypálea (1 weekly; 5hr 30min); Hálki (2 weekly; 1hr 40min); Kálymnos (4 weekly; 2hr 50min); Kastellórizo (2 weekly; 8hr 30min); Kos Kardamena (7 weekly; 40min); Kos Town (6 weekly; 1hr–1hr 40min); Pireás (2 weekly; 17hr 30min); Rhodes (4–5 weekly; 3hr 10min–4hr 45min); Sými (3 weekly; 3–4hr); Tílos (4–5 weekly; 50min).

GETTING AROUND

By bus Free buses from the jetty head up to Emboriós and Nikiá, via Pálli (Mon–Sat 2 daily).
By taxi For a fixed-rate taxi service, call ☎22420 31474.
By car and scooter Rental outlets include Manos K on Mandhráki harbour (☎22420 31029), and Dhiakomihalis in town (☎22420 31459).
By coach Several coach trips set off daily from the jetty to visit the volcano. English-run Enetikon Travel, on the road into town (☎22420 31180), run round-trips every morning from 10.30am (1hr 45min; €6, entrance fee extra).

Mandhráki

The ancient harbour of **MANDHRÁKI**, the capital of Níssyros, silted up centuries ago, creating a fertile patch that now serves as the *kámbos* (community orchard), surrounded in turn by the modern town. Nonetheless, this remains the island's sole ferry port – boats pull in at a concrete jetty to the east, out of sight of the centre. It's an attractive little place, stretching along the seashore slightly further than appears at first glance. Behind the pedestrianized waterfront promenade, to some extent overwhelmed by poor tavernas and souvenir stores aimed at day-trippers, the tangled narrow lanes are lined with whitewashed houses, whose brightly painted balconies and shutters are mandated by law. The ensemble is punctuated by appealing little squares, and offers repeated glimpses of fruit trees to one side, and blue sea to the other.

At its western end, Mandhráki comes to an abrupt halt at a low bluff that's topped by the stout walls of a **Knights' castle**. Though records have been lost, it's known that the Knights Hospitaller occupied Níssyros from 1314 until 1522, and the island is thought to have reached its heyday around 1400. You can't access any more of the castle itself than the corner staircase and gateway that leads to the little **Panayía Spilianí monastery** (generally open daylight hours).

Langadháki, the district immediately below the castle, was badly hit by earthquakes in the 1990s, but little damage is now visible. At sea level, an attractive mosaic footpath leads further west around the headland to reach the short, black-rock beach of **Hokhláki**, which is seldom suitable for swimming.

Archeological Museum

A few blocks back from the sea on the main lane • Tues–Sun 8.30am–3pm • €4 • ☎22420 31588

Níssyros's modern **Archeological Museum** holds assorted treasures from the island's past. The main floor focuses on the pre-Christian era, starting with six-thousand-year-old artefacts created using obsidian from nearby Yialí. Ceramic pieces range from delicate winged figurines of Eros, dating from 350 BC but closely conforming to modern depictions of angels, to a colossal funerary *pithos* (urn) from the sixth century BC. Stelae in the downstairs galleries reveal a Christian presence on the island in the third century.

Paleókastro

Unrestricted access • Walk up the well-signposted path from beneath the cliffs at the west end of Mandhráki waterfront for roughly 20min; once you meet a cement road – also accessible by a much more circuitous drive up from town – turn right and you'll see the castle

The impressive **Paleókastro** is a mighty ancient fortress that's one of the most underrated ancient sites in Greece. On its way up to the castle, the path through the fields passes numerous ancient stairways and ruins. This hilltop was occupied from the eighth century BC onwards; around four centuries later, **Mausolus of Halicarnassus**, the Persian satrap who left us the word "mausoleum", enclosed its inland slopes within 3m-thick walls – the cliffs on the seaward side already formed a natural boundary. If you think of ancient Greek ruins as all graceful white marble columns, prepare to see something different – much older and vaster. Slotted seamlessly together, the colossal trapezoid blocks are reminiscent of Inca masonry. Only the barest outlines of the buildings within the enclosure survive, but visitors can clamber onto the **ramparts** by means of broad staircases to either side of the still-intact **gateway**.

ACCOMMODATION   MANDHRÁKI 8

Haritos ☎ 22420 31322. Small hotel, a short walk from the ferry landing; head left along the coast road rather than towards town. Its eleven rooms have marble-trimmed baths and veneer floors, and the seafront across the road has a terrace restaurant and a geothermic pool. Breakfast included. **€40**

Porfyris ☎ 22420 31376, ⓦ porfyrishotel.gr. Large family-run hotel, well back from the sea in the town centre in a good location overlooking orchards. Most of the 38 basic rooms have twin beds and sea views from private balconies or terraces, and there's a large seawater pool. Breakfast (included) is served on the terrace. **€40**

Romantzo ☎ 22420 31340, ⓦ nisyros-romantzo.gr. Good-value family-run hotel, uphill to the left of the ferry jetty out of sight of the town with a sea-view

terrace. The rooms and apartments, some with rear-view windows, are simple yet comfortable. Breakfast included. **€35**

★**Ta Liotridia** ☎ 22420 31580, ⓔ info@nisyros-taliotridin.com. Two gorgeous suites (sleeping up to four), above the bar of the same name just metres from the sea on the oceanfront footpath in the centre of town. Exposed stone walls incorporating lava boulders, fine wooden furnishings and head-on sea views. Breakfast included. **€100**

Xenon Polyvotis ☎ 22420 31011. Municipally owned hotel on the quayside facing the ferry port; the large rooms are unremarkable, but you can't fault the sea views. It's only open for pre-booked guests, so reserve in advance. Breakfast included. May–Oct. **€40**

EATING AND DRINKING

Essikas ☎ 6947 722 456. Situated along the waterfront, this taverna has an ambitious menu with lots of vegetarian options – try the home-made hummus with home-made bread (€4) or zucchini balls (€5) – as well as daily specials such as chicken with peppers (€6). Daily noon–4pm and 7pm–11pm.

Gleca Onera ☎ 22420 31700. Wonderful cake shop, with outdoor seating, a short walk from Platía Ilikiomenis. The owner, Anna, offers all manner of desserts and ice creams such as her home-made galaktoboureko (Greek custard pie) and cream-and-jelly cake; all desserts €2.50. A popular post-dinner choice. Daily 1–9pm.

Irini ☎ 22420 31365. Lively restaurant, in busy little

tree-shaded Platía Ilikiomenis, inland at the west end of town, offering hearty traditional dishes like aubergine and mince or pepper stuffed with rice for €6–€8. It's popular with the locals, and Irini herself is incredibly hospitable. Daily lunch and dinner.

Kleanthis ☎ 22420 31484. The best seafood restaurant along the waterfront, with bright blue tables and chairs set out on the quayside. Tasty *pittiá* (chickpea croquettes) and other mezes, followed by fish dishes ranging from fried shrimps for €8 to stuffed squid with cheese or swordfish for €16. Daily lunch and dinner.

Proveza ☎ 22420 31618, ⓦ proveza.net. Lively café-bar with extensive comfortable seating on the seafront promenade near *Ta Liotridia*. It's great for a sunset drink, accompanied by an appropriate soundtrack, and also has a row of internet-access computers indoors. Daily 11am–late. **To Lefkandio** ☎ 22420 31304. Poised immediately above the water on the quayside, this restaurant serve local specialities such as Nisyrian cheese (€3) and traditional dishes like moussaka (€6) and green beans in tomato sauce (€5). Daily noon–midnight.

The coast

Níssyros is almost entirely devoid of **beaches**, and only a small proportion of its coast – along the north and northwest shoreline – is even accessible to visitors. While the coast road east from Mandhráki peters out after barely 10km, it does make a pretty **drive** – and you'll have to come this way anyway if you're heading for the volcano. The largest structures en route are a couple of huge abandoned spas, dating back to the Italian era.

Pálli

Four kilometres east of Mandhráki is **PÁLLI**, a fishing village turned low-key resort that can be a welcome retreat when Mandhráki fills with trippers. All summer, the little harbour here is busy enough with pleasure boats – which can't moor at Mandhráki – to support several tavernas. Pálli also has an excellent **bakery**, cranking out tasty brown bread and pies. A reasonable tamarisk-shaded **beach** of reddish-grey sand, kept well groomed, extends east to the derelict Pantelídhi spa, behind which the little grotto-chapel of **Panayía Thermianí** is tucked inside the vaulted remains of a Roman baths complex.

Liés and Pahiá Ámmos

If you keep going east beyond Pálli, along an initially bleak stretch of shore, you'll reach the picturesque cove of **Liés**, home to the summer-only *Oasis* snack-bar. The paved road ends at a car park a little further on, a spot that can also be reached in

---

HIKING ON NÍSSYROS ISLAND

Níssyros is a fabulous destination for **hikers**, with enticing **trails** to suit all abilities. The one drawback is that hiking to and from the volcano from Mandhráki is for most walkers too much to attempt in a single day. It's not so much the distance that's the problem as the fact that you have to climb back out of the island interior on your way home.

VOLCANO TO MANDHRÁKI

About 1km north of the volcano admission booth, a clear, crudely marked path climbs to a pass, then maintains altitude along the north flank of **Káto Lákki** gulch, emerging after an hour and a half at the important monastery of **Evangelístra**, with its giant terebinth tree just outside. Beyond Evangelístra, you have to walk about 1km on the paved access road before the old path kicks in for the final half hour down to Mandhráki. Look sharp at curves to find the old walled-in path. At first it just short cuts the road, then for quite a long stretch it loops above the port well away from the road, before finally curling around to emerge above the local school.

NIKIÁ TO EMBORIÓS

Hiking from **Nikiá to Emboriós** takes just under an hour and a half, with a short stretch of road-walking towards the end. Descend from Nikiá towards the volcano and bear right towards Theológos monastery, then take the left fork by the wooden gate before reaching it. The path ambles along through neglected terraces, without much altitude change, occasionally obstructed by debris and vegetation. You eventually emerge after just under an hour by some utility poles on the modern Emboriós–Nikiá road. Follow the road from there for about 1km (15min) to the turn-off for Lakkí, where the onward trail continues conspicuously uphill into Emboriós.

summer by taxi-boats from Mandhráki. There's a grey-sand beach right here, while another fifteen minutes by trail over the headland brings you to the idyllic, 300m expanse of **Pahiá Ámmos**, where the grey-pink sand is heaped in dunes, there's limited shade at the far end and a large colony of rough campers and naturists congregate in summer.

ACCOMMODATION AND EATING
THE COAST

Afrodite Pálli ☎ 22420 31560. Simple grill and seafood restaurant on the harbour front in Pálli serving seafood such as kalamári (€9) and traditional Greek fare of fried aubergines (€4) and stuffed vine leaves (€6). Daily lunch till late.

★**Apololes Kores** Pálli ☎ 22420 31024. A delightful ouzerí, with basement and garden seating, hidden in a small square opposite Pálli bakery. The menu features organic and local ingredients, with dishes such as buffalo sausages from Northern Greece with fig chutney (€8) and chickpeas with caramelized onions (€7). Vegan friendly. Daily 6pm–11pm.

Hotel Pálli Pálli ☎ 22420 31453. Eight very large rooms, five with sea views, three with garden views, and all with balconies. It's a 10min walk from Pálli bakery, right opposite the beach. Includes breakfast. €40

Mammis Apartments Pálli ☎ 22420 31453. Perched amid hillside gardens a short walk west of Pálli, these ten tasteful self-contained apartments (sleeping four) have large sea-view balconies and their own separate entrances. €40

The interior

If you've come to Níssyros to see the **volcano**, you're already there – the whole island is a volcano. Beyond and behind the steep slopes that climb from the shoreline, the entire centre of the island consists of a vast bowl-shaped depression. The hills end in a slender ridge that's the rim of the caldera, meaning that the two hilltop villages that survive, **Emboriós** and **Nikía**, are long thin strips that enjoy stupendous views both out to sea and down into the maw. The interior is etched almost in its entirety with ancient agricultural terraces, mostly long abandoned but giving a very real sense of the much greater population in antiquity. A side road just beyond Emboriós offers the only road access, and continues south to the craters at the far end.

8

Emboriós

The road up from Pálli winds first past the village of **EMBORIÓS**. As is obvious from the copious ruins that stretch high above the current village centre, the population here once numbered in the thousands; in winter these days it dwindles to just twenty. It's a gorgeous spot though, which is being bought up and restored by Athenians and foreigners. New owners often discover natural volcanic saunas in the basements of the crumbling houses; at the outskirts of the village there's a signposted public **steam bath** (unrestricted access) in a grotto, its entrance outlined in white paint. One can hike down to the caldera floor from Emboriós; a trail drops from behind the little platía, and it's another fifteen-minute walk to the craters.

Some 3km south of Emboriós, a paved drive leads down from the main road to **Panayía Kyrá**, the island's oldest and most venerable monastery, worth a stop for its enchanting, arcaded festival courtyard as much as its church.

The volcano

A steady procession of coach trips from Mandhráki (see p.556) usually keeps the area busy between 11am and 3pm; to enjoy it in solitude, make your own way up early or late in the day – either rent a vehicle or hike there (see box, opposite) • Admission €3

What's loosely referred to as being the "**volcano**" is the eerie conglomeration of cinder cones and deep craters at the far southern end of the summit caldera, reached by a single road that drops down beyond Emboriós. Although the volcano is dormant, and you won't see fiery eruptions or flowing lava, it's disconcertingly alive, with sulphurous steam sprouting from holes and fissures on all sides. There's a snack-bar here, open at peak times only.

As soon as you follow the short trail from the road's-end car park to the fenced overlook, you realize that while the main crater – officially named **Stéfanos** – may look small from a distance, close up it's a massive, hissing, stinking pit. Its striated walls, yellow with sulphur, drop straight down 40m to a flat stained floor that's pockmarked with bubbling fumaroles. You can venture down there via an easy trail that winds along a timeworn groove in the crater wall. Don't get too close to the boiling mud-pots, which sound as though there's a huge cauldron bubbling away beneath you. In legend, this is the groaning of the titan Polyvotis, crushed by Poseidon under a huge rock torn from Kos.

The hillside immediately west holds several steep-sided **cones**, accessible via an obvious and undemanding trail. Climbing up lets you escape the crowds, and also offers a greater thrill of discovery. It seems a shame to reveal what awaits you at the **top**, but rest assured it's worth it.

Nikiá

The village of **NIKIÁ**, overlooking the caldera from high on its southeastern rim, is a gorgeous little place that should figure on any island itinerary. Its spectacular location, 14km from Mandhráki, enjoys panoramic views out to Tílos as well as across the volcano. Tiny lanes lead from the bus turnaround at road's end to railed volcano viewpoints as well as to the diminutive, engagingly round central platía called Pórta. Paved in pebble mosaic, ringed by stone seating for folk dances, and facing a pretty little church, it's all so dazzlingly white that it's hard to keep your eyes open.

A 45-minute **trail** descends from the end of the road to the crater floor. A few minutes downhill, detour briefly to the eyrie-like monastery of **Áyios Ioánnis Theológos**, whose grounds come to life at the September 25–26 evening festival.

ACCOMMODATON AND EATING — THE INTERIOR

Apyria Emboriós ☎ 22420 31377. Excellent little taverna, with a breezy indoor dining room and tables on the platía by the church in peak season, or crammed into a tiny alleyway when it's less busy. Sample delicious local dishes such as meatballs and fried pork (€6), plus fresh honey in July – the friendly owner is a beekeeper. Summer daily lunch and dinner; winter Sun lunch only

★ **Balconi tou Emporiou** Emboriós ☎ 6978 060 289. Opposite the .church, this taverna has sweeping views across the valley below Emboriós – sample dishes such as stuffed peppers with feta (€4) and courgette flowers stuffed with cheese (€4). Daily May–Oct 8am–10pm.

Melalopetra Emboriós ☎ 6978 060 289. ⓦ melanopetra.gr. Two boutique apartments in a renovated old stone house up a narrow, cobbled lane in Emboriós. Designed to the highest standard, the apartments have their own patio or balcony, a fireplace for winter stays, simple decor and an abundance of natural light. Minimum stay 3 nights. **€140**

To Kafeneio tou Nikola Nikiá ☎ 22420 31670. In the church square, this homely taverna is big on locally grown food and produce, serving delicious dishes such as aubergine with melted cheese and tomato (€5.50) or chicken curry with yogurt (€6). Great location to eat amongst the locals in the square. Mid-April to end Oct daily 8.30am–late.

Kos

After Rhodes, **Kos** ranks second among the Dodecanese islands for both size and visitor numbers. The harbour in **Kos Town** is guarded by an imposing **castle** of the Knights of St John, the streets are lined with Italian-built public buildings, and minarets and palm trees punctuate extensive Hellenistic and Roman remains. And while its interior mostly lacks the wild beauty of that of Rhodes, Kos is the most **fertile** island in the archipelago, blessed with rich soil and abundant groundwater.

Mass tourism, catering mainly to package-holiday crowds with all-inclusive complexes comprising tens of thousands of beds, has largely displaced the old agrarian way of life. Like Tílos further south, Kos never had to earn its living from

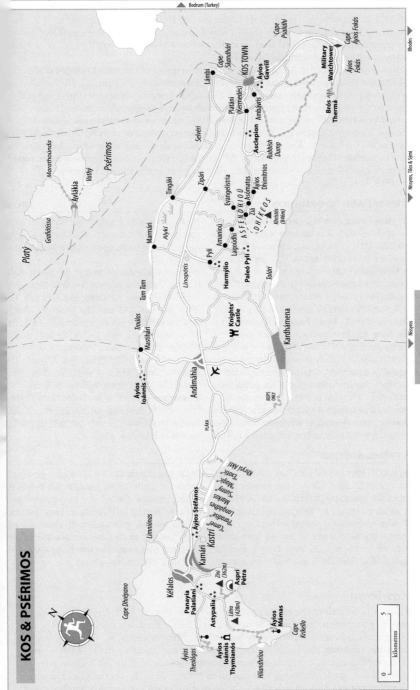

KOS & PSÉRIMOS

Bodrum (Turkey)

Rhodes

Nísyros, Tílos & Sými

Nísyros

8

Marathoúnda

Psérimos

Avlákia

Vathý

Grafiótissa

Platý

Cape Dhtépano

Limniónas

Cape Psalídhi

Cape Áyios Fokás

Áyios Fokás

Military Watchtower

Brós Thermá

Ámbávris

Áyios Gavríl

KOS TOWN

Cape Skandhári

Lámbi

Platáni (Kermedes)

Asclepion

Rubbish Dump

Áyios Dhimítrios

Zià

Psalídhi

Selíveri

Asféndhiou

Evangelístria

Isómatos

Khristós (846m)

Cape Krikello

Hilándhriou

Áyios Theológos

Áyios Ioánnis Thymianós

Astypalia

Panayía Palatiani

Kéfalos

Aspri Pétra

Zíni (362m)

Látra (428m)

Áyios Mámas

Khrysí Aktí

"Exotic"

"Magic"

"Sunny"

"Paradise"

"Camel"

Langádhes

Mórkos

Kamári

Kástri

Áyios Stéfanos

PLÁKA

JEEPS ONLY

Andimáhia

Áyios Ioánnis

Mastihári

Troúlos

Tam Tam

Knights' Castle

Linopótis

Harmýlio

Paleó Pyli

Pyli

Lagoúdhi

Amaniou

Alykí

Marmári

Tingáki

Zipári

Kardhámena

Toidari

N

0   5
kilometres

the sea and consequently has little in the way of a maritime tradition or a contemporary fishing fleet. Except in Kos Town and Mastihári, there are few independent travellers, and from mid-July to mid-September you'll be lucky to find a room without reserving far in advance.

Kos is one of the islands that has been at the forefront of the recent **refugee crisis**. When the refugees first arrived they could be seen around Kos Town: in 2017, however a camp was set up outside the village of Pili, 12km from Kos Town, and new arrivals are taken straight there, so tourists are unlikely to even register their presence. The island experienced further turmoil in July 2017, when an **earthquake** killed two people, damaged the port in Kos Town and destroyed some of the Old Town buildings (see p.564). That said, Kos is still worth a couple of days' time while island-hopping: its few **mountain villages** are appealing, the tourist infrastructure excellent and **swimming** opportunities limitless – about half the island's perimeter is fringed by beaches of various sizes, colours and consistencies.

ARRIVAL AND INFORMATION   KOS

By plane The local airport is just outside Andimahía, in the centre of the island, 24km southwest of Kos Town. Taxis (☎ 22420 23333, ⌨ kostaxi.eu) charge around €37 to Kos Town, and around €25 to Mastihári or Kardhámena. Buses to Kos Town cost €3.20 (4–7 daily; 25min).

Destinations Astypálea, via Léros (2–3 weekly; 1hr 45min); Athens (3 daily; 50min); Iráklio (Heraklion), Crete (3 weekly; 2, 5, 8 or 10hr); Léros, via Kalymnos (2–3 weekly; 1hr); Rhodes (2–3 weekly; 30min); Thessaloníki (2 weekly; 3hr).

By ferry Kos Town port was damaged during the earthquake of July 2017, and at the time of writing is closed to large ferries which currently dock to Kamári in the west of the island: there's a free shuttle bus service back to Kos Town. The catamaran section of Kos port remains unaffected. The ferry port is currently being repaired and is expected to be operational again by the end of 2017. Kos Town domestic connections are listed below; there are also frequent ferry and excursion-boat connections to Bodrum

in Turkey (30–45min). In addition, Mastihári on the north coast has frequent connections with Kálymnos (6 daily; 20min–1hr), and Kardhámena is connected with Níssyros (2 weekly; 40min).

Destinations Astypálea (1 weekly; 4hr 30min); Hálki (3 weekly; 2hr 45min); Kálymnos (2–3 daily; 30min–1hr); Kastellórizo (2 weekly; 9hr 45min); Léros (1–2 daily; 1hr 25min–3hr); Lipsí (2–3 daily; 2hr 10min–4hr 10min); Níssyros (8 weekly; 1hr–1hr 40min); Pátmos (2–4 daily; 1hr 35min–5hr); Pireás (12 weekly; 10–14hr); Rhodes (1–3 daily; 2hr 10min–6hr 15min); Samos (Pythagorion 5 weekly; 3hr 20min; Vathi1 weekly; 3hr 45min); Sými (9 weekly; 1hr 30min–4hr 50min); Syros (2–3 weekly; 5hr 30min); Thíra (2 weekly; 5hr); Tílos (3 weekly; 1hr 50min–2hr 50min).

Information Kos Travel, at Akti Kountouriotou 5 in Kos Town (Mon–Fri 9am–8pm; ☎ 22420 22359) or Voula's Travel, at Korai 3 (Mon–Sat 9am–9pm; ☎ 22420 28477), near *Afendoulis* hotel (see p.565).

GETTING AROUND

By bus KTEL buses are based in Kos Town, with several stops around a triangular park 400m back from the water, and an information booth adjacent at Kleopátras 7 (☎ 22420 22292). Buses between Kos Town and the airport also call at Mastihári.

By bike Bicycles make an excellent way to get around Kos; much of the island is very flat, and Kos Town has an extensive system of cycle lanes. George's Bikes, at Spetson 48 (☎ 22420 24157), has a good selection to rent.

By car and scooter Cars can be rented at the airport and all the resorts. Helpful outlets include Budget in Psalídhi, opposite Grecotel *Kos Imperial Hotel* just outside Kos Town (☎ 22420 28882), and Costa Car Rental (☎ 6948 466 783, ⌨ costascars.com) whose cars are newer than most on the island; they also offer private driver service. For a scooter, try Moto Harley at Kanári 42 (☎ 22420 27693, ⌨ moto-harley.nl).

Kos Town

Home to over half of the island's population of just over 28,000, **Kos Town**, at the far eastern end, radiates out from the harbour and feels remarkably uncluttered. The first thing you see from an arriving ferry is a majestic **Knights' castle**, for once down at sea level, but the town also holds extensive **Hellenistic** and **Roman** remains. Only revealed by an earthquake in 1933, these were subsequently excavated by the Italians, who also planned the "garden suburbs" that extend to either side of the central grid. Elsewhere, sizeable expanses of open space or archeological zones alternate with a hotchpotch of

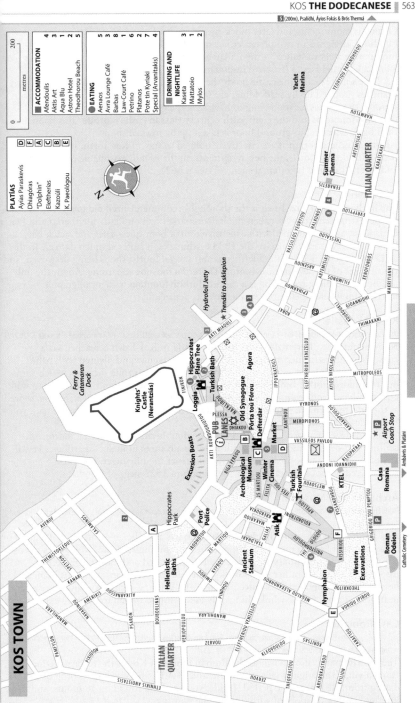

KOS TOWN

S (200m), Psalídhi, Áyios Fokás & Brós Thermá ▲

PLATIAS
Ayías Paraskevís	D
Dhiagóras	F
"Dolphin"	A
Eleftherías	C
Kazoulí	B
K. Paeologou	E

◼ ACCOMMODATION
Afendoulis	4
Aktis Art	3
Aqua Blu	1
Astron Hotel	2
Theodhorou Beach	5

● EATING
Aenaos	5
Avra Lounge Café	3
Barbas	8
Law-Court Café	1
Petrino	6
Platanos	2
Pote tin Kyriaki	7
Special (Arvanitakis)	4

● DRINKING AND NIGHTLIFE
Kaseta	3
Mattatoio	1
Mylos	2

Yacht Marina

Summer Cinema

ITALIAN QUARTER

Hydrofoil Jetty

★ *Trenáki* to Asklepion

Ferry & Catamaran Dock

Knights' Castle (Nerantziás)

Hippocrates' Plane Tree

Loggia

Turkish Bath

Old Synagogue

Agora

Porta toú Fórou

Defterdar

PUB LANES

Market

Excursion Boats

Archeological Museum

Winter Cinema

Turkish Fountain

Casa Romana

Airport Coach Stop

KTEL

Hippocrates Park

Port Police

Hellenistic Baths

Atik

Ancient Stadium

Nymphaion

Western Excavations

Roman Odeion

ITALIAN QUARTER

8

Ottoman monuments and later mock-medieval, Art Deco-ish and Rationalist buildings, designed in two phases either side of the earthquake. As ever, they incorporate a "Foro Italico" – the Italian administrative complex next to the castle – and a Casa del Fascio (Fascist Headquarters).

A little square facing the castle holds the riven trunk of **Hippocrates' plane tree**, its branches propped up by scaffolding; at 700 years of age, it's one of the oldest trees in Europe, though it's far too young to have seen the great healer. Adjacent are two **Ottoman fountains** and the eighteenth-century **Hassan Pasha mosque**, also known as the Loggia Mosque; its ground floor is taken up by rows of shops.

Ferry travellers in transit are effectively obliged to stay in Kos Town. It's a pretty good base, with decent hotels, the best restaurants on the island, reasonable public transport, and several car- and bike-rental agencies (see p.562).

Old town

The liveliest part of Kos Town is the thoroughly commercialized **old town**, which lines the pedestrianized street between the Italian market hall on Platía Eleftherías and Platía Dhiagóras, and is crammed with expensive tourist boutiques, cafés and snack-bars. One of the few areas to survive the 1933 earthquake, it suffered much damage in the 2017 earthquake, with Platía Eleftherías and several tourist shops being destroyed, and the minaret of the seventeenth-century **Defterdar mosque** collapsing. About the only genuinely old thing remaining is a capped **Turkish fountain** with a calligraphic inscription, where Apéllou meets Eleftheríou Venizélou.

Knights' castle

Daily 8am–8pm; Nov–March closed Mon • €4, or €13 for joint ticket including Archeological Museum and Roman House of Kos • ☎ 22420 27927

Known locally as **"Nerantziás"**, the **knights' castle** in Kos Town is reached via a causeway over its former moat, now filled in as an avenue and planted with palms. It's a splendid, tumbledown, overgrown old ruin, where, once inside the gate, which turns out to lead to another broader moat with an inner fortress beyond, you're free to walk and stumble at your own peril over all sorts of walls, battlements and stairways, as well as the odd much more recent and unattractive concrete accretion. At the far end, you find yourself looking out over the ferry quays.

Built in stages between 1450 and 1514, the **double citadel** replaced a fourteenth-century fort deemed incapable of withstanding advances in medieval artillery. Few if any of the many cannonballs lying about were ever fired in anger; the castle surrendered without resistance after the marathon 1522 siege of Rhodes.

Archeological Museum

Platía Eleftherías • Daily 8am–8pm; Nov–March closed Mon • €6, or €13 for joint ticket including Knight's Castle and Roman House of Kos• ☎ 22420 28326

Kos Town's Italian-built **Archeological Museum** has a predictable Latin bias. Centred on an atrium that holds a mosaic of Hippocrates welcoming Asclepios to Kos, it's almost entirely devoted to **statuary**, of which the best preserved and most prominently displayed are Roman rather than Greek. That said, the single most famous item, said to be a statue of Hippocrates, is indeed Hellenistic. With no captions to put the displays in historical context, the whole thing only takes around fifteen minutes to explore.

Casa Romana

Just off Grigoriou Tou Pemptou, near the airport coach stop • Daily 8am–8pm; Nov–March closed Mon • €6, or €13 for joint ticket including Knight's Castle and Archeological Museum • ☎ 22420 28326

The **Casa Romana**, also known as the Roman House of Kos, is the reconstruction of a Roman villa. The original villa was in use until 3 A.D, and was built on top of a site dating from the Hellenistic period. Inside, you can look round its 36 rooms, and three interior courtyards adorned with fine mosaic flooring.

Agora

Unrestricted access in daylight hours

The largest single relic of ancient Kos, the **agora**, occupies a huge open site just back from the harbour. The man who laid it out in 366 BC, Hippodamus, was credited by Aristotle as having "invented the division of cities into blocks". Thanks to **earthquakes** between the second and sixth centuries AD, it's now a confusing jumble of ruins. Scattered through a delightful public park, however, abounding in bougainvillea and palmettos, it's a lovely area in which to stroll, as you admire the crumbling walls, standing columns, and exposed mosaics.

Western excavations

Unrestricted access in daylight hours

Set in pit-like gardens up to 4m below the street level of modern Kos Town, the so-called **western excavations** consist of two intersecting marble-paved streets as well as the Xystos or colonnade of a covered running track. Crumbling plastic canopies at either end of the L-shaped complex shelter **floor mosaics**.

Across Grigoríou toú Pémptou to the south is a small, restored Roman-era **odeion**, which is capable of seating 750 spectators in 14 rows, and was built on the site of a similar Greek theatre.

ACCOMMODATION   KOS TOWN

★Afendoulis Evrypýlou 1 ☎22420 25321, ⓦafendoulishotel.com. Balconied en-suite rooms – including a few family quads – all at excellent prices. Alexis Zikas, brother Ippokrates and wife Dionysia offer real personal service, ensuring a loyal repeat clientele; top-quality breakfast (included) with home-made preserves. **€40**

Aktis Art Vassiléos Yeoryíou 7 ☎22420 47200, ⓦkosaktis.gr. Designer hotel whose futuristic standard doubles or suites, in brown, grey and beige, all face the water. Bathrooms are naturally lit and have butler sinks. There's a gym, conference area, seaside bar and affiliated restaurant. Breakfast included. **€150**

★Aqua Blu Hotel Lambi Beach ☎22420 22440, ⓦaquabluhotel.gr. Luxurious adult-only resort just outside Kos Town, with its own private section of Lambi Beach. There's a pool, plus private plunge pools in the more expensive suites. Breakfast included. **€235**

Astron Hotel Akti Kountouriotou 31 ☎22420 23703, ⓦastron-hotel-kos.gr. This hotel is nothing fancy, but in a good location in Kos Town, 300m from the nearest beach: it has 68 rooms, four suites and eight junior suites, plus a pool, Jacuzzi, café and rooftop terrace where breakfast (included) is served. **€60**

Theodhorou Beach 1200m from the centre, towards Psalídhi ☎22420 22280, ⓦtheodorouhotel.com. Generous-sized units, including suites plus a wing of self-catering studios, with disabled access. A leafy environment includes a lawn pool at the back and a small "private" beach with the *Nostos* day-and-night café-bar. A good choice for families. Breakfast included. **€40**

EATING AND DRINKING

CAFÉS

Aenaos Platía Eleftherías ☎22420 26044. Join the largely local crowd at this café under the Defterdar mosque, and people-watch while refilling your Greek coffee from the traditional *bríki* used to brew it. They also serve a range of teas and flavoured hot chocolates. Daily 9am–late.

Avra Lounge Café Vassiléos Yeoryíou 5 ☎22420 27354. Beachside café set in colonial Italian building near *Aktis Art* (see above). Menu offers breakfasts, salads and pastas such as four cheese linguine (€11). Its own private beach becomes a bar-restaurant at night. Daily 8am–4am.

★Law-Court Café Finikon. Some of the cheapest and best-brewed coffees (€2) in Kos are available (along with cold drinks) under the arches at the rear of the courthouse, with a mostly civil-servant clientele, a few paces from Hippocrates' plane tree. There's no sign outside. Daily 8am–8pm.

Special (Arvanitakis) Vassiléos Yeoryíou ☎22420 22087. This tiny hole-in-the-wall pastry and cake shop, right by the sea, also serves dynamite *gelato* and freshly squeezed orange juice. The a/c interior makes it a refreshing place to stop for a while. Small seating area outside. Daily 10am–7pm.

RESTAURANTS

Barbas Evrypýlou 6 ☎22420 01234. Opposite Hotel Afendoulis (see above), this friendly restaurant serves up simple Greek and international cuisine such as chicken cordon bleu stuffed with cheese (€9.50) and steak with mushroom sauce (€11). The food is average, but served at outdoor tables with attentive service. May–Oct daily noon–midnight.

★Petrino Platía Theológou 1 ☎22420 27251, ⓦpetrino-kos.gr. Elegant garden restaurant with a menu of fish (seabass; €14), shellfish, meat dishes such as pork loin (€12) and the local hard cheese. There are also two cosy indoor salons for winter. Daily 11am–4pm & 6pm–late.

Platanos Platanos Square ☎ 22420 28991. Good choice for people-watching in Platanos Square, overlooking the Hippocrates Plane tree and a short walk from the castle. It's not the cheapest – dishes such as grilled asparagus with Hollandaise sauce (€11.50) and a lemon risotto costs

€16.60 – but you're paying for the location. April–Oc daily 10am–midnight.

Pote tin Kyriaki Pissándhrou 9 ☎ 22420 27872. Meanin "Never on a Sunday", Kos' only genuine ouzerí has a creativ menu (written in school exercise books) with meze delight such as baked feta with honey (€4) – the mussels in tomatoe and red wine sauce (€9) are a favourite. Summer Mon–Sa 8pm–2am; winter Thurs–Sat noon–2pm & 7–10pm.

NIGHTLIFE AND ENTERTAINMENT

Kos Town has a hyperactive nightlife. Visitors from all over the island congregate in the so-called "Pub Lanes", Nafklírou anc Dhiákou, filled with an ever-changing array of generally mediocre bars and clubs. There are newer, better nightlife areas around Platía Dhiagóra (mostly Greeks) and out at Aktí Zouroúdhi towards Lambi.

Kaseta Akti Miaouli 4 ☎ 22420 22352. Great bar on the coast by the police station, popular with locals and tourists alike. Good for a drink during the daytime and evening, and popular for its cocktails (€6–8). Daily 10am–6am.

Mattatoio Aktí Zouroúdhi ☎ 22420 23463. Meaning "slaughterhouse" in Italian, this bar/club on the coast road is

a relaxing place for a drink by day, then transforms into a clul after hours with regular DJ sets and light shows. Dail 10am–6am.

Mylos Aktí Zouroúdhi ☎ 22420 23235. Sprawling around an old seafront windmill, with some tables out on Lambi beach, *Mylos* is Kos Town's top day-and-night-bar, with both live music and DJs. Daily noon–late.

8 Asklepion

4km west of Kos Town • Daily 8am–8pm; Nov–March closed Mon • €8 • ☎ 2242 028763

Native son **Hippocrates** is justly celebrated on Kos; not only does he have a tree, a street, a park, a statue and an international medical institute named after him, but his purported **Asklepion**, one of three in Greece, is a major attraction. Although, in fact, founded just after Hippocrates' death, the Asklepion used and taught Hippocrates' methods. Both a sanctuary of Asclepios (god of healing, son of Apollo) and a renowned curative centre, its magnificent setting on three artificial terraces overlooking Anatolia reflects early concern with the therapeutic environment. Little now remains standing, owing to periodic earthquakes and the Knights filching masonry to build their castle. The **lower terrace** never held many buildings, and was instead the venue for the observance of the Asclepieia – quadrennial athletic/musical competitions in honour of the god. Sacrifices to Asclepios were conducted at an **altar**, the oldest structure here, whose foundations are found near the middle of the **second terrace**. Just east are the Corinthian columns of a second-century AD **Roman temple**, partially re-erected by nationalistic Italians. A monumental staircase leads from the altar to a second-century BC **Doric temple** of Asclepios on the **highest terrace**, the last and grandest of the deity's local shrines.

HIPPOCRATES

Hippocrates (c.460–370 BC) is generally regarded as the father of scientific medicine, even if the Hippocratic oath, much altered from its original form, may well have nothing to do with him. Hippocrates was certainly born on Kos, probably at Astypalia near present-day Kéfalos, but otherwise confirmed details of his life are few. A great physician who travelled throughout the Classical Greek world, he spent at least part of his career teaching and practising on his native island. Numerous medical writings have been attributed to Hippocrates; *Airs, Waters and Places*, a treatise on the importance of environment on health, is generally thought to be his, but others are reckoned to be a compilation found in a medical library in Alexandria during the second century BC. His emphasis on good air and water, and the holistic approach of ancient Greek medicine, now seem positively contemporary.

The east

The shoreline of **eastern** Kos is fringed with good **beaches**, albeit interspersed with marshlands. The best, around Cape Psalídhi in the far east and Lámbi, Tingáki and Marmári on the northern coast, have attracted resort development, but with a bike it's usually possible to find a stretch of sand to yourself: heading for Tingáki or Marmári from Kos Town, the safest route is the minor road from the southwest corner of town. There's almost always a breeze along this stretch of coast, which makes it popular with windsurfers, while the profiles of Kálymnos, Psérimos and Turkey's Bodrum peninsula all make for spectacular offshore scenery. Inland, the rugged **hills** cradle some delightful villages, though sadly many are now empty.

Bros Thermá

East of Kos Town, beyond the huge hotels of Cape Psalídhi, the paved coast road ends after 12km. A dirt track continues for the final kilometre to the massively popular **hot springs** known as **Bros Thermá**. Best experienced at sunset or on moonlit nights, they issue from a grotto and flow through a trench into a shoreline pool formed by boulders, heating the seawater to an enjoyable temperature.

Tingáki

A favourite with British travellers, **TINGÁKI** is 12km west of Kos harbour. Its long narrow beach of white sand improves, and becomes more separated from the frontage road, the further west you go. Thanks to the island of Psérimos just offshore, waves tend to stay small, and the warm shallow waters are ideal for children. There's little accommodation near the beach itself, though medium-sized hotels and studios are scattered amid the fields and cow pastures inland.

Marmári

MARMÁRI lies 3km from Tingáki, beyond the **Alykí** salt marsh, which retains water – and throngs of migratory birds, including flamingos – until June after a wet winter. Marmári has a smaller built-up area than Tingáki, and the beach is broader, especially to the west where it forms little dunes.

The Asfendhioú villages

Accessible via the curvy side road from Zipári, 8km from Kos Town; an inconspicuous minor road to Lagoúdhi; or by the shorter access road for Pylí

The **inland villages of Mount Dhíkeos**, a handful of settlements collectively referred to as **Asfendhioú**, nestle amid the island's only natural forest. Together, these communities give a good idea of what Kos looked like before tourism arrived, and all have been severely depopulated by the mad rush to the coast.

Ziá

There's precious little left of the original village of **ZIÁ**, 7km inland from Tingáki, which now holds barely a dozen resident families. Instead, its heavily commercialized main street and spectacular sunsets make it the target of dozens of tour buses daily, and the general tattiness seems to increase year on year.

Pylí

Both the contemporary village of **Pylí** and the separate ruins of the medieval town can be reached via the road through Lagoúdhi and Amanioú, or from beside the duck-patrolled Linopótis pond on the main island trunk road. Apart from its giant, lion-spouted cistern-fountain (the *piyí*), Pylí's other attraction is the **Harmýlio** ("Tomb of Harmylos"), a fenced-off, subterranean, niched vault that was probably a Hellenistic family tomb.

Paleó Pylí

Paleó Pylí (medieval Pylí), 3km southeast of its modern descendant, was the Byzantine capital of Kos. It's an absolutely wonderful spot, perched on what's now a very isolated peak but still well below the crest of the island's central ridge. Opposite the end of the paved road up, a stair-path leads within fifteen minutes to the roof of the fort. En route you pass the remains of the abandoned town tumbling southwards down the slope.

ACCOMMODATION   THE EAST

Grecotel Kos Imperial Psalídhi ☎22420 58000, ⓦgrecotel.com. Tasteful and classy garden complex with a tropical river novelty pool and spa: the spacious rooms and bungalows are tastefully decorated and come with sound systems. Good package holiday choice. Breakfast included. **€148**

Michals Apartments Studios Psalídhi ☎22420 23829, ⓦmichalisapartments.gr. Situated 1km from the marina and 3km from Kos Town, this welcoming and attentive Greek-Australian family run a superb outfit of twenty large studios and one- and two- bedroomed apartments. There's a pool, snack bar and gym. **€38**

EATING AND DRINKING

★**Ambeli** Tingáki ☎22420 69682. The "Vineyard" is a great local taverna, in a rural setting 2.5km east of the main beachfront crossroads. There's seating both indoors and out, and dishes including *dolmádhes* (€7) and rabbit stew (€8), washed down with wine from their own vineyard. Book ahead in peak season. May–Oct daily lunch and dinner; Nov–April Fri & Sat dinner only, Sun lunch only.

Iy Palia Piyi Pylí ☎22420 41510. Excellent taverna, in a superb setting beside a fountain fed by a natural year-round spring in the upper part of Pylí, 100m west of the

partly pedestrianized square and church. Inexpensive souvláki grilled with onions (€4), home-made tzatzíki, fried-vegetable mezédhes such as courgettes, aubergine and local cheese with local sweet red wine. Daily lunch and dinner.

Oromedon Ziá ☎22420 69983. The best of Ziá's dozen tavernas, this Greek-patronized place is popular for its mushrooms (€3.50) and local sausage with honey (€4) on a roof terrace. Bill Clinton, the Greek president and Turkey's former president have all eaten here. May–Oct daily lunch and dinner.

8

The west

Near the desolate centre of the island, scattered with military installations, a pair of giant, adjacent roundabouts by the airport funnels traffic northwest towards **Mastihári**, northeast Kos Town, southwest towards **Kéfalos** and southeast to **Kardhámena**. Most visitors are bound for the south-coast **beaches**, reached via the Kéfalos-bound turning.

Mastihári

The least "packaged" and least expensive of the north-shore resorts, **MASTIHÁRI**, 8km north of the airport, has a shortish, broad beach extending southwest, with less frequented dunes (and no sunbeds) towards the far end. Ferries and excursion boats from Kálymnos (see p.576) moor close to the centre, which has the feel of a genuine town.

Kardhámena

KARDHÁMENA, 31km from Kos Town and 8km southeast of the airport, is the island's largest package resort after the capital itself. In summer, locals are vastly outnumbered by boozing-and-bonking visitors, predominantly young Brits. A beach stretches to either side – sandier to the southwest, intermittently reefy and hemmed in by a road towards the northeast – but runaway development has banished any redeeming qualities the place might have had. The main reason anyone not staying here would visit is to catch a boat to Níssyros (see p.555).

South-coast beaches

The coastline west of Kardhámena boasts a series of scenic and secluded **south-facing beaches**. Though each has a fanciful English name, they form essentially one long stretch at the base of a cliff, accessed by successive footpaths down from the main road. As the prevailing wind on the island is usually from the north, the water as a rule is gloriously calm.

The longest, broadest and wildest of the beaches, "**Magic**", officially Polémi, has a proper taverna above the car park, no jet skis and a nudist zone ("**Exotic**") at its eastern end. "**Sunny**", signposted as Psilós Gremmós and easily walkable from "Magic", has another taverna and jet skis; **Langádhes** is the cleanest and most picturesque, with junipers tumbling off its dunes and more jet skis. "**Paradise**", alias "**Bubble Beach**" because of volcanic gas-vents in the tidal zone, is small and oversubscribed, with wall-to-wall sunbeds and a large restaurant just above. Jet ski-free "**Camel**" (Kamíla) is the shortest and loneliest, protected by the steep, unpaved drive which runs in past its hillside taverna; the shore here is pure, fine sand, with good snorkelling to either side.

Kamári

The westernmost resort on Kos, **KAMÁRI**, comes just before the high headland at the island's western tip, and is essentially the shoreline annexe of the old town of Kéfalos. More popular with families and older visitors than Kardhámena, Kamári may look from the main road like a long and rather dispiriting strip, but the beach itself is good.

There's also a very lovely spot at its western end, 3km from the centre, where the tiny **Kastrí** islet, topped by a little chapel, stands just off the **Áyios Stéfanos** headland. A public access road leads down to beaches either side of a small peninsula, crowned with the remains of two triple-aisled, sixth-century **basilicas**.

The far west

The village of **KÉFALOS**, 43km from Kos Town, covers a bluff looking down the length of the island. Aside from some lively **cafés** at the south end, it's a dull little place, mainly of note as a staging point for expeditions into the rugged **peninsula** that terminates at **Cape Kríkello**.

The main highlights of a visit there, along the ridge road south, include **Panayía Palatianí** Byzantine church amid the ruins of a larger ancient temple, 1km beyond the village, and the Classical theatre (unrestricted access) and Hellenistic temple of **ancient Astypalia**, 500m further via the side path starting from an unlocked gate. A paved road west just beyond Astypalia leads to windy **Áyios Theológos beach**, 7km from Kéfalos.

ACCOMMODATION AND EATING   THE WEST

Ayios Theologos Taverna Ayios Theológos ☎6974 503 556. High-quality taverna, at the far western tip of the island, from where you can witness incredible sunsets. Fresh home-grown produce used in dishes such as moussaka (€7.50) and bifteki (€8.50) brings in the crowds at weekends. Lunch and dinner: summer daily, winter Sat & Sun.

Grand Café Kamári ☎22420 71290. Large, comfortable café, at the point where Kamári beach briefly disappears and the sea laps directly against the road. As well as drinks, they serve top-quality pastries and sweets from the adjoining bakery. All day: summer daily, winter Sat & Sun.

Kali Kardia Mastihári ☎22420 59289. Reliable taverna, facing the ferry jetty, that's good for fresh fish of the day (€9.50) and mezédhes such as fried aubergines (€4) as well as standards like stifádho (€8), plus great desserts. Daily all day.

Panorama Studios Mastihári ☎22420 59019. Simple studio apartments with a/c, kitchenettes and sea-view balconies, above a small little restaurant just steps from the beach. €52

Psérimos

Were it not so close to Kos and Kálymnos, the little island of **PSÉRIMOS**, filled with remote beaches, might be idyllic. Throughout the season, so many excursion boats arrive that they've had to build a second jetty at little **AVLÁKIA** port. In midsummer, day-trippers blanket the main sandy beach that curves in front of Avlákia's thirty-odd houses and huge communal olive grove; even in May or late September at least eighty visitors daily outnumber the permanent population of 25. Three other beaches are within easy reach: the clean sand-and-gravel strand at **Vathý** is a well-marked, thirty-minute walk east, starting from behind the *Taverna Iy Psérimos*. A forty-five-minute walk north along the main trans-island track leads to the grubbier, pebbly **Marathoúnda**. Best of all is **Grafiótissa**, a 300m-long beach of near-Caribbean quality a thirty-minute walk west of town.

ARRIVAL AND DEPARTURE   PSÉRIMOS

BY FERRY

From Kálymnos Day-trips from Póthia on Kálymnos usually leave at 9.30am daily, and return at 5–6pm.

From Kos Boats from Kos Town operate triangular tours to Platý islet and somewhere on Kálymnos with only a brief stop on Psérimos.

ACCOMMODATION AND EATING

AVLÁKIA

Manola ☎ 22430 51540. Four reasonable studios, most with sea views and some with a/c, facing a very broad segment of the beach from its eastern end. €25

Taverna Manola ☎ 22430 51540. Although it looks more like a bar, and stays open late as the island's main social hub, this beachfront taverna serves good Greek food using produce and animals from their own farm. Specialities include their own goat with red sauce and potatoes (€9) and fresh kalamári (€6). Daily 9am–late.

Tripolitis ☎ 22430 23196. Six simple studio apartments, three of which have sea views, above English-speaking *Anna's* café/snack-bar and directly across from the beach. May–Oct. €40

8

Astypálea

Geographically, historically and architecturally, **Astypálea** really belongs to the Cyclades – on a clear day you can see Anáfi or Amorgós far more easily than any of the other Dodecanese. Its inhabitants are descended from colonists brought from the Cyclades during the fifteenth century, after pirate raids had left the island depopulated, and supposedly Astypálea was only reassigned to the Ottomans after the Greek Revolution because the Great Powers had such a poor map at the 1830 and 1832 peace conferences.

Astypálea's main visitor attractions include a beautiful old **citadel** – not just the castle itself, but also the whitewashed village of **Hóra** beneath it – as well as several good, easily accessible **beaches**. The island may not immediately strike you as especially beautiful: many beaches along its heavily indented coastline have reef underfoot and periodic seaweed, while the windswept heights are covered in thornbush or dwarf juniper. Hundreds of sheep and goats manage to survive, while citrus groves and vegetable patches in the valleys signal a relative abundance of water. Besides the excellent local **cheese**, Astypálea is renowned for its **honey**, **fish** and **lobster**.

There is no **package tourism** on Astypálea, and its remoteness discourages casual trade. During the short, intense **midsummer season** (mid-July to early Sept), however, visitors vastly outnumber the 1500 permanent inhabitants. The one real drawback is that **ferry** connections (see below) are so poor.

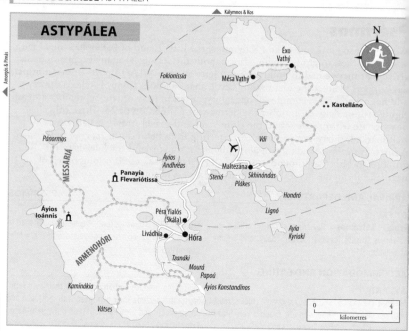

ARRIVAL AND INFORMATION

ASTYPÁLEA

By air Astypálea's tiny airport, 8km northeast of Hóra and Péra Yialós, has frequent connections to Athens (6 weekly) and to Léros, Kalymnos, Kos and Rhodes (3 weekly). Many hotels will pick up and drop off guests, and buses and taxis are available (see below).

By ferry Astypálea's main ferry port, at Áyios Andhréas, 7km north of Péra Yialós, is extremely inconvenient, with no facilities whatsoever, and almost all boats arriving and departing in the dead of night. The only boat that calls in at Péra Yialós, the *Nissos Kalymnos*, serves Kálymnos (2 weekly; 2hr 45min). Ferry tickets can be bought in Péra Yialós from Astypalea Tours

(☎ 22430 61571) and Paradise (☎ 22430 61224).

Destinations Amorgós (4 weekly; 1hr 25min); Dhonoússa (4 weekly; 2hr 20min); Kálymnos (1 weekly; 2hr 30min); Kastellórizo (1 weekly; 15hr 10min); Kos (1 weekly; 3hr 35min); Náxos (4 weekly; 4hr); Níssyros (1 weekly; 6hr); Páros (4 weekly; 5hr); Pireás (5 weekly; 9hr 45min–11hr 35min); Rhodes (1 weekly; 9hr 10min); Tílos (1 weekly; 6hr 35min).

Tourist office There's an information office in one of the windmills at the approach to Hóra (officially June–Sept daily 6–9pm, though in practice hours are erratic; ☎ 22430 61412).

GETTING AROUND

By bus Some 5–6 buses daily connect Péra Yialós with Hóra, Livádhia and Maltezána, and drop passengers at beaches along the way for a fee of €1. Buses takes passengers from the airport to Péra Yialós and Maltezána.

By taxi The island has 2 taxis (☎ 697 570 6365 or ☎ 697 625 6461): fares are reasonable, at around €8–10

from the airport to Péra Yialós.

By car and scooter Rentals are available in Péra Yialós from Astycar (☎ 22430 62265 ⌨ rent-a-car -astypalaia.gr), Kyrannos (☎ 22430 61289, ⌨ astypalaiarentacar.gr) and Vergoulis (☎ 22430 61351), or through several island hotels.

The west

The shape of Astypálea is often compared to a butterfly, in that it consists of two separate "wings" joined by a low narrow isthmus. The only major population centre, made up of the built-up strip that joins the waterfront villages of **Péra Yialós** and **Livádhia** by way of hilltop **Hóra**, is on the southeast coast of its **western** half, well away from both the ferry port and the airport.

Péra Yialós

Astypálea was the first Dodecanese island to be occupied by the Italians, and the little harbour town of **PÉRA YIALÓS** (also known as **SKÁLA**), set in a deeply indented, steep-sided little bay, dates from the Italian era. Only at the head of the harbour, where a broadish gravel beach – fine for families with young children – fronts a row of seafront cafés and restaurants, is there much life or activity. A broad and uninteresting concrete quayside stretches along its southern shore, below Hóra, while the hillsides are dotted with houses and the odd small hotel.

Archeological Museum

June to late Oct Tues–Sun 9am–noon & 6–8pm, though call to check first as opening times are erratic • Free • ☎ 2243 061 500

Just back from the waterfront in the centre of Péra Yialós, the local **Archeological Museum** consists of a single room. Many of its local finds, spanning the Bronze Age to medieval times, are little more than fragments, but it does hold impressive goblets and vases unearthed from two Mycenaean tombs.

Hóra

The delightful, very photogenic ensemble of **HÓRA**, accessible by road as well as steep stair-paths from Péra Yialós, neatly caps a high headland. Beneath the grey walls of the hilltop castle, the village itself is comprised of dazzling bright houses – many restored as holiday homes – threaded along intriguing narrow alleyways. The main approach road is lined with eight picturesque orange-roofed **windmills**.

8

Kástro

Unrestricted access • Free

Astypálea's thirteenth-century **kástro**, among the finest in the Aegean, was erected not by the Knights of St John, but by the Venetian Quirini clan, and modified by the Ottomans after 1537. Rather than purpose-built battlements, its unique "walls" consisted instead of the stacked-up frontages of private houses. Until well into the twentieth century, more than three hundred people lived inside, but depopulation and a severe 1956 earthquake combined to leave only a shell. Reached via a brightly whitewashed passageway beneath its main church of **Evangelístria Kastrianí**, the interior has been laid out with new pathways.

Livádhia

The little resort village of **LIVÁDHIA** occupies the next bay along from Hóra. A long, straight and pebbly **beach**, albeit scruffy with dried vegetation, lines the waterfront, fringed by cafés, restaurants and low-key accommodation. You can walk there from Hóra in fifteen minutes; take the road that drops down to the sea just beyond the *Pylaia Boutique Hotel* (see p.574).

Beyond Livádhia

When the beach at Livádhia is too busy, press on southwest for fifteen minutes on foot to reach the three small fine-pebble coves at **Tzanáki**. Beyond these is **Papoú**, an 80m fine-gravel strand accessible overland by a horrifically steep side track, and then a final path approach around a fenced-off farm.

The third large bay beyond Livádhia, **Áyios Konstandínos**, is a partly shaded, sand-and-gravel cove with a good seasonal taverna. Further afield are the lonely beaches of **Vátses** and **Kaminákia**, which are visited by a seasonal excursion boat from Péra Yialós. By land, **Vátses** has the easier dirt road and is 25 minutes by scooter from Livádhia; sandy, with a basic *kantína*, it's often windy. The track to **Kaminákia**, 8.5km from Livádhia, is rough and steep for the final 2km – best to go in a jeep – but the sheltered, clean and scenic cove, Astypálea's best, repays the effort.

ACCOMMODATION

PÉRA YIALÓS

★Chrysalis Boutique Hotel ☎ 22430 22430 62221, ⓦ chrysalishotel.eu. The best accommodation in Péra Yialós, spilling down the hillside across from the castle, where the first access road down to the harbour drops from the coastal road. It has eight rooms and four suites, all with patios or balconies and Coco-Mat bedding with plush amenities (bathrobes, slippers, toiletries). Local produce breakfast (included) is taken on the terrace with sea and castle views. Room €90, suite €110

Stampalia ☎ 22430 61200, ⓦ facebook.com/ stampaliaStudios. Gorgeous building painted in Cycladic blues and whites, on a left turn before the only petrol station. All eight large suites have a balcony with harbour views plus separate living and bedrooms with Coco-Mat bedding and toiletries: they are well-equipped with coffee machines, local jam and bread and a welcome pack with wine and local honey. €50

HÓRA

Astypalea Palace ☎ 22430 61009, ⓦ astipalea.net. gr. High on the hill road heading out of town towards the airport, *Astypalea Palace* has seven rooms and two suites, all with sleek "Cycladic" interior design and large balconies with castle and sea views: one room has a pool, one a jacuzzi and both suites have jacuzzis. Basic homemade breakfast included. May–Oct. Room €70, suite €110

★Kalderimi ☎ 22430 59843, ⓦ kalderimi.gr. Smart modern complex, just beyond the *Pylaia Boutique Hotel* (see below) on the road out of Hóra: the accommodation is mock-cottage style with rooms and two suites, all with

sweeping views down to the sea. Breakfast included. Roor €75, suite €100

Oneiro Studios ☎ 22430 61351, ⓦ astypalea-hotel .gr. Twelve studios located on the road behind *Astypale. Palace Hotel* (see above). Suitable for families, the sleep 2–4 and are well-equipped for self-catering May–Oct. €50

Pylaia Boutique Hotel ☎ 22430 61070, ⓦ pylaiahotel gr. Spilling down the hillside 200m out of Hóra toward: Livádha, with friendly young management. Slightly toc large to be really "boutique", it has 27 spacious, stylish rooms and suites, most with outdoor space and grea' views, plus a pool and summer-only rooftop restaurant Breakfast included. €90

LIVÁDHIA

★Gerani Studios ☎ 22430 61484, ⓦ astypalaiagerani.gr. Ten very comfortable marble-floored studios with little terraces facing flower-filled gardens, a short walk from the sea. There's Coco-Mat bedding and a welcome pack of local wine, too. Easter to late-Oct. €35

Lilo's Apartments ☎ 22430 61034, ⓦ astypalaia-apartments.de. Family-run apartments located down a side road, a five-minute walk from the beach. Set among lush gardens, all four apartments are generously sized with separate bedroom area, and some have extra sofa beds. Easter–Oct. €40

Mouras Studios ☎ 22430 61227, ⓦ mourastudios.gr. Cute set of individual rental units, right by the beach, each with its own kitchen and balcony, and arranged around a courtyard: some have sea views. Reserve ahead for best rates. €40

EATING AND DRINKING

PÉRA YIALÓS

Akroyiali ☎ 22430 61863. While the food here is pretty good – dishes such as shrimp saganaki (€9) and lamb in lemon sauce (€7.50) – the prime reason this beachfront taverna is so full every night is its unbeatable setting, with tables spreading out onto the sand. Daily 4pm–late.

Akti ☎ 22430 61114. High-quality restaurant, next to *Chrysalis Boutique Hotel* (see above), with tiered seating down the cliff face giving marvellous sea and castle views. It specializes in seafood with dishes like saganaki mussels (€7.50) and grilled kalamári (€12), but also offers a couple of meat dishes such as steak (€17) and grilled chicken (€10). May–Sept daily 5pm–midnight.

★Argo ☎ 22430 59854. Although not on the seafront, *Argo* is a delightful place with a traditional kafenío atmosphere: the tables and chairs are hand-made and painted with different designs, fairy lights adorn the

courtyard and there's a hammock. Meze dishes include its famous potatoes with yogurt (€3.50), falafel (€4.50) and marinated mushrooms (€4.50) in the summer. Live music twice a week in the summer. Daily 10am–late.

Dapia Café ☎ 22430 61590. The pick of the waterfront cafés, with a large well-shaded terrace overlooking the harbour and free wi-fi. Good for full breakfasts, crêpes for €5, juices and infusions, as well as sunset drinks. Daily 8am–late.

HÓRA

Barbarossa ☎ 22430 61577. Located just as the main street starts to climb towards the kástro, this taverna is popular for its warm interior and sea-view terrace, though the food is unexceptional and the salads disappointing – expect dishes such as chicken with blue-cheese sauce (€9.50) or the ubiquitous moussaka (€7). Daily noon–midnight.

afé Kari ☎ 22430 61282. Georgeous, traditional café rving dishes such as feta with honey (€5) and crab melette (€6.50). Conveniently located just beneath the astle with outside seating looking down into town, it's an xcellent place to stop and sip a frappé after a steep climb p. June–Sept daily 9am–late.

★Gerani ☎ 22430 61484. Set inland from the little bridge in the middle of the beach, this taverna serves up Livádhia's best food with sea views from its large tiled terrace. Home-cooked specialities include peppers stuffed with feta (€6.50) and *rabbit stew (€8)*. May–Oct daily 11am–late.

IVÁDHIA

astropelos ☎ 22430 61473. With its large shaded patio, his beachside taverna is a great place to linger over tarters such as split pea dip (€4) or fish cakes (€6.50), hough the seafood can be expensive (seafood pasta €12). une–Sept daily 11am–late.

KAMINÁKIA

Linda ☎ 6972 129 088. Well-run beach taverna, serving honest, rustic fare – salads and a dish-of-the-day such as lamb stew cost around €7. Don't expect a big variety, but the owners are farmers, so all meat is fresh. Late June to early Sept daily noon–6pm.

The east

Astypálea's wilder and less populated **eastern** half is home to the island's airport and a small resort, **Maltezána**, but little else. Apart from a couple of south-coast beaches, the only day-trip worth making over here is the bumpy but spectacular drive out to the huge bay at **Mésa Vathý**.

Stenó and Plákes

Two good but isolated beaches stand on the southern shore of Astypálea's slender central isthmus. At **Stenó** (meaning "narrow", in reference to the isthmus), inviting turquoise shallows stretch away from a sandy shore. There's only limited shade, courtesy of a few tamarisks, but a *kantína* opens up in high summer.

Another kilometre east, the much quieter beach at **Plákes** has no facilities and can only be accessed by walking a few hundred metres down from the main road. It's at the end of the airport runways, but with barely a plane a day that's no problem.

Maltezána

The little resort of **MALTEZÁNA**, Astypálea's second-largest settlement, is 9km northeast of Péra Yialós, under 1km from the airport. Its official name is **ANÁLIPSI**, but it's universally known by the nickname it acquired thanks to medieval Maltese pirates. It's a good spot, though nothing remarkable, with a narrow, exposed, packed-sand beach, a small fishing port at its eastern end, and views south to islets.

ACCOMMODATION AND EATING   MALTEZÁNA

7 Asteira Restaurant ☎ 22430 61957. On the beachfront, this long established family-run taverna is good for simple dishes such as lamb on the spit (€6), young goat with wine (€8), or peppers suffed with rice (€5.50). Feb–Dec daily 11am–9pm.

Astifagia ☎ 22430 64004. On the beachfront, this taverna serves good seafood dishes such as grilled octopus

with fava beans (€15) or kalamári pasta (€12). It's not the cheapest, but worth it. Daily 10am–midnight.

Maltezana Beach ☎ 2243061558, ⓦ maltezanabeach. gr. Astypálea's largest hotel, with 42 large, well-appointed bungalow-rooms – five of which are family-sized apartments – plus a pool and on-site restaurant. Breakfast included. Easter to early Sept. **€60**

Mésa Vathý

Although the main road turns to dirt east of Maltezána, it remains just about passable in an ordinary car, and snakes its way onwards across the exposed hillsides all the way to **MÉSA VATHÝ**, at the head of an utterly magnificent west-facing bay 23km out from Hóra. Much the best way to arrive at this sleepy fishing hamlet would be by boat; it's a popular anchorage for pleasure yachts in summer. There's no town, just one little taverna; walk onwards from the end of the road to reach a small beach.

8

Kálymnos

Despite its size and beauty, the island of **KÁLYMNOS** has long been over-shadowed by Kos. Kálymnos fought in the Trojan War as a vassal of its southern neighbour, and to this day its tourist industry remains largely dependent on the overspill – and the airport – of Kos. In most respects, however, the islands are very different. Kálymnos is much more mountainous, consisting of three high limestone ridges that fan away from the continuous rugged cliffs of its west coast, to create two long sloping valleys that hold most of its settlements and agricultural land.

The island's capital and largest town, the busy port of **Póthia**, faces Kos from the midpoint of its southern shoreline. Most visitors head instead for the west coast, where a handful of small resorts have struggled to survive the collapse of a short-lived experiment in mass tourism. The pick of the pack, **Myrtiés**, stands close to some attractive little beaches. This craggy shoreline has found deserved fame among **climbers** and **hikers**, who keep businesses ticking along in the cooler spring and autumn months. For a beach holiday, you'd do better to head for the separate islet of **Télendhos** (a spectacular sight at sunset), or further north up the coast to **Emboriós**.

The prosperity of Kálymnos traditionally rested on its **sponge industry** (see box, opposite), but blights have now wiped out almost all the eastern Mediterranean's sponges. Only a few boats of the island's thirty-strong fleet remain in use, and most of the sponges sold behind the harbour are imported from Asia and the Caribbean.

ARRIVAL AND INFORMATION

KÁLYMNOS

By air Kálymnos's small airport, 6km northwest of Póthia, is served by a few Olympic, Aegean Airlines and Sky Airways flights. Destinations Astypalea (2 weekly via Léros; 1hr) Athens (6 weekly; 1hr); Léros (2 weekly; 30min); Rhodes, via Kos (2 weekly; 1hr 10min).

By ferry You can buy ferry tickets from Magos Tours (☎22430 28777) and Mahias Travel (☎22430 22909), both based in Póthia. The following schedules are from Póthia; there are also frequent ferries to Télendhos from Myrtiés (see p.580).

Detinations Agathoníssi (5 weekly; 2hr 15min–5hr 30min); Arkioi (4 weekly; 4hr 20min); Astypalea (3 weekly; 2hr 15min–2hr 45min); Halki (1 weekly; 4hr); Kastelórizo (2 weekly; 10hr 15min–13hr); Kos (Kos Town 1–3 daily; 30min–1hr; Mastihari 2 weekly; 20min–1hr); Léros (1–3 daily; 50min–1hr 20min); Lipsi (1–3 daily; 1hr 20min); Níssyros (2 weekly; 2hr 50min); Pátmos (1–3 daily; 1hr 40min–3hr 25min); Pireás (4 weekly; 9hr 40min–14hr 10min); Psérimos (1–2 daily; 20min); Rhodes (1–2 daily; 2hr 40min–8hr 15min); Sámos (5 weekly; 2hr 50min–6hr 50min); Sými (5 weekly; 2hr 10min–6hr 20min); Tílos (3 weekly; 4hr 20min).

Tourist office The municipal tourist office faces the ferry jetty in Póthia (Mon–Fri 8am–3pm; ☎22430 50956, ⓦkalymnosinfo.com).

GETTING AROUND

By bus Buses to the west-coast resorts (9 daily in season; 30min, roughly €1.50), and also northwest to Emboriós (2 daily; 50min, roughly €3) and east to Vathýs (3 daily; 30min; roughly €2), run from two terminals beside the municipal "palace".

By taxi Shared taxis, available at Platía Kyprou, cost less than normal taxis, at roughly €5.

By car and scooter Car rental outlets along Póthia quay include the recommended Auto Market (☎ 22430 51780, ⓦ kalymnoscars.gr), while for scooters check out Kostas (☎ 22430 50110), very close to the tourist office.

Póthia

The long curving waterfront of **PÓTHIA**, Kálymnos's main town and port, may not be architecturally distinguished, but arranged around a huge curving bay it looks fabulous at sunset. The town itself remains vibrant year-round, even if it's not really a tourist destination in its own right. With its houses marching up the valley inland or arrayed in tiers along the surrounding hillsides, it forms a natural amphitheatre that readily fills with noise, whether from souped-up motorbikes or summer sound systems. As well as the usual Italian-era "palace", at the centre of the bay, Póthia also boasts backstreets lined with elegant **Neoclassical houses**, painted the traditional pink or ochre.

Sprawled to either side of the road to the west coast, the built-up area of Póthia stretches northwest up the valley to the suburb of **Mýli**. The whitewashed battlements of the Knights' **Kástro Khryssoheriás** (unrestricted access), 1.2km along, offer wonderful views over town towards Kos. Another 1.5km up is the former island capital, **Hóra**, which is still a large, busy village.

Archeological Museum of Kálymnos
July to mid-Nov daily 9am–3pm • €2 • ☎ 2243 059092

Tucked away in an unremarkable and hard to find new building on Póthia's western hillside, the **Archeological Museum of Kálymnos** provides an excellent overview of local history. Everything is beautifully displayed, with very helpful captions in both Greek and English, and many of its artefacts are quite stunning. Its greatest treasures, discovered

8

SPONGES AND SPONGE DIVING

Sponges are colonies of microscopic marine organisms that excrete a fibrous skeleton. The living sponges that can be seen throughout the Aegean as black, melon-sized blobs, anchored to rocks in three to ten metres of water, are mostly "wild" sponges, impossible to clean or shape with shears. Kalymnian divers seek out "tame" sponges, which are much softer, more pliable, and dwell thirty to forty metres deep.

Sponge fishers were originally **free divers**; weighted with a rock, they'd collect sponges from the seabed on a single breath before being hauled back up to the surface. Starting in the late nineteenth century, however, divers were fitted with heavy, insulated suits (*skáfandhro*). Breathing through an air-feed line connected to compressors aboard the factory boats, they could now attain depths of up to 70m. However, this resulted in the first cases of the "bends". When divers came up too quickly, the dissolved air in their bloodstream bubbled out of solution – with catastrophic results. Roughly half of those early pioneers would leave with the fleets in spring but fail to return in autumn. Some were buried at sea, others, it's said, buried alive, up to their necks in hot sand, to provide slight relief from the excruciating pain of nitrogen bubbles in the joints.

By the time the malady became understood, during World War I, thousands of Kalymnians had died, with many survivors paralysed, deaf or blind. Even though the *skáfandhro* was banned elsewhere as the obvious culprit, it remained in use here until after World War II. After the first **decompression chambers** and diving schools reached Greece, in the 1950s, the seabed was stripped with ruthless efficiency, and the sponge fleets forced to hunt further from home.

Even the "tame" sponge is unusable until processed. The smelly organic matter and external membrane is thrashed out of them, traditionally by being trodden on the boat deck, and then they're tossed for a day or so in a vat of hot seawater. Visitors to Póthia's remaining handful of **workshops** can still watch the sponge vats spin; in the old days, the divers simply made a "necklace" of their catch and trailed it in the sea behind the boat.

To suit modern tastes, some sponges are bleached to a pale yellow colour with nitric acid. That weakens the fibres, however, so it's best to buy the more durable, natural-brown ones.

underwater during the 1990s, are a larger-than-life cast bronze figure of a woman draped in a chiton, thought to date from the second century BC, and the well-preserved bronze head of a ruler, which may have formed part of a colossal equestrian statue.

Municipal Nautical and Folklore Museum

Daily 10am–1pm • €2 • ☎ 2243 051361

Kálymnos's **Municipal Nautical and Folklore Museum**, very near the ferry port on the seaward side of Khristós cathedral, focuses on the sponge fishing past. A large photo shows Póthia in the 1880s, with no quay, jetty, roads or sumptuous mansions, and with most of the population still up in Hóra. You can also see horribly primitive divers' breathing apparatuses, and "cages" designed to keep propellers from cutting air lines.

Péra Kástro

Hóra • Dawn–dusk • Free • Access via a steep stair-path that climbs from the eastern edge of the village

The thirteenth-century Byzantine citadel-town of **Péra Kástro**, a magnificent fortified enclave atop the impressive crag that towers over Hóra, originally served as a refuge from seaborne raiders. Appropriated by the Knights of St John, it remained inhabited until the late 1700s.

Once you've passed through the massive gate and perimeter walls, you're faced with yet more stiff climbing, now through a jumble of overgrown ruins, tumbled stonework, and wild flowers, interspersed with the odd paved walkway. The views are tremendous, but the true highlights are the nine scattered **medieval chapels**, the only complete buildings to survive. Re-roofed and freshly whitewashed, several still have faded frescoes.

8

ACCOMMODATION	PÓTHIA

★**Hotel Apxontiko** ☎ 6942 838 524, ⓦ apxontiko -hotel.com. Tastefully renovated old building by the harbour, with marble floors that keep it cool in summer, and traditional Kálymnos furnishings throughout. All ten rooms have a balcony, five with harbour views, and the owner gives great attentive service. Breakfast included. **€55**

Hotel Panorama Amoudhára ☎ 22430 23138, ⓦ panorama-kalymnos.gr. Simple, well-kept hotel, high on the hillside west of the harbour, where all thirteen rooms have balconies overlooking the port. The

breakfast (included) salon has great views, too. **€45**

Villa Melina Enoria Evangelístria ☎ 22430 22682, ⓦ villa-melina.com. Póthia's quietest and most elegant hotel, set in attractive gardens near the Archeological Museum, just inland from the eastern side of the port. The pink, century-old Italianate villa holds seven high-ceilinged, insect-screened, wood-floored rooms while a further thirteen studios and apartments, sleeping up to six, are laid out around the large swimming pool behind. There's a friendly and very helpful family atmosphere. Breakfast included. **€45**

EATING AND DRINKING

Kafenes Khristós ☎ 22430 28727. Open since the 1950s, this pavement café/ouzerí in the centre of the harbour is popular with locals and tourists alike – try the liver with balsamic sauce (€6.50) or crab salad (€3). Daily 9.30am–3pm & 6pm–late.

O Stukas ☎ 6970 802 346. A traditional taverna, located along the harbour beyond the Town Hall, that serves dishes such as moussaka (€7.50) and lamb *stifado* (€9), along with standard meat and fish grills. Daily 8.30am–late.

Peri Orekseos ☎ 6956 202 534. Tucked away in a small square a few metres from the harbour, this meat and

seafood restaurant serves up traditional food with a twist. The menu is always changing, but expect dishes such as fresh sea urchin with cherry tomatoes (€7) or chicken nuggets with Creten cheese, mushrooms and red wine (€6). Sometimes has live music in summer. Daily 4pm–midnight.

Zaharoplastio O Mihalaras Áyios Nikólaos. A wonderful local cake shop housed in a traditional building on the harbourfront, next to the pharmacy – except delights such as baklava (€6) and Greek rice pudding (€4). Daily 8am–6pm.

Vathýs and Rína

Ten kilometres northeast of Póthia, and accessed via an initially dispiriting coastal road, the long, fertile valley known as **VATHÝS** is Kálymnos' agricultural heartland. Its orange and tangerine groves make a startling contrast to the mineral greys and ochres of the surrounding hills, but visitors only pass this way to visit the fjord port of **RÍNA** at its

outheastern end. Set at the end of a long slender inlet, Rína remains a popular
topover with yachties, and can also be reached by taxi-boats from Póthia. It's a very
cenic spot, with tiny little Christian basilicas perched on the cliffs to either side, while
he total lack of a beach keeps the crowds down. This safe anchorage has been in use
ince Neolithic times; several caves show signs of ancient occupation.

ACCOMMODATION AND EATING · VATHÝS AND RÍNA

Galini Hotel Restaurant Rína ☎ 22430 31241. One of
three similar, largely open-air restaurants clustered around
the harbour at Rína, the friendly *Galina* serves up taverna
food such as lamb chops (€7) and stuffed vegetables (€8).
It also doubles as a ten-room hotel, charging bargain B&B
rates for its clean, simple sea-view rooms. Breakfast
(included) is eaten in the adjoining taverna. Daily 7am–
late. **€35**

Northern Kálymnos

Fringed with wild flowers, and backed by mighty cliffs, Northern Kálymnos is great
hiking and **climbing** territory. **Emboriós** at the road's end makes a great overnight stop, or
you can simply complete a round-island car or scooter tour by heading inland from
Aryinónda, further south, and making your way back to Póthia via Vathýs (see opposite).

Aryinónda to Emboriós

Some 5km beyond Massoúri at the head of its own deeply indented bay, **ARYINÓNDA**
has a clean pebble beach, plus a couple of small tavernas. Keep heading north along the
west coast from here to find several more splendid, isolated beaches, including **Áyios
Nikólaos** and **Kalamiés**. The village of **EMBORIÓS**, at the end of the bus line 20km out
from Póthia, is a pretty little spot that offers a reasonable gravel-and-sand beach, and
a scattering of apartments and tavernas. The little jetty in the middle is served by
excursion boats from Myrtiés, which only run when demand is high enough.

A hundred metres beyond Emboriós, reached by a detour inland of the church, the next
cove along holds the similar, goat-patrolled **Asprokykliá beach**. Follow the rough dirt track
above Asprokykliá to the isthmus by the fish farm, then walk fifteen minutes north on
path and track to reach **Aptíki**, a smallish but perfectly formed pea-gravel cove.

Paliónissos and around

From Skália, 1km or so southeast of Emboriós, a newly paved road – signposted only
in Greek – switchbacks up the west flank of the island and back down the other side.
A steep but safe 5km drive, it stops short of the eastern shoreline, leaving visitors to
walk the final couple of hundred metres along a rough track.

Set at the head of another extravagantly indented fjord-like bay, the yacht anchorage
of **Paliónissos** is more usually reached by excursion boats from Rína (see opposite). It
boasts an ample crescent of shingle beach, with a taverna to either side.

ACCOMMODATION AND EATING · NORTHERN KÁLYMNOS

★**Harry's Paradise** Emboriós ☎ 22430 40062,
ⓦ harrys-paradise.gr. This lovely taverna, set behind
gorgeous flower-filled gardens a short walk from the beach,
serves delicious home-cooked food from a daily-changing
menu, using produce from their own fields – expect dishes
such as leek pie (€4) or a simple omelette (€6). Their small
hotel annexe has six great-value apartments, each with a
kitchenette and balcony – breakfast (included) usually
features eggs from their neighbour's poultry plus home-
made marmalade. April–Nov daily 9am–late. **€60**

The west coast

The mountainous headland that fills Kálymnos's southwest corner is largely
inaccessible. From the moment the island's **west coast** can be reached by road, however,
the shoreline is lined by a succession of small beach communities, though only **Myrtiés**
and **Massoúri** have enough facilities to make worthwhile bases.

Myrtiés to Armeós

Beach tourism on Kálymnos is most heavily concentrated in the twin resorts of **MYRTIÉS** and **MASSOÚRI**. Occupying neighbouring coves that start 8km northwest of Póthia, they face across to towering Télendhos islet (see below), and enjoy dramatic **sunsets**.

They're easy enough to reach on the island's main road, though once it's crossed the island to Pánormos, the road has to climb the Kamári pass before it can zigzag back down to the sea. A lengthy one-way loop then leads drivers through the two resorts. There's no significant gap in the commercial strip of restaurants and hotels that runs through them both, 50m up from the beach, and neither has a historic core or town centre.

The narrow, pebbly **beach** at Myrtiés has a marina at its southern end and the small concrete jetty used by the Télendhos ferries in the middle. The beach at Massoúri, ten minutes' walk north, is broader and sandier; the largest and liveliest on the island, it has a noisy beach-bar vibe in summer. There's also an all-sand beach at **Melitsáhas** cove, 500m south of Myrtiés, but its surroundings have become very run-down; don't reckon on staying there.

Another kilometre north of Massoúri, the coastal village of **Armeós** is the terminus for most local buses. In low season especially, it tends to be dominated by European **rock-climbers**. Several popular cliffs soar overhead – look for the route-inscribed columns at their base – and various businesses cater to climbers' needs.

ACCOMMODATION   THE WEST COAST

Ambiance Hotel Massouri ☎ 22430 59905, ⊛ hhotels. eu. Boutique-style hotel with sixteen clean, comfortable and stylish rooms, all with sea views: guests can eat breakfast (extra) at the *Ambiance Café*, next door. Double **€60**, triple **€70**

Hotel Atlantis Myrtiés ☎ 22430 47497, ⊛ atlantis-kalymnos.gr. Located in Myrtiés Bay, this hotel has seventeen large, well-located studios and apartments, complete with living room, kitchen and panoramic-view balconies looking across to the island of Télendhos. April–Oct. **€25**

Hotel Philoxenia Armeós ☎ 22430 59310, ⊛ philoxenia-kalymnos.com. Simple but good-value hotel, in prime climbing territory at the foot of the roadside hills, a 10min walk north of Massoúri. Plain clean rooms with large balconies, plus a pool with snack-bar; ask in advance if you want dinner. April–Nov. **€50**

Popis Studios Myrtiés ☎ 22430 47741 or ☎ 22430 23117, ⊛ popystudios.gr. Three large, clean, well-equipped studios with galleried sleeping areas. All have balconies with sea views, and are an easy walk to the beach. **€35**

EATING AND DRINKING

Barbayiannis Massoúri ☎ 22430 47215. Terrace restaurant, perched just above the main road in the centre of Massoúri, *Barbayannis* is a long-established taverna with a no-nonsense menu of Greek dishes such as tuna fillet (€9) or meat balls with hand cut chips (€7). April–Oct daily 12.30pm–late.

Ta Linária Linária ☎ 22430 47464. The main attraction of this family-run taverna is the view – it's right on the seafront with the waves lapping beneath.

Expect simple fare such as pork cutlets (€8) and fresh octopus (€6). May–Oct lunch & dinner.

Tsopanakos Armeós ☎ 22430 47929. This friendly meat specialist is the best old-school taverna to survive on the west coast. Whether on the lovely terrace in summer, or in the cosy indoor dining room in winter, feast on dishes such as island-grazed goat in tomato sauce (€8) or domlades (€5). Daily noon–9pm.

Télendhos

The towering pyramid-shaped islet of **TÉLENDHOS**, silhouetted at sunset a few hundred metres west of Myrtiés, was severed from Kálymnos by a cataclysmic earthquake in 554 AD. **Car-free**, home to a mere handful of year-round inhabitants, and blissfully tranquil, it's the single most compelling destination for Kálymnos visitors, and the short row of hotels and restaurants on its east-facing shore makes it a great place to spend a few nights. It's said that somewhere far below the narrow straits between Myrtiés and Télendhos, an ancient town lies submerged.

›eaches

: only takes a few minutes to explore the little built-up strip that stretches in both irections from the boat landing. A narrow **beach** of reasonable sand runs along the ›traight seafront, and the calm shallow water is ideal for kids. Kayaks and beach toys ·re available for rent, while tousled tamarisks provide shade.

To find a more secluded beach, simply keep walking. A few hundred metres north · head right from the boat landing, and keep going after the paved coastal roadway ›eters out to become a dirt path – is the nudist **Paradise** beach, which is peaceful and ·heltered, but at its best in the morning, before the sun disappears for good behind the ·nountain. A ten-minute walk southwest of the village, following a footpath over the idge, will bring you to the pebble beach at **Hokhlakás**, a scenic but more exposed spot ·where the sea tends to be much rougher.

Áyios Vassílios and Ayía Triádha

While all the shoreline buildings are of modern construction, abundant ruins are ;cattered slightly further afield. Closest to the village, north of the boat landing, a ;eafront field holds the ruined outline of the thirteenth-century monastery of **Áyios Vassílios**. On the hillside immediately above Hokhlakás is **Ayía Triádha**, ɔriginally an enormous basilica, though now just a few stones survive. Further up ‡he slopes, wherever you look, giant Cyclopean caves burrow deep into the foot of ‡he central massif.

ARRIVAL AND DEPARTURE

By boat Regular boat-buses shuttle between Myrtiés, on Kálymnos, and Télendhos (8am–midnight every 30min; approx 20min; €2).

ACCOMMODATION TÉLENDHOS

Hotel Porto Potha ☎ 22430 47321, ⊛ telendoshotel .gr. Friendly hotel on the hillside just north of *On The Rocks* (see below), with twelve comfortable and spacious guest rooms, eight self-catering studios, and a large pool, plus what amounts to a private beach. Special offers for hikers and climbers in low season. April to mid-Oct. €̲4̲5̲
On the Rocks ☎ 22430 48260. Three superbly appointed rooms, with balconies and sea views, above

the beachfront restaurant 200m north of the ferry jetty: free kayaks available to borrow. The same friendly owners also rent a studio near Hokhlakás beach, with double-glazing, kitchen and bug screens. Breakfast included. April–Nov. €̲6̲5̲
Zorba's ☎ 22430 48660. Very simple en-suite rooms at bargain prices, above a reasonable taverna a short walk south from the ferry jetty. No wi-fi. €̲4̲5̲

EATING AND DRINKING

Barba Stathis ☎ 22430 47953, ⊛ barba-stathis.gr. Also known as *Tassia's*, this welcoming place is just behind *Zorba's* (see above) en route to Hokhlakás. There's a barbecue every night, with daily specials such as moussaka (€8) or fresh-made *dolmádhes* (€10). Daily 11am–late.
On the Rocks ☎ 22430 48260. Well-located restaurant, with a shaded patio overlooking the beach not far north of the ferry jetty, and run by a very friendly Greek-Australian

family. A full menu of fresh fish and meat dishes such as seafood spaghetti (€15) and lamb stifado (€10). Wednesday night is Greek barbecue, with music and dancing. It also holds a lively bar. Daily 9am–late.
Plaka Next door to, and slightly cheaper than, *On the Rocks* (see above), this large vine-covered terrace, poised just above the beach, is a great place to enjoy inexpensive local dishes such as goat with tomato sauce (€9), or fresh octopus (€10). Daily lunch and dinner.

HIKING ON TÉLENDHOS

Setting out to **hike** right round Télendhos would be a mistake; it's a long and exposed walk with little reward. Devote an hour or two, however, to investigating the islet's **southwest corner**, a little low-lying afterthought. Follow the footpaths through the woods, signed to "Early Christian Necropolis", and in addition to some intact arched sixth-century tombs you'll come to a perfectly sheltered sandy cove that's ideal for swimming and snorkelling.

Léros

As the island of **LÉROS** is indented with deep, sheltered bays, lined with little settlements, it doesn't have an obvious "capital". Ferries arrive at both **Lakkí** on the west coast and **Ayía Marína** on the east, but neither is recommended as a place to stay. Instead visitors congregate in the resorts of **Pandélli** and **Álinda**, and in more refined **Plátanos** up on the hillside. While Léros can be very attractive, however, it doesn't have spectacular **beaches**, so tourism remains relatively low-key.

The island still bears traces of the **Battle of Léros** of November 1943, when German paratroops displaced a Commonwealth division that had occupied Léros following the Italian capitulation. Bomb nose cones and shell casings turn up as gaily painted garden ornaments, or serve as gateposts. After the war, the local economy relied on prisons and sanatoria in former Italian military buildings. During the civil war and the later junta, leftists were confined to a notorious **detention centre** at Parthéni, while **hospitals** at Lecida, 3km from Lakkí, warehoused intractable psychiatric cases and mentally handicapped children. In 1989, a major scandal exposed conditions in the asylums, and most wards were eventually closed: today, the asylums house the relatively small number of refugees who arrive on Léros.

ARRIVAL AND DEPARTURE

By air The tiny airport is near the island's northern tip.
Destinations Astypálea (3 weekly; 25min); Athens (1 daily; 1hr); Kálymnos (3 weekly; 20min); Kos, via Kálymnos (1 daily; 1hr 45min); Rhodes, via Kalymnos or Kos (1 daily; 4–5hr).

By ferry Large ferries and the *Dodekanisos Pride* catamaran arrive at Lakkí; smaller ferries and the *Dodekanisos Express* arrive at Ayía Marína. You can book tickets with Aegean Travel, 9 King George Ave, in Lakkí

LÉROS

(☎ 22470 26000, ⊕ aegeantravel.gr) and Kastis Travel, in Ayía Marína (☎ 22470 22140).
Destinations Agathoníssi (5 weekly; 1hr 10min–4hr); Arkí (5 weekly; 2hr 50min); Kálymnos (1–2 daily; 45min–1hr 15min); Kos (1–3 daily; 1hr 25min–3hr); Lipsí (2–3 daily; 20min–1hr); Pátmos (2–4 daily; 40min–1hr 55min); Pireás (4 weekly; 9–11hr); Rhodes (1–2 daily; 4hr–5hr 15min); Samos (3 weekly; 1hr 55min–5hr 20min); Sými (6 weekly; 3hr 10min–5hr 50min); Syros (2–3 weekly; 5hr 30min).

GETTING AROUND

By bus The island bus starts from the main taxi rank in Platanós, heads north via Ayía Marína, Álinda then turns around to go to the airport, Parthéni, and south to Lakkí and Xirókambos: it runs approx every 30min from 7.30am– 8pm, though times change regularly, so check

with your accommodation.
By car and scooter Take care if you rent a scooter – Lerian roads are particularly narrow, potholed and gravel-strewn, and the low-slung, fat-tyred bikes on offer don't cope well. Try Motoland (Pandélli, ☎ 22470 26400; Álinda, ☎22470 24584) or Rent A Car Léros (Lakkí, ☎22470 22330).

Lakkí and around

Set in a hugely indented bay on Léros's southwest coast, the unusual town of **LAKKÍ** is the arrival port for all the island's large **ferries**. Built in the 1930s as a model town to house 7500 civilian dependants of an adjacent Italian naval base, it's now an incongruous under-populated relic. Sweeping boulevards, out of all proportion to the traffic they see, are lined with Stream Line Modern buildings (see box, opposite) including a round-fronted cinema, but the entire seafront tends to be devoid of life even in high season.

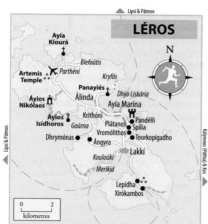

LÉROS

N

Lakkí's nearest approximation to a beach, sand-and-gravel **Kouloúki**, 500m west, has ample trees for shade and supports a seasonal taverna. A kilometre or so beyond is Merikiá, which is a little nicer, and has two tavernas.

War Museum

Merikiá, 2km west of Lakkí • Daily 9am–1.30pm • €3 • ☎ 22470 22109

An interesting little **War Museum**, set in two long arched tunnels that burrow deep into the hillside close to Merikiá beach, commemorates the 1943 Battle of Léros. Part of an enormous Italian-built subterranean complex, the tunnels are crammed with barely World War II documents, models, machine guns and assorted military hardware. To make sense of it all, head first to the far end and watch the archival footage.

Xirókambos

The fishing port of **XIRÓKAMBOS**, 5km south of Lakkí, is served by regular *kaïki* from Myrtiés on Kálymnos. It's a pretty spot, and many visitors swim, but the beach itself is unremarkable, though it does improve as you head west.

In the hillside village of **LEPÍDHA**, 1km short of Xirókambos, a side turning north of the island's campsite leads up to a tiny **acropolis**. Behind the modern summit chapel, you can admire stretches of restored ancient masonry, while the views across to Kálymnos are superb.

ACCOMMODATION AND EATING   XIRÓKAMBOS

Hotel Efstathia ☎ 22470 24099. Studio apartments set 50m back from the beach, with huge, well-furnished doubles with rather basic bathrooms as well as family apartments facing a large pool. Includes breakfast. **€40**

To Aloni ☎ 22470 26048. Xirókambos's best waterfront taverna, where the road meets the sea, with beachside tables shaded by jacarandas. The menu changes daily, but expect dishes like *souvlakí* and grilled meats such as chicken served with mushroom sauce (€9) as well as fresh fish (sea bream €10). Daily 11am–9pm.

8

ITALIAN ARCHITECTURE IN THE DODECANESE

The architectural heritage left by the Italian domination in the Dodecanese has only recently begun to be appreciated. Many structures had been allowed to deteriorate, if not abandoned, by Greeks who would rather forget the entire Italian legacy.

Although the buildings are often dubbed "Art Deco", and some contain elements of that style, most are properly classed as **Rationalist** (or in the case of Léros, **Stream Line Modern**). They drew on various post-World War I architectural, artistic and political trends across Europe, particularly Novecento (a sort of Neoclassicism), the collectivist ideologies of the time, and the paintings of Giorgio di Chirico. The school's purest expressions tended to have grid-arrays of windows (or walls entirely of glass); tall, narrow ground-level arcades; rounded-off bulwarks; and either a uniform brick surface or grooved/patterned concrete. As well as in Italy and Greece, examples can still be found as far afield as Moscow and London (underground stations and blocks of flats), Los Angeles (apartment buildings) and Ethiopia (cinemas).

Italy initially attempted to create a hybrid of Rationalist style and local vernacular elements in the Dodecanese, to evoke a supposed generic "Mediterranean-ness". Every Italian-claimed island had at least one specimen in this "**protectorate**" style, usually the gendarme station, post office, covered market or governor's mansion, but only on the most populous or strategic islands were plans drawn up for sweeping urban re-ordering.

The years from 1936 to 1941 saw an intensified Fascist imperial ideology, an increased reference to the heritage of the Romans and their purported successors the Knights, and the replacement of the "protectorate" style with that of the "**conqueror**". This involved "**purification**", the stripping of many public buildings in Rhodes (though not, curiously, in Kos) of their orientalist ornamentation, its replacement with a cladding of porous stone to match medieval buildings in the old town, plus a monumental severity – blending Neoclassicism and modernism – and rigid symmetry to match institutional buildings (especially Fascist Party headquarters) and public squares across Italy.

Plátanos, Pandélli and around

Five kilometres north of Lakkí, across the island, a continuous built-up strip climbing across a low ridge to connect two east-coast bays nominally consists of three distinct villages. On the shore of the northern bay, **Ayía Marína** stretches along a quayside used by smaller inter-island ferries (see p.582). Immediately above it, older **Plátanos** stands beneath a Knight's castle, while on the bay to the south is **Pandélli**, a busy but attractive little resort.

Plátanos

A 1min taxi ride or 5min walk up from the ferry dock

Draped over the saddle between Ayía Marína and Pandélli, **PLÁTANOS** is a residential community full of fine Neoclassical and vernacular houses. It's a good central base for exploring the island, but short on restaurants or nightlife.

Kástro

May–Oct daily 8.30am–1pm, plus Wed, Sat & Sun 3pm–7pm; Nov–April daily 8.30am–12.30pm • Free

Atop the mighty headland northeast of Plátanos, Léros' **kástro** overlooks virtually the entire island – the reason, of course, why the Knights built a castle up here. Reach it either via a steep stair-path from the central square, or along a zigzagging road that starts its climb 100m back from the beach in Pandélli.

Although the castle's walls and staircases have been stabilized and/or restored, there's little to see; the reason to come is to enjoy the stupendous views from the battlements, especially dramatic at sunset.

Archeological Museum

July–Sept Mon–Sat 9am–2.30pm • €3 • ☎ 22470 24775

Léros's **Archeological Museum**, a short way down towards Ayía Marína, is little more than a single room. Its few artefacts are, however, well laid out, with a good explanation of where each was found, and a clear account of Lerian history.

Pandélli

Ten minutes' walk down from Plátanos, the former fishing village of **PANDÉLLI** is a smart, rather upscale, popular little resort. In summer, there's little room on its small but reef-free, pea-gravel **beach** for anyone other than guests at its beachfront hotels, but it has a good crop of cafés and tavernas. A short way east around the bay, a long cement jetty still serves local fishermen rather than yachts, which in high season must anchor offshore.

Southern beaches

Sadly, the prominent coastal footpath that heads south from Pandélli peters out as soon as it curves out of sight. To reach **VROMÓLITHOS**, 1km south, pedestrians and drivers alike have to follow a higher road, through the village of Spília.

Although the **beach** at Vromólithos is usually less crowded than Pandélli, it's no place to linger, consisting of a long narrow strip of exposed gravel squashed up against the high walls of beachfront properties. The sea is clean, but you have to cross rock seabed at most points to reach deeper water. There's a more secluded, sandier cove southeast towards **Tourkopígadho**, and an even better duo at the end of the side road to **Aï Yiórgi**.

ACCOMMODATION

Castelo Beach Pandélli beach ☎ 22470 23030, ⓦ castelo.gr. With its castellated tiers dominating the west end of Pandélli beach, this hotel is an eyesore, but once inside –in the spacious rooms, many of which have four-poster beds, or in the terrace café, perched just above water – it's a great place to relax. Breakfast included. **€85**

★**Maison des Couleurs** Plátanos ☎ 22470 23341, ⓦ maisondescouleurs.com. This gorgeous Italianate mansion, tucked up on the hillside just a few steps from the centre of Plátanos, holds five irresistibly stylish suites, each decorated in a different colour and featuring antique furnishings such as four-poster beds or clawfoot

...bs. Charming and very helpful hosts, and superb breakfasts (included) out on the terrace. July to mid-...ct. **€80**

Panteli Beach Studios Pandélli beach ☏ 22470 ...6450, ⓦ panteli-beach.gr. Dutch-owned complex of ...ery tasteful and comfortable studios and apartments, ...ll with balcony or terrace. There's no pool, but it opens ...irectly onto the beach. **€50**

Pension Kavos Pandélli beach ☏ 22470 23247.

Family-run studios, at the east end of the harbour by the fishing jetty: it has ten good-sized, airy terraced rooms with sea-view balconies. **€45**

★ **Windmills/Anemomyli** Pandélli ☏ 6936 932 619, ⓦ leroswindmills.com. Lovely little B&B complex, poised above Pandélli on the road up to the castle, and consisting of two galleried windmill apartments and a long cottage, all with stone floors and great views from rear terraces. May–Oct. **€80**

EATING AND DRINKING

★ **Mezedhopolio O Dimitris O Karaflas** Adjoining the *Hotel Rodon* in Spília, between Pandélli and Vromólithos ☏ 22470 25626. One of the best-located ouzerís on the island, mainly because of its sunset views, it serves ample portions of Lerian delicacies such as chunky local sausages (€4), onion rings (€5) and *floyéres* (crispy rolls stuffed with cheese and sometimes ham; €5). Daily lunch and dinner.

★ **Mylos** Ayía Marína ☏ 22470 24894. Excellent restaurant, in a romantic setting by the wave-lapped windmill at the western edge of Ayía Marína. The menu has strong Italian leanings, featuring dishes such as octopus meatballs (€6.50), wild mushroom risotto (€15.50) and couscous with mussels (€11). Book ahead in summer. March–Oct daily 1pm–midnight.

View Café/Bar Apittiki ☏ 6906 454 664. Situated on the hillside just before the castle, this café/restaurant, with a flowered terraced garden, is in a prime location by the windmills, overlooking virtually the whole island. Simple dishes such as bruschetta (€6) or spinach crepe (€5) plus a daily changing menu of sweets made by the owner's family, such as baklava (€4). Late June–Sept daily 9.30am–late.

Zorba's Pandélli beach ☏ 22470 22027. Pandélli's best seafront restaurant, with tables on the beach itself, as well as on a long terrace. It serves mainly seafood, with dishes such as seafood risotto (€8) or lobster spaghetti (€12). Service can be slow at peak times. Reserve ahead in summer. Daily 10am–11.30pm.

NIGHTLIFE

Café del Mar Vromólithos ☏ 22470 24766. Stylish, laidback bar, nestling along a shelf in the hillside just above the north end of Vromólithos beach. Very relaxing in the daytime, but it hots up at night. Daily noon–late.

Meltemi Ayía Marína ☏ 22470 23060. Frequented by locals and tourists alike, this popular bar with a nautical theme has outdoor seating and occasionally hosts live

music. Daily 10am–late.

Savana Pandélli beach ⓦ savanabar-leros.com. Long-standing and very civilized English-Danish bar at the far end of the port. Despite its shaded seafront terrace, it retains a laidback rural feel and is the perfect spot for a late-night musical nightcap (cocktails around €6.50) – things get going from 10pm nightly. Daily noon–late.

Álinda and around

ÁLINDA, 3km northwest around the bay from Ayía Marína, is the longest-established resort on Léros, with development fringing a long, narrow strip of pea-gravel beach. It's also the first area to open in spring and the last to shut in autumn.

Historical and Folklore Museum

Álinda • May–Sept Tues–Sun 9am–noon & 6pm–9pm • €3 • ☏ 22470 25040

Housed in a castle-like seafront mansion, the island's **Historical and Folklore Museum** concentrates on the Battle of Léros. Displays include relics from the sunken *Queen Olga*, a wheel from a Junkers bomber, and a stove made from a bomb casing. There's also a grisly mocked-up clinic (mostly gynaecological tools), assorted rural implements, costumes and antiques.

Beaches

Beaches near Álinda include **Krithóni**, 1.5km south, where its pretty cove gets very crowded in summer. Several more gravelly inlets lie alongside the road that curves around the bay further north, collectively known as **Dhýo Liskária**. From the dead end of the road, a 25-minute scramble north on a faint path brings you to pebbly **Kryfós** cove.

ACCOMMODATION AND EATING

★**Archontiko Angelou** Álinda ☏6944 968 182, ⓦhotel-angelou-leros.com. Grand, atmospheric if slightly faded Italianate villa, a few hundred metres inland from the beach. Nine pretty and very different rooms, with Victorian bath fittings, beamed ceilings and antique furnishings; two have balconies with views of the lovely gardens. A/C rooms (€84) and the vegetarian gluten-free breakfast cost extra. Open most of the year – check winter opening dates. **€70**

Hotel Papafotis Álinda ☏22470 22247, ⓦapartments-studios-leros.com. Some 30 metres from Álinda beach, this father-and-daughter run establishment has fifteen simple, quiet and clean rooms and studios (sleeping up to four), all with balconies or terrace. **€30**

Hotel Princess Álinda ☏22470 24140 ⓦlerosprincess. com. In a huge, oppulant red building, this boutique hotel at the top of Álinda has sweeping views of the bay, a pool and a gorgous breakfast terrace. Staggered down the hillside, the 21 suites all have balconies with either garden, pool or sea views; some have Jacuzzis. Buffet breakfast included. **€152**

★**Nefeli Hotel** Krithóni, between Ayía Marina an[d] Álinda ☏22470 24611, ⓦnefelihotels-leros.com Modern terraced bungalow complex arranged around [a] gorgeous, well-tended garden/bar with 24 individuall[y] styled rooms, tastefully designed in a traditional style. Th[e] local produce-based breakfast (included) is served in th[e] garden room. **€70**

Prima Plora Álinda ☏22470 26122. Along the coas[t] road in Álinda, with tables on the beach, this predominantly fish restaurant serves appetizers such as shrimp pies (€4.50), while main courses include tuna fillet (€12) or bee[f] in lemon sauce (€9). Feb–Dec 11am–midnight.

Vareladiko Dhýo Liskária ☏22470 23726. The last beachfront taverna you come to, at the road's end east of Álinda, where the owners have playfully painted walls and the hillside itself to make it look like a hotel, but all the "rooms" are just facades. As a restaurant, with seaside seating, it serves very simple dishes such as pasta carbonara (€6) or pan-fried chicken with peppers and onions (€9). April–Oct 9am–late.

8

Goúrna and Dhrymónas

The best beach on Léros's west coast is **Goúrna**, at the head of a large bay 2km southwest of Álinda or 3km north of Lakkí. It's the longest sandy beach on the island, hard-packed and gently shelving, if wind-buffeted and somewhat scruffy. A road along the southern shore of the bay ends beside a jetty at little **Dhrymónas**.

ACCOMMODATION AND EATING

Gourna Taverna Goúrna ☏22470 22956. Friendly taverna, with free sunbeds, right in the middle of Goúrna beach. Sample fish dishes such as squid saganaki (€11) or simple grilled meat such as pork steak (€8). Daily 8am–late.

Ouzerí Sotos Dhrymónas ☏22470 24546. This quayside restaurant is so close to the sea that they plant some tables right in the water. It serves good food at good prices with most of the fish caught by Sotios, the owner – expect dishes such as feta with tomatoes and courgettes (€8) and

stuffed or baked squid (€13). Late April–Oct daily noon–late.

Psilalonia Dhrymónas ☏22470 25283, ⓦpsilalonia .com. Lovely, little French-owned B&B, up on the hillside above the far end of the bay at Dhrymónas (turn left at the small chapel where the coast road stops). Three cute, terraced rooms set in a row with fabulous views of the bay. There's no a/c, though their location means they sometimes get a cool breeze in summer. Includes breakfast. April–Oct, except Easter. **€65**

Pátmos

Arguably the most beautiful and certainly the best known of the smaller Dodecanese, **PÁTMOS** has a distinctive, immediately palpable atmosphere. It was in a cave here that St John the Divine (known in Greek as *O Theológos*, "The Theologian", and author of one of the four Gospels) set down the **Book of Revelation**, the final book of the New Testament. The huge fortified **monastery** that honours him remains the island's dominant feature; its monks owned all of Pátmos until the eighteenth century, and their influence remains strong.

Aside from its religious sites, Pátmos's greatest attraction is its **beaches**. With so many attractive strands, you can usually escape the crowds even in high season, though you may need a vehicle to do so. **Day-trippers** exceed overnighters, thanks in art to the island's lack of an airport, nd Pátmos feels a different place once he last excursion boat has left after unset. Among those staying, the island ttracts an upmarket clientele, including ssorted royal and ex-royal families mong repeat visitors, and no single nationality predominates, lending Pátmos a **cosmopolitan** feel almost nique in the Dodecanese.

ARRIVAL AND INFORMATION
PÁTMOS

By ferry All ferries arrive in the heart of Skála.

Destinations Agathonísi (6 weekly; 1hr 50min–2hr 50min); Arkí (6 weekly; 40min); Kálymnos (2–3 daily; 1hr 35min–4hr); Kos (1–3 daily; 1hr 35min–5hr); Léros (2–4 daily; 40min–1hr 55min); Lipsí (1–4 daily; 25–50min); Pireás (4 weekly; 8hr 10min); Rhodes (1–2 daily; 4hr 45min–9hr 45min); Samos (2–4 daily; 1hr–3hr 10min); Sými (7 weekly; 4hr–8hr); Syros (3–5 weekly; 4hr).

Travel agencies Astoria Travel (☎ 22470 31205, ⓦ astoriatravel.com) and Apollon Travel (☎ 22470 31324), both on Skála's main waterfront street.

Information Pátmos has no tourist office, though the Orthodox Culture and Information Center facing the ferry landing (Mon, Tues, Thurs & Fri 9am–1pm & 6–9pm, Sat & Sun 6–9pm) provides information on the island's religious sites, and posts current opening hours. ⓦ patmos-island. com and ⓦ patmosweb.gr are useful websites.

GETTING AROUND

By bus Island buses leave from the quayside to Hóra (11 daily; 25min), Gríkou (8 daily; 25min) and Kámbos (4 daily; 25min); flat fare €1.50. Note, journey times vary according to how many goats are on the road or if the driver stops to have a chat.

By car and scooter Numerous outfits, including Tom &

Gerry (☎ 22470 32066) and Rent-a-Car Express (☎ 6976 220 855): always book ahead in high season.

By excursion boat Boats to Psilí Ámmos and Arkí/ Maráthi leave the quayside from 9.30–10am (10.10–11am to Léros and Lipsí depending on day/season).

Skála

Home to most of Pátmos's 3200 official residents, **SKÁLA** seems initially to contradict any solemn image of the island; the commercial district with its gift boutiques is incongruously sophisticated for such a small town. During peak season, the quay and inland lanes throng with trippers, and visitors still tend to arrive after dark, including those from the huge, humming cruisers that weigh anchor around midnight. Skála becomes a ghost town by early October, when most shops and restaurants close for the winter.

Given time, Skála reveals more enticing corners in the residential fringes to its east and west, where vernacular mansions hem in pedestrian lanes creeping up the hillsides. At the summit of the westerly rise, **Kastélli**, you'll find an ancient acropolis, inside which is a more recently built chapel. An easy ten-minute walk southwest across the flat isthmus, starting from the central market street, brings you to pebbly **Hokhlakás Bay** on the island's west coast. More of a quiet seafront suburb than a beach, it enjoys wonderful sunset views.

ACCOMMODATION

Asteri Near Mérihas cove, Nétia ☎ 22470 32465, ⓦ asteripatmos.gr. The best option in Nétia, set in spacious grounds on a knoll overlooking the bay, just under a 10min walk from the ferry. It has simply furnished rooms of varying sizes, with sea-view balconies; two have wheelchair access. Breakfasts (included) feature own-grown produce. **€40**

Australis Nétia ☎ 22470 32284, ⓦ patmosaustralis.gr. Very friendly, yet somewhat spartan hotel, owned by a helpful Greek-Australian family. Units in the better-standard apartment annexe sleep up to six. Breakfast included. **€45**

Blue Bay Skála ☎ 22470 31165, ⓦ bluebaypatmos.gr. Multitiered Greek-Australian-run hotel on the hillside just above the sea, a short walk south from the jetty just out of sight of Skála. There's no beach, but all the rooms have substantial sea-view balconies. Credit cards only accepted for stays of over two days. Breakfast included. **€40**

Captain's House Konsoláto ☎ 22470 31793, ⓦ captains -house.gr. A fourteen-roomed hotel, moments from the jetty and facing a tiny beach dotted with café tables. The quiet rooms in the rear wing overlook a fair-sized pool and shady terrace. Friendly management and tasteful furnishings including Coco-Mat bedding. Breakfast included. **€60**

Hellenis Netiá ☎ 22470 31275, ⓦ hotelhellinispatmos .gr. This whitewashed forty-roomed hotel is very close to the sea path and just north of a new yacht marina. It has bright, airy common areas and better-than-average rooms

with fridges, balconies and baths. **€30**

Hotel Villa Zacharo Skála ☎ 22470 31529, ⓦ vil˙ -zacharo.gr. Small, ten-roomed family-run hotel on th road to Hóra. The lovely front garden, free tea and coffee the lobby, plus freshly prepared breakfasts using loc produce (included) offset the simply furnished, balconie rooms with tiny bathrooms. **€40**

★**Porto Scoutari** Melói hillside ☎ 22470 33124 ⓦ portoscoutari.com. Although slightly far from the mai town, Pàtmos' premier boutique hotel has rooms sprea around the landscaped gardens: all overlooking the beac and islets. The communal areas are arranged around a larg pool and small spa. Breakfast included. **€65**

Skala Hotel Skála ☎ 22470 31343, ⓦ skalahotel.gr Smart, large, bougainvillea-drenched hotel, set a shor way back from the quayside in the heart of the village, and accessed via a flowery gateway-gazebo. The 78 comfortable rooms have sea-view balconies, and there's a large pool. Breakfast included. **€70**

Studios Mathios Sápsila beach ☎ 22470 32583, ⓦ mathiosapartments.gr. Superior rural accommodation, ranging from five small studios to an entire house, beside an unremarkable beach 2km southeast of Skála, with creative decor and extensive gardens. Owners Iakoumina and Theologos are exceptionally welcoming. Studio **€45**, house **€70**

EATING AND DRINKING

Aigaionesti Skála ☎ 22470 34188. Facing Theológos town beach a short walk along the quayside from the excursion boats, this above-average restaurant has a long menu featuring dishes such as Patmos slow-cooked beef in red wine sauce with mushrooms and mashed potato (€12) or grilled salmon with cauliflower and broccoli sauce (€16.50). As well as enticing tables on the beach, there's seating on the sea-view terrace. Daily 7pm–late.

Helios Skála ☎ 22470 31978. Opposite where the ships disembark, this Italian restaurant has a good menu of *al dente* pasta dishes such as porcini tagliatelle (€9) and salmon farfalle (€9). There's outdoor seating only and, being right by the roundabout it's a little noisy, but the food is worth it. Feb–Sept daily 2pm–late.

Ostria Skála ☎ 22470 31514. The food tends to be run-of-the-mill at this central ouzerí, facing the excursion-boat quay, but – late ferry arrivals take note – it's the only place

serving after 11pm: expect dishes such as stuffed grilled kalamári (€13) or pork steak (€7.50). Live music most summer nights. Daily 10am–late.

To Hiliomodhi Skála ☎ 22470 34179. Cheap and very popular ouzerí, a few metres from the waterfront at the start of the road to Hóra; it serves mezédhes such as fried peppers (€3.50) and seafood delicacies including fresh grilled octopus (€10), plus decent *hýma* wine from Mégara. There's outdoor seating at the back, in an unremarkable pedestrian lane. Daily 6pm–11pm.

★**Votris Restaurant** Skála ☎ 6988 807 376. Just outside Skála on the road to Kambos, this gorgeous balconied restaurant overlooks the marina. Appetizers include hummus with Arabic pitta bread (€5), while mains feature dishes such as caramalized spare ribs (€8). Book ahead in high season. May–Oct daily 6pm–11.30pm.

NIGHTLIFE

Art Café Skála ☎ 22470 33092. Sit inside at the bar, or on the roof terrace overlooking the harbour and monastery of St John at this bohemian-style café next to Rent-a-Car Express, on the harbour. Listen to jazz, blues, rock, old classics, or sometimes live music, while owner Katerina makes cocktails (€8), Baileys smoothies (€6) and desserts

such as lemon pie (€5). Daily 7pm–late.

Café Arion Skála ☎ 22470 31595. This appealing wood-panelled, barn-like place, in the centre of the quayside, is Pátmos's most durable café-bar; all sorts sit outside, dance inside or prop up the long bar. Daily 9am–late.

Ginger Bar Skála ☎ 22470 31009. This small, brightly

rnished place near the *Captain's House* (see opposite) lays the latest tunes, with regular DJ and live performances attracting a slightly younger, Greek crowd. Outside seating at the mosaic tables is a great place to people watch. Daily noon–late.

Koukoumavla Konsoláta ☎ 22470 32325. The "Owl" is a perennially popular, hippy-ish bar near the foot of the main road up to Hóra. Run by a friendly Italian-Greek couple, it has garden seating, wacky decor and live music, and sells crafts as well as snacks and drinks. Daily noon–late.

Apokálypsis monastery

Daily 8am–1.30pm, also Tues, Thurs & Sun 4–6pm. Also opens for cruise ship groups • €2

A ten-minute walk up the hill from Skála, halfway to Hóra, the **Apokálypsis monastery** is built around the cave where St John heard the voice of God issuing from a cleft in the rock, and where he sat dictating to his disciple Prohoros. The cave itself, of course, was once open to the elements, but it's now enclosed within an eleventh-century **chapel**. In a recess in the rock, the place where the saint is said to have rested his head at night is fenced off and outlined in beaten silver. Only if you come first thing in the morning, before the tour groups arrive, can you hope to get a sense of the contemplative peace that inspired St John.

Ayíou Ioánnou Theológou monastery

Daily 8am–1.30pm, also Tues, Thurs & Sun 4–6pm. Also opens for cruise ship groups • Free, museum €6

In 1088, the soldier-cleric **Ioannis "The Blessed" Khristodhoulos** (1021–93) was granted title to Pátmos by Byzantine emperor Alexios Komnenos. Within three years, he and his followers had completed most of what's now **Ayíou Ioánnou Theológou monastery**. Enclosed within its stout hilltop walls, a warren of courtyards, chapels, stairways, arcades, and roof terraces offers a rare glimpse of a Patmian interior. In antiquity, this site held a temple of Artemis, marble columns from which were incorporated here and there in the monastery.

As most of the complex is closed to outsiders – it remains home to a community of around a dozen monks – few visitors spend more than half an hour up here. The diminutive flower-bedecked courtyard just inside the gate opens onto the church itself,

8

SAINT JOHN ON PÁTMOS

Pátmos has been intimately associated with Christianity since **John the Evangelist** – later John the Divine – was exiled here from Ephesus by emperor Domitian in about 95 AD. John is said to have written his **Gospel** on Pátmos, but his sojourn is better remembered for the otherworldly voice that he heard coming from a cleft in the ceiling of his hillside grotto, which bid him to set down its words in writing. By the time John was allowed to return home, that disturbing finale to the New Testament, the **Book of Revelation** (aka the Apocalypse), had been disseminated as a pastoral letter to the Seven Churches of Asia Minor.

Revelation followed the standard Judeo-Christian tradition of apocalyptic books, with titanic battles in heaven and on earth, supernatural visions, plus lurid descriptions of the fates awaiting the saved and the damned following the **Last Judgement**. Open to widely different interpretations, Revelation was being wielded as a rhetorical and theological weapon within a century of appearing. Its vivid imagery lent itself to depiction in frescoes adorning the refectories of Byzantine monasteries and the narthexes of Orthodox churches, conveying a salutary message to illiterate medieval parishioners.

John also combated paganism on Pátmos, in the person of an evil wizard, **Kynops**, who challenged him to a duel of miracles. As the magician's stock trick involved retrieving effigies of the deceased from the seabed, John responded by petrifying Kynops while he was under water. A buoy just off Theológos beach in Skála today marks the relevant submerged rock.

Forever after in the Orthodox world, heights amid desolate and especially **volcanic topography** have become associated with John. Pátmos, with its eerie landscape of igneous outcrops, is an excellent example, as is Níssyros, where one of the saint's monasteries overlooks the volcano's caldera.

where frescoes depict the Apocalypse. Off to one side, the **museum** has a magnificent array of religious treasures, including medieval icons of the Cretan school, and several later donations from Russia. Pride of place among the ancient manuscripts goes to the original chrysobull (edict) signed by Emperor Alexios Komnenos in the eleventh century, granting the island to Khristodhoulos.

Hóra

St John's promise of shelter from pirates spurred the growth of **HÓRA** outside the stout fortifications of the monastery. A magnificent ensemble, it remains architecturally homogeneous, its cobbled lanes sheltering shipowners' mansions from the island's seventeenth to eighteenth-century heyday. High, windowless walls and imposing wooden doors betray nothing of the painted ceilings, *votsalotó* terraces, flagstone kitchens and carved furniture inside. Inevitably, touristic tattiness disfigures the main approaches to the monastery, but by night, when the ramparts are floodlit, it's hard to think of a more beautiful Dodecanesian village. Neither should you miss the view from **Platía Lótza**, particularly at dawn or dusk.

Numerous "minor" churches and monasteries around Hóra contain beautiful icons and examples of local woodcarving; almost all are locked to prevent thefts, but key-keepers generally live nearby. Among the best are the church of **Dhiasózousa**; the convent of **Zoödhóhou Piyís** (daily except Sat 9am–noon), and the convent of **Evangelismoú**, at the edge of Hóra (daily 9–11am).

ARRIVAL AND INFORMATION

By bus Eleven buses from Skála serve Hóra daily (7.40am–9.30pm; roughly 35min).

On foot The 40min walk from Skála to Hóra follows a beautiful old cobbled path. Don't try it in the full heat of the day, and whatever you do, don't walk up the much longer, switchbacking main road. To find the path, head through Skála towards Hokhlakás, then turn left onto a lane that leads uphill to the main road – you'll see the cobbles ahead of you. It's worth noting that nothing is signposted in Hóra, so be prepared to ask locals dor directions.

ACCOMMODATION AND EATING

★**Archontariki** Hóra ☎22470 29368, ⓦarchontariki-patmos.gr. Gorgeous B&B, concealed behind high walls and a blue door in a traditional village house that's been beautifully converted to create four exquisitely furnished, exceptionally comfortable suites and one double. As well as the lovely central courtyard, there's a garden and roof terrace; rates include a superb breakfast. Easter–Sept. **€150**

Loza Platía Loza, Hóra ☎22470 32405. Nicely positioned café/restaurant just below the eponymous platía, close to the main road, where the broad terrace offers sweeping views: as well as hot and alcoholic drinks, the menu features can Quiche Lorraine (€4.50) and country sausages with orange sauce (€7). Daily 8.30am–late.

Pantheon Hóra ☎22470 31226. The village's most authentic restaurant, at the start of the monastery approach. Good atmosphere and music, a lovely old interior, terrace views over the village and friendly management offset the run-of-the-mill mezédhes such as chicken souvláki (€5) or grilled octopus (€7). April–Dec daily 6pm–late.

The rest of the island

Pátmos's **best beaches** are concentrated north of Skála, tucked into the startling eastern shoreline, and accessible from side roads off the main road. Most of the island's west-facing bays are unuseable, owing to the prevailing wind and washed-up debris.

HÓRA FESTIVALS

The best dates to visit Hóra, besides the Easter observances, are September 25–26 for the **Feast of John the Theologian** and October 20–21 for the **Feast of Khristodhoulos**, both of which feature solemn liturgies and processions. The annual **Festival of Religious Music** (late Aug/early Sept) is held in the grounds of the Apokálypsis monastery (see p.589).

Gríkou and Pétra

Not far south of uninspiring Sapsila beach, roads converge at the sandiest part of Gríkou. The beach itself, far from the island's best, forms a narrow strip of hard-packed sand, yielding to sand and gravel, then large pebbles at **Pétra** immediately south. It's not possible to drive any further south along the coast.

Melóï and Agriolívadho

A couple of kilometres northeast of Skála, the large crescent beach at **Melóï** is quite appealing, with tamarisks behind the slender belt of sand, and good snorkelling offshore. It's accessible by road at its southern end, which is home to a taverna. North of Melóï, **Agriolívadho** (Agriolivádhi) is another attractive sheltered bay. Most of the beach is pebbly gravel, but there's a reasonable amount of sand at its broad centre.

Kámbos

Hilltop **KÁMBOS**, 4km north of Skála, is the island's only other real village. Originally built to house the wives and children of lay workers at the monastery, it's surrounded by scattered farms.

Kámbos **beach**, 600m downhill to the east, is a strong contender for the best beach on the island, although it fills with local children in summer. Too deeply indented to be seen from the rest of Pátmos, it offers peaceful sheltered swimming, along with plentiful sunbeds, two tavernas, and beach toys to rent.

Beyond Kámbos

A succession of less busy coves lies **east** of Kámbos. **Vayiá** is a little bay where a few trees overhang a beach of pebbles and coarse sand, there's a snack-bar, and the sea is a particularly enticing shade of turquoise. The double bay at **Lingínou** can only be reached on foot, but has a *kantína*. **Livádhi Yeranoú** is a long stretch of mingled sand and gravel, shaded by tamarisks, and with a delightful islet offshore as a target for swimmers.

8

ACCOMMODATION

THE REST OF PÁTMOS

Patmos Aktis Gríkou Beach ☎22470 32800, ⓦpatmosaktis.gr. This very upmarket, dazzling white 56-room luxury hotel seems incongruous for Pátmos, but there's no disputing the opulence of its rooms, spa and restaurant. Rates includes an award-winning buffet breakfast. Easter to mid-Oct. **€180**

EATING AND DRINKING

Lambi Lámbi Bay ☎22470 31490. Lovely little seafront taverna, founded in 1958, where the roof is held up by elderly tamarisk trees, and some tables are on the beach itself – enjoy dishes such as fresh fish of the day (€9) or simple grilled meats (€6). Easter to mid-Oct daily noon–8pm.

Livádhi Geranoú Taverna Livádhi Geranoú beach ☎22470 32046. Good-value taverna, just up from the beach with a terrace offering sweeping views and a simple, reasonable menu such as fish soup (€4.50) and meatballs (€6). May–Nov daily noon–late.

★**Tarsanas** Patmos Marine boatyard, Dhiakoftí isthmus. The boatyard near the southern tip of the island might not seem the obvious place to find a smart, good-value taverna, but *Tarsanas* is a favourite (year-round) "power lunch" spot for locals. Expect mountainous salads and dishes such as moussaka (€5.50) and roast chicken (€7). The best tables can be found in a permanently grounded boat. Daily lunch and dinner.

Taverna Panagos Kámbos Square ☎22470 31076. Opposite the town square and church, this good-value family-run taverna, popular with tourists and locals, serves dishes of the day such as chickpeas with leeks and dill (€5) and baby goat in tomato sauce (€9). Daily noon–late.

Taverna Stamatis Gríkou Beach ☎22470 31302. Small, family-run taverna with a loyal repeat clientele and tables on the beach, next to *Patmos Aktis* (see above). The menu changes regularly and offers traditional Greek dishes, cooked by the grandmother, such as Patmos goat (€9.50) or simple aubergine imam (aubergines baked with feta cheese in a tomato and white wine sauce; €6.50). Easter–Oct daily 12.30pm–11pm.

Lipsí

The largest, most interesting and most populated of the islets north and east of Pátmos, **LIPSÍ** also has the most significant tourist trade. Out of season, the island still provides an idyllic halt, its sleepy pace almost making plausible a dubious link with **Calypso**, the nymph who held Odysseus in thrall. Once a dependency of the monastery on Pátmos, Lipsí is still conspicuously sown with blue-domed churches. Deep wells water small farms and vineyards, but there's only one flowing spring, and although plenty of livestock can be seen, the non-tourist economy is far from thriving.

ARRIVAL AND DEPARTURE
LIPSÍ

By ferry The island's port is called Lipsi Village. Ferry tickets can be bought from Aegean Travel, tucked away in the central square (Mon–Fri 10am–2pm and 1hr before ferry arrivals; ☎ 22470 41141) and the public ticket office, near the jetty (opens 1hr before ferry arrivals; ☎ 22470 41250).

Destinations Agathoníssi (2 weekly; 2hr 45min); Arkí (3 weekly; 1hr 35min); Kálymnos (1–3 daily; 1hr 20min–2hr 50min); Kos (1–2 daily; 1hr 40min–4hr 10min); Léros (2–3 daily; 25min–1hr 5min); Pátmos (2–3 daily; 20min); Pireás (1–2 weekly; 9hr 45min); Rhodes (1–3 daily; 5hr 10min–8hr 20min); Samos (1 daily; 1hr 30min–4hr 5min); Sými (3 weekly; 4hr 20min–7hr).

GETTING AROUND

By bus Buses leave from the Park (the central square) every 30min in season (10.30am–5.55pm) and go to the various beaches. They are easy to flag down en-route: flat fare €1.
By taxi Gorgos (☎ 6942 409 679) is the only taxi driver on the island. Fares from the harbour to just about anywhere on the island cost €4.
By scooter *Studio Poseidon* (☎ 22470 41130; see opposite) rents scooters and cars.

Lipsí Village and around

Lipsí's only significant population centre, known as **LIPSÍ VILLAGE**, stretches around its large south-facing harbour. From the ferry jetty at its northwestern extremity, the hilltop centre of town is a 600m walk.

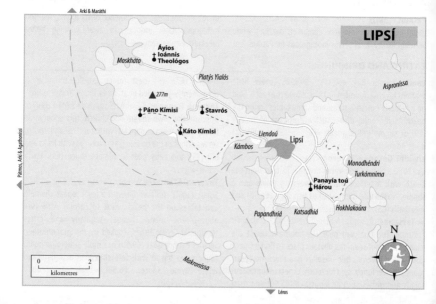

MIRACLE OF LIPSÍ

Flowers on the icon of the church of Theochari are said to blossom only on **22 August**, the day of the **Miracle of Lipsí**, when the event is celebrated around the whole island with parties and traditional dancing until the early hours.

Beaches

None of the **beaches** is more than an hour's walk from the port. The closest, and sandiest, are crowded **Liendoú** and **Kámbos**, but many prefer attractive **Katsadhiá** (sand) and **Papandhriá** (coarse sand-and-gravel), adjacent coves 2km south of the port. Another paved road leads 4km west from town to protected **Platýs Yialós**, a shallow, sandy bay, continuing to sumpy Moskháto fjord (no beach). To reach the isolated east-coast beaches, which lack facilities, rent a **scooter** at the port (see opposite). Hokhlakoúra consists of coarse shingle (finer pebbles at mid-strand); nearby Turkómnima is sandy and much shadier, if mercilessly exposed to the *meltémi*.

ACCOMMODATION   LIPSÍ VILLAGE

Almost all Lipsí's accommodation is in the village: returning regulars make arriving in peak season without reservations unwise.

Aphroditi ☎ 22470 41000, ⓦ hotel-aphroditi.com. Complex of twenty large, tiled-floor studios and apartments, some with kitchens and living room, set slightly back across the road from Liendoú beach. Breakfast included. May–Sept. **€60**

Filoxenia Studios ☎ 22470 41339. Set back from the harbour, but within easy walking distance, these thirteen ground-floor studios are designed to a high standard, with iron double beds, some four-poster. Breakfast included. They also have three villas to rent in the harbour (€200–300 for the whole villa sleeping 5–10 people). **€30**

Galini Apartments ☎ 22470 41212. The first building you see on disembarking, right above the ferry jetty, is a prime budget choice, run by the hospitable Matsouris family. All five units have kitchens and balconies. Nikos sometimes takes guests fishing on request. **€40**

Studio Akrogiali ☎ 6947 218 842. This place has three tastefully decorated, clean and fresh rooms with a harbour-view terrace painted in pastel hues: the bathrooms, however, are on the small side. May–Sept. **€30**

★ **Studio Poseidon** ☎ 22470 41130, ⓦ lipsiposeidon .com. Seven impeccable, roomy, modern studios with large balconies, 150m from the jetty. Three have twin beds, the rest have doubles. Also offers laundry service. **€35**

EATING AND DRINKING

Café du Moulin ☎ 22470 41316. The main daytime hub for travellers and locals, in the central square, is a great place to sit and eat an omelette (€3.50) or simple moussaka (€9) as you watch Lipsí's daily life unfold. Daily 8am–late.

★ **Manolis Tastes** ☎ 22470 41065, ⓦ manolistastes .com. Behind the main square, this award-winning restaurant, housed in what used to be the school, is popular with tourists and locals alike. There's outdoor seating and most of the produce, including the meat, comes from Manolis' land – expect dishes such as chicken fillet with mustard or blue cheese sauce, and huge salads such as fresh avocado and shrimp. Book ahead in August. March–Nov daily 10am–4pm & 5.30pm–late.

Nick & Louli ☎ 698 631 8035. Great little ouzerí with outside tables where mainly locals congregate, right by the harbour square. Choose simple appetizers to share, such as fried courgette flowers (€4) or cod in garlic sauce (€6). May–Oct daily 3pm–late.

To Pefko ☎ 22470 28063. Overlooking the main jetty, this restaurant serves classic Greek cuisine such as mussels with cheese in tomato sauce (€9) and *dolmádhes* (€4.50). May–late Sept daily 6.30pm–late

★ **Yiannis** ☎ 22470 41395. Brightly decorated taverna very near the jetty, next to *Studio Akrogiali* (see above). A good first-night option with main courses such as penne with fresh tuna (€7) or a simple leek pie (€4) as a snack. Mid-May to Oct daily 12.30pm–3pm & 7pm–11pm.

NIGHTLIFE

Angela's ☎ 22470 41177. Next to *Studio Poseidon*, this tiered seating café/bar with views across the port serves regular juices and coffees for €4, then hots up at night with cocktails from €7–12. Daily 8am–late.

★ **The Rock** Lipsí's longest-lasting bar, right by the port, attracts a congenial crowd, with boulder-like host Babis and good tunes. Daily 6pm–late.

8

Arkí and Maráthi

Roughly two-thirds the size of Lipsí, **ARKÍ** is a far more primitive island, lacking proper shops or a coherent village. A mere fifty or so inhabitants eke out a living, mostly fishing or goat/sheep-herding, though servicing yachts attracted by the superb anchorage at Avgoústa Bay – named for the half-ruined Hellenistic/Byzantine **Avgoustínis fortress** overhead – is also important.

Excursion-boat clients swim at the "Blue Lagoon" of **Tiganákia** at the southeast tip, but other **beaches** on Arkí take some finding. The more obvious are the carefully nurtured sandy cove at **Pateliá**, by the outer jetty, and tiny **Limnári** pebble bay (fitting five bathers at a pinch) on the northeast coast, a 25-minute walk away via the highest house in the settlement.

Arkí's nearest large, sandy, tamarisk-shaded beach is a ten-minute boat trip away on **MARÁTHI**, the only inhabited islet (permanent population 3) of the mini-archipelago around Arkí.

ARRIVAL AND DEPARTURE
ARKÍ AND MARÁTHI

By ferry Ferries dock at the jetty on Arkí. Boats to Maráthi run roughly three times a week from Arki (10min); alternatively, take the daily excursion boat from Patmos to Maráthi (1hr 5min).

Destinations from Arkí; Agathoníssi (3 weekly; 1hr); Kálymnos (4 weekly; 5hr 15min); Lipsí (2 weekly; 2hr); Léros (3 weekly; 3hr 20min); Pátmos (3 weekly; 55min); Samos (3 weekly; 2hr 20min).

ACCOMMODATION AND EATING

ARKÍ

Nikolas ☎ 22470 32477. Friendly taverna on the flagstoned harbourside platía, where a mother/son team serve home-made puddings and *mayireftá* such as peppers with goat's cheese for roughly €10 per head. Daily lunch till late.

O Trypas ☎ 22470 32230. Also known as *Tou Manoli*, this waterfront taverna is renowned for its very decent fish meals and *mezédhes*. It also offers mock-trad, stone-floored rental units just up the hillside and doubles as the island's most happening music bar. Daily 1pm–late.

MARÁTHI

Pantelis ☎ 22470 32609, ⓦ marathi-island.gr. The most elaborate and "resort"-like establishment on Maráthi. The beachfront tables outside make a perfect venue to enjoy local free-range goat, freshly-caught fish, or vegetables from the adjacent garden, while the rooms are spacious, airy and tastefully furnished. May–Oct. **€45**

Piratis ☎ 22470 31580 or ☎ 6973 962 462, ⓦ marathi-island.com. Ten simple, adequate a/c en-suite rooms and a full-service taverna with waterside seating and a menu of home-baked classics as well as fresh fish. Barefoot proprietor Mihalis emphasizes his comic-book-pirate persona with a Jolly Roger flag and speedboat named *Piratis*. **€35**

Agathoníssi

The small, steep-sided, waterless islet of **AGATHONÍSSI** is too remote – closer to Turkey than Pátmos, in fact – to be a popular day-trip target. Intrepid Greeks and Italians form its main tourist clientele, along with yachts attracted by excellent anchorage. Even though the *Nissos Kalymnos* (and a summer catamaran) appear regularly, schedules mean you should count on staying at least two days.

Despite the lack of springs, the island is greener and more fertile than apparent from the sea; lentisk, carob and scrub oak on the heights overlook two arable plains in the west. Fewer than a hundred people live here full time, but they make a go of stock-raising or fishing (or rather, fish-farming), and few dwellings are abandoned or neglected.

Most of the population lives in **Megálo Horió** hamlet, just visible on the ridge above the harbour hamlet of **ÁYIOS YEÓRYIOS** and at eye level with tiny **Mikró Horió** opposite. Except for a small shop and two café-restaurants working peak-season nights only in Megálo Horió, all amenities are in the port.

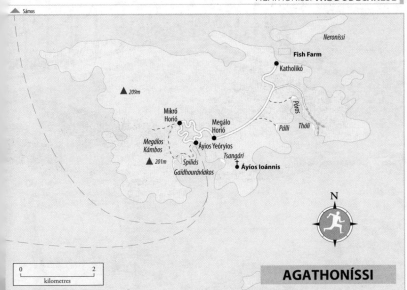

AGATHONÍSSI

With no rental scooters, exploring involves **walking** along the cement-road network, or following a very few tracks and paths – bring plenty of water. If you won't swim at the port, home to the largest sandy **beach**, hike ten minutes southwest to shingle-gravel **Spiliás**, or continue another quarter-hour by path over the ridge to **Gaïdhourávlakos**, another gravel cove. Bays in the east, all reached by paved roads, include tiny **Póros** (45min walk from the harbour), fine sand with lentisk-tree shade at the back; **Thóli** (25min further) in the far southeast, with good snorkelling and some morning shade; and **Pálli** across the same bay, a small but pristine fine-pebble cove reached by a fifteen-minute walk down from the trans-island road.

ARRIVAL AND DEPARTURE

By ferry Ferries dock at Áyios Yeóryios.
Destinations Arkí (3 weekly; 1hr); Kálymnos (4 weekly; 1hr 50min–6hr 35min); Lipsí (4 weekly; 35min–3hr 20min); Léros (4 weekly; 35min–4hr 40min); Pátmos (3 weekly; 2hr 15min); Samos (3 weekly; 1hr 5min).

ACCOMMODATION AND EATING

Rooms Maria Kamitsi ☎ 22470 29065 or ☎ 6932 575 121, ⓦ maryroomsagathonisi.com. Thirteen traditionally decorated rooms at the centre of the beach, by the small port, sharing use of a kitchen and fridges, with a vine-covered patio outside. **€40**

Seagull ☎ 22470 29062. Central taverna, close to the yacht moorings, where the romantic waterside tables are filled every night for a full menu of baked and grilled dishes from €6. Daily lunch and dinner.

To Agnanti ☎ 22470 29019 or ☎ 6974 814 013. Good-value rooms, the newest on the island, above the popular *Memento Bar*, which has a wooden deck reaching out over the water. **€50**

The East and North Aegean

MESTA CHIOS

9

The East and North Aegean

The seven substantial islands and four minor islets scattered off the Aegean coast of Asia Minor form a rather arbitrary archipelago. While there are similarities in architecture and landscape, the strong individual character of each island is far more striking and thus they do not form an immediately recognizable group, and neither are they all connected with each other by ferries. What they do have in common, with the possible exception of Sámos and Thássos, is that they receive fewer visitors than other island groups and so generally provide a more authentic Greek atmosphere. Yet the existence of magnificent beaches, dramatic mountain scenery, interesting sights and ample facilities makes them a highly attractive region of Greece to explore.

Verdant **Sámos** may get the most visitors, but leave behind its crowded resorts and you'll enjoy some of the finest scenery in the entire island group. Quirky **Ikaría** to the west remains relatively unspoilt, if a minority choice, while nearby **Foúrni** is (except in high summer) a haven for determined solitaries, as are the Híos satellites **Psará** and **Inoússes**. **Híos** proper offers far more cultural interest than its neighbours to the south, but far fewer tourist facilities. **Lésvos** may not impress initially, though once you get a feel for its old-fashioned Anatolian ambience you may find it hard to leave. By contrast, few foreigners visit **Áyios Efstrátios**, and for good reason, though **Límnos** to the north is much busier, particularly in its western half. The two islands in the far north are relatively isolated and easier to visit from northern Greece, which administers them: **Samothráki** has one of the most dramatic seaward approaches of any Greek island, and one of the more important ancient sites, while **Thássos** is more varied, with sandy beaches, mountain villages and minor archeological sites.

Due to the proximity of some of these islands to the Turkish mainland – less than 3km, in some cases – they make logical targets for refugees seeking safety within the EU. The **refugee crisis**, which got into full swing in 2015, is still continuing at the time of writing; Híos and Lésvos have borne the brunt of arrivals so far, with "regular" tourism plummeting on both as a result.

Brief history

Despite their proximity to modern Turkey, only Lésvos, Límnos and Híos bear significant signs of an **Ottoman** heritage, in the form of old mosques, hammams and fountains, plus some domestic architecture betraying obvious influences

MÓLYVOS, LÉSVOS

Highlights

❶ Vathý, Sámos The two-wing archeological museum is among the best in the islands. **See p.603**

❷ Foúrni This small fishing island offers numerous deserted coves, a surprisingly lively port and a lovely main street lined with mulberry trees. **See p.614**

❸ Ikaría Western Ikaría has superb beaches, and you can participate in the idiosyncratic nocturnal lifestyle of the Ráhes villages. **See p.617**

❹ Southern Híos The architecturally unique mastic villages have a distinct Middle Eastern feel. **See p.629**

❺ Mólyvos, northern Lésvos This castle-crowned resort village is perhaps the most beautiful of the whole island group. **See p.649**

❻ Límnos villages Atmospheric basalt-built villages with lively central tavernas and great local wines to sample. **See p.652**

❼ Sanctuary of the Great Gods, Samothráki With Mount Fengári as a backdrop, the remote Sanctuary of the Great Gods is blessed with a natural grandeur. **See p.659**

❽ Alykí, Thássos A beautifully situated resort, with fine beaches flanked by ancient and Byzantine archeological sites. **See p.667**

HIGHLIGHTS ARE MARKED ON THE MAP ON P.600

from Constantinople, Macedonia and further north in the Balkans. The limited degree of this heritage has in the past been duly referred to by Greece in an intermittent **propaganda war** with Turkey over the sovereignty of these far-flung outposts – as well as the disputed boundary between them and the Turkish mainland. Ironically, this friction gave these long-neglected islands a new lease of life from the 1960s onward, insomuch as their sudden **strategic importance** prompted infrastructure improvements to support garrisoning, and gave a mild spur to local economies, engaged in providing goods and services to soldiers, something predating the advent of tourism. Yet the region has remained one of the **poorest regions** in western Europe. Tensions with Turkey were periodically aggravated by disagreements over suspected undersea oil deposits in the straits between the islands and Anatolia. The Turks also persistently demanded that Límnos, astride the sea lanes to the Dardanelles, be demilitarized, and since the millennium Greece has finally complied, with garrisons also much reduced on Sámos and Lésvos, as part of the increasing **détente** between the traditional enemies. Indeed, **Turkish tourists** on some of the islands now outnumber Greek conscripts.

Sámos

Sámos is the most perennially popular of the Aegean isles, and indisputably one of the most beautiful. It possesses a greater diversity of scenery than most isles hereabouts, with lush forest, beaches and mountains – one reason for its growing popularity as a hiking destination. Shaped somewhat like a pregnant guppy, it seems to swim away from Asia Minor, to which the island was joined until Ice Age cataclysms sundered it from Mount Mykáli (Mycale) on the Turkish mainland. The resulting 2.5km **strait** provides – bar the outlier of Kastellórizo – the narrowest maritime distance between Greece and Turkey.

Vathý is the island's teeming capital, with appealing beaches peppering the east coast around to the smaller but more tourist-focused town of **Pythagório**. The south coast is craggy and tricky to navigate en route to the beaches out west, with resorts stretching from Órmos Marathokámbou to Limniónas, while a twisting road heads most of the way around gorgeous **Mount Kérkis**, the highest peak on the island. It's beach after beach between **Karlóvassi**, a scruffy, sprawling, wave-beaten town on the north coast, and the capital, though it's worth detouring inland to see a collection of cute hill-villages such as **Manolátes**.

Brief history

The mythical birthplace of Hera, and the actual one of Pythagoras, Sámos has a weightier history than its neighbouring islands. During the Archaic era, it was among the **wealthiest** islands in the Aegean – and, under the patronage of tyrant Polykrates, home to a thriving intellectual community that included Epicurus, Pythagoras, Aristarcus and Aesop. Decline set in when Classical Athens rose, though Sámos' status improved in Byzantine times when it formed its own imperial administrative district. Late in the fifteenth century, the ruling Genoese **abandoned** the island to the mercies of pirates and Sámos remained almost uninhabited until 1562, when it was repopulated with Greek Orthodox settlers from various corners of the empire.

The new Samians **fought** fiercely for independence during the **1820s**, but despite notable land and sea victories against the Turks, the Great Powers handed the island back to the Ottomans in 1830, with the consoling proviso that it be semi-autonomous, ruled by an appointed Christian prince. This period, known as the **Iyimonía** (Hegemony), was marked by a renaissance in fortunes, courtesy of the hemp, leather-tanning and (especially) tobacco trades. However, union with Greece in 1912, an

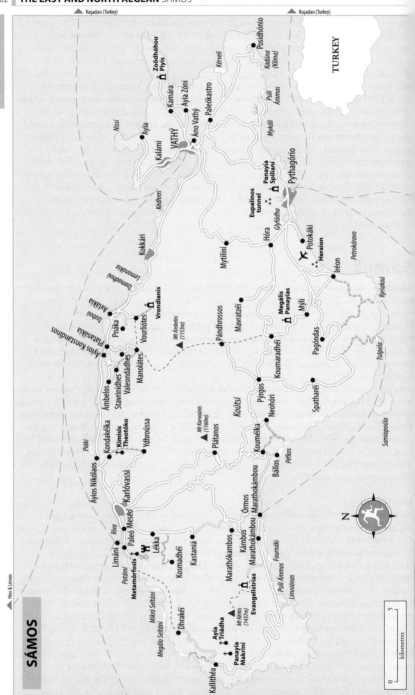

SÁMOS

Kuşadası (Turkey)

Kuşadası (Turkey)

TURKEY

Zoödhóhou Piyís

Kamára
Ayía Zóni
Paleókastro
Posidhónio
Kadína (Klíma)

Nissí
Ayía
Kalámi
VATHÝ
Áno Vathý

Kérveli
Psilí Ámmos
Mykáli

Kédhros

Panayía Spilianí
Pythagório

Kokkári
Lemonákia

Hóra
Eupalínos tunnel
Glyfádha

Potokáki
Heraíon
Iréon

Petrokávo

Myrtiní

Avlákia
Tarsanás
Trabou
Platanákia
Ayios Konstandínos
Pnáka

Vrondianís
Vourliótes
Mt Ámbelos (1153m)

Pándhrossos
Mavratzeí

Megális Panayías
Mýli

Kyriakoú

Pagóndas
Ambelos
Stavrinídhes
Valeondádhes
Manolátes

Koúrtsi
Pýrgos
Neohóri

Spatharéi

Kondakéika
Kímisis Theotóko
Ydhroússa

Mt Karvoúnis (1160m)
Plátanos
Koumaradhéi
Koumékia

Samiopoúla

Ayios Nikólaos
Karlóvassi
Píkki

Kouméika
Bállos
Pélkos

Riva
Paleó Meséo
Lékka

Órmos
Marathókambos

Limáni
Metamórfosis
Kosmadhéi
Kastaniá

Kámbos
Marathókámbou
Foúrnaki

Potámi
Marathókambos
Psilí Ámmos
Limniónas

Dhrakéi
Evangelístrias
Mt Kérkis (1437m)

Mikró Seïtáni
Megálo Seïtáni

Ayía Triádha
Panayía Makriní

Kallithéa

N

0   5
kilometres

Híos & Lésvos

Ikaría & Foúrni

ıflux of refugees from Asia Minor in 1923 and the ravages of a bitter World War II ccupation followed by mass emigration effectively reversed this recovery until tourism ɔok over during the 1980s.

ᴀRRIVAL AND DEPARTURE   SÁMOS

ʏy plane Sámos' airport lies 3km west of Pythagório, ınd some 17km southwest of Vathý. A bus service links p with most domestic (but not international) charter ights; taxi fares to all points are posted on placards, ʰough in high summer these should be booked in dvance. Frequencies for the destinations listed below re for June–Oct.

ᴉestinations Athens (4 daily; 55min); Híos (3 weekly; ᴼmin); Rhodes (3 weekly; 45min); Thessaloníki (6 weekly; ʰr 10min).

ʏy ferry/hydrofoil There are three ferry ports: ʲarlóvassi in the west, plus Vathý and Pythagório in the ᵉast, making the island a major travel hub. All ferries ɔetween Pireás and Sámos call at both Karlóvassi and ᴠathý, while those from the northeast Aegean call at one ɔr the other. Small boats to Kuşadası in Turkey depart from both Vathý and Pythagório, with the latter also ɔffering ferry connections to the Dodecanese islands. ᴛhere are daily services to Foúrni and Ikaría, which can ᴉeave from any of the three ports. Below is a summary of ᴉestinations and summer frequencies.

ᴉestinations from Karlóvassi Áyios Kírykos, Ikaría (2 weekly; 2hr 50min); Évdhilos, Ikaría (6 weekly; 1hr 10min); Foúrni (5 weekly; 1hr 40min–2hr 10min); Híos (1 weekly; 3hr 35min); Lésvos (1 weekly; 6hr 10min); Límnos (1 weekly; 11hr); Mýkonos (5 weekly; 3hr 20min); Pireás (1–2 daily; 6hr 45min–8hr); Sýros (5 weekly; 4hr 20min).

Destinations from Pythagório Agathónissi (3 weekly; 35min–1hr 20min); Áyios Kírykos, Ikaría (3 weekly; 1hr 25min); Foúrni (3 weekly; 1hr–1hr 30min); Lipsí (1–3 daily; 1hr 25min–4hr 40min); Léros (1–3 daily; 1hr 50min–6hr); Kálymnos (1–2 daily; 2hr 35min–7hr 30min); Kos (6 weekly; 3hr 20min–4hr 50min); Kuşadası, Turkey (4 weekly; 1hr 30min); Pátmos (1–4 daily; 1hr–3hr 50min).

Destinations from Vathý Áyios Kírykos, Ikaría (3 weekly; 1hr 50min–2hr 30min); Foúrni (2 weekly; 1hr 45min); Híos (3 weekly; 2hr 30min); Kuşadası, Turkey (3 weekly; 1hr 30min); Lésvos (3 weekly; 5hr–5hr 40min); Límnos (3 weekly; 9hr 30min–11hr); Pireás (4 weekly; 7hr 20min–13hr).

Travel agents The most comprehensive island-wide travel agents, represented in all three ports and some resorts, are By Ship (☎ 22730 22116, ⦿ byshiptravel.gr).

GETTING AROUND

ʙy bus Vathý is the hub of most KTEL routes, with frequent services on weekdays, fewer on Saturdays, and even fewer on Sundays. Aside from the main routes listed here (summer frequencies given), connections are poor, sometimes running just twice a week.

Destinations from Vathý: Kokkári (4–10 daily; 30min); Karlóvassi (3–7 daily; 1hr); Pythagório (4–12 daily; 35min).

By car or motorbike Of the myriad scooter- and car-rental agencies dotted around the island, try Aramis (☎ 22730 23253, ⦿ samos-rentacar.com), with branches island-wide, or Auto Union (☎ 22730 27444, ⦿ autounion

.gr) at Themistoklí Sofoúli 79 in Vathý. Both deliver cars to the airport.

By taxi This isn't a small island so expect to pay around €45 from Pythagório to Karlóvassi.

By kaïki There are several weekly kaïki day-trips (10am–4pm; from €25–30) from Órmos Marathokámbou to the nearby islet of Samiopoúla and inaccessible parts of the south coast.

On a tour Reputable outdoor activities agencies include Samos Outdoor Activities (⦿ samosoutdoors.com) and Sea Kayak Samos (⦿ seakayaksamos.com).

Vathý

Lining the steep northeastern shore of a deep bay, beachless **VATHÝ** (often confusingly referred to as "Sámos") is a busy provincial town which grew from a minor anchorage after 1830, when it replaced Hóra as the island's capital. It's an unlikely, rather ungraceful resort and holds little of interest aside from an excellent museum, some Neoclassical mansions and the hillside suburb of **Áno Vathý**.

Archeological Museum

Off the central park • Tues–Sun 8am–3pm • €3 • ☎ 22730 27469

The only real must-visit in Vathý is the excellent **Archeological Museum**, set behind the small central park beside the nineteenth-century town hall. The collections are

9

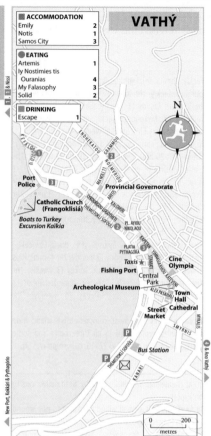

VATHÝ

ACCOMMODATION
Emily 2
Notis 1
Samos City 3

EATING
Artemis 1
Iy Nostimies tis
Ouranias 4
My Falasophy 3
Solid 2

DRINKING
Escape 1

Port
Police
Catholic Church
(Frangoklisiá)
Boats to Turkey
Excursion Kaïkia
Provincial Governorate
PL. AYIOU
NIKOLAOU
PLATIA
PYTHAGORA
Taxis
Fishing Port
Cine
Olympia
Central
Park
Archeological Museum
Town
Hall
Street
Market
Cathedral
Bus Station

0   200
metres

housed in both the old Paschalion building and a modern wing just opposite, constructed for the star exhibit: a majestic, 5m-tall **kouros** discovered out at the Heraion sanctuary. The largest freestanding effigy surviving from ancient Greece, this *kouros* was dedicated to Apollo, but found next to a devotional mirror to Mut (the Egyptian equivalent of Hera) from a Nile workshop.

In the Paschalion, more votive offerings of **Egyptian** design – a hippo, a dancer in Nilotic dress, Horus-as-Falcon, an Osiris figurine – provide evidence of trade and pilgrimage links between Sámos and the Nile valley going back to the eighth century BC. The **Mesopotamian** and **Anatolian** origins of other artworks confirm an exotic trend, most tellingly in a case full of ivory miniatures: Perseus and Medusa in relief; a kneeling, perfectly formed mini-*kouros*; a pouncing lion; and a bull's-head drinking horn. The most famous local artefacts are numerous bronze **griffin-heads**, for which Sámos was the major centre of production in the seventh century BC; they were mounted on the edge of cauldrons to ward off evil spirits.

Áno Vathý

The best inland target on foot, a twenty-minute walk south from town and 150m above sea level, is the atmospheric hill village of **ÁNO VATHÝ**, a nominally protected but increasingly threatened community of tottering, canal-tile-roofed houses: some buildings are being replaced by bad-taste blocks of flats, others are being defaced with aluminium windows and modern tiles. The best of several venerable **churches** is quadruple-domed **Aï Yannáki**, in the vale separating the village's two hillside neighbourhoods.

ARRIVAL AND DEPARTURE   VATHÝ

By ferry Most ferries dock at the new port, almost 3km west of town around the bay (it should be less than €5 by taxi), although boats to Turkey still use the old dock at the north end of the seafront.

By bus Buses stop at the KTEL depot (☎ 22730 27262)

facing the seafront, just south of the centre.

By taxi The taxi rank is in the middle of the seafront (☎ 22730 28404).

By car The southern seafront is the only area for free parking.

ACCOMMODATION

Emily Cnr of Grámmou and 11 Noemvríou, Katsoúni ☎ 22730 24691. Small, well-run two-star hotel with cheerful and comfortable rooms – there's even wall art –

and a roof garden. Breakfast included. March–Nov. €60
Notis Kalistrátou 15 ☎ 22730 22722. This is one of the best options in the good-value area a couple of

ometres north of the port, where the beach is a major awcard. It has plain but comfy studios sporting small lconies and kitchenettes, and greenery all around the mmon areas. **€45**

amos City Themistokli Soufoúli 11 ☎22730 28377,

ⓦsamoshotel.gr. Refurbished behemoth by the ferry dock that's a firm favourite despite the rooms being rather small. Double-glazing against traffic noise, rooftop pool-terrace and a popular café out front. Rudimentary breakfast included. **€65**

ATING AND DRINKING

athý's perennial **nightlife** venue is a "strip" at the start of Kefalopoúlou north of the jetty, with annually changing bars asting sea-view terraces.

OWN CENTRE

rtemis Kefalopoúlou 4 ☎22730 23639. Excellent, ffordable seafood and starters like *fáva*, *hórta* and *seláhi* s well as the usual mains for under €10. Good bulk *robóla* ine from the hill villages, plus indoor and outdoor eating. Mon–Sat 11am–1am.

scape Kefalopoúlou 9 ☎22730 28345. The most urable of the many clubs in the area, playing a fairly tandard mixture of foreign and Greek disco favourites. The rowd switches between the outdoor terrace and a/c ancefloor inside. Daily 9pm–late.

★**My Falasophy** Platía Pythagora ☎22730 40835. Hugely popular with local students, this "hummus bar" evolves around the humble chick pea (hence the quirky ame). Falafel and hummus are available in more ways than ou could imagine from just €2.50; most grab and go, but hey've a couple of tables on the square. Daily noon–1am.

Solid Themistokli Soufoúli 43 ☎22730 24800. The best of the waterfront cafés, with pulsing lounge music and a stylish air to its duplex seating. Good for international lunch dishes such as salmon on rye (€9), though perhaps most notable are the giant homemade pancakes (from €4) – even a "small" serving of the banana-chocolate option will see you waddling out. Daily 8am–1am.

ÁNO VATHÝ

ly Nostimies tis Ouranias Áno Vathý ☎22730 22488. Popular *inomayirío* next to the school, doling out home cooking such as grilled chops and mackerel in summer and more imaginative items at other times, mostly under €10. Try their *bouyiourdí* (pepper-and-cheese hotpot) year-round. Mon–Sat noon–11pm.

The east coast

Striking **Kérveli Bay**, 8km southeast of Vathý via the attractive inland village of Paleókastro, has a small but popular pebble **beach**, with water of crystalline clarity. On the far southeast coast of the island, almost within spitting distance of Turkey and accessed from a turning 1km west of Paleókastro, lie the reasonable beaches of **Mykáli** and **Psilí Ámmos**, both with a mostly mediocre range of facilities.

Zoödhóhou Piyís convent

Accessible on a climbing zigzag road from Kamára, 3km east of Vathý • Daily 8am–2pm & 5–8pm • Free • ☎22730 27469

Around 5km east of Vathý, the ridgetop **Zoödhóhou Piyís convent** gives superb views across the end of the island to Turkey. Held up by four ancient columns from Miletus in Asia Minor, the dome of its *katholikón* enhances the nuns' chanting.

ACCOMMODATION AND EATING   THE EAST COAST

Haravgi Kérveli Bay ☎22730 80757. Right on the beach, with a wide variety of salads, appetisers and mains – try the beef in lemon sauce with cheese (€9.50). Also good for coffee or breakfast, or a bottle of retsina in the evening. May–Sept daily 9am–11pm.

Kerveli Village Kérveli Bay ☎22730 23006, ⓦkerveli.gr. Above the approach road to the beach, this is one of the best hotels in eastern Sámos, with elegantly-decorated rooms – opt for an attic one – a pool with a view, tennis courts and a private lido as well as on-site car rental. May–Oct. **€65**

Klima Paradise Mykáli ☎22730 80017,

ⓦklimaparadise.com. Lovely little place whose studios boast balconies overlooking the beach, some fifty paces away. The rooms have been decorated with rare attention for this price, and there's a charming, end-of-the-road feel. May–Oct. **€55**

Psili Ammos Psilí Ámmos ☎22730 28301, ⓦpsili-ammos.gr. You can expect excellent service, as well as good seafood, salads and meat grills for €10 or less at this taverna, on the far right as you face the sea. May–Oct daily 9am–midnight.

★**Triantafyllos** Paleókastro ☎22730 27860. A

9

little way uphill from the main road in Paleókastro, this is perhaps the best place to eat on Sámos, either in the snazzy inner room, or out on the picturesque square. They bring in a market-fresh haul of excellent seafood, such as *yialisterés* (€8), sea squirts (€8) and eel (€10), early each morning, and you can choose what loo best. Otherwise, it's a great spot even for simple dip which are presented almost like pieces of art. Dai 6am–1am.

Pythagório

Originally called Tigani ("frying pan"), a reference to its reputation as a heat trap, the island's premier resort, **PYTHAGÓRIO**, was renamed in 1955 to honour Pythagoras, ancient mathematician, philosopher and initiator of a rather subversive cult. Sixth-century BC tyrant Polykrates had his capital here, whose sporadic excavation has made modern Pythagório expand northeast and uphill. The village core of cobbled lanes and stone-walled mansions abuts a cosy **harbour**, fitting almost perfectly into the confines of Polykrates' ancient jetty, traces of which are still visible, but today devoted almost entirely to pleasure craft and overpriced café-bars.

Archeological Museum

On the main road from Vathý • Tues–Sun 8am–3pm • €6 • ☎ 22730 62811

Pythagório's splendid **Archeological Museum** has a number of fascinating and well-labelled exhibits laid out over two floors. Star billing on the ground floor goes to the stunning collection of **gold coins** found in the west of the island, plus there's a substantial number of votary objects and some Greek, Hellenistic and Roman statuary. Upstairs is the home for larger statues, such as the Roman Emperor Trajan and a fine *kouros* from 540–530 BC, but the most interesting display is on the subject of **ancient Greek dwellings**. There's also an unlabelled **hoard of gold byzants**, some of more than three hundred imperial coins from the fifth to seventh centuries AD – one of the largest such troves ever discovered. There's also a recently-opened outdoor section, featuring part of the ancient city.

The castle and around

Unrestricted access • Free

Sámos' most complete **castle**, the nineteenth-century *pýrgos* of local chieftain Lykourgos Logothetis, overlooks both town and the shoreline where he, together with a certain "Kapetan Stamatis" and Admiral Kanaris, oversaw decisive naval and land victories against the Turks in the summer of 1824. The final battle was won on Transfiguration Day (Aug 6 – thus the dedication of the **church** by the castle); an annual fireworks show commemorates the triumph. Also next to the castle are the remains of an early **Christian basilica**, occupying the grounds of a slightly larger Roman villa.

Eupalinos tunnel

1km northwest of Pythagório • Daily 8.30am–2.45pm; book by phone at least a day ahead • €8 • ☎ 22730 62813

The **Eupalinos tunnel** is a 1036m-long aqueduct bored through the mountain just north of Pythagório. Designed by Eupalinos of Mégara, and built by slave labour at the behest of Polykrates, it guaranteed the ancient town a siege-proof water supply, and remained in use until late Byzantine times. Even though the work crews started digging from opposite sides of the mountain, the horizontal deviation from true about halfway along is remarkably slight at 8m, and the vertical error nil despite being beneath 170m of rock under the peak of the mountain: a tribute to the competence of ancient surveyors.

9

Panayía Spilianí

1km northwest of Pythagório • Cave open daylight hours • Free

On the way up to the Eupalinos tunnel is a well-marked turning for the monastery of **Panayía Spilianí**. The monastery itself, now bereft of nuns or monks, has been insensitively restored, but behind the courtyard the *raison d'être* of the place is still magnificent: a cool, illuminated, hundred-metre **cave**, at the drippy end of which is a subterranean shrine to the Virgin. This was supposedly the residence of the ancient oracular priestess Phyto, and a hiding place from medieval pirates.

ARRIVAL AND ACTIVITIES PYTHAGÓRIO

By ferry Ferries dock at the jetty towards the western end of the seafront.

By bus The stop for buses is beside the main inland T-junction.

By car Street parking is impossible but there are free car parks near the main T-junction just west of the town beach.

Diving Samos Dive Centre, at K. Kanári 1 (☎ 6972 997 645, ⓦ samosdiving.com), offers scuba diving.

Cinemas The Rex, on the outskirts of Mytiliníi village, 7km to the northwest (late May to mid-Sept; ☎ 22730 51236), is one of the best-maintained outdoor cinemas on the islands, screening quality first-run films, with free *loukoumádhes* (sweet fritters) and cheap pizza at intermission.

ACCOMMODATION AND EATING

Faros On the seafront ☎ 22730 62464. By the beach, away from the main drag (go all the way to the left), this family-run spot is the most renowned place to eat in town – and don't they know it. If you catch them on a good day, the food's pretty good, though you'll pay more than €10 for seafood. Look out for the little fake lighthouse (hence the name), which lights up at night. May–Oct daily 10am–1am.

12 Two blocks inland from seafront ☎ 22730 61369. Named with a nod to local native Pythagoras, this is the best café in town, with outdoor seats on a quiet street, decent coffee, and tasty sandwiches for €3.50. May–Oct daily 7am–11pm.

Polyxeni On the seafront ☎ 22730 61590, ⓦ polyxenihotel.com. Recently repainted a fetching mint green, this hotel is right in the thick of the harbour action, with simple but clean and cosy rooms, most offering sea views. April–Oct. **€58**

Stratos A block inland from the seafront ☎ 22730 61880, ⓦ stratoshotel.com. Boasting perhaps the island's most colourful rooms, this is a good find just back from the shore, with 25 rooms and personable staff who'll make you feel at home. May–Nov. **€40**

West of Pythagório

Just 2km west of Pythagório is the decent sand-and-pebble **Potokáki beach**; although you'll have to contend with hotel crowds and low-flying jets, the beach is well groomed, the water clean and sports available. The coarse-shingle beach of **Iréon** lies 7km further west; at first glance a nondescript, grid-plan resort, its characterful pedestrianized waterfront remains popular. It's home to better tavernas than at Pythagório, and after dark has a more relaxed feel; the restaurants along the shore are especially busy on summer nights around the **full moon**, when Iréon is the best spot on the island to watch it rise out of the sea.

Heraion

5km west of Pythagório • Tues–Sun 8am–3pm • €6 • ☎ 22730 62811

Under layers of alluvial mud, plus today's runway, lies the processional Sacred Way joining ancient Samos with the **Heraion**, a massive shrine of the **Mother Goddess**. Much touted in tourist literature, this assumes humbler dimensions – one surviving column and low foundations – upon approach. Yet once inside the precinct you sense the former grandeur of the temple, never completed owing to Polykrates' untimely death at the hands of the Persians. The site chosen, near the mouth of the still-active Imvrassós stream, was Hera's legendary birthplace and site of her trysts with Zeus; in the far corner of the fenced-in zone you can tread a large, exposed patch of the Sacred Way.

POTOKÁKI

Doryssa Seaside Resort East end of beach ☎22730 88300, ⓦdoryssa.gr. Huge complex including a hotel wing with Philippe Starck-ish rooms and a reconstructed mock-Greek village, with cosy bungalows –there's even a platía with a pricey café. Breakfast included. April to mid-Oct. €165

Seaside Poros Far west end of beach ☎22730 27823. Smart beach bar with a vast wooden deck and free sunbeds for patrons. Lots of cocktails, other drinks and snacks. Daily 10am–midnight (later in high season).

IRÉON

★**Cohyli** One block back from the western seafro▮ ☎22730 95282, ⓦhotel-cohyli.com. The simple h▮ rooms are great value, especially in high season (very go▮ breakfast included), while the excellent taverna ser▮ delights such as urchins, cockles and octopus salad ▮ under €10 in a shady courtyard. Live music twice a week ▮ season. Summer daily 10am–late and some win▮ weekends. €35

Glaros Two-thirds of the way west along the seafro▮ ☎22730 95457. Cult place where the atmosphere a▮ prices are excellent. Home-cooked delights include f▮ soup and okra, alongside standard grills, salads, fri▮ vegetables and barrelled wine. May–Oct daily 2–11pm

The southern hill villages

Between Pythagório and the western beaches, the road rises to connect a series of appealing **hill villages**. Since island bus routes rarely pass through or near the following places, you really need your own vehicle to explore them. Samian "**potter villages**" specialize, in addition to the usual wares, in the *Koúpa toú Pythagóra* or "Pythagorean cup", supposedly designed by the sage to leak over the user's lap if they were overfilled. From Kouméïka, the paved side road going west just before th◂ village is a useful short cut to Órmos Marathokámbou (see opposite) and beyond.

Koumaradhéï and around

The biggest concentration of pottery outlets is at **KOUMARADHÉÏ**, about 7km west of Hóra, along a route with sweeping views. From the village you can descend to th◂ sixteenth-century monastery of **Megális Panayías** (Mon–Sat 10am–1pm & 5.30–8pm; free), or plough on west to the appealing village **Pýrgos**, the centre of Samian honey production.

Plátanos

From the main road between the south coast and Karlóvassi, it's worth detouring up to **PLÁTANOS**, on the flanks of Mount Karvoúnis; at 520m this is one of Sámos' highest villages, with sweeping views west and south. The name comes from the three stout plane trees (*plátanos* in Greek) on its platía, whose spring water in the arcaded fountain-house is immortalized in one of the most popular Samian folk songs. The only special sight is the double-naved thirteenth-century **church of Kímisis Theotókou** (key at house opposite west entrance) in the village centre.

★**Koutouki tou Barba Dhimitri** Central square, Pýrgos ☎22730 41060. A good range of vegetarian mezédhes, as well as the usual meaty grills, in a surprisingly chic environment for such a remote village. Daily 11am–1am.

Orizondes ☎22730 On the main road, Plátanos ☎22730 39215. The most popular restaurant hereabouts with Samians, with a small daily range of fantastic dishes, often cooked to their own recipes; two courses usually run to €15. Daily noon–10pm.

The southwest

The southwestern coast of Sámos boasts some of the island's best beaches, stretching in an almost unbroken line from Bállos in the east to Limniónas out west – some 14km in total. These strands also offer a range of amenities, though there are substantial ifferences in character along the way. The western beaches are presided over by gorgeous **Mount Kérkis**, at 1437m the Aegean's second-highest summit after Mount Fáos on Samothráki.

Bállos

The easternmost beach of note in this area, sandy **BÁLLOS** (also known as "Koumeika") has picturesque rock overhangs at its far eastern end. There are several places to stay and a few tavernas here, all on the shore road, and plenty of more secluded beaches a little way down south.

Órmos Marathokámbou

The port of Marathókambos, **ÓRMOS MARATHOKÁMBOU**, 18km from Karlóvassi, has become something of a mini-resort, though with ample character in its backstreets. Otherwise, the main focus of attention is the pedestrianized quay, home to several tavernas and starting point for excursion boats to the island of Samiopoúla and along the coast.

Kámbos Marathokámbou

Some 2km west around the rise from Órmos is Sámos' most family-oriented resort, **KÁMBOS MARATHOKÁMBOU** (also known as "Votsalákia"), loomed over by Mount Kérkis. It straggles for over 2km along the island's longest beach: to the west is the less crowded **Fournáki**, the collective name for a series of sand-and-pebble **coves** backed by low cliffs.

Psilí Ámmos and Limniónas

The 600m-long **Psilí Ámmos** beach lies 3km west of Kámbos, with a gently-shelving sea – 100m out you're still just knee-deep – that makes it ideal for families with young children. **Limniónas** is a smaller but superior cove 2km further west; yachts and *kaïkia* occasionally call at the protected bay, which offers decent swimming at the east end, away from a rock shelf in the middle.

ACCOMMODATION AND EATING   THE SOUTHWEST

BÁLLOS

Amfilissos On beach ☎ 22730 31669, ⊛ amfilissos.gr. Friendly medium-sized hotel, with functional, adequately furnished rooms, some with sea-view balconies, set behind a landscaped courtyard. Breakfast included. Late May to Sept. **€45**

Esperos Far eastern end of beach ☎ 22730 36451. Restaurant with a small but eclectic menu of mezédhes and fish like *tsipoúra* (€9). Also a relaxed beach bar serving great fruit smoothies. May to early Oct 9am–1am.

CLIMBING MOUNT KÉRKIS

A limestone/volcanic oddity in a predominantly schist landscape, **Mount Kérkis** attracts plenty of legends and speculation. Hermits colonized and sanctified the mountain's many caves in Byzantine times; resistance guerrillas controlled it during World War II; and mariners still regard it with superstitious awe, especially when mysterious lights are glimpsed at night near the cave mouths.

The classic **route up** begins from **Kámbos Marathokámbou**, along the paved but narrow lane leading inland towards the uninhabited Evangelistrías convent. After a 45-minute walk through olive groves, the path begins, more or less following power lines up to the convent, from which a paint-marked **trail** continues even more steeply up to the peak. The views are tremendous, though the climb itself is humdrum once you're out of the trees. About an hour before the top there's a chapel with an attached cottage for sheltering in emergencies, and just beyond, a welcome spring. All told, it's a seven-hour return outing from Kámbos Marathokámbou, not counting rest stops.

9

ÓRMOS MARATHOKÁMBOU

ly Trata Eastern end of Órmos Marathokámbou ☎22730 31859. The most authentic taverna in the resort specializes in fresh local fish (usually caught the same morning) and pork (from their own farm), as well as daily oven dishes for €6–9. May–Oct daily 9am–11pm.

KÁMBOS MARATHOKÁMBOU

★Loukoullos Fournáki ☎22730 37147. Set on the clifftop at the far west of the strand, this welcoming, family-run affair sells a full range of delicious *mayireftá* and home-grown veg dishes (€5–8), best eaten in the garden with wondrous views. They've an atmospheric annexe bar, and the owner makes his own croissants – try them here with home-made jam. May–Sept daily noon–midnight.

Sirena Residence & Spa 300m inland from Kámbos Marathokámbou ☎22730 31035, ⓦsirena.gr. One the island's smartest resorts, with a range of luxury studi and apartments, plus a variety of spa treatments (€15–85 Breakfast included. May–Oct. **€100**

So Nice East end of Kámbos Marathokámbo ☎22730 35636. Cheap but cheerful, with rooms whic are cosy for the price, all featuring balconies an including breakfast. The beach is just a few minute walk away. May–Sept. **€35**

LIMNIÓNAS

★Studios Limnionas Limniónas ☎69781 13883 ⓦstudioslimnionas.com. Boasting some of the bes views on the island, this cheapie is a real steal – rooms wit stylish flooring, leaf-shaded common areas, and a pleasin sense of remoteness. May–Oct. **€40**

The far west

Buses from Karlóvassi (Mon & Fri 4.45am & 1.20pm) stop at Kallithéa (1hr 30min) and Dhrakéï (1hr 50min); they return the same days from Dhrakéï (6.10am & 2.45pm)

From Limniónas, the road rises in not-so-gentle increments, finally cresting on its way to **KALLITHÉA**, a small village with just a simple grill on its tiny square. A newer track (from beside the cemetery) and an older trail both lead up within 45 minutes to a spring, rural chapel and plane tree on the west flank of Kérkis, with path-only continuation for another thirty minutes to a pair of faintly frescoed cave-churches. **Panayía Makriní** stands at the mouth of a high, wide but shallow grotto, whose balcony affords terrific views. By contrast, **Ayía Triádha**, a ten-minute scramble overhead, has most of its structure made up of cave wall; just adjacent, another long, narrow, volcanic cavern can be explored with a torch some hundred metres into the mountain.

Some 7km further northeast, **DHRAKÉÏ** is a minuscule, back-of-beyond village with views across to Ikaría, and a few so-so tavernas. This is the end of the road, and the beginning of a wonderful hiking trail to Karlóvassi (see box, below).

Karlóvassi

KARLÓVASSI, 31km west of Vathý and Sámos' second town, is sleepier and more old-fashioned than the capital, despite having roughly the same population. It's a useful

---

HIKING THE WEST COAST: DHRAKÉÏ TO KARLÓVASSI

From Dhrakéï, a hiking trail of stupendous variety heads north along the west coast to Karlóvassi, passing dense forest, along cliff-faces and through olive groves on its way, as well as mopping up a couple of wonderfully secluded beaches, neither with road access or facilities. After dropping down from Dhrakéï, a lovely trail rises, then curls around a gorge, on its 90min run down to **Megálo Seïtáni** beach (see opposite). The path heading up the cliff at its northern end is a little hard to find, but persevere; it's then another fifty minutes or so to far smaller **Mikró Seïtáni** (see opposite). The path climbs steeply once more before an easy dirt track brings you down to busier **Potámi** beach (see opposite), 45min away. From here you can walk a further 30min to Karlóvassi, or take a cab. It's 8.3km from Dhrakéï to Potámi, with almost 600m of total altitude gain, so this walk is no spring picnic; the foolish can manage it with flip-flops in dry weather, but you're best advised to take sturdy footwear, and enough water for the whole route.

9

ase for enjoying northwestern Sámos' excellent **beaches** or taking a number of ewarding **walks**, though relatively few foreigners stay here. The town sprawls across everal straggly neighbourhoods: farthest west, **Limáni** is the harbour and port district, and home to most tourists on account of its facilities; to its east, **Meséo** tilts appealingly ff a knoll and boasts some good tavernas; while east again is **Néo**, the busiest area and e facto town centre.

anning Museum

etween Meséo and Néo • Tues–Sat 9am–1pm • Free • ☎ 22730 79137

The area between Meséo and Néo is something of a ghost town, its derelict tone-built warehouses, tanneries and mansions providing reminders of the leather ndustry that flourished here until the 1960s. The now-defunct epoch is mmortalized in the modern **Tanning Museum**, which has informative displays on he industry, as well as on tobacco production.

Potámi and around

The closest decent **beach** to Karlóvassi is **Potámi**, thirty minutes' walk away via the coast road from Limáni. This broad arc of sand and pebbles is presided over on the east by the striking modernist clifftop chapel of Áyios Nikólaos from 1971. A streamside path leads twenty minutes inland from Potámi, past the eleventh-century church of **Metamórfosis** – the oldest on Sámos – to a point where the river disappears into a small gorge. Just above the Metamórfosis church, a clear if precipitous path leads up to the remains of a small, contemporaneous **Byzantine fortress**.

Mikró Seïtáni and Megálo Seïtáni

Private water-taxi services can be found in peak season around Karlóvassi port (€10–12 per person to either beach) • Also accessible on a tour (see p.603), or on foot (see box, opposite)

The coast west of Potámi ranks among the most beautiful and unspoilt on Sámos; since the early 1980s it has served as a protected refuge for the rare **monk seal**, still glimpsed occasionally by lucky hikers or bathers. A 45min hike from Potámi (see box, opposite) brings you to **Mikró Seïtáni** ("Little Satan"), a small pebble cove guarded by sculpted rock walls; a fifty-minute walk further along the coast will bring you to **Megálo Seïtáni** ("Big Satan"), the island's finest sand beach, at the mouth of the intimidating Kakopérato gorge. Bring food, water and something to shade yourself, though a swimsuit is optional; these beaches have also become favoured camping and drinking spots with Samians.

ARRIVAL AND DEPARTURE

KARLÓVASSI

By ferry Karlóvassi's dock is out west in Limáni – convenient for those arriving by ferry, or staying at one of the many nearby hotels. Buses to Néo (the town centre) are infrequent but often meet the boats.

By bus Services from Vathý (3–7 daily; 1hr) terminate in Néo, at a hard-to-track-down stop on Seferi.

ACCOMMODATION

Karlovasi Studios Paléo ☎ 69371 33930. Way up above the port, with great views – and extra definition on your calf muscles – guaranteed at this simple spot. All the studios have small kitchenettes, and some have terraces. April–Oct. **€30**

Samaina Inn Limáni ☎ 22730 30400, ⓦ samainahotels.gr. Large and relatively luxurious hotel near the old harbour, offering cheerful, comfortable rooms, some with sea- or pool-facing balconies; they also have a cheaper hotel, the Samaina Port, just to the west. Breakfast included. April–Oct. **€90**

EATING AND DRINKING

★**Ginger** Néo ☎ 22730 33787. The house cocktails (all €7.50) here have won national awards – made with ingredients such as elderflower extract, rose liqueur, hibiscus tea and even wasabi-infused rum, they're really something. It's also good as a café during the day, with plenty of varieties of hot chocolate (€3). Daily 9am–midnight.

9

★ **Hippy's** Potámi beach ☎ 22730 33796, ⓦ hippys. gr. Laidback beach bar, set behind a sunflower garden, with a distinct Indian vibe. It does a limited breakfast and meals menu, plus ample coffee and cocktails. Regular parties and musical events. June to early Sept 10am–late.

O Dionysos Platía 8-Maïoú, Meséo ☎ 22730 30120. Offe creative dishes such as asparagus in mushroom sauce ar richly cooked meat dishes from €10. There's a fancy-lookir interior and outdoor seating on the square (sit in the rig● place and you'll see the nearby church lit up), plus a wine li aspiring to Athenian sophistication. Mon–Sat 11am–1am.

The north coast

The northern coast is studded with beaches almost all the way from Karlóvassi to Vathý. **Kokkári** is the busiest and most popular spot in this area on account of its pristine harbour and splendid range of places to eat and drink, though there are more secluded beaches around if you like peace and quiet more than sunbed carpets and permanently anchored umbrellas.

Áyios Nikólaos

Just 4km east of Karlóvassi, **ÁYIOS NIKÓLAOS** is the tiny seaside annexe of more traditional **Kondakéïka**. A passable pebble beach, **Piáki**, lies ten minutes' walk east past the last studio units.

Kímisis Theotókou

2.5km inland from Kondakéïka along a partly paved road (signposted) • Unrestricted access

Within walking distance of Áyios Nikólaos, the scenic Byzantine church of **Kímisis Theotókou** (left unlocked) is the second oldest and most artistically noteworthy on Sámos. Dating from the late twelfth/early thirteenth century, it has extensive frescoes contemporaneous with the building. The deceptively simple exterior gives little hint of the glorious barrel-vaulted interior, its decoration still vivid except where damp has blurred the images.

Áyios Konstandínos

Some 8km east of Áyios Nikólaos, the small seaside hamlet of **ÁYIOS KONSTANDÍNOS** is a peaceful spot with a collection of mostly warm-toned stone buildings and an over-prettified, surf-pounded esplanade. There are no significant beaches within walking distance, but it's the starting point for the road up to Manolátes (see p.614).

Tzamadhoú

The graceful crescent of **Tzamadhoú** beach is only accessible by paths from the main road just up above, and Lemonákia, the closest beach to Kokkári. The eastern third of the beach, made up of saucer-shaped pebbles, is a well-established gay-friendly nudist zone.

Kokkári

KOKKÁRI is the island's second major tourist centre, covering two knolls behind mirror-image headlands called Dhídhymi ("Twins"). The town's coastal profile remains unchanged, but its identity has been altered by inland expansion across old vineyards and along the west beach; its quaint harbour area is a lively place to hang out, but since the coarse-pebble **beaches** here are buffeted by near-constant winds, it's developd as a successful **windsurfing** resort (see below).

INFORMATION AND ACTIVITIES   **THE NORTH COAST**

Tourist office There's a helpful tourist office on Kokkári's main street, heading inland (May–Sept Mon–Sat 8.30am–1.30pm, plus Mon, Wed & Sat 7–9pm; ☎ 22730 92333).

Windsurfing A windsurfing school thrives just west of Kokkári (☎ 22730 92102, ⓦ samoswindsurfing.gr).

ACCOMMODATION

ÁYIOS KONSTANDÍNOS

Daphne 500m inland from the village ☎ 22730 94003, ⓦ daphnehotel.gr. Set against a leafy backdrop on a hill, this good-value hotel looks, from a distance, like an international conference hotel. Up close, it's more humble, with smart but compact rooms with baths, most boasting great views. Swimming pool and pool tables on site; breakfast included. May–Oct. **€65**

Villa Agios Konstantinos On road to Platanákia ☎ 22730 94000, ⓦ hotelagios.gr. Also known as *Agios Apartments*, this attractive two-storey hotel has a splendid little pool, and sea-facing rooms which are well equipped and sport small balconies. April–Oct. **€45**

TZAMADHOÚ

★ **Armonia Bay** Tzamadhoú ☎ 22730 92279, ⓦ armoniahotels.gr. Directly above the beach, this hotel

sizeable, tastefully decorated rooms with marble-clad baths, as well as a fine pool and attractive communal areas. They often impose a four-night minimum stay. Breakfast included. April–Oct. **€120**

KOKKÁRI

Athena Opposite western beach ☎ 22730 92030, ⓦ hotelathena-samos.gr. Modern, comfortable rooms spread over three buildings, set in beautifully landscaped grounds with a large pool. Very helpful Greek-American owner, and buffet breakfast included. April–Oct. **€55**

Sunrise Beach Behind eastern beach ☎ 22730 92447, ⓦ sunrisebeach.gr. Perched on a green knoll above the beach, this upmarket hotel has airy, spacious rooms, all with sea-view balconies and buffet breakfast included. The hotel also runs the budget Studio Penelope (€35), 200m away. April–Oct. **€75**

EATING AND DRINKING

ÁYIOS NIKÓLAOS

To Arhondospito Kondakéïka village centre ☎ 22730 38072. Popular with students, this convivial ouzerí-cum-taverna rustles up standard grills, some oven dishes and plenty of mezédhes, all for well under €10. Daily 11am–late.

ÁYIOS KONSTANDÍNOS

Aeolos Far west end of seafront ☎ 22730 94021. Terrific fish or grilled meat plus a few daily oven dishes (€5–8), served at photo-worthy tables adjoining a tiny pebble cove, where the sea meets the harbour wall. Their meat and seafood platters (€16 and €18, respectively) will feed two. May–Sept daily noon–11pm.

KOKKÁRI

Cavos On fishing harbour ☎ 22730 92436. Perennially popular place serving up breakfast, snacks, coffees and

cocktails according to the time of day. They also have a big screen for sport-watching. April–Oct daily 8am–late.

Taj Mahal By beach ☎ 22730 92061. Not an Indian restaurant, but a decent café-bar with sunbeds on the beach – it's also the only place on the island where you can puff on a shisha (€5). Daily April–Oct 10am–11pm.

★ **Tarsanas** 100m down lane from western beach ☎ 22730 92337. Wonderful terrazzo-floored 1980s throw-back doing pizzas, a couple of dishes of the day, like *briám* or *dolmádhes*, for €5–6, and their own dynamite red wine. Daily: June–Sept 11am–late; Oct–May 8pm–2am.

Zakore On fishing harbour ☎ 22730 92175. This grill restaurant has an island-wide reputation for its meat dishes, which come from the family butchers': juicy grilled morsels cost €7.50–16, depending on your level of gluttony. Daily April–Oct 1pm–11pm.

Northern hill villages

Inland between Kokkári and Kondakéïka, an idyllic landscape of pine, cypress and orchards is overawed by dramatic mountains. Despite bulldozer vandalism, some of the trail system linking the various **hill villages** is still intact, and walkers can return to the main highway to catch a bus back to base. Those with transport should leave it at Vourliótes and execute a **three-hour loop** via Manolátes, north and down to Aïdhónia, then back up east to your starting point. There is some waymarking, and the final stretch of trail has been rehabilitated.

Vourliótes

VOURLIÓTES, the closest sizeable village to Kokkári, has beaked chimneys and brightly painted shutters sprouting from its typical tile-roofed houses. It central square is a photogenic spot, despite the profusion of restaurant tables. A detour from the road up to tiny **Pnaká**, bisected by a picturesque rivulet, is also rewarding.

9

Manolátes

MANOLÁTES, an hour-plus walk uphill from Vourliótes via a deep river canyon or accessed by a separate link road from the coast, has several excellent and authentic tavernas. The two high-quality *raku* ceramic workshops are not cheap, but worth a look (see below).

EATING AND DRINKING

NORTHERN HILL VILLAGE

AAA Manolátes ☎ 22730 94472. Central taverna offering grilled *mastéllo*, an idiosyncratic version of aubergine *imám*, and meat dishes such as fried liver for €7 – check the blackboard for daily dishes. March–Nov daily 11am–2am, some winter weekends from 8pm.
Iy Pera Vrysi Vourliótes ☎ 22730 93277. This taverna at the village entrance serves a huge range of well-priced, imaginative mezédhes like spinach croquettes or chicken

livers, as well as local *robóla* wine. March–Nov daily noon–1am.
★Pnaka Pnaká ☎ 22730 93297. Traditional *mezedhopolío* revitalized by youthful owners, in a lovely shady setting, where you can enjoy mezédhes like *bouréki* and *bekrí mezé* or more substantial dishes for €8 at most. March–Nov daily 11am–1am.

SHOPPING

Genesis Manolátes ☎ 22730 94645. The best of the village's ceramic shops, with two stores facing each other across a lane just downhill from the central squares. The cups, sourced from the "pottery villages" down south, are

particularly good purchases, and there are cherries to munch while you mull your options. April–Oct daily 10am–9pm.

Foúrni

The straits between Sámos and Ikaría are speckled with a mini-archipelago – once haunted by pirates from various corners of the Mediterranean – of which only two are inhabited. Of these, the largest of the group, **FOÚRNI**, has a growing reputation as a great hideaway; unlike so many small Greek islands, it has a stable population (around 1600), as it is home to a huge fishing fleet and one of the more thriving boatyards in the Aegean.

Apart from remote **Khrysomiliá** hamlet in the north, reached by the island's longest (18km) road, Foúrni's inhabitants are concentrated in the **port** area, and **Kambí** hamlet just over the rise to the south.

The port

The **port** community is larger than it seems from the sea, with a friendly ambience reminiscent of 1970s Greece; the historical pirate connection is reflected in the municipality's official name, Foúrni Korseón ("Fourni of the Corsairs"). The main **market street**, field-stoned and mulberry-shaded, runs 200m inland from the seafront and culminates scenically at a little **platía**, featuring two giant plane trees and a Hellenistic sarcophagus found in a nearby field.

Southern Foúrni

From the primary school near the port, it's a fifteen-minute walk south on a flagstone lane, then over the restored windmill ridge, to **KAMBÍ**, a scattered community overlooking a pair of sandy, tamarisk-shaded coves.

A path system starting at Kambí's last house continues south around the headland to other, more secluded **bays** of varying sizes and beach consistencies. These are also favourite anchorages for passing yachts, but unlike Kambí they have substantial summer communities of rough campers and naturists. In order of appearance they are sand-and-pebble **Áspa**, fifteen minutes along, with a tiny spring seeping from the rocks

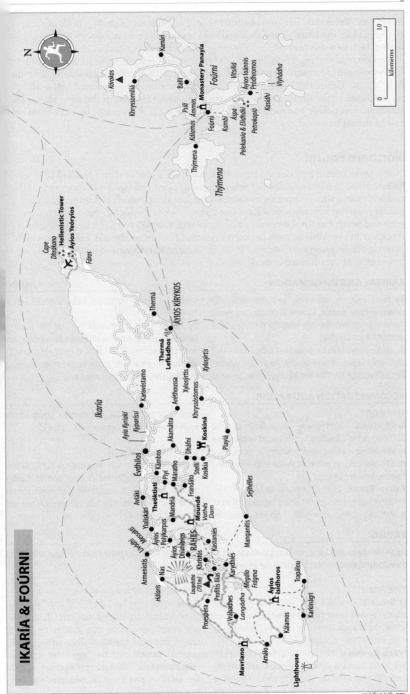

IKARÍA & FOÚRNI

N

0   10
kilometres

Kamári
Khryssomiliá
Kórakas
Balli
Monastery Panayia
Psilí
Kálamos Ámmos
Foúrni
Kambí
Thýmena
Aspa
Pelekánia & Elidháki
Petrokópio
Vitsiliá
Áyios Ioánnis
Pródhromos
Kasídhi
Vlyhádha
Thýmena

Cape
Dhráкano
Hellenistic Tower
Áyios Yeóryios
Fáros
Thermá
Ayía Kyriakí
Kyparíssi
Karavóstamo
Aréthoussa
AYIOS KÍRYKOS
Thermá
Lefkádhos
Xylosýrtis
Akamátra
Dháfni
Koskiná
Playiá
Évdhilos
Kámbos
Pigí
Marathó
Stelli
Kosíkia
Frandáto
Theóktisti
Mandriá
Moundé
Vathés
Dam
Seyhéllés
Avláki
Vlалíkari
Ikaría
Khryssóstomos
Xylosýrtis
Áyios
Polýkarpos
RÁHES
Kastaniés
Mavrianós
Livádhi
Messariá
Áyios
Dhimítrios
Khrístos
Proféttis Ilías
Lагкádha
(701m)
Amenistís
Nás
Hílaris
Proespéra
Vrahádhes
Langádha
Megálo
Frágma
Karydhiés
Kálamos
Amaló
Áyios
Isídhoros
Trapáloù
Karkinágri
Manganítis
Lighthouse

9

just before, **Pelekanía**, five minutes further, and equidistant **Elidháki** – both of these coarse pebble, the latter also with paved road access. The trail is slippery and steep just before Áspa so some may prefer to employ a taxi-boat service (ask at the port).

The side road serving Elidháki from the main island ridge-road also has an option for **Petrokopió** (Marmári) cove, named after its role as a quarry for ancient Ephesus in Asia Minor. The quarry itself, with obvious chisel marks and abandoned half-worked stones down by the shore, proves impressive; the beach is made of the same stone. The southernmost pebble and sand beach of **Vlyhádha** is easily accessible by steps from the end of the asphalt road.

Northern Foúrni

North from Foúrni harbour via steps, then path, are a pair of slightly sullied beaches. **Psilí Ámmos**, in front of a derelict fish-processing plant and equally defunct café at the end with tamarisks, is superior to **Kálamos** further along, which is dominated by a military watchpoint; both now have track access, while the former has a fishermen's jetty and beach bar. In the northeast of the island, **KAMÁRI** too has a beach. Without transport, it's possible to **walk** between town and Kamári on the old *kalderími*, which goes via the ridgetop monastery of Panayía. Isolated **Khrysomiliá** in the far north, however, is of very limited appeal.

ARRIVAL AND INFORMATION

FOÚRNI

By ferry Foúrni is surprisingly well connected, with services to its neighbours, a couple of Cyclades and Pireás. Buy your tickets from the little booth on the road a block south of the market street.

Destinations Áyios Kírykos, Ikaría (1–4 daily; 20min–1hr); Karlóvassi, Sámos (4 weekly; 1hr 40min–2hr 10min); Pireás (2 weekly; 10–11hr 30min); Pythagório, Sámos (3 weekly; 1hr 10min–1hr 30min); Vathý, Sámos (2 weekly; 1hr 40min).

By car or scooter Although much of the island is walkable, you can rent a car or scooter from Escape, just north of the port (☎ 22750 51514, ⓦ fourni-rentals.com).

Services There's an ATM on the market street, and most businesses here take card payments too.

ACCOMMODATION AND EATING

THE PORT

Archipelagos Northern end of seafront ☎ 22750 51250, ⓦ archipelagoshotel.gr. This smart modern hotel by the fishing port has quality fittings in its eighteen doubles and suites, as well as an on-site restaurant during summer. Breakfast included. **€50**

Patras Rooms Central seafront ☎ 22750 51268, ⓦ fourni-patrasrooms.gr. A choice of wood-floored, antique-bed rooms, some with balconies above the owner's laidback café-bar, and fourteen superb hillside apartments, in a tiered complex. April–Oct. **€25**

SOUTHERN FOÚRNI

Studio Rena North side of Kambí ☎ 22750 51364, ⓦ studio-rena.com. Stacked in three tiers on Kambí's northern hillside, these comfortable apartments, painted island blue and white, offer fully equipped kitchens and sea-view balconies. **€24**

EATING

For an island with such a tiny population, there are a lot of places to eat and drink around the port – perhaps uniquely for a Greek island, locals seem to go to bed later on average than tourists.

THE PORT

Iy Drosia Main square ☎ 22750 51678. With tables crowded beneath one of the huge plane trees on the inland square, this is a popular spot for coffee by day or beer by night. Daily 10am–midnight.

Iy Kali Kardhia Just off main square ☎ 22750 51217. The aroma from the superb *kondosoúvli* and *kokorétsi* (both €8) rotating on the huge spits beneath the plane trees is likely to tempt you in, with decent wine ensuring

you stay. April–Oct daily 7pm–late.

Nikos On the shorefront ☎ 22750 51207. The "God of Greek Kitchen" (as claimed out front) is a genial, arm-around-your-shoulder sort, running the best of several shorefront operations. They serve generous *mayireftá* portions, and the large inner room gets quite atmospheric – think the opening chapter of Zorba the Greek – over ouzo on cold evenings. Daily 8am–11pm.

OUTHERN FOÚRNI

ampi Beach Bar Kambí beach ☎ 22750 51647. This ⸱ttle beach bar is a popular sundowner spot, with ⸱eating on a wooden platform overlooking the beach, ⸱nder a large tent, or on deckchairs. May–Oct 9.30am– ⸱unset, sometimes later.

NORTHERN FOÚRNI

Almyra Kamári beach ☎ 6979 141 653. The most accomplished out-of-town taverna on the island rustles up a range of fish at standard prices and various mezédhes for €3–6, with seating right on the beach or in a courtyard. May–Oct 1am–1am.

Ikaría

Skinny but imposing, the island of **IKARÍA** juts out of the sea like the spine of some vast sea monster. At points, its north and south coasts are barely more than 6km apart, but travelling from one to the other is never simple. Rising to over 600m, the twisting 37km road between the main towns – **Áyios Kírykos** on the south coast, and **Évdhilos** in the north – is one of the most hair-raising in the islands. Ikaría's longitudinal ridge enjoys spectacular views from the top though it often wears a streamer of cloud, when the rest of the Aegean is clear.

Named after Icarus – in legend he fell into the sea just offshore, after the wax bindings on his wings melted – Ikaría is less visited than its neighbours. For years the only substantial tourism was generated by a few **hot springs** on the southeast coast; today, there are tourist facilities in and around **Armenistís**, the only resort of note, though the both the main towns, Áyios Kírykos and Évdhilos, make pleasant places to stay. Elsewhere, you can hunt down photogenic **Nas beach** out west, or head up into the **Ráhes villages** for a slice of quintessential Ikaría.

ARRIVAL AND DEPARTURE

IKARÍA

By plane Ikaría airport, which can only handle small domestic planes, is around 12km northeast of Áyios Kírykos, the island capital. Buses sometimes meet the flights in summer, though don't count on them – a taxi costs around €20 to Áyios Kírykos and €35 to Évdhilos. Destinations Athens (1–2 daily; 50min); Iráklio (Heraklion), Crete (2 weekly; 45min); Límnos (6 weekly; 50min).

By ferry Ikaría lies on the main Pireás–Sámos route; ferries alternate between calling at Áyios Kírykos on the south coast, and Évdhilos on the north. Both ports also have services on the northeast Aegean route. Destinations from Áyios Kírykos: Foúrni (6 weekly; 20min–1hr 40min); Híos (2 weekly; 5–6hr); Karlóvassi, Sámos (2 weekly; 2hr 50min); Lésvos (2 weekly; 8–9hr);

THE IKARIAN WAY

Renowned among Greeks for being a little different, many Ikaríans exhibit a lack of obsequiousness and a studied **eccentricity**, which is rather endearing, though some may find it initially offputting. Anti-establishment attitudes predominate and local pride dictates that outside opinion matters little: indeed, the island also hosts some of the most rowdy and musically authentic *paniyíria* in Greece, especially in late summer. In some areas, particularly the Ráhes villages (see p.621), locals are famed for sleeping through much of the day and doing their shopping and socializing at night; tales also abound of bakeries, local stores and the like leaving their counters unstaffed, and relying on honesty-box payment.

One factor behind the odd Ikarían way is that the island – along with Thessaly, Lésvos and the Ionian isles – has traditionally been one of the **Greek left**'s strongholds. This dates from long periods of right-wing domination in Greece, when, as in Byzantine times, the island was used as a place of **exile** for political dissidents, particularly communists, who from 1946 to 1949 outnumbered native islanders. This house-arrest policy backfired, with the transportees (including Mikis Theodhorakis in 1946–47) favourably impressing their hosts as the most noble figures they had ever encountered, worthy of emulation. Earlier in the twentieth century, many Ikarians had emigrated to North America and, ironically, their capitalist remittances kept the island going for decades.

9

Límnos (2 weekly; 13–14hr); Pireás (3 weekly; 11hr); Pythagório, Sámos (3 weekly; 1hr–1hr 30min); Vathý, Sámos (3 weekly; 1hr 50min–2hr 30min).
Destinations from Évdhilos: Híos (1 weekly; 5hr);

Karlóvassi, Sámos (6 weekly; 1hr 10min–2hr); Límnos (weekly; 12hr); Mýkonos (5 weekly; 2hr); Pireás (weekly; 6hr); Sýros (5 weekly; 3hr); Vathý, Sámo (1 weekly; 2hr 30min).

GETTING AROUND

By bus There are one to two cross-island bus services between Áyios Kírykos, Évdhilos and Armenistís, but these are not reliable, bar the frequent local bus from Áyios Kírykos to Thérma (a route which is, in any case, walkable). Check bus times at local travel agencies.
By car or motorbike Aventura (☎22750 31140; ✉aventura@otenet.gr) and Dolihi Tours (☎22750 71122; ✉dolichi@otenet.gr) are the most prominent rental

agencies, with branches in Armenistís, Évdhilos an Áyios Kírykos.
By taxi Taxis can be elusive and are best booked throug a travel agent; a cross-island trip between Áyios Kíryko and Évdhilos usually costs €50.
Hitching Note that hitching is a common and safe practic on this unconventional island.

Áyios Kírykos and around

The south-coast port and capital of **ÁYIOS KÍRYKOS** has little to detain foreign tourists, bar the **archaeological museum** on its periphery. It's a pretty town, though, and not a bad base – especially if you're keen to try one of several local **hot springs** (see box, below). **Thérma** is Ikaría's hot-spring centre, and worth considering as a base, though Áyios Kírykos has a wider range of places to eat and drink – you can walk between the two in half an hour (choose the high road, which has way less traffic).

Archaeological Museum

Above the central hospital • Mon–Wed 8.30am–3pm • €3

Recently reopened, the town's surprisingly large **Archaeological Museum** is worth a peek if can you fit within the window of its restrictive opening hours. It's set in a large, Neoclassical building looking down over the town; artefacts on display include finds from ancient settlements across the island, as well as loot from a few local shipwrecks.

Thérma

With its heyday in the 1960s, the spa hamlet of **Thérma**, 1km northeast of the port, feels a little run-down and forlorn, relying on mostly elderly visitors from July to early October. However, it's worth visiting for the free natural **hot springs** (see box, below) in around the village. There's also a delightful **hammam** here (daily 8am–8pm, though opening hours are haphazard; €4.50), with a *spílio* (**natural sauna**) as well as two mineral-water jacuzzis set into a cave.

HOT-SPRING BATHING IN THÉRMA

As well as taking a dip at the gorgeous hammam (see above), you can also enjoy natural hot spring waters, whenever you like for free. The easiest springs to find are in the open **cave** behind the baths – just a few steps down from the pier you'll be in warm-ish water, though it's better to nestle amongst the rocks beneath the overhang. The adventurous can hunt down the **Palia** springs a 30min hike to the north – the path there is a little tricky to find from the village, so head to Agriolykos Pension (see opposite) and follow the clearer track from there (staff will point the way). After hiking through the scrub, you'll see the ruins of some old Roman baths; don't take the downward path immediately after these, but the next further along. The pools are essentially warm water in holes in the rocky shore, but it's all natural and blissfully remote in feel; the views over to Sámos and Foúrni are quite splendid too.

áros and around

he longest **beach** on the south coast is at **Fáros**, 12km northeast of Áyios Kírykos long a good road which also serves the airport. A colony of summer cottages helters under tamarisks along the sand-and-gravel strand, with a reefy zone to cross efore deep water. From a signposted point just inland from Fáros beach, a dirt rack leads 2km to the trailhead for the round **Hellenistic watchtower** at **Cape Dhrákano**, much the oldest and most impressive ancient ruin on the island (closed ong term for restoration). Right below this to the north, perfectly sheltered in most weathers, is a fantasy-image sand **beach**, with assorted rocks and islets off the cape-tip for contrast.

ACCOMMODATION AND EATING   **ÁYIOS KÍRYKOS AND AROUND**

ÁYIOS KÍRYKOS

Akti Above the eastern quay ☎ 22750 23905, ⓦ pensionakti.gr. A simple place, occupying a commading location on a knoll above the harbour, with comfy a/c rooms, and views of Foúrni from the café-garden. €35

★ **ly Klimataria** two blocks back from seafront ☎ 22750 23686. With tables tucked away on a pedestrianized alley beneath climbing vines, this old favourite does various salads, dips and grills for €6–9 and the odd oven dish, plus fine barrelled wine. April–Oct daily 11am–midnight.

Stou Tsouri Central seafront ☎ 22750 22473. Simple taverna serving up tasty baked dishes like okra, artichokes and stuffed fish for €6 each, plus the usual grilled meat and fish. May–Oct daily 11am–midnight.

THÉRMA

★ **Agriolykos Pension** On north bluff ☎ 22750 22433, ⓦ agriolykos.gr. Wonderful and welcoming place with original artwork, delightfully decorated rooms, a communal kitchen, extensive shady grounds

and direct access to a hidden cove. Breakfast included. April–Oct. €45

Aperanto Galazo A block behind the seafront ☎ 22750 23205. Follow the blue dolphin-markings to this excellent-value guesthouse, with rooms overlooking the bay. Rooms are a little plain, but they do the trick. April–Oct. €25

Meltemi Near the baths ☎ 22750 24178. One of the only reliable eating options here, it's a family affair serving inexpensive souvlaki (€7.50), sardines (€6) and the like. April–Oct daily 10am–10pm.

Marina On south bluff ☎ 22750 22188, ⓦ www .marina-hotel.gr. All the rooms at this friendly little hotel, just above the end of the bay, have fridges, a/c and either balconies or verandas. June–Oct. €55

FÁROS BEACH

Evon's Rooms ☎ 22750 32580, ⓦ evonsrooms.com. The well-equipped a/c rooms here are attractive, especially the pricier galleried ones on the top floor. Right on the beach, with a landscaped garden and private parking. €40

Évdhilos and around

The north-coast port of **ÉVDHILOS** is the island's second town, with most of its facilities packed around a picturesque harbour. With a decent number of places to eat and drink, and locals outnumbering tourists even in high season, this is the most appealing urban base on the whole island.

Kámbos

3km west of Évdhilos

The hamlet of **KÁMBOS** has a small hilltop **museum** (Tues–Sun 8.30am–3pm; €3; ☎ 22750 31300) displaying finds from nearby ancient Oinoe. Adjacent to the museum is the twelfth-century church of **Ayía Iríni**, with column stumps and mosaic patches of a fourth-century basilica defining the entry courtyard. Lower down still are the sparse ruins of a **Byzantine palace** used to house exiled nobles, signposted as "odeion", which earlier structure it encloses.

Monastery of Theóktisti

4km west of Kámbos

Ikaría's outstanding medieval monument is the **monastery of Theóktisti**, 4km up from Kámbos along a twisty road (and an easier 3km road from the cute coastal

9

village of Avláki). The monastery looks over pines to the coast from its perch under a chaos of slanted granite slabs, under one of which is tucked the much-photographed chapel of Theoskepastí. The *katholikón* features damaged but worthwhile frescoes dated to 1688.

ACCOMMODATION
ÉVDHILOS AND AROUND

Atheras On hill behind harbour, Évdhilos ☏ 22750 31434, ⓦ atheras-kerame.gr. The best hotel in town has smart modern rooms arranged around a pool. Its sister hotel, *Kerame*, overlooks the eponymous beach just to the east, with some slightly smarter apartments. April–Oct. **€40**

★**Karimalis Winery** Piyí, 5km southwest of Évdhilos ☏ 22750 31151, ⓦ ikarianwine.gr. Several ancien. luxuriously restored, family-sized cottages make fo perhaps the classiest accommodation on the island Breakfast and port/airport transfers included. Meals anc cooking courses also offered. May–Sept. **€70**

EATING AND DRINKING

Coralli On the west quay, Évdhilos ☏ 22750 31924. This is a good place to feast on large portions of seafood or oven-cooked meat, such as goat *yiouvétsi* or *kokkinistó* for around €8. April–Oct daily 1pm–midnight.

★**Mandouvala** Karavóstamo, 8km east of Évdhilos ☏ 22750 61204. With a delightful patio set above wave-lapped schist rock, this popular taverna provides a range of fish, *mezédhes* and veg delights such as local *soúfiko* (ratatouille) for under €10. A good pit-stop before or after tackling the ridge road. May–Oct daily noon–midnight.

Popi's Main coast road, Fýtema, 2km west of Évdhilos

☏ 22750 31928. Run a by legendary leftist, this place serves some great home cooking – think fried fennel balls (€4), goat with oregano (€8), or beetroot salad with rock samphire (€4.50), all eaten on the shady terrace. May–Oct daily 11am–10pm.

★**Rififi** On the east quay, Évdhilos ☏ 22750 33060. Called "The Robber" (it's next door to a bank), this is by far the coolest of several café-bars around the harbour, and good for crepes, sandwiches and decent coffee by day. At night, however, the place comes into its own – more than 30 beers, 40 whiskies and 20 tequilas to choose from. Daily 8.30am–3am.

Armenistís

Most visitors stay at the north-coast resort of **ARMENISTÍS**, for its two enormous sandy **beaches** battered by seasonal surf: **Livádhi** and **Messaktí** lie five and fifteen minutes' walk east respectively, the latter with several reed-roofed *kantínas*. The sea between here and Mýkonos is the windiest patch in the Aegean, generating consistent summer surf. The waves, which attract Athenian body-boarders, are complicated by strong lateral currents, and summer drownings have (at Livádhi) prompted a lifeguard service and a string of safety buoys.

Armenistís itself is spectacularly set, facing northeast along the length of Ikaría towards sun- and moonrise, with Mount Kérkis on Sámos visible on a clear day. A dwindling proportion of older, schist-roofed houses and ex-warehouses, plus boats hauled up in a central sandy cove, lend the place the air of a Cornish fishing village, though in fact it started out as a smuggler's depot, with warehouses but no dwellings. Just east of Messaktí, the fishing settlement of **Yialiskári** offers alternative facilities and looks out past pines to a picturesque jetty church.

ACCOMMODATION
ARMENISTÍS

★**Cavos Bay** Centre of Armenistís ☏ 22750 71381, ⓦ cavosbay.com.gr. Arranged over six levels, all staring straight at the sea, this is a fantastic spot, with stylish communal areas, colourful rooms with smart linen, and engaging staff. Breakfast included. May–Oct. **€75**

Erofili Beach Above Livádhi beach ☏ 22750 71058, ⓦ erofili.gr. Considered the island's best hotel, though

the communal area and pool, perched dramatically over the beach, impress more than the rooms. Breakfast included. April–Oct. **€80**

Valeta Apartments On the rise between Livádhi and Messaktí beaches ☏ 22750 71252, ⓦ valeta.gr. Above the harbour, these attractive and comfortable studios and quads offer a comparable standard and setting to the hotels, at better rates. May–Oct. **€40**

ATING AND NIGHTLIFE

asmir Livádhi beach. One of the island's most enduring ubs acts as a beach bar during the day and pumps ut foreign and Greek hits by night. June–Sept daily 1am–late.

★ **Kiallaris** Central seafront, Yialiskári ☎ 22750 71227. op place for well-executed *mayireftá* and the freshest fish, ll caught locally – the €7 fish soup and *melitzanosaláta* are especially good. May to early Oct daily 11am–2am.

Paradhosiaka Glyka Main road, Armenistís ☎ 22750 71150. This is one of the Aegean's star *zaharoplastía*,

serving addictive *karydhópita* (walnut cake) and other sweet delights – try the "Ikarian herbs" ice-cream, made with goats' milk, thyme, sage and pennyroyal (€1.50 per scoop). May–Oct daily 8am–1am; reduced hours in winter.

Paskhalis Road to Armenistís harbour ☎ 22750 71302. This long-running and extremely friendly taverna has a sea-view terrace, where you can enjoy tasty home cooking such as veal *stifádho* and roast lamb for around €8. Great barrelled wine too. April–Oct daily 8am–1am.

Nas

Three kilometres west of Armenistís, **NAS** is a rather hippyish hangout where a lush river canyon ends at a deceptively sheltered sand-and-pebble beach. Although no longer a naturist's paradise, in many ways it is the most delightful spot on the island. The little bay is almost completely enclosed by weirdly sculpted rock formations, though it's unwise to swim outside the cove's natural limits – marked here with a line of buoys. The crumbling foundations of the fifth-century BC temple of **Artemis Tavropoleio** ("Artemis in Bull-Headdress") overlook the permanent deep pool at the mouth of the river.

ACCOMMODATION AND EATING   NAS

★ **Thea's** East cliff ☎ 22750 71491, ⓦ theasinn.com. Boasting stunning views, this long-standing favourite has lots of vegetarian options such as *soufikó*, chick-pea puree and pumpkin-filled *pítta*. They also have a few attractive

rooms (giant breakfast included). May–Oct daily 9am–1am (from noon in late July & Aug); Nov–April Sat & Sun 9am–1am. €55

The Ráhes villages

Armenistís was originally the port of four inland hamlets – Áyios Dhimítrios, Áyios Polýkarpos, Kastaniés and Khristós – collectively known as **Ráhes**. Curiously, these already served as "hill station" resorts during the 1920s and 1930s, with three hotels, since long-gone, and the only tourism on the island. Despite the modern, paved access roads through the pines, the settlements retain a certain Shangri-La quality, with older residents speaking a positively Homeric dialect.

On an island not short of foibles, these villages are particularly strange in that most locals sleep until 11am or so, move around until about 4pm, then have

---

WALKING IN WESTERN IKARÍA

Although bulldozers and forest fires have reduced the number of attractive possibilities, **walking** between Ráhes and both coasts on old paths is a favourite visitor activity. An accurate, locally produced map-guide, *The Round of Ráhes on Foot*, shows most asphalt roads, tracks and trails in the west of the island, as well as a **loop-hike** taking in the best of the Ráhes villages. The well-marked route sticks partly to existing paths; it takes a full day for the circuit, with ample rests, though total walking time won't exceed six hours. The highlight is the section from **Khristós to Kastaniés**, which takes in the **Hárakos ravine** with its Spanédhon watermill.

Those wishing to walk across Ikaría are best advised to keep on a "Round of Ráhes" sub-route from Khristós to Karydhiés, from where a historic path crosses the lunar Ammoudhiá uplands before dropping spectacularly to Managanítis on the south coast, a generous half-day's outing from Armenistís.

9

another nap until 8pm, whereupon they rise and spend most of the night shopping eating and drinking, in particular excellent home-brewed **wine** traditionally kept in goatskins.

ACCOMMODATION AND EATING

THE RÁHES VILLAGES

Kapilio Central Khristós ☎ 22750 41517. Right in the main pedestrian zone, this good, inexpensive carnivorous supper option serves grills for around €6–8, with the odd dish from the oven and some simple salads. Daily 6pm–4am.

Olivia Villas Eastern edge of Áyios Dhimítrios ☎ 69721 92323, ⓦ ikaria-olivia.gr. The only reliable place to stay in the area, giving visitors a good crack at

seeing Ráhes by night. The excellent value apartment are huge yet cosy affairs, which sleep up to four. €70

Sto Kampi Main square, Áyios Dhimítrios ☎ 22750 41641. One of the few places in the villages to stay ope throughout the day, selling simple meat dishes (the sausage is good; €6), spaghetti and sandwiches. Daily 10am–1am.

The south coast

The well-paved route south from Évdhilos via Akamátra crosses the island watershed before dropping steadily towards the **south coast**; with your own vehicle this is a quicker and much less curvy way back to Áyios Kírykos compared to going via Karavóstomo. It's an eminently scenic route worth taking for its own sake, the narrow road threading corniche-like through oaks at the pass, and then olives at **Playiá** village on the steep southern slope of the island. Out to sea the islands of Pátmos and Dhonoússa are generally visible, and on really clear days Náxos and Amorgós as well. The principal potential detour, 2km past the castle turning, is the road right (west) to the secluded pebble beach of **Seÿhélles** ("Seychelles"), the best on this generally inhospitable coast, with the final approach by ten-minute hike.

With your own transport, you can visit several villages at the southwest tip of the island. **Vrahádhes** enjoys a natural-balcony setting, while a sharp drop below it, the impact of the empty convent of **Mavrianoú** lies mostly in its setting amid gardens overlooking the sea. Nearby **Langádha** is not actually a village but a lush hidden valley. Note that facilities are scarce over the whole south-coast area, with just the odd erratically opening *kafenío* or seasonal taverna providing refreshment.

Híos

"Craggy Híos", as **Homer** aptly described his putative birthplace, has a turbulent history and a strong identity. This large island, often transliterated as "Chios", grew prosperous in medieval times through the export of **mastic resin**, which is still grown in large quantities today (see box, p.630). Following union with Greece in 1912, several shipping dynasties emerged here; they continue to generate wealth, and someone in almost every family still spends time in the merchant navy.

Unfortunately, the island has suffered more than its share of **catastrophes** since the 1800s. In 1822, the Ottomans massacred thirty thousand Hiots here; this was followed by a violent earthquake, which wrought mass destruction in 1881; and the 1980s saw devastating forest fires compound the effect of generations of tree-felling. From the late 1980s, large-scale tourism gave Híos an alternative source of income, though numbers plummeted in 2015 as a result of the **refugee crisis** (see box, p.787); by 2017, the island was served by a single summer charter flight – from Ljubljana, of all places.

For all this, there's a lot to like about Híos. Its capital, Híos Town, is one of the Aegeans' most intriguing and characterful urban centres, while the nearby beach resorts of **Karfás** and **Ayía Ermióni** cater to sun-seekers. Inland, lie a series of fascinating **mastic villages** – including one decorated with geometric patterning – important **Byzantine monuments**, and some hulking mountains.

9

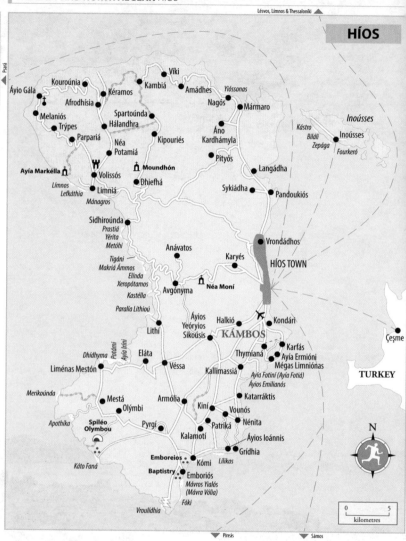

HÍOS

Paná

Áyio Gála
Kouroúnia
Víki
Kambiá
Amádhes
Yióssonas
Kéramos
Nagós
Mármaro
Inoússes
Afrodhísia
Kástro
Biláli
Inoússes
Melaniós
Spartoúnda
Zepága
Fourkeró
Trýpes
Hálandhra
Áno
Parpariá
Kipouriés
Kardhámyla
Néa
Potamiá
Pityós
Langádha
Ayía Markélla
Moundhón
Volissós
Dhiefhá
Límnos
Lefkáthia
Limniá
Sykiádha
Pandoukiós
Mánagros
Sidhiroúnda
Prastiá
Yérita
Metóhi
Vrondádhos
Anávatos
Karyés
HÍOS TOWN
Tigáni
Makriá Ámmos
Elínda
Xeropótamos
Avgónyma
Néa Moní
Kastélla
Paralía Lithioú
Áyios
Yeóryios
Halkió
Kondári
Lithí
Sikoúsis
KÁMBOS
Çeşme
Dhídhyma
Potámi
Ayía Iríni
Eláta
Thymianá
Karfás
Ayía Ermióni
TURKEY
Liménas Mestón
Véssa
Mégas Limniónas
Kallimassiá
Ayía Fotiní (Ayía Fotiá)
Merikoúnda
Áyios Emilianós
Mestá
Armólia
Katarráktis
N
Olýmbi
Kiní
Vounós
Apothíka
Spiléo
Pyrgí
Patriká
Nénita
Olýmbou
Kalamotí
Áyios Ioánnis
Káto Faná
Emboreios
Grídhia
Baptistry
Kómi
Lílikas
Emboriós
Mávros Yialós
(Mávra Vólia)
Fóki
Vroulídhia

0 — 5
kilometres

Pireás
Sámos

ARRIVAL AND DEPARTURE

By plane The airport is 3km south of Híos Town harbour. Frequencies given below for the following destinations are for June–Oct.

Destinations Athens (5–8 daily; 50min); Lésvos (3 weekly; 35min); Sámos (3 weekly; 35min); Thessaloníki (1–3 daily; 1hr).

By ferry Híos is the only stop on the daily superfast service between Pireás and Lésvos and is also on the slower northern mainland to Sámos/Ikaría route, while smaller boats connect it with the satellite islands of Psará and Inoússes, as well as Çeşme in Turkey. All boats leave from Híos Town.

Destinations Áyios Kírykos, Ikaría (2 weekly; 5–7hr); Çeşme (3–4 daily; 20–35min); Inoússes (1–2 daily; 25–50min); Karlóvassi, Sámos (1 weekly; 1hr 45min); Lésvos (1–3 daily; 1hr 20min–2hr 40min); Límnos (2–4 weekly; 6hr 40min–8hr); Pireás (1–3 daily; 6hr 40min–15hr); Psará (4 weekly; 2hr 15min–3hr 45min); Vathý, Sámos (2 weekly; 2hr 40min).

DAY-TRIPS FROM HÍOS

The most popular seasonal **boat excursions** from the main port of Híos Town are to the nearby satellite island of Inoússes (see p.634) and to the Turkish coast. Trips to **Inoússes** usually depart on Sunday at 9am, returning by 5pm at a cost of €20. The longer excursions to Turkey (€25, plus €2 entry tax on the Turkish side) leave daily at 8am for the port of **Çeşme**, where an optional bus transfer (€15) takes you to the city of Izmir, returning by 7pm. You can stay longer, too – a three-day trip including Izmir, Kuşadası and Ephesus will set you back around €160, including accommodation and a guide. Kanaris Tours at Leofóros Egéou 12 (☎ 22710 42490, ⚐ kanaristours.gr) sell tickets for all the above.

GETTING AROUND

By bus Services to the major destinations in the south run quite frequently throughout summer, and there's a decent link to the north, but the northwest is poorly served. All schedules decrease in number on Sundays.

Destinations Katarráktis (3 daily; 45min); Langháda (4 daily; 45min); Mestá (3 daily; 1hr); Pyrgí (3 daily; 45min); Volissós (3 weekly; 1hr 30min).

By car or scooter Of the many rental agencies around the island, the best are Vassilakis/Reliable Rent a Car (☎ 22710 29300, ⚐ rentacar-chios.com), with branches at Evyenías Handhrí 3 in Híos Town, Karfás and Mégas Limniónas; for a scooter try Kovas (☎ 22710 31461, ⚐ kovas.gr), which has an office near the ferry port.

Tours Masticulture (☎ 22710 76084, ⚐ masticulture.com) is an eco-friendly agency that runs tours aimed at independent travellers – kayaking, hiking, cycling and sailing, as well as more left-field ideas like mastic harvesting and star-gazing.

Híos Town

HÍOS TOWN, a brash commercial centre, with a population of 30,000, has few buildings predating the 1881 quake. Yet in many ways it's the most satisfying of the east Aegean ports, with a large and fascinating **marketplace** and several **museums** – not to mention great local nightlife, and a culinary diversity rare in the Aegean. There's currently a sizeable refugee village by the western castle walls; though this is unlikely to result in any problems for tourists, it makes sense to exercise caution in the area, especially at night.

The town forms an amphitheatre of sorts around its **harbour**. The appealing old **kástro** area lies to its north; heading south from here, an attractive **park** functions as the town's lung, and south again is the marvellously lively tradesmen's **bazaar**, where you'll find all sorts on sale (fancy a cast-iron woodstove?) in alleys arrayed off the charming pedestrianized **Aplotarias**.

The kástro

Until the 1881 earthquake, the Byzantine-Genoese **kástro** stood completely intact; thereafter developers razed the seaward walls, filled in the moat to the south and sold off the valuable real estate along the waterfront. Nevertheless, large sections of imposing ramparts remain, with the most dramatic entry to the citadel via the **Porta Maggiora** behind the town hall. Just inside the gate is Platía Kástrou – a good place for coffee – though the most rewarding sight is the restored **Turkish hammam** (Tues–Sun 9am–3pm; free) set under four rose-pink domes in the far north corner. Press further north along the shore and you'll find some renovated examples of the **windmills** for which the island was once famed.

Byzantine Museum

Kanári 12, Platía Vounakíou • Tues–Sun 8am–3pm • €4 • ☎ 22710 26866

The refurbished **Byzantine Museum**, occupying the renovated old **Mecidiye Mosque** with its leaning minaret, has a small but interesting collection, with sections on religious and secular architecture, some splendid murals and icons, as well as various ceramics.

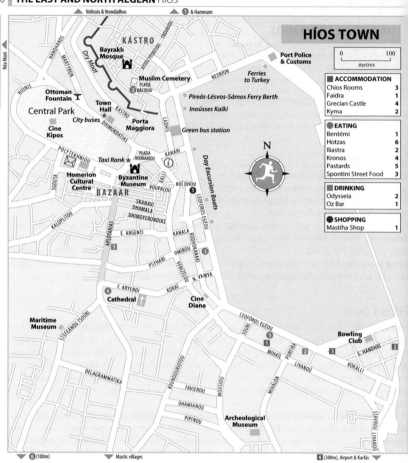

HÍOS TOWN

0	100
	metres

■ ACCOMMODATION

Chios Rooms	3
Faidra	1
Grecian Castle	4
Kyma	2

● EATING

Bentémi	1
Hotzas	6
Iliastra	4
Kronos	4
Pastards	5
Spontini Street Food	3

■ DRINKING

Odysseia	2
Oz Bar	1

● SHOPPING

Mastiha Shop	1

Maritime Museum

Stefánou Tsoúri 20 • Mon–Sat 10am–2pm • Free • ☎ 22710 44139, ⓦ chiosnauticalmuseum.gr

The **Maritime Museum** consists principally of model ships and nautical oil paintings, all rather overshadowed by the mansion containing them. In the foyer are enshrined the knife and glass-globe grenade of Admiral Kanaris, who partly avenged the 1822 massacre by ramming and sinking the Ottoman fleet's flagship, thus dispatching Admiral Kara Ali, architect of the atrocities.

Archeological Museum

Mihálon 10 • Tues–Sun 8.30am–3pm • €2 • ☎ 22710 44239

The **Archeological Museum** has a wide-ranging, well-lit collection from Neolithic to Roman times. Highlights include limestone column bases from the Apollo temple at Faná in the shape of lions' claws; numerous statuettes and reliefs of Cybele (an Asiatic goddess especially honoured here); Archaic faience miniatures from Emborió in the shape of a cat, a hawk and a flautist; a terracotta dwarf riding a boar; and figurines (some with articulated limbs) of *hierodouloi* or sacred prostitutes, presumably from an Aphrodite shrine. Most famous is an inscribed edict of Alexander the Great from 322 BC, setting out relations between himself and the Hiots.

ARRIVAL AND INFORMATION

By air The poky airport lies 3km south of the capital at Kondári, a €5 taxi-ride away; otherwise any blue urban bus on the Híos Town–Karfás route should pass the stop opposite the airport.

By ferry Ferry agents cluster along the north end of waterfront Egéou and its continuation Neoríon.

By bus Blue city buses radiate out from a stop on the north side of Híos Town's central park and serve some nearby

beaches, principally Vrondhádhos and Karfás, but also as far as Ayía Ermióni. For anywhere further afield, buses leave from the "Green bus station" off seafront Egéou.

Tourist information The town's tourist office at Kanári 18 (Mon–Fri 7.30am–3pm; ☎ 22710 44389, ⓦ chios.gr) is one of the most efficient and friendliest in the Aegean; their website has a useful event calendar.

ACCOMMODATION

★**Chios Rooms** Egéou 110 ☎ 22710 20198, ⓦ chiosrooms.gr. These lovingly restored, high-ceilinged rooms are relatively quiet for a seafront location; best is the penthouse "suite" with private terrace. Shared kitchen and book exchange. **€30**

★**Faidra** M. Livanou 13 ☎ 22710 27959. Set in a nineteenth-century building with charming wooden floors, this is a great, homely option. There's only seven rooms – try to nab one of the two with balconies. **€60**

Grecian Castle Bélla Vísta shore avenue ☎ 22710 44740, ⓦ greciancastle.gr. Converted factory towards the

airport with lovely grounds and a sea-view pool, but the smallish main-wing rooms, despite their marble floors, wood ceilings and bug screens, are inferior to the rear "villa" suites. Breakfast included. **€110**

★**Kyma** Evyenías Handhrí ☎ 22710 44500, ⓦ hotelkyma.com. This Neoclassical mansion is like a little trip back in time. Rooms sport handmade wood-and-leather furniture, and those on the sea-facing side have huge terraces; the owner's knowledgeable service really makes the place, and a lavish breakfast is included. **€65**

EATING

Bentémi North of Platía Kástrou ☎ 22710 22720. The best of the kástro square restaurants, with tables beneath mulberry trees in a rose-fringed courtyard. The menu is usually verbal rather than written; expect a choice of sardines, kalamári, and souvláki, all under €10. Live music most Saturdays. Tues–Sun 1pm–midnight.

★**Hotzas** Yeoryíou Kondhýli 3 ☎ 22710 42787. Oldest and most popular taverna in town, with an old-style interior and delightful summer garden. Menu varies seasonally, but expect a mix of vegetarian dishes and *lahanodolmádhes*, sausages, baby fish and *mydhopílafo* (rice and mussels), all well under €10 and accompanied by excellent barrelled wine. Mon–Sat 7pm–late; closed late May to late June.

Iliastra Platía Kástrou ☎ 22710 22322. Appealing place for coffee or desserts such as yoghurt with honey (€3.50);

there's seating within elegant the stone walls, and tables out on the square. Daily 8am–midnight.

Kronos Philippou Argenti 2 ☎ 22710 22311. Well worth tracking down, this ice-cream parlour sells heavenly scoops (from €1.70) made with local mastic, tangerines and the like. Daily 9am–midnight.

★**Pastards** Leoforos Aigaiou 90 ☎ 22710 81466. A great variety of authentic pizza and pasta dishes (from €4.20) at this friendly new restaurant, which looks surprisingly classy considering the low prices. Daily 1pm–1am.

Spontini Street Food 6 Omirou ☎ 22710 80006. Presentable, youthful place offering a mix of wok-fried noodles, pasta dishes and Tex-Mex, of which the latter are best – various fajita and burrito options (€8 or so), tacos, mushroom frittatas and chicken quesadillas. Daily 1.30pm–midnight.

DRINKING

Some 1400 local university students help keep things lively, especially along the waterfront between the two "kinks" in Egéou. You'd think that Hiots invented **ouzo**, such is the profusion of local varieties – many notably drier than the national average. Also worth a mention is **Fresh Chios Beer**, a tasty beverage sold by the bottle at local bars and tavernas, and increasingly seen around the rest of Greece; there's also a porter version.

Odysseia Leofóros Egéou 102 ☎ 22710 20585. Modern, tastefully decorated bar with good live music most nights; they have a full range of Hiot ouzo, plus beer from the local brewery. Daily 10am–late.

★**Oz Bar** Stoa Fragaki ☎ 22710 80326, ⓦ ozcocktailbar.gr. What a great place this skinny venue is. A good spot for

a coffee, juice or brunch by day, it comes into its own at night, with DJs spinning and a range of inventive cocktails (€8–10), many involving local mastic liqueur; they're all detailed on a Monopoly-style menu, and in a cute kitchen-shelf display on one wall. Chios beer also available (€5.50). Daily 10am–3am.

9

THE KÁMBOS

The **Kámbos**, a vast fertile plain carpeted with citrus groves, extends southwest from Híos Town almost as far as the village of Halkió. The district was originally settled by the Genoese during the fourteenth century, and remained a preserve of the local aristocracy until 1822. Exploring the region by two-wheeler may be less frustrating than going by car, since the web of narrow, poorly marked lanes sandwiched between high walls guarantees disorientation and frequent backtracking. Behind the walls you catch fleeting glimpses of ornate old mansions built from locally quarried, rose-and-honey sandstone; their courtyards are often paved in pebbles, or alternating light and dark tiles.

ENTERTAINMENT

Bowling Club Leofóros Egéou 120 ☎ 22710 28517. Popular place with a multitude of pool tables and seven bowling alleys. Daily 10am–late.

Cine Kipos Corner of central park. Film fans are well served by Cine Kipos, with quality/art-house first-run screenings. Late June to early Sept.

Homerion Cultural Centre Iroón Polytekhníou ☎ 22710 44391, ⓦ homerion.gr. Large events hall hosting changing exhibitions and big-name acts.

SHOPPING

Mastiha Shop Egéou 36 ☎ 22710 81600, ⓦ mastihashop.com. Home base of a chain with nine branches in Greece plus others in New York, Paris and Jeddah. Sells all things mastic from chewing gum to shower gel. Daily 8.30am–10pm.

The southeastern coast

Beaches pepper the southeastern coast of Híos, with the first concentration around **Karfás**. To get to the remainder, you'll often have to head up to the main road, and then back down, so it's best just to pick a target and stick to it, rather than trying to join all the dots. Bear in mind that this stretch of coast lies just 8km from Turkey, and is where most of the Hiot refugee landings occur – sadly not all survive the journey.

Karfás and around

The closest decent bathing to the capital is at **Karfás**, 7km south, beyond the airport; most of the large Hiot resort hotels are here, and there's some lively nightlife. Some 2km along the coast, **Ayía Ermióni** is a fishing anchorage that adjoins the next proper beach at **Mégas Limniónas**, a few hundred metres further on: smaller than Karfás but more scenic, it's backed by low, honey-rose-coloured cliffs whose rock is used in the construction of many local buildings. West of Karfás is the delightful **Kámbos** area (see box, above), home to many mansions made with the same rock.

Ayía Fotiní and around

Some 4km further south is the turning for **Ayía Fotiní**, also known as Ayía Fotiá, a 600m pebble **beach** with exceptionally clean water. Cars are excluded from the shore area, and its prettified pedestrian esplanade is lined with various rooms and tavernas. Five kilometres further south, back via the main road, the small fishing village of **Katarráktis** is a laidback spot where locals, French tourists and expats in the know go to eat.

Emboriós and around

The most popular **beaches** at the southern end of Híos are in the vicinity of **Emboriós**, which sits in almost landlocked harbour, 6km southeast of Pyrgí. Ancient **Emboreios**, on the hill to the northeast, has been rehabilitated as an "archeological park" (Tues–Sun am–3pm; €3), while down in modern Emboriós a cruciform early Christian **baptistry** signposted in a field just inland; it's protected by a later, round structure, which remains locked, but everything's visible through the grating.

For **swimming**, follow the road a short way south from Emboriós to an oversubscribed car park and the beach of **Mávros Yialós**, better known as Mávra Vólia, then continue by flagstoned walkway over the headland to more dramatic **Fóki**. Twice as long and backed by impressive cliffs, this pebble strip of purple-grey volcanic stones is part nudist. If you want sand and more amenities go to **Kómi**, 3km northeast of Emboriós, which is the main (albeit low-key) resort for the area.

ACCOMMODATION AND EATING

THE SOUTHEASTERN COAST

KARFÁS AND AROUND

Ankyra Central Mégas Limniónas beach ☎ 22710 32178. All-round reliable *psarotaverna*, serving fish of all categories from €35/kilo and an accompanying range of meat, veg and salads, as well as a fine ouzo selection. May–Oct daily 10am–midnight.

★**Arhondiko Perleas** 1km north of Thymianá ☎ 22710 32217, ⊛ perleas.gr. Set in a huge organic citrus ranch, this classy converted mansion boasts dark wood interiors and original artwork, as well as lavish furnishings. Gourmet breakfast included. **€110**

Melia Sol Above Karfás ☎ 22710 31736, ⊛ meliasolartstudios.gr. Something different to the average resort along this strip, these "art studios" have great visual appeal – decorated along cosy, monochrome lines, they're suitable for families and couples alike. April–Oct. **€85**

Sideratos Apartments Northern end of seafront, Karfás ☎ 69774 37844. Just a few minutes' walk from the beach, there's good value to be had at these spacious apartments, all with private balconies; the hosts are great at the little things which can often add up to so much. April–Oct. **€45**

To Bahari Above the harbour, Ayía Ermióni ☎ 22710 32957. This huge terrace perched on a bluff makes a fine location to enjoy fresh fish (from €40/kilo) plus cheaper meat and veg options. April–Oct daily noon–midnight.

AYÍA FOTINÍ AND AROUND

Asterias Above the harbour, Katarráktis ☎ 22710 61428. Spacious taverna that offers a wide menu of starters, plus grills and cheap fish (mains €7–10).

April–Oct daily 11am–1am.

Iro Apartments On seafront beside the access road, Ayía Fotiní ☎ 22710 30226. Large self-catering studios, with sea views from the balconies, all nicely furnished. Dedicated parking. April–Oct. **€25**

Psarokokkalo On seafront beside the access road, Ayía Fotiní ☎ 22710 51596. Easily the best taverna in the resort, providing tasty *mezédhes*, *souvláki*, pizza, fish and other seafood delights, mostly under €10. Easter–Oct daily 9am–1am.

Sun Rooms Off the southern end of Mégas Limniónas ☎ 22710 33351, ⊛ chiossunrooms.gr. Neat modern block with clean, compact rooms and artistic touches provided by the friendly owner. April–Oct. **€50**

EMBORIÓS AND AROUND

Emporios Bay 50m back from harbour, Emboriós ☎ 22710 70180, ⊛ emporiosbay.gr. This smart modern hotel is a decent bet, with nicely furnished rooms and larger apartments painted in vibrant colours. Breakfast included. April–Oct. **€40**

Karavela East end of Kómi beach ☎ 22710 71054. ☎ 22710 70070. Good all-round taverna near the end of the strip, specializing in grilled fish and meat (under €10) as well as a good line in veg dishes and some decent barrelled wine. Try the grilled local mastelo cheese. May–Oct daily noon–midnight.

Porto Emborios Emboriós ☎ 22710 71306. The best of the tavernas clustered around the harbour serves good seafood at fair prices, a range of salads and dips, plus home-made desserts. March–Oct daily 10am–1am.

The mastic villages

Besides olive groves, southern Híos' gently rolling countryside is home to the **mastic bush**, and the twenty or so **mastihohoriá**, or **mastic villages** (see box, p.630). Since the decline of the mastic trade, the *mastihohoriá* live mainly off their tangerines, apricots and olives, though the villages – the only settlements on Híos spared by the Ottomans in 1822 – retain their architectural uniqueness; they were designed by the Genoese but have a distinctly Middle Eastern feel. The basic plan involves a rectangular warren of tall houses, with the outer row doubling as perimeter fortification, and breached by a limited number of gateways. More recent additions, whether in traditional architectural

9

MASTIC MASTICATION

The **mastic bush** (*Pistacia lentiscus*) is found across much of Aegean Greece, but only in southern Híos – pruned to an umbrella shape to facilitate harvesting – does it produce **aromatic resin** of any quality or quantity, scraped from incisions made on the trunk during summer. For centuries it was used as a base for paints, cosmetics and the chewable jelly beans that became an addictive staple in Ottoman harems. Indeed, the interruption of the flow of mastic from Híos to Istanbul by the revolt of spring 1822 was a main cause of the brutal Ottoman reaction. The wealth engendered by the **mastic trade** supported twenty *mastihohoriá* (mastic villages) from the time the Genoese set up a monopoly in the substance during the fourteenth century, but the demise of imperial Turkey and the development of petroleum-based products knocked the bottom out of the mastic market.

Now it's just a curiosity, to be chewed – try the sweetened Elma-brand gum – or drunk as *mastíha* liqueur. It has had medicinal applications since ancient times; contemporary advocates claim that mastic boosts the immune system and thins the blood. High-end cosmetics, toothpaste and mouthwash are now sold at the Mastiha Shop in Híos Town (see p.628).

style or not, straggle outside the original defences. Of the surviving villages, **Pyrgí**, **Olýmbi** and **Mestá** stand out; the latter two are linked by a delightful hiking path (2.4km; 60min), cutting over a small rise through torched, exposed countryside.

Pyrgí

Church Tue–Sun 8am–3pm • Free

PYRGÍ, 25km south of Híos Town, is the most vividly decorated of the *mastihohoriá*, its houses elaborately embossed with *xystá*, geometric patterns cut into whitewash to reveal a layer of black volcanic sand underneath; in autumn, strings of sun-drying tomatoes add a splash of colour. On the northeast corner of the central square, the twelfth-century Byzantine church of **Áyii Apóstoli**, embellished with later frescoes (probably from 1665), is tucked under an arcade.

Chios Mastic Museum

3km south of Pyrgí • Daily: March–Oct 10am–6pm; Nov–Feb 10am–5pm • €3

One of the island's newest draws, the **Chios Mastic Museum** sits high above Pyrgí, its fancy design inspired by the shelters used by local shepherds, with eco-friendly features – north-facing, it's heated by the sun in summer and cooled by the wind in winter. The airy halls have stylish exhibits pertaining to the production and uses of mastic, as well as the architecture and history associated with it.

Olýmbi and around

OLÝMBI, 7km west of Pyrgí along the same bus route, is one of the less-visited mastic villages but not devoid of interest – keep an eye out for the characteristic **tower-keep**, looming bang in the middle of the platía.

The Spiléo Olýmbou cave

6km southwest of Olýmbi • Tues–Sun: June–Aug 10am–8pm; Sept 11am–6pm • Admission every 30min; guided tours last 20–25min • €5

From Olýmbi, a paved road leads to the well-signed cave of **Spiléo Olýmbou**, near the hamlet of Sykiá. For years it was just a hole in the ground where villagers disposed of dead animals, but since 1985 it has been regularly explored by speleologists. The cavern, with a constant temperature of 18°C, evolved in two phases between 150 million and 50 million years ago, and has a maximum depth of 57m (though tours only visit the top 30m). Its formations, with fanciful names like Chinese Forest, Medusa and Organ Pipes, are among the most beautiful in the Mediterranean.

9

Mestá

Sombre **MESTÁ**, 4km west of Olými, is considered the finest of the mastic villages, exuding a truly kasbah-like air. From its main square, dominated by the **church of the Taxiárhis** with its two icons of the Archangel – one dressed in Byzantine robes, the other in Genoese armour – a maze of dim lanes with anti-seismic tunnels leads off in all directions. Most streets end in blind alleys, except those leading to the six portals; the northeast one still has its original iron gate.

The southwestern beaches

Over on the southwest coast, the closest good, protected beach to Mestá lies 4.7km southwest at **Apothíka**. Others, east of ugly but functional **Liménas Mestón** port, include **Dhídhyma**, 4km away, a double cove guarded by an islet; and **Potámi**, with a namesake stream feeding it.

ACCOMMODATION AND EATING   THE MASTIC VILLAGES

Tourist facilities are relatively sparse in the mastic villages, but stay at least one night and you'll see them at their best – Mestá is the best base, but in all three you'll find signs for private rooms (usually available on spec), as well as simple cafés and tavernas on the main squares.

★ **Lida Mary** Mestá ☎ 22710 76217, ⊕ lidamary.gr. Splendid new boutique hotel right on the main square, with immensely appealing, if rather dungeon-like, rooms. The quirky, cellar-like on-site bar is quite a trip, too. May–Oct. **€55**

Medieval Castle Suites Mestá ☎ 22710 76345, ⊕ mcsuites.gr. Superbly refurbished medieval mansion on a lane just off the main square, with much of the original stone exterior, yet lavishly furnished and equipped with all modern facilities inside. Online deals available. Easter–Oct. **€75**

Mesaionas Mestá ☎ 22710 76050. Excellent home-cooked dishes, such as stewed octopus, moussaka and various veg in sauces for well under €10 each, served on the square. A good lunch-stop. Daily 11am–midnight.

Central Híos

The inland portion of Híos extending west and southwest from Híos Town matches the south in terms of interesting **monuments**, and good roads make touring under your own steam an easy matter. **Avgónyma** has become a popular get-away-from-it-all base of late, while there are also a smattering of good beaches over on the west coast, the main road descending 6km to the sea in well-graded loops.

Néa Moní

15km west of Híos Town • Daily: summer 7am–8pm; winter 8.30am–3pm • ☎ 22710 79391, ⊕ neamoni.gr

Almost exactly in the middle of the island, the monastery of **Néa Moní** was founded by the Byzantine emperor Constantine Monomahos IX ("The Dueller") in 1042 on the spot where a wonder-working **icon** had been discovered. It ranks among the most important monuments on any of the Greek islands; the mosaics, together with those of Dhafní and Ósios Loukás on the mainland, are the finest surviving art of their era in Greece, and the setting – high in partly forested mountains – is equally memorable. Once a powerful community of six hundred monks, Néa Moní was pillaged in 1822 and most of its residents, including 3500 civilians sheltering here, were put to the sword. The 1881 tremor caused comprehensive damage, wrecking many of its outbuildings, while exactly a century later a forest fire threatened to engulf the place until the resident icon was paraded along the perimeter wall, miraculously repelling the flames.

The chapel and museum

Museum: Tues–Sun 8am–1pm • €2

Just inside the **main gate** stands a **chapel/ossuary** containing some of the bones of the 1822 victims; axe-clefts in children's skulls attest to the savagery of the attackers. The restored *katholikón* has a cupola resting on an octagonal drum, a design seen

9

elsewhere only in Cyprus; the famous **mosaics** within have now been restored to their former glory. The narthex contains portrayals of various local saints sandwiched between *Christ Washing the Disciples' Feet* and the *Betrayal*, in which Judas's kiss has unfortunately been obliterated, but Peter is clearly visible lopping off the ear of the high priest's servant. The **museum**, located in the group of buildings behind the chapel, contains an interesting display of ecclesiastical paraphernalia and garments.

Avgónyma and around

Some 5km west of Néa Moní sits **AVGÓNYMA**, a cluster of dwellings on a knoll over-looking the coast; the name means "unproductive pieces of land", an apt description when viewed from the ridge above. Since the 1980s, the place has been restored as a summer haven by descendants of the original villagers, though the permanent population is currently just seventeen. Some 5km north of west of Avgónyma is **Anávatos**, even more minuscule, and with a permanent population of just one – a lady (not even born here) whose house is usually surrounded with plenty of cats and dogs. The views from up here are quite superb.

The west-coast beaches

On the northern stretch of the central west coast, bypass Elínda, alluring from afar but rocky and often murky up close, in favour of the more secluded coves to either side of Metóhi – best of these are **Tigáni** and **Makriá Ámmos**, the latter nudist. Friendly **Lithí** village perches on a forested ledge overlooking the sea towards the southern end of the central west coast. You can eat here but most visitors head 2km downhill to **Paralía Lithioú**, a popular weekend target of Hiot townies thanks to its large but hard-packed, windswept beach.

ACCOMMODATION AND EATING   **CENTRAL HÍOS**

AVGÓNYMA

0 Pyrgos Central square ☎ 22710 42175, ⓦ chiospyrgosrooms.gr. In an attractive arcaded mansion on the main square, with ample courtyard seating, this Greek-American-run taverna serves oven-cooked dishes and grills for €10 or less. Daily 11am–midnight.

Spitakia Various locations around Avgónyma ☎ 22710 20513, ⓦ spitakia.gr. A cluster of small stone cottages sleeping up to five people, plus some rooms, all lovingly restored and tastefully decorated, with good heating for the winter months. €50

PARALÍA LITHIOÚ

Almyriki Apartments ☎ 22710 73124, ⓦ almiriki.gr. Smart complex behind the middle of the beach, with well-appointed rooms sporting modern furniture, TVs and fridges. Chic café-bar on site too. April–Oct. €85

To Akroyiali ☎ 22710 73286. The best of the handful of tavernas here, behind the beach's north end, providing fresh fish, a variety of seafood, simple grilled meat for €6–8 and some tasty mezédhes. May–Sept daily 11am–1am.

Northern Híos

Northern Híos never really recovered from the 1822 massacre, and between Pityós and Volissós the forest's recovery from **fires** in the 1980s has been partly reversed by a bad 2007 blaze. Most villages usually lie deserted, with about a third of the former population living in Híos Town, returning occasionally for major festivals or to tend smallholdings; others, based in Athens or North America, visit their ancestral homes for just a few midsummer weeks.

Langádha and around

Some 16km north of Híos Town, **LANGÁDHA** is probably the first point on the eastern coast road you'd be tempted to stop, though there is no proper beach nearby. Set at the mouth of a deep valley, this attractive little harbour settlement looks across its bay to a pine grove, and beyond to Turkey.

Mármaro and around

Áto Kardhámyla, 37km out of Híos Town, is the island's second town. Better known as MÁRMARO, it's positioned at the edge of a fertile plain rimmed by mountains, which comes as welcome relief from the craggy coastline. However, there is little to attract casual visitors, with the mercilessly exposed port strictly businesslike, and the beach mediocre.

Volissós and around

VOLISSÓS, 42km from Híos Town, was once the market town for a dozen remote hill villages beyond. The buildings around the main square are mostly modern but a host of old stone houses still curl appealingly beneath a crumbling hilltop Byzantine-Genoese fort. Sections of these upper quarters, known as **Pýrgos**, are being restored (usually into quality accommodation), though derelict stores – many with their signs still intact – line the old market street.

Beaches around Volissós

LIMNIÁ (or Limiá), the port of Volissós, lies 2km south of town, bracketed by the local beaches. A 1.5km drive or walk southeast over the headland brings you to **Mánagros**, a seemingly endless sand-and-pebble beach. More intimate, sandy **Lefkáthia** lies just a ten-minute stroll along the cement drive over the headland north of the harbour.

Límnos, the next protected cove 400m east of Lefkáthia, can also be accessed by a direct road from Volissós. Ayía Markélla, 5km further northwest of Límnos, has another long beach, fronting the eponymous, barracks-like pilgrimage **monastery** of Híos' patron saint (festival on July 22).

Monastery of Moundhón

Just outside Dhiefhá village, 2km north of the main Hios Town–Volissós road • For access, seek out the warden, Yiorgos Fokas, in Dhiefhá (☎ 22740 22011)

The engagingly set sixteenth-century **monastery of Moundhón** was second in rank to Néa Moní before its partial destruction in 1822. Best of the naive interior frescoes of the (locked) church is one depicting the *Ouranódhromos Klímax* ("Stairway to Heaven", not to be confused with Led Zeppelin's): a trial-by-ascent, in which ungodly priests are beset by demons hurling them into the mouth of a great serpent symbolizing the Devil, while the righteous clergy are assisted upwards by angels.

ACCOMMODATION AND EATING · NORTHERN HÍOS

LANGÁDHA AND AROUND

Passas On the harbour, Langádha ☎ 22710 74218. The best place to eat on the strip – sit over by the waves or in the covered yard by the huge tree trunk. They usually have fresh squid and octopus on the menu (€8 each), and try Cretan-style ntakos (barley rusk with feta, capers and tomato) for starters. April–Oct daily 10am–midnight.

MÁRMARO AND AROUND

Kardamyla Central Mármaro ☎ 22720 23353. This friendly central hotel has spacious, fan-equipped rooms and a few suites, some with sea views. The restaurant is good too. Breakfast included. June–Sept. €75

VOLISSÓS AND AROUND

Aigiali Beach end of the access road, Límnos ☎ 22740 21856. Attractive, comfortably furnished apartments with well-equipped kitchens and sea-view balconies in a sturdy

modern stone building. The café does great sweets too. May–Sept. €55

★**Fabrika** Just behind main square, Volissós ☎ 22740 22045, ⊛ chiosfabrika.com.gr. This converted olive press, which also has six rooms with quirky decor, serves up superb kondosoúvli and kokorétsi (around €8), as well as a range of daily-changing oven-baked dishes. Seating in the attractive interior or leafy courtyard. Daily noon–2am. €65

Limnos Near access road, Límnos ☎ 22740 22122. Good all-round beachside taverna that dishes up fish grills and specials like kókoras krasáto for €7, as well as delicious mezédhes and highly drinkable wine. May to mid-Oct daily 10am–midnight.

Mavro Provato Main square, Volissós ☎ 22740 22116. Delightful café-restaurant, which does quality coffees, juices and cocktails, as well as good salads, risotto and a few items like burgers (mains around €8). Daily 8am–midnight.

9

Inoússes

INOÚSSES, the closer and more easily accessible of Hios' two satellite islands, has a permanent population of about three hundred, less than half its 1930s figure. For generations this islet, first settled around 1750 by Hiot shepherds, provided Greece with many of its wealthiest **shipping families**: various members of the Livanos, Lemos and Pateras clans were born here.

Inoússes town

Two church-tipped, privately owned islets guard the unusually well-protected harbour of **INOÚSSES TOWN**, which is surprisingly large, draped over hillsides enclosing a ravine. Its illustrious maritime connections help explain the presence of large villas and visiting summer gin-palaces in an otherwise sleepy Greek backwater. Near the quay, the island's only specific sight, the impressive **Marine Museum** (daily 8am–2pm; €1.50; ☎22710 55182), also has a nautical theme and was endowed by various shipping magnates. At the west end of the quay, the bigwigs have also funded a nautical academy, which trains future members of the merchant navy.

Around the island

The southern slope of this tranquil island is surprisingly green and well tended; there are no springs, so water comes from a mix of fresh and brackish wells, as well as a reservoir. The sea is extremely clean and calm on the sheltered southerly shore; among its beaches, choose from **Zepága**, **Biláli** or **Kástro**, respectively five, twenty and thirty minutes' walk west of the port. More secluded **Fourkeró** (or Farkeró) lies 25 minutes east.

ARRIVAL AND DEPARTURE INOÚSSES

By ferry Inoússes can be reached from Híos Town either on a day-trip (see box, p.625) or on the daily ferry (1hr), which departs from Híos in the afternoon and returns in the morning (reduced service in winter). Weekly ferries also stop at the island on their way between Pireás (7hr) and Lésvos (3hr 20min).

ACCOMMODATION AND EATING

Naftikos Omilos Near the jetty ☎22710 55596. This yachtie hangout provides a steady stream of coffee and snacks during the day before morphing into a fairly lively bar by night, as the music volume ramps up. May–Sept daily 9am–2am.

Oinousses Studios Above the harbour ☎22710 55255, ✉oinoussesstudios@gmail.com. Smart modern apartments with fully equipped kitchens and large balconies facing the sea. May–Sept. **€35**

Pateronisso Beside the jetty ☎22710 55311. The best of a small bunch of tavernas dotted on or around the seafront. All the usual fish, meat and salad staples are available, most for under €10. June–Sept daily 7am–midnight.

Thalassoporos On the town's main easterly lane ☎22710 55475. This modest establishment is the island's only bona fide hotel, with small and basic but very clean rooms, mostly affording sea views. May–Sept. **€45**

Psará

Remote **Psará** lies a good 20km west of the northwest tip of Híos and is too far from it to be visited on a day-trip. The birthplace of revolutionary war hero Admiral Konstandinos Kanaris, the island devoted its merchant fleets – the third largest in 1820s Greece – to the cause of independence, and paid dearly for it. Vexed beyond endurance, the Turks landed overwhelming forces in 1824 to stamp out this nest of resistance. Perhaps three thousand of the thirty thousand inhabitants escaped in small boats to be rescued by a French fleet, but the majority retreated to a hilltop owder magazine, blowing it and themselves up rather than surrender. Today, it's a ather bleak place living up to its name ("the mottled things" in ancient Greek), ever really having recovered from the holocaust. The official population now barely xceeds four hundred, and, despite some revitalization since the 1980s, it has never een a tourist boom.

The harbour

ince few buildings in the east-facing harbour community predate the twentieth entury, a strange hotchpotch of ecclesiastical and secular architecture greets you on lisembarking. There's a distinctly southern feel, more like the Dodecanese or the Cyclades, and some peculiar churches, no two alike in style.

Around the island

Psará's **beaches** are decent, improving the further northeast you walk from the port. You quickly pass **Káto Yialós**, **Katsoúni** and **Lazarétto** with its off-putting power station, before reaching **Lákka** ("narrow ravine"), fifteen minutes along, apparently named after its grooved rock formations. **Límnos**, 25 minutes from the port along the coastal path, is big and attractive, but there's no reliable taverna here, or indeed at any of the beaches.

The only real sight on Psará is the **Kímisis (Assumption) monastery**, reached by following the paved road north across the island. Uninhabited since the 1970s, it comes to life only in early August, when its revered icon is carried in ceremonial procession to town and back on the eve of August 5.

ARRIVAL AND DEPARTURE PSARÁ

By ferry Psará has decent ferry links with Híos Town (6 weekly; 2hr 15min–3hr 45min); frequencies drop drastically off season.

ACCOMMODATION

Kato Gialos Apartments Behind Káto Yialós beach ☏ 22740 61178. A mixture of spotless rooms and larger apartments with kitchen facilities, all with sea views and only a minute from the water. June–Sept. **€50**

Psara Studios At the back of the harbour village ☏ 22740 61180. The rooms here are large and furnished well enough, and have functional kitchenettes, plus there's a small garden fringed with palms. May–Sept. **€45**

EATING

Iliovasilema Behind Káto Yialós beach ☏ 22740 61121. Sunset is the best time to dine here on seafood delights such as fried kalamári or octopus with aubergines for €10 or less. A friendly welcome is guaranteed. June–Sept daily 11am–midnight.

★Spitalia Behind Katsoúnis beach ☏ 22740 61376. Located in a restored medieval hospital, this great taverna comes up with specialities such as stuffed goat and other home-style dishes for €7–9, plus grills, salads and good wine. May–Sept daily 11am–1am.

Lésvos

LÉSVOS (also known as Mytilíni), the third-largest Greek island after Crete and Évvia, is the birthplace of the ancient bards Sappho, Aesop, Arion and – more recently – primitive artist Theophilos and Nobel Laureate poet Odysseus Elytis. Despite these **artistic associations**, the island is not at first sight particularly beautiful or interesting: much of the landscape is rocky, volcanic terrain, encompassing vast grain fields, scrubland and saltpans. But there are also oak and pine forests as well as endless olive groves, some more than five centuries old. With its balmy climate and suggestive contours, Lésvos tends to grow on you with prolonged exposure. Lovers of medieval

9

and Ottoman **architecture** certainly won't be disappointed, and castles survive at Mytilíni Town, Mólyvos, Eressós, Sígri and near Ándissa.

Social and political **idiosyncrasies** add to the island's appeal. There is a tendency t vote **communist** (with usually at least one Red MP in office), a legacy of Ottoman-era quasi-feudalism, 1880s conflicts between small and large olive producers and further disruption occasioned by the arrival of many refugees. Breeding livestock, especially horses, remains important, and organic production has been embraced enthusiastically as a way of making Lésvos' agricultural products more competitive; in addition, this is the country's major producer of **ouzo** – perhaps accounting for the island having the highest alcoholism rate in Greece. Lastly, there's the whole **lesbian** connection – the English word derives from the island since it was the home of the poet Sappho, still revered as a symbol of love between women to this day.

Historically, the olive plantations, ouzo distilleries, animal husbandry and fishing industry supported those who chose not to emigrate, but when these enterprises stalled in the 1980s, **tourism** made appreciable inroads. However, it still accounts for only around ten percent of the local economy, and there are few large hotels outside the capital, Skála Kalloní or Mólyvos. Visitor numbers have declined of late, especially since the arrival of refugees from the nearby Turkish shore accelerated in 2015; ironically, the island's major source of tourist growth is now Turks coming here for weekend breaks.

Brief history

In antiquity, Lésvos' importance lay in its artistic and commercial connections rather than in historical events: being on the trade route to Asia Minor, it always attracted merchants and became quite wealthy during **Roman times**. During the late fourteenth century, Lésvos was given as a dowry to a Genoese prince of the Gattilusi clan following his marriage to the sister of one of the last Byzantine emperors – it's

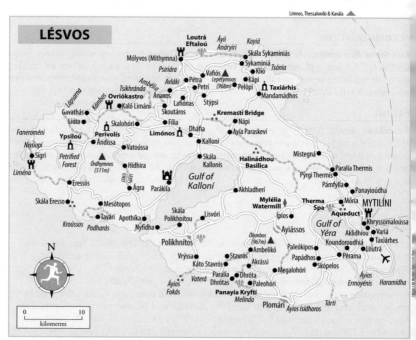

om this period that most of its castles remain. The first two centuries of **Ottoman** ule were particularly harsh, with much of the Orthodox population sold into avery or deported to the imperial capital – replaced by more tractable Muslim olonists, who populated even rural areas – and most physical evidence of the enoese or Byzantine period demolished. Out in the countryside, Turks and Greeks ot along, relatively speaking, right up until 1923; the Ottoman authorities voured Greek *kahayiádhes* (overseers) to keep the peons in line. However, large umbers of the lower social classes, oppressed by the pashas and their Greek lackeys, led across to Asia Minor during the nineteenth century, only to return again after he exchange of populations.

ARRIVAL AND GETTING AROUND LÉSVOS

y plane There are services (frequencies for June–Oct) om Athens (3–5 daily; 55min); Híos (3 weekly, 35min); imnos (3 weekly; 40min); Thessaloníki (2–3 daily; 55min).

y ferry Despite the island's size, all ferries dock n Mytilíni.

Destinations Áyios Kírykos, Ikaría (2 weekly; 8–10hr);

Ayvalık, Turkey (May–Oct 4–6 daily, winter sporadic; 50min–1hr 30min); Évdhilos, Ikaría (1 weekly; 6hr); Híos (1–4 daily; 2hr 15min–3hr 30min); Karlóvassi, Sámos (1 weekly; 4hr 20min); Límnos (2 weekly; 3hr 50min–6hr); Pireás (1–4 daily; 9hr 30min–12hr); Vathý, Sámos (2 weekly; 5hr 35min).

GETTING AROUND

By bus Mytilíni is the hub of all bus routes around the sland, with public buses running once or twice daily to most major towns and resorts, though Lesvos' sheer size makes day-trips from the capital impractical.

Destinations Ándissa (1–2 daily; 2hr); Kalloní (1–3 daily; 45min); Mólyvos (1–3 daily; 1hr 30min); Plomári (1–4 daily; 1hr 15min), Polikhnítos (1–2 daily; 1hr 30min), Skála Eressoú (1–2 daily; 2hr 30min).

Mytilíni Town

MYTILÍNI, the port and capital, sprawls between and around two bays divided by a fortified promontory, and in Greek fashion often doubles as the name of the island. Many visitors are put off by the combination of urban bustle and, in the humbler northern districts, slight seediness. However, several diversions, particularly the marketplace and a few museums within a few minutes' walk of the waterfront, can occupy you for a few hours.

The old town

Between the bazaar and Epáno Skála, Ermoú passes various expensive antique shops near the roofless, derelict **Yéni Tzamí** at the heart of the old Muslim quarter, just a few steps east of a superb, beautifully restored Turkish **hammam**, which unfortunately – like the mosque – is closed unless a special exhibition is being held. Between Ermoú and the castle lies a maze of atmospheric lanes lined with *belle époque* mansions and humbler vernacular dwellings.

The fortress

Just north of port • Tues–Sun 8.30am–3pm; sometimes later in summer • €2 • ☎ 22510 27970

On the promontory sits the Byzantine-Genoese-Ottoman **fortress**, its mixed pedigree reflected in the Ottoman inscription immediately above the Byzantine double eagle at the southern outer gate. Inside you can make out the variably preserved ruins of the Gattilusi palace, a Turkish *medresse* (Koranic academy), a dervish cell and a Byzantine cistern.

Archaeological Museum

8 Noemvríou • Tues–Sun 8.30am–3pm • €4 • ☎ 22510 40223

Mytilíni's excellent **Archaeological Museum** is the town's only real must-see. Much of it is devoted to finds from wealthy Roman Mytilene, in particular the

9

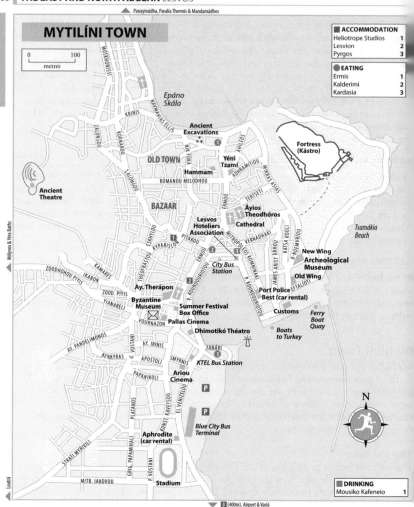

well-displayed **mosaics** – some visible under glass flooring – from second/third-century AD villas. Highlights include a crude but engaging scene of Orpheus charming all manner of beasts and birds, two fishermen surrounded by clearly recognizable (and edible) sea creatures, and the arrival of baby Telephos, son of Auge and Hercules, in a seaborne box, again with amazed fishermen presiding. Earlier eras are represented by Neolithic finds from Áyios Vartholoméos cave and Bronze Age Thermí, but the star exhibits are the minutely detailed late Classical **terracotta figurines**: a pair of acrobats, two *kourotrophoi* figures (goddesses suckling infants, predecessors of all Byzantine *Galaktotrofoússa* icons), children playing with a ball or dogs, and Aphrodite riding a dolphin.

The bazaar area

Inland, the town skyline is dominated in turn by the Germanic-Gothic belfry spire of **Áyios Athanásios cathedral** and the mammary dome of **Áyios Therápon**, both

pressions of the post-Baroque taste of the nineteenth-century Ottoman Greek
bourgeoisie. The interior decor of Áyios Therápon in particular seems more appropriate
to an opera house than a church, with gilt aplenty in the vaulting and ornate column
capitals. They stand more or less at opposite ends of the **bazaar**, whose main
pedestrianized shopping street, Ermoú, links the town centre with the little-used north
harbour of **Epáno Skála**.

Byzantine Museum

Síonos • Mon–Sat 9am–1pm • €2 • ☎ 22510 28916

The well-lit and well-laid-out **Byzantine Museum**, just opposite the entrance to Áyios
Therápon, contains various icons rescued from rural island churches. The most
noteworthy exhibit, and the oldest, is a fourteenth-century icon of Christ *Pandokrátor*;
other highlights include a sultanic *firmáni* or grant of privileges to a local bishop, a rare
sixteenth-century three-dimensional icon of *The Crucifixion* and a canvas of *The
Assumption* by Theophilos (see box, p.640).

ARRIVAL AND DEPARTURE   MYTILÍNI TOWN

By air The town is 7km from the airport; there are regular
buses in the summer, or you can take a taxi (€10).

By ferry Most agencies can make bookings for ferries
within Greece, while Picolo Travel at Koundouriótou
3a (☎ 22510 27000, ⓦ picolotravel.gr) is best for
tickets to Turkey.

By bus There are two bus terminals: long-distance KTEL
buses leave from a small station near Platía
Constandinopóleos at the southern end of the harbour,
while the blue town buses depart from a stand at the top of
the harbour, or the dedicated terminal near the stadium.

By car Car rental can be arranged through one of
the franchises dotted around the harbour, such as reputable
Best at Koundouriótou 87–89 (☎ 22510 37337,
ⓦ best-rentacar.com). Drivers should use the enormous
free public car park a few blocks south of the KTEL or the
oval plaza near the new wing of the Archeological Museum.

ACCOMMODATION

The waterfront **hotels** are noisy and mostly overpriced, but supply usually exceeds demand for the better-value rooms in
the backstreets.

★**Heliotrope Studios** Kyparission 8 ☎ 22510 45388,
ⓦ heliotropestudios.gr. Great value in the town centre,
with colourful, stylish apartments featuring kitchenettes,
washing machines and irons, as well as balconies with
charming views. The garden is a lovely place for coffee, or a
glass of wine. **€50**

Lesvion Koundouriótou 27A ☎ 22510 28177,
ⓦ lesvion.gr. This smart mid-quay hotel is the most
reasonably priced of those on the front, with compact but
comfy rooms. Choose between a noisier harbour view or a
room at the back. **€65**

Pyrgos Eleftheríou Venizélou 49 ☎ 22510 25069,
ⓦ www.pyrgoshotel.gr. Premier in-town hotel in a
renovated nineteenth-century town house, with over-
the-top kitsch decor in the common areas. Most rooms
have a balcony, some have bathtubs and there are three
round rooms in the tower itself. **€115**

EATING AND DRINKING

Ermis Ermoú, Epáno Skála ☎ 22510 26232. This is
the most charming of the ouzerís in this district, with a
belle époque decor (panelled ceiling, giant mirrors,
faded oil paintings) inside and courtyard seating, too.
Prices are fair too (€5 for stuffed courgette flowers), and
they've 25 different types of local ouzo – though the
service can be a little off. Daily noon–2am.

Kalderimi Thássou 2 ☎ 22510 46577. One of the few
surviving ouzerís in the bazaar area, occupying three
picturesque buildings with seating under the shade of
vines; the food is abundant if a bit plainly presented. Mon–
Sat 11am–2am, Sun 11am–4pm.

Kardasia Fanári quay ☎ 22510 41444. Occupying the
prime city-viewing spot on the pedestrianized quay
lane, with various *mayireftá* dishes for €6 or so, plus
good-value fish dishes and wood-fired pizzas. Daily
8am–midnight.

★**Mousiko Kafeneio** Vernardaki 1 ☎ 22510 28827.
Currently, the town's prime hipster spot, its two levels
decorated with plenty of paintings, and moody or jazzy
music played at a volume which encourages
conversation. Good for coffee, tea or juice, and there are
plenty of alcoholic drinks to choose from too. Daily
7.30am–3am.

9

Around Mytilíni

The road heading **north** from Mytilíni towards Mandamádhos follows a rather nondescript coastline, but offers startling views across the straits to Turkey. South of the capital, there are two fine museums at **Variá** and a couple of decent beaches furthe down the peninsula.

Paralía Thermís
12km north of Mytilíni, and linked to the capital by hourly bus (30min)

Although there are no longer any spa facilities around **PARALÍA THERMÍS**, you can see the ruins of a Roman/Byzantine **hammam** just to the south in Pýrgi Thermís; its modern successor sits abandoned near the port. Still, the area has its charms, including a decent (if scrappy) beach, some decent places to sleep and eat, and the cute village of Loutropoli Thermís a twenty-minute walk uphill.

Therma Spa
8km west of Mytilíni, along the main road to Kalloní, and linked to the capital by hourly bus (30min) • Daily 9am–9pm • Indoor bath €3, outdoor bath €5 (plus an extra €5 for the jacuzzi); towels and bathing clothes available to rent • ☎ 22510 41503, ⓦ thermaspalesvos.com

Locals are somewhat divided on the recently renovated **Therma Spa** – some bemoan th fact that it's a little too fancy and non-traditional, while others see it as a successful resuscitation of what was an ailing business. You can take your pick of indoor and outdoor pools – the former are marble-lined affairs in vaulted chambers, with separate facilities for men and women, while the outdoor bath boasts a superlative view out ove the gulf. Massage is available in the plush main hall, where you may be tempted to splash out on an espresso or cocktail before leaving.

Variá
Variá is accessible by hourly bus from Mytilíni (15min)

The most rewarding sights to be visited near Mytilíni are a pair of museums at **VARIÁ**, 5km south of town, which between them hold much of the island's artistic legacy.

Theophilos Museum
Signposted inland from coastal road • Mon–Fri 9am–2pm • €3 • ☎ 22510 41644

The **Theophilos Museum** honours the painter (see box, below), born here in 1873, with four rooms of wonderful, little-known compositions commissioned by his patron Tériade

---

THEOPHILOS HADZIMIHAÏL: THE ROUSSEAU OF GREECE?

The "naive" painter **Theophilos Hadzimihaïl** (1873–1934) was born and died in Mytilíni Town, and both his eccentricities and talents were remarkable from an early age. After wandering across the country from Pílio to Athens and the Peloponnese, Theophilos became one of *belle époque* Greece's prize eccentrics, dressing up as Alexander the Great or various revolutionary war heroes, complete with pom-pommed shoes and pleated skirt. Theophilos was ill and living as a recluse in severely reduced circumstances back on Lésvos when he was introduced to Thériade in 1919; the latter, virtually alone among critics of the time, recognized his peculiar genius and ensured that Theophilos was supported both morally and materially for the rest of his life.

With their childlike perspective, vivid colour scheme and idealized mythical and rural subjects, Theophilos' **works** are unmistakeable. Relatively few of his works survive today, because he executed commissions for a pittance on ephemeral surfaces such as *kafenío* counters, horsecarts, or the walls of long-vanished houses. Facile comparisons are often made between Theophilos and **Henri Rousseau**, the roughly contemporary French "primitive" painter. Unlike "Le Douanier", however, Theophilos followed no other profession, eking out a precarious living from his art alone. And while Rousseau revelled in exoticism, Theophilos' work was principally and profoundly rooted in Greek mythology, history and daily life.

uring the years immediately preceding Theophilos' death. A wealth of detail is evident in elegiac scenes of fishing, reaping, olive-picking and baking from the pastoral Lésvos which Theophilos obviously knew best. The *Sheikh-ul-Islam* with his hubble-bubble (Room 2) seems drawn from life, as does a highly secular Madonna merely titled *Mother with Child* (also Room 2). But in the museum's scenes of classical landscapes and episodes from wars historical and contemporary Theophilos seems on shakier ground.

Tériade Museum

Signposted inland from coastal road • Mon–Fri 9am–2pm • €3 • ☎ 22510 41644

Next door to the Theophilos Museum, the imposing **Tériade Museum** is the legacy of another native son, Stratis Eleftheriades (1897–1983). Leaving the island aged 18 for Paris, he Gallicized his name to Tériade and eventually became a renowned avant-garde art publisher, enlisting some of the leading artists of the twentieth century in his ventures. The displays comprise two floors of lithographs, engravings, ink drawings, wood-block prints and watercolours by the likes of Picasso, Matisse, Le Corbusier, Miró and others: an astonishing collection for a relatively remote Aegean island.

ACCOMMODATION	AROUND MYTILÍNI
Loriet Variá, 4km south of Mytilíni ☎ 22510 43111, ⓦ loriet-hotel.com. A nineteenth-century mansion with modern wings, gardens, fine restaurant and saltwater pool. Rooms vary from blandly modern, marble-trimmed studios to massive suites with retro decor and big bathrooms. **€100**	★**Votsala** Paralía Thermís ☎ 22510 71231, ⓦ votsalahotel.com. This comfortable and relaxing place offers watersports off the beach and well-tended gardens. It prides itself on having no TV in the rooms, and no "Greek nights" or disco. April–Oct. **€56**

Southern Lésvos

Southern Lésvos is indented by two great inlets, the gulfs of **Kallóni** and **Yéra**, the first curving in a northeasterly direction, the latter northwesterly, creating a fan-shaped peninsula at the heart of which looms 967m **Mount Ólymbos**. Both shallow gulfs are landlocked by very narrow outlets to the open sea, which don't – and probably never will – have bridges spanning them. This is the most verdant and productive olive-oil territory on Lésvos, and stacks of pressing-mills stab the skyline.

Pérama

A regular kaïki service (no cars) links Pérama with Koundoroudhiá, which has a blue city bus service to/from Mytilíni

PÉRAMA, disused olive-oil warehouses dotting its oddly attractive townscape, is one of the larger places on the Gulf of Yéra. Although it feels rather forlorn and end-of-the-road, it is easily accessible by public transport from Mytilíni and offers great eating.

Plomári and around

Due south of Mount Ólymbos, at the edge of the "fan", **PLOMÁRI** is the only sizeable coastal settlement hereabouts, and indeed the second-largest municipality on Lésvos. It presents an unlikely juxtaposition of scenic appeal and its famous ouzo industry, courtesy of several local **distilleries**. Despite a resounding lack of good beaches within walking distance, Plomári is popular with Scandinavian tourists; most actually stay at **Áyios Isídhoros**, 3km east, which some deem the best beach on the entire island; there are also two smaller coves between this and the town.

Varvayianni Distillery

1km east of centre • May–Oct Mon–Fri 9am–7pm, Sat 9am–1pm; Nov–April Mon–Fri 8am–4pm • Free • ☎ 22520 32741, ⓦ barbayanni-ouzo.com

The largest and oldest of Plomári's distilleries, **Varvayianni**, offers free tours and tasting, plus a fascinating display of old alembics, presses, storage jars and

9

ROCK-CLIMBING AROUND PLOMÁRI

In 2015, the island's first official **rock-climbing routes** were inaugurated at **Panaíya Kryftí**, just west of Melinda. There are now no fewer than 26 routes on this spectacular, sea-facing limestone cliff; featuring a mix of horiztonal ledges, holes and small cracks, they range in difficulty from 3–7a. Climbs can be made year-round, though in July and August it's best to avoid the middle of the day. For gear rental and climbing advice, contact Plomari Forum (📧 info@plomariforum.gr).

archival material. Best venues for a tipple afterwards are the old *kafenía* on central Platía Beniamín.

Melínda

Melínda, a 700m sand-and-shingle beach at the mouth of a canyon lush with olive trees, lies 6km west of Plomári by paved road. It's an alluring place, with sweeping views west towards the Vaterá coast and the cape of Áyios Fokás, and south (in clear conditions) to northern Híos, Psará and the Turkish Karaburun peninsula.

Panayía Kryftí hot springs

One of the best excursions beyond Melínda is to the **Panayía Kryftí hot springs**. From the first curve of the paved road up to Paleohóri, a dirt track goes 2.8km to a dead end with parking space, with the final 400m on a downhill path to the little chapel just above a protected inlet. On the far side of this you'll see a rectangular cement tank, just big enough for two people, containing water at a pleasant 37–38°C (free access).

Ayiássos and around

AYIÁSSOS, 26km from Mytilíni, nestled in a remote, wooded valley under the crest of Mount Ólympos, is the most beautiful hill town on Lésvos, its narrow cobbled streets lined by ranks of tiled-roof houses, built in part from proceeds of the trade in *tsoupiá* (olive sacks). On the usual, northerly approach, there's no hint of the enormous village until you see huge knots of parked cars at the southern edge of town. Most visitors proceed past endless ranks of kitsch wooden and ceramic souvenirs or carved "Byzantine" furniture, aimed mostly at Greeks, and the central church of the **Panayía Vrefokratoússa** – built in the twelfth century to house an icon supposedly painted by the Evangelist Luke – to the old bazaar. With such a venerable icon as a focus, the local August 15 *paniyíri* is one of the liveliest on Lésvos.

Mount Ólympos

From the southern side of Ayiássos, keen walkers can follow a network of marked paths and tracks for three hours to the **Ólymbos summit**. Approaching from Plomári, there's asphalt road and public transport only up to Megalohóri, with a good dirt surface thereafter up to some air-force radar balls, where paving resumes. Dense woods of oak and chestnut take over from the recovering pine growth beyond the first main ridge.

Mylélia watermill

6km northeast of Ayiássos, signposted along a track near the turning for Ípio • Daily 9am–6pm

Mylélia means "place of the mills", and there were once several hereabouts – the **Mylélia watermill** is the last survivor, restored to working order in the 1990s. The keeper will show you the millrace and paddle-wheel, as well as the flour making its spasmodic exit, after which you can browse the gourmet pastas and other products at the shop, including cheeses, jams, vinegar and salted fish. They also do cooking courses.

Polikhnítos and around

The largest settlement in the southwestern part of southern Lésvos is **POLIKHNÍTOS**, a rather dull, workaday rural centre. It is, however, the point of access to magnificent **Vaterá** beach, the seaside villages of **Skála Polikhnítou** and **Nifídha**, each with its own smaller beach, and the Natural History Museum of **Vrýssa**.

Natural History Museum, Vrýssa

Centre of village • May & June daily 9.30am–3.30pm; July–Sept daily 9.30am–3pm & 4–8pm; Oct–April Wed–Sun 9.30am–3.30pm • €2 • ☎ 22520 61890

Vrýssa, 4km south of Polikhnítos, has a mildly diverting **Natural History Museum** documenting local paleontological finds. In 1997 Athenian paleontologist Michael Dermitzakis confirmed what farmers unearthing bones had long suspected when he pronounced the area a treasure-trove of **fossils**, including those of two-million-year-old gigantic horses, mastodons, monkeys and tortoises the size of a Volkswagen Beetle. Until twenty thousand years ago, Lésvos (like all other east Aegean islands) was joined to the Asian mainland, and the gulf of Vaterá was a subtropical freshwater lake; the animals in question came to drink, died nearby and were trapped and preserved by successive volcanic flows.

Vaterá and around

Vaterá, 9km south of Polikhnítos, is a 7km-long sand **beach**, backed by vegetated hills; the sea here is delightfully calm and clean, the strand itself perhaps the best on Lésvos. Development, mostly seasonal villas and apartments for locals, straggles for several kilometres to either side of the central T-junction but is quite spread out, so the strip does not feel overtly commercialized.

Some 3km west at the cape of **Áyios Fokás** only the foundations remain of a temple of Dionysos and a superimposed early Christian basilica. The little tamarisk-shaded anchorage here has a superb taverna.

ACCOMMODATION AND EATING   SOUTHERN LÉSVOS

PÉRAMA

★ **Balouhanas** ☎ 22510 51948. The northernmost establishment on the front, with a wooden, cane-roofed deck jutting out over the water. Seafood is a strong point, whether grilled or as €6 croquettes, as are regional mezédhes and home-made desserts. Daily 11am–1am.

PLOMÁRI AND AROUND

Maria's Sea end of access road, Melínda ☎ 22520 93239. The restaurant here is excellent, serving a range of fish, meat and mezédhes, all under €10 – occasional music in the evenings, and lovely views around the clock. May–Oct daily 9am–midnight.

Sandy Bay Áyios Isídhoros ☎ 22520 32825, ⓦ sandybay.gr. Focused around the pool with a view, this hotel has a slightly retro feel to its communal areas – though this is no bad thing. The rooms themselves have been decorated with care, but are perhaps a bit small for

the price. Breakfast included. May–Oct. **€60**

★ **Taverna tou Panai** 800m north of Áyios Isídhoros ☎ 22520 31920. Set in an olive grove, this rustic taverna serves fine meat, seafood and *mayireftá* dishes for €6–8 to a mostly Greek clientele. Most produce is home-grown and organic. Daily 10am–late.

AYIÁSSOS

Ouzerí To Stavri Stavrí district ☎ 22520 22936. This quirky little place on the upper north side of town offers a warm welcome and great home-style mezédhes such as cheese croquettes and octopus in vinegar for €4–6. Daily 11am–late.

POLIKHNÍTOS AND AROUND

★ **Akrotiri** Áyios Fokás ☎ 22520 61465. Top-notch little taverna, specializing in seafood delights such as shrimp salad, fish soup or *sardhélles Kallonís*, plus starters

---

POLIKHNÍTOS SPA

If you're after a hot bath, head for the vaulted, well-restored **Polikhnítos Spa** complex (Mon–Sat 2–8pm, Sun 10am–8pm; €4; ☎ 22520 41229, ⓦ hotsprings.gr) 1.5km east of the town of **Polikhnítos**; there are separate, warm-hued chambers for each sex. The water actually gushes out at temperatures up to 87°C, so needs to be tempered with cold.

9

such as cheese croquettes. All cost well under €10 and can be washed down with aromatic wine. April–Oct daily noon–1am.

★**Aphrodite Beach** Towards eastern end, Vaterá ☎ 22520 61288, ⓦ aphroditehotel.gr. Sparkling blue-and-white complex of comfortable units with a/c, fridges and small balconies (buffet breakfast included); there's often a two-night minimum stay in summer. The extremely welcoming family restaurant features tasty dishes such as lamb, *briám*, very palatable wine and occasional live music sessions. May to early Oct 9am–1am. **€60**

Kalamakia Towards eastern end, Vaterá ☎ 22522 61270. Principally a taverna specializing in superb hom cooking such as fish in tomato sauce and stuffed chicke patties, there are also some smart rooms and apartmen at the back. Daily 9am–late. **€30**

O Grigoris Nifídha ☎ 22520 41838. Good seafroi *psarotavérna* with the usual range of fish from €35/ki and seafood, backed up by some salads and veg dishe March–June & mid-Sept to Nov Fri–Sun noon–1ar July to mid-Sept daily noon–1am.

Western Lésvos

The area from the Gulf of Kalloní to the island's west coast is a mostly treeless, craggy region whose fertile valleys offer a sharp contrast to the bare ridges. River mouths form little oases behind a handful of **beach resorts** like Skála Kallonís, Sígri and Skála Eressoú. A few **monasteries** along the road west of Kalloní, plus the occasional striking **inland village**, provide monumental interest.

Ayía Paraskeví and around

A rewarding detour en route to Kalloní is to **AYÍA PARASKEVÍ** village, midway between two important and photogenic monuments from diverse eras: the paleo-Christian, three-aisled basilica of **Halinádhou**, its dozen basalt columns amid pine-and-olive scenery, and the large medieval bridge of **Kremastí**, the largest and best preserved such in the east Aegean, 3km west of Ayía Paraskeví.

Museum of Industrial Olive Oil Production

Southern outskirts of Ayía Paraskeví • Daily except Tues: March to mid-Oct 10am–6pm; mid-Oct to Feb 10am–5pm • €3 • ☎ 22530 32300, ⓦ piop.gr

The eminently worthwhile **Museum of Industrial Olive Oil Production** is housed in a restored communal olive mill. The mill, built by public subscription in the 1920s, only ceased working under the junta; the industrial machinery has been lovingly refurbished and its function explained, while former outbuildings and warehouses are used as venues for secondary exhibits and short explanatory films.

Kalloní and around

KALLONÍ is a lively agricultural and market town in the middle of the island. Some 3km south lies the town's seaside package resort, **Skála Kallonís**, backing a long, sandy but absurdly shallow beach on the lake-like gulf whose water can be turbid. It's mainly distinguished as a **bird-watching** centre during the nesting season (March–May) in the adjacent salt marshes. The local speciality is the gulf's celebrated, plankton-nurtured **sardines**, best eaten fresh-grilled from August to October, though they're available salt-cured all year round.

THE OLIVES OF LÉSVOS

No other Greek island is as dominated by **olive production** as Lésvos, which is blanketed by approximately eleven million olive trees. Most of these vast groves date from after a lethal frost in 1851, though a few hardy survivors are thought to be over five hundred years old. During the first three centuries after the Ottoman conquest, production of olive oil was a monopoly of the ruling pasha, but following eighteenth-century reforms in the Ottoman Empire, extensive tracts of Lésvos (and thus the lucrative oil trade) passed into the hands of the new Greek bourgeoisie, who greatly expanded the industry.

egeon Skála Kallonís ☎22530 22398, ⓦaegeon esvos.gr. Set in a leafy garden, with above-average rnishings for its class, a large pool and friendly owners, ais is the best option among the hotels scattered across ,e western side of the beach strip. **€45**

Dionysos Skála Kallonís ☎22530 28003. The most reliable place to eat on the waterfront, with a good mix of affordable dishes, including local sardines (€6) and Cretan-style *dakos* with feta, tomato and capers (€4.50), as well as a nice location between the beach and harbour areas. April–Oct daily 10am–1am.

.imónos monastery

km west of Kalloní • Museum daily 9.30am–6.30pm, may close at 3pm off season • €2

West of Kalloní, the road winds uphill to **Limónos monastery**, founded in 1527 by the monk Ignatios, whose cell is maintained in the surviving medieval north wing. It's a ambling, three-storey complex around a vast, plant-filled courtyard, home to just a handful of monks and lay workers. The *katholikón*, with its ornate carved-wood ceiling and archways, is traditionally off limits to women; a sacred spring flows from below the south foundation wall. Only the ground-floor **ecclesiastical museum** is currently functioning, with the more interesting ethnographic gallery upstairs still closed.

Hídhira

Seven kilometres south of the beautiful settlement of **Vatoússa**, which boasts a classic plane-shaded square and some fine architecture, stands the hilltop village of **HÍDHIRA**, with a fine winery and interesting museum. The village is a dead end unless you have a jeep capable of continuing across the rough track to Eressós by way of Ágra.

Methymneos Winery

Just below the entrance to Hídhira • Aug–Sept Tues–Sun 10am–2pm, otherwise by appointment • ☎6972 085 371, ⓦmethymneos.gr

The **Methymneos Winery** has successfully revived the local ancient grape variety, decimated by phylloxera some decades ago. Because of the altitude (300m) and sulphur-rich soil (the vineyards lie in a volcanic caldera), their velvety, high-alcohol, oak-aged red can be produced organically, and in 2007 they began to produce bottled white wines, too. They run a highly worthwhile (and free) twenty-minute, English-language **tour** of the state-of-the-art premises.

Monastery of Perivolís

8km west of Vatoússa • Daily 10am–1pm & 5–6pm • Donation expected • No photos

From the main road, a short track leads down to the thirteenth-century monastery of **Perivolís**, built amid a riverside orchard (*perivóli*), which has fine if damp-damaged sixteenth-century frescoes in the narthex. An apocalyptic panel worthy of Bosch (*The Earth and Sea Yield up their Dead*) shows the Whore of Babylon riding her chimera and assorted sea monsters disgorging their victims; just to the right, towards the main door, the Three Magi are depicted approaching the Virgin enthroned with the Christ Child. On the north side there's a highly unusual iconography of Abraham, the Virgin, and the penitent thief of Calvary in paradise, with the four heavenly rivers gushing forth under their feet; just right are assembled the Hebrew kings of the Old Testament.

Ándissa and around

ÁNDISSA, 11km west of Vatoússa, nestles under this parched region's only substantial pine grove; at the edge of the village a sign implores you to "Come Visit Our Square", not a bad idea for the sake of a handful of refreshment options sheltering under three sizeable plane trees.

Gavathás and around

Directly below Ándissa a paved road leads 6km north to **GAVATHÁS**, a village with a shortish, partly protected **beach** and a few places to eat and stay. A side road leads

9

one headland east to huge, dune-dominated, surf-battered **Kámbos** beach, which you may well have to yourself, even in August.

ACCOMMODATION AND EATING

Paradise Gavathás ☎ 22530 56376. This pension-cum-restaurant, 300m back from the seafront, has simple but adequate rooms and serves good fish and locally grown vegetables. May–Sept. **€30**

★**Pedhinon** Ándissa ☎ 22530 56106. The village's

ÁNDISSA AND AROUND

oldest and best taverna, shaded by the largest plan tree, is very friendly and rustles up excellent *mayireftá* such as lamb fricassee and okra. You may even ru into local octogenarian poet Panayiótis Petréllis. Dail 10am–midnight.

Monastery of Ypsiloú

3km west of Ándissa • Museum daily 8.30am–3pm • Donation expected

Two kilometres west of Ándissa there's an important junction. Keeping straight leads you past the still-functioning, double-gated monastery of **Ypsiloú**, founded in 1101 atop an outrider of extinct Órdhymnos volcano. The *katholikón*, tucked in one corner of a large, irregular courtyard, has a fine wood-lattice ceiling but has had its frescoes repainted to detrimental effect. Exhibits in the upstairs **museum** encompass a fine collection of *epitáfios* (Good Friday) shrouds, ancient manuscripts, portable icons and – oddest of all – a *Deposition* painted in Renaissance style by a sixteenth-century Turk.

The petrified forest

5km south of the main Ándissa–Sígrí road • Mon–Thurs & Sat 9am–5pm, Fri 9am–9pm, Sun 10am–5pm • €2

To the west of Ypsiloú begins the 5km side road to the main concentration of Lésvos' overrated **petrified forest**, a fenced-in "reserve" toured along 3km of walkways. For once, contemporary Greek arsonists cannot be blamed for the state of the trees, created by the combined action of volcanic ash from Órdhymnos and hot springs some fifteen to twenty million years ago. The mostly horizontal sequoia trunks average 1m or less in length, save for a few poster-worthy exceptions; there's another more accessible (and free) cluster south of Sígri.

Sígri

SÍGRI, near the western tip of Lésvos, has an appropriately end-of-the-line feel; its bay is guarded both by an Ottoman castle and the long island of **Nissiopí**, which protects the place somewhat from prevailing winds. The eighteenth-century **castle**, built atop an earlier one, sports the reigning sultan's monogram over the entrance, something rarely seen outside İstanbul, evidence of the high regard in which this strategic port with a good water supply was held. The odd-looking church of **Ayía Triádha** is in fact a converted **mosque**, with a huge water cistern taking up the ground floor; this supplied, among other things, the half-ruined **hammam** just south.

Natural History Museum of the Lésvos Petrified Forest

Centre of village • Mon–Thurs & Sat 9am–5pm, Fri 9am–9pm, Sun 10am–5pm • €5 • ☎ 22530 54434, ⓦ www.lesvosmuseum.gr

At the top of town stands the well-executed but overpriced **Natural History Museum of the Lésvos Petrified Forest**, which covers pan-Aegean geology with samples and maps (including, ominously, seismic patterns), as well as the expected quota of petrified logs and plant fossils from when the surrounding hills were far more vegetated.

The beaches

The nearest of several **beaches**, south of the castle headland, is somewhat narrow but is the only one with amenities. The far superior strand of **Faneroméni** lies 3.5km north by a coastal dirt track from the northern outskirts of town. A shorter but equally good beach, **Liména**, can be found 2km south of Sígri at another creek mouth, just off the rough, one-lane, 15km track to Eressós, passable with care in an ordinary car, in 35 minutes.

FROM TOP DRYING SQUID, MÓLYVOS, LÉSVOS (P.649); ARCHAEOLOGICAL SITE, ALYKI (P.667) >

9

ACCOMMODATION AND EATING

Cavo d'Oro ☎22530 54221. The only taverna on the harbour itself (maybe one reason why there's no sign) is a classic for lobster and fish (from €40/kilo), far better than the restaurants around the nearby platía. Daily 11am–2am.

Towerhouse 500m east of the village ☎22530 2290 ⓦtowerhouse.gr. Four spacious antique-furnishe apartments in a *belle époque* folly, set on a landscape hillside setting, with a pool. May–Oct. **€65**

Skála Eressoú

Most visitors to western Lésvos stay at **SKÁLA ERESSOÚ**, reached via a southerly turning between Ándissa and Ypsiloú. Its 3km dark-coloured **beach** almost rivals Vatera's as the best on the island. Behind stretches the largest and most attractive agricultural plain on Lésvos, a welcome green contrast to the volcanic ridges above.

There's not much to central Skála – just a roughly rectangular grid of perhaps five streets by twelve, angling up to the oldest cottages on the slope of Vígla hill above the east end of the beach. The waterfront pedestrian lane is divided midway by a café-lined circular platía with a bust of **Theophrastos**. This renowned botanist hailed from **ancient Eressós** atop Vígla hill – what little remains of the citadel wall is still visible from a distance, and the views reward a scramble up. An even more famous native of ancient Eressós, honoured by a stylized statue on the platía, was **Sappho** (c.615–562 BC), poet and reputed lesbian. There are always conspicuous numbers of gay women about, particularly in the women-only clothing-optional zone of the **beach** west of the river mouth, also home to a small community of terrapins.

ACCOMMODATION

Galini Three blocks inland ☎22530 53138, ⓦhotel-galinos.gr. This welcoming, slightly old-fashioned hotel with a colourful yard outside has cosy, spotlessly clean rooms with little balconies. Breakfast included. **€40**

Kyma Southern tip of town ☎22530 53555,

ⓦfacebook.com/eresoskyma. Right on the edge of town, this is a prime pick at this price level, with presentable rooms – some with balconies right over the water – and a laid-back air quite appropriate to the area. **€60**

EATING, DRINKING AND NIGHTLIFE

With about seven clubs/bars to choose from in peak season, local **nightlife** is the best on the island, and all establishments are gay-friendly. There's also a central, open-air **cinema** (July to early Sept), predictably named after the ancient poet, several blocks inland.

Parasol Eastern seafront ☎22530 52020. Ethnic sounds abound and exotic cocktails flow at one of the resort's most enduring café-cum-bars, with an attractive central seafront location beneath a thatched bamboo roof. May to early Oct daily 10am–1am.

Soulatso Central seafront ☎22530 51105. This psarotaverna is by far the best place for fish on this stretch. Though most seem to go for the sardines (€8), there's plenty more besides, including salted mackerel, meat and veg dishes, all at fair prices. May–Oct daily noon–midnight.

SAPPHIC AND MYSTIC SKÁLA

Through its obvious associations with **Sappho** (see above), Skála Eressoú has for decades been a magnet for lesbians from all over the globe. Various events take place here, most notably the **International Eressos Women's Festival** in September (ⓦwomensfestival.eu). Every day except Sunday from June to late September, barring bad weather conditions, the **Skala Women's Rock Group** hold a swim from beside the *Zorba The Buddha* café (see opposite) to the islet in the middle of the bay and back. This social and non-competitive event is open to women of any sexual orientation.

As evidenced by the name of the café, there is also a perceptible Eastern mystical influence in the village, largely due to the presence of the Osho Afroz Meditation Center (ⓦoshoafroz.com) 3km inland. Consequently, as well as the centre's programmes, there are various yoga, meditation and healing sessions available in Skála. Together, the female and spiritual energies create a unique resort.

Zorba The Buddha Eastern seafront ☎ 22530 3777. Colourful and convivial café-cum-restaurant, with an eastern vibe and a spacious wooden deck where you can enjoy quality teas, juices, ice creams and daily specials like lamb wrapped in vine leaves for €6–8. May–Sept daily 9am–2am.

Northern Lésvos

The northern part of Lésvos is largely fertile and green countryside stippled with poplars and blanketed by olive groves. Occupying the prime position on a promontory in the middle of the coast is one of the northeast Aegean's most attractive resorts, **Mólyvos**, whose castle's cockscomb silhouette is visible for many kilometres around. On either side of it, a number of **coastal resorts** offer superior bathing.

Mólyvos

MÓLYVOS (officially named Míthymna after its ancient predecessor), 61km from Mytilíni, is the island's most beautiful village, with tiers of sturdy, red-tiled houses, some standing with their rear walls defensively towards the sea, mounting the slopes between the picturesque harbour and the Byzantine-Genoese **castle**. A score of weathered Turkish fountains, a mosque and hammam grace flower-fragrant, cobbled alleyways, reflecting the fact that before 1923 Muslims constituted more than a third of the local population and owned many of the finest dwellings.

Modern dwellings and hotels have been banned from the old core, but this hasn't prevented a steady drain of all authentic life from the upper **bazaar**; perhaps four or five "ordinary" shops ply their trade among souvenir shops vastly surplus to requirements. The shingly **town beach** is mediocre, improving considerably as you head towards the sandy southern end of the bay, called **Psiriára**.

The castle

Daily 8.30am–3pm • €2

The imposing ramparts of the **Byzantine castle** of Mólyvos, later repaired by Genoan Francesco Gattelusi, are visible from many kilometres around. Sections can now be accessed from the inside, affording splendid views of the harbour and beyond. Entrance is via the impressive main gate, through which a set of steps leads up to the largely open interior, where a wooden **amphitheatre** is used for occasional summer performances.

ARRIVAL AND GETTING AROUND

MÓLYVOS

By bus or taxi The bus stop and taxi rank are at the southeastern edge of town; it's around €7 to either Pétra or Loutrá Eftaloú. In addition, hop-on, hop-off buses run between Mólyvos and Ánaxos, stopping at various points in between (6 daily in summer; €5).

By car or motorbike There are numerous motorbike and car rental places to the south of the centre, including Kosmos (☎ 22530 71710) and Best (☎ 22530 72145), both offering the option of pick-up here and drop-off in Mytilíni or at the airport. The main car park is at the southeast edge of town; there are further car parks above the port and up by the castle.

ACCOMMODATION

★**Olive Press** Southern edge of town ☎ 22530 71205, ⓦ olivepress-hotel.com. Now this is a relaxing spot, whether it's gazing at the sea from the part-covered communal areas, lounging in the pool, or kicking back in the elegantly designed rooms. Highly recommended. Breakfast included. **€70**

The Schoolmistress With The Golden Eyes In the old centre ☎ 22530 71435, ⓦ mythical-mithymna.com. Worth mentioning for the name alone (it was the title of a Greek novel), this is an appealing option in the upper reaches of town, with a sea of roof tiles – and then the actual sea – visible from balconies. The rooms themselves are almost disappointingly plain, but they're comfy enough. April–Oct. **€40**

Sun Rise 2km east of town ☎ 22530 71713, ⓦ sunrisehotel-lesvos.com. High-class hotel that sprawls in startling white tiers over a hillside. The rooms (of which there are more than a hundred) come in varying sizes, but all are well appointed; on site you'll find two pools, tennis courts, a gym, a sauna and a classy restaurant. Breakfast included. April–Oct. **€75**

9

EATING, DRINKING AND NIGHTLIFE

Apart from a selection of lively bars, there's also an outdoor **cinema** (June–Sept) next to the taxi rank.

Betty's On the road down to the harbour ☎ 22530 71421. Friendly to a fault and with views to die for from the outdoor seats (come around sunset), this is where to head for hearty Greek dishes. You may end up ignoring the menu and seeing what's on offer in the kitchen; dinner specials are usually around €8. May–Oct daily 9am–3pm & 6pm–midnight.

The Captain's Table On the harbour ☎ 22530 71241. Having reinvented itself as more of an ouzerí after complete destruction in a 2014 fire, this enduring spot still produces excellent mezédhes and main courses, mostly under €10. May–Oct daily noon–2am.

★**Conga's Beach Bar** On the main town beach ☎ 22530 72181. There's an almost Caribbean vibe to this chill-out spot, which boasts an impressively wide menu including hangover breakfasts (fried eggs and bacon, plu one cigarette and an asprin; €4.50), mojito-marinate souvláki, burgers, pasta, crepes and waffles. Drinks are little on the pricey side, but they've a wide selection including some house cocktails (from €7). May–Sep dail 10am–3am.

Oxy 2km west of town ☎ 6946 506 178. Massive clu with a swimming pool, state-of-the-art light show an sound system, pumping out the latest techno and danc hits. May–Oct Thurs–Sat 10pm–7am.

Seahorse On the harbour ☎ 22530 71320. This hote restaurant is below average, but worth a visit just for it scrumptious desserts – chocolate soufflé, baklava, walnut cake, apple pie and the like, all around €3.50. May–Oct daily 8am–10pm.

Around Mólyvos

West of Mólyvos there's a string of decent beaches with varying degrees of commercialization, most rampant at **Pétra**. To the east, coastal development is more measured, with some appealing beaches and yet another spa. Inland and southeast, the main paved road via Vafiós curves around 968m, poplar-tufted **Mount Lepétymnos**. You can complete a scenic loop of the mountain via Kápi and Ypsilométopo on its southern flank.

Pétra

Given the limited space in Mólyvos, many package companies operate mostly in **PÉTRA**, 5km due south. The modern outskirts sprawl untidily behind its broad, sandy beach, but two attractive nuclei of old stone houses, some with Levantine-style balconies overhanging the street, extend back from the part-pedestrianized seafront square. Pétra takes its name from the giant, unmissable rock monolith inland, enhanced by the eighteenth-century church of the **Panayía Glykofiloússa**, reached via 114 rock-hewn steps. Other local attractions include the sixteenth-century church of **Áyios Nikólaos**, with three phases of well-preserved frescoes up to 1721, and the intricately decorated **Vareltzídhena mansion** (Tues–Sun 8am–3pm; free).

Ánaxos

ÁNAXOS, 3km south of Pétra, is a higgledy-piggledy package resort fringing by far the cleanest **beach** and seawater in the area: 1km of sand well sown with sunbeds and a handful of tavernas. From anywhere along here you enjoy beautiful sunsets between and beyond three offshore islets.

Loutrá Eftaloú

5km east of Mólyvos • Daily: May–Oct 10am–6pm • €4, plus €1 for towel rental

The **Loutrá Eftaloú** thermal baths are east of Mólyvos, just beyond the end of the paved road. Patronize the hot pool under the Ottoman-era domed structure, rather than the sterile modern tub-rooms. The spa is well looked after, with the water mixed up to a toasty 43°C, so you'll need to cool down regularly; outside stretches the long, good pebble beach of **Áyii Anáryiri**, broken up by little headlands, with the two remotest coves nudist.

Sykaminiá

The exquisite hill village of **SYKAMINIÁ**, just under 10km from Mólyvos, is the birthplace in 1892 of novelist **Stratis Myrivilis**. One of the imposing basalt-built houses below the platía, from which there are views north to Turkey, is marked as his childhood home.

Skála Sykaminiás

A marked trail short cuts the twisting road from just east of Sykaminiá down to **SKÁLA SYKAMINIÁS**, easily the most picturesque fishing port on Lésvos. Myrivilis used it as the setting for his best-known work, *The Mermaid Madonna*, and the tiny rock-top **chapel** at the end of the jetty will be instantly recognizable to anyone who has read the book. The only local **beach** is the one of Kayiá 1.5km east, which has a pebble-on-sand base.

Klió and Tsónia

Some 5km east from upper Sykaminiá is **KLIÓ**, whose single main street leads down to a platía with a plane tree, fountain and more views across to Turkey. The village is set attractively on a slope, down which a wide, paved road descends 6km to **Tsónia** beach, 600m of beautiful pink volcanic sand.

ACCOMMODATION AND EATING — AROUND MÓLYVOS

PÉTRA

Michaelia Southern seafront ☎ 22530 41731. Good-value hotel with smart if slightly cramped rooms, most with balconies facing the sunset. Decent buffet breakfast included. May–Sept. **€45**

Mermaid Far north end of the seafront ☎ 22530 41275. This all-round taverna (whose Greek name, Gorgona, is far more prominent on the signs) provides heaps of inexpensive small and more upscale fish (from €40/kilo), as well as some meat dishes and a variety of starters. April to mid-Oct daily 9am–1am.

ÁNAXOS

Klimataria Northern end of beach ☎ 22530 41864. Tucked under a cliff, this is the best place to eat and sleep in the area, with healthy portions of fresh fish, meat and salads (most items under €10) served in a large, shady courtyard. The twin rooms are adequate, if a little plain. Mid-May to Sept daily 11am–midnight. **€40**

LOUTRÁ EFTALOÚ

Ly Eftalou Behind beach ☎ 22530 71049. The nearest location to the spa to grab a snack or fuller meal, with a shady courtyard, where large meat grills, fish and *mayireftá* cost €10 or under. April–Oct daily 9am–midnight.

SKÁLA SYKAMINIÁS

Anemoessa By the harbour chapel ☎ 22530 55360. This place has the local edge quality-wise, with imaginative starters like stuffed squash blossoms complementing fresh fish, much of which costs €10–14. April–Oct daily noon–1am, plus some winter weekends.

★**Gorgona** Near the harbour ☎ 22530 55301, ⓦ gorgonahotel.gr. Small hotel run by a friendly old couple, whose simple but clean rooms have wraparound balconies. There's a shaded terrace for breakfast (included) and meals are available too. May–Sept. **€35**

Ly Mouria tou Myrivili On the harbour ☎ 22530 55319. Picturesque taverna named after the mulberry tree in which Myrivilis used to sleep on hot summer nights. You can tuck into a standard range of *mezédhes*, salads, meat and seafood dishes, such as octopus in wine sauce for €9. May–Oct daily 11am–1am.

KLIÓ AND TSÓNIA

Ly Apolafsi Near access road, Tsónia ☎ 22530 93700. Homely family taverna, which provides a good range of starters, grills and some *mayireftá* like *exohikó* for €6–8. May–Sept daily 10am–midnight, sometimes later.

Áyios Efstrátios

Áyios Efstrátios (Aï Strátis) is one of the quietest and loneliest islands in the Aegean, with a registered population of under four hundred, only half of whom live here all year round. It was only permanently settled during the sixteenth century, and the land is still largely owned by three monasteries on Mount Áthos. Historically, the only

9

outsiders to visit were those compelled to do so – political prisoners were exiled here both during the 1930s and the civil war years.

Áyios Efstrátios village

ÁYIOS EFSTRÁTIOS village – the island's only habitation – is among the ugliest in Greece. Devastation caused by an earthquake on February 20, 1968, which killed 22 and injured hundreds, was compounded by the reconstruction plan conducted by a junta-linked company, who bulldozed even those structures that could have been repaired. From the hillside, some two-dozen surviving houses of the old village overlook grim rows of prefabs, a sad monument to the corruption of the junta years.

Architecture apart, Áyios Efstrátios still functions as a traditional fishing and farming community, with the prefabs set at the mouth of a wooded stream valley draining to the sandy harbour beach. There are scant tourist amenities.

Around the island

Beyond the village – there are few vehicles and no paved roads – the hilly **landscape**, dotted with a surprising number of oak trees, is deserted apart from rabbits, sheep and the occasional shepherd. **Alonítsi**, on the north coast – ninety minutes' walk from the port following a track due east and over a low ridge – is the island's best **beach**, a 1.5km stretch of sand with rolling breakers and views across to Límnos. South of the harbour lies a series of grey-sand beaches, most with wells and drinkable water, accessible by roundabout tracks. **Áyios Dhimítrios**, an hour-plus distant, and **Lidharió**, ninety minutes away at the end of a wooded valley, are the most popular.

ARRIVAL AND DEPARTURE

ÁYIOS EFSTRÁTIOS

By ferry There are ferry connections with Lávrio (4 weekly; 7hr 30min), Límnos (4 weekly; 1hr 20min) and Kavála

(3 weekly; 6hr 20min). You can also visit from Límnos on one of the overpriced day-trips (2 weekly; €35 return).

ACCOMMODATION AND EATING

There's very little in the way of accommodation on the island, though there are usually a couple of signs for rooms here and there.

Maison Ile ☎ 22540 20141. "Luxury accommodation" is pushing it, but this is the only official place to stay on the island, a large apartment to the south of the town, sleeping

up to four. May–Sept. **€75**

Veranda ☎ 6947 050 153. The best of the island's handful of tavernas, near the port, has super-fresh, if rather pricey fish and seafood, plus a limited range of salads and starters. June–Sept daily noon–midnight.

Límnos

Bucolic **Límnos** is a sizeable agricultural and military island that has become positively trendy of late: there are upscale souvenir shops, old village houses restored by mainlanders as seasonal retreats and music bars during summer at nearly every beach. For all that, the island's remoteness and peculiar ferry schedules protected it until the mid-1990s from most aspects of the holiday trade, and conventional tourism was late in coming because hoteliers lived primarily off the visiting relatives of the numerous soldiers stationed here. Most summer visitors are still Greek, particularly from Thessaloníki, though some Brits and other Europeans now arrive by charter flights.

The island was often the focus of **disputes** between the Greek and Turkish governments, with frequent posturing over invaded airspace, although the detente of recent years has seen such incidences cease. As a result, Límnos' **garrison** of 25,000 soldiers – at the nadir of Greco-Turkish relations during the 1970s and 1980s – is now virtually empty, and used for emergencies only.

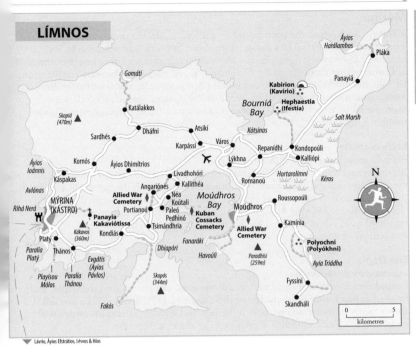

LÍMNOS

Lávrio, Áyios Efstrátios, Lésvos & Híos

The **bays** of **Bourniá** and **Moúdhros**, the latter one of the largest natural harbours in the Aegean, divide Límnos almost in two. The **west** of the island is dramatically hilly, with abundant basalt put to good use as street cobbles and house masonry. The **east** is low-lying and speckled with seasonal salt marshes where it's not occupied by cattle, combine harvesters and vast cornfields. There are numerous sandy **beaches** around the coast – mostly gently shelving – and it's easy to find a stretch to yourself.

Like most volcanic islands, Límnos produces excellent **wine** – good dry white, rosé and retsina – plus ouzo. The Limnians proudly tout an abundance of **natural food products**, including thyme honey and sheep's cheese, and indeed the population is almost self-sufficient in foodstuffs.

ARRIVAL AND DEPARTURE
LÍMNOS

By plane The airport lies 18km east of Mýrina, almost at the geographic centre of the island; there's no shuttle bus into town, so you'll have to take one of the few taxis that always linger outside, and cost at least €25. Frequencies below are for June–Oct.
Destinations Athens (1–2 daily; 50min); Ikaría (6 weekly; 50min); Lésvos (3 weekly; 40min); Thessaloníki (6 weekly; 40min).

By ferry Límnos is on two ferry routes, the one from Lávrio to Kavála and from the northern mainland ports down through the eastern Aegean.
Destinations Áyios Efstrátios (4 weekly; 1hr 20min); Híos (2–3 weekly; 7–8hr); Ikaría (2 weekly; 13hr–15hr 30min); Kavála (5 weekly; 3hr–4hr 30min); Lávrio (5 weekly; 9–13hr); Lésvos (4 weekly; 3hr 50min–6hr 15min); Sámos (2–3 weekly; 11hr).

GETTING AROUND

By bus Buses are fairly infrequent on Límnos, with afternoon departures from Mýrina to many of the more distant villages and 1–2 daily to those nearer the capital.

By car or scooter A vehicle is required for touring; a scooter is quite sufficient for the more touristed western third of the island, although a car is preferable to reach the east of the island.

9

Mýrina

MÝRINA (aka Kástro), the port-capital on the west coast, has the ethos of a provincial market town rather than of a resort. With about five thousand inhabitants, it's pleasantly low-key – if not especially picturesque, apart from a core neighbourhood of old stone houses dating from the Ottoman era, and the ornate Neoclassical mansions backing **Romeïkós Yialós**, the town's beach-lined esplanade. Shops and amenities are mostly found along Kydhá and its continuation Karatzá – which meanders north from the harbour to Romeïkós Yialós – or Garoufalídhi, its perpendicular offshoot, roughly halfway along.

Mýrina castle

Between the town harbour and Romeïkós Yialós • Unrestricted access

Mýrina's main attraction is its Byzantine **castle**, perched on a craggy headland. Ruinous despite later Genoese and Ottoman additions, the fortress is flatteringly lit at night and warrants a climb towards sunset for views over the town, the entire west coast and – in clear conditions – Mount Áthos, 35 nautical miles west. Skittish miniature deer, imported from Rhodes and fed by the municipality, patrol the castle grounds to the amusement of visitors.

The Dápia

In park behind hospital • Unrestricted access

Behind the hospital in a small park is a diminutive, signposted fort, the **Dápia**, built by the Russian Orloff brothers during their abortive 1770 invasion. The fort failed spectacularly in its avowed purpose to besiege and bombard the main castle, as did the entire rebellion, and Ottoman reprisals on the island were severe.

Archeological Museum

Romeïkós Yialós • Tues–Sun 8am–3pm • €2 • ☎ 22540 22900

The **Archaeological Museum** occupies the former Ottoman governor's mansion on the seafront, not far from the site of Bronze Age **Mýrina**. Finds from all of the island's major sites are assiduously labelled in Greek, Italian and English, and the entire place is exemplary in terms of presentation. The star upper-storey exhibits are votive lamps in the shape of sirens, found in an Archaic sanctuary at Hephaestia (Ifestía), much imitated in modern local jewellery. There are also numerous representations of the goddess Cybele/Artemis, who was revered across the island; her shrines were typically situated near a fauna-rich river mouth – on Límnos at Avlónas, now inside the grounds of the *Porto Myrina* resort. An entire room is devoted to metalwork, featuring impressive gold jewellery and bronze objects, both practical (cheese graters, door-knockers) and whimsical-naturalistic (a snail, a vulture).

Town beaches

As town beaches go, **Romeïkós Yialós** and **Néa Mádhitos** (ex-Toúrkikos Yialós), its counterpart to the southeast of the harbour, are not bad. **Rihá Nerá**, the next bay north of Romeïkós Yialós, is even better – shallow as the name suggests ("shallow waters") and well attended by families, with watersports on offer.

ARRIVAL AND INFORMATION

MÝRINA

By bus The bus station is on Platía Eleftheríou Venizélou, at the north end of Kydhá.

By ferry The new jetty is on the far side of the bay – not too far to walk. The most efficient agency for tickets is Sunflight on Platía Eleftheríou Venizélou (☎ 22540 29571).

By car or motorbike Petrides Travel at Karatzá 118 (☎ 22540 29550, ⓦ petridestravel.gr), which also has a branch at the airport, is the best local company for car rental, while Rent a Moto (☎ 22540 25419), on the north side of town at Leofóros Dhimokratías 89, has good rates for two-wheelers.

Tourist information There is no official tourist office, but ⓦ mylemnos.gr is a useful website.

ACCOMMODATION

Apollo Pavilion Frýnis ☎22540 23712, ⊚apollopavilion.gr. In a peaceful cul-de-sac about halfway along Garoufalídhou, this mock classical hotel has three-bed a/c studios with TV and mini-kitchen. Most have balconies, with castle or mountain views. **€60**

Archontiko Cnr of Sakhtoúri and Fariellínon, Romeïkós Yialós ☎22540 29800, ⊚arxontikohotel.gr. Límnos' first hotel, this 1851-built mansion has three floors of small-to-medium-sized wood-trimmed rooms with all mod cons but no balconies. There's an old-fashioned bar/breakfast lounge on the ground floor, filled with antiques. **€80**

Lemnos Limáni Mýrinas ☎22540 22153, ⊚lemnoshotel .com. Standard 1960s-style hotel with average-sized, simply decorated rooms, but the balconies overlooking the fishing harbour and price make it good value. **€35**

EATING, DRINKING AND NIGHTLIFE

Karagiozis Romeïkós Yialós 32 ☎22540 24055. The most established watering hole on the island transforms from laidback café by day to buzzing bar by night, when it sometimes holds theme parties or hosts live bands. Daily 11am–late.

★ **Kosmos** Romeïkós Yialós ☎22540 22050. The most reasonably priced taverna on this popular strip serves up affordable fish dishes (try the huge plate of kalamári, €6.50) and a range of mezédhes accompanied by glorious sunsets across Mt Áthos. April–Oct daily noon–1am.

Nefeli Below the castle ☎22540 23551. Of all the Aegean's café-bars, this arguably has the best view – orange rooftops, craggy hills and a crystalline sea. Good for a frappé after visiting the castle. Daily 9am–midnight.

To Limanaki On the harbour ☎22540 23744. The best and friendliest of the harbourside restaurants, with winning views of the castle and a range of Limnian specialities, including melipasto (a sun-dried goat cheese; €3.50), as well as the regular meats and salads. Daily 9am–midnight.

Western Límnos

Nearly all the tourist amenities are concentrated in the western third of the island, mostly in and around the coastal stretch between Mýrina and the vast Moúdhros Bay. This area includes many of the best **beaches** and most picturesque inland **villages**.

Coast north of Mýrina

Beyond Mýrina's respectable town beaches, the closest good sand lies 3km north at **Avlónas**, unspoilt except for the local power plant a short way inland. Just beyond, the road splits: the right-hand turning wends its way through **Káspakas**, its north-facing houses in neat tiers and a potable spring on its platía, before plunging down to **Áyios Ioánnis**, also reached directly by the left-hand bypass from the capital. The furthest of its three **beaches** is the most pleasant, a curved cove punctuated by a tiny fishing harbour and offshore islet named Vampire Island.

Panayía Kakaviótissa

5km east of Mýrina

A fifteen-minute drive from the capital is the iconic poster image of Límnos: the chapel of **Panayía Kakaviótissa**, tucked into a volcanic cave on the flank of Mt Kákavos (360m). The location is more impressive than the simple collection of icons and brasswork inside.

Sardhés

Some 11km north of the capital, **SARDHÉS** is the highest village on the island, with wonderfully broody sunsets and a celebrated central taverna. The handsome local houses are typical of mountain villages on Límnos in having an external staircase up to the first floor, as the ground floor was used for animals.

Gomáti

Beyond Sardhés and 5km below Katálakkos lies the spectacular, well-signposted **dune** environment at **Gomáti**, one of the largest such in Greece. There are two zones, reached by separate dirt tracks: one at a river mouth, with a bird-rich marsh, and the other to the northwest, with a beach bar and sunbeds. The latter portion especially is a popular outing.

9

Platý

PLATÝ, 2km southeast of Mýrina, has had its traditional profile somewhat compromised by modern villa construction, but it does have two nocturnal tavernas. The long sandy **beach**, 700m below, is popular, with non-motorized **watersports** available at the south end through Babis, below the *Lemnos Village* complex.

Thános and its beaches

Lying just 2km southeast of Platý, **THÁNOS** has more architectural character than its smaller neighbour. Some 1.5km below the town, **Paralía Thánou**, is among the most scenic of southwestern beaches, flanked by volcanic crags and looking out to Áyios Efstrátios island. Beyond Thános, the road curls over to the enormous beach at **Evgátis** (**Áyios Pávlos**), reckoned the island's best, with more igneous pinnacles for definition and Áyios Efstrátios on the horizon.

Kondiás and around

Eleven kilometres east of Mýrina, **KONDIÁS** is the island's third-largest settlement, cradled between hills tufted with Límnos' biggest pine forest. Stone-built, often elaborate houses combine with the setting to make Kondiás an attractive inland village, a fact not lost on the Greeks and foreigners restoring those houses with varying degrees of taste.

Contemporary Balkan Art Gallery

On the main road at the Eastern edge of town • Tues–Sun 9am–2pm & 7–9pm • €2 • ☎ 22540 51425, ⓦ pinakothikikondia.gr

Cultural interest is lent by the imposing **Contemporary Balkan Art Gallery**, which features works by prominent painters from across the Balkans, especially Bulgarian Svetlin Russev. Almost adjacent is the colourful garden studio, where Ukrainian artist Ludmilla Christinitz-Papayiannidhou displays her vibrant works.

ACCOMMODATION AND EATING

WESTERN LÍMNOS

COAST NORTH OF MÝRINA

Aï Yiannis At the end of the first beach, Áyios Ioánnis ☎ 22540 61669. Featuring seating in the shade of piled-up volcanic boulders, this modest *psarotavérna* has fresh fish for under €10/portion. June–Aug daily 10am–midnight.

Aliotida Apartments Behind the third beach, Áyios Ioánnis ☎ 22540 24406, ⓦ www.aliotida-apartments.gr. Bright, well-furnished studios with kitchenettes, tastefully designed amid landscaped grounds. May–Sept. **€35**

SARDHÉS

★**Mantella** Village centre ☎ 22540 61349. The portions here are huge and cost around €7–8 for such rural delights as rabbit *stifádho* and village rooster; the local barrelled wine is superb, too, and the location in the vine-trellised courtyard is atmospheric. Daily noon–1am.

PLATÝ

Grigoris Centre of beach ☎ 22540 22715. With its huge shady courtyard within earshot of the waves, this taverna does good meal deals from €10, and decent meat dishes despite the fact that there are rarely that many people here – try the tasty roast lamb, if they have it. April–Oct 10am–10pm, sometimes later.

Magda Studios 100m back from the beach ☎ 22540 25370, ⓦ magda-studioslimnos.gr. This block of modern studios is well designed, with moderate-sized, comfortable rooms and friendly management; the location, just off the beach, is excellent too. May–Sept. **€35**

★**O Sozos** Just off the main platía ☎ 22540 25085. Local favourite serving up huge portions of succulent *kondosoúvli* and *kokorétsi*, salads and a few *mayireftá* like *dolmádhes*, all well under €10, as well as good *tsípouro* and local barrelled wine. Daily noon–late.

★**Villa Afroditi** 200m back from the beach ☎ 22540 23141, ⓦ afroditi-villa.gr. With splendid topiary, welcoming owners, a pool bar and a mixture of spotless doubles and studios, this is one of the best resorts on Límnos. Free port pick-up and buffet breakfast included. They also run the similar *Ammos Rooms*, 2km south, which is more secluded and far quieter. Mid-May to early Oct. **€65**

THÁNOS AND ITS BEACHES

Beach Bar Pantelis Centre of beach, Paralía Thánou ☎ 22540 22821. By far the most popular beach bar on the island, its deckchairs fill with sun-seekers from early afternoon onwards. It's also a good place for families (before dark, at least), and a cheap sandwich or snack. May to early Sept daily noon–2am.

etradi Studios East end of beach, Paralía nánou ☎ 22540 29905, ⓦ petradistudios.gr. Modern ▪ut tastefully designed two-storey building, warm ochre ▪ colour, with spacious and comfortable rooms. ▪here's a relaxed beach bar on the premises. May–Sept. 30

KONDIÁS AND AROUND

O Hristos Central square, Tsimándhria, 2.5km east of Kondiás ☎ 22540 51278. Old-favourite taverna that dishes up cheap, salubrious grills and a few seafood dishes for €5–8, plus great dips, salads and wine. Daily 9am–1am.

Eastern Límnos

The shores of **Moúdhros Bay**, glimpsed south of the trans-island road, are muddy and best avoided by serious bathers. The bay itself enjoyed strategic importance during World War I, culminating in Allied acceptance of the Ottoman surrender aboard the anchored British warship HMS *Agamemnon* on October 30, 1918. The huge chunk of Límnos east of the bay is little visited but offers some deserted **beaches** and interesting reminders of the island's recent and more distant past.

Moúdhros

MOÚDHROS, the second-largest town on Límnos, is rather a dreary place, with only the wonderfully kitsch, two-belfried **Evangelismós church** to recommend it. The closest decent beaches are at **Havoúli**, 4km south by dirt track, and **Fanaráki**, 4km west, but both have muddy sand and don't really face the open sea. Until recently Moúdhros was quite literally a God-forsaken place, owing to an incident late in Ottoman rule. Certain locals killed some Muslims and threw them down a well on property belonging to the Athonite monastery of Koutloumousioú; the Ottoman authorities, holding the monks responsible, slaughtered any Koutloumousiot brethren they found on the island and set the local monastery alight. Two monks managed to escape to Áthos, where every August 23 until 2000 a curse was chanted, condemning Moúdhros's inhabitants to "never sleep again".

Polyochni (Polyókhni)

10km east of Moúdhros • Tues–Sun 8am–3pm • Free • ☎ 22540 91249

Traces of the most advanced Neolithic Aegean civilization have been unearthed at **Polyochni (Polyókhni)**, on a bluff overlooking a long, narrow beach. Since 1930, Italian excavations have uncovered five layers of settlement, the oldest from late in the fourth millennium BC, predating Troy on the Turkish coast opposite. The town met a sudden, violent end from war or earthquake in about 2100 BC. The **ruins** at the site are well labelled but mostly of specialist interest, though a small, well-presented **museum** behind the entrance helps bring the place to life.

THE WAR CEMETERIES

About 800m along the Roussopoúli road from Moúdhros is an unlocked **Allied military cemetery** maintained by the Commonwealth War Graves Commission, its neat lawns and rows of white headstones incongruous in such parched surroundings. During 1915, Moúdhros Bay was the principal staging area for the disastrous Gallipoli campaign. Of approximately 36,000 Allied dead, 887 are buried here – mainly battle casualties, who died after having been evacuated to the base hospital at Moúdhros. Though the deceased are mostly British, there is also a French cenotaph and – speaking volumes about imperial sociology – a mass "Musalman" grave for Egyptian and Indian troops in one corner, with a Koranic inscription.

There are more graves at another immaculately maintained cemetery behind the hilltop church in **Portianoú**, a little over 1km from the west side of Moúdhros Bay. Among the 348 buried here are two Canadian nurses, three Egyptian labourers and three Maori soldiers. East of Portianoú and Paleó Pedhinó, signposted on a headland, lies the last and strangest of Límnos' military cemeteries: about forty 1920–21 graves of **Kuban Cossacks**, White Army refugees from the Russian civil war.

9

The only really decent beach in the area is **Ayía Triádha**, accessed off the Polyókhni road, with blonde sand heaped in dunes.

Kerós beach

The little village of **Kalliópi**, 8km northeast of Moúdhros via attractive Kondopoúli, has direct access to **Kéros beach**, a 1.5km stretch of sand with dunes and a small pine grove, plus shallow water. It remains popular despite being exposed and often dirty, and attracts plenty of windsurfers (try ⓦsurfclubkeros.com) and foreigners with campervans.

Kótsinas

Some 10km north of Moúdhros, reached via Repanídhi, is the hard-packed beach at **KÓTSINAS**, which is set in the protected western limb of Bourniá Bay. The nearby anchorage offers two busy, seafood-strong tavernas. On a knoll overlooking the jetty stands a corroded, sword-brandishing statue of **Maroula**, a Genoese-era heroine who briefly delayed the Ottoman conquest, and a large church of **Zoödhóhou Piyís** ("the Life-Giving Spring"), where you can see intriguing kitsch icons, a vaulted wooden ceiling and antique floor tiles. Out front, 63 steps lead down through an illuminated tunnel in the rock to the potable (if slightly mineral) spring in question, oozing into a cool, vaulted chamber.

Hephaestia

4.5km from Kondopoúli • Tues–Sun 8am–3pm • Free

Reached via a rough, signposted track from Kondopoúli, the ancient site of **Hephaestia** (present-day Ifestía) offers an admirably reconstructed **theatre** overlooking its former harbour. The name comes from the god Hephaestos, rescued and revered by the ancient Limnians after he crash-landed on the island, hurled from Mt Olympos by Hera.

Kabirion

4km north of main road to Pláka • Tues–Sun 8am–3pm • Free

More evocative than Hephaesia is **Kabirion**, also signposted as "Kabeiroi" (modern Kavírion), on the opposite shore of Tigáni Bay and accessed by a paved road. The **ruins** are of a sanctuary connected with the cult of the Samothracian Kabiroi (see box, p.660), though the site here is probably older. Little survives other than eleven column stumps staking out a *stoa*, behind the *telestirio* or shrine where the cult mysteries took place. A nearby **sea grotto** has been identified as the Homeric Spiliá toú Filoktíti, where Trojan war hero Philoktetes was abandoned by his comrades-in-arms until his stinking, gangrenous leg had healed by application of *límnia yí*, a poultice of volcanic mud still prized on the island. Access to the cave is via steps leading down from the caretaker's shelter, though final access through the narrower of the two entrances involves some wading.

ACCOMMODATION   EASTERN LÍMNOS

Keros Village end of Kéros beach road, Kalliópi ⓣ22540 41059, ⓦsirokowindclub.com. One of the few cheap accommodation options in the far east of Límnos, this remote place has a small garden restaurant, and tidy rooms with balconies. June to mid-Sept. **€35**

Keros Blue Above Kéros beach ⓣ8851 99090, ⓦkerosblue.com. Opened in 2016, this pricey but well-designed hotel has proved popular with the windsurfing set. All rooms sleep up to four, and they've really gone to town with the bathroom decor. June to mid-Sept. **€140**

Samothráki

SAMOTHRÁKI (also known as Samothrace) has one of the most dramatic profiles of all the Greek islands, second only to Thíra (Santorini): its dark mass of granite rises abruptly from the sea, culminating in the 1611m **Mount Fengári**. Seafarers have always been guided by its imposing outline, clearly visible from the mainland, and ts summit provided a vantage point for Poseidon to watch over the siege of Troy. .anding is subject to the notoriously unpredictable weather, but that did not deter pilgrims who, for hundreds of years in antiquity, journeyed to the island to visit the **sanctuary of the Great Gods** and were initiated into its mysteries. The sanctuary remains the main archeological attraction of the island, which, too remote for most tourists, combines earthy simplicity with natural grandeur. The tourist season is relatively short – essentially (late) July and August – but you will find some facilities open as early as Easter and one or two all year round.

Kamariótissa

Ferries dock at the dull village of **KAMARIÓTISSA**. While you're unlikely to want to spend much time here, it does make a convenient base, as some of Samothráki's best hotels lie along or just behind the tree-lined seafront and various rooms for rent can be found in the maze of streets behind; unlike most places these days, owners often meet incoming vessels.

Hóra

HÓRA, also known as **Samothráki**, is the island's capital. Far larger than the portion visible from out at sea would suggest, it's an attractive town of Thracian-style stone houses, some whitewashed, clustered around a hollow in the western flanks of Mount Fengári. It is dominated by the Genoese **Gateluzzi fort**, of which little survives other than the gateway.

The Sanctuary of the Great Gods

Paleópoli, 6km northeast from Kamariótissa and 3km directly north from Hóra • Daily 8.30am–3pm; museum Tues–Sun only • €6, including museum and site • ☎ 22510 41474

Hidden in a stony but thickly wooded ravine between the tiny hamlet of **Paleópoli** and the plunging northwestern ridge of Mount Fengári lie the remains of the **Sanctuary of the Great Gods**. From the late Bronze Age (around the eighth century BC) until the early Byzantine era (fifth century AD), the mysteries and sacrifices of the cult of the

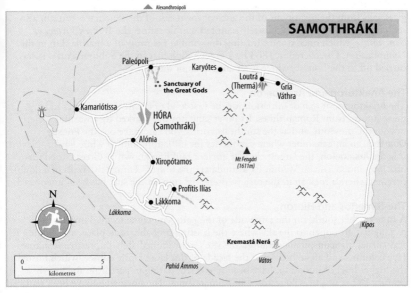

9

> ## THE SAMOTHRACIAN MYSTERIES
>
> The **religion of the Great Gods** revolved around a hierarchy of ancient Thracian fertility figures: the Great Mother Axieros; a subordinate male deity known as Kadmilos; and the potent and ominous twin demons the Kabiroi, originally the local heroes Dardanos and Aeton. When the Aeolian colonists arrived (traditionally c.700 BC) they simply merged the resident deities with their own – the Great Mother became Cybele, while her consort Hermes and the Kabiroi were fused interchangeably with the *Dioskouroi* Castor and Pollux, patrons of seafarers. Around the nucleus of a sacred precinct the newcomers made the beginnings of what is now the sanctuary.
>
> Despite their long observance, the mysteries of the cult were never explicitly recorded, since ancient writers feared incurring the wrath of the Kabiroi (who could reputedly brew up sudden, deadly storms), but it has been established that two levels of **initiation** were involved. Both ceremonies, in direct opposition to the elitism of Eleusis, were open to all, including women and slaves. The lower level of initiation, or *myesis*, may, as is speculated at Eleusis, have involved a ritual simulation of the life, death and rebirth cycle; in any case, it's known that it ended with joyous feasting, and it can be conjectured, since so many clay torches have been found, that it took place at night. The higher level of initiation, or *epopteia*, carried the unusual requirement of a moral standard – the connection of theology with morality, so strong in the later Judeo-Christian tradition, was rarely made by the early Greeks. This second level involved a full confession followed by absolution and baptism in bull's blood.

Great Gods (see box, above) were performed on Samothráki, in ancient Thracian, until the second century BC. Little is known of this dialect except that it was a very old Indo-European tongue, related to and eventually replaced by ancient Greek. The spiritual focus of the northern Aegean, the importance of the island's rituals was second only to the Mysteries of Eleusis in all the ancient world. The well-labelled site strongly evokes its proud past while commanding views of the mountains and the sea.

Archeological Museum

For an explanatory introduction, it is best first to visit the **Archeological Museum**, whose exhibits span all eras of habitation, from the Archaic to the Byzantine. Highlights include a frieze of dancing girls from the propylaion of the Temenos, entablatures from different buildings, and Roman votive offerings such as coloured glass vials from the necropolis of the ancient town east of the sanctuary. You can also see a reproduction of the exquisitely sculpted marble statue, the *Winged Victory of Samothrace*, which once stood breasting the wind at the prow of a marble ship in the Nymphaeum. Discovered in 1863 by a French diplomat to the Sublime Porte, it was carried off to the Louvre, where it remains a major draw.

The Anaktoron and Arsinoeion

The **Anaktoron**, or hall of initiation for the first level of the mysteries, dates in its present form from Roman times. Its inner sanctum was marked by a warning stele, now in the museum, and at the southeast corner you can make out the **Priestly Quarters**, an antechamber where candidates for initiation donned white gowns. Next to it is the **Arsinoeion**, the largest circular ancient building known in Greece, used for libations and sacrifices. Within its rotunda are the fourth-century BC walls of a double precinct where a rock altar, the earliest preserved ruin on the site, has been uncovered.

The Temenos and Hieron

A little further south, on the same side of the path, you come to the **Temenos**, a rectangular area open to the sky where the feasting probably took place, and, edging its rear corner, the conspicuous **Hieron**, the site's most immediately impressive structure. Five columns and an architrave of the facade of this large Doric edifice, which hosted the higher level of initiation, have been re-erected; dating in part from the fourth century BC, it was heavily restored in Roman times. The stone steps have been replaced by modern blocks, but Roman benches for spectators remain *in situ*, along with the sacred stones where confession was heard.

The Nymphaeum (Fountain) of Nike and around
To the west of the path you can just discern the outline of the **theatre**, while just above it, tucked under the ridge, is the **Nymphaeum (Fountain) of Nike**, over which the *Winged Victory* used to preside. West of the theatre, occupying a high terrace, are remains of the main **stoa**; immediately north of this is an elaborate medieval fortification made entirely of antique material.

Loutrá and the far east
With its running streams, giant plane trees and namesake hot springs, **LOUTRÁ** (aka **Thermá**), 6km east of Paleópoli, is a decent enough place to stay, although in late July and August it gets packed, mainly with an incongruous mixture of foreign hippies and elderly Greeks, here to take the sulphurous waters. Far more appealing than the grim **baths** (June–Oct daily 7–10.45am & 4–7.45pm; €3; ☎22510 98229) themselves are the low waterfalls and rock pools of **Gría Váthra**, which are signposted 1.5km up the paved side road leading east from the main Thermá access drive. Loutrá is ghostly quiet for most of the year and its miniature harbour, built as an alternative to Kamariótissa, is never used at all.

   Beaches on Samothráki's north shore are mostly clean but uniformly pebbly and exposed. Some 15km from Loutrá along a corniche road that deteriorates noticeably towards the end is **Kípos beach**, a long strand facing the Turkish island of Gökçeada (Ímvros to the Greeks) and backed by open pasture and picturesque crags. The water is clean and there's a rock overhang for shelter at one end, plus a spring but no other facilities.

The south coast
The warmer south flank of the island, its fertile farmland dotted with olive groves, boasts fine views out to sea – as far as Gökçeada on a clear day. On the way south, beyond sleepy **Lákkoma**, the attractive hill village of **Profítis Ilías** is worth the brief detour.

   From Lákkoma itself, it's less than 2km down to the eponymous **beach**. A further 6km east lies **Pahiá Ámmos**, a long, clean beach with a solitary taverna for sustenance, which does good business with the big summer crowds who also arrive by excursion *kaïkia*. These continue east to **Vátos**, a secluded nudist beach, the **Kremastá Nerá** coastal waterfalls and finally round to Kípos beach (see above).

ARRIVAL AND GETTING AROUND   SAMOTHRÁKI

By ferry The only current connection with the mainland is the ferry from Alexandhroúpoli (2hr 30min; ☎25510 38503, ⓦsaos.gr); its frequency varies from 2–3 daily in July & Aug to 4–5 weekly in winter, and in summer one per week continues on to Límnos (4hr) and Lávrio (15hr).

By kaïki In peak season 1–2 daily excursions run from Kamariótissa to the south-coast beaches. An anticlockwise boat trip also runs round the island from the dock at Loutrá (mid-July to early Sept daily noon–6pm; €20; ☎69740 62054).

By bus There are plenty of buses in season from Kamariótissa along the north coast to Loutrá (6–7 daily; 20min) and inland to Hóra (5–6 daily; 10min), though far fewer in winter.

CLIMBING THE MOON
Loutrá is the prime base for the tough six-hour **climb** up the 1611m **Mount Fengári** (known to the ancients as **Sáos**, a name found on some maps to this day), the highest peak in the Aegean islands; the **path** starts at the top of the village, beside a concrete water tank and a huge plane tree. Tell your accommodation proprietors that you're going. Fengári is Greek for **"moon"** and, according to legend, if you reach the top on the night of a full moon your wish will come true – most of those foolhardy enough to attempt this will just hope to get back down safely.

9

By car or motorbike You can only get to the south and far east of the island with your own transport. The best places to rent wheels are Niki Tours (☎ 25510 41465, ✉ niki_tours@hotmail.com) and Kyrkos car rental (☎ 25510 41628, ✉ akis1kirkos@gmail.com), both on the seafront at Kamariótissa; best book in advance in high season, as supply is short. The only petrol station on the island is 1km above the port, en route to Hóra.

ACCOMMODATION AND EATING

KAMARIÓTISSA

Aeolos Behind northeastern seafront ☎ 25510 41595, ⓦ hotelaiolos.gr. Reasonably well-maintained hotel with a large pool and quiet, spacious rooms. Breakfast is included, and there are good half-board deals in low season. June–Sept. **€55**

Iy Klimataria Towards northeast end of seafront ☎ 25510 41535. With a huge summer terrace, this enduring taverna serves dishes like fried aubergines, oven-baked goat and *soutsoukákia*, all well under €10, plus palatable barrelled wine. June–Sept daily 9am–11pm.

Niki Beach 500m northeast of centre ☎ 25510 41545, ⓦ nikibeach.gr. Newest and smartest hotel near the port, right on the coast, with swish lobby, stylishly furnished rooms, plus a pool and bar. May–Oct. **€60**

HÓRA

★**Taverna 1900** ☎ 25510 41222. Boasting a lovely vine-shaded terrace with stunning views of the kástro and the valley below, this friendly taverna serves stuffed goat for €8 and spicy aubergines. Mid-May to mid-Sept daily noon–1am.

THE SANCTUARY OF THE GREAT GODS

Samothraki Village Paleópoli ☎ 25510 42300, ⓦ samothrakivillage.gr. Smart resort, handily placed for the Sanctuary of the Great Gods, with manicured grounds, neatly furnished rooms, two pools and a bar-restaurant. Price includes half-board. **€95**

LOUTRÁ AND THE FAR EAST

Camping Voradhes 3km east of Loutrá village ☎ 25510 98291. The island's prime municipal campsite has hot-water showers, electricity, a minimarket, restaurant and bar. July & Aug. **€13**

Tasoula Parselia Studios Northwest edge of Loutrá village ☎ 25510 98318, ⓦ samothraki-studios.gr. Attractive rustic studios in a peaceful wooded setting – some of the trees here are 500 years old. Each cosy unit has its own yard or balcony. May–Sept. **€35**

★**To Perivoli T'Ouranou** On the lane to Gría Váthra ☎ 25510 98313. "Heaven's Orchard" aptly describes this leafy taverna. Various dips, types of *saganáki* and spaghetti dishes (€7–8) supplement the usual grills and salads. Regular live traditional music. June to mid-Oct daily 11am–2am.

THE SOUTH COAST

Paradisos Profítis Ilías ☎ 25510 95267. Atmospheric rustic taverna, with a lovely terrace facing sunsets over Thássos. The house speciality is a selection of meats such as lamb, goat and *kondosoúvli* roast on the spit for €7–9, accompanied by fiery *tsípouro* or soothing wine. June to mid-Sept daily 10am–2am.

To Akroyiali Lákkoma beach ☎ 25510 95123. Simple but clean rooms with sea-view balconies are available above a friendly taverna, which serves fresh fish from €35/kilo, some meat and a standard menu of mezédhes and salads. June–Sept. **€30**

Thássos

Just 12km from the mainland, **Thássos** has long been a popular resort island for northern Greeks, and since the early 1990s has also attracted a cosmopolitan mix of tourists, particularly Germans and Scandinavians on packages, as well as an increasing number of people from eastern Europe. They are all entertained by vast numbers of *bouzoúkia* (music halls) and music tavernas, while nature-lovers can find some areas of outstanding beauty, especially inland. Moreover, the island's traditional industries have managed to survive the onslaught of modernity. The elite of Thássos still make a substantial living from the pure-white **marble** that constitutes two-thirds of the landmass, found only here and quarried at dozens of sites in the hills between Liménas and Panayía. Olives, especially the oil, honey, nuts and fruit (often sold candied) are also important products. The spirit *tsípouro*, rather than wine, is the main local tipple; pear extract, onions or spices like cinnamon and anise are added to home-made batches.

Brief history

Inhabited since the Stone Age, Thássos was settled by Parians in the seventh century BC, attracted by **gold** deposits between modern Liménas and Kínyra. Buoyed by revenues from these, and from **silver** mines under Thassian control on the mainland opposite, the ancient city-state here became the seat of a medium-sized seafaring empire. Commercial acumen did not spell military invincibility, however; the Persians under Darius swept the Thassian fleets from the seas in 492 BC, and in 462 BC Athens permanently deprived Thássos of its autonomy after a three-year siege. The main port continued to thrive into Roman times, but lapsed into Byzantine and medieval obscurity.

ARRIVAL AND GETTING AROUND — THÁSSOS

By ferry/hydrofoil Kavála-based ferries (2–5 daily; 1hr 15min) arrive at Skála Prínou, in the northwest of the island. Ferries to the island capital, Liménas (8–12 daily; 40min), leave from Keramotí on the mainland opposite.

By bus The service is fairly good, with frequent buses from Liménas to Panayía and Skála Potamiás (6 daily; 15–30min), Limenária (6 daily; 40min), Theológos (3 daily; 1hr) and Alykí (1 daily; 40min).

By car or motorbike Thássos is small enough to circumnavigate in one full day by rented motorbike or car. Car rental is offered by the major international chains and local Potos Car Rentals (☎ 25930 52071, ⓦ rentacarpotos. gr), with seven branches around the island; try bargaining in the shoulder seasons.

Water-taxi In peak season there are 2 daily services from Liménas to Khryssí Ammoudhía, via intermediate coves.

9

Liménas

Largely modern **LIMÉNAS** (also signposted as Limín or Thássos) is the island's capital, though not the only port. Although it's often plagued with surprisingly clogged traffic, it is partly redeemed by its picturesque fishing harbour and the impressive remains of the **ancient city**. Thanks to its mineral wealth and safe harbour, ancient Thássos prospered from Classical to Roman times. There are substantial remains both above and below the streets, plus a fine archeological museum. Thássos hosts a **summer festival**, with performances of anything from jazz to comedy at the Hellenistic theatre.

The agora

Just back from fishing harbour • Unrestricted access

The largest excavated area is the **agora**; the grassy site is fenced but not usually locked, and is most enjoyably seen towards dusk. Two Roman *stoas* are prominent, but you can also make out shops, monuments, passageways and sanctuaries from the remodelled Classical city. At the far end, a fifth-century BC passageway leads through to an elaborate sanctuary of Artemis, a substantial stretch of Roman road and a few seats of the *odeion*.

Archeological Museum

Next to agora • Tues–Sun 8.30am–3pm • €2 • ☎ 25930 22180

The renovated **Archeological Museum**, close to the agora, contains small but absorbing displays of prehistoric finds, ancient games and archeological methods. Pride of place

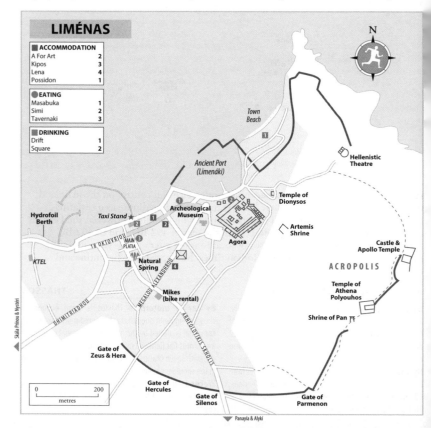

oes to the 4m-tall, seventh-century BC *kouros* carrying a ram, found on the acropolis.
The courtyard contains some impressive sarcophagi and statuary.

Other ancient remains

From a **temple of Dionysos** behind the fishing port, a path curls up to a
Hellenistic theatre, fabulously positioned above a broad sweep of sea. Sadly,
it's only open for performances of the summer festival. From just before the
theatre, the trail winds on the right up to the **acropolis**, where a Venetian-
Byzantine-Genoese fort arose between the thirteenth and fifteenth centuries,
constructed from recycled masonry of an Apollo temple. You can continue,
following the remains of a massive circuit of fifth-century walls, to a high
terrace supporting the foundations of the **Athena Polyouhos** (Athena Patroness of
the City) temple, with Cyclopean walls.

Down from the temple's southern end, a short, level path leads to a cavity
in a nearby rock outcrop that was a **shrine of Pan**, shown in faint relief playing
his pipes. Following the path to the left around the summit brings you to a
precipitous rock-hewn stairway with a metal handrail, which provided a
discreet escape route to the **Gate of Parmenon**, the only gate in the fortifications
to have retained its lintel. From here a track, then a paved lane, descend through
the southerly neighbourhoods of the modern town, completing a satisfying
one-hour circuit. All of these remains offer unrestricted access – though look out
for snakes.

ARRIVAL AND GETTING AROUND   LIMÉNAS

By bus Buses operate from the KTEL office (☏ 25930
22162), facing the seafront a little way west of the centre.
By ferry Ferries from Keramotí dock towards the west end
of the seafront at the New Port. Various operators offer
four-hour boat trips to nearby islands and bays, usually
including a barbecue (€25–30).

By taxi The main taxi rank is just in front of the KTEL office.
By bike or car Bikes can be rented from Mike's on Skala
Ormos Prinou (☏ 25930 71820): car rental is widely
available.
Information There is no official tourist office: the best
online resource is ⓦ thassos-view.com.

ACCOMMODATION

★**A For Art** Off 18 Oktovriou ☏ 25930 58405,
ⓦ aforarthotel.gr. By far the best place to stay in town.
Every inch of its public areas has a glam design; the rooms
are a little more understated, but gorgeous too. Throw in
attentive staff, a hidden pool and a superlative breakfast
(included), and this works out to be a great deal; it's worth
paying for half-board, eating out in the yard and feeling
envy from every passer-by. **€145**
Kipos Cul-de-sac off Arheoloyikís Skholís ☏ 25930
22469, ⓦ kipos.gr. Attractive building with cool lower-
ground-floor doubles and galleried apartments sleeping

up to five upstairs, plus a small pool in the garden. Late
May–Sept. **€43**
Lena Megálou Aléxandhrou ☏ 25930 22933,
ⓔ hotel_lena@hotmail.com. The best-value budget
hotel in town, with compact but clean and comfy rooms;
run by a welcoming Greek-American family. May–Oct.
€30
Possidon Central seafront ☏ 25930 22690, ⓦ thassos-
possidon.com. Unattractive concrete block which greatly
improves inside, with a spacious lobby café and rooms
decorated in bright hues. **€45**

EATING

Masabuka 18 Oktovriou ☏ 25930 23651. This meat
place is quite a sight in the evening, when smoke pours off
the grill and out over the tables in the street. Souvláki sticks
go from just €1 each, though there's a €10 minimum spend
per table. Daily 4pm–midnight.
★**Simi** Behind ancient port ☏ 25930 22517. Recently
spruced up with a bright modern interior (though most
prefer to eat in the courtyard), this taverna has a full

menu of fish, meat and mezédhes, mostly costing
€4–12, along with memorably good wine. Daily
noon–1am.
Tavernaki Northeast corner of main square ☏ 25930
23181. Friendly and traditional taverna with tables lining
the alley outside, where you can feast on succulent grills
and saucy *mayireftá* for under €10, a bit more for most fish.
Daily 10am–1am.

9

DRINKING AND NIGHTLIFE

Drift Miauli 38 ☎ 25930 221133. The town's beach bars are much of a muchness, and rarely rowdy, but this is the prime choice, with mellow music and deckchair seating. Cocktails €7. Daily 10am–late.

Square 18 Oktovriou 11 ☎ 25930 23742. Tourists can b a fickle bunch, and the town's "it" spot changes frequentl This is the current place to hang out, a swanky-looking ba whose chilled daytime vibe becomes more pumping a evening progresses. Daily 9am–late.

The east coast

Much of the busy **east coast** of the island, between Liménas and Alykí, is enclosed by a sheer ripple of rock – splendidly scenic, and dotted with attractive coves any of which wil make a good alternative base to the capital. If you're doing a circuit of the island, it's a good idea to head clockwise, to maximize the sun's presence on the eastern beaches.

Panayía

The first place worthy of a halt southeast from Liménas is **PANAYÍA**, an attractive hillside village overlooking Potamiá Bay. It's a large, thriving place where life revolves around the central square with its huge plane trees, fountain and slate-roofed houses. Up above the village towers the island's highest peak, **Mount Ypsárion**.

Potamiá

POTAMIÁ, much lower than Panayía in the river valley, is far less prepossessing – with modern red tiles instead of slates on the roofs – though it has a lively winter carnival. It's also home to the modest **Polygnotos Vayis Museum** (May–Oct Tues–Sat 9.30am–12.30pm & 6–9pm, Sun 10am–12.30pm; €2; ☎ 25930 61400), devoted to the locally born sculptor; though Vayis emigrated to America when young, he bequeathed most of his works to the Greek state.

Skála Potamiás and Khryssí Ammoudhiá

The road from Potamiá towards the coast is lined with rooms for rent and apartment-type accommodation. A side road some 12km from Liménas takes you down to **SKÁLA POTAMIÁS**, at the southern end of the bay. From the harbourfront a road off to the left brings you to sand dunes extending all the way to **KHRYSSÍ AMMOUDHIÁ**, which makes up the northern end of the bay. Often anglicized to "**Golden Beach**" (referring to the settlement as well as the actual beach), it's a little built up, but preferable to Skála Potamiás in the quality of sand and sea, and also its restaurants and cafés. The beach here can be approached by a direct road that spirals for 5km down from Panayía, or you can walk here along the coast road from Skála Potamiás, though you'll have to duck inland to get around the campsite.

Kínyra and its beaches

The dispersed hamlet of **KÍNYRA**, some 24km south of Liménas, marks the start of the burnt zone which overlooks it, though recovery is under way. Although not having much to recommend it per se, Kínyra is convenient for the superior **beaches** of Loutroú (1km south) and partly nudist Paradise (3km along) – officially called Makrýammos Kinýron – both of which can be reached down poorly signposted dirt tracks. The latter is one of the most scenic beaches on Thassos.

ACCOMMODATION AND EATING

THE EAST COAST

PANAYÍA

Elena Middle of town ☎ 25930 61709. The best place to eat in town, and impossible to miss, especially in the evening when the meats are on the grill (€6–8 or so). Good, aromatic local wine rounds out the picture. Daily noon–midnight.

★ **Thassos Inn** Tris Piyés district near the Kímisis church ☎ 25930 61612, ⓦ thassosinn.gr. Affording superb views over the rooftops, this hotel's bright yellow walls mirror the colour of the mature carp in its fish-pond. The rooms are fine and the terrace cafeteria very relaxing. April–Oct. **€30**

SKÁLA POTAMIÁS AND KHRYSSÍ AMMOUDHIÁ

Alexandra Golden Boutique Just south of the campsite, Skála Potamiás ☎ 25930 58212, ⓦ alexandragoldenhotel.com. It looks a little like Joan Miró has let his paintbrush loose on the buildings surrounding the pool at this blissful, adult-only retreat, with refined and artistic rooms. There's a spa and an excellent restaurant on site too. Late April to Sept. €115

Camping Golden Beach On the beach, half-way between Skála Potamiás and Khryssí Ammoudhiá ☎ 25930 61472, ⓦ camping-goldenbeach.gr. The only official campsite on this side of the island has plenty of shaded pitches, clean baths, laundry facilities and a minimarket. May to mid-Oct. €14

Eric's On main road 400m inland, Skála Potamiás ☎ 25930 61554, ⓦ erics.gr. So called after the owner who widely advertises his resemblance to former footballer Eric Cantona. The rooms and studios are spotless, and there are Premiership matches on satellite TV, plus a swimming pool with bar. €40

Golden Sand Near north end of beach, Khryssí Ammoudhiá ☎ 25930 61771, ⓦ hotel-goldensand.gr. Backing onto the sand after which it is named, this mid-sized resort hotel has smart rooms, most with sea-facing balconies, and a café-bar. April–Oct. €55

Krambousa Near north harbour wall, Skála Potamiás ☎ 25930 61481. In an ideal location by the fishing harbour, they serve oven-baked meat and veg dishes – the best is the *kléftiko* (€12), made with local lamb – and there's decent barrelled wine too. May–Oct daily 8.30am–midnight.

KÍNYRA AND ITS BEACHES

Agorastos On main road behind village ☎ 25930 41225, ⓦ agorastos-thassos.gr. Colourful pension with a leafy terraced garden and cosy, well-furnished rooms, plus a small on-site taverna. April–Oct. €45

Paradise Beach South of Kínyra ☎ 25930 41248. Daytime restaurant on the eponymous beach, serving filling breakfasts, good coffee and a full menu with meat dishes for €8–12. May–Oct daily 8am–10pm.

Southern Thássos

The south-facing coast of Thássos has the balance of the island's best beaches, starting with the prettiest resort, in the shape of **Alykí** – unfortunately it's overlooked by the island's newest expanse of burnt-out land, the area having suffered a major forest fire in 2016. In the southwest corner, **Limenária** is rather dull and functional, although its greater local population means it has more authentic dining choices.

Alykí and around

ALYKÍ hamlet, 35km from Liménas and just below the main road, faces a perfect double bay which almost pinches off a headland. Uniquely, it retains its original whitewashed, slate-roofed architecture, since the presence of extensive antiquities here has led to a ban on any modern construction. Those **ruins** include an ancient temple to an unknown deity, and two exquisite early Christian basilicas out on the headland, with a few columns re-erected.

Of the **beaches**, the sand-and-pebble west bay gets busy in peak season, though you can always head off to the less crowded, rocky east cove, or snorkel in the crystal-clear waters off the marble formations on the headland's far side. Alternatively, head for secluded **Kékes** beach, in a pine grove 1km further southwest.

Convent of Arhangélou Miha'il

5km southwest of Alykí • Open during daylight hours

The **convent of Arhangélou Miha'il** clings spectacularly to a cliff on the seaward side of the road. Though founded in the twelfth century above the spot where a spring had gushed forth, the convent has been hideously renovated by the nuns, resident here since 1974. A dependency of Filothéou on Mount Áthos, its prize relic is a purported nail from the Crucifixion.

Potós and around

Just 1km west of the island's southern tip is a good but crowded beach, **Psilí Ámmos**, with watersports on offer. A few kilometres further, **POTÓS** is the island's prime German-speaking package venue, its centre claustrophobically dense, with the few

9

non-block-booked rooms overlooking cramped alleys. Although the kilometre-long beach is decent enough, there is little to warrant lingering here. **Pefkári**, with its manicured beach and namesake pine grove, 1km west, is essentially an annexe of Potós, with a few mid-range places to stay and better eating options.

Limenária and around

LIMENÁRIA, the island's second town, was built to house German mining executives brought in by the Ottomans between 1890 and 1905. Their remaining mansions, scattered on the slopes above the harbour, lend some character, but despite attempts at embellishing the waterfront, it's not the most attractive place on Thássos.

The nearest good beach is **Trypití**, a couple of kilometres west – turn left into the pines at the start of a curve right. The broad, 800m-long strand is rather marred by the massed ranks of umbrellas and sun loungers for rent. The cleft to which the name refer (literally "pierced" in Greek) is a slender tunnel through the headland at the west end of the beach, leading to a tiny three-boat anchorage.

ACCOMMODATION AND EATING

SOUTHERN THÁSSOS

ALYKÍ AND AROUND

Beautiful Alice Village centre ☎ 25930 31574. The oldest taverna in the village, with a lovely terrace over the sea, where you can choose from a bewildering array of reasonably priced seafood and fish (including sardines cooked in four different ways for €7–9), or simple veggie dishes like stuffed red peppers (€5) and beetroot salad (€4). May–Oct daily 11am–1am.

POTÓS AND AROUND

Camping Pefkari Beach Pefkári ☎ 25930 51190, ⌨ camping-pefkari.gr. With its attractive wooded location and clean facilities, this is undoubtedly the best campsite on Thássos. May–Sept. €14

Thassos Pefkári ☎ 25930 51596, ⌨ hotel-thassos.gr. Accomplished resort hotel just behind the beach with refreshingly colourful and contemporary decor, from its spacious lobby to the well-appointed rooms. There's a pool, tennis court and watersports available too. Breakfast included. €60

LIMENÁRIA AND AROUND

Blionis On seafront ☎ 25930 51178. This attractive café is a great place to go a little Turkish – grab a square of syrupy baklava with a scoop of vanilla ice-cream (€4.50). There are loads of sweets on show, plus good coffee, and even some alcoholic drinks. Mid-April to mid-Oct daily 6.30am–1am, sometimes later.

★**Menel Tree House** On harbour ☎ 25930 53520, ⌨ dhotels.gr. Eco-friendly, artistically-designed hotel, with chunky wood everywhere, bird-cage-like seats to swing in, and deckchairs and a jacuzzi on the roof terrace. The standard of service is high too, making this very good value for the price. April to mid-Oct. €45

★**To Limani** On harbour ☎ 25930 52790. This old-style *tsipourádhiko* is the preferred gathering place for the savvy locals, who accompany the fiery spirit with freshly caught fish from the adjacent sea (from €8 per portion). Daily 11am–midnight.

The west coast

The **west coast**, between Limenária and Liménas, is Thassós' most exposed and scenically least impressive, and the various *skáles* (harbours) such as Skála Kaliráhis and Skála Sotíros – originally the ports for namesake inland villages – are bleak, straggly and windy. **SKÁLA MARIÓN**, 13km from Limenária, is the exception: an attractive little bay, with fishing boats hauled up on the sandy foreshore, and the modern low-rise village arrayed in a U-shape all around with two fine **beaches** on either side.

SKÁLA PRÍNOU has little to recommend it, other than ferry connections to Kavála. **SKÁLA RAHONÍOU**, between here and Liménas, has a smattering of facilities, as well as proximity to **Pahýs beach**, 9km short of Liménas, by far the best strand on the northwest coast. Narrow dirt tracks lead past various tavernas through surviving pines to the sand, partly shaded in the morning.

Pefkospilia West end of Pahýs beach, Skála Rahoníou ☎25930 81051. One of the oldest and most picturesque tavernas on the island, where great traditional cuisine costs well under €10 and is served outside the tiny whitewashed building, almost hidden by firs, as the name ("Fir cave") suggests. Try their eponymous salad, made with orange, fennel and dried tomatoes (€7). May–Sept daily noon–1am.

ension Dimitris On hilltop behind port, Skála Maríon ☎6944 505 064, ✆pension-dimitris.gr. Attractively

designed modern building with smart rooms, a communal kitchen and optional breakfast for a small extra charge. May to mid-Oct. **€50**

Ploumis On beach south of Skála Rahoníou ☎25930 81442. This café-taverna provides everything from breakfast through light snacks to full-blown meals of freshly grilled fish, seafood and meat for around €10. Especially good for watching sunsets. May to mid-Oct daily 9am–midnight.

The interior

Few people get around to exploring inland Thássos – with the post-fire scrub still struggling to revive, it's not always rewarding – but there are several worthwhile excursions to or around the **hill villages**, which, as usual, portray a very different lifestyle to the coastal resorts.

Theológos

THEOLÓGOS, 10km along a well-surfaced but poorly signposted road from Potós, was founded in the sixteenth century by refugees from Constantinople and became the island's capital under the Ottomans. Its houses, most with oversized chimneys and slate roofs, straggle in long tiers to either side of the main street, surrounded by generous kitchen gardens or walled courtyards. A stroll along the single high street, with its couple of *kafenía*, a soldiers' bar, a sandal-maker and traditional bakery, is rewarding.

Kástro

KÁSTRO is the most naturally protected of the island's anti-pirate redoubts: thirty ancient houses and a church surround a rocky pinnacle, fortified by the Byzantines and the Genoese, which has a sheer drop on three sides. Summer occupation by shepherds is becoming the norm after total abandonment in the nineteenth century, when mining jobs at Limenária proved irresistible. Despite its proximity to Theológos as the crow flies, there's no straightforward route to it; especially with a car, it's best to descend to Potós before heading up a rough, 17km dirt track from Limenária.

Sotíras

SOTÍRAS, a steep 3.5km up from Skála Sotíros, is the only interior village with an unobstructed view of sunset over the Aegean, and is thus popular with foreigners, who've bought up about half of the houses for restoration. On the ridge opposite are exploratory shafts left by the miners, whose ruined lodge looms above the church.

The Kazavíti villages

From Prínos (Kalýves) on the coast road, it's a 6km journey inland to the **Kazavíti villages**, which are shrouded in greenery that escaped the fires; they're signposted, albeit poorly, and mapped officially as Megálo and Mikró Prínos but still universally known by their Ottoman name. **MIKRÓ KAZAVÍTI** marks the start of the track for **MEGÁLO KAZAVÍTI**, where the magnificent platía is one of the prettiest spots on the whole island.

EATING AND DRINKING   THE INTERIOR

★Iatrou Theológos village centre ☎25930 31000. This excellent traditional taverna is at its best in the evening when the roasting spits start turning, loaded with

goat and suckling pig (around €7–8). Great barrelled wine too. Daily noon–1am.

The Sporades and Évvia

KASTRO BEACH, SKIATHOS

The Sporades and Évvia

The Sporades lie close to Greece's eastern coast, their hilly terrain betraying their status as extensions of Mount Pílio, directly opposite on the mainland. The three northern islands, Skiáthos, Skópelos and Alónissos, are archetypal Aegean holiday venues, with wonderful beaches, lush vegetation and transparent sea; they're all packed in midsummer and close down almost entirely from October to April. Skýros, the fourth inhabited member of the group, lies well to the southeast, and is much more closely connected – both physically and historically – to Évvia than to its fellow Sporades. These two have far fewer visitors.

Skiáthos, thanks to its international airport and extraordinary number of sandy beaches, is the busiest of the islands, though **Skópelos**, with its *Mamma Mia!* connections, extensive pine forests and idyllic pebble bays, is catching up fast. **Alónissos**, much quieter, more remote and less developed, lies at the heart of a National Marine Park, attracting more nature lovers than night owls. **Skýros** sees fewer foreign visitors, partly because it's much harder to reach, though it's a beautiful island and plenty of domestic tourism means no shortage of facilities. Between Skýros and the mainland, **Évvia** (classical Euboea) extends for nearly 200km alongside central Greece. Although in spots one of the most dramatic of Greek islands, with forested mountains and rugged stretches of little-developed coast, its sheer size and proximity to the mainland means that it rarely has much of an island feel; mainlanders have holiday homes around numerous seaside resorts, but foreigners are very thin on the ground.

An indented coastline full of bays and coves to anchor in, relatively steady winds and the clear waters of the National Marine Park, also make the northern Sporades, rightly, a magnet for **yacht flotillas** and charters. Many companies have bases in Skiáthos, in particular.

ARRIVAL AND DEPARTURE

THE SPORADES AND ÉVVIA

By plane Skiáthos airport receives regular international services from across Europe as well as daily scheduled domestic flights. There are also international charters to Vólos on the nearby mainland (see p.223), while Skýros sees half a dozen flights a week from Athens and Thessaloníki.

By ferry Frequent ferries, fast cats and hydrofoils run from Vólos (see p.223), Áyios Konstandínos (see p.219) and Thessaloníki (see p.268) to Skiáthos, Skópelos and Alónissos; in summer there's also a daily connection between Mandoúdhi in northern Évvia (se p.703). Skýros is accessed from the port of Kými on Évvia (see p.700), where ferries connect with buses from Athens. Two or three times a week in midsummer, this same ferry runs between Kými and Alónissos and Skópelos. For Évvia, local ferries shuttle from various strategic points on the mainland.

By bus and train Évvia is joined to central Greece by two bridges. Buses from Athens run to various points on the island, and there are trains to the island capital, Halkídha.

Skiáthos

Undulating green countryside, some fine rural monasteries and a labyrinthine old town notwithstanding, the real business of **Skiáthos** is **beaches**: by far the best, if also the busiest, in the Sporades. There are over fifty strands (plus a few more on satellite islets),

MAMMA MIA CHAPEL

Highlights

❶ Lalária beach, Skiáthos Glistening white pebbles and turquoise waters, backed by steep cliffs and a natural rock arch, form a photogenic contrast to the island's other, mostly sandy, bays. **See p.677**

❷ Skópelos Town Old-fashioned shops, ornate balconies, domed churches and atmospheric passageways make this one of the most alluring island towns in Greece. **See p.680**

❸ National Marine Park of Alónissos-Northern Sporades Spend a day – or longer – on a boat exploring the islets of this pristine reserve, with their wildlife, monasteries and secluded bays. **See p.690**

❹ Skýros An outrageously pagan carnival, a striking hillside Hóra and wonderfully clear seas are all found on one of the least spoiled islands in the Aegean. **See p.690**

❺ Dhimosári Gorge, southern Évvia Traverse the wildest corner of the island on a mostly cobbled path descending from Mount Óhi. **See p.703**

❻ Paralía Ayíou Nikoláou, northern Évvia The journey to this beautiful cove beach with an excellent taverna is half the point, via sinuous mountain roads through verdant pine forests. **See p.705**

HIGHLIGHTS ARE MARKED ON THE MAP ON P.674

most with fine, pale sand, but still barely enough room for the legions of visitors; Italians and Greeks in summer, Brits and Scandinavians in spring and autumn. The main road along the south and southeast coasts serves an almost unbroken line of villas, hotels, minimarkets and restaurants; although they've not impinged much on Skiáthos' natural beauty, they make it difficult to find anything particularly Greek here But by **hiking** or using a **4WD vehicle**, you can find relative solitude, refreshing vistas and charming medieval monuments in the island's north.

10 ARRIVAL AND DEPARTURE   SKIÁTHOS

BY PLANE

As well as international services, there are regular flights to Athens with Olympic (ⓦolympicair.com; April–Oct 2 daily, Nov–March 3 weekly) and Sky Express (ⓦwww .skyexpress.gr; May–Oct 5 weekly, Nov–April

2–3 weekly). Built on reclaimed land less than 2km eas of Skiáthos Town, Skiáthos airport has an extremely shor runway, and planes come in incredibly low over th harbour. Every Fri, the busiest day for charters, hundreds of people gather by the road at the end of the runway

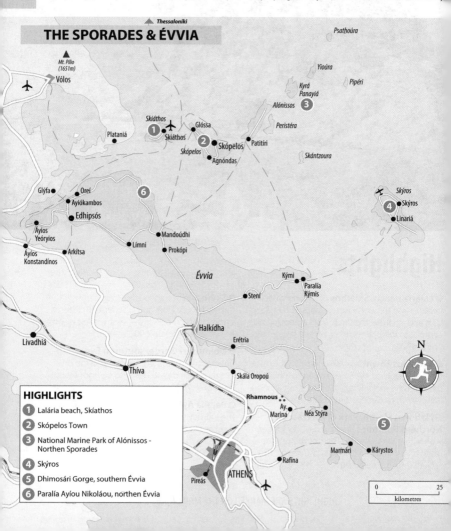

THE SPORADES & ÉVVIA

▲ *Thessaloníki*

Psathoúra

▲ *Mt. Pílio (1651m)*

Vólos

Yioúra

Pipéri

Kyrá Panayiá

Alónissos ③

Skiáthos
① *Skiáthos*

Glóssa

Peristéra

Plataniá

② *Skópelos*

Patitíri

Skópelos

Agnóndas

Skántzoura

Glýfa

Oreí

⑥

Ayiókambos

Edhipsós

Skýros

④ *Skýros*

Linariá

Áyios Yeóryios

Mandoúdhi

Árkitsa

Límni

Prokópi

Áyios Konstandínos

Évvia

Kými

Paralía Kýmis

Stení

Halkídha

Erétria

Livadhiá

N

Thíva

Skála Oropoú

Rhamnous

Ay. Marína

Néa Stýra

⑤

HIGHLIGHTS

① Lalária beach, Skiáthos
② Skópelos Town
③ National Marine Park of Alónissos - Northen Sporades
④ Skýros
⑤ Dhimosári Gorge, southern Évvia
⑥ Paralía Ayíou Nikoláou, northen Évvia

Marmári

Kárystos

Rafína

ATHENS

Pireás

0		25
	kilometres	

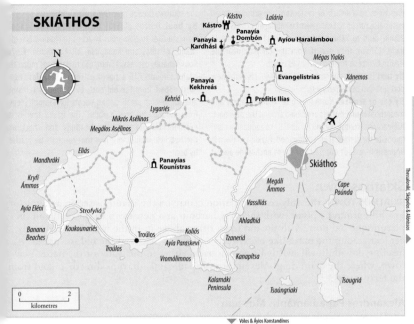

SKIÁTHOS

10

where landing planes pass just a few metres overhead, and the jet blast from those taking off can knock you over; check it out on YouTube.

BY FERRY
Ferries dock right in the centre of Skiáthos Town, virtually opposite the bottom of the main street, Papadhiamándi. In summer, Hellenic Seaways fast catamarans and ferries (w hsw.gr), Aegean Flying Dolphins hydrofoils (w aegeanflyingdolphins.gr) and ANES (w anes.gr) and Aqua (w aquaferries.gr) ferries connect Skiáthos Town daily with Vólos and Áyios Konstandínos on the mainland, and with Skópelos and Alónissos. Less frequently, Hellenic Seaways Flying Cats ply to Thessaloníki, and the ANES ferry *Proteus* to Mandoúdhi in northern Évvia. The rest of the year,

Hellenic Seaways and ANES runs a reduced service of ferries or fast cats to Vólos, Skópelos and Alónissos. Always prebook for the hydrofoils and cats here; when a plane arrives they can be packed.

Tickets and agencies There are ticket booths on the Skiáthos Town dock at busy times; otherwise the Hellenic Seaways agent (☎ 24270 22209) is opposite the jetty at the base of Papadhiamándi and sells tickets for all ferries.

Destinations Alónissos (summer 4–7 daily; winter 3 daily; 1hr–2hr 20min); Áyios Konstandínos (summer 1–3 daily; 1hr 30min–3hr 10min); Mandoúdhi (Évvia; summer 2–7 weekly; 2hr 30min–4hr 20min); Skópelos (summer 4–8 daily, winter 3 daily; 35min–1hr 40min); Thessaloníki (summer 4 weekly, 2hr 45min); Vólos (summer 4 daily, winter 3 daily; 1hr 15min–2hr 45min).

INFORMATION

Tourist information There's no tourist office: the useful w skiathos.gr has extensive accommodation listings.
Services In Skiáthos Town, the National Bank is on

Papadhiamándi, and there are numerous others nearby and around the harbour, many with ATMs. The post office is also on Papadhiamándi.

GETTING AROUND

By bus A superb bus service runs along Skiáthos' coast road, from town to Koukounariés at the western end of the island (daily 7am–12.30am every 20min, more at busy periods; €2); the entire run takes about 30min, but longer in Aug when traffic is chaotic. Despite the number

of buses, it can be hard to get on when everyone is coming home at the end of the day. In town, the terminus is at the eastern (airport) end of the new port, with further stops on the ring road. There are 26 numbered stops, and these numbers are often used when giving

10

directions to a beach or restaurant. In summer, small buses also run up to Evangelístrias monastery (5–8 daily; 20min) and to Xánemos beach, beyond the airport (5 daily; 15min); they depart from the car park near the Health Centre at the top of the old town.

By taxi The main taxi rank (☎ 24270 24461) is at the new port just east of the ferry jetties.

By car or scooter Numerous bike, motorbike, car and motorboat rental outlets are based around the new port; Aegean Car Rental (☎ 24270 22430, ⓦ aegeancars.gr), opposite the ferries, is recommended. Parking in town is impossible, except out past the yacht anchorage and at the southwest edge near the health centre.

By boat Dozens of boat trips are on offer, rangin᠆ from shuttles to numerous beaches (including Tsougr᠆ island, Vassiliás and Kanapítsa, all 10–15min, €2.7᠆ Koukounariés express, 15min, €5) to day-trips round th᠆ island (around €15 a head) or round Skópelos (€20᠆ Most depart from the old port, but various interestin᠆ alternatives, on small sailing yachts for example, leav᠆ from around the new harbour. The island tour is a᠆ excellent way to get your bearings and check ou᠆ the beaches, including a few that can only be reache᠆ by boat.

Skiáthos Town

SKIÁTHOS TOWN, the only real population centre on the island, is set on a couple of low hills around a point, with the ferry harbour and new town to the east, and the picturesque old port, with the old town rising above it, in the west. You can easily get lost among the maze-like backstreets and shady platíes of the old town, but heading downhill will swiftly bring you back, either to the water or the flatter new town, where the main drag, Alexándhrou Papadhiamándi, runs directly inland from the ferry jetties.

Alexándros Papadiamántis Museum

Just off Alexándhrou Papadhiamándi • Tues–Sun 10am–1pm & 5–7pm • €1.50 • ☎ 24270 23843

There are few specific sights in Skiáthos, though the **Alexándros Papadiamántis Museum**, housed in the nineteenth-century home of one of Greece's best-known writers, is worth a look. The upper storey – basically two tiny rooms – has been maintained as it was when the writer, who plainly enjoyed a remarkably ascetic lifestyle, lived (and died) here. The ground floor operates as a bookshop-cum-exhibition area.

Boúrtzi

The peninsula that separates the two harbours, the **Boúrtzi**, makes for an enjoyable stroll. Surrounded by crumbling defences and a few rusty cannon – there was a castle in this obvious defensive position from at least the thirteenth century – it is today a peaceful setting for the one-room **Maritime Museum** (daily 11am–1pm & 6.30–10.30pm, €2), a **café** with great views, and an open-air municipal **theatre**, with regular summertime music and drama performances.

The rest of the island

Skiáthos' **south coast** is lined with beach after beach after beach, almost all of them easily accessible on the bus. If you want to explore the mountainous area north of town, though, or get to the **north coast** beaches, you'll need your own transport or be prepared for some very hot hiking. Be warned that a 50cc moped simply won't make it up some of the exceptionally steep tracks, especially around Kástro. Thanks to the humid climate and springs fed from the mainland, the **interior** is exceptionally green, thick with pine, lentisk, holm oak, heather and arbutus even where (as is all too common) it has been ravaged by forest fires over the years. There are plenty of villas and tourist facilities on the coast, and chapels and farms in the interior, but only **Troúlos** (with another excellent beach) really counts as a village, and even that a tiny one.

vangelístrias monastery

Monastery Daily: April–Oct 9am–9pm; Nov–March 8.30am–3pm • Free • **Museum** Daily: April–Oct 9.30am–8pm; Nov–March 9am–2pm • €2 • From town, you can take the bus (see p.675), drive here in about 10min, or walk in just over an hour; the path takes various short cuts from the road, mostly well signed, starting from the ring road near bus stop 2

The much-revered eighteenth-century **Evangelístrias monastery** is the scene of major pilgrimages at Easter and on August 15, because it was here that the modern Greek flag was first unfurled in 1807. It's a beautiful place, lovingly maintained, and there's an eclectic **museum** comprised of ecclesiastical and rural-folklore galleries plus a vast collection of documents, posters and photos from the independence struggle and Balkan wars. A shop sells the monks' wine, preserves and oil, and there's a traditional café just above the monastery, overlooking a vineyard.

10

SKIÁTHOS' TOP BEACHES

Although almost all the island's **beaches** are sandy, some are very narrow. On the south coast, every one has loungers and at least one bar or taverna pumping out loud music; most have watersports too. To get away from it all, head for the harder-to-reach sands on the north coast. The famous Banana beaches, at the island's southwestern tip, are currently blighted by the development of a vast new resort and hard to access – instead, try some of our favourites listed below, clockwise from town:

Tsougriá An islet in the bay opposite Skiáthos Town, with excursion boats shuttling back and forth from the old port three or four times daily. A favourite of locals, it has two spectacular sand beaches, each with a taverna.

Vromólimnos The prettiest of the Kalamáki peninsula beaches, fine-sand Vromólimnos is a bit of a walk from bus stop 13, and hence a little quieter than many south-coast sands. It has a couple of cafés with fine sunset views, and a busy waterski operation.

Koukounariés Huge stretch of sand at the end of the bus route which is arguably the island's finest beach, and certainly one of its busiest. Wooden walkways traverse the sand to a series of *kantínas*, there's a harbour for excursion boats and every imaginable form of watersport including snorkelling and diving with Skiathos Diving, one of the island's best outfits (☎6977 081 444, ⓦskiathosdiving.gr). Behind the beach, a small salt lake, Strofyliá, sits in the midst of a grove of pine trees – all of it a protected reserve.

Ayía Eléni About 600m from bus stop 25 in Koukounariés, Ayía Eléni is a broad, sandy beach with wonderful views west towards the mountainous mainland. Family-oriented, it has a couple of beach bars and pedaloes and kayaks to rent.

Mandhráki Dunes and a protected pine forest back Mandhráki, a sandy beach with views of Mount Pílio. Among the island's least developed – though it does boast a large snack-bar – it is accessed by a path from bus stop 23 in Koukounariés, or a sandy but driveable track that follows the coast round past Ayía Eléni beach then circles back to join the main road near bus stop 21.

Eliás Next to Mandhráki, and accessed on the same tracks, Eliás lacks the views (it faces north, straight out to sea), but is even more attractive and spacious, with plenty of sand, child-friendly shallow water and a breezy café-bar serving *souvláki*, salads and omelettes. The far end, away from the café, is generally nudist.

Megálos Asélinos From Troúlos village, a side road leads 3.5km north through a lush valley to Megálos Asélinos, a large and exposed beach of gritty sand. There's a big taverna where many excursion boats stop for lunch, but it's a lovely, unspoilt spot at the end of the day when they've all headed home.

Kástro In a small cove set steeply below Kástro (see p.678), this beach can be very crowded in the middle of the day when the tour boats arrive, but is delightful early or late – though it loses the sun early. There's a wonderfully ramshackle snack-bar with a shower of cold river water.

Laláría This famous beach, nestling near the northernmost point of Skiáthos, is only accessible by taxi- or excursion-boat from town. With steep cliffs rising behind a white-pebble shore and an artistic natural arch, it's undeniably beautiful; three sea-grottoes just east rate a stop on most round-the-island trips.

Below the monastery, a signed **path** leads north, past restored **Ayíou Haralámbou** monastery, full of cats and chickens kept by the caretaker, and on past **Panayía Dombó** chapel and then to **Panayía Kardhási** on the way to Kástro.

Kástro
Daily sunrise–sunset • Free

Kástro, occupying a windswept headland at the northernmost tip of Skiáthos, was the island's main population centre throughout the Middle Ages. The **fortified settlement**, established for security from pirate raids, thrived under Byzantine, Venetian and Turkish control until its abandonment around 1830, when the new Greek state stamped hard on piracy, and the population left to build the modern capital. Most of the buildings were dismantled and the materials reused elsewhere, so all that's left now are the remains of the **defences**, half a dozen **churches** (there were once twenty) and a **mosque**. You enter the rocky outcrop across a narrow, stone ridge – a superb natural defence once enhanced by walls and a drawbridge. Inside, the remains are beautifully maintained and well signed; there's fresh spring water and tables where you can picnic.

If you come by boat you're unlikely to escape the crowds; driving or walking involves an exceptionally steep, narrow cobbled track, but does give the chance to arrive early or late, and perhaps get the place to yourself.

ACCOMMODATION
SKIÁTHOS

Much of Skiáthos' accommodation, especially villas and places with pools, is block-booked by package companies; in Skiáthos Town, there are dozens of little pensions and small rooms places scattered throughout the backstreets. You may find it easier to check the island's website (ⓦ skiathos.gr) or go through a local agent. The local room-owners' association kiosk on the quayside (ⓣ 24270 22990) is open long hours in high season. Everywhere is heavily booked in Aug when rates may double; there are plenty of bargains out of season.

SKIÁTHOS TOWN

Atlas Papadhiamándi 39 ⓣ 6987 618 680, ⓦ atlashotelskiathos.gr. Very modern, well-equipped rooms right at the heart of things. Most are in a courtyard set back from the street, so quiet but lacking views; a couple have balconies overlooking the action. **€70**

Architectonika Mitropolítou Ananíou 20 ⓣ ⓣ 24270 23633, ⓦ hotelarchitectonika.gr. Self-styled design hotel, Architectonika has classy modern rooms just a few paces from the Papadiamantis House and close to ferry arrivals. There's a small café in reception and a helpful owner. **€70**

Bourtzi Moraïtou 8 ⓣ 24270 21304, ⓦ hotelbourtzi.gr. Boutique hotel just off Papadhiamándi, with designer decor and a courtyard pool; rooms boast marble floors, flat-screen TVs and all mod cons. Impressive, though the atmosphere can seem more business than island. **€190**

Pension Margarita Ayíou Nikoláou 23 ⓣ 24270 21288, ⓦ pensionmargarita.gr. High on the hill above the new harbour, near the much-signed *Windmill* restaurant, *Margarita* is a traditional rooms place, simply furnished but good value, with a/c and fridge. There are great views from the front rooms and roof terrace, where you can enjoy breakfast or coffee made in the well-equipped communal kitchen. The helpful owner often meets arriving ferries, and will pick up or drop off at the airport. **€45**

Pension Nikolas Evangelístrias ⓣ 24270 23062, ⓦ nikolaspension.gr. Very central place, between Papadhiamándi and the old port, in two buildings facing each other across an internal courtyard, tucked away from the street so reasonably quiet. The simple rooms all have a/c, fridge and TV, with balconies overlooking the courtyard. April–Oct. **€60**

VROMÓLIMNOS

★**Skiathos Holidays** ⓣ 24270 21596, ⓦ skiathos-holidays.com. A group of elegant modern studios, apartments and villas in a great location, in a garden behind the beach. All options have cooking facilities, generous outdoor space and good modern bathrooms, plus there's a garden bar. **€90**

EATING AND DRINKING

By Greek standards – just about any standards in fact – eating in Skiáthos is expensive. The best places also get very busy, so booking is advisable.

KIÁTHOS TOWN

kroyiali Club strip (the coast road beyond the ew harbour) ☎ 24270 21330. Arguably the best seafood in town, with fresh fish laid out on ice to inspect. Attractive eafront setting, too, and reasonable prices; fish priced by weight; fish soup €6.80; octopus €11.30; shrimp spaghetti 13; swordfish souvláki €16.50. Daily noon–11.30pm.

Alexandros Old town backstreets ☎ 24270 22431. raditional Greek old-town restaurant, signposted from Platía Trión Ierarhón but still hard to find, packed every night thanks to some of the lowest prices in town moussaka €7.20; lamb in lemon sauce €9; kalamári €7). There's live Greek music most nights. Service can suffer from the crowds – book or be prepared to wait. Daily 6pm–midnight.

Bakaliko Club strip ☎ 24270 22669. Among the best of the restaurants in the club strip, with mock decor of a traditional Greek grocer's, seating on a deck over the water and decently priced, Turkish-influenced food (taş kebab at €8.80, for example, or Smyrnian meat balls, €8.60); live acoustic Greek music some nights. Daily noon–midnight.

La Cucina di Maria Up the steps from the old port ☎ 24270 24168. Excellent pizza, pasta and creative salads are served at this restaurant behind Trís Ierárhes church. The decor inside is eclectic, though you might prefer to sit out on the balcony, or the courtyard. The downside is price; simple pasta and pizza dishes start from around €12, though portions are large. Daily 6pm–1am.

Marmita Evangelístrias 30 ☎ 24270 2170. Elegant modern Greek restaurant in a courtyard setting in the heart of town, serving traditional dishes alongside more adventurous options. Excellent salads such as rock samphire with tomato, onion and feta (€8.50), and mains including slow-cooked pork marinated with honey and mustard (€13.50), steamed cod with mussels and vegetables (€16.50) or roast rabbit in sweet wine (€14.50). Daily 6–11pm.

Mesoyia Old town backstreets ☎ 24270 21440. As close as Skiathos Town gets to a simple cheap-and-cheerful taverna (though still around €40 for two, with house wine) featuring grilled and mayireftá dishes, plus daily changing seafood, such as prawn yiouvétsi (casserole with pasta). Daily 6pm–midnight.

PROFÍTIS ILÍAS

Platanos 4km from Skiáthos Town ☎ 6932 413 539. Near the island's highest point, Platanos has fabulous views over town and towards Skópelos and Évvia. There's a decent taverna menu (daily specials €8.50–10.50), plus breakfast, omelettes, sandwiches or simply coffee and bakláva; book ahead if you want a decent view in the evening. Daily 10.30am–11pm.

KOLIÓS

Infinity Blue Koliós Bay (bus stop 15) ☎ 24270 49750, ⓦ infinityblue.gr. With lovely vistas from a romantic, hillside setting, Infinity Blue has a Greek/Mediterranean menu and a refined ambience, with proper linen and wine glasses. Fine steaks from €20, plus pasta, risotto and plenty of meat and seafood dishes for €13–18. Daily 6pm–12.30am.

NIGHTLIFE AND ENTERTAINMENT

SKIÁTHOS TOWN

There are plenty of bars and pubs on Papadhiamándi and the nearby old-town backstreets, but the coolest places are overlooking the old port or out on the "club strip" at the start of the coast road beyond the yacht marina.

Attikon Papadhiamándi ☎ 6972 706 305. This summer open-air cinema, at the bottom of Papadhiamándi by the museum, has been showing Mamma Mia! at least three times a week since the film's release; new movies screen on other nights. Jun–Sept; film times vary.

BBC Club strip ☎ 6980 990 741. Club-strip venues seem to be annually changeable, and operate only in July and Aug, but BBC is bigger and longer-lived than most: a riotous crowd inside and a deck jutting out over the shallows to chill out on. Summer Fri–Sun and some weeknights 10pm–6am.

Rock'n'Roll Old port ☎ 24270 22944, ⓦ skiathos-rocknroll.gr. The busiest of a bunch of virtually identical bars on the steps leading up to Platía Trión Ierarhón, Rock'n'Roll has outdoor seating with bean bags and scatter cushions; inside, a DJ serves up mainstream rock, Latin and dance music. May–Sept daily 7pm–4am.

Skópelos

SKÓPELOS is bigger and more rugged than Skiáthos, and its concessions to tourism are lower-key and in better taste, despite a boom in recent years fuelled by the filming here of *Mamma Mia!*. Much of the countryside, especially the southwest coast, really is as spectacular as it appears in the movie, with a series of pretty cove beaches backed by extensive pine forests as well as olive groves and orchards of plums (**prunes** are a local speciality), apricots, pears and almonds. **Skópelos Town (Hóra)** and **Glóssa**, the two main towns, are among the prettiest in the Sporades.

10

ARRIVAL AND DEPARTURE

BY FERRY

In summer, Hellenic Seaways fast catamarans and ferries (Ⓦhsw.gr), Aegean Flying Dolphins hydrofoils (Ⓦaegeanflyingdolphins.gr) and ANES (Ⓦanes.gr) and Aqua (Ⓦaquaferries.gr) ferries run regularly to Alónissos, Skiáthos and the mainland. Some call at Loutráki, the port for Glóssa (and known as Glóssa on ferry and hydrofoil schedules), as well as Skópelos Town. Also in summer Skyros Shipping (Ⓦsne.gr) plies twice a week to Kými on Évvia, via Alónissos, and from there on to Skýros, while the ANES ferry *Proteus* goes from Glóssa to Mandoúdhi in northern Évvia. The rest of the year Hellenic Seaways and ANES run three daily ferries or fast cats to Alónissos, Skiáthos and Vólos, most calling at both of the island's ports. Hydrofoil and fast cat connections to flights in

Skiáthos can be very busy: try to book in advance.

Tickets and agencies There are ticket booths on the doc in Skópelos Town at busy times; otherwise the Hellen Seaways agent (daily 6.30–7.15am & 9am–10pm Ⓣ24270 22767), opposite the harbour gate, sells ticket for all the boats. Many others are nearby, with a couple c agencies by the port in Loutráki.

Destinations Alónissos (summer 4–7 daily, winter 3 daily 20–35min); Áyios Konstandínos (summer 1–3 daily; 2h 50min–4hr 45min); Kými, Évvia (summer 2 weekly; 3h 5min); Mandoúdhi, Évvia (from Glóssa only; summer weekly; 1hr 30min); Skiáthos (summer 4–8 daily, winter daily; 35min–1hr 35min); Skýros (summer 2 weekly; 6h 15min); Thessaloníki (summer 4 weekly, 3hr 40min); Vólo (summer 4 daily, winter 3 daily; 2hr–4hr 25min).

INFORMATION

Tourist information There's no tourist office on the island, but useful sites include Ⓦskopelosweb.gr and Ⓦskopelos.net.

Services Several banks with ATMs are on the quayside in

Skópelos Town; the post office is on Dhoulídhi, just off Platía Plátanos ("Souvláki Square"), directly up from the ferry harbour. English-language newspapers are sold at a shop just off Souvláki Square.

GETTING AROUND

By bus Services run from Skópelos Town across to the island's south coast, then along the south and west coast past all the major beaches; in summer at least a dozen daily buses go via Stáfylos to Kastáni – around half of them continue to Glóssa and Loutráki. The bus terminus is on the seafront by the ferry dock. A free bus for ANES ferry passengers runs between Loutráki and Skópelos Town.

By car and scooter There are numerous car and scooter rental outlets near the ferry dock in Hóra, around the corner of the coast road and the main road heading inland, and along this inland road; they include Magic (Ⓣ22420 23250, Ⓦskopelos.net/magiccars) and Maxi

(Ⓣ24240 24380, Ⓦmaxiautos.gr).

By taxi The central taxi stand is to the left as you leave the ferry dock in Hóra.

By bike Skópelos Cycling (Mon–Sat 10am–2pm & 6–9pm; Ⓣ6947 023 145), with a small shop by the back of the old olive factory, rents out high-quality bikes and runs occasional bike tours.

Boat trips A huge variety of boat trips is on offer around the harbour, at prices ranging from around €10 for a return beach shuttle to €30 for a trip to Alónissos; island circuits, many of them *Mamma Mia!* themed, go for around €20.

Skópelos Town and around

SKÓPELOS TOWN (Hóra) pours off a hill on the west flank of a wide, oval bay: a cascade of handsome mansions and slate-domed churches below the ruined Venetian **kástro**. Away from the waterside commercial strip, the town is endearingly time-warped – indeed among the most unspoilt in the islands – with vernacular domestic architecture and wonderfully idiosyncratic shops of a sort long vanished elsewhere. There are also a couple of **museums**, hard to find in the labyrinthine backstreets.

Folklore Museum

June–Sept Mon–Sat 10am–2pm & 7–10pm, but unreliable • €3 • ☎ 24240 23494

The **Folklore Museum** contains a fine local collection of weaving, embroidery and costumes, mostly from the late nineteenth and early twentieth centuries, with detailed panels explaining local customs and the religious calendar.

Old Skopelitian Mansion Museum

Tues–Sun 10am–2pm & 6–9pm • €3 • ☎ 24240 22940

The **Old Skopelitian Mansion Museum**, also known as the Vakratsa Museum, was the former home of the island's doctor – subsequently occupied by his three daughters, all spinsters and all doctors. Left to the town by the last surviving daughter, it is displayed much as it was when they lived here; a comfortable, bourgeois home full of everyday items, furniture, clothing and books.

10

Beaches

The town **beach** doesn't amount to much, but there are a couple of excellent alternatives very close by: towards **Stáfylos** is a busy road around which cluster many accommodation options; north to **Glystéri** is less populated.

Stáfylos

4km from Hóra • First stop on the bus route round the south coast

Stáfylos is the closest decent beach to Hóra, though it gets very crowded in season. There's a noisy beach bar, so if it's peace you're after, walk to the end of the beach and climb over the headland to larger, more scenic, sand-and-fine-gravel **Velanió**, where there's a summer-only *kantína* and a bit of a nudist scene.

Agnóndas and Limnonári

About 3km and 4km beyond Stáfylos respectively • On the bus route

The beautiful bay of **AGNÓNDAS** has very much the feel of traditional old Greece, with yachts moored and a pretty fishing harbour where the water laps right up to the tables of several tavernas. There's not much of a beach, though, so for that follow the side road to **Limnonári**, about 1km west, for 300m of white sand in a steep-sided bay, one of the island's finest.

Glystéri

Less than 4km northwest of Skópelos Town • Small boats run several times a day (€5 return) in summer from the harbour in Skópelos Town

Glystéri is a small sand-and-pebble beach at the base of an almost completely enclosed bay. Plenty of people brave the narrow, steep road and many more arrive by shuttle boat, so it can get busy.

ACCOMMODATION   SKÓPELOS TOWN AND AROUND

There are numerous rooms for rent in the backstreets of Skópelos Town but in high season everything is very booked up. In midsummer a Rooms Association office (☎ 24240 24567) opens in the lane leading up to Souvláki Square; a wider choice, including apartments and hotels across the island, can be arranged through helpful Madro Travel, by the old port (☎ 24240 22145), or check the useful island websites (see opposite). August prices can be double those for the rest of the year. Most of these places will pick you up from the harbour if you let them know which ferry you're on.

★**Mando** Stáfylos ☎ 24240 23917, ⓦ mandobeachfront.com. Among the best accommodation on the island, *Mando* is friendly and quiet with stone-floored, a/c rooms (plus new superior rooms and a villa) set among manicured lawns where steps lead down to a private swimming platform. There are fridges and tea- and coffee-making equipment in the rooms, plus an outdoor communal kitchen area where an excellent home-made breakfast (included) is served. Room **€60**, villa **€225**

Pension Sotos Harbourfront ☎ 24240 22549, ⓦ skopelos.net/sotos. A budget option, this rambling old house is right at the heart of things, set back from the middle of the harbour behind the giant plane trees.

WALKING ON SKÓPELOS

Away from the main roads there's plenty of **walking** on Skópelos. Long-time resident Heather Parsons battles to maintain paths – volunteer helpers welcome – and leads spring/autumn walks (☎6945 249 328, ✆skopelos-walks.com), as well as publishing a hiking guide, *Skopelos Trails*. Among the better hikes are those east of Skópelos Town, where three historic **monasteries**, Metamórfosis, Evangelístrias and Prodhrómou (all open daily roughly 8am–1pm & 5–8pm), stand on the slopes of Mount Paloúki. Near Glóssa, there's a beautiful 45-minute trail to the renovated village of **Palió Klíma**, via the island's oldest settlement, **Athéato** (Mahalás), which is slowly being restored by outsiders, and the foreigner-owned hamlet of **Áyii Anáryiri**.

10

Inside, the pine furnishings seem redolent of the 1970s, though all the simple rooms have a/c; go for the quieter ones at the back. There's a communal kitchen and sunny courtyards. **€30**

Seaview Studios Glyfonéri ☎6972 383 019, ✆skopelosweb.gr/en/studios/seaviews. Modern block of studios and apartments on the hillside above Glyfonéri beach (on the Glystéri road less than 1km from the kástro in town, but steeply uphill), with stunning views towards Alónissos. Newly furnished, they often have exceptionally good off-season deals. **€40**

Skopelos Village Town Beach ☎24240 22517, ✆skopelosvillagehotel.com. Self-catering complex, 600m east around the bay, with luxurious studios and suites set among landscaped grounds with two pools and a restaurant. The "Seabreeze" suites are worth the extra for their modern design and sleek bathrooms, though it's only good value if you get an off-season deal. **€150**

Sofia's Garden Studios Old town ☎24240 22218. In the heart of the old town, hidden in the backstreets above Souvláki Square, *Sofia's* has three storeys of good-value a/c studios of various sizes tucked away in a lovely garden setting (some on the top floor have sea views). **€45**

★ **Thea Home** Ring road ☎24240 22859, ✆theahomehotel.com. Lovely rooms (some pretty small) and a family apartment are set in the old house, all with fridge, a/c and sweeping views from the top of the town; modern studios and a pool are immediately below. Bikes are available (free) and there's an excellent home-made breakfast (extra). Room **€60**, apartment **€100**

EATING AND DRINKING

The seafront is lined with cafés and tavernas, the best of which are up at the old port end; for something more modest, aptly nicknamed Souvláki Square is packed with decent fast-food outfits.

Glyfoneri Taverna Glyfonéri Beach ☎24247 70020. Barely a kilometre out of town towards Glystéri (though steeply up and down), this is a classic Greek beachfront taverna, perfect for whiling away a slow afternoon with the added bonus of free loungers on the beach and views of Alónissos. Well-prepared classics such as moussaka and kalamári (both €8.50) plus fresh fish (sardines €8; fish of the day €12–15). Daily 9am–10.30pm.

Gorgones Old town ☎24240 24709. Popular place (beside the well-signed *Oionos Blue Bar*), with tables in a stepped alley, garden courtyard and an indoor space. There's a short menu of good Greek food at fair prices (Skopelos cheese pie €5.50; spit-roasted pork €8.50), though occasionally erratic service. Daily 7pm–midnight.

Kymata Old port ☎24240 22381. About the oldest taverna on Skópelos and practically the last on the harbour, this is a shrine of quality traditional cooking such as papoutsákia (€7) or veal yiouvétsi (casserole with pasta; €11). Daily lunch and dinner.

Kyratso's Kitchen Old port ☎24240 23184. Named after Kyratso, the matriarch of the family, this is a wonderful traditional taverna (relocated from Glystéri beach), where the daily specials are displayed in the kitchen. Simple dishes like goat with fresh tomato (€14.50) or pork with prunes (€12) are best, or try the speciality, black fish (€15). There's live music every evening from 7.30pm. Daily noon–11.30pm.

★ **Mouria** Agnóndas ☎6991 230 230. One of three simple harbourside tavernas, *Mouria* is a big, unpretentious place with fair prices for fish (priced by weight) and plenty of well-prepared Greek dishes (kalamári or moussaka €8.50; stuffed squid €16.50; shrimp spaghetti €12.50), plus a decent house wine. Free sun-loungers for customers. Daily lunch and dinner.

★ **Mousses** Beyond the town beach ☎24240 24414. Classy, slightly upmarket place on the coast road east of town; in the evenings, you'll need to book for the waterside tables, looking back over the bay towards the houses. There's excellent fish and traditional Greek dishes – try stuffed squid (huge portion €16), fish *stifádho* (€15) or pork with plums (€15). Daily 11am–12.30am.

Perivoli Old town ☎24240 23758. A beautiful spot in the garden courtyard of an old house, up an alley just above Souvláki Square. The Greek/Mediterranean menu includes innovative starters and salads (€7–7.50) followed by pasta and risotto or modern Greek dishes like grilled lamb with oghurt and coriander (€12) or shrimp and chicken *souvláki* (€11) – plus a selection of wines by the glass. Daily pm–midnight.

oupa Old Olive Factory ☎ 24240 24494. Classy, modern reek place in the Old Olive Factory area, where there's

also a good Italian restaurant, and pizza/burger take-away. Starters include the likes of tzatzíki with lemon and wild fennel (€6.20); mains from range moussaka or meatballs with wild rice (both €11.50) to local goat chops (€13.90), plus pasta and risotto. Daily 6.30pm–12.30am.

NIGHTLIFE

Anatoli Kástro ☎ 24240 22851. Veteran rembétika musician Yiorgos Xintaris performs at this tumbledown place on top of the kástro, where there's live music nightly from late June to early Sept. They also serve food, and by day there's a café with incomparable views. Daily 10am–late.

Merkourio (Mercurius) Between Souvláki Square and the Folklore Museum ☎ 24240 24593. Just up from the ferry jetty, this cool bar has views over the harbour and a

gallery often featuring local artists. Cocktails are served on candlelit terraces, to a soft-rock and Latin soundtrack; also open during the day for breakfast and coffee. Easter–Sept daily 7pm–4am.

Oionos Blue Bar Old town ☎ 6942 406 136. Small, often crowded bar in an old house, well signed inland from the centre of the harbour, with a jazz, blues and world-music playlist, plus a staggering variety of imported beers and whiskies. Outdoor seating in the alley too. Daily 10am–2am.

10

Around the island

Many of the island's best, and certainly the most accessible, **beaches** lie just off the main road and bus route, which heads south across the island from Hóra and then up the west coast to Glóssa. The island's **northeast coast** is harder to reach, with just a couple of paved roads from Glóssa to Perivolioú or Áyios Ioánnis Kastrí.

Pánormos

PÁNORMOS is the biggest resort outside Skópelos Town, though still very understated and low-key. An extensive pebble beach lines the expansive bay, with plenty of tavernas (most offering free loungers for customers), shops and rooms. Adjoining **Blo** inlet is a beautiful, quiet anchorage, though there's no beach here.

Miliá and the Mamma Mia! beaches

The wide-open spaces of **Miliá**, immediately beyond Pánormos, comprise two 400m sweeps of grey sand and pebbles opposite Dhassía islet, divided by a headland; each has a seasonal bar/kantína. Having found fame as the *Mamma Mia!* beach, **Kastáni**, almost adjacent to Miliá, has become very crowded, with a big beach bar pumping out dance music. Nonetheless, it's a beautiful place, with fine sand and crystal-clear water. Beyond unattractive **Élios** (**Néo Klíma**), isolated **Armenópetra** boasts two spectacular beaches either side of a point. There's no shade and no facilities, but great views of Glossá on the hillside above.

Glóssa

Skópelos' second town, **GLÓSSA**, 26km from Hóra near the northwest tip of the island, is spectacularly arrayed in stepped, hillside tiers, high above the coast. A traditional, rural place where many of the houses have overhanging balconies and lush gardens, it is explored along narrow, steep, mostly **car-free lanes** (there's an unsigned car park behind the church on the main road), with breathtaking **views** around almost every corner. Apart from wandering the photogenic alleys and grabbing a coffee or meal, there's not a great deal to do here, and the only official accommodation in town is in rented houses (rarely available locally); there is a small **Folklore Museum** just above the main square, though (10am–2.30pm & 5.30–9pm, Thurs 10am–2.30pm only, closed Mon; free).

Loutráki

LOUTRÁKI, some 3km steeply down a serpentine road from Glóssa (or on foot by a shorter, well-signed *kalderími*), is a pretty little place with views of Skiáthos. The port of the larger town, it has a line of cafés and tavernas around the ferry dock, an archeological kiosk with information on local sites and island history, lots of **yachts** at anchor and a narrow pebble beach.

Perivolioú

A narrow, winding road through mature pine forest leads to beautiful little **Perivolioú** beach, some 7km from Glóssa and close to the island's northern tip. There's ice-clear water and no development at all at this sandy cove, nor at nearby **Hondroyiórgis** beach, reached along a driveable track. Continue on this track, and you'll join the road down to Áyios Ioánnis Kastrí.

Áyios Ioánnis Kastrí

The tiny sand cove at **Áyios Ioánnis Kastrí** is one of the busiest on the island, thanks to its position at the base of the *Mamma Mia!* wedding chapel. Perched on a rock monolith (105 steps lead up), the chapel is almost ridiculously photogenic, and attracts tour boats from Skiáthos as well as being an essential halt on the round-island trip. Late afternoon, when they've all left, is generally the quietest time. There's an excellent **snack-bar** (summer daily 10am–sunset) here, where they serve a mean Greek salad.

ACTIVITIES   **AROUND THE ISLAND**

Watersports There are ski boats offering all the usual rides at Pánormos, Miliá and Kastáni. An excellent kayaking outfit, Kayaking Skopelos (☎6983 211 298, ⓦkayakinggreece.com), based in Glóssa, runs day-trips, sunset paddles and longer expeditions.

ACCOMMODATION AND EATING

Adrina Beach Hotel Between Pánormos and Miliá ☎24240 23371, ⓦadrina.gr. Beautiful, ivy-clad, four-star bungalow complex tumbling down a hillside to its own private beach. Wonderful sea views from many of the rooms and duplex maisonettes, plus there's a seawater pool and taverna. Adjacent is the still more glamorous, five-star *Adrina Resort & Spa*, with the same management and contact details. **€180**

★**Agnanti** Glóssa ☎24240 33606, ⓦagnanti.com.gr. Traditional taverna, well signposted in the heart of the old town, with upmarket dishes served indoors and on a terrace with spectacular views; book ahead to be sure of the view. Starters (€4–7.50) include the likes of black taramasaláta or octopus with fáva; mains might be chicken dolmádhes (€13), slow-cooked pork with prawns (€11) or

kingfish fillet (€19). Daily 11am–11pm.

Milia Apartments Miliá ☎24242 23998, ⓦmiliaapartments.com. Modern complex with double studios and triple and duplex quad apartments, most with great views; breakfast (included) is served on the terrace, and there's a decent taverna nearby. Before the crowds arrive, you have your own private beach. **€85**

Selenunda Hotel Loutráki ☎24240 34073, ⓦhotelselenunda.com. High above the harbour at Loutráki, the peaceful *Selenunda* has stunning views from every room. All the simple tile-floor rooms come with a/c, TV and kitchenette, and bigger family apartments are available. Steps lead down to the waterfront, but with luggage you may want to call to be picked up. **€50**

Alónissos

The end of the line for ferries and hydrofoils, **ALÓNISSOS** is more rugged and wild than its neighbours, and attracts significantly fewer visitors. Some of Greece's cleanest sea surrounds the island, and while the **beaches** rarely match those of Skópelos or Skiáthos for sand or scenery, the white pebbles on most of them further enhance the impression of gin-clear water. The cleanliness of the sea is partly thanks to Alónissos' relative isolation, but largely due to its being the only permanently inhabited member of a mini-archipelago at the east end of the Sporades which has been designated a marine park (see p.690). Inland, it's green; pine forest, olive groves and fruit orchards cover the southern half, while a dense maquis of arbutus, heather, kermes oak and lentisk cloaks the north.

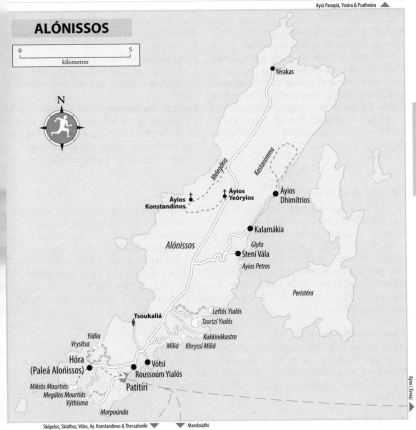

Kyrá Panayiá, Yioúra & Psathoúra

ALÓNISSOS

0 — 5
kilometres

N

Yérakas

10

Meleyákia

Kostanórema

Áyios Konstandínos
Áyios Yeóryios
Áyios Dhimítrios

Kalamákia

Alónissos

Glyfa
Stení Vála

Ayios Petros

Peristéra

Leftós Yialós
Tzortzí Yialós

Tsoukaliá

Kokkinókastro

Yidália
Vrysítsa

Miliá   Khryssí Miliá

Hóra
(Paleá Alónissos)
Vótsi
Roussoúm Yialós

Mikrós Mourtiás
Megálos Mourtiás
Výthisma
Patitíri

Marpoúnda

Skópelos, Skiáthos, Vólos, Áy. Konstandínos & Thessaloníki   Mandoúdhi

Kými (Évvia)

ARRIVAL AND DEPARTURE

BY FERRY

All ferries to Alónissos dock at the harbour in Patitíri. In summer, Hellenic Seaways fast catamarans and ferries (⟨w⟩ hsw.gr), Aegean Flying Dolphins hydrofoils (⟨w⟩ aegeanflyingdolphins.gr) and ANES (⟨w⟩ anes.gr) and Aqua (⟨w⟩aquaferries.gr) ferries run regular daily services to Skópelos, Skiáthos and the mainland. Also in season, Skyros Shipping (⟨w⟩ sne.gr) runs twice a week to Kými on Évvia and from there on to Skýros, while the ANES ferry Proteus plies to Mandoúdhi in northern Évvia. The rest of the year Hellenic Seaways and ANES offer three daily ferries or fast cats to Skópelos, Skiáthos and Vólos. Hydrofoil and fast cat connections to or from flights in Skiáthos can be very busy: try to book in advance.

ALÓNISSOS

Operators and tickets There are numerous travel and ticket agencies facing the harbour in Patitíri, which sell tickets for all ferries and hydrofoils; most helpful and efficient is Albedo Travel (☎ 24240 65804, ⟨w⟩ alonissosholidays.com), at the bottom of the western (left-hand) street.

Destinations Áyios Konstandínos (summer 1–3 daily; 2hr 25min–5hr 30min); Kými, Évvia (summer 2 weekly; 2hr 20min); Mandoúdhi, Évvia (summer 2 weekly; 1hr 50min); Skiáthos (summer 4–6 daily, winter 3 daily; 1hr 10min–2hr 30min); Skópelos (summer 4–6 daily, winter 3 daily; 20–30min); Skýros (summer 2 weekly; 5hr 30min); Thessaloníki (summer 4 weekly; 4hr 10min); Vólos (summer 3–4 daily, winter 3 daily; 2hr 40min–5hr 15min).

INFORMATION

Services There's a bank with an ATM and a post office on the eastern shopping street leading up from the harbour in Patitíri. English-language newspapers are sold near the bottom of the western shopping street in Patitíri.

Tourist information There's no tourist office on the island, but useful sites include ⟨w⟩ alonissos.gr and ⟨w⟩ alonissosholidays.com.

10

By bus There are just two summer-only bus routes on Alónissos: from Patitíri up to Hóra (daily 9am–2pm & 5pm–midnight roughly hourly, more in early evening; €1.60) and to Stení Vála (3 daily; €1.70). In Patitíri the bus stop is on the harbour at the bottom of the eastern inland street; tickets cannot be bought on the bus, so get them from the *Avra Café*, opposite the stop, or from shops in Hóra or Stení Vála. In high season Alonissos Transport (☎ 6972 282 848), with a harbourfront booth, runs return trips to a different beach every day (€5–10), and to Hóra in the evening.

By taxi The taxi stand in Patitíri is on the harbour opposit the bus stand.

By car and scooter There are numerous car and scoote rental outlets near the harbour, including Albedo Trave (see p.685) and others in the inland street immediatel' beyond it.

Boat trips and excursions Various boat trips are on offe around the harbour; the best marine park (see p.690) tour cost around €40 a head (including lunch and drinks), bu check their itinera ries, as some don't go far in. Albedo Trave (see p.685) runs walking, diving and sea-kayak excursions.

Patitíri and around

The island's southeastern corner contains almost its entire population and most of its visitors. **PATITÍRI**, port and de facto capital, occupies a sheltered bay flanked by steep, pine-tufted cliffs and ringed by bars, cafés and tavernas. It's a bit soulless – much is modern, built after the 1965 earthquake (see below) – but it has tried to compensate with a stone-paved waterfront and general tidy-up, while the unassuming streets shelter some unexpectedly fancy shops. The waterfront **MOM Information Centre** (daily 10am–4pm; free; ⓦmom.gr), above the *Avra Café*, next to the *Alkyon Hotel*, has models and multimedia displays about the endangered **monk seal** (see p.689).

Alonissos Museum

Harbour • Daily: May & Sept 11am–6pm; June–Aug 11am–7pm • €4 • ⓦalonissosmuseum.com

In an unmissable stone building above the western side of the harbour, the **Alonissos Museum** is crammed with local artwork, traditional costumes, reconstructed island interiors, war memorabilia, wine-making equipment, and exhibits on piracy and seafaring.

Roussoúm Yialós and Vótsi

Immediately outside Patitíri, **ROUSSOÚM YIALÓS** and adjoining **VÓTSI**, each with a little fishing harbour, are virtually suburbs. You can walk to the **beach** at Roussoúm, down steps from town, which is considerably more pleasant than swimming in Patitíri itself. Both offer pleasant, good-value rooms and tavernas.

Hóra

HÓRA (Paleá Alónissos), the island's original settlement, was severely damaged by a Sporades-wide earthquake in March 1965, after which most of the reluctant population was compulsorily moved to Patitíri; the issue was essentially forced in 1977 by the school's closure and cutting off of electricity. Outsiders later acquired the

---

HIKING ON ALÓNISSOS

Although its often harsh, rugged landscape might suggest otherwise, of all the Sporades, Alónissos caters best to **hikers**. Fifteen routes have been surveyed, numbered and signposted (though signs and waymarks are starting to deteriorate): many provide just short walks from a beach to a village or the main road, but some can be combined to make meaty circular treks. The best of these are trail #11 from Áyios Dhimítrios, up the Kastanórema and then back along the coast on #15 (2hr 30min), or trails #13 plus #12, Melegákia to Áyios Konstandínos and Áyios Yeóryios (just over 2hr, including some road walking to return to the start). A couple of local walking guides are available in shops in town.

abandoned houses for virtually nothing and restored them; only a few locals still live here, which gives the village a very twee, un-Greek atmosphere, abetted by multiple knick-knack and crafts shops. But it's stunningly picturesque, with great views as far as Mount Áthos in clear conditions. For much of the year, there are more hedgehogs than people about; the place only really comes to life – noisily so – on midsummer evenings. As an alternative to the bus ride, you can walk on a well-preserved *kalderími*, or footpath (45min uphill, 30min down), signposted off Patitíri's western inland street, almost at the edge of town.

10

Southern beaches

Numerous small cove beaches surround Alónissos' southern tip. Closest to Patitíri is **Výthisma** – less than 1km down a track off the road to **Marpoúnda** beach (monopolized by an all-inclusive Italian complex) and then a scramble down into the cove. The grey sand-and-pebble beach is pretty, and part nudist, but without facilities or shade. **Megálos Mourtiás** is just a short swim further round, and there is a path which continues that way, but most people get here on the steep paved road from Hóra. With bright white pebbles and two tavernas, it's crowded and noisy. **Mikrós Mourtiás**, just west, is served by a well-maintained footpath from Hóra (#1), or you can get most of the way down on a driveable dirt track: another enclosed cove, it claims to be a nudist beach – though in practice it doesn't seem to be. Immediately north of Hóra, visible tucked into their respective finger-like inlets, are compact **Vrysítsa** and **Yiália** (with a picturesque windmill), both of which have more sand than pebbles, but no facilities.

ACCOMMODATION	PATITÍRI AND AROUND

Most accommodation is in or around Patitíri; the local room-owners' association (☎ 24240 66188, ⓦ alonissos-rooms.gr) has a booth on the waterfront, while Albedo Travel (☎ 24240 65804, ⓦ alonissosholidays.com) and other nearby travel agents handle hotels, studios and villas across the island: some of the best houses in Hóra can be found at ⓦ alonissos-homes.eu. Most places will offer transport up the steep streets if you let them know when you're arriving.

PATITÍRI

Angelos Apartments Western side of town ☎ 6973 955 267, ⓦ angelosalonissos.com. Lovely, well-equipped modern studios and apartments, almost all with balconies offering fine views. In town but peaceful, and with an exceptionally friendly welcome. **€60**

Ikion Eco Hotel High up on the eastern side of town, behind the Town Hall ☎ 24240 66360, ⓦ ikion.com. Boutique-style hotel, classily decorated in shades of cream and white. Standard rooms are fairly small, but some have great views, which the larger superior rooms mostly lack; all have fridge, a/c and TV. Excellent home-made breakfast included. **€95**

Nereides Hotel Paliohorafína, above the western edge of town ☎ 24240 65643, ⓦ nereides. gr. This pleasant complex offers stunning views, a small pool, and studios and family apartments with flat-screen TVs, modern wooden furniture, and quality bathrooms. Very good deals out of season. Breakfast included. **€85**

Pension Nina Above the eastern side of the harbour ☎ 24240 66127, ⓦ ninna.gr. Lovingly refurbished studios whose balconies – especially in the deluxe upper-floor rooms – have tremendous views of the comings and goings in the harbour. Very well-equipped, with full kitchens. **€65**

HÓRA

Elma's Houses Upper part of the village ☎ 24240 66108, ⓦ elmashouses.com. Two exquisitely restored studios (a one-bed and a two-bed) and two houses (sleeping up to four), all beautifully furnished from the owner's Gorgona antique shop. Upmarket, but worth it. **€105**

★**Konstantina Studios** Lower part of the village ☎ 24240 65900, ⓦ konstantinastudios.gr. Exceptionally comfortable and well-presented studios, elegantly decorated and fully equipped – all enjoy spectacular views. There's a lovely garden and a home-made breakfast is included. **€95**

VÓTSI

Pension Oniro Overlooking the harbour ☎ 24240 65368, ⓦ pension-oniro.gr. An unmistakable, lilac-painted traditional pension, whose simple rooms all have a/c and TV, plus kitchenettes in the studio; there's also a new family apartment with a huge terrace. Fine views from the balconies down over Vótsi and out to sea, too, and a very friendly welcome. **€60**

EATING AND DRINKING

Though there's no shortage of **places to eat** in Patitíri, only a couple stand out from the crowd. **Nightlife** consists of few music bars on the western side of the harbour, below the museum. There's generally better, if pricier, food, and more night-time activity, up in Hóra. Hóra's main street is lined with restaurants, many with wonderful views, but few that are good value or particularly high quality. Locals and those in the know tend to eat further down, or in the backstreets.

PATITÍRI

Archipelagos Bottom of the western street, on the waterfront ☎ 24240 65031. The best of the waterfront restaurants, popular with locals for its good mezédhes, fish and traditional Greek cooking (chicken in lemon sauce €7.50; swordfish *souvláki* €12; stuffed kalamári €12) – plus excellent home-made chips. Daily lunch and dinner.

Helios On a terrace overlooking the harbour ☎ 24240 65667. *Helios* has great harbour views and a menu with some alternative flavours, such as chicken stir-fry or pork with prunes (both €10), as well as pasta, quesadillas and sandwiches. Occasional live music: book if you want the view in the evening. Daily 6pm–midnight.

To Kamaki On the eastern street, 150m from the waterfront ☎ 24240 65245. Authentic, welcoming ouzerí where the seafood-heavy menu encompasses unusual dishes like crab croquettes or octopus stifádho, plus plenty more standard dishes which you can inspect in the kitchen. Meze €4–6, mains €8–13.50. Live Greek music Tues, Thurs & Sat from 9pm. Dinner daily, plus lunch Sat & Sun.

HÓRA

Astrofeyia Near the lower square ☎ 24240 65182. Expat favourite serving unusual (for Greece) dishes like Thai green curry or chilli con carne (€12 each) as well as vegetarian options and excellent salads, all served on a terrace with a friendly welcome and great view. Daily 7pm–midnight.

★**Hayiati** At the end of the main street ☎ 24240 66244, ⓦ hayiati.com. *Hayiati* has probably the best view in Hóra; an unbeatable setting to sip coffee and try traditional sweets like *kazandibí* (Turkish-style milk pudding). Later, it becomes a piano bar with easy-listening music nightly and occasional live events. Cocktails are pricey, but not too bad considering the location, though it can be very busy. Daily all day.

VÓTSI

Dendrolimano Overlooking the harbour ☎ 24240 65252. Cool, modern, upmarket Greek restaurant/bar with a gorgeous terrace above the water. Expect unusual combinations like stewed goat with fresh goat cheese (€14), excellent pasta (spring lobster with orzo €24) plus simpler grills and steaks (around €20). Daily 7pm–midnight.

Northern Alónissos

A single road runs northeast from Patitíri up the spine of the island, giving access to **beaches** which are almost exclusively on the **east coast**. There are great views across to the substantial islet of Peristéra (see p.690) much of the way, and many of the marked hiking trails (see box, p.686) start from the road.

Tsoukaliá

The first turning on the northbound road heads westwards to **Tsoukaliá**, a scruffy cove signed as an archeological site; there was an ancient kiln here, and pottery continued to be made until recently, so thousands upon thousands of potsherds are strewn across the closed, fenced site and beach.

East-coast beaches

First of the **east-coast beaches** are **Miliá** and **Khryssí Miliá**: the former is busy, with white pebbles, piney cliffs and a *kantína*; the latter beautifully sandy and shallow (ideal for kids) and hence very busy, with loungers, taverna and beach bars. Next up is scenic **Kokkinókastro**, named for the red-rock cliffs which overlook it. Scramble down to reach pebbles on a red-sand base extending both sides of a promontory, with a seasonal bar. Another road leads to **Leftós Yialós** and **Tzórtzi Yialós**: the pretty white-pebble beach at Leftós, with its tavernas and loud beach bars, attracts plenty of day-trip boats; Tzórtzi is smaller and less attractive, but much quieter.

STENÍ VÁLA is the biggest settlement away from the island's southern corner, though still barely a village. There are plenty of rooms, while the harbourfront shops and

THE MEDITERRANEAN MONK SEAL

The **Mediterranean monk seal** (*Monachus monachus*) has the dubious distinction of being the most endangered European mammal. Fewer than six hundred survive, around half of them in Greek waters, of which fifty or more inhabit this part of the northern Sporades; the rest are mainly off the Turkish coast or around islands off the coast of West Africa.

Females have one **pup** about every two years, which can live for 45 years. As **adults**, they can grow to 2m in length and weigh over 200kg. Formerly, pups were reared in the open, but disturbance by man led to whelping seals retreating to isolated sea caves with partly submerged entrances. Without spending weeks on a local boat, your chances of seeing a seal are slim (marine-park cruises are far more likely to spot dolphins); if seals are spotted (usually dozing on the shore or swimming in the open sea), keep a deferential distance.

Monk seals can swim 200km a day in search of food – and compete with fishermen in the overfished Aegean, often destroying nets. Until recently, fishermen routinely killed seals; this occasionally still happens, but the establishment of the **National Marine Park of Alónissos-Northern Sporades** has helped by banning September–November fishing northeast of Alónissos and prohibiting it altogether within 1.5 nautical miles of Pipéri. These measures have won local support through the efforts of the **Hellenic Society for the Protection of the Monk Seal** (Ⓦmom.gr; see p.686), even among Sporadean fishermen, who realize that the restrictions help restore local fish stocks. The society has reared several abandoned seal pups (bad weather often separates them from their mothers), who are subsequently released in the sea around Alónissos.

10

tavernas attract yachts and day-trip boats. A long pebble beach – **Glýfa** – lies immediately north, and a better, partly sandy one, **Áyios Pétros**, is a ten-minute walk south. **KALAMÁKIA**, the next hamlet north, has no beach but does have a timeless fishing-port feel and some great waterfront tavernas. At **Áyios Dhimítrios**, the final beach easily accessible by road, brilliantly white pebbles stretch around both sides of a narrow point; the south-facing side has loungers and a couple of café/bars, while the other is quite undeveloped. **Yérakas**, almost at the island's northern tip, is the end of the road and feels like it; there's a tiny fishing harbour in the deep bay and a dirty-white pebble beach where a snack truck parks in summer – the water, however, is spectacularly clean and clear.

ACTIVITIES   NORTHERN ALÓNISSOS

Scuba diving There's a good diving outfit, Ikion Diving   (☎24240 65158, Ⓦikiondiving.gr), at Stení Vála.

ACCOMMODATION AND EATING

4 Epohes Stení Vála ☎24240 66101, Ⓦ4epochesalonnisos.com. The *4 Epohes* (*4 Seasons*) is a modern studio complex set around a good-sized pool just above Stení Vála; very comfortable, well-equipped rooms, and a pool bar and roof-garden. **€60**

Eleonas Leftós Yialós ☎24240 66066, Ⓦeleonas-alonissos.gr. Set in an olive grove behind the beach, this is the better of the popular beach bar/tavernas at Leftós Yialós. Alónissos pies are their speciality, from excellent plain cheese (€8.50) to more exotic octopus and goat varieties (€14). Prices are relatively high but portions big – a single pie and a salad makes a substantial lunch for two. Daily lunch and dinner.

Margarita Kalamákia ☎24240 65738. The best of four tavernas lined up along the quayside, each with its own fishing boat, *Margarita* serves excellent fish (priced by weight), mezédhes and simple Greek classics; stuffed peppers €5.50, moussaka €6, kalamári €10. They also have a/c rooms at the back (€40). Daily lunch and dinner.

★**Milia Bay Hotel & Apartments** Miliá ☎24240 66032, Ⓦmilia-bay.gr. In a stunning position high above Miliá beach and in a handy location for town, these studios and apartments have views out to sea over the landscaped grounds. All have kitchens and are furnished somewhat eccentrically with antiques from the family collection. There's a pool and pool-bar, open to the public, where a delicious breakfast is served (extra). **€90**

Sossinola Sténi Vála ☎24240 65776, Ⓦsossinola.gr. Harbourfront taverna that also has modern, a/c rooms, studios and apartments, with balconies looking out over the harbour or out to sea. There's plenty of fish on the taverna menu, plus Alónissos pies (€7) and a meaty goat in tomato sauce (€9). Restaurant daily 9am–11.30pm. **€40**

National Marine Park of Alónissos-Northern Sporades

Ⓦ alonissos-park.gr

Founded in 1992, the **National Marine Park** protects monk seals, dolphins, wild goats and rare seabirds in an area encompassing Alónissos plus a dozen **islets** speckling the Aegean to the east. None of these has any significant permanent population, but a few can be visited by excursion boats, weather permitting. **Pipéri** islet forms the core zone of the park – an off-limits seabird and monk-seal refuge, approachable only by government-authorized scientists. **Peristéra**, opposite Alónissos, is uninhabited, though some Alonissans cross to tend olive groves in the south; it's little visited by excursion craft except for a brief swim-stop at the end of a cruise. Well-watered **Kyrá Panayiá**, the next islet out, has a tenth-century monastery whose old bakery and wine/olive presses, restored in the 1990s, are maintained by one farmer-monk. Nearby **Yioúra** has a stalactite cave which mythically sheltered Homer's Cyclops, plus the main wild-goat population, but you won't see either as *kaïkia* must keep 400m clear of the shore. Tiny, northernmost **Psathoúra** is dominated by its powerful lighthouse, the tallest in the Aegean; some excursions stop for a swim at a pristine, white-sand beach.

Skýros

Despite its natural beauty, **SKÝROS** has a relatively low profile. There are few major sites or resorts, and access, wherever you're coming from, is awkward. Those in the know, however, realize it's worth the effort, and there are increasing numbers of millenial Athenians and Thessalonians taking advantage of domestic flights – and making Skýros Town a much more cosmopolitan place than you might expect – plus steadily growing international tourism. The New Age **Skyros Centre**, pitched mostly at Brits, has also effectively publicized the place. There are plenty of **beaches**, but few that can rival the sand of Skiáthos or film-set scenery of Skópelos. There's also a substantial **air-force presence** around the airport in the north, and a big **naval base** in the south; almost all the accommodation and tourist facilities cluster around Skýros Town in the centre of the island.

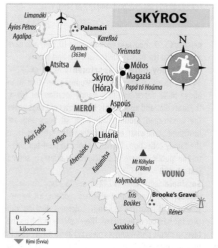

A position bang in the centre of the Aegean has guaranteed the island a busy **history**: it was occupied from prehistory, with a truly impressive Bronze Age settlement currently being excavated, was a vital Athenian outpost in the Classical era, and an equally important naval base for the Byzantines and under Venetian and Turkish rule, when it was a crucial staging post on the sea lanes to Constantinople.

ARRIVAL AND DEPARTURE   SKÝROS

By plane Olympic (Ⓦ olympicair.com) connects Skýros with Athens while Sky Express (Ⓦ www .skyexpress.gr) operates summer flights to Thessaloníki. The airport is about 10km from town; some Olympic flights are met by a bus, but normally you'll have to take a taxi or rent a car – a Pegasus car rental booth opens at flight times (see p.692).

FROM TOP SKÝROS; KOUKOUNARIÉS BEACH, SKIÁTHOS (P.677) >

10

CARNIVAL ON SKÝROS

Skýros has a particularly outrageous *apokriátika* (pre-Lenten) **carnival**, featuring its famous **goat dance**, performed by groups of masked revellers in the streets of Hóra. The leaders of each troupe are the **yéri**, menacing figures (usually men but sometimes sturdy women) dressed in goat-pelt capes, weighed down by huge garlands of sheep bells, their faces concealed by kid-skin masks, and brandishing shepherds' crooks. Accompanying them are their "brides", men in drag known as **korélles** (maidens), and **frángi** (maskers in assorted "Western" garb). When two such groups meet, the *yéri* compete to see who can ring their bells longest and loudest with arduous body movements, or even get into brawls using their crooks as cudgels.

These rites take place on each of the four weekends before **Clean Monday** (see p.45), but the final one is more for the benefit of tourists, both Greek and foreign. The Skyrians are less exhausted and really let their (goat) hair down for each other during the preceding three weeks. Most local hotels open for the duration, and you have to book rooms well in advance.

Destinations Athens (3–6 weekly; 40min); Thessaloníki (summer 2 weekly; 45min).

By ferry Skyros Shipping (ⓦ sne.gr) sails daily from Kými, on Évvia (see p.700), to Linariá, Skýros' port. The ferry leaves Kými every evening, returning from Skýros early in the morning (afternoon on Sun). Direct KTEL buses to Kými leave from Athens' Liossíon bus station in the early afternoon arriving in time to connect with the ferry.

Destinations Alónissos (July & Aug 2 weekly; 5hr 20min); Kými, Évvia (daily, more in summer, especially weekends; 1hr 40min); Skópelos (July & Aug 2 weekly; 6hr).

Agents and tickets Ferry tickets are sold from an office at the back of the Town Hall in Skýros Town (☎ 22220 91790) and from a booth by the harbour in Linariá (☎ 22220 94365). For plane tickets and most other queries, try Skyros Travel (☎ 22220 91600, ⓦ skyrostravel.com), about 100m above the platía on the main street in Skýros Town (Mon–Fri 9.30am–2.30pm & 6.30–10pm, Sat 10am–1pm & 7–9pm; timetables and other useful info displayed outside); they can also arrange taxi or minibus transfers between Kými and Athens airport.

INFORMATION

Tourist information The Visit Skyros website (ⓦ visit-skyros.gr) has impressive interactive mapping.

Services The post office and National Bank (with ATM) are on the platía in Skýros Town, and there's a further ATM higher up the main street and another in Linariá. English-language newspapers are sold from a hut opposite the platía in Skýros Town.

GETTING AROUND

By bus Buses run three times daily between Skýros Town and Linariá (€1.60), connecting with the ferries; in town the bus stop is near the bottom of the main street, by the school. In summer a couple of daily buses also go to Magaziá and Mólos.

By taxi There are plenty of taxis (☎ 22220 91666) to meet the ferries, with taxi stands by the main square in town, and near the bus stop.

By car and bike There's good car and bike rental (motor and pedal) from Anemos in Mólos (☎ 22220 93705, ⓦ anemos-skyros.gr), while Skyros Travel/Pegasus (see p.690) rents cars too, or you can get scooters from several places including Scoot & Scoot (☎ 22220 96096, ⓦ skyrosrental.gr) in Linariá. All will deliver a vehicle to you.

Boat trips and tours Various boat trips are available, including excursions to the islet of Sarakinó, with its white-sand beach, stopping at various sea caves en route: other activities include hiking and birdwatching. All can be arranged through feel in greece (☎ 22220 93100, ⓦ feelingreece.gr) in Skýros Town.

Skýros Town and around

Once through the rather scruffy outskirts, **SKÝROS TOWN (Hóra)** is a beautiful place, its Cycladic-style flat-roofed white houses clinging to the inland slope of a pinnacle rising precipitously from the coast. In legend, King Lykomedes raised the young Achilles in his palace here, and also pushed Theseus to his death from the summit. A single main street leads up to a central platía; beyond that, cobbled and increasingly narrow and **traffic-free**, lies a 150m stretch lined with almost everything

ou'll need – shops, many of them selling classy jewellery, crafts and antiques,
estaurants, banks and sophisticated bars. Wander off the main street and the place
s suddenly bigger than it first seemed. There are fascinating glimpses everywhere
- covered passageways, churches and front doors open to reveal **traditional house
interiors** with gleaming copperware, antique embroideries and the proud local crafts
of painted ceramics and elaborately carved wooden furniture.

Kástro

10

The Byzantine-Venetian **kástro** atop the ancient **acropolis** above town is a very steep
climb through the picturesque old quarter. It was badly damaged by an earthquake in
2001 and the upper part of the castle is still being restored. You can enter the Byzantine
monastery of Áyios Yeóryios, though, which occupies the lower half (daily
10am–1.30pm, free; ☎6973 538854). An arched passageway leads in through the
walls, giving a real sense of the impregnability of the place, and it's a wonderfully calm
space, with glorious views.

Rupert Brooke memorial

On the northern edge of town • ⓦ rupertbrookeonskyros.com • Follow the main street uphill and take the signed left fork, or walk up
steps from Magaziá

The British poet Rupert Brooke is always associated with Skýros, though in fact he
spent only a few days here, arriving as a **naval officer** off the south of the island on
April 17, 1915, and dying six days later of blood poisoning on a French hospital ship.
He lies buried in an olive grove above the bay of Trís Boúkes (see p.696). The **Rupert
Brooke memorial** comprises a nude bronze statue of "Immortal Poetry", in a quiet
square with wonderful seaward views.

Archeological Museum

Below the Rupert Brooke memorial • Tues–Sun 8am–3pm • €2 • ☎ 22220 91327

Skýros' two-room **Archeological Museum** is far better than you might expect, with
the added bonus of a lovely setting above the sea. The highlights are early Bronze
Age pottery, obsidian axe-heads and stone blades and tools from Palamári (see
p.695); later artefacts include a Geometric-era ceramic rhyton (drinking vessel) in
the form of a Skyrian pony, and a vase with eight ducks being beset by snakes.
There's also a side room in the form of a traditional Skyrian house, with carved
wooden screen and furniture.

Manos Faltaïts Museum

Below the Rupert Brooke memorial • Daily 10am–2pm & 6–9pm • €2 • ☎ 22220 91232

An early nineteenth-century mansion built over a bastion in the ancient walls houses
the eccentric **Manos Faltaïts Museum**, in the family home of a prolific local painter.
Along with his own works, it's an Aladdin's cave of local history and folklore, with
traditional furnishings and costumes, curios and books.

Magaziá and Mólos

Immediately below Skýros Town, reached by a direct stairway or more roundabout
roads, is the beach hamlet of **MAGAZIÁ**. From here, a long sandy beach, the island's
best, extends to **MÓLOS**; these days the two are pretty much joined by low-key,
low-rise development – much of the island's **accommodation** is down here, along
with plenty of **restaurants** and a couple of lively beach **bars**. Around the point
beyond Mólos, a much more exposed beach is punctuated by rock outcrops whose
weird, squared-off shapes are the result of Roman (and later) quarrying rather than
natural erosion; one monolith, by the cape with its snack-bar/windmill, has a
rock-hewn chapel inside.

10

Linariá and around

LINARIÁ, where the ferries dock, is a delightfully chilled-out place where the day's big excitement is the arrival and departure of the ferry. A few intrepid yachties make it here and there are some excellent places to eat and drink, though little else to do. The next small bay, about fifteen minutes' walk away, is **Aheroúnes**, a peaceful spot with a much better beach.

ACCOMMODATION

SKÝROS TOWN

★**Nefeli** On the main road as you enter town ☎ 22220 91964, ⊚ skyros-nefeli.gr. The island's plushest hotel has lovely designer rooms, studios and split-level apartments, arrayed around a large saltwater pool. There's a small gym and hammam, plus free bikes for guests. Breakfast (included) is served on an outdoor terrace, and much of what is served in the restaurant comes from the hotel's own farm. **€125**

Pension Nicolas On the southern edge of town ☎ 22220 91778, ⊚ nicolaspension.gr. In a quiet location, 5min walk out of town, this friendly establishment offers double and quad rooms; the latter have hand-carved traditional wooden sleeping platforms, and all have a/c and TVs. **€45**

MAGAZIÁ AND MÓLOS

Angela Mólos ☎ 22220 91764, ⊚ angelahotelskyros .com. Large complex of simple rooms and studios, near the beach at the northern end of Mólos, beyond the harbour, in extensive gardens around a pool. All with a/c, TV and fridge, and some with kitchenette. **€60**

Georgia Tsakami Magaziá ☎ 22220 91357, ⊚ georgiashouse.gr. Plain traditional rooms, recently redecorated, with fridge and electric ring, in a great position directly behind the beach. Most have a private balcony at the

SKÝROS TOWN AND AROUND

back, and there's a communal terrace at the front. **€40**

★**Perigiali** Magaziá ☎ 22220 92075, ⊚ perigiali.com. Sparkling modern complex of rooms, studios and family apartments around a good-sized pool, in a narrow lane behind the beach at the southern end of Magaziá. A few have sea views, though most look over the gardens; all have a/c and fridge, some have cooking facilities. **€80**

★**Vina Beach Hotel** Mólos ☎ 22220 93111, ⊚ skyroshotel.gr. Right on the beach at the far end of Mólos, with a pool at the edge of the sand, these delightful, spacious modern rooms and apartments all have sea views, a/c, TV and fridge, some with cooking facilities. Free kayaks and sunloungers for guests. **€80**

LINARIÁ AND AHEROÚNES

Lykomides Linariá ☎ 22220 93249, ⊚ lykomides.gr. Spotless, newly renovated *dhomátia* with wooden-shuttered balconies; some look right over the harbour, others are higher and quieter. All have fridge, a/c and TV, and some include cooking facilities; there's also a large apartment. **€40**

Pegasus Aheroúnes ☎ 22220 93442, ⊚ skyros -pegasus.gr. A variety of well-maintained studios and apartments, most with good views, in a tranquil spot behind the beach. All come with kitchenette, a/c, TV and a friendly welcome; there's also a café on site. **€50**

EATING, DRINKING AND NIGHTLIFE

Skýros Town has plenty of bars and fast food, pizza or *souvláki* places, but surprisingly few good restaurants. Food tends to be better on the coast, especially in the excellent psarotavernés (fish restaurants) surrounding the harbour in Linariá.

SKÝROS TOWN

Akamatra Main square ☎ 22220 29029. Large, fancy bar on two floors, with leather seating and terraces overlooking both the platía and street. Open during the day for coffee, and till the early hours for regular DJ events. Daily 10am–2am.

O Pappous ki Ego Near the top of the main street ☎ 22220 93200. "My Grandfather and I" serves traditional Skyrian dishes such as fried bread with Skyrian cheese (actually more like a giant cheese pie), squid with aniseed, and excellent meatballs with ouzo; mostly smaller, meze-style dishes (€3.50–6.50, with a few mains for around €8). It's designed to be reminiscent of a traditional village store, and classier than your average Greek taverna. Daily from 7pm.

MAGAZIÁ AND MÓLOS

Asterias Mólos ☎ 22220 93008. Excellent restaurant on the waterfront platía with a pretty beachfront terrace and sunbeds below for customer use. There's no printed menu – usually a good sign – just half a dozen daily specials reeled off by the waiter (generally €8–10), plus the usual salads and sides. Live Greek music on Thursday evenings. Daily 10am–3am.

★** Iy Istories tou Barba** Mólos ☎ 22220 91453. In a lovely setting, with blue chairs on a blue terrace above the Magaziá end of Mólos beach, this ouzerí serves traditional and interesting meze along with mains including cuttlefish with fennel (€7.50), meatballs (€7) and seafood spaghetti (€12). The atmosphere is equally traditional, with black-and-white photos of old island

...e stuck in the menu. Daily 1pm–midnight.

...icy Beach Bar Magaziá ☎ 22220 93337. Beach ...ar with loungers, umbrellas and watersports, plus a ...rrace with food (sandwiches, crêpes, pasta), ...ices and smoothies, free wi-fi and a bar. Quiet ...usic by day, cranked up at night with summer ...vents such as a full-moon party. Daily breakfast till ...he early hours.

...tefanos Magaziá ☎ 22220 91272. Attractive, ...raditional taverna with wooden tables on a terrace ...anging out over the sand at the southern end of Magaziá ...each. Standard dishes such as *moussaka* (€7) or lamb with ...otatoes (€8.50) are deliciously prepared. Daily ...45am–11.30pm.

...halassa Mólos beach ☎ 22220 92044. Beach bar by ...ay (with wi-fi, sunbeds, bar and snacks), cocktail bar ...nd club at night, when there's a huge dance space, ...hough that only really gets busy in Aug. Daily ...9am–3am.

LINARIÁ

Kavos ☎ 22220 93213. All-day bar tumbling down a rocky cliff on a series of terraces, with steps down to a private swimming area below. Quiet daytime sounds are turned up loud to greet the evening ferry; there's wi-fi, drinks and light meals, plus late-night revelry in mid-season. April, May & Sept Mon–Fri 2pm–2am, Sat & Sun 10am–2am; June–Aug daily 10am–2am.

★**Marigo** ☎ 22220 96010. From the people who run *O Pappous ki Ego*, a modern take on a traditional fish taverna. Fresh fish by the kilo, but also less usual dishes like cuttlefish couscous (€8) or goat in lemon sauce (€8.50), plus good daily specials. Daily 9am–midnight.

★**Psariotis** ☎ 22220 93250. Probably the best of the traditonal tavernas around Linariá's harbour, *Psariotis* has its own boat to catch fish, which is noticeably less expensive than elsewhere, with some of the cheapest lobster in Greece (at least out of season). They also do a good fish soup (€12), plus plenty of standard Greek dishes at regular prices (moussaka or *souvláki* €6). Daily 11am–1am.

Merói

A single paved road loops around Skyros's northern half, **Merói**. Heading anticlockwise from Hóra, the first possible stop is at secluded **Kareflóu** beach, 1.5km down a poorly signed rough track. Sandy and extensive, it's also exposed and has no facilities at all.

Palamári

3km down a dirt road • Mon–Fri 7.30am–2.30pm • Free

The early Bronze Age settlement of **Palamári**, inhabited from around 2800 to 1650 BC, and then lost for 3500 years, sits on the ridge of a low cape at the northeastern edge of the island, above a beach and a river which once formed a lagoon and natural harbour. The site, still being excavated, is extraordinary: you can make out the houses, streets, drainage and walls of a well-organized and powerfully **fortified city**, which must have been at the heart of Aegean trading in the Minoan era. Informative signage and a small exhibition fill in the background.

Atsítsa and around

Past the airport at the island's northern tip, the west coast is infinitely greener, heavily forested in pine. Around 2.5km of rough track leads to a couple of the island's most scenic and remote beaches: nudist **Áyios Pétros**, more respectable **Limanáki**, right by the airport almost at the end of the runway, and still more isolated **Agalípa**. **Atsítsa** itself is well-known as the home of the **Skyros Centre** (✆ skyros.com) and the attractive, pine-fringed bay here is sheltered by an islet and has lovely clear water for swimming.

Beyond Atsítsa, you can head back across the centre of the island on a good dirt road through the woods, or carry on around the coast, through an area devastated by forest fire in 2007 and still not fully recovered. **Áyios Fokás**, in the heart of this area, is a quiet beach that makes a great lunch spot; while the descent through woods to deeply indented **Péfkos**, the best of the southwest-coast bays with a fine, long, sandy beach, offers spectacular views.

EATING AND DRINKING   MERÓI

★**Perasma** Near Palamári ☎ 22220 92911. Excellent, reasonably priced taverna at the junction of the airport road not far from Palamári; apparently in the middle of

nowhere, but with plenty of custom from local air-force families. The family-style cooking is based on local produce, much of it organic and produced in the taverna's

10

own fields, served beneath a shady awning. There's no menu, just a short list of daily specials and grilled meats at around €5 for starters and salads, €7–8 for mains. Daily lunch and dinner.

Taverna tis Kyra Kalis Áyios Fokás. A wonderfully out-of-the-way lunch spot, with octopus (€9) and sardines (€7) thrown on a charcoal grill on the beach and simple Greek home-style cooking. Lush vines and pot plants compensate for the burnt slopes roundabout. Daily lunch and dinner.

Vounó

South of Skýros Town, you turn off at **Aspoús**, where there's a decent grey-sand beach, to reach **Vounó**. Much of this southern half of the island, especially as you ascend **Mount Kóhylas**, is almost eerily barren, home only to goats and a few stunted trees, but it's here – high on the mountain – that you're most likely to see wild Skyrian horses and other **wildlife**, including abundant Eleonora's falcon. En route there's an extensive pebbly strand at **Kalamítsa**.

Brooke's grave

Follow the turning to the naval base for just over 1km; it's in an olive grove off to the left of the road

The one sight down on the southern tip of the island (though it's tricky to spot) is **Rupert Brooke's grave** at **Trís Boúkes**, a simple marble tomb inscribed with his most famous poem, *The Soldier* ("If I should die, think only this of me / That there's some corner of a foreign field / That is for ever England...").

EATING AND DRINKING | VOUNÓ

Mouries Fléa ☎ 6947 465 900. A big, traditional taverna in this tiny hamlet on the road between Aspoús and Kalamítsa. They serve local lamb, goat and wine under the namesake mulberries; the kid in lemon sauce is great (€10). It's very popular at weekends when they often have live Greek music, and over the road they run a riding centre with pony-and-trap rides (see box, above). Daily lunch and dinner.

Évvia

The second-largest of the Greek islands after Crete, **ÉVVIA (Euboea)** – separated only by a narrow gulf from central Greece – often feels more like an extension of the mainland than an entity in its own right. At **Halkídha**, the old drawbridge spans a mere 40m channel where Évvia was mythically split from Attica and Thessaly by a blow from Poseidon's trident. Easy access from Athens means that in summer Évvia can seem merely a beach annexe for Athens and the mainland towns across the Gulf.

Nevertheless, Évvia is an island, often a very beautiful one, and in many ways its problems – long distances to cover, poor communications, few concessions to tourism – are also its greatest attractions, ensuring that it has remained out of the mainstream of tourism. Exceptionally **fertile**, Évvia has always been a quietly prosperous place that would manage pretty well even without visitors. The classical name, Euboea, means "rich n cattle", and throughout history it as been much coveted. Today griculture still thrives, with plenty of cal goat and lamb on the menu, long with highly rated local retsina.

Évvia divides naturally into three ections, with just a single road onnecting the northern and southern arts to the centre. The **south** is mountainous, barren and rocky; highlights are low-key Kárystos and hiking the nearby mountains and gorges. The **centre**, with the sprawling island capital at Halkídha, is green, wealthy and busy with both industry and agriculture. There are plenty of beaches but for visitors its mainly a gateway, with the bridges at Halkídha and onward transport to Skýros from the easterly port of Kými. In the **north**, grain fields, olive groves and pine forest are surrounded by the bulk of the island's resorts, most dominated by Greek holiday homes.

ARRIVAL AND DEPARTURE   ÉVVIA

By ferry Ferries make the short crossing from the mainland to Évvia at various points all the way up the coast: from Ráfina to Marmári, Ayía Marína to Néa Stýra, Skála Oropoú to Erétria, Arkítsa to Edhipsós, Áyios Konstandínos to Áyios Yeóryios and Glýfa to Ayiókambos. Which you choose depends on where you are heading on Évvia; most run very frequently – details are given under the individual ports.

By car Two bridges link Évvia to the mainland, the old drawbridge right in the heart of Halkídha and a suspension bridge on the outskirts. If you are driving you can use these or any of the ferries (more expensive, but the mainland motorway is far faster than roads on the island if you're heading to the north or south).

By bus KTEL buses run direct from Athens' Liossíon bus station to many destinations on Évvia including Halkídha (every 30min most of the day; @ ktelevias. gr), Kárystos, Kými, Límni and Edhipsós. There are also buses from Athens to all the mainland ports above.

By train Frequent trains connect Athens with Halkídha (@ trainose.gr).

GETTING AROUND

By bus and car Most places in Évvia can be reached by bus, but services tend to run just a couple of times a day, so if you want to explore you'll need a car. There are fewer rental offices in Halkídha and the resorts than you

might expect: try Car'n Motion (@ 210 802 4787, @ carnmotion.gr), with local bases and options for pick-ups or drop-offs at the ferries. If you're bringing a hire car from the mainland, tell the rental company.

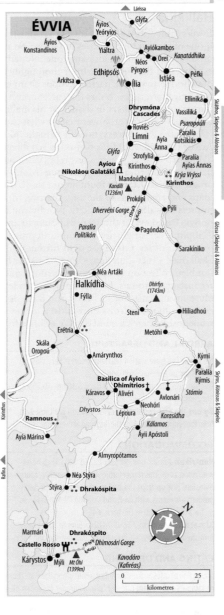

10

Halkídha

Évvia's capital, **HALKÍDHA** (ancient Chalkis), has a population of over 100,000, making it one of the ten biggest cities in Greece. So it's not entirely surprising if it often has an urban feel, rather than an island one. Nonetheless, the centre is compact and easy to explore, and the busy waterfront thoroughly attractive. Right at the centre, beneath the drawbridge across the narrow **Évripos channel** to the mainland, the gulf-water swirls by like a river; every few hours the current reverses. Aristotle is said to have thrown himself into the waters in despair at his inability to understand what was happening; there is still controversy over exactly what causes the capricious currents.

An impressive **fortress**, floodlit at night, protects Halkídha from the mainland side. Across the bridge, Odhós Kótsou heads directly uphill towards the centre through the old **Kástro** district, where a few relics of an older city survive. Chief among these is a handsome fifteenth-century **mosque** (Mon, Wed, Fri & Sun 10am–2pm; free), with an ornate carved **Ottoman fountain** out front. The mosque now houses an exhibition of maps and engravings of the city, charting the gradual decline from its heyday as an impressive walled Venetian city. Nearby you can see the tower of the beautiful church of **Ayía Paraskeví**, at the corner of Stamáti and Tzavára (daily 7am–noon & 5.30–7.30pm; free): originally a Dominican priory, founded around 1250, it retains many original features. Off to the right further up Kótsou you'll find the **Folklore Museum** at Skalkóta 4 (Tues–Sun 8am–3pm; €3; ☎ 22210 21817) housed in the old jail, with a jumbled collection of costumes, furniture and local traditions in a series of reconstructed rooms. Higher up still, then left on the main street, the **Archeological Museum** at Venizélou 13 (Tues–Sun 8am–3pm; €2; ☎ 22210 25131) offers a pleasant escape from the raucous surrounds; a tortoise roams the statuary in the shady garden, while inside there's a good display of finds from across the island.

ARRIVAL AND DEPARTURE HALKÍDHA

By train The train station (🖰 trainose.gr) is very close to the bridge on the mainland side.
Destination Athens (at least 10 daily 5.30am–10.20pm; 1hr 20min).
By bus The KTEL bus station (🖰 ktelevias.gr) is almost 2km from the centre at Stíron 1, on the ring road at the southeastern edge of town; local buses will take you in to the market area, but it's much easier to use a taxi (about €5).
Destinations Athens (every 30min 6am–10.30pm; 1hr 15min); Edhipsós (1 daily; 2hr 30min); Erétria (12 daily; 30min); Kárystos (1 a day; 3hr); Kými (6 daily; 2hr); Límni (3 daily; 2hr).

ACCOMMODATION

Kentrikon Angéli Govíou 5 ☎ 22210 22375, 🖰 hotel-kentrikon.com. This rather forbidding nineteenth-century mansion, just up from the bridge, conceals unexpectedly modern a/c rooms with wi-fi and satellite TV. No views, so go for a quieter room at the back. **€45**
Kimata Liáska 1 ☎ 22210 74724. Simple, minimally furnished rooms above a busy main road overlooking the port; modern double glazing and a/c keep out most of the noise, and it's good value for the location. **€40**
Paliria Eleftheríou Venizélou 2 ☎ 22210 28001, 🖰 paliria-hotel.gr. Big, business-style three-star whose main attraction is the amazing view across the water, so be sure to get a room at the front. Basic buffet breakfast included. **€65**

EATING AND DRINKING

A long line of cafés and restaurants extends along the waterfront to the north of the bridge; there are plenty of fancy seafood restaurants and elegant café-bars plus a number of simpler places. Prices are lower inland towards the centre, though.

Apanemo Ethníkis Symfilíosis 78, Fanári ☎ 22210 22614. Very popular seafood restaurant in a lovely seaside setting with tables on the beach; good value fish (by weight), or try the seafood pasta (€10.50), red mullet (€12) or octopus (€11). It's a good 30min walk from the centre in a quiet suburb, just before the lighthouse at the far north end of the shoreline, so you may want to book, and/or take a taxi. Daily noon–midnight.
Paralia Voudóuri 10 ☎ 22210 87932. Long-established, old-fashioned, waterfront *psistariá*, serving up large portions of grilled meat at very reasonable prices (€7–9 a large portion); salads and oven-baked dishes too. The next door fish restaurant is jointly run, so you can order from their menu too. Daily 11am–midnight.

af Papanastasíou 3 ☎6948 180 857. An imposing one building, off Platía Agorás near the top of Kótsou, ouses this bustling ouzerí, with good fish and mezédhes (portions of fish from €9, meze €4–8). It's popular with locals, hence busiest late in the evening. Daily 2pm–midnight.

Central Évvia

The **coast road** southeast of Halkídha heads through industrial suburbs to a coastline of second homes, small hotels and beaches which make popular escapes from the city. At **Lépoura** it forks, to the right for the south of the island, left to curl around towards the east coast and **Kými**. The west-coast coves and beaches en route, facing open sea, are prized by locals for the cleanliness of the water. Beyond Kými you can cut back across the mountainous heart of the island via **Metóhi** and **Stení**.

Erétria

Modern **ERÉTRIA** is a dull-looking resort on a grid plan; for most travellers its main asset is a ferry service across to Skála Oropoú in Attica. The place deserves a closer look, though. For a start it boasts some of the best **beaches** on this stretch of coast, to the east of the harbour, and more importantly it preserves the remains of **Ancient Eretria**, the most impressive site on the island. Eretria was an important city from the eighth century BC to the sixth century AD, flourishing above all around 400 BC following the decline of Athens.

Archeological Museum

On the inland edge of town by the main road · Tues–Sun 8.30am–3pm · €2 · ☎22290 62206

First stop on your exploration should be the **Archeological Museum**, where you can pick up a leaflet with a map showing all the main sites around town. Among the museum's displays of ceramics, statues and jewellery, labelled mainly in Greek and French, the tenth-century BC Lefkandi Centaur stands out – a lovely piece and one of the earliest known examples of **figurative pottery**. There are also fascinating models of the ancient city.

House of Mosaics

It's worth crossing the road from the museum to see the overgrown West Gate and **theatre**, but of the other sites, many of them locked, the unarguable highlight is the **House of Mosaics**. Here, under a modern cover, four magnificent mosaic floors dating from around 370 BC have been preserved, vividly depicting animals and mythical scenes. Ask at the Archeological Museum about access.

ARRIVAL AND DEPARTURE   ERÉTRIA

By ferry Ferries shuttle the short crossing to Skála Oropoú every 30min in summer (7am–10pm; 25min; ☎22290 64990, or ☎22950 37270 in Skála Oropoú; ☜eretriaferries .blogspot.co.uk).

By bus Erétria is linked to Halkídha (12 daily; 30min) and there are frequent services from Athens to Skála Oropoú (15 daily; 1hr 15min; ☜ktelattikis.gr).

ACCOMMODATION

Eviana Beach Oníron ☎22290 62113, ☜evianabeach.gr. Smart hotel at the start of the beach road, right behind the beach, handy for town and with great sea views; all the rooms have a/c, TV and balcony, some are newly renovated. **€65**

Kálamos

The most accessible of a number of beautiful coves on the west coast is **KÁLAMOS**, about 7km down narrow lanes from Neohóri on the main road. This stretch of the main road is dotted with medieval remains – Byzantine chapels and watchtowers which gave warning of approaching pirates. Kálamos itself is a tiny but stunning cove enclosing a sandy **beach**, surrounded by half a dozen tavernas and rooms establishments. In August it's packed; the rest of the year often deserted. South of

Kálamos a paved road, alarmingly steep and narrow in places, heads past a series of other small cove beaches with no facilities at all to the little resort and fishing village of **Áyii Apóstoli**, from where you can rejoin the main road south of Lépoura.

ACCOMMODATION AND EATING   KÁLAMOS

Tota Marinou ☎ 22230 41881. One of many rooms places right behind the beach, with exceptional value small, simple rooms with a/c and fridge, most with sea view. They also have a huge parking area and a welcoming waterfront taverna (mains €6–8) with loungers for customers. June–Sept; restaurant daily 9am–11pm. **€30**

10

Kými

KÝMI consists of two parts: the ferry port, properly known as Paralía Kýmis, and the upper town, 4km up a spectacularly winding road. The port offers plenty of accommodation and a long row of harbourfront restaurants and cafés that might come in handy should you be waiting for a ferry, though the upper town is far more attractive, with great views towards Skýros from its lush, green hillside location.

Folklore Museum

Paralías 14, in the upper town on the road up from the harbour • Wed 10.30am–1pm, Sat & Sun 10.30am–2pm • €2 • ☎ 22220 22011

There's a small **Folklore Museum** displaying weaving and embroidery, costumes, rural implements and old photos recording the doings of Kymians both locally and in the US, home to a huge emigrant community. Among them was **Dr George Papanikolaou**, deviser of the "Pap" cervical smear test, who is honoured with a statue up on the platía.

ARRIVAL AND DEPARTURE   KÝMI

By bus Buses generally drop off in the upper town, except for those connecting with Skýros ferries.
Destinations Halkídha and Athens (6 daily; 2hr/4hr).
By ferry Skyros Shipping (☎ 22220 22020, ⓦ sne.gr) sail every evening to Linariá on Skýros, returning from Skýros early in the morning. The ticket office is on the quayside. Athens buses connect with all the ferries.
Destinations Alónissos (summer 2 weekly; 2hr 20min); Skópelos (summer 2 weekly; 3hr 5min); Skýros (1 daily, more in summer, especially weekends; 1hr 40min).

Stení

At bustling Néa Artáki, 5km north of Halkídha, a side road leads east to **STENÍ**, a village-cum-hill-station at the foot of Mount Dhírfys, Évvia's highest summit where traces of snow survive till early summer. It's a beautiful place in a cleft in the mountains, cool in summer and full of rushing streams, and is striving to make itself something of a centre of **activity tourism**: there are marked hiking trails up the mountain, mountain-bike routes, and even a ski lift in winter. Stení also marks pretty much the halfway point of the wonderfully scenic **road to Kými**, all paved except for a short section just outside Metóhi; Kými is 51km or an hour and 35 minutes' drive away (follow signposts for Metóhi if starting from Kými).

ACCOMMODATION AND EATING   STENÍ

Numerous tavernas specializing in meaty fare line the road as it passes through Stení, all popular for weekend outings, and there are more options in the village itself.
Steni ☎ 22280 51221, ⓦ hotelsteni.gr. Cosy, welcoming hotel looking across at the village, with spectacular views from its sumptuous common areas and comfortable if rather small rooms, some recently renovated and all with mountain views. **€50**
Vrahos ☎ 6906 262 673. An atmospheric place with firewood stacked outside and views of the village goings-on. The menu offers standard Greek fare and delicious barbecued meats – try the *kondosoúvli* (hunks of spit-roasted pork; €9) or rotisserie chicken (€7). Daily lunch and dinner.

Southern Évvia

So narrow that you can sometimes see the sea on both sides, mountainous **southern Évvia** is often barren, bleak and windswept. The single road from the north is narrow and winding

ADVENTURE TOURISM ON ÉVVIA

Mountainous, wild and empty, with a beautiful little-known interior, Évvia is a great place for **hiking**, **mountain-biking** and **climbing**. Stení is the centre of much of this, with events like the **Dirfys Trail**, an annual run up the mountain, but there's also excellent walking around Kárystos (see below) and in the north (see p.703). A number of hikes are detailed on the Anavasi map of Évvia and Evia Adventure Tours (☎6973 856 793, ⓦeviatours.com) can organize highly recommended mountain-biking, trekking, climbing and canyoning **tours** all over the island, especially around Stení.

n places – most people who come here arrive by ferry, and though Greeks have holiday homes in numerous coastal spots there's really just one attractive resort, at **Kárystos**.

Heading south by road, you'll pass what maps mark as **Lake Dhýstos**; these days it has been largely reclaimed as farmland, and there's barely any water. Atop conical Kastrí hill on the east shore are sparse fifth-century BC ruins of **ancient Dystos** and a medieval citadel. At **STÝRA**, 35km from Lépoura, three impressive **dhrakóspita** ("dragon houses") are signposted up a daunting but driveable track. So named because only dragons were thought capable of installing the enormous masonry blocks, their origins and purpose remain obscure. The shore annexe of **NÉA STÝRA**, 3.5km downhill, is a locals' resort, pretty enough, but worth knowing about mainly for its handy ferry connection to Ayía Marína. Much the same is true of **MARMÁRI**, 20km south, except here the link is with Rafína. Both have plenty of food and accommodation should you be stuck waiting for a bus or ferry.

ARRIVAL AND DEPARTURE SOUTHERN ÉVVIA

By ferry In high summer, at least seven ferries daily shuttle between Néa Stýra and Ayía Marína (45min; information ☎22240 41533), and four to six a day link Marmári and Rafína (1hr; information ☎22240 31222); around half that number run through the winter. Ferry tickets are sold on the quaysides.

By bus Most ferries in Marmári are met by a bus to Kárystos. Connecting buses link Athens Mavrommatéon terminal with both Rafína (see p.120) and Ayía Marína.

Kárystos

KÁRYSTOS is a delightfully old-fashioned, thoroughly Greek resort, strung out along a broad bay flanked by good (if often windy) beaches. It's a quiet place – even in August, when thousands of Greeks descend, they're a fairly staid crowd – but its attractions grow on you; graceful Neoclassical buildings in the centre, endearingly old-fashioned shops and tavernas, and a magnificent setting. On the main town **beach**, west of the centre, there are beach bars, sunbeds and kayak rental; further out this way, and around the bay to the east, there are plenty of empty patches of sand.

Though a place of some importance in antiquity, mentioned by Homer and a rival of Athens, there's very little trace now of this history: only a fenced-in **Roman heroön** (mausoleum), a block from the water at the corner of Kotsíka and Sakhtoúri, and the thirteenth-century, waterfront **Boúrtzi** (locked except for special events), all that's left of once-extensive fortifications. Just uphill from this small Venetian tower, the tiny but well-explained **Archeological Museum of Karystos** (Tues–Sun 8.30am–3pm; €2; ☎22240 29218) displays statues, temple carvings and votive objects from the region.

ARRIVAL AND INFORMATION KÁRYSTOS

By bus The bus stop is on Amerikís, next to the Town Hall, about three blocks in and one east from central Platía Amalías.

Destinations Halkídha (1 daily, 3hr); Marmári (4 daily, 20min).

Tourist information There's a tourist information booth on the waterfront, open on summer evenings, while helpful South Evia Tours at Platía Amalías 7 (daily 9am–11pm; ☎22240 26200, ⓦeviatravel.gr) sells ferry tickets, rents cars and bikes, finds lodging, arranges excursions and also has a shop selling souvenirs, maps and foreign newspapers.

10

GETTING AROUND

By bike Karystos Bikes at the corner of Sakhtoúri and Platía Amalías (☎ 22240 26530, ⓦ karystosbikes.gr) rent out high-quality mountain bikes by the hour or day, and offer suggested routes.

By taxi There's a taxi office (☎ 22240 26500) on Platí... Amalías.

ACCOMMODATION

Galaxy Odysséos 1 ☎ 22240 22600, ⓦ galaxyhotelkaristos.com. Big old hotel at the western end of the waterfront with a friendly, family atmosphere. Not very modern, but comfortable and good value. Breakfast included. **€40**

Karystion Kriezótou 3 ☎ 22240 22391, ⓦ karystion.g... A lovely spot on a quiet, pine-covered promontory wit... direct access to the adjacent beach. The modern exterio... and elegant public areas are fancier than the room... though these are gradually being renovated. **€45**

EATING, DRINKING AND NIGHTLIFE

Seafront Kriezótou is lined with cafés and touristy tavernas, though you'll generally find better value away from th... front. Theohári Kótsíka, one of the lanes leading inland from here to parallel Sakhtoúri, just to the west of the platí... has several *psistariés* and takeaway kebab places, as does I. Kótsika, between Platía Amalías and the Town Hall. Ther... are also plenty of wonderful old-fashioned food stores, such as *Galaktopoleío Stani* (see below).

Aeriko West beach ☎ 22240 23745. Lounge bar behind the beach with a beach bar area on the sand; probably the best of a selection of bar/clubs behind the beach here. Live music and club nights in summer. Daily 9am–4am.

★**Cavo D'oro** Paródos Sakhtoúri ☎ 22240 22326. Despite the name, this is an absolutely traditional Greek taverna, always busy, serving the likes of cheese-stuffed peppers, home-made tzatzíki and goat in tomato sauce (mains €8–9). There's no menu, so choose from the bubbling pots or raw ingredients in the kitchen. You'll find it in the first alley off the waterfront west of the square. Noon–4.30pm & 7pm–late; closed Tues.

Galaktopoleío Stani Sakhtoúri 100 ☎ 22240 24448. Just west of Platía Amalías, this dairy store sells virtually nothing but traditional home-made yoghurt and rice pudding. Mon–Sat 8am–1pm; Tues, Thurs & Fri also 6–9pm.

Hovoli Kriezótou 118 ☎ 22240 23927. Elegant café or the waterfront serving coffee and sweets by day, wine by the glass and beer at night; somewhat pricey, but offset by the delicious traditional snacks that come with each drink. Daily all day till late.

To Kyma Káto Aetós ☎ 22240 23365. Big seaside restaurant 2km east of town, with a terrace above the water and another further up. Plenty of fresh fish (priced per kilo) as well as all the usuals – kalamári €8, lamb in lemon sauce €8.50, moussaka €6.50. It's a popular weekend excursion for big parties, so best to book ahead. Fri–Sun noon–11pm.

Mýli and the south-east

MÝLI, a lovely place full of rushing water, lies just 3km inland from Kárystos, and is a natural first stop on any trip east. The one real sight here is medieval **Castello Rosso** (**Kokkinókastro**; usually open daylight hours in summer), a stiff climb above the village; seen from Kárystos, the castle looks amazingly well preserved, but up close it's mostly semi-ruined apart from the restored gatehouse. The sweeping views make the trip worthwhile, however.

Mount Óhi

Alpine club shelter ☎ 22240 22472 to get the keys

Mount Óhi (1399m), inland from Kárystos, is Évvia's third-highest peak and the focus of trails of sufficient quality to attract overseas trekkers. From Mýli, it's a three-hour-plus **hike** up the bare slopes of Óhi, mostly by a good path short-cutting the road; about forty minutes along are various finished and half-finished cipollino marble **columns**, abandoned almost two thousand years ago. The Romans loved the greenish, veined material and extensively quarried southern Évvia, shipping the marble back to Italy. The path reaches an **alpine club shelter**, with spring water outside, just below the summit, and a **dhrakóspito** ("dragon house"), even more impressive than the Stýra trio (see p.701), which seemingly sprouts from the mountainside.

himosári Gorge

he one unmissable excursion in southern Évvia is the three-hour hike down the
himosári Gorge. The descent northeast from Mt Óhi, mostly in deep shade, past
arious springs and watermills, follows a good, mostly cobbled path as far as the farming
amlet of Lenoséi, then a track to **Kallianós** village, with another path just before the
tter down to a beach. South Evia Tours (see p.701) and others organize guided treks
ere in summer; otherwise you'll have to arrange a taxi transfer back, or hitch.

10

Northern Évvia

eaving Halkídha to the north, the main road snakes steeply over a forested ridge, with
pectacular views back over the city and the narrow strait, and then down through the
hervéni Gorge, gateway to Évvia's green and forested northwest.

ARRIVAL AND DEPARTURE
NORTHERN ÉVVIA

y ferry Eight or more ferries a day shuttle between
dhipsós and Arkítsa (45min; ☎ 22260 23330,
ⓦ ferriesedipsos.gr), and six between Ayiókambos and
lýfa (25min; ☎ 22260 31680, ⓦ ferriesglyfa.gr); there are
so more seasonal services from Áyios Konstandínos to
yios Yeóryios (25min; ☎ 22260 33460). Tickets are sold on
ne quayside, and buses from Athens' Liossíon 260 terminal

serve the mainland ports. There's also a ferry from the port
of Mandoúdhi on the west coast to Alónissos and Skópelos,
twice weekly in summer (ⓦ anes.gr), with connecting
buses to and from Athens.
By bus Edhipsós has three daily links to Athens via the
ferry (3hr), and just one to Halkídha (2hr 30min). Three
buses a day run between Halkídha and Límni and Roviés.

Prokópi and the Church of St John the Russian

PROKÓPI, in a broad wooded upland where the road emerges from the gorge, is famous
for its hideous 1960s pilgrimage **Church of St John the Russian**, actually a Ukrainian
soldier captured by the Ottomans early in the eighteenth century and taken to central
Anatolia, where he died. His mummified body began to work miracles, leading to
canonization; the saint's relics were brought here in the 1923 population exchange (see
p.781). A vast pilgrimage in late May sees people walking from Halkídha (and beyond)
and camping all around the church; you're likely to see pilgrims walking on the road at
any time of year, though.

Límni and around

LÍMNI, a well-preserved Neoclassical town and sheltered port, with magnificent views west
to the mainland, rivals Kárystos as the most characterful resort on Évvia. The main
drawback is a lack of decent beaches, though there are plenty of pebble strands all around.
   Immediately west of Límni, the hamlets of **Sipiádha** and **Khrónia** are virtually
suburbs, each with a good pebbly beach and a choice of accommodation. **ROVIÉS**,
7km from Límni, is a bigger place, famous for its olives and with a picturesque, ruined
medieval tower at its heart.

Folklore Museum

Límni • Tues–Sat 10am–1pm, Sun from 10.30am • €2 • ☎ 22270 31335

Behind Límni's waterfront is a maze of unnamed alleys; on one such is the little
Folklore Museum. This traces the history of the place from Mycenaean times – ancient
Elymnia was an important city in Euboea – to the twentieth century, with some
wonderful old photos, and it's a fun visit, where you're likely to get a personal tour
from the curator, who speaks little English.

Ayíou Nikoláou Galatáki

7km southeast of Límni • Daily: winter 9am–noon & 2–5pm; summer 9am–noon & 5–8pm • Free • Knock for entry; strict clothing rules apply

The beautiful monastery of **Ayíou Nikoláou Galatáki** perches on the burnt-out slopes of
Mount Kandíli. Much rebuilt since its original Byzantine foundation atop a temple of

Poseidon, the convent retains a thirteenth-century anti-pirate tower and a crypt; its recent miraculous escape from fires that devastated the countryside all around offers further proof to locals of the sanctity of the place. One of the six resident nuns will show you **frescoes** dating from a sixteenth-century renovation. Especially vivid, on the right, is the *Entry of the Righteous into Paradise*: the virtuous ascend a perilous ladder to be crowned by angels and received by Christ, while the wicked miss the rungs and fall into the maw of Leviathan.

10

Dhrymóna cascades

Inland from Roviés, a beautiful drive leads up towards Mt Xiró and a group of small waterfalls known as the **Dhrymóna cascades**. A well-maintained circular path will take you past the falls in less than 15 minutes, but it's a lovely spot, popular with locals for paddling and picnics. There's a café here and an excellent restaurant on the way up (see below).

ARRIVAL AND DEPARTURE   LÍMNI AND AROUND

By bus Buses stop on Límni's central waterfront near the bottom of the main street, Angéli Govioú. Tickets are sold at the nearby kafenío.

ACCOMMODATION

★**Eleonas** Roviés ☎ 22270 71619, ⓦ eleonashotel. com. Classy, peaceful place in a secluded olive grove outside town, with ground-floor a/c garden rooms or first-floor ones with balconies. Set back some way from the sea, north of town, but with fine views. Rooms have a/c, fridge (stocked with drinks at supermarket prices) and basic cooking facilities, and a superb home-made breakfast is included. **€75**

Graegos Studios Límni ☎ 22270 31117, ⓦ graegos. com. Four comfortable a/c studios, with well-equipped kitchens, right at the eastern end of the waterfront. The two at the front have fabulous big balconies with views of the fishing port. **€65**

Kaminos Límni ☎ 22270 31640, ⓦ kaminoshotel.com On the waterfront a couple of kilometres south of Límni this stunning conversion of a magnetite processing factory has luxurious suites, each with kitchenette and classy modern furnishings. There's also a pool and an excellent retro-industrial style restaurant in the old warehouse Breakfast included. **€125**

EATING AND DRINKING

Alonia Forest Kalamoúdhi ☎ 22270 71167. A traditional rural taverna, signed off the road to the waterfalls, serving earthy country food on a terrace with wonderful views. There's no menu, and service can be slow, especially at weekends when it's a popular local outing, but the grilled local meats and selection of daily specials (€6–9) are worth the wait; great salads and home-made pies too. Summer daily noon–10pm; winter Sat & Sun only.

Lambros Límni ☎ 22270 31351. Immaculate setting with a waterfront terrace and steps down to the water in a

tranquil spot, 500m out of town on the road to the monastery. Food is the regular Greek taverna array, with plenty of fish, cooked with care; mains €6.50–8.50. Daily 6pm–11.30pm.

Platanos Límni ☎ 22270 31686. Lovely taverna/ *tsipourádhiko* shaded by an ancient plane on the waterfront in the heart of town. Simple dishes like sardines or kalamári (€8) and a wide range of *ráki* and *tsipoúro* served with *pikilía* (small selection €8, large €16). Daily noon–midnight.

Edhipsós

EDHIPSÓS (aka **LOUTRÁ EDHIPSOÚ**, the baths of Edhipsós) is one of Greece's most popular **spa** towns, with a line of grand hotels gracing the front and plenty of places to eat and drink. The sulphurous **natural hot springs** here, with water gushing to the surface at up to 75°C, were well known in antiquity, but reached their modern heyday in the 1930s, when the likes of Winston Churchill and Greta Garbo took to the waters here. Today, the place's faded glory is undergoing something of a revival. If your wallet doesn't stretch to services at the *Thermae Sylla Spa* (see below), you can bathe for free at the adjacent public **beach**, where geothermal water pours into an artificial set of cascades. There are more free, open-air hot springs at **Ília**, 8km east, where the water is channelled into ad hoc pits by shovel-wielding locals.

ARRIVAL AND DEPARTURE **EDHIPSÓS**

By ferry Ferries arrive on the central seafront.

By bus The bus station is a couple of blocks south on Thermopotámou, the main street inland from the waterfront.

Taxis The taxi stand (☎ 22260 23280) is directly opposite where the ferry docks.

ACCOMMODATION AND EATING

Kaliva Thermopotámou & Plutárhou ☎ 22260 22735. Inland at the top of the bus station street, *Kaliva* has tables in a mulberry-shaded courtyard, serving some of the best traditional Greek food in town, at fair prices. Meze €4–5, meat dishes €6–8. Daily noon–11.30pm.

Kentrikon 25th Martíou 14 ☎ 22260 22302, ⌨ kentrikonhotel.com. Friendly hotel one street back from the seafront: it's excellent value given the facilities, which include comfortable modern rooms, gym and indoor and outdoor spa pools. Breakfast included. **€50**

Thermae Sylla Waterfront ☎ 22260 60100, ⌨ thermaesylla.gr. Five-star complex at the northern end of the seafront promenade that's by far the grandest of the surviving hotels, with indoor and outdoor pools plus a spa with a huge variety of treatments, also available to non-guests. **€170**

The north and west coasts

Beyond Edhipsós and round to the **west coast** stretches a string of small resorts, on the whole consisting of long, exposed pebble beaches, backed by hamlets of second homes and small hotels; if you want a quiet escape to old-fashioned Greece, there's plenty to like here, though very little to do except when the Athenians turn up in August. Between villages, the driving is often steep and winding, the scenery green and spectacular.

The cape immediately east of Edhipsós, off the main road, is particularly quiet and scenic, the venue of Greek family holidays and an incongruous Club Med. **ÁYIOS YEÓRYIOS** is the one coastal settlement of any size, with summer ferries from Áyios Konstandínos. On the main road, heading clockwise from Edhipsós, you come first to **AYIÓKAMBOS**, with regular **ferry** connections to Glýfa on the mainland. **NÉOS PÝRGOS** and **OREÍ**, next up, pretty much merge together into a single resort; the latter has good restaurants around its attractive harbour. **ISTIÉA**, inland, is the biggest town in the region, with a confusing slew of roads in and out and a fine beach nearby, surrounded by wetlands, at **Kanatádhika**. **PÉFKI** is another small, pleasant resort with extensive, windswept beaches either side, good for kitesurfing (see below).

Beyond Péfki, the road mainly heads inland. **Paralía Ayíou Nikoláou**, signed from the village of **ELLINIKÁ**, is a lovely, sandy cove overlooked by tavernas and by a tiny white chapel on a little islet. At **Psaropoúli**, steeply below the town of **VASILIKÁ**, there's a vast, barely developed bay of grey sand and pebbles. **PARALÍA AYÍAS ÁNNAS**, by contrast, is a substantial resort on a couple of kilometres of brownish sand, with showers and loungers at the resort end, and plenty of empty space beyond. Finally, at the tiny hamlet of **KRÝA VRÝSSI**, there's a lovely brown-sand beach with the ruins of ancient **Kirinthos** at its southern end.

ACTIVITIES **NORTH COAST**

Kitesurfing The winds at Péfki beach are exploited by the excellent kitesurfing school, Kites Guru (☎ 6977 245 438, ⌨ kitesguru.gr).

ACCOMMODATION AND EATING

Aenaon Studios Kanatádhika Beach ☎ 22260 55461, ⌨ aenaonstudios.gr. Simple one- and two-room studios in a garden setting behind the beach. It's the warmth of the welcome that sets it apart, along with the activities, from yoga, cooking or movie nights in the garden, to bird-watching in the surrounding wetlands, or hiking and fishing further afield. Excellent home-made breakfast for €6. **€40**

Paradisos Paralía Ayíou Nikoláou ☎ 22260 42257. In a wonderful setting among the pines on the point above the beach – the food is good hearty Greek staples, with plenty of local veg, and spit-roast joints at weekends; mains €6.50–8.50. Daily 9am–11pm.

To Steki tis Yiannas Oreí ☎ 22260 71540. One of a string of excellent tavernas in Oreí, with a lovely seaside location by the harbour, serving fresh fish (by kilo, or around €12 a portion), octopus and kalamári, plus daily oven-baked specials (€7–10). Daily lunch and dinner.

10

The Ionian islands

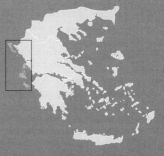

FISKÁRDHO, KEFALONIA

The Ionian islands

The six core Ionian islands, which shepherd their satellites down the west coast of the mainland, float on the haze of the Ionian Sea. Their lush green contours, a result of heavy winter rains, come as a shock to those more used to the stark outlines of the Aegean. The west coasts of the larger islands also boast some of Greece's most picturesque cliff-backed beaches, whose sands are caressed by a band of milky turquoise water leading to the deeper azure sea.

11

Tourism is the dominant influence these days, as it has been for decades on **Corfu** (Kérkyra), which was one of the first Greek islands established on the package-holiday circuit, though the continuing downturn means it does not feel as swamped as in the past. And while parts of its coastline are among the few stretches in Greece with development to match the Spanish *costas*, the island is large enough to contain parts as beautiful as anywhere in the group. The southern half of **Zákynthos** (Zante) has also gone down the same tourist path, but elsewhere the island's pace is a lot less intense. Little **Paxí** lacks the water to support large-scale hotels and has limited facilities tucked into just three villages, which means it gets totally packed in season. The most rewarding trio for island-hopping are undoubtedly **Kefaloniá, Itháki** and **Lefkádha**. Although connected to the mainland by a causeway and iron drawbridge, and boasting some excellent beaches along its stunning west coast, Lefkádha still has quite a low-key straggle of tourist centres and only two major resorts. Kefaloniá offers three "real towns" and further gorgeous beaches, as well as a selection of worthwhile attractions, while Itháki – Odysseus's rugged home – is protected from a tourist influx by an absence of sand. Although officially counted among the Ionians and constituting the seventh of the traditional *eptánisos* (heptanese or "seven islands"), rugged Kýthira is geographically quite separate from the six main islands. Only accessible from the southern Peloponnese, it is covered in Chapter 2 (see p.152).

Brief history

The Ionian islands were the Homeric realm of Odysseus, centred on Ithaca (modern Itháki), and here alone of all modern Greek territory the Ottomans never held sway – except on Lefkádha. After the fall of Byzantium, possession passed to the **Venetians**, and the islands became a keystone in Venice's maritime empire from 1386 until its collapse in 1797. Most of the population remained immune to the establishment of Italian as the official language and the arrival of Roman Catholicism, but Venetian influence remains evident in the architecture of the island capitals, despite damage from a series of earthquakes.

On Corfu, the Venetian legacy is mixed with that of the **British**, who imposed a military "protectorate" over the Ionian islands at the close of the Napoleonic Wars, before ceding the archipelago to Greece in 1864. There is, however, no question of the islanders' essential Greekness: the poet Dhionyssios Solomos, author of the national anthem, hailed from the Ionians, as did Nikos Mantzelos, who provided the music, and the first Greek president, Ioannis Kapodhistrias.

LOGGERHEAD TURTLE, OFF ZÁKYNTHOS

Highlights

❶ Corfu Town Venetian fortresses, beautiful churches, fine museums and appealing Venetian architecture. **See p.711**

❷ Longás beach, Corfu Shaded till early afternoon and backed by sheer red cliffs, this beach is an excellent hangout. **See p.724**

❸ Andípaxi Some of the Ionians' best swimming and snorkelling is on offer at the exquisite beaches of Paxí's little sister. See p.730

❹ Lefkádha's west coast Between Áï Nikítas and Pórto Katsíki lie some of the archipelago's finest and least crowded beaches. See p.739

❺ Mount Énos, Kefaloniá The highest point in the Ionians offers stunning vistas of surrounding islands and the mainland – it's also home to a unique species of pine. **See p.743**

❻ Melissáni Cave, Kefaloniá Take a boat trip inside this once-enclosed underwater cave and see dappled sunlight on the water amid rock formations. **See p.746**

❼ Itháki's Homeric sites Relive the myths on Odysseus's island by visiting locations described by Homer. **See p.750**

❽ Boat tour around Zákynthos The best way to see the impressive coastline, including the Blue Caves and Shipwreck Bay, is to cruise from Zákynthos Town. **See p.755**

HIGHLIGHTS ARE MARKED ON THE MAP ON P.710

Corfu

Dangling between the heel of Italy and the west coast of mainland Greece, green, mountainous **CORFU (Kérkyra)** was one of the first Greek islands to attract mass tourism in the 1960s. Indiscriminate exploitation turned parts into eyesores but a surprising amount of the island still consists of olive groves, mountains or woodland. The

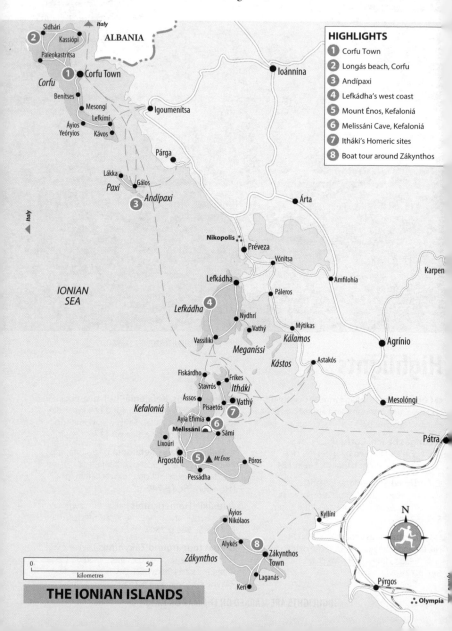

HIGHLIGHTS

1. Corfu Town
2. Longás beach, Corfu
3. Andípaxi
4. Lefkádha's west coast
5. Mount Énos, Kefaloniá
6. Melissáni Cave, Kefaloniá
7. Itháki's Homeric sites
8. Boat tour around Zákynthos

THE IONIAN ISLANDS

majority of package holidays are based in the most developed resorts and unspoilt terrain is often only a few minutes' walk away.

Corfu is thought to have been the model for Prospero and Miranda's place of exile in Shakespeare's *The Tempest*, and was certainly known to **writers** such as Spenser, Milton and – more recently – Edward Lear and Henry Miller, as well as Gerald and Lawrence Durrell. Lawrence Durrell's *Prospero's Cell* evokes the island's "delectable landscape" still evident in some of its beaches, the best of the whole archipelago.

The staggering amount of **accommodation** on the island means that competition keeps prices reasonable even in high season, at least in many resorts outside of Corfu Town. Prices at restaurants and in shops also tend to be a little lower than average for the Ionians.

ARRIVAL AND DEPARTURE

CORFU

By plane Corfu's airport, 2km south of Corfu Town, receives seasonal charters and a few scheduled flights from different parts of northern Europe, as well as scheduled year-round and seasonal domestic services (see p.716).

By ferry and hydrofoil The vast majority of domestic services, all those to Italy and the hydrofoil to Albania run from Corfu Town (see p.716), although there are a few boats to the mainland from Lefkímmi.

GETTING AROUND

By bus Corfu's bus service radiates from the capital (see p.7160). Island-wide services stop operating between 6 and 9pm, suburban ones between 9 and 10.30pm. Printed English timetables are available for both and can be picked up at the respective terminals.

By car or motorbike Many people rent vehicles to get around the island, and there are numerous international and local companies in Corfu Town (see p.716) and around the resorts.

11

Corfu Town

The capital, **CORFU TOWN**, has been one of the most elegant island capitals in the whole of Greece since it was spruced up for the EU summit in 1994. Although many of its finest buildings were destroyed by Nazi bombers in World War II, two massive forts, the sixteenth-century church of Áyios Spyrídhon and some buildings dating from French and British administrations remain intact. As the island's major port of entry by ferry or plane, Corfu Town can get packed in summer.

The city comprises a number of distinct areas. The **Historic Centre**, the area enclosed by the Old Port and the two forts, consists of several smaller districts: **Campiello**, the oldest, sits on the hill above the harbour; **Kofinéta** stretches towards the Spianádha (Esplanade); **Áyii Apóstoli** runs west of the Mitrópolis (Orthodox cathedral); while, tucked in beside the Néo Froúrio, is what remains of the old **Jewish quarter**. These districts and their tall, narrow alleys conceal some of Corfu's most beautiful architecture. The **New Town** comprises all the areas that surround the Historic Centre.

Historic Centre

The most obvious sights in the **Historic Centre** are the forts, the **Paleó Froúrio** and **Néo Froúrio**, whose designations (*paleó* – "old", *néo* – "new") are a little misleading, since what you see of the older structure was begun by the Byzantines in the mid-twelfth century, just a hundred years before the Venetians began work on the newer citadel. They have both been damaged and modified by various occupiers and besiegers – the last contribution was the Neoclassical shrine of St George, built by the British in the middle of Paleó Froúrio during the 1840s.

CORFU TOWN COMBINATION TICKET

A handy **combination ticket** covers five of Corfu Town's main attractions: the Paleó Froúrio, Antivouniotissa Museum, Asiatic Museum, Archaeological Museum (if open) and the Paleopolis Museum in Mon Repos. The ticket costs €14 and is available at any of the included sights.

Néo Froúrio

Daily 8am–3pm · Free · ☎ 26610 27370

Looming above Old Port's west side, the **Néo Froúrio** is the more architecturally interesting of Corfu Town's two forts. The entrance, at the back of the fort, gives onto cellars, dungeons and battlements, with excellent views over the town and bay; there's a small gallery and seasonal café at the summit.

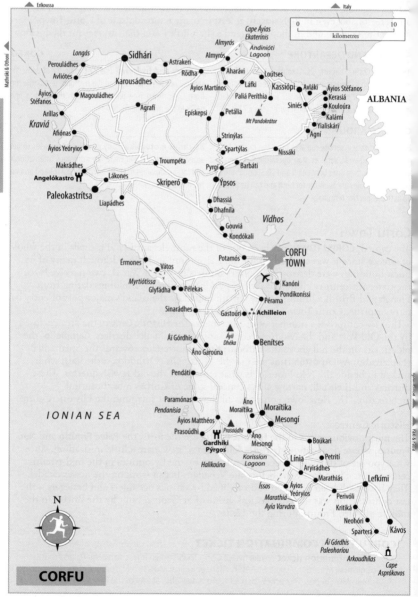

CORFU

aleó Froúrio

oril–Oct Mon–Sat 8am–8pm, Sun 8.30am–3pm; Nov–March daily 8am–3pm • €6 (or included in combination ticket) • ☎ 26610 48310

he **Paleó Froúrio**, on the east town, is not as well preserved as the Néo Froúrio and contains some incongruous modern structures, but it has a small, interesting **Byzantine Museum** just inside the gate, and even more stunning views from the central Land Tower. It also hosts daily *son et lumière* shows.

he Listón and Spianádha

ust west of the Paleó Froúrio, the focus of town life is the **Listón**, an arcaded café-lined treet built during the French occupation by the architect of the Rue de Rivoli in Paris, and the green **Spianádha** (Esplanade) it overlooks. The cricket pitch, still albeit rarely n use at the northern end of the Spianádha, is another British legacy, while at the southern end is the **Maitland Rotunda**, built to honour the first British High Commissioner of Corfu and the Ionian islands. The neighbouring statue of Ioannis Kapodhistrias celebrates the local hero and statesman (1776–1831) who led the diplomatic efforts for independence and was made Greece's first president in 1827.

11

Palace of SS Michael and George

Listón • **Asiatic Museum** Daily 8am–8pm • €6 (or included in combination ticket) • ☎ 26610 30443, ⓦ matk.gr • **Municipal Gallery of Corfu** Daily 8.30am–3pm • Free • ☎ 26610 48690 • ⓦ artcorfu.com

At the far northern end of the Listón is the nineteenth-century **Palace of SS Michael and George**, a solidly British edifice built as the residence of their High Commissioner (one of whom was the future British prime minister William Gladstone) and later used as a palace by the Greek monarchy. The former state rooms house the **Asiatic Museum**, a must for aficionados of oriental culture. Amassed by Corfiot diplomat Gregorios Manos (1850–1929) and others, it includes Noh theatre masks, woodcuts, wood and brass statuettes, samurai weapons and artworks from Thailand, Korea and Tibet, as well as some exquisite garments and jewellery from Central Asia in the Jason Deighton-Sartzetakis collection. The adjoining **Municipal Gallery of Corfu** holds a small collection of contemporary Greek art.

Antivouniotissa Museum

Arseníou • Tues–Sun 8.30am–3pm • €2 (or included in combination ticket) • ☎ 26610 38313 • ⓦ antivouniotissamuseum.gr

Up a short flight of steps on Arseníou, the **Antivouniotissa Museum** (often still known by its former name, the Byzantine Museum) is housed in the restored church of the Panayía Andivouniótissa. It houses church frescoes, sculptures and sections of mosaic floors from the ancient site of Paleópolis, just south of Corfu Town. There are also some pre-Christian artefacts, and a collection of icons dating from between the fifteenth and nineteenth centuries.

Solomos Museum

Theodhórou Mákri, off Arseníou • Mon–Fri 9.30am–2pm • €1 • ☎ 26610 30674

This hidden **Solomos Museum** is dedicated to modern Greece's most famous nineteenth-century poet, **Dhionysios Solomos**. Born on Zákynthos, Solomos was author of the poem *Amnos stín Eleftheria* ("*Hymn to Liberty*"), which was to become the Greek national anthem. He studied at Corfu's Ionian Academy and lived in a house on this site for much of his life.

Áyios Spyrídhon

Spyrídhonos • Daily 8am–9pm • Free

A block behind the Listón is the sixteenth-century church of **Áyios Spyrídhon**, whose maroon-domed campanile dominates the town. Here you will find the silver-encrusted coffin of the island's patron saint, **Spyrídhon** – Spyros in the diminutive – after whom seemingly half the male population is named. Four times a year (Palm Sunday and the following Sat, Aug 11 and the first Sun in Nov), to the

11

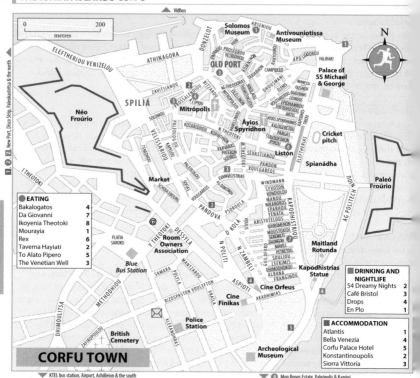

CORFU TOWN

EATING
Bakalogatos	4
Da Giovanni	7
Ikoyenia Theotoki	8
Mourayia	1
Rex	6
Taverna Hayiati	2
To Alato Pipero	5
The Venetian Well	3

DRINKING AND NIGHTLIFE
54 Dreamy Nights	2
Café Bristol	3
Drops	4
En Plo	1

ACCOMMODATION
Atlantis	1
Bella Venezia	4
Corfu Palace Hotel	5
Konstantinoupolis	2
Siorra Vittoria	3

accompaniment of much celebration and feasting, the relics are paraded through the town streets. Each of the days commemorates a miraculous deliverance of the island credited to the saint – twice from plague, once from a famine and, in the eighteenth century, from the Turks.

Mitrópolis

Platía Mitropóleos • Daily 8am–7pm • Free

After Áyios Spyrídhon, the next most important of the town's many churches, is the **Mitrópolis** (Orthodox cathedral), which is perched at the top of its own square opposite the Old Port. It also houses the remains of a saint, in this case St Theodora, the ninth-century wife of Emperor Theophilos. The building dates from 1577, and the plain exterior conceals a splendid iconostasis, as well as some fine icons, including a sixteenth-century image of *Saint George Slaying the Dragon*.

Vídhos

Hourly shuttle *kaïkia* run from the Old Port (daily 8am–1.30am; €2 return)

Vídhos, the wooded island visible from the Old Port, is a quieter day-trip destination than Vlahérna or Pondikoníssi (see p.716). It makes a particularly enjoyable summer evening excursion, when there is often live music at the restaurant near the jetty.

New Town

There are a couple of noteworthy sights in the **New Town** which surrounds the Historic Centre. This area also encompasses much of Corfu Town's commercial heart, centred around busy **Platía Saróko**.

Archeological Museum

Vráïla 1 • Closed until 2018; likely opening hours Tues–Sun 8.30am–3pm • €3 (or included in combination ticket) • ☎ 26610 30680

At the time of writing, Corfu Town's **Archeological Museum** was nearing the end of extensive renovations: it's reopening is scheduled for 2018. Entry details and some exhibits may have changed, but you can be sure it will still include the star attraction, a massive (17m) **Gorgon pediment** excavated from the Doric temple of Artemis at Paleópolis, just south of Corfu Town, as well as a fine range of neolithic and classical treasures.

British cemetery

nr of Zafiropoúlou and Kolokotróni • 24hr • Free

Just south of Platía Saróko, the well-maintained **British cemetery** features some elaborate civic and military memorials. It's a quiet green space away from the madness of Saróko and, in spring and early summer, comes alive with dozens of species of orchids and other exotic blooms.

The outskirts

Each of the sights on the sprawling **outskirts** of the city can easily be seen in a morning or afternoon, and you could conceivably cover several in one day. Mon Repos and the remains of Paleópolis are the most worthwhile sights at which to spend some time.

Mon Repos estate and around

Estate Daily 8am–7.30pm • Free • **Paleópolis Museum** Daily 8.30am–3.30pm • €4 • ☎ 26610 41369

About 1.5km around the bay from the Rotunda and the Archeological Museum, tucked behind Mon Repos beach, the area centred on the **Mon Repos estate** contains the most accessible archeological remains on the island, collectively known as **Paleópolis**. Within the estate, thick woodland conceals two **Doric temples**, dedicated to Hera and Poseidon. The Neoclassical **Mon Repos villa**, built by British High Commissioner Frederic Adam in 1824 and handed over to Greece in 1864, is the birthplace of Britain's Prince Philip and has been converted into the **Paleópolis Museum**. As well as various archeological finds from the vicinity, including some fine sculpture, it contains previous residents' period furniture and temporary modern art exhibitions.

Other remains worth a peek outside the confines of the estate include the **Early Christian Basilica** (Tues–Sun 8.30am–3pm; free) opposite the entrance, the **Temple of Artemis** (open access; free), a few hundred metres west, and the eleventh-century church of **Áyii Iáson and Sosípater**, back towards the seafront on Náfsikas.

THE IONIAN SCHOOL OF PAINTING

The Ionian islands have a strong tradition of excellence in the fine arts, particularly iconography. Once occupied by the Venetians and later the British, the islands spent centuries more in touch with developments in western Europe than in the Ottoman empire.

Until the late seventeenth century, religious art in the Ionians, as elsewhere, was dominated by the stylistic purity and austerity of the Cretan School. The founder of the **Ionian School of painting** is **Panayiotis Dhoxaras**, who was born in the Peloponnese in 1662 but, after studying in Venice and Rome, moved to Zákynthos and later lived and worked in Lefkádha and Corfu until his death in 1729. From his travels, Dhoxaras absorbed the spirit of Italian Renaissance art, and brought a greater degree of naturalism into iconography by showing his subjects, usually saints, in more human poses amid everyday surroundings. He also introduced the technique of **oil painting** into Greece in place of the older method of mixing pigments with egg yolk.

Dhoxaras' work was carried on by his son, **Nikolaos** (1710–1775), and over the next two centuries the tradition flourished through the skilled brushwork of a host of talented artists, such as Corfiot **Yioryios Khrysoloras** (1680–1762), Zakynthian **Nikolaos Kandounis** (1768–1834) and three generations of the Proselandis family, starting with **Pavlos Proselandis** (1784–1837).

Vlahérna and Pondikoníssi

Bus #2 leaves Platía Saróko every 30min for Vlahérna convent; boats frequently leave Vlahérna dock for Pondikoníssi (€3 return)

The most famous excursion from Corfu Town is to the islets of **Vlahérna and Pondikoníssi** 2km south of town below the hill of Kanóni, named after the single cannon trained out to sea atop it. Reached by a short causeway, the tiny, white convent of Vlahérna is one of the most photographed images on Corfu. Pondikoníssi, tufted by greenery from which peeks the small chapel of Panayía Vlahernón, is identified in legend with a ship from Odysseus's fleet, petrified by Poseidon in revenge for the blinding of his son Polyphemus.

Achilleion

Gastoúri, 6km south of Corfu Town • Daily 8am–7pm (Nov–April till 4pm) • €8, including headset • ☎ 26610 56245, ⓦ www.achillion-corfu .gr • Bus #10

Just south of Corfu Town, past the resort sprawl of Pérama sits the bizarre **Achilleion**, a palace built in a mercifully unique blend of Teutonic and Neoclassical styles in 1890 by Elizabeth, Empress of Austria. Henry Miller considered it "the worst piece of gimcrackery" that he'd ever laid eyes on and thought it "would make an excellent museum for surrealistic art". The house is predictably grandiose but the **gardens** are pleasant to walk around and afford splendid views in all directions.

ARRIVAL

CORFU TOWN

By plane The airport is 2km south of the town centre. Dedicated bus #15 connects with central Corfu Town hourly, or you can flag down blue city buses #5 and #6 at the junction 500m north of the terminal. Taxis charge a rather steep €10 into town.

Domestic destinations Athens (3–4 daily; 1hr); Kefaloniá (summer 2–3 weekly; 1hr 25min); Préveza (summer 5 weekly; 30min); Thessaloníki (summer 2 weekly; 1hr); Zákynthos (summer 2–3 weekly; 2hr 20min).

By bus There are two bus terminals: the islandwide KTEL green bus service (also for Athens and Thessaloníki) operates from a new terminal 1.5km southwest of the centre at Ethnikís Lefkímis 13 (☎ 26610 28900, ⓦ greenbuses.gr); the suburban blue bus system, which also serves nearby resorts such as Benítses and Dhassiá, is based in Platía Saróko (☎ 26610 31595, ⓦ corfucitybus. com). Buses to Athens (3 daily; 7hr 30min–8hr) and Thessaloníki (1–2 daily; 5hr 30min–6hr) board the ferry from the New Port; schedules are year-round.

By ferry All vessels dock at the New Port (Néo Limáni), just west of the Néo Froúrio. The Old Port (Paleó Limáni), east of the New Port, is used only for day excursions. Most of the ferry offices are on the main road opposite the New Port; if you're travelling to Italy, go to Igoumenítsa for more options as the number of ferries direct to Italy has been severely reduced. The port authority (domestic ☎ 26610 32655, international ☎ 26610 30481) can advise on services. For the destinations below, frequencies given are for the summer season and are greatly reduced or nonexistent in winter.

Destinations Ancona (2 weekly; 15hr); Bari (10 weekly; 8hr–10hr 45min); Brindisi (6 weekly; 7–12hr); Eríkoussa/ Mathráki/Othoní (3 weekly; 2–4hr); Igoumenítsa (every 15min–1hr; 1hr 15min–2hr).

By hydrofoil Hydrofoils dock at the eastern end of the New Port and run for most of the tourist season.

Destinations Gáïos (Paxí; May–Oct 1–3 daily; 50min); Sarande (Albania; 1–2 daily; 30min).

By car Most of the international car rental chains have outlets at the airport and New Port. Among the more competitive local companies are Sunrise (Ethnikís Andístasis 6, ☎ 26610 44325, ⓦ corfusunrise.com) or Ionian Travel (☎ 26610 80444, ⓦ ioniantravel.gr), based in nearby Gouviá but happy to bring vehicles to the airport or your accommodation.

By motorbike or scooter Motorbikes and scooters can be rented from Moto Atlantis, Xenofóndos Stratigoú 52 (☎ 26610 23665), in the New Port.

ACCOMMODATION

Accommodation in Corfu Town is busy all year, and expensive. The Room Owners' Association at D. Theotóki 2A (Mon–Fri 9am–1.30pm, plus summer Tues, Thurs & Fri 6–8pm; ☎ 26610 26133, ⓔ oitkcrf@otenet.gr) can help find rooms.

Atlantis Xenofóndos Stratigoú 48 ☎ 26610 35560, ⓦ atlantis-hotel-corfu.com. Large and spacious a/c hotel in the New Port; with its functional 1960s ambience, it rather lacks character, but the rooms are perfectly adequate. **€85**

★**Bella Venezia** Zambéli 4 ☎ 26610 46500, ⓦ bellaveneziahotel.com. Smart, yellow Neoclassical building which blends elegance with a cosy atmosphere. The sophisticated rooms are furnished and decorated in warm hues. Breakfast in the airy conservatory included. **€113**

orfu Palace Hotel Leofóros Dhimokratías 2 ☎ 26610 9485, ⓦ corfupalace.com. The most luxurious hotel on he island, with sweeping staircases up from the lobby, ▪door and outdoor pools, landscaped gardens, a highly-ated French restaurant and well-appointed rooms, each ✓ith a marble bath. Breakfast included. **€220**

▪onstantinoupolis Zavitsiánou 11 ☎ 26610 48716, Ͻ konstantinoupolis.gr. A classy hotel in the Old Port with tasteful decoration and comfortable rooms, most with fine harbour views. Good discounts out of high season. Buffet breakfast included. **€108**

Siorra Vittoria Stefánou Pandová 36 ☎ 26610 36300, ⓦ siorravittoria.com. Boutique hotel converted from an 1823 mansion that exudes class all over, from its period lounge to the lavishly furnished rooms. There is also a lovely garden, a rarity in Corfu Town. Breakfast included. **€166**

EATING

▪akalogatos Alipíou 23 ☎ 26613 01721, ⓦ mpakalogatoscorfu.gr. Deservedly popular retro-style ͆sipourádhiko in Spiliá which serves a variety of veg, cheese, meat and fish mezédhes all under €7, plus microbrewery beer and local wine. Daily 11am–2am.

▪a Giovanni Kapodhístriou 6 ☎ 26610 44055, ⓦ dagiovanni.net. Among the town's many Italian ▪restaurants, this one serves perhaps the most authentic food and enjoys a fine location opposite the Spianádha. Fine antipasti, pizzas and meat or seafood spaghetti dishes cost €10–17. Daily noon–1am.

Ikoyenia Theotoki Alkiviádhou Dhárri, Garítsa ☎ 26610 35004, ⓦ tavernatheotokis.com. By far the best of the several establishments tucked behind the seafront park, this popular family taverna serves excellent mezédhes, meat and good-value fish dishes for around €10 or less. March–Oct daily noon–2am.

★**Mourayia** Arseníou 15–17 ☎ 26610 33815, ⓦ mouragia.gr. An unassuming, good-value taverna near the Byzantine Museum that does a range of tasty mezédhes for €6–8, including sausage or seafood such as mussels and shrimp in exquisite sauces. It also boasts views of passing ferries and Vídhos island. March–Nov daily noon–midnight.

Rex Kapodhistríou 66 ☎ 26610 39649, ⓦ rexrestaurant .gr. Rather pricey, owing to its location just behind the Listón, but this place has some of the best food in town, especially the delicious oven dishes, such as pork stuffed with plum and fig (€18). Daily noon–9pm.

Taverna Hayiati New Port ☎ 26610 21740. Conveniently located for ferry departures, this welcoming place has an old-fashioned feel and serves up simple grills like chops, plus some oven dishes, for well under €10. Daily 10.30am–10pm.

To Alato Pipero Dhoná 17 ☎ 6942 263 873. This ouzerí in Spiliá is one of the best places to have sprung up in recent years; it serves a moderate range of delicious mezédhes, such as sausages and saganáki (most €4–6), plus mains all for under €10. Daily noon–2am.

★**The Venetian Well** Platía Kremastí ☎ 26615 50955, ⓦ venetianwell.gr. Tucked in a tiny square a few alleys north of the cathedral, this classy place provides superb quality Greek nouvelle cuisine. Main dishes such as lamb cooked with aubergine purée, fig chutney and baby potatoes cost over €20, while starters like the superb lobster and crayfish soup go for around €14. Easter–Oct daily 7pm–midnight.

11

DRINKING, NIGHTLIFE AND ENTERTAINMENT

There are some hip youth-oriented bars in town and a dwindling number of clubs on the once famed "disco strip" of Ethnikís Andistáseos, a couple of kilometres north past the New Port, though action has mostly shifted to the resorts.

CAFÉ-BARS

Café Bristol Platía Vrahlióti ☎ 6936 660 101. Well-established town centre favourite with quirky decor, old-fashioned floor tiles and reasonably priced cocktails. Daily 9am–late.

En Plo Faliráki jetty ☎ 26610 27000. This popular café boasts an unbeatably brilliant, breezy setting, with views of the Paleó Froúrio. A fine place for a preprandial ouzo or late-night brandy. Daily 10am–late.

CLUBS

54 Dreamy Nights Emborikó Kéndro, Ethnikís Andistáseos 54 ☎ 6940 645 436, ⓦ facebook .com/54dreamynights. This huge club has outlasted all its rivals in and around the Emborikó Kéndro shopping centre, with the latest sounds, a retractable roof and

frequent fireworks. Daily 10pm–late.

Drops Leofóros Dhimokratías 14 ☎ 6944 912 947. A popular place, perched above the yacht harbour with super views of the Old Fort, that buzzes till the wee hours with the clink of glasses and the latest trendy sounds. Daily 8pm–late.

CINEMAS

Cine Finikas Akadhimías ☎ 26610 39768. Down the cul-de-sac extension of Akadhimías, the town's open-air summer cinema is a lovely place to take in a film. June–Sept, showings usually 9pm & 11pm.

Cine Orfeus Akadhimías, at Aspióti ☎ 26610 39768. Corfu's winter cinema has comfy seats and a big screen. Oct–May, times vary.

The northeast

The **northeast**, at least beyond the suburban resorts near Corfu Town, is the most typically Greek part of Corfu – it's mountainous, with a rocky coastline chopped into pebbly bays and coves, above wonderfully clear seas.

Dhassiá

Six kilometres from Corfu Town, the coastline begins to improve at **Dhafníla** and **DHASSIÁ**, set in adjacent wooded bays with pebbly beaches. The latter, the first worthwhile place to stop in this direction, is much larger and contains nearly all the area's facilities, including a couple of major **watersports** enterprises.

Ýpsos

Ýpsos, 2km north of Dhassiá, can't really be recommended to anyone but hardened bar-hoppers, though it is home to a diving centre (see opposite). The thin pebble beach lies right beside the busy coast road, and the resort is generally pretty tacky.

11

Barbáti

At **BARBÁTI**, 4km north of Ýpsos, you'll find the sandiest beach on this coast, though its charm has been somewhat diminished recently by the construction of the gargantuan *Riviera Barbati* apartment complex. The beach is a favourite with families, and much accommodation is prebooked in advance.

Agní and Yialiskári

The first of a series of idyllic pebbly coves you encounter when travelling north from largely missable Nissáki is **AGNÍ**, a favourite mooring spot for yachties, largely because of its well-established reputation as something of a gourmet's paradise. The even more scenic, facility-free bay of **YIALISKÁRI** can be reached in ten minutes by a path from Agní.

Kalámi and Kouloúra

KALÁMI, around 3km north of Agní, is somewhat commercialized, but the village is still small and you can imagine how it would have looked in the year Lawrence

---

MOUNT PANDOKRÁTOR

Mount Pandokrátor, Corfu's highest mountain, is crowned by **Pandokrátoras monastery**, whose main sanctuary, built in the seventeenth century, is open to visitors; nothing remains of the original buildings from three centuries earlier.

The most direct route from the south is signposted via Spartýlas and then the village of **Strinýlas**, a popular base for walkers and served by buses from Corfu Town. An alternative approach from the north coast goes via Loútses to the charming ghost village of **Paliá Períthia**, with the crumbling remains of half a dozen churches and some good restaurants – from here, the summit is a steep 5km climb, or you'll need a four-wheel drive. The main westerly route ascends via **Láfki** to **Petália**, just south of which a paved road leads the final 5km east to the summit.

A useful **map** of the mountain by island-based cartographer Stephan Jaskulowski or one of Hilary Whitton-Paipeti's walking books are available from the better English-language bookshops in Corfu Town.

ACCOMMODATION AND EATING

★**The Merchant's House** Paliá Períthia ☎ 26630 98444, ⓦ merchantshousecorfu.com. Superb renovated old stone house, with warmly painted suites, which can sleep four, and stylish furniture. This boutique B&B offers comfort, great views and a fine breakfast. April–Oct. **€165**

★**Old Perithia** Paliá Períthia ☎ 26630 98055. Worth climbing any mountain for, this traditional taverna is renowned for its succulent goat (€8) and home-produced feta cheese. The views are splendid too, of course. Noon–midnight: May–Sept daily; Oct–April Sat & Sun.

Durrell spent here on the eve of World War II. The **White House**, where Durrell wrote *Prospero's Cell*, is now split in two: the ground floor is an excellent taverna (see p.720), while the upper floor houses exclusive accommodation. The tiny harbour of **KOULOÚRA**, barely a kilometre north of Kalámi, has managed to keep its charm intact, set at the edge of an unspoilt bay with nothing to distract from the pine trees and *kaïkia* apart from its idyllically located taverna (see p.720).

Áyios Stéfanos

The most attractive resort on this stretch of coast, 3km down a lane from Siniés on the main road, is **ÁYIOS STÉFANOS** (officially Áyios Stéfanos Sinión to distinguish it from its namesake in northwest Corfu). The delightful bay bends almost at a right angle, the northern section of which contains the beach, beyond the string of restaurants.

ARRIVAL AND GETTING AROUND | THE NORTHEAST

By bus Green buses between Corfu Town and Kassiópi serve all resorts, along with some blue suburban buses as far as Dhassiá.

By boat In Áyios Stéfanos, Giannis Boats (☎ 26630 81532, ⓦ giannisboats.gr) rents out vessels of varying sizes from €50/day.

11

ACTIVITIES

Diving Ýpsos beach is home to one of the island's major diving centres, Waterhoppers (☎ 26610 93867, ⓦ waterhopperscorfu.gr).

Watersports 2001 is the most prominent water-sports outfit in Dhassiá (☎ 26610 47525, ⓔ 2001skiclub@in.gr).

ACCOMMODATION

Kalami Tourist Services, based in the eponymous village (☎ 26630 91062, ⓦ kalamibay.com), manages a range of properties in Kalámi and Agní.

DHASSIÁ AND DHAFNÍLA

Dassia Beach/Dassia Margarita Dhassiá ☎ 26610 93224, ⓦ dassiahotels.gr. These two almost adjacent sister hotels both have attached restaurants and balconied guest rooms. The *Margarita* is much cheaper, while the plusher *Beach* has a new annexe. Breakfast included. April–Oct. **€40**

★ **Dionysus Camping Village** Dhafníla ☎ 26610 91417, ⓦ dionysuscamping.gr. Corfu's top campsite has tents pitched under terraced olive trees, and bungalow huts for rent, plus a pool, shop, bar and a restaurant. Camping **€16.50**, bungalow **€24**

BARBÁTI

Paradise Barbáti ☎ 26630 91338, ⓦ corfu-paradise.gr. Up above the main road and set amid a colourful tiered garden, this place offers decent-sized rooms that have

balconies with bird's-eye sea views. April–Oct. **€55**

AGNÍ AND YIALISKÁRI

★ **Orchard Villas** Yialiskári ☎ 0777 166 0035 (UK), ⓔ sales@theorchardvillas.com. Four superbly constructed luxury villas of varying sizes, perched on the hillside above a deserted beach. All are beautifully furnished, fully equipped and have individual pools. They even have UK sockets. May–Oct. **€175**

ÁYIOS STÉFANOS

Kochili ☎ 26630 81700, ⓦ kochilitaverna.com. This fine family taverna, which serves good home-style oven food and grills for €7–8, also has the only independently bookable rooms in the village, simply furnished but with lovely bay views. May–Oct. **€40**

EATING, DRINKING AND NIGHTLIFE

DHASSIÁ

EDEM Dhassiá ☎ 26630 93013, ⓦ edemclub.com. Corfu's prime beach nightclub draws revellers from far and wide. International DJs play cutting-edge techno, trance and other dance genres to a lively crowd. Also hosts occasional rock and other theme nights. May–Sept daily 9pm–late.

Karydia Dhassiá ☎ 26630 93562. A good restaurant on the main road, with a verdant garden, serving well-prepared versions of Corfiot specialities such as *sofríto* (beef

fried in garlic sauce) and *pastitsádha* (pasta-and-meat dish) for under €10, accompanied by decent barrelled wine. April–Oct daily 2pm–midnight.

AGNÍ AND YIALISKÁRI

★ **Nikolas** Agní ☎ 26630 91243, ⓦ agnibay.com. The oldest and best taverna of the renowned Agní trio. Superb home-style dishes (around €10–12) such as lamb *kléftiko* are served with a smile, and there are plenty of tasty *mezédhes* to choose from. Also has accommodation. April–Oct daily 9am–1am; Nov–March Fri–Sun noon–1am.

KÁLAMI AND KOULOÚRA

Kouloúra Kouloúra ☎ 26630 91253, ⓦ tavernakouloura .com. This taverna dates from 1960 and is deservedly popular for its romantic location right by the water and its excellent fresh fish – unusually, the more expensive species are sold by the portion, from €22. April–Oct noon–midnight.

White House Kalámi ☎ 26630 91040, ⓦ thewhitehouse.gr. Located in the old Durrell house and

recommended for its specials, such as mussels and swordfish with garlic (€13–23), though it's also good for simple grills, salads and a variety of *mezédhes*. Noon–1am: April–Oct daily; Nov–March Fri–Sun.

ÁYIOS STÉFANOS

★**Fagopotion** ☎ 26630 82020. With a deck right on the quay, this place serves finely prepared seafood, plus dishes such as rabbit *stifádho* and unusual items such as *zogorítiki* (soufflé with four cheeses). Most mains €10–20. Noon–1am: April–Oct daily; Nov–March Fri–Sun.

The north coast

The north coast between **Kassiópi** and **Sidhári** is blessed with some of the island's best stretches of sand and, as a direct result, is also home to a few of Corfu's most crowded package-tourism resorts, which vary in degrees of development but still have plenty to offer the independent traveller.

Kassiópi

At the far east end of the north coast is **KASSIÓPI**, a fishing village that's been transformed into a major party resort. The Roman emperor Tiberius had a villa here, and the village's sixteenth-century Panayía Kassópitra church is said to stand on the site of a temple of Zeus once visited by Nero. Little of Kassiópi's past survives, apart from an abandoned Angevin kástro on the headland – most visitors come for the nightlife and the five **pebbly beaches**, the largest of which is **Kalamiónas**, close to the coast road.

Almyrós beach and Aharávi

Little-developed **Almyrós beach**, around 10km west along the marshy, overgrown coastline from Kassiópi, is one of the longest on the island, with only a few apartment buildings and one huge new resort dotted sporadically behind it. The **Andinióti lagoon**, a haven for birds and twitchers, backs Cape Ayías Ekaterínis to the east, which marks the northern end of the Corfu Trail (see box, p.727).

At the western end of Almyrós beach, the old village of **AHARÁVI** is tucked on the inland side of the busy main road in a quiet crescent. The village serves as a base for those seeking alternative routes up onto **Mount Pandokrátor** (see box, p.718). Roads to small hamlets such as Áyios Martínos and Láfki continue onto the mountain, and even a stroll up from the back of Aharávi will find you on the upper slopes in under an hour.

Folklore Museum of Acharávi

Western end of main road • Daily 10am–2pm; phone for out of hours visits • €3 • ☎ 26630 63052, ⓦ museum-acharavi.webs.com

Aharávi's impressive **Folklore Museum of Acharávi** spreads across two large floors, with the ground level displaying dozens of old photos, maps, ornaments and furniture. In the basement, you can look round well-designed reconstructions of various shops such as a barber and a doctor's surgery, as well as typical period rooms, all with the original furnishings and equipment, such as a well-worn olive press.

Ródha and Sidhári

RÓDHA, barely 3km west of Aharávi, has tipped over into overdevelopment, and is not the place to come for a quiet time, though it does offer some handy facilities. "Old Ródha" is a small warren of alleys between the main road and the seafront, where you'll find the best restaurants and bars.

At the west end of the north coast, **SIDHÁRI** is totally dominated by British package tourists; its small but pretty town square, with a bandstand set in a small garden, is lost a welter of restaurants, bars and shops. The **beach** is sandy but not terribly clean, and many people tend to head just west to the curious coves, walled by wind-carved sandstone cliffs, around the vaunted Canal d'Amour. Sidhári also has its own modest **water park** (Ⓦsidariwaterpark.com; €5), a good place to keep the kids happy.

GETTING AROUND   THE NORTH COAST

By car or motorbike Vlasseros Travel (☎ 26630 95695, Ⓔ vlaseros@gmail.com) is Sidhári's biggest general tourist agency and handles car rental. In Ródha, Myron offers good rates for motorbike rental (☎ 26630 63477).

By boat Voyager in Ródha (☎ 6932 908 173) has boat rental from €15/hr.

ACTIVITIES

Diving Kassiópi is home to one of the island's most reliable diving operations, Corfu Divers (☎ 26630 81218, Ⓦ corfu-divers.com), which is partly British-run.

Horseriding Costas in Ródha offers horseriding (☎ 6944 160 011; €15/hr per person for groups of five or more), as does Vlasseros Travel in Sidhári (€15/hr; see above).

ACCOMMODATION

11

KASSIÓPI

★ Kastro ☎ 26630 81045, Ⓦ kastrokassiopi.com. Overlooking the beach behind the castle, these smart a/c apartments have balconies with sweeping views, as does the attached restaurant, which does excellent fresh food. May to mid-Oct. **€50**

Panayiota Apartments ☎ 26630 81063, Ⓦ panayotakassiopi.com. Bargain studios, quite small and simply furnished, one block behind Kalamíones beach on the west side of the castle's peninsula. April–Oct. **€35**

ALMYRÓS BEACH AND AHARÁVI

Akti Anastasia Almyrós Beach ☎ 6977 972 280, Ⓦ aktianastasia.gr. The ideal place for a peaceful escape, this squat rectangular block sits on a grassy plot close to the

quiet beach and has sea-facing balconies. May–Oct. **€40**

Dandolo Aharávi ☎ 26630 63557, Ⓦ dandolo.gr. Set in lush grounds on the edge of the old village, the refurbished complex contains fair-sized studios with well-equipped kitchens and verandas. April–Oct. **€45**

RÓDHA AND SIDHÁRI

Afroditi Ródha ☎ 26630 63103, Ⓔ just_2beautiful @yahoo.gr. The independently rented rooms at this sizeable seafront hotel all have balconies overlooking the sea and a fridge. Breakfast included. May–Oct. **€40**

Roda Camping Ródha ☎ 26630 93120, Ⓦ rodacamping. gr. Around 2km east of the resort, one of the island's best campsites offers a plethora of amenities, including a pool, restaurant and minimarket. May–Sept. **€15.50**

EATING, DRINKING AND NIGHTLIFE

KASSIÓPI

Calypso ☎ 26630 81000. Low-key cocktail bar by the main village junction that gets livelier later on with a mixture of 1960s, 1970s and 1980s music. April–Oct daily 9am–late.

Janis ☎ 26630 81082, Ⓦ janisrestaurant.com. Where Kalamíones beach meets the coast road, this huge taverna has an extensive menu of starters, salads, veg and meaty main courses for €8–10, plus pricier fish and lobster you can choose from a tank. April–Oct daily 9am–2am.

The Old School Taverna ☎ 26630 81211. Fish restaurant at the harbour, which offers deals on the daily catch, plus meat dishes such as *stifádho* and *sofríto* for €8–9 and all the standard dips. May–Oct daily 11am–1am.

ALMYRÓS BEACH AND AHARÁVI

★ Theritas Aharávi ☎ 26630 63527. This taverna in the old village is the most authentic in the area, serving good home-cooked dishes (€7–9) such as *sofríto*, grills and various starters as well as very palatable wine. May–Oct daily noon–1am.

Votsalakia Aharávi ☎ 26630 63346. At the western end of Aharávi beach, this is the best of the seafront restaurants, serving fresh fish and seafood, from around €8, as well as the usual array of salads and mezédhes. May–Oct daily 10am–midnight.

RÓDHA AND SIDHÁRI

Dolphin Ródha ☎ 26630 63431. This seafront taverna in Old Ródha is the best place for fish or seafood (mostly €9–12), which you can enjoy beside the waves that lap below the patio, accompanied by some good local barrelled wine. May–Oct daily 11am–1am.

Kavvadias Sidhári ☎ 26630 99032. By far the resort's most authentic taverna, on the eastern stretch of beach. It dishes up all the Greek favourites, mostly under €10, and makes the odd foray into Asian cuisine. Try their homemade ouzo. April–Oct daily 10am–midnight.

Talk of the Town Sidhári ☎ 26630 99113. Snazzy Brit-run bar, on the main strip, which features a variety of music, some live shows, and has an upmarket restaurant on one side of the premises. Open all year. Daily noon–late.

Corfu's satellite islands

Only three of Corfu's quintet of **Dhiapóndia islands**, scattered up to 20km off the northwest coast, are inhabited: Eríkoussa, Othoní and Mathráki. Each of them supports a tiny year-round community but they only really come alive in summer and even then the islands remain a relaxed backwater.

Flattish **Eríkoussa** is the sandiest and most visited of the three. There is an excellent golden sandy beach right by the harbour and quieter **Bragíni beach**, reached by a path across the wooded island interior. **OTHONÍ** is the largest island and has a handful of places to stay and eat in its port, **Ámmos**, which has two pebbly beaches. The village of **Horió** in the island's centre and sandy but deserted **Fýki Bay** are worth visiting if you stay. Hilly, densely forested and with the long, almost invariably deserted **Portéllo beach**, beautiful **MATHRÁKI** has the fewest inhabitants, though it is gradually gearing up towards visitors.

ARRIVAL AND DEPARTURE
CORFU'S SATELLITE ISLANDS

Day-trips Some travel agencies in the northern resorts offer day-trips to Eríkoussa, while a trip taking in all three islands from Sidhári or Áyios Stéfanos is excellent value. Vlasseros Travel in Sidhári (see p.721) run trips to Eríkoussa (4 weekly; €20), while on the west coast, day-trips run several times a week in season (€30 per person) from Áyios Stéfanos to all three islands.

By kaïkia and ferry There are passenger services from Áyios Stéfanos on the Aspiotis lines *kaïki* (Mathráki/Othoní 3 weekly; Eríkousa 2 weekly; €12–15 return; ☎ 26630 41297, ⓦ aspiotislines.gr). The twice-weekly ferry from Corfu Town (2–4hr) is the least efficient way to get there.

ACCOMMODATION, EATING AND DRINKING

On Othoní **rooms** are rented by local islanders such as Tassos Kassimis (☎ 26630 71700; €35) and Khristos Aryiros (☎ 26630 71652; €40), both based on Portéllo beach.

Erikousa Eríkoussa ☎ 26630 71555, ⓦ hotelerikousa. gr. Busy throughout the season by virtue of being the island's sole hotel, with simple but adequate rooms, *Erikousa* also has the only bona fide taverna. Breakfast included. May–Sept. **€65**

Hotel Calypso Othoní ☎ 26630 72162, ⓦ othonoi.gr. Some 200m east of the jetty, Othoní's only hotel has neat, comfortably furnished rooms with balconies plus a small bar. May–Sept. **€60**

La Locanda dei Sogni Othoní ☎ 26630 71640, ⓦ othoni. com. Quality but not unreasonably priced Italian restaurant, which does a line in authentic antipasti, pasta and pizza dishes for €10 or less, plus plenty of Greek items. They also rent out some rooms (€45). May–Sept daily noon–1am.

Port Centre Mathráki. Good restaurant on the harbour that specializes in freshly caught fish at very decent prices, plus a few simple salads and mezédhes. Most dishes under €10. Late May to Sept daily noon–midnight.

Paleokastrítsa

PALEOKASTRÍTSA, a sprawling village 23km west of Corfu Town, surrounded by dramatic hills and cliffs, has been identified as the Homeric city of Scheria, where Odysseus was washed ashore and escorted by Nausicaa to the palace of her father Alkinous, king of the Phaeacians. It's a stunning site, as you would expect, with a delightful centre, though it's one that's long been engulfed by tourism.

Beaches

The focal point of the village is the largest and least attractive of three **beaches**, home to sea-taxis and *kaïkia* (see box, below). The second beach, to the right, is stony with

---

> ### BOAT TRIPS FROM PALEOKASTRÍTSA
>
> From Paleokastrítsa's first beach, you can get a boat trip (€10/40min) to some nearby seawater caves, known as the "**blue grottoes**", which is worth taking for the spectacular coastal views. Boats also serve as a taxi service to three neighbouring **beaches**, Áyia Triánda, Palatákia and Alípa, which all have snack-bars.

lear water, but the best of the three is a small, unspoilt strand reached along the path
y the *Astacos Taverna* (see below). Protected by cliffs, it's almost entirely undeveloped.

Corfu Aquarium

t the neck of the promontory • April–Oct daily 10am–7pm • €6 • ☎ 26630 41339, ⓦ corfuaquarium.com

The attractive log-and-stone structure of the **Corfu Aquarium** contains a comprehensive
election of local fish species, as well as lobster, squid and octopus. There is also a
election of exotic snakes and reptiles, which are enthusiastically presented by the staff.

Theotókou monastery

On the rocky bluff above the village • Daily 7am–1pm & 3–8pm • Free, donations welcome

The **Theotókou monastery** is believed to have been established in the thirteenth
century. There's a **museum** here, resplendent with icons, jewelled bibles and other
impedimenta of Greek Orthodox ritual, though the highlight is the **gardens**, from
which there are spectacular coastal views.

Angelókastro

Around 6km north up the coast from Paleokastrítsa • June–Oct daily 8.30am–2pm • €2

Paleokastrítsa's ruined Byzantine castle, the **Angelókastro**, is only approachable by a
path from the hamlet of **Kríni**. En route, there are a couple of outstanding spots around
the village of **Makrádhes** for a snack or drink while you take in the whole vista of
Paleokastrítsa's promontory. The **fortress** itself has been partially restored for visitor
safety and is worth the steep climb for the stunning, almost circular views of the
surrounding sea and land from the battlements.

11

ACCOMMODATION AND EATING

PALEOKASTRÍTSA

Astacos Taverna ☎ 26630 41068, ⓦ astacos.biz.
Highlights at this friendly taverna, just behind the second
beach, include the lobster after which the restaurant is
named (€70/kilo), or more pocket-friendly moussaka.
There are also some well-appointed studios just behind
(€51). May–Sept daily 9am–late.

Dolphin Snackbar ☎ 26630 41035, ✉ dolphin@
gmail.com. Just down some steps from the main road
and above Alípa beach, the simple rooms here are
adequate, with easy beach access. The terrific Greek food
on offer, such as the substantial garlic swordfish, is a

snip at €9. April–Oct daily 8.30am–midnight. **€35**

Paleo Camping ☎ 26630 41204,
ⓦ campingpaleokastritsa.com. Just off the main road,
almost a 30min walk from the centre, this campsite has
good facilities, shady if slightly cramped tent pitches and a
mini-market. May–Sept. **€15**

Vrahos ☎ 26630 41128. This upmarket taverna, opposite
the aquarium, with starched tablecloths and rather stiff
service, offers pricey top-of-the-range fish, Italian cuisine
and some unusual dishes like artichokes. Most mains €12–
18. April to mid-Oct daily noon–1am.

The northwest coast

The northwest conceals some of the island's most dramatic coastal scenery, with violent
interior mountainscapes jutting out of the verdant countryside. North of Paleokastrítsa,
the densely olive-clad hills conceal good sandy beaches, such as **Áyios Yeóryios** and
Áyios Stéfanos.

GETTING AROUND

THE NORTHWEST COAST

By bus Public transport between west coast resorts is
difficult: virtually all buses ply routes from Corfu Town to

single destinations and rarely link resorts.

Áyios Yeóryios and Afiónas

Like many of the west-coast resorts, **ÁYIOS YEÓRYIOS**, around 9km north of
Paleokastrítsa, isn't actually based around a village, though it is sometimes referred to as
Áyios Yeóryios Pagón after the inland village of Payí to avoid confusion with its
southern namesake. The resort has developed in response to the popularity of the large

sandy bay, and it's a major **windsurfing** centre, especially towards the northern end, where boats can also be rented.

The village of **AFIÓNAS**, perched high above the north end of Áyios Yeóryios bay, has been suggested as the likely site of **King Alkinous' castle** – there are vestigial Neolithic remains outside the village – and the walk up to the lighthouse on Cape Aríllas affords excellent views over Áyios Yeóryios and Aríllas Bay to the north.

Áyios Stéfanos and around

The northernmost of the west coast's resorts, **ÁYIOS STÉFANOS** is low-key, popular with families and a quiet base from which to explore the northwest and the Dhiapóndia islands (see p.722), visible on the horizon. Officially named Áyios Stéfanos Avlióton to distinguish it from its namesake in the northeast, its small harbour lies a good kilometre south of the long sandy beach.

Some 4km north of Áyios Stéfanos, in Corfu's northwest corner, **Avliótes** is a handsome hill town with the odd *kafenío* and tavernas but few concessions to tourism. The town is useful for its accessibility to the small, quiet village of **Perouládhes** in the very northwest and stunning **Longás beach** below, bordered by vertical reddish layer-cake cliffs that make for shady mornings.

11

ACCOMMODATION, EATING AND DRINKING **THE NORTHWEST COAST**

ÁYIOS YEÓRYIOS AND AFIÓNAS

★**Ostrako** Áyios Yeóryios ☎26630 96028. This gaily painted taverna has a terrace overlooking the southern end of the beach, and it's unbeatable for seafood such as squid and octopus for only €10 or less. The eclectic recorded folk music helps create a delightful atmosphere. May–Oct daily 11am–1am.

Panorama Afiónas ☎26630 51846, ⓦpanoramacorfu. com. Friendly family restaurant on the west side of the village which serves tasty meals made from organic produce for €7–9 and has great views from its terrace; it also has some good-value apartments (€40). May–Sept daily 10am–1am.

Pension Vrahos Áyios Yeóryios ☎26630 51323, ⓦvrachospension.com. At the far northern end of the beach, under the eponymous cliff, this pension offers bright, good-value rooms in the building behind its taverna, which serves Greek and international cuisine. They prefer to rent by the week. May–Oct. **€40**

ÁYIOS STÉFANOS AND AROUND

Nafsika Áyios Stéfanos ☎26630 51051, ⓦnafsikahotel.com. Located behind the southern strip of beach, the resort's oldest hotel has been renovated in soothing marine colours. It has comfy rooms, a popular restaurant and gardens with a pool and bar. May–Oct. **€60**

★**O Manthos** Áyios Stéfanos ☎26630 52197. The oldest taverna, behind the southern beach, is still the best, and serves Corfiot specialities such as *sofríto* and *pastitsádha* for around €8. Ask the venerable owner to show you his memorabilia. There's music and dance every Sat. May–Oct daily noon–1am.

Panorama Longás beach ☎26630 51846. The taverna's name gives the game away – perched on the cliff above the beach, its garden terrace is a great spot for a sunset dinner or cocktail at the attached *7th Heaven Café*. Main dishes like shrimp *saganáki* cost €11–14. May–Sept daily 11am–midnight.

Central Corfu

Much of **central Corfu** is occupied by the **plain of Rópa**, whose fertile landscape backs onto some of the best beaches on the west coast, such as delightful **Myrtiótissa**, as well as the island's only mountain resort, **Pélekas** – all a quick bus ride across the island from Corfu Town. The only place of note on the central east coast is **Benítses**.

Érmones and Myrtiótissa

ÉRMONES, around 15km south of Paleokastrítsa by road, is one of the busiest resorts on the island, its lush green bay backed by the mountains above the Rópa River but rather marred by the ugly tiered *Érmones Beach Hotel* and its private funicular.

Far preferable to the gravelly sand of Érmones is the idyllic strand of **MYRTIÓTISSA**, about 3km south. In *Prospero's Cell*, Lawrence Durrell described Myrtiótissa as "perhaps the loveliest beach in the world"; for years it was a well-guarded secret but is now a firm favourite, especially with nudists who gather at the southern end. Indeed it gets so busy summer that it supports three *kantínas*, meaning it's at its best well out of high season. Above the north end of the beach is the tiny, whitewashed **Myrtiótissa** monastery, dedicated to Our Lady of the Myrtles.

Pélekas and around

PÉLEKAS, inland and 5km southeast of Érmones, has long been popular for its views – the **Kaiser's Throne** viewing tower, just above the town, was Wilhelm II's favourite spot on the island. On the small square, the **Odhiyítria church**, renovated in 1884, is worth a peek. Pélekas' sandy **beach** is reached down a short path, though sadly it's been rather spoilt by the monstrous *Pelekas Beach* hotel that now looms over it.

The inland area around Pélekas holds some of Corfu's most traditional villages. This atmosphere of days gone by is best reflected in **SINARÁDHES**, around 4km away, which houses the **Folklore Museum of Central Corfu** (Tues–Sun 9.30am–2pm; €3; ☎26610 54962) in an authentic village house, complete with original furniture and full of articles and utensils that once formed an intrinsic part of daily rural life.

Áï Gordhis and Áyii Dhéka

Around 7km south of Pélekas, **ÁÏ GORDHIS** is one of the major party beaches on the island, largely because of the activities organized by the startling *Pink Palace* complex (see p.726), which dominates the resort. Inland from Áï Górdhis is the south's largest prominence, the humpback of **ÁYII DHÉKA** (576m), reached by path from the hamlet of Áno Garoúna; it is the island's second-largest mountain after Pandokrátor. The lower slopes are wooded, and it's possible to glimpse buzzards wheeling on thermals over the higher slopes. The monks at the tiny monastery just below the summit lovingly tend a bountiful orchard.

Áyios Matthéos

In south-central Corfu, the town of **ÁYIOS MATTHÉOS**, 3km inland, is still chiefly an agricultural centre, although a number of *kafenía* and tavernas offer a warm welcome. On the other side of Mount Prasoúdhi, 2km by road, is the **Gardhíki Pýrgos**, the ruins of a thirteenth-century castle built in this unlikely lowland setting by the despots of Epirus.

Benítses

South of Corfu Town on the east coast, there's nothing to recommend before **BENÍTSES**, a once-notorious bonking-and-boozing resort, whose old centre at the north end has long since reverted to a quiet bougainvillea-splashed Greek village, popular with eastern Europeans. There are a couple of minor attractions, namely the modest ruins of a **Roman bathhouse** at the back of the village and the small but impressive **Shell Museum** (daily: March–May & Oct 10am–6pm, June–Sept 9am–8pm; €4; ☎26610 72227).

ACCOMMODATION, EATING AND DRINKING   **CENTRAL CORFU**

ÉRMONES AND MYRTIÓTISSA

★**Myrtia** Myrtiótissa ☎26610 94113, ✉sks_mirtia @hotmail.com. Just before the path down to the beach, this delightful taverna has an olive-shaded garden, where they serve tasty home-style cooking for €6–10 and offer a few simple but clean and cosy rooms (€45). May–Oct daily noon–midnight.

Nafsica Érmones ☎26610 94911. Perched just above the southern end of the beach, with a huge terrace, *Nafsica* provides good, filling mezédhes and main courses of both meat and fish for under €10. April–Oct daily 11am–1am.

Philoxenia Érmones ☎26610 94091, ⊕hotelphiloxenia.gr. Far better value than the *Ermones Beach Hotel*, this spacious modern hotel on the south side

of the creek has two pools and a bar, and all the rooms face the sea. May to mid-Oct. **€80**

PÉLEKAS AND AROUND

Pension Paradise Pélekas ☎26610 94530. Located on the road in from Vátos, this ochre-tinted year-round *pension* run by a friendly old couple has simple homely rooms at bargain rates. **€30**

★**Pink Panther** Pélekas ☎26610 94360. The imaginative dishes on the menu here (all under €10), with a refreshing array of peppery sauces, can be enjoyed along with a glass or two of aromatic local wine while gazing at the splendid view from the lofty terrace. Easter–Oct daily 11am–1am.

11

AÏ GORDHIS

★**Elena's** Aï Górdhis ☎ 26610 53210, ⓦ elenasapartments.com. A variety of rooms and apartments in the village is available through this seafront taverna, which is painted marine blue and white and serves excellent home-style cuisine at low prices, such as beef in mustard sauce for €8.50. April–Oct. **€35**

Pink Palace Aï Górdhis ☎ 26610 53103, ⓦ thepinkpalace.com. Legendary year-round backpackers' haunt, with pools, games courts, restaurants, a shop and a disco. As well as dorms (sleeping five or six), there are compact singles and doubles. Rates include breakfast and an evening buffet. Dorm **€26**, double **€52**

BENÍTSES

Benitses Arches ☎ 26610 7211 ⓦ hotelbenitsesarches.com. Pretty bougainville adorned hotel, with quiet rooms set a couple of blocks ba~ from the main road. April–Oct. **€50**

★**Klimataria** ☎ 26610 71201, ⓦ klimataria restaurant.gr. Locals flock from Corfu Town and beyond t~ this top quality but not overly expensive *psárotavern~* where the cheaper species of fish and seafood go for €10 c~ less, while the pricier ones are set at fair market rate~ Reservations recommended. Feb–Nov daily noon–1am.

O Paxinos ☎ 26610 72339. Intimate taverna in the ol~ village, specializing in Corfiot dishes such as *sofríto* an~ *pastitsádha*, not cheap at €12 a pop but expertly prepared an~ washed down with fine barrelled wine. Daily noon–1am.

Southern Corfu

Corfu's **southwest coast** offers perhaps the island's finest stretches of sand, from the peaceful **Korissíon lagoon** on down, almost unbroken to the island's tip. On the east side, there is a mixture of resorts, ranging from peaceful enclaves like **Boúkari** to the full-on party antics of **Kávos**, accessible via Corfu's second-largest settlement, traditional **Lefkími**.

Moraïtika and Mesongí

On the east coast, roughly 20km south of the capital, the first real development after Benítses is **MORAÏTIKA**, whose main street is an ugly strip of bars, restaurants and shops, but its beach is the best between Corfu Town and Kávos. The original village, **Áno Moraïtika**, is signposted a few minutes' hike up the steep lanes inland and is virtually unspoilt, its tiny houses and alleys practically drowning in dazzling bougainvillea. The resort has become very popular with eastern Europeans.

Commencing barely a hundred metres on from the Moraïtika seafront and separated only by the Mesongí River, **MESONGÍ** continues this stretch of package-tour-oriented coast but is noticeably quieter and has a range of accommodation deals.

Boúkari and Petrití

Little more than a handful of tavernas, a shop and a few small, family-run hotels, **BOÚKARI** is linked to Mesongí by a quiet road that follows the seashore for about 3km, often only a few feet above it. It's an out-of-the way idyllic little strip of unspoilt coast and is handily placed for exploring the wooded region inland around **Aryirádhes**, rarely visited by tourists and perfect for quiet walks.

Four kilometres south of Boúkari, the village of **PETRITÍ**, only created in the 1970s when geologists discovered the hill village of Korakádhes was sliding downwards, fronts onto a small but busy harbour. It is mercifully free of noise and commerce, with a beach of rock, mud and sand set among low olive-covered hills. Barely 2km south of Petrití are the picturesque, but little-visited, rocky coves of **Nótos beach**.

The southwest coast

Over on **the southwest coast**, one of the island's most distinctive geographical features is the **KORISSÍON LAGOON**, home to turtles, tortoises, lizards and numerous indigenous and migratory birds. Its northern section, which is over 5km long and 1km wide at its centre, is separated from the sea by the dunes of **Halikoúna beach**, an idyllic spot for swimming and rough camping, while more touristic **Íssos beach** borders the southern end.

Far pleasanter than **Áyios Yeóryios**, the main Brit-dominated but rather brash resort on the coast south of the Korissíon lagoon, are **MARATHIÁ** and **AYÍA VARVÁRA**, both essentially forming a single resort further southeast along the same continuous strand. They are separated by a stream that you can easily cross on the beach but each settlement is approached by different roads. The most direct route to Marathiá beach is signposted from the tiny village of **Marathiás**, a couple of kilometres southeast of Aryirádhes on the main road, while Ayía Varvára is signposted from the village of Perivóli further south.

Lefkími

Anyone interested in how a Greek town works away from the bustle of tourism shouldn't miss **LEFKÍMI**, towards the island's southern tip. The second-largest settlement after Corfu Town, it's the administrative centre for the south of the island as well as the alternative ferry port for Igoumenítsa. The town has some fine architecture including several striking churches: **Áyii Anáryiri**, with a huge double belfry, **Áyios Theódhoros**, on a mound above a small square, and **Áyios Arsénios**, with a vast orange dome that can be seen for miles.

11

Kávos and around

There are no ambiguities in **KÁVOS**, 6km south of Lefkími: either you like 24-hour drinking, clubbing, bungee-jumping, go-karts and chips with everything, or you should avoid the place altogether. Visitor numbers have dropped in recent years, however, and in summer 2017 the police started to clampdown on licensing hours and music volume levels, in the wake of the murder of a tourist in Zákynthos (see p.757) and campaigning by a local residents' group.

Beyond the limits of Kávos, where few visitors stray, there is plenty of unspoilt countryside and coast worth exploring: a thirty-minute walk south of Kávos along unpaved roads, then a path, takes you to the cliffs of **Cape Asprókavos** and the crumbling **monastery of Arkoudhílas**. The cape looks out over the straits to Paxí, and down over deserted **Arkoudhílas beach**, which can be reached by road or path from **Sparterá**, a quiet village 3km west of Kávos. Even more attractive is **Áï Górdhis Paleohoríou beach**, 3km southwest of Sparterá, one of the least visited on the island and not to be confused with the eponymous beach further north. A municipal café provides the only refreshment. The Cape is also the southern starting point for the **Corfu Trail** (see box, below).

ARRIVAL AND DEPARTURE	SOUTHERN CORFU
By ferry Lefkími has a year-round ferry connection to Igoumenítsa (4–6 daily; 40min).	**By bus** Lefkími is on the frequent bus route from Corfu Town to Kávos (10 Mon–Fri, 8 Sat, 5 Sun; 1hr 20min).

WALKING THE CORFU TRAIL

The **Corfu Trail**, 200km in length, covers the whole island from **Cape Asprókavos** in the south to Áyios Spyrídhon beach, next to **Cape Ayías Ekaterínis** in the far north. The route takes walkers across a variety of terrain – from beaches to the highest peaks – passing by Lefkími, Korissíon lagoon, Áyii Dhéka, Pélekas, Myrtiótissa, Paleokastrítsa, Áyios Yeóryios Pagón, Spartýlas and Mount Pandokrátor.

Paths along the entire route are **waymarked** with yellow aluminium signs. As usual, ramblers are advised to wear headgear and stout footwear and carry ample water and provisions, as well as all-weather kit in all but the high summer months. Strong walkers can cover the route in ten days.

Hilary Whitton Paipeti's excellent *Companion Guide to the Corfu Trail* (Ⓦcorfutrailguide.com; €10) contains detailed **maps** and descriptions of the route, divided into ten daily sections. A proportion of the profits goes towards maintenance of the trail, and anyone using the trail is asked to contribute €3 for the same reason. Also, check Ⓦtravelling.gr/corfutrail for organized walking packages including accommodation.

ACCOMMODATION, EATING AND DRINKING

MORAÏTIKA AND MESONGÍ

Bella Vista Áno Moraïtika ☎ 26610 75460. The menu here is fairly simple but the food excellent, with grills and Corfiot specialities for €7–9 plus fresh salads. It justifies its name with a lovely garden, splendid sea views and refreshing breezes. March–Nov daily noon–midnight.

Charlie's Bar Moraïtika. Opened in 1939, the village's oldest bar is a meeting place for locals and tourists alike, with a central location on the main road. Light snacks are available and the music consists of old rock from the owner's huge collection. Daily noon–late.

Christina Beach Mesongí ☎ 26610 76771, ⓦ hotelchristina.gr. Few hotels have rooms so close to the sea. Those facing the water cost around twenty percent more than the ones looking onto the garden. Breakfast included and three-course evening meals for residents cost only €10. May–Sept. **€53**

Firefly Moraïtika ☎ 26610 75850, ⓦ fireflyhotel.eu. On one of the northernmost lanes down to the beach, this taverna has a good range of meat, fish, salads and dips (all well under €10), plus it rents out whatever rooms are not booked by Romanian tour operators (€30). May–Sept daily 11am–late.

Spiros on the Beach Mesongí ☎ 26610 75285. Beachfront restaurant, good for tasty fish soup plus other seafood dishes, many under €10: it also has various carnivorous and vegetarian options. May to mid-Oct daily 11am–2am.

BOÚKARI AND PETRITÍ

★**Boukari Beach** Boúkari ☎ 26620 51791, ⓦ boukaribeach.gr. Right on the sea, 1km north of Boúkari's harbour, is one of Corfu's best tavernas. It offers delicious home cooking, fresh fish and live lobster from €45/65 per kilo, plus many dishes under €10. The friendly family also run the smart and comfortable *Penelopi* (€35) hotel and *Villa Alexandra*, with huge self-catering suites, plus the eponymous new apartments (see below). April–Nov daily 9am–late.

★**Panorama Villas** Nótos beach ☎ 26620 51612, ⓦ panoramacorfu.gr. A wonderfully friendly haven worth making the detour to, whether to stay in the compact b comfy rooms or for the fine shady restaurant, renowned f its excellent home cooking, such as moussaka for € Breakfast included. **€40**

Stamatis Petrití ☎ 26620 51920. The best of the bun clustered around the harbour, this year-round local taverr rustles up goodies like mussels and small fish for aroun €7–10. Daily noon–1am.

★**Villa Boukari Beach** Boúkari ☎ 26620 5126 ⓦ villaboukaribeach.com. Up behind the superb famil restaurant (see above), these smart new apartments ar both spacious and comfortable, with modern furnishings well-equipped kitchens and large balconies. Breakfas included. **€55**

THE SOUTHWEST COAST

Akroama Marathiá ☎ 26620 52736. Good family-rur taverna serving treats like swordfish and local sausage fo €8–10, which can be enjoyed from the terrace on a lov cliff. They also have some comfortable rooms (€35). May– Sept daily 11am–1am.

Family Studios Marathiá ☎ 26620 51192, ⓦ family-studios.com. This homely family-run complex runs some spanking new studios and the excellent *Perfect Ten* taverna stretching back from the lively seafront *Bright Blue* beach bar. May–Sept. **€40**

LEFKÍMI

Cheeky Face Lefkími ☎ 26620 22627. The old couple who run this simple year-round *estiatório*, by the bridge over the canal in the lower part of town, provide inexpensive staples such as *pastítsio* for €6.50 and have a few equally basic rooms nearby (€40). Daily 10am–11pm.

KÁVOS AND AROUND

Future Kávos ☎ 01772 923989. The resort's premier superclub, with imported north European DJs, the renowned Club Trinity night, state-of-the-art sound-and-light systems, shots galore and a constant parade of the scantily clad. May–Oct daily 10pm–late.

Paxí and Andípaxi

Unusually verdant and still largely unspoilt, **PAXÍ (Paxos)** has established a firm niche in Greece's tourist hierarchy, despite being the smallest of the main Ionian islands at barely 12km by 4km, with only mediocre beaches and no historical sites. Yet it has become so popular that it is best avoided in high season. It's a particular favourite of yachting flotillas, whose spending habits have brought the island an upmarket reputation and made it just about the most expensive place to visit in the Ionian islands. The capital, **Gáïos**, is quite cosmopolitan, with delis and boutiques, but northerly **Lákka** and tiny **Longós** are where hard-core Paxophiles head, while by far the best swimming is at Paxí's little sister island, **Andípaxi**.

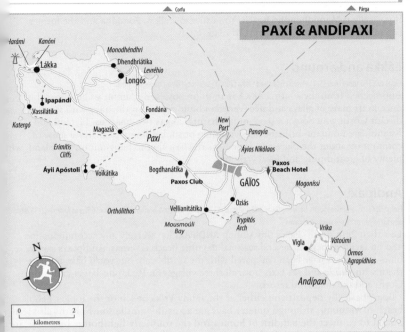

Gáïos

The island's capital, **GÁÏOS**, is a pleasant town built around a small square in the middle of an elongated seafront overlooking two islands, Áyios Nikólaos and Panayía. Nearly all the town's facilities are to be found on the seafront or within little over 100m of it.

Folk Museum

Seafront • June to mid-Sept daily 10am–2pm & 7–10pm • €2 • ☎ 26620 32247

Gáïos' only museum, the **Folk Museum**, is housed in an old school building on the sea-front about 200m south of the main square. One room is set up as an eighteenth-century bedroom with some period furniture and costumes. Other items on display from different epochs include kitchen implements, musical instruments, china, stationery and guns.

Around Gáïos

Inland are some of the island's oldest settlements, such as Oziás and Vellianitátika, in prime walking country but with scarcely any facilities. The **coast south** of Gáïos is punctuated by the odd shingly cove, none ideal for swimming, until matters improve towards the tip at **Mogoníssi beach**, which shares some of Andípaxi's sandier geology.

Longós and around

LONGÓS is the prettiest village on the island, though it's dominated by the upmarket villa crowd. Its scruffy beach is favoured by local grannies for the sulphur springs, so most people swim off **Levrehió beach** in the next bay south. Longós is at the bottom of a steep winding hill, which makes **walking** a bit of a chore, but the short circuit around neighbouring **Dhendhriátika** provides spectacular views and allows access to the small but excellent **Monodhéndhri beach**. You can also walk to **Fondána** and the former capital of **Magaziá**, back on the main road.

Lákka and around

Buses run 3–5 times Mon–Sat between Gáïos and Lákka (20min), and most divert through Longós

Approached from the south, **LÁKKA** is an unprepossessing jumble of buildings, but once in its maze of alleys and neo-Venetian buildings or on the quay with views of distant Corfu, you do get a sense of its charm. Lákka's two **beaches**, Harámi and Kanóni, are none too brilliant for swimming or sunbathing, but there's a sense of community about the place and overall it's the best spot to hang out on the island, with plenty of great dining and local walking.

Andípaxi

Frequent seasonal *kaïkia* shuttle between Gáïos and Andípaxi (€12 return); the glass-bottomed boat from Gáïos to Andípaxi (€15 return) also takes you to its sea stacks and caves

Less than 2km south, Paxí's tiny sibling **ANDÍPAXI** has scarcely any accommodation and no facilities beyond several seasonal daytime beach tavernas. Andípaxi's sandy, blue-water coves have been compared with the Caribbean, but you'll have to share them with *kaïkia* and sea taxis from all three villages on Paxí, plus larger craft from Corfu and the mainland resorts.

Boats basically deposit you either at the sandy **Vríka beach** or the longer pebble beach of **Vatoúmi**, although quieter bays are accessible to the south. Paths also lead inland to connect the handful of homes and the southerly lighthouse, but there are no beaches of any size on Andípaxi's western coastline and thick thorny scrub makes access difficult.

ARRIVAL AND DEPARTURE

PAXÍ AND ANDÍPAXI

By ferry/hydrofoil Both ferries and hydrofoils dock at the new port of Gáïos on Paxí, 1km north of the town centre. Tickets are available at travel agencies around the island and booths at the dock prior to departure.

Destinations Corfu Town (hydrofoil; May–Sept 1–3 daily; 50min); Igoumenítsa (summer 1–2 daily, less frequently in winter; 1hr).

WALKS AROUND LÁKKA

Lákka is perfectly sited for the finest walking on Paxí. For a simple, short hike, take the track leaving the far end of Harámi beach. This mounts the headland and leads on to the **lighthouse**, where a goat track descends through tough scrub to a sandy open-sea beach with rollers best left to confident swimmers.

Another good walking route heads west into the hills above the village to **Vassilátika**, high on the west-coast cliffs, with stunning views out to sea. From here, the path to the left of the blue-painted stone archway leads on to the most dramatic cliff-edge views (vertigo sufferers beware) and continues to **Magaziá** in the centre of the island, where you can flag down a bus or taxi.

The best **walk** on Paxí, however, is to the church at **Áyii Apóstoli**, almost halfway down the west coast, next to the hamlet of **Voïkátika**, which has a decent taverna. The rough track is signposted a few hundred metres south of Magaziá, and takes less than half an hour on foot. The church and surrounding vineyards overlook the sheer 150m **Erimítis cliffs**, which at sunset are transformed into a seaside version of Ayers Rock, turning from dirty white to pink and gold and brown. If you visit Áyii Apóstoli at sunset, take a torch for the return trip. The *Sunset* bar, next to the church, can provide a welcome drink to augment the natural splendour and sometimes even hosts full-moon parties during the warmer months.

Noel Rochford's **book**, *Landscapes of Paxos*, lists dozens of walks on the island; this and cartographers Elizabeth and Ian Bleasdale's *Paxos Walking Map* are on sale in most travel agencies.

CCOMMODATION

there are only three bona fide hotels and much of the accommodation on Paxí is booked by foreign tour companies, ⊃ms and villas are best booked through one of the island's **travel agencies**: Gaïos Travel (☎ 26620 32033 or UK 01964 543750, ⓦ gaiostravel.co.uk) and New Plans (☎ 6980 344 759, ⓦ newplans.gr), both on the capital's seafront; or ⊔utsis (☎ 26620 31807, ⓦ routsis-holidays.com) and British-owned Planos Holidays (☎ 26620 31744 or UK ☎ 01373 ▌3022, ⓦ planos.co.uk), both based in Lákka, for northern Paxí.

┆mfitriti **Hotel** Lákka ☎ 26620 30011, ▶ amfitritihotel.gr. Hidden among olive groves behind ┘arámi beach, the least expensive of Paxí's three hotels ⁻fers comfortable rooms with private balconies and ⁻tchenettes. May–Oct. **€85**

★**Paxos Beach Hotel** Gáïos ☎ 26620 32211, ⊃ paxosbeachhotel.gr. Attractive en-suite bungalows ⌄ith balconies on a hillside above a pebbly beach 2km

south of town; amenities include a saltwater pool, yoga sessions, tennis court and mini-golf. Free shuttle bus. Breakfast included. May–Oct. **€140**

Paxos Club Gáïos ☎ 26620 32450, ⓦ paxosclub.gr. Nearly 2km inland from Gáïos, this luxury resort set in lavish gardens offers large, well-furnished rooms and suites with kitchens, as well as a classy restaurant, pool and bar. Breakfast included. May–Sept. **€100**

EATING, DRINKING AND NIGHTLIFE

GÁÏOS

▌odos ☎ 26620 32265, ⓦ dodos-paxos.blogspot.co.uk. ⊔et in a garden inland from the Anemoyiannis statue ⊔owards the southern end of the seafront, this old favourite ⊔erves a full range of mezédhes and main courses, mostly ⌄nder €10. June to early Oct daily noon–midnight.

★**Genesis** ☎ 26620 32495. Convivial, brightly decorated ▌averna-cum-café, by far the best of the seafront establish-ments, right opposite the Anemoyiannis statue, serving ⌄ood wine and home-cooked dishes, such as several types ⌄f *stifádho* including octopus for around €10. May–Oct daily 10am–1am.

Phoenix Disco ☎ 26620 32210. On a hill over-looking the bay, with a large outdoor dancefloor and the usual mix of foreign and Greek disco hits. The island's premier nightclub. June–Sept daily 10pm–late.

LONGÓS

0 Gios ☎ 26620 31735. A simple and relatively cheap taverna in the middle of the harbour, where you can get great grills for €7–8, the odd oven dish and some basic salads and dips. June–Sept daily noon–midnight.

★**Vassilis** ☎ 26620 30062. Friendly port-side restaurant, where the bus has to squeeze past the pavement tables. Terrific seafood dishes, such as corals of sea urchins, cuttlefish risotto and shrimps with ouzo for €12–18, outlined on a memorable newspaper-style menu. May–Oct daily 11am–1am.

LÁKKA

★**Alexandros** Platía Edward Kennedy ☎ 26620 30045. Very friendly taverna tucked in the southwest corner of the village, great for fresh fish, *gourounópoulo*, creamed mushrooms and pork roll (mains around €10). May–Oct daily 1pm–1am.

Harbour Lights ☎ 26620 31412. This perennially favourite bar in the middle of the harbour is most likely to stay open the longest hours. There's a good range of drinks accompanied by well-known pop and rock sounds. May–Oct daily noon–late.

La Rosa di Paxos ☎ 26620 31471, ⓦ larossadipaxos. gr. Slightly upmarket seafront restaurant, which does good risottos, ravioli and pasta dishes for €10–15, plus a variety of salads and some more standard Greek favourites. Mid-May to mid-Oct daily noon–1am.

ANDÍPAXI

Bella Vista Vatoúmi beach ☎ 26620 31766. Perched on a cliff overlooking the cove, this taverna justifies its name and also dishes up fresh fish and meat grills for €10 or less, plus a range of salads and mezédhes. June–Sept daily noon–6pm.

Spiros Vríka beach ☎ 26620 31172. The oldest taverna on the island has great grilled and oven food, mostly €7–9. They can also arrange self-catering accommodation up in Vígla, Andípaxi's settlement, on a weekly basis. Late May to mid-Sept daily 11am–7pm.

11

Lefkádha

LEFKÁDHA (Lefkás) is an oddity, which is exactly why it is some people's favourite Ionian island. Connected to the mainland by a long causeway through lagoons and a 30m pontoon bridge, Lefkádha was long an important strategic base. As you approach the causeway, you'll pass a series of fortresses which climax in the fourteenth-century castle of **Santa Maura** – the Venetian name for the island. These defences were too close to the mainland to avoid an

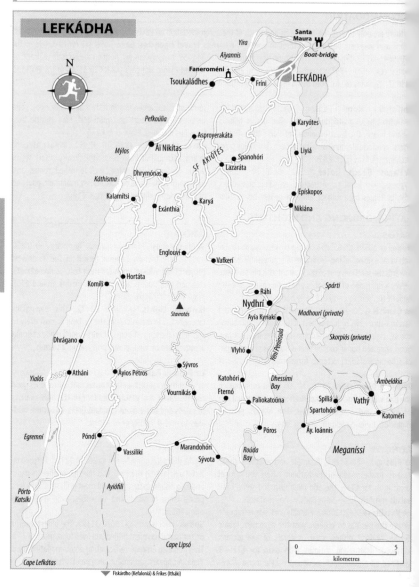

LEFKÁDHA

N

Yíra
Aïyannis
Santa Maura
Boat-bridge
Faneroméni
Tsoukaládhes
Fríni
LEFKÁDHA

Pefkoúlia
Karyótes

Asproyerakáta
Liyiá
Mýlos
Áï Nikítas
SF AKIÓTÉS
Spanohóri
Káthisma
Dhrymónas
Lazaráta
Kalamítsi
Exánthia
Karyá
Epískopos
Nikiána

Englouví
Vafkerí

Hortáta
Komíli
Ráhi
Spárti
Nydhrí
Madhourí (private)
▲
Stavrotás
Ayía Kyriakí
Skorpiós (private)
Dhrágano
Vlyhó
Yén Peninsula
Yialós
Atháni
Áyios Pétros
Sývros
Katohóri
Dhessími Bay
Ambelákia
Vournikás
Fternó
Paliokatoúna
Spiliá
Vathý
Áy. Ioánnis
Spartohóri
Katoméri
Egremní
Póndi
Póros
Roúda Bay
Meganíssi
Vassilikí
Marandohóri
Sývota
Pórto Katsíki
Ayiófili

Cape Lipsó
0   5
kilometres
Cape Lefkátas
▼ Fiskárdho (Kefaloniá) & Frikes (Itháki)

Ottoman tenure, which began in 1479, but the Venetians wrested back control a couple of centuries later. They were in turn overthrown by Napoleon in 1797 and then the British took over as Ionian protectors in 1810, until reunification with Greece in 1864.

The whiteness of its **rock strata** – *lefkás* has the same root as *lefkós*, "white" – is apparent on its partly bare ridges. While the marshes and boggy inlets on the east coast can lead to a mosquito problem, the island is a fertile place – it supports cypresses, olive groves and vineyards, particularly on the western slopes. The rugged **west coast**, however, is the star attraction and boasts some of the finest beaches in the archipelago.

y plane Lefkádha itself does not have an airport but is ss than 20km from the one at Préveza, which receives any charters and a few scheduled flights from northern rope. There is no dedicated airport bus, but KTEL services om Préveza stop on the main road 200m from the rminal entrance and taxis are readily available.

omestic destinations Athens (5 weekly; 50min); Corfu ummer 5 weekly; 30min); Kefaloniá (summer 3 weekly; 0min); Zákynthos (summer 3 weekly; 1hr 15min).

y bus The bus station is out past the marina, around km from the centre of Lefkádha Town (☎ 26450 22364, ⓦ ktel-lefkadas.gr).

Destinations Athens (5 daily; 5hr); Igoumenítsa (1 daily; 2hr); Pátra (2 weekly; 3hr); Préveza (6 daily; 30min); Thessaloníki (1 daily; 5hr).

By ferry Until the completion of the new harbour at Vassilikí, expected sometime in 2018, all ferries departing from Lefkádha leave from Nydhrí; the summer schedules below are reduced drastically in the low season.

Destinations Fiskárdho (Kefaloniá; summer 2–3 daily; 1hr); Fríkes (Itháki; summer 2 daily; 1hr 30min).

Information Check out ⓦ lefkas.net, the most comprehensive website on the island.

y bus There are services from Lefkádha Town to almost every illage on the island, with frequent daily schedules to Nydhrí, Vassilikí and Áyios Nikítas/Káthisma, especially in summer.

By car or motorbike The best outlet for car and motor-bike

rental in the capital is Santas (☎ 26450 25250, ⓦ ilovesantas .gr), next to the *Ionian Star* hotel. There are numerous other rental agencies at the main resorts, such as Alex Rane A Car in Vassilikí (☎ 26450 31580, ⓦ alexrentacar.eu).

11

Lefkádha Town

LEFKÁDHA TOWN sits at the island's northernmost tip, right where the causeway joins it to the mainland. Like other capitals in the southern Ionian, it was hit by the earthquakes of 1948 and 1953, and the town was devastated, with the exception of a few Italianate churches. It's a small town – you can cross it on foot in little over ten minutes – and still very attractive, especially around the main square, **Platía Ayíou Spyridhónos**, and the arcaded high street of Ioánnou Méla. The largely pedestrian-only centre boasts over half a dozen richly decorated private family **churches**, best visited around services as they are usually locked at other times. Many contain rare works from the Ionian School of painting, including work by its founder, Zakynthian Panayiotis Doxaras.

Phonograph, Radio and Tradition Museum

Panayióti Políti 1–3 • May–Oct daily 10am–2pm & 7pm–midnight • Free • ☎ 26450 21088

You can catch a glimpse of the old way of life at the quaint little **Phonograph, Radio and Tradition Museum**, which is dedicated to antique phonographs, radios and an astounding array of bric-a-brac. It also sells recordings of rare traditional music and a few assorted souvenirs.

Archeological Museum

Cnr of Sikelianoú & Svorónou • Tues–Sun 8am–3pm • €3 • ☎ 26450 21635

On the northwestern seafront, the modern cultural centre houses the newly expanded **Archeological Museum**, which contains interesting, well-labelled displays on aspects of

---

LEFKÁDHA'S SUMMER FESTIVALS

Lefkádha has been home to various literati including two prominent Greek poets, Angelos Sikelianos and Aristotelis Valaoritis, and the American writer Lafcadio Hearn. Fittingly, each summer for over fifty years, Lefkádha has hosted two parallel and wide-ranging cultural festivals, the **International Folklore Festival** and **Speech & Arts Events**. From June to September, troupes from around the world perform mainly at Santa Maura castle near Lefkádha Town, but also in villages around the island. The island and mainland Greece respond with troupes of their own musicians, dancers and theatrical companies. For details, contact ☎ 26450 26711 or see ⓦ lefkasculturalcenter.gr.

daily life, religious worship and funerary customs in ancient times, as well as a room o prehistory dedicated to the work of eminent German archeologist Wilhelm Dörpfeld.

ACCOMMODATION LEFKÁDHA TOW

The Lefkádha Room Owners Association (☎ 26450 21266; from €30) can help find rooms in Lefkádha Town.

Boschetto Dörpfeld 1 ☎ 26450 20244, Ⓦ boschettohotel.com. Quality boutique hotel looking across the lagoon to Ayía Mávra fortress. The rooms are all decked out with classy soft furnishings in soothing shades. April–Oct. **€90**

Ionian Star Panágou 2 ☎ 26450 24672, Ⓦ ionion-star. gr. As well as its own pool and a games room, the island's

top hotel has comfortable spacious rooms, many with se view balconies. Breakfast included. **€60**

Pension Pirofani Dörpfeld ☎ 26450 2584 Ⓦ pirofanilefkada.com. This smallish *pension*, just on th sea side of the main square, boasts a smart new receptio and comfortable rooms, decorated in a snazzy moder fashion. May–Oct. **€65**

EATING AND DRINKING

Burano Golémi ☎ 26450 26025. Smart *mezedhopolío* on the seafront almost opposite the marina, which has candlelit tables within, as well as pavement seating to enjoy the wide range of modest-sized dishes available (mostly €5–8). May–Oct daily noon–1am.

★**Eftyhia** Alley just off Dörpfeld ☎ 26450 24811. A fine little old-fashioned *estiatório* where you can choose from the mostly baked delights, such as stuffed marrow (€7), once you've perused the glass window in the kitchen. April–Oct daily, plus occasional winter days 11am–11pm.

Ev Zin Filarmonikís 8 ☎ 6974 641 160. Self-proclaime "soul food place" with a slightly bohemian atmosphere imaginative decor and unusual dishes such as Tex-Mex risotto and Roquefort steak for around €15. April–Oc daily noon–1am.

Lighthouse Filarmonikís 14 ☎ 26450 25117. Behind the brash bright blue exterior lies a solid family taverna with seating indoors or in the shady garden. Plenty o starters such as *saganáki* are available, as well as many meat and fish mains for £7–9. March–Nov daily 7pm–1am.

NIGHTLIFE AND ENTERTAINMENT

Cäsbäh Platía Ayíou Spyridhónos ☎ 26450 25486. One of the most enduring café-bars in town, which echoes its name by playing some ethnic sounds and having touches of eastern decor. Daily 11am–late.

Eleni Faneroménis 51 ☎ 26450 24550. The town's outdoor cinema has two showings of mostly English films. Programmes

change daily. May to mid-Oct daily from 9pm.

Lagoon Sikelianoú 3 ☎ 6995 781 351. With views over the peaceful eponymous lagoon opposite, this is a relaxed place playing ethnic music by day – then sip a cocktail or down shots to the latest dance tunes as the night wears on. May–Oct 11am–late.

Around Lefkádha Town

Lefkádha has the best swimming options close to town of any Ionian capital, thanks to the sandy lagoon borders at **Yíra** and **Aïyánnis**. Inland, there is also the attractive **Faneroméni monastery** and there are some traditional mountain villages centred around **Karyá**.

Yíra and Aïyánnis

There is a decent and lengthy shingle-and-sand beach west of the lagoon at **YÍRA**, a thirty-minute walk from the centre of Lefkádha Town. Roughly 4km long, the beach is often virtually deserted even in high season. Its western extension, **AÏYÁNNIS**, is a popular yet relaxed spot with several restaurants.

Faneroméni monastery

Fríni • Daily 8am–2pm & 4–8pm • Free

The uninhabited **Faneroméni monastery** is reached by any of the west-coast buses or by a steep 45-minute hike on foot from town through the hamlet of Fríni. There's a small museum and chapel, and an ox's yoke and hammer, used when Nazi occupiers forbade the use of bells.

aryá and the interior

ne island's **interior** offers imposing mountainscapes and excellent walking between llages only a few kilometres apart. **KARYÁ** is at the centre of the interior, and offers me rooms. This is the centre of the island's lace and weaving industry, with the small ut fascinating **Folklore Museum** set in a former lacemaker's home (April–Oct daily am–9pm; €4; ☎26450 41590). The historic and extremely scenic villages of **Vafkerí** nd **Englouví** are within striking distance, with the west-coast hamlets of **Dhrymónas** nd **Exánthia** a hike over the hills.

CCOMMODATION AND EATING · AROUND LEFKÁDHA TOWN

ilos Beach Resort Yíra ☎26450 21332, milosbeach.gr. Spreading out around their long-.tablished club in a disused windmill on the beach, this is)w a fully fledged windsurfing and kitesurfing resort with variety of studios. May–Sept. €70

a Platania Karyá ☎26450 41247. The best of the trio of avernas that fringe the beautiful plane-shaded square,

here they dish up ample portions of mostly meat dishes such as *frigadhéli* for around €6–8. Daily 11am–1am.
Tilegraphos Aïyánnis ☎26450 24881, ⓦtilegrafos.eu. With a shady elongated garden, this restaurant serves a decent range of *mezédhes* and seafood, mostly under €10. There is also a mellow yellow block of simple but comfy rooms (€40). May–Oct daily 9am–late.

11

The east coast

Anchored by the island's busiest resort of **Nydhrí**, Lefkádha's east coast is the most ccessible and most developed part of the island, much more so, in fact, than the nearby mainland coast. The beaches are mostly shingly and unspectacular, with the exception of **Dhessími** and **Rouda** bays, until you reach the long strand on the bay of **Vassilikí**.

Northeast coast

The stretch of the **northeast coast** between the capital and Nydhrí is a rather unprepossessing sprawl of seaside villages linked by almost unbroken development. Unless you choose to camp at **Karyótes**, there's little point stopping before the small fishing port of **Liyiá**. Further on lies **Nikiána**, another reasonably picturesque fishing village. Beaches all along this part of the coast tend to be pebbly and small.

Nydhrí

Most package travellers will find themselves in **NYDHRÍ**, the island's biggest resort by far and also the jumping-off point for Meganíssi (see p.738). It's an average resort but has a lovely setting and a reasonable pebble beach which offers watersports.

Dhessími Bay and Roúda Bay

Just south of Nydhrí, beyond somnolent **Vlyhó**, the neck of the Yéni peninsula to the east joins the main body of the island. Across this thin but steep strip of land, sizeable **Dhessími Bay** is perhaps the prettiest spot on the whole east coast, carved out by deep pine-ridged promontories. Just south of the quiet village of **Póros** is the increasingly busy beach resort of **Roúda Bay**, officially Mikrós Yialós, some 10km from Nydhrí.

BOAT TRIPS FROM NYDHRÍ

Nydhrí is the base for myriad **boat trips** around the nearby **satellite islands** and further afield to **Itháki** and **Kefalloniá**. The boats leave from the quay each morning between 9 and 10am, and return late afternoon. Tickets are around €15 per person for local trips, €20 for longer distances. Most craft to the nearby islets are small fibreglass *kaïkia*, with bars, toilets and open seating areas – some take in the sea caves of Meganíssi and others not, so check before booking: Eptanisos Cruises (☎26450 92218, ✉lefkadacruises@gmail.com) is a reliable bet.

Sývota

Around 14km south of Nydhrí, the fjord-like inlet of **SÝVOTA**, 2km down a steep hill from the main road, cuts a deep gash into the coastline. This is one of the most popul stops for yachting flotillas. There's no beach except for a remote cove, but there are some fine tavernas which mostly specialize in fish.

Vassilikí, Póndi and around

Around 5km due west of Sývota but longer by the winding road, **VASSILIKÍ**, the island's premier **watersports resort**, lies at the east end of a huge bay, cut off from the rest of the east coast by the barren peninsula of Cape Lipsó. Winds in the bay draw vast numbers of windsurfers, with light morning breezes for learners and tough afternoon blasts for advanced surfers.

The **beach** at Vassilikí is stony and poor but improves 1km west at tiny **Póndi**. Most non-windsurfers, however, use the daily *kaïki* trips to superior beaches on the sandy west coast, though there is now an unpaved shortcut to Pórto Katsíki (see p.739).

11

ACTIVITIES

THE EAST COAS

Windsurfing In Vassilikí: the largest of the three beach windsurf centres, British-run Club Vassiliki (☎ 26450 31588, ⓦ clubvass.com) offers all-in windsurfing tuition and accommodation deals; Wildwind is another UK-base operation (☎ 6979 110 665, ⓦ wildwind.co.uk).

ACCOMMODATION, EATING AND DRINKING

NORTHEAST COAST

Kariotes Beach Camping Karyótes ☎ 26450 71103, ⓦ campingkariotes.gr. The nearest campsite to Lefkádha Town has shady pitches, a small shop and a good pool – handy, as the local beach is poor. May–Oct. **€15.50**

Pantazis Nikiána ☎ 26450 20273. ⓦ pantazis-studios. gr. A good fish restaurant, serving fresh fish from €45 per kilo, at the south end of the small curved beach: it also has simple rooms to let in a row of adjoining bungalows at the back. May–Sept 11am–late. **€45**

NYDHRÍ

The Barrel ☎ 26450 92906. At the northern end of the busy quayside, this restaurant has a huge patio, where you can enjoy a wide range of mezédhes and main courses from €7 for the basics up to €16 for steak in cream sauce. April–Oct 11am–1am.

★**Ionian Paradise** ☎ 26450 92268, ⓦ ionianparadise. gr. Set in a lush garden only a minute along the Ráhi turning from the main road, this hotel complex has rooms with smart furniture and kitchenettes. A swimming pool is planned for 2018. May–Oct. **€40**

DHESSÍMI BAY AND ROÚDA BAY

Beach Camping Santa Maura Dhessími Bay ☎ 26450 95007, ⓦ campingsantamaura.com. This is marginally the better of the two huge campsites that dominate the olive groves behind Dhessími Bay. April–Oct. **€15**

Pirofani Dhessími Bay ☎ 26450 95700. This beach taverna in between the two Dhessími Bay campsites is very good, dishing up exquisite mezédhes such as octopus in wine sauce and *koloukythopittákia* (little courgette pies mostly under €10. May to mid-Oct dail 11am–midnight.

Póros Beach Camping Roúda Bay ☎ 26450 95452 ⓦ porosbeach.com.gr. One of the smartest campsites i the archipelago, with a bar, post office, shop, pool, vehicle rental and forty spanking new studios. May–Oct. Camping **€18**, studio **€45**

SÝVOTA

★**12 Gods** ☎ 26450 31880. Each chair is named after one of the twelve Olympian deities at this excellent two-storey taverna, located in an old store-house. The huge menu includes fine fresh fish and a tasty selection of mezédhes, veg and meat dishes in the €8–12 bracket. May–Oct daily 11am–1am.

Asterida Apartments ☎ 26450 23548, ⓦ asterida.gr. Just above the middle of the harbour, these delightful studios and apartments all have fully equipped kitchens and bay views. May–Sept. **€45**

VASSILIKÍ, PÓNDI AND AROUND

Abraxas Tunnel Rock Bar Vassilikí ☎ 6972 875 333. By far the best place to hang out with the locals and enjoy a decent and fair-priced selection of beers, ciders and spirits accompanied by rock music from different eras. Daily 8pm–late.

Akroyiali Póndi ☎ 26450 31569. A welcoming old couple run this beachside taverna, which offers delights such as garlic prawns and steak Diane for around €10, as well as fine barrelled wine. May–Oct daily 11am–1am.

Anemos Luxury Villas Póndi ☎6972 551 378, ⓦanemosluxuryvillas.gr. Set on a hillside around 1km beyond Póndi, with sweeping views of the bay, these smart new self-catering villas are extremely comfortable and well-equipped. May to mid-Oct. **€65**

Pension Holidays Vassilikí ☎26450 31011, ⓔpensionholidays@hotmail.com. Round the corner from the harbour, this remains the best-value option in Vassilikí, w: bright cosy rooms, all boasting sea-facing balconies. **€30**

★**Vangelaras** Vassilikí ☎26450 31224. We established taverna on the eastern quay, which offers t: resort's most authentic selection of Greek cuisine (€7–1: and a variety of wines, as well as a fine waterside locatio April–Oct daily 11am–1am.

Lefkádha's satellites

Lefkádha has four satellite islands clustered off its east coast, although only one, **Meganíssi**, the largest and most interesting, is accessible. **Skorpiós**, owned by the Onassis family, fields armed guards to deter visitors. **Madhourí**, owned by the family of poet Nanos Valaoritis, is private and similarly off limits, while tiny **Spárti** is a large scrub-covered rock. Day-trips from Nydhrí skirt all three islands (see box, p.735), and some stop to allow swimming in coves. Though officially a dependency of Lefkádha, the more remote island of **Kálamos** is only accessible from the mainland.

Meganíssi

Ferries run from Nydhrí (7 daily; 20min)

Meganíssi is a sizeable island with a decent number of facilities and a magical, if somewhat bleak and scrubby, landscape. The locals – many returned émigrés from Australia – live from farming and fishing and are genuinely welcoming. There are two **ports**, the main one of **Vathý** in the north, and **Spiliá** on the west coast, ten minutes' steep walk below **Spartohóri**, an immaculate village with whitewashed buildings and an abundance of bougainvillea. The walk between the two docks takes little over an hour, by way of the attractive inland village of **Katoméri**. From here, paths lead from Katoméri to remote beaches including popular **Ambelákia**.

ACCOMMODATION, EATING AND DRINKING | MEGANÍSSI

Esperides Resort Hotel Spartohóri ☎26450 22170, ⓦesperides-resort.gr. The island's poshest resort sits atop a headland 500m from the village and offers splendidly stylish rooms, as well as a pool, two jacuzzis and two bar-restaurants. May–Sept. **€85**

Meganissi Katoméri ☎26450 51240, ⓦhotelmeganisi .gr. The island's longest-established hotel is a relaxed place with decent-sized, comfortable rooms, a restaurant and pool, and is handily located for exploring. May–Sept. **€45**

Rose Garden Vathý ☎26450 51216, ⓦrosegardenvathi. com. A popular place tucked into the corner of the square and seafront, where you can get good fresh fish or a few meat or veg options from the oven, mostly €7–9. There is also a small block of rooms (€40). May–Sept daily noon–midnight.

The west coast

Lefkádha's **west coast** can compete with anywhere in Greece in its display of dramatic coastal scenery. On both sides of **Áï Nikítas**, the only real resort, mountainous roads rise and descend from the sea, offering tantalizing glimpses of the stunning sandy beaches, sandwiched between imposing cliffs and turquoise lapping waves.

Áï Nikítas and around

Jammed into a picturesque gorge 12km southwest of Lefkádha Town is **ÁÏ NIKÍTAS**, the prettiest resort on Lefkádha, a jumble of pedestrianized lanes and small wooden buildings. Sea taxis (€4 one way) ply between Áï Nikítas and **Mýlos beach**, a delightful cove just round the southern promontory. A couple of kilometres north is sand-and-pebble **Pefkoúlia beach**, one of the longest on the island.

áthisma beach

45min walk or a short (under 10min, several daily in season) bus ride from Áï Nikítas

he most popular beach on the coast, **Káthisma**, is a shadeless kilometre of fine sand,
hich becomes nudist and a lot less crowded beyond the large jutting rocks halfway
long. Freelance camping still goes on at this end too.

tháni and around

outh of Kalamítsi, past the hamlets of Hortáta and Komíli, the landscape becomes
lmost primeval. At 38km from Lefkádha Town, **ATHÁNI** is the island's most remote
pot to stay. Three of the Ionian's choicest **beaches** are accessible from Atháni: the
earest, reached by a 4km paved road, is **Yialós**, followed by **Egremní**, down a steep
ncline unpaved for the last 2km, though at the time of writing this was blocked due to
arthquake damage. Further south, an asphalted road leads to the dramatic and
opular twin beach of **Pórto Katsíki**.

| ACCOMMODATION, EATING AND DRINKING | THE WEST COAST | 11 |

ÏÏ NIKÍTAS AND AROUND

aptain's Corner Áï Nikítas ☎ 26450 97493. Near the
each, this is the liveliest drinking venue in the village, with a
ub-style atmosphere, a decent selection of drinks, snacks
nd mostly rock tunes. May to mid-Oct daily 11am—late.

Deck Pefkoúlia beach ☎ 26450 97070. Buzzing café-
restaurant halfway along the huge beach, with a selection of
coffees and cocktails, plus sandwiches, salads and other light
meals to choose from for €5—10. They also rent out some well-
equipped studios (€50). May—Sept daily 9am—late.

Klimataria Áï Nikítas ☎ 26450 97383. Halfway along
the main street and with a leafy courtyard, this place serves
good traditional cuisine, including favourites like *pastítsio*
for €7—10. May—Sept daily noon—1am.

O Lefteris Áï Nikítas ☎ 26450 97495. Simple grilled fish
and meat dishes for €7—9, accompanied by the expected
choice of salads, dips and starters, and washed down
with quaffable local wine. May to mid-Oct daily
11am—midnight.

★**Pension Ostria** Áï Nikítas ☎ 26450 97300,
✉ ostrialefkada@hotmail.com. Set in a beautiful blue-
and-white building above the village, this *pension* is
decorated in a mix of beachcomber and ecclesiastical

styles, with compact but comfortable rooms and a snack-
bar with terrace. May—Oct. **€40**

KÁTHISMA BEACH

Club Copla ☎ 26450 29411, ⊛ copla.gr. Beach bar-
cum-club that has long established itself as a favourite
with the night-time crowd; they hold regular parties and
raves to a techno soundtrack. May—Sept daily
11am—late.

Kathisma ☎ 26450 97050, ⊛ kathisma.com. Vast
taverna at the north end of the beach, with a extensive menu
of Greek staples for €7—10 and some smart apartments to
rent (€50). May—Oct daily 10am—midnight.

Politia Hotel ☎ 26450 97498, ⊛ politiahotel.gr. Large
blue and yellow complex up where the road turns towards
Kalamítsi, with comfortable good-value rooms, sizeable
pool and a decent taverna. **€45**

ATHÁNI AND AROUND

★**John's Eatery** Just south of Atháni ☎ 26450 33070,
⊛ panorama-athani.com. Superb and very friendly
Armenian restaurant with a shady patio, where you can
enjoy delightfully spiced kebabs and sausages for €7—9, as

LOVERS' LEAP

Fourteen kilometres south along the main road from Atháni, barren **Cape Lefkátas** drops
abruptly 75m into the sea. **Byron's Childe Harold** sailed past this point, and "saw the evening
star above, Leucadia's far projecting rock of woe: And hail'd the last resort of fruitless love". The
fruitless love is a reference to Sappho, who in accordance with the ancient legend that you
could cure yourself of unrequited love by leaping into these waters, leapt – and died. In her
honour, the locals termed the place **Kávos tis Kyrás** ("lady's cape"), and her act was imitated
by the lovelorn youths of Lefkádha for centuries afterwards. And not just by the lovelorn, for
the act (known as *katapondismós*) was performed annually by scapegoats – always a criminal
or a lunatic – selected by priests from the Apollo temple whose sparse ruins lie close by. This
purification rite continued into the Roman era, when it degenerated into little more than a
fashionable stunt by decadent youth. These days, in a more controlled modern re-enactment,
Greek hang-gliders hold a tournament from the cliffs every July.

well as standard Greek meat and fish dishes. May–Oct daily 10am–midnight.

★**Serenity** Atháni ☎26450 33639, ⍵serenity-th.com. Run by two Israeli women, this unique retreat and

health spa is beautifully constructed in stone on the hillsi 500m south of the village. The five rooms are decorated ethnic style, and there are chill-out tents and an infin pool. May–Oct. **€100**

Kefaloniá

KEFALONIÁ (also known in English as Cephalonia) is the largest of the Ionian islands, a place that has real towns as well as resorts. Like its neighbours, Kefaloniá was overrun by Italians and Germans in **World War II**; the "handover" after Italy's capitulation in 1943 led to the massacre of over five thousand Italian troops on the island by invading German forces, as chronicled by Louis de Bernières in his novel, *Captain Corelli's Mandolin* (see p.807). Virtually all its towns and villages were levelled in the **1953 earthquake**, and these masterpieces of Venetian architecture had been the one

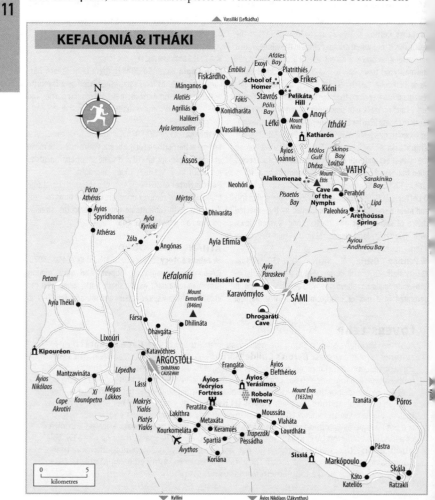

KEFALONIÁ & ITHÁKI

)uch of elegance in a severe, mountainous landscape. Seismic events are still a regular
henomenon – the strong quake of January 2014 caused severe damage on the Lixoúri
eninsula and in Argostóli, but mercifully no loss of life.

Until the late 1980s, the island paid scant regard to **tourism**; perhaps this was partly due
o a feeling that Kefaloniá could not be easily marketed. A more likely explanation,
owever, for the island's late emergence on the Greek tourist scene is the Kefalonians'
egendary reputation for insular pride and stubbornness, plus a good measure of
ccentricity. There are, however, definite attractions here, with some **beaches** as good as any
n Greece and the fine local wines of Robola. Moreover, the island seems able to soak up a
ot of people without feeling at all crowded, and the magnificent scenery speaks for itself.

RRIVAL AND DEPARTURE

KEFALONIÁ

y plane Kefaloniá airport lies 7km south of Argostóli:
here are 5–6 daily bus connections into the capital or it's
15 by taxi.
omestic destinations Athens (2–3 daily; 1hr); Corfu
summer 3 weekly; 1hr 20min), Préveza (summer 3 weekly;
30min) and Zákynthos (summer 3 weekly; 25min).
y ferry Kefaloniá has three ports that provide ferry
connections with neighbouring islands and the mainland.
Below are summer schedules, most of which are reduced
drastically in winter; any services that stop altogether are

indicated by months of operation. There is only a scanty bus
service at Pessádha and none at Áyios Nikólaos (on
Zákynthos) port, so you'll have to hitch or take an expensive
taxi in most cases.
Destinations Astakós (from Sámi, 2 daily; 2hr 30min);
Áyios Nikólaos, Zákynthos (from Pessádha, 2 daily May–
Sept; 1hr 30min); Kyllíni (from Póros, 5–7 daily; 1hr
15min); Pisaetós, Itháki (from Sámi, 3 daily; 40min).
By bus Buses run from Argostóli to Athens via Póros (3
daily; 6hr 30min–7hr) and via Pátra (1 daily; 4hr).

GETTING AROUND

y bus Kefaloniá's basic KTEL bus network radiates out
from Argostóli (see below). There are two or three services
to all the main island destinations Mon–Fri, one or two on
Sat and one to most places on Sun.

By car or motorbike Ainos (☎ 26710 22333,
ⓦ ainostravel.com) and CBR (☎ 26710 27125, ⓦ cbr-
rentacar.com) are reliable outlets, with branches in
Argostóli and other resorts.

Argostóli

ARGOSTÓLI, Kefaloniá's capital, is a large and thriving town – virtually a city – with a
marvellous position on a bay within a bay. The causeway connecting the two sides of
the inner bay, known as Dhrápano owing to its sickle shape, was initially constructed
by the British in 1813 and is now a pleasant pedestrian route. The town was totally
rebuilt after the 1953 earthquake, but has an enjoyable atmosphere that remains
defiantly Greek, especially during the evening *vólta* around **Platía Valianou** (formerly
Platía Metaxá) – the nerve centre of town – and along the pedestrianized **Lithóstroto**,
the main shopping street which runs parallel to the seafront.

Korgialenio History and Folklore Museum

Ilía Zervoú 12 • Mon–Sat 9am–2pm • €3 • ☎ 26710 28835, ⓦ corgialenios.gr

The **Korgialenio History and Folklore Museum**, behind the Municipal Theatre, has a rich
collection of local religious and cultural artefacts including photographs taken before
and after the 1953 earthquake. At the time of writing it was closed due to staffing
difficulties: check the website for the latest on its re-opening.

Focas-Cosmetatos Foundation

Valiánou 1 • Mon–Sat 9.30am–12.30pm, plus June–Sept 7–9.30pm • €4, including the Botanical Gardens • ☎ 26710 26595, ⓦ focas-
cosmetatos.gr

Insight into how the island's nobility used to live can be gained from a visit to the
Focas-Cosmetatos Foundation, opposite the provincial government building. It
contains elegant furniture and a collection of lithographs and paintings including
works by nineteenth-century British artists Joseph Cartwright and Edward Lear.

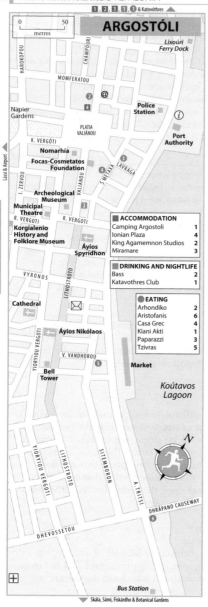

ARGOSTÓLI

Map legend:

ACCOMMODATION
Camping Argostoli	1
Ionian Plaza	4
King Agamemnon Studios	2
Miramare	3

DRINKING AND NIGHTLIFE
Bass	2
Katavothres Club	1

EATING
Arhondiko	2
Aristofanis	6
Casa Grec	4
Kiani Akti	1
Paparazzi	3
Tzivras	5

Skála, Sámi, Fiskárdho & Botanical Gardens

Archeological Museum

Y. Vergóti • Tues–Sun 8.30am–3pm • €3 • ☎ 26710 28300

The refurbished **Archeological Museum** has a sizeable collection of pottery, jewellery, funerary relics and statuary from prehistoric, through Mycenaean to late Classical times. Unfortunately, it suffered extensive damage in the 2014 earthquake and was closed at the time of writing.

Botanical Gardens

2km south of the centre • May–Oct Mon–Sat 9am–2pm • €4, including the Focas–Cosmetatos Foundation • ☎ 26710 26595, Ⓦ focas-cosmetatos.gr

The pleasantly relaxing **Botanical Gardens** have been transformed under the stewardship of the Focas-Cosmetatos Foundation into a diverse collection of the island's flora, arranged in a natural fashion with a stream running through the middle.

ARRIVAL AND DEPARTURE   ARGOSTÓLI

By bus The KTEL bus station (☎ 26710 22276, Ⓦ ktelkefallonias.gr) is 100m south of the Dhrápano causeway in the south of town. The frequencies given below are drastically reduced off season.
Destinations Fiskárdho (Mon–Sat 1–2 daily; 1hr 45min); Lássi (summer at least hourly; 30min); Póros (Mon–Sat 3–5 daily; 1hr); Sámi (Mon–Sat 4 daily; 45min); Skála (Mon–Sat 2 daily; 1hr)
By ferry There are frequent flat-bottomed boats to Lixoúri (Mon–Sat every 30min, Sun hourly; 20min).

ACCOMMODATION

The Kefalonia & Federation of Lodgings (☎ 26710 29109, Ⓦ kefalonia-ithaca.gr) can arrange rooms in Argostóli and around the island, as well as on Itháki (see p.749).

Camping Argostoli 2km north of town ☎ 26710 23487, Ⓦ camping-argostoli.gr. Although it's inconveniently out of town, just beyond the Katavóthres sea mills, this campsite has decent facilities including a minimarket. May–Sept. **€15**

★**Ionian Plaza** Platía Valiánou ☎ 26710 25581, Ⓦ ionianplaza.com. One of the ritziest hotels on the island, with designer decor throughout, from the lobby up to the chic bathroom fixtures. Breakfast included. **€126**

King Agamemnon Studios I. Metaxá 36 ☎ 26710 24260, Ⓦ kingagamemnon.gr. Basic modern studios with kitchenettes, in a brightly painted block north of the Lixoúri ferry dock, all with a/c and TV, some with sea-facing balconies. **€30**

Miramare I. Metaxá 2 ☎ 26710 25511, Ⓦ miramarehotelargostoli.com. Reasonably smart and comfortably furnished hotel, north of the Lixoúri ferry dock, offering several seafront rooms with balconies. **€50**

ATING, DRINKING AND NIGHTLIFE

RESTAURANTS AND CAFÉS

★**Arhondiko** Rizospastón 5 ☏ 26710 27213. Classy stone building with a small patio out front, where the friendly owner serves tasty dishes such as *exohikó*, *trapatsádha* and *biftéki* in Roquefort sauce, mostly for under €10. Daily noon–1am.

Aristofanis A. Trítsi 10 ☏ 26710 28012. Right by the Dhrápano bridge, this once simple old-style *kafenío* morphs into an excellent ouzerí by night serving main courses for around €10 from 7pm onwards. Daily 8am–midnight.

Casa Grec S. Metaxá 12 ☏ 26710 24091. With a smart interior and lovely courtyard, this chic restaurant adds a touch of nouvelle cuisine to Greek standards, serving the likes of pork shank, chicken with prawns and grilled haloúmi, though many mains cost €15 or more. Daily noon–midnight.

★**Kiani Akti** A. Trítsi ☏ 26710 26680. Unmissable dining experience on a large wooden deck jutting out over the water by the cruise-ship dock, about 400m north of Platía Valianou. Specializes in seafood such as razor clams in mustard sauce and shrimps in ouzo for around €10–12, plus super fresh fish. Daily 1pm–2am.

Paparazzi Lavrága 2 ☏ 26710 22631. Just southeast of Platía Valiánou, this Italian-run restaurant serves delights such as prosciutto with melon and veal stuffed with ham and mozzarella in a mushroom sauce for €12–18. May–Oct daily 7.30pm–1am.

Tzivras V. Vandhórou 1. A classic daytime *estiatório* with an impressive range of staples from the oven, which come in large portions. These include a lot of vegetarian options such as *briám*, with most meat dishes costing €8. Daily 10am–5pm.

BARS AND CLUBS

Bass P. Valiánou ☏ 26710 25020, ⊛ bassclub.gr. Opposite the archeological museum, this is the town's main late-night indoor club, whose hi-tech interior shakes to the latest vibes of various dance genres and hosts occasional live acts. Daily 10pm–late.

Katavothres Club 2km north of town ☏ 26710 22221. Up by the eponymous *katavóthres* (sinkholes), this smart new place gets more hopping as the night goes on, with live acts and a roster of well-known DJs. By day there is a decent restaurant Daily 1pm–2am.

Livathó peninsula

The bulge of land southeast of Argostóli known as the **Livathó peninsula** is a patchwork of small villages and agricultural land bordered by some attractive coastline. Many package travellers will find themselves staying in **Lássi**, a short bus ride or half-hour walk from town. The only other reason you might come to this corner of the island is for the summer ferry link with Zákynthos from **Pessádha** (see p.741).

Áyios Yeóryios

The best inland excursion from Argostóli is to **ÁYIOS YEÓRYIOS**, the medieval Venetian capital of the island, 7km southeast of Argostóli but not connected by public transport. The old town here supported a population of fifteen thousand until its destruction by an earthquake in the seventeenth century: substantial ruins of its **castle** (Tues–Sun 8.30am–3pm; free) can be visited on the hill above the modern village of Peratáta, a steep 1km walk below on the main southeast bus routes.

Mount Énos and around

At 15km from a point halfway along the Argostóli–Sámi road, **Mount Énos** isn't really a walking option, but roads nearly reach the official 1632m summit. The mountain has been declared a **national park**, to protect the *Abies cephalonica* firs named after the island, which clothe the slopes. There are no facilities on or up to the mountain, but the **views** from the highest point in the Ionian islands out over Kefaloniá's neighbours and the mainland are wonderful. At any time other than summer, the weather can deteriorate with terrifying speed.

Áyios Yerásimos monastery and Robola winery

Monastery Daily 9am–1pm & 4–8pm • Free • **Winery** April–Oct daily 7am–8.30pm; Nov–March Mon–Fri 7am–3pm • Free • ⓦ robola.gr

If you're coming from Argostóli and heading for Mount Énos, there's a doubly rewarding detour via a turning on the right (not far west of the mountain) towards Frangáta. First, there's the huge and lively **Áyios Yerásimos monastery**, which hosts two of the island's most important festivals (Aug 15 and Oct 20); the most interesting feature is the double cave beneath the back of the sanctuary, where the eponymous saint meditated for lengthy periods. Right behind the monastery is the **Robola winery**, which offers a free self-guided tour and generous wine tasting.

Lixoúri and its peninsula

Ferries run from Argostóli to Lixoúri till well after midnight (summer Mon–Sat every 30min, Sun hourly; winter hourly; 20min)

Across the water from Argostóli, the town of **LIXOÚRI** was flattened by successive **earthquakes** and hasn't risen much above two storeys since – a wise decision which has kept damage to manageable levels, most recently in January 2014. It's a little drab but has good restaurants, quiet hotels and is favoured by those who want to explore the eerie quake-scapes left in the south and the barren north of the peninsula.

Beaches around Lixoúri

Xi and Mégas Lákkos are served by buses from Lixoúri (2–3 daily; 15–20min)

Lixoúri's nearest beach, a 2km walk south, is **Lépedha**, composed of rich-red sand and backed by low cliffs, as are **Xi** and **Mégas Lákkos** (the name means "big hole") beaches, both of which have good facilities. Around 4km southwest lies the quieter beach at **Kounópetra**, site of a curious rock formation. Until the 1953 earthquake, this "rocking stone" (as the name signifies in Greek) had a strange rhythmic movement that could be measured by placing a knife into a gap between the rock and its base. However, after the quake, the rock became motionless. Some 2km further west, in an area known as Vátsa, the last beach of any size on the southern tip of the peninsula is sandy **Áyios Nikólaos**, a very quiet and scenic strand.

The western coast

Those with transport can strike out for the rugged western coast of the peninsula. First you can visit the monastery at **Kipouréon** (daily 8am–6pm; free), now home to just a single aged monk, before heading north to the spectacular beach at **Petaní**, one of the best in the Ionians. Tucked in the fold of the **Áyios Spyrídhonas** inlet further north is the beach of **Pórto Athéras**, which serves the traditional village of Athéras a short way inland and is another fine strip of sand with shallow water.

ACCOMMODATION AND EATING   **LIXOÚRI AND ITS PENINSULA**

★**Akrogiali** Lixoúri ☎ 26710 92613. Wonderful unpretentious taverna on the seafront, which draws admirers from all over the island for its excellent and inexpensive grilled and baked meat, fish and seafood, mostly well under €10. Daily noon–1am.

La Cité Lixoúri ☎ 26710 92701, ⓦ lacitehotellixouri .gr. Four blocks back from the seafront, this great-value hotel has a uniquely shaped pool in its exotic garden, while the rooms are spacious and colourfully furnished. April–Oct. **€45**

O Yialós Pórto Athéras ☎ 26710 69315. Set at the back of the beach, this good all-round taverna serves mostly grills for €7–8. Their garden acts as home for families with camper vans and can be used for camping.

May–Sept daily noon–1am.

★**Spiaggia** Áyios Nikólaos ☎ 6977 631 053, ⓦ vatsa.gr. Atmospheric restaurant with an attractive wood-and-bamboo deck, where you can tuck into excellent pasta, seaweed salad and seafood for around €10. There are four well-equipped chalets and two luxury villas behind (€70). May–Oct daily 11am–late.

★**Xouras** Petaní ☎ 26710 97458, ✉ petanoi@gmail .com. By far the better of the two tavernas here, where the friendly Greek-American owner Dina serves a fine selection of grills, salads and some oven-cooked dishes, all under €10. There are comfortable studios attached too (€50). May–Oct daily 9am–midnight.

Southeast Kefaloniá

Southeast Kefaloniá contains some fine beaches and much of the island's package tourism, from smaller resorts such as **Lourdháta** and **Káto Kateliós** east via the busiest foreign enclave of **Skála** to the port resort of **Póros**. One or two of the villages strung along the main Argostóli–Póros road, which follows the southern contours of Mt Énos, are also worth a brief halt, especially **Markópoulo**.

Lourdháta and Trapezáki

From the sprawling village of Vlaháta, around 15km east of Argostóli, a couple of turnings bear 2km down the mountainside to **LOURDHÁTA**, which has a kilometre-long shingle beach, mixed with imported sand. Another fine beach, reached by a turning from Moussáta, 2km west of Vlaháta, is **Trapezáki**, a relatively slim but appealing strand with just one fancy restaurant by the small jetty.

Markópoulo

The inland village of **MARKÓPOULO** witnesses a bizarre snake-handling ritual every year on August 15, on the occasion of the **Assumption of the Virgin Festival**, when a swarm of harmless snakes "appears" in commemoration of a legend that the nuns of the former convent here prayed to be turned into snakes to avoid an attack by pirates. The **church** at which the ritual is enacted is well worth visiting at any time of year.

11

Káto Kateliós and around

Some of the finest sandy beaches on the island are to be found around the growing micro-resort of **KÁTO KATELIÓS**, which already has a couple of hotels, and below the village of **Ratzaklí**, just before the resort of Skála. The coast around Káto Kateliós is also Kefaloniá's key breeding ground for the loggerhead **turtle** (see p.757); camping on the nearby beaches is therefore prohibited.

Skála

SKÁLA is a low-rise, mostly package resort with little independent accommodation, set among handsome pines above a few kilometres of good sandy beach. A **Roman villa** (daily 10am–2pm & 5–8pm, longer hours in summer; free) and some mosaics were excavated here in the 1950s, on the western edge of the village, and are open to the public.

Póros

Connected to Skála by a lovely 12km coastal route that at times seems to skim across the shallow sea, **PÓROS** was one of the island's earliest resorts, though it has now certainly seen better days. The town's small huddle of hotels and apartment blocks is not enhanced by a scruffy seafront and thin pebbly beach. Póros is actually made up of **two bays**: the northern one, where most tourists are based, and the harbour bay, a few minutes over the headland, with connections to Kyllíni on the Peloponnesian coast.

ACCOMMODATION, EATING AND DRINKING — **SOUTHEAST KEFALONIÁ**

LOURDHÁTA AND TRAPEZÁKI

Christina Studios Lourdháta ☎26710 31130, ⓦchristinastudio.gr. Fully equipped kitchen-studios with side views to the sea are available at this lovely building set into the lush vegetation behind the beach. May–Oct. **€40**

Denis Seaside Trapezáki ☎26710 31454. Beautifully remodelled with a spacious patio including water feature and candlelit tables. The presentation of the dishes is equally stylish, with specials like goat in red sauce (€12–15). May–Oct daily 11am–11pm.

★**Lorraine's Magic Hill** Lourdháta ☎26710 31605, ⓦlorrainesmagichilllourdas.com. With a lovely airy terrace, on the hill just behind the beach, this relaxed joint serves a wide range of home produce, including tender calves' liver and succulent goat for €10 or less. Also does cocktails in its alter ego as a bar. May–Oct daily noon–late.

Trapezaki Bay Hotel Trapezáki ☎26710 31503, ⓦtrapezakibayhotel.com. This luxury hotel 500m uphill from the beach has all mod cons, including a spa and beauty treatments. The fixed price all summer means good value in peak season and the rate includes airport transfer and breakfast. May–Oct. **€115**

KÁTO KATELIÓS

Blue Sea ☎ 26710 81122. Seafront taverna renowned for the freshness and quality of its fish (from €50/kg) and lobster (€70/kg). Also does the usual accompanying dishes, plus pizza and pasta. May–Oct daily 11am–1am.

Cozy ☎ 26710 81031. This little bar with a fitting name, at the west end of the seafront, is the prime drinking location in the area, where you can enjoy a beer or cocktail accompanied by some laidback summer sounds. Mid-May to Oct daily 10am–late.

Maria's ☎ 26710 81765. Located at the western end of the seafront, this ouzerí-cum-taverna offers a wide selection of dishes such as stuffed pork or baked swordfish for around €8. May–Oct daily noon–1am.

Odyssia ☎ 26710 81615, ⓦ odyssia-apartments.gr. These smart and comfortable apartments, run by a welcoming family, enjoy a convenient and quiet location behind the east end of the harbour. May–Oct. **€45**

SKÁLA

★ **Captain's House** ☎ 26710 83389, ⓦ captainshous .net. On the road parallel to the main street to the eas' *Captain's House* has warmly decorated rooms and studios plus a cute little bar outside. April–Oct. **€40**

Paspalis ☎ 26710 83140. This well-establishe beachside favourite serves fish and home-cooked meat an vegetable dishes, mostly under €10. Especially popula during the day, as it has a pool for patrons. May–Oct daily 11am–midnight.

Ta Pitharia ☎ 26710 83567, ⓦ tavernatapitharia -skala.com. The best taverna in the village provides a range of mezédhes, oven dishes and roasts like *kondosoúvl* (spit-roasted pork) for under €10, or you can go for a massive €20 steak. May–Oct daily 10am–1am.

PÓROS

Agrapidos ☎ 26710 72480. With fine views across the harbour from the headland above it, this all-purpose taverna does a good range of dips, starters, salads and main courses such as moussaka in the €7–10 range. April–Oct daily 11am–midnight.

Santa Irina ☎ 26740 72017, ✉ maki@otenet.gr. By the crossroads inland, this medium-sized *pension* has basic but clean rooms offered at superb value. Breakfast included. Mid-May to Sept. **€30**

Sámi and around

Most boats to the island dock at the large and functional port town of **SÁMI**, near the south end of the Itháki straits, more or less on the site of **ancient Sami**. This was the capital of the island in Homeric times, when Kefaloniá was part of Ithaca's maritime kingdom. Ironically, today the administrative hierarchy is reversed, with Itháki considered the backwater. In more recent times, Sámi was used as the set for much of the filming of *Captain Corelli's Mandolin* (see p.807). The long sandy beach that stretches round the bay to the village of **Karavómylos** is perfectly adequate, but 2km further east, beyond ancient Sami, lies a more dramatic pebble beach, **Andísamis**, set in a stunning curved bay.

Dhrogaráti Cave

5km southwest of Sámi • April–Oct daily 9am–7pm, sometimes later in peak season • €4 • ☎ 26740 23302

Signposted just off the Sámi–Argostóli road lies a very impressive stalagmite-bedecked chamber, known as the **Dhrogaráti Cave**. The cave, which reaches a depth of 60m and was discovered over 300 years ago, is occasionally used for concerts thanks to its marvellous acoustics.

Melissáni Cave

3km northwest of Sámi • Daily 8am–7pm, sometimes later in peak season • €7 • ☎ 26740 22997

The **Melissáni Cave**, on the road north from Sámi, is partly submerged in brackish water, which, amazingly, emerges from an underground fault extending the whole way under-neath the island to a point near Argostóli. At that point, known as Katavóthres, the sea gushes endlessly into a **subterranean channel** – the fact that the water ends up in the cave has been shown with fluorescent tracer dye. The beautiful textures and shades created by the light pouring through the collapsed roof of the cave make the short boat excursion into it a must.

̖yía Efimía

̖m north of Sámi

̖YÍA EFIMÍA, reachable from Sámi via a scenic coastal drive that includes coves such as ̖yía Paraskeví, is a small fishing harbour popular with package operators, yet with no ̖najor developments. Its main drawback is its beaches, or lack thereof – the largest, ̖bsurdly named Paradise beach, is a pathetic 20m of shingle. It is, however, home to ̖ne of the island's few **scuba-diving** enterprises (see below).

̖RRIVAL AND GETTING AROUND

̖y ferry The main dock is towards the southern end of the ̖ong seafront, though Itháki ferries depart from the central ̖ection.

̖y bus Island buses congregate outside the KTEL office ̖bout 100m from the dock.

SÁMI AND AROUND

By car and motorbike Sami Wheels, a block behind the port, (☎26740 22455) rents out motorbikes at fair rates, and Island (☎26740 23084, ⓦkefaloniaislandrentals. com) is a reliable local car rental company.

ACTIVITIES

11

Diving The Aquatic Scuba Diving Club in Ayía Efimía (☎26740 62006, ⓦaquatic.gr) is the island's premier

scuba-diving outfit. It runs courses, does wreck diving and offers introductory dives.

ACCOMMODATION, EATING AND DRINKING

SÁMI

Akrogiali ☎26740 22494. At the far northern end of the seafront, this family taverna has seating right above the beach and serves a range of the cheaper fish and meat dishes like *kreatópita* for around €7–9. They also have rooms from €35. May–Sept daily noon–midnight.

Athina ☎26740 22779 ⓦathinahotel.gr. Fairly large hotel at the Karavómylos end of the beach, with smallish, simple rooms, two cafés and various sports facilities such as tennis courts. May–Oct. **€65**

★Camping Karavomilos Beach Karavómylos ☎26740 22480, ⓦcamping-karavomilos.gr. Just 1km along the beach from Sámi, the better of the island's two campsites has over three hundred well-shaded spaces, a taverna, shop and bar. May–Oct. **€20**

Karnagio ☎6939 582 041. With a decent selection of vegetable and meat dishes from €6–9, including the famous local meat pie, this is the best of the central bunch of port-side tavernas. April–Oct daily 11am–1am.

Melissani ☎26740 22464, ⓦmelissanihotel.gr. Up a couple of blocks behind the main dock, this slightly old-fashioned but welcoming hotel has cosy, great-value rooms, many with good views from their balconies. May–Sept. **€30**

AYÍA EFIMÍA

Amalia ☎26740 61088. Round the headland past the harbour, this is the place for moderately priced island cuisine such as small fried fish and local sausage (€7–8). May–Sept daily noon–1am.

Odyssey ☎26740 61089, ⓦhotelodyssey.gr. This spanking hotel lies round the headland from the harbour, with spacious modern rooms plus a restaurant, bar, spa and huge pool. Two night minimum stay. May–Sept. **€55**

Spiros ☎26740 61739. A wide range of specials such as lamb *kléftiko* and beef ragout with yoghurt sauce can be enjoyed for under €10 at this taverna that's halfway along the harbour. May–Sept daily noon–1am.

Northern Kefaloniá

Northern Kefaloniá offers some splendid beaches, an architecturally attractive village in **Fiskárdho**, and some amazing coastal scenery. Indeed, the northern half of the coast road between Argostóli and Fiskárdho, starting at the point where a side road peels off to the long sandy beach of **Ayía Kyriakí**, is the most spectacular ride in the Ionian archipelago.

Mýrtos beach and around

Four kilometres by paved road below the main north–south artery, stunningly photogenic **Mýrtos** is regarded by many as the most dramatic beach in the Ionian islands – a splendid strip of pure-white sand and pebbles. Sadly, it has no natural shade for most of the day and gets mighty crowded in high season, with just a couple of seasonal snack-shacks for refreshment. Back at the crossroads, the small settlement of **Dhivaráta** has the nearest amenities to Mýrtos.

Ássos

Six kilometres beyond Dhivaráta, as you head north from Argostóli, is the turning for the atmospheric village of **ÁSSOS**, clinging to a small isthmus between the island and a huge hill crowned by a ruined fort. It can get a little claustrophobic, but there's nowhere else quite like it in the Ionians. Ássos has a small pebble beach and three tavernas on a plane-shaded village square backed by mansions, mostly now restored after being ruined in the 1953 quake.

Fiskárdho and around

FISKÁRDHO, on the northernmost tip of the island, sits on a bed of limestone that buffered it against the worst of the quakes. Two **lighthouses**, Venetian and Victorian, guard the bay, and the headland ruins are believed to be from a twelfth-century chapel begun by Norman invader Robert Guiscard, who gave the place its name. The nineteenth-century harbour frontage is occupied by chic restaurants and boutiques.

There are two good pebble beaches close to Fiskárdho – **Émblisi** 1km back out of town and **Fókis** just to the south – and a nature trail on the northern headland. It's also worth exploring the coastal region west of **Mánganos**: **Alatiés** has a tiny beach tucked in between folds of impressive white volcanic rock, while the real gem is the small bay of **Ayía Ierousalím**, whose gravel-and-sand beach with crystal clear waters is home to one of the island's best tavernas (see opposite).

ACTIVITIES   **NORTHERN KEFALONIÁ**

Kayaking You cant rent single or tandem kayaks from €40 for half a day from Fiskardo Kayaks (☎ 6982 871 608, ⓦ fiskardokayaks.com).

Scuba diving The only dive operator in the far north of the island is Fiskardo-Divers (☎ 26740 23832, ⓦ fiskardo-divers.com).

ACCOMMODATION, EATING AND DRINKING

MÝRTOS BEACH AND AROUND

Minas Apartments Dhivaráta ☎ 26740 61515, ⓦ minasapartments.gr. Just above the main junction, these large and well-appointed studios with kitchenettes are the best accommodation close to Mýrtos beach. April–Oct. **€40**

ÁSSOS

Cosi's Inn ☎ 26740 51420, ⓦ cosisinn.gr. Brightly decorated, well-furnished and good-value rooms are the attraction at this cosy hillside inn on the approach road to the centre. Breakfast included. April–Oct. **€50**

Kanakis Apartments ☎ 26740 51631, ⓦ kanakisapartments.gr. Very smart studios and spacious maiso-nettes which share a pool and are equipped with all mod cons. Only 100m from the heart of the village. April–Oct. **€60**

Nefeli ☎ 26740 51251. With its prime location on the quay beside the beach, this taverna does a decent line in seafood, mezédhes and salads. Most main courses around €10–12. April–Oct daily 10am–1am.

★ **Platanos** Set just back from the seafront under a huge plane tree, hence the name, this place is good for grilled meat and fish, as well as oven food, mostly €10 and up. There's also a wide selection of salads and starters, plus aromatic local wine. April–Oct daily 11am– midnight.

FISKÁRDHO

Archontiko ☎ 26740 41342. Beautiful traditional stone mansion that has been converted into luxurious rooms above and behind a harbourfront mini-market. The furniture is period style, but all the equipment, such as the TVs, is cutting edge. April–Oct. **€90**

Kastro Club ☎ 26740 41010. Up behind the main bypass road, the oldest club in northern Kefaloniá has tiered terraces and a big outdoor dancefloor. The isolated location allows the volume to be jacked up on the usual mix of international and Greek hits. July–Sept daily 10pm–late.

Lagoudera ☎ 26740 41275. With two premises, one on the harbour, the other just off the small square, *Lagoudera* specializes in tasty oven-baked food for €9–10 but also does grills and all the usual side dishes. April–Oct daily noon–2am.

Lord Falcon ☎ 26740 41072. One block back from the harbour, the Ionians' first Thai restaurant serves up a fine array of soups, stir-fries and red, green and Penang curries for around €10–14. May–Oct Mon–Sat 6.30pm–midnight, Sun 1–4.30pm.

★ **Regina's** ☎ 26740 41125, ⓦ regina-studios.gr. Up by the car park, these friendly family-run studios are compact but great value. Some have balconies looking over the village to the bay, and there's a lovely courtyard. They can arrange motorboat rental too. April–Oct. **€40**

YÍA IEROUSALÍM

Odisseas Ayía Ierousalím, 26740 41133. The extremely friendly brother-sister-mum trio who run *Odisseas* serve up exquisite traditional dishes made with free-range meat (most under €10) and do a line in olive bread and other baked goodies, plus jams and preserves. They also allow camping on their grounds. April–Oct daily noon–midnight.

Itháki

Rugged **ITHÁKI**, Odysseus's legendary homeland, has yielded no substantial archeological discoveries, but it fits Homer's description to perfection: "There are no tracks, nor grasslands … it is a rocky severe island, unsuited for horses, but not so wretched, despite its small size. It is good for goats." Despite its proximity to Kefaloniá, there's relatively little tourist development due, in part, to a dearth of beaches beyond a few pebbly coves: the island, however, is good walking country, and indeed the interior, with its sites from **The Odyssey**, is the real attraction. In the scheme of modern Greek affairs, Itháki is a real backwater, and its inhabitants rather resentful that it is officially a subsection of Kefaloniá prefecture.

11

ARRIVAL AND DEPARTURE — ITHÁKI

By ferry Surprisingly for such a small island, Itháki has three active ports. The following are summer schedules, which are reduced drastically in winter.

Fríkes destinations Lefkádha, see p.732 (May–Oct 1 daily; 1hr 30min).

Pisaetós destinations Astakós (1–2 daily; 2hr 30min); Sámi, Kefaloniá (3 daily; 40min).

Vathý destinations Astakós (1–2 daily; 1hr 30min).

GETTING AROUND

By bus There is effectively no public transport on the island, though you might be able to flag down the school bus during term.

By taxi Taxis are available, especially at Vathý's square.

By car and motorbike Cars and motorbikes can be rented through travel agencies in Vathý, including Polyctor Tours (26740 33120, ithakiholidays.com).

Vathý and around

Itháki's main port and capital is **VATHÝ**, enclosed by a bay within a bay so deep that few realize the mountains out "at sea" are actually the north of the island. This snug town is compact, relatively traffic-free and boasts the most idyllic seafront setting of all the Ionian capitals. Like its southerly neighbours, it was heavily damaged by the 1953 earthquake but some fine examples of pre-quake architecture remain. Vathý has a small **archeological museum** on Kalliníkou (Tues–Sun 8.30am–3pm; free; 26740 32200), a short block back from the quay. Near the corner of the quay behind the Agricultural Bank, there is also the moderately interesting **Folklore & Cultural Museum** (April–Oct Mon–Fri 10am–2pm & 7.30–9.30pm; €1).

Beaches around Vathý

There are two reasonable pebble **beaches** within fifteen minutes' walk of Vathý: **Dhéxa**, over the hill above the ferry quay, and tiny **Loútsa**, opposite it around the bay. The better beaches at **Sarakíniko** and **Skínos** are an hour's trek along paved roads leaving the opposite side of the bay. In season, daily *kaïkia* ply between the quay and remote coves.

Pisaetós

The harbour of **PISAETÓS**, around 5km west of Vathý via a steep route across the island's neck, has a fair-sized rocky beach that's all right for a pre-ferry swim and popular with local rod-and-line fishermen. Little goes on here except during the busy period around ferry arrivals, when a small canteen on the quay is the focus of activity.

ODYSSEUS SIGHTS AROUND VATHÝ

Three of the main **Odysseus** sights are just within walking distance of Vathý: the Arethoússa Spring, the Cave of the Nymphs and ancient Alalkomenae, although the last is best approached by **moped** or **taxi**.

ARETHOÚSSA SPRING

The walk to the **Arethoússa Spring** – allegedly the place where Eumaeus, Odysseus's faithful swineherd, brought his pigs to drink – is a three-hour round trip along a track signposted next to the seafront telecoms office. The unspoilt but shadeless landscape and sea views are magnificent but some of the inclines can be slippery.

Near the top of the lane leading to the spring path, a signpost points up to what is said to have been the **Cave of Eumaeus**. The route to the spring continues for a few hundred metres, and then branches off onto a narrow footpath through steep gorse-covered cliffs. Parts of the final downhill track involve scrambling across rock fields (follow the splashes of green paint), and care should be taken around the small but vertiginous ravine that houses the **spring**. The ravine sits below a crag known as **Kórax** (the raven), which matches Homer's description of the meeting between Odysseus and Eumaeus. In summer it's just a dribble of water.

THE CAVE OF THE NYMPHS

The **Cave of the Nymphs** (Marmarospíli) is about 2.5km up a rough but navigable road sign-posted on the brow of the hill above Dhéxa beach. The cave is atmospheric, but it's under-whelming compared to the caverns of neighbouring Kefaloniá and, these days, is illuminated by coloured lights. The claim that this is *The Odyssey's* Cave of the Nymphs, where the returning Odysseus concealed the gifts given to him by King Alkinous, is enhanced by the proximity of **Dhéxa beach**.

ALALKOMENAE

Alalkomenae, Heinrich Schliemann's much-vaunted "Castle of Odysseus", is signposted on the Vathý–Pisaetós road, on the saddle between Dhéxa and Pisaetós, with views over both sides of the island. The actual site, however, some 300m uphill, is little more than foundations spread about in the gorse, and in fact the most likely contender for the site of Odysseus's castle is above the village of **Stavrós** (see opposite).

INFORMATION

Tourist information An excellent website on the island is ⓦ ithacagreece.com.

ACCOMMODATION

The best source of rooms, studios or villas around the capital or all over the island are the two main quayside travel agencies.

★ **Captain Yiannis** ☎ 26740 33311, ⓦ captainyiannis. com. Complete with tennis court and pool with bar, this great-value resort round the east side of the bay is spread over several blocks of modern rooms and apartments. Breakfast included. Mid-May to Sept. **€55**

Mentor ☎ 26740 32433, ⓦ hotelmentor.gr. The town's oldest hotel, in the southeast corner of the harbour, was refurbished a few years ago and its comfortable rooms have balconies either with direct or side views of the water. **€74**

Omirikon Residence ☎ 26740 33596, ⓦ omirikonhotel.com. Stylish boutique hotel, yet with a personal, family-run touch. All its rooms are classed as suites, and are spacious and well furnished with sea-view balconies. Breakfast included. May–Oct. **€85**

EATING AND DRINKING

O Nikos ☎ 26740 33039. Just off the square, this is a good old-fashioned *estiatório*, where you can feast on heaps of oven-baked goodies (€6–8), on show behind the glass panel within. Pavement seating in summer. Daily 11am–midnight.

★ **To Kohili** ☎ 26740 33565. By far the best of the half-dozen harbourside tavernas, with seating on the quay or in the leafy garden round the corner. They serve a good range of mezédhes, as well as tasty meat dishes such as lamb *kléftiko*, *yiouvétsi* and *soutzoukákia*, plus grills and pasta for under €10. Daily 11am–1am.

Trehantiri ☎ 26740 33444. Tucked a block back from the seafront, this family-run taverna does a good line in home cooking, from fish soup to slow-cooked pork and goat dishes on display in trays (around €10). April–Oct daily noon–1am.

Northern Itháki

The main road out of Vathý continues across the isthmus and takes a spectacular route to the northern half of Itháki, which is based around **Stavrós**. This is excellent scooter country, and the close proximity of the settlements, small coves and Homeric interest also make it good rambling terrain. As with the rest of Itháki, there are only limited tourist facilities, concentrated mostly in **Fríkes** and **Kióni**.

Stavrós

STAVRÓS, the second-largest town on Itháki, is a steep 2km above the nearest beach at Pólis Bay. It's a pleasant enough town, with *kafenía* edging a small square dominated by a rather fierce statue of Odysseus.

Stavrós Museum

Off the road to Platrithriés • Tues–Sun 8.30am–3pm • Free

The tiny **Stavrós Museum** displays local archeological finds. Most of these come from the early Helladic site on the side of **Pelikáta Hill**, where remains of roads, walls and other structures have been suggested as the possible site of Odysseus's palace.

11

Anoyí

Some 5km southeast of Stavrós along a scenic mountain road is **ANOYÍ**, which translates roughly as "upper ground". Once the second-most important settlement on the island, it is almost deserted today. The centre of the village is dominated by a freestanding Venetian campanile, built to serve the church of the **Panayía**, which features heavily restored Byzantine frescoes. The church comes alive for the annual *paniyíri* on August 14, the eve of the Virgin's Assumption; at other times, enquire at the *kafenío* about access. In the surrounding countryside are some extremely strange rock formations, the biggest of which is the 8m-high Iraklis (Hercules) rock, just east of the village.

Monastery of Katharón

3km south of Anoyí • Free

The **monastery of Katharón** boasts stunning views down over Vathý and the south of the island. It houses an icon of the *Panayía* (Madonna), discovered by peasants clearing scrubland in the area. The monastery celebrates its festival on September 8 with services, processions and music.

Afáles Bay area

Afáles Bay, the largest cove on the entire island, with an unspoilt and little-visited pebble-and-sand beach, can be accessed by a track down from the outskirts of **Platrithriés**. This quiet yet rather spread-out village lies on the less direct westerly route from Stavrós to Fríkes, which first loops below the hill village of Exoyí. Just off the start of the road up to Exoyí, a signpost points about 1km along a rough track to the supposed **School of Homer**, where excavations still in progress have revealed extensive foundations, a well as ancient steps. The site is unfenced and well worth a detour for its views of Afáles Bay as much as the remains.

Fríkes

Wedged in a valley between two steep hills, **FRÍKES** was only settled in the sixteenth century and emigration in the nineteenth century almost emptied the place – as few as two hundred people live here today – but the protected harbour is a natural port. There are no beaches in the village, but plenty of good, if small, pebble **coves** a short walk away towards Kióni. When the ferries and their cargoes have departed, Fríkes falls quiet – this is its real charm.

Kióni

KIÓNI sits at a dead end 5km southeast of Fríkes. On the same geological base as the northern tip of Kefaloniá, it avoided the very worst of the 1953 earthquake and so retains some fine examples of pre-twentieth-century **architecture**. It's an extremely pretty village, wrapped around a tiny harbour, and tourism here is dominated by British blue-chip travel companies and visiting yachts. The bay has a small **beach**, 1km along its south side, a sand-and-pebble strand below a summer-only snack-bar.

ACCOMMODATION AND EATING
NORTHERN ITHÁKI

STAVRÓS

Margarita ☎26740 31229. This large, friendly *zaharoplastío* is a good place for a coffee, a refreshing drink or to sample the local sweet *ravaní*. Also has sport on TV. Daily 8am–11pm.

★ **0 Tseligas** ☎26740 31596. Not easy to miss thanks to its bright yellow building and awnings, this welcoming place dishes up great *mezédhes*, *kondosoúvli* and *kokorétsi* on the spit, but is best known for the speciality *tserépa* (chicken or lamb baked with potatoes and peppers). May to early Oct 11am–midnight.

FRÍKES

Frikes Bay Suites ☎6977 700 377, ✉frikesbaysuites @gmail.com. These smart and airy bayside apartments, very close to the harbour, are spacious, tastefully furnished in modern style and come with fully equipped kitchens. May–Oct. **€85**

Nostos ☎26740 31644, 🌐hotelnostos-ithaki.gr. Around 100m from the seafront, the only conventional hotel in northern Itháki has a pool in its relaxing grounds and smart, spacious rooms. Buffet breakfast included. May to mid-Oct. **€80**

★ **Rementzo** ☎26740 31719. In the corner of the quay, this friendly taverna serves a selection of fresh fish, baked

meat and vegetable dishes, salads and pizza, plus good wine and ouzo (mains €6–10). April–Oct daily 10am–1am.

Ulysses ☎26740 31733. A popular restaurant in the middle of the seafront that specializes in succulent home-style cuisine for around €10: it also serves plenty of snacks, sweets and beverages. May–Oct daily 11am–midnight.

KIÓNI

Avra ☎26740 31453. Harbourside taverna that offers the usual selection of fresh salads, some dips and a good choice of mainly grilled meat for €8–10, plus fish courses to suit all budgets. May–Sept daily 11am–1am.

Calypso ☎26740 31066. Popular taverna in the middle of the tiny bay, which has imaginative dishes like spicy pork with mashed potato for €12.50, plus some very drinkable aromatic wine. May–Oct daily noon–midnight.

Captain's Apartments ☎26740 31481, 🌐captains -apartments.gr. Set up above the village, with sweeping views of the bay, these roomy apartments are decorated in warm rustic colours. May–Sept. **€55**

Kioni Apartments ☎26740 31144, 🌐ithacagreece.eu. Tucked into the rocks that fringe the harbour, these six compact but comfortable studios are built in traditional style and have sea-facing balconies or flagstone patios. May–Sept. **€70**

Zákynthos

ZÁKYNTHOS (Zante), southernmost of the six core Ionian islands, is divided between relative wilderness and indiscriminate commercialization. However, much of the island is still green and unspoilt, with only token pockets of tourism, and the main resorts seem to be reaching maximum growth without encroaching too much on the quieter parts. The island has **three distinct zones**: the barren, mountainous northwest; the fertile central plain; and the eastern and southern resort-filled coasts. The biggest resort is **Laganás**, on Laganás Bay in the south, a 24-hour party venue that doesn't stop for breath during the busy summer season. There are smaller, quieter resorts north and south of the capital, and the southerly Vassilikós peninsula has some of the best countryside and beaches, including exquisite **Yérakas**.

The island still produces fine **wines**, such as the white Popolaro, as well as sugar-shock-inducing *mandoláto* **nougat**, whose honey-sweetened form is best. Zákynthos is also the birthplace of **kantádhes**, the Italianate folk ballads which can be heard in tavernas in Zákynthos Town and elsewhere. In addition, the island harbours one of the key breeding sites of the endangered **loggerhead sea turtle** at Laganás Bay (see box, p.757).

ARRIVAL AND DEPARTURE
ZÁKYNTHOS

By plane Zákynthos' airport is 4km southwest of the capital.

Domestic destinations Athens (4–5 daily; 55min); Corfu (summer 3 weekly; 2hr); Kefaloniá (summer 3 weekly; 25min); Préveza (summer 3 weekly; 1hr 15min).

By bus KTEL buses from Zákynthos Town (see below) to the mainland destinations below are timed to connect with ferry sailings. You can board the bus at the station or by the ferry itself.

Destinations Athens (4 daily; 4hr 30min–5hr); Pátra (4 daily; 2hr 30min); Thessaloníki (3 weekly; 8–9hr).

By ferry The island is well connected from Zákynthos Town year-round with Kyllíni on the Peloponnesian coast (5–7 daily; 1hr 30min) and has a seasonal ferry link with Pessádha on Kefaloniá (2 daily May–Sept; 1hr 30min) from the northern Áyios Nikólaos (aka Skinári).

GETTING AROUND

By bus The local KTEL network radiates out from Zákynthos Town with frequent summer services to the busiest tourist resorts, especially Argási, Kalamáki and Laganás, but few or no buses to the far north or the west coast.

By cars and motorbike There are many rental outlets around the island, such as Eurosky (☎ 26950 26278, ⊚ eurosky.gr), whose head Zákynthos Town office is at Makrí 6, two blocks south of the main square. Diamond Cars, based at Sarakinádho and Tsiliví (☎ 26950 25961, ⊚ diamond-carrentals.gr), will bring a vehicle to your accommodation.

By taxi Taxis are widely available and can be called on ☎ 26950 48400.

Zákynthos Town

The town, like the island, is known as both **ZÁKYNTHOS** and Zante. This former "Venice of the East" (*Zante, Fior di Levante*, "Flower of the Levant", in an Italian jingle), rebuilt on the old plan after the 1953 earthquake, has bravely tried to re-create some of its style, though reinforced concrete can only do so much.

The town stretches beyond the length of the wide and busy harbour, its main section bookended by the grand, recently renovated **Platía Solomoú** at the north, and the church of **Áyios Dhionýsios**, patron saint of the island, at the south. Zákynthos is a working town with limited concessions to tourism, although there are sufficient facilities and it's the only place to stay if you want to see the island by public transport.

Áyios Dhionýsios

Southern end of seafront • **Church** Daily 8am–1pm & 5–10pm • Free • **Museum** Daily: May–Sept 8am–11pm; Oct–April 9am–noon & 5–8pm • €2

The church of **Áyios Dhionýsios** is well worth a visit for the dazzling giltwork and fine modern murals inside, which were completely repainted at the turn of the millennium. Behind the church there is also a **museum**, which has some fine paintings and icons.

Platía Solomoú

Platía Solomoú is named after the island's most famous son, the poet Dhionysios Solomos, the father of modernism in Greek literature, who was responsible for establishing demotic Greek (as opposed to the elitist *katharévousa* form) as a literary idiom. He is also the author of the lyrics to the national anthem, an excerpt from which adorns the statue of Liberty in the square.

Platía Solomoú is home to the massive Museum of Zakynthos and the town **library**, which has a small collection of pre- and post-1953 quake photography. On the seaward corner of the square stands the squat restored church of **Áyios Nikólaos tou Mólou**, where the vestments of St Dhionysios are kept.

Museum of Zakynthos

Platía Solomoú • Tues–Sun 8am–3pm • €4 • ☎ 26950 42714

The **Museum of Zakynthos**, also known as the Byzantine Museum, is notable for its collection of artworks from the **Ionian School** (see box, p.715), the region's post-Renaissance art movement, spearheaded by Zakynthian painter Panayiotis Doxaras. The movement was given impetus by Cretan refugees, unable to practise their art under Turkish rule. It also houses some secular painting and a fine model of the town before the 1953 earthquake.

Museum of D. Solomos and Eminent People of Zákynthos

Platía Ayíou Márkou • Daily 8am–2pm; summer also 8–10pm • €4 • ☎ 26950 48982

The impressive **Museum of D. Solomos and Eminent People of Zákynthos** is devoted to the life and work of Solomos and other Zakynthian luminaries. It shares its collection of manuscripts and personal effects with the other museum dedicated to the poet on Corfu (see p.713), where Solomos spent most of his life. There are also plenty of photographs and paintings of notable islanders.

The kástro

Bóhali • Daily: June–Sept 8am–8pm; Oct–May 8.30am–3pm • €4

Zákynthos' massive **kástro** broods over the hamlet of Bóhali on its bluff above the town. The ruined **Venetian fort** has vestiges of dungeons, armouries and fortifications, plus stunning views in all directions. Its shady carpet of fallen pine needles makes it a great spot to relax or picnic.

ARRIVAL AND INFORMATION

ZÁKYNTHOS TOWN

By bus The bus station is inconveniently located some 2km up from the seafront, near the hospital (☎ 26950 22255, ⓦ ktel-zakynthos.gr), with buses to mainland destinations and the main resorts.

By ferry The ferry quay is at the southern end of the town's seafront (see p.753).

Tourist information The tourist police, in the main police station halfway along the seafront, can supply basic information and keep a list of accommodation (May–Oct daily 8am–10pm; ☎ 26950 24482), or check the informative website ⓦ zante-paradise.com.

ACCOMMODATION

The Federation of Rented Rooms (☎ 26950 49498, ⓦ zanterooms.gr) can be contacted for accommodation around town and all over the island. Some of the best hotels are in the quiet Repára district, just north of the centre.

Egli Loútzi ☎ 26950 28317. Smallish hotel whose entrance is just off the seafront, tucked in beside the gargantuan *Strada Marina*, though some of its clean, compact rooms face the harbour. **€40**

★Palatino Kolokotróni 10, Repára ☎ 26950 27780, ⓦ palatinohotel.gr. Classy and surprisingly good-value place, which has beautifully furnished rooms with all mod cons and ritzy common areas. Ample buffet breakfast included. **€80**

Plaza Kolokotróni 2, Repára ☎ 26950 45733, ⓦ plazazante.gr. Barely 50m from the town beach, this snazzy four-storey hotel has comfortable, modern rooms, some with sea-facing balconies, and a relaxing lobby café. Breakfast included. **€60**

BOAT TRIPS FROM ZÁKYNTHOS TOWN

At least ten pleasure craft offer **day-trips** around the island from the quay in Zákynthos Town (around €25). All take in sights such as the **Blue Caves** at Cape Skinári, and moor in **Tó Naváyio (Shipwreck Bay)** and at the Marathiá caves at **Cape Kerí** in the southwest. Choose the trip with the most stops, as eight hours bobbing round the coast can become a bore, and check that your operator will actually take you into the caves. Additionally, there are shorter trips to **Kerí** and turtle-spotting in **Laganás Bay** for €15, including on one vessel with underwater seating. **Cavo Grosso** at Lombárdhou 22 (☎ 26950 48308, Ⓦ cavogrosso.gr) offers a range of excursions.

EATING AND DRINKING

Komis Bastoúni tou Ayíou ☎ 26950 26915. Across the quay from Áyios Dhionýsios, this restaurant is an upmarket favourite serving unusual seafood dishes like clams and urchins, mostly over €10, along with multiple mezédhes and good barrelled wine. Daily noon–2am.

★ **Malanos** Ayíou Athanasíou 38, Kípi ☎ 26950 45936. A superb rustic taverna off the Kalamáki road, that serves quality home-style cooking, as well as grills and ample fresh salads, mostly under €10. Live music on Fri & Sat, or nightly in high season. Daily 10am–4pm & 8pm–1am.

Stathmos Filitá 42 ☎ 26950 24040. The former bus station, just a block behind the seafront, has surpisingly become a delightful old-style *inomayirío*, serving a fine selection of *mezédhes* such as *saganáki* and seafood or meaty main courses for under €10. Daily noon–midnight.

Varkarola Lombárdhou 78 ☎ 26950 26999. Attractively designed establishment that offers dishes such as soufflé and roast pork for €6–8, plus good lunchtime deals. The best place in town to come for its nightly *kantádhes*. Daily 11am–2am.

NIGHTLIFE

Base Platía Ayíou Márkou ☎ 26950 42409, Ⓦ basecafe. gr. In a prime location and boasting a snazzy cocktail bar on the roof, this perennially busy favourite plays an eclectic dance mix at night, while its daytime café ambience is more rock and ethnic sounds. Daily 11am–late.

Bliss 21 Maïou 23 ☎ 26950 22004. Trendy place with a chilled café-style space downstairs and a bar that often features live music upstairs. Genres vary from rock through jazz to Latin. Daily 10am–late.

The Vassilikós peninsula

The busy southern end of Zákynthos' most noticeable feature is the **Vassilikós peninsula**, which points in somewhat phallic mimicry of Florida towards the Peloponnese. It is headed by the package resort of **Argási**, but its treasures really lie in the succession of sandy beaches, mostly on the eastern side, which culminate in the stunning strand of **Yérakas**.

Argási

Barely 4km south of Zákynthos Town, **ARGÁSI** is the busiest resort on this coast, sprawling for over a kilometre behind a beach that is scarcely a few feet wide in parts. Although the rest of the peninsula is far more appealing, it does offer a wide choice of facilities, including a popular concentration of clubs, and is a closer base for exploring the rest of the island.

The east coast

The first two coves south of Argási are **Kamínia** and the more scenic **Pórto Zóro**. The main road dips and dives along the east coast of the peninsula, with short access roads descending to these and longer beaches further south, such as **Iónio** and **Banana** – a free summer bus service runs to both beaches from Zákynthos Town and Laganás. Above these contiguous strands, the only facilities away from the coast are to be found at the rather formless village of **Áno Vassilkós**. The coast ends up at the well-established hamlet of **Áyios Nikólaos**, which has a good beach and a range of facilities including the best **watersports** on the peninsula: a free bus service runs here in season from Argási, Kalamáki and Laganás.

The west coast

At the very southwestern tip of the peninsula, **Yérakas** is the star attraction: a sublime crescent of golden sand. It's also a key loggerhead **turtle breeding ground**, and is therefore off limits between dusk and dawn, as well as being subject to strict rules on the number and placement of umbrellas. The excellent **Mediterranean Marine Life Centre** (April–Oct daily 8am–8pm; free; ⊕facebook.com/earthseasky.ioniannatureconservation), about 200m in from the beach, provides interesting background on these and other sea creatures, and also has a small zoo with donkeys, goats and the like.

Further north along the rugged west coast of the peninsula, accessed by the only (partly unpaved) road which crosses it, is **Dháfni**, home to a couple of tavernas.

ACTIVITIES

Watersports St Nicholas Beach Watersports in Áyios Nikólaos (☎ 6937 107 652) rents equipment for a range of

THE VASSILIKÓS PENINSULA

activities including windsurfing, parasailing and scuba diving.

ACCOMMODATION, EATING AND NIGHTLIFE

ARGÁSI

Barrage ☎ 6955 586 878, ⊕barrageclub.com. The biggest of the clubs that line the road from Zákynthos Town into Argási, with a huge garden and two indoor spaces, where well-known DJs play house, techno and other dance vibes to a crowd of gyrating bodies. May to mid-Oct daily 10pm–late.

The Beer Academy ☎ 26950 43903. Up the main road that runs inland, this is a great place to come for cheap drinks, a game of pool and football or other sporting events on multiple screens. Decent bar food too. April–Oct daily 9pm–late.

Ethnic ☎ 6978 267 094. Nicely fitted out Greek–Australian grill house, on the main strip, which can rustle up comfort food like liver and onions, as well as the usual grills, for €8–10. April–Oct daily 11am–1am.

★**Windmill Bay** ☎ 26950 24810, ⊕windmillhotelszante.com. At the far southern end, this spanking new hotel has huge, beautifully decorated apartments. There's also a large kidney-shaped pool with a snack bar, while the *Anadalis* restaurant serves superb Greek nouvelle cuisine from 6pm. Breakfast included. April–Oct. **€70**

THE EAST COAST

★**Levantino Studios & Apartments** Kamínia ☎ 26950 35366, ⊕levantino.gr. Well-equipped units of varying sizes, set in carefully manicured grounds behind the beach. They also have a snack-bar and free sunbeds with umbrellas. May–Oct. **€50**

Logos Áno Vassilkós ☎ 26950 35296. Legendary rustic club which occupies a large space in the pine woods, where night owls dance to a mixture of rock and disco sounds and sip exotic cocktails. June–Sept Mon, Wed, Fri & Sat 9pm–late.

Porto Zorro Pórto Zóro ☎ 26950 36013, ⊕portozorro. gr. This good-value hotel, right on the eponymous beach, has decent-sized rooms whose stark white linen is tempered by the brown wood-panelling. The attached taverna offers a full menu. **€45**

Vasilikos Beach Áyios Nikólaos ☎ 26950 35325, ⊕hotelvasilikosbeach.gr. Huge beach-resort complex that has a variety of rooms as well as a pool, jacuzzi and watersports among its many amenities. Buffet breakfast included. May–Oct. **€55**

THE WEST COAST

Antonis Dháfni ☎ 6984 184 332, ⊕antonistaverna. com. Fine taverna-cum-bar, where you can have a light snack and sip a sunset cocktail, or enjoy a full meal of fresh fish or home-cooked meat for under €10. June–Sept daily 10am–10pm.

Belvedere Luxury Suites Yérakas ☎ 26950 36061, ⊕belvederezante.com. Upmarket complex on the hill around 1km up from the beach, with top quality rooms and suites, plus a huge pool and flashy restaurant on wooden decks in the garden. May–Oct. **€80**

★**Triodi** Yérakas ☎ 26950 35215. Excellent taverna with a leafy garden, great for fresh fish or well-prepared meat dishes (mostly under €10), plus all the usual salads, dips and good local wine. May–Oct daily 11am–1am.

Laganás Bay

The large sweep of **Laganás Bay**, anchored on the major party resort of **Laganás** itself, dominates southern Zákynthos. **Kalamáki** is another busy resort at the eastern end, while delightful **Límni Kerioú** in the southwest completes the picture. As the bay is also a prime home to the **loggerhead turtle**, there has long been an uneasy coexistence between mass tourism and conservation (see box below).

LOGGERHEAD TURTLES

The Ionian islands harbour the Mediterranean's main concentration of **loggerhead sea turtles**, a sensitive species which is under direct threat from the tourist industry. These creatures lay their eggs at night on sandy coves and, easily frightened by noise and lights, are uneasy cohabitants with rough campers and late-night discos. Each year, many turtles fall prey to motorboat injuries, nests are destroyed by bikes and the newly hatched young die entangled in deckchairs and umbrellas left out at night.

The Greek government has passed laws designed to protect the loggerheads, including restrictions on camping on some beaches, but local economic interests tend to prefer a beach full of bodies to a sea full of turtles. On **Laganás**, nesting grounds are concentrated around the 14km bay, and Greek marine zoologists are in angry dispute with the tourist industry. The turtles' nesting ground just west of **Skála** on Kefaloniá is another important location, although numbers have dwindled to half their former strength and now only about eight hundred remain. Ultimately, the turtles' best hope for survival may rest in their potential draw as a unique tourist attraction in their own right. The Sea Turtle Protection Society of Greece has a wealth of information about **turtle protection programmes** and how to volunteer on its website at ⓦarchelon.gr.

While capitalists and environmentalists are still at, well, loggerheads, the **World Wide Fund for Nature** has issued guidelines for visitors:

- Don't use the beaches of Laganás and Yérakas **between sunset and sunrise**.
- Don't stick **umbrellas** in the sand in the marked nesting zones.
- Take your **rubbish** away with you – it can obstruct the turtles.
- Don't use **lights** near the beach at night – they can disturb the turtles, sometimes with fatal consequences.
- Don't take any **vehicle** onto the protected beaches.
- Don't **dig** up turtle nests – it's illegal.
- Don't pick up the **hatchlings** or carry them to the water.
- Don't use **speedboats** in Laganás Bay – a 9kph speed limit is in force.

11

Laganás

A large percentage of the hundreds of thousands of people who visit Zákynthos each year find themselves in **LAGANÁS**. Set amid the fine 9km beach that runs almost the entire length of the bay, it offers entertainments from watersports to ballooning, and even an occasional funfair. Beachfront **bars and restaurants** stretch for well over 1km, the bars and restaurants on the main drag another kilometre inland. Some stay open around the clock; others just play music at deafening volume until dawn, and the competing video and music bars can make Laganás at night resemble the set of *Blade Runner*. However, following the brutal **murder** of an American tourist in a bar in summer 2017, the police have started clamping down on some of the excesses and opening hours – it remains to be seen how long this will remain in force.

Kalamáki

Neighbouring Laganás to the east, **Kalamáki** has a better, much wider beach than its westerly neighbour and is altogether quieter, with a slightly more family-oriented feel. Even the bars are more laidback, although it does suffer from some airport noise.

Límni Kerioú

Límni Kerioú, at the southwestern end of Laganás Bay, has gradually evolved into a relaxing and picturesque resort, with a pleasant if not spectacular beach and a couple of diving operations. It's reached by a turning that branches off the main road before it climbs up towards the west coast, after the hill village of **Lithakiá**.

ACTIVITIES

Diving Límni Kerioú is home to Diving Center Turtle Beach (☎26950 49424, ⓦdiving-center-turtle-beach.com).

Horseriding Laganas Horse Riding (☎6977 875 792,

ⓦlaganahorseriding.gr), on the road between Lagan and Kalamáki, can arrange riding trips inland or on th beach.

ACCOMMODATION, EATING, DRINKING AND NIGHTLIFE

LAGANÁS

Rescue Club ☎26950 51612, ⓦrescueclub.net. Claiming to be the biggest club on the island, this place, in the middle of the main strip, has an outdoor bar area and huge indoor dancefloor with top sound and lighting equipment to enhance the nonstop dance favourites played by famous DJs. May–Oct daily 10pm–late.

★**Sarakina** ☎26950 51606, ⓦsarakinahotel.gr. Best taverna in the area, serving tasty dishes such as pork in wine sauce for around €10 and featuring nightly *kantádhes*. A free minibus shuttles diners from Laganás to its leafy location nearly 2km inland. It also has a hotel with rooms from €40. May–Oct daily 6pm–2am.

Zeros ⓦzerosclubzante.com. Massive club, on the main strip, with state-of-the-art sound systems and top DJs, which hosts various big events through the summer and regular foam parties and other themes. May–Oct daily 9pm–late.

KALAMÁKI

Cave Club ☎26950 48278, ⓦcavebar.tripod.com. Set in a real cave on the hillside above the village, with a leafy patio garden where you can enjoy a cocktail to the mostly laidback rock sounds. May–Oct daily 9pm–3am.

Crystal Beach ☎26950 42788, ⓦcrystalbeach.gr. Large resort hotel, which has smart rooms for independent travellers as well as package holiday-makers, plus restaurant, bar, pool and watersports on the beach. Breakfast included. May–Oct. **€65**

Stani ☎26950 26374. Both branches of this wel established taverna have extensive menus of Greek an international dishes (mostly under €10), although the on by the beach is predictably busier during the day than th *Stani* on the main strip. May–Oct daily 11am–1am.

LÍMNI KERIOÚ

Camping Tartaruga ☎26950 51967, ⓦtartaruga camping.com. Easily the best campsite on the island though reaching it requires a vehicle as it's on a remote stretch of Laganás Bay below Lithákia. Shady pitches, a pebble beach and minimarket are all to hand. May–Oct **€12**

Nikolas ☎26950 48752. The best of severa establishments that line the seafront south of the harbour, this friendly place dishes up great starters, salads, meat dishes and succulent swordfish: most mains are under €10. May–Oct daily noon–1am.

★**Pansion Limni** ☎26950 48716, ⓦpansionlimni. com. Disarmingly friendly and great-value family guest-house, with comfortable self-catering rooms and a shared wraparound balcony that has sea views. They also run the *Porto Tsi Ostrias* pension, 200m inland, with larger, beautifully designed apartments. **€35**

Rock Café ☎26950 23401. Chilled-out joint with an airy wooden balcony overlooking the beach, a well-stocked bar and, as the name suggests, a decent line in rock sounds. May–Oct daily noon–2am.

Western Zákynthos

At the far southwest end of Laganás Bay, the landscape ascends into the mountains around **Kerí**, the first of a series of pretty villages along the sparsely inhabited **west coast** which contain some of the island's best architecture, including some especially splendid churches.

ARRIVAL AND DEPARTURE

By car and motorbike The bus system does not reach the wild western side of the island, so a rental car or sturdy

motorbike is required to get there.

Kerí

Hidden in a fold above the cliffs at the island's southernmost tip, the village of **KERÍ** retains several pre-quake Venetian buildings including the **Panayía Kerioú** church; the Virgin is said to have saved the island from marauding pirates by hiding it in a sea mist. A road leads 1km on to the lighthouse, with spectacular views of the sea, rock arches and stacks.

Maherádho

MAHERÁDHO boasts impressive pre-earthquake architecture set in beautiful arable uplands, surrounded by olive and fruit groves. The church of **Ayía Mávra** has an impressive freestanding campanile and, inside, a splendid carved iconostasis and icons. The town's major **festival** – one of the biggest on the island – is the saint's day, which falls on the first Sunday in June. The other notable church in town, that of the **Panayía**, commands breathtaking views over the central plain.

Kilioméno and around

KILIOMÉNO is the best place to see surviving pre-earthquake domestic architecture, in the form of the island's traditional two-storey houses. The town was originally named after its church, **Áyios Nikólaos**, whose impressive campanile, begun over a hundred years ago, still lacks a capped roof. The road from Kilioméno passes through the nondescript village of Áyios Léon, from where two turnings lead through fertile land and down a paved loop road to the impressive rocky coast at **Limniónas**, where there is a tiny bay.

Kambí

The tiny clifftop hamlet of **KAMBÍ** is popular with day-trippers who come to catch the sunset over the sea; there are extraordinary views to be had of the 300m-high cliffs and western horizon from Kambí's three clifftop tavernas.

Mariés and around

Set in a wooded green valley 5km north of Kambí, the tiny village of **MARIÉS** is the only other place with coastal access on this side of Zákynthos: a 7km track leading down to the rocky inlet of **Stenítis Bay**, where there's a taverna and yacht dock. Another steep road leads to the uninspiring **Vrómi Bay**, from where speedboats run trips to Shipwreck Bay (see p.761), while the main road continues north towards Volímes (see p.761).

ACCOMMODATION AND EATING | **THE WEST COAST**

KERÍ

Apelati ☎ 26950 43324, ✉ apelatidenia @gmail.com. Just off the main road before the incline east of the village, this farm-like taverna serves home-style dishes from fresh ingredients for well under €10 and has a few simple rustic rooms (€30). May–Oct 11am–midnight.

Lighthouse ☎ 26950 43384, 🌐 liveris.gr. Scenically situated taverna, 1km west of the village, where people flock for sunset dinners in the large and lush patio garden. The food is standard fare (mains €8–10), but the view unsurpassed. May–Sept daily noon–midnight.

KILIOMÉNO AND AROUND

Porto Limnionas Limniónas, ☎ 6977 258 541. Perched on a rocky outcrop just above the tiny harbour, this *psarotavérna* is known for its high-quality if rather pricey fish at €50 per kilo minimum, and also has a huge selection of tasty mezédhes. May–Oct daily noon–11pm.

KAMBÍ

Stavros ☎ 6977 258 541. Perched on the hill just below the famous landmark of the huge cross (*stavrós* in Greek), this solid taverna draws in the crowds, especially for sunset dinners, with mains such as pork chops around €10. May–Oct daily noon–11pm.

The northeast

The amalgamated resorts of **Tsiliví** and **Plános**, a few kilometres north of Zákynthos' capital, are the touristic epicentre of this part of the island. Further north, they give way to a series of tiny beaches, while picturesque villages punctuate the lush landscape inland. Beyond **Alykés**, as you approach the island's tip at **Cape Skinári**, the coast becomes more rugged, while the mountains inland hide the weaving centre of **Volímes**.

Tsiliví and around

North and inland from Zákynthos Town, the roads thread their way through luxuriantly fertile farmland, punctuated with tumulus-like hills. **TSILIVÍ**, 5km north of the capital, is the first beach resort here and is in effect one with the hamlet of **Plános**; the resultant conglomeration rivals Argási for development.

The beaches further along this stretch of coast become progressively quiet and more pleasant, and all have at least some accommodation and restaurants to choose from. Good choices include **Pahiá Ámmos** and **Dhrossiá**.

Alykés Bay

Alykés Bay, 12km north of Tsiliví, is a large sandy bay with lively surf and the northeast's two largest resorts. The first, **ALIKANÁS**, is a small but expanding village, and much of its accommodation is foreign-owned villa rentals. The second, **ALYKÉS**, named after the spooky saltpans behind the village, has the best beach north of the capital.

Katastári and around

Two kilometres inland from Alykés, **KATASTÁRI** is the largest settlement after the capital. Precisely because it's not geared towards tourism, it's the best place to see Zakynthian life as it's lived away from the usual racket. Its most impressive edifice is the huge rectangular church of Iperáyia Theotókos, with a twin belfry and small new amphitheatre for festival performances.

A couple of kilometres south of Katastári, the tiny hamlet of **PIGHADHÁKIA** is the unlikely setting for the **Vertzagio Cultural Museum** (March to early Nov daily 9am–2pm & 5–8pm; €3), which houses an interesting array of agricultural and folk artefacts and can be reached by road on the little train from Alikanás and Alykés (€12.50 including museum entry and refreshments at *Kaki Raki*; ☎6937 126 391, ⊛trainaki.com). Nearby, the diminutive **Áyios Pandeléïmon** chapel has the unusual feature of a well, hidden beneath the altar.

AYÍA MARÍNA, a few kilometres southwest of Katastári, has a **church** with an impressive Baroque altar screen and a belfry that's being rebuilt from the remnants left after the 1953 earthquake. As in most Zákynthos churches, the bell tower stands detached, in Venetian fashion. In the upper part of the village is **Helmi's Natural History Museum** (daily 9am–6pm: Nov–April closes at 2pm; €2; ☎26950 65040, ⊛museumhelmis.gr), which displays plenty of stuffed birds and mammals, seashells and the largest ammonite found in Greece. You can also watch an informative film about turtles.

Makrýs Yialós and around

Tiny **Xygiá beach**, cut into a deep cove 4km north of Alykés, has sulphur springs flowing into the sea – follow the smell – which provide the odd sensation of swimming in a mix of cool and warm water. The next somewhat longer beach of **Makrýs Yialós** also makes for an extremely pleasant break on a tour of the north. Just to the north of Makrýs Yialós, you'll come to a pretty promontory with a small harbour, called **Mikró Nissáki**.

Áyios Nikólaos and around

Ferries to Pessádha on Kefaloniá run twice a day May–Sept (1hr 30min); there's no bus connection from Zákynthos Town though.

Just over 20km from Zákynthos Town, **ÁYIOS NIKÓLAOS** is a small working port with a daily summer ferry connection to Pessádha on Kefaloniá. It's also known to locals as **Skinári** (after the nearby inland village) to avoid confusion with its namesake on the Vassilikós peninsula.

The Blue Caves

Potamitis Boat Trips (☎26950 31241, ⊛potamitisbros.gr) run daily in season from Cape Skinari every 15min 9am–7.30pm • €7.50; €15, combined with Shipwreck Bay

The **Blue Caves** are some of the more realistically named of the many contenders in Greece. They're terrific for snorkelling, and when you go for a dip here your skin ill appear bright blue. To reach them, follow the road as it snakes onwards from yios Nikólaos through a landscape of gorse bushes and dry-stone walls until it nds at the lighthouse of **Cape Skinári**, from below which the cheapest **boat trips** perate.

olímes and around

Divided into three contiguous parts, **VOLÍMES** is the centre of the island's embroidery ndustry and numerous shops sell artefacts produced here. With your own transport, ou could make it to the **Anafonítria monastery**, 3km south, thought to have been the ell of the island's patron saint, Dhionysios, whose festivals are celebrated on August 24 nd December 17.

A paved road leads on from Volímes to the cliffs overlooking **Shipwreck Bay** (To Naváyio), with hair-raising views down to the shipwreck, a cargo ship which was mistaken for a drug-running vessel and run aground by the coastguard in the 1960s.

ACCOMMODATION AND EATING

THE NORTHEAST

11

TSILIVÍ AND AROUND

Zarkadis Beach Apartments Tsiliví ☎ 26950 23332, ⓦ zarkadis.gr. Very comfortable, well-equipped apartments in an attractive building with spacious leafy grounds behind the beach. April–Oct. __€45__

To Limenaki Tsiliví ☎ 26950 44740. This fine seafront psarotavérna towards the harbour is one of the most authentic places to eat in the area. An ample slice of swordfish costs €9, meat dishes a little less, plus there are plenty of mezédhes to choose from. May–Oct daily noon–1am.

Asian Feast Plános ☎ 6946 828 614. The resort's prime ethnic restaurant serves both Indian and Chinese cuisine, with dishes such as chicken vindaloo, lamb phall and Peking duck (all €6.50–11). May–Oct daily noon–midnight.

ALYKÉS BAY

Astoria ☎ 26950 83533, ⓦ astoriazante.com. Large but friendly seafront establishment with standard rooms, run by returnees from New York – hence the Statue of Liberty images and the like. Easter–Oct. __€40__

★**To Paradosiako** ☎ 26950 83412. On the main road coming in from the south, this restaurant lives up to its name, meaning "traditional", by appealing to locals. It has unusual dishes like swordfish in tarragon sauce for only €9. May–Oct daily 9am–1am.

MAKRÝS YIALÓS

Pilarinos ☎ 26950 31396. This good taverna on the flattish hillock behind the beach does a decent line in grills, fish and the usual accoutrements, mostly under €10, plus there's a makeshift campsite on the grounds. May–Oct daily 11am–midnight.

ÁYIOS NIKÓLAOS AND AROUND

★**Anemomilos** Cape Skinári ☎ 26950 31132, ⓦ potamitisbros.gr. Two expertly converted windmills make for a unique place to stay. There are also some cheaper, more conventional rooms, a snack-bar, and the same family run the excellent To Faros taverna nearby. May–Oct. __€55__

Panorama Áyios Nikólaos ☎ 26950 31013, ⓔ panorama-apts@ath.forthnet.gr. These friendly studios are a good-value option if you are leaving on the morning ferry to Kefaloniá or want a northern base. Breakfast included. April–Oct. __€35__

PIGHADHÁKIA

★**Kaki Rahi** ☎ 26950 83670. Traditional family-run taverna, which serves tasty local cuisine from home-grown ingredients for under €10, plus its own fine barrelled wine. At lunchtime, you can get here on the little train from Alykés. Live music Sat evenings. May–Oct daily 11am–midnight.

ERECHTHEION TEMPLE, ATHENS

Contexts

History

reece's position at the heart of the eastern Mediterranean and at the rossroads of Europe, Asia and Africa, has long presented it with unique pportunities and dangers. The Greeks are a people who have suffered alamities, yet they have also achieved the highest reaches of human ccomplishment. In the areas of politics, philosophy, literature, science and rt, Greece has influenced Western society more than any other nation in istory; in the twenty-first century, it seems their economic policy may have o be added to that list.

Prehistoric Greece: to 2100 BC

Evidence of human habitation in Greece goes back half a million years, as demonstrated by the skeleton of a **Neanderthal** youth in the **Petralóna Cave**, 50km east of the northern city of Thessaloníki, along with the earliest known site of a man-made fire in Europe.

Only very much later, about **40,000 years ago**, did **Homo sapiens** make their first appearance in Greece after migrating out of Africa. At several sites in **Epirus** in northwest Greece, Homo sapiens used tools and weapons of bone, wood and stone to gather wild plants and hunt. Even between **20,000 and 16,000 years ago**, when the Ice Age was at its peak, **Stone Age man** continued to make a home in Greece, though only when the glaciers finally receded about **10,000 BC** did a considerably warmer climate set in, which altered the Greek environment to something more like that of present times.

The Neolithic period

Agricultural communities first appeared in northern Greece around **6500 BC**. Whether agriculture developed indigenously or was introduced by migrants from Asia Minor is much debated: what is certain, however, is its revolutionary effect.

An assured supply of food enabled the Stone Age inhabitants of Greece to settle in fixed spots, and they built mud-brick houses on stone foundations. Though still reliant on stone implements, this new farming culture marked a significant break with the past, so a "new stone age" or **Neolithic period** is said to have begun. As the flint needed for weapons and tools was rare in Greece, mainlanders imported obsidian from the island of **Melos** (Mílos) in the southern Cyclades. The earliest **seaborne trade** known anywhere in the world, this clearly involved a mastery of building and handling boats.

Cycladic culture and the beginnings of the Greek Bronze Age

Around **3000 BC** a new people settled in the **Cyclades**, probably from Asia Minor, bringing with them the latest metallurgical techniques. While continuing the old trade in obsidian, they also developed a **trade in tin** and were making prodigious voyages westwards as far as Spain by 2500 BC. The mining of **gold and silver** in the Cyclades

c. 40,000 BC	c. 6500 BC	c. 3000 BC
Stone Age Homo sapiens arrives in Greece	Permanent communities and the world's earliest seaborne trade herald the Neolithic era	In the Cycladic islands, a new people introduce striking new art forms. The dawn of the Bronze Age

may have dated from this period, too. Long before Crete or the Greek mainland, these new islanders became specialists in **jewellery-making**, **metalwork** and **stone-cutting**. From the abundant marble of the Cyclades, they sculpted statuettes, mostly of female figures. Slender, spare and geometric, these **Cycladic sculptures** are startlingly modern in appearance, and were exported widely, to Crete and mainland Greece, along with other ritual objects.

In about 3000 BC, the introduction of bronze technology to the mainland, also from the Cyclades, marked the start of the **Bronze Age** in Greece. By **2500 BC** the widespread use of bronze had transformed farming and fighting throughout the Eastern Mediterranean and the Middle East. Because tin (which when alloyed with copper creates bronze) came from so far afield – in the east from the Caucasus, Persia and Afghanistan, in the west from Cornwall, Brittany, northwest Spain and northern Italy – the Aegean became an important trade route. This resulted in a burst of development along the eastern coast of **central Greece** and the **Peloponnese**, and on the **Aegean islands** which linked the Greek mainland to Asia Minor and the Middle East.

It is uncertain what **language** was spoken at this time, but one thing is clear: it was not yet Greek. Indeed, when **Greek-speaking people** did arrive on the mainland in about 2100 BC, their destructive impact paralysed its development for five hundred years.

The coming of the Greeks

The destruction of numerous mainland sites in about **2100 BC**, followed by the appearance of a new style of pottery, has suggested to archeologists the violent arrival of a **new people**. They domesticated the horse, introduced the potter's wheel and possessed considerable metallurgical skills. These newcomers replaced the old religion centred on female fertility figures with **hilltop shrines**, thought to have been dedicated to the worship of male sky gods like Zeus. And with them came a new language, an early form of **Greek**, though they were obliged to adopt existing native words for such things as olives, figs, vines, wheat and the sea, suggesting that these new migrants or invaders may have come from distant inland steppes where they had been pastoral highlanders, not farmers, fishermen or sailors.

Minoan and Mycenaean civilizations: 2100–1100 BC

The history of the Aegean during the second millennium BC can be seen as a struggle between the **Mycenaean culture** of the Greek mainland and the **Minoan culture** of Crete. Situated halfway between mainland Greece and Egypt, Crete exploited the Bronze Age boom in trade to become the dominant power in the Aegean by the start of the second millennium BC. Its influence was felt throughout the islands and also on the mainland, where the Greek-speaking invaders were "Minoanized", gradually developing a culture known as Mycenaean (after Mycenae, a principal mainland Bronze Age site) that owed a lot to Crete.

Minoan Crete

Living on a large and fertile island with good natural harbours, the people of **Crete** raised sufficient crops and livestock to export surplus quantities of oil and wool. Among their most impressive tools, literally at the cutting edge of new technology, was

c. 2100 BC	c. 2000 BC	c. 1700 BC	c. 1500 BC
The Greek language is heard in Greece for the first time	On Crete, the great Minoan palaces are built	Knossós and the other palaces are destroyed by earthquake, but rebuilt even more grandly	Mainland Mycenaeans gain control of Crete

metre-long bronze saw that readily converted the forest-clad mountains into an ample source of **timber for ships**. Some timber was probably also exported, most likely to treeless Egypt, while metalwork, jewellery and pottery of superb Cretan craftsmanship were shipped to the mainland and beyond. **Kamares ware**, as Cretan pottery of this period is known, was especially valued; it has been found all along the Cretans' 1175km-long maritime trade route to the East – on the Aegean islands of Rhodes and Sámos, on the coast of Asia Minor at Miletus, and in Syria and Egypt.

On Crete itself, Minoan power was concentrated on three vast **palace complexes** – at Knossós, **Phaestos** and **Malia**, all in the centre of the island. First built around 2000 BC, their similarity of plan and lack of defences suggest that some form of confederacy had replaced any regional rivalries on the island, while Minoan sea power induced a sense of security against foreign invasion. Not that prosperity was confined to the palace centres; the numerous remains of villas of the Minoan gentry, and of well-constructed villages, show that the wealth generated by the palaces was redistributed among the island's population. Following an **earthquake** around 1700 BC, the palaces at Knossós and Phaestos were rebuilt, and a more modest palace constructed at **Zakros** on the east coast. This activity coincided with an apparent centralization of power at Knossós, which gave rise to a **Minoan golden age**.

Mycenaean dominance

Suddenly, however, around **1500 BC**, the Mycenaeans gained control of the palace of Knossós and were soon in full possession of Crete. How this happened is unknown, but it probably marked the culmination of a growing rivalry between the Mycenaeans and the Minoans for control of the Aegean trade, which perhaps coincided with a **volcanic explosion** on the island of Thera (Thíra/Santoríni) and its consequent **tsunami**.

Greek now became the language of administration at Knossós and the other former Minoan palaces, as well as on the mainland – indeed, this is the earliest moment that

---

THE TROJAN WAR

For the Greeks, the story of the **Trojan War** was the central event in their early history, and in their minds Homer's **Iliad** was not just a poem of heroic deeds sung at noble courts, but the epic of their first great national adventure.

Excavations in the late nineteenth century by Heinrich Schliemann (see p.790) uncovered many Troys of several periods, but the layer known as **Troy VIIa** clearly suffered violent destruction in about 1220 BC. The Mycenaeans are the likeliest perpetrators, though the abduction of a Greek beauty called **Helen** would not have been the only reason they launched a thousand ships against the Trojans. Mycenaean prosperity greatly depended on trade with the Eastern Mediterranean, where increasingly unsettled conditions made it imperative that they secure their lines of **trade and supply**. Troy commanded a strategic position overlooking the Hellespont, the narrow waterway (today called the Dardanelles) dividing Europe and Asia and linking the Aegean to the Black Sea, where it controlled important trade routes.

The capture of Troy was the last great success of the Mycenaeans, and perhaps for that reason it was long remembered in poetry and song. It inspired later generations of Greeks to dream of overseas expansion, culminating in the fourth century BC when Alexander the Great carried a copy of the *Iliad* as he marched across Asia, founding Greek cities as he went, and stood with his army on the banks of the Indus River.

---

c. 1220 BC	**c. 1150 BC**	**c. 1100 BC**
Trojan War; events are immortalized by Homer and enter the realm of myth	The so-called Sea Peoples sweep across Greece, ushering in a new Dark Age	The first iron tools and weapons begin to transform agriculture and warfare

Greek language can definitely be identified, as the palace records on Crete are from now on written in a script known as **Linear B**, which, when deciphered in 1953, was shown to be a form of Greek. Having wrested control of the Aegean trade from the Minoans, the **Mycenaeans** were dominant for another three hundred years. At the end of that period, in about 1220 BC, they famously laid siege to, and destroyed, yet another rival, the city of **Troy**.

Yet within a generation, the Mycenaean world was overwhelmed by a vast **migration** of northerners from somewhere beyond the Black Sea. Probably victims of a catastrophic change in climate that brought drought and famine to their homelands, these **Sea Peoples**, as the ancients called them, swept down through Asia Minor and the Middle East and also crossed the Mediterranean to Libya and Egypt, disrupting trade routes and destroying empires as they went. With the palace-based Bronze Age economies destroyed, the humbler **village-based economies** that replaced them lacked the wealth and the technological means to make a mark in the world. Greece was plunged into a Dark Age, and knowledge of the Minoan and Mycenaean civilizations slipped into dim memory.

The Dark Age and the rise of the city-state: 1150–491 BC

The poverty and isolation that characterized Greece for the next five hundred years did have one lasting effect: **emigration**. Greeks spread to the Dodecanese islands, to Cilicia along the south coast of **Asia Minor**, and to **Cyprus**, which now became Greek-speaking. Later, around 1000 BC, they also settled in large numbers along the western coast of Asia Minor. Even in the Dark Age there were a few glimmers of light: **Athens**, for example, escaped the destruction that accompanied the fall of Mycenaean civilization, and maintained trading links abroad. It became the route through which the **Iron Age** was introduced to mainland Greece with the importation of iron weapons, implements and technological know-how around 1100 BC. A new cultural beginning was also made in the form of pottery painted in the **Geometric style**, a highly intricate and

---

THE ILIAD AND THE ODYSSEY

The **Iliad** and the **Odyssey**, the oldest and greatest works in Greek literature, were the brilliant summation of five centuries of poetic tradition, first developed by nameless bards whose recitations were accompanied by music. Completed by 725 BC, they are far older than the *Pentateuch*, the first five books of the Old Testament, which achieved their finished form only around 400 BC. The whole Greek world knew the **Homeric epics**, and their influence upon the subsequent development of Greek literature, art and culture in general cannot be overstated. Few works, and probably none not used in worship, have had such a hold on a nation for so long.

The *Iliad* is the story of a few days' action in the tenth and final year of the **Trojan War**, which in its tales of heroic exploits recalls the golden age of the Mycenaeans. The *Odyssey* begins after the war and follows the adventures of **Odysseus**, who takes ten years to return to his island home of Ithaca on the western side of Greece. The story of his voyages demonstrates the new Greek interest in the area around the Black Sea and in Italy and Sicily to the west. They are also a celebration of an emerging **Hellenic identity**, of a national adventure encompassing both shores of the Aegean and beyond.

900–700 BC	c. 800 BC	776 BC	750–650 BC
Geometric Period	Revival of trade between Greece and the Middle East kick-starts an economic revival	The first Olympic Games are staged at Olympia	Greeks colonize the Eastern Mediterranean, from Italy to Asia Minor

ontrolled design that would lie at the heart of later Greek architecture, sculpture and ainting. But it was the **Phoenicians**, sailing from Sidon and Tyre in present-day ebanon, who really re-established trading links between the Middle East and the egean world in the eighth century BC, and Greeks followed swiftly in their wake.

With wealth flowing in again, Greek civilization developed with remarkable rapidity; o other people achieved so much over the next few centuries. The institution most esponsible for this extraordinary achievement, the **city-state** or **polis**, came into being t a time of rapidly growing populations, greater competition for land and resources, increasing productivity and wealth, expanding trade and more complex relationships with neighbouring states. The birthplace of **democracy** and of equality before the law, he city-state became the Greek ideal, and by the early seventh century BC it had pread throughout Greece and wherever Greeks established colonies overseas.

Trade also acted as a cultural stimulus; contact with other peoples made the Greeks aware of what they shared among themselves, and led to the development of a **national entiment**, notably expressed and fostered by the **panhellenic sanctuaries** that arose during the eighth century BC, of Hera and Zeus at **Olympia** and of Apollo and Artemis t **Delos**, as well as the **oracles** of Zeus at **Dodona** and of Apollo at **Delphi**.

Expansion and colonization

Around 750 BC, Greeks began to found **colonies** in the Western Mediterranean – in **Sicily** and **southern Italy** especially – while a century later, around 650 BC, further colonies were established round the shores of the **Black Sea**. By the fifth century BC, Greeks seemed to sit upon the shores of the entire world, in Plato's words like "frogs around a pond".

One impetus for expansion was competition between the Greeks and the Phoenicians over trade routes; but there was also rivalry among the Greek city-states themselves. **Chalkis**, **Eretria** and **Corinth** were the major colonizers in the west, while the **Ionian Greeks** were the chief colonizers around the Black Sea. When the Spartans needed more land, they conquered neighbouring Messenia in 710 BC, but generally land shortage drove Greeks overseas. Thus colonists were sent from Santoríni (Thíra) to found Cyrene in North Africa, and were forbidden to return on pain of death. Whatever the reason for their foundation, however, most colonies kept up close relations with their mother cities.

Democracy, tyranny and slavery

Meanwhile, at home in the city-states, political tensions were building between the **aristocratic rulers** and the **people**. A large class of farmers, merchants and the like was excluded from political life but forced to pay heavy taxes. The pressure led to numerous reforms and a gradual move towards **democracy**. Ironically, the transition was often hastened by **tyrants**. Despite the name – which simply means they seized power by force – many tyrants were in fact champions of the people, creating work, redistributing wealth and patronizing the arts. **Peisistratos**, tyrant of Athens during the sixth century BC, is perhaps the archetype. Successful and well-liked by his people, his populist rule ensured Athenian prosperity by gaining control of the route into the Black Sea. He also ordered that Homer's works be set down in their definitive form and performed regularly, and encouraged the theatrical festivals where Greek drama was born.

c. 725 BC	700–480 BC	621 BC	c. 620–570 BC
The Iliad and Odyssey, hitherto retold as oral sagas, are set down in writing	Archaic Period	Draco's reforming "draconian" law code is published in Athens	Lifetime of the great poet Sappho, from whom we get the words sapphic and lesbian (after her birthplace, Lésvos), lived and wrote

Athens and the Golden Age: 490–431 BC

Democracy was a very long way from universal. The population of **Athens** and surrounding Attica amounted to some 400,000 people, of whom about 80,000 were slaves, 160,000 foreigners, and another 160,000 free-born Athenians. Out of this last category came the **citizens**, those who could vote and be elected to office, and their number amounted to no more than 45,000 adult men.

Yet if the powers of democracy were in the hands of the few, the energy, boldness an◄

BIG IDEAS: SOCRATES, PLATO AND ARISTOTLE

The Golden Age of Athens under Pericles, and the city-state rivalry after the Peloponnesian War, saw the **birth of Western philosophy** under the towering figures of Socrates, Plato and Aristotle.

SOCRATES (C.470–399 BC)

The son of an Athenian sculptor, **Socrates** was for a time a sculptor himself, and fought bravely for Athens as a hoplite in the Peloponnesian War. In his twenties, he turned to philosophy, which he practised in his own peculiar style, asserting ceaselessly, the supremacy of reason. Often, in the streets of Athens, he would ask some self-regarding Athenian of the older generation questions, then pick his answers to pieces, until he came up with a definition that held water or, more likely, the victim confessed his own **ignorance** before crowds of Socrates' mirthful young supporters.

By this "Socratic method" he asked for definitions of familiar concepts such as piety and justice; his technique was to expose the ignorance that hid behind people's use of such terms, while acknowledging his own similar ignorance. Indeed, when the Delphic oracle proclaimed that no man was wiser than Socrates, he explained this by saying wisdom lies in knowing how little one really knows. Because he valued this question-and-answer process over settling on fixed conclusions, Socrates never wrote anything down. Yet his influence was pivotal; before his time, philosophical enquiry concerned itself with speculations on how the natural world was formed and how it operates; afterwards, it looked to **ethics** and the **analysis of concepts**.

Socrates' method could be irritating, especially when he questioned conventional morality, and this, coupled with powerful friendships with unpopular oligarchs, led to a backlash. Having tried him for impiety and corrupting the young, and sentenced him to death, the city gave him the option of naming another penalty, probably expecting him to choose exile. Instead, Socrates answered that if he was to get what he deserved, he should be maintained for life at public expense. At this the death penalty was confirmed, but even then it was not to be imposed for two months, with the tacit understanding that Socrates would escape. Instead Socrates argued that it was wrong for a citizen to disobey even an unjust law, and in the company of his friends he drank the cup of hemlock. "Such was the end," wrote Plato, "of our friend; of all the men of his time whom I have known, he was the wisest and justest and best."

PLATO (C.427–C.347 BC)

As a young man, **Plato** painted, composed music and wrote a tragedy, as well as being a student of Socrates. He intended a career in politics, where his connections would have ensured success, but Socrates' death made Plato decide that he could not serve a government that had committed such a crime, and his mission became to exalt the memory of his teacher. In Plato's writings, many of them **dialogues**, Socrates is frequently the leading participant,

---

546 BC	**498 BC**	**490 BC**
Peisistratos seizes power in Athens	Rebellious Ionian Greeks burn the city of Sardis, provoking a Persian invasion of Greece	Victory by the Athenians and Plataeans at the Battle of Marathon ends the first Persian campaign. Pheidippides runs to Athens to convey the good news

reative spirit that it released raised Athens to greatness. Throughout the **fifth century BC** the political, intellectual and artistic activity of the Greek world was centred on the ity. In particular, Athens was the patron of **drama**, both tragedy and comedy. Athenian ragedy always addressed the great issues of life and death and the relationship of man o the gods. And the Athenians themselves seemed to be conscious of living out a high rama as they fought battles, argued policy, raised temples and wrote plays that have ecided the course and sensibility of Western civilization.

while at the **Academy** in Athens, which Plato founded, the Socratic question-and-answer method was the means of instruction.

Plato's philosophy is elusive, though certain themes recur. He believed that men possess **immortal souls** separate from their mortal bodies. **Knowledge**, he believed, was the recollection of what our souls already know; we do not gain knowledge from experience, rather by using our reasoning capacity to draw more closely to the realm of our souls. The true objects of knowledge are not the transient, material things of this world, which are only reflections of a higher essence that Plato called **Forms** or **Ideas**. Forms are objects of pure thinking, cut off from our experience; but Forms also motivate us to grasp them, so that the reasoning part of us is drawn to Forms as a kind of mystic communion.

Plato's notion of a mystic union with a higher essence would play an important role in later religious thought. But, more immediately, his teachings at the Academy concerned themselves with logic, mathematics, astronomy and above all **political science**, for its purpose was to train a new ruling class. Prominent families sent him their sons to learn the arts of government. Plato taught that the best form of government was a constitutional monarchy, at its head a wise and just philosopher-king. Though it was a utopian vision, Plato's political philosophy helped prepare the intellectual ground for the acceptance of an absolutist solution to the increasing uncertainties of fourth-century BC Greece.

ARISTOTLE (384–322 BC)

Aristotle grew up in Pella, the capital of an increasingly powerful Macedonia, where his father was doctor to King Amyntas II; it is therefore not unlikely that Amyntas' son, the future Philip II, and Aristotle were boyhood friends. Aged seventeen, Aristotle was sent to Plato's Academy in Athens, and he remained there, first as a student, then as a teacher, a faithful follower of Plato's ideas. His independent philosophy matured later, during the years he spent at Pella, as tutor to Alexander the Great, and later still, after 335 BC, when he founded his own school, the **Lyceum**, in Athens.

Aristotle came to reject Plato's dualism. He did not believe that the soul was of a substance separate from the body, rather that it was an aspect of the body. Instead of Plato's inward-looking view, Aristotle sought to explain the physical world and human society from the viewpoint of an outside observer. Essentially a **scientist and realist**, he was bent on discovering the true rather than establishing the good, and he believed sense perception was the only means of human knowledge. His vast output covered many fields of knowledge – logic, metaphysics, ethics, politics, rhetoric, art, poetry, physiology, anatomy, biology, zoology, physics, astronomy and psychology. Everything could be measured, analysed and described, and he was the first to classify organisms into **genera and species**.

The exactitude of Aristotle's writings does not make them easy reading, and Plato has always enjoyed a wider appeal owing to his literary skill. All the same, Aristotle's influence on Western intellectual and scientific tradition has been enormous.

480 BC	480 BC	480 BC	480–323 BC
Greek defeat at the Battle of Thermopylae, scene of heroic Spartan defiance	Persians sack and burn Athens	Battle of Salamis; the Persian fleet is destroyed and supply lines cut	Classical period

The Persian Wars

The wars between Greece and Persia began with a revolt by Ionian Greeks in Asia Minor. Athens and Eretria gave them support, burning the city of Sardis in 498 BC. Provoked by their insolence, **Darius**, the Persian king, launched a punitive expedition. The **Persians'** unexpected repulse at **Marathon** in 490 BC persuaded Darius to hurl his full military might against Greece, to ensure its subjection once and for all to the Persian Empire.

After Darius died in 486 BC, his son **Xerxes** took over. In 483 BC, he began preparations that lasted two years and were on a fabulous scale. Bridges of boats were built across the Hellespont for Persia's vast imperial army to parade into Europe, and a canal was cut for the fleet through the Athos peninsula. Though the Greek historian **Herodotus** claimed that Xerxes' army held one million eight hundred thousand soldiers, his figure is probably a tenfold exaggeration. Even so, it was a massive force, an army of 46 nations, combined with a fleet of eight hundred triremes carrying almost as many sailors as there were soldiers in the army.

Despite their numerical superiority, the might of Asia was routed both at sea off **Salamis** in 480 BC and on land at **Plataea** the following year. Within a few days of that second battle came another naval victory at **Mycale**, off Sámos, when Xerxes' subject Ionians defected to join their fellow Hellenes. Xerxes could do no more than return to Susa, his capital deep in Persia, leaving the entire Aegean free.

This sudden shift in the balance of power between East and West, notwithstanding occasional reversals, endured for the next 1500 years. Within 150 years, **Alexander the Great** (see p.774) achieved in Asia what Xerxes had failed to achieve in Europe, and the Persian Empire succumbed to a Greek conqueror.

Themistocles and the rise of sea power

The greatest Athenian statesman, and architect of the victory over Persia, was **Themistocles**. Following the Ionian revolt, he understood that a clash between Persia and Greece was inevitable, and he had the genius to recognize that Athens' security and potential lay in its command of the sea. Thus he began in 493–492 BC to develop **Piraeus** (Pireás) as the harbour of Athens. Though his initial pretext was the hostility of the island of Aegina (Égina), his eyes were always on the more distant but far greater Persian danger.

When the Persians marched into Attica in the late summer of 480 BC, the oracle at Delphi told the Athenians to trust in their wooden wall. Many took that to mean the wooden wall around the citadel of the Athenian Acropolis, but Themistocles argued that it referred to the Athenian fleet. Determined to fight at sea, Themistocles warned his Peloponnesian allies against retreating to the Isthmus, where they too had built a wall, threatening that if they did, the entire citizenry of Athens would sail to new homes in southern Italy, leaving the rest of Greece to its fate. On the eve of the **Battle of Salamis**, as the Persians stormed the Acropolis, slaughtering its defenders and burning down its temples, the taunt came back from the Peloponnesians that Athens had no city anyway. Themistocles replied that so long as the Athenians had two hundred ships, they had a city and a country.

The naval victory at Salamis that he masterminded cut the Persians' maritime lines of supply and contributed to their defeat at Plataea the following year. It gave Athens and

479 BC	458 BC	447–438 BC	431–415 BC
Persians are defeated at the Battle of Plataea and forced out of Greece	Aeschylus produces the Oresteia trilogy in Athens	Parthenon, the symbol of Athens' Golden Age, is constructed	Spartan victory in Peloponnesian War marks the end of Athens' ascendancy

s allies command of the sea, ensuring their eventual victory throughout the Aegean. or his pains the Athenians later drove Themistocles into exile.

Rise of the Athenian Empire: 478–431 BC

The first consequence of the Greek victory against the Persians was not, as might have been expected, the rise of **Sparta**, the pre-eminent Greek military power, whose soldiers had obediently sacrificed themselves at Thermopylae and won the final mainland battle at Plataea. Instead, many Greek city-states voluntarily placed themselves under the leadership of Athens.

This Aegean confederation was named the **Delian League**, after the island of Delos where the allies kept their treasury. Its first task was to protect the Greeks of Asia Minor against a vengeful Xerxes. This was the opposite of the policy proposed by Sparta and its Peloponnesian allies, which called for the abandonment of Greek homes across the Aegean and the resettlement of Asian Greeks in northern Greece.

That typified the Spartan attitude throughout the Persian crisis, in which Sparta had shown no initiative and acted only at the last minute. Its policy was provincial, protecting its position in the Peloponnese rather than pursuing the wider interests of Greece. Sparta persistently lacked vision, adventure and experience of the sea, believing that what could not be achieved by land was impossible. Thus, over the coming decades Sparta lost prestige to Athens, which Themistocles had established as a maritime power and whose imperial potential was realized under Pericles.

This was the **Athenian Golden Age**, and indeed a golden age for all Greece. The fifty years following Salamis and Plataea witnessed an extraordinary flowering in architecture, sculpture, literature and philosophy, whose influence is felt to this day.

GREEK TRAGEDY

Greek tragedy has its roots in a fertility ritual celebrating the life and death of Dionysus, the god of the vine. Because goats were sacrificed in his honour, this ritual, in which a chorus danced and sang, was called *trag-odia*, a goat-song. Around 520 BC, an actor was introduced who came and went, changing costumes and playing different roles in successive episodes.

Aeschylus transformed matters by introducing a second actor and increasing the amount of dialogue, while reducing the size and role of the chorus. Thus tragedy became drama, driven by exchanges of words and actions. That Aeschylus had fought at Marathon and, probably, Salamis, may explain the urgency of his play, *The Persians*, the oldest surviving Greek tragedy. Although a religious man who believed in the overwhelming power of the gods, Aeschylus makes clear that it is man himself, through the free choices he makes, who steps into the appalling conflicts of the tragic situation. His later work, the *Oresteia*, a great drama of revenge, focused on Agamemnon's return home from the Trojan War and his murder. By now, Aeschylus was using a third actor and painted scenery, ideas taken from **Sophocles**, his younger rival.

Sophocles' innovation made it possible to present plots of considerable complexity. His was a world of inescapable consequences – in *Oedipus Rex*, for example, to be unseeing is not enough, while *Antigone* presents the ultimate tragic conflict, between right and right.

The effect of the tragedies of Aeschylus and Sophocles was to leave their audiences with an enhanced sense of pity or of terror. The unspoken moral was "You are in this too", the cathartic experience leaving everyone stronger – as though Athens, democratic, confident and imperial, was preparing itself to meet the blows of destiny.

429 BC	**399 BC**	**380 BC**	**371 BC**
Death of Pericles brings uncertainty to Athens	Socrates condemned to death for corrupting the minds of the youth of Athens	Plato establishes his Academy in Athens	Sparta defeated by Thebes at the Battle of Leuctra

Greeks of the time recognized the historical importance of their experience and gave it realization through the creative impulse. Just as **Herodotus**, the "father of history", made the contest between Europe and Asia the theme of his great work, so **Aeschylus**, who fought at Marathon, made Xerxes the tragic subject of *The Persians* and thereby brought the art of drama to life. Indeed, in the intoxicating Athenian atmosphere, the warriors who turned back the Persian tide seemed to have fought in the same cause as Homer's heroes at Troy. In thanksgiving and celebration, the temples upon the Acropolis that the Persians had destroyed were rebuilt – most notably with the building of the **Parthenon**.

Yet Athens was still just one among numerous city-states, each ready to come together during a common danger but reasserting its sovereignty as the foreign threat receded. This was illustrated by the ten-year struggle from 461 BC onwards between Athens and various **Peloponnesian states**, itself a warning of a yet greater war to come between Athens and Sparta.

Pericles

In 461 BC, **Pericles** (c.495–429 BC) was first elected to Athens' most important elected position, of *strategos* (general). The ten *strategoi* proposed the legislation that was then voted on in the Assembly. Pericles was so brilliant at winning over audiences in a society where the people were sovereign, that in practice he governed the state for around thirty years; with only two exceptions, he was annually re-elected until his death in 429 BC.

Among his early triumphs – in the face of conservative opposition – was to make **peace with Persia** in 449 BC, the better to turn his attention to **Sparta**. Pericles believed that Athenian power was not only Greece's best defence against Persia but also the best hope for the unification of Greece under enlightened rule.

Ultimately, the jury remains out as to whether Pericles preserved Athens' greatness for as long as possible or hurried its demise. On the one hand, many believe that it was thanks to Pericles that Athens was able to avoid **war with Sparta** for as long as it did. Thucydides, the historian of the Peloponnesian War, greatly admired Pericles for his integrity and for the restraint he exercised over Athenian democracy. Others hold him responsible for passing up the opportunity to create an institution more generous, and more inclusive, than the city-state. Pericles supported the parochial and populist demand that **Athenian citizenship** should not be extended to its allies, thereby stoking up the flames of envy and foregoing the chance of creating a genuine and enduring Greek confederacy.

Decline of the city-state: 431–338 BC

The **Peloponnesian War** that began in **431 BC** was really a continuation of earlier conflicts between Athens and its principal commercial rivals, Corinth and Aegina and their various allies in the Peloponnese. Sparta had earlier stood aside, but by 432 BC, when Corinth again agitated for war, the **Spartans** had become fearful of growing Athenian power.

The Athenian empire was built on trade, and the city was a great sea power, with 300 triremes. The members of Sparta's **Peloponnesian League**, meanwhile, had powerful armies but no significant navy. Just as Themistocles had sought to fight the Persians by sea, so Pericles followed the same strategy against Sparta and its allies, avoiding major battles against superior land forces. Athens and Piraeus were protected by their walls, but the Peloponnesians and their allies were allowed to invade Attica with impunity

362 BC	359 BC	338 BC	336 BC
Epaminondas of Thebes killed at the Battle of Mantinea	Philip II becomes king of Macedonia.	Philip II's victory at Chaeronia unites Greece under Macedonian rule	Alexander the Great succeeds his father, and within 6 years has conquered all of Persia

THUCYDIDES: THE FIRST MODERN HISTORIAN

The writing of history began among the Greeks, first with **Herodotus**, then with Thucydides. Whereas Herodotus gives the impression that he prefers telling a good story, and that he still inhabits Homer's world of epic poetry, for **Thucydides** the paramount concern is to analyse events. In that sense Thucydides is the first modern historian; wherever possible he seeks out primary sources, and his concern is always with objectivity, detail and chronology. Not that there is anything dry about his writing; its vividness and insight make reading him as powerful an experience as watching a Greek drama.

Thucydides began writing his history at the outset of the **Peloponnesian War**. He intended to give an account of its whole duration, but for reasons unknown, he abruptly stopped writing in the twentieth year, though he is thought to have survived the war by a few years, living until about 400 BC. Born into a wealthy, conservative Athenian family in around 455 BC, he was a democrat and an admirer of Pericles; his reconstruction of Pericles' speeches presents the most eloquent expression of the Athenian cause. But when Thucydides was **exiled** from his city seven years into the war, it was the making of him as a historian. As he put it, "Associating with both sides, with the Peloponnesians quite as much as with the Athenians, because of my exile, I was thus enabled to watch quietly the course of events".

Thucydides was himself a **military man**, who understood war at first hand. Hence his concern for method in his research and analysis in his writing, for he intended his book to be useful to future generals and statesmen. For these reasons, we have a better understanding of the Peloponnesian War than of any ancient conflict until Julius Caesar wrote his own first-hand accounts of his campaigns. And for these reasons too, Thucydides' history stands on a par with the greatest literature of ancient Greece.

nearly every year, and Thrace saw constant warfare. On the other hand, the Peloponnesians lacked the sea power to carry the fighting into Asia Minor and the Aegean islands or to interfere with Athens' trade, while the Athenians used their maritime superiority to launch attacks against the coasts of the Peloponnese, the Ionian islands and the mouth of the Gulf of Corinth, hoping to detach members from the Peloponnesian League. So long as Athens remained in command of the sea, it had every reason to expect that it could wear down its enemies' resolve.

Pericles' death in 429 BC was an early blow to the Athenian cause. Although **Kleon**, his successor, is widely blamed for Athens' eventual defeat, after Pericles the city was in fact always divided into a peace party and a military one, unable to pursue a consistent policy. The final straw came in 415 BC, when a bold operation designed to win Sicily to the Athenian cause turned into a catastrophic debacle. Though not entirely defeated, Athens was never to be a major power again.

City-state rivalries

The Peloponnesian War left **Sparta** the supreme power in Greece, but those whom the Spartans had "liberated" swiftly realized that they had simply acquired a new and inferior master, one that entirely lacked the style, ability and intelligence of Athens. Meanwhile, Athens had lost its empire but not its trade, and as it rapidly rebuilt its navy, its mercantile rivals faced no less competition than before.

Adding to the intrigues between Persia, Athens and Sparta was a bewildering and unstable variety of alliances involving other Greek states. The most important of these

335 BC	326 BC	323 BC	323–146 BC
Aristotle founds the Lyceum in Athens	Alexander's army reaches India	Death of Alexander	Hellenistic Period

was **Thebes**, which had been an ally of Sparta during the Peloponnesian War but came round to the Athenian side, and then for a spectacular moment under its brilliant general **Epaminondas** became the greatest power in Greece, in the process dealing Sparta a blow from which it never recovered. Theban supremacy did not survive the death of Epaminondas, however, and Greece subsequently found itself free for the first time in centuries from the dictates of Persia or any over-powerful Greek city-state. Exhausted and impoverished by almost continuous war, it was an opportunity for Greece to peacefully unite. But the political and moral significance of the city-state had by now eroded, and with the **rise of Macedonia** came the concept of an all-embracing kingship.

The Macedonian Empire

Despite its large size and population, **Macedonia** played little role in early Greek affairs. Many in Greece did not consider the Macedonians to be properly Greek; not in speech, culture or political system. They did not live in city-states, which Aristotle said was the mark of a civilized human being, but as a tribal people, led by a king, and were closer to the barbarians. Such attitudes still rankle today, and inform some of the bitter debate over the name and status of the FYROM, the Former Yugoslav Republic of Macedonia.

Towards the middle of the fourth century, however, the power of Macedonia grew under the leadership of **Philip II**. Philip was determined to Hellenize his country; borrowing from Greek ways and institutions, he founded the city of **Pella** as his capital and lured teachers, artists and intellectuals to his court, among them **Aristotle** and **Euripides**. An admirer of Athens, Philip sought an alliance that would make them joint masters of the Greek world. But the Athenians opposed him, and he took matters into his own hands.

In **338 BC**, Philip brought about the unity of the mainland Greeks by force, defeating the Thebans and Athenians at **Chaeronia** with one of the most formidable fighting units the world has ever seen: the **Macedonian phalanx**. Armed with the *sarissa*, an eighteen-foot pike tapering from butt to tip, its infantrymen were trained to move across a battlefield with all the discipline of a parade-ground drill. Instead of relying on a headlong charge, its effectiveness lay in manipulating the enemy line – seeking to open a gap through which the cavalry could make its decisive strike.

Alexander the Great

After Chaeronia, Philip summoned the Greek states to Corinth and announced his plans for a panhellenic conquest of the Persian Empire. But Philip was murdered two years later and his father's plans for an **Asian campaign** fell to his son **Alexander** – throughout which, it is said, he slept with the *Iliad* under his pillow.

In the East too there was an assassination, and in 335 BC the Persian throne passed to **Darius III**, namesake of the first and doomed to be the last king of his line. Using essentially his father's tactics, Alexander led his army through a series of astonishing victories, usually against greater numbers, until he reached the heart of the Persian Empire. Alexander crossed the Hellespont in May of **334 BC**, with thirty thousand foot soldiers and five thousand horses. By autumn, all the Aegean coast of **Asia Minor** was his; twelve months later he stood on the banks of the Orontes River in **Syria**; in the winter of 332 BC, **Egypt** hailed him as pharaoh; and by the spring of 330 BC the great Persian cities of **Babylon**, **Susa**, **Persepolis** and **Pasargadae** had fallen to him in rapid succession until, at **Ecbatana**,

c. 300 BC	c. 287 BC	215–213 BC	200–197 BC
Euclid's Elements published; its thirteen volumes create the basis of much of modern maths and science	Mathematician, inventor and scientist Archimedes is born on the Greek colony of Sicily	First Macedonian War extends Roman influence in Greece	Second Macedonian War, culminating in the Roman victory at Cynoscephalae

e found Darius in the dust, murdered by his own supporters. Alexander wrapped the corpse in his Macedonian cloak, and assumed the lordship of Asia.

Hellenistic Greece

No sooner had **Alexander** died, at Babylon in 323 BC, aged 33, than Athens led an alliance of Greeks in a **war of liberation** against Macedonian rule. But the Macedonians had built up a formidable navy which inflicted heavy losses on the Athenian fleet. Unable to lift the Macedonian blockade of Piraeus, Athens surrendered and a pro-Macedonian government was installed. The episode marked the end of Athens as a sea power and left it permanently weakened.

Greece was now irrevocably part of a new dominion, one that entirely altered the scale and orientation of the Greek world. Alexander's strategic vision had been to see the Mediterranean and the East as two halves of a greater whole. Opened to Greek settlement and enterprise, and united by Greek learning, language and culture, if not always by a single power, this **Hellenistic Empire** enormously increased international trade and created unprecedented prosperity.

Asked on his deathbed to whom he bequeathed his empire, Alexander replied "To the strongest". Forty years of warfare between his leading generals gave rise to three dynasties, the **Antigonid** in Macedonia, which ruled over mainland Greece, the **Seleucid** which ultimately centred on Syria and Asia Minor, and the **Ptolemaic** in Egypt, ruled from Alexandria, founded by Alexander himself, which in wealth and population, not to mention literature and science, soon outshone anything in Greece.

Meanwhile, in the Western Mediterranean, **Rome** was a rising power. **Philip V** of Macedonia had agreed a treaty of mutual assistance against Rome with Hannibal. After Hannibal's defeat, Rome's legions marched eastwards, and routed Philip's army at **Cynoscephalae** in Thessaly in 197 BC.

Roman Greece: 146 BC–330 AD

Rome was initially well disposed towards Greece, which was regarded as the originator of much of Roman culture, and granted autonomy to the existing city-states. However, after a number of uprisings, the country was divided into **Roman provinces** from 146 BC.

During the first century BC, Rome was riven by civil wars, many of whose climactic battlefields were in Greece: in 49 BC, **Julius Caesar** defeated his rival Pompey at **Pharsalus** in Thessaly; in 42 BC, Caesar's assassins were beaten by **Mark Antony** and **Octavian** at **Philippi** in Macedonia; and in 31 BC, **Antony** and his Ptolemaic ally **Cleopatra** were routed by **Octavian** in a sea battle off **Actium** in western Greece. The latter effectively marked the birth of the **Roman Empire** – an empire that in its eastern half continued to speak Greek.

By the first century AD, Greece had become a **tourist destination** for well-to-do Romans; they went to Athens and Rhodes to study literature and philosophy, and toured the country to see the temples with their paintings and sculpture. They also visited the by now thoroughly professional **Olympic Games**. When the emperor **Nero** came to Greece in AD 67, he entered the Games as a contestant; the judges prudently declared him the victor in every competition, even the chariot race, in which he was thrown and failed to finish.

146 BC	86 BC	31 BC		49–52 AD
Greece divided into Roman provinces	Romans, led by Sulla, sack Athens	Defeat of Antony and Cleopatra at the Battle of Actium brings all of Greece and the Middle East under Roman sway		St Paul lives and preaches in Corinth and Athens; he introduces Greece to Christianity

Barbarian incursions

During the mid-third century, the **Heruli**, a tribe from southern Russia, succeeded in passing through the Bosphorus and into the Aegean. Ravaging far and wide, they plundered and burned **Athens** in 267. New city walls were built with the marble rubble from the wreckage, but their circumference was now so small that the ancient Agora, littered with ruins, was left outside, while what remained of the city huddled round the base of the Acropolis. It was a familiar scene throughout Greece, as prosperity declined and population fell. Only in the north along the **Via Egnatia**, the Roman road linking ports on the Adriatic with Thessaloníki on the Aegean, did Greece continue to thrive.

Byzantine and medieval Greece: 330–1460 AD

The **Byzantine Empire** was founded in May 330 when the **emperor Constantine** declared Nova Roma (as he called the city of Byzantium – known today as Istanbul) the new capital of the Roman Empire. Founded on the banks of the Bosphorus by Greek colonists in the seventh century BC, Byzantium occupied a commanding point from where the entire trade between the Black Sea and the Mediterranean could be controlled. **Constantinople**, the city of Constantine, as it became popularly known, was perfectly positioned for the supreme strategic task confronting the empire: the defence of the Danube and the Euphrates frontiers. Moreover, the new capital stood astride the flow of goods and culture from the East, that part of the empire richest in economic resources, most densely populated and rife with intellectual and religious activity.

Christianity takes hold

Constantine's other act with decisive consequences was to **legalize** and patronize the **Christian Church**. Here again Constantinople was important, for while Rome's pagan traditions could not yet be disturbed, the new capital was conceived as a Christian city. Within the century, Christianity was established as the religion of state, with its liturgies (still in use in the Greek Orthodox Church), the Creed and the New Testament all in Greek.

In 391, emperor **Theodosius I** issued an edict banning all expressions of **paganism** throughout the empire. In Greece, the mysteries at Eleusis ceased to be celebrated the following year, and in 395 the Olympic Games were suppressed, their athletic nudity an offence to Christianity. Around this time too, the Delphic oracle fell silent. The conversion of pagan buildings to Christian use began in the fifth century. Under an imperial law of 435, the Parthenon and the Erechtheion on the Acropolis, the mausoleum of Galerius (the Rotunda) in Thessaloníki and other temples elsewhere became churches. Even this did not eradicate pagan teaching: philosophy and law continued to be taught at the Academy in Athens, founded by Plato in 385 BC, until prohibited by the emperor Justinian in 529.

In 395, the Roman Empire split into **Western and Eastern empires**, and in 476 **Rome fell** to the barbarians. As the Dark Ages settled on Western Europe, Byzantium inherited the sole mantle of the empire. Latin remained its official language, though after the reign of Justinian (527–565), the emperors joined the people in speaking and writing Greek.

Thessaloníki, the second city of the Byzantine Empire, was relatively close to Constantinople, yet even so the journey by land or sea took five or six days. The rest of Greece was that much farther and Attica and the Peloponnese grew decidedly

117–138	267	395
The reign of Emperor Hadrian, a Hellenophile who left many monuments, above all his great library and monumental arch in Athens	Barbarians pillage Athens	Roman Empire splits; Greece becomes part of the eastern, or Byzantine, Empire; Olympic Games suppressed

provincial. Conditions worsened sharply in the late sixth century when Greece was devastated by **plague**. In Athens, after 580, life came almost to an end, as the remaining inhabitants withdrew to the Acropolis, while at Corinth the population removed itself entirely to the island of Égina. Only Thessaloníki fully recovered.

The rise of Islam and the Crusades

The advent of **Islam** in the mid-seventh century had its effect on Greece. The loss to the Arabs of the Christian provinces of Syria in 636 and Egypt in 642 was followed by an attack by an Arab fleet in 677 on Constantinople itself. In 717–18, a combined Arab naval and land force beleaguered the city again, while in 824, the Arabs occupied Crete.

In 1071, the **Byzantine army** was destroyed at **Manzikert**, a fortress town on the eastern frontier, by the **Seljuk Turks** who went on to occupy almost all Asia Minor. After the Byzantine emperor turned to the West for help, the Roman Catholic pope replied by launching the **First Crusade** in 1095. Together, the Crusaders and the Byzantines won a series of victories over the Seljuks in Asia Minor, but the Byzantines, wary of possible Crusader designs on the empire itself, were content to see their Latin allies from the West advance alone on Jerusalem, which they captured in 1099.

The worst fears of the Byzantines were borne out in 1204 when the **Fourth Crusade** attacked and sacked **Constantinople** itself. Greece was shared out between Franks, Venetians and many others in a bewildering patchwork of feudal holdings. Amid endless infighting in the West, a new Turkish dynasty, the **Ottomans**, emerged in the late thirteenth century. By 1400, they had conquered all of Byzantine Greece except Thessaloníki and the Peloponnese. In 1452, they invaded the Peloponnese as a diversion to the main attack on **Constantinople**, which fell on May 23, 1453. In 1456, the Ottomans captured **Athens** from the Venetians and turned the Parthenon church

THE ORIGINS OF THE ORTHODOX CHURCH

The split between the Orthodox and Catholic Churches is traditionally dated to the "**Great Schism**" of 1054. But in practice the Churches had been diverging for centuries, and arguably the final break came much later. The causes of the split were as much linguistic – following the division of the Roman Empire, the language of the Church in Rome was Latin, while in the East it was Greek – and political as they were doctrinal, though there were certainly significant theological differences. Chief among these were the **iconoclastic controversy** – over the use of images in worship – the use of leavened (in the East) or unleavened bread (in the West) in the liturgy, and the Roman adjustment of the Creed, in 1014, to include the word "filioque" (and the Son).

The final schism was precipitated by the pope's claim to **supremacy over the Church**. While the patriarch in Constantinople and other Orthodox leaders accepted the bishop of Rome as "first among equals", they were not prepared to accept his ultimate authority over all the Church – or his subsequent claims to infallibility. In 1054, papal legates went to Constantinople to press the patriarch, Michael Celaurius, to accept Rome's claims. When he refused, Cardinal Humbert, leader of the Latin contingent, excommunicated Celaurius, who responded by in turn excommunicating Humbert and his colleagues.

Any hope of reconciliation disappeared with the sacking of Constantinople during the Fourth Crusade, when Orthodox churches were looted by Catholic crusaders and forcibly converted to Catholic worship, and by the centuries of separation which followed the fall of Constantinople, when much of the Orthodox East came under Ottoman rule.

435	600–700	730
Parthenon and other Greek temples converted to churches	For historians and classicists, the Christianization of Greece in the sixth century marks the end of the Ancient Greek era	Icons and other images banned in the Orthodox Church for being idolatrous; the height of the iconoclastic controversy

into a mosque, and in 1460 they conquered the **Peloponnese**. **Trebizond** fell the following year, and the Byzantine Empire was no more.

Greece under Ottoman occupation: 1460–1821

Western possessions in Greece after 1460 amounted to **Rhodes** – held by the Knights of St John – and, under **Venetian rule**, the Peloponnesian ports of **Koróni**, **Methóni** and **Monemvasiá** and the islands of **Évvia**, **Crete**, **Corfu** and **Égina**. In 1522, the Ottomans drove the Knights of St John from Rhodes, and within two more decades they had captured all the Venetian mainland colonies in Greece, leaving them only Crete.

Although the Greeks refer to the Ottoman Turkish occupation as *sklaviá* – "slavery" – in practice, in exchange for submitting to Muslim rule and paying tribute, the Greeks were free to pursue their religion and were left very much in charge of their own religious and civil affairs. The essence of the Ottoman administration was **taxation**. Tax collection was often farmed out to the leaders of the Greek communities, and some local magistrates profited sufficiently to exercise a dominant role not only within their own region but also in the Ottoman Empire at large.

The other important institution within Greece was the **Orthodox Church**. The Church was wealthy and powerful; Greeks preferred to give their lands to the monasteries than have them occupied by the Turks, while the Muslims found it easier to work with the Church than to invent a new administration. Though often corrupt and venal, the Church did at least preserve the traditional faith and keep alive the written form of the Greek language, and it became the focus of Greek nationalism.

Western resistance

In 1570, Ottoman troops landed on **Cyprus**. Nicosia was swiftly captured, and thirty thousand of its inhabitants slaughtered. Turkish brutality in Cyprus horrified Europe, and the **Holy League** was formed under the aegis of the pope. Spain and Genoa joined Venice in assembling a fleet led by Don John of Austria, the bastard son of the Spanish king, its lofty aim not only to retake the island but to recapture all Christian lands taken by the Ottomans. In the event, it was utterly ineffectual, yet out of it something new arose – the first stirrings of **Philhellenism**, a desire to liberate the Greeks whose ancient culture stood at the heart of Renaissance thought and education.

There was, too, the encouragement of a naval victory, when in 1571 Don John's fleet surprised and overwhelmingly defeated the much larger Ottoman fleet, at its winter quarters at **Lepanto** on the Gulf of Corinth in western Greece. Two hundred and sixty-six Ottoman vessels were sunk or captured, fifty thousand sailors died, and fifteen thousand Christian galley slaves were freed. Throughout Europe the news of Lepanto was received with extraordinary rejoicing; this was the first battle in which Europe had triumphed against the Ottomans, and its symbolic importance was profound. Militarily and politically, however, the Ottomans remained dominant. They finally took **Crete** in 1669, marking the end of the last bastion of Byzantine culture.

Greek nationalist stirrings

During the eighteenth century, the islanders of **Ýdhra** (Hydra), **Spétses** and **Psará** built up a merchant fleet that traded throughout the Mediterranean, where thriving colonies

824–961	1071	1095	1204
Arab occupation of Crete; a warning of things to come	Byzantine army defeated by the Turks	First Crusade drives back the Turks	Fourth Crusade sacks Constantinople; much of Greece taken over by western European powers

f Greeks were established in many ports. Greek merchant families were also well stablished, often in important administrative positions, throughout the Ottoman empire.

These wealthier and more educated Greeks enjoyed greater than ever opportunities or advancement within the Ottoman system, while the Greek peasantry, unlike the mpire's Muslim inhabitants, did not have to bear the burden of military service. Nevertheless, the Greeks had their grievances against the Ottoman government, which mostly concerned the arbitrary, unjust and oppressive system of taxation. But among the Greek peasantry it was primarily religion that set them against their Muslim neighbours – as much as one-fifth of the population – and their Ottoman overlords. Muslim leaders had long preached hatred of the infidel, a view reciprocated by the priests and bishops of the Orthodox Church.

War of Independence: 1821–32

The **ideology** behind the **War of Independence** came from the Greeks of the diaspora, particularly those merchant colonies in France, Italy, Austria and Russia who had absorbed new European ideas of nationalism and revolution. Around 1814, assorted such Greeks formed a secret society, the **Filikí Etería** (Friendly Society). Their sophisticated political concepts went uncomprehended by the peasantry, who assumed the point of an uprising was to exterminate their religious adversaries. And so when war finally broke out in **spring 1821**, almost the entire settled **Muslim population of Greece** – farmers, merchants and officials – was **slaughtered** within weeks by roaming bands of Greek peasants armed with swords, guns, scythes and clubs. They were often led by Orthodox priests, and some of the earliest Greek revolutionary flags portrayed a cross over a severed Turkish head.

The war

While the Greeks fought to rid themselves of the Ottomans, their further aims differed widely. Landowners sought to reinforce their traditional privileges; the peasantry saw the struggle as a means towards land redistribution; and westernized Greeks were fighting for a modern nation-state. Remarkably, by the end of **1823**, the Greeks appeared to have won their independence. Twice the sultan had sent armies into Greece; twice they had met with defeat. Greek guerrilla leaders, above all **Theodoros Kolokotronis** from the Peloponnese, had gained significant military victories early in the rebellion, which was joined by a thousand or so **European Philhellenes**, almost half of them German, though the most important was the English poet, **Lord Byron**.

But the situation was reversed in 1825, when the Peloponnese was invaded by formidable Egyptian forces loyal to the sultan. Thus far, aid for the Greek struggle had come neither from Orthodox Russia, nor from the Western powers of France and Britain, both wearied by the Napoleonic Wars and suspicious of a potentially anarchic new state. But the death of Lord Byron from a fever while training Greek forces at **Mesolóngi** in 1824 galvanized European public opinion. When Mesolóngi fell to the Ottomans in 1826, Britain, France and Russia finally agreed to seek autonomy for certain parts of Greece, and sent a combined fleet to put pressure on the sultan's army in the Peloponnese and the Turkish-Egyptian fleet harboured in Navaríno Bay. Events

1453	1522	1571	1669
Constantinople falls to the Ottoman Turks, followed by much of Greece	Knights of St John driven from Rhodes	Battle of Lepanto – the first significant military defeat for the Ottoman Empire	Iráklio falls to the Ottomans – the end of a brutal 25-year conquest of Crete

took over, and an accidental naval battle at **Navaríno** in October 1827 resulted in the destruction of almost the entire Ottoman fleet. The following spring, Russia itself declared war on the Ottomans, and Sultan Mahmud II was forced to accept the existence of an autonomous Greece.

At a series of conferences from 1830 to 1832, **Greek independence** was confirmed by the Western powers, and borders were drawn in 1832. These included just eight hundred thousand of the six million Greeks living within the Ottoman Empire, and territories that were largely the poorest of the classical and Byzantine lands: **Attica**, the **Peloponnese** and the islands of the **Argo-Saronic**, the **Sporades** and the **Cyclades**. The rich agricultural belt of **Thessaly**, **Epirus** in the west and **Macedonia** in the north remained in Ottoman hands, as did the Dodecanese and Crete.

The emerging state: 1832–1939

Modern Greece began as a **republic**. **Ioannis Kapodistrias**, its first president, concentrated his efforts on building a viable central authority. Almost inevitably he was assassinated, and perhaps equally inevitably the "Great Powers" – Britain, France and Germany – stepped in. They created a **monarchy**, setting a Bavarian prince, Otto (Otho), on the throne, with a new capital at Athens. By 1834, Greece also had its own national, state-controlled **Orthodox Church**, independent from the Patriarchate in Constantinople; at the same time, two-thirds of the monasteries and convents were closed down.

Despite the granting of a constitution in 1844, **King Otto** proved autocratic and insensitive, filling official posts with fellow Germans and ignoring all claims by the landless peasantry for redistribution of the old estates. When he was forced from the country by a popular revolt in 1862, the Europeans produced a new prince, this time from Denmark. The accession of **George I** (1863–1913) was marked by Britain's decision to hand over the **Ionian islands** to Greece. During his reign, Greece's first roads and railways were built, its borders were extended, and land reform began in the Peloponnese.

The Great Idea and expansionist wars

From the start, Greek foreign policy was motivated by the **Megáli Idhéa** (Great Idea) of redeeming ethnically Greek populations outside the country and incorporating the old territories of Byzantium into the new kingdom. There was encouragement all around, as Ottoman control was under pressure across the Balkans.

In 1881, revolts broke out among the Greeks of **Crete**, **Thessaly** and **Epirus**, aided by guerrillas from Greece. Britain forced the Ottoman Empire to cede Thessaly and Arta to Greece, but Crete remained Ottoman. When Cretan Greeks set up an independent government in 1897, declaring *énosis* (union) with Greece, the Ottomans responded by invading the mainland and came within days of reaching Athens. The Great Powers came to the rescue by warning off the Turks and placing Crete under an international protectorate. Only in 1913 did **Crete** unite with Greece.

It was from Crete, nonetheless, that the most distinguished modern Greek statesman emerged: **Eleftherios Venizelos**, having led a civilian campaign for his island's liberation, was elected as Greek prime minister in 1910. Two years later he organized an alliance of Balkan powers to fight the **Balkan Wars** (1912–13), campaigns that saw the Ottomans virtually driven from Europe, and the Bulgarian competition bested in the

1821	**1824**	**1827**	**1832**
Rebellion breaks out in various parts of the empire; much of Greece liberated	Lord Byron dies, becoming a Greek national hero in the process	Ottoman fleet destroyed at the Battle of Navaríno, encouraging Great Power intervention	Independent Greek state established, with its capital in Náfplio

ulmination of a bitter, four-decade campaign for the hearts and minds of the Macedonian population. With Greek borders extended to include the **northeast Aegean islands, northern Thessaly, central Epirus** and parts of **Macedonia**, the Megáli Idhéa was approaching reality.

World War I

Divisions appeared with the outbreak of **World War I**. Although Venizelos urged Greek entry on the Allied side, hoping to liberate Greeks in Thrace and Asia Minor, the new king, **Constantine I**, who was married to the German Kaiser's sister, imposed neutrality. Eventually, Venizelos set up a revolutionary government in Thessaloníki, polarizing the country into a state of **civil war**. In 1917, Greek troops entered the war to join the French, British and Serbians in the Macedonian campaign against Bulgaria and Germany. Upon the capitulation of Bulgaria and the Ottoman Empire, the Greeks occupied **Thrace**, and Venizelos presented demands at Versailles for predominantly Greek **Smyrna** (modern Izmir), on the Asia Minor coast, to become part of the Greek state.

The Katastrofí and its aftermath

The demand for Smyrna triggered one of the most disastrous episodes in modern Greek history, the so-called **Katastrofí** (Catastrophe). Venizelos was authorized to move forces into Smyrna in 1919, but a new Turkish nationalist movement was taking power under Mustafa Kemal, or **Atatürk**. After monarchist factions took over when Venizelos lost elections in 1920, the Allies withdrew support for the venture. Nevertheless, the monarchists ordered Greek forces to advance upon Ankara, seeking to bring Atatürk to terms. The Greeks' **Anatolian campaign** ignominiously collapsed in summer 1922 when Turkish troops forced the Greeks back to the coast. As the Greek army hurriedly evacuated from **Smyrna**, the Turks moved in and **massacred** much of the Armenian and Greek population before burning most of the city to the ground.

For the Turks, this was the successful conclusion of what they call their War of Independence. The borders of modern Turkey, as they remain today, were established by the **1923 Treaty of Lausanne**, which also provided for the **exchange of religious minorities** in each country – in effect, the first large-scale regulated ethnic cleansing. Turkey was to accept 390,000 Muslims resident on Greek soil. Greece, with a population of under five million, was faced with the resettlement of over **1.3 million Christian refugees** from Asia Minor.

The Katastrofí had intense and far-reaching consequences. The bulk of the agricultural estates of **Thessaly** were finally redistributed, to Greek tenants and refugee farmers, and huge shanty towns grew into new quarters around **Athens**, **Pireás** and **Thessaloníki**, spurring the country's then almost nonexistent industry. Politically, reaction was even swifter. By September 1922, a group of Venizelist army officers "invited" King Constantine to abdicate and executed six of his ministers held most responsible for the debacle. Democracy was nominally restored with the proclamation of a **republic**, but for much of the next decade, changes in government were brought about by factions within the armed forces. Meanwhile, among the urban refugee population, unions were being formed and the **Greek Communist Party** (**KKE**) was established.

1834	1881	1896	1912–13
Capital transferred to Athens	Following military action and treaties, much of northern Greece added to the new nation	Inspired by Baron Pierre de Coubertin, the first modern Olympics are held in Athens	Balkan Wars extend Greece's borders close to its modern extent; Crete also becomes part of the new nation

Rise of Metaxás

In 1935, a plebiscite restored the king, **George II**, to the throne, and the next year he appointed **General John Metaxás** as prime minister. Metaxás had opposed the Anatolian campaign, but had little support in parliament, and when KKE-organized strikes broke out, the king dissolved parliament without setting a date for new elections. This blatantly unconstitutional move opened the way for five years of ruthles and at times absurd **dictatorship**. Metaxás proceeded to set up a state based on the **fascist** models of the era. Left-wing and trade-union opponents were imprisoned or forced into exile, a state youth movement and secret police were set up, and rigid censorship, extending even to passages of Thucydides, was imposed. But it was at least a Greek dictatorship, and while Metaxás was sympathetic to fascist organizational methods and economics, he utterly opposed German or Italian domination.

World War II and civil war: 1939–1950

When World War II broke out, the most immediate threat to Greece was **Italy**, which had invaded Albania in April. Even so, Metaxás hoped Greece could remain neutral, and when the Italians torpedoed the Greek cruiser *Elli* in Tínos harbour on August 15, 1940, they failed to provoke a response. **Mussolini**, however, was determined to have a war with Greece, and after accusing the Greeks of violating the Albanian frontier, he delivered an ultimatum on October 28, 1940, to which Metaxás famously if apocryphally answered "**ohi**" (no). Galvanized by the crisis, the Greeks not only drove the invading Italians out of Greece but managed to gain control over the long-coveted and predominantly Greek-populated area of northern Epirus in southern Albania. ("Ohi Day" is still celebrated as a national holiday.)

Mussolini's failure, however, only provoked Hitler into sending his own troops into Greece, while the British rushed an expeditionary force across the Mediterranean from Egypt. Within days of the **German invasion**, on April 6, 1941, the German army was pouring into central Greece. Outmanoeuvred by the enemy's highly mechanized forces and at the mercy of the Luftwaffe, resistance was soon broken. When the Germans occupied Crete in May, King George and his ministers fled to Egypt and set up a government-in-exile. Metaxás himself had died before the German invasion.

Occupation and resistance

The joint Italian-German-Bulgarian **occupation of Greece** was among the most bitter experiences of the European war. Nearly half a million Greek civilians starved to death over the winter of 1941–42, as all food was requisitioned to feed the occupying armies. In addition, entire villages throughout the mainland, but especially on Crete, were burned at the least hint of resistance, and nearly 130,000 civilians were slaughtered up to autumn 1944. In their northern sector, which included Thássos and Samothráki, the Bulgarians demolished ancient sites and churches to support any future bid to annex "Slavic" Macedonia.

No sooner had the Axis powers occupied Greece than a spontaneous resistance movement sprang up in the mountains. The National Popular Liberation Army, known by its initials **ELAS**, founded in September 1941, quickly grew to become the most effective resistance organization, working in tandem with **EAM**, the National

1923	1924	1935	1936–41	1940
Following a disastrous campaign against Turkey, over one million Christian refugees are resettled in Greece	Plebiscite abolishes the monarchy and establishes a republic	Monarchy restored under George II	Fascist-style dictatorship of Ioánnis Metaxás	Italian invasion of Greece is successfully repelled

GREEK JEWS AND WORLD WAR II

Following the German invasion of Greece, Jews who lived in the Italian zone of occupation were initially no worse off than their fellow Greeks. But after Italy capitulated to the Allies in September 1943 and German troops took over from the Italians, the **Jewish communities** in Rhodes and Kos in the Dodecanese, as well as in Crete, Corfu, Vólos, Évvia and Zákynthos, were exposed to the full force of **Nazi racial doctrine**. The Germans applied their "**final solution**" in Greece during the spring and summer of 1944, with the **deportation** of virtually the entire Jewish population, about eighty thousand in all, to **extermination camps** in Poland. Thessaloníki alone contained fifty-seven thousand, the largest Jewish population of any Balkan city.

Greek Christians often went to extraordinary lengths to protect their persecuted countrymen. Thus, when the Germans demanded the names of the Jews of Zákynthos prior to a roundup, Archbishop Khrysostomos and Mayor Loukas Karrer presented them with a roster of just two names – their own – and secretly oversaw the **smuggling** of all the island's 275 Jews to remote farms. Their audacious behaviour paid off, as every Zakynthian Jew survived the war. In Athens, the police chief and the archbishop arranged for false identity cards and baptismal certificates to be issued. Elsewhere, others were warned in good time of what fate the Germans had in store for them, and often took to the hills to join the partisans.

Liberation Front. Communists formed the leadership of both organizations, but opposition to the occupation and disenchantment with the prewar political order ensured they won the support of many non-communists. By 1943 ELAS/EAM controlled most areas of the country, working with the British SOE, Special Operations Executive, against the occupiers.

But the Allies were already eyeing the shape of postwar Europe, and British prime minister **Winston Churchill** was determined that Greece should not fall into the communist sphere. Ignoring advice from British agents in Greece that ELAS/EAM were the only effective resistance group, and that the king and his government-in-exile had little support within the country, Churchill ordered that only right-wing groups like **EDES**, the National Republican Greek Army, should receive British money, intelligence and arms. In August 1943, a resistance delegation asked the Greek king, George, in Cairo, for a postwar coalition government in which EAM would hold the ministries of the interior, justice and war, and requested that the king himself not return to Greece without popular consent expressed through a plebiscite. Backed by Churchill, King George flatly rejected their demands.

Liberation and civil war

As the Germans began to withdraw from Greece in September 1944, most of the ELAS/EAM leadership agreed to join an interim government headed by the liberal anti-communist politician **George Papandreou**, and to place its forces under that government's control, which effectively meant under command of the British troops who landed in Greece that October. But many partisans felt they were losing their chance to impose a communist government and refused to lay down their arms. On December 3, 1944 the police fired on an EAM demonstration in Athens, killing at least sixteen. The following day, vicious **street fighting** broke out between members of the Greek Communist Party (KKE) and British troops which lasted throughout the

1941	1944–49	1952	1952
German invasion rapidly overruns the country; mass starvation in the Greek cities in the winter	German withdrawal is promptly followed by the outbreak of bitter civil war	Greece, now firmly part of the Western bloc, joins NATO	New constitution establishes a parliamentary democracy, with king as Head of State

month, until eleven thousand people were killed and large parts of Athens destroyed. In other large towns, ELAS rounded up its most influential and wealthy opponents and marched them out to rural areas in conditions that guaranteed their deaths.

After Papandreou resigned and the king agreed not to return without a plebiscite, a **ceasefire** was signed on February 12, 1945, and a new British-backed government agreed to institute democratic reforms. Many of these were not implemented, however. The army, police and civil service remained in right-wing hands, and while collaborators were often allowed to retain their positions, left-wing sympathizers were excluded. A KKE boycott of elections in March 1946 handed victory to the parties of the right, and a **rigged plebiscite** followed that brought the king back to Greece. Right-wing gangs now roamed the towns and countryside with impunity, and by the summer of 1946, eighty thousand leftists who had been associated with ELAS had taken to the mountains.

By 1947, guerrilla activity had again reached the scale of a **full civil war**, with ELAS reorganized into the Democratic Army of Greece (DSE). In the interim, King George had died and been succeeded by his brother Paul, while the **Americans** had taken over the British role and began implementing the Cold War **Truman Doctrine**, in which massive economic and military aid was given to an amenable Greek government. In the mountains, American military advisors trained the initially woeful Greek army for campaigns against the DSE, while the cities saw mass arrests, courts martial and imprisonments. From their stronghold on the slopes of Mount Grámmos, on the border of Greece and Albania, the partisans waged a losing guerrilla struggle. At the start of 1948, Stalin **withdrew Soviet support**, and in the autumn of 1949, after Tito closed the Yugoslav border, denying the partisans the last means of outside supplies, the remnants of the DSE retreated into Albania, and the KKE admitted defeat by proclaiming a supposedly temporary suspension of the civil war.

Reconstruction and dictatorship: 1950–74

After a decade of war that had shattered much of Greece's infrastructure (it is said that not one bridge was left standing by 1948) and had killed twelve percent of the 1940 population, it was a demoralized, shattered country that emerged into the Western political orbit of the 1950s. Greece was **American-dominated**, enlisted into the **Korean War** in 1950 and **NATO** not long after. The US embassy – still giving the orders – foisted an electoral system on the Greeks that ensured victory for the right for the next twelve years. Overt leftist activity was banned (though a "cover" party for communists was soon founded), and many of those who were not herded into political "re-education" camps or dispatched by firing squads, legal or vigilante, went into exile throughout Eastern Europe, to return only after 1974. The 1950s also saw the wholesale **depopulation of remote villages** as migrants sought work in Australia, America and Western Europe, or the larger Greek cities.

Constantine Karamanlis and Cyprus

The American-backed right-wing **Greek Rally** party, led by **General Papagos**, won the first decisive post-civil-war elections in 1952. After the general's death, the party's leadership was taken over – and to an extent liberalized – by **Constantine Karamanlis**.

1955	1960	1964	1964
Karamanlis becomes prime minister	Cyprus gains independence	King Constantine II succeeds his father, Paul	The film of Zorba the Greek released, its soundtrack going on to grace (or blight) every Greek restaurant ever since

Under his rule, stability of a kind was established and some economic advances registered, particularly after the revival of Greece's traditional German markets.

The main ongoing crisis in foreign policy was **Cyprus**, where Greek Cypriots demanding *énosis* (union) with Greece waged a long terrorist campaign against the British. Turkey adamantly opposed *énosis* and said that if Britain left Cyprus, it should revert to Turkish rule. A 1959 compromise granted independence to the island and protection for its Turkish Cypriot minority but ruled out any union with Greece.

By 1961, unemployment, the Cyprus issue and the presence of US nuclear bases on Greek soil were changing the political climate, and when Karamanlis was again elected, there was strong suspicion of intimidation and fraud carried out by right-wing elements and the army. After eighteen months of strikes and protest demonstrations, Karamanlis resigned and went into voluntary exile in Paris.

George Papandreou and the colonels

New elections in 1964 gave the **Centre Union Party**, headed by **George Papandreou**, an outright majority and a mandate for social and economic reform. The new government was the first to be controlled from outside the right since 1935, and in his first act as prime minister, Papandreou sought to heal the wounds of the civil war by **releasing political prisoners** and allowing exiles to return. When King Paul died in March and his son came to the throne as **Constantine II**, it seemed a new era had begun.

But soon **Cyprus** again took centre stage. Fighting between Turkish and Greek Cypriots broke out in 1963, and only the intervention of the United States in 1964 dissuaded Turkey from invading the island. In the mood of military confrontation between Greece and Turkey – both NATO members – Papandreou questioned Greece's role in the Western alliance, to the alarm of the Americans and the Greek right. When he moved to purge the army of disloyal officers, the army, with the support of the king, resisted.

Amid growing tension, elections were set for May 1967. It was a foregone conclusion that Papandreou's Centre Union Party would win, but **King Constantine**, disturbed by the party's leftward shift, was said to have briefed senior generals for a coup. True or not, the king, like almost everyone else in Greece, was caught by surprise when a group of unknown **colonels** staged their own **coup** on April 21, 1967. In December, the king staged a counter-coup against the colonels, and when it failed he went into exile.

The junta announced itself as the "**Revival of Greek Orthodoxy**" against corrupting Western influences, not least long hair on men and miniskirts. Political activity was banned, independent trade unions were forbidden to recruit or meet, the press was so heavily censored that many papers stopped printing, and thousands of communists and others on the left were arrested, imprisoned and often tortured. Culturally, the colonels put an end to popular music and inflicted ludicrous censorship on literature and the theatre, including a ban on the production of classical tragedies. In 1973, chief colonel **Papadopoulos** abolished the monarchy and declared Greece a republic, with himself as president.

Restoration of democracy

The colonels lasted for seven years. Opposition was voiced from the start by exiled Greeks in London, the US and Western Europe, but only in 1973 did demonstrations break out openly in Greece – the colonels' secret police had done too thorough a job of

1967	1974	1975
Colonels' coup marks the start of 7 years of repressive military rule	Greek-backed attempted coup in Cyprus leads to Turkish invasion and the division of the island; and to the end of the colonels' regime. Monarchy abolished by a plebiscite and a republic declared	New constitution provides for parliamentary government with president as Head of State

infiltrating domestic resistance groups and terrifying everyone else into docility. After students occupied the **Athens Polytechnic** on **November 17**, the ruling clique sent armoured vehicles to storm the gates. A still-undetermined number of students (estimates range from twenty to three hundred) were killed. Martial law was tightened and Colonel Papadopoulos was replaced by the even more noxious and reactionary **General Ioannides**, head of the secret police.

The end came within a year, when the dictatorship embarked on a disastrous adventure in **Cyprus**. By attempting to topple the Makarios government, the junta provoked a **Turkish invasion** and occupation of forty percent of Cypriot territory. The army finally mutinied and **Constantine Karamanlis** was invited to return from Paris to resume office.

Karamanlis swiftly negotiated a ceasefire in Cyprus, and in November 1974 he and his **Néa Dhimokratía** (New Democracy) party were rewarded by a sizeable majority in elections. The chief opposition was the new Panhellenic Socialist Movement (PASOK), led by **Andreas Papandreou**, son of George.

Europe and a new Greece: 1974–2000

To Karamanlis's enduring credit, his New Democracy party oversaw an effective return to **democratic stability**, even legalizing the KKE (the Greek Communist Party) for the first time. Karamanlis also held a **referendum on the monarchy**, in which seventy percent of Greeks rejected the return of Constantine II. So a largely symbolic presidency was instituted instead, occupied by Karamanlis from 1980 to 1985, and again from 1990 to 1995. In 1981, Greece joined the **European Community**.

In the same year, the socialist party, **PASOK**, and its leader **Andreas Papandreou** swept to power. The new era started with a bang as long overdue **social reforms** were enacted; wages were indexed to the cost of living, civil marriage was introduced and equal rights legislation passed. By the time PASOK was voted in again in 1985, it was apparent the promised economic bonanza was not happening: hit by low productivity, lack of investment (not helped by anti-capitalist rhetoric from the government) and world recession, **unemployment** rose, **inflation** hit 25 percent and the **national debt** soared.

In the event, it was the **European Community**, once Papandreou's bête noire, which rescued him, with a huge **loan** on condition that an **austerity programme** was maintained. Forced to drop many of his populist policies, the increasingly autocratic Papandreou turned on his former left-wing allies. Combined with the collapse of Soviet rule in Eastern Europe, his own very public affair with an Olympic Airways hostess half his age, and a raft of economic scandals, PASOK's hold on power was, unsurprisingly, weakened. For over two decades from 1989, when **New Democracy** was elected once more, the two parties exchanged power on a regular basis.

The 1990s were not easy, with an economy riven by unrest and division, and huge foreign policy headaches caused by the break-up of the **former Yugoslavia** and the ensuing wars on Greece's borders. Alone among NATO members, Greece was conspicuous for its open support of **Serbia**.

By the end of the 1990s, the economy was apparently stabilizing, with inflation consistently in single figures, and in 1997 national morale was further boosted with the award of the 2004 Olympic Games to Athens. In addition, a dramatic and unexpected change in Greece's always distrustful **relations with Turkey** came when a severe

1981	1982	1991	1999
Greece joins the EU and Andreas Papandreou wins first of successive elections for PASOK	The Rough Guide to Greece, the first ever Rough Guide, published	Yugoslav Republic of Macedonia declares independence; Greece objects to use of the name Macedonia	Athens earthquake; rapprochement between Greece and Turkey

earthquake struck northern Athens on September 7, 1999, killing scores and rendering almost a hundred thousand homeless. Coming soon after a devastating earthquake in northwest Turkey, it spurred a thaw between the two historical rivals, as they came to each other's aid. Soon afterwards, foreign minister George Papandreou (son of Andreas) announced that Greece had dropped its opposition to EU financial aid to Turkey and that Greece would no longer oppose Turkish candidacy for the EU.

The twenty-first century: boom … and bust

Greece entered the twenty-first century on a high; entry to the **eurozone** in 2001 was seen as hugely prestigious, while the **2004 Olympic Games** and unexpected Greek victory at the **Euro 2004 football championships** were considered national triumphs. EU funds and Olympic investment kick-started widespread infrastructure improvements but these ostensibly positive developments turned out to be symptomatic of Greece's problems. It was an open secret that the figures had been massaged to ensure Greece met the strict criteria for entry to the euro – the extent of that fix only became apparent later. The Olympics had also incurred huge debts and a lack of legacy planning left many venues to rot.

In December 2008, **rioting** and weeks of unrest broke out in Athens, provoked by the police shooting a 15-year-old student: these were the first sign of Greece's deep-rooted

---

IMMIGRATION AND THE REFUGEE CRISIS

Since 1990, well over a million **immigrants** have arrived in Greece, a huge burden for a country of just over ten million citizens, creating a permanent economic underclass. The three largest groups are Albanians, Bulgarians and Romanians, followed by Poles, Pakistanis, Bangladeshis, Syrians, Filipinos, Ukrainians, Russians, Equatorial Africans, Kurds and Georgians.

Since the summer of 2015, numbers have increased exponentially with the flood of **refugees** escaping the war in Syria and other turmoil in the Middle East. These desperate people risked life and limb to make the crossing in flimsy boats from the Turkish coast to the closest Greek islands, with Lésvos (see p.635), Híos (see p.622) and Kos (see p.560) bearing the brunt of the arrivals. Many did not survive the journey, such as the toddler Alan Kurdi, the image of whose drowned body provoked an international outcry. Those who did were initially put up in makeshift camps on the islands, with many then moved to larger but poorly equipped camps outside Athens, Thessaloníki or near the Macedonian border.

At first, the majority of the refugees stayed in Greece only temporarily before heading, often on foot, towards northern Europe. When this "**Balkan corridor**" was closed in March 2016, however, around 60,000 people were effectively trapped in squalid conditions, putting further strain on Greece's ailing economy. Although Greece has been granted more than €400 million in aid to deal with the **refugee crisis**, the situation remains critical.

The Greek response has been decidedly mixed, with some openly welcoming and helping the refugees, and others protesting against programmes to integrate their children into the national education system. Overall, the Albanians and other eastern Europeans have become largely established in Greece and are not as reviled as they were originally, yet immigrants are still blamed for all manner of social ills. For the first time, **crime** – especially burglary and mugging – is a major issue. Equally worryingly, the understandable concerns of ordinary Greeks have been accompanied by a significant rise in support for the utterly repugnant **fascist party** Golden Dawn, who constantly seek to stoke fears and create divisions.

2002	2004	2008
Greece adopts the euro, consigning Europe's oldest currency, the drachma, to history after some 3000 years	Athens Olympics pass off triumphantly and Greece's football team unexpectedly win Euro 2004 in Portugal	Rioting breaks out in Athens, bringing the country's economic crisis to world attention

troubles and impending **crisis**. When PASOK returned to power in 2009, led by **George Papandreou**, the extent of the economic problems began to be fully revealed, with a **national debt** of €262 billion and a deficit running at 12.7 percent of GDP (against a euro limit of 3 percent). As Greece's huge public sector, lax tax collection and allegedly widespread corruption came under scrutiny, government attempts to increase revenue and cut spending ran up against popular opposition and economic downturn.

Following Papandreou's resignation and a brief government of "national unity", a cross-party coalition led by New Democracy chief **Antonis Samaras** came to power after two elections in quick succession in summer 2012. They accepted the terms of fresh **EU bailouts** in exchange for even harsher **austerity measures**, but popular displeasure with the continued hardship led to the election in January 2015 of a coalition government led by the new radical leftwing party **SYRIZA**, who had come a narrow second in 2012.

Led by dynamic young **Alexis Tsipras**, SYRIZA opposed all EU-imposed bailout terms, and their charismatic finance minister **Yiannis Varoufakis** set about negotiations with the country's debtors. The dreaded "troika" of the EU, World Bank and IMF hardly budged though and demanded continued austerity in exchange for further bailouts, resulting in Varoufakis' resignation. In a bizarre turn of events in summer 2015, Tsipras put the terms of the bailout to a national **referendum**, which the majority rejected, yet he was subsequently forced to accept them to stave off total economic collapse and possible expulsion from the EU. A further strain on the country's resources was caused by the massive influx of **refugees** from the Middle East (see box, p.787), which began in summer 2015.

Despite the enormous setback of continuing austerity and the loss of 25 MPs who were unequivocally opposed to the bailout terms, Tsipras managed to win snap elections in September 2015 and form another **coalition government**, again supported by Panos Kammenos and his Independent Greeks party. SYRIZA have since defied the odds by staying in power, despite the population's mounting **disillusionment** with further bailout terms, increased taxes (especially on property) and a general resignation that the country's recovery remains a distant dream.

2012	2015	2017
Uneasy New Democracy-led coalition agrees to bailout with imposed austerity measures	A coalition led by radical leftwing SYRIZA wins two elections but is forced to continue many austerity measures	Another €8.5 billion is released from Greece's €86 billion third bailout package amidst continuing austerity

Archeology

Until the second half of the nineteenth century, archeology was a very hit-and-miss, treasure-hunting affair. The early students of antiquity went to Greece to draw and make plaster casts of the great masterpieces of Classical sculpture. Unfortunately, a number soon found it more convenient or more profitable to remove objects wholesale and might be better described as looters than scholars or archeologists.

Early excavations

The **British Society of Dilettanti** was one of the earliest promoters of Greek culture, financing expeditions to draw and publish antiquities. Founded in the 1730s as a reputedly drunken club for young aristocrats who had completed the Grand Tour (among them Sir Francis Dashwood, founder of the Hellfire Club), the society was the first body organized to sponsor systematic research into Greek antiquities, though it was initially most interested in Italy, as Greece was then still a backwater of the Ottoman Empire.

One of the first expeditions sponsored by the society was that of two young artists, **James Stuart** and **Nicholas Revett**, who spent three years in Greece, principally in and around Athens, drawing and measuring the antiquities. The publication of their exquisite illustrations and of **Johann Winckelmann**'s *History of Art* in 1764, in which the **Parthenon** (see p.69) and its sculptures were exalted as the standard for architectural beauty, gave an enormous boost to the study (and popularity) of all things Greek; many European Neoclassical town and country houses date from this period.

The Dilettanti financed a number of further expeditions to study Greek antiquities, including one to Asia Minor in 1812. While waiting in Athens for a ship to Turkey, the party employed themselves in excavations at **Eleusis** (see p.123), where they uncovered the **Temple of Demeter**. After extensive explorations in Asia Minor, the participants returned via Attica, where they excavated the **Temple of Nemesis** at **Ramnous** (see p.121) and examined the **Temple of Poseidon** at **Soúnio** (see p.119).

Pilfering and preservation

Several other antiquarians of the age were less interested in discoveries for their own sake. A French count, **Choiseul-Gouffier**, removed part of the **Parthenon frieze** in 1787, and his example prompted **Lord Elgin** to detach much of the rest in 1801. These were essentially acts of looting – "Bonaparte has not got such things from all his thefts in Italy", boasted Elgin – and their legality was suspect even at the time (see box, p.70).

Other discoveries of the period were more ambiguous. In 1811, a party of English and German travellers, including the architect **C. R. Cockerell**, uncovered the **Temple of Aphaea** on **Égina** (see p.336) and shipped away the pediments. They auctioned off the marbles for £6000 to Prince Ludwig of Bavaria, and, inspired by this success, returned to Greece for further finds. This time they struck it lucky with 23 slabs from the **Temple of Apollo Epikourios** at **Bassae** (see p.177), for which the British Museum laid out a further £15,000. These were huge sums for the time and highly profitable exercises, but they were also pioneering archeology for the period. Besides, removing the finds was hardly surprising: Greece, after all, was not yet a state and had no public museum, so antiquities discovered were invariably sold by their finders.

The new nation

The Greek War of Independence (1821–28) and the establishment of a modern Greek nation changed all this. As a result of the selection of Prince Otto of Bavaria as the first king of modern Greece in 1832, the **Germans**, whose education system stressed classical learning, were at the forefront of archeological activity. In 1834, **Ludwig Ross** began supervising the excavation and restoration of the **Acropolis** (see p.65), and later dismantled the accretion of Byzantine, Frankish and Turkish embellishments that obscured its Classical structure.

The Greeks themselves had begun to focus on their ancient past when the first stirrings of the independence movement were felt. In 1813, the **Philomuse Society** was formed, aiming to uncover and collect antiquities, publish books and assist students and foreign philhellenes. In 1829, an orphanage on the island of Égina became the first **Greek archeological museum**.

In 1837, the **Greek Archeological Society** was founded by **Kyriakos Pittakis**, a remarkable figure who during the War of Independence had used his knowledge of ancient literature to discover the Klepsydra spring on the Acropolis – thus solving the problem of lack of water during the Turkish siege. In the first four years of its existence, the Archeological Society sponsored excavations in Athens at the **Theatre of Dionysos** (see p.70), the **Tower of the Winds** (see p.76), the **Propylaia** (see p.68) and the **Erechtheion** (see p.70).

The great Germans

Although King Otto was deposed in 1862 in favour of a Danish prince, Germans remained leaders of Greek archeology in the 1870s. Two men dominated the scene: Ernst Curtius and Heinrich Schliemann.

Ernst Curtius was a traditional classical scholar. He had come to Athens originally as tutor to King Otto's family and in 1874 returned to Greece to secure permission to conduct excavations at **Olympia** (see p.187). He set up a **German Archeological Institute** in Athens and negotiated the **Olympia Convention**, under the terms of which the Germans were to pay for and have total control of the dig; all finds were to remain in Greece, though the excavators could make copies and casts; and all finds were to be published simultaneously in Greek and German.

This was an enormously important agreement, which almost certainly prevented the treasures of Olympia and Mycenae following those of Troy to a German museum. But other Europeans were still in acquisitive mode: **French consuls**, for example, had been instructed to buy any "available" local antiquities in Greece and Asia Minor, and had picked up the Louvre's great treasures, the **Venus de Milo** and **Winged Victory of Samothrace**, in 1820 and 1863 respectively.

At **Olympia**, digging began in 1875 on a site buried beneath river mud, silt and sand. Only one corner of the **Temple of Zeus** was initially visible, but within months the excavators had turned up statues from the east pediment. Over forty magnificent sculptures, as well as terracottas, statue bases and a rich collection of bronzes, were uncovered, together with more than four hundred inscriptions. The laying bare of this huge complex was a triumph for official German archeology.

While Curtius was digging at Olympia, another German was standing archeology on its head. **Heinrich Schliemann** had amassed a private fortune through various Midas-like enterprises and had embarked on the **search for Troy** and the vindication of his lifelong belief in the truth of Homer's tales of prehistoric cities and heroes. Although most of the archeological establishment, led by Curtius, was unremittingly hostile, Schliemann achieved spectacular success in 1873 by unearthing the so-called **Treasure of Priam**, a stash of gold and precious jewellery and vessels. To his mind, this vindicated his search for Homer's city of Priam and Hector.

Three years later, Schliemann turned his attentions to **Mycenae** (see p.135), again inspired by Homer, and once more following a hunch. Alone among contemporary scholars, he sought and found the legendary graves of Mycenaean kings inside the

:isting Cyclopean wall of the citadel rather than outside it, in the process unearthing
‚e magnificent treasures now displayed in the Mycenaean Halls of the National
rcheological Museum in Athens (see p.85). In 1884, Schliemann returned to Greece
‚ excavate another famous prehistoric citadel, this time at **Tiryns** (see p.139).
Almost single-handedly, and in the face of continuing academic obstruction,
chliemann had revolutionized archeology and the study of Greek history and
vilization. Although some of his results have been shown to have been deliberately
lsified in the sacrifice of truth to beauty, his achievements remains enormous.

The last two decades of the nineteenth century saw the discovery of other important
Classical sites. Excavation began at **Epidaurus** (see p.145) in 1881 under the Greek
rcheologist **Panayiotis Kavvadias**, who made it his life's work. Meanwhile, at **Delphi**
see p.206), the **French** began digging at the **sanctuary of Apollo**. Their excavations,
vhich continued nonstop from 1892 to 1903, revealed the extensive site visible today;
vork on the site has continued sporadically ever since.

TOP ARCHEOLOGICAL SITES

In a country with such a wealth of ancient remains as Greece, it's hard to pick out a definitive
list of highlights, but here are some of the most famous and unmissable sites.

THE CLASSICS

The Acropolis, Athens Can rightfully claim to be one of the most iconic images of Western
civilization. See p.65

Mycenae The citadel of King Agamemnon and cavernous tholos tombs never fail to impress.
See p.135

Knossós The part-reconstructed Minoan palace contains some beautiful ancient frescoes.
See p.459

Delphi Known as the earth's navel, this extensive mountainside site still enchants visitors.
See p.206

Delos Guarded by majestic lions, the treasury of the Athenian Empire occupied the entire
island. See p.396

Vergina The dazzling wealth of the Macedonian dynasty is on display beneath an apparently
mundane earth mound. See p.288

Olympia The birthplace of the Olympic Games is a vast and impressive site, centred around
the ancient stadium. See p.187

Epidaurus An ancient theatre with incredible acoustics, where performances of Classical
drama are a highlight of the annual Athens and Epidaurus Festival. See p.145

Festós The second of the great Minoan palaces, with no reconstruction and far fewer crowds.
See p.463

THE BEST OF THE REST

Sanctuary of the Great Gods, Samothráki An idyllically located site that was a major
centre of an ancient mystery cult. See p.659

Akrotíri, Santoríni Newly re-opened, the remains of the Minoan outpost on Santoríni, long
buried under lava, are astonishing, their setting unique. See p.443

Ólynthos One of the best examples of an ancient town, all laid out in neat grids. See p.302

Bassae This superbly well-preserved temple is enhanced by its stunning location in the
Arcadian mountains. See p.177

Philippi Extensive site that was equally important in Roman and early Christian history. See p.312

Temple of Aphaea, Égina A wonderfully complete temple, in a hilltop island setting with
views of Athens. See p.336

Paleópolis, Corfu Relatively few people visit the scattering of temples and basilicas in the
suburbs of Corfu Town. See p.715

Tiryns This squat Mycenaean period citadel boasts some of the most impressive Cyclopean
walls ever built. See p.139

Palamári, Skýros If only as evidence that new discoveries can still be made, Palamári, a
fortified Bronze Age settlement at the heart of the Aegean, is extraordinary. See p.695

Evans and Knossós

The early twentieth century saw the domination of Greek archeology by an Englishman, **Sir Arthur Evans**. An egotistical maverick like Schliemann, he too was independently wealthy, with a brilliantly successful career behind him when he started his great work at **Knossós** (see p.459) on **Crete**. There he discovered one of the oldest and most sophisticated of Mediterranean societies, which he christened Minoan.

Evans first visited Crete in 1894 and headed for the legendary site of Knossós, which had earlier attracted the attention of Schliemann. Evans succeeded in buying the site, and in March 1900 began excavations. Within a few days, evidence of a great complex building was revealed, along with artefacts that indicated an astonishing cultural sophistication: elegant courtyards and verandas, colourful wall-paintings, pottery, jewellery and sealstones – the wealth of a civilization which dominated the eastern Mediterranean 3800 years ago.

For the next thirty years, Evans continued to excavate at Knossós, during which time he established, on the basis of changes in the pottery styles, the **system of dating** that remains in use today for classifying **Greek prehistory**: Early, Middle and Late Minoan (Mycenaean on the mainland). Like Schliemann, Evans attracted criticism and controversy for his methods – most notably his decision speculatively to reconstruct parts of the palace in concrete – and for many of his interpretations. Nevertheless, his discoveries and his dedication put him near the pinnacle of Greek archeology.

Into the twentieth century: the foreign institutes

In 1924, Evans gave the site of Knossós and all other lands within his possession on Crete to the **British School at Athens** (it was only in 1952 that Knossós became the property of the Greek State). At the time, the British School was one of several foreign archeological institutes in Greece; founded in 1886, it had been preceded by the **French School**, the **German Institute** and the **American School**.

Greek archeology owes much to the work and relative wealth of these foreign schools and others that would follow. They have been responsible for the excavation of many of the most famous sites in Greece: the **Heraion** on **Sámos** (German; see p.607); the sacred island of **Delos** (French; see p.396); sites on **Kos** (see p.560) and in southern **Crete** (both Italian); **Corinth** (see p.132), **Samothráki** (see p.659) and the **Athenian Agora** (all American; see p.72), to name but a few.

One of the giants of this era was **Alan Wace** who, while director of the British School at Athens from 1913 to 1923, conducted excavations at **Mycenae** and proposed a new chronology for prehistoric Greece, which put him in direct conflict with Arthur Evans. Evans believed that the mainland citadels had been ruled by Cretan overlords, whereas Wace was convinced of an independent Mycenaean cultural and political development. Wace was finally vindicated after Evans's death, when in the 1950s it emerged that Mycenaean Greeks had conquered the Minoans in approximately 1450 BC.

The period between the world wars saw many new discoveries, among them the sanctuary of **Asklepios** (see p.566) and its elegant Roman buildings on **Kos**, excavated by the Italians from 1935 to 1943, and the Classical Greek city of **Ólynthos** (see p.302), in northern Greece, which was dug by the American School from 1928 to 1934. After the wholesale removal of houses and apartment blocks that had occupied the site, the American School also began excavations in the **Athenian Agora**, the ancient marketplace, in 1931, culminating in the complete restoration of the **Stoa of Attalos** (see p.74).

More recent excavations

Interrupted by World War II and the Greek Civil War, it was not until 1948 that excavations were resumed with a Greek clearance of the **Sanctuary of Artemis** at **Brauron** in Attica, and in 1952 **Carl Blegen** cleared **Nestor's Palace** (see p.185) at

ylos in Messenia. Greek archeologists began work at the Macedonian site of **Pella** (see p.281), the capital of ancient Macedonia, and at the **Nekromanteion of Ephyra** in Epirus.

In comparison to earlier digs, these were minor operations, reflecting a modified approach to archeology which laid less stress on discoveries and more on **documentation**. However, that's not to say there were no spectacular finds. At **Mycenae**, in 1951, a second circle of graves was unearthed, and at Pireás, a burst sewer in 1959 revealed four superb Classical bronzes. In 1961, the fourth great **Minoan palace** of **Káto Zákros** (following the unearthing of Knossós, Festós and Mália) was revealed by torrential rains at the extreme eastern tip of Crete.

At **Akrotíri** (see p.443) on the island of **Santoríni** (Thíra), **Spyros Marinatos** revealed, in 1967, a Minoan-era site that had been buried by volcanic explosion in either 1650 or 1550 BC – the jury is still out on that one. Its buildings were two or three storeys high and superbly frescoed. Marinatos was later tragically killed while at work on the site when he fell off a wall, and is now buried there.

A decade later came an even more dramatic find at **Vergina** (see p.288) – **ancient Aegae** – in northern Greece, the early capital of the Macedonian kingdom, which later became its necropolis. Here, **Manolis Andronikos** found a series of royal tombs dating from the fourth century BC which contained an astonishing hoard of exquisite gold treasures. Andronikos showed this to have been the **tomb of Philip II** of Macedon, father of Alexander the Great.

Today, archeologists are still at work in the field, although the emphasis is often as much about **conservation** as exploration. All too often newly discovered sites are inadequately fenced off or protected, and a combination of the elements, greedy developers and malicious trespassers – sometimes all three – has caused much damage and deterioration. On a happier note, new discoveries are still being made: expansion of the **Athens metro** has led to scores of small finds, many of which have been artfully incorporated into displays at the respective stations, such as Panepistimio, Syndagma and Akropoli, while important ongoing excavations include the Bronze Age fortified port of **Palamári** (see p.695) on **Skýros**, and what may be the largest ancient tomb ever discovered in Greece, at **Amphipolis**, not far from Thessaloníki (see box p.313).

Wildlife

For anyone who has seen Greece only at the height of summer with its brown parched hillsides and desert-like ambience, the richness of the wildlife – in particular the flora – may come as a surprise. As winter warms into spring, the countryside transforms itself into a mosaic of coloured flowers, which attract a plethora of insect life, followed by birds. Isolated areas, whether islands or remote mountains such as Olympus, have had many thousands of years to develop their own individual species. Overall, Greece has around six thousand species of native flowering plants – nearly four times that of Britain, over the same land area. Many are unique to Greece, and make up about a third of Europe's endemic plants.

Plants

Whereas in temperate northern Europe plants flower from spring until autumn, the arid summers of Greece confine the main **flowering period** to the spring, a narrow window when the days are bright, the temperatures not too high and the groundwater supply is still adequate. In Rhodes and eastern Crete this begins in early March, western Crete in early April, the Peloponnese and eastern Aegean mid- to late April, and the Ionian islands in early May, though a cold dry winter can cause several weeks' delay. In the high mountains the floral "spring" arrives in summer, with the alpine zones of central and western Crete in full flower in June, and mainland mountain blooms emerging in July.

The delicate flowers of early spring – orchids, fritillaries, anemones, cyclamen, tulips and small bulbs – are replaced as the season progresses by more robust shrubs, tall perennials and abundant annuals, but many of these close down completely for the fierce **summer**. A few tough plants, like shrubby thyme and savory, continue to flower through the heat and act as magnets for butterflies.

Once the worst heat is over, and the first showers of **autumn** arrive, so does a second "spring", on a much smaller scale but no less welcome after the brown drabness of summer. Squills, autumn cyclamen, crocus in varying shades, pink or lilac colchicum, yellow sternbergia and other small bulbs all come into bloom, while the seeds start to germinate for the following year's crop of annuals. By the new year, early spring bulbs and orchids start to flower in the south.

Coastal species

Plants on the **beach** grow in a difficult environment: fresh water is scarce, salt is in excess and dehydrating winds are often very strong. Feathery **tamarisk** trees are adept at surviving this habitat, and consequently are often planted to provide shade. On hot days or nights you may see or feel them sweating away surplus saltwater from their

---

THE FIRST NATURALISTS

Despite an often negative attitude to wildlife, Greece was probably the first place in the world where it was an object of study. **Theophrastos** (372–287 BC) from Lésvos was the first recorded botanist and a systematic collector of general information on plants, while his contemporary, **Aristotle**, studied the animal world. During the first century AD, the distinguished physician **Dioscorides** compiled a herbal study that remained a standard work for over a thousand years.

oliage. Sand dunes also provide shelter for a variety of colourful small plants as well as ant reed or **calamus**, a bamboo-like grass reaching up to 6m in height and often cut or use as canes. It frequently grows in company with the shrubby, pink- or white-flowered and highly poisonous **oleander**.

Meadow and hill plants

Arable fields can be rich with colourful weeds: scarlet poppies, blue bugloss, yellow or white daisies, wild peas, gladioli, tulips and grape hyacinths. Small, unploughed **meadows** may be equally colourful, with slower-growing plants such as orchids in extraordinary quantities.

The rocky earth makes cultivation on some **hillsides** difficult and impractical. Agriculture is often abandoned and areas regenerate to a rich mixture of shrubs and perennials – known as **garigue**. With time, a few good wet winters, and in the absence of grazing, some shrubs will develop into small trees, intermixed with tough climbers – the much denser **maquis** vegetation. The colour yellow often predominates in early spring, with brooms, gorse, Jerusalem sage and giant fennel followed by the blues, pinks and purples of bee-pollinated plants. An abundance of the pink and white of Cistus rockroses is usually indicative of an earlier fire, since they are primary recolonizers. A third vegetation type is **phrygana** – smaller, frequently aromatic or spiny shrubs, often with a narrow strip of bare ground between each hedgehog-like bush. Many aromatic herbs such as lavender, rosemary, savory, sage and thyme are native to these areas.

Orchids

Nearly 190 species of **orchid** are believed to occur in Greece; their complexity blurs species' boundaries and keeps botanists in a state of taxonomic flux. In particular, the Ophrys bee and spider orchids have adapted themselves, through subtleties of lip colour and false scents, to seduce small male wasps. These insects mistake the flowers for a potential mate, and unintentionally assist the plant's pollination. Though all species are officially protected, many are still picked.

High-altitude plants

The **higher mountains** of Greece have winter snow cover, and cooler weather for much of the year, so flowering is consequently later than at lower altitudes. The **limestone peaks** of the mainland, and of islands such as Corfu, Kefaloniá, Crete, Rhodes, Sámos and Samothráki, hold rich collections of attractive **rock plants**, flowers whose nearest relatives may be from the Balkan Alps or the Turkish mountains. **Gorges** are another spectacular habitat, particularly rich in Crete. Their inaccessible cliffs act as refuges for plants that cannot survive the grazing, competition or more extreme climates of open areas. Many of Greece's endemic plants are confined to cliffs, gorges or mountains.

Much of the surviving **original woodland** is in mountain areas. In the south it includes cypress: native to the south and east Aegean. The cooler shade of woodland provides a haven for plants that cannot survive full exposure to the Greek summer, including peonies and numerous ferns.

With altitude, the forest thins out to scattered individual conifers and kermes oak, before finally reaching a limit at around 1500–2000m on the mainland – much lower on the islands. Above this tree line are **summer meadows**, and then bare rock. If not severely grazed, these habitats are home to many low-growing, gnarled, but often splendidly floriferous plants.

Birds

Migratory species that have wintered in East Africa move north, through the eastern Mediterranean, from around **mid-March to mid-May**. Some stop in Greece to breed; others move on into the rest of Europe. The southern islands are the first landfall after a long sea crossing, and smaller birds recuperate for a few days before moving on. Larger

GREECE'S BEST WILDLIFE SPOTS

Samariá Gorge Crete's most famous ravine hides some of Greece's rarest plants, though other nearby gorges feel far wilder. See p.501

Préspa Lakes Straddling the Albanian border, these serene bodies of water provide refuge for a host of waterfowl. See p.292

Laganás Bay Though much of it is touristic, the bay is still a prime breeding ground for the loggerhead turtle. See p.757

Mount Olympus The mountain of the Gods is also home to over 1600 species of plants. See p.282

Dhadhiá National Park This haven contains some of Greece's last virgin forest, which hosts 36 species of birds of prey. See p.324

North Píndhos The wooded valleys of this natural wilderness are the place to spot Greece's largest mammals, including wolves and brown bears. See p.250

birds such as storks and ibis often fly very high, and binoculars are needed to spot them as they pass over. In autumn, birds return, but usually in more scattered numbers. Although some are shot, there is not the wholesale slaughter that takes place in some other Mediterranean countries.

At night, the tiny **scops owl** has a very distinct, repeated single-note call, very like the sonar beep of a submarine; the equally diminutive **little owl**, with a weird repertoire of cries, may be visible by day in ruined buildings. Near wooded streams, the most evocative nocturnal bird is the **nightingale**, most audible in the May mating season.

Larger raptors occur in remoter areas and prefer mountain gorges and cliffs. **Buzzards** are the most abundant, and often mistaken by optimistic birdwatchers for the rarer, shyer **eagles**. **Griffon vultures**, however, are unmistakeable, soaring on broad, straight-edged wings, whereas the **lammergeier** (bearded vulture) is a state-of-the-art flying machine with narrow, swept wings, seen over mountain tops by the lucky few; the remaining ten or so pairs in Crete are now the Balkans' largest breeding population.

In lowland areas, **hoopoes** are a startling combination of pink, black and white, obvious when they fly and the only natural predator of the processionary caterpillar, a major pest of pine forests. The shy **golden oriole** has an attractive song but is adept at hiding its brilliant colours among the olive trees. Multicoloured flocks of elegant bee-eaters fill the air with their soft calls as they hunt insects. Brightest of all is the **kingfisher**, more commonly seen sea fishing here than in northern Europe.

In areas of wetland that remain undrained and undisturbed, such as salt marshes, coastal lagoons, estuaries and freshwater ponds, **ospreys**, **egrets**, **ibis**, **spoonbills**, **storks**, **pelicans** and many **waders** can be seen feeding. **Flamingos** frequently appear, as lone individuals or small flocks, in the eastern Aegean saltpans and the westerly Amvrakikós Gulf, between December and May.

Mammals

Greece's small **mammal** population ranges from rodents and shrews to hedgehogs, hares and squirrels (including the dark-red Persian squirrel on Lésvos). Medium-sized mammals include badgers and foxes and the persecuted golden jackal, but the commonest is the ferret-like stone (or beech) marten, named for its habit of decorating stones with its droppings to mark territory.

In the mainland **mountains**, mostly in the north, are found the shy chamois and wild boar, with even shyer predators like lynx, wolves and brown bear. Occasionally seen running wild in Crete's White Mountains, but more often as a zoo attraction, is an endemic ibex. Formerly in danger of extinction, a colony of them was established on the offshore islet of Dhía, where they thrived and exterminated the rare local flora.

~eptiles and amphibians

~eptiles, the commonest of which are **lizards**, flourish in the hot dry summers of ~reece. Most of these are small, agile and wary, rarely staying around for closer ~spection. They're usually brown to grey, subtly spotted, striped or tessellated, though ~ adult males the undersides are sometimes brilliant orange, green or blue. The more ~bust green lizards, with long whip-like tails, can be 50cm or more in length, but are ~qually shy and fast-moving unless distracted by territorial disputes with each other.

Nocturnal **geckos** are large-eyed, short-tailed lizards. Their spreading toes have claws ~nd ingenious adhesive pads, allowing them to cross house walls and ceilings in their ~earch for insects, including mosquitoes. The rare **chameleon** is a slow-moving, swivel-~yed inhabitant of eastern Crete, Yiálova and some eastern Aegean islands such as Sámos. ~ssentially green, it has the ability to adjust its coloration to match the surroundings.

Once collected for the pet trade, **tortoises** can be found on much of the mainland, ~nd some islands, though not Crete. Usually their noisy progress through hillside scrub ~egetation is the first signal of their presence, as they spend their often long lives grazing ~he vegetation. Closely related **terrapins** are more streamlined, freshwater tortoises that ~ove to bask on waterside mud by streams or ponds. Usually only seen as they disappear ~nder water, their numbers have declined steeply on many islands due to pollution.

Sea turtles occur mostly in the Ionian Sea, but also in the Aegean. The least rare are ~he loggerhead turtles (*Caretta caretta*), which nest on Zákynthos and Kefaloniá, the ~eloponnese, and occasionally in Crete. Their nesting grounds are disappearing under ~ourist resorts, although they are a protected endangered species (see p.757).

Snakes are abundant in Greece and many islands; most are shy and non-venomous. Several species, including the Ottoman and nose-horned vipers, do have a venomous ~bite, though they are not usually aggressive; they are adder-like and often have a very distinct, dark zigzag stripe down the back. Snakes are only likely to bite if a hand is put in the crevice of a wall or a rock face where one of them is resting – but if bitten, seek immediate treatment. Most snakes are not only completely harmless to humans but beneficial, since they keep down populations of pests such as rats and mice.

Frogs and toads are the commonest and most obvious amphibians throughout much of Greece, particularly during the spring breeding season. Frogs prefer the wettest places, and the robust marsh frog revels in artificial water-storage ponds, whose concrete sides magnify their croaking impressively. Tree frogs are tiny emerald-green jewels, with huge and strident voices at night, sometimes found in quantity on the leaves of waterside oleanders. Toads are most visible in May.

TOURISM AND THREATS TO WILDLIFE

Since the 1970s, **tourist developments** have ribboned along **coastlines**, sweeping away both agricultural plots and wildlife havens as they do so. These expanding resorts increase local employment, often attracting inland workers to the coast; the generation that would once have herded sheep on remote hillsides now works in tourist bars and tavernas. Consequently, the pressure of domestic **animal grazing**, particularly in the larger islands, has been significantly reduced, allowing the regeneration of tree seedlings; Crete, for example, has more woodland now than at any time in the last five centuries. However, **forest fires** remain a threat everywhere. Since 1980, blazes have destroyed much of the tree cover in Thássos, southern Rhodes, Kárpathos, Híos, Sámos and parts of the Peloponnese; the trees may well regenerate eventually, but by then the complex shade-dependent ecology will be (or already is) irrecoverably lost.

In the mainland interior, increasing demand for power brings huge **hydroelectric schemes** to remote rivers and gorges with little chance for opposition to be heard. Even the **Orthodox Church**, whose lands once often provided wildlife with a refuge from hunters, now looks to capitalize on their value for major tourist developments. In the north, the forests of sacred **Mount Áthos** are being surrendered to commercial logging. On the bright side, the **Kárla marsh-lake** near Vólos has been allowed to partially refill again, to the delight of migratory birds.

FLORA AND FAUNA FIELD GUIDES

In addition to the **guides** listed below, there are many local guides, of varying quality but sometimes excellent. These are available to buy in local stores, especially on the islands.

FLOWERS

Christopher Grey-Wilson and Marjorie Blamey *Wild Flowers of the Mediterranean*. Comprehensive field guide, with coloured drawings; recent and taxonomically reasonably up to date.

Karl Peter Buttler *Orchids of Britain and Europe*. A comprehensive, though now rather dated guide, published in 1991. Pierre Delforge's Collins guide, with the same title, was more up to date, but now out of print.

John Fielding & Nicholas Turland *Flowers of Crete*. Coffee-table volume with 1900 coloured photos of the Cretan flora, much of which is also widespread in Greece.

BIRDS

George Handrinos and T. Akriotis *The Birds of Greece* (o/p). A comprehensive guide that includes island birdlife, though images are mainly black-and-white, so not a field guide.

Lars Jonsson et al *Collins Bird Guide*. The ornithologist's choice for the best coverage of Greek birds (it covers the whole of Europe), with excellent descriptions and illustrations.

MAMMALS

MacDonald and Barrett *Mammals of Britain and Europe* (o/p). The best field guide on its subject, sadly now hard to find.

REPTILES

Arnold, Burton and Ovenden *Reptiles and Amphibians of Britain and Europe*. An excellent guide, though it excludes the Dodecanese and east Aegean islands.

INSECTS

Michael Chinery *Insects of Britain and Western Europe*. Although Greece is outside the geographical scope of the guide, it provides generic identifications for many of the insects you might see there.

Tom Tolman and Richard Lewington *Collins Butterfly Guide*. A thorough and detailed field guide that illustrates most of the species seen in Greece.

MARINE LIFE

W. Luther and K. Fiedler *Field Guide to the Mediterranean Sea Shore* (o/p). Very thorough, if now very old; includes most Greek shallow-water species.

Insects

Greece teems with insects: some pester, like flies and mosquitoes, but most are harmless to humans. **Grasshoppers** and **crickets** swarm through open areas of vegetation in summer, with larger species that are carnivorous and can bite if handled. Larger still are grey-brown locusts, flying noisily before crash-landing into trees and shrubs. The high-pitched, endlessly repeated chirp of house crickets can drive one to distraction, as can the summer whirring of cicadas on the trunks of trees.

From spring through to autumn, Greece is full of **butterflies**. Swallowtail species are named for the drawn-out corners of the hindwings, in shades of cream and yellow, with black and blue markings. The unrelated, robust brown-and-orange pasha is Europe's largest butterfly. In autumn, black-and-orange African monarchs may appear, sometimes in large quantities. However, the "butterflies" occurring in huge quantity in sheltered sites on islands such as Rhodes, Níssyros and Páros are in fact tiger moths, with their black-and-white forewings and startling bright orange hindwings.

Other insects include the camouflaged **praying mantis**, who hold their powerful forelegs in a position of supplication until another insect comes within reach. The females are notorious for eating the males during mating. Hemispherical **scarab beetles** collect balls of dung and push them around with their back legs.

Corfu and the Epirot mainland opposite are famous for extraordinary **fireflies**, which flutter in quantities across meadows and marshes on May nights, speckling the darkness with bursts of cold light to attract partners; look carefully in nearby hedges, and you may spot the less flashy, more sedentary glow-worm.

Other non-vertebrates of interest include the **land crabs**, which are found in the south and east of Greece. They need water to breed, but can surprise when seen crawling across remote hillsides.

Music

Music is ubiquitous in modern Greek culture; even the most indifferent visitor can't fail to notice it in tavernas and other public spaces. Like so many aspects of the country, it amalgamates "native" and eastern styles, with occasional contributions from points west, and flourishes alongside and often in preference to Western pop. Many traditional songs can trace their roots back to Byzantine religious chants or to the popular music of the Ottoman Empire, though more nationalist-minded musicologists claim their original descent from the now-lost melodies of ancient Greece.

Folk music and instruments

The best opportunities to hear live Greek folk music are the numerous summer *paniyíria* (saints' day festivals) or more tourist-oriented **cultural programmes**, when musicians, based in Athens clubs during winter, tour the islands and villages. Various high-quality revival groups are attempting to recapture the musicianship of the old-timers, fortunately well archived on CD.

Island music

The arc of southern Aegean islands comprising **Crete, Kássos, Kárpathos** and **Hálki** is one of the most promising areas to hear live music. The dominant instrument here is the **lýra**, a lap-fiddle related to the Turkish *kemençe*. It is played not on the shoulder but balanced on the thigh, with a loose bow that can touch all three strings simultaneously, which makes double chords possible. The contemporary **Cretan lýra** is larger, tuned lower (like a Western violin), and played with a much tauter bow. Usually, the *lýra* is backed up by a **laoúto**, which closely resembles a mandolin, with a long fretted neck and four sets of double strings.

In parts of the southeastern Aegean, most notably **Kálymnos** and northern **Kárpathos**, you also find a simple, **droneless bagpipe** – the **askomandoúra** or *tsamboúna*. The **sandoúri** (hammer dulcimer) – promoted in Greece by refugees from Asia Minor – has seen increased popularity in recent decades.

On most Aegean islands, particularly the **Cyclades**, the *lýra* is replaced by a more familiar-looking **violí**, essentially a Western violin. Accompaniment was provided until recently by *laoúto* or *sandoúri*, though these days you're most likely to be confronted with a bass guitar and rock drums.

Island folk songs – **nisiótika** – feature melodies which, like much folk music the world over, rely heavily on the pentatonic scale. Lyrics, especially on smaller islands, touch on the perils of the sea, exile and thwarted love.

Lésvos occupies a special place in terms of island music, having absorbed melodies and instrumentation from various nationalities of neighbouring Anatolia; it is the only island with a vital **brass band** tradition, and nearly every Greek dance rhythm is represented in local music.

By way of contrast, the **Ionian islands** (except Lefkádha), the only modern Greek territory never to have seen Turkish occupation, has a predominantly Western musical tradition. Their indigenous song-form is Italian in name – **kantádhes** – and in instrumentation (guitar and mandolin) and vocalization (major scales, choral delivery); it's most often heard now on Lefkádha, Kefaloniá and Zákynthos.

Mainland music

In the **Peloponnese** and **central/western Greece**, many folk songs – known as **paliá dhimotiká** – hark back to the Ottoman occupation and the War of Independence; others, in a lighter tone, refer to aspects of pastoral life. Their essential instrument is the **klaríno** (clarinet), which reached Greece during the 1830s, introduced either by Gypsies or King Otto's Bavarian entourage. Backing was traditionally provided by a *koumpanía* consisting of *kythára* (guitar), *laoúto*, *laoutokythára* (a hybrid instrument) and *violí*, with *toumberléki* (lap drum) or *défi* (tambourine) for rhythm.

Many mainland melodies are **dances**, divided by rhythm into such categories as *kalamatianó* (a line dance), *tsámiko*, *hasaposérviko* or *syrtó*, the quintessential circle dance of Greece. Those that aren't danceable include the slow, stately *kléftiko*, which relate, baldly or in metaphor, incidents or attitudes from the Ottoman era and the figh^t for freedom.

The folk music of **Epirus** (**Ípiros**) shows strong resemblances to that of neighbouring Albania and the Republic of Macedonia, particularly in the **polyphonic pieces** sung by both men and women. The repertoire divides into three categories, also found further south: *mirolóyia* or laments; drinking songs or *tís távlas*; and various danceable melodie^s as noted above, common to the entire mainland and many islands too.

Macedonia and Thrace in the north remained Ottoman territory until the early 1900s, with a bewilderingly mixed population, so music here still sounds more generically Balkan. Worth special mention are the **brass bands** peculiar to western Macedonia, introduced during the nineteenth century by Ottoman military musicians. Owing to the huge, post-1923 influx of Anatolian refugees, these regions have been a treasure-trove for collectors and ethnomusicologists seeking to document the old music of Asia Minor.

Among Thracian instruments, the **kaváli** (end-blown pastoral flute) is identical to the Turkish and Bulgarian article, as is the local drone bagpipe or **gáïda**, made like its island counterpart from goat skin. The **zournás**, a screechy, double-reed oboe similar to the Islamic world's *shenai*, is an integral part of weddings or festivals, played along with the deep-toned *daoúli* drum as a typically Gypsy ensemble. Other percussion instruments like the *daïrés* or tambourine and the *darboúka* provide sharply demarcated dance rhythms such as the *zonarádhikos*. The *klaríno* is present here as well, as are two types of *lýra*, but the most characteristic melodic instrument of Thrace is the **oúti** (oud), whose popularity received a boost after refugee players arrived.

Rembétika

Often known as the Greek "blues", **rembétika** began as the music of the urban dispossessed. It has existed in some form in **Greece**, **Smyrna** and **Constantinople** since at least the very early 1900s – probably a few decades earlier. But its evolution is as hard to define as American blues, with which half-useful comparisons are often made. Although rembétika shares marked similarities in spirit with that genre, there's little or none in its musical form.

The 1919–22 Greco–Turkish war and the subsequent **1923 exchange of populations** were key events for rembétika; they resulted in the influx to Greece of over a million Asia Minor Greeks, many of whom settled in shanty towns around Athens, Pireás and Thessaloníki. Here, a few men would sit around a charcoal brazier in a so-called *tekés* or stoners' shanty, toking from a *nargilés* (hookah) filled with hashish. One might improvise a tune on the *baglamás* or **bouzoúki** (a long-necked, fretted, three-stringed lute) and begin to sing songs of illicit or frustrated love, disease and death; their tone – resignation to the singer's lot, coupled with defiance of authority – will be familiar to old-time blues fans.

By the early 1930s, key (male) musicians had emerged from the *tekés* culture. Foremost among them was a Pireás-based quartet: the beguiling-voiced **Stratos Payioumtzis**; composer and lyricist **Anestis Delias** (aka **Artemis**), who died in the street of a drug

THE SOUND OF THE UNDERGROUND

This "**Golden Age**" of rembétika was short-lived, as the music's association with a **drug-laced underworld** would prove its undoing. During the strait-laced **Metaxas dictatorship** (see p.782), tangos and frothy Italianate love songs were encouraged instead, and musicians with uncompromising lyrics and lifestyles were blackballed. In Athens, even possession of a *bouzoúki* or *baglamás* became a criminal offence, and several performers did jail time. Others went to Thessaloníki, where the local police chief was a big fan of the music and allowed its practitioners to smoke in private.

The unfortunate rembétes incurred disapproval from the puritanical left as well as the puritanical right; the growing **Communist Party** of the 1930s considered the music and its habitués hopelessly decadent and politically unevolved. Despite this, rembétika was strangely popular among the rank-and-file on both sides of the 1946–49 civil war – perhaps the only taste uniting a fatally polarized country.

Ironically, the original rembétika material was rescued from oblivion by the 1967–74 **colonels' junta**. Along with various other features of Greek culture, most rembétika verses were banned. The generation coming of age under the dictatorship took a closer look at the forbidden fruit, derived solace and deeper meanings from the nominally apolitical lyrics. When the junta fell in 1974 – even a little before – there was an outpouring of reissued recordings of the old masters.

overdose in 1943; *baglamá*-player Yiorgos Tsoros, better known as **Batis**, an indifferent musician but another excellent composer; and **Markos Vamvakaris**, who became the linchpin of the group. Though a master instrumentalist, he initially considered that his voice, ruined perhaps from too much hash-smoking, wasn't fit for singing. But he soon bowed to the encouragement of record label Columbia, and his gravelly, unmistakeable delivery set the standard for male rembétic vocals until the 1940s.

In the late 1940s, several *rembétisses* (female rembétika vocalists) sang with **Vassilis Tsitsanis**, the most significant composer and *bouzoúki* player after Vamvakaris. Tsitsanis performed almost up to his death in 1984 – his funeral in Athens was attended by nearly a quarter of a million people.

The éntekhno revolution

The "Westernization" of rembétika that began with Tsitsanis preceded the rise of the **éntekhno music** that emerged during the late 1950s. *Éntekhno*, literally "artistic" or "sophisticated", was an orchestral genre where folk or rembétika instrumentation and melodies became part of a much larger symphonic fabric, but with a still recognizably Greek sound.

Its first and most famous exponents were **Manos Hatzidhakis** and **Mikis Theodhorakis**, both classically trained musicians. They not only combined rembétic and Byzantine influences with orchestral arrangements, but also successfully used the country's rich **poetic tradition** for lyrics.

The downside of increased sophistication was an inevitable distancing from indigenous roots, in particular the modal scales which had been used since antiquity. And with its catchy tunes, *éntekhno* fell prey to the demands of the local film industry – writing a soundtrack became a composer's obligatory rite of passage – and at its worst degenerated to Muzak cover versions.

Laïká: son of rembétika

Diametrically opposed to *éntekhno* was the **laïká** ("popular") music of the 1950s and 1960s, its gritty, tough style directly linked to rembétika, undiluted by Western influences. *Laïká* used time signatures common in Turkey and was mistakenly known overseas as belly-dance music. Once again, these "debased" oriental influences were much to the chagrin of those who also objected to the apolitical, decadent, escapist song content.

The most notable *laïká* performer was **Stelios Kazantzidhis** (1931–2001), whose volcanic, mournful style was never equalled. His work, often in duets with **Marinella** and **Yiota Lidhia**, immortalized the experiences of the Greek working class that emerged from the 1940s faced with a choice of life under restrictive regimes or emigration. "Stellaras" inspired fanatical devotion in his fans over a fifty-year career: truck drivers emblazoned their cabs with a single word, "Yparho" (the name of his biggest hit). On the day he died nearly every CD player in the land played Kazantzidhis songs in tribute, and thousands thronged his funeral in industrial Elefsína.

Singer-songwriters and folk-rock

The first significant musician to break the *bouzoúki* mould was Thessalonian **Dhionysis Savvopoulos**, who emerged in 1966 with a maniacal, rasping voice and angst-ridden lyrics, his persona rounded out by shoulder-length hair and outsized glasses. Savvopoulos' work soon became impossible to pigeonhole: perhaps equal parts twisted northern Greek folk, Bob Dylan and Frank Zappa at his jazziest. Though briefly detained and tortured, he resumed performing, and became something of a touchstone for late 1960s Greek youth.

Despite a modest discography, Savvopoulos had a considerable effect on younger artists, and during his brief tenure as a record producer, he gave breaks to numerous younger artists, many of them also from northern Greece. Among his protégés were **Nikos Xydhakis** and **Manolis Rasoulis**, whose landmark 1978 album, *Iy Ekdhíkisi tis Yiftías* (The Revenge of Gypsydom), subverted the pretentiousness of 1960s and 1970s *éntekhno* and other "politically correct" music. More recently, Thessalonians **Nikos Papazoglou** and **Sokratis Malamas** have come to the fore.

Contemporary music

Eleftheria Arvanitaki, who began her career on a Savvopoulos album, and continued with rembétika revival group Opisthodhromiki Kompania, went on to dabble in various genres, and is still performing today. Look out too for **Ross Daly** who frequently appears live in Greece or tours abroad, offering fusion interpretations of traditional pieces plus his own improvisations. Of Irish descent, he plays numerous traditional Greek instruments and has absorbed influences not just from Crete, where he has long been resident, but from throughout the Near East. Two other exports from Crete are mandolinist **Loudhovikos ton Anoyeion**, originally an artist on Manos Hatzidhakis' late-1980s Seirios label, and innovative lyra player **Stelios Petrakis**.

Various other, less durable groups have attempted to explore foreign influences on Greek music with mixed success. Often this eclecticism has gone too far, with bells, sitar, ney and synthesizer resulting in a bland, New Age-y sound not identifiably Greek. Individuals who have managed to avoid this trap include innovative young clarinettist **Manos Achalinotopoulos**; *oud* player **Haig Yagdjian**; the group **Notios Ihos**, led by Ahilleas Persidhis; singer **Savina Yiannatou**; singer/composer **Hristi Stassinopoulou**; and the **Greeks & Indians** fusion concerts and recordings coordinated by visionary Alexandhros Karsiotis of Saraswati Records.

Discography

The following CDs are among the best available for each of the genres detailed above: ★ denotes a particularly strong recommendation. Unless otherwise specified, all are Greek pressings. Athens has several good Greek CD stores (see p.115). Online, you'll find some of our choices at Amazon, but rather more at Thessaloníki-based Studio 52 (see p.280), which operates a worldwide online order service, and also at Athens-based Xylouris (ⓦxilouris.gr).

FOLK

COMPILATIONS

★ **Lesvos Aiolis** *Tragoudhia ke Hori tis Lesvou/Songs & Dances of Lesvos* (2 CDs). Field recordings (1974–96) of this island's last traditional music, supervised by musicologist Nikos Dhionysopoulos. The quality and uniqueness of the pieces, and lavishly illustrated booklet, merit the expense.

Thalassa Thymisou: Tragoudhia ke Skopi apo tis Inousses. Superb result of Thessaloníki music school in Khordais' "field trip" to Inoússes, a small islet near Híos; live sessions in Inoussan tavernas plus studio recordings.

ARTISTS

★ **Khronis Aïdhonidhis** *T'Aïdhonia tis Anatolis: Songs of Thrace and Asia Minor*. Flawlessly produced 1990 session featuring the top singer of material from Thrace and western Asia Minor, plus an orchestra directed by Ross Daly, and guest Yiorgos Dalaras. Epikranthi (2006; rare) is an unrivalled interpretation of ecclesiastical hymns and popular laments from Orthodox Holy Week recorded with his designated disciple, Nektaria Karantzi.

★ **Petro-Loukas Halkias** *Petro-Loukas Chalkias and Kompania* (World Network, Germany). Halkias and his *kompanía* (group) of *laoúto, violí*, guitar and percussion realize the true sense of the *kompanía*: tight coordination, yet clearly articulated instrumental voices.

Xanthippi Karathanasi *Tragoudhia ke Skopi tis Makedhonias/Songs and Tunes of Macedonia*. A native of Halkidhikí, Karathanasi is a foremost interpreter of north-mainland material – and her sidemen are so good they almost steal the show.

Andonis Xylouris (Psarandonis) *Palio Krasi In'íy Skepsi Mou* and *Idheon Antron*. Psarandonis – shunned by other Cretan musicians – has an idiosyncratically spare and percussive *lýra* style, but here unusual instruments are well integrated into a densely textured whole. Daughter Niki executes a gorgeous rendition of "Meraklidhiko Pouli" on *Idheon Antron*, and also steals the show on his more recent *Andartes ton Vounon*.

REMBÉTIKA

COMPILATIONS

★ **Rembetika; Rembetika 2; Vassilis Tsitsanis 1 & 2** (JSP Records, UK). Compiled by veteran rembetophile Charlie Howard, these are currently the benchmark collections for rembétika up to the 1950s. Poor liner notes, but you get four CDs with nearly 80min each of superbly remastered music in each box set.

★ **Greek Orientale: Smyrneic-Rembetic Songs and Dances** (Arhoolie-Polylyric, US). Superb collection spanning 1911 to 1937, with Roza, Rita, Marika Papagika and Dhimitris Semsis.

Lost Homelands: The Smyrneic Song in Greece 1928–35 (Interstate/Heritage, UK). Exceptional sound quality and literate liner notes give this collection the edge over rivals.

★ **Rough Guide to Rebetika** (World Music Network, UK). The best single introduction to the genre, with performers from its earliest recorded days to current revivalists.

ARTISTS

Dhimitris Moustakydhis *16 Rebetika Paigmena se Kithara*. Thessalonian revivalist gem: 16 classics, mostly from the 1920s and 1930s, accompanied by guitar instead of *bouzoúki*.

Roza Eskenazi *Rembetissa* (Rounder, US). Ace renditions of standards and rare gems with her usual sidemen Semsis, Tomboulis, and Lambros on *kanonáki*.

★ **Marika Ninou** *Stou Tzimi tou Hondrou/At Jimmy the Fat's*. Poor sound quality – it was a clandestine recording – but still a classic: one of the few documents of a live rembétic evening, with Ninou and Tsitsanis performing at their habitual club in 1955.

Rebetiki Kompania *Pos Tha Perasi ly Vradhia*. The easiest-found offering from a group that spearheaded the late-1970s rembétika revival.

Vangelis Papazoglou 1897–1943 1920s/30s compositions sung by the era's top stars, including Stellakis Perpiniadhis, Roza Eskenazi, Kostas Roukounas and Rita Abatzi. Poor sound quality, but several versions of his classic "ly Lahanadhes".

Vassilis Tsitsanis *Vassilis Tsitsanis 1936–1946* (Rounder, US). Mostly male singers, but includes several rare (for him) *mastoúriaka*. The twenty hits of *Ta Klidhia* – look for the ring of three keys (*klidhiá*) on the cover – pair him with such mid-1960s stars as Grigoris Bithikotsis, Kaity Grey and Poly Panou.

Markos Vamvakaris *Bouzoúki Pioneer 1932–1940* (Rounder, US). Excellent sound quality, good notes and unusual material.

★ **Stavros Xarhakos** *Rembetiko*. Soundtrack to the eponymous 1984 film which helped repopularise rembétika, and virtually the only "original" rembétika composed in the last sixty years. Lyrics by Nikos Gatsos.

ÉNTEKHNO

Manos Hatzidhakis *Athanasia*. Most essential recording by this artist, still much played and covered since his death in 1994; *Laïki Agora*, with lyrics by Nikos Gatsos is also a must.

★ **Yannis Markopoulos** *Rizitika*. The French subtitle "*La Chante Profonde de Crète*" – says it all: stirring anthems such as "*Pote Tha Kamei Xasteria*", which launched Nikos

Xylouris' *éntekhno* career. *Thiteia*, with lyrics by Manos Eleftheriou, is also much loved, as is *Anexartita*, released just before the junta fell, with top star Viky Moskholiou on many tracks.

★**Mikis Theodhorakis** *Epitafios/Epifaneia* with Bithikotsis and Hiotis, and *To Axion Esti* with Manos Katrakis, are among his most influential, reputation-justifying works, in white-boxed remasters of the original sessions. Also re-issued, *Enas Omiros* marks the debut, aged 19, of his long-time collaborator Maria Farandouri, with settings of Brendan Behan poetry, while *Thalassina Fengaria* is a much-loved song cycle with Bithikotsis, Farandouri Moskholiou interpreting lyrics by poet Nikos Gatsos.

Stavros Xarhakos *Syllogi*. More lyrics by Nikos Gatso Nikos Xylouris's crystalline voice and orchestra (includin funky electric guitar licks), conducted by Khristodhoulo Halaris, make this a 1973 landmark.

★**Nikos Xylouris** *Itane mia Fora* (2 CDs). A 40-trac selection of Xylouris' best 1970s work, with Yianni Markopoulos and others, making clear why he is sti worshipped four decades after his tragically early death.

LAÏKÁ

★**Haris Alexiou** Start with *Ta Tragoudhia tis Haroulas*, with lyrics by Manolis Rasoulis and Manos Loïzos, which established her as alto queen of 1980s *laïká*, then grab *Kalimera Ilie* (with Manos Loïzos), whose title track was for years the PASOK anthem. *Ta Tsilika* has her rembétika interpretations; *Yirizondas ton Kosmo* is a more recent live *éntekhno*/pop disc.

★**Eleftheria Arvanitaki** *Tragoudhia yia tous Mines* is upbeat and *laïká*-based; in *Ektos Programmatos* Eleftheria gets rootsily down in lively sessions at Athens and Thessaloníki clubs.

Yiorgos Dalaras *Tragoudhia me Ousies*. Live recording o a summer 2007 concert at Athens' Iródhio. A double set crammed full of *laïká* and rembétika favourites whose linking theme is *ousíes* or "(controlled) substances", with singing from a host of other stars and phenomenal musicians. Also available with a DVD of the performance.

Glykeria (Kotsoula) *Me ti Glykeria stin Omorfi Nhykhta*. A live recording which showcases this versatile *laïká* singer and rembétika/*nisiótika* revivalist, active during the 1980s.

Stelios Kazantzidhis *Iy Zoi Mou Oli* (2 CD). Retrospective of all the classic hits that made him a national institution.

SINGER-SONGWRITERS

★**Himerini Kolymvites** Evergreen band who write all their own material. Their eponymous first CD (1981), is laced with often surreal lyrics plus richly textured, drunken melodies; *23 Kokkina Fota* (2009) is the best since.

★**Sokratis Malamas** *Ena*. A 2000 release that embodies his mature, confident style, with just voice and guitar; 1992's *Tis Meras ke tis Nykhtas*, with Melina Kana, was the big breakthrough for both; they continued their partnership rewardingly in *Perasma* (2010).

Thanassis Papakonstandinou He's not for everyone, but arguably among the most original musicians working in Greece. If you like his trend-setting *Vrahnos Profitis* (2000), carry on to *Agrypnia* (2002), where he reprises "*Ayia Nostalgia*", title track of his utterly different 1993 debut.

Nikos Papazoglou *Synerga*. A gentle, mystical album; 2005's *Maïssa Selini* is rootsier and broke a long recording silence.

Dhionysis Savvopoulos *Trapezakia Exo* (Lyra MBI). The catchiest outing from the man who set off the folk-rock movement.

Nena Venetsanou This female singer has a deep, earthy voice lending itself to a number of genres. *Ikones* reworks everything from Hatzidhakis (including some premieres) to *nisiótika* to chanson; *Zeïbekika* is a surprisingly successful recasting of rembétika as "profane prayers", performed in French chapels.

★**The Rough Guide to Greek Café** (World Music Network, UK). Never mind the silly title – this has got almost all the stars and trends, in innovative Greek music, from the early 1980s to 2010, including pretty much everyone mentioned above.

FOLK REVIVAL AND FUSION

★**Bosphorus** (Fanari tis Anatolis) *Beyond the Bosphorus*. This tour de force, with guests Mode Plagal, revisits Constantinopolitan and Anataloian melodies, with Vassiliki Papayeoryiou on vocals. Vassiliki's 2013 disc *Ellinotourkika* is just that – selected Greek, Turkish and Kurdish songs, backed by superb musicians.

Greeks & Indians (9 vols to date): This series (vol 3, *Ta Ipirotika*; vol 4, *Ta Pondiaka*; and vol 8, *Ta Laïka*★) sees top performers of Greek regional music – including Petro-Loukas Halkias, Ross Daly, Nikos Saragoudhas, Sofia Papazogou, Yiorgos Amarantidis and Yiorgos Koros – joining forces with some of the best North Indian musicians around.

Haïnidhes *Haïnidhes* (MBI) and *Kosmos ki Oneiro ine Ena* (MBI) are this Cretan band's first two, and arguably best, albums, with folk-influenced original compositions taking precedence over old standards.

Hristi Stassinopoulou *Greekadelia* Greek folk material, startlingly updated by the country's premier (self-described) "ethno-trance" practitioner.

Loudhovikos Ton Anoyion *O Erotas stin Kriti ine Iangolikos* helped rescue the Cretan mandolin from its rthm-backing ghetto; *Pyli tis Ammou* exemplifies evolution in a larger group, with guests Malamas, Dazoglou and Venetsanou.

Mode Plagal *Mode Plagal II*. The best of several solo albums; folk tunes meet funky guitar and saxophone licks à la Coltrane and Miles Davis improvisations/compositions.

Stelios Petrakis *L'Art de la Lyra/The Art of the Lyra* French release sees Stelios return to his Cretan roots, with both songs and dances, backed by *laoúto*, percussion and voice.

Savina Yiannatou *Anixi sti Saloniki/Spring in Salonika*. Ladino Sephardic songs, with crisp backing from Kostas Vomvolos' orchestra; Savina's voice (and trademark vibrato) can take some getting used to, though.

Books

The best books in this selection are marked by a ★ symbol; titles currently out of print are indicated as "o/p". Recommended specialist Greek booksellers include, in the UK, the Hellenic Bookservice (ⓦhellenicbookservice.com) and in Canada, Kalamos Books (ⓦkalamosbooks.com).

TRAVEL/IMPRESSIONS

★**Kevin Andrews** *The Flight of Ikaros.* Intense, compelling account by a sensitive young archeologist wandering the backcountry during the civil war. Five decades on, still one of the best books on Greece as it was before "development".

★**Gerald Durrell** *My Family and Other Animals.* Delightful evocation of Durrell's 1930s childhood on Corfu, where his family settled, and where he developed a passion for the island's fauna while elder brother Lawrence entertained Henry Miller and others.

Lawrence Durrell *Prospero's Cell* and *Reflections on a Marine Venus.* The former constitutes Durrell's Corfu memoirs, from his time there as World War II loomed. *Marine Venus* recounts his 1945–47 colonial-administrator experiences of Rhodes and other Dodecanese islands.

★**Patrick Leigh Fermor** *Roumeli: Travels in Northern Greece* and *Mani: Travels in the Southern Peloponnese.* Sir Patrick – knighted in 2004 for his writing and contribution to British-Greek relations – is an aficionado of rural Greece's vanishing minorities and customs. These two volumes, written in the late 1950s and early 1960s respectively, are scholarly travelogues interspersed with strange yarns. Despite self-indulgent passages, they remain among the best books on modern Greece.

Eleni Gage *North of Ithaka.* Eleni is the namesake and granddaughter of the Eleni whose murder her son Nicholas famously set out to avenge. A New York journalist, she decided to spend most of 2002 in her grandmother's old Epirot village in Epirus, rebuilding the family house – and more. Her open-hearted account takes in village life and travels from Albania to Árta.

Roy Hounsell *The Papas and the Englishman: From Corfu to Zagoria.* Roy and wife Effie forsake the usual expat arenas and settle in Koukoúli under Mount Gamíla, renovating an ancient, crumbled mansion.

John Humphrys and Christopher Humphrys *Blue Skies and Black Olives: A Survivor's Tale of Housebuilding and Peacock Chasing in Greece.* The irascible BBC presenter and his son, a cellist with a Greek orchestra, give their contrasting versions of the frustrations involved in building a holiday home in the Peloponnese. Enjoyable, if all a bit familiar.

Edward Lear *The Corfu Years, The Cretan Journal* and *Journals of a Landscape Painter in Greece and Albania*

(latter o/p). Highly entertaining journals – the first two beautifully illustrated – from the 1840s and 1850s.

Peter Levi *The Hill of Kronos.* Finely observed landscape, monuments, personalities and politics, as poet and classical scholar Levi describes his first journeys to Greece in the 1960s before being drawn into resistance against the colonels' junta.

John Lucas *92 Acharnon Street.* Fond memories of Athens in the 1980s, beautifully told by a writer with a poetic turn of phrase.

★**Willard Manus** *This Way to Paradise: Dancing on the Tables.* American expat's memoir of nearly four decades in Líndhos, Rhodes, which begins long before the region's submersion in tourism. Wonderful period detail, including bohemian excesses and cameos from the likes of S.J. Perelman, Germaine Greer and Martha Gellhorn.

Christopher Merrill *Things of the Hidden God: Journey to the Holy Mountain.* Merrill, an accomplished poet and journalist, first came to Áthos in the wake of a traumatic time reporting on the breakup of Yugoslavia. With fine black-and-white photographs, this is probably the best contemporary take on Áthos, and on Orthodoxy.

Henry Miller *The Colossus of Maroussi.* Corfu, Crete, Athens and the soul of Greece in 1939, with Miller completely in his element; funny, sensual and transporting.

Dilys Powell *An Affair of the Heart* and *The Villa Ariadne.* Powell accompanied archeologist husband Humfry Payne on excavations at the Hereon of Perahóra, and after his sudden death in 1936 maintained strong links with the local villagers, described in *An Affair….* The clearer-eyed, less sentimental *The Villa Ariadne* chronicles her 1950s travels to Crete.

Leon Sciaky *Farewell to Salonica.* Memoir of a *belle époque* boyhood in a middle-class Sephardic Jewish family, before their 1915 emigration to the US. The Sciakys had close ties with Bulgarian peasants in Kukush (now Kilkís) – and Leon is far more sympathetic to Bulgaria than to the Greek regime which assumed control of cosmopolitan Salonica in 1912.

Tom Stone *The Summer of My Greek Taverna.* Enjoyable cautionary tale for those fantasizing about a new life in the Aegean sun. Moving to Pátmos in the early 1980s, Stone tries to mix friendship and business at a beach taverna, with predictable (for onlookers anyway) results.

chard Stoneman, ed A Literary Companion to Travel in eece. Ancient and medieval authors, plus Grand Tourists an excellent selection.

Patricia Storace Dinner with Persephone. A New York et, resident for a year in Athens (with forays to the ovinces), puts the country's 1990s psyche on the couch. orace has a sly humour and an interesting take on reece's "imprisonment" in its imagined past.

ohn L. Tomkinson, ed Travellers' Greece: Memories of 1 Enchanted Land. Seventeenth- to nineteenth-century

(mostly English) travellers' impressions of islands and mainland, ranging from the enraptured to the appalled; ideal for dipping into.

★**Sofka Zinovieff** Eurydice Street. An anthropologist and journalist by training, Zinovieff first came to Greece in the early 1980s, then returned in 2001 with her diplomat husband and two daughters to live in Athens. With sharp observations on nationalism, Orthodoxy, politics, November 17 and leisure (to cite just a few topics), this is the best single account of life in today's urban Greece.

ICTION

OREIGN FICTION

★**Louis de Bernières** Captain Corelli's Mandolin. Set n Kefaloniá during the World War II occupation and ftermath, this accomplished 1994 tragi-comedy quickly cquired cult, then bestseller, status in the UK and US. But n Greece it provoked a scandal once islanders, Greek left ntellectuals and surviving Italian partisans woke up to its virulent disparaging of ELAS. It seems the novel was based on the experiences of Amos Pampaloni, an artillery captain on Kefaloniá in 1942–44 who later joined ELAS, and who accused De Bernières of distorting the roles of both Italians and ELAS on the island. The Greek translation was abridged to avoid causing offence.

Meaghan Delahunt To The Island. Novel about an Australian woman travelling with her young son to Náxos, to visit the father she has never met. On her journey she encounters her father's past, as a political activist tortured by the junta. Not your usual travelogue.

Oriana Fallaci A Man (o/p). Gripping tale of the junta years, based on the author's involvement with Alekos Panagoulis, the army officer who attempted to assassinate Colonel Papadopoulos in 1968 – and who himself died in mysterious circumstances in 1975.

★**John Fowles** The Magus. Fowles' biggest and best tale of mystery and manipulation – plus Greek island life – based on his stay on Spétses as a teacher during the 1950s. A period piece that repays revisiting.

Victoria Hislop The Island and The Thread. The former leper colony of Spinalonga forms the backdrop to The Island, a huge-selling novel about a young woman discovering her Cretan roots. A good story is marred by the slightly cloying nature of its telling. The Thread attempts a similar uncovering of little-known history interwoven with family secrets, set in Thessaloníki.

Olivia Manning The Balkan Trilogy, Volume 3: Friends and Heroes. Wonderfully observed tale, in which Guy and Harriet Pringle escape from Bucharest to Athens, in the last months before the 1941 invasion.

Steven Pressfield Gates of Fire and Alexander: The Virtues of War. Two of several Greek-set historical novels by Pressfield. Gates of Fire, his bestselling first, is a stirring tale of the Spartans at Thermopylae; later books, including

Alexander: The Virtues of War – in which Alexander the Great recounts his warrior's life to brother-in-law Itanes in a first-person narrative – are rather more measured.

Evelyn Waugh Officers and Gentlemen. This second volume of Waugh's brilliant, acerbic wartime trilogy includes an account of the Battle of Crete and subsequent evacuation.

Sofka Zinovieff The House on Paradise Street. A beautifully written novel by someone who knows Greece well (see above), this is a family drama set against the backdrop of the Nazi occupation of Greece and the subsequent civil war.

GREEK FICTION

★**Apostolos Doxiadis** Uncle Petros and Goldbach's Conjecture. Uncle Petros is the disgraced family black sheep, living reclusively in outer Athens; his nephew discovers that Petros had staked everything to solve a theorem unsolved for centuries. Math-phobes take heart; it's more a meditation on how best to spend life, and what really constitutes success.

Vangelis Hatziyannidis. Hatziyannidis' abiding obsessions – confinement, blackmail, abrupt disappearances – get a workout in his creepy debut novel Four Walls, set on an unspecified east Aegean isle, where a reclusive landowner takes in a fugitive woman who convinces him to revive his father's honey trade – with unexpected consequences. His next novel, Stolen Time, revisits the same themes, as an impoverished student gets a tidy fee from a mysterious tribunal for agreeing to spend two weeks in the hotel from Hell.

★**Panos Karnezis.** Karnezis has become the most accessible, and feted, Greek writer since the millennium. He grew up in Greece but now lives in London and writes in English; however, his concerns remain utterly Greek. Little Infamies is a collection of short stories set in his native Peloponnese during the late 1950s and early 1960s; The Maze is a darker-shaded, more successful novel concerning the Asia Minor Catastrophe. More recent works include The Birthday Party, based on events in the life of Aristotle Onassis and daughter Christina, and The Convent, a gentle whodunnit with nuns.

THE CLASSICS

Many of the classics make excellent companions for a trip around Greece; reading Homer's Odyssey when battling the vagaries of island ferries puts your own plight into perspective. Most of these good beginners' choices are published in a range of paperback editions. Particularly outstanding translations are noted.

★**William Allan** *Classical Literature: A Very Short Introduction.* Exactly as it promises: an excellent overview.

Herodotus *The Histories.* Revered as the father of narrative history – and anthropology – this fifth-century BC Anatolian writer chronicled both the causes and campaigns of the Persian Wars, as well as the assorted tribes and nations inhabiting Asia Minor.

★**Homer** *The Iliad* and *The Odyssey.* The first concerns itself, semi-factually, with the late Bronze Age war of the Achaeans against Troy in Asia Minor; the second recounts the hero Odysseus's long journey home, via seemingly every corner of the Mediterranean. The best prose translations are by Martin Hammond, and in verse Richmond Lattimore. For a stirring if very loose verse *Iliad*, try also Christopher Logue's recent version, *War Music*.

Ovid *The Metamorphoses.* Ovid was a first-century AD Roman poet, but his masterpiece includes accessible renditions of the more piquant Greek myths, involving transformations as divine blessing or curse. Excellent verse

translation by David Raeburn; prose version A.D. Melville.

Pausanias *The Guide to Greece.* Effectively the first-ever guidebook, intended for Roman pilgrims to central mainland and Peloponnesian sanctuaries. Invaluable for later archeologists in assessing damage or change to temples over time, or (in some cases) locating them at all. The two-volume Penguin edition is usefully annotated with the later history and nomenclature of the sites.

Plato *Apology.* The most accessible of Plato's works relates the fascinating defence put up by his mentor Socrates against the state charges of corrupting the youth, as well as his dignified acceptance of the death penalty.

★**Thucydides** *History of the Peloponnesian War.* Bleak month-by-month account of the conflict, by a cashiered Athenian officer whose affiliation and dim view of human nature didn't usually obscure his objectivity.

Xenophon *The History of My Times.* Thucydides' account of the Peloponnesian War stops in 411 BC; this eyewitness account continues events until 362 BC.

Nikos Kazantzakis *Zorba the Greek; The Last Temptation of Christ; Christ Recrucified/The Greek Passion; Freedom and Death; The Fratricides;* and *Report to Greco.* Kazantzakis can be hard going, yet the power of his writing shines through. *Zorba the Greek* is a dark, nihilistic work, worlds away from the two-dimensional film. By contrast, the movie version of *The Last Temptation of Christ* – specifically Jesus's vision, once crucified, of a normal life with Mary Magdalene – provoked riots among Orthodox fanatics in Athens in 1989. *Christ Recrucified* (*The Greek Passion*) resets the Easter drama against the backdrop of Christian/Muslim relations, while *Freedom and Death,* perhaps his most approachable, chronicles the rebellions of nineteenth-century Crete. *The Fratricides* portrays a family riven by the civil war. *Report to Greco* is an autobiographical exploration of his Cretan-ness.

Artemis Leontis (ed) *Greece: A Traveler's Literary Companion.* A nice idea, brilliantly executed: various

regions of the country as portrayed in (very) short fiction or essays by modern Greek writers.

★**Petros Markaris** *The Late Night News* (*Deadline in Athens* in US)*; Zone Defence;* and *Che Committed Suicide.* Inspector Haritos is an unmistakeably Greek cop, and these detective tales, while thoroughly engrossing on their own, also offer a real insight into the realities of life in modern Greece.

Alexandros Papadiamantis *Tales from a Greek Island* and *The Murderess.* The island is Skiáthos, Papadiamantis' birthplace. These quasi-mythic tales of grim fate come from a nineteenth-century writer ("the inventor of modern Greek fiction") comparable to Hardy and Maupassant.

★**Dido Sotiriou** *Farewell Anatolia* (o/p). A perennial favourite since publication in 1962, this chronicles the traumatic end of Greek life in Asia Minor, from World War I to the 1922 catastrophe, as narrated by a fictionalized version of Sotiriou's father.

ANCIENT GREECE

★**Mary Beard and John Henderson** *The Classics: A Very Short Introduction.* A brilliant short introduction to all elements of Classics: art, architecture, history and mythology.

★**Walter Burkert** *Greek Religion: Archaic and Classical.* Superb overview of deities and their attributes and antecedents, the protocol of sacrifice and the symbolism

of festivals. Especially good on relating Greek worship to its predecessors in the Middle East.

A.R. Burn *Penguin History of Greece* (o/p). A classic account; packed and informative on everything from philosophy to military history.

Paul Cartledge *Alexander the Great: The Truth Behind The Myth.* An evocative, meticulous and accessible iography, stinting neither on the man's brutality nor his achievements.

aul Cartledge *Cambridge Illustrated History of ncient Greece* or *Ancient Greece: A Very Short ntroduction*. Two excellent general introductions to ncient Greece; choose between brief paperback or large llustrated tome.

★**Paul Cartledge** *The Spartans: An Epic History*. Reassessment of this much-maligned city-state which was secretive and a source of outsider speculation even in its own time.

James Davidson *Courtesans and Fishcakes: The Consuming Passions of Classical Athens*. Absorbing book on the politics, class characteristics and etiquette of consumption and consummation – with wine, women, boys and seafood – in Classical Athens. His more recent *The Greeks And Greek Love: A Radical Reappraisal of Homosexuality in Ancient Greece*, is less successful.

★**M.I. Finley** *The World of Odysseus*. Reprint of a 1954 warhorse, pioneering in its investigation of the historicity (or not) of the events and society related by Homer. Breezily readable and stimulating.

★**Robert Graves** *The Greek Myths*. Definitive account and analysis of the myriad alternative ancient Greek myths. His wonderful *The Golden Fleece* is an imaginatively expanded version of Jason's voyage with the *Argo*.

Simon Hornblower *The Greek World 479–323 BC*. An erudite, up-to-date survey of ancient Greece at its zenith, from the end of the Persian Wars to the death of Alexander.

Mary Lefkowitz *Greek Gods, Human Lives: What We Can Learn from Myths*. Rather than being frivolous, immoral or irrelevant, ancient religion and its myths, in their bleak indifference of the gods to human suffering, are shown as being more mature than the later creeds of salvation and comfort.

Oswyn Murray *Early Greece*. The story of Greece from the Minoans and Mycenaeans through to the beginning of the Classical period.

Robin Osborne *Greece in the Making 1200–479 BC* and *Greek History: The Basics*. The former is a well illustrated paperback on the rise of the city-state; the latter a short new introduction to ancient Greek history. Both are scholarly, if at times a little hard-going.

Robin Lane Fox *Alexander the Great*. An absorbing study that mixes historical scholarship with imaginative psychological detail.

Robin Lane Fox *The Classical World: An Epic History of Greece and Rome*. A racy and entertaining romp through several centuries, written by someone who knows his stuff.

F.W. Walbank *The Hellenistic World*. An historical overview of Greece under the sway of the Macedonian and Roman empires.

MEDIEVAL AND MODERN HISTORY

Timothy Boatswain and Colin Nicolson *A Traveller's History of Greece*. Well-written overview of crucial Greek periods and personalities, from earliest times to the end of the twentieth century.

★**Richard Clogg** *A Concise History of Greece*. If you read only one title on "modern" Greek history, this should be it: a remarkably clear account, from the decline of Byzantium to the economic crisis, with numerous maps and feature captions to the well-chosen artwork.

C.M. Woodhouse *Modern Greece: A Short History*. Woodhouse was a key liaison officer with the Greek Resistance during World War II, and later a Conservative MP. Writing from a more right-wing perspective than Clogg, his account – from the foundation of Constantinople to 1990 – is briefer and drier, but scrupulous with facts.

BYZANTINE, MEDIEVAL AND OTTOMAN GREECE

David Brewer *Greece, the Hidden Centuries: Turkish Rule from the Fall of Constantinople to Greek Independence*. Readable yet authoritative history of this little-explored era of Greek history.

Nicholas Cheetham *Mediaeval Greece* (o/p). A general survey of the period's infinite convolutions in Greece, with Frankish, Catalan, Venetian, Byzantine and Ottoman struggles for power.

★**Roger Crowley** *Constantinople: The Last Great Siege, 1453*. Thrillingly readable narrative of perhaps the key event of the Middle Ages and its repercussions throughout Europe and the Islamic world.

★**John Julius Norwich** *Byzantium: The Early Centuries*; *Byzantium: the Apogee* and *Byzantium: The Decline*. Perhaps the main surprise for first-time travellers to Greece is the fascination of its Byzantine monuments. This is an astonishingly detailed yet readable – often witty – trilogy of the empire that produced them. There's also an excellent, one-volume abridged version, *A Short History of Byzantium*.

INDEPENDENT GREECE

David Brewer *The Greek War of Independence*. The finest narrative of revolutionary events (with some black-and-white illustrations), strong on the background of Ottoman Greece as well as the progress of the war.

★**John S. Koliopoulos and Thanos M. Veremis** *Greece: The Modern Sequel*. Thematic rather than chronological study that pokes into corners rarely illuminated by conventional histories; especially good on Macedonian issues, brigandage and the communists.

★**Michael Llewellyn Smith** *Ionian Vision: Greece in Asia Minor, 1919–22*. Still the best work on the disastrous Anatolian campaign, which led to the population exchanges between Greece and Turkey.

Giles Milton *Paradise Lost: Smyrna 1922 – The Destruction of Islam's City of Tolerance*. Highly readable account of the events that led to what is still known in Greece as the Katastrofí; and which explains much about modern Greek-Turkish relations.

WORLD WAR II AND THE CIVIL WAR

★**David H. Close** *The Origins of the Greek Civil War*. Excellent, even-handed study that focuses on the social conditions in 1920s and 1930s Greece that made the country so ripe for conflict; draws on primary sources to overturn various received wisdoms.

Nicholas Gage *Eleni*. Controversial account by a Greek-born *New York Times* correspondent who returns to Epirus to avenge the death of his mother, condemned by an ELAS tribunal in 1948. Good descriptions of village life, but the book has its agenda and its political "history" is at best selective.

Iakovos Kambanellis, translated by Gail Holst-Warhaft *Mauthausen*. Kambanellis was active in the resistance, caught, and sent to Mauthausen concentration

camp. There are harrowing atrocities in flashback aplenty but the book dwells equally on post-liberation, as the initially idealist inmates realize that the "New World Order" will be scarcely different from the old. The basis of a play and the eponymous Theodhorakis oratorio.

★**Mark Mazower** *Inside Hitler's Greece: The Experience of Occupation 1941–44*. Eccentrically organized, but the scholarship is top-drawer and the photos magnificent. This book demonstrates how the utter demoralization of the country and incompetence of conventional politicians led to the rise of ELAS and the onset of civil war.

★**Eddie Myers** *Greek Entanglement* (o/p). The inside story of sabotaging the Gorgopotamos viaduct by the British brigadier who led it, and lots else about co-ordinating the resistance from 1942–44. Myers comes across as being under no illusions about the various Greek guerrillas he dealt with.

★**C.M. Woodhouse** *The Struggle for Greece, 1941–49* (o/p). Masterly, well-illustrated account of the so-called "three rounds" of resistance and rebellion, and how Greece emerged without a communist government.

ART AND ARCHEOLOGY

Mary Beard *The Parthenon*. Compelling, readable reassessment of the building, both in terms of its real purpose and the possible meaning of its relief sculptures, in light of the discoveries made during its ongoing reconstruction.

John Boardman *Greek Art*. An evergreen study in the *World of Art* series, first published in 1964. For more detailed treatment, there are three period volumes entitled *Greek Sculpture: Archaic Period, Classical Period* and *The Late Classical Period*.

A.R. and Mary Burn *The Living Past of Greece: A Time Traveller's Tour of Historic and Prehistoric Places* (o/p). This wide-ranging guide covers sites from Minoan through to Byzantine and Frankish, with good clear plans and lively text.

Mary Gere *Knossos and the Prophets of Modernism*. Effective debunking of the Knossos restoration, demonstrating in particular how the "Minoan" frescoes are in fact mostly 1920s works by Piet de Jong and Émile Gillieron, heavily influenced by the Art Nouveau and Art Déco movements.

Paul Hetherington *Byzantine and Medieval Greece: Churches, Castles and Art of the Mainland and Peloponnese* (o/p). A gazetteer of all major mainland sites – readable, authoritative and with useful plans. His more recent *The Greek Islands: Guide to Byzantine and Medieval Buildings and their Art*, is equally good, with more illustrations, though there are some peculiar omissions.

BOOKS FOR KIDS

The Greek myths and legends are perfect holiday reading for kids; they're available in a huge number of versions aimed at all ages, often lavishly illustrated.

Terry Deary *Groovy Greeks; Greek Tales;* and the *Fire Thief* trilogy. The first of these is from Deary's familiar *Horrible Histories* series, the three books of *Greek Tales* take a sideways look at famous myths, and the *Fire Thief* is a comedy-fantasy series based on Prometheus, who stole fire from the gods.

Caroline Lawrence *The Roman Mysteries*. The final two volumes of this authentically detailed series of Roman-era mystery books for 8- to 11-year-olds, *The Colossus of Rhodes* and *Fugitive from Corinth*, are set in Greece.

Mary Renault *The King Must Die; The Last of the Wine; The Masks of Apollo; The Praise Singer;* and *The Alexander*

Trilogy. The style may be a tad dense and dated, but these retellings of great Greek stories remain classics of historical fiction.

Rick Riordan *Percy Jackson* series. A modern setting infused with Greek mythology as Percy Jackson, 12 years old and dyslexic, discovers he is the modern-day son of a Greek god. Gripping bestselling tales.

Francesca Simon *Helping Hercules*. Fans of *Horrid Henry* will enjoy this clever retelling of Greek myths by the same author, where young heroine Susan sorts out the not-so-heroic heroes.

GREEK POETRY

Modern Greece has an intense and dynamic **poetic tradition**. Two Greek poets – George Seferis and Odysseus Elytis – have won the Nobel prize in literature; along with C.P. Cavafy, from an earlier generation, and Yiannis Ritsos they are the great names of modern Greek poetry. Good English translations of pretty much all their work are widely available, or try these anthologies:

Peter Bien, Peter Constantine, Edmund Keeley, Karen Van Dyck, eds *A Century of Greek Poetry, 1900–2000* (o/p). Superb bilingual anthology, with some lesser-known surprises alongside the big names.

Nanos Valaoritis and Thanasis Maskaleris, eds *An Anthology of Modern Greek Poetry* (o/p).

English-only text, but excellent biographical info on the poets and good translations by two native Greek-speakers.

Karen Van Dyck, ed *Austerity Measures*. Another wonderful bilingual anthology featuring mostly angst-ridden poetry from the past decade since Greece's economic and social crisis took hold.

Reynold Higgins *Minoan and Mycenaean Art*. Concise, well-illustrated roundup of the culture of Mycenae, Crete and the Cyclades, part of the *World of Art* series.

J. Alexander MacGillivray *Minotaur: Sir Arthur Evans and the Archaeology of the Minoan Myth*. Taking as its starting point Evans' manipulation of the evidence at Knossós to fit his own prejudices and beliefs, this is also a

fascinating look at the development of modern archeology and the history of Crete.

R.R.R. Smith *Hellenistic Sculpture*. Appraisal of the art of Greece under Alexander and his successors; another *World of Art* title.

James Witley *The Archaeology of Ancient Greece*. An excellent, not overly academic overview of current scholarship.

PEOPLE AND CULTURE

★**Bruce Clark** *Twice a Stranger: How Mass Expulsion Forged Modern Greece and Turkey*. The build-up to and execution of the 1923 population exchanges, and how both countries are still digesting the experience nearly a century later. Compassionate and readable, especially the encounters with elderly refugees and oral histories.

Rae Dalven *The Jews of Ioannina* (o/p). History and culture of the thriving pre-Holocaust community, related by the poet-translator of Cavafy, herself an Epirot Jew.

Renée Hirschon *Heirs of the Greek Catastrophe: the Social Life of Asia Minor Refugees in Piraeus*. Ethnography of a district in Kokkinia which maintained a separate identity for three generations after 1923. It's inevitably nostalgic, as increasing wealth has largely dissolved the community, but helps explain why Athens is so higgledy-piggledy.

★**Gail Holst** *Road to Rembetika: Music of a Greek Subculture*. The most intriguing Greek urban musical style of the past century, evocatively traced by a Cornell

University professor and long-term observer of the Greek music scene.

Anastasia Karakasidou *Fields of Wheat, Hills of Blood*. Controversial work establishing how Macedonia only became "Greek" politically and ethnically in the early twentieth century, through an official Hellenization process. Initially declined for publication by Cambridge University Press after ultra-nationalists' threats both in Greece and the diaspora.

John Cuthbert Lawson *Modern Greek Folklore and Ancient Greek Religion: A Study in Survivals*. Exactly as it says: a fascinating, thorough study still applicable a century after first publication.

Mark Mazower *Salonica, City of Ghosts: Christians, Muslims and Jews 1450–1950*. Beautifully written book that masterfully records how this multi-ethnic port, the most cosmopolitan European city under Ottoman rule, became homogeneously Greek Orthodox.

FOOD AND WINE

Andrew Dalby *Food in the Ancient World from A to Z; Siren Feasts: A History of Food and Gastronomy in Greece* (o/p); and *Tastes of Byzantium: The Cuisine of a Legendary Empire* (o/p). All scholarly works, the first of these is literally an A–Z, laid out encyclopedia-style, of ancient foods and food terms. *Siren Feasts* demonstrates just how little Greek cuisine has changed in three millennia, and is also excellent on the introduction and etymology of common vegetables and herbs. *Tastes of*

Byzantium adds the influences of Rome, Turkey and the Middle East.

★ **Diane Kochilas** *The Food and Wine of Greece*. More than 250 classic and modern recipés from the mainland and islands. Kochilas lives much of the year on Ikaría, where she conducts frequent food and cooking workshops.

Konstantinos Lazarakis *The Wines of Greece*. An excellent overview of what's happening in Greece's eleven recognized wine-producing regions, updated in early 2018.

Greek

So many Greeks have lived or worked abroad that you will find English-speaker in the tiniest island village. Add the thousands attending language schools or working in the tourist industry – English is the lingua franca of most resorts – and it's easy to see how so many visitors return home having learned only minimal restaurant vocabulary. You can certainly get by this way, but it isn't very satisfying, and the willingness and ability to say even a few words will transform your status from that of dumb "tourístas" to the more honourable one of "xénos/xéni", which can mean foreigner, traveller and guest all combined.

Learning basic Greek

Greek is not an easy language for English-speakers but it is a very beautiful one, and even a brief acquaintance will give you an idea of the debt owed to it by Western European languages. Greek **grammar** is predictably complicated; **nouns** are divided into three genders, all with different case endings in the singular and in the plural, and all adjectives and articles have to agree with these in gender, number and case. To simplify things, all adjectives are cited in the neuter form in the lists on the following pages. **Verbs** are even more complex; they're in two conjugations, in both active and passive voices, with passively constructed verbs often having transitive sense. As a novice, it's best to simply say what you want the way you know it, and dispense with the niceties.

TEACH-YOURSELF GREEK COURSES

Anne Farmakides *A Manual of Modern Greek, 1, for University Students.* If you have the discipline and motivation, this is among the best for learning proper, grammatical Greek.

Hara Garoufalia et al *Read & Speak Greek for Beginners* (book & CD). Unlike many quickie courses, this provides a good grammatical foundation; new in 2008.

David Holton et al *Greek: A Comprehensive Grammar of the Modern Language.* A bit technical, so not for rank beginners, but it covers almost every conceivable construction.

Alison Kakoura and Karen Rich *Talk Greek* (book and 2 CDs). Probably the best in-print product for beginners' essentials, and for developing the confidence to try them.

Aristarhos Matsukas *Complete Greek: Teach Yourself* (book and optional cassettes or CDs). Another complete course; touches on idiomatic expressions as well.

PHRASEBOOKS AND DICTIONARIES

Collins Pocket Greek Dictionary Harry T. Hionides. Very nearly as complete as the *Pocket Oxford* and probably better value for money. The inexpensive *Collins Gem Greek Dictionary* (UK only) is palm-sized but identical in contents – the best day-pack choice.

The Pocket Oxford Greek Dictionary J. T. Pring. A bit bulky for travel, but generally considered the best Greek–English, English–Greek paperback dictionary.

Rough Guide Phrasebook: Greek Current, accurate and pocket-sized, with phrases that you'll actually need. The English–Greek section is transliterated, though the Greek–English part requires mastery of the Greek alphabet.

The Greek alphabet: transliteration and accents

Besides the usual difficulties of learning a new language, Greek has an entirely separate **alphabet**. Despite initial appearances, this is in practice fairly easily mastered – a skill that will help enormously in getting around independently. In addition, certain combinations of letters have unexpected results. This book's **transliteration system** (see below) should help you make intelligible noises, but remember that the correct **stress** marked throughout the book on any words of more than one syllable with an acute accent or sometimes dieresis) is crucial. With the right sounds but the wrong stress people will either fail to understand you, or else understand something quite different.

The **dieresis** (¨) is used in Greek over the second of two adjacent vowels to change the pronunciation; often in this book it can function as the primary stress. In the word *caïki* (caique), the use of a dieresis changes the pronunciation from "keh-key" to "ka-ee-key". In the word *païdhákia* (lamb chops), the dieresis changes the sound of the first syllable from "peh" to "pah-ee", but in this case the primary stress is on the third syllable. It is also, uniquely among Greek accents, used on capital letters in signs and personal-name spellings in Greece, and we have followed this practice on our maps.

GREEK	TRANSLITERATION	PRONOUNCED
Α, α	a	*a* as in father
Β, β	v	*v* as in vet
Γ, γ	y/g	*y* as in yes except before consonants or a, o or ou when it's a breathy *g*, approximately as in gap
Δ, δ	dh	*th* as in then
Ε, ε	e	*e* as in get
Ζ, ζ	z	*z* sound
Η, η	i	*i* as in ski
Θ, θ	th	*th* as in theme
Ι, ι	i	*i* as in ski
Κ, κ	k	*k* sound
Λ, λ	l	*l* sound
Μ, μ	m	*m* sound
Ν, ν	n	*n* sound
Ξ, ξ	x	*ks* sound, never *z*
Ο, ο	o	*o* as in box
Π, π	p	*p* sound
Ρ, ρ	r	*r* sound, lightly rolled as in Scottish
Σ, σ, ς	s	*ss* sound, except *z* before m or g
Τ, τ	t	*t* sound
Υ, υ	y	*i* as in ski
Φ, φ	f	*f* sound
Χ, χ	h before vowels, denoted kh before consonants but pronounced the same	harsh *h* sound, like *ch* in loch
Ψ, ψ	ps	*ps* as in lips
Ω, ω	o	*o* as in box, indistinguishable from *o*

COMBINATIONS AND DIPHTHONGS

ΑΙ, αι	e	*e* as in get
ΑΥ, αυ	av/af	*av* before voiced consonants and vowels *af* before voiceless consonents
ΕΙ, ει	i	*i* as in ski
ΕΥ, ευ	ev/ef	*ev* before voiced consonants and vowels *ef* before voiceless consonents
ΟΙ, οι	i	*i* as in ski
ΟΥ, ου	ou	*ou* as in tourist
ΓΓ, γγ	ng	*ng* as in angle; always medial
ΜΠ, μπ	b/mb	*b* at start of a word, *mb* if medial
ΝΤ, ντ	d/nd	*d* at start of a word, *nd* if medial

THE QUEST FOR "PURE" GREEK

When Greece achieved independence in 1832, its people were mostly illiterate, and the spoken language – **dhimotikí**, "demotic" or "popular" Greek – had undergone enormous change since the Byzantine and Classical eras. The vocabulary had numerous loan words from the languages of the various invaders and conquerors – especially Turks, Venetians and Slavs – and the grammar had been considerably streamlined since ancient times.

The leaders of the new Greek state, filled with romantic notions of Greece's past glories, set about purging the language of foreign words and reviving its Classical purity. Accordingly, they created what was in effect an artificial language, **katharévoussa** (literally "cleansed" Greek). Long-forgotten words and phrases were reintroduced and complex Classical grammar reinstated. *Katharévoussa* became the language of the schools, government, business, the law, newspapers and academia. Everyone aspiring to membership in the elite strove to master it.

The split between *katharévoussa* and *dhimotikí* quickly took on a **political** dimension, with intellectuals and left-wing politicians championing the demotic form, while the right, notably the colonel's junta of 1967–74, insisted on the "purer" *katharévoussa*. *Dhimotikí* returned permanently after the fall of the colonels, though the Church and the legal profession still persist with *katharévoussa*.

All this has reduced, but not eliminated, confusion. The Metaxás dictatorship of the 1930s changed scores of village names from Slavic, Turkish or Albanian words to Greek ones – often reviving the name of the nearest ancient site. These official **place names** still hold sway on most road signs and maps – even though the local people may use the *dhimotikí* or non-Greek form. Thus for example you will see "Plomárion" or "Ypsoúnda" written, though everyone actually says "Plomári" or "Stemnítsa" respectively.

Polite forms and questions

Greek makes the distinction between the **informal** (*essý*) and **formal** (*essís*) second person, like the French "tu" and "vous". Young people and country people often use *essý* even with total strangers, though it's best to address everyone formally until/unless they start using the familiar with you, to avoid offence. By far the most common greeting, on meeting and parting, is *yiásou/yiásas* (literally "health to you").

To ask a **question**, it's simplest, though hardly elegant, to start with *parakaló* (please), then name the thing you want in an interrogative tone.

GREEK WORDS AND PHRASES

ESSENTIALS

Hérete/Yiásas	Hello	Pos se léne?	What's your name?
Kaliméra	Good morning	Me léne …	My name is …
Kalispéra	Good evening	Kýrios/Kyría	Mr/Mrs
Kaliníkhta	Goodnight	Dhespinís	Miss
Adío	Goodbye	Parakaló, o …?	Where is the …?
Tí kánis/Tí kánete?	How are you?	Dhen xéro	I don't know
Kalá íme	I'm fine	Tha se dho ávrio	See you tomorrow
Ke essís?	And you?	Kalí andhámosi	See you again
Ne	Yes	Páme	Let's go
Óhi	No	Parakaló, na me voithíste	Please help me
Parakaló	Please	(Dhen) Trógo/píno	I (don't) eat/drink
Efharistó (polý)	Thank you (very much)	(Dhen) Mou aréssi	I (don't) like
Sygnómi	Sorry/excuse me	Stinyásas!	Cheers!
Miláte angliká?	Do you speak English?	Málista	Certainly
(Dhén) Katalavéno	I (don't) understand	Endáxi	OK, agreed
Parakaló, na milísate pió sigá	Speak slower, please	Anikhtó	Open
		Klistó	Closed
Pos léyete aftó sta Ellinká?	How do you say it in Greek?	Méra	Day
		Níkhta	Night
		Edhó	Here

kí	There
irígora	Quickly
igá	Slowly
ou?	Where?
os?	How?
óte?	When?
iatí?	Why?
Ti óra … ?	At what time … ?
Ti íne/Pió íne … ?	What is/Which is … ?

ACCOMMODATION

Parakaló, éna dhomátio	We'd like a room
yiá éna/dhýo/tría átoma	for one/two/three people
yiá mía/dhýo/tris vradhiés	for one/two/three nights
me dhipló kreváti	with a double bed
me dous	with a shower
Xenodhohío	Hotel
Xenónas	Guesthouse
Xenónas neótitas	Youth hostel
Zestó neró	Hot water
Krýo neró	Cold water
Klimatismós	Air conditioning
Anemistíra	Fan
Boró na to dho?	Can I see it?
Boroúme na váloume ti skiní edhó?	Can we camp here?
Kámping/Kataskínosi	Campsite

SHOPPING AND SERVICES

Póso (káni)?	How much (does it cost)?
Tí óra aníyi/ klíni?	What time does it open/close?
Parakaló, éna kiló portokália?	May I have a kilo of oranges?
Póssi, pósses or póssa?	How many?
Aftó	This one
Ekíno	That one
Kaló	Good
Kakó	Bad
Megálo	Big
Mikró	Small
Perisótero	More
Ligótero	Less
Lígo	A little
Polý	A lot
Ftinó	Cheap
Akrivó	Expensive
Mazí (me)	With (together)
Horís	Without
Magazí	Shop
Farmakío	Pharmacy
Tahydhromío	Post office
Gramatósima	Stamps
Venzinádhiko	Petrol station
Trápeza	Bank
Leftá/Khrímata	Money
Toualéta	Toilet
Astynomía	Police
Yiatrós	Doctor
Nosokomío	Hospital

ON THE MOVE

Parakaló, o dhrómos yiá … ?	Can you show me the road to … ?
Aeropláno	Aeroplane
Leoforío, poúlman	Bus, coach
Aftokínito, amáxi	Car
Mihanáki, papáki	Motorbike, scooter
Taxí	Taxi
Plío/vapóri/karávi	Ship, ferry
Tahyplóö, katamarán	High-speed boat, catamaran
Dhelfíni	Hydrofoil
Tréno	Train
Sidhirodhromikós stathmós	Train station
Podhílato	Bicycle
Otostóp	Hitching
Mé ta pódhia	On foot
Monopáti	Trail, path
Praktorío leoforíon KTEL	Bus station
Stási	Bus stop
Limáni	Harbour
Ti óra févyi?	What time does it leave?
Ti óra ftáni?	What time does it arrive?
Póssa hiliómetra?	How many kilometres?
Pósses óres?	How many hours?
Pou páte/pas?	Where are you going?
Páo sto …	I'm going to …
Thélo na katévo sto …	I want to get off at …
O dhrómos yiá …	The road to …
Kondá	Near
Makriá	Far
Aristerá	Left
Dhexiá	Right
Katefthía/ísia	Straight ahead
Éna isitírio yiá …	A ticket to …
Éna isitírio apló/ mé epistrofí	A ticket one-way/return
Paralía	Beach
Spiliá	Cave
Kéndro	Centre (of town)
Eklissía	Church
Thálassa	Sea
Horió	Village

GREEK'S GREEK

There are numerous words and phrases which you will hear constantly, even if you don't have the chance to use them. These are a few of the most common.

Éla! Come (literally) but also Speak to me! You don't say! etc.

Oríste! Literally, Define!; in effect, What can I do for you? Say that again, when used interrogatively. Also used as phone response.

Embrós! More phone responses
/Léyete!

Tí néa? What's new?

Tí yínete? What's going on?

Étsi k'étsi So-so

Ópa! Whoops! Watch it!

Po-po-po! Expression of dismay or concern, like French "O là là!"

Pedhí moú My boy/girl, sonny, friend, etc.

Maláka(s) Literally "wanker", but often used (don't try it!) as an informal term of address

Sigá sigá Take your time, slow down

Kaló taxídhi Bon voyage

NUMBERS

énas/mía/éna	1
dhýo	2
tris/tría	3
tésseri/tésseres/téssera	4
pénde	5
éxi	6
eftá	7
okhtó	8
ennéa (or, in slang, enyiá)	9
dhéka	10
éndheka	11
dhódheka	12
dhekatrís/ía	13
dhekatésseri/es/a	14
dhekapénde	15
íkossi	20
íkossi éna	21
triánda	30
saránda	40
penínda	50
exínda	60
evdhomínda	70
ogdhónda	80
enenínda	90
ekató	100
ekatón penínda	150
dhiakóssies/ia	200
pendakóssies/ia	500
hílies/hília	1000
dhýo hiliádhes	2000
prótos/próti/próto	first
dhéfteros/i/o	second
trítos/i/o	third

TIME AND DAYS OF THE WEEK

Tóra	Now
Argótera	Later
Símera	Today
Ávrio	Tomorrow
Khthés	Yesterday
Tó proï	In the morning
Tó apóyevma	In the afternoon
Tó vrádhi	In the evening
Kyriakí	Sunday
Dheftéra	Monday
Tríti	Tuesday
Tetárti	Wednesday
Pémpti	Thursday
Paraskeví	Friday
Sávato	Saturday
Tí óra íne?	What time is it?
Mía iy óra/dhýo iy óraa /trís iy ór	One/two/three o'clock
Tésseres pará íkossi	Twenty minutes to four
Eftá ke pénde	Five minutes past seven
Éndheka ke misí	Half past eleven
Se misí óra	In half an hour
S'éna tétarto	In a quarter-hour
Se dhýo óres	In two hours

MONTHS AND SEASONS

Yennáris/Ianouários	January
Fleváris/Fevouários	February
Mártis/Mártios	March
Aprílis	April
Maïos	May
Ioúnios	June
Ioúlios	July
Ávgoustos	August
Septémvris/ios	September
Októvris/ios	October
Noémvris/ios	November
Dhekémvris/ios	December
Therinó dhromolóyio	Summer schedule
Himerinó dhromolóyio	Winter schedule

A food and drink glossary

BASICS

Katálogos	Menu
O logariasmós	The bill
Merídha	Portion
Zestó	Hot
Krýo	Cold
('Horís) ládhi	(Without) oil
Hýma	Bulk (wine, olives etc)
Varelísio/a	Barrelled wine/beer
Hortofágos	Vegetarian
Kréas	Meat
Lahaniká	Vegetables
Neró	Water
Psári(a)	Fish
Thalassiná	Seafood
Mezédhes	Small plates of various food, dips etc
Orektiká	Starters
Pikilía	Mixed selection on plate
Aláti	Salt
Pipéri	Pepper (condiment)
Avgá	Eggs
Méli	Honey
Psomí ...	Bread ...
Olikís	Wholemeal
Sikalísio	Rye
Kalambokísio	Corn
Tyrí	Cheese
Yiaoúrti	Yoghurt
Záhari	Sugar
Zaharíni	Sweetener

FOOD SHOPS, RESTAURANTS AND BARS

Baráki	Bar
Estiatório/Inomayiría	Old-style restaurant mainly featuring baked dishes
Exohikó kéndro	Out-of-town restaurant
Foúrnos	Bakery
Galaktopolío	Café specializing in dairy products
Mezedhopolío	Restaurant specializing in mezédhes
Ouzerí	Restaurant specializing in ouzo and mezédhes
Patsatzídhiko	Restaurant specializing in tripe soup
Psarotavérna	Specialist fish taverna
Psistariá	Grill house
Souvlatzídhiko	Souvláki shop
Tsipourádhiko	Restaurant specializing in *tsípouro* and mezédhes

Zaharoplastío	Patisserie, confectionary shop

COOKING TERMS

Akhnistó	Steamed
Frikasé	Stew, either lamb, goat or pork, with celery
Iliókafto	Sun-dried
Kokkinistó	Cooked in tomato sauce
Kourkoúti	Egg-and-flour batter
Krasáto	Cooked in wine sauce
Ladherá	Vegetables cooked in an oily sauce
Ladholémono	Oil and lemon sauce
Makaronádha	Any spaghetti/pasta-based dish
Mayireftá	Traditional oven-baked dish
Pastó	Fish marinated in salt
Petáli	Butterflied fish, eel, shrimp
Psitó	Roasted
Saganáki	Cheese-based red sauce; also fried cheese
(Tis) Skáras	Grilled
Sti soúvla	Spit-roasted
Sto foúrno	Baked
Tiganitó	Pan-fried
Tís óras	Grilled/fried to order
Yakhní	Stewed in oil and tomato sauce
Yemistá	Stuffed (squid, vegetables, etc)

SOUPS, STARTERS AND SNACKS

Avgolémono	Egg and lemon soup
Bouréki, bourekákia	Courgette/zucchini, potato and cheese pie
Dolmádhes, yaprákia; yalantzí	Vine leaves stuffed with rice and mince; with vegetables
Fasoládha	Bean soup
Fáva	Purée of yellow peas
Féta psití	Baked feta cheese slabs with chilli
Galotýri	Curdled creamy dip
Hortópita	Pastry stuffed with greens
Kápari	Pickled caper leaves
Kopanistí, khtypití	Pungent, fermented cheese purée
Kreatópita	Meat pie, usually with mince

Lahanodolmádhes	Stuffed cabbage leaves
Loukanoukópita	Sausage roll
Mavromátika	Black-eyed peas
Melitzanosaláta	Aubergine/eggplant dip
Piperiés florínes	Marinated sweet peppers
Rengosaláta	Herring salad
Revythokeftédhes	Chickpea/garbanzo patties
Skordhaliá	Garlic dip
Soúpa	Soup
Spanakópita	Spinach pie, usually with cheese
Strapatsádha	Eggs scrambled with tomato and onions
Taramosaláta	Cod roe pâté
Tiganópsomo	Toasted oiled bread
Trahanádhes	Crushed wheat and milk soup, sweet or savoury
Tyrokafterí	Cheese dip with chilli
Tyrópita	Cheese pie
Tyropitákia	Small fried cheese pies
Tzatzíki	Yoghurt and cucumber dip
Tzirosaláta	Cured mackerel dip

VEGETABLES

Ambelofásola	Runner beans
Anginá res	Artichokes
Angoúri	Cucumber
Ánitho	Dill
Bámies	Okra/ladies' fingers
Briám, tourloú	Ratatouille
Domátes	Tomatoes
Fakés	Lentils
Fasolákia	French (green) beans
Fasóles	Small white beans
Horiátiki (saláta)	Greek salad (with olives, feta, etc)
Hórta	Steamed greens
Kolokythákia	Courgette/zucchini
Koukiá	Broad fava beans
Láhano	Cabbage
Maroúli	Lettuce
Melitzánes imám/ Imám baïldí	Aubergine/eggplant slices baked with onion, garlic and copious olive oil
Patátes	Potatoes
Patzária	Beetroot
Piperiés	Peppers
Pligoúri, pinigoúri	Bulgur wheat
Radhíkia	Wild chicory
Róka	Rocket, arugula
Rýzi/Piláfi sáltsa	Rice (usually with sauce)
Saláta	Salad
Spanáki	Spinach
Yígandes	White haricot beans

FISH AND SEAFOOD

Ahini, foúskes	Sea urchins
Astakós	Lobster
Atherína	Sand smelt
Bakaliáros	Cod or hake, usually latter
Barbóuni	Red mullet
Fangrí	Common bream
Galéos	Dogfish
Garídhes	Shrimp, prawns
Gávros	Mild anchovy
Glóssa	Sole
Gónos, gonákia	Any hatchling fish
Gópa	Bogue
Hokhlí	Sea snails
Kakaviá	Bouillabaisse
Kalamarákia	Baby squid
Kalamária	Squid
Karavídhes	Crayfish
Koliós	Chub mackerel
Koutsomoúra	Goatfish (small red mullet)
Lakérdha	Light-fleshed bonito, marinated
Lithríni	Red bream, pandora
Melanoúri	Saddled bream
Ménoula	Sprat
Mýdhia	Mussels
Okhtapódhi	Octopus
Petalídhes	Limpets
Platý	Skate, ray
Psarósoupa	Fish soup
Sardhélles	Sardines
Sargós	White bream
Seláhi	Skate, ray
Sfyrídha	White grouper
Skáros	Parrotfish
Skathári	Black bream
Skoumbrí	Atlantic mackerel
Soupiá	Cuttlefish
Strídhia	Oysters
Thrápsalo	Large, deep-water squid
Tónos	Tuna
Tsipoúra	Gilt-head bream
Xifías	Swordfish
Yermanós	Leatherback
Yialisterés	Smooth Venus shellfish

MEAT AND POULTRY

Arní/arnáki	Lamb
Bekrí mezé	Pork chunks in spicy pepper sauce

iftéki	Hamburger
rizóla hiriní	Pork chop
rizóla moskharísia	Beef chop
xohikó/Kléftiko	Lamb baked in tin foil or in pastry
rigadhéli	Minced meat dumplings
Gourounópoulo	Suckling pig roast on a spit
Hirinó	Pork
Kalamáki	Small kebab on a wooden skewer
Katsíki/Yídha	Goat
Keftédhes	Meatballs
Kókoras krasáto	Coq au vin
Kokorétsi	Liver/offal roulade, spit-roasted
Kondosoúvli	Spit-roasted pork
Kopsídha	(Lamb) shoulder chops
Kotópoulo	Chicken
Kounéli	Rabbit
Loukánika	Spicy course-ground sausages
Moskhári	Veal
Moussakás	Aubergine/eggplant, potato and lamb-mince casserole with béchamel topping
Païdhákia	Rib chops, lamb or goat
Pantséta	Pork belly
Papoutsákia	Stuffed aubergine /eggplant "shoes"
Pastítsio	Macaroni "pie" baked with minced meat
Pastourmás	Cured, highly spiced beef
Patsás	Tripe soup
Patsitsádha	beef with pasta in wine sauce
Provatína	Female mutton
Psaronéfri	Pork tenderloin medallions
Salingária	Garden snails
Sofríto	beef fried in garlic sauce
Soutzoukákia	Minced meat rissoles/ beef patties
Souvláki	Any type of kebab
Spetzofáï	Sausage and pepper stew
Stifádho	Meat stew with tomato and boiling onions
Sykóti	Liver
Tiganiá	Pork chunks fried with onions
Yiouvétsi	Baked clay casserole of meat and pasta
Yíros	Rotisserie meat, usually pork

SWEETS AND DESSERT

Baklavás	Honey and nut pastry
Bergamóndo	Bergamot
Bougátsa	Sweet cream pie served warm with sugar and cinnamon. Can be savoury in north.
Galaktoboúreko	Custard pie
Glyká koutalioú	Spoon sweet (syrupy fruit preserve)
Halvás	Semolina- or sesame-based sweet
Kataïfi	Honey-soaked "shredded wheat"
Karydhópita	Walnut cake
Kréma	Custard
Loukoumádhes	Dough fritters in honey syrup and sesame seeds
Pagotó	Ice cream
Pastélli	Sesame and honey bar
Ravaní	Sponge cake, lightly syruped
Rizógalo	Rice pudding
Sandiyí	Whipped cream

FRUITS

Akhládhi	Big pear
Aktinídhi	Kiwi fruit
Fystíkia	Pistachio nuts
Fráoules	Strawberries
Karpoúzi	Watermelon
Kerásia	Cherries
Krystália	Miniature pears
Kydhóni	Quince
Lemóni	Lemon
Mílo	Apple
Pepóni	Melon
Portokáli	Orange
Rodhákino	Peach
Sýka	Figs
Stafýlia	Grapes

CHEESE

Ayeladhinó	Cow's-milk cheese
Féta	Salty, creamy white cheese
(Kefalo) graviéra	(Extra-hard) Gruyère-type cheese
Katsikísio	Goat cheese
Kasséri	Medium-sharp cheese

Myzíthra	Sweet cream cheese
Próvio	Sheep cheese

DRINKS

Boukáli	Bottle
Býra	Beer
Gála	Milk
Galakakáo	Chocolate milk
Kafés	Coffee
Krasí	Wine
áspro/lefkó	white
kokkinélli/rozé	rosé

kókkino	red
Limonádha	Lemonade
Metalikó neró	Mineral water
Portokaládha	Orangeade
Potíri	Glass
Rakí/Tsikoudhiá	Clear Cretan spirit
Retsína	Wine made with added pine resin
Tsáï	Tea
Tsáï vounoú	"Mountain" (mainland sage) tea
Tsípouro	Clear strong spirit

Glossary

Acropolis Ancient, fortified hilltop.

Agora Market and meeting place of an ancient Greek city; also the "high street" of a modern village (**agorá** in modern Greek).

Amphora Tall, narrow-necked jar for oil or wine.

Áno Upper; common prefix of village names.

Apse Curved recess at the east end of a church nave.

Archaic period Late Iron Age period, from around 750 BC to the start of the Classical period in the fifth century BC.

Arhondikó A lordly stone mansion, often restored as boutique accommodation.

Astikó (Intra) city, municipal, local; adjective applied to phone calls and bus services.

Ayíasma A sacred spring, usually flowing out of church foundations.

Áyios/Ayía/Áyii (m/f/plural). Saint or holy. Common place-name prefix (abbreviated Ag or Ay), often spelled **Agios** or **Aghios**.

Basilica Colonnaded, "hall-" or "barn-" type church adapted from Roman models, most common in northern Greece.

Bema Rostrum for a church oratory.

Bouleuterion Auditorium for meetings of an ancient town's deliberative council.

Bouzoúki Most common Greek stringed musical instrument.

Capital The flared top, often ornamented, of a column.

Cavea Seating curve of an ancient theatre.

Cella Sacred room of a temple, housing the cult image.

Classical period From the end of the Persian Wars in 480 BC until the unification of Greece under Philip II of Macedon (338 BC).

Conch Concave semi-dome surmounting a church apse, often frescoed.

Corinthian Decorative columns, festooned with acanthus florettes; any temple built in this order.

Dhimarhío Town hall.

Dhomátia Rooms for rent in purpose-built block, without staffed reception.

Dorian Northern civilization that displaced and succeeded the Mycenaeans and Minoans through most of Greece around 1100 BC.

DIALECTS AND MINORITY LANGUAGES

Ancient **dialects** survive in many remote areas of Greece, some quite incomprehensible to outsiders. The dialect of Sfákia in Crete is one such; Tsakónika of the east-central Peloponnese is another, while the dialect of the Sarakatsáni shepherds is apparently the oldest, related to the language of the Dorian settlers.

The language of the Sarakatsáni's traditional rivals, the **Vlachs**, is not Greek at all, but derived from early Latin, with strong affinities to Romanian. In the regions bordering the Republic of Macedonia and southwestern Bulgaria, you can still hear **Slavic Macedonian** spoken, while small numbers of Sephardic Jews in the north speak **Ladino**, a medieval form of Spanish. Until a few decades ago, **Arvanítika** – a dialect of medieval Albanian – was the first language of many villages of inland Attica, southern Évvia, northern Ándhros, and much of the Argo-Saronic; lately the clock has been turned back, so to speak, as throngs of Albanian immigrants circulate in Athens and other parts of the country. In Thrace, there is a substantial **Turkish-speaking** population, as well as some speakers of **Pomak** (a derivative of Bulgarian with a large Greco-Turkish vocabulary), while Gypsies countrywide speak Romany.

Doric Minimalist, unadorned columns, dating from the Dorian period; any temple built in this order.

Drum Cylindrical or faceted vertical section, usually pierced by an even number of narrow windows, upholding a church cupola.

Entablature The horizontal linking structure atop the columns of an ancient temple; same as **architrave**.

Eparhía Subdivision of a modern province, analogous to a county.

Exedra Display niche for statuary.

Exonarthex The outer vestibule or entrance hall of a church, when a true **narthex** is present.

Forum Market and meeting place of a Roman-era city.

Frieze Band of sculptures around a temple. Doric friezes consist of various tableaux of figures (**metopes**) interspersed with grooved panels (**triglyphs**); Ionic ones have continuous bands of figures.

Froúrio Medieval citadel; nowadays, can mean a modern military headquarters.

Garsoniéra/es Studio villa/s, self-catering apartment/s.

Geometric period Post-Mycenaean Iron Age era named for its pottery style; starts in the early eleventh century BC with the arrival of Dorian peoples. By the eighth century BC, with development of representational styles, the **Archaic period** begins.

Hammam Domed "Turkish" bath, found on Rhodes and certain northeast Aegean islands.

Hellenistic period The last and most unified "Greek empire", created in the wake of Alexander the Great's Macedonian empire and finally collapsing with the fall of Corinth to the Romans in 146 BC.

Heroön Shrine or sanctuary-tomb, usually of a demigod or mortal; war memorials in modern Greece.

Hóra Main town of an island or region; literally it means "the place". A hóra is often known by the same name as the island.

Ierón The sanctuary between the altar screen and the apse of a church, reserved for priestly activities.

Ikonostási Wood or masonry screen between the nave of a church and the altar, supporting at least three icons.

Ionic Elaborate, decorative development of the older **Doric** order; Ionic temple columns are slimmer, with deeper "fluted" edges, spiral-shaped capitals and ornamental bases.

Kafenío Coffee house or café.

Kaïki (plural **kaïkia**) Caique, or medium-sized boat, traditionally wooden and used for transporting cargo and passengers; now refers mainly to island excursion boats.

Kalderími A cobbled mule-track or footpath.

Kámbos Fertile agricultural plain, usually near a river mouth.

Kantína Shack, caravan or even a disused bus on the beach, serving drinks and perhaps sandwiches or quick snacks.

Kástro Any fortified hill, but most often the oldest, highest, walled-in part of an island hóra, intended to protect civilians.

Katholikón Central church of a monastery.

Káto Lower; common prefix of village names.

Kendrikí platía Central square.

Kouros Nude Archaic statue of an idealized young man, usually portrayed with one foot slightly in front of the other.

Megaron Principal hall or throne room of a Mycenaean palace.

Meltémi North wind that blows across the Aegean in summer, starting softly from near the mainland and hitting the Cyclades, the Dodecanese and Crete full on.

Metope see **Frieze**.

Minoan Crete's great Bronze Age civilization which dominated the Aegean from about 2500 to 1400 BC.

Moní Formal term for a monastery or convent.

Moreas Medieval term for the Peloponnese; the peninsula's outline was likened to the leaf of a mulberry tree, *mouriá* in Greek.

Mycenaean Mainland civilization centred on Mycenae and the Argolid from about 1700 to 1100 BC.

Naos The inner sanctum of an ancient temple; also, the central area of an Orthodox Christian church.

Narthex Western vestibule of a church, reserved for catechumens and the unbaptized; typically frescoed with scenes of the Last Judgement.

Neolithic Earliest era of settlement in Greece; characterized by use of stone tools and weapons together with basic agriculture. Divided arbitrarily into Early (c.6000 BC), Middle (c.5000 BC) and Late (c.3000 BC).

Néos, Néa, Néo "New" – a common prefix to a town or village name.

Nomós Modern Greek province – there are more than fifty of them. Village bus services are organized according to their borders.

Odeion Small theatre, used for musical performances, minor dramatic productions or councils.

Orchestra Circular area in a theatre where the chorus would sing and dance.

Palaestra Gymnasium for athletics and wrestling practice.

Paleós, Paleá, Paleó "Old" – again a common prefix in town and village names.

Panayía Virgin Mary.

Pandokrátor Literally "The Almighty"; generally refers to the stern portrayal of Christ in Majesty frescoed or in mosaic in the dome of many Byzantine churches.

Paniyíri Festival or feast – the local celebration of a holy day.

Paralía Beach, or seafront promenade.

Pediment Triangular, sculpted gable below the roof of a temple.

Pendentive Triangular sections of vaulting with concave sides, positioned at a corner of a rectangular space to support a circular or polygonal dome; in churches, often adorned with frescoes of the four Evangelists.

Períptero Street kiosk.

Peristereónes Pigeon towers, in the Cyclades.

Peristyle Gallery of columns around a temple or other building.

Pinakothíki Picture gallery, ancient or modern.

Pithos (plural **pithoi**) Large ceramic jar for storing oil, grain, etc. Very common in Minoan palaces and used in almost identical form in modern Greek homes.

Platía Square, plaza.

Polygonal masonry Wall-building technique of Classical and Hellenistic periods, using unmortared, closely joined stones; often called "Lesvian polygonal" after the island where the method supposedly originated. The much-(ab)used term **Cyclopean** refers only to Bronze Age mainland sites such as Tiryns and Mycenae.

Propylaion Monumental columned gateway of an ancient building; often used in the plural, **propylaia**.

Pýrgos Tower or bastion; also tower-mansions found in the Máni or on Lésvos.

Skála The port of an inland island settlement, nowadays often larger and more important than its namesake, but always younger since built after the disappearance of piracy.

Skyládhiko Rough-and-ready live bouzouki club.

Squinch Small concavity across a corner of a column-less interior space, which supports a superstructure such as a dome.

Stele Upright stone slab or column, usually inscribed with an edict; also an ancient tombstone, with a relief scene.

Stoa Colonnaded walkway in Classical-to-Roman-era marketplaces.

Távli Backgammon; a favourite café pastime, especially among the young. There are two more difficult local variations (*févga* and *plakotó*) in addition to the standard international game (*pórtes*).

Telestirion Shrine associated with ancient mystery rituals.

Témblon Wooden altar screen of an Orthodox church, usually ornately carved and painted and studded with icons; more or less interchangeable with **ikonostási**.

Temenos Sacred precinct of ancient temple, often used to refer to the sanctuary itself.

Theatral area Open area found in most of the Minoan palaces with seat-like steps around. Probably a type of theatre or ritual area.

Tholos Conical or beehive-shaped building, eg a Mycenaean tomb.

Triglyph see **Frieze**.

Tympanum The recessed space, flat or carved in relief, inside a pediment.

Votsalotó Mosaic of coloured pebbles, found in church or house courtyards of the Dodecanese and Spétses.

Yperastikó Long-distance – as in bus services.

ACRONYMS

ANEK Anónymi Navtiliakí Etería Krítis (Shipping Co of Crete, Ltd), which runs most ferries between Pireás and Crete, plus many to Italy.

EAM National Liberation Front, the political force behind ELAS.

ELAS Popular Liberation Army, the main Resistance group during World War II and predecessor of the Communist army during the civil war.

ELTA Postal service.

EOS Greek Mountaineering Federation, based in Athens.

EOT Ellinikós Organismós Tourismoú, National Tourist Organization.

KKE Communist Party, unreconstructed.

KTEL National syndicate of bus companies; also refers to individual bus stations.

LANE Lasithiakí Anónymi Navtiliakí Etería (Lasithian Shipping Company Ltd), based in eastern Crete.

ND Conservative (Néa Dhimokratía) party.

NEL Navtiliakí Etería Lésvou (Lesvian Shipping Co).

OSE Railway corporation.

OTE Telecommunications company.

PASOK Socialist party (Pan-Hellenic Socialist Movement).

SEO Greek Mountaineering Club, based in Thessaloníki.

SYRIZA Synaspismós tis Rizospastikís Aristerás (Coalition of the Radical Left) – alternative, "Euro"-Socialist party.

Rough Guide credits

Editor: Amanda Tomlin
Layout: Ankur Guha
Cartography: Katie Bennett and Rajesh Mishra
Picture editors: Yoshimi Kanazawa and Aude Vauconsant
Managing editor: Monica Woods

Cover photo research: Nicole Newman
Photographers: Chris Christoforou, Geoff Garvey and Michelle Grant

Publishing information

This fifteenth edition published May 2018 by
Rough Guides Ltd

Distribution

UK, Ireland and Europe
Apa Publications (UK) Ltd; sales@roughguides.com
United States and Canada
Ingram Publisher Services; ips@ingramcontent.com
Australia and New Zealand
Woodslane; info@woodslane.com.au
Southeast Asia
Apa Publications (SN) Pte; sales@roughguides.com
Worldwide
Apa Publications (UK) Ltd; sales@roughguides.com
Special sales, content licensing and co-publishing
Rough Guides can be purchased in bulk quantities
at discounted prices. We can create special editions,
personalized jackets and corporate imprints tailored to
your needs. sales@roughguides.com
roughguides.com
Printed in China

840pp includes index
A catalogue record for this book is available from the
British Library
ISBN: 978-0-2-4130-642-0
The publishers and authors have done their best to
ensure the accuracy and currency of all the information in
The Rough Guide to Greece, however, they can accept
no responsibility for any loss, injury, or inconvenience
sustained by any traveller as a result of information or
advice contained in the guide.
1 3 5 7 9 8 6 4 2

Help us update

We've gone to a lot of effort to ensure that the fifteenth
edition of **The Rough Guide to Greece** is accurate and up-
to-date. However, things change – places get "discovered",
opening hours are notoriously fickle, restaurants and
rooms raise prices or lower standards. If you feel we've got
it wrong or left something out, we'd like to know, and if
you can remember the address, the price, the hours, the
phone number, so much the better.

Please send your comments with the subject line
"**Rough Guide Greece Update**" to mail@uk.roughguides
.com. We'll credit all contributions and send a copy of the
next edition (or any other Rough Guide if you prefer) for
the very best emails.

ABOUT THE AUTHORS

Nick Edwards Since graduating in Classics & Modern Greek from Oxford, Nick spent many years living in Athens and travelling widely, especially in India. He later settled in Pittsburgh with spouse Maria, until they returned to his native south London in 2008. He's a lifelong Spurs fan, psych music aficionado and believer in universal Oneness.

John Fisher was one of the authors of the first ever Rough Guide – to Greece – and has been inextricably linked with the series ever since, much of the time stuck in the office. Now living in London with his wife, Adrienne, and two sons, he is a freelance writer, editor and dispute mediator.

Rebecca Hall divides her time between her native UK and Greece. She teaches English part time, is a travel writer, and proud contributor to the Rough Guide series. Her debut novel *Girl Gone Greek* can be found on Amazon, and you can follow her adventures at www.lifebeyondbordersblog.com.

John Malathronas is a travel writer and photographer who has published three travelogues with Summersdale Publishing and co-authored ten guidebooks for Michelin and the Rough Guides. He has written for *CNN Travel*, the *Daily Telegraph*, *The Daily Mail*, *The Independent*, *The Sunday Times* and *National Geographic Traveller*, as well as for publications in the US, Canada and Australia. He has a popular blog, *The Jolly Traveller*, speaks several languages and is active on social media, tweeting and blogging as he moves around our planet.

Martin Zatko has written or contributed to over thirty Rough Guides, including those to Korea, China, Japan, Vietnam, Myanmar, Taiwan, Turkey, Morocco, Europe and Fiji. Some of those guides have been written in Greece, a land whose beaches, floral fragrances and general tranquillity Martin finds rather conducive to clarity of thought.

Acknowledgements

Nick Edwards would like to thank the following people and establishments for hospitality along the way: The Excelsior Hotel and Hoppy Pub in Thessaloníki; Maria & Vassilis of Papanikolaou Hostel and Vangelis of To Pazari in Litóhoro; Theodoros of Irtha & Edessa in Édhessa; Petros of Keletron, Xenia & Yiorgos of Allahou Guest House and Mihalis of Nostalgia in Kastoriá, the Imaret, O Kanados and Gorgones ke Manges in Kavála; on Corfu, Kostas of Boukari Beach, Petros & Mariana in Horepiskopi, Christos of Fagopotion in Áyios Stéfanos, the Palia Perithia taverna, and the Venetian Well; on Lefkádha, Spyros of Pension Holidays and Nassia of Vangelaras in Vassilikí, 12 Gods in Syvota, John's Eatery in Atháni and Maria of Ionian Paradise in Nydhrí; on Kefaloniá, Andronikos of Kyani Akti in Argostóli for the super seafood feast, and Lagoudera and Regina's in Fiskárdho; Martha, Deni and family of Pansion Limni on Zákynthos. Special thanks to old pals Graham and Gordon & co for expert driving and company on various islands. Cheers to Steve & Yiota, Vasso & Yiorgos, Emmie & Fotis, Yiannis & Eleftheria, Vassilis & Rhea (plus families) and Tracey for making the post-RG tour very enjoyable. Finally, thanks for continuing support to Maria.

Rebecca Hall would like to thank the people of the Dodecanese islands who made sure that her research was enjoyable and taught her the Greek way of relaxing, with a frappé in hand watching the world; special thanks to Adriana of Triton Tours in Rhodes, for her unprecedented knowledge of ferries and ticketing advice: also thanks to the people of Kos who worked tirelessly to help all tourists after the 2017 earthquake; and to Angela and Nikos who have become like family; and, of course, the Rough Guides editors and team who helped her through the process of this new edition.

John Malathronas would like to thank Dudley der Parthog, Olivia Eftaxopoulos, Birgit Feger, Argy Kakissis, Anastassia Deligianni, Makis Bitsios, George Tziachris, Stephanie Milliken, Effie Moskofoglou, Maria & Stelios Parasiri , Phoebe Irving, Yannis Klaras, Dimitris Lianos, Vassilia Orfanou, Natasha Sá Osório, Eleni Politou, Theodoros & Thanasis Drakakis, Thanassis Kranas and Yorgos Troullos.

Martin Zatko would like to thank the owners and staff at every place he stayed at for their kindness and useful advice, including Stefanos and Elli on Samos, Gavriil on Fourni, Triantafillia on Ikaria, Theodore and George on Hios, Iannis and Argiris on Lesvos, Afroditi on Limnos, Eleni on Thassos, Dita in Kalambaka, Ioannis in Metsovo, Antonios in Dilofo, Lichnos Beach in Parga, Jenny and Christina in Nafpaktos, Chrisoula in Galaxhidi, Giorgos and Efi in Delphi, and Andrinos and Miltos in the Pelion. He would also like to thank Amanda Tomlin for her editing work, and Monica Woods for giving him the chance to work on such an exciting project.

Readers' updates

Thanks to all the readers who have taken the time to write in with comments and suggestions (and apologies if we've inadvertently omitted or misspelt anyone's name):

David Authers; Anait Chrysafi; Rob Coleman; Chris Dawes; Carl Dawson; Dominic Green; Ivan Helmer; Frank James; Paul Hansen; Ian Jennings; Martin Nan; Manolis Petinarakis; Steve Scoffield; Carola Scupham; Brian Shepherd; Nicholas Sloan; Monica Tweddell; Triantafyllos Vaitsis; and Sue Wake.

Photo credits

Cover Firostefáni, Santoríni **AWL Images** Gerhard Zwerger-Schoner

1 AWL Images Ltd: Robert Birkby
2 AWL Images: Neil Farrin
4 iStockphoto: Getty Images / Kisa Markiza
5 Shutterstock: leoks
9 Shutterstock: TalyaPhoto (tr); Anastasios71 (b)
10 iStockphoto: Getty Images / BDphoto
11 Superstock: robertharding (t); iStockphoto: Getty Images / Paul Cowan (c); Getty Images / mango2friendly (b)
12 Shutterstock: Mila Atkovska
13 iStockphoto: Getty Images / Simon Bradfield (t); Getty Images / AlbertoLoyo (b)
14 iStockphoto: Getty Images / Freeartist (t); Shutterstock: Pierdelune (b)
15 Getty Images: Robert Harding / Stuart Black (t); Corbis / Ted Horowitz (b)
16 iStockphoto: Getty Images / f8grapher (t); Getty Images: LOOK-foto / Juergen Richter (bl); Shutterstock: Veniamakis Stefanos (br)
17 Getty Images: Roger Wilmshurst (t); iStockphoto: Getty Images / Siempreverde22 (c)
18 Shutterstock: elgreko (t); iStockphoto: Getty Images / Panos Karapanagiotis (b)
19 iStockphoto: Getty Images / vasiliki (t); Getty Images / Starcevic (br)
20 iStockphoto: Getty Images / Lemonan (tl); Getty Images / efilippou (tr); Getty Images / Saso Novoselic (b)
21 SuperStock: KokkasIML (t); iStockphoto: Getty Images / Jana Janina (c); Shutterstock: Anton Zelenov (b)
22 Shutterstock: Zenobillis
59 Shutterstock: Lefteris Papaulakis
73 Shutterstock: Milan Gonda (tl); EQRoy (b)
107 Getty Images: Paul Panayiotou (tl); Robert Harding Picture Library: Alvaro Leiva (tr)
124–125 iStockphoto: Getty Images / efesenko
127 Shutterstock: Anastasios71
147 Shutterstock: PitK (t); iStockphoto: Getty Images / alxpin (b)
163 Alamy Images: Peter Eastland
189 Shutterstock: sebos
200–201 Shutterstock: WitR

203 Shutterstock: sssanchez
215 iStockphoto: Getty Images / mango2friendly (t); Shutterstock: Valery Bocman (b)
231 iStockphoto: Getty Images / fotofritz16
255 Shutterstock: Alberto Loyo (t); Photoshot: Stuart Black (b)
264–265 SuperStock: Peter Schickert
267 4Corners Images: Aldo Pavan
287 Shutterstock: Nicram Sabod (t); iStockphoto: Getty Images / fotofritz16 (b)
326–327 iStockphoto: Getty Images / Sergey Borisov
329 Sutterstock: Constantinos Iliopoulos
354–355 Shutterstock: EGUCHI NAOHIRO
357 iStockphoto: Getty Images / Freeartist
379 iStockphoto: Getty Images / papadimitriou
407 Getty Images: Jean-Pierre Lescourret (t)
435 4Corners: Günter Gräfenhain/Huber (t); Shutterstock: Aerial-motion (b)
446–447 iStockpho: Getty Images / Arsty
449 Alamy Images: Gareth McCormack
510–511 iStockphoto: Getty Images / Freeartist
527 Shutterstock: Mariusz Switulski (tl); Getty Images: Corbis: Atlantide Phototravel (b)
567 iStockphoto: Getty Images / nejdetduzen (t)
596–597 Getty Images: Izzet Keribar
599 Getty Images: Gallo Images / Danita Delimont
623 Shutterstock: kostasgr (t); Robert Harding Picture Library: Stuart Black (b)
647 Getty Images: Gallo Images / Danita Delimont (t); Shutterstock: Porojnicu Stelian (b)
670–671 Shutterstock: Mila Atkovska
673 iStockphoto: Getty Images / Saso Novoselic
691 Shutterstock: Milan Gonda (t); iStockphoto: Getty Images / sangriana (b)
706–707 Robert Harding Picture Library: ImageBROKER / Gerhard Zwerger-Schoner
709 Shutterstock: Vladislav Sinelnikov
737 Shutterstock: Pawel Kazmierczak (tl); iStockphoto: Getty Images / chatsimo (tr); Getty Images / Saso Novoselic
762 iStockphoto: Getty Images / Devasahayam Chandra Dhas

Index

Maps are marked in grey

B

C

Map symbols

The symbols below are used on maps throughout the book

International boundary	International airport	Monastery	Swamp/marsh
State boundary	Domestic airport	Church (regional)	Spring
Chapter boundary	Transport stop	Observatory	Waterfall
Main road	Helipad	Synagogue	Lighthouse
Minor road	Metro/subway	Place of interest	Windmill
Motorway	Tram stop	National Park	Vineyard
Pedestrianised road	Boat	Fountain	Gorge
Steps	Post office	Mountain refuge	Steep slope
Unpaved road	Internet access	Ruin	Shipwreck
Railway	Hospital	Castle	Bridge
Cable car	Information centre	Skiing	Building
Tram line	Toilet	Arch	Church (town)
Funicular	Parking	Gate	Stadium
Coastline	Fuel/gas station	Viewpoint	Park
Path	Campsite	Mountain range	Christian cemetery
Wall	Statue	Mountain peak	Muslim cemetery
Ferry	Mosque	Cave	Beach

Listings key

- Accommodation
- Eating
- Drinking/nightlife
- Shopping

Find the real Greece

The Sunvil Promise
· Handpicked accommodation · Personal service
· Value for money · Local knowledge
· Holidays tailored to your taste

Visit **sunvil.co.uk** or call
020 8568 4499

ABTA
Travel with confidence
ABTA No.V6218

ssured

sunvil
find the real country